WORLD CONGRESS ON NEURAL NETWORKS- SAN DIEGO

1994 INTERNATIONAL
NEURAL NETWORK SOCIETY
ANNUAL MEETING

TOWN & COUNTRY HOTEL
SAN DIEGO, CALIFORNIA USA
JUNE 5-9, 1994

VOLUME 3

Lawrence Erlbaum Associates, Inc., Publishers
365 Broadway
Hillsdale, New Jersey 07642

ISBN 0-8058-1745-X

Books published by Lawrence Erlbaum Associates are printed on acid-free paper, and their bindings are chosen for strength and durability.

Printed in the United States of America

WCNN '94 ORGANIZING COMMITTEE

Paul Werbos, Chairman, *National Science Foundation*

Harold Szu, *Naval Surface Warfare Center*

Bernard Widrow, *Stanford University*

WCNN '94 SPECIAL SESSION CHAIRS

BIOMEDICAL APPLICATIONS OF NEURAL NETWORKS
David G. Brown, *Center for Devices and Radiological Health,*
US Food and Drug Administration
John N. Weinstein, *National Cancer Institute, US National Institutes of Health*

**COMMERCIAL AND INDUSTRIAL APPLICATIONS OF
NEURAL NETWORKS**
Bernard Widrow, *Stanford University*

**FINANCIAL AND ECONOMIC APPLICATIONS OF
NEURAL NETWORKS**
Guido J. Deboeck, *World Bank*

**APPLICATION OF NEURAL NETWORKS IN THE
CHEMICAL PROCESS INDUSTRIES**
Thomas McAvoy, *University of Maryland*

MIND, BRAIN, AND CONSCIOUSNESS
John G. Taylor, *King's College London*

WCNN '94 PROGRAM COMMITTEE

WCNN '94 PROGRAM COMMITTEE

Thomas McAvoy, *University of Maryland*
Thomas McKenna, *Office of Naval Research*
Larry Medsker, *American University*
Erkki Oja, *Lappeenranta University of Technology*
Robert Pap, *Accurate Automation Corporation*
Barak Pearlmutter, *Siemens Corporate Research*
Richard Peterson, *Georgia Tech Research Institute*
Gerhardt Roth, *Brain Research Institute*
David Rumelhart, *Stanford University*
Mohammad Sayeh, *Southern Illinois University*
Dejan Sobajic, *Electric Power Research Institute*
Harold Szu, *Naval Surface Warfare Center*
John G. Taylor, *King's College London*
Brain Telfer, *Naval Surface Warfare Center*
Shiro Usui, *Toyohashi University of Technology*
John N. Weinstein, *National Cancer Institute*
Paul Werbos, *National Science Foundation*
Bernard Widrow, *Stanford University*
Takeshi Yamakawa, *Kyushu Institute of Technology*
Lotfi A. Zadeh, *University of California at Berkeley*
Mona Zaghloul, *George Washington University*

CONGRESS SPONSOR

The International Neural Network Society (INNS) is the sponsor of WCNN '94 - San Diego.

PRESIDENT   **Walter J. Freeman**, *University of California at Berkeley*
PRESIDENT-ELECT   **John G. Taylor**, *King's College London*
PAST PRESIDENT   **Harold Szu**, *Naval Surface Warfare Center*
SECRETARY   **Gail Carpenter**, *Boston University*
TREASURER   **Judith Dayhoff**, *University of Maryland*

BOARD OF GOVERNORS:

Shun-ichi Amari, *University of Tokyo*
James A. Anderson, *Brown University*
Andrew Barto, *University of Massachusetts*
David Casasent, *Carnegie Mellon University*
Leon Cooper, *Brown University*
Rolf Eckmiller, *University of Bonn*
Kunihiko Fukushima, *Osaka University*
Stephen Grossberg, *Boston University*
Mitsuo Kawato, *Advanced Telecommunications Research Institute*
Christof Koch, *California Institute of Technology*
Teuvo Kohonen, *Helsinki University of Technology*
Bart Kosko, *University of Southern California*
Christoph von der Malsburg, *University of Southern California*
Alianna Maren, *Accurate Automation Corporation*
Paul Werbos, *National Science Foundation*
Bernard Widrow, *Stanford University*
Lotfi A. Zadeh, *University of California at Berkeley*

ORDER OF APPEARANCE

TECHNICAL AREAS continued

TABLE OF CONTENTS

Presenting author is listed first.

VOLUME 1

Plenaries

Special Session: Biomedical Applications of Neural Networks

Oral

ix

Special Session: Commercial and Industrial Applications of Neural Networks

Special Session: Application of Neural Networks in the Chemical Process Industries

Special Session: Mind, Brain, and Consciousness

Oral

Applications

Oral

TABLE OF CONTENTS continued

TABLE OF CONTENTS continued

Machine Vision

Oral

TABLE OF CONTENTS continued

Neural Fuzzy Systems

TABLE OF CONTENTS continued

TABLE OF CONTENTS   continued

Prediction and System Identification

Oral

Poster

Mathematical Foundations

Hardware Implementations

TABLE OF CONTENTS   continued

Biological Neural Networks

Oral

Poster

TABLE OF CONTENTS continued

TABLE OF CONTENTS continued

Supervised Learning

Oral

TABLE OF CONTENTS   continued

TABLE OF CONTENTS continued

Associative Memory

TABLE OF CONTENTS   continued

Unsupervised Learning

Oral

Biological Vision

TABLE OF CONTENTS continued

Circuits and System Neuroscience

Oral

Links to Cognitive Science & Artificial Intelligence

Oral

Speech and Language

Oral

TABLE OF CONTENTS   continued

Cognitive Neuroscience

Oral

Neurodynamics and Chaos

Oral

TABLE OF CONTENTS continued

Signal Processing

Session Chairs: Bernard Widrow
Horacio Bouzas

ORAL PRESENTATIONS

Nonlinear Adaptive Signal Processing
for Inverse Control

Bernard Widrow   Michel Bilello*

Stanford University Department of Electrical Engineering, Stanford, CA 94305-4055

Abstract

A plant can track an input command signal if it is driven by a controller whose transfer function approximates the inverse of its transfer function. A stable inverse can be obtained even if the plant is nonminimum-phase. No direct feedback is used, except that the plant output is monitored and utilized to adapt the parameters of the controller. A model-reference inverse control system can learn to approximate a desired reference-model dynamics.

Control of internal plant disturbance is accomplished with an optimal adaptive disturbance canceller. It does not affect plant dynamics, but feeds back plant disturbance in a way that minimizes disturbance power at the plant output.

Similar principles can be utilized to control nonlinear systems. Neural networks are used to build a model of the plant and to construct its inverse.

1   Introduction

This paper presents techniques for solving adaptive control problems by means of adaptive filtering.

Many problems in adaptive control can be divided into two parts: (a) control of plant dynamics, and (b) control of plant disturbance. Very often, a single system is utilized to achieve both of these control objectives. Our approach however treats each problem separately. Control of plant dynamics can be achieved by preceding the plant with an adaptive controller whose transfer function is the inverse of that of the plant. Control of plant disturbance can be achieved by an adaptive feedback process that minimizes plant output disturbance without altering plant dynamics.

The principle of control of plant dynamics can be extended to deal with nonlinear plants. In that case, tapped delay lines and neural networks are used in place of linear adaptive filters.

2   Adaptive Inverse Control for Linear Plants

2.1   Direct Plant Identification

Adaptive plant modeling or identification is an important function. Fig. 1 illustrates how this can be done with an adaptive FIR filter. The plant input signal is the input to the adaptive filter. The plant output signal is the *desired response*, the target signal for the filter output. The adaptive algorithm, LMS [1] or RLS [2], minimizes mean square error, causing the model $\hat{P}$ to be a best least squares match to the plant P for the given input signal and for the given set of parameters (weights) allocated to $\hat{P}$.

*This work was sponsored by NSF under grant NSF IRI 91-12531, by ONR under contract no N00014-92-J-1787, and by EPRI under contract RP:8010-13

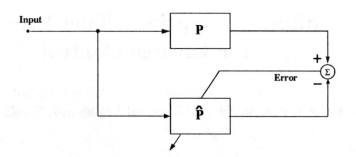

Figure 1: Direct plant identification.

2.2 Inverse Plant Identification

Another important function is inverse plant identification. This technique is illustrated in Fig. 2(a). The plant input is as before. The plant output is the input to the adaptive filter. The desired response for the adaptive filter is the plant input in this case. Minimizing mean square error causes the adaptive filter $\widehat{P^{-1}}$ to be a best least squares inverse to the plant P for the given input spectrum and for the given set of weights of the adaptive filter. The adaptive algorithm attempts to make the cascade of plant and adaptive inverse behave like a unit gain. This process is often called deconvolution.

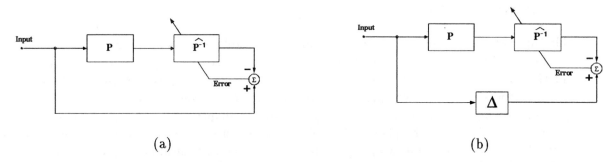

(a)   (b)

Figure 2: Inverse identification. (a) for minimum-phase plants. (b) for nonminimum-phase plants

For sake of argument, the plant is assumed to have poles and zeros. An inverse, if it also had poles and zeros, would need to have zeros where the plant had poles and poles where the plant had zeros. Making an inverse would be no problem except for the case of a nonminimum-phase plant. It would seem that such an inverse would need to have unstable poles, and this would be true if the inverse were causal. If the inverse could be noncausal as well as causal however, then a two-sided stable inverse would exist for all linear time-invariant plants in accord with the theory of two-sided Laplace transforms.

A causal FIR filter can approximate a delayed version of the two-sided plant inverse, and an adaptive FIR filter can self-adjust to this function. The method is illustrated in Fig. 2(b). The time span of the adaptive filter (the number of weights multiplied by the sampling period) can be made adequately long so that the mean square error of the optimized inverse would be a small fraction of the plant input power. To achieve this objective with a nonminimum-phase plant, the delay Δ needs to be chosen appropriately. The choice is generally not critical however.

The inverse filter is used as a controller in the present scheme, so that Δ becomes the response delay of the controlled plant. Making Δ small is generally desirable, but the quality of control depends upon the accuracy of the inversion process which sometimes requires Δ to be of the order of half the length of the adaptive filter, or less.

A model-reference inversion process is shown in Fig. 3. A reference model is used in place of the delay of Fig. 2(b). Minimizing mean square error with the system of Fig. 3 causes the cascade of the plant and its "model-reference inverse" to approximate closely the response of a model M. Much is known about the design of model reference systems [3]. The model is chosen to give a desirable response to the overall system. Some delay may need to be incorporated into the model in order to achieve low error.

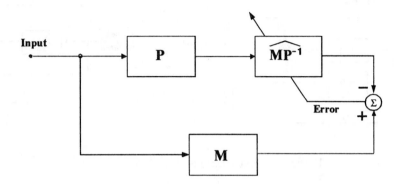

Figure 3: Model-reference plant inverse.

2.3 Adaptive Control of Plant Dynamics

Now having the plant inverse, it can be used as a controller to provide a driving function for the plant. This simple idea is illustrated in Fig. 4(a) for minimum-phase plants. Fig. 4(b) shows the corresponding scheme for nonminimum-phase systems. Many simulation examples have been performed, with consistently good results, as long as the plant is stable or is first stabilized by feedback. Extensive analysis will be presented in the forthcoming book by Widrow and Walach [4].

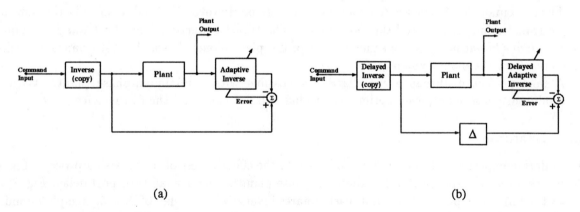

(a)   (b)

Figure 4: Inverse control scheme. (a) for minimum phase plants. (b) for nonminimum-phase plants.

2.4 Adaptive Plant Disturbance Cancelling

The systems of Fig. 4 only control and compensate for plant dynamics. The disturbance appears at the plant output unabated. The only way that the plant output disturbance can be reduced is to obtain this disturbance from the plant output and process it, then feed it back into the plant input. The system shown in Fig. 5 does this.

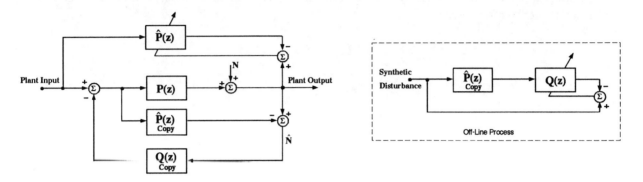

Figure 5: Disturbance cancelling system.

In Fig. 5, an exact copy of $\hat{P}$ is fed the same input signal as the plant P. The output of this $\hat{P}$ copy is subtracted from the plant output. Assuming that $\hat{P}$ has a dynamic response essentially identical to that of the plant P, the difference in the outputs is a close estimate of the plant disturbance. This disturbance is filtered by Q and then subtracted from the plant input. The filter Q is generated by an off-line process that delivers new values of Q almost instantaneously with new values of $\hat{P}$, which adapts continually to keep up with changes in the plant P.

The filter Q is essentially the best inverse (without delay) of P. The *synthetic disturbance* used to train Q should have a spectral character like that of the plant disturbance. It is shown in the Widrow and Walach book [4] that the disturbance cancelling system of Fig. 5 adapts and converges to minimize the plant disturbance at the plant output. As such, it is an optimal linear least squares system. There is no way to further reduce the plant disturbance.

The system of Fig. 5 appears to be a feedback system. However, if $\hat{P}$ is dynamically the same as P, the transfer function around the loop is zero. The transfer function from the *Plant Input* point to the *Plant Output* point is the same as that of the plant alone. Thus, the disturbance canceller does not affect the plant dynamics.

Almost perfect disturbance cancellation is possible with a minimum-phase plant. With a nonminimum-phase plant, even optimal cancelling will not cancel all the disturbance.

2.5 Example

A simulation experiment has been done to illustrate the effectiveness of the inversion process. Fig. 6 shows the impulse response of a nonminimum-phase plant having a small transport delay. Fig. 7(a) shows the impulse reponse of the best least squares inverse with a delay of $\Delta = 50$ sample periods. Fig. 7(b) is a convolution of the plant and its inverse impulse response. The result is essentially a unit impulse at a delay of 50.

Fig. 8 show results of a plant disturbance cancellation experiment. Although the plant in this case was nonminimum-phase, the results are quite good.

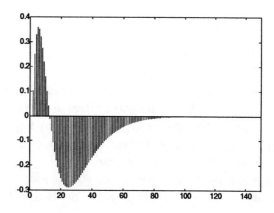

Figure 6: Impulse response of nonminimum-phase plant.

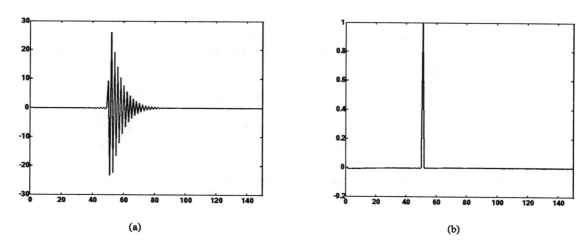

(a)   (b)

Figure 7: (a) Impulse response of delayed inverse. (b) Convolution of plant with delayed inverse.

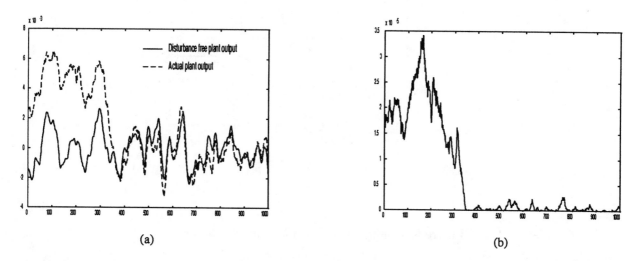

(a)   (b)

Figure 8: (a) Output of undisturbed plant and output of disturbed plant, with and without disturbance canceller. (b) Instantaneous power of plant output disturbance. (Canceller turned on at $k = 300$.)

3 Nonlinear Inverse Control

The principles of inverse control can be extended to deal with nonlinear systems. Nonlinear systems behave quite differently from their linear counterparts. A major difference is that whereas a linear system possesses a unique inverse, nonlinear systems have only local inverses if at all, valid only in a bounded region of the signal space. As linear adaptive filters are used to control linear plants, the inverse controller for nonlinear plants involves a type of recurrent neural network. The ability of multilayered neural networks to approximate nonlinear mappings over compact regions as detailed in [5] makes them useful in identifying direct and inverse models.

The inverse control of nonlinear plants involves a two-stage process where a model of the plant is first constructed (identification) and second the plant model is inverted.

3.1 Plant Identification

The system is modelled through the use of a feedforward multilayered neural network fitted with tapped delay lines at its input and output and a feedback loop. This is the nonlinear equivalent of a linear IIR filter. With an appropriate number of hidden neurons, such a neural network can represent a system of the form

$$y_k = f(y_{k-1}, y_{k-2}, \ldots, y_{k-n}, u_{k-1}, \ldots, u_{k-p})$$

over a bounded region of input space. The choice of the integers n and p is part of the modelling design and follows from requirements of model accuracy. The identification scheme, illustrated in Fig. 9, is founded on a standard technique, which is the nonlinear equivalent of the equation-error formulation described in [6], and is called a *series-parallel* model in [7]. The choice of this formulation allows the use of the standard backpropagation algorithm suited to training feedforward neural networks.

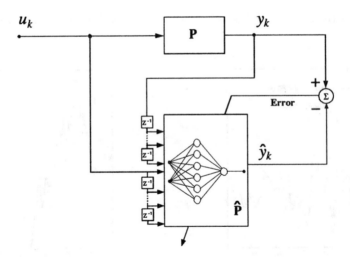

Figure 9: Configuration for plant identification.

3.2 Computing the Inverse

The second step is the design of the controller. Once the plant identification has been performed and a model of the plant obtained, the controller, also implemented as a recurrent neural network, is trained to behave like the inverse of the system. The algorithm used for training the controller is a variant of the recurrent backpropagation algorithm [8]. The controller is trained upstream from the plant model and the error signal is backpropagated through the plant model as illustrated in Fig. 10.

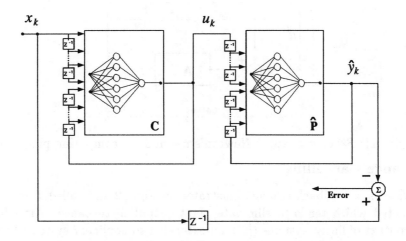

Figure 10: Configuration for training of inverse controller.

Newton's method Although the previous algorithmic scheme performs well, it is advantageous to consider an alternate procedure based on Newton's method for solving nonlinear equations.

The motivation for this procedure is the desire to increase speed and precision by training the inverse of the plant model using standard backpropagation as opposed to a recurrent version thereof. To do so, a desired controller output needs to be derived.

The desired controller output is simply the input to the plant that would yield the desired plant output. Thus, we want to solve the equation $y^{(d)} = \mathcal{F}u$, where $y^{(d)}$ is the target (desired) signal and $\mathcal{F}$ is the nonlinear discrete-time plant mapping.

Let A be the first derivative of $\mathcal{F}$ evaluated at the origin. We iteratively apply the following algorithm:

$$
\begin{aligned}
u^{(0)} &= A^{-1}y^{(d)} \\
u^{(n+1)} &= u^{(n)} + A^{-1}(y^{(d)} - \mathcal{F}(u^{(n)})), n \geq 0
\end{aligned}
$$

In the above equations, the sequences $u^{(m)}$ are finite for obvious practical reasons. However, it should be pointed out that under certain conditions, the convergence of this algorithm is guaranteed even in the infinite dimensional case. Of course, no matrix inversion needs to be performed here. In fact, since A is lower-triangular in virtue of causality, only a triangular system of linear equations, $Ae^{(n)} = y^{(d)} - \mathcal{F}(u^{(n)})$, is solved at each time step by forward substitution.

The procedure is carried out according to Fig 11. Note that the $u^{(j)}$ are entire sequences and not time samples. Data is gathered from the actual plant and then processed off-line to supply the next input sequence. If the inverse of the plant model is to be computed, the whole computation can be performed off-line with the plant model in place of the physical plant. At the end of the iterative procedure, $u^{(d)}$ is obtained, the desired output for training the inverse controller.

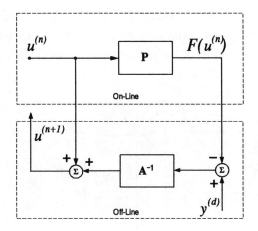

Figure 11: Scheme to apply Newton's method for computing plant input.

3.3 Disturbance Cancelling

As for linear systems, a feedback scheme, illustrated in Fig. 12 and called *Internal Model Control* can be implemented which tends to eliminate plant output disturbance. After being thoroughly studied in the context of linear systems ([9]), an extension to nonlinear systems has been suggested ([10]). The underlying idea is the same as in the linear case. An estimate of the output disturbance is produced by comparing the plant output and the plant model output. The estimated disturbance is then fedback to the controller input. It turns out that if the closed-loop system is stable, and if the controller is chosen to be the inverse of the plant model, then the disturbance can be cancelled.

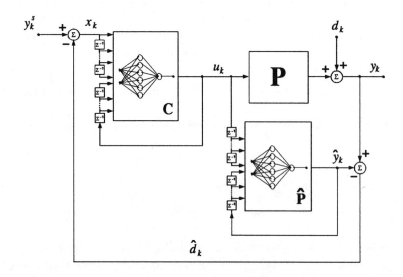

Figure 12: Internal Model Control for cancelling output disturbance.

3.4 Examples

Example 1 Let's consider the nonlinear plant suggested in [7] and defined by the equation:

$$y_k = \frac{y_{k-1}}{1 + y_{k-1}^2} + u_{k-1}^3$$

III-10

The input signal is confined in the interval $[-2, 2]$. The plant model in training configuration (Fig. 9) had two inputs, the external input u and the output from the real plant, and one output. It had one hidden layer with 10 units. The result of the plant identification is displayed in Fig. 13(a). Specifically, the outputs of the plant and plant model are compared when the same test signal is fed to their inputs.

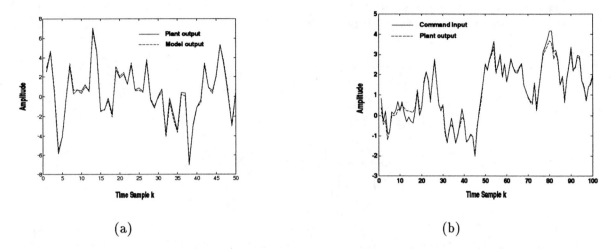

(a)   (b)

Figure 13: Example 1. (a) Result of plant identification (b) Performance of inverse controller.

The neural network controller had a two-tap tapped delay line as input, a hidden layer with 10 units and one output which is fed to the plant model. The error is backpropagated through the plant model using on-line recurrent backpropagation. The time plots of Fig. 13(b) show the command input fed to the trained inverse controller and the plant output. Although there are errors, the agreement between the two signals is very good. The important thing to note is that the controller is trained to be an inverse to the plant model and not the plant itself. Consequently, good performance of the controller is contingent on building an accurate model for the plant.

Next, we demonstrate the efficacy of the Internal Model Control in cancelling the output disturbance. The inverse controller and the plant model have been inserted in the control structure according to Fig. 12. The result of this experiment in the form of the power of the disturbance at the plant output before and after the feedack loop is closed is shown in Fig. 14.

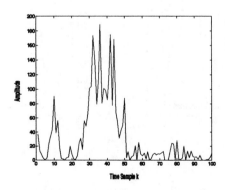

Figure 14: Instantaneous power of disturbance at plant output (feedback loop closed at $k = 50$).

Example 2 As a second example, we modify the previous system equation and now consider:

$$y_k = \frac{y_{k-1}}{1 + y_{k-1}^2} + \sin(u_{k-1})$$

We will use this example to illustrate the use of Newton's method to train the inverse controller.

We start with the process of plant identification. The plant model neural network has similar characteristics to the previous example's. Using a random signal uniformly distributed in the interval $[-1, 1]$, we obtain the results displayed in Fig. 15.

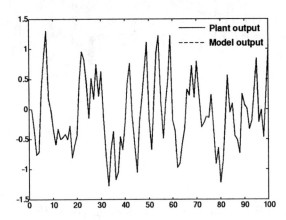

Figure 15: Result of nonlinear plant identification for example 2.

Next, the inverse model is train using the two different methods discussed earlier. The inverse controller is then placed in cascade with the real plant to evaluate tracking performance. The results in Fig. 16(a) were produced by an inverse controller trained with standard backpropagation after the desired controller output had been solved for using the Newton-like method. By comparison, an inverse controller trained with recurrent backpropagation through the plant model yielded the results of Fig. 16(b). The plots demonstrate better performance with the former method.

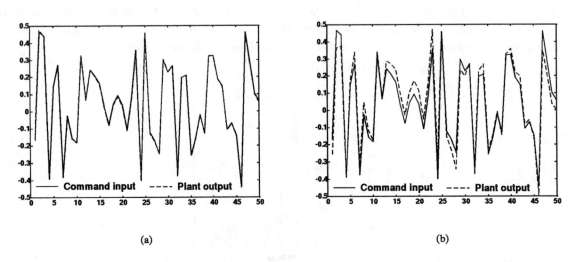

(a)   (b)

Figure 16: Tracking performance for plant of example 2. (a) using Newton method and standard backpropagation. (b) using recurrent backpropagation.

4 Conclusion

Methods for adaptive control of plant dynamics and for control of plant disturbance for unknown linear plants have been described. In addition extension of control of plant dynamics to nonlinear plants using neural networks have been presented. For their proper application, the plant must be stable. An unstable plant could first be stabilized with feedback, then adaptively controlled.

References

[1] Bernard Widrow and Samuel D. Stearns. *Adaptive Signal Processing*. Prentice-Hall, Englewood Cliffs, NJ, 1985.

[2] Simon Haykin. *Adaptive Filter Theory*. Prentice-Hall, Englewood Cliffs, NJ, 2 edition, 1991.

[3] I. D. Landau. *Adaptive Control. The Model Reference Approach*. Marcel Dekker, New York, 1979.

[4] Bernard Widrow and Eugene Walach. *Adaptive Inverse Control*. Prentice-Hall, Englewood Cliffs, NJ, 1994. (in press).

[5] K. Hornik, M. Stinchcombe, and H. White. Multilayer feedforward networks are universal approximators. *Neural Networks*, 2:359–366, 1989.

[6] John J. Shynk. Adaptive IIR filtering. *IEEE ASSP Magazine*, April 1989.

[7] Kumpati S. Narendra and Kannan Parthasarathy. Identification and control of dynamical systems using neural networks. *IEEE Transactions on Neural Networks*, 1(1):4–27, March 1990.

[8] R. J. Williams and D. Zipser. A learning algorithm for continually running fully recurrent neural networks. ICS Report 8805, Institute for Cognitive Science, University of California at San Diego, La Jolla, CA 92093, October 1988.

[9] Manfred Morari and Evanghelos Zafiriou. *Robust Process Control*. Prentice Hall, Englewood Cliffs, NJ, 1989.

[10] Constantin G. Economou and Manfred Morari. Internal model control 5. extension to nonlinear systems. *Ind. Eng. Chem. Process Des. Dev.*, 25:403–411, 1986.

THE USE OF CALIBRATION LAYERS IN A SLIDING NETWORK ARCHITECTURE

Gavin R. Peacock
ITRI, University of Brighton, England

ABSTRACT

Some neural network problems may seem to require a large frame size compared to frame number, which would ordinarily lead to large statistical problems. Given the right assumptions, a sliding architecture may be used to overcome these difficulties. Sometimes these assumptions are partially broken thus producing non-optimum results. This paper describes one such case where some of the input signals are of unknown calibration. A solution is suggested and then put to the test using an artificial problem. This produced up to a factor of 10 improvement on the errors when compared to the case of a simple sliding architecture.

1 INTRODUCTION

Take a typical multi-layer perceptron problem: an input $x(k)$ is provided where k indicates which frame of data the input is taken from; and a required output $y^{req}(k)$ is provided to which the actual output of the net $y(k)$ must converge through the iterative setting of the weights of the network. Let the maximum number of available frames n_k be much smaller than the number of elements of the input vector n_i. This would normally lead to severe statistical errors (including over-learning in an mlp [Chauvin 1990]) without a redesign of the network architecture or of the data set. For a given problem, it may be possible to make the following two approximations.

The *local* approximation: y_i^{req} can only be associated with $x_i^{local} = (x_{i - \Delta i / 2} \cdots x_{i + \Delta i / 2})$.

The *location independence* approximation: the mapping formed between the two is by the nature of the problem independent of i.

If this is the case then a sliding architecture can be used (see figure 1). This improves the ratio of frame size to frame number by a factor of about n_i^2 / Δ_i. This turns a large number of inputs into an advantage by producing many more frames from them. Such an architecture is equivalent to the windowing of visual or other data for classification problems such as character recognition. In Hand et al. [1992] this type up break down is used to retrieve the positions of the eyes in the picture of a face. For many problems this is the simple and obvious approach. Although its use here is intended for function estimation problems rather than classification, this is not a novel architecture.

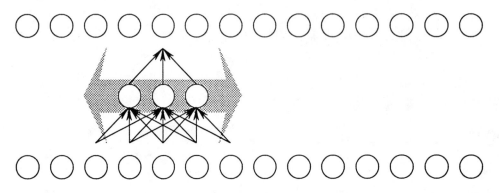

Figure 1   Sliding Network Architecture

Because of the large improvement, it can be tempting to use this architecture even if the two approximations are broken to some extent. However, it may often be possible to adapt the architecture so that this frame size to number ratio improvement is still obtained, while still complying with the approximations.

This case arose from an application of neural networks to the measurement of the sound pressure response of small rooms [Allison 1972, 1976; Bodlund 1976; Craik 1990]. Four sets of input data and one set of required output was available with 1024 frequency points per signal (and so i represented the frequency). Because the number of rooms with which to provide frames of data would always be small (in this case 48, half of which would have to be reserved for testing), there is an inherent problem with the frame size to number ratio. However, it was a reasonable approximation to make that an output at frequency i could only be associated with inputs of frequency close to i. This width of input was defined by the resonances present in a room [Kuttruff 1973, chapter III]. Each mode of resonance had a certain frequency bandwidth over which it could be excited, and this bandwidth provides the possibility of associating the output with inputs of slightly different frequency. This works out to around 10 frequency points out of 1024. Given there were four sets of inputs, each output had to be associated to 40 inputs. Although there were problems in doing so, it was also useful to use the location independence approximation because this lead to a network that would extrapolate for rooms of different sizes.

Thus these two approximations led to the use of a sliding network architecture, where the network slid over the frequency range steadily filling in the outputs. In doing so, the frame size to number ratio was improved by the order of 100,000 enabling the use of neural networks as a solution.

However, in this example the calibration of three of the inputs was uncertain. This breaks the location independence approximation. For a fully connected network, the uncalibrated nature of the input signal does not present a problem because the network can calibrate itself to the input signal. This is not possible with a sliding network because the calibration is dependent on i, whereas the network is independent of i.

2 SOLUTION

In this case, the solution is quite simple and effective. Assuming that the required calibration for input x_i is essentially linear and independent of all other inputs, then the calibration of the input can be carried out by what will be termed a *calibration layer*. A calibration layer is a layer of single links that processes the uncalibrated input nodes to produce a new set of nodes representing a calibrated input: $x_i^{cal} = w_i^{cal} x_i + \theta_i$. The sliding network can then slide along this new set of nodes oblivious of the calibration. Thus these links are fixed to each input instead of sliding along with the net, and can therefore provide a processing dependent on i. In principle, the required output can represent a signal also of unknown calibration, and so an output calibration layer can also be used. This new architecture is shown in figure 2.

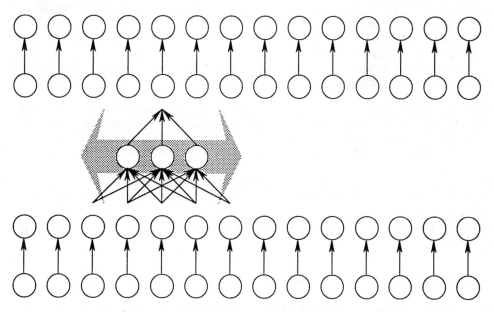

Figure 2   Sliding Network with Calibration Layers

Assuming that the sliding net would ordinarily be taught using some method of gradient descent of back-propagated errors [Rumelhart, McClelland 1986; Werbos 1988], this learning scheme can easily be extended to train the calibration layers. Thus while the network is positioned at output y_i and frame k the output calibration link to y_i can be taught as part of the net, and also those input calibration links connected to x_i^{local}.

There are three points to note.

Although each output calibration link will only have k frames from which to learn, and each input link $k\Delta i$ frames, this will not result in the learning problems encountered before the use of a sliding net architecture, because each calibrated node only has access to a single input.

Although the architecture shown in figure 2 is a network containing four layers of weights, the problems normally associated with deep nets when using backpropagation will not be present. This is because the errors back-propagated through the output calibration links are not dispersed by the layer, and so remain specific to a given output.

The weights of a feedforward network are usually initialised at random. This is because it is not possible to say what the nodes that these weights connect to, represent. However, in the case of the calibration layers, the roles of the nodes involved is well defined. Thus the weights and thresholds can be initialised according to the means and standard deviations (with respect to the training set of frames) of the inputs and required output.

3 EXPERIMENT

To test the performance of such a system, an artificial problem was devised.

The input was 20 floating point numbers set to rectangular noise between 0 and 1. The required output was set according to:

$$y_i^{req} = x_i x_{i+1} .$$ (1)

Three other vectors of 20 elements were also provided as input. These were also set with rectangular noise. The required output was unrelated to these other inputs. This increased the size of the input so that it was comparable to the number of frames used and so forces the use of a sliding architecture.

These vectors formed one frame of data. There were 46 such frames constructed for the purposes of training.

From the input layer upwards, the network was constructed as follows.

Each input node was connected by a permanent calibration link to a calibrated input node. There was no output function on the activation of these nodes.

The first layer of the sliding net connects 4 inputs from each input vector (16 in total) to the 7 nodes of the first layer which performed a weighted summation on these connections followed by a logistic sigmoid output function to provide the network with a non-linear response.

These nodes lead on to the second layer which consisted of just one node operating another weighted summation, but this time without a further output function.

This node then connected to one of the links of the output calibration layer. The nodes of the output calibration layer had no output function.

The initialisation procedure for the calibration layers described earlier was used. This served to produce the unknown calibration of the input and output. Because this was carried over the 46 frames of the training set, this lead to a statistical error in this initialisation of about 15%. The test will work if the network can remove this error.

All other weights and thresholds were initialised randomly according to a rectangular distribution between -1 and $+1$.

Learning was carried out using backpropagation with momentum [Rumelhart, McClelland 1986; Jacobs 1988] throughout the network. A constant of 0.9 was used for the momentum. The momentum term was initialised to zero in all cases.

The learning rates were applied layer by layer producing four learning rates: r_{in}, r_1, r_2, r_{out}; in that order from input to output.

4 RESULTS

Best results were obtaining with learning rates of about: $r_{in} = 0.001$, $r_1 = 0.1$, $r_2 = 0.1$, $r_{out} = 0.001$. Figures 3 and 4 compare the learning curves for these values of the calibration learning rates against the case of no learning in the calibration layers. These results were obtained using a further frame of data, not part of the 46 frames of the learning set, thus requiring the network to predict. Note that the values used for the other rates not specified in the graphs are those given above.

These results show a factor of ten improvement in the network's prediction through using input calibration learning, and a factor of two improvement using output calibration learning.

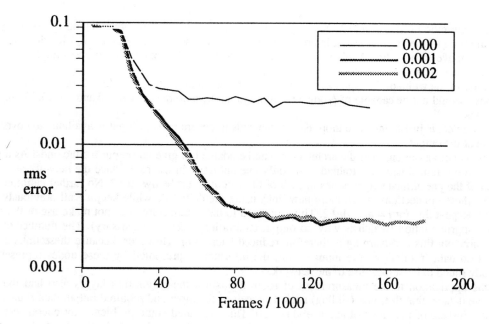

Figure 3   Effect of Input Calibration
Values shown are for r_{in}

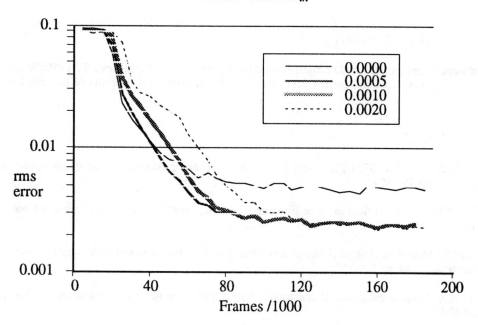

Figure 4   Effect of Output Calibration
Values shown are for r_{out}

5 CONCLUSIONS

The calibration learning proved to be an effective method of introducing a input node specific adjustment dependent on position without reintroducing the frame size to number problem.

The values of the calibration learning rates was smaller than that of the main sliding part of the net by a factor of 100. Any rates much higher than this produced results worse than the case of no calibration learning. It appears that the calibration has to wait for the main network to produce a rough mapping before it can start to converge, whilst the main network can start to converge before the calibration layers. Although once the calibration layers have started to learn, this should feed back to enable the main net to learn a more accurate mapping, the learning in the calibration layers would remain subordinate to the main net. Thus this method can only be used if either the calibration of the original signal is not too poor, or if there are enough frames (n_k) for the initialisation procedure used above to be valid. If this is not the case, then it would be difficult for an initial mapping to be formed, and so neither part of the system would converge.

Because of the width of the input, Δi, is larger than the width of the output (which is just 1), the network as described above would not be capable of producing an output at the extremes of i ($i \approx 0$ and $i \approx n_i$). There are two ways around this.

The simplest is just to measure more data at the ends to ensure enough input is available to cover for the required range of the output.

If this is not an option, then the architecture can be adapted to give an output for the ends. As a starting point, take the fully trained network, trained using only one output as in figure 2. Place the network at $i = \Delta i / 2$. Connect each of the pre-ultimate layer nodes to each of the output nodes below $\Delta i / 2$. No further calibration links are needed for these connections. Train these new links using the delta rule while keeping all previously trained links constant. Repeat this for $i = n_i - \Delta i / 2$. This extension to the architecture does not make use of the location independence approximation (which is why no output calibration links are necessary). The number of frames available to carry out this end-learning is therefore reduced back to n_k. However, because these links are using nodes trained on data from across the input vector, the information presented by these nodes represent those features already found to be of most use to the network.

In the application to the measurement of room acoustics, the calibration layers also had the role of normalising the data so that the main (sliding) network received the input and required output data roughly in the range of 0 to 1 instead of the range of about −90 to −50. This presented some problems not encountered in the experiment outline earlier. To get a convergent behaviour from the calibration layers, the threshold adjustments had to be scaled down on the input calibration links. Also, the momentum term had to be taken off the threshold update rule.

ACKNOWLEDGEMENTS

This work forms part of a PhD project funded jointly by a SERC CASE award and B&W Loudspeakers (Worthing, England). This work was carried out at the IT Research Institute (University of Brighton) and at B&W Loudspeakers.

REFERENCES

Allison, R. F., Berkovitz, R. (1972) The sound field in home listening rooms, *journal of the audio engineering society, vol 20, no 6*, pp 459-469

Allison, R. F. (1976) The sound field in home listening rooms II, *journal of the audio engineering society, vol 24, no 1*, pp 14-19

Bodlund, K. (1976) Statistical characteristics of some standard reverberant sound field measurements, *journal of sound and vibration, vol 44*, pp 539-557

Chauvin, Y. (1990) Dynamic behaviour of constrained back-propagation networks, *neural information processing systems 2*, pp 642-649

Craik, R. J. M. (1990) On the accuracy of sound pressure level measurements in rooms, *applied acoustics, vol 29, part 1*, pp 25-33

Hand, C. C., Evans, M. R., Ellacott, S. W. (1992) A neural network feature detector using a multi-resolution pyramid, *In R. Linggard, D. J. Myers, C. Nightingale (Ed.) neural networks for vision, speech and natural language*, Chapman & Hall

Jacobs, R. A. (1988) Increased rates of convergence though learning rate adaptation, *neural networks, vol. 1*, pp 295-307

Kuttruff, H. (1973) *Room Acoustics*, Applied Science Publ.

Rumelhart, D. E., McClelland J. L., PDP Research Group (1986) *Parallel Distributed Processing, Vol 1*, MIT Press.

Werbos, P. J. (1988) Backpropagation - past and future, *proceedings of the IEEE international conference on neural networks*, pp 343-353

Partial Recurrent Time Delay Neural Network Channel Equalizer

Xiaolin Yang and Anthony Kuh *
Department of Electrical Engineering
University of Hawaii at Manoa
2540 Dole Street, Holmes 483
Honolulu, Hawaii 96822

Abstract

In this paper, we propose a Partial Recurrent Time Delay Neural Network. The architecture is quite similar to a Recursive Adaptive filter and can be trained as a channel equalizer. Results show that the proposed architecture gives good results for several simulation channels. For tests conducted, it outperforms the DFE equalizer and the best available neural equalizer. For a nonminimum phase channel, the neural equalizer performs well, while traditional equalizers do not perform well.

1 Introduction

The problem to be considered in channel equalization is that of utilizing the information represented by the observed channel output $y_t, y_{t-1}, \ldots, y_{t-m+1}$ to produce an estimate of the input symbol $x_{t-\tau}$. A system which performs this function is known as an equalizer, which compensates for unwanted channel features and presents the receiver with a sequence of samples that have in a sense "cleaned-up" the effects of Intersymbol Interference (ISI) and noise. Equalizers can be classified into two categories; the symbol-decision and sequence-estimation equalizer [8]. A linear transversal equalizer(LTE) is a symbol-decision equalizer as the operation of this equalizer at each sample t is based on the m most recent channel observations. A decision is made regarding the transmitted symbol at sample $t - \tau$. The integer m and τ are known as the equalizer order and delay respectively. A powerful technique to improve the performance of the symbol-decision equalizer is to include past detected symbols into its input vector, this equalizer is called a decision feedback equalizer (DFE) [8]. The best known sequence-estimation equalizer is the maximum likelihood sequence estimator (MLSE) [8]. The MLSE is optimal for detecting the entire transmitted sequence and provides the best attainable performance for any equalizer [2]. High complexity and the deferring of decisions are two drawbacks of the MLSE. Although the concept of adaptive equalization has been known for many years [9], neural networks have only recently being used as nonlinear adaptive filters for the channel equalization problem [6]. Some researchers have use neural networks as a channel equalizer by using basic neural network architectures and algorithms [3] [2]. The Time Delay Neural Network architecture has not been used in channel equalization before.

In the paper, we will extend the Time-Delay Algorithm to a partial recurrent Time-Delay algorithm. The new architecture and algorithm are more flexible than the original models, and can implement more powerful functions. In order to avoid overfitting the training data, penalty functions are used. After estimating the channel characteristics, the neural networks will be used as a channel equalizer. Our neural channel equalizer is tested on these channels and comparison results are made with other neural channel equalizers and the DFE.

2 Motivation and Proposed Architecture

In this paper, we will mainly discuss the partial recurrent network instead of the fully recurrent architecture. We use a partially recurrent architecture since these networks can incorporate information about past states

*The authors acknowledge support from NSF grant EET-8857711

III-20

and learning algorithms are much simpler than full recurrent networks. The algorithms that we proposed are similar to the Jordan Elman network [5] shown in Figure 1. In the partial recurrent architecture, the input layer is divided into two parts: the true input units and the context units (the feedback units) [13]. The context units simply hold a copy of the value of state variables from the previous time step.

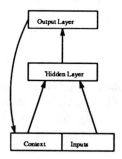

Figure 1: Partial Recurrent Neural Network Architecture

The modifiable connections are all feedforward, and can be trained by a feedforward learning scheme. If the state variables are delayed values of the output from the output layer, the state variables accumulate a weighted moving average of the past values they see. The architecture can be used to implement a non-linear *Autoregressive Moving Average* (ARMA) predictor [12] or a non-linear recursive adaptive equalizer. The feedforward network is a special case of the recurrent form, which can be used to implement a non-linear traversal adaptive equalizer [3]. The recurrency in a partial recurrent network lets the network remember cues from the recent past, but does not appreciably complicate the training as *real-time recurrent learning(RTRL)* proposed by Williams and Zipser [5] and *time-dependent recurrent back-propagation* proposed by Pearlmutter [7].

A Time Delay Neural Network (TDNN) [11] is typically described as a layered network in which the outputs of a layer are buffered several time steps and then fed fully connected to the next layer. The TDNN architecture can be viewed as an FIR filter network, i.e. each connection in the static feedforward architecture becomes an FIR filter [12].

In a partial recurrent architecture, delayed versions of computational nodes can serve as inputs to the network. We will consider only the case where delayed versions of output nodes are inputs to the network. This network is a nonlinear version of a linear infinite impulse response (IIR) filter. The proposed Partial Recurrent Time Delay Neural Network (PRTDNN) architecture is a TDNN with partial recurrent architecture. The TDNN proposed by Waibel [11] is a special case of a PRTDNN. The PRTDNN is trained using a variation of the backpropagation algorithm using regularization methods.

The simplest weight regularization method is to use an exponential weight decay. While this method discourages use of large weights; the penalty of one large weight is much more than many small ones. This can be cured by using a different penalty term, such as [5] which normalizes the effects of different magnitude weights by decaying larger magnitude weights more rapidly. This method is called the weight elimination method and is used in conjunction with the backpropagation algorithm.

We note that the PRTDNN architecture has the following advantages over more conventional neural architectures:

1. Temporal properties can be stored to improve learning ability. This is important for short sequence reproduction task.

2. The learning algorithm is an extension of the backpropagation algorithm, therefore, the partial recurrent architecture will not complicate the learning process. The feedback connections are fixed, all modifiable weights are in feedforward connections, so backpropagation or other feedforward learning algorithms may easily be used for training.

3. Feeding back the output will provide more information to train the network, which makes the network remember cues from the recent past.

The drawbacks of the architecture are:

1. More connections may result in poor generalization or overtraining. Weight decay or other pruning techniques must be used to prevent overly complex networks. Network architecture size can be estimated follow Baum [1].

2. Training is usually slow. This is because the networks are larger with more weights and inputs to represent time delays.

3   Channel Equalization

In this section, the channel equalization problem is tackled by using different neural network models including our proposed PRTDNN architecture. First, several typical channels are presented, then the network architecture and parameters are discussed. Finally, comparison results are shown.

3.1   Channel Characteristics

The input samples are chosen from $\{-1, 1\}$ with equal probability and are assumed to be independent of one another. The additive noise samples n_i are chosen independently from a Gaussian distribution with mean 0 and variance σ_n^2. The above system has been used to model a variety of communication systems, such as HF communication channels [3]. The task of the equalizer is to recover the transmitted symbols based on the channel observation, with the performance measure being the error probability. For easy comparison, we use the same channels as [3] [10] [2]. The following are the Z-transforms of the channels that we used:

$$A) \quad H(z) = 0.3482 + 0.8704z^{-1} + 0.3482z^{-2} \tag{1}$$

$$B) \quad H(z) = 0.4084 + 0.8164z^{-1} + 0.4084z^{-2} \tag{2}$$

$$C) \quad H(z) = 0.7255 + 0.5804z^{-1} + 0.3627z^{-2} + 0.0724z^{-3} \tag{3}$$

Channel A is a nonminimum phase channel, channel B is a near catastrophic nonminimum phase channel and channel C is a minimum phase channel. A channel is called catastrophic if there exists two infinite length paths that diverge from a state (never remerging) with finite distance in minimum squared Euclidean distance [8]. Channel A has one zero outside the unit circle in the Z-plane. Channel B has two zeros close to the unit circle. All zeros of channel C lies within the unit circle.

All the channel transfer functions are normalized, that is , for transfer function

$$H(Z) = \sum_{i=0}^{n} h_i z^{-i}$$

we have

$$\sum_{i=0}^{n} h_i^2 = 1$$

The signal to noise ratio (SNR) is then given by

$$SNR = 1/\sigma_n^2$$

where σ_n^2 is the noise variance.

The decision device is simply a hard-limiter.

Gibson [3] propose the idea of applying neural networks to the channel equalization problem. He uses a standard three layer feedforward neural network with the backpropagation algorithm as a training algorithm. For minimum phase channels, the neural equalizer performs well in high noise environments. The LTE (Linear Traversal Equalizer) works fine for high SNR. For nonminimum phase channels, the neural equalizer outperforms the LTE because the neural equalizer can form a nonlinear decision boundary. He uses 5-9-3-1 perceptron as an equalizer for channel A. A good method to improve the performance is to introduce feedback. Siu [10] propose the first DFE (Decision Feedback Equalizer) neural network based on Gibson [3]. The same channel is tested by 4-9-3-1 network with one decision feedback. The performance improvement can be seen clearly at high SNR (above 15db). He finds that the MSE decreases as the training samples increase.

Usually, we use 1000 training samples. These papers compare the neural equalizer with conventional LTE or DFE. Better performance can be achieved by MLSE (Maximum-likelihood Sequence Estimation) with a long decision delay. Chen [2] propose a Bayesian neural equalizer using a Radial Basis Function(RBF) architecture. He applied the neural equalizer to channels B and C. The result shows that when the neural equalizer and MLSE with Viterbi algorithm have the same decision delay, the BEPs (Bit Error Probability) are comparable. The MLSE only offers superior performance when it has a long decision delay. In general the Bayesian neural equalizer can not achieve the performance bound set by the MLSE since it is only a symbol-decision equalizer. Based on the above architecture, we apply the time delay neural architecture to all three channels.

3.2 Neural Equalizer Structures and Comparison Result

The network architecture is selected according to channel transfer function and heuristic experimentation.
The activation function for the PRTDNN is

$$\frac{e^x - e^{-x}}{e^x + e^{-x}}$$

The simulation results are shown in Figure (2 - 4). The curves are $Log_{10}BEP$ versus SNR for each channel. The result is quite near the MLSE bound. The BEP for ISI free channel is $Q(1/\sigma)$, $BEP_{DFE} = Q(h_0/\sigma)$, $BEP_{MLSE} = Q(d_{min}/2\sigma)$ where $Q(x) = 1/\sqrt{2\pi} \int_x^\infty e^{-y^2/2} dy$ [2] [8].

For channel A the BEP achieved by PRTDNN is better than that of LTE or MLP(LTE) in Gibson [3] because of the feedback architecture. Results show that the PRTDNN is also better than that of Siu [10] in high SNR. There is 3db gain at BEP= 10^{-4}. Compared with Chen [2], there is 1.5db gain at BEP= 10^{-4}. PRTDNN outperforms other methods for channel A.

For channel B the BEP achieved by PRTDNN and Chen is comparable. In high SNR environments, PRTDNN performs slightly better. For low SNR, both of them approximate the MLSE bound. MLSE need a very long delay to get good performance because of the near catastrophic channel. Conventional DFE does not work well for nonminimum phase channel A and B as shown in Figure 2 and 3.

For channel C the time delay neural equalizer works better than that of Chen [2], but not as good as using the Viterbi algorithm with long decision delay, the MLSE bound. For this channel the conventional DFE works fairly well and usually converges faster than neural equalizers.

The simulation shows for minimum phase channel, the conventional DFE works fine, but for nonminimum phase channel, neural equalizer works better than conventional DFE. The PRTDNN not only considered decision feedback, but also included the temporal relationship between current observation and that of the recent past, which results in it outperforming other methods.

4 Summary

In the paper, we showed a partial recurrent time delay architecture and algorithm. We have explored the use of the proposed algorithm as applied to three channel equalization problems. We compared the performance of the algorithm in terms of Bit Error Probability (BEP). We found that the proposed algorithm works better for channel equalization problems than other neural equalizers. For the sequence reproduction and the sequence recognition problem, examples include channel equalization problems, the partial recurrent architecture is worthy of further investigation. This is because the architectures and algorithms are not very complex as compared to real time recurrent architectures and test results are improved over simple feedforward networks by introducing feedback and delay.

Further research would include optimizing parameters via regularization techniques and testing channels with additive non-Gaussian noise and also channels that are time varying.

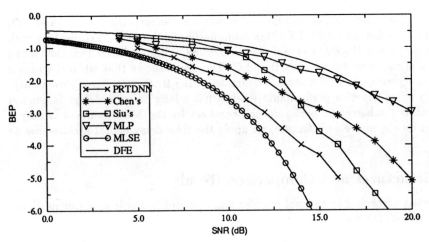

Figure 2: BEP for channel $0.3482 + 0.8704Z^{-1} + 0.3482Z^{-2}$

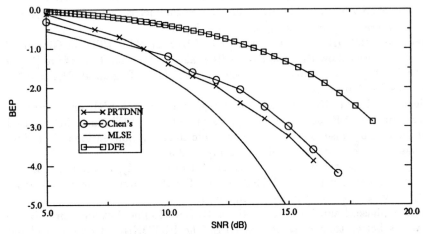

Figure 3: BEP for channel $0.4084 + 0.8164Z^{-1} + 0.4084Z^{-2}$

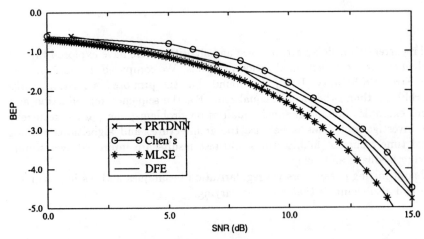

Figure 4: BEP for channel $0.7255 + 0.5804Z^{-1} + 0.3627Z^{-2} + 0.0724Z^{-3}$

References

[1] Baum E. and Haussler D., (1989). "What size net gives valid generalization?" *Neural Computation.*

[2] Chen, S. Mulgrew, B. McLaughlin, S. (1993) "Adaptive bayesian equalizer with decision feedback" *IEEE transactions on signal processing* 41(9) pp 2918

[3] Gibson G, Siu S, Cowan C.F.N (1991) "The application of nonlinear structures to the reconstruction of binary signals" *IEEE transactions on signal processing* 39(8) pp 1877

[4] Jordan, M.I. (1986). "Attractor Dynamics and Parallelism in a Connectionist Sequential Machine," In *Proceedings of the Eighth Annual Conference of the Cognitive Science Society* Amherst (1986), 531-546. Hillsdale: Erlbaum.

[5] Hertz, J., Krogh, A., and Palmer, R.G., (1991) *"Introduction To The Theory Of Neural Computation,"* Addison-Wesley.

[6] Nerrand, O., Roussel-Ragot P, Personnaz L. Dreyfus G. (1993) "Neural networks and nonlinear adaptive filtering: unifying concepts and new algorithms" *Neural Computation* 5, 165-199.

[7] Pearlmutter, B.A. (1989a). "Learning State Space Trajectories in Recurrent Neural Networks" In *International Joint Conference on Neural Networks* (Washington 1989), vol. II, 365-372. New York: IEEE

[8] Proakis, John G. (1989) *Digital communications* New York : McGraw-Hill, McGraw-Hill series in electrical engineering. Communications and signal processing 2nd ed.

[9] Qureshi, S. (1985) "Adaptive equalization" *Proceedings of the IEEE*, 73, (9),1349-1387.

[10] Siu, S. Gibson, G.J. Cowan, C.F.N.(1990) "Network structures and performance comparison with standard architecture" *IEE Proceedings* 137, (4), 221-225.

[11] Waibel A., Hanazawa T., Hinton G.,Shikano K., Lang K, (1989) "Phoneme recognition using time-delay neural networks," *IEEE Trans. on ASSP* 37, (3), 328-339

[12] Wan, E. (1992) "Finite impulse response neural networks for autoregressive time series prediction" *Proceedings of the NATO Advanced Workshop on Time Series Prediction and Analysis,* (Sante Fe, NM, May 14-17 1992) Ed. by A.Weigend and N.Gershenfeld, Addison-Wesley, 1993

[13] Williams, R.J. and D.Zipser (1989a). "A Learning Algorithm for Continually Running Fully Recurrent Neural Networks" *Neural Computation* 1, 270-280.

Image Compression using Multi-layer Perceptron with Block Classification and SOFM Coding

Kwang Bo Cho, Cheol Hoon Park, and Soo-Young Lee
Department of Electrical Engineering,
Korea Advanced Institute of Science and Technology
373-1 Kusong-Dong Yusong-Gu Taejon 305-701, Korea (South)
Tel: +82-42-869-3431 / Fax: +82-42-869-3410 / E-mail: sylee@eekaist.kaist.ac.kr

ABSTRACT: Image compression based on neural networks is presented with block classification and coding. Multilayer perceptron with error back-propagation learning algorithm is used to transform the normalized image data into the compressed hidden values by reducing spatial redundancies. Image compression can basically be achieved with smaller number of hidden neurons than the numbers of input and output neurons. Additionally, the image blocks can be grouped for adaptive compression ratios depending on the characteristics of the complexity of the blocks. The quantized output of the hidden neuron can also be entropy coded or vector quantized for an efficient transmission. Self-organizing featuremap shows better performance than vector quantization. In computer simulation, about 25:1 compression ratio was achieved using the entropy coding without much degradation of the reconstructed images, and about 40-45:1 compression ratio using vector quantization or self-organizing feature map.

1. Introduction

Because of its massive parallelism, global operation, adaptive learning, noise robustness, and generalization property, neural networks is a good candidate in signal processing applications where high computational power is required[1,2]. In particular, some recent contributions of neural networks have been reported for the image data compression applications[1-4].

Multilayer neural networks with error back-propagation learning algorithm are used to transform the image data into the compressed data in the outputs of hidden neurons by the reduction of spatial redundancy[1]. The number of neuron units at the hidden layer is smaller than those of the input and output layers. We propose an adaptive compression method, which classifies image blocks to compress at different ratios according to the characteristics of the blocks for higher compression ratios and good generalization property. Also coding methods of the outputs of the hidden neurons are proposed for more compression and efficient transmission of the compressed image data for reconstruction. Section 2 describes briefly a typical compression method that employs two-layer neural networks and proposed adaptive image compression/reconstruction processes. The proposed method divides image blocks into four classes by the classification algorithm. And the quantized outputs of the hidden neurons can be coded by entropy coding, vector quantization, or self-organizing featuremap(SOFM). Section 3 defines the evaluation criteria and the compression ratio, and section 4 shows computer simulation results. Finally section 5 concludes the paper.

2. Image Compression/Reconstruction by Neural Networks

The image compression/reconstruction architecture based on neural networks is shown in Fig. 1. We use two-layer neural networks, where the hidden neurons are duplicated for data transmission. Data compression can basically be achieved with smaller number of hidden neurons than the numbers of input and output neurons, which are assigned the same values of image data normalized with 8 bits during learning. All outputs of the hidden neurons with sigmoid characteristics are quantized uniformly with 6 bits[1].

The image compression/reconstruction processes are shown in Fig. 2. We use the original images that are divided into 8x8 pixel blocks. First, the block classifier classifies blocks of each image, then each pixel value is normalized and its value is inputted to neural networks. At the transmission channel, hidden values of neural networks are coded by entropy coding , VQ, or SOFM. The processes are reversed for the reconstruction. Now we explain these processes more in detail.

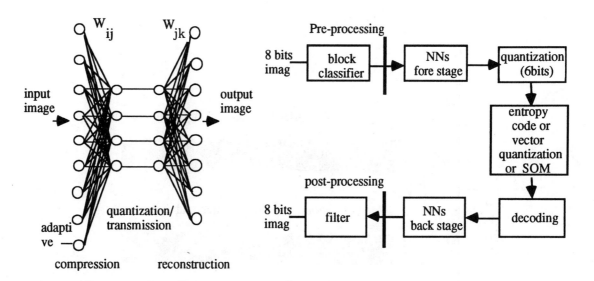

Fig. 1. Neural network architecure for compres-   Fig. 2. Image compression/reconstruction processes.
sion and reconstruction.

2.1 Preprocessing stage - block classifier

The image block classifier is proposed so that compression is carried out by two-layer neural networks with different sizes, of the hidden layers according to the complexity of the blocks. The classification algorithm including gradient calculation and edge detection[4,5] is used with some simplification. The image blocks are classified into four categories: the shade (class 1: no significant gradient), the complicated (class 2: definite mixed edge), the edged (class 3: definite single edge - horizontal, vertical, or diagonal), and the midrange block (class 4: moderate gradient, no edge).

The shade block is based on the well-known fact that intensity changes smaller than the Weber fraction T_s are not visible[5] - this property was proved by Weber's law through psycovisual experiments. Weber's law states that the noticeable difference depends on intensity. So we compressed the Shade block as only one average gray level value. The other blocks are compressed at different ratios with different numbers of hidden neurons. Examples of the classified blocks of the Lena image are shown in Fig. 3.

2.2 Mapping stage - main compression/reconstruction

The values of 8 bit image data are normalized from -1.0 to 1.0 as input values of neural networks. The normalized image block is fed into the input layer on the compression side(fore stage), and reconstructed image block is obtained from the output layer on the reconstruction side(back stage). Class 1 blocks need no neural network, while class 2, 3, and 4 blocks are applied to the corresponding neural networks with the 8, 6, and 4 hidden neurons respectively. All output values of hidden layers are quantized as 6 bits.

2.3 Coding - entropy coding, vector quantization, and self-organizing feature map

The quantized output of the hidden neurons can be coded for more compression by entropy coding, vector quantization or self-organizing feature map. In case of entropy coding, the differential output values of hidden neurons are entropy encoded to achieve lossless compression. One approach is to construct a variable-length code, such as a modified Huffman code[6]. To encode the hidden values with a modified Huffman code, that is matched to the statistics of the differential hidden values, we define the entropy H by

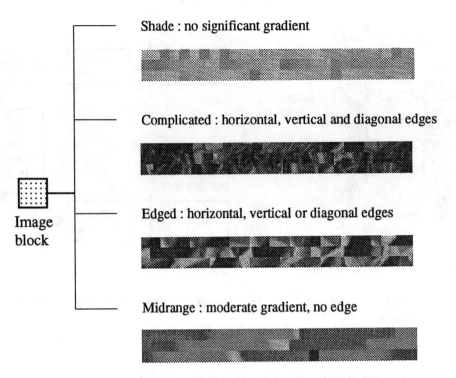

Shade : no significant gradient

Complicated : horizontal, vertical and diagonal edges

Edged : horizontal, vertical or diagonal edges

Midrange : moderate gradient, no edge

Fig. 3. Examples of the classified blocks.

$$H = -\sum_{i=1}^{L} p_i \log_2 p_i \qquad (4)$$

where P_i is the probability that the message will be the ith value. Since $\sum_{i=1}^{L} p_i = 1$, it can be shown that $0 \le H \le \log_2 L$. From the information theory, the entropy H in (4) is the theoretically minimum possible average bit ratio required for coding a message. Supposing the average bit ratio using the codewords that we have designed is the same as the entropy[7], we use entropy coding in simulation.

In vector quantization(VQ), the hidden neuron activations are decomposed into n-dimensional vectors. These n x 1 hidden vectors are vector quantized according to the codebook. The LBG algorithm was used in training the vector quantizers[8].

In self-organizing feature map (SOFM), the hidden neuron activations of the two-layer neural networks are input vectors of the SOFM. Once the SOFM has been trained, the weight vectors will be organized into an approximation of the distribution function of the input vectors. This is compared as VQ. The hybrid structure using MLP and SOFM is shown in Fig. 4.

2.4 Postprocessing - filter

When the compression ratio is very high, the boundaries of adjacent blocks become quite distinguishable, which is called the blocking effect due to independent coding of each block. To reduce the blocking effect one usually filters the image after reconstruction[7]. A low pass filter is used to improve the quality of reconstructed images and typically applied only at or near the block boundaries to avoid unnecessary image blurring. We don't use, however, this postprocessing in simulation for the comparison of compression performance.

As a summary, the compression processes have two coding schemes:(1) lossy coding using neural networks which is a quantization of hidden neuron activations, and (2) lossless coding using an entropy code with the differences of hidden values or lossy coding using VQ or SOFM.

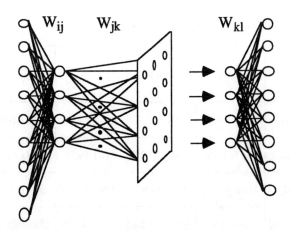

Fig. 4. Hybrid structure using MLP and SOFM.

3. Evaluation Criteria and Compression Ratio

We make use of mean-squared error(MSE) and peak signal-to-noise ratio(PSNR) as error measure of reconstruction.

$$MSE = \frac{1}{N^2} \sum_{x=0}^{N-1} \sum_{y=0}^{N-1} e^2(x,y) \tag{5}$$

$$PSNR = 10\log(\frac{\sum 255^2}{\sum e^2}) \tag{6}$$

The compression ratio(*CR*) without and with entropy coding are measured by equations (7) and (8).

$$CR = \frac{1}{block\#} \sum_{block} (\frac{N^2 \times N_i}{H \times N_h + \log_2 class\#}) \tag{7}$$

$$CR_{entropy} = \frac{1}{block\#} \sum_{block} (\frac{N^2 \times N_i}{H \times entropy + \log_2 class\#}) \tag{8}$$

where N^2 is block size and H is the number of hidden neurons, N_i and N_h are the numbers of bits used in the input and hidden layers, respectively. In vector quantization, CR_{vq} is calculated from the entropy in the Shade blocks, code size in the vector quantizer, and code for classifying class. In self-organizing featuremap, CR_{som} is calculated from the entropy in the Shade blocks, the size of output neurons for SOFM, and code for classifying class.

4. Simulation Results

In simulation, four images of 8 bit gray levels, i.e. Lena, Bridge, Boat, and Train, are used. At first we had tried the simple neural networks approach without any coding, which are trained by the Lena image and tested by the other three images. We try two cases with 8 hidden neurons and 4 hidden neurons which give about 10:1 and 21:1 compression ratio, respectively. Because the Bridge image is very complicated, PSNR is very low.

Now let's look at performance improvements by added features at the presented architectures. The class distribution for each image is shown in Table 1. For example, about 6% blocks are Shade blocks in the Lena image. We note the Bridge image is the most complicated with about 58% of Complicated blocks.

At the second experiments, the neural networks are trained by the classified blocks of the Lena image and tested by the other three images and the entropy is calculated from 6 bit output values of hidden neurons.

Table 1. Class Distribution of each image.

Image class	Lena	Bridge	Boat	Train
1 (Shade)	259 (6.3%)	46 (1.1%)	541 (13.2%)	203 (4.9%)
2 (Complicated)	586 (14.3%)	2366 (57.8%)	814 (19.9%)	339 (8.3%)
3 (Edged)	576 (14.1%)	734 (17.9%)	829 (20.2%)	987 (24.1%)
4 (Midranged)	2675 (65.3%)	950 (23.2%)	1912 (46.7%)	2567 (62.7%)

Shade blocks need no neural network, while the Complicated, Edged, and Midrange blocks are applied to the corresponding neural networks with 8, 6, and 4 hidden neurons, respectively. We get about 25:1 compression ratio without much degradation.

At the third experiment, the same neural networks are used, but values of hidden activations are quantized using vector quantization. For learning of the vector quantizer of 1024 codewords of each class, we use the standard LBG algorithm in training vector quantizer with the hidden values of the Lena and Bridge images.

At the fourth experiment, we use SOFM instead of VQ. The size of input vectors is the same as VQ. The number of output neurons is 1024. Simuation results are shown in Table 2.

Table 2. Results with Block Classification and SOFM Coding

Image	MSE		PSNR: (dB)		Compression Ratio (CR $_{som}$)	
	class 2 4 x 1	class 2 8 x 1	class 2 4 x 1	class 2 8 x 1	(class 2 : 4 x 1)	(class 2 : 8 x 1)
Trained Lena	79.77	89.89	29.112	28.594	39.04:1 (0.20 bpp)	43.82:1 (0.18 bpp)
Trained Bridge	299.99	325.06	23.360	23.011	28.90:1 (0.28 bpp)	42.87:1 (0.19 bpp)
Boat	141.39	162.64	26.627	26.016	38.42:1 (0.21 bpp)	45.15:1 (0.18 bpp)
Train	75.34	89.78	29.361	29.004	40.70:1 (0.20 bpp)	43.57:1 (0.18 bpp)

The major advantage of this approach is its good performancefor un-trained images, and the image compression using the block classifier and coding is more effective at high compression ratio. All the simulation results for the Lena image are summarized in Fig. 5. N is neural networks, E is entropy coding, B is block classifier, V is vector quantization, and SOFM is self-organizing map. In this figure, the JPEG(Joint Photographic Expert Group)[10] is very good, below 30:1 compression ratio, but performance drops very rapidly for higer compression. Interpolative/Residual VQ(I/RVQ)[10] can achieve higher compression ratio, but its PSNR is not good. Although performance of the simple neural network approach is very limited, better performance may be achieved by block classification and coding based on vector quantization and SOFM.

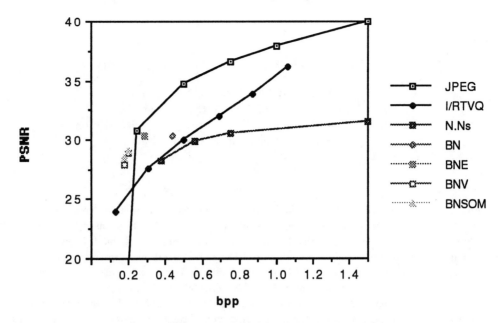

Fig.5 PSNR vs. bpp (bit per pixel) for the Lena image

6. Conclusion

In this paper, we present a new method of image compression and reconstruction using neural networks, block classification, entropy coding, VQ, and SOFM. We got about 25:1 compression ratio without much degradation of the reconstructed images in entropy coding and about 40-45:1 compression ratio with some degradation in VQ or SOFM. Also we propose hybrid model with MLP and SOFM which shows good performance in high compression ratio region. As future work, we are concerned with color image compression and video coding using neural networks.

Acknowledgement: This research was supported by Korean Ministry of Science and Technology through Korea Advanced Institute of Science and Technology.

REFERENCES

[1] N. Sonehara, M. Kawato, S. Miyake, and K. Nakane, "Image Data Compression Using a Neural network Model," *IJCNN*, vol.2, pp. 35-40, Washington, 1989.

[2] C.H. Park, "Neuro-fuzzy information processing," *Proc. of 91' Korean Scientist and Engineer Summer Symposium*, pp. 90-94, Seoul, Korea, 1991.

[3] F.Arduini,S.Fioravanti and D.Giusto, "Adaptive Image Coding using Multilayer neural Networks," *ICASSP*, vol.2, pp. 381-384, San Francisco, 1992.

[4] K.B. Cho, C.H. Park, and S.Y. Lee,"Classified Image Compression and Coding using Neural Networks," *Proc. of APCC*, pp. 414-417, Taejon, Korea, 1993.

[5] B.Ramamurthi and A.Gersho,"Classified Vector Quantization of Images," *IEEE Trans. Commun.*, vol.34, Nov. 1986.

[6] M. Rabbani and P. W. Jones, *Digital Compression Techniques*, SPIE, Washington, 1991.

[7] J. S. Lim, *Two-Dimensional Signal and Image Processing*, Prentice-Hall, USA, 1990.

[8] Y. Linde, A. Buzo, and R. Gray, "An Algorithm for Vector Quantizer Design," *IEEE Trans. Commun.*, vol. COM-28, no. 1, pp. 84-95, Jan. 1980.

[9] C. H. Park and K. B. Cho, "Image Compression using Neural Networks and Sub-sampling," *JNNS*, Iizuka, Japan, Aug. 1993.

[10] M. Rabbani and P.W. Jones, *Digital Compression Techniques*, SPIE, Washington, 1991.

On the convergence of the Least Mean Squares algorithm to rational expectations equilibria

Emilio Barucci†   Leonardo Landi‡

†DIMADEFAS, Università di Firenze
Via C. Lombroso 6/17, 50134 Firenze, Italy.
‡Dipartimento di Sistemi e Informatica, Università di Firenze
Via S. Marta 3, 50139 Firenze, Italy.

Abstract

We study the convergence of the *Least Mean Squares* learning algorithm in *self-referential linear stochastic* models when agents form their expectations according to a misspecified version of the model itself. The law of motion *perceived* by the agents influences the *actual* law of motion of the model. In this framework, agents experience a learning activity by which they update their estimates. The so called *rational expectations equilibrium* is obtained if agents take their expectations consistently with the "true" model. We assume that agents update their estimates by a "modified" *Least Mean Squares* learning algorithm. The convergence of this algorithm to the *rational expectations equilibria* of the model is analyzed and a general convergence result is obtained. The point to which the algorithm converges is dependent on the strength of the noise signal which affects the model and on the characteristics of the function which weighs the noise signal itself. The main difference with respect to similar studies about convergence of learning mechanisms to *rational expectations equilibria* in *self-referential linear stochastic* models, lies in the algorithm that is not the *Ordinary Least Squares* usually adopted in the literature.

1 Introduction

In this paper, we address an interesting problem in economic theory: the interaction between the evolution of a *Self-Referential Linear Stochastic* (SRLS) model dependent on agents' beliefs and a learning process for the agents based on a misspecified version of the model itself.

If the agents know the "true" model, then, the *Rational Expectations Equilibrium* (REE) is the solution of the system. At the REE, agents use optimally their private information consistently with the "true" model and the expectation errors conditioned on the available information set, have zero mean. If the agents form their expectations by a misspecified model, then expectation errors have not zero mean and a learning activity takes place.

In the literature [1], it has been assumed that agents believe in a linear model, characterized by the parameter matrix $\mathcal{B}$, and that they update their estimates by the means of the *Recursive Ordinary Least Squares* (ROLS) algorithm. In [1], it has been proved that, with the ROLS mechanism, the convergence is always to the REE point but that it is guaranteed only for a restricted set of functions and parameters of the model.

In this study, we assume that agents update their estimates by a "modified" version of the *Least Mean Squares* (LMS) algorithm [2]. We analyze the convergence of the LMS algorithm for a general class of SRLS models. Inside this framework, it is necessary to modify the "classical" LMS algorithm by using a decreasing learning factor. Convergence is proved by deriving the ordinary differential equation associated with the "modified" LMS updating rule, see [3]. The convergence is *in probability*. We prove that the "modified" LMS algorithm converges to an equilibrium point of the differential equation but that such point can differ from the REE according both to the strength of the noise signal and to the type of function which weighs the noise signal itself inside the SRLS model.

The paper is organized as follows. In section 2, SRLS models are briefly described. In section 3, the LMS algorithm is applied to this framework. Then, convergence results are discussed.

2   Self-referential linear stochastic models

Following [1], we denote with two subvectors of $z_t \in \Re^n$, not necessarily disjoint, the set of variables that the agents are interested in, i.e., $z_{1t} \in \Re^{n_1}$, and the set of variables, i.e., $z_{2t} \in \Re^{n_2}$, that the agents think are relevant to predict the variables in z_{1t}.

In the literature, the linear law of motion for z_{1t} *perceived* by the agents, at time t, is usually described by:

$$z_{1t}^e = \mathcal{B}_t^T z_{2(t-1)} + \mu_t \tag{1}$$

where $\mathcal{B}_t \in \Re^{n_2 \times n_1}$ is the parameter matrix representing the *perceived* law of motion of z_{1t} and $\mu_t \in \Re^{n_1}$ is a noise vector. The agents' beliefs in (1) cause the *actual* law of motion for the entire vector z_t to be given, in a general setting, by:

$$z_t = \begin{bmatrix} z_{1t} \\ z_{1t}^c \end{bmatrix} = \begin{bmatrix} 0 & T(\mathcal{B}_t)^T \\ & A(\mathcal{B}_t)^T \end{bmatrix} \cdot \begin{bmatrix} z_{2(t-1)}^c \\ z_{2(t-1)} \end{bmatrix} + \begin{bmatrix} V(\mathcal{B}_t)^T \\ B(\mathcal{B}_t)^T \end{bmatrix} \cdot u_t \tag{2}$$

where the superscript c expresses the complement with respect to z_t, $u_t \in \Re^n$ is a stationary white noise, $T(\mathcal{B}_t)$ is the application which, given $\mathcal{B}_t$, describes the *actual* law of motion for z_{1t} at time t, i.e., $T : \mathcal{B}_t \to T(\mathcal{B}_t) \in \Re^{n_2 \times n_1}$. The function $V(\mathcal{B}_t)$ modulates the noise term in the SRLS model according to the agents' estimations represented by $\mathcal{B}_t$, $V : \mathcal{B}_t \to V(\mathcal{B}_t) \in \Re^{n \times n_1}$. The other applications are defined as:

$$A : \mathcal{B}_t \to A(\mathcal{B}_t) \in \Re^{n \times n_2}, \ B : \mathcal{B}_t \to B(\mathcal{B}_t) \in \Re^{n \times n_2}.$$

Note that the agents' estimation which is represented by $\mathcal{B}_t$ in (1), defines together with the features of the model, the *actual* law of motion in (2).

A REE of the SRLS model in (2) is a fixed point of the application $T(\mathcal{B})$, i.e., $\mathcal{B}^*$ such that $T(\mathcal{B}^*) = \mathcal{B}^*$.

The data generating process in (2) does not imply that z_t is a stationary stochastic process. Although the LMS learning algorithm has been applied also in non-stationary environments [4], we restrict our study to the stationary case. Let us define the set D_s where the SRLS model (2) is a stationary stochastic process.

$$D_s = \{\mathcal{B} \in \Re^{n_2 \times n_1} \,|\text{the eigenvalues, i.e., } \lambda_i, \text{ of}$$
$$\begin{bmatrix} 0 & T(\mathcal{B})^T \\ & A(\mathcal{B})^T \end{bmatrix}$$
$$\text{are less than unity in absolute value, i.e., } |\lambda_i| < 1\}$$

In the literature, the algorithm used to update the estimates of the parameter $\mathcal{B}$ is the ROLS, see [1]. Convergence of such algorithm to the REE of the SRLS model has been analyzed using the ordinary differential equation associated with the ROLS updating rule, following [3]. It has been proved that agents succeed in reaching the REE of (2) when the ordinary differential equation is stable, see [1]. Let us remark that the ROLS algorithm is not sensitive neither to the noise term u_t nor to the type of function $V(\mathcal{B})$ which weighs the noise signal itself.

In the following, a similar procedure will be used to prove the convergence of the "modified" LMS algorithm.

3   The Least Mean Squares algorithm in self-referential linear stochastic models

The ROLS mechanism has been used to update agent estimates because it guarantees a good performance being the "Best Linear Unbiased Estimator". However, the agents' model is misspecified inside the SRLS framework. An alternative learning procedure deriving from the engineering literature on the adaptive signal processing, is the LMS algorithm [2]. In order to apply such mechanism to the SRLS framework and to use it as a learning mechanism for the agents to update the parameters $\mathcal{B}$, it is necessary to define how agents estimate the vector of variables z_{1t}.

We define the following linear *perceived* law of motion for the agents:

$$z_{1t}^e = \mathcal{B}_t^T z_{2(t-1)} . \tag{3}$$

Let us remark that (3) represents a deterministic *perceived* law of motion and does not include a noise component as (1). However, a stochastic component in (3) does not affect the convergence analysis carried out below.

In order to apply the LMS algorithm to the SRLS model, the *instantaneous* error $\varepsilon_t \in \Re^{n_1}$ shall be computed, i.e., $\varepsilon_t = z_{1t}^e - z_{1t}$, where:

- z_{1t}^e is the forecasted value of z_{1t} by the means of (3),
- z_{1t} is the *actual* law of motion generated by (2) as $z_{1t} = T(\mathcal{B}_t)^T z_{2(t-1)} + V(\mathcal{B}_t)^T u_t$.

Let us define $\beta_i \in \Re^{n_2}$ the i-th column of the parameter matrix $\mathcal{B}$. Let us express the functions $T(\cdot)$ and $V(\cdot)$ when evaluated at β_i, for $i = 1, \ldots, n_1$: $T_i : \beta_i \to T_i(\beta_i) \in \Re^{n_2}$ is the i-th column vector of the matrix $T(\mathcal{B})$ and $V_i : \beta_i \to V_i(\beta_i) \in \Re^n$ is the i-th column vector of the matrix $V(\mathcal{B})$.

The LMS algorithm updates the parameter matrix $\mathcal{B}$ to minimize the *Mean Square Error* (MSE) related to the SRLS model in (2). The MSE is given by the mean value, taken over time, of the square of the *instantaneous* error ε_t. Let us fix the parameter matrix, i.e., drop the subscript t. Because it has been assumed that $E\{\varepsilon_{t_i} \varepsilon_{t_j}\} = 0$ for $i \neq j$, then the MSE, expressed by $\xi(\mathcal{B})$, has its i-th component equal to $\xi_i(\beta_i) = E\{\varepsilon_{t_i}^2\} = E\{(z_{1t_i} - z_{1t_i}^e)^2\}$. Using the agents' estimations in (3) the i-th MSE is expressed as

$$\xi_i(\beta_i) = E\{z_{1t_i}^2\} + \beta_i^T E\{z_{2(t-1)} z_{2(t-1)}^T\}\beta_i - 2E\{z_{1t_i} z_{2(t-1)}^T\}\beta_i , \quad i = 1, \ldots, n_1 .$$

Let us introduce the matrices $M_{z_{2t}}(\beta_i) = E\{z_{2(t-1)} z_{2(t-1)}^T\} \in \Re^{n_2 \times n_2}$, $M_{u_t} = E\{u_t u_t^T\} \in \Re^{n \times n}$ and $C_t(\beta_i) = E\{u_t z_{2(t-1)}^T\} \in \Re^{n \times n_2}$. Because of the restriction to stationary stochastic processes, the statistics of the process z_t and u_t are time invariant, i.e., $M_{z_{2t}}(\beta_i) = M_{z_2}(\beta_i)$, $M_{u_t} = M_u$ and $C_t(\beta_i) = C(\beta_i)$ for $\mathcal{B} \in D_s$. Note that the assumption $C(\beta_i) = 0$, usually done in economics, implies that the MSE function is given by the sum of two quadratic forms:

$$\xi_i(\beta_i) = (T_i(\beta_i) - \beta_i)^T M_{z_2}(\beta_i) (T_i(\beta_i) - \beta_i) + V_i(\beta_i)^T M_u V_i(\beta_i) , \quad i = 1, \ldots, n_1 . \tag{4}$$

Depending on functions $T(\cdot)$ and $V(\cdot)$, the function $\xi_i(\beta_i)$ can have more than one *global* maximum/minimum, *local* maximum/minimum and *saddle* points. Note that a REE is a minimum for the first quadratic form in (4) but is not necessarily a minimum of the MSE function.

We have to remark that the LMS algorithm looks for *minima* and *saddle* points of the MSE function that can be not *global* minimum. In order to compute the *stationary* points of the MSE function, let us evaluate the gradient of the i-th MSE component. The gradient of the i-th MSE function is:

$$\nabla \xi_i(\beta_i) = 2 \left(\frac{\partial T_i(\beta_i)}{\partial \beta_i} - I \right)^T M_{z_2}(\beta_i) (T_i(\beta_i) - \beta_i) + 2 \frac{\partial V_i(\beta_i)}{\partial \beta_i}^T M_u V_i(\beta_i) , \quad i = 1, \ldots, n_1 .$$

As a result, β_i^* such that $\beta_i^* = T_i(\beta_i^*)$ is not necessarily a *critical* point of the i-th MSE surface.

If the noise component of the model u_t, which agents do not take into account in their signal extraction activity, enters directly the model and is weighed by a constant function $V(\mathcal{B})$ which is not dependent on their beliefs, then a REE is a minimum of the MSE. Otherwise, if the noise term enters the SRLS model weighed by the function $V(\mathcal{B})$, i.e., $V(\mathcal{B})^T u_t$, which depends on the agents' estimate $\mathcal{B}$, then the minimum of the MSE, depending on the noise component, is different from the REE. In this case, the LMS learning mechanism is not able to reach the REE but deviates to a non-REE.

Let us remark that the LMS algorithm always converges to a point that can be either a non-REE or a REE, depending on the net noise signal. On the contrary, the ROLS algorithm can also diverge regardless the characteristics of the net noise signal.

In [5], we have proved the convergence *on average* of the LMS algorithm to the REE when applied to SRLS models where $T(\cdot)$ is a linear function of $\mathcal{B}$ and $V(\cdot)$ is independent of $\mathcal{B}$. To analyze the convergence of the LMS learning algorithm for a more general class of SRLS models, we have to restrict the attention to the convergence *in probability* by applying the framework introduced by Ljung [3]. Moreover, the "classical" LMS algorithm is modified by assuming a decreasing learning factor γ_t instead of a fixed η.

In the following, the reasons that cause the "classical" LMS algorithm not to converge *on average* in a more general class of SRLS models, are briefly sketched. Then, the LMS algorithm is modified and the convergence to the minimum of the MSE is proved.

Let us recall the LMS expression used to update the i-th parameter column β_{t_i} [2],

$$\beta_{t+1_i} = \beta_{t_i} - 2\eta\varepsilon_{t_i}\frac{\partial\varepsilon_{t_i}}{\partial\beta_{t_i}} \ , \quad i = 1,\ldots,n_1 \tag{5}$$

where η is a positive constant such that $\eta \in \Re$, $\varepsilon_{t_i} \in \Re$ is the *instantaneous* error, i.e., $\varepsilon_{t_i} = z_{1t_i} - z_{1t_i}^e$ and $\frac{\partial\varepsilon_{t_i}}{\partial\beta_{t_i}} \in \Re^{n_2}$. Recalling the SRLS model in (2), then the derivative of the *instantaneous* error is given by:

$$\frac{\partial\varepsilon_{t_i}}{\partial\beta_{t_i}} = \left(\frac{\partial T_i(\beta_{t_i})}{\partial\beta_{t_i}} - I\right)^T \cdot z_{2(t-1)} + \frac{\partial V_i(\beta_{t_i})}{\partial\beta_{t_i}}^T \cdot u_t \ , \quad i = 1,\ldots,n_1 \ .$$

As a result the "classical" LMS updating rule for the SRLS model in (2), is given by:

$$\begin{aligned}
\beta_{t+1_i} &= \beta_{t_i} - 2\eta\left(T_i(\beta_{t_i}) - \beta_{t_i}\right)^T z_{2(t-1)} \cdot \left[\left(\frac{\partial T_i(\beta_{t_i})}{\partial\beta_{t_i}} - I\right)^T z_{2(t-1)} + \frac{\partial V_i(\beta_{t_i})}{\partial\beta_{t_i}}^T u_t\right]\\
&\quad - 2\eta V_i(\beta_{t_i})^T u_t \cdot \left[\left(\frac{\partial T_i(\beta_{t_i})}{\partial\beta_{t_i}} - I\right)^T z_{2(t-1)} + \frac{\partial V_i(\beta_{t_i})}{\partial\beta_{t_i}}^T u_t\right] \ , \quad i = 1,\ldots,n_1 \ .
\end{aligned} \tag{6}$$

The rule in (6) updates the parameter β_{t_i} according to two terms: one includes the product $(T_i(\beta_{t_i}) - \beta_{t_i})^T z_{2(t-1)}$ and the other includes $V_i(\beta_i)^T u_t$. Let us subtract from both sides of (6) the value of the REE point β_i^*. Let us take the average of the resulting terms, assuming, for example, that both $V(\cdot)$ and $T(\cdot)$ are linear functions of $\mathcal{B}$ so that their derivatives are constants and assuming that $\mathcal{B}$ is independent of z_2 and u_t.

$$\begin{aligned}
E\{\beta_{t+1_i} - \beta_i^*\} &= E\{\beta_{t_i} - \beta_i^*\} - 2\eta\left(\frac{\partial T_i(\beta_{t_i})}{\partial\beta_{t_i}} - I\right)^T M_{z_2}(\beta_i)E\left\{T_i(\beta_{t_i}) - \beta_{t_i}\right\}\\
&\quad - 2\eta\frac{\partial V_i(\beta_{t_i})}{\partial\beta_{t_i}}^T M_u E\{V_i(\beta_{t_i})\} \ , \quad i = 1,\ldots,n_1 \ .
\end{aligned}$$

Let us analyze such expression as $t \to \infty$. It can be noted that two series arise. The first one, originated from the signal z_{2t} vanishes while parameters β_i converge to the REE while the second one, which includes the noise term, does not vanish but takes the parameter $\mathcal{B}$ away from the REE making the overall process diverging *on average*, from the REE.

In order to use the LMS algorithm as agents' learning mechanism in SRLS models where the function $V(\cdot)$ is dependent on $\mathcal{B}$, it is necessary to modify the "classical" LMS updating rule which assumes η a positive constant, with the following "modified" LMS rule where η has been substituted with γ_t which is a decreasing function as $t \to \infty$. The decreasing positive values given by γ_t are used to reject the noisy observations. Let us modify the LMS learning algorithm defining the parameter matrix $\bar{\mathcal{B}} = \{\bar{\beta}_i, i = 1,\ldots,n_1\}$ as follows:

$$\bar{\beta}_{t+1_i} = \beta_{t_i} - 2\gamma_{t+1}\varepsilon_{t_i}\frac{\partial\varepsilon_{t_i}}{\partial\beta_{t_i}} \ , \quad i = 1,\ldots,n_1 \ . \tag{7}$$

As a consequence, the "modified" LMS algorithm in (7), when applied to the SRLS model in (2), reduces to the following updating rule:

$$\begin{aligned}
\bar{\beta}_{t+1_i} &= \beta_{t_i} - 2\gamma_{t+1}\left[\left(\frac{\partial T_i(\beta_{t_i})}{\partial\beta_{t_i}} - I\right)^T z_{2(t-1)}z_{2(t-1)}^T\left(T_i(\beta_{t_i}) - \beta_{t_i}\right)\right.\\
&\quad + \left(\frac{\partial T_i(\beta_{t_i})}{\partial\beta_{t_i}} - I\right)^T z_{2(t-1)}u_t^T V_i(\beta_{t_i}) + \frac{\partial V_i(\beta_{t_i})}{\partial\beta_{t_i}}^T u_t z_{2(t-1)}^T\left(T_i(\beta_{t_i}) - \beta_{t_i}\right)\\
&\quad \left. + \frac{\partial V_i(\beta_{t_i})}{\partial\beta_{t_i}}^T u_t u_t^T V_i(\beta_{t_i})\right]
\end{aligned} \tag{8}$$

According to [3], let the sets D_2 be closed and D_1 open and bounded with $D_2, D_1 \subset \Re^{n_2 \times n_1}$ and $D_2 \subset D_1 \subset D_s$. The final algorithm for generating beliefs $\mathcal{B}_t = \{\beta_{t_i}, i = 1,\ldots,n_1\}$ is:

$$\mathcal{B}_{t+1} = \begin{cases} \bar{\mathcal{B}}_{t+1} & \text{if } \bar{\mathcal{B}}_{t+1} \in D_1 \\ \text{some value in } D_2 & \text{if } \bar{\mathcal{B}}_{t+1} \notin D_1 \end{cases} \tag{9}$$

The most natural candidate for "some value in D_2" is $\mathcal{B}_{t'}$ where t' is the last time that the parameter $\mathcal{B} \in D_2$, but any other point in D_2 is acceptable. When $D_2 = D_1 = \Re^{n_2 \times n_1}$, then $\bar{\mathcal{B}} = \mathcal{B}$ for all t.

Besides the decreasing learning factor γ_t, the "modified" algorithm defined by (8-9) deviates from that in (6) because it invokes a "projection facility" (9) that prevents the estimator from ever leaving the set determined by D_1. In this way, the observations that drive $\mathcal{B}$ outside of D_1 are ignored. The "projection facility" is used as to verify more easily the hypotheses used in the Ljung's framework, see [3].

In order to study the convergence of such algorithm, we apply the method suggested by Ljung in [3]. Accordingly, we compute the differential equation associated with (8-9). Using matrices $M_{z_2}(\beta_i)$ and M_u, it is given by:

$$\frac{d\beta_i}{dt} = -2\left[\left(\frac{\partial T_i(\beta_i)}{\partial \beta_i} - I\right)^T M_{z_2}(\beta_i)\left(T_i(\beta_i) - \beta_i\right) + \frac{\partial V_i(\beta_i)}{\partial \beta_i}^T M_u V_i(\beta_i)\right] \, , \quad i = 1, \dots, n_1 \, . \quad (10)$$

Let us define the set D_a as the "domain of attraction" of the equilibrium point of the differential equation in (10) that is a minimum point ($\mathcal{B}^{min}$) of the MSE. In order to prove the convergence of the "modified" LMS learning mechanism in (8-9) by the means of the associated differential equation in (10), the following assumptions on the model in (2) are employed. These conditions have been stated following the guidelines in [1] as to satisfy hypothesis of Theorem 1 in [3] on the convergence of recursive algorithms.

A.1 The ordinary differential equation has a unique fixed point $\mathcal{B}^{min}$,

A.2 $T(\cdot)$ and $V(\cdot)$ are twice differentiable, and $A(\cdot)$, $B(\cdot)$ have one derivative in D_s,

A.3 the covariance matrices M_{z_2} and M_u are nonsingular,

A.4 for all t, $\gamma_t > 0$ and $\gamma_t \to 0$ as $t \to \infty$,

A.5 the vector u_t consists of n stationary random variables, u_t is serially independent. Further $E\{|u_{i_t}|^p\} < \infty$ for all $p > 1$, for $i = 1, \dots n$.

A.6 Suppose that there exist an event Ω_0 with $P(\Omega_0) = 1$ such that for each $\omega \in \Omega_0$ there is one random variable $C_1(\omega)$ and a subsequence $\{t_k(\omega)\}$ such that $\forall \, t_k(\omega) \, |z_{2_{t_k}}| < C_1(\omega)$.

A.7 Let D_2 be a closed set and D_1 be an open and bounded set, with $D_2 \subset D_1 \subset D_s$. Assume that the trajectories of the ordinary differential equation with initial condition $\mathcal{B}_0 = \{\beta_{0_i}, i = 1, \dots, n_1\} \in D_2$ never leave a closed subset of D_1.

Assumption $A.1$ is made solely to simplify the demonstration. From [3], it is clear that our results can be extended to a model with multiple minima of the MSE.

Proposition 3.1 *Let $\mathcal{B}$ be given by the learning mechanism in (8-9). Let $\mathcal{B}^{min}$ be unique point of attraction of the ordinary differential equation in (10) and let D_a be the domain of attraction of $\mathcal{B}^{min}$. Let the initial condition $\mathcal{B}_0$ be in D_2. Assume A.1 to A.7 are satisfied. If*

$$D_1 \subset D_a, \text{ so that } D_2 \subset D_1 \subset \left(D_s \bigcap D_a\right)$$

then $\mathcal{B} \to \mathcal{B}^{min}$ with probability one as $t \to \infty$.

Proof. In order to prove the proposition above, we use Theorem 1 in [3]. Moreover, let us refer to the assumptions $B.1$–$B.11$ in [3]. Note that:

- assumptions $B.1$ and $B.2$ in [3] are implied by our $A.5$,
- assumptions $B.3$, $B.4$ and $B.5$ in [3] are implied by the smoothness assumptions on $T(\cdot)$, $A(\cdot)$, $B(\cdot)$ and $V(\cdot)$ in our $A.2$,
- assumption $B.6$ in [3] is satisfied because the following limits exist:

$$\lim_{t\to\infty} E\left\{\left[(T_i(\beta_i) - \beta_i)^T z_{2(t-1)} + V_i(\beta_i)^T u_t\right]^T \cdot \left(\frac{\partial T_i(\beta_i)}{\partial \beta_i} - I\right)^T z_{2(t-1)}\right\} =$$
$$= \left(\frac{\partial T_i(\beta_i)}{\partial \beta_i} - I\right)^T M_{z_2}(\beta_i)\left(T_i(\beta_i) - \beta_i\right)$$
$$\lim_{t\to\infty} E\left\{\left[(T_i(\beta_i) - \beta_i)^T z_{2(t-1)} + V_i(\beta_i)^T u_t\right]^T \cdot \frac{\partial V_i(\beta_i)}{\partial \beta_i}^T u_t\right\} =$$
$$= \frac{\partial V_i(\beta_i)}{\partial \beta_i}^T M_u(\beta_i) V_i(\beta_i)$$

where β_i is fixed and z_{2t} is evaluated for a solution of the difference equation.

- Assumption $B.7$ is implied by our $A.5$ and $A.2$ where the Lipschitz constants $\mathcal{K}_1$ and $\mathcal{K}_2$ in [3] are, respectively the norms of the first and second derivatives of

$$\left[\left(\frac{\partial T_i(\beta_{t_i})}{\partial \beta_{t_i}} - I\right)^T z_{2(t-1)} z_{2(t-1)}^T \left(T_i(\beta_{t_i}) - \beta_{t_i}\right) + \left(\frac{\partial T_i(\beta_{t_i})}{\partial \beta_{t_i}} - I\right)^T z_{2(t-1)} u_t^T V_i(\beta_{t_i})\right.$$
$$\left. + \frac{\partial V_i(\beta_{t_i})}{\partial \beta_{t_i}}^T u_t z_{2(t-1)}^T \left(T_i(\beta_{t_i}) - \beta_{t_i}\right) + \frac{\partial V_i(\beta_{t_i})}{\partial \beta_{t_i}}^T u_t u_t^T V_i(\beta_{t_i})\right]$$

with respect to β_i and z_{2t}.

- Finally assumptions $B.8$ to $B.11$ are implied by our $A.4$.

Finally if $A.7$ is satisfied, then since $z_{1t} = T_i(\beta_{t_i})^T z_{2(t-1)} + V_i(\beta_{t_i})^T u_t$ it follows that there exists a subsequence of $\{t_k\}$ such that $|z_{1t_k}|$, $|z_{2t_k}|$ and $\beta_{t_{k_i}}$ are bounded along this subsequence; therefore (20) in [3] is satisfied and we can apply the Theorem 1, which states the convergence of the solution of the differential equation associated with a general recursive stochastic algorithm. $\square$

Note that proposition 3.1 does not cover the case in which, at some points on the boundary of D_1, trajectories of (10) point away from the interior of D_1. Trajectories that leave D_1, are not allowed to do so by the virtue of the "projection facility" in (9). In order to comply with this fact the following corollary is stated.

Corollary 3.1 *Assume that $A.1$-$A.6$ are satisfied, $\beta_i \in D_1 \subset D_s$, and that D_1 is open and bounded. Assume that $D_1 \subset D_a$. Given that:*

$$P_1 = P(\beta_i \to \beta_i^*)$$
$$P_2 = P(\beta_{t_{k_i}} \to (D_1 - D_2) \text{ for a subsequence } \{t_k(\omega)\})$$

then $P_1 + P_2 = 1$.

Proof. Elementary. $\square$

There is an important class of models in which it is possible to verify analytically the required behaviour of the trajectories of the ordinary differential equation (10) at the boundary of D_1. These classes are those for which z_2 is exogenous in the sense that $A(\cdot)$ and $B(\cdot)$ in (2) are independent of $\mathcal{B}$. Note that in this case $M_{z_2}(\beta_i) = M_{z_2}$.

4 Conclusions

We have studied the convergence of a "modified" version of the LMS algorithm to the REE of SRLS models when agents believe in a misspecified model. The analysis has been carried out associating with the "modified" LMS updating rule the ordinary differential equation. This algorithm has been proved to converge to a point which can differ from the REE. This is dependent on the strength of the noise signal which affects the model and on the characteristics of the function which weighs the noise signal itself.

The "modified" LMS algorithm converges always to a point while other learning procedures such as the ROLS algorithm can diverge. These features make the "modified" LMS mechanism more natural and plausible to model agents' beliefs in SRLS models.

References

[1] A. Marcet and T. J. Sargent. Convergence of least squares learning mechanisms is self-referential linear stochastic models. *Journal of Economic Theory*, 48:337–368, 1989.

[2] B. Widrow. Adaptive filters. In R. E. Kalman and N. De Claris, editors, *Aspects of Network and Systems Theory*, pages 563–587, New York, 1971. Holt and Rinehart and Winston.

[3] L. Ljung. Analysis of stochastic algorithms. *IEEE Transactions on Automatic Control*, AC-22(4):551–575, August 1977.

[4] B. Widrow, J. M. McCool, M. G. Larimore, and C. R. Johnson. Stationary and nonstationary learning characteristics of the lms adaptive filter. *Proceedings of the IEEE*, 64(8):1151–1162, 1976.

[5] E. Barucci and L. Landi. Least mean squares learning algorithm in self referential linear stochastic models. In *Proceedings of ICANN'94*, Salerno, Italy, May 1994.

A NOVEL APPROACH TO NOISE-FILTERING BASED ON A GAIN-SCHEDULING NEURAL NETWORK ARCHITECTURE.

T. TROUDET [1] and W. MERRILL
Advanced Control Technology Branch
NASA Lewis Research Center
Cleveland, Ohio 44135

Abstract.

A Gain-Scheduling Neural Network Architecture is proposed to enhance the noise-filtering efficiency of feedforward neural networks, in terms of both nominal performance and robustness. The synergistic benefits of the proposed architecture are demonstrated and discussed in the context of the noise-filtering of signals that are typically encountered in aerospace control systems. The synthesis of such a gain-scheduled neurofiltering provides the robustness of linear filtering, while preserving the nominal performance advantage of conventional non-linear neurofiltering. Quantitative performance and robustness evaluations are provided for the signal processing of pitch rate responses to typical pilot command inputs for a modern fighter aircaft model.

1. Introduction.

The capability of feedforward neural networks to serve as noise-filters for complex systems with varying characteristics and/or changing modes of operation was recently analyzed for the noise-filtering of signals that are typically encountered in aerospace control and diagnostic systems [1]. For such systems, the nominal dynamics of the signals are a simplified version of the actual dynamics, due to modelling approximations, system uncertainties, and/or changing modes of operation. As a result, the desired neurofilter should not only provide satisfactory signal processing over the nominal dynamic range of the signals, but should also be robust and maintain its performance in the presence of changes in the nominal dynamics of the signals. From that perspective, linear and non-linear feedforward neural networks were trained to filter noise by learning to map sequences of noisy input data onto the exact values of the most recently sampled data [1]. Comparative performance/robustness evaluations indicated that the synthesized non-linear neurofilter performed better than the linear neurofilter within the nominal dynamic range of signals; whereas the linear neurofilter was more robust in the presence of substantial variations in the parameters of the signal generating process. This result pointed to the need for a more global neural architecture with a potential to synergistically combine the complementary benefits of linear neurofiltering and conventional non-linear neurofiltering.

To address that issue, a gain-scheduling neural network (GSNN) architecture is proposed to find the optimal combination of linear and non-linear neurofiltering that provides the best signal estimates from input sequences of noisy data. The system functionality of the gain-scheduled neurofilter is briefly introduced in section 2, while section 3 describes the gain-scheduling training architecture itself. In Section 4, the nominal performance and robustness of the gain-scheduled neural network are compared to those of the linear and non-linear neurofilters separately, while Section 5 discusses possible extensions towards performance/robustness enhancement, non-linear adaptive neurofiltering, and neurosmoothing.

2. System Functionality of the Neurofilter.

The system functionality of the neurofilter is illustrated in Fig.1 in the context of an aerospace control system application. The signals to be filtered are the simulated pitch-rate responses to both pitch rate and velocity commands. The closed-loop system includes a *non-linear* neurocontroller designed in Refs.[2-3] to provide independent control of pitch-rate/airspeed for a state-space representation of a modern fighter aircraft [4]. The plant model consists of an integrated airframe/propulsion linear model, a fuel flow actuator modelled as a linear second order system with position and rate limits, and a thrust vectoring actuator modelled as a linear first order system with position and rate limits. As a result, the signal generating process represented by the closed-loop control system of Fig.1 contains nonlinearities due to the actuator position/rate limits, and the nonlinear structure of the neurocontroller. For the purpose of this study, the

---

[1] Sverdrup Technology, Inc., 2001 Aerospace Parkway, Brook Park, Ohio, 44142.

noise source has been placed outside of the control loop so that a clean baseline signal would be available for comparison. The purpose of the trained neurofilter is to provide an estimate of the actual data values that have been corrupted by noise in order to enhance any subsequent processing by *out-of-the-loop* peripheral modules such as failure-detectors and failure-identifiers (e.g. Ref.[5]), off-line/on-line system-identifiers (e.g. Ref.[6]), damage estimators (e.g. Ref.[7]), etc.

In this simulation, the information needed to synthesize the neurofilter is provided by closed-loop pitch rate responses to input commands $\bar{z}_{SEL}(t) = (q_{SEL}(t), v_{SEL}(t))$, where $q_{SEL}(t)$ is the pitch rate command input, and $v_{SEL}(t)$ is the velocity command input. The pitch rate command input $q_{SEL}(t)$ is a doublet randomly centered at a time t_c between 2.5s and 5s such that $q_{SEL}(t \leq t_c) = Q_0$, $q_{SEL}(t_c < t \leq 2t_c) = -Q_0$, and $q_{SEL}(2t_c < t) = 0$, as indicated in Fig.2a. The concurrent velocity command input is the step function $v_{SEL}(t \leq 0) = 0$ and $v_{SEL}(0 < t) = V_0$, as indicated in Fig.2b. These commanded inputs $q_{SEL}(t)$ and $v_{SEL}(t)$, which represent the frequency-content of typical pilot command inputs, were subsequently filtered through a *prefilter-for-command-shaping* (Fig.1) in order to generate the commanded trajectories $\bar{z}_c(t) = (q_c(t), v_c(t))$ that are to be tracked by the closed-loop control system. The commanded pitch rate response $q_c(t)$ and the commanded velocity response $v_c(t)$ corresponding to a doublet pitch rate command input $q_{SEL}(t)$ and a step velocity command input $v_{SEL}(t)$ are represented in the diagrams of Fig.2. The maximum intensities $|Q_0|$ and $|V_0|$ of the randomly selected input commands were bounded by $Q_{max} = 3$deg/sec (corresponding to 0.5 inches of pilot stick deflection), and $V_{max} = 20ft/s$. The pitch rate responses to such randomly generated pilot command inputs were sampled every $\Delta = 10ms$ over $T = 14s$, and they were corrupted with additive gaussian white noise with a standard deviation $\sigma_{training} = 0.3deg/sec$ before being passed to the training architecture of the neurofilter.

3. Gain-Scheduling Training Architecture.

The proposed neurofilter consists of a linear neural network and a non-linear neural network with optimized internal configurations, and whose outputs are modulated by a gain-scheduling feedforward neural network. The optimized linear neural network and the optimized non-linear neural network used in this simulation were trained in Ref.[1] with the training architecture shown in Fig.3. During training, the inputs of these two neurofilters consisted of sequences of the fifty most recently sampled noisy data, and the target values were the exact values of the last sampled data. In Fig.3, the notation $F^A(p, h, 1)$ represents a feedforward neural network with p input units, a single hidden layer of h sigmoidal neurons, and a single linear output neuron. Both linear and non-linear neurofilters were trained to minimize the error $(\hat{q} - q)^2(t)$ between the filter output $\hat{q}(t)$ and the exact value $q(t)$ of the pitch rate signal generated as in Section 2. The optimized network configurations of these two types of neurofilters were $F^A(50, 30, 1)$ for the non-linear neurofiltering (i.e. 50 inputs, 30 hidden sigmoidal neurons, and 1 linear output neuron), and $F^A(50, 1)$ for the linear neurofiltering (i.e. 50 inputs, and 1 linear output neuron).

As shown in Fig.4, the "fusion" of the optimized linear and non-linear neurofilters is achieved by training a gain-scheduling neural network to minimize the error $(\hat{q}_{GSNN} - q)^2(t)$ between the *Gain-Scheduled Neural Network* output $\hat{q}_{GSNN}(t)$ and the exact value $q(t)$ of the pitch rate signal generated as in Section 2. As indicated in Fig.4, the gain-scheduled neurofilter estimate $\hat{q}(t)_{GSNN}$ is an adaptive combination of the non-linear neurofilter estimate $\hat{q}(t)_{non-linear}$, and the linear neurofilter estimate $\hat{q}(t)_{linear}$:

$$\hat{q}_{GSNN}(t) = g(t) \times \hat{q}(t)_{non-linear} + (1 - g(t)) \times \hat{q}(t)_{linear} \tag{1}$$

where the gain $g(t)$ is the output of the non-linear gain-scheduling neural network. The role of the gain-scheduling neural network is therefore to find the optimal combination of linear and non-linear neurofiltering that extracts the best signal estimates from input sequences of noise-corrupted data. In order to facilitate this "classification", the inputs of the gain-scheduling neural network were chosen to be filter estimates of the exact signal values instead of the original noisy data values. These filter estimates were furthermore chosen to be the computed outputs of the linear neurofilter, in light of the robustness advantage that linear filtering has over conventional non-linear neurofiltering. The configuration of the gain-scheduling neural network chosen in this application consisted of twenty five input units, ten hidden sigmoidal neurons, and a linear output neuron with the thresholding activation function $y(x)$:

$$y(x < 0) = 0; \quad y(0 \leq x \leq 1) = x; \quad y(1 < x) = 1 , \tag{2}$$

and training was performed with the backpropagation algorithm [8-9].

III-39

4. Comparative Nominal Performance and Robustness Evaluations.

The ability of the linear, non-linear, and gain-scheduled neurofilters to remove the noise from the pitch rate response to a given pilot commanded input "c" is measured by the ratio R_c

$$R_c = \frac{\sqrt{\Sigma_{k=0}^{T/\Delta}(\hat{q}(t_k) - q(t_k))^2}}{\sqrt{\Sigma_{k=0}^{T/\Delta}\hat{n}(t_k)^2}}, \tag{3}$$

T being the duration of the pilot command input, and Δ the sampling time of the vehicle outputs. In Eq.(3), $q(t_k)$ is the exact pitch rate response, $\hat{n}(t_k)$ is the white noise fluctuation added to $q(t_k)$, and $\hat{q}(t_k)$ is the filter output corresponding to an input sequence of p sampled noisy data, i.e. $\{q(t_{k-i})+\hat{n}(t_{k-i}), \, min(k,p) \geq i \geq 0\}$.

To compare the performances of the aforementioned neurofilters, two measures "R" and "r" based on Eq.(3) are introduced [1]. The R-measure is a statistical average of R_c calculated over the whole dynamic range of pilot command inputs as characterized in Section 2 by (Q_0, V_0, t_c) where Q_0, V_0, and t_c are uniformly distributed over $[-Q_{max}, +Q_{max}]$, $[-V_{max}, +V_{max}]$, and $[2.5s, 5s]$ respectively. The r-measure is the value of R_c for a most demanding case of pilot command input corresponding to the pitch rate doublet $Q_{SEL}(t \leq 5sec) = Q_{max}$, $Q_{SEL}(5sec < t \leq 10sec) = -Q_{max}$, $Q_{SEL}(10sec < t) = 0$; and the velocity step $V_{SEL}(t < 0) = 0$ and $V_{SEL}(0 < t) = V_{max}$. The R-measure grades the average efficiency of a neurofilter in removing the noise over an exhaustive set of pilot command inputs, whereas the r-measure estimates the filtering efficiency for one of the worst cases of pilot command inputs. To test the ability of the neurofilters to operate at noise levels other than that used in training, the R- and r- measures were evaluated with gaussian white noise of various standard deviations ranging from $\sigma_{min} = 0$ to $\sigma_{max} = 1deg/sec$. The values of the R- and r- measures corresponding to the nominal dynamic range of the signals are plotted in Figs.5a & 6a respectively. The results show that the gain-scheduled neurofilter outperforms both the optimized linear filter and the optimized non-linear neurofilter, not only at the noise level used in training, but also at all noise levels between $\sigma_{min} = 0$ and $\sigma_{max} = 1deg/sec$.

To further compare the robustness of the gain-scheduled neurofilter with the robustness of the optimized linear neurofilter and non-linear neurofilter respectively, the R- and r-measures were also evaluated on a test set extending beyond the nominal dynamic range of the signals (used for training) and generated as follows. The matrix elements of the A, B, and C matrices of the vehicle model [4] were randomly varied within $\pm 50\%$ of their nominal values, with the sole requirement that the stability of the closed-loop system be preserved [2]. Due to the severity of the deviations of the A, B, C matrices from their nominal values, the closed-loop system responses to typical pilot command inputs presented significant deviations from the nominal responses. The statistical evaluations of "R" and "r" are plotted in Figs.5b & 6b respectively for a typical set of A, B, and Cs leading to large variations of the vehicle model. The results show that the gain-scheduled neurofilter still outperforms the optimized linear filter and the optimized non-linear neurofilter at all noise levels. This is graphically illustrated in Fig.7 by the filtering of the pitch rate response to the most demanding pilot command input of the vehicle model with the same set of off-nominal A, B, and C matrices as that used for the evaluations of the R- and r-measures plotted in Figs.5b & 6b respectively. As shown by the plots of Fig.7a, 7b & 7c, additive gaussian white noise is more efficiently removed from the noisy closed-loop signals by the gain-scheduled neurofilter (7c) than by the optimized linear neurofilter (7a) or the optimized non-linear neurofilter (7b) separately. The synergistic benefits of the newly proposed gain-scheduling architecture are even more apparent when comparing Figs.7a, 7b & 7c in light of the plot of the gain-scheduling neural network output (identical to the output gain of the non-linear neurofilter) shown in Fig.7d. This comparison indicates that the gain-scheduled neurofiltering presents the characteristics of linear neurofiltering around 1 sec and 6 sec, i.e. when the pitch rate estimates of the linear neurofilter are better than those of the non-linear neurofilter. More specifically, Fig.7d also indicates that, around 1 sec, the gain-scheduled neurofilter estimate consists of about 80 % of linear neurofilter estimate, and about 20 % of non-linear neurofilter estimate. Around 6sec, the gain-scheduled neurofilter estimate is 100 % of the linear neurofilter estimate. Otherwise, the gain-scheduled neurofilter estimate is for the most given by the non-linear neurofilter estimate, e.g. above 12 sec where it is 100 % of the non-linear neurofilter estimate.

5. Conclusion.

A Gain-Scheduling Neural Network Architecture has been proposed to enhance the robustness of feed-forward neurofilters, and was analyzed in the context of the noise-filtering of pitch rate responses to pilot command inputs for a modern fighter aircraft model. The proposed architecture consists of an optimized linear feedforward neurofilter, an optimized non-linear feedforward neurofilter, and a gain-scheduling feed-forward neural network which is trained with backpropagation to synergistically combine the complementary benefits of the linear and non-linear neurofilters. The resulting gain-scheduled neurofilter consistently performed better than each neurofilter separately, within the nominal as well as off-nominal dynamic range of the simulated signals.

Future areas of research would include possible extensions of the functionality and scope of the proposed gain-scheduling neural network architecture. Of particular interest would be the possibility of further enhancing neurofiltering through the gain-scheduling of a collection of linear filters that would have been separately optimized on the disjoint elements of a partition of the space of the input signals. The synthesis of the multi-output gain-scheduler(s) required for the fusion of such optimized linear neurofilters could benefit from the robustness of genetic algorithms or even fuzzy rule-based scheduling, or from training algorithms like those developed for the hierarchical mixing of expert neural networks [10].

Of additional interest would be the possibility to extend the proposed architecture to achieve *non-linear adaptive neurofiltering* through the synergy of supervised and unsupervised training schemes, and by taking advantage of the on-line learning capabilities of neural networks. An important practical issue to be addressed in that regard would be whether neural networks can be trained in unsupervised training modes to efficiently gain-schedule the supervised training of a partition of individual neurofilters of the type proposed in Ref.[11].

Of further interest would be the possibility to extend the proposed architecture to the smoothing of noisy signals by training a neural network to gain-schedule optimized linear and non-linear *neurosmoothers* that would have been previously trained to map sequences of p successively sampled noisy data onto the exact values of any of the previous $(p-1)$ samples input to the network. Such gain-scheduled *neurosmoothers* would be expected to provide better signal estimates than their *neurofilter* counterparts in view of the additional information provided [11-12], yet at the expense of the time corresponding to the delay needed for the signals to be available. How to reach the best compromise between "accuracy" and "time" would therefore depend upon the computational requirements and characteristics of the specific post-processing to be performed on the signals.

Finally, future comparative analysis with other traditional techniques, such as Extended Kalman Filtering [13], could also provide insight on how to improve the performance and broaden the applicability of the proposed Gain-Scheduling Neural Network approach.

References.

[1] Troudet, T., and Merrill, W., "A Comparative Robustness Evaluation of Feedforward Neurofilters", *32nd AIAA Aerospace Sciences Meeting*, Reno, NV, January 1994.

[2] Troudet, T., "Robustness Enhancement of Neurocontroller and State Estimator", *World Congress on Neural Networks*, Vol. III, pp. 163-167, Portland, July 1993.

[3] Troudet, T., Garg, S., and Merrill, W., "Design and Evaluation of a Robust Neurocontroller for a Multivariable Aircraft Control Problem", *Int. Joint Conf. on Neural Networks*, Baltimore, MD, June 1992.

[4] Garg, S., Mattern, D.L., and Bullard, R.E.,"Integrated Flight/Propulsion Control System Design Based on a Centralized Approach", *Journal of Guidance, Control and Dynamics*, Vol.14, No.1, 1991.

[5] Duyar, A., and Merrill, W., "Fault Diagnosis of the Space Shuttle Main Engine", *Journal of Guidance, Control, and Dynamics*, Vol.15, No.2, pp.384-389, 1992.

[6] Troudet, T., and Merrill, W., "Neuromorphic Learning of Continuous-Valued Mappings from Noise-Corrupted Data", *IEEE Trans. on Neural Networks*, Vol.2, No.2, pp.294-301, 1991.

[7] Troudet, T., and Merrill, W., "A Real Time Neural Net Estimator of Fatigue Life", *Inter. Joint Conf. On Neural Networks*, Vol.2, pp.59-64, San Diego, 1990.

[8] Werbos, P., "Beyond Regression: New Tools for Prediction and Analysis in the Behavioral Sciences", *Thesis in Applied Mathematics*, Harvard University (August, 1974).

[9] Rumelhart, D., Hinton, G., and Williams R., "Learning Internal Representations by Error Propagation", *Parallel Distributed Processing: Explorations in the Microstructures of Cognition*, ed. by D. Rumelhart, J. McClelland, et al., Vol.I, pp.318-362, MIT Press, 1986.

[10] Jordan, M. I., and Jacobs, R. A., "Hierarchical Mixtures of Experts and the EM Algorithm", *MIT Preprint*, Submitted to *Neural Computation*; and References therein.

[11] Klimasauskas, C., "Neural Nets and Noise Filtering", *Dr. Dobb's Journal*, p.32, Jan. 1989.

[12] Anderson, B., and Montgomery, D., "A Method for Noise-Filtering with Feed-forward Neural Networks: Analysis and Comparison with Low-pass and Optimal Filtering", *Int. Joint Conf. on Neural Networks*, Vol.I, pp.209-214, San Diego, 1990.

[13] Gelb, A., "Applied Optimal Estimation", *The MIT Press*, 1974.

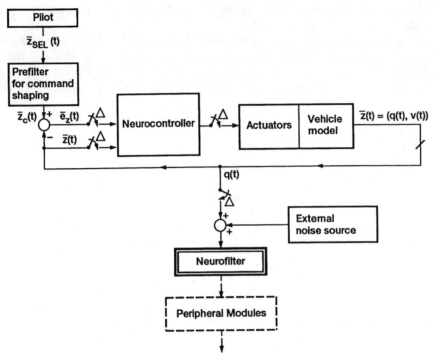

Figure 1.—Functional system diagram of the trained neurofilter.

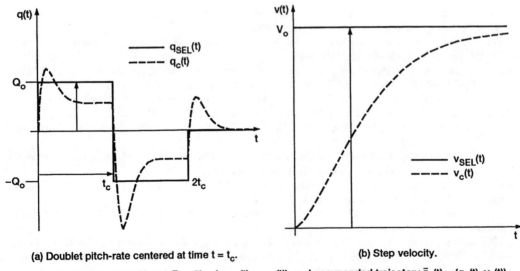

(a) Doublet pitch-rate centered at time $t = t_c$.

(b) Step velocity.

Figure 2.—Pilot command input, $\bar{z}_{SEL}(t) = (q_{SEL}(t), v_{SEL}(t))$, and commanded trajectory $\bar{z}_c(t) = (q_c(t), v_c(t))$.

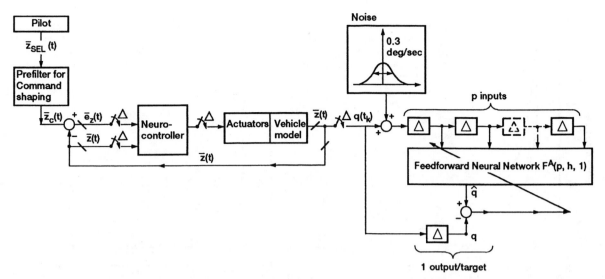

Figure 3.—Training architecture of asymmetric neurofilters F^A (p, h, 1) with p input units, one linear output, and a single hidden layer of h sigmoidal neurons.

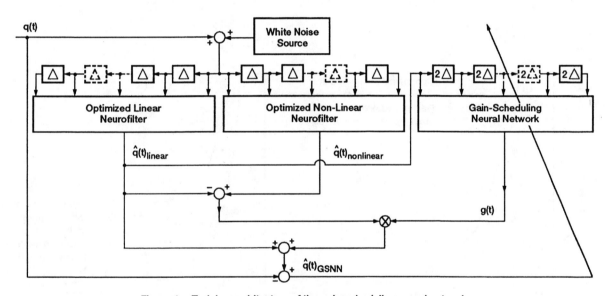

Figure 4.—Training architecture of the gain-scheduling neural network.

III-43

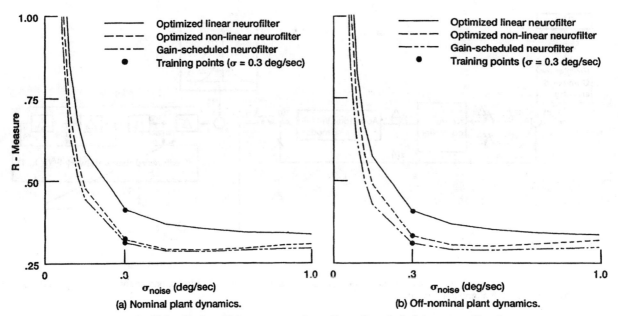

(a) Nominal plant dynamics.

(b) Off-nominal plant dynamics.

Figure 5.—Noise filtering efficiency averaged over the entire set of pilot command inputs.

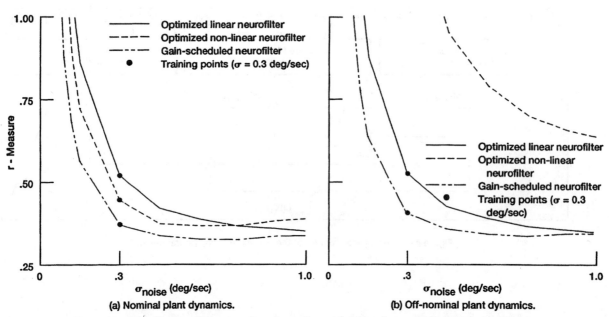

(a) Nominal plant dynamics.

(b) Off-nominal plant dynamics.

Figure 6.—Noise filtering efficiency averaged over the most demanding case of pilot command input.

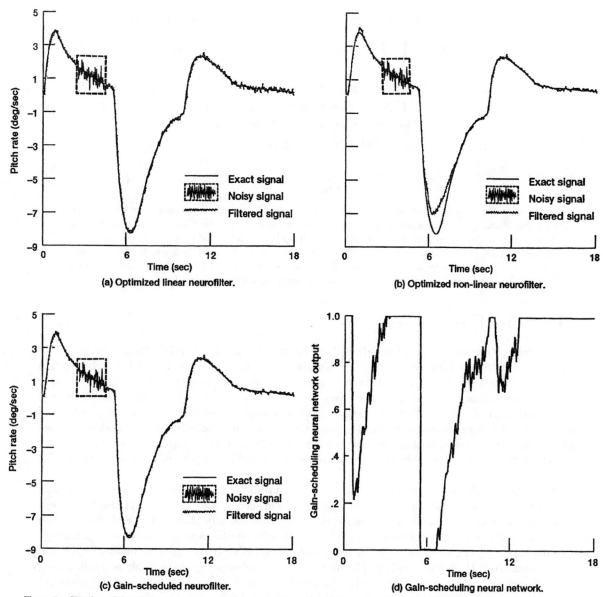

Figure 7.—Filtering of the pitch rate response to the most demanding pilot command input with off-nominal plant dynamics.

III-45

A Multiresolution Learning Method for Back-Propagation Networks

Lai-Wan Chan, Wing-Chung Chan
Department of Computer Science
The Chinese University of Hong Kong
Shatin, N.T., Hong Kong

Abstract

A multiresolution learning method for back-propagation networks is proposed in this paper. With this learning method, a series of back-propagation networks are built to learn the same set of input vectors under different resolutions. After a network has been trained on a particular resolution of input vectors, the connection weights are transformed into the next network which is responsible to learn a higher resolution of input vectors. The objective of it is to improve the convergence rate of the networks. Experimental results were used to demonstrate the ability of this approach.

1 Introduction

The back-propagation network has been studied for many years and many researchers have applied it to a wide variety of problems successfully [9]. Unfortunately, it is shown that the back-propagation algorithm, which adopts the steepest descent technique, is slow to converge in a multilayer network [3, 4]. Such limitation prohibits the use of back-propagation network on large scale problems, e.g. problems with high dimensionality input space. The multilayer perceptron assumes the individual input neuron acts independently from the other neurons. In fact, in some problems, for example, image recognition problems, use images as the grey level input to the network. The input neurons do have some correlations with their neighboring neurons. However, a multilayer perceptron has not taken this into account.

On the other hand, the human visual system, as an optimal image processor, can process a huge amount of information quickly. Studies of such system have shown that the retina of the human eye is an structured array so as to see a wide angle in a low-resolution way using peripheral vision, while simultaneously allowing high-resolution, detailed perception by the fovea in a small central portion of the viewing region [5]. This finding triggered significant interest in multiresolution signal decomposition and some researchers [1, 8] have applied this multiresolution technique in many fields of applications, e.g. edge detection, data compression, surface interpolation, and shape analysis. Recently, several researchers incorporate this technique with neural networks [10, 12].

A multiresolution representation of a signal provides a simple hierarchical framework for interpretating the information. In some sense, the signal at a coarse resolution provide the "context" of the signal. It is natural to analyze first the signal at a coarse resolution and then gradually increase the resolution. It is believed that such coarse-to-fine strategy provides a possibility for reducing the computational cost of signal operations [8].

In this paper, we propose a problem-independent learning method, which adopts the multiresolution signal decomposition technique, for back-propagation networks in order to alleviate the shortcomings of this kind of networks described above. With this multiresolution learning method, a series of back-propagation networks are trained on a set of training data under different resolutions and we believe that the convergence rate of back-propagation networks can be improved, e.g. the convergence rate is faster than the original one.

2 Multiresolution Approximation of $L^2(R)$

In this section, we review the basic concept of multiresolution analysis introduced by Mallat [6, 7]. Suppose that the original signal $f(x)$ described in this paper is measurable and has a finite energy: $f(x) \in L^2(R)$. According to Mallat's definition, we can define the multiresolution approximation of $L^2(R)$.

Definition The approximation of a signal $f(x)$ at a resolution r can be defined as an estimate of $f(x)$ derived from r measurements per unit length. These measurements are computed by uniformly sampling at a rate r the function $f(x)$ smoothed by a low-pass filter whose bandwidth is proportional to r.

In an approximation operation, when removing the details of $f(x)$ smaller than r, the highest frequencies of this function is suppressed. In the following, we discuss only the approximation of a function on a dyadic sequence of resolution $\left(2^j\right)_{j \in Z}$.

The approximation of the signal $f(x)$ at the resolution 2^j, $A_{2^j} f(x)$, is characterized by the set of inner products as,

$$A_{2^j}^d f = \left(\langle f(u), \phi_{2^j} \left(u - 2^{-j} n \right) \rangle \right)_{n \in Z}, \tag{1}$$

where $\phi_{2^j}(x) = 2^j \phi(2^j x)$ and $\phi(x) \in L^2(R)$ is a unique function called a scaling function. $A_{2^j}^d f$ is called a discrete approximation of $f(x)$ at the resolution 2^j. In practice, a physical measuring device can only measure a signal at a finite resolution. For normalization purposes, it is supposed that this resolution is equal to 1 and let $A_1^d f$ be the discrete approximation at the resolution 1 that is measured.

Let H be a discrete filter whose impulse response is $h(n) = \langle \phi_{2^{-1}}(u), \phi(u-n) \rangle$ and let $\tilde{H}$ be the mirror filter with impulse response,

$$\tilde{h}(n) = h(-n). \tag{2}$$

Then, it can be shown that the discrete approximation of $f(x)$ at a resolution 2^j, $A_{2^j} f$, can be calculated by filtering $A_{2^{j+1}} f = \left(\langle f(u), \phi_{2^{j+1}} \left(u - 2^{-j-1} k \right) \rangle \right)_{n \in Z}$ with the discrete filter $\tilde{H}$ and keeping every other sample of the convolution product,

$$A_{2^j}^d f = \left(\sum_{k=-\infty}^{+\infty} \tilde{h}(2n - k) \langle f(u), \phi_{2^{j+1}} \left(u - 2^{-j-1} k \right) \rangle \right)_{n \in Z}. \tag{3}$$

All the discrete approximations $A_{2^j}^d f$, for $j < 0$, can thus be computed from $A_1^d f$ by repeating this process. This operation is called a pyramid transform and the set of discrete approximations $\left(A_{2^j}^d f \right)$ was called a Gaussian pyramid by Burt and Adelson [1].

3 The Multiresolution Learning Method

The multiresolution learning method we proposed involves a series of back-propagation networks. Each network is responsible to learn on the same set of input vectors but under different resolutions. The sequence of training processes to be carried out by the set of back-propagation networks is from the coarsest resolution to the finest resolution. After a network has been trained on a particular resolution of input vectors, it transfers the learned information, that is the connection weights, to the upper level network which is required to learn a higher resolution of input vectors.

3.1 Input Vector Representation

Firstly, let us define how input vectors are represented under different resolutions. Let $\{\vec{x}_i\}$ be a set of N-dimensional input vectors where $\vec{x}_i = (x_{i1}, x_{i2}, \ldots, x_{iN})$ and $x_{ij} \in \Re$. It has been mentioned in Section 2 that $A_1^d f$ is the discrete approximation at the resolution 1 and contains a finite number of samples. Then, we can define the discrete approximation of $\vec{x}_i$ at the resolution 1, $A_1^d \vec{x}_i$, as,

$$A_1^d \vec{x}_i = (x_{in})_{1 \leq n \leq N}. \tag{4}$$

A set of N-dimensional input vectors $\{A_1^d \vec{x}_i\}$ can thus be formed.

By choosing a suitable discrete filter H and applying Equation 3, the discrete approximation of $\vec{x}_i$ at the resolution 2^j, $A^d_{2^j}\vec{x}_i$, can also be defined as,

$$A^d_{2^j}\vec{x}_i = \left(\sum_{k=-\infty}^{+\infty} \tilde{h}(2n-k) A^d_{2^{j+1}}\vec{x}_i(k) \right)_{1 \le n \le 2^j N}, \tag{5}$$

where $A^d_{2^{j+1}}\vec{x}_i(k)$ being the k-th element of $A^d_{2^{j+1}}\vec{x}_i$. Hence, all the discrete approximations $A^d_{2^j}\vec{x}_i$, for $j < 0$, can thus be computed from $\vec{x}_i$ by repeating this process.

In order to avoid border problems when computing the discrete approximations $A^d_{2^j}\vec{x}_i$, it is supposed that the original input vector $A^d_1\vec{x}_i$, is symmetric with respect to $n = 1$ and $n = N$, i.e.,

$$A^d_1\vec{x}_i(n) = \begin{cases} A^d_1\vec{x}_i(-n+2) & \text{if } -N+2 < n < 1 \\ A^d_1\vec{x}_i(2N-n) & \text{if } N < n < 2N-1 \\ 0 & \text{if } n \le -N+2 \text{ or } n \ge 2N-1 \end{cases} \tag{6}$$

If the chosen discrete filter H is even, e.g., $\tilde{H} = H$, each discrete approximation $A^d_{2^j}\vec{x}_i$ will also be symmetric with respect to $n = 1$ and $n = 2^j N$.

3.2 Back-Propagation Network Architecture

After several sets of the input vectors under different resolutions, $\left(\{A^d_{2^j}\vec{x}_i\} \right)_{J \le j \le 0}$, have been generated, we build a group of back-propagation networks $(B_{2^j})_{J \le j \le 0}$ and each back-propagation network B_{2^j} is responsible to learn a set of discrete approximations $\{A^d_{2^j}\vec{x}_i\}$. The size of the input layer for each network will be the same as the dimension of vectors of this particular resolution, that is $2^j N$; while the size of the output layer represents the number of categories to be classified in the input vectors and is the same for all networks generated.

The required number of neurons in the hidden layer greatly depends on the nature of the problem to be solved [3]. With some specific knowledge about the structure of the problem, and a fundamental understanding of how the back-propagation networks might go about implementing this structure, one can sometimes form a good estimate of the proper network size. Like the size of the output layer, the size of the hidden layer is the same among all back-propagation networks created.

3.3 Training Procedure Strategy

With some sets of vectors under different resolutions and a series of corresponding back-propagation networks, we can start the training procedure. First of all, the lowest level network B_{2^J} (the network with the coarser resolution of vectors as input) is trained first. We initialize the connection weights of this network with small random numbers [9] and start the training process. Traditionally, the training process of a back-propagation network is repeated until a minimum on sum squared error (SSE) or a point sufficiently close to the minimum is found. However, such a minimum may not be found in the networks we defined except the highest level one B_1 (the one with the original input vectors $\vec{x}_i$ as input). It is because some information of the original input vectors is lost during the approximation process.

As a result, we define an intermediate stopping criteria for terminating the training processes of the back-propagation networks $(B_{2^j})_{J \le j \le -1}$ which are trained on the discrete signals $\left(\{A^d_{2^j}\vec{x}_i\} \right)_{J \le j \le -1}$. Let M be the number of hidden neurons, $2^j N$ be the number of input neurons, w_{pq} be the connection weight between hidden neuron q and input neuron p and it will be updated with Δw_{pq} in the current training cycle. Hence, a term $W(t)$ is defined as,

$$W(t) = (2^j N M)^{-1} \sum_{q=1}^{M} \sum_{p=1}^{2^j N} \left| \frac{\Delta w_{pq}}{w_{pq}} \right| + \rho W(t-1), \tag{7}$$

where $0 < \rho < 1$, called a history factor, and $(2^j N M)^{-1}$ is used for normalization purpose. The intermediate stopping criteria is then defined as,

$$W(t) < \delta, \tag{8}$$

where $\delta > 0$.

3.4 Connection Weight Transformation

After the intermediate stopping criteria is satisfied in one network B_{2j}, we transfer the connection weights of it to the next network B_{2j+1} with higher resolution. From the lower level network, we have two sets of connection weights, $\{w_{pq}\}$ and $\{v_{qr}\}$, where w_{pq} is a connection weight from input neuron p to hidden neuron q and v_{qr} is a connection weight from hidden neuron q to output neuron r.

Since the sizes of the hidden layer and the output layer are the same on both networks, we can simply assign $\{v_{qr}\}$ to the higher level network as the connection weights between hidden layer and output layer.

However, the sizes of their input layers are different and we need to do some transformations on $\{w_{ij}\}$. If a discrete signal $A_{2j}^d \vec{x_i}$ is passed to the lower level network, the hidden neuron q will receive,

$$\sum_{p=1}^{2^j N} w_{pq} A_{2j}^d \vec{x_i}(p),\tag{9}$$

as its input. In order to maintain the same status after transformation, the following condition must be held for each hidden neuron,

$$\sum_{o=1}^{2^{j+1} N} \left(w'_{oq} A_{2j+1}^d \vec{x_i}(o)\right) = \sum_{p=1}^{2^j N} \left(w_{pq} A_{2j}^d \vec{x_i}(p)\right),\tag{10}$$

where w'_{oq} is the connection weight of the higher level network from input neuron o to hidden neuron q. We can worked out from Equation 5 and 10 that the connection weights w'_{oq} are equal to,

$$w'_{oq} = \begin{cases} \sum_{p=1}^{2^j N} \tilde{h}(2p-1) w_{pq} & \text{if } o = 1 \\ \sum_{p=1}^{2^j N} \left(\tilde{h}(2p-o) + \tilde{h}(2p+o-2^{j+2}N) + \tilde{h}(2p+o-2)\right) w_{pq} & \text{if } 2 \le o \le 2^{j+1}N - 1 \\ \sum_{p=1}^{2^j N} \tilde{h}(2p-2^{j+1}N) w_{pq} & \text{if } o = 2^{j+1}N \end{cases}.\tag{11}$$

4 Experimental Results

In this section, we show some computational results to illustrate the performance of the proposed learning method. A numeric recognition problem is used as an example. For this problem, 10 binary patterns of numbers, from 0 to 9, were selected as training examples and the size of them was 32×32.

Two experiments were carried out with two different sets of initial connection weights for back-propagation networks. In each experiment, we selected 3 history factors ρ and 2 intermediate stopping criteria δ, i.e., $\rho = 0.8$, $\rho = 0.5$, $\rho = 0.2$, $\delta = 0.0005$, and $\delta = 0.001$, for the training processes of the proposed learning method. To demonstrate our method, two sets of network structure were used, $(B_{2j})_{-2 \le j \le 0}$ and $(B_{2j})_{-1 \le j \le 0}$, and were called the 3-level network set and the 2-level network set respectively. Also, a 1-level network B_1 was built to compare the performance with the 3-level and the 2-level network sets. The training processes of all networks were repeated until the SSE was smaller than 0.01, that is $\varepsilon = 0.01$. Hence, for each experiment, there was a total of 13 training jobs to be carried out.

As shown in Equation 5 and 11, we must first define the impulse response $\tilde{h}(n)$ before the input vectors can be represented under different resolutions and the connection weight transformation can be carried out. In other words, $h(n)$ must be defined since $\tilde{h}(n) = h(-n)$ from Equation 2.

There are many ways of choosing these coefficients $h(n)$ [11], as long as $\sum_{n=-\infty}^{+\infty} h(n) = 1$. Here, we adopted the suggestion from Daubechies [2],

$$h(n) = \begin{cases} \frac{1+\sqrt{3}}{8} & \text{if } n = -2 \\ \frac{3+\sqrt{3}}{8} & \text{if } n = -1 \\ \frac{3-\sqrt{3}}{8} & \text{if } n = 0 \\ \frac{1-\sqrt{3}}{8} & \text{if } n = 1 \\ 0 & \text{otherwise} \end{cases}.\tag{12}$$

With the use of the coefficients shown in Equation 12, Equation 5 and 11 can then be simplified into,

$$A_{2^j}^d \vec{x}_i = \left(\sum_{k=2n-2}^{2n+1} \tilde{h}(2n-k) A_{2^{j+1}}^d \vec{x}_i(k) \right)_{1 \le n \le 2^j N} , \qquad (13)$$

and,

$$w'_{oq} = \begin{cases} \tilde{h}(1)w_{1q} & \text{if } o = 1 \\ \tilde{h}(0)w_{1q} + \tilde{h}(2)w_{1q} + \tilde{h}(2)w_{2q} & \text{if } o = 2 \\ \tilde{h}(-1)w_{\frac{o-1}{2},q} + \tilde{h}(1)w_{\frac{o+1}{2},q} & \text{if } o = 3, 5, \cdots, 2^{j+1}N - 3 \\ \tilde{h}(0)w_{\frac{o}{2},q} + \tilde{h}(2)w_{\frac{o+2}{2},q} & \text{if } o = 4, 6, \cdots, 2^{j+1}N - 2 \\ \tilde{h}(-1)w_{2^jN-1,q} + \tilde{h}(-1)w_{2^jN,q} + \tilde{h}(1)w_{2^jN,q} & \text{if } o = 2^{j+1}N - 1 \\ \tilde{h}(0)w_{2^jN,q} & \text{if } o = 2^{j+1}N \end{cases} . \qquad (14)$$

Since the binary patterns used in the experiments were all in two dimensions, the multiresolution technique described in Section 2 cannot be applied to them directly. However, it has been shown that the two-dimensional multiresolution transform can be seen as a one-dimensional multiresolution transform along the x and y axes [6]. We first convolve the rows of binary patterns with a one-dimensional filter H, retain every other row, convolve the columns of the resulting signals with another one-dimensional filter and retain every other column. Hence, two sets of binary patterns can be collected with size 16×16 and 8×8 and they are used as input vectors for networks B_{2-1} and B_{2-2} respectively. For all networks in each experiment, the sizes for the hidden layer and the output layer were set to 15 and 10 respectively.

All of the experiments were run on a SPARCstation 10/30 with 32MB memory. Table 1 shows the training results of the two experiments. The convergence time for each training job is presented and a performance index, a ratio to the convergence time of the 1-level network, is calculated.

Table 1: Training results of the three experiments.

Job no.	Network Type	ρ	δ	Experiment 1		Experiment 2	
				Convergence Time (sec)	Performance Index	Convergence Time (sec)	Performance Index
1	3-level	0.8	0.0005	662.52	11.16	635.35	8.61
2	3-level	0.8	0.001	853.30	8.67	741.85	7.38
3	3-level	0.5	0.0005	955.62	7.74	932.52	5.87
4	3-level	0.5	0.001	1424.62	5.19	1384.48	3.95
5	3-level	0.2	0.0005	1274.13	5.81	1297.30	4.22
6	3-level	0.2	0.001	1983.52	3.73	2008.87	2.72
7	2-level	0.8	0.0005	2354.70	3.14	1780.05	3.07
8	2-level	0.8	0.001	2841.17	2.60	2139.13	2.56
9	2-level	0.5	0.0005	2986.17	2.48	2305.78	2.37
10	2-level	0.5	0.001	3190.02	2.32	2646.95	2.07
11	2-level	0.2	0.0005	2995.55	2.47	2542.80	2.15
12	2-level	0.2	0.001	3268.58	2.26	2936.73	1.86
13	1-level	—	—	7396.93	1.00	5472.72	1.00

It is shown in Table 1 that the multiresolution learning method improves the training performance of back-propagation networks significantly, from the least improvement of 1.86 times faster in the Experiment 2 to the best improvement of 11.16 times faster in the Experiment 1. Generally, the training performance increases as the network level increases, e.g., the convergence time for a 3-level network is shorter than the one for a 2-level network. As ρ increases or δ decreases, the convergence rate of the network will also increase.

5 Discussion and Conclusion

First of all, let us investigate why the training performance of a back-propagation network will be improved when the multiresolution learning method is used. With the use of the low level network in the the learning method, the training examples can be learned in a lower resolution. Since the architecture of the low level networks is always simpler than the one of the high level networks, the low level networks often take less time in the training processes. Even though the examples cannot be fully generalized in this level, the low level networks can actually reduce the overhead for the high level networks in some extents. The function of the high level networks is to refine the generalization rather than start it from the beginning.

As it is shown in Table 1, the convergence rate increases as ρ increases or δ decreases. It is quite easy to be understood that such improvement is expected. In this case, the low level network, say B_{2j} contributes more in the whole training process with a large value of ρ or a small value of δ and is allowed to learn the information of $\{A_{2j}^d \vec{x}\}$ as much as possible. The main objective of the high level network B_{2j+1} is to learn the difference of information between $\{A_{2j+1}^d \vec{x}\}$ and $\{A_{2j}^d \vec{x}\}$. Usually, the computational cost for B_{2j} is smaller than the one of B_{2j+1}.

In this paper, we proposed a problem-independent learning method, which adopts the multiresolution signal decomposition techniques, for back-propagation networks in order to alleviate the shortcomings of this kind of networks, i.e., the convergence rate is slow. Experimental results has shown that our proposed learning method improves the training performance of back-propagation networks significantly.

References

[1] Peter J. Burt and Edward H. Adelson. "The Laplacian pyramid as a compact image code". *IEEE Transactions on Communications*, 31(4):532–540, 1983.

[2] I. Daubechies. "Orthonormal bases of compactly supported wavelets". *Communications on Pure and Applied Mathematics*, 41:909–996, 1988.

[3] Don R. Hush and Bill G. Horne. "Progress in supervised neural networks". *IEEE Signal Processing Magazine*, pages 8–29, January 1993.

[4] R.A. Jacobs. "Increased rates of convergence through learning rate adaptation". *Neural Networks*, 1(4):295–308, 1988.

[5] Martin D. Levine. *Vision in Man and Machine*, chapter 3, pages 59–99. McGraw-Hill, 1985.

[6] Stephane G. Mallat. "A theory for multiresolution signal decomposition: the wavelet representation". *IEEE Transactions on Pattern Analysis and Machine Intelligence*, 11(7):674–693, 1989.

[7] Stephane G. Mallat. "Multifrequency channel decompositions of images and wavelet models". *IEEE Transactions on Acoustics, Speech, and Signal Processing*, 37(12):2091–2110, 1989.

[8] A. Rosenfeld, editor. *Multiresolution Image Processing and Analysis*. Springer-Verlag, 1984.

[9] D.E. Rumelhart, G.E. Hinton, and R.J. Williams. "Learning internal representations by error propagation". In D.E. Rumelhart and J.L. McClelland, editors, *Parallel Distributed Processing: Explorations in the Microstructure of Cognition*, volume 1: Foundations, pages 318–362. Bradford Books/MIT Press, 1986.

[10] Michael Sabourin and Amar Mitiche. "Modeling and classification of shape using a Kohonen associative memory with selective multiresolution". *Neural Networks*, 6(2):275–283, 1993.

[11] Gilbert Strang. "Wavelets and dilation equations: a brief introduction". *SIAM Review*, 31(4):614–627, 1989.

[12] Stephan R. Yhann and Tzay Y. Young. "A multiresolution approach to texture segmentation using neural networks". In *Proceedings of International Conference on Pattern Recognition*, volume 1, pages 513–517, Atlantic City, NJ, 1990.

A NEURAL NETWORK DEMODULATOR FOR BANDWIDTH EFFICIENT WAVEFORMS

Dr.Kenneth S. Schneider and Ruben H. Nazario
Telebyte Technology, Inc.
270 Pulaski Road
Greenlawn, NY 11740

ABSTRACT

The work is intended to motivate further research in the application of neural networks to demodulation. An example is provided of improved demodulation of bandwidth efficient waveforms with a three layer neural network. Simulation results of the probability of error with this demodulator are discussed.

The intent here is to tie together two important technological areas, neural networks and demodulation in digital communications. The paper is motivational in its goal . The result is presented, with the hope that this will spark further work in this area.

At first glance the connection between neural networks and digital communications seems obvious. In digital communications, discrete time, quantized, information samples are respresented by or modulate individual waveforms. These waveforms are sent through a transmission channel where they are usually disturbed by noise and/or other interference and/or distortion caused by dispersive phenomena or a variety of other deleterious effects. At the receiving end the disturbed modulation waveform is presented to a demodulator which attempts to extract, without error, the information sample represented. Demodulation can be viewed as detection or estimation of the information from the received waveform. However, alternatively, demodulation can also be viewed as a simple pattern classification problem, with the received, disturbed, modulation waveform being the pattern and the information sample represented being the prototype. This is a task well suited to a neural network.

Yet, despite the obvious connection there have been relatively few reports of a neural network approach to demodulation. True, the adaptive equalizer which is really a demodulator has been in existence for several decades and is a neural network. But, it is a very primitive neural network having only a single layer and not really exploiting any nonlinearity. An examination of the

open literature has shown very little work in applying "modern,"
multilayer, neural networks or Hopfield networks to the problem
of demodulation. References [1], [2] and [3] provide some
connection but hardly represent much attention from the community
as a whole.

How then to begin? It would seem that neural networks would
provide the greatest advantage to demodulation when the channels
themselves are nonlinear and/or non-Gaussian. These are
channels disturbed by intermodulation, limiter based distortion,
co-channel interference and dispersive effects. After all the
nonlinearities present in neural networks may be brought to bear
on this communication situation in the same way they are brought
to bear on nonlinear control problems. Furthermore, the existing
techniques for demodulating in such circumstances are far from
optimal. However, this is what we hope to motivate and is beyond
the scope of the present paper.

Rather, the problem is picked up by looking at the standard
Additive White Gaussian Noise (AWGN) channel and applying a
neural network to getting greater bandwidth efficiency. AWGN
channels are linear. The issue of bandwidth efficiency,
(modulation schemes which represent more bits per Hz) is itself
important as the information age explodes and the electromagnetic
spectrum is taxed to the limit in both cable and wireless
communications.

Let us begin our motivational work by looking at the problem of
binary digital communication on the AWGN channel. Specifically,
consider the situation where information is transmitted using
binary orthogonal signals. In particular consider the set of
signals illustrated in Figure 1. Here, the upper signal
represents the binary digit "0" and the lower signal represents
the binary digit "1." A bit is transmitted every T seconds. If
T=1/R and B= the modulation signal bandwidth then the spectral
efficiency is R/B bits per Hz. The actual bandwidth varies with
the definition used. However, in any measure B varies inversely
with the signal "on-time" which in this example is T/2 seconds.
This signal set is, of course, a version of pulse position
modulation. In baseband communications it is often referred to
as Manchester encoding and preferred for its synchronization
capabilities.

In the AWGN channel this binary orthogonal modulation set is
optimally demodulated by a pair of matched filter correlators,
one matched to $S_0(t)$ and one matched to $S_1(t)$. The index of the
correlator output which is largest is the bit decision. The
probability of error versus Signal-to-Noise Ratio (SNR) resulting
from this optimal approach is available in many references, (see
for example [4]) and indeed is the same for any pair of
orthogonal signals in these circumstances.

Consider now a slightly altered version of this waveform set,
namely the binary waveform set illustrated in Figure 2. Here,

the first modulation waveform has been extended to the right and
the second to the left, each by T/2, one quarter of a Baud
period. The on-time has been extended. Consequently, the
bandwidth is reduced by approximately 33 1/3%. This is a
significant increase in spectral efficiency. Of course, one
could have gone to binary antipodal signalling (PSK) and gotten a
100% increase. But, we can say that this would "break the rules"
by not allowing negative amplitude values.

The waveforms in this new set are correlated. They are no longer
orthogonal. A bank of matched filter correlators is no longer
the optimal demodulator. How should these, more bandwidth
efficient, waveforms be demodulated? One could do nothing. That
is, employ the now sub-optimal matched filter correlators. In
the output of the "incorrect" matched filter correlator there is
now cross-talk. In the present example this amounts to an
equivalent reduction of SNR by about 5 db. This is a significant
penalty to get the increased spectral efficiency.

One could also resort to an improved but still sub-optimal
technique of somehow estimating the cross-talk and subtracting it
from the "incorrect" matched-filter correlator output. This is
like performing a Gram-Schmidt orthonormalization on the
modulation waveform set and using the resulting waveforms for
correlation. A technique employing this was reported in Ref. [5]
and is essentially a type of spacial equalizer. However,
estimation of the cross-talk itself involves noise. Hence, there
is an enhancement of the effective noise and a reduction in
equivalent SNR. This is always a phenomenon associated with
equalization. The penalty in reduced SNR is not as great as the
case of doing nothing. The increased spectral efficiency does
come with some penalty but not anything like 5 db.

We have investigated the use of a three (3) layer neural network
for demodulating the bandwidth efficient modulation waveform set
illustrated in Figure 2. But before describing the architecture
and results it is appropriate to ask why this is even worth
considering. That is, why is this an alternative to the suboptimal techniques just described and an alternative worth
investigating. Those suboptimal techniques were based on matched
filter correlation. Correlation is an exploitation of first
order statistics, moments. A two (2) layer neural network can
automatically do this. The addition of a third, hidden, layer
allows higher order statistics to be dealt with and features not
captured in correlation processing.

The three (3) level neural network architecture which we
investigated as a demodulator is illustrated in Figure 3. The
architecture consists of only 13 neurons. The input layer
captures eight (8) uniformly spaced samples of the received
waveform. These are designated as $\{S*(i), i=1,...8\}$. They are
uniformly spaced every T/8 seconds beginning at 0+. There is no
nonlinear processing in the input layer. The hidden layer
consists of four (4) neurons. To avoid an overly complicated

figure we have only shown a few of the branches with corresponding weights. Each neuron in the hidden layer uses a sigmoid as the activation with parameter 2. The neurons in this layer are represented by circles with heavy black dots in the center. The third or output layer is a single neuron with the same type of sigmoid behavior. The output, Z, for purposes of training is kept as a real number. In operation it is quantized to either zero (0) or one (1) based upon nearest neighbor.

This neural network was trained using back propagation. An error acceptance parameter of 0.2 and a convergence parameter of 0.2 were used throughout training. All weights were initialized randomly.

We examined the behavior of the network as a demodulator using simulation. This was accomplished by fixing the SNR and fixing the size of the SNR and fixing the size of the training set. A specific training set of size, N (an even number) was generated as follows. The first two waveforms in the set were the noise-free modulation waveforms, $S_0(t)$ and $S_1(t)$. (N/2)-1 additional waveforms were then generated by taking $S_0(t)$ and perturbing it by samples of randomly generated AWGN at the SNR. The same number of additional waveforms were generated by perturbing $S_1(t)$. For a given SNR and training set we measured the probability of error using 30,000 randomly generated testing waveforms. This limitation arose because simulation was executed on a 386 PC with an accelerator board.

The simulation results are shown in Figure 4. Each curve corresponds to a different SNR and shows the variation of simulated probability of error with the size of the training set. Rather, than make each curve a "smooth" interpolation of simulated measurements we have preserved the actual randomness. Nonetheless, we can still reach a firm conclusion which is our essential result. It appears that in each case the probability of error approaches that for binary orthogonal signalling with increasing training set size. This is an interesting result. We are able to get a significant improvement in bandwidth efficiency with no penalty in SNR, provided training is sufficiently long.

What should be the next step? Before proceeding to more complicated, non-linear channels, one should look at the same problem of bandwidth efficiency but with larger modulation waveform sets. In particular, it would be nice to derive, at least by simulation, the equivalent of a Shannon Coding Theorem for neural networks. That is, what degree of bandwidth efficiency can be obtained while still having an orthogonal signalling probability of error?

REFERENCES

[1]   Hampshire II, J.B., "A Differential Theory of Learning for Efficient Statistical Pattern Recognition," Ph.D. Thesis, Carnegie Mellon University, Carnegie Institute of Technology, 1993.

[2]   Midwinter, J.E. and Selviah, D.R., "Digital neural networks, matched filters and optical implementations," in Neural Computing Architectures, M.I.T. Press, 1989 pp 258-278.

[3]   Lippmann, Richard P. and Beckman, Paul, "Adaptive Neural Net Preprocessing for Signal Detection in Non-Gaussian Noise," in NIPS Proceedings Advances in Neural Information Processing Systems I, Morgan Kaufman, San Mateo, Calif, 1989, pp 124-132

[4]   Proakis, John G., Digital Communications, McGraw-Hill, New York, 1983, p 153.

[5]   Schneider, Kenneth S., "Crosstalk Resistant Receiver for M-ary Multiplexed Communications," IEEE Transactions on Aerospace and Electronic Systems, July 1980 pp 426-433

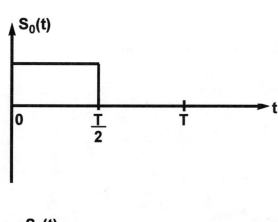

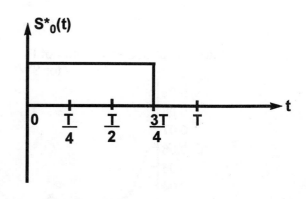

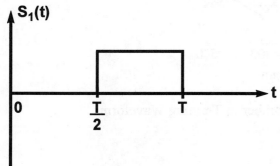

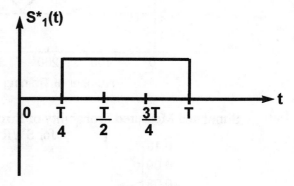

Figure 1
Example set of binary orthogonal signals

Figure 2
Binary modulation waveform set which is
not orthogonal

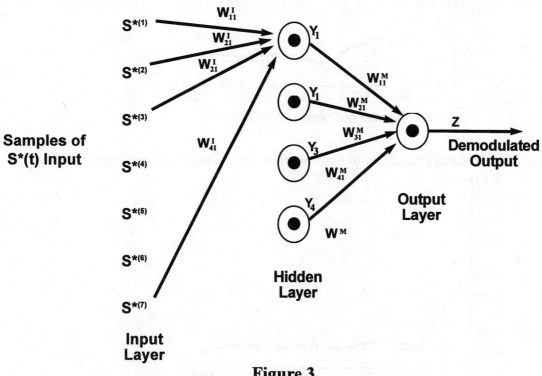

Figure 3
Architecture of Neural Network Demodulator

Figure 4

a. Simulated Measured Probability of Error vs Number of Training Waveforms for SWR=6dB

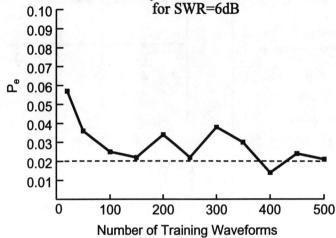

b. Simulated Measured Probability of Error vs Number of Training Waveforms for SWR=6.5dB

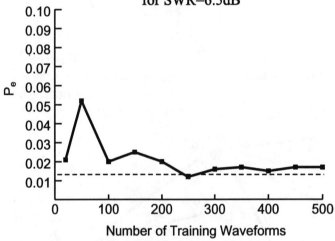

c. Simulated Measured Probability of Error vs Number of Training Waveforms for SWR=7dB

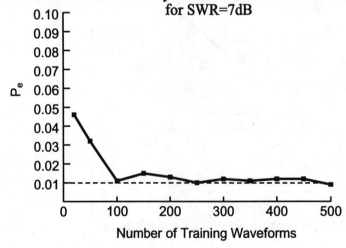

An Edge-Preserving Neural Network For Image Compression

Mahmoud R. El-Sakka and Mohamed S. Kamel[1]

Department of Systems Design Engineering
University of Waterloo
Waterloo, Ontario, Canada, N2L 3G1

Abstract

When conventional BP ANN is employed for image encoding the decoded images usually exhibit some degradation of the edges. This is due to the fact that edge pixels usually represent a small portion of the entire image and BP learning algorithms do not differentiate between edge and non-edge pixels. In this paper, a novel Edge-Preserving ANN learning algorithm is proposed. This learning algorithm pays more attention to edge information. The error between the computed and desired output value is multiplied by a weighting factor which is proportional to the amount of edge information in the corresponding input pixel. The algorithm is implemented and its performance is assessed by comparing it to the conventional BP.

1 Introduction

Successful image compression using back propagation neural networks has been demonstrated in [1] [2]. In these systems the decoded image usually suffers from degraded edges. The human visual system contains special cells in the brain which are very sensitive to edges [3]. This suggests that in order to obtain a good quality image, edge information has to be preserved.

ANNs are mathematical models of theorized mind and brain activity [4]. Typically, these models differ in their topology, way of learning, and way of recalling information [5] [6] [7]. For instance, BP ANN, [8], which is a supervised, feedforward network learns by making weight connection adjustments according to the error between the computed and desired output values. All output values receive the same attention regardless of the information they represent. However, in order to avoid edge degradation, it would be desirable for edge pixels to receive more emphasis (while learning) than the rest of the pixels.

In the next section, a novel ANN learning algorithm which preserves edge information is proposed. To justify this proposed learning algorithm, simulation experiments were carried out. These experiments and results are described in section 3, a discussion of the results is presented in section 4, and the paper is summarized in the concluding section 5.

2 Edge-Preserving ANN model

In this model, the error between the computed and desired output value is multiplied by a weighting factor which is proportional to the amount of edge information in the corresponding input pixel. These proposed weighting factor can be calculated by using the Laplacian operator which is a second-order derivative operator and can be implemented by convolving the mask shown in Figure 1

---

[1] Correspondence should be addressed to: mkamel@watnow.uwaterloo.ca (e-mail) and/or (519)888-4567 ext. 5761 (phone).

```
        0    1    0
        1  - 4    1
        0    1    0
```

Figure 1: Mask used to compute the Laplacian

with the image. Then, the absolute value of this Laplacian of each pixel is normalized by dividing it by the maximum absolute Laplacian value from all pixels of the image. Finally, a value of 1 is added to each pixel of the absolute normalized Laplacian image to get a weighting factor for each image pixel between 1 and 2. The purpose of the added 1 is to maintain the effect a non-edge pixel has in adjusting ANN weights. So, when the proposed weighting factor is close to 1 for a pixel that has almost no edge information, its effect on changing ANN weights is the same as the conventional BP learning algorithm. On the other hand, when it is close to 2 for a pixel that represents part of an edge, its effect on changing ANN weights is almost double what it would be using the conventional BP learning algorithm. Figure 2 (a) shows Laplacian edge-effect enhanced during learning.

After learning, an image block is compressed by forward propagating it through the network, then, quantizing and saving the hidden layer unit activations instead of saving the original block pixel values. To uncompress an image block, these quantized values are presented to the second half of the network then the reconstructed block is generated from the output layer unit activations. Figure 2 (b) shows a diagram for the compression and decompression operations.

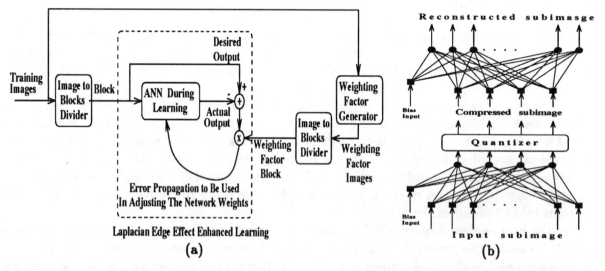

Figure 2: The proposed learning: (a) Proposed Laplacian edge-effect enhanced during learning, (b) The compression and decompression operations.

3   Experimental Results

The main purpose of this experiment is to test the proposed learning algorithm and compare its performance with the conventional BP learning algorithm. In this experiment, two three-layer BP

ANNs were used. Each ANN consists of 16 input units, 4 hidden units, and 16 output units. The only difference between these two ANNs is their learning algorithm. In the first ANN the proposed modified learning is employed while the conventional BP learning is employed in the second ANN. The input to these two ANNs are 16 values representing a 4 by 4 image block pixel values.

The learning rate and the number of learning iterations are selected identical in both ANNs. The learning data set is generated from the *terminal* image, shown in Figure 3 (a). The testing data set is generated from the *hotel* image, shown in Figure 3 (b).

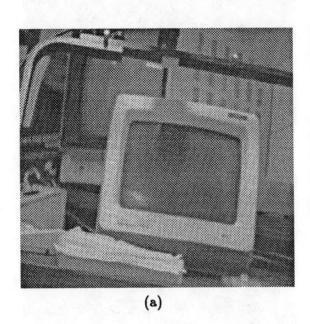
(a)

(b)

Figure 3: (a) Learning image, (b) Testing image.

Figure 4 (a),(b),(c), and (d), shows the reconstructed learned image and the absolute error after performing compression / decompression using both of the ANN learning algorithms. Six bits were used to quantize the activation of each hidden unit. The absolute error image is enhanced by adding a value of 128 to each pixel value. Figure 4 (e) shows a table for the mean squared error of the reconstructed learned image for both learning algorithms. This table demonstrates the effect of using various quantization levels.

Figure 5 (a) and Figure 5 (b) show a zoomed section of the reconstructed testing image after performing compression / decompression using both of the ANN learning algorithms with six bits quantization. Figure 5 (c) shows a table for the mean squared error of the reconstructed testing image for both learning algorithms.

4 Discussion

The proposed Laplacian edge-effect enhanced learning shows better performance in the form of less mean squared error, as well as appearing to produce better quality of reconstructed image. When Laplacian edge effect enhanced learning is employed the edges are preserved more than when regular BP learning is employed. This is because the proposed learning algorithm gives more importance to the learning of edge information in the image.

As shown in Figure 4 (e) and Figure 5 (c), error for proposed Laplacian edge-effect enhanced learning is consistently lower than that obtained using regular BP learning for any number of

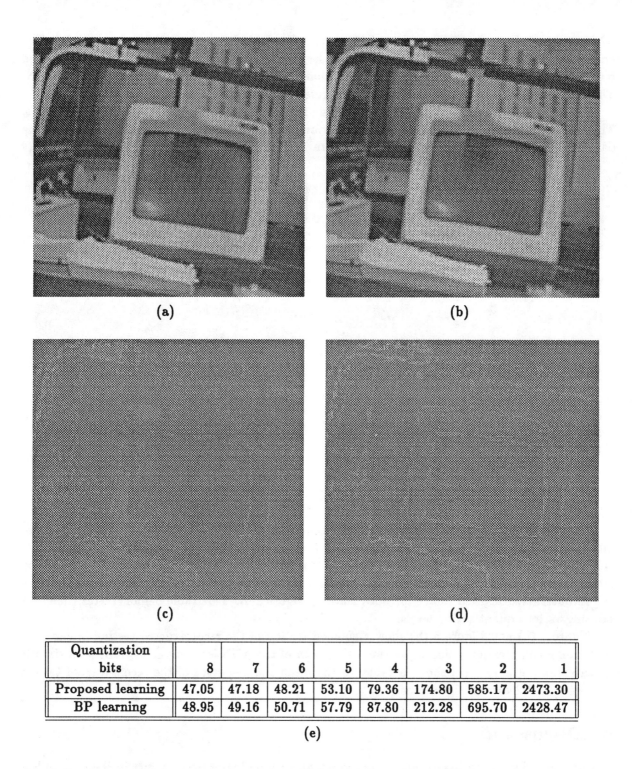

Quantization bits	8	7	6	5	4	3	2	1
Proposed learning	47.05	47.18	48.21	53.10	79.36	174.80	585.17	2473.30
BP learning	48.95	49.16	50.71	57.79	87.80	212.28	695.70	2428.47

(e)

Figure 4: (a) and (b) Reconstructed taught image after performing compression / decompression using the proposed learning algorithm and the BP learning algorithm respectively with 6 bits quantization, (c) and (d) absolute error in image (a), (d) respectively, and (e) Reconstruction mean squared error for different quantization levels .

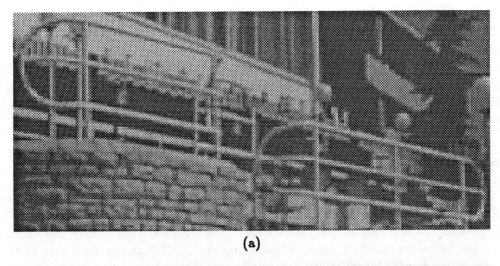

(a)

(b)

Quantization bits	8	7	6	5	4	3	2	1
Proposed learning	112.82	113.05	114.36	119.53	144.33	239.35	527.14	1861.18
BP learning	135.31	135.51	136.31	140.1	156.82	255.51	591.37	1456.55

(c)

Figure 5: (a) and (b) Zoom on a part of the reconstructed testing image after performing compression / decompression using the proposed learning algorithm and the BP learning algorithm respectively with 6 bits quantization, (c) Reconstruction mean squared error for different quantization levels .

quantization bits used except with 1 bit quantization. However, in the latter case, it does not really matter which method is better since fidelity would be extremely low for both due to high mean square error.

Otherwise, the error slightly increases with decreasing quantization level for the hidden layer unit activations. This is true down to a certain level of quantization (4 bits in this case), after which the error increases dramatically. Below this quantization and with the current learning level, the network is no longer able to encode the image successfully.

5   Conclusion

Trained ANNs are able to extract the desired information in a given image and encode it according to a predetermined criterion. This criterion is given to the ANNs during learning in the form of training examples and the learning algorithm. Edge degradation during the compression / decompression processes can be reduced by adapting the ANN learning algorithm so that it can pay more attention to edge information. Potentially, this method could be used to emphasize other image features such as texture.

References

[1] G.W.Cottrell, P.Munro, and D.Zipser, "Image Compression by Back Propagation: An Example of Extensional Programming", in *Models of Cognition: A Review of Cognition Science*, by N.E.Sharkey (Ed.), Ablex Publishing Corporation, 1989.

[2] N.Sonehara, M.Kawato, S.Miyake, and K.Nakane, "Image Data Compression Using A Neural Network Model", *International Joint Conference on Neural Networks*, Vol.II, pp.35-41, June 1989.

[3] M.Kunt, A.Ikonomopoulos, and M.Kocher, "Second-Generation Image-Coding", *Proceedings of the IEEE*, Vol.73, pp.549-574, April 1985.

[4] P.D.Wasserman, *Neural Computing: Theory and Practice*, Van Nostrand Reinhold, 1989.

[5] P.K.Simpson, *Artificial Neural Systems: Foundations, Paradigms, Applications, and Implementations*, McGraw-Hill, 1990.

[6] R.P.Lippmann, "An Introduction to Computing With Neural Nets", *IEEE Acoustics, Speech and Signal Processing Magazine*, Vol.4, pp.4-22, April, 1987.

[7] G.E.Hinton, "Connectionist Learning Procedures", *Artificial Intelligence*, Vol.40, pp.143-150, 1989.

[8] D.E.Rumelhart, G.E.Hinton, and R.J.Williams, "Learning Representations by Back-Propagating Errors", *Nature*, Vol.323, pp.533-536, October 1986.

A Neural Net for the Separation of Nonstationary Signal Sources

Kiyotoshi MATSUOKA and Mitsuru KAWAMOTO
Department of Control Engineering
Kyusyu Institute of Technology
Sensui 1-1, Tobata, Kitakyusyu, 804 Japan

Abstract This paper proposes a neural network that learns to recover the original random signals from their linear mixtures observed by the same number of sensors. The network acquires the function without using any information about the statistical properties of the sources and the coefficients of the linear transformation, except the assumption that the source signals are statistically independent and nonstationary. The learning rule is formulated as a steepest descent minimization of a time-dependent cost function that takes the minimum only when the network outputs are uncorrelated with each other.

1. Introduction

This work deals with the problem of how the original signals generated by some stochastic sources (e.g., voices uttered by two persons) can be separated from their linear mixtures observed by the same number of sensors (e.g., output voltages of two microphones). Such a signal separation is called "blind separation", when it must be performed in the absence of any special information about the statistical properties of the sources and the coefficients of the linear transformation, except the fact that the source signals are statistically independent of each other.

It can be shown that the blind separation is impossible if the sources are stationary, gaussian processes. The method proposed here assumes that the source signals are nonstationary, while the conventional methods stipulate that they are nongaussian [1, 2, 3, 4, 5].

This paper proposes an adaptive linear network which acquires the function of blind separation. It is achieved by iteratively modifying the network's parameters so as to minimize a time-dependent cost function that takes the minimum only when the network outputs are uncorrelated with each other. It is shown that the equilibrium of the learning dynamics is uniformly asymptotically stable. A computer simulation is also given to demonstrate the validity of the method.

2. Signal Sources

Suppose that random signals $x'_j(t)$ ($j=1,...,N$) are generated by N statistically independent sources, and their linear mixtures (affine transformation) $s'_i(t)$ ($i=1,...,N$) are observed by N sensors:

$$s'_i(t) = \sum_{j=1}^{N} a_{ij}x'_j(t) + a_i \tag{1}$$

where a_{ij} and a_i are constants independent of time t. Putting $x_j(t) = x'_j(t)-\langle x'_j(t)\rangle$ and $s_i(t) = s'_i(t)-\langle s'_i(t)\rangle$ ($\langle * \rangle$ denotes the ensemble average of $*$), (1) can be rewritten as

$$s_i(t) = \sum_{j=1}^{N} a_{ij}x_j(t) \tag{2}$$

We here assume that $\langle x'_j(t)\rangle$ ($j=1,...,N$) are constant with time, implying that $\langle s'_i(t)\rangle$ ($i=1,...,N$) are also constant. Then, $s_i(t)$ can also be considered an observable signal because $\langle s'_i(t)\rangle$ can easily be estimated by a time average of $s'_i(t)$. Henceforth, we call $x_j(t)$ and $s_i(t)$ as source signal and sensor signal, respectively. (2) can be expressed in vector notation as

$$s(t) = A x(t) \tag{3}$$

where $s(t) = [s_1(t),...,s_N(t)]^T$, $x(t)=[x_1(t),...,x_N(t)]^T$, and $A=[a_{ij}]$.

The objective of this paper is to propose a neural network that learns to recover the original signals $x_j(t)$ (j=1,...,N) from the sensor signals $s_i(t)$ (i=1,...,N) in the absence of any special information about the properties of $\mathbf{A}$ and $\mathbf{x}(t)$, but it should be noted that this definition of signal separation has an ambiguity. Namely, if $x_j(t)$ (j=1,...,N) are source signals, then $d_1 x_{p_1}(t)$, ..., $d_N x_{p_N}(t)$ can also be considered as source signals, where $\{p_1,...,p_N\}$ is an arbitrary permutation of $\{1,...,N\}$ and $d_1,...,d_N$ are arbitrary nonzero constants. It is because $d_1 x_{p_1}(t)$, ..., $d_N x_{p_N}(t)$ are also statistically independent and $s_i(t)$ can be expressed by their linear combination with coefficients $a_{i,p_1}/d_1$, ..., $a_{i,p_N}/d_N$. Henceforth, we therefore define the signal separation as a process providing any of the following type of signals:

$$\overline{\mathbf{x}}(t) = \mathbf{D}\mathbf{P}\mathbf{x}(t) \tag{4}$$

where $\mathbf{P}$ is a permutation matrix and $\mathbf{D}$ a diagonal matrix with nonzero diagonal elements.

The assumptions we need for blind separation are very modest ones, as follows.

Assumption 1 Matrix $\mathbf{A}$ is nonsingular.

Assumption 2 $x_j(t)$ (j=1,...,N) are statistically independent with zero mean.

This implies that the covariance matrix $\mathbf{R}(t)$ of $\mathbf{x}(t)$ is a diagonal matrix:

$$\mathbf{R}(t) = \text{diag}\{r_1(t),...,r_N(t)\} = \text{diag}\{<x_1^2(t)>,.....,<x_N^2(t)>\} \tag{5}$$

where diag{...} represents a diagonal matrix with diagonal elements {...}.

Assumption 3 $r_i(t)$ (i=1,...,N) are linearly independent functions.

Namely, the following equation holds only when $c_i = 0$ (i=1,...,N).

$$\sum_{i=1}^{N} c_i r_i(t) = 0 \tag{6}$$

Here, time-varying functions $r_i(t)$ (i=1,...,N) are considered to be defined in the time interval during which the sensor signals are observed. [We shall stipulate a slightly stronger condition in §4.]

The last assumption is important because Assumptions 1 and 2 are not sufficient to realize the signal separation in general; if, for example, $\mathbf{x}(t)$ is a stationary, gaussian process, then signal separation is essentially impossible (see §6). Under Assumptions 1-3 we can prove that, if the same sensor signal $\mathbf{s}(t)$ is produced by source signal $\overline{\mathbf{x}}(t)$ as well as by $\mathbf{x}(t)$, then the relation (4) must hold. It means that, about the definition of the source signals, we need not to take into account any other ambiguity than the one mentioned above.

3. Signal Separation Network

For signal separation we consider a recurrent network shown in Fig.1, which receives sensor signals $s_i(t)$ (i=1,...,N) as input and produces outputs $y_i(t)$ (i=1,...,N). The dynamics of each output unit is given by the following first-order linear differential equation

$$\tau\frac{dy_i(t)}{dt} + y_i(t) = s_i(t) - \sum_{j=1}^{N} c_{ij}y_j(t) \qquad (i=1,...,N) \tag{7}$$

Here, $-c_{ij}$ (i, j=1,...,N; i≠j) represent the strengths of the mutual connections between the output units, and they change slowly according to an adaption rule which will be shown later. The output units have no self connection; $c_{ii}=0$. (7) is expressed in vector notation as

$$\tau\frac{d\mathbf{y}(t)}{dt} + \mathbf{y}(t) = \mathbf{s}(t) - \mathbf{C}\mathbf{y}(t) \tag{8}$$

where $y(t) = [y_1(t),...,y_N(t)]^T$, $C = [c_{ij}]$, and τ is a time constant. If $-(I+C)$ is a stable matrix and time constant τ is sufficiently small, then the network function (8) can be replaced by the following static input-output relation, which will be assumed in the sequel.

$$y(t) = (I + C)^{-1}s(t) \qquad (9)$$

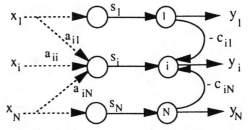

Fig. 1 Signal separation network

Our objective is now to determine C such that $y_i(t)$ is proportional to $x_{pi}(t)$, where $\{p_1,...,p_N\}$ is a permutation of $\{1,...,N\}$. We call C so determined as signal separation operator. The general form of signal separation operator is $C = APD-I$, where P is an arbitrary permutation matrix and D is an arbitrary diagonal matrix with nonzero diagonal elements. It is assured as $y(t) = (C+I)^{-1}s(t) = D^{-1}P^TA^{-1}\cdot Ax(t) = D^{-1}P^Tx(t)$, which is essentially equivalent to (4). Moreover, the constraints $c_{ii}=0$ leads to $D = [diag\{AP\}]^{-1}$ (diag$\{*\}$ denotes the matrix made by putting the nondiagonal elements in matrix $*$ to be zeros). Thus, the general form of the signal separation operator under the condition $c_{ii}=0$ is given by

$$C = AP[diag\{AP\}]^{-1} - I \qquad (10)$$

This result, however, cannot be used for constructing the signal separation network, because we are assuming that matrix A is unknown. Here, we give the following theorem which is useful to obtain the signal separation operator by a learning process.

Theorem 1 The following three statements are equivalent.
  (i) C is given by (10).
  (ii) $<y_i(t)y_j(t)>$ $(i,j=1,...,N; i\neq j)$ are zero at any time t.
  (iii) The following nonnegative scaler function takes zero at any time t.

$$Q(C,R(t)) = \frac{1}{2}\{\sum_{i=1}^{N} \log <y_i^2(t)> - \log \left|<y(t)y(t)^T>\right|\} \qquad (11)$$

4. Learning Process

From Theorem 1 it is found that the signal separation can be realized by determining C so that $Q(C, R(t))$ will take the minimum value at *any* time. In order to achieve this we consider the following dynamics

$$T\frac{dc_{ij}}{dt} = -\frac{\partial Q(C,R(t))}{\partial c_{ij}} \qquad (i,j = 1,...,N; i\neq j) \qquad (12)$$

By calculating the derivative in the right-hand side we have

$$T\frac{dC}{dt} = (I + C^T)^{-1}\{(diag<y(t)y(t)^T>)^{-1}<y(t)y(t)^T> - I\} \qquad (13)$$

Note that diagonal elements in both sides of this equation ($Tdc_{ii}/dt = ...$) are immaterial; c_{ii}'s are always zero. It can be seen that (12) or (13) is to attain the minimum of $Q(C, R(t))$ by a steepest descent method. The behavior of this leaning dynamics, however, is not so simple because $Q(C, R(t))$ includes a time-varying function $R(t)$, but we can prove the following theorem.

Theorem 2 Every *equilibrium* of equation (13) takes the form of (10), and it is (locally) uniformly asymptotically stable under the following condition. [*Equilibrium* defined here indicates the state at which $\mathbf{C}$ does not change at *any* time.]

Assumption 3' For some t_0, T_0 (>0), and ε (>0), the following inequality holds for any unit vector $[q_1, q_2]$ ($q_1^2 + q_2^2 = 1$) and for any time t ($\geq t_0$).

$$\frac{1}{T_0} \int_t^{t+T_0} \left(\sqrt{\frac{r_j(\tau)}{r_i(\tau)}} q_1 + \sqrt{\frac{r_i(\tau)}{r_j(\tau)}} q_2 \right)^2 d\tau \geq \varepsilon > 0 \tag{14}$$

This condition is easily attained if $r_i(t)$ ($i=1,...,N$) continue to fluctuate somewhat independently.

In order to actually realize (13), we need to estimate $\langle \mathbf{y}(t)\mathbf{y}(t)^T \rangle$ in real time. To this end we can use the following moving average $\Phi = [\phi_{ij}]$ of $\mathbf{y}(t)\mathbf{y}(t)^T$ under a certain condition.

$$T' \frac{d\Phi(t)}{dt} + \Phi(t) = \mathbf{y}(t)\mathbf{y}(t)^T \tag{15}$$

So, (13) becomes

$$T \frac{d\mathbf{C}}{dt} = (\mathbf{I} + \mathbf{C}^T)^{-1} \{ (\text{diag}\Phi(t))^{-1}\Phi(t) - \mathbf{I} \} \tag{16}$$

5. A Special Case: N=2

Here, we shall consider the special case of N=2, for which (13) reads

$$T \frac{dc_{12}}{dt} = \frac{1}{(1 - c_{12}c_{21})} \frac{\langle y_1(t)y_2(t) \rangle}{\langle y_1^2(t) \rangle} \quad , \quad T \frac{dc_{21}}{dt} = \frac{1}{(1 - c_{12}c_{21})} \frac{\langle y_2(t)y_1(t) \rangle}{\langle y_2^2(t) \rangle} \tag{17}$$

According to (10), it has two equilibria given by

$$c_{12} = \frac{a_{12}}{a_{22}}, c_{21} = \frac{a_{21}}{a_{11}} \ (P = \begin{bmatrix} 1 & 0 \\ 0 & 1 \end{bmatrix}) \quad \text{or} \quad c_{12} = \frac{a_{11}}{a_{21}}, c_{21} = \frac{a_{22}}{a_{12}} \ (P = \begin{bmatrix} 0 & 1 \\ 1 & 0 \end{bmatrix}) \tag{18}$$

According to Theorem 2, both the equilibria are stable in terms of the *learning dynamics* (13), but it should be noted that the *network dynamics* (7) must also be stable for the equilibrium. It can be shown that only one of these satisfies the condition $|c_{12}c_{21}| < 1$ which allows the network dynamics to be stable.

We next consider a simplified learning dynamics obtained by eliminating the common terms $1/(1-c_{12}c_{21})$ appearing in the right-hand sides of (17)

$$T \frac{dc_{12}}{dt} = \frac{\langle y_1(t)y_2(t) \rangle}{\langle y_1^2(t) \rangle} \quad , \quad T \frac{dc_{21}}{dt} = \frac{\langle y_2(t)y_1(t) \rangle}{\langle y_2^2(t) \rangle} \tag{19}$$

An interesting feature of this learning rule is that it is a variant of an anti-Hebbian rule [6]; the connection weight $-c_{ij}$ *decreases* proportionally to the product of $y_1(t)$ and $y_j(t)$ but with time-varying rate $1/\langle y_i^2(t) \rangle$. Obviously, (19) has the same equilibria (18) as the original dynamics (17), but the stability becomes a little different; one equilibrium satisfying $|c_{12}c_{21}| < 1$ is solely stable. Namely, only the equilibrium for which the *network dynamics* is stable is stable also with respect to the *learning dynamics*.

We here show a computer simulation, in which the differential equations previously given are transformed into difference equations, using the Euler approximation. For source signals $x_i(k)$ and $x_2(k)$, the following stationary and nonstationary, gaussian white signals are used, respectively:

$$x_1(k) = u_1(k) \quad , \quad x_2(k) = \eta(k)u_2(k)$$

where $u_1(k)$ and $u_2(k)$ are both the gaussian white signal with zero mean and unity variance, and

$\eta(k)$ was given by $\eta(k) = 3 \sin(\pi/200)k$. Matrix $\mathbf{A}$ is given as

$$\mathbf{A} = \begin{bmatrix} 1 & 0.5 \\ 0.5 & 1 \end{bmatrix}$$

(15) and (17) become, respectively,

$$\phi_{ij}(k+1) = \alpha\phi_{ij}(k) + (1-\alpha)y_i(k)y_j(k) \qquad (i, j = 1,2)$$

$$c_{12}(k+1) = c_{12}(k) - \beta \cdot \frac{\phi_{12}(k)}{\phi_{11}(k)} \quad , \quad c_{21}(k+1) = c_{21}(k) - \beta \cdot \frac{\phi_{21}(k)}{\phi_{22}(k)}$$

The values of $y_i(k)$ are assumed to be given by the static input-output relation (9). The parameters of the learning dynamics are chosen as $\alpha = 0.9$ and $\beta = 0.001$, and the initial values of c_{12}, c_{21}, and ϕ_{ij} ($i=1,2$) are set at 0, 0, and 1, respectively.

Fig. 2 shows the plots of $x_i(k)$ and $y_i(k)-x_i(k)$ ($i = 1,2$). Theoretically, the network should learn to provide the output as $y_i(k) = x_i(k)$ ($i = 1,2$). One can see that the network acquires the desired function in about a thousand steps.

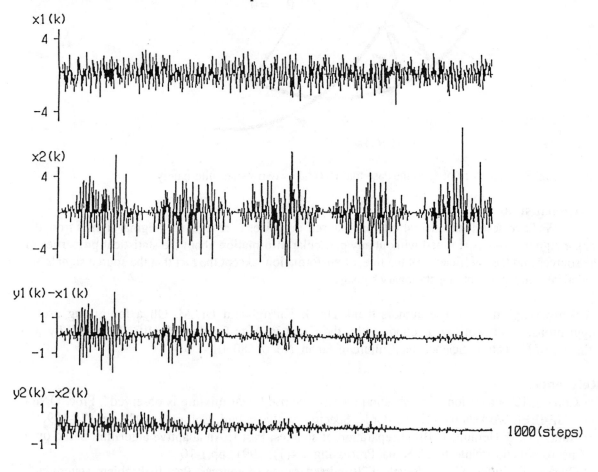

Fig. 2 The plots of $x_i(k)$ and $y_i(k)-x_i(k)$

6. Discussion

Suppose that $\mathbf{x}(t)$ in (3) obeys a *stationary* gaussian process with constant covariance matrix $\mathbf{R} = \{r_1,...,r_N\}$. Then, we can see that the source signal $\overline{\mathbf{x}}(t)=[\overline{x}_1(t),...,\overline{x}_N(t)]^T$ and the linear transform $\overline{\mathbf{A}}$ given below yield the same sensor signal $\mathbf{s}(t)$,

$$\overline{\mathbf{x}}(t) = \mathbf{D}\mathbf{E}^T\mathbf{R}^{-1/2}\mathbf{x}(t) \tag{20}$$

III-69

$$s(t) = \overline{\mathbf{A}}\,\overline{\mathbf{x}}(t) = \mathbf{A}\,\mathbf{R}^{1/2}\mathbf{E}\mathbf{D}^{-1}\overline{\mathbf{x}}(t) \tag{21}$$

where $\mathbf{D}$ is a diagonal matrix, $\mathbf{E}$ an orthogonal matrix, and $\mathbf{R}^{1/2} = \mathrm{diag}\{r_1^{1/2},...,r_N^{1/2}\}$. Note that $<\overline{\mathbf{x}}(t)\overline{\mathbf{x}}(t)^{\mathrm{T}}> = \mathbf{D}^2$ is a diagonal matrix, i.e., $\overline{x}_i(t)$ ($i=1,...,N$) are independent of each other because noncorrelation is equivalent to independence in gaussian processes. The arbitrariness of $\mathbf{E}$ implies that it is essentially impossible to recover $\mathbf{x}(t)$ from $s(t)$ with the ambiguity of (4). This fact means that $\mathbf{C}$ minimizing $Q(\mathbf{C}, \mathbf{R})$ is not an isolated point but forms a hypersurface in $N(N-1)$ dimensional space of c_{ij}'s ($i \neq j$). So, along with learning, $\mathbf{C}$ approaches any point on the surface, depending on its initial value.

If $\mathbf{R}(t)$ changes with time, the situation becomes different. Let us, for example, consider the case that $\mathbf{R}(t)$ ($N=2$) takes $\mathbf{R}_1$ and $\mathbf{R}_2$ alternately (see Fig.3). When $\mathbf{R}(t)=\mathbf{R}_1$, $\mathbf{C}$ moves to the curve determined by $Q(\mathbf{C},\mathbf{R}_1)=0$, and when $\mathbf{R}(t)=\mathbf{R}_2$, $\mathbf{C}$ moves toward the curve $Q(\mathbf{C}, \mathbf{R}_2)=0$. As a result, $\mathbf{C}$ converges to a cross point of the two curves, i.e., the desired equilibrium (10).

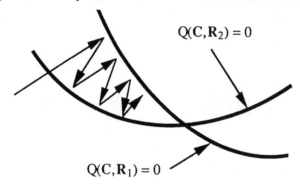

Fig. 3 Trajectory of $\mathbf{C}$ in the case that $\mathbf{R}(t)$ takes two values alternately

7. Conclusion

We have described a neural network that self-organizes to recover the original signals from the sensor signals. It is performed without any particular information about the statistical properties of the sources and the coefficients of the linear transformation, except the fact that the source signals are statistically independent, nonstationary signals.

Acknowledgement   The authors thank Dr. S. Kurogi and Dr. M. Ohya for giving useful suggestions. This work was supported by the Grant-in-Aids for the Scientific Research by the Ministry of Education, Science and Culture of Japan, No. 05680301.

References

[1] Comon, P."Separation of stochastic processes whose linear mixture is observed", Proc. ONR-NSF-IEEE Workshop on Higher-Order Spectral Analysis, Vail, Colorado, 1989, pp.174-179.

[2] Jutten, C. & Herault, J."Blind separation of sources, Part I: An adaptive algorithm based on a neuromimetic architecture", Signal Processing, 24(1), 1991, pp.1-10.

[3] Comon, P., Jutten, C., & Herault, J."Blind separation of sources, Part II: Problem statement", Signal Processing, 24(1), 1991, pp.11-20.

[4] Sorouvhyari, E."Blind separation of sources, Part III: Stability analysis", Signal Processing, 24(1), 1991, pp.21-29.

[5] Burel, G."Blind separation of sources: a nonlinear neural algorithm", Neural Networks, 5, 1992, pp.937-947.

[6] Matsuoka, K. & Kawamoto, M. "A neural network that self-organizes to perform three operations related to principal component analysis", Neural Networks, to appear.

OPTIMAL LOCAL ESTIMATION OF RBF PARAMETERS

STEFANIA MARCHINI* and N. ALBERTO BORGHESE**
*Dipartimento di Scienze dell'Informazione, University of Milano, I.
**Institute Neuroscience Bioimages C.N.R., Via Mario Bianco 9, 20131 Milano, I

ABSTRACT

Radial Basis Functions have been recently proposed as an effective method for the reconstruction of continous functions, starting from a not evenly sampled set of points. This approach allows a convenient representation of the reconstructing function through neural networks. As far as gaussian radial basis are concerned, the parameters that completely define the reconstructing function are the coordinates of the center and the variance of each gaussian and their number. We propose here, a method to automatically determine these parameters starting from the distances between the sampled data. Preliminary results are reported for small sets of bidimensional points.

INTRODUCTION

The reconstrunction of a continous curve $g(x)$ starting from a set of points by means of a parametric function $f(x) = F(x,w)$, with w a set of unknown parameters, is an ill-posed problem that allows an infinite number of solutions, all compatible with the data. To obtain the solution optimal to the problem, a classical approach is to introduce soft constraints that do not specify exact desired values of the function $F(x,w)$ but only a tendency of it in the definition domain. One of the most promising classes of reconstructing functions has been recently proposed by Poggio and Girosi (1989); it allows to write the function $F(x,w)$ as a linear combination of radial (gaussian) functions:

$$F(x,w) = \sum_{i=1}^{N} c_i G(x; d_i / \sigma_i) \qquad (1)$$

where c_i, d_i e σ_i are the parameters w to be determined, respectively: the amplitude coefficient, the center and the variance of the gaussian G_i; N is the number of different gaussian functions employed; $N \leq M$, where M is the number of the sampled points $P_i = (x_i; y_i)$.

In this paper we propose a method for the automatic setting of these parameters as a function of the distances between the points, to achieve the optimal reconstructing function. The behaviour of the method has been tested comparing the different curves obtained from a set of randomly generated points.

This algorithm can be easily extended to multi-dimensional functions and it is well suited for a hardware neural network implementation.

METHOD

First, the optimal number of gaussian functions is determined, then the optimal values of the coefficient parameters is computed.

The coefficeints c_i can be determined analytically imposing that $F(x,w)$ passes through the M sampled points.

$$\sum_{i=1}^{M} c_i G(x_i; d_i / \sigma_i) = y_i \qquad (2)$$

in matrix notation: $Y = G \times C$ where $[Y]_i = y_i, [C]_i = c_i, [G]_{ij} = G(x_i; x_j)$.

If the sampled points are close enough one to the other and the number of the centers is equal to the number of the gaussians ($N = M$), the matrix G is close to singular and the obtained solution for the coefficients c_i is heavily affected by computational errors. It is therefore mandatory to reduce the number of gaussians. Moreover, the use of a number of gaussian basis functions smaller than the number of sampled points, prevents overfitting the data: $F(x,w)$ will not follow the ripples caused by the noise on the points and a better approximation of the original signal is produced with a greater ability of generalizing to similar signals. In Figure 1 the reconstructing curve is shown for a set of M points ($N=M$) and different values of the variance σ. Notice the high value of the coefficients and the high oscillations in the curve, above all when σ assumes a low value.

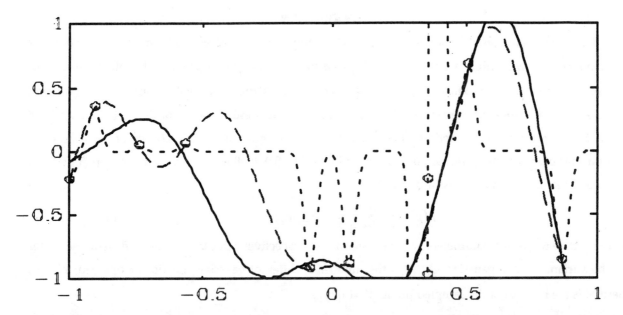

Figure 1: *Three different reconstructing functions F(x,w) with different values of the variance σ. With solid line is reported the approximating curve with σ = 0.1; relative coefficients are: {3.34; -6.06; 3.19; 0.67; -11.32; 18.12; -12.77; -12.72; 21.36; -5.63}. With dashed line is reported the approximating curve with σ = 0.05; relative coeficients are: { -7.01; 10.55; -6.30; 2.62; -1.82; 1.83; -1.54; -1.54; 2.91; -1.07}. With dot lines is reported the curve obtained with σ = 0.0006; relative coefficients are:{-0.014; 0.021; 0.002; 0.004; -0.057; -0.055; -37.167; 37.130; 0.041; -0.053}. Points coordinates are: {(-1.00, -0.23); (-0.74, 0.04); (0.51, 0.66); (-0.08, -0.93); (0.06, -0.89); (-0.56, 0.06); (-0.91, 0.34); (0.04, -0.98); (0.36, -0.23); (0.09, -0.87)};*

For these reasons it is numerically efficient, to reduce the number of gaussian basis functions adopted and therefore the number of coefficeints c_i. The problem can be summarized as: *How many and which gaussians should be eliminated, and how?*

We propose here an iterative procedure to determine the number and the values of the centers. Initially, the abscissas of the centers are set coincident with the abscissas of the sampled points. At every iteration step one gaussian is eliminated as follows: the pair of gaussians whose centers are the nearest ones is determined and a gaussian with the abscissa equal to mean value of the abscissas of the two centers is substituted to them. This procedure is ended when all the centers result are separated by a distance greater than a predermined threshold, related to the desired degree of smoothness for the curve.

Alternatively, an analytical solution can be carried out. The optimal number of gaussians is determined using the properties of the singular value decomposition. This analytical technique decomposes the matrix G (NxM) into the product of three matrixes: $G = UWV^T$ where U and V are orthonormal (NxM and MxM) and W is a diagonal matrix (MxM) which contains the singular values [Golub and Van Loan (1989)]. The number of effective centers is the range of G that is equal to the number of singular values of W, significatively different from zero. For the same points reported in Figure 1, a significant reduction in the value of the coefficients is obtained reducing from 10 to 8 the number of centers. Moreover some ripples, that can be easily attributed to noise, are filtered out as can be seen in Figure 2.

Once the number of gaussians, N, has been determined, the optimal value of the coefficients can be determined as [Poggio e Girosi (1989)]:

$$C = \left(G^T G + \lambda g\right)^{-1} G^T Y \qquad (3)$$

with C, Y and G are the vectors and matrix defined in equation (2) and g the matrix defined as follows: $[g]_{ij} = G(x_i; x_j)$. The parameter λ regulates the degree of smoothness of the reconstructing function. The smaller is the value of λ, the nearer to the points will be the reconstructing function F(x,w) and it will also undergo to undesiderable oscillations that will yield a poor generalization capability. The bigger is the value of λ, the smoother is the funtion. In this case the frequency content of the reconstructed signal will be reduced [Oppeheim and Shafer (1975)], operating a low-pass filtering that will eventually filter out possible rippels.

The parameter λ is therefore global over the entire definition domain of F(x,w). Alternatively, we can play with the value of the variance of the gaussians that is used in the reconstructing function. It is also related to the degree of smoothness in the reconstructing curve; as can be noted from Figure 1, the curve becomes smoother as the variance of the gaussians increases.

The variance can be automatically computed following the heuristic of *global first nearest-neighbor* proposed by Moody and Darken (1989). The variance is set to the mean of the minimal distances between each center and its nearest point P_i.

The sum of the mean square distance between F(x,w) and the sampled points can give an idea on the performance of the reconstructing function. In Table 1, this distance is plotted as a function of both λ and the variance of the gaussians; it increases with the increase of both λ and σ but the curve becomes evidently smoother.

variance σ \ λ	0	0.1	0.5	1	5
0.05	0.4238	0.4136	0.767	1.0083	1.8422
0.08	0.4377	0.6489	1.0517	1.2613	2.0189
0.1	0.4449	0.7937	1.1747	1.3734	2.1057
0.25	1.2398	1.3326	1.7243	1.9103	2.4464
0.3845	1.1634	*1.688*	2.0079	2.14	2.5707
0.5	2.3728	1.9056	2.1401	2.2485	2.635
0.75	2.4181	2.1323	2.2938	2.3801	2.7209
1	2.5269	2.2534	2.3768	2.4548	2.7738
5	2.6675	2.5524	2.6631	2.7277	2.9792

Table 1: The data of this table are referred to the function F(x,w) constituted of 8 gaussians used to reconstruct the curve through a set of 10 points as shown in figure 2. Mean square distance as a function of the smoothness parameter λ and of the variance of the gaussians are reported. In italics the variance as computed using global first nearest-neighbor is highlighted.

We may get a better approximation of the function considering that the frequency property of the signal to be reconstructed, may not be equal over all the definition domain. This can be obtained by choosing gaussians of different variances; each variance σ_i will be a function of the distances between the sampled points and it is set equal to the mean distance of its center from those points that falls into a certain region around its center; this region has the function of a receptive field for each gaussian. The reconstructing curve obtained with gaussian of different variances, is plotted in figure 2 and the mean square distance reported in Table 2. It should be remarked that the advantage of this procedure becomes apparent for large set of data.

Variance									Distance	
0.2023	0.2775	0.3773	0.2948	0.359	0.3582	0.1775	0.1752			1.3461

Table 2: The data of this table are referred to the function F(x,w) constituted of 8 gaussians used to reconstruct the curve through a set of 10 points as shown in figure 2. Mean square error as a function of the variances of the gaussians are reported. The smoothness parameter λ is set to 0. The amplitude of the interval to determine the variance is set to ± 0.5.

CONCLUSION

Although λ can, alone, regulate the degree of smoothness of the reconstructing function, it can be used when analytical solutions are feasible. The reconstruction of functions from large sets of data (surfaces, multi-dimensional temporal sequences), requires the use of numerical solutions. Gaussian basis functions allow to naturally partition the definition domain into regions (*receptive fields*), that ease numerical solutions. The parameters to be tuned are affected only from the behaviour of the data belonging to a small sub-region of the definition domain. Taking advantage of this property, our method can achieve an optimal reconstruction of functions of large data sets.

Moreover, this approach is particularly suited to be implemented with neural networks: it allows to define its topology and to locally tune its parameters for a huge amount of data.

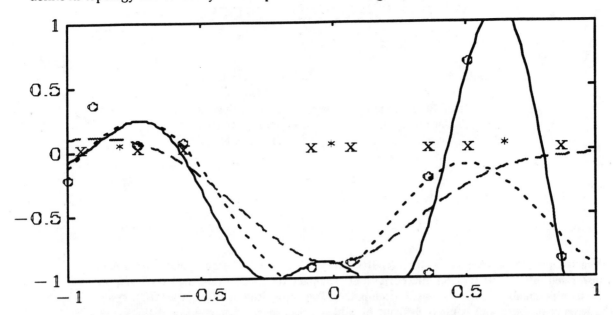

Figure 2: *Approximation of a curve starting from the same set of points as in Figure 1, through a reduced set of gaussians. The sampled points are represented with ○. Solid line represents the approximation function obtained with 8 gaussians centered in ×: {-0.74; 0.51; -0.08; 0.07; -0.56; 0.87; 0.36; -0.95} with relative coefficients:{ -2.06; 22.78; -13.59; 20.84; 3.36; -5.88; -27.62; 0.26} and variance σ = 0.1 equal for all gaussians. Dashed line represents the approximation function obtained with 3 gaussians centered in * : { -0.01; -0.8; 0.65} with relative coefficients:{ -0.70; 0.11; -0.03} and variance σ = 0.1 equal for all gaussians. Dot line represents the approximation function obtained with 8 gaussians centered in ×, with relative coefficients: {6.2530; 0.8655; -2.3784; -3.8514; -0.9216; -2.3840; 4.0225; -3.6141} and variance reported in Table 2.*

REFERENCES

G. H. Golub and C. F. Van Loan, *Matrix Computation*, 2nd ed. Baltimore: Johns Hopkins University Press (1989).

J. Moody and C. Darken, *Neural Comput.* 1, 281 (1989).

T. Poggio and S. Edelman, *Nature* 343, 263 (1990).

T. Poggio and F. Girosi, *Artif. Intell. Memo 1140* (Artificial Intelligence Laboratory, Massachussets Institute of Technology, Cambridge, 1989).

T. Poggio and F. Girosi, *Science* 247, 978 (1989).

Oppenheim and Shafer, *Digital signal processing*, Prentice Hall (1975)

A Neural Network Approach to High Accuracy Optical Character Recognition

Thanh A. Diep
102 Durand
Dept. of Electrical Engineering
Stanford University
Stanford, CA 94305

Hadar I. Avi-Itzhak
102 Durand
Dept. of Electrical Engineering
Stanford University
Stanford, CA 94305

Abstract--Optical character recognition (OCR) refers to a process whereby printed documents are transformed into ASCII files for the purpose of compact storage, editing, fast retrieval, and other file manipulations through the use of a computer. The recognition process of an OCR system is a challenging problem and is made difficult by added noise, image distortion, and the various character typefaces, sizes, and fonts that a document may have. In this study a neural network approach is introduced to perform high accuracy recognition on multi-size and multi-font characters; a novel centroid-dithering training process with a low noise-sensitivity normalization procedure is used to achieve high accuracy results. The study consists of two parts. The first part focuses on single size and single font characters, and a two-layered neural network is trained to recognize the full set of 94 ASCII character images in 12-pt Courier font. When tested on a database of 1,072,452 characters, this neural network has zero recognition errors. The second part trades accuracy for additional font and size capability, and a larger two-layered neural network is trained to recognize the full set of 94 ASCII character images for all point sizes from 8 to 32 and for 12 commonly used fonts. No errors were incurred while testing this network on a database of 347,000 characters of 12 fonts and four different point sizes. When tested on the database of 1,072,452 Courier 12 point characters, this neural network had one recognition error.

I. Introduction

In today's world of information, countless forms, reports, contracts, and letters are generated each day; hence, the need to archive, retrieve, update, replicate, and distribute printed documents has become increasingly important[1,2]. An available technology that automates these tasks on computer media is optical character recognition (OCR); printed documents are transformed into ASCII files, which enable compact storage, editing, fast retrieval, and other file manipulations through the use of a computer. An overview of the OCR process is illustrated below:

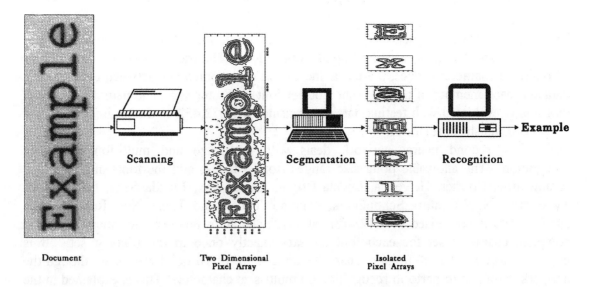

Figure 1: The Optical Character Recognition Process

An essential requirement for OCR lies in the development of an accurate recognition algorithm by which digitized images are analyzed and classified into corresponding characters. Published literature report error rates in the order of one percent for single-font recognition and higher error rates for multi-fonts [3,4]. While an error rate in the order of one percent may appear impressive, it would generate 30 errors on an average page containing 3000 characters. Such error rates limit the usefulness in many applications and illustrate the need for a more accurate recognition algorithm.

The study proposes using neural networks to perform high accuracy character recognition and consists of two parts. The first part focuses on single size and single font characters, and a two-layered neural network is trained to recognize the full set of 94 ASCII character images in 12-pt Courier font[1]. The second part trades accuracy with additional font and size capability, and a larger two-layered neural network is trained to recognize the full set of 94 ASCII character images for all point sizes from 8 to 32 and for 12 commonly used fonts.

II. Neural Network Implementation

The neural network used to recognize single-size and single-font character images has 3000 inputs, 20 neurons in the first layer, and 94 neurons in the second or output layer. The neural network used to recognize multi-size and multi-font character images has 2500 inputs, 100 neurons in the first layer, and 94 neurons in the output layer. Both networks are fully connected and feedforward with the sigmoidal function generating the nonlinearity. The training algorithm used in this study is the backpropagation algorithm[6,7].

---

[1]Courier font is important because it is the font most often used in legal documents. The technique used in the development of a neural network for Courier font is general and can be applied to any other single font.

A. *Database*

The first neural network deals with single-size and single-font character recognition, and the training and testing data is of 12 point Courier font. The training data is comprised of 94 digitized character images; there is a one-to-one correspondence between each training data and each member of the 12 point Courier font character set. The neural network is thoroughly evaluated with testing data, comprising of 1,072,452 character images from a library of English short stories.

The second neural network deals with multi-size and multi-font character recognition. The allowable point size ranges from 8 to 32, and the fonts include Arial, AvantGarde, Courier, Helvetica, Lucida Bright, Lucida Fax, Lucida Sans, Lucida Sans Typewriter, New Century Schoolbook, Palatino, Times, and Times New Roman. The training data is comprised of 1,128 (or 94 x 12) character images; each member of the complete character set for each font appears exactly once in the training set. It is important to note that all training character images are of 16 point size, even though the network is trained to perform recognition on multi-size characters. This is explained in the next section. The testing data consists of 347,712 characters or 28,976 characters for each font and has an even mixture of 8, 12, 16, and 32 point sizes.

B. *Data Preprocessing and Normalization*

Before it is fed to the neural network, the digitized image is preprocessed and normalized. The preprocessing and normalization procedure serves several purposes; it reduces noise sensitivity and makes the system invariant to point size, image contrast, and position displacement.

The reduction of noise sensitivity is achieved by *thresholding*. Thresholding removes the low-level background noise, which is caused by inherent paper nonuniformity, specks, and other paper defects. The input image is filtered by zeroing those pixels whose values are less then 20% of the peak pixel value, while the remaining pixels are unchanged. The threshold setting is heuristic and has been empirically shown to work well for white paper. The threshold setting should be adjusted accordingly when a different paper product is used, e.g. newspaper.

Following thresholding, the resultant image is centered by positioning the centroid of the image to the center of a fixed size frame. The centroid $(\bar{x}, \bar{y})$ of an image is defined as follows:

$$\bar{x} \overset{def}{=} \frac{\sum_x x \sum_y pixel(x,y)}{\sum_x \sum_y pixel(x,y)} \tag{1}$$

$$\bar{y} \overset{def}{=} \frac{\sum_y y \sum_x pixel(x,y)}{\sum_y \sum_x pixel(x,y)} \tag{2}$$

For the 12 point Courier font case, a frame size of 50-by-60 pixels has been found to be adequate in enclosing all character images. For the multi-size and multi-font case, a frame size of 50-by-50 pixels is employed, and an additional scaling process must be applied to the images. The scaling entails initially computing the radial moment M_r:

$$M_r \stackrel{def}{=} \sqrt{\frac{\sum_x \sum_y [(x-\bar{x})^2 + (y-\bar{y})^2] pixel(x,y)}{\sum_x \sum_y pixel(x,y)}} \qquad (3)$$

Next, the image is enlarged or reduced with a gain factor of $\dfrac{10}{M_r}$, producing images of constant radial moments. The value of this constant radial moment is linked to the selected frame size of 50-by-50. From a broader perspective, this scaling process is equivalent to a point-size normalization procedure and enables a neural network to treat all character images the same way regardless of the point size. An illustration of the thresholding, scaling, and centering operations is shown below:

(a) Single-Size and Single-Font Preprocessing

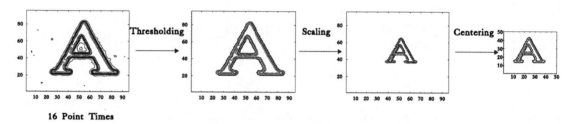

(b) Multi-Size and Multi-Font Preprocessing

Figure 2: Preprocessing

The next step in the preprocessing and normalization procedure is to convert the two-dimensional images into vectors. The conversion is achieved by concatenating the rows of the two-dimensional pixel array. It follows that the vector for the single-size and single-font case has 3,000 elements and that the vector for the multi-size and multi-font case has 2,500 elements. Additionally, each vector is normalized to unit power:

$$\vec{v}_{normalized} \stackrel{def}{=} \frac{\vec{v}}{\|\vec{v}\|} \qquad (4)$$

The normalization reduces sensitivity to varying scanner gains (image-to-background contrast) as well as different toner darkness (shades of ink). This unit-norm vector is then fed into the neural network.

During training, there is an additional step performed on the input data: *centroid dithering*. The centroid dithering process applies to both the single-size and single-font case as well as the multi-size and multi-font case. The process involves dithering the centroid of the two-dimensional input image. After centering and scaling, the input image is displaced randomly and independently in both the horizontal and vertical directions over the range of [-2,+2] pixels in each dimension; the image is shifted at random in one of twenty-five possible displacement positions. The resultant image is then converted into a vector, normalized, and fed into the network as previously described.

Centroid dithering effectively creates many "different" images from a single image. The neural network is exposed to the same character at different displacement positions, making the recognition system invariant to input displacements. It is important to emphasize that the dithering is performed exclusively during training and not during testing. There are several other added advantages of using this technique. For example, the approach does not increase the number of training data, and the amount of training data can be kept at a minimum. The approach also enables the network to tolerate width variations in character strokes which might be caused by different printer setting, toner levels, and variations in font implementation. This is particularly useful when bold face characters are encountered.

C. *Training and Testing*

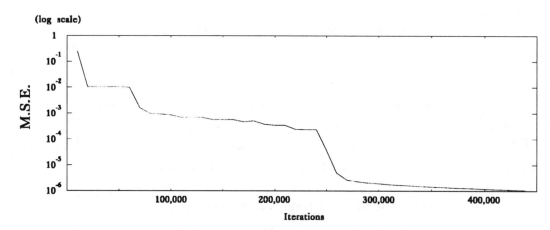

Figure 3: Learning Curve of the Single-Size and Single-Font Neural Network

The training is performed using the backpropagation algorithm with an initial learning-rate parameter of $\mu=10$ for both the single-size and single-font neural network and the multi-size and multi-font neural network. The learning progress is monitored by computing the mean squared error (m.s.e.) for each output neuron:

$$m.s.e. = \frac{C}{\begin{bmatrix} no.\ of \\ shift\ positions \end{bmatrix} \cdot \begin{bmatrix} no.\ of \\ training\ patterns \end{bmatrix} \cdot \begin{bmatrix} no.\ of \\ fonts \end{bmatrix} \cdot \begin{bmatrix} no.\ of \\ output\ neurons \end{bmatrix}} \qquad (5)$$

where C is the cost function defined by:

$$C \stackrel{def}{=} \sum_{\substack{training \\ pattern\ p}} \left(e^2\right)_p \stackrel{def}{=} \sum_{\substack{training \\ pattern\ p}} \left(\sum_{\substack{output \\ neuron\ i}}^{N} (d_i - y_i)^2\right)_p \qquad (6)$$

Here, d_i and y_i designate the desired and actual outputs of the ith neuron in the last layer in response to the pth input pattern. N is the number of neurons in the output layer (N=94).

The m.s.e. at the onset of training is predictable. Since they are randomly initialized over the interval [-10^{-10} , $+10^{-10}$], all weights may be approximated as zeros. Hence, all neurons assume the value of Sgm(0) = 0.5 in the initial m.s.e. calculations, irrespective of the input pattern. With a desired value of either 1 or 0, each output neuron generates an error of ± 0.5, and the resultant mean squared error is 0.25.

The m.s.e. values as a function of training iterations are plotted and shown in Figure 3 for the single-size and single-font neural network. The single-size and single-font neural network was trained with 430,000 iterations, and the final m.s.e. is approximately 10^{-6}. The multi-size and multi-font neural network was trained with 8,650,000 iterations, and the final m.s.e. is approximately $2 \cdot 10^{-6}$.

D. *Postprocessing*

Postprocessing refers to a simple procedure by which the output of the neural network is analyzed and modified. An important task of postprocessing pertains to the detection of invalid character inputs. More specifically, the detection is accomplished by observing the occurrence of small responses on *all* output neurons. This is an intrinsic property of a trained neural network and is very useful in discounting bad images which might result from segmentation errors or other defects.

The second function of postprocessing involves recovering lost information from scaling and centering multi-size and multi-font character images and is used for the multi-size and multi-font system only. The characters c, C, k, K, o, O, p, P, s, S, v, V, w, W, x, X, z, and Z of certain fonts lose their case information after scaling and are therefore recognized by the neural network without an affirmative upper/lower case identification. This case information, however, can easily be reconstructed by a context-based approach. The technique resorts to examining the radial moments of the original character images prior to scaling and is best explained by an example. Without loss of generality, it is assumed that the neural network identifies an image as the character "c." The first step is to deduce the point size of this "c" by computing the gain $10 / M_r{}^*$, where $M_r{}^*$ is the radial moment of a neighboring character that is case distinguishable. The next step is to calculate the radial moments of a fabricated upper case "C" and a fabricated lower case "c" of this point size. The case information is then obtained by comparing the radial moment of the input character "c" with those of the fabricated ones.

Commas and single quotes of certain fonts also become indistinguishable after centering and scaling. The discrimination between these two characters is made by comparing the centroid location of the input character image before preprocessing to the height of the line. Finally, the numeral zero cannot be reliably distinguished from the letter

"O" in some fonts, and similarly the numeral "1", lower case "L", upper case "I", and vertical bar "|" are ambiguous for some fonts. Under these circumstances the characters are left as they are without any postprocessing.

III. Recognition Performance

A. *Results*

In order to determine the recognition performance, a computer program is used to compare the output of the recognition system with the ASCII files which were used to generate the testing data. The computer program examines each and every output character, and all discrepancies excluding spaces, tabs, and carriage return are recorded. The discrepancies are individually examined and classified as either an "erroneous" or a "correct" recognition.

There are two situations where discrepancies are classified as correct recognition. The first case involves image corruption which renders the invalid images unrecognizable. Figure 4 provides examples of invalid inputs due to segmentation error, scanning error, and paper residue. As explained in Section II Part D, the neural network automatically generates small responses on all the output neurons to indicate "bad" inputs. Such occurrence is detected during postprocessing, and the discrepancy is not counted as a recognition error. The second case involves characters that are indistinguishable. These include the numeral "0", letter "O", lower case "L", upper case "I", numeral "1", and the vertical bar "|" in some fonts. The ambiguity arises from the fact that one character from one font looks identically to a *different* character of another font. Henceforth, the neural network may output any of the ambiguous characters when the input is ambiguous, and it is not counted as an error. Any other discrepancies which do not fall into one of these two categories are counted as recognition errors.

The character-ambiguity problem does not apply to the single-size and single-font experiment, since all characters of the Courier font are distinguishable. All discrepancies except those of corrupted images are treated as errors. The neural network is required to recognize all 94 characters including the difficult distinction between the lower case L ("l") and the numeral one ("1"). The single-size and single-font neural network is tested with 1,072,452 characters of 12 point Courier font, and a perfect recognition accuracy has been achieved. This recognition performance exceeds any previously known results by at least an order of magnitude.

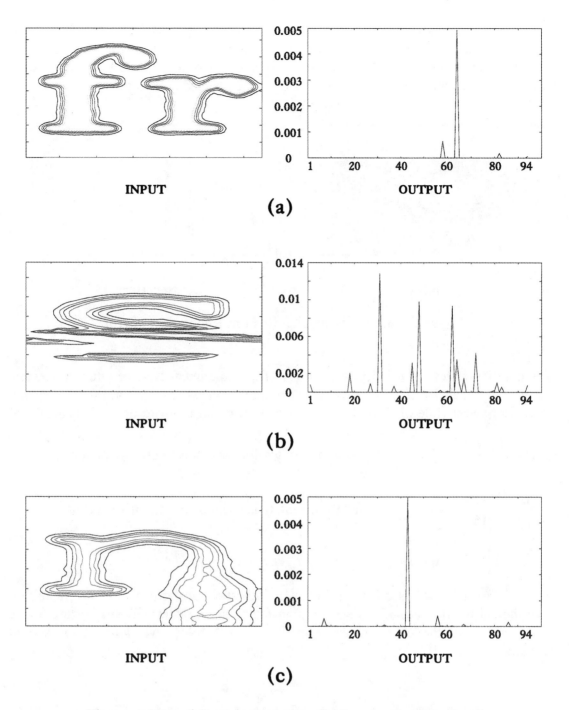

Figure 4. Neural Responses to Invalid Images as a Result of
(a) Segmentation Error, (b) Scanning Error, and (c) Paper Residue

The multi-size and multi-font neural network was tested with 347,712 characters or 28,976 characters for each of the following fonts: Arial, AvantGarde, Courier, Helvetica, Lucida Bright, Lucida Fax, Lucida Sans, Lucida Sans Typewriter, New Century Schoolbook, Palatino, Times, and Times New Roman. The testing data consists of an even mixture of 8, 12, 16, and 32 point sizes. Using the performance criteria as previously described, the multi-size and multi-font neural network has achieved a perfect recognition accuracy. The same network was also tested with the data used for the single-size and single-font neural network. There was one recognition error among the 1,072,452 testing characters of 12 point Courier font. The error is documented in Figure 5.

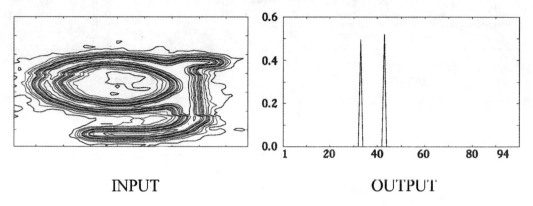

INPUT   OUTPUT

Figure 5. Multi-Size and Multi-Font Recognition Error

B. *Analysis*

The question arises: if n independent trials of an experiment have resulted in success, what is the probability that the next trial will result in success? In this context, we employ Laplace's Special Rule of Succession[13] which yields an estimate of the probability of

success $p = \dfrac{n+1}{n+2}$. For the single-size and single-font neural network, we obtain

$p = \dfrac{1,072,453}{1,072,454} = 99.99991\%$, and for the multi-size and multi-font neural network,

$p = \dfrac{347,713}{347,714} = 99.99971\%$.

Alternately, we introduce the following statistical analysis in order to quantify a lower bound for the recognition accuracy on future testing data. Given a testing image corresponding to the pth character where $p \in \{1,2,...,94\}$, we define two random variables:

$$\mathbf{A}_p \overset{def}{=} y_p \tag{7}$$

$$\mathbf{B}_p \overset{def}{=} \underset{k \neq p}{Max}[y_k] \tag{8}$$

where y_p is the output of the pth neuron of the output layer. The correct recognition of a character requires that $\mathbf{A}_p > \mathbf{B}_p$. The conditional probability of error given an input image of the pth character is derived below.

$$Prob(error \mid p) = Prob(\mathbf{A}_p < \mathbf{B}_p \mid p) \tag{9}$$

$$\leq Prob(\mid \mathbf{A}_p - \mathbf{B}_p - E(\mathbf{A}_p - \mathbf{B}_p) \mid > \mid E(\mathbf{A}_p - \mathbf{B}_p) \mid \mid p) \tag{10}$$

III-84

$$\leq \frac{\mathrm{Var}(A_p - B_p)}{[E(A_p - B_p)]^2} \qquad (11)$$

$$\approx \mathrm{Var}(\mathbf{A_p} - \mathbf{B_p}) \qquad (12)$$

Inequality (11) invokes the Chebyshev inequality, and inequality (12) approximates A_p as 1 and $\mathbf{B_p}$ as 0. These assumptions are verified by the sample averages obtained from testing data.

To illustrate the concept, we apply the Chebyshev lower bound to the four most frequent characters in our data: "e", "t", "a", and "o". These letters are all in lower case except the letter "o". Since it is an ambiguous character, the samples could also be an upper case or a zero. The following tables summarize the sample averages and variances computed during the test run and the resultant bound on the probability of error.

Character	Samples	$E(A_p - B_p)$	$\mathrm{Var}(A_p - B_p)$ ($\approx$ Chebyshev upper bound)
"e"	113,060	0.99	$1.7 \cdot 10^{-5}$
"t"	80,273	0.99	$5.8 \cdot 10^{-5}$
"a"	72,565	0.99	$2.9 \cdot 10^{-5}$
"o"	70,423	0.98	$5.6 \cdot 10^{-5}$

Table 1. Chebyshev Upper Bound for the Probability of Error for the Single-Size and Single-Font Neural Network

Character	Samples	$E(A_p - B_p)$	$\mathrm{Var}(A_p - B_p)$ ($\approx$ Chebyshev upper bound)
"e"	38,784	0.99	$3.9 \cdot 10^{-5}$
"t"	25,920	0.99	$1.1 \cdot 10^{-4}$
"a"	24,528	0.99	$3.2 \cdot 10^{-4}$
"o"	26,112	0.99	$9.2 \cdot 10^{-5}$

Table 2. Chebyshev upper Bound for the Probability of Error for the Multi-Size and Multi-Font Neural Network

The Chebyshev bound is known in general to be a conservative bound, and the upper bounds on the probabilities of error in Tables 1 and 2 are much higher than those estimated by the Laplace Rule of Succession.

IV. Conclusions

The study presents a neural network scheme with centroid dithering and a low noise-sensitivity normalization procedure for high accuracy optical character recognition. The single-size and single-font neural network has been successfully trained to recognize 12 point Courier font characters. The neural network was trained with a database of 94 character images. The neural network was tested on a database of 1,072,452 character images and achieved perfect recognition. Based on the experience of this network, a larger neural network was successfully designed and trained to recognize characters of 12 commonly used fonts and point sizes from 8 to 32. The latter neural network was trained with 1,128 character images, and it achieved perfect recognition on a testing database of 347,712 multi-size and multi-font characters. To gauge the tradeoff between the two networks, the multi-size and multi-font neural network was tested on the 1,072,452 Courier character database, and one error was incurred.

Acknowledgment

We would like to thank the Fannie and John Hertz Foundation and the United States Air Force for their fellowship funding and to acknowledge Canon Research Center America, Palo Alto, California for providing the OCR data.

References

[1]   G. R. Cote and B. Smith, "Profiles in Document Managing," *Byte*, September 1992, pp. 198-212.

[2]   L. Grunin, "OCR Software Moves into the Mainstream," *PC Magazine*, pp. 299-350, October 30, 1990.

[3]   S. Kahan, T. Pavlidis, and H. S. Baird, "On the Recognition of Printed Characters of Any Font and Size," *IEEE-PAMI* 9, 2, pp. 274-288, 1987.

[4]   S. Mori, C. Y. Suen, and K. Yamamoto, "Historical Review of OCR Research and Development," *IEEE Proceedings*, Vol. 80, No. 7, pp. 1029-58, July 1992.

[5]   E. Parzen. *Modern Probability Theory and Its Applications*. John Wiley & Sons, Inc., N.Y., 1960.

[6]   D. E. Rumelhart, G.E. Hinton, and R.J. Williams , "Learning Representation by Error Backpropagation," In *Parallel Distributed Processing*, vol. 1, MIT Press, Cambridge, MA, 1986, Chap. 8, pp. 318-362.

[7]   B. Widrow and M. Lehr, "30 Years of Adaptive Neural Networks: Perceptron, Madaline, and Backpropagation," *Proceedings of the IEEE*, Vol. 78, No. 9, pp. 1445-1442, September 1990.

Two-Layer Linear Structures for Fast Adaptive Filtering

Françoise Beaufays, Bernard Widrow*

Abstract

The LMS algorithm invented by Widrow and Hoff in 1959 is the simplest, most robust, and one of the most widely used algorithms for adaptive filtering. Unfortunately, it suffers from high sensitivity to the conditioning of its input autocorrelation matrix: the higher the input eigenvalue spread, the slower the convergence of the adaptive weights.

This problem can be overcome by preprocessing the inputs to the LMS filter with a fixed data-independent transformation that, at least partially, decorrelates the inputs. Typically, the preprocessing consists of a DFT or a DCT transformation followed by a power normalization stage. The resulting algorithms are called DFT-LMS and DCT-LMS. A fast and robust implementation of the DFT or the DCT preprocessing stage is itself obtained by using an adaptive filter based on the LMS algorithm. The overall structure is thus a fully adaptive two-layer linear filter, which achieves better speed performance than pure LMS while retaining its low computational cost and its extreme robustness.

Introduction

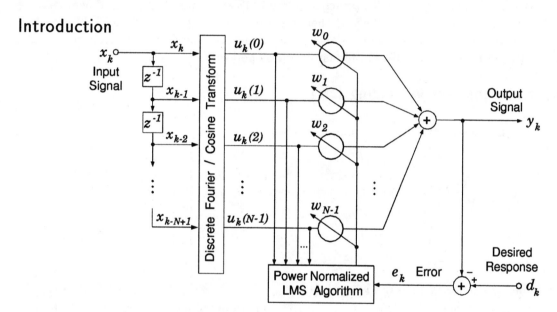

Figure 1: **The DFT-LMS and DCT-LMS algorithms: block diagram.**

The DFT-LMS and DCT-LMS algorithms are represented in Fig.1. The signal x_k is passed through a tap-delay line whose outputs are transformed by a DFT or a DCT. This transformation splits the signal into different frequency components that are approximately uncorrelated. The outputs of the DFT/DCT, $u_k(\cdot)$, are then fed to the adaptive filter, whose weights are adjusted using the power normalized LMS algorithm (*i.e.* a version of the LMS algorithm where each weight has a learning rate that is inversely proportional to the estimated power of its input). The DFT/DCT

*The authors are with the Department of Electrical Engineering, Stanford University, Stanford, CA 94305-4055. This research was sponsored by EPRI under contract RP8010-13, by NSF under grant NSF IRI 91-12531, and by ONR under contract N00014-92-J-1787.

preprocessing along with the power normalization tend to make the equivalent input autocorrelation matrix close to identity and, consequently, to improve the convergence speed of the LMS filter weights. This approach is to be contrasted with recursive least squares algorithms where the inputs are whitened by an estimate of their inverse autocorrelation matrix.

The performance of algorithms based on data-independent transformations clearly depends on the orthogonalizing capabilities of the transform used. No general proof exists that demonstrates the superiority of one transform over the others. DFT-LMS first introduced by Narayan [1] is the simplest algorithm of this family, mainly because of the exponential nature of the DFT. It is our experience though that in most practical situations DCT-LMS performs much better than DFT-LMS [2]. In addition, it has the advantage of being real-valued.

Since the signals $x_k, x_{k-1}, \ldots$ come from a tap-delay line, their DFT/DCT at a given iteration can easily be calculated recursively from the DFT/DCT at the previous iteration. This is sometimes refered to as the *sliding DFT/DCT*, and requires only $\mathcal{O}(N)$ operations per iteration, where N is the length of the LMS filter. However, in this approach, the propagation and accumulation of errors due for example to round-off noise in floating point arithmetic makes it necessary to often reset the DFT/DCT. This increases the overall number of computations and adds to the complexity of the circuitry. The *LMS spectrum analyzer* [3] provides another way of computing a DFT recursively in $\mathcal{O}(N)$ operations, but because it relies on an *adaptive* technique, it automatically adjusts for possible errors.

In the next sections, we will recall the principle of the LMS spectrum analyzer and demonstrate its robustness to noise propagation. We will then generalize it to the case of the DCT. We will conclude by presenting a fully adaptive two-layer linear structure: the first layer preprocesses the inputs to the second layer, which effects the fast filtering operation.

LMS spectrum analyzer vs. sliding DFT

The DFT of the signals $x_k, x_{k-1}, \ldots, x_{k-N+1}$ is given by

$$DFT_k = \sqrt{\frac{1}{N}} \begin{bmatrix} 1 & 1 & 1 & \ldots & 1 \\ 1 & \alpha^{-1} & \alpha^{-2} & \ldots & \alpha^{-(N-1)} \\ 1 & \alpha^{-2} & \alpha^{-4} & & \\ \vdots & \vdots & & \ddots & \vdots \\ 1 & \alpha^{-(N-1)} & & \ldots & \alpha^{-(N-1)(N-1)} \end{bmatrix} \cdot \begin{bmatrix} x_{k-N+1} \\ x_{k-N} \\ \vdots \\ \vdots \\ x_k \end{bmatrix}, \quad (1)$$

where $\alpha \triangleq e^{j\frac{2\pi}{N}}$, and $j = \sqrt{-1}$.

Let us define the complex phasor $F_k \triangleq \sqrt{\frac{1}{N}} [1 \ \ \alpha^k \ \ \alpha^{2k} \ \ \ldots \ \ \alpha^{(N-1)k}]^T$, where T denotes the transpose. The series of phasors $F_0, F_1, \ldots F_{N-1}, F_N, \ldots$ is periodic of period N (*i.e.* $F_N = F_0$, $F_{N+1} = F_1$, etc.) and $\{F_0, F_1, \ldots F_{N-1}\}$ form an orthonormal basis in the N-dimensional space:

$$F_k^T \overline{F}_l = \frac{1}{N} \sum_{m=0}^{n-1} \alpha^{m(k-l)} = \begin{cases} 0 & \text{if } k \neq l \\ 1 & \text{if } k = l, \end{cases} \quad (2)$$

where $\overline{F}_l$ is the complex conjugate of F_l. Eq.1 can be rewritten as

$$DFT_k = \sqrt{\frac{1}{N}} \begin{bmatrix} 1 \\ 1 \\ 1 \\ \vdots \\ 1 \end{bmatrix} x_{k-N+1} + \sqrt{\frac{1}{N}} \begin{bmatrix} 1 \\ \alpha^{-1} \\ \alpha^{-2} \\ \vdots \\ \alpha^{-(N-1)} \end{bmatrix} x_{k-N} + \ldots + \sqrt{\frac{1}{N}} \begin{bmatrix} 1 \\ \alpha^{-(N-1)} \\ \alpha^{-2(N-1)} \\ \vdots \\ \alpha^{-(N-1)(N-1)} \end{bmatrix} x_k \quad (3)$$

$$= \sum_{m=k-N+1}^{k} x_m \overline{F}_{m-k+N-1} = \sum_{m=k-N+1}^{k} x_m \overline{F}_{m-k-1} \tag{4}$$

$$= P^k \sum_{m=k-N+1}^{k} x_m \overline{F}_{m-1}, \tag{5}$$

where we have defined the diagonal matrix $P \triangleq \mathrm{diag}\{1, \ \alpha, \ \alpha^2, \ldots \alpha^{N-1}\}$.

Sliding DFT. – The DFT at time $k+1$ is easily related to the DFT at time k:

$$DFT_{k+1} = P^{k+1} \sum_{m=k+1-N+1}^{k+1} x_m \overline{F}_{m-1} \tag{6}$$

$$= P^{k+1}\left[\sum_{m=k-N+1}^{k} x_m \overline{F}_{m-1} + (x_{k+1} - x_{k-N+1}) \overline{F}_k \right] \tag{7}$$

$$= P\left[DFT_k + (x_{k+1} - x_{k-N+1}) P^k \overline{F}_k \right] \tag{8}$$

$$= P\left[DFT_k + (x_{k+1} - x_{k-N+1}) \overline{F}_0 \right]. \tag{9}$$

Each element of the DFT at time $k+1$ is obtained by adding to the same element at time k the contribution of the newest data sample, x_{k+1}, removing the contribution of the oldest one, x_{k-N+1}, and multiplying by a phase factor. The update from time k to $k+1$ of the whole DFT (N components) requires thus $\mathcal{O}(N)$ operations. This is to be contrasted with the conventional DFT, which is $\mathcal{O}(N^2)$, or its butterfly counterpart, the FFT, which is $\mathcal{O}(N \log N)$.

LMS spectrum analyzer. – The LMS spectrum analyzer [3] is represented in Figure 2. The signal to be transformed, d_k^F (we will see shortly how d_k^F relates to x_k), is used as the desired output of an adaptive filter. The input to the filter at time k is the complex phasor F_k.

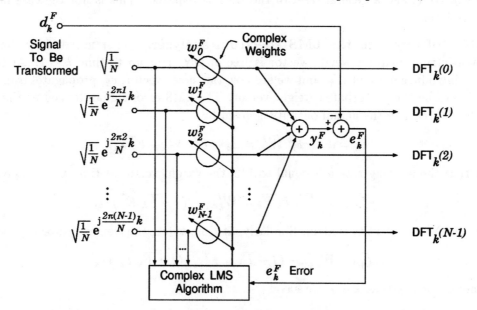

Figure 2: **The LMS spectrum analyzer for calculating the DFT.**

The adaptive weights of the spectrum analyzer are updated with the complex LMS algorithm [4] :

$$W_{k+1}^F = W_k^F + 2\mu \, e_k^F \, \overline{F}_k, \tag{10}$$

where W_k^F and e_k^F are respectively the weight vector and the error signal at time k, and μ is the learning rate. The error e_k^F is defined as the difference between the desired output d_k^F and the actual output y_k^F, $e_k^F = d_k^F - y_k^F = d_k^F - F_k^T W_k^F$. Replacing e_k^F in the weight update formula, chosing the initial weight vector W_0^F to be equal to zero and the learning rate μ to be equal to $1/2$, and using the periodicity and orthonormality properties of the complex phasors F_k, it can be shown [3] that

$$W_k^F = \sum_{m=k-N}^{k-1} d_m^F \overline{F}_m = \sum_{m=k-N+1}^{k} d_{m-1}^F \overline{F}_{m-1}. \tag{11}$$

Comparing with the DFT formula (Eq.5), it is clear that if we choose $d_{m-1}^F \triangleq x_m$, the DFT and the LMS analyzer weights are related by the simple formula: $DFT_k = P^k W_k^F$. *At each instant k, the weight vector of the LMS filter is proportional to the DFT of the past N data samples.* Note that the elements of the multiplicative diagonal matrix P^k are precisely equal to the inputs of the filter. The DFT components are thus simply obtained by pulling output lines from the adaptive weights (see Fig.2).

If we compare the expressions for the weight vector (Eq.11) at times k and $k+1$ as we did for the DFT, we find that

$$W_{k+1}^F = W_k^F + (x_{k+1} \overline{F}_k - x_{k-N+1} \overline{F}_k), \tag{12}$$

which is identical to Eq.9 since the DFT and the weight vector at time k differ only by the multiplicative factor P^k. Of course, this algorithm is also $\mathcal{O}(N)$.

Although the sliding DFT and the spectrum analyzer look very similar, they differ in how they handle round-off errors. In both algorithms the DFT is computed recursively; noise appearing in the DFT at time k thus propagates to the DFT at time $k+1, k+2, \ldots$ Because in the sliding DFT (Eq.9) the elements of the multiplicative diagonal matrix P all have modulus one, those errors will propagate unattenuated, and will accumulate over time until the calculated DFT is too different from the true DFT, and a general reset of the DFT is required. This is not the case in the LMS spectrum analyzer.

Propagation of errors in the LMS spectrum analyzer. – Let us consider the situation where the spectrum analyzer weight vector is free of any error up to time $k-1$. At time k, we deliberately introduce noise in W_k, and we see how this noise vector, ϵ_k, propagates over time. Let $\widetilde{W}_k^F = W_k^F - \epsilon_k$ be the perturbated weight vector. The LMS error signal defined as the difference between the desired and the actual outputs is given by

$$\tilde{e}_k = d_k - F_k^T \widetilde{W}_k^F = d_k - F_k^T W_k^F + F_k^T \epsilon_k. \tag{13}$$

Assuming that the learning rate μ is equal to $1/2$, the weight vector at time $k+1$ is given by

$$\widetilde{W}_{k+1}^F = \widetilde{W}_k^F + \tilde{e}_k \overline{F}_k = W_{k+1}^F - (I - \overline{F}_k F_k^T) \epsilon_k, \tag{14}$$

where I is the $N \times N$ identity matrix. Similarly, at time $k+2$, the weight vector is given by

$$\widetilde{W}_{k+2}^F = W_{k+2}^F - (I - \overline{F}_{k+1} F_{k+1}^T)(I - \overline{F}_k F_k^T) \epsilon_k, \tag{15}$$

and in general, for any time $k+j$, we have[†]

$$\widetilde{W}_{k+j}^F = W_{k+j}^F - \prod_{m=0}^{j-1} (I - \overline{F}_{k+m} F_{k+m}^T) \epsilon_k, \tag{16}$$

[†]It can be verified that the order in which the matrix multiplies are effected is irrelevant. This justifies the otherwise ambiguous notation $\prod_m$.

Without lost of generality, we can assume that $k = N$ so that

$$\widetilde{W}^F_{N+j} = W^F_{N+j} - \prod_{m=0}^{j-1} (I - \overline{F}_{N+m} \, F^T_{N+m}) \, \epsilon_N \qquad (17)$$

$$= W^F_{N+j} - \prod_{m=0}^{j-1} (I - \overline{F}_m \, F^T_m) \, \epsilon_N. \qquad (18)$$

Let us now examine how the multiplication by the matrix $(I - \overline{F}_m \, F^T_m)$ affects the error vector ϵ_N. The vectors $\{X_0, \, X_1, \ldots X_{N-1}\}$, and therefore also the vectors $\{\overline{F}_0, \, \overline{F}_1, \ldots \overline{F}_{N-1}\}$, form an orthonormal basis in the N-dimensional space. Any error vector ϵ_N can be decomposed into its N components in this last basis:

$$\epsilon_N = \sum_{n=0}^{N-1} \epsilon_N(n) \, \overline{F}_n. \qquad (19)$$

The product $(I - \overline{F}_m \, F^T_m) \, \epsilon_N$ can be evaluated as:

$$(I - \overline{F}_m \, F^T_m) \, \epsilon_N = (I - \overline{F}_m \, F^T_m) \sum_{n=0}^{N-1} \epsilon_N(n) \, \overline{F}_n = \epsilon_N - \epsilon_N(m) \, \overline{F}_m. \qquad (20)$$

The multiplication of the error by $(I - \overline{F}_m \, F^T_m)$ eliminates its mth component, and leaves the other components unchanged. Multiplying the residual error vector by $(I - \overline{F}_{m+1} \, F^T_{m+1})$ will cancel out its $(m+1)^{\text{th}}$ component, and so on. As iterations go by, the modulus of the error vector decreases monotonically. After N iterations, all its components have been cancelled, and the error is reduced to zero.

In software and hardware implementations, errors occur at each iteration. While the sliding DFT lets these errors accumulate over time and requires periodic resets of the DFT, the LMS spectrum analyzer can be run without interruption, as long as required by the application.

LMS spectrum analyzer for the DCT

As pointed out previously, it is our experience that in many applications the DCT-LMS algorithm achieves better results than the DFT-LMS. There exist many different discrete cosine transforms [5], the one of interest here is defined as

$$DCT_{N-1}(p) = \sqrt{\frac{2}{N}} \, k_p \sum_{m=0}^{N-1} x_m \, \cos \left(\frac{p(m + 1/2)\pi}{N} \right), \qquad (21)$$

where $DCT_{N-1}(p)$ is the pth component of the DCT at time $N - 1$, and the constant $k_p = 1/\sqrt{2}$ for $p = 0$ and 1 otherwise. Because this DCT has a period $2N$ instead of N like the DFT, special care must be taken in deriving an LMS cosine-spectrum analyzer. The pth component of the DCT at arbitrary time k can be written as

$$DCT_k(p) = \sqrt{\frac{2}{N}} \, k_p \sum_{m=k-N+1}^{k} x_m \, \cos \frac{p(m - k + N - 1 + 1/2)\pi}{N} \qquad (22)$$

$$= \sqrt{\frac{2}{N}} \, k_p \, (-1)^p \, \cos \frac{pk\pi}{N} \sum_{m=k-N+1}^{k} x_m \, \cos \frac{p(m - 1 + 1/2)\pi}{N} \qquad (23)$$

$$+ \sqrt{\frac{2}{N}} \, k_p \, (-1)^p \, \sin \frac{pk\pi}{N} \sum_{m=k-N+1}^{k} x_m \, \sin \frac{p(m - 1 + 1/2)\pi}{N}.$$

In order to obtain a fully adaptive structure for DCT-LMS, the two sums in Eq.24 must be evaluated using LMS spectrum analyzers. The LMS spectrum analyzer for the DFT was based on the fact that the input vectors, F_k, had the double property of being N-periodic ($F_k \equiv F_{k+N}$) and forming an orthonormal basis in the N-dimensional space. It is easy to verify that the following vectors have the same properties:

$$C_k = D_k \sqrt{\frac{2}{N}} [k_0 \cos \frac{0(k+1/2)\pi}{N}, k_1 \cos \frac{1(k+1/2)\pi}{N}, \ldots, k_{N-1} \cos \frac{(N-1)(k+1/2)\pi}{N}], \quad (24)$$

$$S_k = -D_k \sqrt{\frac{2}{N}} [k_1 \sin \frac{1(k+1/2)\pi}{N}, k_2 \sin \frac{2(k+1/2)\pi}{N}, \ldots, k_N \sin \frac{N(k+1/2)\pi}{N}], \quad (25)$$

with

$$D_k = \begin{cases} I & \text{if } k \in [nN \quad (n+1)N[\quad \text{and } n \text{ is even} \\ D & \text{if } k \in [nN \quad (n+1)N[\quad \text{and } n \text{ is odd,} \end{cases} \quad (26)$$

where I is the identity matrix and the diagonal matrix $D \triangleq \text{diag}\{1, -1, 1, \ldots\}$. Note that S_k was not obtained by only replacing "cos" by "sin" in C_k, the indices were also "shifted" (i.e. the first component starts with index 1 instead of 0). This was necessary to ensure the orthogonality of the S_k vectors. The constants $k_1, \ldots k_{N-1}$ are equal to 1 as before, $k_N = 1/\sqrt{2}$.

By analogy with the DFT case, two spectrum analyzers taking for desired output x_k, and for input C_k or S_k have the following weight vectors:

$$W_k^c = \sum_{m=k-N+1}^{k} x_m C_{m-1}, \qquad W_k^s = \sum_{m=k-N+1}^{k} x_m S_{m-1}. \quad (27)$$

Let us also define two other LMS spectrum analyzers. Their desired signal is

$$\hat{x}_k = \begin{cases} x_k & \text{if } k \in [nN \quad (n+1)N[\quad \text{and } n \text{ is even} \\ -x_k & \text{if } k \in [nN \quad (n+1)N[\quad \text{and } n \text{ is odd,} \end{cases} \quad (28)$$

and the input vecrors are C_k and S_k respectively. The weight vectors are given by

$$\widehat{W}_k^c = \sum_{m=k-N+1}^{k} \hat{x}_m C_{m-1}, \qquad \widehat{W}_k^s = \sum_{m=k-N+1}^{k} \hat{x}_m S_{m-1}. \quad (29)$$

Comparing Eq.24 with Eq.27 and 29, and using the definitions for C_k and S_k (Eq.24 and 25), we get the desired result:

$$DCT_k(p) = \begin{cases} \cos \frac{pk\pi}{N} W_k^c(p) + \sin \frac{pk\pi}{N} W_k^s(p) & \text{if } p \text{ is even} \\ \cos \frac{pk\pi}{N} \widehat{W}_k^c(p) + \sin \frac{pk\pi}{N} \widehat{W}_k^s(p) & \text{if } p \text{ is even} \end{cases} \quad (30)$$

Instead of using one complex LMS filter as in the DFT, we used four real LMS filters of which only half of the weights (the even or the odd ones) were retained. The four filters can of course be run in parallel. As in the case of the DFT, noise rejection is ensured by the adaptive nature of the LMS spectrum analyzer.

A Two-layer Linear Adaptive Structure

Let us now incorporate the LMS spectrum analyzer into the DFT-LMS algorithm. The resulting structure is shown in Fig.3. It has two cascaded layers of adaptive weights, but nonetheless it remains a linear filter. The two-layer DCT-LMS structure is slightly more complicated than the DFT-LMS one but it is based on the same principle.

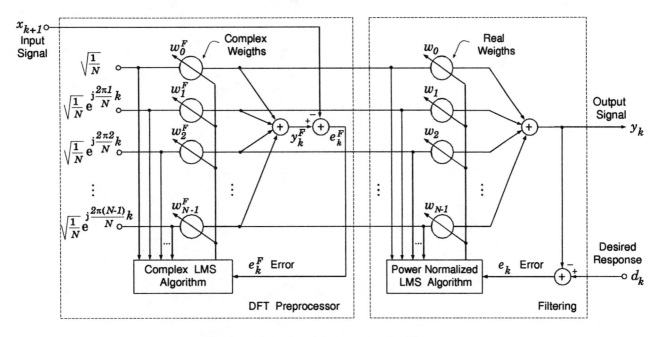

Figure 3: **A two-layer linear adaptive filter.**

The two-layer adaptive filter shown above and its DCT counterpart are simple linear structures containing only two or three LMS blocks. They achieve faster convergence of the filtering weights than pure LMS. They use a minimum of computations, about three times the amount for LMS alone, and offer excellent robustness properties. Recursive least squares algorithms offer even better convergence properties, but only in time-invariant systems. They are far more complicated and can be unstable. All in all, the two-layer DFT-LMS and DCT-LMS algorithms should find increased use in practical real-time applications.

References

1. S.S. Narayan, A.M. Peterson, M.J. Narasimha. Transform Domain LMS Algorithm. *IEEE Trans. on Acoustics, Speech, and Signal Proc.* Vol. ASSP-31. No. 3. June 1983.

2. F. Beaufays. Orthogonalizing Adaptive Algorithms: RLS, DFT/LMS, and DCT/LMS. In *Adaptive Inverse Control.* B. Widrow, E. Walach. Prentice-Hall, Englewood Cliffs, NJ. In prints.

3. B. Widrow, Ph. Baudrenghien, M. Vetterli, P.F. Titchener. Fundamental Relations Between the LMS Algorithm and the DFT. *IEEE Trans. on Circuits and Systems.* Vol. CAS-34. No. 7. Pp. 814-819. July 1987.

4. B. Widrow, J.M. McCool, M. Ball. The complex LMS algorithm. *Proc. IEEE.* Vol. 63. Pp. 719-720. April 1975.

5. K.R. Rao, P. Yip. *Discrete Cosine Transform.* Academic Press, Inc., San Diego, CA. 1990.

Pattern Recognition

**Session Chairs: Teuvo Kohonen
Brian Telfer**

ORAL PRESENTATIONS

Physiological Model for the Self-Organizing Map

Teuvo Kohonen
Helsinki University of Technology
Neural Networks Research Centre
Rakentajanaukio 2 C, FIN-02150 Espoo, Finland

Abstract. The role of the Self-Organizing Map (SOM) algorithm as a genuine "distributed" neural-network model has recently strengthened, when it has become apparent that this algorithm has a neurophysiologically justifiable interpretation. First, a laterally interconnected planar network of neural cells can act as a very effective, self-resetting winner-take-all circuit if one describes its cells using a simple nonlinear dynamic model. Second, the Hebbian law of synaptic plasticity can be modified such that if the nearby synapses are made to interact in a particular way, the synaptic vectors become normalized. Third, the lateral interaction between neighboring cells in the network in learning may be implemented partly neurally, partly through diffuse chemical agents. The adaptive, self-organizing process taking place in such a physiological model can then be shown to be almost identical with that defined by the simpler SOM algorithms.

1 Introduction

The Self-Organizing Map (SOM) algorithm [1,2] may take on many forms depending on the particular vector-space metrics used for the decoding of signal patterns by the neural cells. In simple biologically inspired mathematical neuron models, a cell is usually activated by the incoming signals in proportion to their weighted sum, whereby the weights are thought to represent synaptic efficacies. A version of the SOM that makes use of such cells can be defined in the following way:

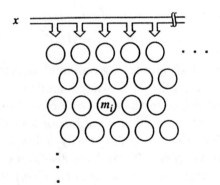

Fig. 1. Layout of a Self-Organizing Map

Assume a planar network of cells (Fig. 1), all of which receive the same input signals represented by the vector $x = (\xi_1, \xi_2, \ldots, \xi_n)^{\mathrm{T}} \in \Re^n$. Let each cell i have its own input weight vector $m_i = (\mu_{i1}, \mu_{i2}, \ldots, \mu_{in})^{\mathrm{T}} \in \Re^n$. By means of lateral feedback connections (cf. Ch. 3) the cell with index $i = c$ becomes the "winner" and is switched into the high activity state if

$$m_c^{\mathrm{T}} x = \max_i \{m_i^{\mathrm{T}} x\} \,, \tag{1}$$

whereas, due to the same lateral interactions, the activity of all the other cells is suppressed to a low value. This switching state lasts for a short period, after which it is automatically reset (cf. Ch. 3).

"Learning" in the above network means that the cells around the "winner" c are adapted to the input x at a rate h_{ci}, where h_{ci} is a function of lateral distance of cells c and i in the network, and possibly of time, too. One learning law that is compatible with (1) may be expressed (in discrete-time steps t) as

$$m_i(t+1) = \frac{m_i(t) + h_{ci}(t) \cdot x(t)}{\text{norm of numerator}} , \qquad (2)$$

and if the adaptation steps are small, the first terms of the Taylor series with $||m_i(t)|| = 1$ yield

$$m_i(t+1) \approx m_i(t) + h_{ci}(t) \cdot [x(t) - m_i(t)m_i^{\mathrm{T}}(t)x(t)] . \qquad (3)$$

It will be pointed out in Ch. 4 that with *arbitrary* $m_i(0)$, (3) tends to normalize the m_i.

A physiological SOM model that behaves like the algorithm defined by (1) and (2), or (1) and (3) must include and implement the following functions: (i) a winner-take-all (WTA) function that selects the "winner" and switches its activity on, (ii) a reset function that, after a small delay, automatically suppresses the "winner", (iii) adaptation of the synaptic weights resembling the law (3), and (iv) interaction of neighboring cells in the network during learning that resembles the effect of h_{ci} in (3).

2 A simple nonlinear dynamic model for the neurons

The output activity η_i (spiking frequency) of neuron i may be described by an effective simplified differential equation

$$d\eta_i/dt = I_i - \gamma(\eta_i) \qquad (4)$$

where I_i is the combined effect of all inputs, e.g., afferent inputs as well as feedbacks, on cell i eventually embedded in a network of cells [3]. In simple modeling, without much loss of generality, I_i may be thought to be proportional to the dot product of the signal vector and the synaptic efficacy vector. Let $\gamma(\eta_i)$ describe the resultant of all loss or leakage effects that oppose to I_i. This is an abbreviated way of writing: since $\eta_i \geq 0$, (4) only holds when $\eta_i > 0$, or when $\eta_i = 0$ and $I_i - \gamma(\eta_i) \geq 0$, whereas otherwise $d\eta_i/dt = 0$. We have also found that for stable convergence in a system of interconnected cells, $\gamma(\eta_i)$ must be convex, i.e., $\gamma''(\eta_i) > 0$.

It should be noticed that (4) may also define a "sigmoid"-type transfer function: in the stationary state, with I_i constant in time and $d\eta_i/dt = 0$, we have

$$\eta_i = \gamma^{-1}(I_i) \qquad (5)$$

in the domain where η_i is defined; γ^{-1} may, for instance, saturate at high input. However, (4) is a more general model law, because it can be used to describe dynamic phenomena as well.

3   The WTA function

Consider now Fig. 2 that delineates the cross section of a two-dimensional network [4]. The larger circles represent "principal" neurons, such as the pyramidal cells in the cortex, and they receive external inputs to which they have to yield a selective response. The smaller circles, the "reset neurons", are inhibitory neurons that have a longer time constant, and in the simplest model each of them feeds back to the same principal neuron to which it is assigned. Their purpose is to suppress the "winner" after a certain delay.

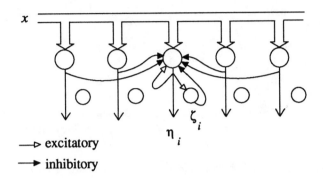

Fig. 2.   Simplified model of a distributed neural network (cross section of a two-dimensional array). Each location consists of an excitatory principal input neuron and an inhibitory interneuron that feeds back locally. The lateral corrections between the principal input neurons may or may not be made via interneurons.

In a more complete model [6] the principal neurons may be interconnected through a great many excitatory and inhibitory interneurons, whereas each solid arrow in Fig. 2 only approximates this "polysynaptic" interconnection between cell i and cell k by an effective static coupling strength g_{ik}. For $k \neq i, g_{ik} < 0$, while $g_{ii} > 0$. This approximation is justified as long as the time constants of the interneurons, let alone the "reset neurons," are small or at least of the same order of magnitude as those of the principal neurons [6].

Referring to the more complete discussion in [4] we write the systems equations as

$$
\begin{aligned}
d\eta_i/dt &= I_i - a\zeta_i - \gamma(\eta_i) \\
d\zeta_i/dt &= b\eta_i - \gamma_1(\zeta_i)
\end{aligned}
\tag{6}
$$

where a and b are constants, and similar hard-limiting restrictions as in (4) must apply to the right-hand sides. Moreover we assume that I_i is decomposed as $I_i = I_i^e + I_i^f$, where

$$
I_i^e = m_i^T x = \sum_j \mu_{ij}\xi_j \text{ is the "external" input, and}
$$

$$
I_i^f = \sum_k g_{ik}\mu_k \text{ represents the lateral feedback, respectively.}
\tag{7}
$$

In Fig. 3 we approximate the loss function $\gamma_1(\zeta_i)$ by another constant θ. This circuit will be seen to operate in *cycles*, where each cycle can be thought to correspond to one discrete-time phase in (2) or (3). During each cycle the cell corresponding to the "winner" (maximum $m_i^T x$) will take over and suppress the other cells. Normally the input would be changed during each new cycle; however, if the input is held steady for a longer time, the next cycle activates the "runner-up", after which the "winner" is activated again, etc.

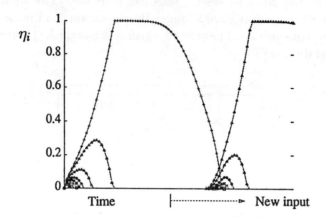

Fig. 3.   Demonstration of the WTA function provided with automatic reset. The first inputs were applied at time zero. New inputs were applied as indicated by the dotted arrow. The network consisted of 20 cells, and the inputs $I_i^e = m_i^T x$ were selected as random numbers from the interval (0, 1). The g_{ii} were equal to 0.5 and the $g_{ik}, i \neq k$, were -2.0, respectively. The loss function had the form $\gamma(\eta) = 0.1\ln\frac{1+\eta}{1-\eta}$; other simpler laws can also be used. The feedback parameters were $a = b = 1, \theta = 0.5$. The network operates as follows: The first "winner" is the cell that receives the largest input; its response will first stabilize to a high value, while the other outputs tend to zero. When the activity of the "winner" is temporarily depressed by the dynamic feedback, the other cells continue competing. The solution was obtained by the classical Runge-Kutta numerical integration method, using a step size of 10^{-5}.

It may be necessary to emphasize that the single-winner WTA circuit described above was obtained when the excitatory feedback connection (g_{ii} above) is only made to the same principal cell. In biological networks it is more plausible that excitatory feedbacks extend to a greater group of neighboring neurons, making the activity in, say, several hundreds of nearby cells correlate strongly. Such "bubbles" of activity have been simulated [1,5], whereas a full mathematical analysis has so far been carried out for single-winner WTA networks only.

4 A non-Hebbian law for synaptic modifiability

The Hebbian adaptation law for a neuron with input signals ξ_j and output activity η_i means that for the adaptive changes at synapses we assume $d\mu_{ij}/dt \sim \xi_j \eta_i$. Quite apparently the pure Hebbian law is unsatisfactory since μ_{ij} would grow monotonically. In order to make reversible changes possible, we must take into account the mutual interference between nearby synapses in the same cell. If this interference is mediated by postsynaptic coupling by nearby synapse r, one of the simplest and most natural thinkable laws for such a reversible or "active forgetting" effect would read

$$d\mu_{ij}/dt \sim (\xi_j - \lambda\mu_{ij} \sum_r \mu_{ir}\xi_r) \cdot \eta_i \tag{8}$$

where λ is a decay constant, $\mu_{ir}\xi_r$ is the postsynaptic effect at synapse r, which proportionally reduces the synaptic strength μ_{ij} at synapse j, and index r runs over nearby synapses on the same cell.

In order to implement a SOM process, the law (8) must still be modified in order to take into account the interaction of neighboring cells during learning. Such an interaction could be implemented by another system of short-range lateral neural connections that do not contribute to the output activities η_i but only modulate the modifiability of synapses of a neighboring neuron (like the chemical transmitter norepinephrine does), or alternatively, this interaction may be controlled by nonspecific chemical agents, acting like messengers to nearby neurons. Whatever the nature of such a spatial modulatory interaction is, it may be described at neuron i by a sum term $\sum_l h_{il}\eta_l$, where the h_{il} are interaction strengths during learning, and l runs laterally over the neighborhood of cell i in the network. Finally we thus get for the form of the non-Hebbian adaptation law to be used to describe learning effects in the SOM,

$$d\mu_{ij}/dt = (\xi_j - \lambda\mu_{ij}\sum_r \mu_{ir}\xi_r)\sum_l h_{il}\eta_l \ . \tag{9}$$

It may already be discernible from (9), but it has further been justified in [4], that (9) and (3) are very similar expressions: (9) in discrete time, (3) in continuous time. As a matter of fact, (6), (7), and (9) together define a continuous-time self-organizing process that has very similar properties as the SOM. Illustrative solutions for the $\eta_i(t)$ and $\mu_{ij}(t)$ that confirm this have been obtained by numerical simulation (Ch. 5), whereby formation of self-organizing maps has been observed, in a similar fashion as by the SOM algorithm, (1) and (3).

Relating to (9), we may now consider a local subset of synapses at the cell's membrane, such as the synapses of a large apical dendrite branch of a pyramidal cell, over which index r runs, and denote the input to this subset by $x = (\xi_1, \xi_2, \ldots, \xi_r)^{\mathrm{T}}$, with $m_i = (\mu_{i1}, \mu_{i2}, \ldots, \mu_{ir})^{\mathrm{T}}$ the corresponding synaptic weight vector. Further it seems reasonable to resort to a kind of "mean field" approximation, whereby, from the point of view of cell i, the factor $\sum_l h_{il}\eta_l$, which we denote by α, shall not depend on η_i, or depends on it only weakly. Then (9) can be written in vector form,

$$dm_i/dt = \alpha x - \beta m_i m_i^{\mathrm{T}} x \ , \tag{10}$$

with $\beta = \lambda\alpha$. This is a *matrix Riccati equation*, and the author has solved it in his book of 1984 [1]. With time, every m_i becomes normalized to the same length $\bar{x}\sqrt{\alpha}/\|\bar{x}\|\sqrt{\beta}$, where $\bar{x}$ is the mean of its input! This is exactly what is needed to make (9) compare with (2) and (3).

It should further be emphasized that the cyclic operation of the WTA function, as described in Ch. 3, in effect *samples* the input signals. The physiological model, although originally written in continuous time, then acts as if the signals were expressed as a discrete-time series! Thus the analogy of the physiological model and the algorithmic SOM is even closer.

5   Animation

Fig. 4 shows three frames from a film that describes the continuous-time self-organizing process, based on (6), (7) and (9). The input vector x was two-dimensional and had a uniform distribution over the square frame; this example corresponds to the standard SOM-experiments found, e.g., in [1], where the weight vectors coincide with the nodes of this net. It took three weeks to run this simulation on a Silicon Graphics R3000 computer, because the stepwise solution of the differential equations (with relative step size 10^{-5}) was extremely slow. The corresponding learning process based on the SOM algorithm (1) and (2) takes only a few dozen seconds.

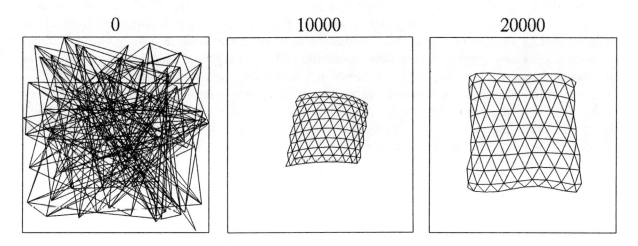

Fig. 4.

It should also be mentioned that the last frame in Fig. 4 does not yet represent the final converged state, but is still somewhat "shrunk"; we stopped the program after three weeks of running.

6 Conclusion

We have been able to show that the SOM algorithm may describe the behavior of a neurophysiological system rather accurately, while the original algorithm is computationally on the order of 30000 times faster than the more naturalistic description studied in this paper.

References

[1] T. Kohonen, *Self-Organization and Associative Memory*, Heidelberg: Springer, 1984, 3rd ed. 1989.

[2] T. Kohonen, "The self-organizing map," *Proc. IEEE*, vol. 78, pp. 1464-1480, September 1990.

[3] T. Kohonen, "An introduction to neural computing," *Neural Networks*, vol. 1, pp. 3-16, 1988.

[4] T. Kohonen, "Physiological Interpretation of the Self-Organizing Map Algorithm," *Neural Networks*, vol. 6, pp. 895-905, 1993.

[5] T. Kohonen, "The 'Neural' Phonetic Typewriter," *Computer*, vol. 21, pp. 11-22, March 1988.

[6] S. Kaski and T. Kohonen, "Winner-Take-All Networks for Physiological Models of Competitive Learning," to appear in *Neural Networks*, a special issue on Models of Neurodynamics and Behaviour.

Adaptive Wavelet Networks for Pattern Recognition

Brian A. Telfer and Harold H. Szu
Naval Surface Warfare Center, Dahlgren Division, Code B44
Silver Spring, MD 20903

Abstract

The utility and robustness of wavelet features is demonstrated through three practical case studies of detecting objects in multispectral electro-optical imagery, sidescan sonar imagery and acoustic backscatter. Emphasis is placed on choosing proper waveforms for particular applications, on advantages of using multiple waveform-types to detect local features in an object, and on adaptively computing the waveforms and their dilation and shift parameters to optimize classification accuracy.

1   Introduction

In any pattern recognition application, proper choice of features is a critical issue. It is well known that for practical applications with finite training data, increasing the number of features up to a point reduces the test set misclassification error, while increasing beyond that point increases the error because too many trainable classifier parameters causes overfitting [1]. Thus, it is important to choose a small number of features that contain the most discriminatory information. Just as important for practical applications, the features must be robust to data variations not necessarily exhibited in the training set. We have found in several real applications that information at different resolution scales provided by wavelet features leads to highly discriminating, robust classifiers. Additionally, adapting the wavelets to specific applications using neural networks results in a small number of features that reduces the effects of overfitting.

Wavelets are attractive features for their ability to examine data at different scales and frequencies. Additionally, unlike windowed Fourier transforms, the wavelet transform allows a choice of basis. Thus, in using wavelet features, the proper wavelet waveform and a small number of shifts and dilations should be chosen to provide significant discriminatory information. To address this, we have combined wavelets and neural networks to adaptively compute a superposition-wavelet filter that is optimized for classification [2]. Others have also studied wavelet networks, but for function approximation rather than as classifiers of wavelet-based features [3-8]. ([8] implements the promising approach of determining class boundaries using wavelets, but this differs from using wavelet features.) Selecting wavelet features for classification is quite different than for approximation and representation. The different considerations that are important for classification are: 1) features must contain information that differs between classes, rather than the information in common to the data, 2) orthogonality is not as important as are waveforms that match the application to extract the most discriminatory information, 3) selecting the best features need not be real-time since it is an off-line process.

After a brief mention of the central ideas of wavelets, three case studies are presented. The first [9], detecting objects from multispectral electro-optical imagery, demonstrates the power of an on-center, off-center filter to remove background clutter and camera nonuniformities, within the context of wavelets to process the data at different scales. The emphasis in the second study [10] with sidescan sonar imagery was to demonstrate the utility of composite wavelet features, that is, groups of different wavelet waveforms to identify different local features in an object. The evidence provided by each feature-type is then fused with a neural network to produce a decision. Both of these studies employed user-specified wavelets, although the obvious utility of adaptivity will be described. The third study [11], based on detecting objects in active sonar returns, demonstrates the ability of a combination of wavelet feature detectors and a neural network to adaptively determine wavelet features that provide the most discriminatory information.

2   Wavelets

The wavelet transform (WT) is a powerful technique for representing data at different scales and frequencies through constant-Q bandpass filters, e.g. [12]. Wavelets are especially attractive from the standpoint of neural networks because the human ear computes an approximate WT [13], and the eye has been shown to have wavelet-like receptive fields [4]. In 1-D, the continuous WT is given by

$$W_s(a, b) = \int g^* \left(\frac{t-b}{a} \right) s(t) \, dt/a, \tag{1}$$

where $g(t)$ is the wavelet, a and b are dilation and shift parameters, and we have adopted a $1/a$ normalization rather than the conventional $1/\sqrt{a}$ to allow for unbiased frequency interpretation [14]. The work in Section 3.3 is based on a Morlet wavelet given by

$$g(t) = \exp(-t^2/2 + j5t). \tag{2}$$

One of the powerful properties of the WT is the freedom to choose a wavelet basis, with the primary requirement being that the wavelet have 0 mean. Of course, for classification features, we do not compute a full WT, but only compute the wavelet or wavelet-derived features needed. The completeness of the WT is unneeded, since there is no need to reconstruct the original signal for classification. In our work, we have sampled the continous WT at discrete shifts and dilations. Although a wavelet chosen to fit a particular application are similar to banks of scaled matched filters, wavelets often perform better because of their 0-mean nature which eliminates background areas through sensitivity to edges of particular shapes [15]. This is demonstrated in Sec. 3. Also, a formulation has been developed to linearly combine the wavelet function at different dilations to produce scale-invariant wavelet functions [16], which avoid the additional computation required by a bank of filters.

The discrete WT has received tremendous attention (see [12] for an overview) and a fast O(N) algorithm exists. We do not consider that here, except to note that work is ongoing to allow more freedom to choose a particular wavelet waveform while still allowing a fast algorithm [17,18].

3   Case Studies

3.1   Multispectral Imagery

One band from a set of six-band multispectral imagery [9] is shown in Fig. 1a. The six 480×720-pixel spectral bands have wavelengths evenly spaced between 400-900nm. In the foreground are the blob-shaped objects we wish to detect, and various types of clutter are visible.

For comparison, a perceptron with two layers of weights was trained with the six spectral values from one pixel forming a feature vector. The training set consisted of 21 target pixels (the centers of half the targets) and 279 clutter pixels. The classification of all pixels (training and test) is shown in Fig. 1b. The classification results are poor, with some blobs not detected and many false alarms, especially along the boundaries between ground types. Blobs on the right side of the image are missed or poorly detected because a camera nonuniformity causes the right side of the image to appear slightly lighter than the left.

For the wavelet processing, the wavelet was chosen to have a positive central elliptical area matching the blobs in Figure 1a, with a surrounding negative area so that the function integrates to zero (on-center, off-surround). We have chosen one wavelet with only a single scale and orientation since we know the target size and orientation for this application. A straightforward method of detecting other scales would be to use other wavelet dilations. A preferable alternative has been developed to linearly combine the wavelet function at different dilations to produce scale-invariant wavelet features [16]. The wavelet was correlated with each spectral band, and another perceptron with two layers of weights was trained on the wavelet-preprocessed spectral bands in the same manner as before. The classification results are shown in Fig. 2c. Every blob has been detected and the only false alarms are a few small areas of a resolution chart. Even these few false alarms could be eliminated by discarding detections that contain only 2-3 pixels (at the cost of missing a few of the blobs). Thus, wavelet preprocessing significantly improves over classification of the raw data, and is robust to the camera nonuniformity and diverse clutter types present in the image.

Although we did not test adaptive wavelet techniques for this case study, these would be beneficial in optimizing the size of the wavelet's negative area, in adapting the waveform to different sensors, and in computing additional wavelets to reject clutter.

3.2 Sidescan Sonar Imagery

A sidescan sonar image is shown in Fig. 2a [10]. Objects, predominantly in the righthand-side of Fig. 2a, appear as highlights with shadows extending in the direction of sound propagation. As in Section 3.1 and as expected, neural network classification of the raw data produced poor results. In applying wavelets to this problem, two wavelet filters were selected, one with an on-center, off-surround form to detect highlights, and the other a similar but horizontally elongated filter to detect shadows. Each wavelet at different scales was correlated with the input image. A single-layer perceptron with two weights (one corresponding to a pixel in the highlight correlation image and one to a pixel in the shadow correlation image) was trained to fuse evidence from the two correlation images at a particular scale. It was shown that the same neural network would also properly fuse the correlation images at different scales. The classification output is shown in Fig. 2b, produced with wavelets at a scale matching most of the targets. The results are excellent. (The responses in the central swath would normally be gated out, but are included in this image.) Wavelets at different scales, in conjunction with the neural network, were demonstrated to detect objects at different scales (results shown in [10]). Again, the wavelet features are demonstrated to be robust to a wide range of clutter levels and types.

3.3 Acoustic Signals

Fig. 3a shows representative acoustic backscatter from a metallic object and natural clutter when ensonified with a linear-FM transmit signal [11]. The two signal classes have similar strengths and durations, and there is significant intraclass variation, which creates a challenging pattern recognition task. Synthetic reverberation noise (20dB) was added to all signals to increase realism. The data was divided into training and test sets with 222 and 216 returns, respectively (multiple aspects and multiple days of collection). Fig. 3 shows corresponding wavelet transform magnitudes, computed with a Morlet wavelet.

To find the groupings of wavelet features, the algorithm adapts Gaussian patches in the time-scale magnitude space. In that sense, it is similar to a radial basis classifier, but adaptively computes wavelet features rather than finding boundaries in an existing feature space. The classifier output v_n for the nth training sample is given by

$$v_n = \gamma \left\{ \sum_k w_k \sum_i \sum_j \exp\left[-\frac{1}{2} \left(\left(\frac{a_i - m_{ak}}{\sigma_{ak}} \right)^2 + \left(\frac{b_j - m_{bk}}{\sigma_{bk}} \right)^2 \right) \right] \|W_n(a_i, b_j)\| \right\}, \qquad (3)$$

where w_k, m_{ak}, m_{bk}, σ_{ak} and σ_{bk} are the weight, mean and standard deviations of the kth Gaussian patch, and $\gamma(z) = 1/[1 + \exp(-z)]$ (normally denoted by σ, but changed here to avoid notational conflict). The classification parameters are optimized by minimizing the mean squared error between the actual and desired outputs using gradient descent.

The resulting adaptive wavelet classifier (with 30 Gaussian patches) gives a test set error rate of 0.083 vs 0.130 from classifying power spectral features. (This is one result from numerous tests at different levels of reverberation noise, which all have the same qualitative difference.) This difference is not surprising, since the wavelet classifier makes use of time and frequency information, whereas the power spectral classifier only uses frequency information. The adaptive wavelet features are robust, in that they generalize well to the test data that has considerable intraclass variation from the training data, and also contains reverberation noise. Fig. 4 displays the adaptive wavelet classifier weights corresponding to the time/frequency information in Fig. 3b. The Gaussian patches can be seen as well as the areas that are given heaviest weight for classification, particularly the trailing edge of the return. Ongoing work for this application emphasizes computing a small set of wavelet-based features that can be quickly computed, rather than integrating sets of WT magnitudes.

4   Conclusion

The three case studies summarized here demonstrate the promise of wavelet and adaptive wavelet classifiers for practical applications that require robust features. This work is heading toward classifiers that use multiple adaptive wavelet waveforms to provide discriminatory information that is local in time/space and frequency/scale. The wavelet waveforms are adaptive to particular applications, and can incorporate scale invariance through appropriate combination of wavelet coefficients.

(a)

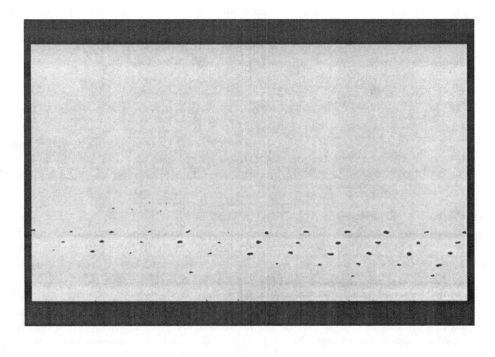

(b)

Figure 1: a) 400nm band of multispectral electro-optical imagery, b) detections by neural network operating on spectral data, c) detections by neural network operating on wavelet-preprocessed data.

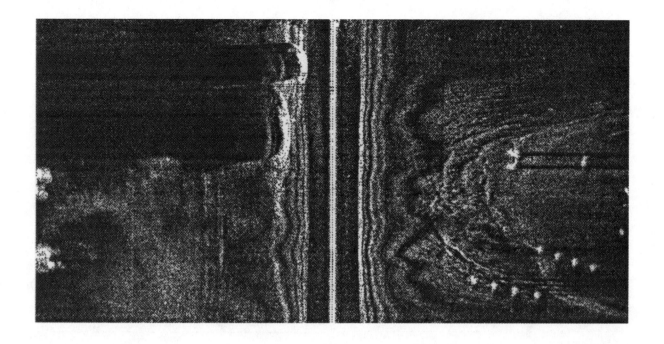

(a)

(b)

Figure 2: a) sidescan sonar image, b) detections by neural network fusing evidence from preprocessing with highlight and shadow wavelets.

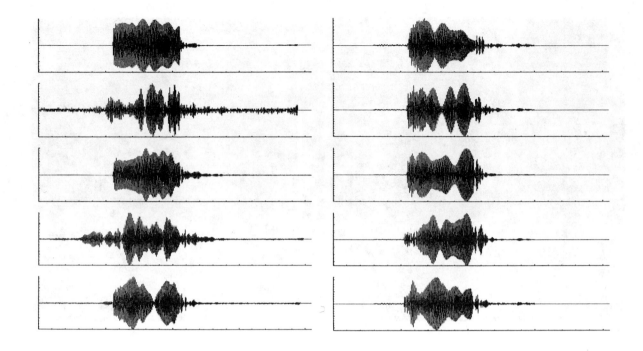

(a)

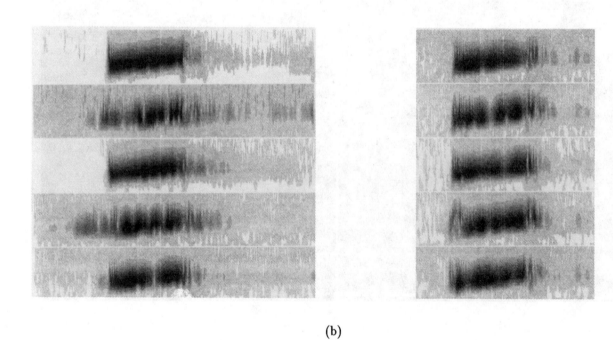

(b)

Figure 3: a) acoustic backscatter time series from metallic object (left) and natural clutter (right) at different aspect angles, b) corresponding wavelet transform magnitudes (frequency vs. time).

Figure 4: Adaptive wavelet classifier weights (frequency vs. time).

Acknowledgement

We thank our colleagues who have participated in the individual application studies: A. Dubey, N. Witherspoon (Sec. 3.1); J. Garcia, H. Ko (Sec. 3.2); G. Dobeck (Sec. 3.3). This work was supported by the NSWCDD Independent Research Program; the Marine Corps Systems Command, Amphibious Warfare Technology Directorate; and the Office of Naval Research, Code 32, Contract N0001493WX4B340. The sidescan sonar image is from the Naval Image Database compiled by the NSWC Coastal Systems Station, Panama City FL, Code 130A.

References

[1] R.O. Duda, P.E. Hart, *Pattern Classification and Scene Analysis*. New York: John Wiley and Sons, 1973.

[2] H. Szu, B. Telfer, S. Kadambe, "Adaptive Wavelets for Signal Representation and Classification," *Optical Engineering*, vol. 31, 1907-1916, Sept. 1992.

[3] S. Mann, S. Haykin, "Adaptive 'Chirplet' Transform: an Adaptive Generalization of the Wavelet Transform," *Optical Engineering*, vol. 31, 1243-1256, June 1992.

[4] J. Daugman, "Complete Discrete 2-D Gabor Transforms by Neural Networks for Image Analysis and Compression," IEEE Trans. ASSP, vol. 36, 1169-1179, July 1988.

[5] Q. Zhang, A. Benveniste, "Wavelet Networks," *IEEE Trans. Neural Nets.*, vol. 3, 889-898, Nov. 1992.

[6] B. Bakshi, G. Stephanopoulos, "Wavelets as Basis Functions for Localized Learning in a Multiresolution Hierarchy," *Proc. Int. Joint Conf. Neural Networks*, II 140-145, June 1992.

[7] Y. Pati, P. Krishnaprasad, "Analysis and Synthesis of Feedforward Neural Networks using Discrete Affine Wavelet Transforms," *IEEE Trans. Neural Networks*, vol. 4, 73-85, Jan. 1993.

[8] T.I. Boubez, R.L. Peskin, "Wavelet Neural Networks and Receptive Field Partitioning," *Proc IEEE Int. Conf. Neural Networks*, 1544-1549, Mar. 1993.

[9] B. Telfer, H. Szu, A. Dubey, N. Witherspoon, "Detecting Blobs in Multispectral Electro-optical Imagery using Wavelet Techniques," *Proc. SPIE*, vol. 1961, 377-385, April 1993.

[10] J. Garcia, B. Telfer, H. Ko, H. Szu, "Composite Wavelet Features for Image Recognition," Proc. SPIE, vol. 2242, April 1994.

[11] B. Telfer, H. Szu, G. Dobeck, "Adaptive Wavelet Classification of Acoustic Backscatter," Proc. SPIE, vol. 2242, April 1994.

[12] I. Daubechies, *Ten Lectures on Wavelets*. Philadelphia: SIAM, 1992.

[13] X. Yang, K. Wang, S. Shamma, "Auditory Representations of Acoustic Signals," *IEEE Trans. IT*, vol. 38, 824-839, Mar. 1992.

[14] B. Telfer, H. Szu, "New Wavelet Transform Normalization to Remove Frequency Bias," *Optical Engineering*, vol. 31, 1830-1834, Sept. 1992.

[15] Y. Sheng, D. Roberge, H. Szu, "Optical Matched Filters for Shift-Invariant Pattern Recognition," *Optics Letters*, vol. 18, 299-301, Feb. 15 1993.

[16] H. Szu, X. Yang, B. Telfer, Y. Sheng, "Neural Network and Wavelet Transform for Scale-Invariant Data Classification," *Physical Rev. E*, vol. 48, no. 2, 1497-1501; NSWCDD Invention Disclosure, case no. 75380.

[17] H. Szu, B. Telfer, "Foundations of Adaptive Wavelet Transform," *Proc. SPIE*, vol. 2242, April 1993.

[18] P. Abry, A. Aldroubi, "Designing Multiresolution Analysis-type Wavelets and their Fast Algorithms," submitted for publication.

Comparison of Sequences Generated by a Self-Organizing Feature Map using Dynamic Programming

Marc Lalonde and Jean-Jules Brault
Laboratoire Scribens
Département de Génie Électrique et Génie Informatique
École Polytechnique de Montréal,
C.P. 6079 Succ. centre-ville
Montréal, QC, Canada H3C 3A7
Email: brault@scribens.polymtl.ca

Abstract

The presentation of a series of patterns to a Kohonen network (Self-Organizing Feature Map) is known to generate a "trajectory" that may itself carry meaningful information. Handwritten signature verification is a typical application in which each pattern represents a specific portion of a given signature. An efficient way to compare an unknown trajectory to a reference trajectory consists in using a string comparison technique developed by Wagner & Fischer (and related to dynamic programming). Editing costs (for insertions/deletions/substitutions) are determined according to the response of the feature map following presentation of the sequences to be compared. An example in signature verification is given to illustrate the method.

I. Introduction

The neural network model called Self-Organizing Feature Map (SOFM - described by Kohonen in [3], [4], [5] and [6]) has been successfully applied to pattern classification (along with LVQ) and vector quantization problems. However, in several situations, sequences of patterns must be dealt with in addition to the recognition of the patterns themselves. Upon presentation of such a sequence, specific cells are activated one after the other, thus generating a trajectory over the entire map that is typical of the input sequence. [5] has pointed out the above-described phenomenon when studying the feature map in speech recognition; other applications may produce the same results: character recognition based on the analysis of successive letter segments ([11], [12]), study of EEG signals during sleep [14], signature verification [9], etc. These applications show the importance of evaluating the correctness of a test trajectory generated over a SOFM compared to reference trajectories.

This paper is mainly aimed at the signature verification problem, even though the proposed technique could be applied to other types of sequences. Let us consider a set of reference signatures obtained from an individual; these signatures are segmented into various elements from which feature vectors are extracted; the vectors are then grouped to form a training set for a SOFM; after learning, each cell of the SOFM is tuned to the shape and velocity profiles of a specific portion of the individual's signature; when a test signature is to be validated, the resulting trajectory (potentially distorted) must be compared to those of the references, taking into account possible erroneous, missing or additional elements.

The rest of the paper is divided into six sections. Section II describes the type of SOFM used. Section III presents sequence comparison problems as well as solutions already proposed in the literature. In section IV, we present a brief summary of the Wagner & Fischer algorithm and the necessary ajustments are explained. Finally, in section V, an example using simple signatures illustrates the trajectory comparison process.

II. Description of the SOFM

The SOFM network is seen as a tool for the visualization of metric-topological relationships in a multidimensional vector space. It can be used in pattern classification, clustering and vector quantization since prototype vectors are formed during learning and correspond to the centroid of sub-domains within the overall space (these prototypes are actually weight vectors associated to the cells). When an input vector $\vec{I}(t)$ is presented to the network, cells compete against each other and the cell having its weight vector $\vec{W}(t)$ closest to $\vec{I}(t)$ outputs the strongest response that allows the inhibition of all the others (the cell is said to win the competition). The usual measures of proximity include the Euclidian distance and the dot product between $\vec{I}(t)$ and $\vec{W}(t)$. The dot product will be used here and the justification will be given later in section IV. The activation of a cell (namely cell i) is then given by:

$$Act_i(t) = \vec{I}(t) \cdot \vec{W}_i(t) \tag{1}$$

where $\vec{I}(t)$ and $\vec{W}(t)$ are normalized. Learning is carried out in a classical manner ([4], [5], [6] and [13]):

- presentation to the SOFM of a vector drawn from the training set;
- determination of the winning cell c such that $Act_c = \max_i \{Act_i\}$
- adaptation of the weight vectors associated to cells belonging to neighborhood $N_c(t)$ centered on cell c:

$$\vec{W}_i(t+1) = \begin{bmatrix} \dfrac{\vec{W}_i(t) + h(r,t)I(t)}{\| \vec{W}_i(t) + h(r,t)I(t) \|}, & \forall\, i \in N_c(t) \\\\ \vec{W}_i(t) & \text{otherwise} \end{bmatrix} \tag{2}$$

with $N_c(t) \rightarrow c$; furthermore,

$$h(r,t) = \alpha(t) e^{-\frac{r^2}{\sigma^2}} \tag{3}$$

where $\alpha(t) \rightarrow 0$ with t increasing, and r is the distance between cell i and cell c within a neighborhood $N_c(t)$ of diameter σ^2. Cells are labelled with a code (e.g. a letter); upon recall, a given sequence would produce the activation of a series of cells which may be summarized by a string of codes (e.g. "a e f d c b").

The question now is how to compare such a sequence to a reference sequence.

III. Methods for sequence comparison

Since a sequence possesses an underlying structure (it is made of a symbol 'a' followed by a symbol 'b', etc.), one could consider the use of a syntactic method (i.e. grammar). Production rules would be extracted from the references, and test sequences would be recognized depending on whether they fit the constructed grammar or not. However, many reasons prevent us from resorting to this technique:

difficulty to extract production rules. Extra rules should be added to the set of basic production rules in order to handle missing or additional elements: this is a type of problem that syntactic methods have always had trouble to cope with.

difficulty to deal with variations inherent in the use of feature maps. This turns out to be a key problem since patterns of a test sequence are often perceived as more or less pronounced variations of those of reference sequences. If the variations are significant, the expected cells will remain inactive: their neighbors will come out (according to the fact that the mapping produced is said to be "topology-preserving", as shown in [4], which implies that neighboring cells possess contiguous weight vectors in the weight space). Constructing a coherent grammar capable of handling all possibilities is nearly impossible.

Another approach would favor the use of other neural networks with sequence processing capabilities. Networks like that of Tank & Hopfield [15], the Time-Delay of [10] or recurrent architectures (e.g. [1]) could be considered. Although some of them were designed to process distorted sequences (whether by using temporal windows [15] or by learning [10]), the "variations problem" remains unsolved: these nets expect specific input patterns or features, and no substitutes are allowed.

We can finally draw ideas from the study of string comparison: how to optimally transform a test string into a reference string by using simple editing operations (insertions/deletions/substitutions) associated to costs. The general string comparison algorithm is derived from dynamic programming (DP) techniques and it has been used for tackling a large number of problems (see [7] and [8] for a review of these techniques and their applications). The same concept has been explored independently by Wagner & Fischer (in [16]) when they addressed the issue of comparing string typed on a keyboard with reference keywords. They came up with a similar approach to DP that computes a distance between two strings based on specific costs (depending on the probability of typing error, for example; in that regard, the cost for confusing 'r' and 'e' should obviously be much lower than that of confusing 'r' and 'p'). The analogy with the problem explained in introduction is striking: the feature map may be seen as a keyboard where a sequence of keys making up a word corresponds to a sequence of activated cells. As two neighbouring keys can be substituted with high probability, in the same way two neighboring cells represent (by their weight vectors) similar shapes or patterns: therefore the cost for their substitution could be a function of their activations before competition.

This analogy naturally leads to the use of the Wagner & Fischer algorithm as a means of measuring the dissimilarity between two sequences generated by a feature map.

IV. Wagner & Fischer algorithm

Here is a brief summary of the Wagner & Fischer algorithm:

Let A and B be two strings.
$A = \{a_i\}$; $i = 1 .. \text{length}(A)$
$B = \{b_j\}$; $j = 1 .. \text{length}(B)$

In order to transform A into B, three operations are allowed:
· substitution $a_i \rightarrow b_j$; cost = $\gamma (a_i \rightarrow b_j)$
· insertion $\lambda \rightarrow b_j$; cost = $\gamma (\lambda \rightarrow b_j)$
· deletion $a_i \rightarrow \lambda$; cost = $\gamma (a_i \rightarrow \lambda)$
where λ is the null string.

The distance between strings A and B is the accumulation of small distances D(i, j) given by:

$$D(i,j) = \min \begin{bmatrix} D(i-1,j-1) + \gamma(a_i \rightarrow b_j) \\ D(i-1,j) + \gamma(a_i \rightarrow \lambda) \\ D(i,j-1) + \gamma(\lambda \rightarrow b_j) \end{bmatrix} \qquad (4)$$

The cost function γ must obey fundamental properties so that the distance can be considered a metric [7]:

1. $\gamma(a_i \rightarrow b_j) \geq 0$: nonnegative costs
2. $\gamma(a_i \rightarrow a_i) = 0$: cost = 0 for two identical symbols
3. $\gamma(a_i \rightarrow b_j) = \gamma(b_j \rightarrow a_i)$: symmetry
4. $\gamma(a_i \rightarrow b_j) \leq \gamma(a_i \rightarrow \lambda) + \gamma(\lambda \rightarrow b_j)$: triangular inequality condition

The determination of costs is a key issue. We set costs $\gamma(\lambda \rightarrow b_j)$ and $\gamma(a_i \rightarrow \lambda)$ to 1: they are considered as editing costs resulting from the deletion or the insertion of an element with respect to one of the sequences under analysis. As for the substitution cost $\gamma(a_i \rightarrow b_j)$, it should remain low if the element corresponding to a_i activates a nearby cell instead of that activated by the element corresponding to b_j, or become high for the alternate case. Intuitively, it is reasonable to suggest:

$$\gamma(a_i \rightarrow b_j) = Act_c - Act_{ref} \qquad (5)$$

where Act_c =   activation of the winning cell (symbol a_i) after presentation of a test vector
       Act_{ref} =   activation of the cell (symbol b_j) that should have won according to reference B
Moreover, knowing that $Act_c > Act_{ref}$ since c is the winning cell, then it follows that $0 < \gamma(a_i \rightarrow b_j) < 2$.

If the winning cell is the same as the expected cell, then the corresponding patterns from the two strings match together and can be substituted with no cost; on the other hand, if the corresponding patterns do not sustain comparison, the activation of the expected cell will be much lower than that of the cell c, thus yielding a high substitution cost that is likely to favour a deletion or an insertion operation. It is important to point out that this cost is bounded since the activation of the winning cell c is less or equal to 1 (with normalized vectors $\vec{I}(t)$ and $\vec{W}(t)$). This fact ensures that the property of triangular inequality is respected. In addition, one can easily notice that all properties stated in section IV are respected, except that of symmetry: given that comparisons are made between test sequences and known references, only the test vectors are supposed available (it is not necessary to keep the feature vectors that produced the reference sequences). As a consequence, a comparison between a reference sequence and a test sequence cannot be performed. In any case, it is mentioned in [7] that an asymmetric distance is accepted in situations where an unknown sequence is compared against template sequences (in speech recognition, for example).

V. An example

In order to illustrate the idea, a basic experiment has been conducted with signatures made of simple straight lines (figs. 1-2). Points joined by the lines are actual segmentation points. Feature vectors are then constructed with specific measures obtained from the curves (depicted in fig. 3), thus carrying the following information:

$$Vector = \left[\frac{l_1}{\sqrt{l_1^2 + l_2^2}} , \frac{l_2}{\sqrt{l_1^2 + l_2^2}} , \sin\theta , \cos\theta \right] \qquad (6)$$

Note that pairs of segments are overlapping: segment #1 joined to segment #2, segment #2 joined to segment #3, etc. so that elements are chained together. Due to the selected coding, each segment is described with respect to the prior segment by angle θ. Since the features are comparable (they are piecewise normalized so that the vector length remains constant), the vector can be transformed into a unit vector, as required by the feature map learning algorithm. Learning begins with $\alpha(0) = 0.9$ and $N_c(0) =$ 90% of map surface (a 4x4 map). The training vectors are those extracted from references R1 and R2. The so obtained map (sketched in figure 4) sets up an analysis framework specific to the genuine signer. Note that in more advanced signature verification systems the vector (5) is more complete since the varying curvature of the pen trace between segmentation points along with its dynamics is taken into account [9].

Reference and test sequences generated trajectories shown in fig. 5. A careful study of test signatures Ti reveals that T1 is similar to R1 and R2, T2 counts an extra segment, and T3 is totally different from R1 or R2. We expect:

- small distance between T1 and Rj
- distance between T2 and Rj at least greater to 1 (the cost due to the deletion of the additional segment)
- large distance between T3 and Rj

Comparisons have been made using the Wagner & Fischer algorithm (described in section IV) and the optimal matching paths appear in figs. 6 to 8. We see that T1 fully matches any reference; the additional segment in T2 has been removed; deletion of elements in T3 and insertion of others are such that the resulting signatures now look similar. Moreover, distance measures compiled in table 1 confirm our estimations. This simple example shows that comparison of sequences generated by a feature map can be done with a DP technique: in a classification context, an unknown sequence could be compared against a set of prototype sequences and the smallest distance would indicate the class the input sequence probably belongs to.

Distance Ti vs Rj	Reference #1	Reference #2
Test #1	0.0234	0.0280
Test #2	1.2494	1.2786
Test #3	4.3052	4.3052

Table 1. Distances between "signatures" as computed by the DP algorithm

VI. Discussion

The major constraint limiting the wide application of the algorithm is undoubtedly the requirement about unit feature vectors, which is sometimes difficult to meet (particularly in our example where the feature vector was a set of interrelated geometrical measurements). Another definition of activation for the feature map cells would be possible provided that normalization of the overall map response is made in order to guarantee a set of costs that is in agreement with the previously stated triangular inequality principle. An alternate activation function for each cell (sigmoidal instead of the standard linear in recall mode) could do the job, but the gain and the inflexion point of the sigmoid would become critically important parameters.

Other pertinent adjustments may also affect the choice of costs: in some cases, elements of a sequence could have more importance than others, e.g. in signature verification, where the various portions of a signature may exhibit very different sizes, and thus unequal importance. The retained cost values should be weighted so that the importance of each element is considered.

VII. Conclusion

In this paper, we showed that a string comparison technique related to dynamic programming (namely the Wagner & Fischer algorithm) was capable of measuring the dissimilarity between two sequences generated by a SOFM neural network. Costs associated to editing operations are chosen according to the map response.

References

1. Elman, J.L., 1990 "Finding Structure in Time", *Cognitive Science*, **14**, 179-211.
2. Gonzalez, R.C., Thomason, M.G. *Syntactic Pattern Recognition: an introduction*. Addison-Wesley, 1978.
3. Kohonen, T. "Self-organized formation of topologically correct feature maps". *Biol. Cybern*, **43** (1982), pp. 59-69.
4. Kohonen, T. *Self-Organization and Associative Memory*. Springer-Verlag, 3rd ed., 1988.
5. Kohonen, T. "The 'Neural' Phonetic Typewriter". *IEEE Computer*, March 1988. pp. 11-22.
6. Kohonen, T. "The Self-organizing Map". *Proceedings of the IEEE*, **78** (1990), n 9. pp.1464-1480.
7. Kruskal, J.B. "An Overview of Sequence Comparison" in Sankoff, D. "*Time Warps, String Edits, and Macromolecules: the Theory and Practice of Sequence Comparison*". Addison-Wesley, 1983.
8. Kruskal, J.B., Sankoff, D. "An Anthology of Algorithms and Concepts for Sequence Comparison" in Sankoff, D. "*Time Warps, String Edits, and Macromolecules: the Theory and Practice of Sequence Comparison*". Addison-Wesley, 1983.
9. Lalonde, M., Brault, J.J. "On the use of Self-Organizing Maps in Dynamic Signature Verification". In preparation (1993).
10. Lang, K.J., Waibel, A.H. "A Time-Delay Neural Network Architecture for Isolated Word Recognition". *Neural Networks*, **3** (1990), pp. 23-43.
11. Morasso, P. "Neural Models of Cursive Script Handwriting". *Proc. Int. Joint Conf. on Neural Networks '89*, Wash. DC, v 2, pp. 539-542.
12. Morasso, P., Barberis, L., Pagliano, S., Vergano, D., "Recognition of Experiments of Cursive Dynamic Handwriting with Self-Organizing Networks", *Pattern Recognition*, **26**, (1993), n 3, pp. 443-450.
13. Ritter, H., Kohonen, T., "Self-Organizing Semantic Maps", *Biol. Cybern.*, **61** (1989), pp. 241-254.
14. Roberts, S., Tarassenko, L. "Analysis of the sleep EEG using a multilayer network with spatial organisation". *IEE Proc. -F*, v 139 n 6, Dec. 1992. pp. 420-425.
15. Tank, D.W., Hopfield, J.J., "Neural Computation by Concentrating Information in Time", *Proc. Natl. Acad. Sci. USA*, **84**, pp. 1896-1900.
16. Wagner, R.A., Fischer, M.J. "The String-to-String Correction Problem". *Journal of the ACM*, **21**, no 1, Jan. 1974. pp. 168-173.

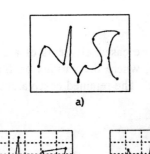
a)

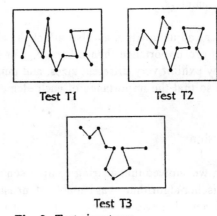
Test T1   Test T2

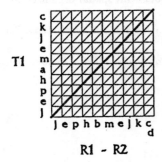
b)   c)

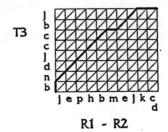
Test T3

Fig. 1 a) Sample of reference signatures
b) Reference R1
c) Reference R2

Fig. 2 Test signatures

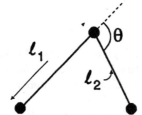

Fig. 3 Segment coding

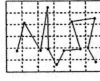

Fig. 4 Weight ordering
after learning

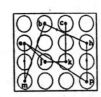

R2: ʃ e p h b m e ʃ k c̃
T1: ʃ e p h a m e ʃ k c̃
T2: ʃ e k n d e m e ʃ k c̃
T3: b n d ʃ c c b ʃ
R1: ʃ e p h b m e ʃ k c̃

Fig. 5   Sequences generated by
signatures Ti and Rj

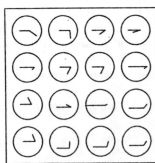
T1

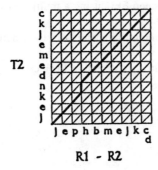
T2

T3

R1 - R2   R1 - R2   R1 - R2

Fig. 6 Optimal path: T1 vs Rj   Fig. 7 Optimal path: T2 vs Rj   Fig. 8 Optimal path: T3 vs Rj

Handwritten Digit Recognition Using Fuzzy ARTMAP Network

Natalya Markuzon[1]

Department of Cognitive & Neural Systems

Boston University, 111 Cummington St., Boston, MA 02215, USA

Abstract

Fuzzy ARTMAP is a supervised learning system which includes nonlinear dynamics in the learning process. A modified learning rule which enables 'forgetting' of insignificant information is introduced. A handwritten digit recognition task is applied to evaluate the performance of the network in a real, noisy environment. Two different preprocessing algorithms, based on either positional or directional information extracted from the image, are used. The latter algorithm is more successful. The fuzzy ARTMAP network is compared to the K Nearest-Neighbor (KNN) algorithm. Although the modified learning rule improves the performance of fuzzy ARTMAP, KNN still performs somewhat better. However, the amount of memory and the length of recognition time required by fuzzy ARTMAP are significantly smaller.

ARTMAP, KNN, and the ZIP Code Database

ARTMAP [Carpenter, Grossberg and Reynolds, 1991] is a neural network architecture that performs incremental supervised learning of recognition categories and multidimensional maps in response to binary input vectors presented in an arbitrary order. Fuzzy ARTMAP [Carpenter et al., 1992] incorporates fuzzy logic [Zadeh, 1965] to classify inputs by a fuzzy set of features indicating the extent to which the feature is present. To evaluate the performance of the system on a difficult problem, the handwritten digit recognition task was proposed. Digits were obtained from the *United States Postal Office of Advanced Technology Handwritten ZIP Code Database (1987)* which consists of five-digit ZIP codes. Separation of digits, beyond the scope to this project, was performed manually.

The K Nearest-Neighbor classifier has been examined on handwritten recognition tasks [Lee, 1991]. Compared to a backpropagation network which uses local receptive fields and shared weights, and to radial basis function networks, it provides a similarly low error rate. However, KNN requires a very large amount of memory, and is slow in classification. The KNN algorithm chooses a winning category based on the K training points that lie nearest to a test point. It is used for comparison with fuzzy ARTMAP performance.

Noisy images are passed through several steps of preprocessing before being presented to the recognition network. First, the background noise is removed from figures and transformation of images into a scale-rotation invariant representation is performed. Then, two

---

[1]Supported in part by British Petroleum (BP 89A-1204)

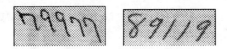

Figure 1: Examples of ZIP codes from *United States Postal Office of Advanced Technology Handwritten ZIP Code Database (1987)*.

types of preprocessing are applied to construct a one-dimensional input vector for the classifier. The first method incorporates positional information while the second incorporates directional information. Both fuzzy ARTMAP and KNN show slightly better performance with the directional preprocessor than with the positional preprocessor. Thus directional preprocessing is used to compare system performance. Simulations show that there is a trade-off between the predictive accuracy and the number of nodes created by the classifiers. The following sections describe the preprocessing steps, the classifiers, and simulation results.

ZIP code data and preprocessing steps

ZIP codes from the postal service data base use a great variety of sizes, styles, and instruments. Both the training set and the test set contain numerous examples that are ambiguous, extremely noisy, and can be misclassified by people. Gray scale images consist of five digits, and some extraneous marks may also be present, such as pieces of letters from the address label or underlining. Digits in a zip code may overlap and they are surrounded by the background noise. Some examples are shown in Figure 1.

Most of the background noise has lower intensity than the digits and was removed by thresholding. The level of the threshold was automatically defined by the analysis of histograms of images, computed as an average over the image intensity plus empirical value that defines the range of noise intensity fluctuations. After thresholding, small spots of high intensity, several pixels in width that do not belong to digits may remain in the image. A median filter removed these points. This filter substitutes the pixel intensity value by the middle value over its neighbors, removing isolated fluctuations of intensity in small areas.

Digits in ZIP codes have different inclinations (Figure 1). To allow separation and to remove rotation uncertainty, digits were transformed into an invariant vertical position. The main direction was defined as the one with the highest activity obtained during convolution of the image with orientation selective filters of different orientations. The affine

Figure 2: Digits transformed to a vertical position, with background noise removed.

transformation with the center in the left upper corner of the image transforms the image to make the main direction vertical. This positions digits in an upright position (Figure 2). After manual separation, a linear transformation fit each digit to the $16 * 16$ box. To transform 2-D into a 1-D classifier input, *coarse coding* [Seibert, Waxman, 1990] and *directional preprocessing* were used. In coarse coding, a featural component is the convolution of pixel intensities in the image with large overlapping Gaussian-weighted receptive field. The receptive field was truncated at a diameter of $3 - 4$ pixels, and fields overlapped by half.

Orientation selective filters in the form of difference-of-Gaussians were used in directional preprocessing. The image was divided into 16 cells of $4 * 4$ pixels size. The image in each cell was convolved with filters of several orientations, the number of orientations was fixed at 6 throughout. Then, for each cell and each filter the maximum activity over the resulting image was defined, and it was considered as one feature in the input vector to classifier. This procedure provides a network with the information about directional preferences of digits in different locations. Input vectors obtained with the positional and the directional preprocessings contained 49 features and 64 features respectively.

Fuzzy ARTMAP and modified learning rule

Fuzzy ARTMAP (Figure 3) includes a pair of Fuzzy ART modules (ART_a and ART_b) [Carpenter, Grossberg and Rosen, 1991] linked together via an inter-ART associative memory F^{ab} that is called a *map field*. During supervised learning, ART_a receives a stream $\{\mathbf{a}^{(p)}\}$ of input patterns and ART_b receives a stream $\{\mathbf{b}^{(p)}\}$ of patterns, where $\mathbf{b}^{(p)}$ is the correct prediction given $\mathbf{a}^{(p)}$. These modules are linked by an associative learning network and an internal controller that ensures autonomous system operation in real time. The controller is designed to create the minimal number of ART_a recognition categories needed to meet accuracy criteria.

Vigilance parameter ρ_a calibrates the minimum confidence that ART_a must have in a recognition category, or hypothesis, activated by an input $\mathbf{a}^{(p)}$ in order to ART_a to accept that category, rather than search for a better one through an automatically controlled process of hypothesis testing. Lower values of ρ_a enable larger categories to form. These lower ρ_a values lead to a broader generalization and a higher degree of code compression. A predictive failure at ART_b increases ρ_a by the minimum amount needed to trigger hypothesis testing at ART_a, using a mechanism called *match tracking*. Match tracking sacrifices the minimum amount of generalization necessary to correct the predictive error. Hypothesis

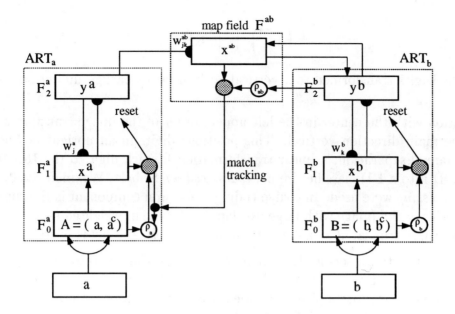

Figure 3: Fuzzy ARTMAP.

testing leads to the selection of a new ART_a category, which focuses attention on a new cluster of $\mathbf{a}^{(p)}$ input features that is better able to predict $\mathbf{b}^{(p)}$. Match tracking allows a single ARTMAP system to learn a different prediction for a rare event than for a cloud of similar frequent events in which it is embedded.

An ARTMAP voting strategy is based on the observation that fast learning typically leads to different adaptive weights and recognition categories for different orderings of a given training set, even when the predictive accuracy of all simulations is similar. The different internal category structures cause the set of test set items where errors occur to vary from one simulation to the next. The voting strategy uses an ARTMAP system that is trained several times on one input set with different orderings. The final prediction for a given test set item is the one made by the largest number of simulations.

Once an ART_a category (J) is chosen whose prediction of the actual ART_b category is correct, match tracking is disengaged, and resonance occurs at ART_a. During resonance, learning occurs at ART_a according to the equation

$$\mathbf{w}_J^{(\text{new})} = \beta(\mathbf{I} \wedge \mathbf{w}_J^{(\text{old})}) + (1 - \beta)\mathbf{w}_J^{(\text{old})}, \tag{1}$$

where fast learning corresponds to setting $\beta = 1$.

The categories created during learning may be represented geometrically as multidimensional "boxes" in the space of input vectors [Carpenter et al., 1992]. The important feature of learning rule (1) is that it allows only increases in the size of these boxes during learning. However, such a rule results in a great dependency on early training vectors in how categories are formed. A modified learning rule introduced here reduces this dependency. In the process of learning, the winning category (J) is now allowed to both expand and shrink:

$$\mathbf{w}_J^{(\text{new})} = (1 - \beta)\mathbf{w}_J^{(\text{old})} + \beta\mathbf{I}, \tag{2}$$

preprocessing	# simulations	avg. # of categories	% correct test set predictions	
			without voting	with voting
directional	5	484	89.7-91.6	92.5 - 93.0
positional	5	509	89.5-90.0	91.9 - 92.2

Table 1: Fuzzy ARTMAP performance with directional and positional preprocessing. The system was trained on 9720 training exemplars and tested on the remaining 2426 exemplars.

where β is relatively small (around 0.2). Simulations have shown that the recognition ability of the network with learning rule (2) is slightly increased at the expense of reduced code compression.

Parameters and results

Preliminary simulations were used to choose parameters for recognition methods. In the KNN algorithm a Euclidean (L_2) metric was used, and the number of neighbors (K) was fixed at 5.

ART dynamics are determined by a choice parameter $\alpha > 0$, a learning rate parameter $\beta \in [0,1]$, and a baseline vigilance parameter $\overline{\rho_a} \in [0,1]$. All simulation used $\overline{\rho_a} = 0$ and choice parameter $\alpha = 1.0$. Fast learning with $\beta = 1$ was used in all simulations with fuzzy ARTMAP as a classifier; for ARTMAP with the learning rule (2), slow learning with $\beta = 0.2$ was employed. All inputs were normalized, as well as complement coding [Carpenter, Grossberg and Rosen, 1991] was used; the number of voters was equal to 7.

The performance was measured on the test set of 2426 exemplars after the system was trained in the off-line regime on 9720 training exemplars presented to the system in the random order. Most fuzzy ARTMAP learning occurs during the first epoch, and the system achieves 100% of correct prediction on the training set in about 20 epochs, while more than 99% is achieved in $10 - 15$ epochs. The results of fuzzy ARTMAP performance on the testing set are shown in Table 1 for both types of preprocessing. The network performed better with the directional preprocessing: recognition and the compression rate are slightly higher. The same relation was obtained while using K Nearest-Neighbor classifier - with the coarse coding preprocessing 93.7% of test exemplars were correctly recognized, compare to 94.7% with the directional preprocessing.

Table 2 shows a comparative performance of kNN classifier, fuzzy ARTMAP, and fuzzy ARTMAP with modified learning rule (2). All the results were obtained with the directional preprocessing by using the same training and testing sets. Trained on 9720 inputs, KNN correctly recognized 94.7% of the test set compare to 92.8% achieved by fuzzy ARTMAP and 93.8% achieved by fuzzy ARTMAP with the modified learning rule. However, fuzzy ARTMAP compressed memory by factor of 20, or by factor of 8 with the modified learning rule, resulting in a comparable speed-up of test set recognition time. This comparison shows a trade-off between the number of nodes in the network and the level of performance on the test set.

	fuzzy ARTMAP	fuzzy ARTMAP + modified learning rule	KNN
average % of correct test set predictions	92.8	93.8	94.7
average number of committed nodes	484	1261	9720
test set classification time (hours)	0.3	0.5	5.1

Table 2: Performance for three classifiers on handwritten letter recognition task. The directional preprocessing was used in all three cases. The training (9720 inputs) set and the test set (2462 inputs) were the same for all networks.

Acknowledgment:

I would like to thank Professor Gail A. Carpenter for valuable help and fruitful discussions. The database was made available by the Office of Advanced Technology, United States Postal Service.

References

[Carpenter, Grossberg and Reynolds, 1991] Carpenter, G.A., Grossberg, S. and Reynolds, J.H. (1991). ARTMAP: Supervised real-time learning and classification of nonstationary data by a self-organizing neural network. *Neural Networks*, **4**, 565-588.

[Carpenter et al., 1992] Carpenter, G.A., Grossberg, S., Markuzon, N., Reynolds, J.H., and Rosen, D.B. (1992). Fuzzy ARTMAP: A neural network architecture for incremental supervised learning of analog multidimensional maps. *IEEE Transactions on Neural Networks*, **3**, 698-713.

[Carpenter, Grossberg and Rosen, 1991] Carpenter, G.A., Grossberg, S., and Rosen, D.B. (1991). Fuzzy ART: Fast stable learning and categorization of analog patterns by an adaptive resonance system. *Neural Networks*, **4**, 759-771.

[Lee, 1991] Lee, Y. (1991) Handwritten Digit Recognition Using K Nearest-Neighbor, Radial-Basis Function, and Backpropagation Neural Networks. *Neural Computation*, **3**, 440-449

[Seibert, Waxman, 1990] Seibert, M., Waxman, A.M. (1990). Learning aspect graph representations of 3D objects in a neural network. *Proceedings of the 1990 International Joint Conference on Neural Networks*. Wash DC. Hillsdale, NJ: Lawrence Erlbaum Associates. **II**, 233-236.

[Zadeh, 1965] Zadeh, L. (1965). Fuzzy sets. *Information Control*, **8**, 338–353.

The Adaptive Feature Extraction Nearest Neighbor Classifier

Waleed Fakhr[*]*, M. Kamel*[**]*, and M.I. Elmasry*[*]
[*]VLSI Research Group, Electrical and Comp. Eng. Dept.
[**]PAMI Research Group, System Design Eng. Dept.
University of Waterloo, Waterloo, Ontario, Canada

ABSTRACT

In this paper an adaptive feature extraction nearest neighbor classifier "AFNN" is proposed. The AFNN consists of a linear adaptive feature extractor "AFE", mapping the original I-dimensional input to a lower L-dimensional feature space which is applied to an adaptive nearest neighbor classifier "ANNC". Both the AFE and ANNC parameters are learned simultaneously by maximizing the mutual information of the overall classifier. A stochastic complexity criterion is developed to estimate the optimal number of features and prototypes required for a certain task. Results of two experiments show the advantages of using the AFNN framework.

1. Introduction

Distance-based classifiers can be very demanding from the computational and storage aspects depending on two factors: the number of prototypes and the input dimensionality. The reduced Parzen classifier [1], the learning vector quantization "LVQ" [2], and the condensed versions of the nearest-neighbor classifier [3], attempt to use a small number of prototypes while retaining the classification optimality. Although these techniques may lead to significant reduction in complexity over traditional methods such as the nearest neighbor classifier "NNC", and the Parzen window classifier [1], greater reduction can still be obtained by reducing the input dimensionality. Not only does the large input dimensionality add complexity, it also deters the performance, especially for small data sets [4]. This drawback may be overcome by extracting a small set of features from the original attributes, without losing the discriminative information in the data. Feature extraction techniques vary according to their main objective, which may be either compression or classification. The Karhunen-Loeve transform "KLT" is optimal in data compression applications such as transform coding, where uncorrelated features result with only few of them containing most of the probability information required to reconstruct the data [1]. The KLT, however, may be far from optimal for classification, since it does not address the issue of discrimination between classes. This fact is demonstrated here, as well as in [1].

In this paper an adaptive feature extraction nearest neighbor classifier "AFNN" is proposed, aiming to overcome the above drawbacks. It is composed of two parts. The first part is an adaptive feature extractor "AFE", with a linear singular transform from the original I dimension to a smaller L dimension. The second part is an adaptive nearest neighbor classifier "ANNC" [5,6], which operates on the L-dimensional space, and has a codebook of K_j prototypes for the j_{th} class. Both the transform weights of the AFE and the prototype parameters of the ANNC are learned together, starting from random values, by maximizing the mutual information of the overall classifier. The MMI learning is used since it directly minimizes an upper bound of the classifier's probability of error [7]. For the AFNN architecture to be defined we have to estimate two unknowns, namely: the optimal number of extracted features, and the optimal number of prototypes. Following the Bayesian model selection framework [8], we derive an expression for the stochastic complexity criterion for classification "SCC" in the AFNN classifier. This allows us to compare different combinations of the number of features and prototypes, and select the best one: with the least SCC. The AFNN is tested with two classification experiments. A 2-dimensional synthetic problem, which demonstrates the drawbacks of the KLT in classification, and a 16-dimension printed letter recognition problem between the letters I and J.

2. Adaptive Feature Extraction Nearest Neighbor Classifier: AFNN

The AFNN is a hybrid architecture which consists of two parts: the adaptive feature extractor "AFE", and the adaptive nearest neighbor classifier "ANNC" as shown in figure(1) for a 2-class case.

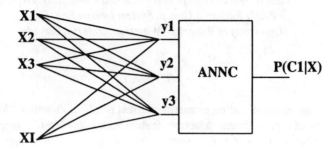

Fig(1): The AFNN

In the AFE, the I-dimensional input vector x is transformed by a linear singular transform to the L-dimensional hidden vector y. This hidden vector is the reduced dimensionality feature vector, which is used as the input pattern to the ANNC. The linear transform w has $(I.L)$ weights, where the weight connecting the x_i input to the y_l hidden node or feature is denoted by w_{li}. When the n_{th} input pattern is applied, the l_{th} feature is given by:

$$y_l(n) = \sum_{i=1}^{I} w_{li} \, x_i(n) \tag{1}$$

The ANNC, as discussed in [5,6], is a nearest neighbor classifier, with a small number of prototypes per class which adapt their locations to maximize the mutual information criterion, for a given set of training data. For a two-class case, let the codebook of the ANNC contains K_1 and K_2 prototypes for class 1 and 2 respectively. Each prototype is an L-dimensional vector with each component denoted by m_{lj}, where j is the class index, and l denotes the l_{th} component in the vector. When an input pattern x is applied, a feature pattern y results, and the nearest prototypes to that pattern (in the Euclidean sense) are m_j where j is 1 and 2 for both classes respectively, which may also called the winner prototypes. A probabilistic approximation of the ANNC presented in [6], assumes that each prototype is the center (mean vector) of a Gaussian window, and that for a given pattern y, each class probability density function "PDF" is approximated by the Gaussian centered at the winner prototype. For simplicity, we assume that all Gaussians are radially symmetric with equal standard deviation σ. In that case, the winner prototype with the least distance to the input pattern, corresponds to the Gaussian with highest value. Following this formulation, the j_{th} class probability density approximation for the feature vector y, is given by:

$$P(y|\theta_j, M_j, C_j) = (2\pi\sigma^2)^{-\frac{L}{2}} \exp - \frac{1}{2\sigma^2} \sum_{l=1}^{L} (y_l - m_{lj})^2 \tag{2}$$

where j is 1 or 2, and m_{lj} is the l_{th} component of the winner prototype in the j_{th} class. Now let us consider how the AFNN can be used to perform optimal classification. The linear transform maps the data of the j_{th} class to K_j clusters in the feature space, where K_j is the number of prototypes in that class codebook. The adaptation of the transform weights, and these cluster centers, is aimed to make the clusters of opposite classes linearly separable, so that the ANNC classifier can form optimal piece-wise-linear decision boundaries. The capability of the AFNN depends on the number of features L, and the number of prototypes per class K_j, where there is always a minimal combination of both which is sufficient for the classifier to be optimal. In order to learn the transform and the prototype locations we maximize the mutual information for the AFNN classifier, employing the probabilistic formulation presented above.

3. MMI Training of the AFNN

For the 2-class case, the large sample approximation of the mutual information for the AFNN is given by:

$$G_{MI} = \frac{1}{N} \left(\sum_{n=1}^{N_1} \log P(C_1|\theta,y_n,M) + \sum_{n=1}^{N_2} \log P(C_2|\theta,y_n,M) \right) \tag{3}$$

where θ is the ANNC parameter vector, and $P(C_j|\theta,y_n)$ is the posterior class probability model for the j_{th} class, given by:

$$P(C_j|\theta,y_n) = \frac{P(y_n|\theta_j,M_j,C_j)}{P(y_n|\theta_1,M_1,C_1) + P(y_n|\theta_2,M_2,C_2)} \tag{4}$$

The MI defined in (3) is an implicit function of the original input x and the transform weights w. Since the feature vector y is their linear combination, (3) becomes:

$$G_{MI} = \left(\sum_{n=1}^{N_1} \log P(C_1|\theta,w,x_n,M) + \sum_{n=1}^{N_2} \log P(C_2|\theta,w,x_n,M) \right) \tag{5}$$

where the posterior class probability is defined in (4), but with y being substituted as a function of x and w, as given in (1). The MI is maximized with respect to the weights and the prototype centers by a gradient-ascent algorithm. For a given pattern x_n from the j_{th} class the MMI weight updating equation is given by:

$$\Delta w_{li} = \mu_w \frac{P_k}{(P_1 + P_2)} \frac{x_{in}}{\sigma^2} (m_{lj} - m_{lk}) \tag{6}$$

where μ_w is the learning gain, P_k is the PDF of the opposite class, m_{lj} and m_{lk} are the l_{th} components of the winner prototype mean vectors for the j_{th} class and the opposite k_{th} class respectively. Now we turn our attention to the learning equations for the mean vectors of the winning prototypes. For an input x_{in} from the j_{th} class, there is one winning mean vector per class, namely m_j and m_k, from the correct and incorrect class codebooks respectively. The MMI updating equations for these mean vector components are given by:

$$\Delta m_{lj} = \mu_m \frac{P_k}{(P_1 + P_2)} \frac{1}{\sigma^2} (y_l - m_{lj}) \,, \quad \Delta m_{lk} = -\mu_m \frac{P_k}{(P_1 + P_2)} \frac{1}{\sigma^2} (y_l - m_{lk}) \tag{7}$$

where μ_m is the learning gain. These learning equations push the mean vector either closer to or farther from the feature vector, for the correct and incorrect class codebooks respectively. It is to be noted that both weights and prototypes updating is done after the whole epoch is presented (batch mode).

It is well known that the more complex the model is, the more flexible it becomes, and hence can form arbitrary decision boundaries. However, there is always a certain model complexity level over which it starts to overfit the given training data, resulting in poor generalization to new data. We propose a stochastic complexity criterion for classification "SCC", which is derived from the Bayesian model selection framework, to find the optimal number of features and prototypes in the AFNN.

4. SCC for the AFNN

The stochastic complexity criterion for classification [6] is given by: $SCC = -\log P(D_c|M)$, where M denotes the model under consideration, D_c denotes the classifier data (i.e., the training data patterns and their class labels), and $P(D_c|M)$ is the evidence for the classification data given the model, which is also the data-model likelihood of the classifier, and is given by:

$$P(D_c|M) = \iint_{\theta w} P(\theta,w|M) \prod_{n=1}^{N} P(C_j|x_n,\theta,w,M) \, d\theta \, dw \tag{8}$$

where j is the class index of the data pattern x_n, and $P(\theta,w|M)$ is the prior probability distribution of the parameters of the model, which are namely, θ of the ANNC part and w of the transform part. The SCC of the AFNN model, which needs to be minimized, is approximated by [6]:

$$SCC = -G_{MI}(\theta_{MI}, w_{MI}) + \frac{1}{2N} \log \det[\, I(w_{MI})\,] - \frac{|W|}{2N}[\log(2\pi) - \log N] + DSCC_{annc} \qquad (9)$$

where $|W|$ is the number of weights, N is the number of training patterns, and: (1) $G_{MI}(\theta_{MI}, w_{MI})$ is the mutual information of the AFNN classifier, at the MMI parameters estimates, (2) $I(w_{MI})$ is the observed Fisher information matrix for the weights, which is a symmetric matrix of dimension $|W|$. If we order the weights of the adaptive transform network in a vector of a dimension $|W|$, then the mi_{th} element of the Fisher matrix, for the AFNN architecture, can be simplified to:

$$f_{mi} = \frac{Q}{N} \sum_{n=1}^{N} \frac{\delta G_{MI}}{\delta w_i} \frac{\delta G_{MI}}{\delta w_m} \qquad (10)$$

where $Q = P_1/P_2$ for class-1 data, and its inverse for class-2 data. From (10), the second derivatives needed for the Fisher matrix can be computed by the gradient information directly, which are already available from the learning equations, hence simplifying the computational complexity of the SCC significantly, and, (3) The $DSCC_{annc}$ is the discrete SCC approximation for the ANNC part of the classifier, which is given in [5,6]. Note that uniform prior probabilities for all the parameters were assumed.

Many combinations of the number of features and prototypes for the AFNN are trained by the MMI, their SCC are computed, and the one with the least SCC is selected as the best candidate among the competing ones.

5. Experimental Results

Two 2-class classification experiments were used to test the AFNN. Here, the results emphasize on the ability of the SCC to find the optimal AFNN model, and on the comparison between these different models.

5.1. Experiment 1

This experiment is designed to demonstrate the inability of the KLT to perform useful dimensionality reduction in the context of classification. Here we have two classes of data, with 100 patterns each, as shown in figure(2).

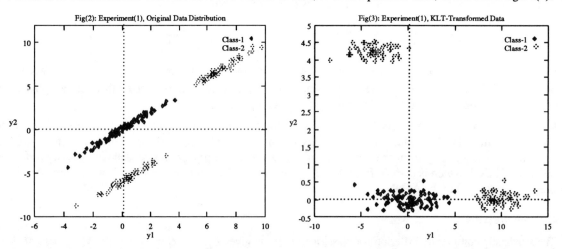

The first class has one cluster, while the second has two clusters, and the two classes are totally separable, however, nonlinearly, and the optimal attainable classification performance is 100%. The KLT is applied to this data, which is a 2 by 2 matrix of entries [0.707, 0.707, 0.707, -0.707], and the resulted transformed data with is shown in figure(3). From this figure we see clearly that if one tries to choose only one KLT-extracted feature, the two classes would be grossly overlapped. More specifically, if the y_1-axis feature is extracted, class-1 data and class-2 upper-cluster data will be projected on the y_1 axis on top of each others, and a very poor classification results. Similarly, if y_2-axis feature is extracted, class-1 data and the right-most cluster of class-2 will be projected on the chosen axis on top of each others, and er poorer classification is obtained.

The AFNN was first applied with two extracted features (similar to the KLT), and two prototypes per class. The resultant transform matrix has entries[1] [0.7788, -0.326, -0.495, 0.197], which are totally different from the KLT weights. The resulted transformed data is shown in figure(4), where AFNN(2.2) means 2 features and 2 prototypes are used. It is clear that class-2 data is transformed to a single cluster, and that the two classes are linearly separable.

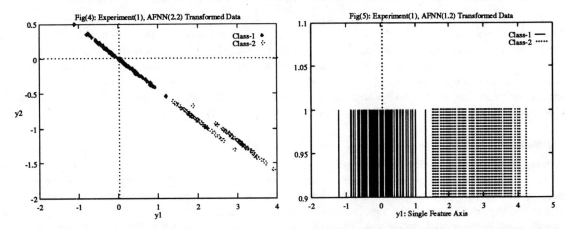

This obviously means that there exists a line which when this transformed data is projected on, they are still separable, i.e., only one extracted feature is sufficient. Now, we apply an AFNN with only one feature and two prototypes per class. Indeed, the AFNN obtained an optimal 100% classification solution, with weights [0.843,-0.533], where the data is projected along a line where they are separable, as shown in figure(5), where each projected data point is represented by an impulse. This experiment shows clearly that the KLT cannot in general be used for classification purposes, since it is not designed to do so. Instead, we should use a classification-oriented feature extraction transform, such as the AFNN.

5.2. Experiment 2: 2-Letter Problem

This experiment is a printed letter recognition task, where 16-dimensional patterns for the letters I and J are used. These 16 dimensions are high-level extracted attributes as discussed in [10], however, as the results show, much less number of adaptively extracted features is sufficient. In this problem, we also used 100 patterns per class for training and 400 per class for testing, and the AFNN is compared to the MLP, the LVQ, the probabilistic neural network "PNN", and the NNC.

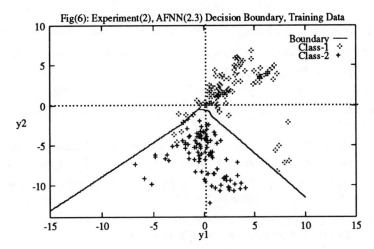

---

[1] Which are the transform weights

Table 1: Experiment 2, Summary of Results

Classifier	AFNN(2,3)	MLP(10)	MLP(20)	MLP(40)	LVQ(3)	NNC	PNN
%Test	93	90.4	90.5	90.6	90.6	92.9	93
#Parameters	46	190	380	760	96	3200	3200

In this experiment, the AFNN(2,3) has the least SCC, thus is chosen here for comparison with other classifiers. The transformed training data with the decision boundary for the AFNN(2,3) is shown in figure(6). This figure shows how the opposite classes data are transformed to piece-wise-linearly separable clusters in the feature space. The conclusions of this experiment are: (1) The AFNN(2,3) has outperformed all other classifiers in both the performance and the reduction of complexity, and, (2) Although the MLP, the NNC, and the PNN have performed well, they are inferior to the AFNN in the performance (MLP), or in complexity (NNC and PNN).

6. Summary and Conclusions

A novel hybrid classifier; the AFNN, is proposed, which is composed of two parts. The first part is a linear transform which extracts a minimum number of features from the input attributes, while the second uses these features in an ANNC-type classifier. An MMI learning algorithm is developed to estimate the weights of the transform and the ANNC prototypes simultaneously. An SCC criterion is also developed to estimate the optimal combination of features and prototypes, based on the MMI trained AFNN. The results show that high-dimensionality problems can be mapped into much smaller dimensionality, which results in very compact ANNC stage, and very compact overall AFNN classifiers. It also shows that, because of the optimal training used, the AFNN performs as well or better than the traditional NNC. The conclusions of this paper are: The KLT should not, in general, be used for supervised classification purposes when dimensionality reduction is sought. It is argued intuitively, and shown experimentally, that the KLT may lead to very poor classification results, for certain problems. The AFNN, on the other hand, is designed to find a set of features, which are optimal from the classification perspective, thus will not suffer from the KLT problems. It was surprising to find that only very few extracted features are sufficient for a classification performance as well as, or better, than a classical classifier such as the NNC. If this trend is valid for many large-dimensionality classification problems, it may prove to be extremely useful in many ways. Firstly, the overall learning time is small. And secondly, the overall size is minimal, since it uses the minimal number of features, and the minimal number of prototypes. Finally, the developed SCC criterion is successful in estimating the best combination of the number of features and prototypes among many trained AFNN architectures.

References

[1] K. Fukunaga; "Introduction to Statistical Pattern Recognition", Second Edition, Academic Press, Inc. 1990.

[2] T. Kohonen; "The Self-Organizing Map", Proc. of the IEEE, Vol.78, No.9, pp.1464-80, Sept. 1990.

[3] Jean Voisin and Pierre A. Devijver; "An Application of the Multiedit-Condensing Technique to the Reference Selection Problem in a Print Recognition System", Pattern Recognition, Vol.20, No.5, pp.465-474, 1987.

[4] Anil K. Jain and R. Dubes; "Feature Definition in Pattern Recognition with Small Sample Size", Pattern Recognition, Vol.10, pp.85-97., 1978.

[5] Waleed Fakhr, M. Kamel and M.I. Elmasry; "Optimal Discriminative Training of Adaptive Nearest Neighbor Classifiers with Minimum Number of Prototypes". Submitted to the Neural Computation Journal, July 1993.

[6] Waleed Fakhr; "Optimal Adaptive Probabilistic Neural Networks for Pattern Classification", Ph.D. Thesis, University of Waterloo, Waterloo, Ont., Canada, Sept. 1993.

[7] Martin E. Hellman and Josef Raviv; "Probability of Error, Equivocation, and the Chernoff Bound", IEEE Trans. on Information Theory, Vol.16, No.4, pp.368-372, July 1970.

[8] J. Rissanen; "Stochastic Complexity in Statistical Inquiry", World Scientific, 1989.

[9] P.W. Frey and D.J. Slate; "Letter Recognition Using Holland Style Adaptive Classifiers", Machine Learning, Vol. 6, pp.161-182, 1991.

PARALLEL CONSENSUAL NEURAL NETWORKS WITH OPTIMALLY WEIGHTED OUTPUT *

J.A. Benediktsson, J.R. Sveinsson
Laboratory for Information Technology and Signal Processing
University of Iceland
Hjardarhagi 2-6, 107 Reykjavik, Iceland.

O.K. Ersoy and P.H. Swain
School of Electrical Engineering
Purdue University
W. Lafayette, IN 47907, U.S.A.

Abstract

A recently proposed neural network architecture, the parallel consensual neural network, is applied in classification of data from multiple data sources. The parallel consensual neural network (PCNN) architecture is based on statistical consensus theory and involves using stage neural networks with either non-linearly transformed input data or different initializations for the stage networks. When non-linear transformations are applied, the input data are transformed several times and the different transformed data are used as if they were independent inputs. The independent inputs are classified using stage neural networks and the outputs from the stage networks are then weighted and combined to make a decision. Optimization methods are proposed to compute the weights for the stage networks. The given experimental results show the superiority of the optimization approach as compared to conjugate-gradient backpropagation in classification of test data.

1 Introduction

The recent resurgence of research in neural networks has resulted in the development of new and improved neural network models. These new models have been trained successfully to classify complex data. In pattern recognition applications, the question of how well neural network models perform as classifiers is very important. In previous papers [1],[2], it has been shown that neural networks compared well to statistical classification methods in classification of multisource remote sensing/geographic data and very-high-dimensional data. The neural network models were superior to the statistical methods in terms of overall classification accuracy of training data. However, statistical methods based on consensus from several data sources outperformed the neural networks in terms of overall classification accuracy of test data. Thus it would be very desirable to combine certain aspects of the statistical consensus theory approaches and the neural network models. However, it is very difficult to implement statistics in neural networks. In [3] parallel consensual neural networks (PCNNs) were proposed and implemented as stage-wise neural network algorithms. The network models in [3] do not use prior statistical information but are somewhat analogous to the statistical consensus theory approaches. In this paper the methods proposed in [3] are extended to include optimal weights for the stage networks. The paper begins with a short overview of consensus theory followed by a discussion of the PCNNs. Finally, experimental results are given.

---

*This research is supported in part by the Icelandic Council of Science, the National Aeronautics and Space Administration Contract No. NAGW-925 and the Research Fund of the University of Iceland

2 Consensus Theory

Consensus theory [4],[5] is a well-established research field involving procedures for combining single probability distributions to summarize estimates from multiple data sources with the assumption that the data sources are Bayesian. In most consensus theoretic methods, the data from each source are at first classified into a number of source-specific data classes [1]. The information from the sources is then aggregated by a global membership function and the data are classified according to the usual maximum selection rule into a number of user-specified information classes. The combination formula obtained in consensus theory is called a consensus rule. Several consensus rules have been proposed. Probably the most commonly used consensus rule is the linear opinion pool which has the following form for the information class if n data sources are used:

$$C_j(Z) = \sum_{i=1}^{n} \alpha_i p(\omega_j | z_i) \tag{1}$$

where $Z = [z_1, \ldots, z_n]$ is a pixel, $p(\omega_j | z_i)$ is a source-specific posterior probability and α_i's $(i = 1, \ldots, n)$ are source-specific weights which control the relative influence of the data sources. The weights are associated with the sources in the global membership function to express quantitatively our confidence in each source [4]. The linear opinion pool is simple but has several shortcomings, e.g., it is not externally Bayesian since it is not derived from class-conditional probabilities using Bayes' rule. Another consensus rule which overcomes the shortcomings associated with the linear opinion pool is the logarithmic opinion pool:

$$L_j(Z) = \prod_{i=1}^{n} (p(\omega_j | z_i))^{\alpha_i}. \tag{2}$$

The logarithmic opinion pool has performed well in classification of data from multiple sources [4].

It is desirable to implement consensus theoretic approaches in neural networks since consensus theory has the goal of combining several opinions and a collection of different neural networks should be more accurate than a single network in classification. It is important to note that neural networks have been shown to approximate class-conditional probabilities, $p(\omega_j | z_i)$, at the output in the mean square sense [6]. Using this property of neural networks it becomes possible to implement consensus theory in the networks.

3 Neural Networks with Parallel Stages

A block diagram of the parallel consensual neural network (PCNN) architecture is shown in Figure 1. Each stage neural network (SNN) has the same number of outputs neurons as the number of information classes and is trained for a fixed number of iterations or until the training procedure converges. When the training of the first stage has finished, the classification error is computed. Then another stage is created. The input data to the second stage are obtained by non-linearly transforming (NLT) the original input vectors. That stage is trained in a fashion similar to the first stage. When the training of the second stage has finished, the consensus for the SNNs is computed. The consensus is obtained by taking class-specific weighted averages of the output responses of the SNNs using source-specific weights [4], similar to the ones in equations (1) and (2). Error detection is then performed and the consensual classification error is computed. In neural networks it is very important to find the "best" representation of input data and the consensual method attempts to average over the results from several input representations or different initializations for the stages. Also, in the consensual neural networks, classification of test data can be done in parallel with all the stages receiving data simultaneously, which makes this method attractive for implementation on parallel machines.

The PCNN is self-organizing in the following sense: If the consensual classification error is lower than the classification error for the first stage, another stage is created and trained in a way similar to the second stage, but with another non-linear transformation of the input data or another initialization of the stage neural network. Stages are added in the consensual neural network as long as the consensual classification error decreases or a tolerance limit is reached. If the consensual classification error is not decreasing or is lower than the tolerance limit, the training is stopped. Using this architecture it can be guaranteed that the PCNNs should do no worse that single stage networks, at least in training. To be able to guarantee such

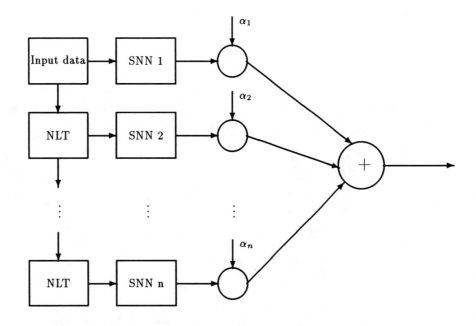

Figure 1: Parallel consensual neural network architecture

performance in classification of test data, cross-validation methods can be used. Also, it has been shown [7] that if all the networks in a collection of neural networks arrive at the correct classification with a certain likelihood $1 - p$ and the networks make independent errors, the chances of seeing exactly k errors among N copies of the network is:

$$\left(\begin{array}{c} n \\ k \end{array} \right) p^k (1-p)^{n-k}$$

which gives the following likelihood of a sum of network outputs being in error:

$$\sum_{k>n/2} \left(\begin{array}{c} n \\ k \end{array} \right) p^k (1-p)^{n-k}$$

which is monotonically decreasing in N if $p < 1/2$. This implies that using a collection of networks reduces the expected classification error if the networks have equal weights and make independent errors. It has also been shown [8] that the standard deviation of the classification of a portfolio of neural networks (such as the PCNN) decreases as the number of stage networks increase.

In [3] two versions of the PCNN were proposed. Both PCNNs combine the information from separate inputs and can be considered neural network implementations of the consensus rules in equations (1) and (2). Here we concentrate on the PCNNS, the consensual neural network version of the linear opinion pool which will be referred to below as the PCNN.

Related neural network architectures to the PCNN have been proposed by Hansen and Salamon [7], Ersoy and Hong [9], Deng and Ersoy [10], Valafar and Ersoy [11], Alpaydin [12], and Nilson [13]. However, the PCNN architecture is different from all of these. It uses non-linear transformation between stages and weights the output from all the SNNs.

4 Optimal Weights

The weight selection schemes in the PCNN should reflect the goodness of the separate input data, i.e., relatively high weights should be given to input data that can be classified with good accuracy. There are at least two possible weight selection schemes. The first one is to select the weights such that they weight

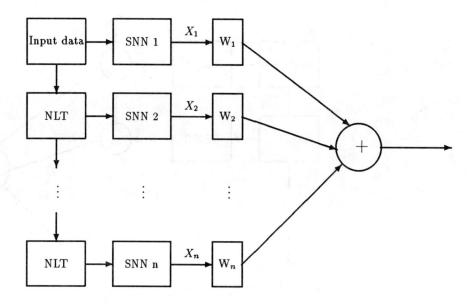

Figure 2: PCNN with weighted individual stages

the individual stages but not the classes within the stages. This scheme is shown in Figure 1. In this case one possibility is to use equal weights for all the outputs of the SNNs and effectively take the average of the outputs from the SNNs. Another possibility is to use reliability measures which rank the SNNs according to their goodness. These reliability measures are, e.g., stage-specific classification accuracy of training data, overall separability and equivocation [1].

The second scheme is to choose the weights such that they not only weight the individual stages but also the classes within the stages. This scheme is depicted in Figure 2. In the case of the PCNN the combined output response Y can be written in a matrix form as

$$Y = XW$$

where X is a matrix containing the output of all the SNNs and W contains all the weights. Assuming that X has full column rank, the above equation can be solved for W using the pseudo-inverse of X or a simple delta rule.

Let's now look at the problem of choosing the weights such that they not only weight the individual stages but also the classes within the stages. In order to find the optimal weights in Figure 2 we define

$$X = [X_1 \ X_2 \ \dots \ X_n],$$

$$W = \begin{bmatrix} W_1 \\ W_2 \\ \vdots \\ W_n \end{bmatrix}$$

where X_i $i = 1, \dots, n$ are $m \times p$ matrices. Each row of X_i represents an output vector of each stage network SNN i. W_i $i = 1, \dots, n$ are $p \times p$ matrices representing the weight of each stage network SNN i. If $Y = D$ is the desired output of the whole network we have

$$XW = D.$$

W is an unknown matrix, and its least square estimate W_{opt} is sought to minimize the square error

$$\|XW - D\|^2.$$

This is a well known problem from linear regression, signal processing and adaptive filters. The formula for W_{opt} uses the pseudo-inverse of W, i.e.,

$$W_{opt} = (X^T X)^{-1} X^T D$$

where X^T is the transpose of X, and $(X^T X)^{-1} X^T$ is the pseudo-inverse of X if $X^T X$ is non-singular. In the case that X is not of full column rank this solution becomes ill-conditioned. In that case one can use dummy augmentation to make W a full column rank matrix in a higher dimensional space and then solve the problem. There are at least two other suboptimal methods for solving the optimization problem above. The rest of this section will be denoted to these methods.

The first method is to use sequential formulas to compute the optimal W. Let the ith row vector of the matrix X be x_i^T and the ith row of the matrix D be d_i^T, then W can be calculated iteratively using the sequential formula

$$
\begin{aligned}
W_{i+1} &= W_i + P_{i+1} x_{i+1} \left(d_{i+1}^T - x_{i+1}^T \right) \\
P_{i+1} &= P_i - \frac{P_i x_{i+1} x_{i+1}^T P_i}{1 + x_{i+1}^T P_i x_{i+1}} \qquad i = 0, 1, \ldots, m
\end{aligned}
$$

where W_m is the least square estimate of W_{opt}. The initial conditions to the sequential formula are $W_0 = 0$ and $P_0 = \beta I$, where β is a positive large number.

The second method solving the least square error problem is to choose unitary W which minimizes $\|D - XW\|$. We compute

$$\|D - XW\|^2 = \|D\|^2 - 2 <D, XW> + \|X\|^2$$

where $<D, XW> = \text{tr}(DW^T X^T)$ and tr returns the trace of of its argument matrices. If

$$X^T D = V \Sigma U^T$$

is a singular value decomposition (SVD) of $X^T D$ then

$$
\begin{aligned}
\text{tr}(DW^T X^T) &= \text{tr}(X^T D W^T) \\
&= \text{tr}(V \Sigma U^T W^T) \\
&= \text{tr}(\Sigma U^T W^T V) \\
&= \sum_{i=1}^{p} \sigma_i(X^T D) t_{ii}
\end{aligned}
$$

where $T = [t_{ij}] = U^T W^T V$ is a unitary matrix. This sum is maximized when all $t_{ii} = 1$, that is when $W_{opt} = V U^T$.

5 EXPERIMENTAL RESULTS

The PCNNs were used to classify a data set consisting of the following 4 data sources:

1. Landsat MSS data (4 data channels)

2. Elevation data (in 10 m contour intervals, 1 data channel)

3. Slope data (0-90 degrees in 1 degree increments, 1 data channel).

4. Aspect data (1-180 degrees in 1 degree increments, 1 data channel)

Each channel comprised an image of 135 rows and 131 columns, all channels were co-registered. The area used for classification is a mountainous area in Colorado. It has 10 ground-cover classes which are listed in Table 1. One class is water; the others are forest types. It is very difficult to distinguish between the forest types using the Landsat MSS data alone since the forest classes show very similar spectral response [1]. Reference data were compiled for the area by comparing a cartographic map to a color composite of

Table 1: Training and Test Samples for Information Classes in the Experiments on the Colorado Data Set

Class #	Information Class	Training Size	Test Size
1	Water	301	302
2	Colorado Blue Spruce	56	56
3	Mountane/Subalpine Meadow	43	44
4	Aspen	70	70
5	Ponderosa Pine 1	157	157
6	Ponderosa Pine/Douglas Fir	122	122
7	Engelmann Spruce	147	147
8	Douglas Fir/White Fir	38	38
9	Douglas Fir/Ponderosa Pine/Aspen	25	25
10	Douglas Fir/White Fir/Aspen	49	50
Total		1008	1011

the Landsat data and also to a line printer output of each Landsat channel. By this method 2019 reference points (11.4% of the area) were selected comprising two or more homogeneous fields in the imagery for each class. It has been shown [2],[3] that neural networks are sensitive to having representative training samples. In order to see how well the PCNNs compared to a backpropagation neural network with a representative training sample, the training samples were selected uniformly spaced apart in the experiments. Around 50% of the samples were used for training and the rest to test the neural networks (see Table 1). Two versions of the PCNN were applied in classification of the Colordado data, i.e., PCNN with equal weights and optimized weights. (The optimal approach reported here was the inverse method but the suboptimal methods gave similar results.) The PCNN algorithms were implemented using one-layer conjugate-gradient delta rule neural networks (CGLC) [2],[14] as its SNNs. The conjugate-gradient versions of the feedforward neural networks are computationally more efficient than conventional gradient descent neural networks. The original input data were Gray-coded but that representation has previously given the best results for this particular data set [2]. Using the Gray-code and 8 bits for each input stage expanded the dimensionality of input data to 56 dimensions. Therefore, each SNN had 57 inputs (one extra input for the bias), and 10 outputs. In these experiments the Gray-code of the Gray-code was the non-linear transformation selected. This is the same non-linear transformation used in [3]. Each SNN was trained for 200 iterations. In order to get comparison to the results of the PCNN, the single-stage conjugate-gradient backpropagation (CGBP) algorithm with two layers [14] was trained on the same data with a variable number of hidden neurons. The CGBP neural networks had 57 inputs, 8, 16, 24 and 32 hidden neurons and 10 output neurons. Eleven experiments were run for the PCNN with different numbers of stages. The highest number of SNNs used in each PCNN was fifteen. All the neural networks used the sigmoid activation function. The experiments were run on a SUN SPARCstation 10/41.

The average results of the experiments with the PCNN are shown in Figure 3 for the two weight selection schemes and the standard deviation of the training accuracy for the PCNNs is shown in Figure 4. The results with the CGBP (for different number of hidden neurons) are shown in Figure 5 as a function of the number of training iterations. From these figures it is clear that the PCNN methods outperformed the single stage CGBP in terms of classification accuracy of test data. Also, the difference between the equal weight selection and the optimal weighting method became very clear in the experiments. The optimal approach clearly outperformed the equal weighting approach in terms of training accuracy. In fact, for training data, the optimal weighting approach did show monotonically increasing overall accuracy as a function of the number of stages. This result was expected since the weights in the PCNN were optimized based on the training data. On the other hand, the PCNN methods showed very similar test accuracies after 15 stages. On the average, the optimal approach achieved 80.77% overall accuracy for test data as compared to 80.74% for the equal weighting approach. In comparison, the CGBP method achieved the maximum accuracy of 77% for test data. It is also important to note that the test results with both PCNNs are better than the best statistical result achieved in [4].

As Figure 4 displays, the standard deviation of the classification went down as a function of the number of stages used. Overall, the PCNN results in these experiments were very satisfying.

6 CONCLUSIONS

In this paper optimized weights were computed for the stage networks in the PCNN architecture. The results obtained showed the PCNN architecture to be a desirable alternative to conjugate-gradient backpropagation for multisource classification when representative training data are available. The results for the PCNN outperformed all other methods (applied now and previously on the data set used) in terms of classification accuracy of test data. The results using the optimized weights were very promising and it is important to note that the new optimized weighting approach can also be used for the networks proposed in [11] and [12]. Although binary input data were used in the experiments, the PCNN with optimized weights works both for analog and binary input data.

At this point, the PCNNs require to be tested extensively. Different non-linear transformations and the various weight-selection schemes proposed here need to be explored more thoroughly. Also, different types of PCNN architectures are being investigated. These architectures include PCNNs with different non-linear transforms for each stage and different number of iterations for the stages. The most important remaining problem in the research concerning the PCNN architecture is the selection of the non-linear transformations. In this paper we did not concentrate on that problem but used somewhat an ad hoc method, i.e. the Gray-code of the Gray-code. Using an optimal non-linear transformation could be critical to the performance of the PCNN.

ACKNOWLEDGEMENT

The Colorado data set was originally acquired, preprocessed and loaned to us by Dr. Roger Hoffer of Colorado State University. Access to the data set is gratefully acknowledged.

References

[1] J.A. Benediktsson, P.H. Swain and O.K. Ersoy, "Neural Network Approaches Versus Statistical Methods in Classification of Multisource Remote Sensing Data," *IEEE Transactions on Geoscience and Remote Sensing*, vol. GE-28, no. 4, pp. 540-552, July 1990.

[2] J.A. Benediktsson, P.H. Swain and O.K. Ersoy, "Conjugate-Gradient Neural Networks in Classification of Multisource and Very- High Dimensional Remote Sensing Data," *International Journal of Remote Sensing*, vol. 14, no. 15, pp. 2883-2903, October 1993.

[3] J.A. Benediktsson, J.R. Sveinsson, O.K. Ersoy and P.H. Swain, " Parallel Consensual Neural Networks", *Proceedings of the 1993 IEEE International Conference on Neural Networks*, vol. 1, pp. 27-32, San Francisco, 1993.

[4] J.A. Benediktsson and Philip H. Swain, "Consensus Theoretic Classification Methods," *IEEE Transactions on Systems Man and Cybernetics*, vol. 22, no. 4, pp. 688-704, July/August 1992.

[5] C. Genest and J.V. Zidek, "Combining Probability Distributions: A Critique and Annotated Bibliography," *Statistical Science*, vol. 1. no. 1, pp. 114-118, 1986.

[6] D. W. Ruck, S.K. Rogers, M. Kabrisky, M.E. Oxley, and B.W. Suter, "The Multilayer Perceptron as an Approximation to a Bayes Optimal Discrimination Function," *IEEE Transactions on Neural Networks*, vol. 1, no. 4, pp. 296-298, 1990.

[7] L.K. Hansen and P. Salamon, "Neural Network Ensembles," *IEEE Transactions on Pattern Analysis and Machine Intelligence*, vol. 12, no. 10, pp. 993-1001, 1990.

[8] G. Mani, "Lowering Variance of Decisions by Using Artificial Neural Network Portfolios," *Neural Computation*, vol. 3, pp. 484-486, 1991.

[9] O.K. Ersoy and D. Hong, "Parallel, Self-Organizing, Hierarchical Neural Networks," *IEEE Transactions on Neural Networks*, vol. 1, no. 2, pp. 167-178, 1990.

[10] S-W. Deng and O.K. Ersoy, "Parallel, Self-Organizing, Hierarchical Neural Networks with Forward-Backward Training," *Circuits, Systems and Signal Processing*, vol. 12, no. 2, 1993.

[11] H. Valafar and O.K. Ersoy, Parallel, Self-Organizing, Consensual Neural Network, Report No. TR-EE 90-56, School of Electrical Engineering, Purdue University, 1990.

[12] E. Alpaydin, "Multiple Networks for Function Learning", *Proceedings of the 1993 IEEE International Conference on Neural Networks*, vol. 1, pp. 9-14, San Francisco, 1993.

[13] N. Nilsson, Linear Machines, McGraw-Hill, New York, 1965.

[14] E. Barnard, "Optimization for Training Neural Nets,"*IEEE Transactions on Neural Networks*, vol. 3, no. 2, pp. 232-240, March 1992.

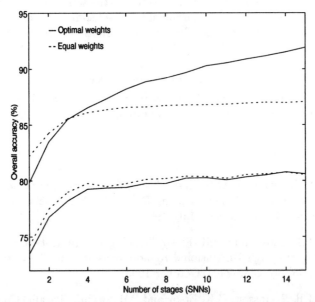

Figure 3: Average results for the PCNN with equal and optimal weights as a function of the number of SNNs. The upper curves represent training results and the lower curves test results.

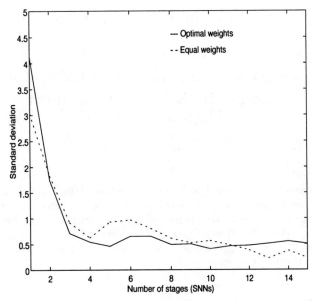

Figure 4: Standard deviation for the training results of the PCNN methods.

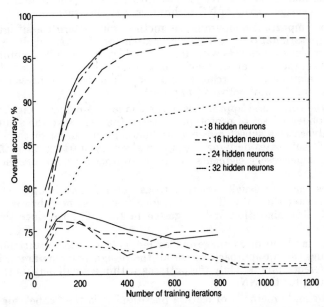

Figure 5: Experimental results for the CGBP with a variable number of hidden neurons. The upper curves represent training results and the lower curves test results.

Efficient Nearest Neighbor Classification

Nagarajan Ramesh and Ishwar K. Sethi
Vision & Neural Networks Laboratory
Computer Science Department
Detroit, MI 48202

Abstract

In this paper we propose an efficient and flexible method of finding the nearest neighbor using a CMAC. A subset of design patterns are selected as probable candidates amongst which the nearest neighbor is searched for. This reduces the number of distance computations compared to the traditional approach. Unlike many other efficient techniques, this system can be trained on additional design patterns at a later time without affecting the previous learning. Experimental results are presented to demonstrate the efficiency of the proposed approach.

1   Introduction

Since its formal introduction as a classification tool by Cover and Hart in 1967 [1], the Nearest Neighbor (NN) rule is being applied in a large number of areas and is still an interesting topic of research [2]. In its simple form, it deals with the problem of associating a new pattern with the label of any one of the other design patterns already known. As the name implies, the label of the pattern of the nearest neighbor, measured using a suitable distance metric, is the one chosen to be associated with the new pattern. An extension of this rule is the k-NN rule which considers the classes of k nearest neighbors before such an association is made. The NN rule is not only intuitive, but is also bounded at the upper limit by at most twice the Bayesian error [1] which makes is attractive for use with patterns whose distributions are not known. For an excellent and comprehensive survey of NN techniques, see Dasarathy [3].

In spite of serving as an important nonparametric method for pattern classification, the NN approach has a major problem: computational complexity. The search for the NN involve a large number of distance computations whose complexity increases with dimensionality. As a result, a number of techniques have been proposed to reduce this computational complexity, most of which can be classified under one of the following categories: "condensed" approach, "hierarchical" approach, "pattern preprocessing" approach, "feature space partitioning" approach, and "neural network" approach.

Among the earliest of the condensed approaches is the condensed nearest neighbor (CNN) rule [4], which is a method to derive a condensed set of prototype patterns that will give the same result at the original set. While this approach advocates a subset growing methodology, a similar method called the reduced nearest neighbor (RNN) rule [5] advocates deriving the minimal set by starting off with the complete original set and iteratively deleting unnecessary elements. In both approaches however, the goal of minimal subset is not guaranteed.

Hierarchical approaches that are usually referred to as "branch and bound" techniques, have to do with constructing a tree to cluster the data. The search for the nearest neighbor is reduced because only a few branches are examined. The algorithm first suggested in 1975 [6] have since then undergone a number of improvements [2].

Preprocessing the data has been often suggested as reducing the computational complexity of the actual NN search. Sethi [7] suggests an approach where all the design patterns are ordered with respect to their distances from three reference points. Only the patterns within a small neighborhood of the new pattern are considered while searching for the NN.

Among the earlier and simple methods of feature partitioning is the "cube" algorithm of Yunck [8]. Here the nearest neighbor of a new pattern is searched for within a hypercube that surrounds the pattern. Use of a k–d tree [9] is a more recent method used to reduce the search complexity. Partitioning the feature space perpendicular to each axis in such a manner as to maintain an equal (or near equal) number of patterns on each side of the partition is the central idea to this scheme. The partition is done recursively until a small number of samples remain within each partition. An incremental search starting from the root node is then used for search for an arbitrary set of m nearest neighbors.

Recently, the k-NN rule has been implemented using artificial neural networks (ANN) [10] built on four blocks; matching network, k-maximum network, counting network and 1–maximum network. In the matching network the training patterns are stored in the interconnections. The matching scores between a new

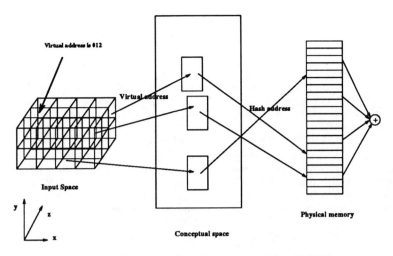

Figure 1: Conceptual architecture of the CMAC

pattern and the stored patterns are computed by this block are fed into the subsequent layers to compute the k–nearest neighbors. When the number of training patterns and the value of k is known apriori, the parallelism offered by the network can be exploited by hardware. However if these parameters are not known, the network has to be redesigned each time, and simulating it in software offers no advantage over the traditional k–NN classifier,

In this paper, we present a method to reduce the complexity of search for the nearest neighbors by associating with a new pattern, only a small set of design patterns amongst which to look for the nearest neighbor. The selection of this small set is facilitated by a model called the CMAC (Cerebellar Model Articulation Controller/ Cerebellar Model Arithmetic Computer) which was introduced as a controller for a robotic manipulator [11]. Later the CMAC found applications in shape recognition [12], and neural network domains [13]. We adapt the model for the nearest neighbor determination. The use of CMAC in computing the nearest neighbor offers two major advantages – efficiency and flexibility. Efficiency is offered in terms of the CMAC providing a small subset of patterns for distance computations, while flexibility is offered in terms of the CMAC's ability to update its database of design patterns without having to go through the "learning" process again. While a number of methods described in the literature to compute the nearest neighbor are efficient, few offer the flexibility of not having to retrain the system when new design patterns have to be added.

2 The CMAC

2.1 Architecture

The CMAC (Cerebellar Model Articulation Controller/ Cerebellar Model Arithmetic Computer) was first introduced in 1972 by James Albus. See [14] for a good introduction to the model. It is a serious attempt to model the functionality of the human brain while maintaining a simplified but close structural relationship to it.

The CMAC is a system that can be trained to learn even nonlinear transformations. As most neural network models [15], it operates in two phases; a training phase during when a set of patterns are presented to the system, and a testing phase when it responds to the inputs presented. Again, as in a neural network, the input to output transformation is learnt by the system and need not be known apriori. The effectiveness of the system is gauged by its ability to provide correct or near correct responses to slightly corrupted inputs.

In applications that use the CMAC, three basic properties are exploited. First, when provided with an input pattern similar to an exemplar pattern that was learnt in the training phase, it produces an output that is similar to the response that should have been produced by the exemplar pattern. Second, to produce such an output, it sums up the contents of distributed memory locations. This distribution of information enhances the robustness of the system. Third, the CMAC uses overlapping low resolution blocks in the input space to aid in its input/output mapping.

These concepts are illustrated in Figure 1. The input space is divided into a number of "blocks". In the case of the three dimensional input space shown in the figure, each of the axis is divided at regular intervals, with each interval labelled with a unique address. Therefore, each block is uniquely addressable. For example, if along each axis the numbering begins from 0, the address of the block indicated by the thick arrow is 012. A set of non-overlapping blocks that partition the input space is called a *level*. Another set of non–overlapping blocks with a small offset along each axis, can be generated to encompass the same input space. That would constitute another *level*.

If the address of a block is determined by the limits within which it falls along each feature axis, the range of block addresses can be enormous. This address range that is often termed *conceptual memory*, can grow even bigger with increasing dimensions and increasing resolutions of the blocks. In reality, an address in the conceptual memory, called *virtual address* is mapped to physical address in physical memory by hashing. The address of the block into which a pattern falls, is the virtual address of the pattern. Each level is assigned it own memory partition and generates a virtual address for the pattern encountered. The output corresponding to the pattern is distributed over hashed physical addresses over all the memory partitions.

A CMAC works as follows. When a training pattern is presented to the system, a virtual address for the pattern is determined for each level. This is merely the address of the block into which the pattern falls. A hash algorithm would then give a physical address corresponding to each level. The current contents of the physical addresses are summed to give an output. The difference between the actual and current outputs is then used as a correction term, a proportion of which (depending upon the learning rate) is added or subtracted equally amongst the physical addresses. Thus if a training pattern is presented to the system repeatedly, its output gets closer and closer to the actual output, until training is stopped or no change in memory content take place. Recent studies have proved the convergence of the algorithm [16].

In the testing phase, if a new pattern is slightly shifted with respect to one of the training patterns the output error will be determined by the contents of the virtual addresses that are not common between the new pattern and the previously trained pattern. A consequence of this scheme is that slightly corrupted inputs will give slightly corrupted outputs.

2.2 Modifications to the CMAC

We modified the CMAC to be used as a NN classifier. Briefly, the design patterns to be learnt by the CMAC are identified by their an index and stored. When a new pattern is presented, a subset of the learned design patterns is retrieved, amongst which the nearest neighbor is computed. The number of patterns retrieved is a function of four parameters of the CMAC; the memory partition size, the block size, the number of levels, and the offset of the levels with respect to each other.

The CMAC as a NN classifier operates in two phases; a learning phase and a classification phase. In the learning phase, the the design patterns indexed by their sequence number are input to the system. The sequence numbers used are just to identify the design patterns and their ordering has no effect on the performance of the system. For each design pattern, the system computes a virtual address, which is mapped to a physical address. The physical addresses are organized as a sequence of bits. A "1" in the ith bit indicates that the ith design pattern has been hashed into this physical address, while a "0" indicates an absence of such a hash. At the hashed physical address, the bit that corresponds to the index of the design pattern, is set. The virtual to physical address hashing and bit setting is done for each level of the CMAC. In addition, the design patterns are stored in an array in the sequence they are encountered.

In the classification phase the virtual address of the new pattern is first computed for each level which is then mapped to a physical address. The indices of all the bits that are set to "1" at that physical address are retrieved since they correspond to patterns that are in the neighborhood (defined by the block size) of the current pattern. This retrieval is done for each level and a count of the number of retrievals for each index is kept. The indices selected the most number of times are probable candidates for the nearest neighbor. If more than one maximum exists, all of the maximums are selected and the distance between the new pattern and each of the retrieved patterns is computed. The smallest amongst these distances is the nearest neighbor. Note that it is not necessary for the system to retrieve the same number of samples for each new pattern.

A number of properties of the CMAC, make it attractive for use as a NN classifier. The training is "one shot" and and does not involve any intense computation. The ordering of the design samples is not important and they can be input to the system even incrementally without affecting the previously learnt patterns. The retrieval of a subset of design patterns reduce the number of distance computations making the CMAC an efficient NN classifier. The size of the retrieved subset of patterns can be controlled by the user to a limited extent by specifying the various CMAC parameters.

3 Experimental Details

The CMAC NN classifier was implemented on a Sparc station 2 running the 4.3BSD UNIX operating system using C language. The system performance was graded on two measures - *efficiency* and *recognition rate* which are described in the next section. Three data sets were used in the experiments, the details of which are described in section 3.2. In Section 3.4 we report the effects of some CMAC parameters on the performance.

3.1 Performance measures

As indicated in the earlier sections, the CMAC is an efficient NN classifier. It is therefore natural to choose to measure the computational gain obtained on the data. The measure chosen should be data independent as much as possible. The *efficiency*, η, is defined for this purpose as, $\eta = 1 - \frac{N_c}{N_n}$ where N_c is the number of distance computations using CMAC, and N_n is the number of distance computations using traditional NN classifier. Though data dependent, we also report the *recognition rate*, γ, which is defined as $\gamma = \frac{N_q}{N_t}$ where N_q is the number of correct nearest neighbors determined and N_t is the total number of test patterns.

3.2 Data

The "vowel" data set, used for speech recognition, has often been used as a benchmark ANN systems to compare the performance of different networks. The data which was collected by Deterding [17] consists of 11 steady state vowels uttered by 15 speakers, 8 males and 7 females, with each speaker repeating a vowel 6 times. Of the 90 sets, the first 48 sets were used for training and the other 42 sets were used for testing. In effect, there are 528 training samples and 462 testing samples. The actual data is a 10–dimensional vector whose components are based on the log area ratios. The published literature [18] indicates that classification based on this data has been difficult and the "best" classification rate obtained so far is 56% using the NN approach.

The second set of data called the "sonar" data was first used by Gorman et. al [19]. The data was obtained from sonar returns bouncing off two types of materials; metal cylinder and roughly cylindrical rock, at various angles and under various conditions. Each pattern is a 60 dimensional vector whose components are in the range [0,1]. Each component represents the integrated energy over a particular frequency band. There are 104 training patterns and 104 testing patterns.

The third set, called the "fingerprint" data, consists of 2000 training patterns and 2000 test patterns each belonging to one of 5 classes. Each pattern has 112 components. The data was obtained from images of fingerprint impressions following feature extraction. Direction vectors served as features. The initial correlated 1680 dimensional vector was reduced to 112 by performing the Karhunen–Loeve transform.

3.3 Classification on large data set

Though a recognition rate of 100% can be obtained by adjusting the parameters of the CMAC, we also want to achieve computational gains. Therefore, subjecting the three sets of data to the CMAC NN classifier, we tabulate what we consider our best results.

Data set	Efficiency, η	recognition rate, γ	1–NN recognition rate
fingerprint data	0.99	74.95	82.85
sonar data	0.98	67.30	91.34
vowel data	0.91	50.21	56.27

With all the data sets, the CMAC NN classifier is able to perform at over 90% efficiency with slight degradation in recognition rate. Even though the recognition rate of the sonar data using the traditional NN classifier seems much higher, that same rate can be obtained at the cost of some efficiency. As indicated above, these values do not reflect the best recognition rates but rather the compromise between efficiency and recognition rates.

3.4 Effect of number of levels and block size

Figure 2 is a plot of the average number of retrievals versus the number of levels while Figure 3 is the plot of recognition rate versus the number of levels in the CMAC. These plots are for the "vowel" data. As the number of levels increase, there is a drastic reduction in the number of samples retrieved initially, after which it becomes more or less uniform. Also, depending upon the pattern distribution, in general, the smaller the initial set retrieved, the less the probability of finding the nearest neighbor in the retrieved set. This causes the reduction in recognition rate with increased number of levels as seen in Figure 3. The isolated peaks in the figure, we believe are caused by the distribution of data, and the main point to note here is the general decrease in performance.

Figures 4 and 5 indicate the plot of the average number of retrievals and recognition rate with increase in block size. The block size is indicated as a percentage of the maximum range of the input vector component. As the block size increases, more and more patterns tend to be retrieved as one would expect and therefore the average number of initial retrievals increase, and recognition rate increases. Again, peaks in the performance curve are caused by the distribution of the design patterns.

While it is possible to obtain a good recognition rate by increasing the number of retrievals, for applications where the exact nearest neighbor is not so crucial, a reasonably good performance can be achieved by retrieving only a small set of design patterns. Thus one can establish a tradeoff between accuracy and computational complexity.

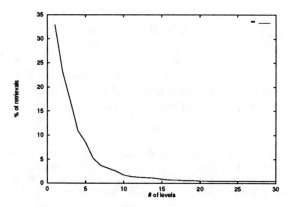

Figure 2: Average number of retrievals as a function of number of levels

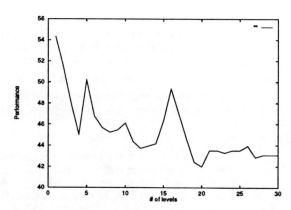

Figure 3: Recognition rate as a function of number of levels

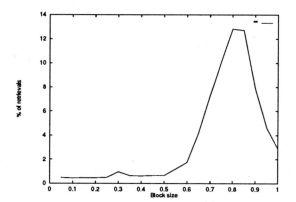

Figure 4: Average number of retrievals as a function of block size

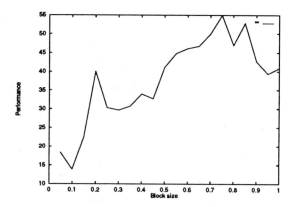

Figure 5: Recognition rate as a function of block size

3.5 Computational savings

The fingerprint data serves to illustrate the performance of the CMAC NN classifier on a data set that is large and has a high dimensionality. The table below compares the performances of the CMAC NN classifier with the traditional NN classifier. With little degradation, the the average number of retrievals for distance computation is reduced drastically. As indicated earlier, in applications where computational speed is more important than a slight loss in accuracy, the CMAC NN classifier is best suited.

	Performance	Avg # of distance computations	time (in seconds)
Brute force NN	82.85%	2000	1639
CMAC NN	74.95%	6.686	423

3.6 Interpretation of results

The results of our experiments with real–world data point to a number of useful features. Learning is a one shot process that requires no preprocessing, or ordering of the data, which eliminates the computation for "preparing" the data that is usually associated with fast retrieval methods. This method can work with a limited memory, the only effect of using limited memory would be that the retrieved sample set increases. The number of initial index retrievals can be controlled to a certain extent by specifying the parameters of the CMAC. For example, if a large set is needed, the block size can be increased.

There is a compromise between the initial number of indices of patterns retrieved and the computational complexity. For example if more number of indices are retrieved, a larger search for the nearest neighbor is required amongst the retrieved pattern, while if a small set is retrieved, there is a chance that the actual nearest neighbor is not in that small set. In applications where the exact nearest neighbor is not crucial, this method can help reduce the computation by a large factor.

4   Conclusions and future research

We have presented a new method for finding the nearest neighbor of a pattern, using the CMAC model. The nearest neighbor is searched for, amongst a small set of retrieved indices of initially stored patterns. By controlling the parameters of the CMAC, we can control the size of this set. While a large retrieved set will required a lot of computations to search for the nearest neighbor, a small set will tend not to have the actual nearest neighbor present. Depending upon the application, a suitable compromise can be reached.

At present, we are looking into two possible extensions of this approach. One is to be able to specify hyper–spherical shaped blocks, so that, while using the Euclidean distance metric, unnecessary sample patterns are not retrieved. The second extension is to order the retrieved small set to obtain the k–NN's of the new pattern. This is a rather simple extension, though at the moment we have not implemented it.

Acknowledgments: We acknowledge the use of the NIST database for the "fingerprint" data, and the University of California, Irvine's repository of machine learning databases for the "sonar" and "vowel" data.

References

[1] T. M. Cover and P. E. Hart, "Nearest neighbor pattern classification," *IEEE Trans. Information Theory*, vol. 13, Jan 1967.

[2] Q. Jiang and W. Zhang, "An improved method for finding nearest neighbors," *Pattern Recognition*, vol. 14, pp. 531–536, July 1993.

[3] B. Dasarathy, ed., *Nearest Neighbor(NN) norms: NN pattern classication techniques*. IEEE Computer Society Press, 1991.

[4] P. E. Hart, "Condensed nearest neighbor rule," *IEEE Trans. Information Theory*, vol. 14, pp. 515–516, 1968.

[5] G. W. Gates, "The reduced nearest neighbor rule," *IEEE Trans. Information Theory*, vol. 18, pp. 431–433, May 1972.

[6] K. Fukunaga and P. M. Narendra, "A branch and bound algorithm for computing k-nearest neighbors," *IEEE Trans. on Computer*, vol. 24, pp. 750–753, 1975.

[7] I. K. Sethi, "A fast algorithm for recognizing nearest neighbors," *IEEE Trans. Systems, Man, and Cybernetics*, vol. 11, pp. 245–248, Mar 1981.

[8] T. P. Yunck, "A technique to identify nearest neighbors," *IEEE Trans. Systems, Man, and Cybernetics*, vol. 6, Oct 1976.

[9] A. J. Broder, "Strategies for efficient incremental nearest neighbor search," *Pattern Recognition*, vol. 23, no. 1/2, pp. 171–178, 1990.

[10] A. K. Jain and J. Mao, "A k-nearest neighbor artificial neural network classifier," in *Proc. IJCNN, vol-2*, (Seattle), pp. 515–520, July 1991.

[11] J. S. Albus, "A new approach to manipulator control:the cerebellar model articulation controller (CMAC)," *J. Dynamic Systems, Measurements and Control*, pp. 220–227, Sept. 1975.

[12] F. H. Glanz and W. T. Miller, "Shape recognition using a CMAC based learning system," in *Proc. SPIE Intelligent Robot and Computer Vision:Sixth in a Series*, pp. 294–298, SPIE, 1987.

[13] W. T. Miller, F. H. Glanz, and L. G. Kraft, "CMAC: An associative neural network alternative to backpropagation," *Proc. IEEE*, vol. 78, pp. 1561–1567, Oct 1990.

[14] J. Albus, *Brain, Behavior and Robotics*. BYTE Books, 1981.

[15] J. McClelland and D. Rumelhart, *Parallel Distributed Processing — Explorations in the Microstructure of Cognition*, vol. 1. Cambridge, MA: MIT Press, 1986.

[16] C. Lin and C. Chiang, ch. Theoretical foundation for CMAC technique, pp. 11–19. Proc. ANNIE'93, St.Louis, Missouri: ASME Press, Nov14-17 1993.

[17] D. H. Deterding, *Speaker normalisation for automatic speech recognition*. PhD thesis, University of Cambridge, 1989.

[18] A. J. Robinson, *Dynamic error propagation networks*. PhD thesis, University of Cambridge, 1989.

[19] R. P. Gorman and T. J. Sejnowski, "Analysis of hidden units in a layered network trained to classify sonar targets," *Neural Networks*, vol. 1, pp. 75–89, 1988.

Reduction of Input Nodes for Shift Invariant Second Order Neural Networks using Principal Component Analysis(PCA)

Bong-Kyu Lee , Dong-Kyu Kim,Yoo-Kun Cho
Dept. of Computer Engineering
Seoul National University,Shinlim-Dong,Gwanak-Ku
Seoul 151-742,KOREA
e-mail : bklee@dosa1.snu.ac.kr

Heong-Ho Lee
Dept.of Electrical Engineering
Chung Nam University,Daejeon,Korea

Hee-Yeung Hwang
Dept of Electrical Engineering
Hoseo University,Chunan,Korea

Abstract

When two dimensional images are used as input to a neural network, the noise from the input device and small deformations in the end parts that occur in the processes of separating each pattern and size normalization lead to images shifted from the original learned image being input to the neural network which is a maijor cause of misrecognition. In existing multi-layer perceptrons using standard EBP, it is difficult to solve shift invariant problems because pattern pixel values are presented directly to the neural network input nodes. Second order neural network inputs consist of geometrically related nonlinear combinations of two pixels, and can be used for shift invariant pattern recognition. But the number of Second order neural network input nodes increases in proportion to N^2, where N is the dimension of the input patterns, even if we only consider shift invariance. Such large number of input nodes lead to slower learning and recognition.

In this paper, we propose a method for reducing the number of shift invariant second order neural network input nodes using combinations of input pattern pixels and PCA(Principle Component Analysis). Using the proposed method, we are able to implement a shift invariant second order neural network with 2/5*N nodes. Due to the reduced number of input nodes, a 50% reduction in the learning and recognition time was obtained.

I. Introduction

Multi-layer perceptrons using EBP(Error Back Propagation) learning rule have attracted a great deal of interest recently in the field of pattern recognition where solutions using existing algorithmic methods, because of it's simplicity and superior problem solving capabilities. But the perceptron has a low rate of recognition for patterns which has been geometrically transformed (rotation, scaling, shifting). This shows that the multi-layer perceptron model has a weak point in recognizing geometrically transformed patterns, one of the basic problems of pattern recognition[2]. Geometric invariance is important in pattern recognition because the target location and orientation is usually unknown. Among all the variations, shift variation generally occurs in two dimensional pattern recognition. Shift variation refer to the shifting of the entire extracted pattern as a result of a small amount of noise at the end points of the pattern that occur during the process of extracting indivisual patterns from the entire scene[1].

To overcome such geometric variations, researches on using higher order neural networks, which can learn variations by itself, have been actively conducted. Recent research has shown that because invariances can be built into the architecture of higher order neural networks, they can be effectively used for invariant pattern recognition[2,3]. But straightforeward use of higher order neural networks is limited in actual implementations because of the combinatorial explosion of the number of input layer nodes in proportion to the input pattern dimension. If the input pattern to be learned is of dimension N, the number of input layer nodes increases in

$O(N^2)$, even if we only consider the second order neural networks. This is the major obstacle to actual implementation. Also, such large number of input nodes lead to slower learning and recognition[5,7].

There have been many approaches which maintain the geometric invariance properties of higher order networks while reducing the number of input nodes. For example, sigma-pi networks use a hidden layer of higher order nodes[10]. This strategy retains the higher order network properties, but its learning speed is slower. Another approach is to use a priori information to remove the terms which are irrelevant to the problem in a single layer of higher order nodes[5,7]. However since it is often difficult to find the properties of input pattern space a priori, this stretegy has limited applications.

Recently, the problems of the above methods have been overcome be representing pixel combinations in the same relation in the context of the invariance wanted by a single representative node[1,4,6]. Using such methods allow an O(N) implementation of high order neural networks with N dimensional input patterns. For example, shift invarient second order neural networks have 2*N input nodes for N dimensional input patterns. But even such methods still need a large number of input nodes necessitating longer learning and recognition time.

In this paper, as a part of an on going research to reduce the number of high order neural network input nodes, we propose a method for reducing the number of shift invariant second order neural network input nodes to close to the input pattern dimension N using PCA(Principal Component Analysis) and pattern pixel combinations. Using the proposed method, we are able to implement a shift invariant second order neural network only with 2/5*N nodes. Experiments using the implemented neural network on shifted Korean Munjo character set resulted in about 95% recognition rate. Due to reduced number of input nodes, reduction in the learning and recognition time was also obtained.

The rest of the paper is structured as followes. In section II, we show an O(N) shift invariant second order neural network implementation using pixel combinations. Section III details the process of implementating a further reduced shift invariant second order neural network using principal component analysis on the pixel combinations obtained in section II. Section IV presents the experimental results that show the proposed reduced second order neural network is superior to the existing non-reduced second order neural network. The paper ends with a conclusion in section V.

II. Shift Invariant Second Order Neural Network using Pixel Combinations.

Second order neural networks have the lowest order among higher order neural networks and have shift and size invariant properties. These properties are due to the fact that second order neural networks perceives the relationship between two pixels combinations.

The operation equation for second order neural network is shown in equation (1). To obtain shift invariance, we need only to take the two dimentional corelation terms of equation (1) into account. Equation (2) shows the terms of equation (1) that affect the relative positions of the inputs, only these terms need be taken into account for shift invariance[2,3].

$$h_i = \sum_{j=1}^{n} W_{i(jj)}\xi_j^2 + \sum_{j=1}^{n-1}\sum_{k=j+1}^{n} W_{i(jk)}\xi_j\xi_k + \sum_{j=1}^{n} W_{ij}\xi_j + W_i \tag{1}$$

$$h_i = \sum_{j=1}^{n-1}\sum_{k=j+1}^{n} W_{ijk}\xi_j\xi_k \tag{2}$$

For shift invariant learning, weights in shifted positions are updated simultaneously according to equation (3). So equation (2) can be rewritten as equation (4).

$$W_{ijk} = W_{i|j-k|} \tag{3}$$

$$h_i = \sum_{j=1}^{n-1}\sum_{k=j+1}^{n} W_{i(k-j)}\xi_j\xi_k \tag{4}$$

In shift invariant second order neural networks, since all weights in shifted positions have the same values, all the two pixel combinations are added beforehand and the cumulative value can be represented by a single input node of the second order neural network. This feature, summation of all the two pixel combinations for given relative position, is called SOP(Summation Of Products) or second order feature[1,7].

$$SOP = \sum[\prod(\xi_{jk}\xi_{kl}.....)] \qquad (5)$$

In obtaining second order features, the direction must be taken into account. There are four directions which two pixel combinations can have. So, second order feature can be represented by a 2*N - (L+M) dimensional vector with each element representing the numbers of the relative position pixel combinations. Fig 1. shows the possible directions of two pixel combinations and an example of the second order feature.

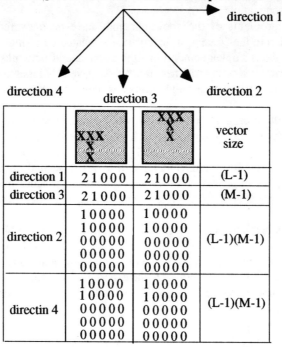

			vector size
direction 1	2 1 0 0 0	2 1 0 0 0	(L-1)
direction 3	2 1 0 0 0	2 1 0 0 0	(M-1)
direction 2	1 0 0 0 0 1 0 0 0 0 0 0 0 0 0 0 0 0 0 0 0 0 0 0 0	1 0 0 0 0 1 0 0 0 0 0 0 0 0 0 0 0 0 0 0 0 0 0 0 0	(L-1)(M-1)
directin 4	1 0 0 0 0 1 0 0 0 0 0 0 0 0 0 0 0 0 0 0 0 0 0 0 0	1 0 0 0 0 1 0 0 0 0 0 0 0 0 0 0 0 0 0 0 0 0 0 0 0	(L-1)(M-1)

Fig 1. Directions of two pixel combinations and example of second order feature

As can be seen above, shift invariant second order neural network can be implemented by first order multi-layer perceptron which has about 2*N input nodes when using the second order features.

III. Reduction of Second order Neural Network using PCA(Principal Component Analysis)

Shift invariant second order neural network using second order features considering position and directional correlations has O(N) input nodes. But the size of the neural network increases twice as fast as the dimension of the real pattern. To be realistically applied to pattern recognition systems, the learning and recognition process must be achieved as quickly as possible. Thus it is preferable to reduce the number of input nodes of second order neural networks as much as possible.

PCA(Principal Component Analysis) is a statistical tool which yields substantial data reduction by representing each pattern in terms of a relatively small subset of orthonormal features(Principal Component) extracted from the input set[8,9]. The Principal Components are eigenvectors of the covariance matrix formed from the pattern set. Each eigenvalue is equal to the variance of the projections of the patterns onto the corresponding principal component. The principal components can be obtained by using the diagonal terms from the diagonalized covariance matrix. Then the values obtained from the PCA are equivalent to the variance of each dimension of each pattern. So, the variances of each dimension can be used as Principal Components[8,9].

Fig. 2 shows the top 80% of the variance of each dimension from 990 chracter patterns from the Korean Munjo chracter set. As can be seen from Fig 2. dimensions of smaller variances differ very little for most of the patterns. Therefore such dimentions only increase the learning and recognition time while contributing very little to the overall recognition rate. By eliminating these dimension from the second order features, improvement for learning and recognition time can be obtained without adversely affecting the recognition rates.

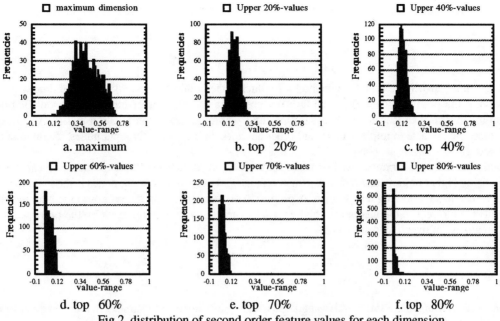

Fig 2. distribution of second order feature values for each dimension

IV. Experimental results

Second order neural networks reduced to 2*N input nodes using pixel combinations are shown to be further reducible by using PCA without adversely affecting the recognition rate through experiments of 990 patterns from the Korean Mungjo charcter set. The experiments compared the results of using a fixed percentage of the second order features with the highest variance values. We have conducted experiments using the top 10%, 20%, 30%, 40%, 50%, 70%, and 100% of the second order features. Fig. 3 shows the resulting recognotion rate, learning time and recognition time.

First of all, using second order neural networks rather than first order neural networks show a far higher recognition rate proving that theshift invariance problem has been overcome. Also, comparing the results of using the top 20% with the results of using all second order features, we can see that using only the top 20% of the features results in a 80% reduction in the number of the input nodes and a 50% reduction in learning and recognition time.

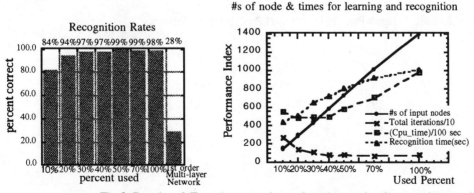

Fig 3. Results of Experiments using reduced second order neural networks.

From the experimental results, we can see that the second order features obtained through pixel combination still has redundant information that does not contribute to improving the recognition rate.

Eliminating such redundant information through PCA can lead to a further reduction in the number of input nodes without adversely affection the recognition rate while also improving the learning and recognition speed.

V.Conclusion

In this paper, we propose a method for reducing the number of second order neural network input nodes for solving the problems caused by the $O(N^2)$ increase in the number of input nodes -- difficulties in implementations, increases in learning and recognition time -- through pixel combination and PCA. Using the proposed method, we are able to implement second order network with only 2/5*N input nodes. Reduction in the learning and recognition time is also obtained.

Because geometric invariances are important for the pattern recognition, there are many researches being conducted on using higher order neural network. But combinatorial explosion of input nodes is the main obsticle to research. So, researches for solving this problem is progressively increasing. In the proposed method, we adopt a statistical tool(PCA) to reduce the number of higher order neural network input nodes. So the proposed method can be used regardless of the given pattern class.

References

[1] B.C. Kim,H.Y. Kwon,D.K. Kim, H.Y.Hwang,D.S. Cho, " Shift invariant character feature extraction using second order neural network characteristics," WCNN'93 , vol. IV , pp. 28 - 32.

[2] S.J. Perantonis ,P.J.G. Lisboa , "Translation,Rotation,and Scale Invariant Pattern Recognition by Higher order Neural Networks and Moment Classifier," IEEE Transactions on Neural Network,March,vol. 3 , No. 2, pp. 241-251,1992.

[3] C.L. Giles ,T. MAxwell, "Learning,invariance,and generalization in high-order neural networks," Applied Optics,vol. 25,pp. 4972 - 4978,1987.

[4] Y. Shin , J. Fhosh , "The pi-sigma network : an Efficient Higher-Order Neural Network for pattern classification and function approximation," , Proc. IJCNN 91 , vol. , pp. 13 - 18.

[5] L. Spirkovska , M.B. Reid, "Connectivity Strategies for Higher-Order Neural Networks applied pattern recognition,"Proc. IJCNN 90,vol.1 , pp. 21 - 26.

[6] W. A.C. Schmidt , J.P. Davis, "Pattern Recognition Properties of various feature spaces for higher order Neural Networks," IEEE Transaction on PAMI , vol. 15,No. 8, pp. 795 - 801,1993.

[7] H. Yang , C.C. Guest, "High order Neural Networks with reduced numbers of interconnection weights," Proc. IJCNN 91 , vol. 3 , pp. 281 - 286.

[8] J. Hertz, A. Krogh , R.G. Palme , Introduction to the Theory of Neural Computation, Addision-Wesely , 1991.

[9] S.D. Hyman , T.P. Vogl , K.T. Blackwell , G.S. Barbour , J.M. Irvine , D.L. Alkon, "Classification of Japanese Kanji using Principal Component Analysis as a preprocessor to an artificial neural network,",IJCNN 91,vol.1 , pp.233- 238.

[10] D.E. Rumelhart and J.L. McClelland, Parallel Distributed Processing,MIT,1986.

#s of node & times for learning and recognition

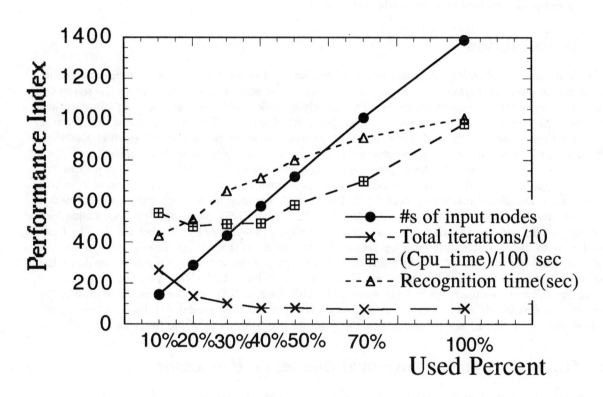

Temporal Sequence Processing Based on the Biological Reaction-Diffusion Process

Hillol Kargupta and Sylvian R. Ray
Department of Computer Science
University of Illinois at Urbana-Champaign
Urbana Illinois 61801[1]

Abstract

Temporal (spatiotemporal) sequences are a fundamental form of information both in natural and engineered systems. The biological control process which directs the generation of iterative structures from undifferentiated tissue is a type of temporal sequential process. A quantitative explanation of this temporal process is **reaction-diffusion**, initially proposed by Turing[1952] and later widely studied and elaborated.

We have adapted the reaction-diffusion mechanism to create a novel network and algorithm based on a chemical "neuron" model, which performs storage, associative retrieval and prediction for temporal sequences. Experiments demonstrate the ability of the device to achieve any desired *depth*, limited only by storage capacity, to remember and predict on the basis of count to any length, and to learn an embedded Reber grammar to 98% accuracy and permit retrieval with controllable redundancy.

1 Introduction

A fundamental class of biological mechanisms is widely believed to control the growth of repetitive structures such as insect leg segments, periodic patterns such as the stripes of a zebra, and similar sequences which are largely but not exactly repetitive. The underlying biological process has been explained quantitatively by the reaction-diffusion process consisting of a set of partial differential equations that describe the space-time concentration of chemical morphogens responsible for stimulation of growth. Reaction-diffusion is, in a word, a natural spatiotemporal sequential process which we wish to exploit.

On the engineering side of the ledger, the storage and retrieval of spatiotemporal sequences has received a good deal of attention by reason of their fundamental place in the simulation of cognitive processes. A few of the many proposals for TSP(temporal sequence processing) are time-delay neural nets, recurrent multilayer feedforward nets[Elman 1990, Jordan 1987], gamma delay networks[deVries & Principe 93], and the gaussian delay network, TEMPO2 [Bodenhausen & Waibel 1991]. The basic problem is to find a viable procedure for projecting the history of a sequence into the present so that the past, back to some 'depth', can be made to influence the present or future. Of course, we desire the device or network to be as fundamentally simple as possible and also biologically plausible.

In the following sections, we will (1) discuss the objectives of TSP and some previous efforts, (2) explain how reaction-diffusion operates biologically, (3) define our TSP model, (4) discuss some experimental tests of the model and (5) summarize the qualities and limitations of the Re-Di model.

2 Objectives for a Temporal Sequence Processor

The two distinct ways that we want to apply the TSP to process sequences are reviewed next.

1. **Embedded Sequence Recognition (ESR)** – A number of short pattern sequences, $PS = (ps_1, ps_2, \ldots)$, are to be learned by the device. An unbounded argument sequence ARGSEQ, is compared to the set, PS, to determine if any one of the stored pattern sequences is embedded in the ARGSEQ. The stored patterns could be meaning-bearing features of signals and the objective is to identify the existence of features in a semi-infinite signal. The process of matching a specific external sequence to internal stored states we will call *guided sequence retrieval*.

---

[1]Communication: ray@cs.uiuc.edu

2. **Sequence-Addressable Sequence Memory (SASM)** – A 'long' sequence(s), ST, is stored. Short address sequences are to be compared to ST for the purpose of locating regions of ST which match the applied address sequence ('address comparison', a variant of guided sequence retrieval). If a sufficiently exact match to the address sequence is found, we optionally want to read the continuation of ST from the match point without further external guidance (*free sequence retrieval).*

Upon close examination, storage, guided sequence retrieval, address comparison, and free sequence retrieval all exert their special requirements on the engineering of the network. Note also that free sequence retrieval is equivalent to *prediction.* For example, when the long stored sequence, ST, is a musical melody or financial time series, free sequence retrieval amounts to using similar past behavior to project the expected future.

Class Flexibility – It is also highly desireable in many applications of TSPs that the system has controllable tolerance to variations in the time of symbol occurrence.

In this sense, the stored sequences act as exemplars of classes, a useful condition often found in neural nets.

We propose to explain how the Re-Di TSP deals with all of these foregoing objectives.

3 Biological Reaction-Diffusion

A well-studied biological experiment consists of the surgical removal of an internal segment of a cockroach tibia followed by regrafting of the distal and proximal parts as illustrated in Fig.1 [Meinhardt 1982]. If the original tibia consisted of a sequence of similar but not identical segments numbered 123456789, and the segment, 4567, were removed, it is found that after one or two moults, the internal segment sequence is regenerated, in this case, in its original order. This experiment implies the existence of control information and a controlled growth process which stores and retrieves sequences. How is this to be explained? The quantitative explanation was set forth some 40 years ago[Turing 52] as a set of p.d.e.'s which are self-stabilized and which specify the growth and decay of morphogens stimulating the regenerative growth of the segments. An example of reaction-diffusion equations are given.[2]

$$\frac{\delta g_i}{\delta t} = \frac{c_i g_i^2}{r} - \alpha g_i + D_{g_i} \frac{\delta^2 g_i}{\delta x^2} \tag{1}$$

$$\frac{\delta r}{\delta t} = \sum_i c_i g_i^2 - \beta r + D_r \frac{\delta^2 r}{\delta x^2} \tag{2}$$

g_i represents the concentration of the ith morphogen which excites the growth of the ith segment of the tibia, r is the concentration of the common reactant chemical, and the coefficients are constants. The D's are the diffusion coefficients. Assume that segment 8 emits morphogen g_7. If r=1, $\delta g_7/\delta t$ will grow by positive feedback for some time and the diffusion term (containing D_g)will diffuse the chemical into the segment 8/segment 3 interface, stimulating growth of segment 7 material. At farther locations, the reactant r, which is set to diffuse rapidly, will suppress growth of g_7. Thus the strongest stimulus for growth of segment 7 will occur at the edge of the segment 8 material. Notice that reactant r is generated in proportion to the sum of squares of morphogens present (eqn.2, 1st term on right), and, by appearing in the denominator of term 1 of eqn.1, suppresses the growth of all morphogens.

After segment 7 has grown, it emits g_6 which excites the regeneration of segment 6, etc. until the surgically removed tibia segments regenerate(Fig. 1, rightmost sketch).

The reaction-diffusion equations permit calculation of the growth, diffusion and decay of each morphogen in turn which effectively carries the history of previous activity forward in time while distributing the information spatially by diffusion. This is the natural biological mechanism which we shall imitate to engineer a temporal sequence processor.

---

[2]These equations are somewhat simplified here, hence less than fully accurate, by reason of the limited space available for explanation. See [Meinhardt 1982] for the complete equation set.

4 The Re-Di Temporal Sequence Processor

4.1 The Basic Cell

A basic cell of the Re-Di processor or network has the following properties:

(1) The cell has a single label which specifies the chemical(morphogen) which it emits, i.e., the cell labelled **m** emits g_m.

(2) When activated, the cell emits one unit of its chemical into the medium.

(3) The cell has K receptors. Each receptor specifies the chemical vector which will activate the cell. The kth receptor has values, $V_j^k = (v_1, v_2, \ldots, v_N)$ where N is the maximum number of chemicals and v_i corresponds to chemical g_i. A cell is activated when the chemical concentration vector, $G = (g_1, g_2, \ldots)$ at the location of the cell is sufficiently near equal one of the K receptors (V vectors) of the cell. More precisely, cell C is activated if

$$\min_j \sum_{k=1}^{N} |(g_k(x) - V_{jk})| < \sigma \qquad j = 1, \ldots, K$$

At birth, all cell labels are blank and all V-vectors equal 0.

4.2 The Architecture of the TSP

A general TSP is composed of a number of basic cells distributed randomly in a volume suffused by a medium which supports diffusion of the chemicals(see Fig.2). In the present report, we will assume the basic cells are distributed on an x,y plane at integer locations. In general, there may be any number of cells with the same label but we will limit ourselves to one cell for each label, that is, there is one source for each chemical. The network is capable of generating the reactant chemical, r(x,y), at any position (x,y) where a basic cell exists. It is also assumed possible to locate the particular cell corresponding to an external symbol.

The growth, decay and diffusion of chemicals in the TSP are governed by the following equations.

The Reaction-Diffusion (Re-Di) Equations

$$\frac{\delta g_p^2(z)}{\delta t} = \frac{\epsilon g_p^2(z)}{r} - \alpha g_p(z) + D_g\left(\frac{\delta^2 g_p(z)}{\delta z^2}\right) \tag{3}$$

$$\frac{\delta r(z)}{\delta t} = \gamma \sum_{p=1}^{N} g_p^2(z) - \beta r(z) + D_r\left(\frac{\delta^2 r(z)}{\delta z^2}\right) \tag{4}$$

Operation of the TSP is best described with an example which follows.

4.3 Storing a Sequence (Training the Processor)

Assume the processor is in its virgin state and we will follow the steps of storing the sequence, $s_1 s_2 s_3 \ldots$ = **cdddf**. The chemical concentration, $\vec{G} = 0$, everywhere. We will assume a 5 x 5 array of cells located at $x = 1, \ldots, 5$, $y = 1, \ldots, 5$.

Upon applying $s_1 = $ **c**, one cell is recruited randomly and assigned the label, **c**. Suppose it is at x=3, y=3. C(3,3) is labelled the active cell(AC), it emits one unit of g_c, and the Re-Di equations are applied, diffusing g_c throughout the medium.

Upon applying $s_2 = $ **d**, another blank cell is recruited (say at x,y = 2,3), it is labelled d, flagged as the AC, and one of its receptors (V registers) is set or trained to the value of the chemical environment at its location at that moment. Only chemical g_c will be non-zero. The AC then emits one unit of g_d and the Re-Di equations are stepped to simulate growth or decay and diffusion of all chemicals in the system.

Upon applying $s_3 = $ **d**, the cell labelled 'd' is located, namely C(2,3), which continues as the AC. If none of the V-registers of C(2,3) is within the σ tolerance zone of the *current* $\bar{g}(2,3)$, an unused V-register of C(2,3) learns (is set to) $\bar{g}(2,3)$. Then one unit of g_d is emitted and the Re-Di equations are applied.

When $s_4 = $ **d** is applied, the procedure for s_3 is repeated. If σ is sufficiently small, the fact of a different chemical environment for each transition results in a unique activation vector for each transition. That is, the 2nd **d** to the 3rd **d** is distinguished from the 3rd to the 4th **d**.

Finally upon applying $s_5 = $ **f**, a new cell it recruited, labelled **f**, and set to recognize the $\bar{g}$ which carries the history of the sequence. Eventually, the chemical concentrations decay to zero. The device generates a chemical 'alphabet soup' *capable of uniquely representing the historical context of every transition.*

Retrieval of a sequence follows the same procedure as the storage process except no V-registers are altered.

Upon future reapplication of the same sequence for the purpose of recognizing the stored sequence, if the chemical concentrations are noiseless and applied with the same timing, the conditions stored in the V-registers will be exactly recapitulated causing the same cell activation sequence to reemerge.

Even if there is some noise or the timing varies, use of a wider tolerance window (greater σ) can still permit the stored sequence to be recognized.

5 Examples

5.1 Count (or Depth) Test

The ability of the network to count can be tested directly by demonstrating that the sequence, $cd^{n}e$ can be distinguished from $cd^{n+1}f$, that is, the occurrence of n **d**'s is distinct from n+1 **d**'s. The test consists of storing a sequence such as **cddddddd...** and noting the point where successive **d**'s are not distinguished by utilizing a new V-register. This experiment was performed with various values of tolerance, σ. The results are shown below.

COUNTING TEST

σ	n (largest depth)
0	∞
.01	10
.02	6
.04	4
.05	3

Metaphorically, larger values of σ correspond to paying less attention to the precise count. As the count or depth increases, the penalty is a proportionate increase in the required storage capacity which can be defined as: Capacity $= N_c N_V$ where $N_c = $ the number of cells and $N_V = $ the average number of occupied V registers (activation condition registers) per cell.

5.2 Embedded Reber Grammar

An embedded Reber grammar was generated with all transition probabilities $= 0.5$. The network was trained with 500 strings and tested with 500 different strings. Sequence length was unrestricted; string lengths as long as 29 symbols were observed. We used a hard-line accuracy requirement, namely, every transition in a string must be predicted by the network in order to score a Pass. Usually prediction of the penultimate symbol (t or p) by correlation to the second symbol (t or p) is the goal.

Variation of the activation tolerance measure, σ, demonstrates the range of generalization possible during storage of sequences. In the limit as $\sigma \to 0$, every transition was learned uniquely which required about 600 V-registers to record an average 4683 transitions. Every sequence which has ever been presented is uniquely retrievable when $\sigma = 0$ during storage. When σ increases, some distinct strings may be stored as equivalent but fewer V registers are used (e.g., about 300 V registers when $\sigma = 0.005$). Ultimately when $\sigma = 0.5$, the representation became context-free, that is, no history was stored — any transition between Reber grammar symbols was permitted. Similarly, during Test phase, the acceptable tolerance for each transition, σ_{TST} was varied. With $\sigma = .001, \sigma_{TST} = .005$, 98.4% of strings were recognized. Accuracy for various combinations of storage and test tolerance are summarized in Fig. 3.

5.3 Time Flexibility

In the foregoing cases, retrieval was performed with the same timing used during storage. If retrieval is performed at a rate slower or faster than the rate during storage, the chemical concentrations will be different. In this experiment, the storage(training) algorithm was performed with a unit time between each symbol by using a unit step of decay and diffusion. To simulate retrieval at a slower rate than storage, we performed two or three steps of the Re-Di equations between symbols. In Fig. 4, the error rate is the percentage of sequences in which at least one transition was not correctly signalled. The error rate can be reduced by increasing the activation tolerance, σ_{TST}. Almost any sequence could be retrieved with $\sigma_{TST} = 0.2$. Increasing σ_{TST} permits an increasing number of transitions to be seen as permissible, even some which may not have been explicitly seen during the storage operation. Thus, the cost of retrieving at a rate different from the rate used during storage is that one must accept a higher level of uncertainty that the object sequence was, in fact, precisely the one that was stored. On the other hand, temporal spacing in the stored sequence can be distinguished in the retrieval process, if desired, by using both a small σ and small σ_{TST} at the cost of storage capacity.

5.4 Sequence Addressable Sequence Memory

SASM entails the storage of comparatively 'long' strings addressed by shorter sequences. The storage algorithm is independent of the lengths of sequences being stored.

An experiment was designed to test the ability of the Re-Di TSP to perform in SASM style. Six simple musical melodies averaging about 20 notes duration were encoded in a form which represents *both the note and its duration*.[3] All of the melodies had a common internal subsequence, the objective being in part to demonstrate that the sequences could still be completely distinguished downstream from the common point.

After storing the melodies, a brief (3 to 6 note) initial string from an arbitrary stored string was used as the address. The address was presented in Guided Sequence Retrieval mode. At that point, having developed the chemical distributions corresponding to the initial part of one of the stored strings, the system reverted to Free Sequence Retrieval meaning that each successive activated node was decided competitively by selecting the unique (usually) node with the largest activation. In all cases except one special condition, the expected sequence was correctly retrieved all the way to its terminal symbol.

6 Summary and Conclusions

Temporal sequence processing fundamentally requires memory of the history of the sequence, usually supplied by a delay kernel. In the current paper, we have explained how history be carried by a mechanism analogous to chemicals growing, decaying and diffusing according to the reaction-diffusion process. This obviates the need to propose ad hoc shapes or specifications for the delay kernel. The proposed system provides full control of depth during storage by a single parameter, σ. Increasing depth increases required storage capacity; decreased depth amounts to expanding class generalization (decreased resolution)of sequences during storage. Another similar parameter, σ_{TST}, can be set to various degrees of tolerance of transitions during retrieval. The system is capable of counting to any magnitude (i.e., has arbitrary depth). Large depth carries the cost of larger memory capacity, however. The Re-Di system attained an accuracy of 98% in the severe test posed by an unrestricted-length embedded Reber grammar. The system is also capable of reading back at a rate different from that during storage but at a cost of increasing error tolerance as the difference between storage and retrieval

---

[3]Unfortunately, space does not permit the full explanation of the encoding and the experiment details. A full description is in preparation.

rates increase. It is also possible to store and retrieve not only the spatial vector sequence but also the duration of each vector.

REFERENCES

Bodehausen, Ulrich and Waibel, Alex(1991). Learning the Architecture of Neural Networks for Speech Recognition. IEEE Proceedings of the ICASSP,**1**, 117-124.

deVries, B., & Principe,J.C.(1992). The gamma model – A new neural net model for temporal processing. Neural Networks, **5**, 565-576.

Elman, Jeffrey(1990). Finding Structure in Time. Cog.Sci. **14** (179-211).

Jordan, M.I.(1987). Attractor dynamics and parallelism in a connectionist sequential machine. In *Proceedings of 8th Annual Conf. of the Cognitive Science Society*(pp.531-546).

Meinhardt,Hans (1982). Models of Biological Pattern Formation. Academic Press, Inc.

Turing, Alan(1952). The Chemical Basis of Morphogenesis. Phil. Trans. of the Royal Soc. of London, Ser. B, **237**,37-72.

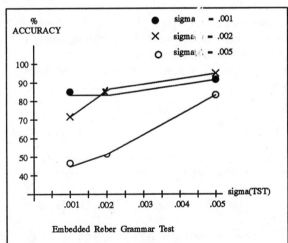

Fig. 1: Regeneration of Sequential Segments of Cockroach Tibia

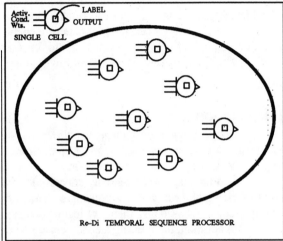

Fig. 2: Architecture of the Re-Di Processor: Randomly Distributed Array of Basic Cells

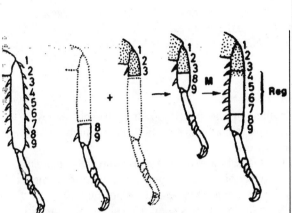

Fig. 3: Retrieval Accuracy as a Function of Storage and Retrieval Tolerances

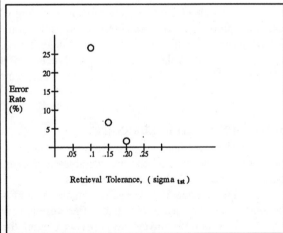

Fig. 4: Percentage Erroneous Sequences vs. σ_{TST} - Retrieval Speed = 50% of Storage Speed

A Language for Connectionist Pattern Recognition

Tim Cooper (timc@cs.su.oz.au)
Sydney University Computer Science Dept
Sydney 2006 Australia

Abstract

In this paper we present a computer language that allows you to create neural nets, not by training them but by programming them.

The language constructs allow you to program at a high-level, schema level. It actually looks a little like Prolog. However, it is based on a theory which is at odds with the idea of symbolic logic and predicate calculus.

The idea was born out of the realisation that from a software engineering point of view, the best way of creating a perceptual recognition network may be to program it rather than to coax a learning algorithm into learning examples and generalising appropriately.

The language is designed for pattern recognition tasks, e.g. character / speech / face recognition. A digit recogniser is presented in the paper to illustrate the general principles.

The Connectarine Development Environment is implemented in C under MS-DOS.

Introduction

Connectarine is a language that allows you to explicitly program neural-nets at the schema level. The program consists mainly of a set of productions that have a similar syntax to Prolog, which interact to generate all the neurons and all the connections in the network.

The language was originally conceived from the realisation that from a software development point of view, the best way of producing a character recogniser or speech recogniser may be to connect one up manually, based on a theory of feature detectors, rather than to use a learning algorithm.

In addition, the resulting neural nets are editable, their operation is comprehensible (they are not 'black boxes' like most other neural nets) and they are very efficient (they are sparsely connected and the neurons are systematically created). They may even exhibit better performance, because of the element of design in their construction.

A Connectarine program takes a set of input neurons and a set of 'productions'. It uses these to generate more neurons, and these neurons to generate further neurons, until the productions don't generate any more neurons. The weights are generated at the same time as the neurons.

The author believes that neural nets are the most natural and efficient way to do fuzzy recognition tasks, whether they are trained or programmed.

Introduction to Connectarine

The basic unit in Connectarine is the neuron. A neuron is specified as an identifier with various parameters. The productions use variables and expressions in place of the parameters to define new neurons and their connections and weights.

The language allows you to create layered networks, general feed-forward networks, feedback networks, and it even allows you to define infinite networks.

In order to convey the concepts behind the Connectarine language, let's look at a piece of Connectarine code and skeleton:

```
<< input: on(1..12,1..19) >>

edgelet("-",x,y)  :- on(x-1,y),on(x,y),on(x+1,y),
                          -on(x,y-1),  -on(x,y+1).
```

```
...etc...
<< output: digit(0..9) >>
```

The line at the beginning and the one at the end interface a Connectarine program with the outside world. They define the input neurons and output neurons. In the middle there is a list of productions.

In this case, 'on(x,y)' are the input neurons. We also say that they represent the activation values of those neurons. For example, 'on(3,4)' specifies the activation value of position (3,4) on the bit-map.

The neurons are feature detectors. We often call a neuron a 'concept detector', because they are used to represent concepts in the more general sense - visual features, complex visual objects, semantic objects, etc. (We take the unorthodox view that 'meanings' can be assigned to neurons in this way in the computer as well as the brain. However, our reasons and our qualifications are not discussed here).

For example, "edgelet("-",x,y)" represents a short horizontal edge at position (x,y). Neuron expressions, where variables are substituted for the parameters, are used in the productions. A production is something of the form:

<neuron-expr> :- <list of neuron expressions>.

Connectarine starts with the input neurons. It tries to fit them in into all possible places in the right-hand-side of a production. This 'fitting it in' involves assigning values to the respective variables. These values then allow us to evaluate the parameters in the left-hand-side and create a neuron with those parameters.

The Connectarine system calculates the activation level of a neuron in the usual way of summing together the efferent neurons (on the right-hand-side) and passing the result through a sigmoidal response function. The programmer has control over the steepness and the threshold of the sigmoid function, (the 'threshold' referring to the x-position of the inflection point).

Connectarine also supports fuzzy logic, however it is the author's view that connectionist logic, where values are summed and sigmoided and two half-true statements can add to each other, is more effective and natural in this domain than fuzzy logic. For example, for these purposes it is better that (0.5 or 0.5) > (0.5 or 0), than (0.5 or 0.5) = (0.5 or 0).

We assume that any neuron not in the database of neurons has an activation of zero. (Actually, this is an oversimplification of the algorithm, but it is generally true).

Programming a Digit-Recogniser with Connectarine

The input to a character recogniser is a matrix of bit-map pixel activations. By creating a level of edge detectors as illustrated in the last section, we can make a start on the full network.

These edgelets get put together into 'cornerlets' (little corners) and 'curvelets' (little curves) and 'edges' (medium-sized edges). There are also detectors for line-endings.

These features get built together to form medium-sized corner-detectors and curve-detectors of every possible orientation, and so on. Eventually we get up to more complex features such as 'The top of a 5' and 'a J-type curve', and finally to '2' and '8' and so on, which are the output neurons.

At each stage, we reduce the resolution of the image by combining together neurons in the same areas of the bit-map. At each stage we get detectors for more complex features, with larger receptive fields. Ultimately, we get full digit-detectors whose receptive field is the entire bit-map, and these form the output layer. The final neural net has about 11 layers.

Here are extracts from a digit-detector program:

```
<< Sigmoid(70%,6) >>
edgelet("|",x,y) :- on(x,y-1), on(x,y), on(x,y+1), -on(x-1,y), -on(x+1,y).
edgelet("/",x,y) :- 2*on(x-1,y-1), 2*on(x,y), 2*on(x+1,y+1), -on(x,y+1),
                    -on(x-1,y), -on(x+1,y), -on(x,y-1).

<< Sigmoid(35%,8) >>
cornerlet("|_",x/2,y/2) :- edgelet("|",x,y+1), edgelet("|",x+1,y+1),
```

edgelet("-",x+2,y-1), edgelet("-",x+2,y).
curvelet("_",x/2,y/2) :- edgelet("\",x-1,y+1), edgelet("_",x+1,y).
curve("_/",x/2,y/2) :- fuzzy_curvelet("_",x-1,y), fuzzy_curvelet("_/",x+1,y).

{ --- character-specific neurons ----}
lines7 :- edge("7",x,y), edge("7",x,y+1).
bottom5 :- curve("_/",x,y), fuzzy_curve(")",x,y+2).

{ ---- Output neurons ---- }
digit("2") :- top2("2",x,y), cusp2(x,y-1).
digit("5") :- side5(x,y), top5(x,y), curve("5",x2,y2).

In all things, we do not regard features as either being there or not. They just have a higher or lower activation value. For example, the feature detector for a cross will get activated by the tiny serif at the bottom of a '1'. Even these very small activations play a part in the overall process. They might represent some feature which should be there, but because of bad printing or bad handwriting isn't properly there. They can still affect the overall outcome.

This network will recognise a character no matter where on the bit-map it is situated. It recognises characters of different sizes, within upper and lower limits; this is a consequence of rules such as:

curve("_/",x,y) :- curve("_",x-1,y), curve("_",x,y), curve("_/",x+1,y), curve("_/",x+2,y).

where the sigmoid response function is tuned to respond when just some of these are activated. When every level of the network has rules such as this, it causes recognition to occur regardless of size, except above a certain size and below a certain size.

It will also cope with a certain degree of rotation, as an intrinsic feature of having feature detectors that accept distortions. In fact, you can look at what happens as you rotate the digit: the activation strength of the output neuron representing that digit is at a maximum when the character is near its normal orientation. As you move it around, the activation strength drops off, until there is no recognition (activation ≈ 0).

A Digit-recogniser in perspective:

This program recognises single digits from bit-maps. It takes the image as an input vector, and has 10 output neurons corresponding to the 10 digits. All the neurons in the middle represent various features at various positions. For example, if you do a query to look at the activation of the horizontal edge-detectors on an image such as:

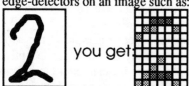 you get

The activation of each of the 10 output neurons corresponds roughly to the probability it is that digit. You can either look for the highest activation, or look for the highest activation but require that it be significantly higher than the next highest, or just take all the output neurons and feed them into a higher-level network.

If you want to put it into the context of something like a post-code recogniser, you might need digit-detectors with position parameters so that at each position of the bit-map (at a low resolution, however), you have neurons detecting each digit. You should get something like this:

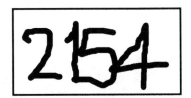

```
2-detectors:        -==--    ---
1-detectors:   --- -=-    -   --
5-detectors:   --     - -===-   -
4-detectors:   ---   --    -===--
```

There is interest at the moment in recognising characters from stroke information. In other words, you get a full description of the trajectory of a pen rather than a bit-map representation of a character. This is a very important component of the new pen-based notebook computers. This is no problem for a character recogniser of the type described above. You just get rid of the first layer, and have the edgelet layer as the input layer. So the stroke-information is translated directly into activations of each of these edgelets, by software outside the net, and then exactly the same network can be used to do the character recognition.

This neural net recognises characters based on the juxtapositions of the various features, (not by merely looking at sets of features, e.g. "it has a cross and a horizontal concavity"). If the goal of a neural net is to recognise words, this idea can also be taken further by allowing the neural net to look at the characters surrounding a given character in order to help categorise it. In other words, the various activation values for potential characters feed into a 'frequent English syllable recogniser', which then outputs a single identifier or goes back to the letter level to output the individual characters.

If we go up the next level to word-root or word recognition, we can even recognise misspelt words, just as we recognise distorted characters.

According to the author's theory, tasks such as text recognition and speech recognition should be done in this way, rather than by a process of hypothesis testing. Each level outputs a set of possibilities with various activation values into the next level, and 1 or more neurons in the next level will fire. In other words, a feed-forward neural net is sufficient for these tasks. The fact that humans can recognise handwritten text pre-attentively supports this theory.

Of course, the language also supports recurrent networks, so a hypothesis-testing model could also be explored.

Results:

A Connectarine interpreter and development environment has been implemented, in C, in MS-DOS. A Connectarine compiler (compiling Connectarine to C or object-code) is planned.

The digit-recogniser described in this paper has been implemented. It has not been tested on any public database of character bitmaps, however it is 99% accurate on one set of 100 12x19 digit bitmaps. The first 50 digit bitmaps were used to develop the program, and the remaining ones were used to test the program with no further development. This full database is reproduced below, so the reader can verify that the digits represent a variety of possible digit bit-maps and the recogniser can cope with distortion and noise (as well as translations and differences in size).

This program consists of 550 lines of Connectarine code (including comments etc). The development of the digit recogniser was a non-trivial task, and one requiring the author to acquire a certain amount of expertise in the methodology. The program is far from perfect, but also far from plateauing out. As the 3 days of programming progressed, recognition rates improved steadily as bitmap quality decreased.

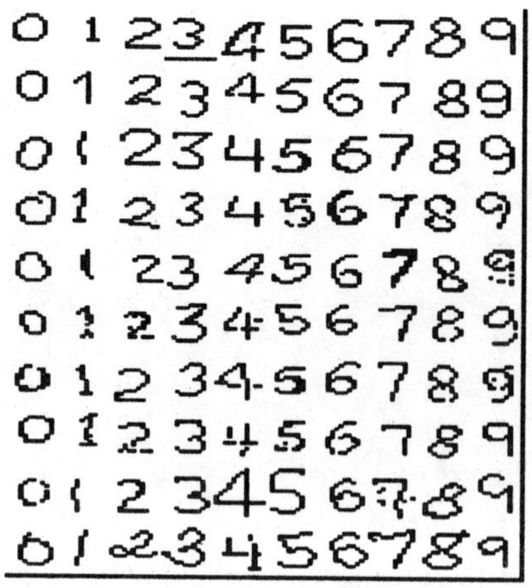

In other words, given the Connectarine development environment, a general tool for all fuzzy recognition tasks, a fully functional optical digit recogniser was created after just 3 days' work.

Relation to Other Work:

This is the only project we know of which uses the idea of explicit programming of neurons and feature detectors, or implementing production rules as neurons. There has been a lot of work done on hybrid connectionist expert/production systems, [Gal88] and [Kas90]. The need for a toolbox of alternative methods is expressed in [Kan92]. Connectarine could be viewed as a forward-chaining Prolog with connectionist logic (or fuzzy logic which is also supported) and with arithmetical unification. However, the issues raised by the language are not related to traditional logic programming.

Fukushima's 'Neocognitron' deals with feature detectors and pattern recognition in a similar way [Fuk88], [Fuk88b]. This project involved the creation of a deep neural network capable of recognising hand-written digits in a translation-, size- and distortion- independant way. In this case, the network was created by providing it with training sets of intermediate features at several levels, and having it learn to recognise these given the processing from the lower levels. There was an explicit architecture of alternating generalisation and categorisation levels, which is in a sense how this digit recogniser works.

Other approaches to handwritten character recognition are given in [Jak88] and [Nak92]. In these systems, a single layer of preprogrammed feature detectors is created by traditional programming methods and then fed into a neural net. This first layer would presumably take longer to develop without a language such as Connectarine than in Connectarine. Also, the performance of the neural net from that point upward might suffer from being a shallow net, when the problem intrinsically requires a deep neural net to avoid combinatorial explosions.

There are programs which allow you to create neural nets by wiring up and calibrating individual neurons or tracts of neurons, for example MacBrain for the Macintosh, but these are not suitable for serious use on a neuron-by neuron basis. These systems, and numerous other systems, allow one to configure broad connectivity patterns, but the idea there is to work with learning rules which do all the real work.

* * * * *

There are many opportunities to combine this kind of approach with other approaches to neural nets. A network like this could be combined with trained neural nets by concatenating neural nets along layers. For example, Connectarine might be better at doing the lower levels or higher levels of a perceptual network. Conversely, Connectarine could benefit from training algorithms in certain ways. Connectarine could also be used to define a good starting point for a learning algorithm, because it creates networks that are already close to some kind of local or global minimum.

There are not many techniques for creating deep neural nets. Connectarine is one such technique. Deep neural nets are appropriate for tasks such as this, because the variety of transformations that recognition is supposed to be invariant under would otherwise lead to a combinatorial exsplosion. The Neocognitron is one such system, but this requires the collation of large sets of intermediate features.

Connectarine could also be applied to other categorisation problems, the type expert systems are more commonly used for. It has the advantage that its operation is not opaque, that it is possible to analyse the network and to validate that it will not generate wildly inappropriate responses.

Connectarine has enabled the author to study the theory of perception in a neural net with a view to explaining, although not mimicking, the human perceptual cortex.

However, the system in itself is primarily intended as a serious tool for performing fuzzy pattern recognition. The next development will be to apply it to another domain, such as speech recognition or recognition of pathologies in cytology slides.

References:

[Fuk88]: Fukushima, Kunihiko: "A Neural Network for Visual Pattern Recognition", *IEEE*, (March 1988).

[Fuk88b]: Fukushima, Kunihiko: "Neocognitron: A Hierarchical Neural Network capable of Visual Pattern Recognition", *Neural Networks* Vol 1 pp119-130, (1988)

[Gal88]: Gallant, Stephen I: "Connectionist Expert Systems" *Communications of the ACM*, 31, pp152 (1988)

[Guy89]: Guyon, L.: "Comparing different Neural Network Architectures for Classifying Handwritten Digits", *Proceedings of the International Joint Conference on Neural Networks*, Vol 2, pp127-132, IEEE press, New York, June (1989)

[Jac88]: Jackel L.D., Graf H.P., Hubbard W., Denker J.S. & Henderson D., "An Application of Neural Net Chips: Handwritten Digit Recognition", *IEEE Conference on Neural Nets*, Vol II, pp 107-115 (1988)

[Kan92]: Kanal L. & Raghavan S., "HYBRID SYSTEMS - A Key to Intelligent Pattern Recognition", *Proceedings of the International Joint Conference on Neural Nets*, Vol IV pp 177-183 IEEE (1992)

[Kas90]: Kasabov, Nikola: "Hybrid Connectionist Rule Based Systems", *Artificial Intelligence - Methodology, Systems, Applications*, 227-235 (1990)

[Nak92]: Nakayama K., Chigawa Y. & Hasegawa O., "Handwritten Alphabetic and Digit Recognition using Feature Extraction Neural Network and Modified Self-Organising Map", *Proceedings ot the Joint Conference on Neural Nets*, Vol. IV, pp 235-240, IEEE (1992)

A Neural Network for Recognizing Characters Extracted from Moving Vehicles

Jang-Hee Yoo, Byung-Tae Chun
Artificial Intelligence Division
Systems Engineering Research Institute
P.O. Box 1, Yoosung, Taejeon, 305-333, Korea
email : jhyoo@serims.seri.re.kr

Dong-Pil Shin
Korea Information Networks
Yoido-Dong 14-24, Youngdeungpo-Ku
150-101, Seoul, Korea

Abstract

In this paper, described are a neural network model and system implementation for recognizing characters extracted from license plates of moving vehicles. A method for selecting features appropriate for recognition is proposed based on relationships between character features and recognition rate, and an enhanced back-propagation algorithm is also proposed which effectively selects training patterns and dynamically modifies learning rate. Based on the proposed algorithm, a character recognition system for license plate is developed and tested against real data. In the test performed on vehicles running on the roads, the system demonstrated recognition rate higher than 95 percent.

1. Introduction

Neural networks have been successfully employed in various applications of pattern recognitions. Especially, neural network has demonstrated good performance in recognizing noise-stained characters and hand-written characters, and thus neural network implementation might be appropriate for recognizing characters extracted from moving vehicles[5, 6, 7]. Real-time recognition of characters for vehicle license plates is very difficult, as the size of characters varies depending upon the position of the image extraction, motion of the camera, and speed of the vehicle. The required complexity of the system is very close to that of recognizing hand-written characters.

Researches on developing neural network-based character recognition systems have mainly used features extracted based on heuristics. However, the feature extraction methods currently being used have not proved their validity through systematic analysis, and the features tend to lose its distinctive features, because of the uncertainty involved in feature extraction and overlapped features. In addition, the number of features is so large that recognition requires enormous computation time and thus makes it almost impossible to implement on current hardwares.

Back-propagation has been known to be useful in training multi-layered neural networks. However, disadvantages of the algorithm are that it requires a large computational time for training, possibly converges into local minimum, and forgets previously learned weights in the process of training[3, 4, 9].

In this research, a back-propagation algorithm is employed to recognize characters in the license plate of moving vehicle in real-time. Input-node removal method is proposed as an effective way of extracting features from the object, and an enhanced back-propagation algorithm is employed based on selective training pattern to prevent oscillation and to facilitate fast convergence. The proposed methods were successfully employed in recognizing characters in the license plate of moving vehicles.

2. Neural Network Design for Character Recognition

Character recognition system based on neural networks consists of four sequential steps: preprocessing, feature extraction, training, and recognition. Preprocessing step is comprised of segmentation, noise filtering, and normalization[7, 9]. Feature extraction is a process to determine how to explicitly describe the character pattern, generally by constructing feature vectors representing characters, and thus have a strong influence on overall recognition rate. Improperly selected features frequently lead to low recognition rate and require complex recognition algorithms[1, 7, 9].

Analysis on the relationship between features and overall recognition rate in back-propagation algorithm can lead to performance improvement of the recognition system by selecting relevant features. As the features propagate its influence up to the output nodes, a direct relationship between input features and recognition rate can be analyzed by activating neural networks, purposefully removing relevant input nodes, and then measuring recognition rate. Although an attempt has been made to measure the influence of input features by analyzing distributions of weights in hidden layers[2], the interpretation of weight vectors is very difficult.

Removal of irrelevant input nodes can be done by setting values of those input nodes to zeros, which in turn sets the weighted summation of hidden nodes, $net_j (= \Sigma w_{ji} x_i)$ zero and thus lead to none contribution to output values. Accordingly, we propose that the influence of extracted features on recognizing characters can be known by the analysis of the relationship between the removed input node and the recognition rate, thus system performance can be improved by effective feature selection.

─Box-1 : Enhanced Back-propagation Algorithm─

Step I: Selective Learning
  current_tss = 0.0;
  Loop number_of_input for each pattern
    compute_actual_output();
    compute_error();
    current_tss = current_tss + current_error;
    If current_error > average_error Then
        adjust_weights();
    end_if
  end_of_loop

Step II: Adapt Learning Rate
  average_error$_t$ = current_tss / number_of_input;
  delta_error = average_error$_{t-1}$ - average_error$_t$;
  *tolerance = - number_of_output * number_of_input / E6;*
  If delta_error > tolerance Then
    oscillation = oscillation + 1;
  end_if
  oscillation_criterion = epoch mod number_of_input;
  If oscillation_criterion = 0 Then
    *learning_rate = initial_learning_rate * oscillation / number_of_input;*
    oscillation = 0;
  end_if

In back-propagation algorithm, the dynamic modification of learning rate and the effective selection of training patterns can improve system performance. The effective selection of training patterns can be done in the following operations: divide the total error sums obtained in the forward pass by the number of training patterns to calculate an average error, and then train patterns which have error larger than average error in the backward pass. This process is described in *step I* in Box-1. In general, training the partial set of input patterns would lead to oscillation and it can be solved by dynamic modification of learning rate. Dynamic modification of learning rate can be implemented by counting the number of oscillation when the error size increases over the predetermined range, reflecting the ratios in setting learning rate, and eventually decreasing learning rate in case of oscillations, while increasing learning rate in case of convergence, to get the faster convergence of the training. Box-1 describes enhanced back-propagation learning algorithm.

In the enhanced learning algorithm, tolerance value, in addition to the initial learning rate and momentum, must be determined to measure error increase for detecting oscillation. Also, periods of modifying learning rate should be determined. In the algorithm, the learning rate should be modified whenever the number of epochs increased is equal to the number of training patterns, as described in *step II* in Box-1. Selective training patterns might reduce computation complexity in each epoch, and dynamic modification of learning rate might effectively prevent oscillation frequently encountered in back-propagation algorithm. Both mechanisms might improve convergence speed and degree of generalization. In the applications of real world problems, the enhanced back-propagation algorithm effectively solved a set of complex training patterns. In case of easy training patterns the number of epochs in the enhanced algorithm tends to become larger than in the conventional algorithm. However, the total training time in enhanced algorithm was reduced through effective decreases of computation time each epoch.

3. Recognizing Characters in Vehicle License Plate

Currently, in Korea the vehicle license plate consist of eight characters, except some special use. The first two characters in the upper row are Hangul(Korean script) characters (geographical regions), and the third character in the upper row is a numeral (vehicle class). The first character in the lower row is a Hangul character, while the next four characters in the lower row are four numerals as in the Figure-1. Part (a) in Figure-1 depicts a license plate in 512*480 gray-scaled vehicle image captured by CCD camera, while part (b) depicts digitized result of license plates after operations of segmentation and preprocessing for each character. The resolution ratio of preprocessed character strings, except four numerals of relatively large size in the lower row, is very low, which imposes complexities and inherent difficulties on pattern recognition. In the review of 200 images of license plates in the experiment it was found that the size of Hangul characters in the upper row varies from 13*15 to 27*29 pixels, and the size of Hangul characters in lower row takes various ranges of 16*23 to 38*47 pixels. The size of numerals varies too; numerals in the upper row change the size from 8*17 to 20*24 pixels, while numerals in lower row change from 10*49 to 29*60 pixels.

a) License Plate in Vehicle Image   b) Segmentation and Digitized Result

Figure-1: Korean Vehicle License Plate

The first two Hangul characters in the upper row indicate geographical region, one of the six registration cities and nine registration provinces. Five out of the six types of Hangul syllable[8] are included in the composition of the two characters. The resolution of two characters' image is so low that it is very difficult to separate vowels and consonants, and to extract features via Bar Masking. When combining two characters into a complete pattern after separately recognizing individual character was attempted, the uncertainty exponentially increases. Therefore, method of simultaneous recognition of two characters as a single pattern was employed. The first Hangul character in the lower row has the structure of "consonant + vowel", generating 84 different character patterns. In the Hangul character recognition, a single character is divided into vowel and consonant. A structural method was employed for vowel recognition, while neural network was employed for consonant recognition. The vertical consonants of Hangul characters are written in the simplified form but horizontal consonants are written in the cursive style. It is advisable to divide consonants into horizontal consonants and vertical consonants, and to recognize each of them. Numerals are comprised of 10 different patterns from 0 to 9, and it is more effective to divide numerals into small size numerals and large size numerals and recognize each of them. Figure-2 depicts Hangul characters and numerals which are used in Korean vehicle license plates.

서울, 부산, 대전, 광주, 대구, 인천, 경기, 강원, 충북, 충남, 경북, 경남, 전북,
전남, 제주, 가, 나, 다, 라, 마, 바, 사, 아, 자, 차, 카, 타, 파, 하, 거, 너, 더, 러,
머, 허, 고, 노, 도, 로, 모, 보, 소, 오, 조, 초, 코, 토, 포, 호, 구, 누, 두, 루, 무, 부,
수, 우, 주, 추, 쿠, 투, 푸, 후, 그, 느, 드, 르, 므, 브, 스, 으, 즈, 츠, 크, 트, 프, 흐,
1, 2, 3, 4, 5, 6, 7, 8, 9, 0

Figure-2 : Characters used in Korean Vehicle License Plates

In this research of neural network application, constructed are five neural networks, each for: geographical regions, small size numerals, large size numerals, vertical consonants, and horizontal consonants of Hangul characters. Out of 300 license plates extracted from vehicles running on the roads, 200 license plates were used for training and another 100 license plates were used for testing recognition rate. For the purpose of network architecture, the number of input nodes was determined by the features, the number of hidden nodes was by experience, and the number of output nodes was by the number of output codes.

4. Experiments and Results

In the experiments, training was done until recognition of training patterns was 100 percent correct, and then variations of recognition rate with removals of input nodes was investigated. Investigation on the geographical region codes showed that 15 features out of 34 features, when they were removed, did not have a strong impact on recognition rate, generally less than 1 percent. In particular, 5 features had completely no influence on the recognition rate. However, when all of the 15 features were removed simultaneously, the recognition rate was lowered to 59 percent and therefore it was revealed that the overall recognition rate was greatly influenced by the removal of irrelevant nodes. The recognition rate was easily recovered by adjusting weights with a small number of iterations. With the respect of feature selection, only small number of training patterns can effectively determine features of trainable patterns. Table-I shows the architecture of neural network employed in the experiment, number of patterns, the number of features for each character, and test results of characters recognition of vehicle license plates.

Table-1: Experimental Results of Characters Recognition

Items \ Characters	Neural Nets Topology (input*hidden *output)	Experimental Patterns		Feature Selection			Recognition Rate (%)
		Number of Training Patterns	Number of Test Patterns	Number of Featutres	Number of Removable Features	Number of Detemined Features	
Geographical Region	29 * 29 * 15	200	100	34	15	29	96.0
Small Size Numeral	25 * 25 * 10	200	100	37	15	25	95.0
Vertical Consonant	14 * 14 * 14	152	78	16	6	14	94.9
Horizontal Consonant	14 * 14 * 14	48	22	16	7	14	90.9
Large Size Numeral	25 * 25 * 10	800	400	37	14	25	98.3

In the Table-1, the number of removable features, having no impact on overall recognition rate even with the removal of the features, was determined in the beginning step considering that even simultaneous removal of some features would not have any impact on recognition rate. In case of numeral recognition, relatively many features could be removed without a significant impact. However, in case of Hangul characters and regional codes, because of the low resolution, all the features showed relevant to the overall recognition rate.

In this research, the enhanced back-propagation algorithm was employed for neural network application. The algorithm was useful and effective for overcome local minima reached possibly when the regional code "경기 (Kyunggi)" was trained as "경북(Kyungbuk)" for similar character pattern, and for speeding up the convergence. The newly developed algorithm demonstrated much improved performance level when applied to complex and difficult patterns, but showed almost equal performance to conventional algorithms when applied to easy patterns. It was found that the tolerance value used for determining error increase to detect oscillations is very sensitive to learning speed. The degree of generalization was much enhanced and better results were demonstrated in the experiment when the training patterns were uniformly distributed and the size was large.

5. Conclusion

In this paper, an enhanced back-propagation algorithm and feature selection method are described for improving convergence speed and were employed in an character recognition systems of license plates extracted from moving vehicles. The proposed algorithm can enhance system performance through effective feature extraction, reduction of recognition time and learning speed, and increased recognition rate. The vehicle license plates recognition system implemented in T800 Transputer-based environment[10] showed that the time for a complete recognition required only 0.09-0.11 seconds after digitized and segmentation, which was not problematic in real world applications. The recognition rate, even though varied depending on the results of preprocessing step, was generally above 95 percent, relatively high performance. This research requires further experiments on training more samples, especially needs further research on new feature extraction methods and improving the degree of generalization.

[References]

[1] A. Rajavelu, M. T. Musavi, and M. V. Shirvaikar, "A Neural Network Approach to Character Recognition," *Neural Networks*, Vol.2, pp.387~393, 1989.

[2] Caudill M., "Using Neural Nets: Representating Knowledge," *AI Expert*, pp.34~41, Dec. 1989.

[3] Don R. Hush and Bill G. Horne, "Progress in Supervised Neural Networks," *IEEE Signal Processing Magazine*, pp.8~39, Jan. 1993.

[4] David E. Rumelhart, Geooffney E. Hinton, and R. I. Willians, "Learning Internal Representations by Error Propagation," in David E. Rumelhart, James L. McClelland, and PDP Research Group (Eds.), *Parallel Distributed Processing*, Vol.1, pp.318~362, MIT Press, 1986.

[5] F. Lisa, J. Carrabina, C. Perez-Vicente, N. Avellana, and E. Valderrama, "Two-bit Weights Are Enough To Solve Vehicle License Recognition Problem," *in Proceedings of International Conference on Neural Networks*, San Francisco, Vol.III, pp.1242~1246, Apr. 1993.

[6] Luisa DE VENA, "Number Plate Recognition by Hierarchical Neural Networks," *in Proceedings of 1993 International Joint Conference on Neural Networks*, Nagoya, Vol.III, pp.2105~2108, Oct. 1993.

[7] Robert Schalkoff, *Pattern Recognition : Statistical, Structural and Neural Approaches*, John Wiley & Sons, Inc., 1992.

[8] Sung-Bae Cho and Jin H. Kim, "Recognition of Large-Set Printed Hangul(Korean Script) by Two-Stage Backpropagation Neural Classifier," *Pattern Recognition*, Vol.25, No.11, pp.1353~1360, Nov. 1992.

[9] Yoh-Han Pao, *Adaptive Pattern Recognition and Neural Networks*, Addison-Wesley Publishing Company, 1989.

[10] INMOS Ltd, *The Transputer Data Book*, inmos, 1989.

Dual-Use Neural Network Pattern Recognition For Automated Imagery Database Query

Tim Rainey, Dean Brettle, and Fred Weingard

Booz, Allen and Hamilton Inc.
8283 Greensboro Drive, Room 594
McLean, VA 22102-3838
Tel : 703 - 902 - 5546
Fax : 703 - 902 - 3663
email : rainey@picard.jmb.bah.com

Robert Sibert and Eric Birnbaum

Federal Bureau of Investigation
Ninth Street & Pennsylvania Ave. N.W.
Washington, DC 20535
Tel : 202 - 324 - 1327
Fax : 202 - 324 - 8201

ABSTRACT

A dual-use neural network technology, called the Statistical - Multiple Object Detection and Location System (S-MODALS), has been developed by Booz•Allen & Hamilton, Inc. over a 5-year period, funded by various Air Force organizations for Automatic Target Recognition (ATR). This conference paper will detail improvements in the MODALS neural network architecture that led to the Statistical - MODALS architecture which has a natural extension to multi-sensor fusion (Visible, IR, SAR) and multi-look evidence accrual for tactical and strategic reconnaissance. Since S-MODALS is a learning system, it is readily adaptable to object recognition problems other than ATR as evidenced by this S-MODALS investigation into the automated database query of DRUGFIRE forensic imagery. The pattern matching problem of microscopic marks for DRUGFIRE shell casings is analogous to the pattern matching problem of targets for the Visible component of the S-MODALS design. That is to say, the physics; phenomenology; discrimination and search strategies; robustness requirements; and error level and confidence level propagation are all of a similar nature.

1.0 Overview of the MODALS Approach

The Multiple Object Detection and Location System (MODALS) distinguishes itself from many classical Automatic Target Recognition (ATR) approaches because it simultaneously detects, segments, and identifies multiple targets in an image [1-4]. Classical ATR approaches carry these operations out independently in a sequential fashion. This sequentially independent approach can result in mistakes at each step, thus reducing the overall system performance to the product of the performances of each step. MODALS consists of three layers each working together to bring about a target identification. The conceptual methodology behind MODALS is quite simple: find features that distinguish the training targets from each other, associate the positions of these features for each training target, and try to find the same set of target features in the same geometry in the test images.

Based on a training target, MODALS learns a set of distinct features. Several features, small squares of pixels, are learned for each training target perspective. These features are used to estimate whether a target occurs at a given location. However, features must be successfully acquired that are effective for both discriminating one target from another and discriminating the targets from background. This discrimination capability is accomplished in MODALS using a neural network learning technique. After learning the features, each feature type and feature location is associated with the desired target type to produce a final neural network ATR performance system, MODALS.

The MODALS performance network consists of three layers: the Feature Extraction Layer, the Spatial Location Layer, and the Object Detection Layer. The Feature Extraction Layer computes matches between each feature and all areas of the test image using a similarity metric. The Feature Extraction Layer's similarity metric is based on minimizing the error between the learned feature and the test image. The similarity metric is invariant to changes in ambient illumination and robust to changes in directional illumination, rotation, scaling, and noise. The Spatial Location Layer locates the best feature matches in locations close to where features were learned in training. These locations are defined by Spatial Location Layer masks. The size and shape of each mask is a function of the desired amount of robustness to rotation and scale. The Spatial Location Layer produces both the position and value of these feature matches for all possible target locations. The last layer of the MODALS system, the Object Detection Layer, is responsible for target detection and identification. Feature and position information corresponding to each training target perspective is combined to accumulate detection evidence for a training target perspective. In parallel to the combination of feature errors, the Object Detection Layer also computes whether the positions of the best feature matches correspond to a valid rigid body rotation. This computation involves the calculation of a Positional Mean Square Error (PMSE), a measure of how much the locations of the detected features correspond to a rigid body rotation of the training target. The combination of feature errors and positional errors results in an error measure for every training target perspective at every possible target location. This error measure can be interpreted as the overall error between the image at that location and each training target perspective. The Object Detection Layer evidence for each training target perspective is spatially competed, resulting in one or more spatially separated potential target detections. After the training target perspective competition, an Object Detection threshold controls which target error measures are low enough to be considered detections. This threshold shifts the ATR system operating characteristics along the classic probability of detection/false alarm ROC curve.

2.0 Probabilistic Modification of MODALS

The Feature Extraction Layer similarity metric is a measure of each feature's normalized mean square error (mse). To obtain the training target perspective output response, MODALS simply averages the normalized mean square errors across the features in a training perspective. This evidence accrual method produces the Object Detection Layer output. Different objects consist of different numbers of features and averaging in error space was the method chosen to measure overall target error in a consistent way. However, this evidence accrual method has two drawbacks. First, it does not take into account the different statistics of different features. For instance, an mse value of 0.1 for a complicated feature may be highly indicative of a target, whereas the same mse value may be a very common response to background for a relatively uniform feature. Second, averaging a few poor mse values with many good mse values can have an unwarranted effect. These few outliers can bias the Object Detection output to the point where it equals the average of many mediocre mse values caused by the background. One of the most evident results of this combination anomaly was the initial, relatively poor performance of MODALS on occluded targets versus unoccluded targets [1]. An evidence accrual method was needed which would compensate for the differences in the statistics of different features, and would not allow a few poor mse values (caused by occluded features) to spoil the Object Detection output.

Ideally, the Feature Extraction output would represent the probabilities that each feature is present, and the Object Detection output would represent the probability that the target is present. If this was the case then, given certain assumptions, Probability Theory provides the following equation for combining the Feature Extraction output:

$$P_O = 1 - \prod(1 - P_{F_j})$$

P_O is the probability that the target is present, P_{F_j} is the probability that feature j is present, and j is 1 to N features.

To interpret this equation, remember that P_{F_j} is the probability that feature j is present, so $(1-P_{F_j})$ is the probability that feature j is absent. $\prod(1-P_{F_j})$ is the probability that all features are absent (assuming independence). So, $1-\prod(1-P_{F_j})$ is the probability that not all features are absent (i.e. at least one feature is present). Therefore, if we can determine the probability that each feature is present, we have a method for determining if the target is present.

Can we determine P_{F_j} given the mse output of the Feature Extraction similarity metric (f_j)? In Probability Theory, this is called a conditional probability and is given by the formula:

$$P(F_j \mid f_j) = P(f_j \mid F_j) \, P(F_j) \, / \, P(f_j)$$

where $P(F_j \mid f_j)$ is the probability that feature j is present given an mse of f_j, $P(f_j \mid F_j)$ is the probability distribution of f_j if the feature is actually present, $P(F_j)$ is the probability that the feature is actually present regardless of the mse value (i.e. the target density), and $P(f_j)$ is the probability distribution of f_j regardless of whether the feature is present or not.

All measured mse values can be used to approximate the distribution $P(f_j)$. However, only those mse values measured in the presence of the feature can be used to approximate the distribution $P(f_j \mid F_j)$. In order to accurately approximate the function $P(f_j \mid F_j)$, it is necessary to have a large number of examples of each feature for training. This implies a large number of examples of training target perspectives. In its current form, MODALS requires only a small number of training target perspectives. This characteristic is one of its advantages. It is both undesirable and impractical to attempt to directly approximate the function $P(f_j | F_j)$ by increasing the number of training images required. Something other than $P(F_j | f_j)$ must be used to compute the Object Detection output.

As mentioned above, $P(f_j)$ is a distribution which is fairly easy to approximate, however, it is a probability *distribution* and not a raw probability. $P(mse < f_j)$, called the *cumulative* probability, is the integral of $P(f_j)$ from zero to f_j. $P(mse < f_j)$ represents the probability of observing an mse value less than f_j (regardless of whether the feature is present or not). Since the features are taken from the target and the features are rare in the background, the mse and $P(mse < f_j)$ will be lower when the feature is present than when it is absent. The S-MODALS evidence accrual method uses (as the Object Detection output) the probability of observing a set of mse values which are less than the measured set of mse values :

$$o = \prod P(mse < f_j)$$

Here, a high Object Detection output indicates that doing better than all the measured mse values is fairly common. A low Object Detection output indicates that doing better than all the measured mse values is rather uncommon. So, low Object Detection outputs indicate targets, while high Object Detection outputs indicate background. Note that a $P(mse < f_j)$ close to one (e.g. from an occluded feature) will have little effect on the product, whereas a very small $P(mse < f_j)$ will have an extreme effect.

The advantage to using $P(mse < f_j)$ instead of the mse value f_j can be seen in the following example. Consider two features F_1 and F_2 both taken from the same target perspective. F_1 is not very distinctive (e.g. almost entirely uniform), and F_2 is very distinctive (e.g. a corner or edge). Clearly an mse value of 0.1 for F_1 is much less indicative of a target than an mse value of 0.1 for F_2. The probability of getting an mse value less than 0.1 for F_1 might be 90% whereas the probability of getting an mse value less than 0.1 for F_2 might be 5%. Moreover, the probability of both mse values being less than 0.1 is 0.05*0.90=4.5%. Note that combining the mse values directly would have meant assigning equal confidence to the presence of both features, when in fact their is much less confidence in the presence of F_1 than F_2.

Until now in this discussion, we have been assuming that the Spatial Location Layer mask is only one pixel (i.e. there is no difference between the Spatial Location output and the Feature Extraction output). We will now remove this assumption. In the original formulation of MODALS, the Spatial Location output was simply the minimum Feature Extraction mse over some elliptical region. If we continue to do this, a method is needed for appropriately combining Spatial Location values. We can not combine Spatial Location values directly, but we can combine the probability of getting lower than a Spatial Location value the same way we combined the probability of getting lower than an Feature Extraction value.

$$o = \prod P(\min mse < s_j)$$

How is $P(\min mse < s_j)$ related to $P(mse < f_j)$ if s_j is the minimum of f_j over some region? $P(\min mse < s_j)$ is the probability that the minimum mse is less than the observed minimum mse (i.e. s_j). This would be true if one or more mses in the region were less than s_j. Put another way, this would be true if not all mses in the region are more than s_j. The probability that any one mse in the region is greater than s_j is

$$1 - P(mse < s_j)$$

The probability that all mses in the region are more than s_j is

$$(1 - P(mse < s_j))^{N_j}$$

where N_j is the number of pixels in the region for feature j. The probability that not all mses in the region are greater than s_j is

$$P(\min mse < s_j) = 1 - (1 - P(mse < s_j))^{N_j}$$
$$1$$

so, the formula for the Object Detection output becomes (Note that this degenerates to our earlier formula when N_j equals one.)

$$o = \prod (1-(1-P(mse < s_j))^{N_j})$$

The above formula represents the theoretical basis for the Statistical - MODALS evidence accrual technique. This evidence accrual method compensates for the differences in the statistics of different features, and does not allow a few poor mse values (caused by occluded features) to spoil the Object Detection output. Figure 1 shows a set of representative S-MODALS test imagery and Figure 2 shows the improvement of S-MODALS versus MODALS on occluded targets. The same evidence accrual technique can also combine evidence from different sensors, different representations, and over time. This formula provides S-MODALS with the ability to perform multi-sensor and multi-look evidence accrual for tactical reconnaissance.

3.0 DRUGFIRE

Recognizing the benefits which could be derived from the application of state-of-the-art computer technologies to the discipline of forensic firearms identification, the FBI has developed the DRUGFIRE system. DRUGFIRE is presently a database driven multimedia imaging system which significantly increases the effectiveness of forensic laboratories in maintaining and searching either their own individual or shared multi-agency unsolved case firearms evidence files. In the latter case, this new technology supports the establishment of regional computerized firearms evidence clearinghouse operations which facilitate the sharing and linking of forensic information between regionally clustered forensic laboratories. In so doing, it materially extends the capabilities of forensic firearms identification examiners.

Since the introduction of the ballistic comparison microscope in 1925, which allows side-by-side examination of the microscopic marks on two bullets or cartridge cases, firearms examinations have been limited to the simultaneous comparison of two specimens on the same microscope. DRUGFIRE seamlessly integrates a relational database, video, digital image processing and manipulation, audio and telecommunication technologies in a manner which emulates and augments the functions of the ballistic comparison microscope. In the old microscopic technique, two cartridge cases are presented in the same field of view under the microscope. An optical hairline divides the two cartridge case images from each other. When similar microscopic markings are found on both cartridge cases, the analyst can overlay the two images in an attempt to create a continuous image of the particular marks being analyzed. The overlay is accomplished by manipulating the optical hairline, cartridge case holders and lights of the comparison microscopes. The DRUGFIRE system digitally emulates this manual process on the workstation monitor. Through the use of software, digital and video cartridge case imagery can be manipulated in the same fashion as having the two physical shell casings under the microscope. The software permits the scaling, rotating, and translating of the imagery, as well as edge enhancement and contrast/brightness control. The digital images of the microscopic marks on representative fired cartridge cases and shotshell casings are stored in a relational database and linked to the appropriate alphanumeric encodings for the descriptive forensic firearms identification characteristics such as caliber type, firing pin impression type, and breech/bolt face mark type. The images, which depict the highly reproducible microscopic features that cannot be effectively classified by alphanumeric encodings, are captured in accordance with standardized DRUGFIRE system formats and protocols and are annotated so as to indicate their orientation and the presence of distinctive features. A database query based on the descriptive forensic firearms identification characteristics returns the cartridge case images in a tile (5 images x 5 images) format for the analyst to visually inspect and select the most similar images for more comprehensive side-by-side comparison.

It has been recognized that the effectiveness of the DRUGFIRE system could be substantially improved through additional automation of the querying process. The querying of the database and the searching of a large number of images is still a rather labor-intensive process in the present system. This automated enhancement will greatly increase the effectiveness of searching the microscopic marks in the DRUGFIRE system, particularly when stored image files become voluminous and difficult to search using only the descriptive forensic firearms identification characteristics of the current DRUGFIRE system. For the DRUGFIRE application, the pattern recognition capabilities of S-MODALS directly exploits the highly reproducible microscopic marks that cannot be effectively classified by alphanumeric encodings unlike the quantitative descriptive forensic firearms identification characteristics.

4.0 DRUGFIRE Image Database Query With S-MODALS

In conjunction with the FBI, Booz•Allen's Advanced Computational Technologies Practice investigated the application of S-MODALS to the imagery data from the DRUGFIRE Imagery Database. The objective of the investigation was to closely approximate the hit performance level of a firearms examiner using an automated pattern recognition system. S-MODALS was trained on the image of the primer area of only one fired cartridge case from a particular criminal case. S-MODALS then processed all of the other candidate cartridge case images of the same firearm caliber type retrieved from the DRUGFIRE Imagery Database. The S-MODALS database query produces a prioritized list of cartridge case image matches for the forensic expert from best match to worst match. The investigation included testing 9 cartridge case images covering four different firearm caliber types (.40S&W, 10mm Auto, .32 Auto, and .380 Auto), where each firearms caliber type had a different number of test cartridge case images (45, 26, 30, 176). In each test the top match returned by S-MODALS was the training image. The next match returned by S-MODALS was an actual DRUGFIRE hit. For the .380 Auto fired cartridge case image, S-MODALS returned the two known hits as the top two candidates among 176 cartridge case images. In each instance where there was more than one cartridge case to match with the training image, S-MODALS reduced the imagery search space down to its smallest achievable amount, except in one incident. The exception was that S-MODALS rejected one of the actual DRUGFIRE hits because the cartridge case image's magnification was much smaller than its labeling in the database. In this incident S-MODALS actually performed quality control on the imagery.

Based on the promising potential expressed by this investigation the FBI is presently "blind" testing the S-MODALS technology under a three phase test. Each phase includes searching a database of 200 9mm Luger cartridge case images for hits with four unknown cartridge case images. Since twenty-five cartridge case images make up one tile, the test consists of a potentially common operational condition where a firearms examiner must search 8 tiles of imagery. Upon recently completing phase one, the performance of the S-MODALS pattern recognition capabilities has ranked all of the DRUGFIRE hits within the top five matches except for one instance when a catridge case was placed on the second tile as the 38th match overall. Figure 3 shows the top four S-MODALS candidates for one of the unknown cartridge case tests. The top three candidates are related DRUGFIRE hits. The fourth match is the next best match.

5.0 Conclusion

A neural network technology, called the Statistical - Multiple Object Detection and Location System, was developed for multi-sensor fusion (Visible, IR, SAR) and multi-look evidence accrual for tactical and strategic reconnaissance. Since S-MODALS is a learning system, it is readily adaptable to object recognition problems other than ATR as evidenced by this S-MODALS investigation into the automated database query of DRUGFIRE forensic imagery. The pattern matching problem of microscopic marks for DRUGFIRE shell casings is analogous to the pattern matching problem of targets for the Visible component of the S-MODALS design. Other on-going investigations include applying S-MODALS to face recognition and medical imagery for the Air Force.

6.0 References

1. W. A. Thoet, T. G. Rainey, D. W. Brettle, L. A. Slutz, F. S. Weingard, "ANVIL neural network program for three-dimensional automatic target recognition," *Opt. Eng.* 31(12), 2532-2539 (1992).

2. W. A. Thoet, T. G. Rainey, L. A. Slutz, F. S. Weingard, "Recent Results From The ANVIL Neural Network Program For 3D Automatic Target Recognition," *Proc. 2nd Automatic Target Recognizer Systems and Technology Conf.*, Vol 1, 329-342 (1992).

3. W. A. Thoet, T. G. Rainey, L. A. Slutz, F. S. Weingard, "Interim Results From A Neural Network 3D Automatic Target Recognition Program," *in OE/Aerospace Sensing, Proc. SPIE* 1700, 64-72 (1992).

4. Tim Rainey, William Thoet, Dean Brettle, Russell Leighton, "Recent Results From The Multi-Sensor Fusion Neural Network Program For Tactical Reconnaissance," *Proc. 3rd Automatic Target Recognizer Systems and Technology Conf.*, Vol 2, 1-12 (1993).

5. ATRWG, "Appendix 1 To Automatic Target Recognizer Definitions and Performance Measures: ATR Truth Normalized Performance Measures Beyond Level 1 Discrimination", ATRWG No. 88-005 (1988).

6. ATRWG, "Target Recognizer Definitions and Performance Measures," ATRWG No. 86-001 (February 1986).

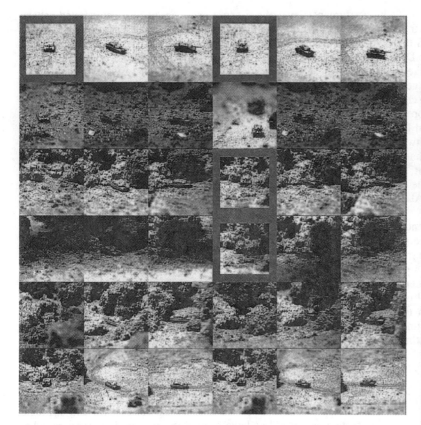

Figure 1. Sample of S-MODALS test imagery

Figure 3. S-MODALS output for DRUGFIRE imagery

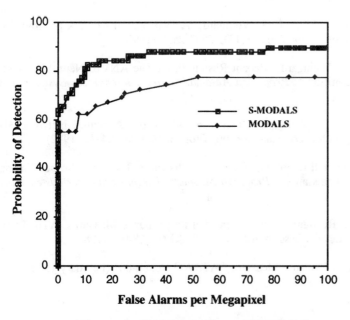

Figure 2. S-MODALS vs. MODALS for Occluded Targets

III-172

Medial Axis Transform Based Features and a Neural Network for Human Chromosome Classification

Lerner, B., Rosenberg, B., Levinstein, M., Guterman, H., Dinstein, I. and Romem, Y.*
Department of Electrical and Computer Engineering
Ben-Gurion University of the Negev
Beer-Sheva, Israel 84105

* The Institute of Medical Genetics, Soroka Medical Center
Beer-Sheva, Israel 84105

Abstract

Medial axis transform (MAT) based features and a two-layer feedforward neural network were used in this study for human chromosome classification. Two approaches to the MAT, the "skeleton" and the piecewise linear (PWL), were examined. The medial axis based on the "skeleton" approach, as well as, the chromosome classification results based on this approach were slightly better than these of the PWL approach. Several chromosome features, like the density profile, the centrometric index and the length of the chromosome, as well as, combinations of them, were tested. The probability of correct training set classification using all the available features and the neural network classifier was almost perfect (99.3-99.6%). The probability of correct test set classification was greater than 97% using features based on the "PWL" approach and over 98% using features based on the "skeleton" approach.

1. Introduction

Human chromosome inspection is a vital task in cytogenetics, especially in clinical prenatal analysis, genetical syndrome diagnosis (e.g., Down's syndrome), cancer pathology research and environmentally induced mutagen dosimetry [7], [10]. Cells used for chromosome inspection are taken mostly from amniotic fluid or blood samples. One of the inspection aims is to detect deviations from normal cell structure. Abnormal cells can have an excess or deficit of a chromosome and/or structural defects like breaks, fragments or translocations (exchange of genetic material between chromosomes). However, even today this inspection is performed manually in most of the cytogenetic laboratories in a time consuming, repetitive and expensive procedure [9], [10].

Efforts to develop automatic chromosome classification techniques have been made through the last 40 years. However, all the efforts to make the chromosome analysis automatic had limited success and poor classification results compare to those of a trained cytotechnician [2], [7], [9], [10]. Some of the reasons for the poor performances are the inadequate use of the expert knowledge and experience and the insufficient ability to make comparisons and/or eliminations among chromosomes within the same metaphase. In addition, the systems always require the operator interaction to separate touching and/or overlapping chromosomes and to verify the classification results [7], [10].

Neural networks make it possible to overcome most of these limitations. This is mainly because they permit application of expert knowledge and experience through network training. Furthermore, human chromosome classification based on neural networks requires no *a priori* assumptions or knowledge of the data to be classified as some conventional methods need. Finally, it is well known that the problems best solved by neural networks are those that humans do well, and classification of chromosomes is one of them.

\# This work was supported in part by the Paul Ivanier Center for Robotics and Production Management, Ben-Gurion University, Beer-Sheva, Israel.

2. Feature description

Appropriate feature description is considered to be one of the most important part of classification procedures, and in human chromosome classification it is probably the most important one. In some studies, global features, like the histogram of gray levels [3] or the 2D Fourier transform components [4], have been used. In this study, we have employed 3 types of features: the density profile (d.p) along the medial axis [1], [5], [7], the centrometric index (c.i) (the ratio of the short arm length to the whole chromosome length) [2], [5], [7] and the length (lng) of the chromosome [5], [7]. The Medial Axis Transform (MAT) is almost always required for the extraction of these features.

2.1 The MAT

The MAT is widely used as a convenient transformation for elongated objects, e.g., in character recognition or chromosome analysis where the width of the objects contains little (if any at all) useful information. The MAT of an object cannot only reduce storage and time requirements, but also to preserve the topological properties of the object.

Two different approaches to MAT were used in this work, namely, the "skeleton" and the PWL approaches [5]. The "skeleton" approach is based on finding a preliminary medial axis of chromosome via the realization of the fire front's propagation and extinction [11]. This preliminary medial axis is further processed to get one extended continuous medial axis. Removing irrelevant points of the preliminary medial axis on one hand and completion of necessary points on the other hand complete the postprocessing of the medial axis in this approach. The second approach employs a piecewise linear (PWL) approximation [2], [5] to the medial axis. The PWL is preferred over the use of existing polynomial approximation techniques whenever a chromosome is not straight [2].

2.2 Feature extraction

The MAT in both approaches enables us to transform the 2D image of the chromosome to 1D representation. By calculating lines perpendicular to the medial axis points we can integrate (or average) the intensities (gray levels) of all the image pixels along these lines and to obtain a density profile (d.p).

The method we have used in this study to calculate the centrometric index (c.i) is based on searching for the closest pair of opposite contour points on the clipped contours of a chromosome [5], similarly to the method described in [2]. However, instead of using an exhaustive search for the closest pair we searched for the closest pair along the lines perpendicular to the medial axis. No fundamental difference in results of the two methods is expected. However, our method is faster than the method in [2] (there is no exhaustive search of all the pairs of opposite points). The length of the chromosome was calculated along the medial axis.

All the features were further normalized. The d.p feature vector was normalized both in length and in value. Normalizing in length yields suitable feature representation (all classified vectors are in the same dimension) and invariance to scale change. The length of the normalized d.p vector was set to be 64 both from chromosome length and from practical considerations. The 64 values of the d.p vector, the centrometric index and the chromosome length were normalized into the [-0.5,0.5] range, in agreement with the MLP requirements.

3. The neural network classifier

In this research, a two-layer feedforward neural network trained by the backpropagation (bp) learning algorithm [8] was chosen for the chromosome classification. The bp algorithm is an error driven parameter estimation algorithm where the objective is to minimize the output squared error function by adjusting interconnection weights and node thresholds. The network was initialize using random weights in the [-1,1] range. The number of hidden units of the network was set according to the Principal Components Analysis (PCA), applied to the feature vectors. The number was set to be the number of the largest eigenvalues, the sum of which accounts for more than a pre-specified percentage of the sum of all the eigenvalues [6]. This pre-specified percentage has been called by us "var". In the implementations, the "var" parameter was set to values of 70-90%.

4. Data set

Images of amniotic fluid cells were acquired from the Institute of Medical Genetics of Soroka Medical Center, Beer-Sheva. The pictures were obtained with the aid of a light microscope and captured by a CCD camera (Cohu). The pictures were digitized with a frame grabber (VISIONplus-AT). The size of the digitized picture was 512 X 768 pixels and each pixel was represented by 1 byte (256 gray levels). No pre-processing techniques were applied. The segmentation was done manually using a graphical software package on a 486 PC computer. Chromosomes of 5 different types, namely types "2", "4", "13", "19" and "x" were extracted [3], [4] from more than 150 different cells.

For each chromosome the MAT was extracted and the 66 features (64 d.p + c.i + lng) were computed using the procedure described in [5]. Several variations of features were tested to evaluate their importance to the classification procedure, e.g., d.p alone, d.p + c.i, d.p + c.i + lng and c.i + lng. The d.p features were extracted both using the integral representation and the average representation and in both approaches: "skeleton" and PWL.

5. Results

The input vector to the neural network was either 2 or 64-66 dimensional (depend on the type of the features). The output vector was 5 dimensional with one component set to "1" (actually 0.9) for the correct classification and "0" (actually 0.1) elsewhere.

Optimization of the neural network parameters regarding the chromosome data is described elsewhere [6]. The learning rate (μ) was set to be 0.026, the momentum constant (α) to be 0.97 and the training cycle was set to be 4000 epochs, although only 500-1000 epochs were required to get almost the best results. Training and test vectors were chosen randomly from the same data set where the number of training vectors was 70-90% of all the vectors (depending on the experiment) and the remaining vectors were reserved for testing. All the simulations were repeated (at least) 3 times, with the same network parameters but with different sets of randomly chosen training vectors, and the results were averaged.

5.1 The PWL vs. the "skeleton" approach to the MAT

Two major conclusions can be made [5] while comparing the PWL and the "skeleton" approaches.

(a). (b).

Figure 1. A comparison of the (a). "skeleton" and (b). PWL approaches to the MAT.

The first is that the medial axis of the "skeleton" approach is finer than the axis of the PWL approach and follows very accurately the chromosome band pattern (Figure 1). The second conclusion, which can be concluded from Figure 2, is that while the probability of correct training set classification is similar in both approaches, the probability of correct test set classification is larger using the "skeleton" features (in about 3-5%). Both conclusions seem to be very close related. Figure 2 depicts the classification results of an experiment in which the percentage of training vectors ("per") is 70-90% of all the vectors and the "var" parameter is set to be 70-90%.

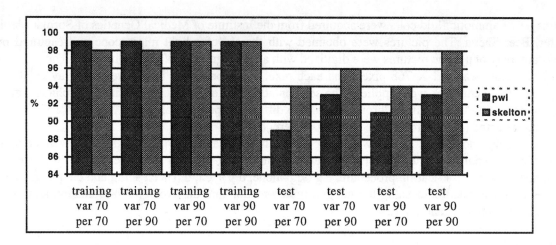

Figure 2. Classification based on the density profile features.

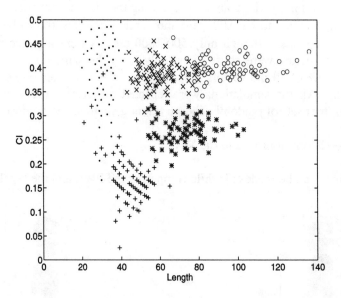

Figure 3. Chromosome clustering into a 2-dimensional feature space spanned by the centrometric index (c.i) and the chromosome length (lng). ("o"- chromosome type "2", "∗"- chromosome type "4", "+"- chromosome type "13", "·"- chromosome type "19" and "x"- chromosome type "x").

5.2 Feature evaluation

The relative importance for the classification procedure of four sets of features was examined. The first set includes only the density profile (d.p) features, while the second set includes, in addition, the centrometric index (c.i). The length of the chromosomes (lng) is the additional feature in the third set. The forth set includes only the (c.i) and the (lng) features. To learn about the significance of these two last features, we have plotted in Figure 3 the two of them one against the other for the entire data set. We can see that these two important features are almost sufficient for the classification of the chromosome data into it 5 types. However, these two features would not be enough when we will try to classify the chromosome data to all its 24 types.

The probability of correct classification of the neural network, using the 4 sets of features, for the PWL approach, is given in Figure 4. The probability of correct classification in the training and in the test sets using the first set of features (d.p) was 99.15-99.5% and 89.3-92.9%, respectively, for various combinations of the two parameters- "per" and "var". The probability of classification of the second set of features (d.p + c.i) was 99.3-99.5% and 92.1-96.45% for training and test, respectively, and this of the third set (d.p + c.i + lng) was 99.3-99.6% and 94.2-97.2% for training and test, respectively. The probability, using only the (c.i) and the (lng) features, was 93.05-94.4% for training and 86.9-92.9% for the test. These results indicate that the 2 features are almost equally important as the 64 d.p features for the classification of the 5 particular classes (types of chromosomes). This conclusion will be definitely changed whenever all the 24 chromosome types will be used. The probabilities achieved using the "skeleton" approach were equal or little higher compare to these of the PWL. It can be clearly seen from the figure the importance of combining different features, especially whenever the "var" is relatively low (small amount of information is retained by the PCA).

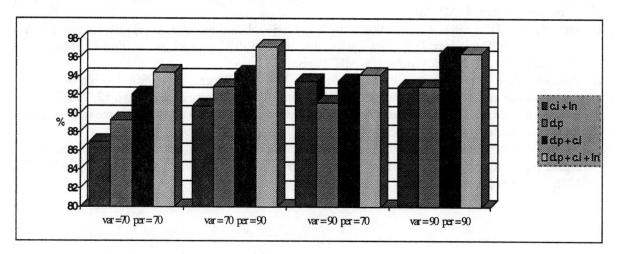

Figure 4. The probability of correct test classification using the 4 sets of features and the PWL approach to the MAT.

6. Discussion and Conclusions

Medial axis transform based features and a two-layer feedforward neural network were used in this study for human chromosome classification. Two approaches to the MAT, the "skeleton" and the PWL, were examined. The medial axis based on the "skeleton" approach, as well as, the chromosome classification results based on this approach were slightly better than these of the PWL approach. Several typical chromosome features, like the density profile, the centrometric index and the length of the chromosome, as well as, combinations of them, were tested. When classifying only 5 types of chromosomes, as was done in this study, the relative importance of the centrometric index and of the length of the chromosome is very high. The probability of correct training set classification using all the available features and the neural network classifier was almost perfect (99.3-99.6%). The probability of correct test set classification was greater than 97% using features based on the PWL approach and over 98% using features based on the "skeleton" approach.

7. References

1. Granlund, G.H. (1976). Identification of human chromosome by using integrated density profile. *IEEE Transactions on Biomedical Engineering*, **BME-23**, 182-192.
2. Groen, F.C.A., ten Kate, T.K., Smeulders, A.W.M. & Young, I.T. (1989). Human chromosome classification based on local band descriptors. *Pattern Recognition Letters*, **9**, 211-222.
3. Lerner, B., Guterman, H. & Dinstein, I. (1992). On classification of human chromosomes. *Neural Networks for Learning, Recognition and Control*, a research conference at Boston University, May 14-16.
4. Lerner, B., Guterman, H., Dinstein, I. & Romem, Y. (1993). Classification of human chromosomes by two-dimensional Fourier transform components. *WCNN'93*, Portland, July 11-15, 793-796.
5. Lerner, B., Guterman, H., Dinstein, I. & Romem, Y. (1993). Medial axis transform based features and a neural network for human chromosome classification. (Submitted for publication).
6. Lerner, B., Guterman, H., Dinstein, I. & Romem, Y. (1993). Human chromosome classification using multilayer perceptron neural network. (Submitted for publication).
7. Piper, J., Granum, E., Rutovitz, D. & Ruttledge, H. (1980). Automation of chromosome analysis. *Signal Processing*, **2**, 203-221.
8. Rumelhart, D.E., Hinton, G.E. & Williams, R.J. (1986). Learning internal representations by error propagation. In Rumelhart, D.E., McClelland, J.L. and the PDP research group, *Parallel Distributed Processing*, vol. 1, chap. 8, Cambridge: MIT Press.
9. Vanderheydt, L., Oosterlinck, A., Van Daele, J. & Van Den Berghe, H. (1980). Design of a graph-representation and a fuzzy-classifier for human chromosomes. *Pattern Recognition*, **12**, 201-210.
10. Wu, Q., Suetens, P. & Oosterlinck, A. (1987). Toward an expert system for chromosome analysis. *Knowledge-Based Systems*, **1**, 43-52.
11. Xia, Y. (1989). Skeletonization via the realization of the fire front's propagation and extinction in digital binary shapes. *IEEE Transactions on Pattern Analysis and Machine Intelligence*, **11**, 1076-1086.

Neural Network Classifier to Threshold Images from 3D Microcomputed Tomography

L. A. Feldkamp, G. Jesion, G. V. Puskorius, and D. J. Kubinski

Research Laboratory, Ford Motor Company
3135 Scientific Research Laboratories Building
P.O. Box 2053
Dearborn, Michigan 48121-2053

ABSTRACT

We describe the use of neural networks to perform context dependent thresholding of grayscale three-dimensional images of trabecular and cortical bone as measured *in vitro* by high-resolution x-ray computed tomography ("micro-CT"). Classifiers are constructed on the basis of a simple model of the blurring necessarily associated with the tomographic measurement. We discuss the procedure used for training and testing and illustrate the application to actual experimental data.

1 Introduction

The ability to measure with high (better than 100 micrometer) resolution the three-dimensional structure of small specimens of human and animal bone has the potential for substantially increasing understanding of many aspects of growth, remodeling, and mechanics of bone [1–3]. Typical cross-sectional slices extracted from full data sets are shown in Fig. 1. For purposes of the present discussion, it is sufficient to regard the measuring system as generating an estimate of density at each point of a three-dimensional lattice superimposed on the object of interest. In the present case, the lattice spacing is 50 μm and a typical cross-sectional dimension of a bone specimen is somewhat less than 1 cm (i.e., 10000 μm). The density estimates, which were reconstructed from two-dimensional images, are approximately the convolution of the actual density of the object with a spatially isotropic resolution function. The full width at half maximum (FWHM) of the system as considered here is approximately 59 μm.

Many structures of interest in trabecular bone, which is often described as consisting of plates and rods, are of order 100–200 μm, i.e., not much larger than the resolution of the measuring system. The accessible structures in cortical (dense) bone are the marrow cavities, which can have dimensions smaller than 100 μm. Though both trabecular and cortical structures are typically clearly visible in images such as Fig. 1, quantitative analysis such as by use of stereological techniques requires each sample point to be labelled as foreground (bone) or background (non-bone). A simple threshold, either that used in Fig. 1 or any other, is easily seen to be inadequate. The underlying cause is the interaction of measurement resolution with structures of different sizes and degrees of curvature. For equal intrinsic bone mineral densities, the measured density (or gray level) that distinguishes bone from non-bone will be higher in the vicinity of a flat or concave bone surface than near a convex surface. For example, the image gray level in the center of an easily visible cortical cavity is as high as that of much of the bone in the trabecular region. Our approach is thus to base our estimate of a particular lattice point's classification not only on its own measured density values but also on its spatial context, i.e., on the densities of its close neighbors.

2 Construction of Input Vectors

Input vectors are obtained by moving a volumetric window through the data. On the basis of preliminary experiments, we have chosen a 33-element input vector, consisting of the central point and the 32 neighbors located within 2 lattice spacings. This choice is a compromise between retaining as much context information as possible and minimizing the number of network parameters by restricting the number of input variables.

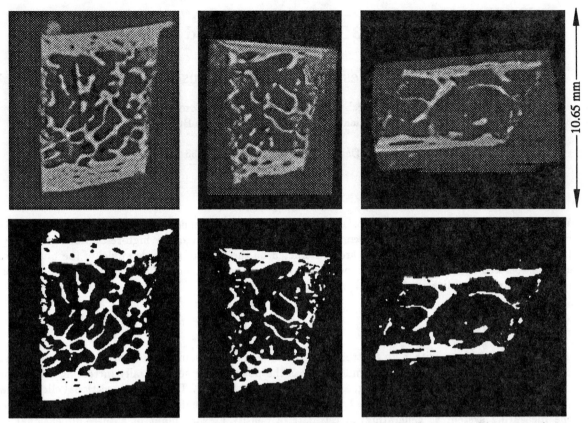

10.65 mm

Figure 1: Tomographically reconstructed slices from three different human iliac crest core biopsy specimens are shown in the top panels. A fixed-threshold binary version of each slice is also shown. Within each specimen cortical bone appears at the top and bottom, while the open structure of trabecular bone occupies the remainder of the volume. The plastic in which the specimens were embedded is visible, as is debris resulting from the process of obtaining the specimens. The scale of size is the same for the horizontal and vertical directions.

3 Generation of Training and Testing Sets

It was not feasible to obtain experimentally a large, representative selection of **correctly labelled** examples, since available higher resolution imaging methods, e.g., light microscopy, are largely limited to two dimensions. (We have, however, used direction microscopic examination as a standard in evaluating analyses based on data thresholded by earlier methods [3].) As an alternative, we have generated input-output training pairs from mathematical "phantoms" constructed to possess curvatures and structural thicknesses that are representative for this application. Such a phantom, shown in Fig. 2, consists of a set of concentric spherical shells of unit density. Spherical symmetry was chosen to avoid embedding unwarranted anisotropy into the classifier. Both locally convex and locally concave foreground/background interfaces are present. This is important, since trabecular surfaces are frequently convex, while the bone surface as viewed from cortical cavities is predominantly concave.

The phantom is folded with isotropic Gaussian resolution (FWHM 59 μm). An input vector is generated by sampling the blurred phantom at a selected central position and at 32 neighboring samples on a 50 micrometer lattice. The corresponding target output value is the binary value of the unblurred phantom at the central point. Both training and testing instances are generated by selecting randomly placed instances. Our initial trial utilized uniformly distributed training instances. We observed, however, that most errors in testing came from the regions very close to the foreground-background interfaces and disproportionately represented regions of low radius of curvature. Hence, we adopted an alternative procedure in which we preferentially select training instances from regions that straddle the interface radii. This has the effect

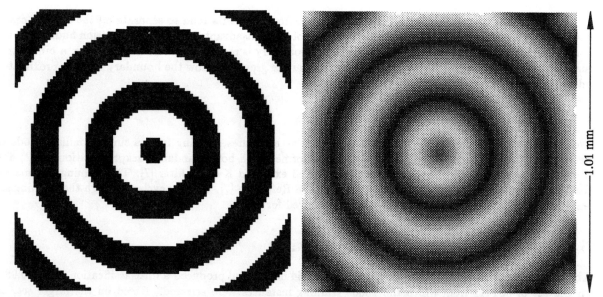

Figure 2: The center slices of the phantom from which training vectors are obtained. The binary phantom at left is subjected to Gaussian resolution to produce the blurred phantom on the right. The thickness of the shells represents 100 μm.

of excluding from training the approximately 40 percent of possible instances that are centered on largely uniform regions. Further, we give more weight to instances near surfaces of high curvature by selecting the regions that straddle each interface with equal probability. In the results reported here, we used training sets of 20000 instances. For testing we employed 531441 instances selected uniformly from a similar phantom whose interface radii interleave those of Fig. 2.

4 Networks

4.1 Binary Tree Network

Our implementation of a binary-tree network, based on ideas presented in [4], was described briefly in [5]. Using a conjugate-gradient algorithm, each node of the network generates for the collection of instances presented to it the Fisher linear discriminant direction in the space of the input vector. The instances are then projected onto this direction. A splitting point along this direction is determined on the basis of minimum entropy [4] or minimum number of misclassifications. If the node branches, the entropy criterion is employed; if the node is terminal, the minimum errors criterion is used. One way for the node to be terminal is for the split to be pure (i.e., for the instances presented to the node in training to be linearly separable), in which case the two criteria yield the same split point. If the split is not pure, the node may still be made terminal if it yields insufficient entropy reduction or if fewer than a specified number of instances would be propagated to each of its prospective branches. Finally, a branch of a nonterminal node may itself be made terminal if too few instances are assigned to it or if the entropy of the ensemble of instances is smaller than a specified value.

Such termination criteria are an attempt to optimize the generalization capability of the resulting network by not overfitting the training data. Determining the optimal growth of binary tree classifiers has been the subject of considerable discussion [6], and we recognize that *a priori* criteria are likely to be less than optimal. In the present case, however, we have plentiful examples beyond those used directly for training, permitting us to perform a simple backward pruning to minimize the misclassification rate. (In order that a node made terminal in the pruning process can be given the split point that minimized errors on the original training set, we retain during training both the bias weight that corresponds to the split for minimum entropy and the bias weight for minimum number of errors.)

A potential advantage of tree networks is that the first few nodes tend to separate off the obvious cases, saving time in training, testing, and application. A potential disadvantage is that the decision boundaries are constructed from hyperplanes. If a curved decision boundary is required for best performance, a binary tree may run out of training instances before enough nodes are grown to allow the boundary to be approximated adequately.

4.2 Layered Networks

We trained conventional layered networks of several architectures, ranging from a single nonlinear node to networks with two hidden layers. Training was performed with both standard backpropagation (SBP) and a method, called NDEKF, based on a node-decoupled extended Kalman filter [7]. The training parameters for NDEKF were the default parameters described in Reference [7]. Twenty cycles through the training set were used for NDEKF, while 200 cycles were employed for SBP.

5 Results of Training and Testing

The binary tree generated from the training set had 44 nodes, and produced a misclassification rate of 0.98% on the set of 531441 from which the 20000 training instances were selected. Based on the larger set, an optimal pruning was carried out, reducing the tree to 34 nodes and the misclassification rate to 0.94%. When applied to the 531441 independent instances of the testing phantom, the error rate was 2.2%.

Taken together, the nodes beyond the root node make a small but important contribution to classification accuracy, at a cost of somewhat in excess of a factor of two in the average computation time required to classify an instance; if the tree is restricted to the root node, the misclassification rates are 1.4% and 2.5% on the original and testing phantoms, respectively.

Using the NDEKF approach, a single nonlinear node yields an error rate of 0.11% on the original phantom and 0.18% on the testing phantom. Standard backpropagation did not do quite this well, but the error rates of 0.29% on the original phantom and 0.31% on the testing phantom are still very good. (It must be mentioned that many trials were required before we found SBP parameters that led to effective training.)

We also employed SBP and NDEKF to train single-hidden-layer networks containing 2, 3, and 4 hidden nodes and various networks with two hidden layers. Though several performed very well, none of these larger networks proved more effective at generalization than the single-node NDEKF-trained classifier.

The weights of both the first node of the tree network and the single node of the network trained by NDEKF display considerable cubic symmetry, reflecting the symmetry of the phantom which is used to generate the training sets. This suggests that a symmetrized version of the weight vector of the single-node network would be effective. Carrying out the symmetrization by averaging appropriate weights resulted in approximately the same performance on the testing set as noted above. By averaging input-vector elements related by symmetry, the input vector can be reduced to 5 elements. We did this and retrained single-node classifiers using both SBP and NDEKF. Training proceeds more rapidly and the misclassification rates in testing are virtually identical to those reported above.

In order to assure that the outstanding performance of the NDEKF-trained single-node classifier is not overly sensitive to the resolution used in creating the training and testing instances, we repeated the testing with instances generated with resolutions smaller (54 μm) and larger (64 μm) than the original. The error rates were very good, 0.34% and 0.21%, respectively, indicating a considerable degree of robustness. In a further test, the foreground and background of the original phantom were reversed. The error rate for this was 0.11%.

6 Application to Experimental Data

From the standpoint of neural networks, the relevant generalization has already been discussed. However, from a practical standpoint, the important consideration is performance on experimentally obtained data. This performance, in turn, is influenced by several factors that are not addressed by the evaluation of network performance just presented. Primary among these is the degree to which the simple model used in creating the phantom reflects the true transfer function of the measurement process. In particular, our model as

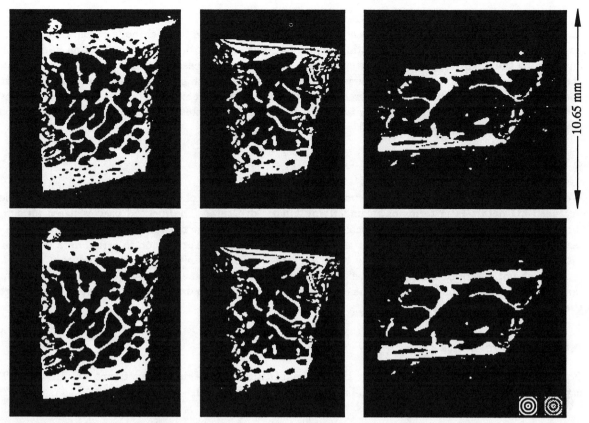

Figure 3: The slices of Fig. 1 classified by the binary-tree network (top) and by the NDEKF-trained single-node network (bottom). For reference, images of the phantom in binary and blurred forms are shown in proper scale in the bottom-right corner.

presented does not include statistical noise, which is certainly present experimentally. Further, the phantom used to generate examples for training and testing does not model either spatial variations in the intrinsic mineral density or variations in the density of the material in non-bone regions.

With these cautions in mind, the trained networks can be applied to experimental data. The density (more properly, linear attenuation coefficient) range of the data must be scaled to the range of densities of the blurred phantom. This is accomplished by creating density histograms for the entire 3D experimental data set and the 3D phantom, and then matching central measures of their respective foreground and background peaks. This permits the same trained network to be applied to a succession of data sets for which the relation between mineral density and measured attenuation coefficient varies, as might be caused by slightly different x-ray primary energies.

In Fig. 3 we display the results of applying the optimally pruned binary tree and the NDEKF-trained single-node classifier to the data of Fig. 1. It should be noted that, because of the volumetric window, the network classifiers make use of more information than appears in the gray-scale images shown. Though the two classifiers yield slightly different results, each is successful in preserving cortical cavity structure without unduly thinning the delicate trabecular structure.

7 Discussion

The weight pattern of the single-node classifier has a particularly simple structure. The central value is large and positive, the nearest neighbors are much smaller and positive, and the remainder negative. The sum of the elements, together with the bias, determines the threshold for a uniform region and is found to be perfectly reasonable, i.e., right in the middle of the density range.

An obvious extension to the binary tree procedure, which should be useful for many other applications, is to use NDEKF as an alternative means of determining the weights for each node of the binary tree. A possible scheme, which we are investigating, would be to generate both the Fisher direction and the LMS direction by the NDEKF procedure. The split point would then be chosen, as mentioned above, on the basis of either minimum entropy or minimum errors, with the better direction used in either case. This elaboration does not appear to be required in the present application, since a single node, determined by NDEKF, leaves little to be desired. However, extension to cases with anisotropic resolution or other complications would likely require more than a single node.

8 Conclusions

We have described the application of neural networks to the problem of classifying the points of resolution-degraded 3D data sets in terms of an underlying binary structure. The method used is based on simple models for the resolution and the physical structures of interest. The networks employed perform well on test instances generated in the same way as those used for training. Application to actual data is also quite satisfactory, and this method is currently being used as the first step in an analysis procedure.

Though not described here, the model with which examples are generated has been extended to include noise. This is found to be useful when the classifier must be applied to data in which the noise level is higher than in the data shown here.

Acknowledgements

Portions of this work were supported by the National Institutes on Aging under Grant AG-07542-03. The experimental data were taken by Ms. S. Lang of Henry Ford Hospital.

References

[1] L. A. Feldkamp and G. Jesion, "3-D X-Ray Computed Tomography," in *Review of Progress in Quantitative Nondestructive Evaluation* 5A, 555–566, Plenum, 1986.

[2] L. A. Feldkamp, S. A. Goldstein, A. M. Parfitt, G. Jesion, and M. Kleerekoper, "The Direct Examination of Three Dimensional Bone Architecture In Vitro by Computed Tomography," Journal of Bone and Mineral Research 4, 3–11, 1989.

[3] J. L. Kuhn, S. A. Goldstein, L. A. Feldkamp, R. W. Goulet, and G. Jesion, "Evaluation of a Microcomputed Tomography System to Study Trabecular Bone Structure," Journal of Orthopaedic Research 8, 833–842, 1990.

[4] C. Koutsougeras and C. A. Papachristou, "Training of a Neural Network for Pattern Classification Based on an Entropy Measure," Proc. ICNN, I247–I254, 1988.

[5] K. A. Marko, L. A. Feldkamp, and G. V. Puskorius, "Automotive Diagnostics Using Trainable Classifiers: Statistical Testing and Paradigm Selection," Proceedings of the International Joint Conference on Neural Networks, San Diego, I33–I38, 1990.

[6] L. Breiman, J. H. Friedman, R. A. Olshen, and C. J. Stone, *Classification and Regression Trees*, Wadsworth, Belmont, CA, 1984.

[7] G. V. Puskorius and L. A. Feldkamp, "Decoupled Extended Kalman Filter Training of Feedforward Layered Networks," submitted for these proceedings; S. Singhal and L. Wu, "Training Multilayer Perceptrons with the Extended Kalman Algorithm," in *Advances in Neural Information Processing Systems* 1 (Denver 1988), D. S. Touretzky, ed., 133–140, Morgan Kaufmann, San Mateo, CA, 1989.

Pattern Recognition

Session Chairs: Teuvo Kohonen
Brian Telfer

POSTER PRESENTATIONS

An Iterative Algorithm to Find the Energy Function Coefficients of a Recurrent Neural Network

Fatih A. Unal

National Semiconductor, Embedded Systems Division
2900 Semiconductor Dr., Santa Clara, CA, 95051

Abstract

A new iterative algorithm is proposed to compute the energy function coefficients of a Hopfield Network. The coefficients specify the relative weights of the energy function components. The components, typically, correspond to an objective function and some constraints when solving optimization problems. The energy function components compete and cooperate with each other as the network settles down to a stable state. The Hopfield Network's Liapunov function is mapped to the energy function to derive the connection weights and the bias inputs for the neurons. The descending capability of the Liapunov function is shared by the energy function components based on the relative weights of their coefficients as the Hopfield Network evolves towards a final solution state with a minimum energy. Attention must be paid as to how these energy function coefficients are found since they directly affect the validity and the quality of the solution into which the network converges. Determining the right set of coefficients is nontrivial when analytical methods are employed. The iterative algorithm treats the energy function components as errors and adjusts the coefficients iteratively to minimize the errors. The validity of the algorithm is verified with a dynamic time warping Hopfield Network which can be used in the pattern matching phase of a pattern recognition system.

1. Introduction

Hopfield Network is a fully connected, recurrent neural network with symmetric connection weights [6]. It found applications in various fields such as optimization [7], [26], pattern recognition [12], [25] and signal processing [11]. Moreover, the similarities between the Hopfield Networks and spin glasses attract physicists to describe the disordered media [14]. The existence of a Liapunov function for the Hopfield Network, which is analogous to the energy function, permits the use of statistical physics methods to determine the stability points [27]. It is possible to construct a Hopfield Network with predefined dynamically stable configurations and consequently the network can be used as an associative or content addressable memory [13]. The Hopfield Networks provide a basic model for the cognitive and computational neuroscience fields [27]. Furthermore, it is feasible to implement the Hopfield Network in silicon with the present analog VLSI technology [20].

This paper describes a new iterative algorithm to compute the energy function coefficients that specify the relative weights of the energy function components which could be an objective function and some associated constraints when solving an optimization problem using a Hopfield Network. Once the energy function is defined, it can be mapped to the Liapunov function of the Hopfield Network to determine the connection weights and the bias input for the neurons. Finding the proper set of coefficients is critical since these coefficients directly affect the connection weights and the bias inputs which in turn determine the validity and the quality of the solution into which the Hopfield Network converges. Thus, attention must be paid as to how these coefficients are determined. In most of the studies reported, these energy coefficients are found empirically [1], [4], [7], [21]. Recently, some researchers proposed that the eigenvalues and the eigenvectors of the connection weight matrix can be exploited to find the energy coefficients when the nonlinear system equations for the Hopfield network are approximated by linear functions [3]. Others suggested that useful relationships among the energy coefficients can be obtained and the ranges for the energy coefficients can be found by analyzing the stability of the dynamical fixed points [9]. The proposed algorithm provides a systematic means to compute the energy function coefficients directly. There is no need to approximate the network nonlinearities nor analyze the stability of the dynamical fixed points to apply the algorithm. The new algorithm is tested with a dynamic time warping (DTW) Hopfield Network which was reported previously [22], [23]. The DTW is an optimization algorithm which compares patterns to find an optimal match under some constraints. It is used in pattern recognition applications such as speech recognition, speaker identification and speaker verification [16], [17], [19].

Solving optimization problems using a Hopfield Network is explained in the next section . The new iterative algorithm to find the energy function coefficients is presented in Section 3. Section 4 describes the DTW using Hopfield Network. The experimental results verifying the validity of the approach are given in Section 5. Finally, the conclusions are drawn in Section 6.

2. Solving Optimization Problems with a Hopfield Network

Table 1 summarizes a procedure which can be used to set up a Hopfield Network to solve an optimization problem:

Step 1. Find a neural network representation for the problem
Step 2. Determine a number representation with the neurons
Step 3. Define a Liapunov Function L(v) for the Hopfield Network
Step 4. Devise an energy function E(v) for the optimization problem
Step 5. Derive the connection weights **W** and the bias inputs **b** by equating L of Step 3 and E of Step 4
Step 6. Compute the energy function coefficients **c**

Table 1: A General Procedure to Solve an Optimization Problem with a Hopfield Network.

In step 1, a neural representation scheme is found. It is necessary to assign a meaning to every neuron or group of neurons as to what these neuron outputs depict when the neural network converges to a final state. Then, a number representation scheme with the neurons is determined in step 2, since most problems require their solutions to be in numerical form [21]. Step 3 requires the definition of a Liapunov function. The majority of the studies utilize the following quadratic function which was proposed by Hopfield [6] as $L(\mathbf{v}) = -1/2 \, \mathbf{v}^t\mathbf{W}\mathbf{v} - \mathbf{b}^t\mathbf{v} + \tau^{-1}\Sigma_i \int d\alpha g^{-1}$ where the integral is from 0 to v_i and i ranges from 0 to N-1. The outputs of the neurons are represented collectively by the vector **v**, the connection weights between the neurons by the matrix **W**, the bias inputs by the vector **b** and the activation functions of the neurons by g. In step 4, an energy function consisting of an objective function , possibly with some constraints is defined. This function is minimized to obtain the best solution under the constraints. The characteristics of this function should match that of the Liapunov function of the Hopfield network since there will be a mapping between the two to determine the connection weights and the bias inputs for the neurons. Typically a quadratic function would be suitable but any other class of functions could also be used as long as a corresponding Liapunov function is found for the network. The constraints can be added to the objective function to make the mapping easier between these two functions. It has been shown that inequality, as well as equality constrained optimization problems can be effectively solved by means of the Hopfield Network [2]. In general, the energy function can be devised in the form $E(\mathbf{c},\mathbf{v}) = 1/2 \, c_0 E_0(\mathbf{v}) + 1/2 \, c_1 E_1(\mathbf{v}) + ... + 1/2 \, c_K E_K(\mathbf{v})$ where the E_0 component corresponds to the objective function and the remaining components E_1 through E_K represent the constraints. There is no straightforward method to find the energy function for a given problem. Each problem requires a different approach and the energy function for a particular problem is not unique. The Liapunov function L(v) and the energy function E(v) are equated to each other in step 5, and the connection weights **W** and the bias inputs **b** for the neurons are found by comparing the linear and the quadratic parts. During this derivation, the integration component of the Liapunov function is ignored since its contribution is negligible because of the high gain of the activation function [6]. Also, the constant term in the energy function E(v) is ignored since it does not have any effect on the result while minimization is taking place. Note that the connection weights and the bias inputs which are found by equating the energy function to the Liapunov function assure the minimization of the objective function along with the constraints by enforcing the neuron outputs to follow a monotonically decreasing energy path as the network evolves. Consequently, when the network reaches a minimum energy state, a solution to the optimization problem is achieved. Step 6 is explained in the following section.

3. Computation of the Energy Function Coefficients

The energy function coefficients c_i weigh the objective function, and the associated constraint components, and specify their relative shares in the descending capability of the Liapunov function L(v) as the Hopfield Network evolves towards a final solution state with a minimum energy. These energy components cooperate and compete with each other during the iterations of the neural network. Since they control the energy function directly they determine the quality of the solution into which the network converges.

Figure 1 shows a schematic representation of the algorithm. The objective is to adjust the energy function coefficients c_i in such a way that the energy function components E_i (that are treated as errors in this context) are pushed towards their minima so that high quality solutions are achieved while maintaining the validity of the result.

The energy function components descend as the network converges to a stable state since the connection weights **W** and the bias inputs **b** are computed by equating the energy function $E(v)$ to the Liapunov function $L(v)$ which monotonically decreases during the iterations. This also guarantees the convergence of the algorithm that is confirmed by the computer simulations performed in Section 5.

To be able to use this algorithm, for each constraint component E_i, the maximum and the minimum values (E_i^{MAX} and E_i^{MIN}) have to be calculated. Then the error ranges can easily be found as shown in Table 2. Also, one has to decide on the training set and determine what values to use for the parameters validity threshold N_1 (the number of times the neural network has to converge to a valid solution in a row), and the adjustment factor Δc.

The selection of the training set depends on the application field and the quality-validity tradeoff. The ideal training set would be all possible combinations of the inputs. For some problems, this approach may not practical due to the abundance of input data. In such cases, the use of a representative subset can be sufficient as we did for the DTW applications in this work. The optimal selection of the training set can be quite complicated and is beyond the scope of this study.

The initial values of the energy function coefficients are selected as $c_0 = 0$, $c_1 = 1$, $c_2 = 1$, $c_3 = 1$, $c_4 = 1$, $c_5 = 1$. This way, the competing effect of the objective function with the constraints is eliminated at the beginning. Having one as the value for the constraint coefficient gives equal effect to every energy function constraint component. During the iterations of each run of the neural network, the constraint components are examined whether they reach their minima and the coefficient with the highest relative error is updated in accordance with the proposed algorithm. Once the network achieves N_1 times valid results in a row (in the algorithm, "valid" is the counter used for this purpose) then the objective function coefficient is updated to push the network towards finding better quality results. With this new value of the objective function coefficient the above process is repeated until the network reaches an invalid final state. Once this occurs, the value of the objective function coefficient is kept constant and the constraint coefficients are updated as before until the network achieves N_1 times valid solutions in a row again. When this validity threshold is exceeded, the network is ready for a higher objective function coefficient. This continues until no further improvement is possible for the objective function coefficient. The improvement is measured by means of the objective function to constraint coefficients ratios (c_0 / c_i) as defined in Table 2. In this study, if any of these ratios decreases then the algorithm terminates. Better improvement checking mechanisms can be developed by considering more than one decrease in a row (checking the average of the ratios over a few runs rather than halting at the first decrease) , the rate of change of the ratios and so forth. The selection of the validity threshold N_1 depends on the application. If the invalid solutions do not degrade the performance of the system significantly as reported in [22], [24] , then this value can be chosen smaller. This results in a larger objective function coefficient which in turn promotes higher quality solutions but more often invalid results. If the quality of the solution is not the primary concern (having a valid solution is of higher priority) then the validity threshold N_1 can be set to a large value which suppresses the enlargement of the objective function coefficient. In our experiments, the validity threshold N_1 is picked as 10. The adjustment factor Δc is another parameter of the algorithm which is used to calibrate the energy function coefficients. A constant adjustment factor, namely $\Delta c = 0.1$, is used in this study. Analytical methods can be developed to find more precise values which would elicit better tuning of the energy function coefficients. It should be noted that this parameter does not have to be a constant. Faster and better results might be achieved by employing an adaptive adjustment factor during the iterations.

4. Dynamic Time Warping Using a Hopfield Network

DTW is a pattern matching algorithm which is used to compare an input test pattern with a reference pattern template and obtain an optimum match subject to certain constraints [8]. The associated distance between the two patterns is also determined during the process. The DTW algorithm eliminates the nonlinear x-axis variations to compensate for the nonlinear temporal distortions which might arise due to the variations in the speaking rates of the speakers in speech processing applications. Consequently a better comparison is achieved as opposed to an ordinary direct template matching procedure which might yield a larger distance between the two patterns despite the similarity. It is widely utilized in pattern recognition areas such as speech recognition, speaker verification and recognition and contributes significantly to the performances of these speech processing systems [16], [17], [19]. While effective in pattern recognition the DTW algorithm is lacking in that the processing time becomes a major consideration for real time applications as the number and the size of the patterns increase. A parallel computing architecture becomes the only avenue to achieve the high computational rate demanded. A possible remedy toward this end is the use of a Hopfield Network.

The DTW algorithm can be formulated as a minimum cost path problem as illustrated in Figure 2. This way the problem is transformed to finding an optimal alignment path $m = w(n)$ between a reference pattern $r(n)$ and a test pattern $t(m)$ over a 2-D finite cartesian grid of size N x N, where N is the length of the patterns, n and m are the discrete time scale indices for the reference and the test patterns respectively. Each grid node $v(n,m)$ has a specified cost $d(r(n),t(m))$ which corresponds to the distance between the reference pattern sample $r(n)$ and the test pattern sample $t(m)$. The problem is to obtain the minimum cost path from $v(0,0)$ to $v(N-1,N-1)$. Note that, the patterns $r(n)$ and $t(m)$ could be multidimensional feature vectors representing the data to be compared.

In order to implement an effective and efficient DTW algorithm, it is necessary to specify a number of factors and constraints on the solution which could vary depending on the application field [15]. These are typically endpoint constraints, local and global path constraints, axis orientation and distance measure specification. The endpoint constraints match the boundary points of the test and reference patterns (i.e., $w(0) = 0$, $w(N-1) = N-1$). The local path constraints [8] allow only the arcs with slopes 0, 1 or 2, and avoid consecutive zero slope arcs. These constraints guarantee that the average slope of the warping function $w(n)$ lies between 1/2 and 2, provide path monotonicity and prevent excessive compression or expansion of the time scales of the patterns as depicted in Figure 2. The endpoint and the local path constraints give rise to the global path constraints. The global path constraints define the domain of the matching operation which is a parallelogram (indicated by a dashed line) as shown in Figure 2. The axis orientation may affect the performance of the system If the path constraints and/or the distance measure are asymmetric [18]. In this study the reference pattern is mapped to the abscissa, and the test pattern is mapped to the ordinate as shown in Figure 2. The absolute difference metric $d(r(n),t(m)) = |r(n) - t(w(n))|$ is used as the distance measure. So, the total distance along the optimal path $w(n)$ from the grid point (0,0) to the grid point (N-1,N-1) can be written as $D = \min_{w(n)}\{\sum_n d(r(n), t(w(n)))\}$ where n runs from 0 to N-1. The type of the distance measure used by the DTW algorithm may affect the matching results depending on the properties of the patterns compared [5]. A succinct review of the distance measures can be found in [10].

With all these constraints in mind, we can reiterate the definition of the DTW problem as finding an optimal warping path $m = w(n)$ through the grid points $v(n,m)$ (in Figure 2) to match the reference pattern $r(n)$ with the test pattern $t(m)$ subject to the constraints such that the total distance D is minimized. Thus, for the particular example illustrated in Figure 2, the optimal warping path $m = w(n)$ (indicated by the solid line) goes through the grid nodes $v(0,0)$, $v(1,1)$, $v(2,1)$, $v(3,3)$, $v(4,4)$ and $v(5,5)$ and corresponds to the best match between the two patterns with the associated total distance 10 (2+1+2+0+2+3). Note that none of the other valid paths (which satisfy the constraints) within the parallelogram have smaller total distance.

To be able to realize the DTW algorithm using the Hopfield Network, the procedure given in Table 1 is followed: Every grid point on the (n,m) plane in Figure 2 can be naturally represented by a neuron. Thus, a two dimensional array (of size N x N) representation is used for the neural network with a total number of N^2 neurons. The neuron outputs will be denoted by v_{xi} with subscripts x (for ordinate m) and i (for abscissa n) showing the row and the column indices respectively. The optimal path $m = w(n)$, which corresponds to the optimal match between the test and the reference patterns, will be determined by the neurons which have outputs 1 when the network converges to a stable state.

The second step of the procedure given in Table 1 can be omitted since there is no need to find a number representation with the neuron groups for the implementation of the DTW algorithm. The neuron outputs of the continuous Hopfield Network stays in the range 0 through 1 and the neuron outputs with binary states 0 and 1 are sufficient to represent the warping path $m = w(n)$. To ensure the validity of the path, the neurons are forced to have binary values 0 or 1 by means of an appropriate constraint component in the DTW energy function. As a result of this constraint, the neuron states converge to either 0 or 1 outputs when the Hopfield Network reaches a minimum energy stable state which corresponds to one of the corners of the NxN dimensional hypercube.

Hence, by scrutinizing the warping path $m = w(n)$ through the grid nodes in Figure 2, and considering the objective function D (total distance along the optimal path $w(n)$), and the DTW constraints described, the following energy function $E(v)$ can be constructed for the DTW algorithm

$$E(v) = \frac{c_0}{2} \sum_{x=0}^{N-1} \sum_{i=0}^{N-1} \sum_{y=0}^{N-1} \left[\left(d_{x,i} + d_{y,i+1} \right) v_{x,i} v_{y,i+1} + (d_{x,i} + d_{y,i-1}) v_{x,i} v_{y,i-1} \right]$$

$$+ \frac{c_1}{2} \sum_{\substack{x=0 \\ }}^{N-1} \sum_{\substack{i=0 \\ }}^{N-1} \sum_{\substack{y \neq x \\ y \neq x+1 \\ y \neq x+2}}^{N-1} v_{x,i} v_{y,i+1} + \frac{c_2}{2} \sum_{x=0}^{N-1} \sum_{i=0}^{N-1} \sum_{y \neq x}^{N-1} v_{x,i} v_{y,i} + \frac{c_3}{2} \left(\sum_{x=0}^{N-1} \sum_{i=0}^{N-1} v_{x,i} - N \right)^2$$

$$+ \frac{c_4}{2} \sum_{x=0}^{N-1} \sum_{i=0}^{N-1} \sum_{\substack{j \neq i \\ |i-j| \neq 1}}^{N-1} v_{x,i} v_{x,j} - \frac{c_5}{2} \sum_{x=0}^{N-1} \sum_{i=0}^{N-1} \left(1 - 2 v_{x,i} \right)^2$$

where modulo N is used for the subscripts wherever applicable (i.e., N = 0.). The detailed explanation of the energy function and the derivations of the connection weights and the bias inputs can be found in [22].

The last step of the procedure given in Table 1 is the computation of the energy function coefficients c. By using the energy function $E(v)$, and the following equations (With N=10), the number of the neurons at each column and the total number of neurons -including the boundary neurons if any - within the boundary of the parallelogram (An example for N=6 is shown in Figure 2) can easily be calculated. The number of neurons at column n is $m_H (n) - m_L (n) + 1$ and the total number of neurons are equal to $\sum_n [m_H (n) - m_L (n) + 1]$ where n = 0,..., N-1. Hence, starting with column 0, the number of neurons at each column are 1, 3, 4, 6, 6, 6, 6, 4, 3, 1 which adds up to 40. Now, in the succeeding paragraphs, we will analyze each component of the DTW energy function $E(v)$, and calculate the numerical values of the error ranges for the energy function constraints.

The component E_0 (weighted by $c_0 /2$) corresponds to the objective function that minimizes the total distance D between the two patterns along the warping path $w(n)$ through the grid points.

The component E_1 (weighted by $c_1 /2$) stands for the Itakura path slope constraint. The slopes of the arcs between the grid nodes are pushed to 0, 1, or 2 by this component. It takes its minimum value zero when all neurons have output zero. The maximum value is reached if all neuron outputs are one. For column i, there can be 7 allowable arcs (with slopes other than zero, one or two) connecting adjacent neurons at column i+1. Therefore 7x10x10=700 is the maximum value of the function for the entire NxN grid. If we consider only the parallelogram, then it is 0+4+12+20+21+20+12+4+0+0=93. Therefore the error range for this energy function component is 93 -0=93.

E_2 (weighted by $c_2 /2$) forces every sample of the reference pattern to be visited once during matching with the test pattern. It becomes minimum (zero) when all neurons outputs are zero. The maximum value is reached if all neuron outputs are one. For column i, there are 9 possible multiplications. Therefore 9x10x10=900 is the maximum value of the function for the NxN grid. For parallelogram, it is 1x0+3x2+4x3+6x5+6x5+6x5+6x5+4x3+3x2+1x0=156. So, the error range is 156-0=156.

Because of E_3 (weighted by $c_3 /2$), the network ends up having N active neurons (output value one) when a stable state is reached. E_3 has the minimum value zero if all neurons have zero outputs. The maximum value is attained when all neuron outputs are one. Thus, is the maximum the function can get for the complete NxN grid. For the parallelogram, it is $(40-10)^2 = 900$. Consequently, the error range is 900-0=900.

Successive zero slope arcs in each row are avoided by the component E_4 (weighted by $c_4/2$). It reaches its minimum value zero if all neuron outputs are equal to zero. The maximum value is acquired when all neuron outputs are equal to one. For row x, there are 8 neuron couples (for which the outputs are to be multiplied). Hence the maximum value of the function for the whole NxN grid can be 8x10x10=800, and for the parallelogram, beginning with row zero, is 0+2+12+12+12+12+12+2+0=76. The error range for this component is 76-0=76.

E_5 (weighted by $c_5/2$) helps the neurons to have 0 or 1 output when the network converges to a minimum energy state. E_5 reaches its minimum value -100 for the NxN grid when all neuron outputs are either zero or one. For the parallelogram, it is -40 since there are 40 neurons inside (including the border) the parallelogram. The maximum value is obtained if all neuron outputs are 0.5 which is the fuzziest state for the neurons with (1-2x0.5)=0, and the error range is 0-(-40)=40.

5. Experimental Results

The dynamical behavior of the Hopfield Network is represented by the differential equation $\dot{\mathbf{u}} = \mathbf{Wv} + \mathbf{b}$. The number of equations is equal to the number of the neurons in the network, and the operation of the neural network is simulated by solving these differential equations simultaneously. The equations are solved numerically using Euler's method [22], [23].

First, to elucidate the operation of the new iterative algorithm (given in Table 2), an illustrative experiment is carried out with the adjustment factor $\Delta c = 0.2$, and the validity threshold $N_1 = 5$. The reference pattern $\mathbf{r}$ and the test pattern $\mathbf{t}_1$ shown in Figure 5 (a) are used as the training input. Figure 3 shows the progress of the energy function components E_i, (i = 0,...,5) per run for 100 runs (50 iterations each). The energy function coefficients converged to $c_0 = 0.8$, $c_1 = 4.0$, $c_2 = 4.8$, $c_3 = 1.2$, $c_4 = 1.4$, $c_5 = 1.6$ at the end of 100 runs. The initial values used for the energy function coefficients were $c_0 = 0$, $c_1 = 1$, $c_2 = 1$, $c_3 = 1$, $c_4 = 1$, $c_5 = 1$ as suggested in the algorithm. Note that the energy function components descend smoother and more consistently during the iterations as the coefficients are adjusted at each run.

Next, to carry out the subsequent experiments, the algorithm is run with the adjustment factor $\Delta c=0.1$ and the validity threshold $N_1 = 10$. The reference $\mathbf{r}$ and the test patterns $\mathbf{t}_1$ and $\mathbf{t}_2$ shown in Figure 5 (a) and (c) are utilized as the training input. At the end of the training, the energy function coefficients are computed as $c_0 = 2.0$, $c_1 = 13.8$, $c_2 = 13.8$, $c_3 = 4.5$, $c_4 = 6.3$, $c_5 = 1.5$. The initial values of the coefficients were $c_0 = 0$, $c_1 = 1$, $c_2 = 1$, $c_3 = 1$, $c_4 = 1$, $c_5 = 1$ as suggested in the algorithm.

To evaluate the performance of the network, uniformly distributed random reference and test signals are generated. From these signals a distance matrix $\mathbf{d}$ is produced (absolute differences between the signal samples as shown in Figure 2). The distances are normalized to the unit square. Using $\mathbf{d}$, the optimal warping path corresponding to the global minimum total distance and the path with the global maximum distance are determined by going through all of the possible paths within the parallelogram, as shown in Figure 2. Then the DTW Hopfield Network is employed to find the optimal path. A distance measure is defined to compare the results as $d_{GM} = (min_{NN} - min_G)/(max_G - min_G)x100$, where min_G and max_G are the global minimum and maximum distances corresponding to the best and worst warping paths and min_{NN} is the minimum distance corresponding to the optimal path found by the network. d_{GM} is the percentage of the distance to the global minimum and represents the independent variable on the horizontal axis in Figure 4 (a) and (b). The y-axis denotes the number of times d_{GM} occurred out of 500 runs. Two tests are run to measure the performance of the DTW Hopfield Network with the constraints coefficients $c_1 = 13.8$, $c_2 = 13.8$, $c_3 = 4.5$, $c_4 = 6.3$, $c_5 = 1.5$. In the first test, the numerical value of the objective function coefficient is taken as $c_0 = 2.0$. Then the same test is repeated with a more aggressive objective function coefficient, $c_0 = 4.0$, to demonstrate its impact on the solution validity and quality. Figure 4 (a) shows the test results with the energy function coefficients $c_0 = 2.0$, $c_1 = 13.8$, $c_2 = 13.8$, $c_3 = 4.5$, $c_4 = 6.3$, $c_5 = 1.5$. The network converged to a valid solution 96 % of the time and reached the global minimum 20 times. In our previous study (without using the new iterative algorithm) the results were 85 % and 6 times respectively [23]. With the energy function coefficients $c_0 = 4.0$, $c_1 = 13.8$, $c_2 = 13.8$, $c_3 = 4.5$, $c_4 = 6.3$, $c_5 = 1.5$, the result summarized in Figure 4 (b) is obtained. Using this set, the DTW Hopfield Network reached a valid solution 72 % of the time and converged to the global minimum 56 times which were 63 % and 27 previously [23]. In this case, the quality of the paths found are superior to the prior case as expected. The reason for this is that while the constraint coefficients c_1, c_2, c_3, c_4, c_5 enforce the validity of the warping path the objective function coefficient c_0, competes with them to minimize the total distance associated with the path. Thus, the quality of the DTW path can be improved by increasing the value of c_0 but this results in more frequent invalid paths. For both cases, the network converges to a valid solution in less than 50 iterations (peaking around 20) and the results achieved show that the network is capable of matching the reference and test patterns effectively.

The purpose of the last experiment is to demonstrate the superiority of the pattern matching performed by the DTW Hopfield Network over the ordinary direct template matching. First, the direct template matching is applied to the reference pattern r and the test patterns t_1, t_2 which are shown in Figure 5 (a) and (c). The absolute difference distance metric ($|x|$) is used to calculate all distances. The distance between r and t_1 is found as 62 (20-14 + 15-3 + 5-1 + 4-0 + 11-4.9 + 14.9-13 + 20-14 + 19-15 + 16-5 + 7-0), and the distance between r and t_2 is found as 55 (20-15 + 15-15 + 12.5-5 +10-0 + 10-4.9 + 14.9-10 + 20-10 + 15-7.5 + 5-5 + 5-0). Thus, according to the direct template matching, the test pattern t_2 is more similar to the reference pattern r than the test pattern t_1. Next, the DTW Hopfield Network (with the energy function coefficients $c_0 = 4.0$, $c_1 = 13.8$, $c_2 = 13.8$, $c_3 = 4.5$, $c_4 = 6.3$, $c_5 = 1.5$) is used to find the distances between the same patterns. This time the distance between r and t_1 is found as 1.93 (in 14 iterations) and the distance between r and t_2 is found as 3.77 (in 20 iterations). Figure 5 (b) and (d) illustrate the effect of DTW clearly. As the results show, the DTW Hopfield Network can compare patterns more intelligently and achieve better solution than that of the ordinary direct template matching.

6. Conclusions

The main objective of this study is to show that the proposed iterative algorithm can be used to compute better energy function coefficients for a Hopfield Network. A DTW algorithm, which compares two patterns to obtain the best match under some constraints, is used to verify the validity of the approach. The idea behind this algorithm is to find the optimal balance among the energy function components to obtain a high quality result while maintaining the validity of the solution. The algorithm has the flexibility to accommodate different quality requirements of diverse optimization problems. The results provided in Section 5 verify that, this algorithm finds a good set of energy coefficients which induces a superior pattern match than that of the ordinary direct template matching. The same set of energy function coefficients was also used to measure the performance of the DTW Hopfield Network relative to the traditional DTW algorithm. Using the DTW Hopfield Network along with the new iterative algorithm, more satisfactory results are achieved in comparison to our previous study [23].

The procedure given in Section 2 provides a methodical approach to solve optimization problems using the Hopfield Network. Most of the steps in this procedure are straightforward, except the neural network representation and the definition of the energy function. There can be more than one valid neural network representation and energy function for a given problem. The DTW energy function $E(v)$, defined in Section 4, is neither unique nor claimed to be the best energy function for the DTW problem. Combining some of the constraint components and/or incorporating them into the objective function would reduce the number of energy function coefficients. But then it would not be possible to control the effects of these components independently. It should be noted that the components of the energy functions compete and cooperate with each other, while the neural network descends with the Liapunov function, as dictated by the energy function, toward a stable minimum energy state. The energy function coefficients c_0 through c_5 define the characteristics of this falling motion. There is a delicate balance among these components which are weighted by the energy function coefficients. It would be interesting to study the effects of changing the energy function coefficients dynamically (as a function of energy) as the neural network evolves toward a solution state. This could aid the DTW Hopfield Network to reach lower minima with faster convergence rates.

The effect of the objective function (relative to the constraint components) could be reduced by calibrating the energy coefficients if maintaining a valid result has a higher priority than the quality of the solution. For the signal recognition system described in [24], the quality of the path was the main concern (validity of the path had secondary importance) since only uncorrelated signals pulled the network to the invalid state space. When the signals were similar, the neural network remained in the valid state space.

References

[1] B. Abbiss, B. J. Brames and M. A. Fiddy, "Superresolution Algorithms for a Modified Hopfield Neural Network," IEEE Trans. on Signal Processing, vol. 39, pp. 1516-1523, July 1991.

[2] Abe, J. Kawakami and K. Kotaroo Hirasawa, "Solving Inequality Constrained Combinatorial Optimization Problems by the Hopfield Neural Networks," Neural Networks, vol. 5, no. 4, pp. 663-670, 1992.

[3] V. B. Aiyer, M. Niranjan and F. Fallside, "A Theoretical Investigation into the Performance of the Hopfield Model," IEEE Trans. Neural Networks, vol. 1, pp. 204-215, June 1990.

[4] Chiu, C. Y. Maa and M. A. Shanblatt, "Energy Function Analysis of Dynamic Programming Neural Networks," IEEE Trans. Neural Networks, vol. 2, no. 4, pp. 418-426, July 1991.

[5] H. Gray and J. D. Markel, "Distance Measures for Speech Processing," IEEE Trans. Acoust., Speech, Signal Processing, vol. 24, no. 5, pp. 380-391, October 1976.

[6] J. Hopfield, "Neurons with graded response have collective computational properties like those of two-state neurons," Proc. Nat. Acad. Sci. USA, vol. 81, pp. 3088-3092, May 1984.

[7] J. Hopfield and D. W. Tank, "Neural computation of decisions in optimization problems," Biolog. Cybern., vol. 52, pp. 1-25, 1985.

[8] Itakura, "Minimum prediction residual principle applied to speech recognition," IEEE Trans. Acoust., Speech, Signal Processing, vol. ASSP-23, pp. 67-72, Feb. 1975.

[9] Kamgar-Parsi and B. Kamgar-Parsi, "Dynamical Stability and Parameter Selection in Neural Optimization ," IJCNN 92 Proceedings, vol. 4, pp. 566-571, Baltimore, Maryland, June 7-11, 1992.

[10] Kohonen, Self-Organization and Associative Memory (Springer Series on Information Sciences). Springer-Verlag, 1989.

[11] Kosko, Neural Networks for Signal Processing. Englewood Cliffs, NJ: Prentice-Hall, 1992.

[12] P. Lippmann, "An introduction to computation with neural nets," IEEE Acoustics, Speech, and Signal Processing Magazine, vol. 4, pp. 4-22, April 1987.

[13] A. N. Michel and J. A. Farrel, "Associative Memories via Artificial Neural Networks," IEEE Control Systems Magazine, pp. 6-17, April 1990

[14] Muller and J. Reinhardt, Neural Networks-An Introduction. Berlin Heidelberg, Germany: Springer-Verlag, 1991.

[15] Myers, L. R. Rabiner and A. E. Rosenberg, "Performance Tradeoffs in Dynamic Time Warping Algorithms for Isolated Word Recognition," IEEE Trans. Acoust., Speech, Signal Processing, vol. 28, pp. 623-635, Dec. 1980.

[16] M. Naik, "Speaker Verification: A Tutorial," IEEE Communications Mag., pp. 42-48, Jan. 1990.

[17] O'Shaughnessy, "Speaker Recognition," IEEE ASSP Mag., pp. 4-17, Oct. 1986.

[18] R. Rabiner, A. E. Rosenberg and S. E. Levinson, "Considerations in Dynamic Time Warping for Discrete Word Recognition," IEEE Trans. Acoustics, Speech, Signal Processing, vol. 26, pp. 575-582, December 1978.

[19] F. Silverman and D. P. Morgan, "The Application of Dynamic Programming to Connected Speech Recognition," IEEE ASSP Mag., pp. 6-25, July 1990.

[20] S. Sinencio and R. W. Newcomb, eds. Special Issue on Neural Network Hardware, IEEE Trans. on Neural Networks, vol. 3, no. 3, May 1992.

[21] Takeda and J. W. Goodman, "Neural networks for computation: number representations and programming complexity," Appl. Opt., vol. 25, pp. 3033-3046, Sept. 1986.

[22] F. A. Unal, Pattern Matching Using an Artificial Neural Network, Ph.D. Dissertation, Florida Institute of Technology, Melbourne, FL, 1992.

[23] F. A. Unal and N. Tepedelenlioglu, "Dynamic Time Warping Using an Artificial Neural Network," IJCNN'92 Proceedings, vol. 4, pp. 715-721, Baltimore Maryland, June 7-11, 1992.

[24] F. A. Unal and N. Tepedelenlioglu, "Signal Recognition Using a Dynamic Time Warping Neural Network," WCNA-92 Proceedings, Tampa, Florida, August 19-26, 1992.

[25] F. A. Unal and N. Tepedelenlioglu, "Temporal Pattern Recognition Using an Artificial Neural Network," to be published in Progress in Neural Networks, Special Volume on Motion Detection and Temporal Pattern Recognition by J. Dayhoff, December 1993.

[26] Takefuji, Neural Network Parallel Computing. Norwell, MA: Kluwer Academic Publishers, 1992.

[27] Weisbuch, Complex Systems Dynamics. Redwood City, CA: Addison Wesley, 1990.

Find error ranges E_i^R for constraints:

$E_i^R \leftarrow E_i^{MAX} - E_i^{MIN}$; i=1,...,K

/* K: Number of energy function constraints */
Initialize energy function coefficients:

$c_i \leftarrow 1$; i=1,...,K /* constraint coefficients */

$c_0 \leftarrow 0$ /* relax objective function coefficient */

Initialize improvement ratios:

$c_{0/i}^{OLD} \leftarrow c_0/c_i$; i=1,...,K

$c_{0/i}^{NEW} \leftarrow c_0/c_i$; i=1,...,K

While (training is not sufficient)
  Apply an input to network from training set
  While $(c_{0/i}^{NEW} - c_{0/i}^{OLD} \geq 0)$; i=1,...,K

  $valid \leftarrow 0$ /* reset validity in a row counter */
  Find connection weights W and bias inputs b
  While $(valid < N_1)$ /* below validity threshold */

    Initialize neurons and run network

    if $E_i = E_i^{MIN}$; i=1,...,K

    then /* valid result */
    $valid \leftarrow valid + 1$
    else /* invalid result */
    {
    $valid \leftarrow 0$
    Find max normalized error and its index j

    $\max_i \dfrac{E_i}{E_i^R}$, i=1,..,K; j

    Adjust c_j: $c_j \leftarrow c_j + \Delta c$

    Find W and b
    }
  end While
  Adjust c_0: $c_0 \leftarrow c_0 + \Delta c$

  Update improvement ratios:

  $c_{0/i}^{OLD} \leftarrow c_{0/i}^{NEW}$; i=1,...,K

  $c_{0/i}^{NEW} \leftarrow c_0/c_i$; i=1,...,K

  end While
end While
Stop

Table 2: An Iterative Algorithm to Find the Energy Function Coefficients $c_0,...,c_K$

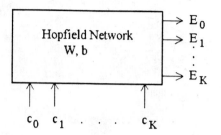

Figure 1: A Schematic Representation of the Iterative Algorithm that Finds the Energy Function Coefficients

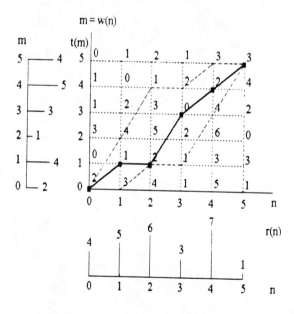

Figure 2: A DTW Example Depicting an Optimal Alignment Path m = w(n) to match r(n) to t(m)

III-195

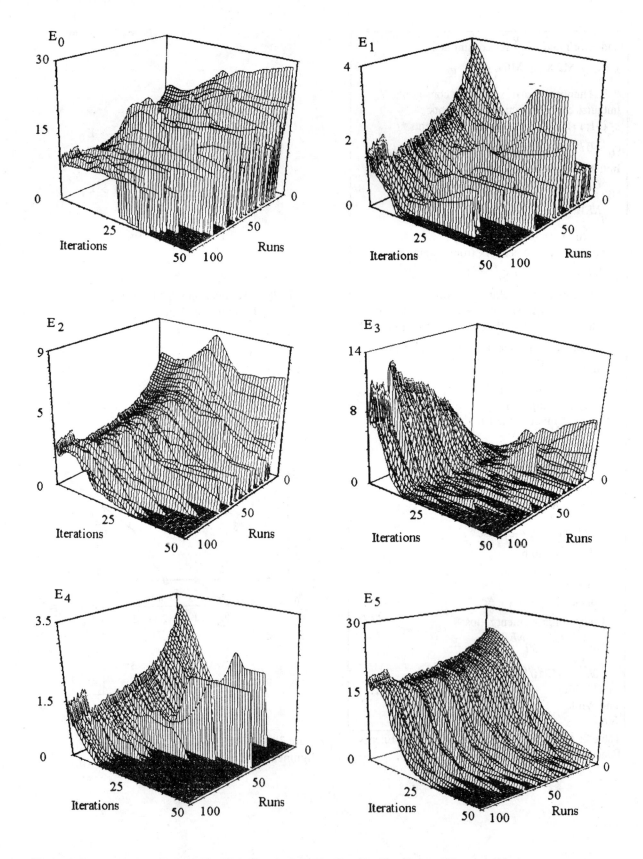

Figure 3: Progress of the Energy Function Components E_0, E_1, E_2, E_3, E_4, and E_5

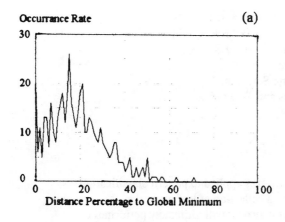

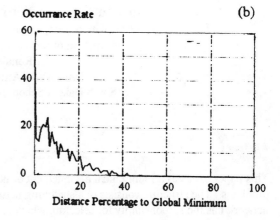

Figure 4: DTW Hopfield Network Performance Measurement Results

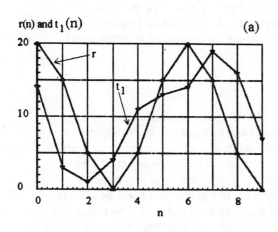

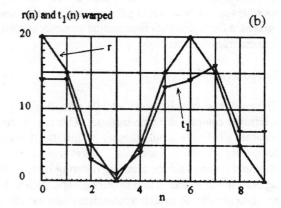

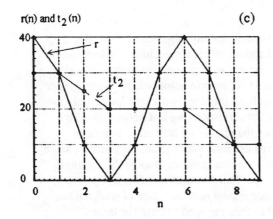

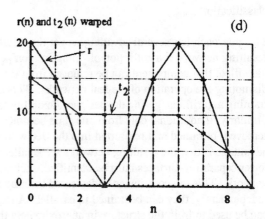

Figure 5: The Reference and Test Patterns Before and after DTW

A Multi-Stage Neural Network Classifier

Edward Corwin, Sterling Greni, Antonette Logar, Karen Whitehead
Department of Mathematics and Computer Science
Ronald Welch
Institute for Atmospheric Sciences
South Dakota School of Mines and Technology

Abstract

This paper explores a hierarchical arrangement of neural networks applied to pattern classification problems. The structure consists of a switching network and a collection of leaf networks. The switching network has the responsibility for selecting which of the leaf networks will ultimately perform the classification. The number of leaf networks, as well as the classes assigned to each leaf network, is determined by iterative application of a clustering algorithm. The iterations terminate when an objective function is minimized. The advantage of this method is the modularization of the network structure which dramatically reduces training time and allows locally confined network maintenance. For the multi-font character recognition problem considered here, classification accuracy remained comparable to that of a single back propagation network and training time was reduced by a factor of 20. Greater speedups can be achieved if parallel training and clustering are used. A classification problem is also presented for which the classification accuracy exceeds that of a single back propagation network and reduces training time.

Introduction

The usefulness of neural networks for classification problems is based upon a network's ability to construct arbitrarily complex decision surfaces. This is frequently accomplished by training a single network to separate all classes simultaneously. Thus, the training algorithm must find a single set of weights which accurately classifies all samples. This is analogous to sorting a million names by moving all of them at once and hoping that the resulting ordering is closer to a sorted list. People sort large lists by first separating the elements into smaller groups, such as by the first letter in a name. The resulting sublists are then sorted. A similar approach is taken with the network structure described here. The classes are first grouped into clusters and a separate neural network, a "leaf" network, is associated with each cluster. A "switching network" is responsible for selecting the appropriate leaf network to perform the final classification task.

This approach has several advantages over the traditional monolithic training algorithm. First, the resulting network is a collection of "plug-in" components. If a more efficient switching network can be identified, that component can be removed from the tree and replaced with the new network without disrupting the operation of the leaf networks. This structure does not require homogeneous topologies or training algorithms, giving the designer flexibility to attack localized problems with appropriate solutions. Similarly, if additional data from one class becomes available, the corresponding leaf network can be removed, retrained and reinserted into the tree without affecting the remaining networks. A second advantage is that the resulting networks are smaller and thus require less time to train. In addition, since fewer separating surfaces must be identified, each network has a simpler problem to solve than a single network. This too contributes to decreased training requirements. Third, since the networks operate independently, they can be trained in parallel. A multi-processor system or a collection of workstations can be used to train the structure in approximately the amount of time required to train the largest network in the structure.

The idea of creating a hierarchical structure of neural networks is not new. Tree structures have been used to decompose problems as well as to increase reliability through combining decisions from multiple branches of a classification tree [2]. Of particular interest are the CART algorithms, which generate neural tree classifiers, and have been shown to be very effective [1][7][10][11][12][13]. Neural tree classifiers combine classification trees with neural networks by utilizing relatively small neural networks at the interior nodes of the tree to identify splitting rules. The CART (classification and regression tree) method for constructing classification trees proceeds in two phases. First is the growing phase which recursively finds splitting rules at interior nodes by optimizing a criterion such as an impurity measure. Traditionally, the splitting rules have been based on single features or linear combinations of features. Neural networks have been used to generalize this method by finding nonlinear combinations of features on which to base the splitting rules[5]. The second phase is a pruning phase in which a subtree is selected based on minimization of an error-complexity criterion. Leaf nodes are associated with a single class. Our approach is to associate leaf nodes not with single classes but with clusters of classes. A neural network serves as a switching device to select the correct leaf network. A leaf network is then used to perform the classification within the cluster. One advantage of this approach is a reduction in the height of the tree and an accompanying reduction in classification time. More importantly, the switching network and all of the leaf networks can be trained in parallel which greatly reduces training time.

Method

The structure consists of four components : the switching network, the leaf networks, the clustering algorithm, and the error recovery algorithm. Note that a single decision network may not be appropriate for every problem. A hierarchy of switching networks was also implemented, and while effective, was not necessary for the problems studied. However, other classification tasks may benefit from an additional layer of switches.

The algorithm can be described as follows :
> *step 1* :Cluster the classes
> *step 2* :Train a switching network to classify a vector as a member of a given cluster
> *step 3* :Train each leaf network to discriminate between the classes for which it is responsible. Note that all of the leaf networks and the switching network can be trained simultaneously.
> *step 4* : Present a testing vector to the switching network. The switching network will select a leaf network. The leaf network will classify the vector or have an insufficient response to make a classification. In that event, the switching network selects the next most likely candidate and repeats step 4.

The first step, determining the number of leaf networks and the class distribution, can be accomplished by a clustering algorithm. A maximum distance clustering algorithm was the most effective of the well known algorithms we investigated [3][6]. However, we introduce a variation designed to produce a relatively even distribution of class assignments. Three competing elements must be balanced in selecting the proper network topology : the number of leaf networks, the difficulty of the classification task each must perform, and the difficulty of selecting the correct leaf network. As the number of leaf networks increases, the difficulty of the individual tasks decreases but that difficulty is simply transferred to the switching network. Alternatively, if too few leaf networks are used classification accuracy suffers and as the network sizes increase so does the training time. The algorithm presented below seeks to balance these competing interests.

The clustering algorithm used here can be summarized as follows :
> *step 1* : Select an initial value, n, for the number of clusters. This is an artificial starting point and will be adjusted by successive applications of the algorithm.
>
> step 2 : Select cluster seeds. The process of selecting seeds for the desired number of clusters is described inductively. The first two seeds, s_1 and s_2, are chosen so that $d(s_1,s_2)=\|s_1-s_2\|$ is a maximum. Suppose $S_k=\{s_1,s_2,...,s_k\}$ is the set of seeds chosen for the first k clusters. Select $x \notin S_k$ such that :

$$\prod_{i=1}^{k}\|x-s_i\|$$

is a maximum and set s_{k+1}=x. Repeat the process until all n seeds have been selected.

step 3 : Select a point p to add to a cluster. Each point not yet assigned to a cluster is considered in turn. A point is temporarily added to cluster C_j and :

$$\sum_{x\in C_j, y\in C_j}\|x-y\|$$

is computed . The point is assigned to the cluster for which the above sum is minimized. One additional consideration must be explored. If a point p is a member of a class c, and p has been assigned to cluster C_j what does that imply about other elements of c? One possibility is to allow individual points to be assigned without reference to prior assignments of other elements of c. This implies that more than one leaf network may be responsible for classifying vectors in a given class. This is only practical if a sufficient number of training samples is available for each leaf network. Another possibility is to force all elements of a class to be grouped in the same cluster. This can be done by assigning one element in a class using the technique described above then assigning all other elements of that class to the same cluster. An alternative method is to perform the above calculation using classes instead of individual points.

Steps 1-3 can be computed in parallel for a variety of n values. To determine an optimal number of clusters, compute the average cluster tightness, where average cluster tightness is defined by :

$$T_n = \frac{1}{n}\sum_{i=1}^{n}\frac{2}{n_i(n_i-1)}\sum_{x\in C_i, y\in C_i}\|x-y\|$$

where n is the number clusters and n_i is the number of points in cluster C_i. Let $N = \Sigma n_i$, the total number of points. As n increases from 1 to N, T_n decreases, first rapidly and then more slowly until $T_n = 0$. Judgment is used to select that value of n for which ΔT_n, that is $T_{n+1} - T_n$, is sufficiently small.

In these experiments all networks were trained with back propagation, but it is not necessary to do so or even to have all networks trained using the same algorithm. One of the advantages of the "plug-in" components is that any type of network can be inserted at any point in the tree.

An error recovery algorithm is necessary to handle situations in which the wrong leaf network was selected by the switching network. In many situations, if a network is not able to classify a vector, it will produce small output at each of the output nodes. The current solution is to set a threshold value and if none of the outputs reaches the threshold value, the current leaf network is declared to be inappropriate and an alternate selection is made. The leaf network which received the second largest output value from the switching network is selected and the process is repeated.

Experimental Results

A Sample Problem

A sample problem was devised to test the effectiveness of this algorithm relative to a single back propagation network. The data was produced by generating random points within fourteen overlapping spheres. The elements of each of the fourteen classes were randomly divided in half with one group used for training and the other for testing. The clustering algorithm was applied to the data and produced four clusters, each with three or four classes. Note that the classes are not linearly separable. The topology used for this experiment was a switching network and four leaf networks each with three input nodes, four hidden nodes and 4 output nodes.. The back propagation network consisted of 3 inputs nodes, a single hidden layer with 8 nodes, and 14 output nodes. The number of hidden units in the back propagation network was varied from 6 to 13 with the best classification accuracy produced by a 3-8-14 network. The accuracy for the back propagation network was 95% correct on the testing data while the hierarchical network was able to classify 100% of the test vectors correctly. The switching network made the correct selection on the first try 100% of the time. Training time was reduced by a factor of two without using parallel training. We report this experiment to demonstrate that problems do exist for which this network can reduce training time and improve classification accuracy relative to a single back propagation network.

Character Recognition

A more difficult problem is that of multi-font character recognition. Computer generated characters in six fonts were digitized and a feature extraction mechanism was used to create 156 vectors, each containing 14 elements [4][8]. These were divided into groups of 78 vectors. One group contained vectors representing each character in three fonts and was used for training The other group of 78 vectors contained the remaining three fonts and was used for testing.

The clustering algorithm produced four clusters each with six or seven classes. The switching network used was a neural network trained using back propagation and consisted of 14 input nodes, a single hidden layer with 4 hidden nodes and 4 output nodes. Each of the four leaf networks was also trained with back propagation and contained 14 input nodes, 6 hidden nodes and 7 output nodes. A single back propagation network with 14 input nodes, 20 hidden nodes and 26 output nodes was trained. This topology produced the best results for the multi-font character data set as reported in [8].

Several criteria were used to compare this approach to a single back propagation network. First, consider the size of the network. A network with 14 input nodes, 20 hidden nodes and 26 output nodes contains 60 nodes and, including bias weights, 846 weights. The number of weights is particularly important since each must be updated for one iteration. Training was stopped at 700 iterations by the criteria that the change in the error over a 100 iteration period was smaller than a predefined epsilon. This resulted in a total of 592,200 weight updates. Since weight updates are the most expensive part of the algorithm, this is a good measure of relative speed. In contrast the decision tree neural network with its five networks contained 130 nodes and 636 weights. However, since each leaf network is assigned a simpler task, fewer training iterations were required. The average number of iterations for all five networks was 400, resulting in 254,400 weight updates. In this case, the decision tree neural network required approximately 25% less storage for weights and reduced the number of weight updates by approximately 42%.

Timings were also conducted using a Sun Workstation. The single network required 5.39 seconds/iteration to train, or a total of 3773 seconds. Two timings must be considered for the decision tree network. First, code was written to train the networks on a single processor machine. The total time was 402.8 seconds However, one of the advantages of this architecture is that all five networks can be trained in parallel. Thus, a five processor machine, or five processes running on five dedicated workstations, can produce the weights in approximately 168.4 seconds, or the maximum of the five independent training times. Thus, training times were reduced by 89% for the single processor implementation and 95% using parallel training. Note that the number of weight updates is reduced by 42% while training time is reduced by 89% even for the sequential implementation. This difference can be attributed to the fact that the amount of time required for a weight update is dependent upon the size of the network.

Classification accuracy was also measured. The single network had an accuracy of 100% on the training vectors and 90% on the testing vectors. The multi-stage network also classified 100% of the training vectors and 90% of the training vectors correctly. Thus, performance was not affected and the time and space required to achieve this performance were significantly reduced. Note also that the switching network was able to identify the correct leaf network on the first attempt 100% of the time for the training data and 98.7% times for the testing data.

Conclusion

This research attacks the problem of pattern classification when the number of classes is large and rapid training time is necessary. An emphasis was placed on designing a topology which could exploit large-grain parallelism or benefit from a distributed computing environment. The approach is to cluster the classes, use a neural network as a switch to select the appropriate cluster, and utilize neural networks to build intracluster separating surfaces. The switching network and the leaf networks can be trained in parallel as can instances of the clustering algorithm with different numbers of seed points. Experiments using this topology have produced classification accuracy comparable to that generated by a monolithic back propagation network and training times have been consistently reduced. For the multi-font character data, a speedup of a factor of 20 was achieved including the time required to generate the clusters. An additional benefit of this structure is the creation of "plug-in" components, that is, individual networks can be removed and replaced with more effective structures or retrained as additional data becomes available without affecting the remaining networks in the hierarchy. Not all of our experiments have been reported here, but our results consistently show accuracy comparable to that achieved by the best monolithic back propagation networks with significant training time reductions.

Future work will concentrate on finding faster and more effective clustering algorithms as well as making improvements to the network learning rules. One planned addition to the leaf networks is the incorporation of the "don't care" training algorithm. In a don't care network, the separating surfaces are combinations of surfaces which separate pairs of classes rather than the traditional approach of separating one class from all others. The algorithm is fully described in [9] and has proven very effective in a variety of applications. As with the structure described above, don't care networks build complicated separating surfaces from simple components, each of which is easier and quicker to identify than the single separating surface. Further reductions in training time should be possible with this method.

Bibliography

[1] Atlas, Les, Ronald Cole, Yeshwant Muthusamy, Alan Lippman, Jerome Connor, Dong Park, Mohammed El-Sharkawi, and Robert Marks, "A Performance Comparison of Trained Multilayer Perceptrons and Trained Classification Trees", *Proceedings of the IEEE*, Volume 78, Number 10, October 1990.

[2] Benediktsson, J.A., J.R. Sveinsson, O.K. Ersoy, P.H. Swain, "Parallel Consensual Neural Networks", *Proceedings of the 1993 IEEE International Conference on Neural Networks*, Volume 1, pp. 27-32, San Francisco, CA, 1993.

[3] Duda and Hart, Pattern Classification and Scene Analysis, John Wiley & Sons, 1973.

[4] Fuji and Morita, "Recognition Systems for Handwritten Letters Simulating Visual Nervous System", Pattern Recognition and Machine Learning, pp 56-69, Plenum Press, New York, 1971.

[5] Guo, Heng, and Saul Gelfand, "Classifier Trees with Neural Networks Feature Extraction", Proceedings of the IEEE Computer Society Conference on Computer Vision and Pattern Recognition, Champaign, IL, 1992.

[6] Hartigan, John A., *Clustering Algorithms*, John Wiley and Sons 1975.

[7] Lee, James Shih-Jong, Jenq-Neng Hwang, Daniel Davis, and Alan Nelson, "Integration of Neural Networks and Decision Tree Classifiers for Automated Cytology Screening", *Proceedings of the International Joint Conference on Neural Networks*, Seattle, WA, 1991.

[8] Logar, Corwin and Oldham, "A Performance Comparison of Classification Techniques for Multi-Font Charactc. ecognition", to appear International Journal of Man Machine Studies.

[9] Logar, Corwin, Watters, Weger and Welch, "A Don't Care Back Propagation Algorithm Applied to Satellite Image Recognition", Proceedings of National SAC/ACM Conference, March 1994.

[10] Park, Youngtae and Jack Sklansky, "Fast Tree Classifier", *Proceedings of the 10th International Conference on Pattern Recognition*, Atlantic City, NJ, 1990.

[11] Perrone, Michael and Nathan Intrator, "Unsupervised Splitting Rules for Neural Tree Classifiers", *Proceedings of the International Joint Conference on Neural Networks*, Baltimore, MD, 1992.

[12] Sethi, Ishwar, "Entropy Nets : From Decision Trees to Neural Networks", *Proceedings of the IEEE*, Volume 78, Number 10, pp. 1605-13, 1990.

[13] Stromberg, Jan-Erik, Jalel Zrida, and Alf Isaksson, "Neural Trees - Using Neural Nets in a Tree Classifier Structure", *Proceedings of the International Conference on Acoustics, Speech and Signal Processing, Toronto*, 1991.

A Modular, Cyclic Neural Network for Character Recognition

M. Costa, E. Filippi and E. Pasero

Dept. of Electronics, Politecnico di Torino
C.so Duca degli Abruzzi, 24 - 10129 TORINO - ITALY

Abstract

We present a multi-layer feed-forward neural network that has been built up for pattern recognition purposes. Since we put special emphasis onto the aptitude towards hardware implementation, we provided it with a modular architecture of partially connected subnets. At its turn, this special organization makes it possible to avoid random initialization of the weights. The learning strategy is characterized by the adaptation of the learning rate coupled with an intermediate "batching" of the error back-propagation. To test the performance of the net in the classification of hand-written numerals, we fed the input units with grey-shaded patterns obtained from a large data set of the US National Institute of Standards and Technology (NIST). The original samples have been subjected only to scaling operations. The results up to now obtained seem quite interesting. In fact, in this application our recognizer ranks well among the ten best-rated OCR systems which competed in a world-wide contest organized by NIST itself in June 1992.

1 Introduction

Multi-Layer Perceptrons (MLPs) are presently used in a large variety of pattern recognition tasks, so they really constitute a clear example of general-purpose devices. However, when dealing with real-world applications like OCR, MLPs are seldom utilized in a plain form: in fact they are usually tailored to specific requirements, and sometimes they become part of more complex classifying systems.

This stems from the fact that, although its operation principle is quite straightforward, yet the design of an efficient MLP classifier constitutes a complex task, since at least three main issues are to be considered:

1) Experimental results clearly show that performance cannot be set free from the way information is encoded into the examples. *Data Preprocessing* strategy thus assumes major relevance, in that it can dramatically affect the final result as well as the amount of resources that suffices to achieve it;

2) Given the application, we would like to determine the optimal *Network Architecture* by means of few specifications and design rules. As a matter of fact, such process instead relies upon heuristic choices;

3) The *Learning Procedure* usually involves several parameters. Again, their values must be determined mainly on a trial-and-error basis, especially if advanced techniques like *weight decay*[1] are adopted.

It is thence evident that additional hints are needed in order to properly address the design strategy. In fact, several solutions have been proposed that exploit suggestions often provided by the application itself. For instance, several works are concerned with prior extraction of relevant features from the raw data: this is done by means of traditional algorithms[2], by setting up hybrid networks[3,4], or via highly constrained architectures with several hidden layers[5] that apply to MLPs some ideas owned by the Neocognitron[6]. An alternative interesting approach leads to the definition of MLP committees in conjunction with data resampling and the generation of synthetic patterns[7].

On the other side, we must take into account the existence of conventional techniques that already proved to be very effective, especially in the OCR field[8]. Compared to them, Artificial Neural Networks can rely on their own intrinsic, massive parallelism; but this winning characteristic cannot be exploited by software simulations on serial processors. So we think that it is required to give priority importance to the *hardware feasibility* of the proposed solutions. This concept, while forcing us to cope with stringent constraints, amazingly turned into a guideline along the formulation of those answers to the above issues that are described in the following sections.

2 Data Preprocessing

For our training experiments we chose a database of hand-written digits collected by the US National Institute of Standards and Technology (NIST). It consists of 223125 samples stored as binary images inside matrices of 128*128 pixels each.

We performed only scaling operations on the original data to produce patterns with specified dimensions and number of grey levels. For this purpose we developed two different algorithms: the first one forces the character to "touch" all four borders of the output image, while the other one preserves its original aspect ratio.

At first we utilized such procedures to build two distinct training sets of 16*16 binary patterns. We then carried out several simulations using two copies of the same MLP to assess the best alternative solution. Unfortunately, in any case we did not obtain encouraging results. However, we achieved substantial improvements by averaging the responses of the two nets. This fact suggested the opportunity of feeding a single MLP with both versions of the same data. In order to reduce the number of input components without losing information, we decided to use smaller patterns (8*8) with an higher number of grey levels (64).

Fig. 1 shows some examples of patterns that have been subjected to this kind of twofold preprocessing (only 5 grey levels are displayed).

Fig. 1

3 Network Architecture

In view of future hardware implementation, we identified three primary requirements to be followed in the architectural definition of the net:

1) Every neuron must have a limited number of synapses (we imposed a maximum of 32 plus the threshold);

2) Interconnections must be planned so as to allow an easy routing of the communication lines;

3) No additional constraints specifically related to OCR are to be imposed, so in principle the same solution can be directly utilized for other classification tasks, or scaled to fit their requirements.

We therefore designed a MLP provided with modular architecture. The number of modules equals that of the classes to be distinguished. Every module can be viewed as a partially connected subnet with only one output neuron.

Fig. 3 emphasizes the general organization of the net: in particular, it can be seen that different modules do not share any connection. We can take great advantage of this, because we can plan to physically realize only few modules and then multiplex them. Their actual number can be settled to allow an efficient pipelining of the preprocessing stage with proper MLP operation. Moreover, this highly parallelizable structure guarantees low spatial cross-talk among hidden neurons, thus resulting in a fairly high convergence rate during the training phase[9].

Fig. 4 shows the inner structure of the single module. The output neuron is completely connected with the hidden layer of 32 elements. At its turn, each hidden unit has access to only 28 input components in a cyclic, sequential fashion: i.e., inputs 1-28 are connected to the first neuron, inputs 29-56 are connected to the second neuron, .., inputs 113-128 and 1-12 are connected to the fifth neuron (that depicted dark in the figure), and so on. These choices take care of two important features: first, each module covers the input vector an integer number of times, so that the very same connection scheme is preserved along the network; second, different hidden neurons in the same module are connected with different subsets of the input vector.

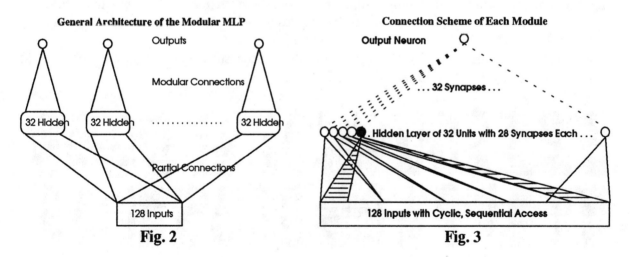

General Architecture of the Modular MLP

Outputs

Modular Connections

32 Hidden   32 Hidden   ....   32 Hidden

Partial Connections

128 Inputs

Fig. 2

Connection Scheme of Each Module

Output Neuron

... 32 Synapses ...

. Hidden Layer of 32 Units with 28 Synapses Each ...

128 Inputs with Cyclic, Sequential Access

Fig. 3

4 Learning Procedure

The special architecture of the net had a profound impact on the learning strategy itself. In fact, we noted that in this case random initialization of the weights could be avoided. We therefore started with null values (an entire class of MLPs with logistic neurons and generic number of hidden layers can be initialized in this way. Details are in [10]). Such a chance carries some interesting properties:

1) We get rid of one heuristic parameter, i.e. the maximum absolute value of the initial random weights;

2) Since neurons are provided with logistic transfer function, they lie in the farthest state from saturation. In other words, they are maximally sensitive to the error signal.

Of course, it was necessary to avoid the sudden spreading of weight values towards a substantially random distribution after few updatings. To do this, two solutions appeared that took the serious drawback of slowing down of the system evolution. That is:

1) Performing a *by epoch* training;

2) Using low learning rate.

Concerning the first point, we found a satisfactory trade-off by making one update every 100 patterns presented to the net, thus realizing an intermediate "batching" of the error back-propagation.

We then started with low learning rate (0.01), and then changed its value according to the Vögl adaptive technique[11]. After 100 training epochs, we halved all the weights and kept on with the same procedure for 50 additional epochs. Although this operation can be considered a very crude form of *weight decay*, nevertheless it have already proven to be quite effective[12].

Figures 4 and 5 show the behaviours of the learning rate and of the Mean Square Error (MSE) on the outputs vs. the number of training epochs. It should be noted that, as long as the learning rate increases, MSE tends to saturate until it stops decreasing. When this happens, the learning rate gets halved, thus allowing narrower zones of the error surface to be explored. As a result, MSE starts going down again.

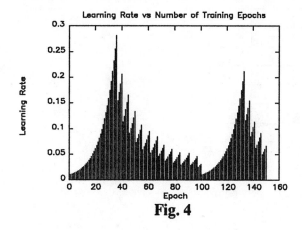

Fig. 4

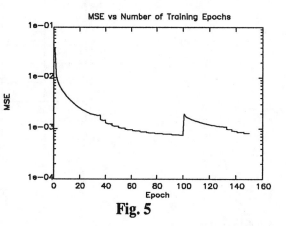

Fig. 5

5 Performance Evaluation

In June 1992, NIST organized a world-wide contest with the purpose of evaluating the state of the art in the OCR field. For what concerns hand-written numerals, NIST provided a suggested training set (the one we previously described) and a test set of 58646 samples purposely taken from a very different population. Therefore, recognition performance on the latter database is very revealing about the generalization capability of the system. We preprocessed such samples in the same way we did for their training counterparts (except for the fact that in this case we used only 16 grey levels), and then we tried to classify them by means of our modular MLP.

In particular, we were mainly interested in checking the behaviour of the net when constraints on the resolution of both memory and computing elements are applied[13,14]. We then quantized all the weights using 6 bits, and the transfer function of the hidden neurons using 4 bits. Here output neurons are not involved. In fact, since their transfer function is monotonic, we can determine the winning class directly on their activations. In analog implementations these quantities are usually expressed in terms of currents, and very simple circuits can be designed to select the highest one[15].

With this configuration, when we forced the net to take a decision anyway, we achieved 3.69% error rate on the NIST Test Set. It is worth nothing that performance worsening is very limited in comparison with the usage of floating-point weights and neurons, since it amounts to about 0.1%. This stems from the fact that weight values result more uniformly distributed once decay is applied and additional training epochs performed.

We then rejected the most dubious cases by imposing lower thresholds onto the winning outcome: clearly this is not the most effective solution, since the amount of information provided by the net is not fully taken into account. However, it has been chosen for its simplicity. Fig. 6 summarizes the results we obtained: dots in the graph show the behaviour of the error rate with regard to the percentage of rejected samples.

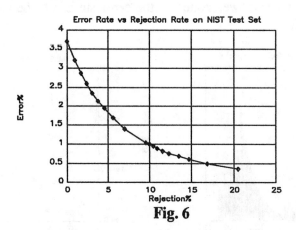

Fig. 6

6 Conclusions

We showed how a large, real-word task like the recognition of hand-written numerals may be efficiently and economically accomplished by means of a rather general-purpose MLP. In fact, our classifier correctly recognized more than 96.3% of the samples contained in the NIST Test Set.

Therefore, it ranks sixth in the corresponding graduated list even in the presence of the constraints we imposed for hardware feasibility purposes.

We want to point out here the plainness of the solutions that allowed us to achieve this result: no complex features are extracted from the raw data, no "a priori" knowledge about the problem to be solved is used in the architectural definition of the net. Moreover, the system has a total amount of 9610 free parameters: so it is about as large as a completely connected MLP with 128 inputs, one hidden layer of only 69 units, 10 outputs.

Acknowledgements

This work is partly supported by Italian "Programma Nazionale di Ricerca sulle Tecnologie per la Bioelettronica"

References

[1] Krogh A. and Hertz J. A., "A Simple Weight Decay can Improve Generalization", in Advances in Neural Information Processing Systems 4, Moody J. E., Hanson S. J. and Lippmann R. P. (eds.), Morgan Kauffman Publishers, San Mateo, California, 1992

[2] Garris M. D., Wilkinson R. A. and Wilson C. L., "Methods for Enhancing Neural Network Handwritten Character Recognition", in Proc. of the International Joint Conference on Neural Networks, Vol. 1, San Diego, California, 1991

[3] Costa M. and Pasero E., "FNC: a Fuzzy Neural Classifier with Bayesan Engine", in Proc. of Italian Workshop on Neural Nets, Vietri sul Mare (SA), Italy, 1993

[4] Iwata A., Tohma T., Matsuo H. and Suzumura N., "A Large Scale Neural Network "CombNET" and its Application to Chinese Character Recognition", in Proc. of the International Neural Network Conference, Vol. 1, Paris, France, 1990

[5] LeCun Y., Boser B. E., Denker J. S., Henderson D., Howard R. E., Hubbard W. and Jackel L. D., "Handwritten Digit Recognition with a Back-Propagation Network", in Advances in Neural Information Processing Systems 2, Touretzky D. S. (ed.), Morgan Kauffman Publishers, San Mateo, California, 1990

[6] Fukushima K. and Wake N., "Handwritten Alphanumeric Character Recognition by the Neocognitron", in IEEE Transactions on Neural Networks, Vol. 2, No. 3, May 1991

[7] Drucker H., Schapire R. and Simard P., "Improving Performance in Neural Networks Using a Boosting Algorithm", in Advances in Neural Information Processing Systems 5, Hanson S. J., Cowan J. D., Giles C. L. (eds.), Morgan Kauffman Publishers, San Mateo, California, 1993

[8] Mori S., Ching Y. S. and Yamamoto K, "Historical Review of OCR Research and Development", in Proceedings of the IEEE, Vol. 80, No. 7, July 1992

[9] Jacobs R. A., Jordan M. I. and Barto A. G., "Task Decomposition through Competition in a Modular Connectionist Architecture: the What and Where Vision Tasks", COINS Technical Report No. 90-27, Dept. of Computer & Information Science, University of Massachusetts, 1990

[10] Costa M., "Sulle Topologie di Connessioni in Percettroni Multistrato che Consentono di Inizializzare a Zero i Pesi della Rete", Internal Report No. DE-930715, Dept. of Electronics, Politecnico di Torino, 1993

[11] Vogl T. P., Mangis J. K., Rigler A. K., Zink W. T. and Alkon D. L., "Accelerating the Convergence of the Back-Propagation Method", in Byol. Cybern. 59, 1988

[12] Vassallo G., Gioiello M., Condemi C. and Sorbello F., "Neural Solutions for the Handwritten Character Recognition Task", submitted to Conference on Computer Vision and Pattern Recognition, Seattle, Washington, 1994

[13] Boser B. E., Sackinger E., Bromley J., LeCun Y. and Jackel L. D., "Hardware Requirements for Neural Network Pattern Classifiers", in IEEE Micro, February 1992

[14] Reyneri L. M. and Filippi E., "An Analysis on the Performance of Silicon Implementations of Backpropagation Algorithms for Artificial Neural Networks", in IEEE Transactions on Computers, Vol. 4, No. 12, December 1991

[15] Vittoz E., "Analog VLSI Implementation of Neural Networks", in Proc. of Journées d'Électronique - Réseaux de Neurones Artificiels / Artificial Neural Networks, Lausanne, Switzerland, 1989

Self-Organization of Feature Maps for Recognition of Unconstrained Handwritten Numerals

Sukhan Lee[1,2] and Yeongwoo Choi[1]

Dept. of EE-Systems[1]
University of Southern California
Los Angeles, CA 90089-0781

Jet Propulsion Laboratory[2]
California Institute of Technology
Pasadena, CA 91109

Abstract

A novel method for recognizing unconstrained handwritten numerals based on the self-organization of local feature maps is presented. The proposed network is hierarchically configured with three blocks of layers. The bottom layer has local feature maps that represent distinct shapes and locations of local features of individual numerals. Those feature maps are self-organized into groups to represent the fundamental composition of individual numerals. The middle layer has maximum selection networks, which generate an output from each feature group as the matching score of a local feature that has maximum matching with the given input sample. Finally, the top layer is a backpropagation network for making a final decision based on the outputs of individual feature groups of each numeral. The proposed network achieves robustness to translation, rotation, and scaling by defining areas of feasible feature locations in the feature maps defined in both the Cartesian and Polar coordinates. Distortion is handled by a number of representative shapes generated by self-organization of each feature group. The self-organization of feature maps is accomplished by automatically recruiting local features and by describing their correlations from training samples based on the evaluation of network performance. The experimentation with the CEDAR[1] data base demonstrates that the proposed method is superior to the existing benchmark results [1, 2].

1 Introduction

Handwritten zip codes and character data manifest that real data are subject to large amounts of distortion, scaling, and rotation. But, many of the previous approaches developed for off-line handwritten character recognition can only provide a partial solution to those real-world problems. Thus, it is essential to develop a recognition system robust to various forms of deformations present in real data, yet computationally efficient for real-time applications.

As a means of achieving the above goal, we have proposed a *Dual Cooperative Neural Network* (DCN) in which a *Cartesian Network* (CN) and a *Log-Polar Network* (LPN) cooperatively determine the pattern class [3]. DCN is intended to combine the strengths of the Cartesian and polar coordinate data representations: for instance, rotated and/or scaled input patterns in Cartesian coordinates appear in polar representation as horizontally or vertically shifted patterns, which can be easily detected by *nearby horizontal or vertical shift invariant feature detecting cells* in polar coordinate feature maps. Furthermore, the discrimination power of DCN is increased by the two sets of local feature maps that are selected independently as the most salient geometric features in the Cartesian and polar coordinates, respectively. The proposed DCN has been shown effective in handling handwritten numeric patterns corrupted by translation, rotation, scaling, and distortion, as demonstrated in [3].

In this paper, a new network architecture is proposed for DCN with the emphasis on the self-organization of local feature maps. The proposed network architecture has a hierarchical structure with three blocks of layers: *a local feature map layer, a maximum selection/correlation layer,* and *a decision layer with back-propagation networks (BPNs).* In network learning, not only the weights of BPNs in the decision layer are

---

[1]The Center of Excellence for Document Analysis and Recognition, SUNY, Buffalo

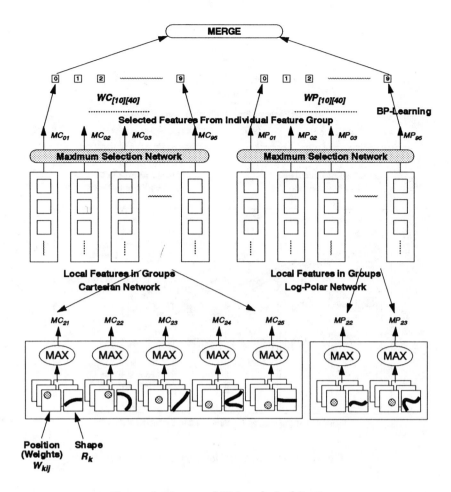

Figure 1: Proposed Network Architecture

iteratively updated, but also the features of the local feature map layer are automatically recruited for each feature group whenever necessary for improving the network performance. The proposed self-organization of feature maps avoids the difficulties of selecting shape features in Neocognitron approach [4], and of determining the number of required hidden units or local features in the backpropagation based network approaches [1, 2]. The network achieves the robustness to translation, rotation, and scaling variations based on the tolerance of feasible feature locations in the feature maps defined in the Cartesian and polar coordinates. Whereas, the robustness to distortion and thickness variations comes from a variety of representative feature shapes defined in the maps by self-organization. The proposed network has been successfully tested with the standard *CEDAR* data base.

2 Network Architecture

Fig. 1 illustrates the proposed network architecture. At the bottom layer are the local feature maps. The local feature maps are to represent distinct shapes and locations of local features of individual numerals. To represent the fundamental composition of individual numerals, local feature maps are organized into groups. For instance, there are 5 feature groups defined for the numeral 2 in CN, and 4 feature groups in LPN. For the entire numerals, 47 feature groups are defined in CN and 41 in LPN. Each group provides a single matching score to be used for the final decision.

A feature map, composed of a shape map and a position map, represents a cluster of features similar in shape and location. The shape map specifies the representative shape of the feature map, and the position

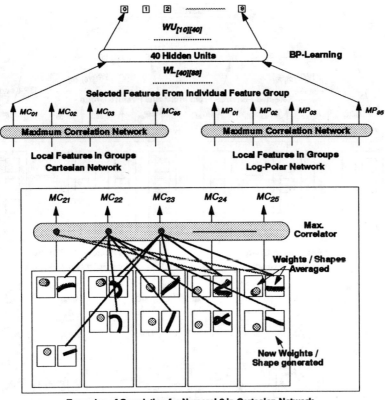

Examples of Correlation for Numeral 2 in Cartesian Network

Figure 2: Alternative Network Architecture

map defines the tolerance in position based on the weights assigned to each cell of the feature map. The network recruits feature maps for each group based on self-organization.

At the middle layer is the maximum selection/correlation network. It simply generates an output from each feature group as the maximum matching score with the given input sample, or, as the matching score of a feature map that provides the maximum correlation with the given input sample in a global context, as a more sophisticated matching scheme. At the top layer are BPNs for the final decision based on the outputs of individual feature groups of each numeral. A BPN can be defined for CN and LPN either individually or as a whole.

Fig. 1 illustrates a network architecture with three layers, where the maximum selection network is used for the middle layer, and single layer BPNs are used for generating outputs of CN and LPN, respectively. The outputs of CN and LPN are merged at the top for a final decision under the consideration of the rank of individual numerals. This network architecture emphasizes simplicity so that the network can show a high degree of generalization.

Fig. 2 illustrate an alternative, but more sophisticated, network architecture. First, it uses maximum correlation networks, instead of maximum selection networks, at the middle layer. The maximum correlation network maintains the correlation connections of feature maps among individual groups of a numeral, and generates an output from each group that provides the maximum correlation with the input. The correlation among feature maps for numeral 2 in CN is shown in Fig. 2, where each correlation node, MC_{ij}, connects the feature maps of different groups to represent the contextual information among feature maps. Each correlation node makes a sum of the matching scores of its feature maps, and the matching scores of the feature maps corresponding to the correlation node which scores maximum are selected for the input to the next layer. The correlation nodes are also self-organized. In addition, at the top layer, a 2-layer BPN is used for making a final decision.

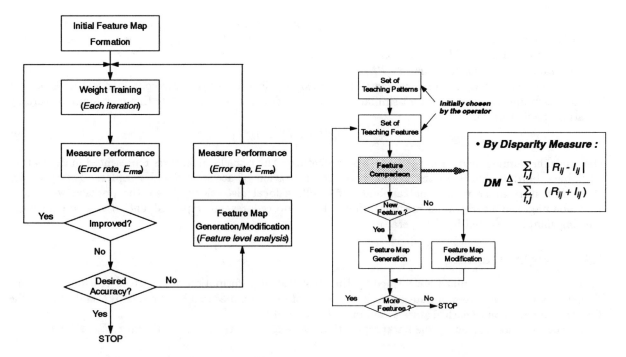

Figure 3: (a) Overall Learning Scheme (b) Initial Feature Map Generation

3 Network Self-Organization

The overall learning scheme is shown in Fig. 3(a). Initial feature maps are self-organized from the local features selected by the operator. Then, based on the initial feature maps, the weights, WC and WP, of BPNs are trained by the backpropagation learning to reduce the error. The weight training continues as long as the performance of the network shows any improvement. When the network performance is saturated, either we generate new feature maps, or reinforce the existing feature maps based on the rejected and incorrect samples. This process is iterated until the network performance reaches a desired value. In what follows, we describe the above procedure in more detail.

3.1 Initial Feature Map Generation

In this stage, initial feature maps are self-organized in each feature group of the numeral from teaching samples and their features selected by an operator. Fig. 3(b) shows the initial feature map generation. Some examples of teaching feature selection are shown in Fig. 7, and their generated features for numeral 2 are shown in the first row of Fig. 5.

Initially, there exists no feature map in each feature group. The number of feature maps in each feature group are increased by feature comparison. When a teaching sample is given, the first teaching feature, I, is compared to the existing reference features of the corresponding feature group. Feature comparison is done by measuring the *similarity* (SM) between the input and the reference features. The SM is defined by $SM \triangleq 1 - DM$, and DM is a disparity measurement with normalized sizes. If a similar feature dose not exist in the corresponding feature group, that is, the SM is less than the given threshold (in our experiment, the threshold is set at 0.8), the input feature is recruited as a new reference feature, R_k. Thus, a new feature map is generated by copying $R_k = I$ and by initializing the corresponding position weight, $W_{k_{ij}}$, the i,jth cell of the kth feature map,

$$W_{k_{ij}}^{new} = \begin{cases} \frac{1}{m} & \text{if } W_{k_{ij}}^{old} = 0 \\ W_{k_{ij}}^{old} + \frac{1}{n}(\frac{1}{m} - W_{k_{ij}}^{old}) & \text{otherwise} \end{cases} \tag{1}$$

where m is the number of the teaching features for each numeral, and n is the number of updates of the corresponding weight. Also, the position weights of the nearby cells, $W_{k_{pq}}$, are initialized by $W_{k_{pq}} = G(p,q)W_{k_{ij}}$ where $G(p,q)$ is a slightly decreasing function by the cell position, and has the highest value in i,jth position. *These neighboring weights are initialized together to tolerate positional errors in CN and to tolerate scale and rotational errors in LPN.*

Then, the next input feature is compared to the existing features of the corresponding feature group. If there exist similar features, the most similar feature is modified to accommodate this new input feature by updating the feature map :

$$R_k^{new} = R_k^{old} + \frac{1}{n}(I_r - R_k^{old}), \tag{2}$$

where n is the number of updates for that reference feature. Thus, the local features represented in the feature maps have blurred shapes as the result of the generalization of accommodated samples. This provides the local feature maps with some capability of handling local distortions. Also, the position weights of corresponding and nearby cells are reinforced. These procedures are repeated until there are no more teaching samples selected by the operator.

3.2 Weight Training

Since the initial feature maps are formed by the local feature information of the given teaching patterns, the network needs to accommodate global information of teaching patterns by training WC and WP for the different contribution of each feature group in each numeral.

The weights are trained by the backpropagation learning [5] to reduce network error, E_p, defined by

$$E_p = \frac{1}{2}\sum_i (t_{p_i} - o_{p_i})^2. \tag{3}$$

Here, t_{p_i} is the desired output value (1 for true, -1 for others) and o_{p_i} is the actual output value for the ith output unit of the pth teaching pattern with a sigmoidal activation function. And, the overall network error, E_{rms}, is defined by

$$E_{rms} = \sqrt{\frac{2}{MN}\sum_{p=1}^{N} E_p}, \tag{4}$$

where M is the total number of class, and N is the total number of training patterns. Weights are updated by

$$\Delta_p W_{ij} = \frac{\partial E_p}{\partial W_{ij}} = \eta(1 - o_{p_i}^2)(t_{p_i} - o_{p_i})MC_{ij}, \tag{5}$$

where η is a learning coefficient (0.01 in our experiment), and MC_{ij} (or MP_{ij}) is a maximum matching score of each feature group.

During the experiment, the patterns were repeatedly presented in a constant order. The weights were updated after each presentation of a single pattern rather than updated by a *true* gradient procedure (averaging over the whole training set before updating the weights), due to a large redundancy in the data base [1].

3.3 Self-Organization of Feature Maps

After each iteration of weight updates, the error rate and E_{rms} were measured. If the error rate was improved, weight updates were continued. But, when there is no more improvement in error rate with iterative weight training, the network may need new shape features from the rejected and incorrect training samples. For the selection of optimal or near optimal features, a self-organization of local feature sets for individual characters, as a part of supervised network learning process, is needed. Thus, new shape features are captured and added to the network, and similar features are accommodated to the existing features of the network from the training samples.

Fig. 4 shows examples of the feature map generation/modification. Initially, only the first 2, which was selected by the operator, was registered in the network as a reference sample. Assuming that the second 2 is given to the network and the network result is unclear (possible for rejection) or incorrect, then new feature

III-214

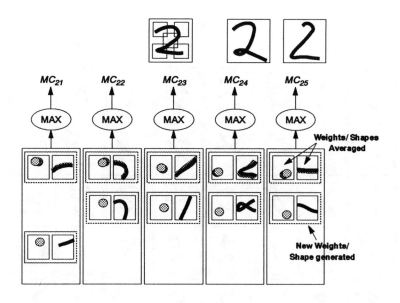

Figure 4: Examples of Feature Map Generation/Modification

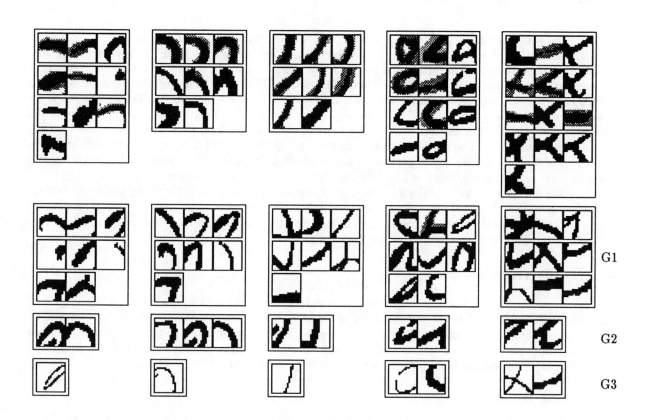

Figure 5: Generated Reference Features for Numeral 2 in CN

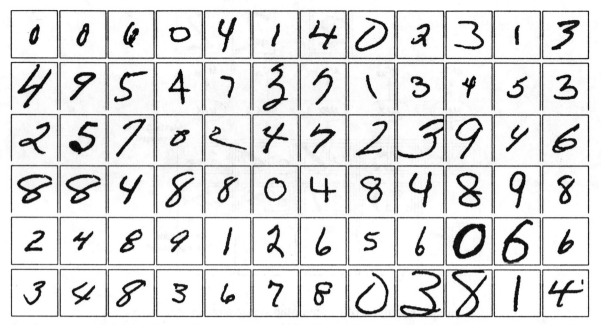

Figure 6: Unconstrained Handwritten Numerals from Zip Codes (Examples of correctly recognized test patterns)

maps can be generated from this sample. Firstly, the output response of each feature group is examined. To select a position of a new feature in each feature group, the position with the highest matching score among the currently registered feature maps is selected. And, a new feature is captured from the rejected or incorrect pattern according to that position information. Then, the shape of the captured feature is compared to the existing features in the same feature group. If there exists a similar feature, the shape and positions (weights) are accommodated by averaging. If not, this feature is registered as a new feature in that feature group by creating a new feature map (shape and positions). Thus, for the second 2, one feature is blurred to the existing similar feature, and four features are generated and registered in each feature group. For the third 2, only one feature is generated, and four other features are accommodated to the existing features. This process is continued until all the rejected and incorrect patterns are examined.

Fig. 5 shows the generated reference features for numeral 2 in CN with 200 training patterns. Features in the first row show the generated reference features in each feature group from the operator given teaching features. G1 indicates the first generation of new features after the 30th iterations of weight updates, and G2 and G3 show the next generations of new features.

4 Experiment

In this experiment, the proposed network with maximum selection network and single layer BPNs in each CN and LPN was implemented and tested. Weights, WC and WP, are fully connected with 10 output units, and each corresponding outputs of the networks are merged by adding output score and rank together. When an input pattern is given, it is size normalized to 58×58 for CN and log-polar transformed to 23×70 for LPN (instead of 23×60 to handle boundary portions of the transformed input).

4.1 Data Base

Real handwritten zip code data provided by *CEDAR* were used for the experiment. These are binary handwritten digits segmented from zip codes with a resolution of 300 ppi (12 pixels/mm). Some examples are shown in Fig. 6. It can be seen that the data usually contain *distortion, scaling, thickness variations, rotation, translation, noise, etc.* From this data base, the initial 2000 patterns (200 for each numeral) were used for training, and 2213 patterns[2] were used for testing in this experiment.

---

[2] *CEDAR* recommended test set

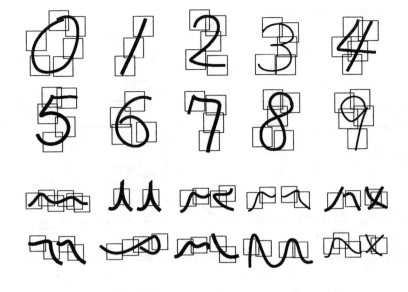

Figure 7: Examples of Feature Selection in CN and LPN

Table 1: Generated Reference Features in CN and in LPN

CN	Initial	G1	G2	G3
0	7 8 5 11 9 6	10 9 6 14 12 7	10 9 7 15 12 7	11 9 7 16 13 7
1	4 4 5	7 7 8	7 7 8	7 7 8
2	10 8 8 11 13	18 15 15 19 22	20 18 17 21 24	21 19 18 23 26
3	10 9 10 9 12	12 11 12 9 12	14 12 14 9 13	15 12 14 10 14
4	18 20 18 17 13	22 24 22 20 16	25 25 24 21 19	25 25 25 21 19
5	12 18 19 15 16	15 19 22 17 17	16 20 22 17 17	16 21 23 18 18
6	11 14 15 17	14 16 21 21	14 16 21 21	15 17 22 22
7	15 11 11 11	18 14 12 13	19 15 13 13	19 18 13 14
8	20 21 14 15 17	31 33 25 27 29	31 33 25 27 29	33 35 28 29 30
9	16 15 20 11 11	20 20 27 16 14	21 22 28 16 14	21 23 28 16 14
Total (Ave. No.)	590 (12.5)	790 (16.8)	828 (17.6)	865 (18.4)
LPN	Initial	G1	G2	G3
0	15 16 9 11 12 10	18 18 10 12 14 10	19 18 10 13 14 10	19 18 10 13 14 10
1	5 4	7 6	7 6	7 6
2	16 21 14 14	24 29 19 21	24 29 20 22	26 32 21 23
3	15 18 17 18	21 24 21 20	23 27 22 22	24 27 22 22
4	15 13 9 14	20 19 13 17	21 23 13 17	23 23 13 17
5	17 12 15 15	26 18 22 21	29 19 26 24	34 20 28 25
6	9 11 19 20	13 14 21 24	15 15 23 26	16 15 24 31
7	11 15 9 9	15 20 12 13	15 21 12 13	15 22 12 14
8	18 19 17 15	28 28 26 25	30 30 28 26	31 32 29 27
9	16 16 17 9 12	24 21 24 13 15	29 25 26 15 17	31 25 28 18 17
Total (Ave. No.)	567 (13.8)	766 (18.7)	824 (20.1)	865 (21.1)

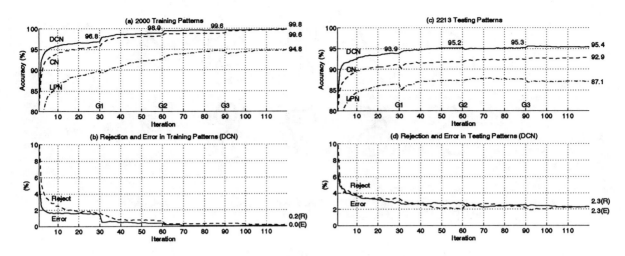

Figure 8: Network Performance : with rejection when the difference of two strongest outputs are within 5%.

Table 2: Various Test Results for 2213 Test Patterns

End of	Initial	G1	G2	G3
w/o rejection	95.2 0.0 4.8	96.3 0.0 3.7	96.4 0.0 3.6	96.7 0.0 3.3
rejection w/ 5%	93.9 3.3 2.8	95.2 2.0 2.8	95.3 2.2 2.6	95.4 2.3 2.3
2.0% error	92.9 5.1 2.0	93.5 4.5 2.0	94.8 3.3 2.0	95.0 3.0 2.0
1.0% error	87.3 11.7 1.0	90.6 8.4 1.0	92.5 6.5 1.0	93.0 6.0 1.0

4.2 Results

Initial networks were formed with about 20 to 30 training samples of each numeral in each network. Examples of operator selection of teaching features are shown in Fig. 7. The number of selected features are different depending on the numeral. 47 features were selected in CN and 41 in LPN. Table 1 shows the number of generated reference features in each feature group of the numeral with 2000 training patterns. At G1, many new feature were generated, but at G2 and G3, only small number of new features were generated and added.

The network performance is shown in Fig. 8. Each iteration involves presentation of 2000 training samples. In Fig. 8(a), DCN (solid line) represents merged results of CN (broken line) and LPN (dotted line). From the initial networks, after 25 iterations of weight updates, the network performance was almost saturated, that is, no more improvement in accuracy was obtained. Thus, at G1, new features were generated from the rejected and incorrect patterns by the network self-organization. By recruiting new necessary features, the network performance was immediately improved both for training and testing patterns. Fig. 8(b) shows the rejected and incorrect training patterns as learning progresses. Fig. 8(c) and (d) show the results with 2213 test patterns. We can see the effectiveness of the dual cooperation of networks by the performance improvement particularly in the testing patterns. Test results show 95.4% of accuracy with 2.3% rejection and 2.3% error for test patterns, and 99.8% of accuracy with 0.2% rejection for training patterns.

But, for a practical and accurate evaluation of the proposed network, and for a fair comparison with [1], we have measured the accuracy and rejection rate for 1% and 2% error of the test patterns. Those results are shown in Table 2. We can see the robustness of the proposed network particularly in 2% and 1% error measurement. At the end of G3, our system rejected 3.0% for a 2.0% error and 6.0% for a 1.0% error, which is about 3% better than [1] in recognition rate. Fig. 9 shows incorrectly recognized test patterns for the 1% error (Fig. 9(a)), for 2% error (Fig. 9(a-b)), and for rejection within 5% (Fig. 9(a-c)). Some of the patterns were incorrectly recognized mainly due to their large size.

With this experiment, we can conclude that the network performance can be greatly improved 1) by combining the iterative weight training of BPNs and the automatic recruitment of local feature maps in each

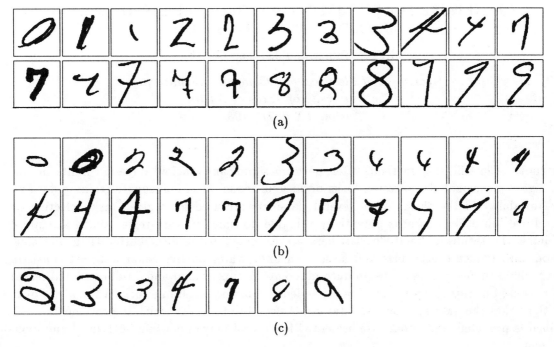

(a)

(b)

(c)

Figure 9: Incorrectly Recognized Test Patterns : (a) 1% error, (a-b) 2% error, and (a-c) rejection w/ 5%

feature group, and 2) by combining two independent, cooperative networks, CN and LPN. Comparing to other works [1, 2, 4], our proposed network with a new learning scheme was tested with totally unconstrained handwritten numerals *without* any complex rotation and/or thickness normalization steps and *without* any noise removal process.

5 Conclusion

In this paper, a new hierarchical network structure based on self-organization of feature maps to recognize unconstrained handwritten numerals has been discussed, and very promising results were obtained. Our approach can give robustness to various deformations such as translation, rotation, scaling, and even distortion and thickness variation. Complete experiments by including the maximum correlation layer and by adding more training patterns are in progress.

References

[1] Y. LeCun, B. Boser, J. S. Denker, D. Henderson, R. E. Howard, W. Hubbard, and L. D. Jackel. Backpropagation applied to handwritten zip code recognition. In *Neural Computation*, volume 1, pages 541–551, 1989.

[2] Gale L. Martin and James A. Pittman. Recognizing hand-printed letters and digits using backpropagation learning. In *Neural Computation*, volume 3, pages 258–267, 1991.

[3] Sukhan Lee and Yeongwoo Choi. Recognition of unconstrained handwritten numerals based on dual cooperative neural network. In *3rd International Workshop on Frontiers in Handwriting Recognition, Buffalo*, pages 1–10, May 1993.

[4] Kunihito Fukushima and Nobuaki Wake. Handwritten alphanumeric character recognition by the neocognitron. In *IEEE Trans. on Neural Networks*, volume 2, no. 3, pages 355–365, 1991.

[5] D. E. Rumelhart, G. E. Hinton, and R. J. Williams. Learning internal representations by error propagation. In *Parallel Distributed Processing*, volume 1, pages 318–362. D.E. Rumelhart and J.L. McClelland (Eds.), Cambridge, MA: MIT Press, 1986.

A FRAMEWORK FOR ESTIMATING PERFORMANCE IMPROVEMENTS IN HYBRID PATTERN CLASSIFIERS

Kagan Tumer and Joydeep Ghosh

Department of Electrical and Computer Engineering
The University of Texas at Austin
Austin, TX 78712-1084

Abstract: Classification methods often perform significantly below Bayesian limits in complex, high-dimensional classification tasks because of model bias, inadequate training data and noise/variability in the data. When several classifiers are used for a given task, selecting one method over all others discards potentially valuable information. Strategies aimed at suitably combining the results of multiple classifiers are expected to perform better than any single method, and reduce overall bias and noise. An underwater passive sonar data set consisting of over 1000 samples processed to produce different 25-dimensional and 24-dimensional feature vectors is used in this study to examine an evidence combination framework. An analysis of the conditions that the data sets must satisfy, and the conditions under which improvements can be obtained is provided, and results are presented for hybrid networks using both local and global classifiers.

1 Introduction

Supervised feed-forward neural networks have been applied to numerous classification problems in signal processing and pattern recognition [5]. These include the Multi-Layer Perceptron (MLP) employing sigmoidal "hidden units," as well as kernel-based classifiers such as those using Radial or Elliptical Basis Functions (EBFs) [2, 6]. Such networks can serve as nonparametric, adaptive classifiers that learn through examples [5], without requiring a good *a priori* mathematical model for the underlying signal characteristics.

Finding the best-suited network and the optimal selection of features for classification is not generally possible beforehand. Concatenating all types of signal descriptors into a single input vector is undesirable for several reasons. First, a large input layer may lengthen the training time and complicate parameter selection. Second, mixing conceptually different features may decrease the relative importance of the most discriminating features. Therefore, it may be beneficial to train separate networks on distinct data sets obtained from the same physical signal by using qualitatively different feature extractors. Similarly, different types of FFNs have different characteristics. For example, EBFs are more locally tuned than MLPs. Furthermore each network introduces some bias, and combining different networks can reduce the bias and make the classifier more robust [7].

In the context of supervised feedforward networks, interpretation of network outputs as Bayesian a posteriori probabilities [8] provides a sound basis for combining the results from multiple classifiers to yield more accurate classification [1, 3, 4]. The concept of stacked generalization, an inductive approach to combining generalizers, has been recently introduced by Wolpert [9]. A framework for hybrid neural networks in regression estimates was discussed in [7].

In this paper, we focus on the statistical aspects of such combining methods. Errors made by different classifiers are labeled and used in estimating potential improvements. First we provide a motivating example and analyze the properties of both correctly and incorrectly classified patterns. Then, we present a framework in which combination results can be studied. Finally, we show how the theory can be applied to the data set of Section 2.

2 A Motivating Real Life Example

In this section we motivate the combination framework by studying a real life classification problem, where the objective is to correctly identify different underwater acoustic signals. Since neither the important features of the data, nor the best classifier to process them is known beforehand, two classifiers and two features sets are used in the study.

Table 1: Data Description.

		Feature Set 1		Feature Set 2	
Class	Description	Training	Testing	Training	Testing
1	Porpoise whistle	116	284	142	284
2	Ice cracking	116	175	175	175
3	Whale cry 1	116	129	129	129
4	Whale cry 2	148	235	118	235
Total		496	823	564	823

The first classifier (C1) is a fully connected MLP with a single hidden layer consisting of 50 units, and the second classifier (C2) is an EBF with 50 kernels. In the first feature set (FS1), each sample is represented by a 25-dimensional vector comprising of 16 Gabor wavelet coefficients, 8 other temporal descriptors and 1 signal duration indicator [1]. The second feature set (FS2) contained 24-dimensional vectors each comprising of 10 reflection coefficients of energy segments obtained through short time windows, 10 reflection coefficients computed over the entire window, 3 temporal descriptors, and 1 signal duration indicator. Table 1 shows the number of classes, and the number of training and test samples available for each feature set. The test patterns in each feature set represent the *same* raw data.

Table 2: Results of Individual Classifiers.

Classifier/ Feature set	% Correctly Classified	Standard Deviation	95% Confidence Interval
C1/FS1	92.66	.63	92.21–93.11
C1/FS2	88.60	.73	88.08–89.12
C2/FS1	91.30	.64	90.84–91.76
C2/FS2	82.02	2.22	80.43–83.61

Table 2 provides the classification results for each individual classifier/feature set pair. The best performance is achieved by C1 using FS1. A naive approach is to select this combination and ignore the other three. An important fact that must be remembered however is that since each pattern is assigned to the class whose output unit has the largest activation value, valuable information may be discarded during this "max" selection step. A more scrutinizing look reveals that there are significant fluctuations in the activation values of the winning classes, depending on the classifier used and on whether the class chosen was in fact the correct one or not. Since these activation values approximate a posteriori probability distributions [8], they can be used to combine information in different ways. Two such combiners will be examined in this study. The first combiner (AVE) will average the output activities of the sources and select the maximum. The second combiner (MAX) will assign the pattern to the class whose output has the largest activation among both sets of output vectors. In the following section we provide a framework in which the combination results can be interpreted and studied.

3 Combining Framework

In this section we formalize the conditions that are necessary for a combiner to improve the classification rate of different classifiers. Given any data set, the first stage in classification tasks is to extract the features that will be used as inputs to the classifier. Different feature sets will capture different aspects of the data. Similarly different networks will emphasize different properties of the input space. If a combiner is to improve the results, it must utilize all the pieces of information that are available through the individual classifiers. This section develops a framework highlighting the conditions under which such improvements can be expected.

Let D be a data set, and let D_{tr} and D_{tst} be a partition that represents the training and test sets respectively. A network f assigns a pattern $x \in D_{tst}$ to class C_i if the ith output unit $f(x)_i$, has the largest activation value among all output units. Let $d(\cdot, \cdot)$ be a distance metric in the pattern space. An ϵ-neighborhood $N(x; \epsilon)$ of x is the set of all points y such that $d(x, y) < \epsilon$. A deleted ϵ-neighborhood $N^*(x; \epsilon)$ of x is $N(x; \epsilon) - \{x\}$, i.e., the point x is removed.

Definition 1 *A data set D, partitioned into n classes $C_1, \ldots, C_n$, is <u>consistent</u> if $\forall x \in D$, $\exists$ a deleted ϵ-neighborhood $N^*(x; \epsilon)$ of x s.t. $\forall y \in N^*(x; \epsilon)$, $x \in C_i \Rightarrow y \in C_i$. Furthermore, $N^*(x; \epsilon) \bigcap D_{tr} \neq \phi$ and $N^*(x; \epsilon) \bigcap D_{tst} \neq \phi$.*

A data set is consistent if there are no point–classes, i.e. classes consisting of single isolated points. It is important to note that consistency does not require classes to be contiguous, just that two points sufficiently close belong to the same class, and that the training and test sets represent the data equally well.

Definition 2 *Let $E[f(x)_i]$ and $E[f(z)_i]$ represent the average activations of the outputs corresponding to the correct class, computed over $N(x; \epsilon)$ and $N(z; \epsilon')$ respectively. A data set D is <u>balanced</u> with respect to a given function f, if $E[f(x)_i] = E[f(z)_i]$, for any two arbitrary $N(x; \epsilon)$ and $N(z; \epsilon')$.*

A data set is balanced if the expected activation value of correctly classified outputs is independent of the samples chosen.

Definition 3 *A network f is <u>properly trained</u> if $\forall x \in D_{tst}$ that has been assigned to class C_i, $f(x)_i$ is a monotonically non-increasing function of $d(x, y)$, where $y \in C_i$, $y \in D_{tr}$. Moreover $\forall z \in D_{tr}$, $d(x, y) \leq d(x, z)$.*

A network is properly trained if the largest activation value of the output for a test pattern is a non-increasing function of its relative distance of the pattern to the closest training pattern of the correct class.

Theorem 1 *A network properly trained on a balanced, consistent data set will have higher expected activation values for correctly classified patterns than for incorrectly classified patterns.*

Proof: Let $x \in D_{tst}$. Further, let x be misclassified in class C_i (target class was $j \neq i$). Let $y \in D_{tr}$ be the closest pattern in C_i to x. Since the data set is consistent, there exists a deleted ϵ-neighborhood $N^*(y; \epsilon)$ of y such that $N^*(y; \epsilon) \subseteq C_i$. Since $x \notin C_i$, we also have $x \notin N^*(y; \epsilon)$. Therefore $d(x, y) \geq d(z, y)$, $\forall z \in N^*(y; \epsilon)$, and, since f is properly trained $f(z)_i \geq f(x)_i$, $\forall z \in N^*(y, \epsilon) \bigcap D_{tst}$. So, $E[f(z)_i] \geq f(x)_i$ where $E[\cdot]$ is computed over $N(y, \epsilon) \bigcap D_{tst}$. Now, for all the erroneously classified patterns x, such a neighborhood exists. Furthermore since the data set is balanced the expected valued of the activation for correct patterns is constant. Therefore $E[f(z)_i] \geq f(x)_i$, for all erroneously classified patterns x, on any neighborhood $N(z, \epsilon) \subseteq D_{tst}$. Therefore $E[f(z)_i] \geq E[f(x)_i]$, where z and x are correctly and incorrectly classified patterns respectively. □

Definition 4 *Two data sets D_1 and D_2 are $\underline{mutually\ balanced}$ if both are balanced with respect to f and $E[f(x)_i] = E[f(z)_i]$, for any two arbitrary $N(x; \epsilon) \subseteq D_1$ and $N(z; \epsilon') \subseteq D_2$.*

It is important to use mutually balanced data sets with combiners in order to avoid overemphasizing one classifier over another. If the output activations of two classifiers differ greatly, selecting the output with the largest value, or performing an arithmetic average will not necessarily improve the results. The contribution of Theorem 1 is that it predicts the possible improvements after a simple examination of the classifier outputs. If the average output activation of correctly classified patterns is higher than the average output activation of incorrectly classified patterns, then the AVE or MAX combiners are expected to correct errors where at least one of the classifiers provided the correct response[1].

4 Results

The previous section provided a framework in which combination results can be anticipated. Furthermore, Theorem 1 provides some insight on when improvements can be expected, namely when on an average, the activation values for the correctly classified patterns are higher than the activation values for the incorrectly classified patterns, for both classifier/feature sets that will be combined.

Since the basis for combining is that correctly classified patterns carry more weight (or more information) than incorrectly classified patterns, it stands to reason that as long as the correctly classified patterns are more dependable, combining will improve results. Table 3 provides the average activation value for the highest outputs (winning classes) of each network and data set combination for which the correct classification percentages were presented in Table 2. The

---

[1]If the values are very similar, hypothesis testing may be conducted to estimate how many patterns can be expected to be corrected.

Table 3: Average Output Activation Values.

Classifier / Data Set	Correctly Classified Patterns		Incorrectly Classified Patterns	
	Activation	Variance	Activation	Variance
C1 – FS1	.9723	.0121	.7811	.0666
C1 – FS2	.9537	.0260	.5901	.1628
C2 – FS1	.7739	.0720	.4786	.0315
C2 – FS2	.6346	.1432	.3850	.0709

averages are computed over correctly and incorrectly classified patterns. For example, the first row says that when $C1$ was used on $FS1$, the average activation value of a correctly classified pattern was .9723, while the average activation value for an incorrectly classified pattern was .7811.

Table 4: Combination Results

	BEST	AVE	MAX	LIMIT
C1-FS1/C1-FS2	92.66	95.24	93.46	97.21
C2-FS1/C2-FS2	91.30	93.34	91.76	96.96
C1-FS2/C2-FS1	91.30	92.95	92.10	96.84
C1-FS1/C2-FS1	92.66	93.03	93.35	95.02
C1-FS2/C2-FS2	88.60	89.14	88.60	92.71
C1-FS1/C2-FS2	92.66	93.92	93.68	96.96

With four different ways of processing the data, there are six possible pairs of combinations. Table 4 shows the combination results for each of the six pairs, using the MAX and AVE combiners. The best result of the two sources (BEST) provides the base to measure the improvements due to combination. The last column provides a theoretical limit on the improvements, as obtained by a combiner that corrects all patterns that are correctly classified by at least one classifier. The combinations that provided statistically significant improvements for at least one of the combiners are given in the first two rows. The combination in the third row provided marginal improvements that were at the threshold of statistical significance. An analysis of Table 3 reveals that for the two combinations that provided statistically significant results, the activation value for the correctly classified patterns in each sources was larger than the activation value for the incorrectly classified patterns on both sources. For the third combination the average activation of incorrectly classified patterns in one classifier was statistically comparable to the average activation of correctly classified patterns in the other classifier ($77.39 \sim 78.11$, statistically). For the remaining three combinations where there weren't any statistically significant improvements, the average activation of one classifier on incorrectly classified patterns was higher than the average activation of the correctly classified patterns on the other classifier.

5 Discussion

A framework predicting combining results was developed and the predictions were tested using underwater acoustic signals. The results reveal that the the framework was successful in predicting when combining would provide significant improvements. However, the improvements were short of the limits predicted by the theory. This discrepancy is mainly due to the fact that the two feature sets are not totally independent, and noise and bias are not the only reasons a pattern is incorrectly classified. Outliers, for example, are incorrectly classified regardless of the features extracted to represent them. Furthermore, signal classes are not necessarily disjoint. Thus, a more general framework where independence of classifiers and feature sets is not used, needs to be developed. Furthermore this framework has to handle not only disjoint class memberships, but also probabilistic classification, where only the likelihood of class membership may be known.

Acknowledgements: This research was supported in part by ONR contract N00014-92-C-0232.

References

[1] S. Beck and J. Ghosh. Noise sensitivity of static neural classifiers. In *SPIE Conf. on Applications of Artificial Neural Networks SPIE Proc. Vol. 1709*, Orlando, Fl., April 1992.

[2] D.S. Broomhead and D. Lowe. Multivariable functional interpolation and adaptive networks. *Complex Systems*, 2:321–355, 1988.

[3] J. Ghosh, S. Beck, and C.C. Chu. Evidence combination techniques for robust classification of short-duration oceanic signals. In *SPIE Conf. on Adaptive and Learning Systems, SPIE Proc. Vol. 1706*, pages 266–76, Orlando, Fl., April 1992.

[4] J. Ghosh, L. Deuser, and S. Beck. A neural network based hybrid system for detection, characterization and classification of short-duration oceanic signals. *IEEE Jl. of Ocean Engineering*, 17(4):351–363, october 1992.

[5] R. P. Lippmann. Pattern classification using neural networks. *IEEE Communications Magazine*, pages 47–64, Nov 1989.

[6] J. Moody and C. J. Darken. Fast learning in networks of locally-tuned processing units. *Neural Computation*, 1(2):281–294, 1989.

[7] M.P. Perrone and L. N. Cooper. When networks disagree: Ensemble methods for hybrid neural networks. In R. J. Mammone, editor, *Neural Networks for Speech and Image Processing*. Chapmann-Hall, 1993.

[8] M.D. Richard and R.P. Lippmann. Neural network classifiers estimate bayesian a posteriori probabilities. *Neural Computation*, 3(4):461–483, 1991.

[9] D. H. Wolpert. Stacked generalization. *Neural Networks*, 5:241–259, 1992.

An Adaptive Resonance Theory (ART) Neural Network for Synthetic Aperture Radar Target Recognition and Classification

T. Owens Walker III, Murali Tummala and Robert Voigt

Department of Electrical and Computer Engineering, Code EC/TU
Naval Postgraduate School, Monterey, California

Abstract - An Adaptive Resonance Theory (ART) neural network algorithm is used to aid the human operator in the recognition and classification of target images from a synthetic aperture radar (SAR). The plasticity-stability properties of ART allow realtime classification of both familiar and unfamiliar images. Computer simulation demonstrates that the effectiveness of this approach in a noisy environment is dependent on proper utilization of model parameters. The goal is an intelligent system which is capable of classifying surface ship combatants while autonomously adapting in realtime to unexpected changes in the real world.

I. Introduction

Neural networks have been touted as a powerful solution for many pattern recognition applications [1], [6]. The concept of a "trainable" computer holds a great deal of potential for command and control systems that need to dynamically adjust to continuously changing and unforeseen circumstances. One of the desired objectives for neural networks is the ability to aid the human decision making process by off–loading some of the information processing that must be accomplished prior to making a decision.

In combat systems today, there is usually no shortage of information. In fact, there is usually more raw data than one person can process in a reasonable amount of time without some additional analysis aids. The military is continually searching for the best decision aids, assuming that they are reliable, so that operators may perform more effectively, especially in a combat situation. The ability of the computer to do certain tasks, such as spatial and temporal pattern recognition, at which the human brain is adept, leads us to artificial neural networks which attempt to assimilate those functions that the operator is too busy to do.

In [3], Carpenter and Grossberg apply the adaptive resonance theory (ART) to pattern recognition of binary data. They have also applied ART 2 to pattern recognition of analog data in [2]. Srinivasa and Jouaneh [8] utilize a combined invariance net and ART 1 network to achieve pattern recognition of binary inputs. In this paper, we will explore a particularly useful application of the ART neural network to combat systems target detection, recognition and classification. The input data used for this application are synthetic aperture radar images. The SAR provides unique target signatures that can be converted to binary patterns for classification using ART 1. The goal of this project is to devise an intelligent system which is capable of classifying surface ship combatants while autonomously adapting in realtime to unexpected changes the real world scenarios.

The original adaptive resonance theory algorithm developed by Carpenter and Grossberg is a two layer neural network with interacting layers [3]. It was designed for the learning of recognition categories. The significant feature of the ART network is that it learns or adapts to new inputs while at the same time attempts to retain its previously learned information in some stable state. This ability to learn while retaining old information is known as the plasticity-stability dilemma [1]. Essentially, the ART should be able to process and learn unfamiliar events while remembering familiar events without re-classifying them. The ART used for this paper is basic ART 1, which uses binary data for its inputs. ART 2, which will be discussed later, is a follow on to ART 1 and allows for analog as well as binary input data.

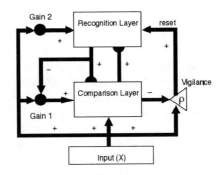

Figure 1. A Typical ART 1 Architecture [2]

The one significant difference between an ART architecture and other learning schemes is that it is designed to learn quickly and stably in realtime in response to a changing world with an unlimited number of inputs until it runs out of memory. An ART network can classify information by adding neurons to its recognition layer dynamically [3]. New learning does not replace previously learned situations and the vigilance parameter can be adjusted to allow for a realistic number of neurons to be used in the structure of the network.

II. Application of ART in a Synthetic Aperture Radar Environment

For the purposes of this paper, several assumptions and generalizations are made concerning the characteristics of the synthetic aperture radar [7]. It is assumed that the radar is capable of providing adequate resolution to accurately train the network. The radar return is approximated by a silhouette of some arbitrary surface vessel. Five different types of ships were processed with significantly different silhouettes for classification. To investigate the effect of varying target angles, these silhouettes were also rotated in perspective views. In all, each ship was presented from 6 different target angles.

The silhouette of the ship becomes the input to the ART. In actual practice, the return would be processed prior to analysis using equipment onboard the SAR platform. A 16 by 36 grid is overlaid on the silhouette (see Figure 2(a)). This grid is processed so that a square is represented as a binary one if more than 50% of that square contains some return of the silhouette. The result is a 16 by 36 grid of ones and zeros which is, effectively, a binary representation of the radar return (see Figure 2(b)).

The grid is assumed to be sized to the target in order to maximize the target usage of the grid from several different target angles. The grid can be sized based on the range to the target and the target's approximate size based on the return. The inherent assumption is that the SAR has a fine enough resolution return to accurately represent the same class of ship from different target angles over a wide range of distances to the target. Each of these target angles would be classified differently according to the ART; however, they are correlated at the output by some post-processing mechanism to give the operator the target classification, distance and approximate target angle. Since each neuron classifies an individual target angle (six per ship), a simple logical OR of the six applicable neurons for a specific ship would give immediate classification.

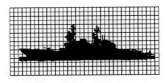

(a) Ship with grid overlay

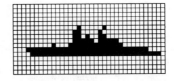

(b) Simulated, processed radar return from target

Figure 2. Grid Overlay for Target Data

The grid sizes are proportional to the distance to the target. Obviously as the target gets farther away, it becomes increasingly difficult to achieve accurate granularity on the grids. One solution to this problem is to change the element size, such as combine four grid elements into one outside of certain ranges and then reclassify based on this new data. The problem is that outside a certain range, all targets start to look the same and classification may not be attainable. This is a problem inherent to the nature of the SAR itself [7].

In summary, the ART network will receive the processed radar data in the form of a two dimensional array of ones and zeros. The grid provides the ART network with a binary array which the network converts to a column vector for analysis.

There could be additional pre-processing done of the raw SAR data, such as classification of targets by size. This would be a simple way to eliminate two targets of dissimilar sizes with similar superstructures. For example, separate ART 1 networks could be set up for ships between certain lengths so that a single ART 1 would not have to be particularly large in terms of neurons to cover all ships.

In the processed radar return, there may appear to be a considerable amount of white space around the target. This white space is to allow for different target angles of the same ship and for the high noise area around the hull of the ship where sea return is a major factor in signal loss and scattering. Significant pre-processing of the raw radar data should give a clean grid similar to the one in Figure 2.

III. ART 1 Network Design and Implementation

The ART 1 network was implemented using MATLAB 4.0 [5]. A flowchart of the basic algorithm for this problem is illustrated in Figure 3.

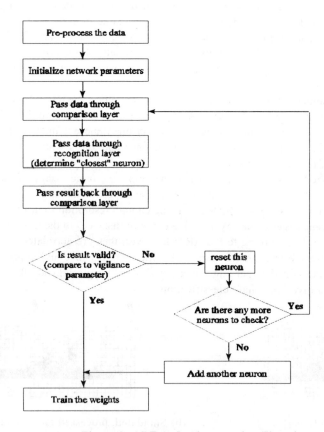

Figure 3. ART 1 Implementation Flowchart

The comparison layer is composed of a hardlimiter with three inputs: the input vector, the results of layer two weighted by the layer 1 weight vector, and a bias (or gain) vector. The hardlimiter evaluates the sum of these three vectors to produce a vector of ones and zeros. The bias vector is initialized to zeros, but switches to a value of -1.5 for the second run through this layer to check the validity of the winning neuron.

The recognition layer is composed of a competition algorithm with two inputs: the results from layer one weighted by the layer 2 weight vector and a bias vector. This bias vector is used to eliminate neurons that have been disqualified by the vigilance parameter. If a neuron is disqualified, its element in the bias vector will be set to -100, thus effectively removing it from further competition. The Instar training algorithm [5] is used to adjust both weight vectors of the winning neuron.

The vigilance parameter is set by the user, and it reflects the result of a bitwise AND operation between the input vector and the pattern of the chosen neuron. The elements of the resulting vector are summed and divided by the sum of the input vector elements. In this way, the vigilance parameter measures the percentage of ones in the proper places.

Preprocessing

A grid of size 16 x 36 is superimposed on the radar image. The grid squares are then marked "1" if there is a RADAR return, "0" otherwise. The result is a 16 x 36 matrix of "1"'s and "0"'s representing a rough image of the target. The size of this grid is crucial and will be discussed later.

The rows of this matrix are concatenated to form one long vector. This vector is then checked to determine if it is all zeros (i.e.. no target present). In this event, it is designated as no target, and the algorithm terminates. Otherwise, the vector is entered into the network to be classified.

Parameters

There are two crucial user defined parameters in the network: the vigilance and the maximum number of neurons. These two values are interrelated and are most easily determined by a bit of trial and error. Once set, they both become network constants.

The vigilance parameter determines the coarseness of the classifications [3]. In this problem, the vigilance parameter can range from 0 to 1, with the higher values representing more strict classifications. Typical values seem to range from .6 to .99 for this problem.

The maximum number of neurons also affects the classification of the inputs. In the world of computer simulation, the number of neurons can be unlimited, but in the real world factors such as cost and availability will limit the maximum number [4]. By limiting the number of neurons, we are setting a limit on how many different groups of classifications we are allowing. This number must be within the tolerances determined by the vigilance parameter.

IV. Results

The key to successful results was the proper choice of the vigilance parameter. To begin with, the vigilance parameter must be chosen to provide proper discernability in the classifications. This tends to lead to a fairly high value, in our case from approximately 0.8 to 0.99. These settings are too high in actual practice due to noise in the radar return which creates new target classifications based on the added noise. One solution is to alter the vigilance parameter once the network has been satisfactorily "trained". By lowering the value, the network becomes more tolerant of noise in the input. The effect of varying the vigilance parameter is illustrated in Figure 4. The network was initially trained at a vigilance of 0.95, and then the images were corrupted by noise and tested at various settings for the vigilance. It is clear that the optimum value for operation is closer to 0.6, and the performance deteriorates rapidly around 0.85.

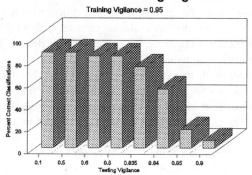

Figure 4. Testing Vigilance Results

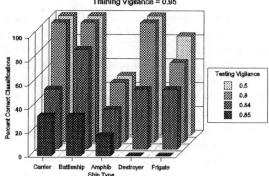

Figure 5. Ship Classification Results

A very low value (0.10) for the vigilance parameter was chosen for a second set of test cases to illustrate the effect of coarse classification. The images tend to be classified into a few, broad categories. Testing with this value for this vigilance yields consistent results due to the broad range of the resultant groupings.

Figure 5 points out that the success rate of the classifications is dependent on the ship type. In general pattern recognition, this means that the percentage of successful classifications of a pattern is dependent on the pattern itself. Using our silhouettes, the amphibious ship fared the worst while the battleship and the carrier seemed to do the best. This can be attributed to, in part, the fact that the carrier and battleship silhouettes contain more distinguishing features than the other vessels.

In practice, a network is also limited by the maximum number of neurons available. In implementation, the number of neurons is proportional to the amount of "memory" needed. In our test runs, if the number of neurons chosen is too low, the network is unable to classify all of the images. This is because the network does not modify the weights of an existing neuron if the result is out of tolerance (set by the vigilance parameter).

Thus, in field applications, the maximum number of neurons and the vigilance parameter are crucial and difficult quantities to determine. In practice, they need to be set by a qualified technician and considered fixed to the user in the field. Any changes in these values could lead to "instability" in the network.

It should be noted, once the network has stabilized to a given set of neurons, it will precisely classify the original set of training vectors. This is because the network will not alter the weight vectors if the result is a perfect match.

VII. Conclusions

ART 1 networks are well suited for target classification and recognition. The ability to learn and classify targets proved to work well for this application. The SAR target information was classified into separate categories when the vigilance parameter was set to a proper value.

The difficulty in developing the system lies primarily in the implementation and the choice of the network parameters. The vigilance parameter tends to be highly sensitive and difficult to determine other than by trial and error. In addition, varying levels of noise would require different degrees of classifications and, thus, different values for the vigilance parameter. A possible solution is to present the network a library of known images at a high vigilance parameter and then send it out to the field with a lower value for the noisy environment.

A limiting factor in the implementation is the maximum number of neurons available. If the network cannot place an image within the required tolerance, it will need to utilize another neuron. If no neuron is available, the network will fail to classify the image rather than corrupting a previous category.

There are two major areas that can be further explored: the redefinition of the vigilance parameter and the adaptation of the problem to an ART 2 model.

The vigilance parameter can be modified to take advantage of certain a priori knowledge in the working environment. Rather than using a single value, the vigilance parameter can consist of a vector of values. This would allow the operator to utilize different criteria for different sections of the image. Specifically, the operator can make use of the fact that for a surface target, the top 1/3 of the radar return will consist of the superstructure, the middle 1/3 would emphasize the hull, and the bottom 1/3 would be dominated by noise from sea return. The vigilance parameters could be varied to emphasize the general hull outline and superstructure characteristics while deemphasizing the sea clutter.

To take advantage of the varying signal return strength, this problem is ideally suited to application of an ART 2 network. An ART 2 network is capable of handling continuous analog input as well as binary data [2]. The gray-scale levels inherent in a SAR image presentation could be used to further classify the image, essentially adding a 3 dimensional knowledge to the classification. The different gray-scale levels can be attributed to different relative ranges, as well as different target material [7]. Unfortunately, the price for this capability is the increased complexity [4]. The typical ART 2 network processes a discrete number of values over a certain finite range and requires a great deal of pre-processing of the data [6] before it is accepted by the network. Furthermore, the analog data presents additional noise problems that would necessitate a significant amount of signal processing.

References

[1] Gail A. Carpenter and Stephen Grossberg, "A Massively Parallel Architecture for a Self-Organizing Neural Pattern Recognition Machine," *Computer Vision, Graphics and Image Processing*, Vol. 37, 1987, pp. 54-115.

[2] Gail A. Carpenter and Stephen Grossberg, "ART 2: Self-Organization of Stable Category Recognition Codes for Analog Input Patterns," *Applied Optics*, Dec. 1, 1987, pp. 4919-4930.

[3] Gail A. Carpenter and Stephen Grossberg, "The ART of Adaptive Pattern Recognition by a Self-Organizing Neural Network," *IEEE Computer*, Vol. 21, No. 3, March 1988, pp. 77-88.

[4] Maureen Caudill and Charles Butler, *Naturally Intelligent Systems*, MIT Press, Cambridge Massachusetts, 1990.

[5] Howard Demuth and Mark Beale, *Neural Network Toolbox User's Guide*, Mathworks Inc., 1992.

[6] Dan Hammerstrom, "Working with Neural Networks", *IEEE Spectrum*, July 1993, pp. 46-53.

[7] S. A. Hovanessian, Introduction to Synthetic Array and Imaging Radars. Dedham, MA: Artech House, Inc, 1980.

[8] Narayan Srinivasi and Musa Jouaneh, "A Neural Network for Invariant Pattern Recognition," *IEEE Transactions on Signal Processing*, Vol. 40, No. 6, June 1992, pp. 1595-1599.

Learning Categorical Error Bounds
as well as Prototypes with
Error Correcting Adaptive Resonance Networks

Robert A. Baxter

Baxter Research

8 Bernard Street

Newton, MA 02161

e-mail: rab@world.std.com

Abstract

Error Correcting Adaptive Resonance Theory (ECART) networks represent differences between inputs and templates explicitly. This class of ART networks generalizes the attentional vigilance parameter of other ART networks into an *attentional vigilance vector*. The attentional vigilance vector allows independent control of the vigilance associated with each input element. Raising the vigilance of an input element corresponds to lowering the acceptable categorical error tolerance associated with that element. Four sets of rules are required to define the function of an ECART network: (1) a code selection rule, (2) a resonance or reset rule, (3) template learning rules, and (4) initial conditions. Different sets of rules can be chosen to make the ECART network functionally equivalent to a number of different classifiers, including ART 1, ART 2a, Fuzzy ART, and the supervised forms of each of these. The focus of this paper is on the ability of ECART networks to learn not only the category representatives but also the variability associated with each category. From a statistical point of view, learning category prototypes and their variability is similar to estimating means and variances. Learning both categorical prototypes and their variability provides robust recognition of patterns in noisy environments.

1. Introduction

The basic principles of Adaptive Resonance Theory (ART) were introduced by Grossberg (1976). A number of ART networks have been introduced and studied since then (Carpenter and Grossberg, 1987a, 1987b; Carpenter, Grossberg, and Rosen, 1991; Carpenter, Grossberg, and Reynolds, 1991; Carpenter, Grossberg, Markuzon, Reynolds, and Rosen, 1991). Baxter (1991a, 1991b) introduced a class of adaptive resonance networks which explicitly compute errors between input vectors and learned templates. Such networks are referred to as ECART (Error Correction Adaptive Resonance Theory) networks. ECART networks can operate as unsupervised or supervised pattern recognition machines. Unsupervised ECART networks represent *coding errors* – errors between input vectors and learned feature templates. Supervised ECART networks represent both coding errors and *predictive errors*. In these networks predictive errors encode differences between learned outcomes and actual outcomes, and, in the absence of coding errors, determine the appropriate number of coding cells to use to represent the training set. One additional flexibility of ECART networks over other networks that comes naturally from explicit representation of errors is the generalization of the concept of attentional vigilance. ECART networks allow the formation of a set of attentional vigilance parameters, referred to as the *attentional vigilance vector*. The attentional vigilance vector allows independent control of the vigilance associated with each input element. Raising the vigilance of an input element corresponds to lowering the acceptable categorical error tolerance associated with that element.

In statistical pattern classification problems, categories can be represented by a number of parameters. The most commonly-used parameter is the category prototype, e.g. the mean. A number of classifiers only use a prototypical representation of categories. Categories can also be represented by their boundaries. It is often necessary to represent categories by more than one type of representation in order to capture key informational aspects. Consider the problem of classifying exemplars generated by two different Gaussian distributions. Only two categories and two parameters for each category (the mean and variance) are necessary to represent and classify the exemplars generated by the two distributions. If these two parameters are estimated correctly for each category, the Bayesian optimum classification performance can be obtained. ART networks represent categories by prototype (as in ART 1 and ART 2) or by boundaries (as in Fuzzy ART). In this paper, unsupervised and supervised ECART networks that represent categories by both prototypes and boundaries are described.

2. ECART network function and architecture

Figure 1 depicts the flow of signals in an ECART network. The major components of an ECART network are an input field, a competitive coding field, a coding error field, a predictive error field, and a novelty detector. ECART networks can be implemented as massively parallel networks for extremely fast processing.

Four sets of rules are required to define an ECART network: (1) a code selection rule, (2) a resonance or reset rule, (3) learning rules, and (4) initial conditions (initial template values). Many possible variations of ECART networks are possible by choosing different sets of rules; two unsupervised variations are described in the following paragraphs.

Bidirectional ECART

The first variation has feature templates with elements that can increase and decrease in value; this variation will be referred to as *Bidirectional ECART*. Let the scaled input pattern be denoted by $\mathbf{x}$, the elements of the scaled input pattern are denoted by x_i (x_i are scaled such that their values lie on the closed interval $[0, 1]$), adaptive feature template j is denoted by $\mathbf{w}_j$, and the elements of the adaptive feature templates are denoted by w_{ji}. Feature codes of the feature templates are indexed by j. The selected code for a given input pattern is denoted by J and is the code with the maximum s_j over all codes $j \in \bar{R}$, where

$$s_j = -\sum_i \left(e_i^+ + e_i^- \right)^p \tag{1}$$

and where $e_i = x_i - w_{ji}$, $e_i^+ = [e_i]^+$, and $e_i^- = [-e_i]^+$. The notation $[e_i]^+$ indicates the rectification function $\max(e_i, 0)$. The value of p is either 1 or 2; an L_1 norm is obtained with $p = 1$, whereas an L_2 (Euclidean) norm is obtained with $p = 2$. $\bar{R}$ is the set of all previously-learned codes that have not been reset for the current input pattern.

The novelty detector determines whether an input pattern is novel or familiar. If a pattern is sufficiently familiar, the network is said to be in the resonant state and the most similar feature template is adapted to better match the current input pattern. The resonance criterion is given by

$$r = \sum_i \left[e_i^+ + e_i^- - E_i \right]^+ = 0 \tag{2}$$

where the E_i are the allowable error tolerances. Since x_i and w_{ji} lie in the closed interval $[0, 1]$ the E_i are related to the elements of the vigilance vector by $\rho_i = 1 - E_i$. A small value of E_i corresponds to a high vigilance for element i. If all $E_i = 0$, every unique input pattern will create a unique template. If $r > 0$, then the novelty detector resets the selected code (J is removed from $\bar{R}$) and the search for a better code ensues. If no existing templates are sufficiently familiar, then a new template is created.

The discrete-time form of the learning rule is given by

$$w_{Ji}(t+1) = w_{Ji}(t) + \lambda_J e_i(t) \tag{3}$$

where λ_j is the learning rate associated with code j and is restricted to positive values. In Bidirectional ECART, the initial values of the elements of $\mathbf{w}_j$ are set to zero.

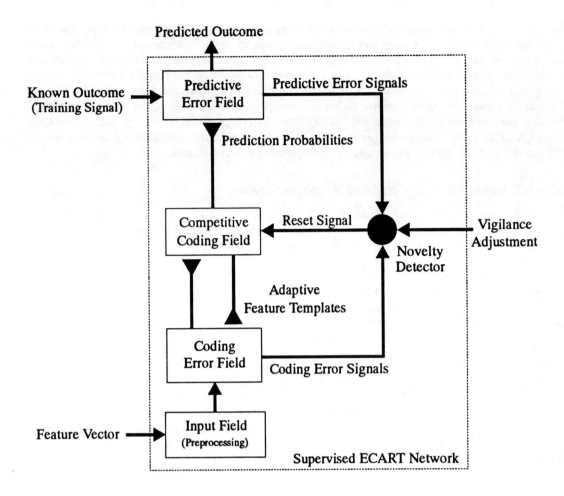

Figure 1: ECART networks consist of an input field, a competitive coding field, a coding error field, a predictive error field, and a novelty detector. The black triangles represent long-term memory weights.

The value of λ_j affects the stability of the feature codes. Bidirectional ECART is equivalent to the *leader algorithm* if λ_j is initially set to unity and is set to zero after the first update of $\mathbf{w}_j$. A more general rule is to initially set λ_j to unity, and decrease λ_j each time code j is selected by a decay factor. If the decay factor does not change, this rule results in an exponential decay in the learning rate as a function of the number of times the code is chosen. Note that the templates in a Bidirectional ECART represent category prototypes. If λ_j is a small constant and learning involves many passes through the training set, the prototypes will approach the category means.

Unidirectional ECART

The templates of the Bidirectional ECART network can oscillate; therefore, the feature codes may not be stable for some sets of input patterns unless λ_j decays sufficiently fast during training. Several ways of making λ_j decay during training were discussed in the previous paragraph. An alternative method of stabilizing the templates is to restrict the direction in which the templates can change. This variation of ECART is referred to as Unidirectional ECART. Unidirectional ECART requires two set of weights which will be denoted by w_{ji}^+ and w_{ji}^- with initial values 0 and 1, respectively. The coding errors in Unidirectional ECART are given by

$$e_i^+ = \left[x_i - w_{ji}^+\right]^+ \tag{4}$$

$$e_i^- = \left[w_{ji}^- - x_i\right]^+ \tag{5}$$

and the learning rules are given by

$$w_{ji}^+(t+1) = w_{ji}^+(t) + \lambda_J e_i^+(t) \tag{6}$$

$$w_{ji}^-(t+1) = w_{ji}^-(t) - \lambda_J e_i^-(t) \tag{7}$$

The code selection and resonance criteria remain unchanged.

In Unidirectional ECART the templates represent categorical boundaries and can be described geometrically as *hyper-rectangles*. If an input vector falls within one of the existing hyper-rectangles, it belongs to that cluster and no learning takes place. If an input vector does not lie within an existing hyper-rectangle, it will cause the most similar hyper-rectangle (defined by s_j) to expand to include that vector – provided the resonance criterion is satisfied. If the resonance criterion is not satisfied, a new cluster is created.

Different code selection and resonance criteria are possible. For example, with the code selection function

$$s_j = \frac{\sum_i \min(x_i, w_{ji}^+) + \max(x_i, w_{ji}^-)}{\beta + \sum_i w_{ji}^+ + w_{ji}^-} \tag{8}$$

and the resonance criterion

$$r = \frac{\sum_i \min(x_i, w_{ji}^+) + \max(x_i, w_{ji}^-)}{\sum_i x_i} > \rho \tag{9}$$

the Unidirectional ECART network is functionally equivalent to Fuzzy ART (Carpenter, Grossberg, and Rosen, 1991).

3. Learning prototypes and error bounds

The Bidirectional and Unidirectional ECART networks can be combined to form a network that represents category error bounds as well as prototypes. The simplest way of combining the two networks is simply to let them operate independently in parallel and use the templates of the Bidirectional ECART network as the prototypes and those of the Unidirectional ECART network as the error bounds. The problem with this method is that the two networks may not generate the same number of categories; thus, a one-to-one correspondence between prototypes and error bounds is not guaranteed (and is unlikely in many cases).

An preferable method is to use three different types of coding errors and templates with the following learning rules

$$w_{Ji}(t+1) = w_{Ji}(t) + \lambda_J e_i(t) \qquad (10)$$
$$w_{Ji}^+(t+1) = w_{Ji}^+(t) + \mu_J e_i^+(t) \qquad (11)$$
$$w_{Ji}^-(t+1) = w_{Ji}^-(t) - \mu_J e_i^-(t) \qquad (12)$$

where

$$e_i = x_i - w_{ji} \qquad (13)$$
$$e_i^+ = \left[x_i - w_{ji}^+\right]^+ \qquad (14)$$
$$e_i^- = \left[w_{ji}^- - x_i\right]^+ \qquad (15)$$

The code selection and resonance criteria are the same as before. If $\mu_J = \lambda_J$, this method guarantees that the prototype templates w_{ji} are in one-to-one correspondence with the error bound templates $w_{ji}^\pm$. In this method, the code selection and resonance criteria depend exclusively on the category boundaries ($w_{ji}^\pm$).

Alternatively, the category prototypes can be used to select the most appropriate codes and to generate reset signals. More generally, the code selection and resonance criteria can make use of some combination of the category prototypes and boundaries in order to select the most appropriate code. For example, the code selection criterion can be generalized to determine the code with the maximum s_j,

$$s_j = -\alpha \sum_i \left(e_i^+ + e_i^-\right)^p - \beta \sum_i |e_i|^p \qquad (16)$$

and, similarly, the resonance criterion can be generalized to the form

$$r = \sum_i \left[\alpha \left(e_i^+ + e_i^-\right) + \beta |e_i| - E_i\right]^+ = 0 \qquad (17)$$

Here, α and β determine how much emphasis is placed on categorical prototypes and boundaries, respectively, in the code selection and resonance processes.

4. Summary

Several methods of extending ECART networks to learn categorical prototypes and error bounds have been discussed. The extensions are combinations of Bidirectional and Unidirectional ECART networks. The category prototypes may have chaotic trajectories but, with appropriate restrictions, they can be guaranteed to be bounded from above and below by the categorical boundaries. These techniques can be applied to both unsupervised and supervised ECART networks.

References

[1] R. A. Baxter, "Supervised adaptive resonance networks," in *ANNA-91: Analysis of Neural Network Applications*, (New York), pp. 123–137, Association of Computing Machinery, May 1991.

[2] R. A. Baxter, "Error propagation and supervised learning in adaptive resonance networks," in *International Joint Conference on Neural Networks*, (New York), pp. 423–429, IEEE, July 1991.

[3] S. Grossberg, "Adaptive pattern classification and universal recoding. II: Feedback, expectation, olfaction, and illusion," *Biological Cybernetics*, vol. 23, pp. 187–202, 1976.

[4] G. A. Carpenter and S. Grossberg, "A massively parallel architecture for a self-organizing neural pattern recognition machine," *Computer Vision, Graphics, and Image Processing*, vol. 37, pp. 54–115, 1987.

[5] G. A. Carpenter and S. Grossberg, "ART 2: Self-organization of stable category recognition codes for analog input patters," *Applied Optics*, vol. 26, no. 23, pp. 4919–4930, 1987.

[6] G. A. Carpenter, S. Grossberg, and D. B. Rosen, "Fuzzy ART: Fast stable learning and categorization of analog patterns by an adaptive resonance system," *Neural Networks*, vol. 4, pp. 759–771, 1991.

[7] G. A. Carpenter, S. Grossberg, and J. H. Reynolds, "ARTMAP: Supervised real-time learning and classification of nonstationary data by a self-organizing neural network," Tech. Rep. CAS/CNS-TR-91-001, Boston University, Boston, MA, 1991.

[8] G. A. Carpenter, S. Grossberg, N. Markuzon, J. H. Reynolds, and D. B. Rosen, "Fuzzy ARTMAP: A neural network architecture for incremental learning of analog multidimensional maps," Tech. Rep. CAS/CNS-TR-91-016, Boston University, Boston, MA, 1991.

Robustness of Pattern Recognition in a Noniteratively Trained, Unsupervised, Hard-Limited Perceptron

Chia-Lun J. Hu, Professor
Electrical Engineering Department
Southern Illinois University at Carbondale
Carbondale, IL 62901

ABSTRACT

When a set of raw image data is preprocessed properly, the training of an artificial-perceptron pattern-recognizer may be achieved in a noniterative manner. The noniterative training is not only very fast (e.g., 2 seconds for training 4 hand-written characters), but may also be very robust (e.g., the recognization could be rotation-invariant, size-invariant, and location-invariant even though the perceptron is trained with only unrotated standard patterns.). The high robustness of this noniteratively trained perceptron is due to the optimum noniterative training scheme and the Fourier-transform preprocessing scheme we adopted in our design. This paper reports the theoretical origin and the experimental results of this novel perceptron pattern recognition system. An unedited video movie of the whole training/recognition process is recorded in real time for demonstration purpose.

Key words: Pattern Recognition, Non-Conventional Unsupervised Learning

I. INTRODUCTION

Preprocessing of raw image data is generally a very important part in pattern recognition schemes employing artificial perceptrons. Preprocessing must not be too detail nor too coarse in order to achieve high robustness in recognition while still preserve the differentiation capability of recognizing different training patterns. Fourier descriptors have been used in preprocessing the raw data by many pattern-recognition researchers [1,2]. Once when a proper preprocessing scheme is selected, the training of the perceptron and the recognition of the untrained patterns can generally be achieved very efficiently by applying a **noniterative** training scheme to a one-layered, hard-limited structure [3,4,5]. The theory and the experiments of this novel **compound perceptron learning system** is reported in detail in the following.

II. FOURIER TRANSFORMS USED IN PREPROCESSING

Global Properties v.s. Local Properties

When we look at the two characters shown in Fig. 1, we can recognize them immediate as A and B. The reason that our brains can immediately recognize these characters is **NOT** that we have inspected carefully all the detailed small variations such as the crooked parts in A or the fuzzy lines in B. But instead, we have picked up the general structures or the coarse variations of the images which allow us to make the immediate decisions. These general structures are **NOT** **LOCAL** properties of the images. They are **GLOBAL** properties of the images. That is, if some crooked parts of A are changed or some fuzzy lines of B are changed, etc., locally, this makes quite a difference in the image. But, as a whole, it does not affect our brain decisions at all. Consequently, in the design of an artificial character recognition scheme which we wish to have a robustness approaching as close as possible to that of our biological recognition system, two factors must be taken into account:

I. It must be able to automatically extract global properties of the images.

II. It must be able to filter out the small variations in the images.

Fourier transforms of the image functions with high (spatial) frequency components truncated off seem to be able to meet both of these conditions. This is so because each Fourier component is calculated from the **whole** image function, not from a local part of the image. Therefore it is a global property, not a local property. Also if we truncate off all high frequency Fourier components, we are filtering out all small spatial variations in the images.

In addition to satisfy these conditions, if we separate the r-function from the θ-function in the Fourier analysis as shown below, we may also obtain **rotation-invariant robustness** in the recognitions.

Fourier Transforms in a Polar Coordinate

Suppose we have a digitized image in the form of black and white (blank) pixels and the x, y coordinates of each (black) pixel are known. Then we can find the x, y coordinates of the centroid of the black pixels. If we use this centroid point as the center, we can draw a polar coordinate with maximum radius equal to the maximum r of all the pixels (Fig. 2). Each dot in Fig. 2 represents the center of each black pixel. Counting the number of dots in each ring will give us a radial vector V_r and counting that in each sector will give us an angular vector V_θ. If there are J rings and K sectors in the polar coordinate, then these two vectors are, respectively, J-dimension and K-dimension analog vectors of integer components. These vectors can also be represented by quantized analog scalar functions $f_1(r)$ and $g(\theta)$ with integer quantization levels such as the ones shown in Fig. 3. If we normalize each level in f_1 with respect to the area of each ring, and normalize r with respect to r_{max}, and call the new function f(r), then we can apply the following **Hankel and Fourier transformations** to f and g respectively to get the **spatial frequency components** F_m and G_n of these two functions. (Hankel transform is equivalent to Fourier transform of a circularly symmetric function along the radial direction of the polar coordinate [6].)

$$F_m = 2\pi \int_0^1 rf(r)J_0(2\pi mr)dr \qquad (1)$$

where J_0 is the zeroth order Bessel function of first kind.

$$G_n = \left| \frac{1}{2\pi} \int_{-\pi}^{\pi} g(\theta) e^{-j2\pi n\theta} d\theta \right|$$ (2)

where | | means taking the magnitude of the complex number enclosed inside. Notice that the phase angle in the Fourier transform in (2) is ignored.

The physical meanings of these Fourier components are the following. F_m represents the **variation** of the **radial structure** of the **whole image** in the "detail range m" (or frequency range m). Similarly, G_n represents the **variation** of the **angular structure** of the **whole image** in the detail range n. With higher frequency components truncated off, these F_m and G_n then constitute an analog word and this analog word is the input word we use for training the perceptron. Notice that when the image is rotated, this analog word will **not change** at all. (The rotation invariance of F_m is obvious because f(r) does not depend on θ. The rotation invariance of G_n is due to the fact that if θ in (2) is replaced by $\theta+\theta_0$ where θ_0 is any rotation angle, the **magnitude** of the complex integration will NOT depend on the initial phase θ_0.)

Because of the quantized nature of the f and g functions shown in Fig. 3, the actual computation of the integrals is converted to finite, weighted sums of the quantization data. These finite sums are called the **segmented Fourier transforms** which are very easy and very fast to handle in digital computations. These transforms are very similar to the conventionally used FFT.

III. THE NONITERATIVELY TRAINED HARD-LIMITED PERCEPTRON

The perceptron we use for training and recognition is very similar to the ones we reported previously [3, 4, 5]. We use also the **optimal** one-step learning scheme we reported in [4] such that the training vectors are located with equal noise distances to any dichotomization plane in the N-space. But instead of applying this optimum scheme to a supervised learning scheme, we apply it to an **unsupervised learning scheme** to elimnate the illegality problems we occasinally encountered in a **supervised** learning system. The general theory of this one-step learning scheme is briefly reviewed here.

If the input-output mapping vectors to be learned are $\{U_m \rightarrow V_m, m=1 \text{ to } M\}$ where U_m is an N-dim analog vector and V_m is a P-bit binary vector, then the goal of learning is to find the connection matrix a_{ij} in the following simmultaneous nonlinear algebraic equations.

$$v_{mi} = Sgn(\sum_{j=1}^{N} a_{ij} u_{mj}), \qquad i=1 \text{ to } P, m=1 \text{ to } M$$ (3)

where u_{mi}, v_{mi} are components of U_m and V_m. For a supervised learning problem, U_m, V_m are given. If we multiply both sides of (3) by v_{mi} which is = either 1 or -1, (3) is then changed to

$$\sum_{j=1}^{N} a_{ij} v_{mi} u_{mj} > 0, \qquad i=1 \text{ to } P, m=1 \text{ to } M$$ (4)

(the property that $v_{mi}Sgn(X)=Sgn(v_{mi}X)$ is used in the above derivation.) Since j is the only running index in (4), (4) can be re-written in the form of the inner product between two vectors:

$$A_i \bullet Y_{mi} > 0 \qquad\qquad m=1 \text{ to } M, \text{ i fixed.} \qquad\qquad (5)$$

where A_i is an N-dim vector representing the i-th row of a_{ij} matrix; and $Y_{mi} = v_{mi}U_m$ = the m-th input vector dichotomized according to the i-th output bit in the m-th mapping pair. Whenever $\{U_m \rightarrow V_m\}$ mapping is given, Y_{mi} are given, and A_i can be solved from the M simultaneous inequalities shown in (5). The solution may or may not exist. The **if-only-if** condition that solution exists in (5) is, by Farkas Lemma, that

$$\text{all } \{Y_{mi}, \text{ i fixed, m=1 to M}\} \text{ are } \textbf{positively linearly independent} \text{ (or PLI).} \qquad (6)$$

PLI means that **no positive real constants** $\{p_m > 0, m=1 \text{ to } M\}$, except all 0's, satisfy the following linear relation among all Y_{mi}'s

$$\sum_{m=1}^{M} p_m Y_{mi} = 0 \qquad\qquad \text{i fixed.} \qquad\qquad (7)$$

For a supervised learning problem, $\{Y_{mi}\}$ are fixed when $\{U_m \rightarrow V_m\}$ mapping is given. (6) may be violated and the solution of a_{ij} may not exist at all. This mapping is called an illegal mapping for the **supervised learning** in the one-layered perceptron (OLP). That means, no matter what learning rule we use to train OLP, we cannot realize the given mapping at all if (6) is violated in a supervised learning scheme. On the other hand, if each training U_m represents a different pattern to be recognized, then we can use the **unsupervised approach** to assign each V_m in such a way that all the M $U_m \rightarrow V_m$ mapping pairs become legal. Therefore solutions of (5) **definitely exists.** The algorithm for solving (5) is then trivial and the solution can be obtained by **one matrix-operation step.** This unsupervised one-step learning scheme is what we adopted in our present design.

IV. EXPERIMENTAL RESULTS

We use a mouse in Microsoft Visual Basic (loaded to a 486 PC) to write any free-hand letters such as the ones shown in Fig. 4. A program written in Visual Basic then digitizes the image and stores the x,y positions of each quantized pixel in a data file. Recalling the data file and apply it to an event-driven, interacting program we designed according to the above discussion then allows us to preprocess the data as well as to train the neural network or to test the image. We use a one-layered, hard-limited perceptron with 32 channels of analog input. The output is a 2-bit binary vector. We used the regularly hand-written letters such as the four letters shown in Fig. 4-1 for training. Then we can test any free-hand writings such as the ones shown in Fig. 4-2. With more than 80% successful rate, these free-hand writings can be recognized correctly in the test. Notice that the test patterns include script letters and rotated letters which are **not** included in the training set.

V. CONCLUSION

Applying a special Fourier-transform preprocess scheme to an **unsupervised** learning in a one-layered, hard-limited perceptron allows us to obtain high robustness when the perceptron is switched to the recognition mode. The training of the perceptron is very fast (4 patterns in 2 seconds,) because the training is noniterative and one-step. The recognition of the perceptron is very robust because we apply an optimum training scheme to the preproccesed global properties of the image. An unedited video movie is recorded for a real-time demonstration of the training and the recognition experiments.

REFERENCES

[1] Persoon, E and Fu, K. S., (1977), "Shape Discrimination Using Fourier Descriptors," **IEEE Trans. Systems Man Cyb.**, SMC-7, #2, 170-179, 1977.

[2] Zahn, C.T. and Roskies, R.Z. (1972), "Fourier Descriptors for Plane Closed Curves," **IEEE Trans. Comput.**, C-21, #3, 269-281, 1972.

[3] Hu, C.J., (1990), "A Novel, One-Step, Geometrical Supervised Learning Scheme," **Proceedings of the 1990 International Joint Conference on Neural Networks, Washington, D.C.**, vol. I, I-635 to I-638, Jan. 15-19, 1990

[4] Hu, C.J., (1992), "A Deterministic Method of Solving Supervised Learning Problems," **Intelligent Engineering Systems Through Artificial Neural Networks**, ASME Press, Vol. 2, 91-96, 1992.

[5] Hu, C.J., (1993), "Recognizing the Untrained Patterns in a Noniterative Perceptron Learning Scheme," **Procs. of SPIE International Conference on Science of Artificial Neural Networks**, vol. II, 218-224, April, 1993.

[6] Goodman, J. W., "**Introduction to Fourier Optics**," p.12, McGraw Hill, 1968.

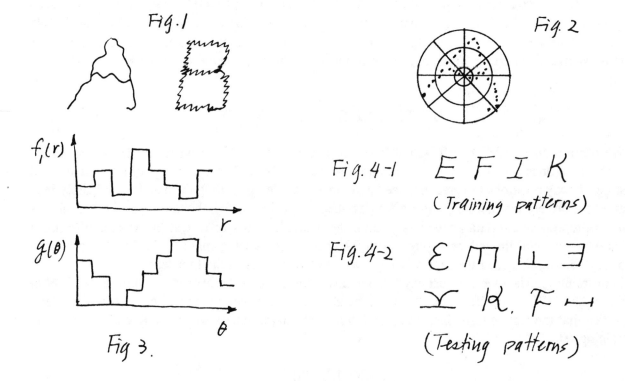

On Modifying The Weights
In
A Modular Recurrent Connectionist System

by
H. Elsherif & M. Hambaba
Intelligent Systems Laboratory
Electrical Engineering & Computer Science Department
Stevens Institute of Technology
Hoboken, NJ 07030
email: helsheri@vaxa.stevens-tech.edu
Tel# 201-216-5618
email: mhambaba@vaxa.stevens-tech.edu
Tel# 201-216-5050

ABSTRACT

A modular recurrent connectionist architecture is proposed to classify binary and continuous patterns. This system consists of three networks: one feed-forward Back-Propagation (**BP**) network and two Self-Organization Map (**SOM**) networks. The feed-forward (*basic*) network is trained until a saturation error level occurs. Simultaneously, the first **SOM** (*input control*) network and the last **SOM** (*output control*) are defining the mapping features for the given input/output patterns. The resultant features are used by a **Gaussian** potential function to adjust the weights of the *basic* network and to classify the given patterns.

Summary

A connectionist system can be evaluated in terms of its capability to represent the knowledge (patterns) in terms of input-output mapping function. An accurate representation of this mapping depends on many issues including the system architecture, the type of the connections, the number of neurons in the hidden units, the type of activation functions, the learning algorithm, and the input set representation. These issues are important to find the optimal parameters of the network to represent the given knowledge. In this research, the *connectionist system architecture* and the *dynamic weights* are the main issues to be explored and examined.

Although many psychologist and biologists [1] believe that the brain has a modular architecture, only a few researchers have applied the idea of modularity in the connectionists. There are several advantages of the modular architecture over a single-network architecture [2,3] including a higher learning speed, an easier interpreted, debugged, and extended pattern representations, a reduced hardware implementation, and a better generalization.

The generalization is a measure of how well the network performs on the actual patterns once the training is complete. Making the weights dynamic is the biggest parameter in improving the generalization. Several researches have been developed towards making the weights dynamic. These include Grossberg's shunting model [4] and Nowlan and Hinton 's model for soft weights sharing [5]. In addition to these researchers, some studies combined the concept of dynamic weights with modular architecture, including Pollack's cascaded back-propagation model [6] and Jacobs's mixed expert network [2].

In our research, we are developing novel modular architectures based on the dynamic of the connections. Previously, a modular feed-forward architecture [7,8] based-on a back-propagation (*basic*) network and a self-organization mapping (*control*) network was proposed and examined (Figure-1). The *basic* network uses the Back-propagation learning algorithm [9] and has only one-hidden layer (i.e. $s=3$) with (k) hidden-units. This network updates the weights $w_{ij}(t)$ during the learning phase by the Back-propagation rule.

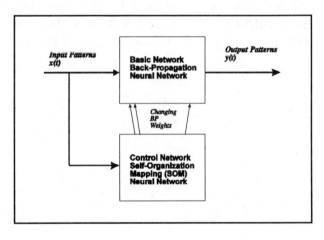

(Figure-1) A Modular Feed-Forward Architecture

At the same time, the *control* network (Self-Organization Map [10]) finds a mapping from the input pattern space $x \in \Re^n$ onto a regular two-dimensional array ($n*k$). With every node i in this array, a parametric reference vector $m_i \in \Re^n$ is associated. An input pattern may be compared with all the m_i in the smallest of the Euclidean distance $\|x-m_i\|$ to represent the best-matching node which is signified by c as:

$$\|x-m_c\|=\min_i\{\|x-m_i\|\}$$

Note that every input pattern x_j is mapped onto the node c relative to the parameter m_i.

The feed-forward modular architecture [7] uses the best-matching node in the two-dimensional array (i.e., c) to update the weights of the outputs of the *basic* network by Δw_{ij} which is given by:

$$\Delta w_{ij}=\chi*x_i*\|x_j-m_c\|$$

It also updates the weights in the hidden layer of the *basic* network by Δw_{ij} which is given by:

$$\Delta w_{ij}=\chi*x_i*\exp(\|x_j-m_i\|)$$

Where χ is a normalization factor.

In this paper, a modification has been provided to the above architecture to give the flexibility to find also the mapping features in the desired outputs, as shown in Figure-2. The *input control* network finds a mapping from the input pattern space $x \in \Re^n$ onto a regular two-dimensional array ($n*k$).

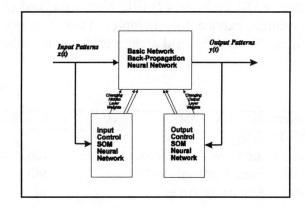

(Figure-2) A Modular Recurrent Architecture

As shown in Figure-2, another Self-Organization Map (**SOM**) network (*the output control*) is added to find a mapping from the desired output pattern space $y \in \Re^q$ onto an array ($q*d$), where d is the number of the desired outputs. While the *input control* network finds the best-matching nodes in the input patterns, the *output control* network tries to find the best-matching nodes in the output patterns which can be represented as:

$$\|y-m_b\|=\min_d\{\|y-m_d\|\}$$

The Learning phase of this architecture has two steps. In the first step, the *basic* network updates the weights until the error reaches a saturation level (0.0001 of error versus the epoch). The *input* and the *output control* networks finds the best matching nodes for both of the input patterns and the desired outputs. In the second step, the *control* networks updates the weights of the outputs of the *basic* network using a **Gaussian** potential function by Δw_{ij} which is given by :

$$\Delta w_{ij} = \chi * y_i * \exp(\|y_j - m_b\| / 2\sigma^2)$$

Where χ is an output normalization factor and σ is the standard deviation for the desired outputs.

At the same time , it updates the weights in the hidden layer of the *basic* network by Δw_{ij} which is given by:

$$\Delta w_{ij} = \eta * x_i * \exp(\|x_j - m_c\| / 2\psi^2)$$

Where η is an input normalization factor and ψ is the standard deviation for the given input patterns.

This modular recurrent architecture and its learning algorithm test three examples: (1) Exclusive-OR Problem, (2) IRIS plant data, and (3) 3-partition nonlinear functions (e.g., logarithmic, exponential, multiply). Table-1 shows a comparison between three architectures: the modular feed-forward architecture, the modular recurrent architecture, and Jacobs's mixed networks model.

Problem/Network Type	No. of Epoch	RMS. Output Error %
XOR-Problem		
Mixed Expert Networks(Jacobs)	1267	8%
Modular Feed-Forward Arch.	843	3.5%
Modular Recurrent Arch.	904	2.3%
IRIS Data		
Mixed Expert Networks(Jacobs)	4389	14.1%
Modular Feed-Forward Arch.	2493	12.6%
Modular Recurrent Arch.	1783	9.8%
3-Partition Function		
Mixed Expert Networks (Jacobs)	659	2.1%
Modular Feed-Forward Arch.	672	3.2%
Modular Recurrent Arch.	865	1.9%

(Table-1) Simulation Results

Conclusion

In this research, we have designed a connectionist system by combining the dynamic weights with the modular recurrent architecture to classify binary and continuous patterns. This system includes the dynamic weights as a multiplicative **Gaussian** function connections which allows it to determine the mapping from the given patterns to the output patterns and switch between different input spaces. Currently, we are still testing more non-linear dependent patterns in different signal processing application. At the same time, more mathematical analysis are being studied to prove some theories.

References

[1] J. Fodor, *"The Modularity of Mind"*, Cambridge, MA: The MIT Press.

[2] R. Jacobs, M. Jordan, S. Nowlan, and G. Hinton, *"Adaptive Mixtures of Local Experts"*, Neural Computation, Vol 3, pp 79-87, 1991.

[3] A. Waibel, *"Modular Construction of Time-Delay Neural Networks for Speech Recognition"*, Neural Computation, Vol. 1, 1989, pp. 39-46.

[4] S. Grossberg, *"Nonlinear Neural Networks: Principles, Mechanisms, and Architectures"* Neural Networks, Vol 1, pp 17-62, 1988.

[5] S. Nowlan and G. Hinton, *"Simplifying Neural Networks by Soft Wight-Sharing"*, Neural Computation, Vol 4, pp. 473-493, 1992.

[6] J. Pollack, *"Cascaded Back-Propagation on Dynamic Connectionist Networks"*, in Proc. Ninth Annual Conference Cognitive Science Society, pp 391-404, 1987.

[7] H. Elsherif and M. Hambaba, *"A Modular Neural Network Architecture for Pattern Classification"*, IEEE Workshop on Neural Networks for Signal Processing 1993 (NNSP '93), pp 232-239, Sept. 7-9, 1993, Baltimore, MD.

[8] H. Elsherif and M. Hambaba, *"A Modular Neural Network Architecture for Pattern Classification"*, accepted to be in Boston '1993, SPIE Workshop, Sept.1993, Boston, MA.

[9] D. Rumelhart, G. Hinton, and R. Williams, *"Learning Representation by Back-Propagation Errors"*, Nature, Vol 323, pp 533-536, 1988.

[10] T. Kohonen, *"Self-Organization and Associative Memory (3rd Ed)"*, Berlin: Springer-Verlag, 1989.

Learning Curves and Optimization of a Multilayer Perceptron Neural Network for Chromosome Classification

Lerner, B., Guterman, H., Dinstein, I. and Romem, Y.*
Department of Electrical and Computer Engineering
Ben-Gurion University of the Negev
Beer-Sheva, Israel 84105

* The Institute of Medical Genetics, Soroka Medical Center
Beer-Sheva, Israel 84105

Abstract

The use of multilayer perceptron (MLP) neural network (NN) as human chromosome classifier was studied. The MLP NN classifier was optimized in the sense of learning rate, momentum constant and training cycle, to the chromosome data. The MLP classifier learning curves were examined by measuring the probability of correct test set classification for an increasing number of training examples. Only 10-20 examples were required to the MLP NN classifier to reach it ultimate performance regarding the number of features used. To compare the results to relevant theory, we have calculated the entropic error (loss). The empirical dependence of the entropic error on the number of examples is highly comparable to the 1/t function that is a universal learning curve.

1. Introduction

Human chromosomes are responsible for about 50% of early fetal losses, 5% of late fetal losses and 20% of birth defects [16]. No wonder that karyotyping, the procedure of chromosome analysis, is a corner stone of prenatal diagnosis. The Canadian Workload Measurement System [3] allocates 465 minutes for karyotyping amniocytes, the most common diagnostic activity in cytogenetics. Most of the time is dedicated to microscopy, a tedious, eye straining task requiring meticulous attention to details. Obviously it needs highly qualified, therefore, well-paid personal. As today, the analysis of chromosomes is the limiting factor in the wide application of cytogenetics as a diagnostic tool. The commercially available computerized systems for chromosome sorting are of great help but still inadequate. The systems are definitely inferior to the human performer. First and most important, these are expensive, non automatic devices that need human assistance throughout the process.

Neural networks make it possible to overcome most of these limitations. This is mainly because they permit application of expert knowledge and experience through network training. The neural network classifier has the advantage of being fast (highly parallel), easily trainable and capable of creating arbitrary partitions of the feature space. Multilayer perceptron neural networks have been used in several studies of biological object classification. In a research to evaluate the growth of tumors in mice, an MLP neural network trained by the backpropagation learning algorithm [14] was able to distinguish among seven stages in tumor growth [4]. In another investigation [15], the MLP trained to classify cervical cell images, as either normal or abnormal. The classifier correctly classified 96% of the cell images in the test set. In a similar study, an MLP NN used to classify cells for cancer diagnosis with probability of correct classification of about 96% [12]. An attempt to train an MLP NN to define and detect DNA-binding sites was done [13], with 80% probability of correct detection. The only known effort to classify human

---

This work was supported in part by the Paul Ivanier Center for Robotics and Production Management, Ben-Gurion University, Beer-Sheva, Israel.

chromosome images using NN, besides the work of our group [5]-[10], is described in [2]. This reference is an abstract only. The classification was made using the Fourier coefficients of the medial axis and an MLP NN and yielded 92.5% probability of correct classification for the test set.

An effort was made through the last two years to utilize neural networks as a human chromosome classifier [5]-[10]. This effort has been mainly concentrated on the feature extraction and selection issues. This research, on the other hand, has focused on the optimization of an MLP NN as a human chromosome classifier of 5 chromosome types. In addition, the learning curves of the MLP classifier were empirically investigated and compared to the theory.

2. The MLP classifier

In this research, a two-layer feedforward neural network trained by the backpropagation (bp) learning algorithm [14] was chosen for the classification. The bp algorithm is an error driven parameter estimation algorithm where the objective is to minimize the output squared error function by adjusting interconnection weights and node thresholds. Learning is controlled by the values selected for the learning rate and the momentum constant. No rule for selecting the optimal values of these parameters exists and usually they are chosen empirically according to the training data. The number of hidden layers and the number of hidden units in each hidden layer affects the shape of the decision regions of the classifier, therefore affects the classification performance and complexity. In this study, two layer perceptron was considered. The network was initialize using random weights in the [-1,1] range. The input vector was 64-dimensional and the output vector was 5 dimensional with one component set to "1" (actually 0.9) for the correct classification and "0" (actually 0.1) elsewhere [9]. The number of hidden units of the network was set according to the Principal Component Analysis (PCA), applied to the feature vectors. The number was set to be the number of the largest eigenvalues, the sum of which accounts for more than a pre-specified percentage of the sum of all the eigenvalues [9]. In all the simulations, this number was set according to a pre-specified percentage of 90%.

3. Learning curves

Learning curves show how fast the behavior of a machine improves as the number of training examples increases. There are several approaches to this problem, e.g., the statistical-mechanical approach, the information-theoretic approach and the statistical approach. All of these approaches suggest that the average error decreases universally in the order of 1/t, where t is the number of training examples. A universal property, that irrespective of the machine architecture, the average entropic loss decreases asymptotically as d/t, where d is the number of modifiable parameters of the classifier, has been proved [1]. The average entropic loss is the average of the logarithm of the probability of correct classification for the next new pattern after a classifier has been trained by t training examples. Moreover, when the classifier error tends to zero (or the probability of correct classification tends to 1) the average entropic loss and the generalization error are almost identical [1].

In this study, we measured the probability of correct test set classification while the number of training examples increased. The maximum number of examples was set by the minimum number of training vectors over all classes (chromosome types). The experiment was repeated with a different number of features selected by the "knock-out" algorithm. The "knock-out" algorithm is a feature selection method, where the best features among the extracted features are selected using the effectiveness (scattering) criterion of "minimum variance" [17].

In addition, the entropic error (loss) e*(t) [1],

1) $$e^*(t) = -\log(P_{test})$$

was calculated and compared to the theoretical curve (P_{test} is the probability of correct test set classification).

4. Results

4.1 The MLP NN optimization

A description of the methodology and the features we have used appears elsewhere [5]-[9]. Three parameters of the classifier, namely the training cycle (in epochs units), the momentum constant (α) and the learning rate (μ) were checked in order to find the best network. All the simulations were repeated (at least) 3 times, with the same network parameters but with different sets of randomly chosen training vectors, and the results were averaged. The probability of correct training and test sets classification is plotted, in Figure 1, against the training cycle (epochs). Training is made in batch mode, which mean that the network weights are changed only after each presentation of all the vectors to the network (epoch). We can see that the ultimate learning is obtained for the first 500-1000 epochs (and with Sum Square Error (SSE) of less than 4). However, training cycle in all the simulations was kept to be 4000 epochs.

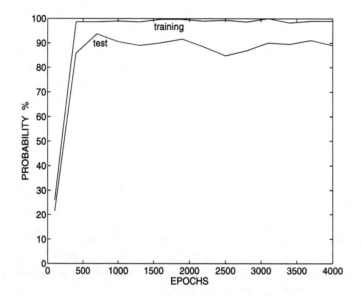

Figure 1. The probability of correct test classification.

The sensitivity of the classification procedure to the momentum constant (α) and to the learning rate (μ) is shown in figure 2 and Figure 3, respectively. Best generalization was obtained when the momentum constant and the learning rate were equal to 0.97 and 0.026, respectively. Therefore, all the simulations were held with these 3 values of parameters: training cycle of 4000 epochs, α=0.97 and μ =0.026.

Using these parameters, the MLP classifier was almost perfectly (99.3-99.6%) trained to classify chromosomes of 5 types and yielded over 98% of probability of correct test classification [7], [9].

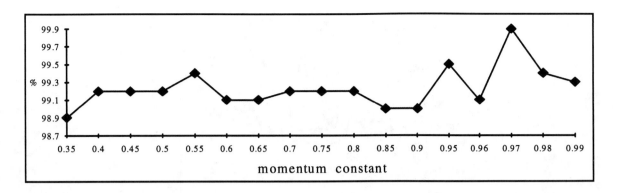

Figure 2. The correct test set probability vs. the momentum constant.

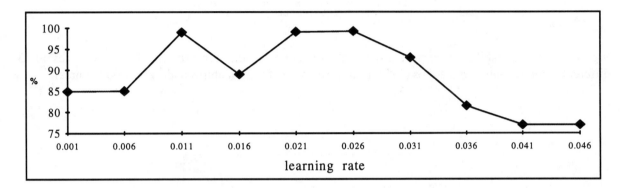

Figure 3. The correct test set probability vs. the learning rate and for the optimal momentum constant yielded at Figure 2.

4.2 Learning curves

The probability of correct test set classification was measured when the number of training examples increased. The maximum number of examples was 84 that is the smallest number of training vectors in one of the chromosome classes. First, the MLP network was trained using only one example for each chromosome type and the probability of correct test set classification was calculated. Then, another example for each chromosome type was added to the training set and the new probability of correct test set classification was calculated. The procedure continued until all available examples (84) were used. The experiment was repeated 3 times for a different number of selected features, namely 10, 20 and 60 features. In each case, the features were the "best" features we can select according to the "knock-out" algorithm [17]. The results are shown in Figure 4. Only 10-20 examples are required to the MLP NN classifier to reach it ultimate performance regarding the number of features used. The entropic error (loss) has been calculated in order to compare the results to the theory outlined before. The dependence of the entropic error on the number of examples is shown, for the best 60 features, in Figure 5. The results are very close approximated by the 1/t function which is a universal learning curve [1].

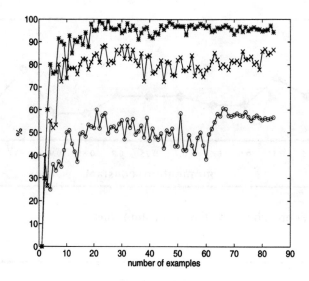

Figure 4. The probability of correct test set classification vs. the number of training examples for 3 different values of selected features ("o" for 10 features, "x" for 20 features and "*" for 60 features).

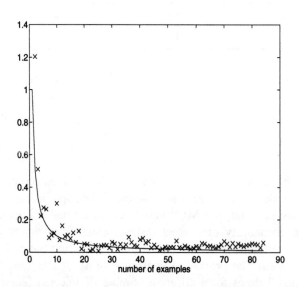

Figure 5. The entropic error (loss) vs. the number of training examples, for the best 60 features ("x"), compared to a universal learning curve in the order of 1/t (solid line).

5. Discussion

The multilayer perceptron (MLP) neural network (NN) was used to classify human chromosomes. The NN classifier was optimized to the chromosome data in the sense of training cycle, learning rate and momentum constant. On the basis of this optimization, the MLP NN classifier was almost perfectly

(99.3-99.6%) trained to classify chromosomes of 5 types and yielded over 98% of probability of correct test classification [7].

The MLP classifier learning curves were investigated by the calculation of the probability of correct test set classification where the number of training examples was increased. Only 10-20 examples were required to the MLP NN classifier to reach it ultimate performance regarding the number of features used. To compare the results to a relevant theory, we have calculated the entropic error (loss). The dependence of the entropic error on the number of examples is highly comparable to the 1/t function which is a universal learning curve [1].

6. References

1. Amari, S. (1993). A universal theorem on learning curves. *Neural Networks*, **6**, 161-166.
2. Becker, R., Lefkowitz, W., Hohmann, L., Christopher, K. and Surana, R. (1991). Identification of metaphase human chromosomes from axial densitometric tracings using a backpropagation neural network. *Laboratory Investigation*, **64**, 121A.
3. Canadian Workload Measurement System. (1986). Minister of Supply and Services Canada, Toronto, p. 88.
4. Egbert, D.D., Rhodes, E.E and Goodman, P.H. (1988). Preprocessing of biomedical images for neurocomputer analysis. *IEEE Int. Conf. of Neural Networks*, San Diego, CA, vol. I, 561-568, July 24-27.
5. Lerner, B., Guterman, H. & Dinstein, I. (1992). On classification of human chromosomes. *Neural Networks for Learning, Recognition and Control*, a research conference at Boston University, May 14-16.
6. Lerner, B., Guterman, H., Dinstein, I. & Romem, Y. (1993). Classification of human chromosomes by two-dimensional Fourier transform components. *WCNN'93*, Portland, July 11-15, 793-796.
7. Lerner, B., Guterman, H., Dinstein, I. & Romem, Y. (1993). Medial Axis Transform based features and neural network classifier for human chromosome classification. (Submitted for publication).
8. Lerner, B., Rosenberg, B., Levinstein, M., Guterman, H., Dinstein, I. & Romem, Y. (1993). Feature selection and chromosome classification using an MLP neural network. (Submitted to *ICNN'94*).
9. Lerner, B., Guterman, H., Dinstein, I. & Romem, Y. (1993). Human chromosome classification using multilayer perceptron neural network. (Submitted for publication).
10. Lerner, B., Guterman, H., Dinstein, I. & Romem, Y. (1993). A Comparison of Multilayer Perceptron Neural Network and Bayes Piecewise Classifier for Chromosome Classification. (Submitted to *ICNN'94*).
11. Lerner, B., Guterman, H., Dinstein, I. & Romem, Y. (1993). "Tailored" Neural Networks to Improve Image Classification. (Submitted to *WCNN'94*).
12. Moallemi, C. (1991). Classifying cells for cancer diagnosis using neural networks. *IEEE Expert*, December, 8-12.
13. O'neill, M.C. (1991). Training backpropagation neural networks to define and detect DNA-binding sites. *Nucleic Acids Research*, **19**, 313-318.
14. Rumelhart, D.E., Hinton, G.E. & Williams, R.J. (1986). Learning internal representations by error propagation. In Rumelhart, D.E., McClelland, J.L. and the PDP research group, *Parallel Distributed Processing*, vol. 1, chap. 8, Cambridge: MIT Press.
15. Ricketts, I.W. (1992). Cervical cell image inspection- a task for artificial neural networks. *Network*, **3**, 15-18.
16. Simpson, J.L. (1990). Incidence and timing of pregnancy losses. *American Journal of Medical Genetics*, **35**, 165-173.
17. Sambur, M.R. (1975). Selection of acoustic features for speaker identification. *IEEE Transactions on Acoustics, Speech and Signal Processing*, **ASSP-23**, 176-182.

NEURO-MUSCULAR SIGNAL DECOMPOSITION FOR DIAGNOSIS AND PROSTHESIS CONTROL USING HOPFIELD NEURO-CHIP

Mohammad Bodruzzaman, Saleh Zein-Sabatto, Mohan Malkani

Center for Neural Engineering
Tennessee State University
Nashville, TN 37209-1561

Harold Szu
Naval Surface Warfare Center Dahlgren Division, Code R44
Silver Spring, MD 20903

Richard Saeks
Accurate Automation Corporation
Chattanooga, TN 37406

Abstract

A neuro-muscular signal, during muscle contraction, is composed of multiple train of randomly distributed (Poisson process) action potentials innervated by a number of motor units from spinal cord. In order to study the motor control strategy and diagnosis of various neuro-muscular diseases, many investigators have used techniques of pattern recognition to decompose the muscle signal into its constituent action potential trains. In this work, a Hopfield network model is used, for its real-time chip fabrication possibility, to solve this inverse problem of neuro-muscular system by decomposing muscle signal. A muscle signal is simulated which is composed of five different patterns of action potential trains. The shapes of the simulated action potentials are derived from typical real muscle signals. Signal templates, one from each class of action potentials, are converted into its bipolar bitmap patterns and are used to compute the network weights and biases. Each detected action potential in the signal is then converted to its equivalent bitmap pattern and then presented to the Hopfield network for iterative stabilization to its closest attractor in the network state space. The system is performing very good recognition with 94% detection rate even when the entire signal was corrupted with 20% noise for a normal clinical measurement environment. The result is very promising for real-time implementation. Applying this method to surface muscle signals, there is a good potential to develop multiple spike train-based biological control algorithms for prosthesis.

1 Introduction

A neuro-muscular signal, also called myoelectric (ME) or electromyographic (EMG) signal, arises from the depolarization of muscle fibers following the discharge of the innervating motor neuron. The depolarization wave, called an action potential (AP), propagates along the muscle fibers. In normal skeletal muscle, the fibers never contract as individuals. Instead, a small groups of them contract in concert. Such a group of muscle fibers is supplied by the terminal branches of the nerve fiber or axon whose cell body is in the anterior horn of the spinal grey matter. This nerve cell body, plus the long axon, plus its terminal branches and all the muscle fibers together constitute a motor unit (MU). The action potential of a MU is called a motor unit action potential (MUAP).

In a sustained muscle contraction, the motor units must be repeatedly activated. The resulting sequence of MUAPs is called a motor unit action potential train (MUAPT). The waveform of the MUAPs within a MUAPT will remain constant provided that the geometric relationship between the electrode and the active muscle fibers, the properties of the recording electrode, and the biochemical properties of the muscle tissue all remain constant.

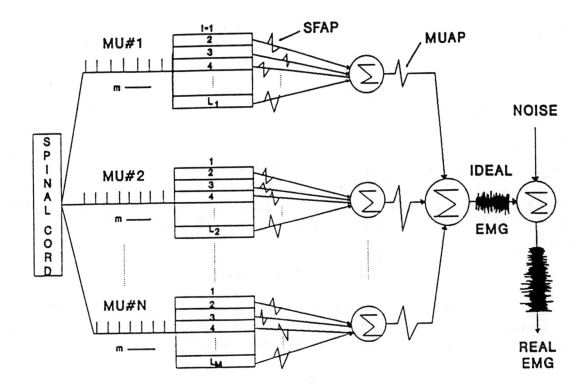

Figure 1: A Schematic of a Neuromuscular System

The muscle fibers belonging to the same motor unit are distributed randomly within the muscle rather than being clustered together, and can be spread throughout a territory occupying as much as 30% of the muscles cross sectional area. As a result, neighboring muscle fibers generally belong to different motor units, and in any small region there can be fibers from as many as 50 motor units. Therefore, a single MUAPT is observed when the fibers of only one motor unit in the vicinity of the electrode are active. Such a situation occurs only during a very weak muscle contraction. As the force output of a muscle increases, motor unit having fibers in the vicinity of the electrode become activated, and several MUAPTs will be detected simultaneously.

One of the the research goals in this field is that how to decompose or inverse process the muscle signal into its constituent MUAPTs in order to study the motor control strategy and to improve the diagnostic accuracy of the clinical EMG examination. Many investigators have used modern techniques of pattern recognition to decompose the muscle signal into its constituent MUAPTs. In this work, a Hopfield network model is used, for its real-time chip fabrication possibility, to solve this inverse problem of neuromuscular system by decomposing muscle signal and proposed an idea for developing decomposed multiple impulse train-based prosthesis or robot controller.

2 Neuromuscular System Model

A schematic of a neuromuscular system model is shown in the Figure 1. The Dirac delta impulses $\delta_i(t)$ are fired by the alpha-motoneurones which travel down the axons and then stimulate the associated muscle fibers. Let us assume that there are L_n muscle fibers connected with n^{th} motor unit and M_n be the total number of firings in a contraction time T_c, fired by the nth motor unit.

The minimum level of system configuration is a muscle fiber connected to a nerve branch. The system input is an impulse and the output of this system is an impulse response which is called single fiber action potential (SFAP). Thus the input train of impulses can be represented as:

$$\delta_n(t) = \sum_{m=1}^{M_n} \delta(t - t_m^n) \tag{1}$$

where

$$t_m = \sum_{j=1}^{m} x_j \quad for \quad m, j = 1, 2, 3, \ldots, M_n \tag{2}$$

In the above expressions, t is the continuous time variable, t_m represents the time locations of the impulses x_j. Therefore, the equation for the impulse response train of a single muscle fiber (l^{th}) is given by:

$$u_{nl}(t) = \sum_{m=1}^{M_n} h_{nlm}(t - t_{mn}) \tag{3}$$

Where h is the impulse response of muscle fibre. A impulse response train, also called MUAPT, from all the muscle fibers belonging to the nth motor unit is then obtained by the spatial summation over all the muscle fibers, L_n, innervated by the nth motor unit as:

$$u_n(t) = \sum_{l=1}^{L_n} \sum_{m=1}^{M_n} h_{nlm}(t - t_{mn}) \tag{4}$$

Again the EMG signal as they are detected by the electrode is the spatial summation of MUAPTs from all N motor units resulting a multi-train EMG signal and can be represented as:

$$emg(t) = \sum_{n=1}^{N} u_n(t) = \sum_{n=1}^{N} \sum_{l=1}^{L_n} \sum_{m=1}^{M_n} h_{nlm}(t - t_{mn}) \tag{5}$$

The signal given by the above expression is the physiological EMG signal and is not observable. When the signal is detected, an electrical measurement noise $w(t)$ is introduced from various sources. The detected signal will also be affected by the spatio-temporal convolution by the nerve-muscle fibers belonging to a number of MU. Thus the resulting observable EMG signal can be expressed as:

$$EMG(t) = \sum_{n=1}^{N} s_n(t) * u_n(t) + w(t) \tag{6}$$

where $s_n(t)$ is the point spreading function in space and time sparse in discrete index n.

In a continuously force varying contraction the parameters M_n and N are directly force dependent. Therefore, the final EMG signal will be a function of both time t and muscle force F. This EMG signal can be detected by intramuscular or by surface electrodes. In the clinical EMG laboratory, the conventional bipolar and monopolar needle electrodes are usually used.

3 Brief History of EMG Decomposition Problem

The problem of decomposition of any multi-train signal is an important issue for the pattern recognition and signal processing society. It is important because by decomposing such a signal, during muscular contraction, the clinical electromygraphers are able to observe the recruitment pattern of each motor unit that has been recruited. In the following, a brief history of EMG decomposition is presented.

Bergmans [1] has described an on-line computer program that can identify individual MUAPs automatically. The program stores the first potential it detects, may be either a valid MUAP or a superimposition, and compares it with the next six potentials. If it matches one of them, it is assumed to be a valid MUAP; if it doesn't, it is assumed to be a superimposition. Up to five unique MUAPs are collected per recording site, and histograms of their amplitude, durations, numbers of phases (fluctuations that cross the baseline) are compiled. The program compares MUAPs automatically on the basis of maximum sample-to-sample difference after alignment by threshold crossing points.

Prochazka *et al.* [2] have described a computer method for clinical firing pattern analysis. The EMG is recorded during a low level contraction using a bipolar wire electrode and is analyzed interactively off-line. The operator plays back the EMG at slow speed and selects up to four distinct MUAPs as templates. The program then attempts to identify the subsequent potentials by template matching, using a least-square-error criterion, and is able to resolve superimpositions involving two MUAPs automatically.

LeFever, Mambrito and De Luca [3, 4] have developed a method for studying motor-unit firing behavior during maximal contractions by decomposing the EMG signal recorded by a selective multipolar needle electrode. The method is primarily intended for physiological investigations rather than for clinical use, and is designed to perfectly identify every firing up to eight simultaneously active MUAPs. The method uses three data channels, obtained between different lead-off pairs of the multipolar electrode, to increase MUAP distinguishability. It identifies the MUAPs using a template matching procedure that takes into account both waveshape and relative firing likelihood given the past firing history, and it can resolve superimpositions involving two MUAPs. It can track slow changes in MUAP waveshape, firing rate, and firing-rate variability. Only records derived from attempted isometric contractions have been decomposed. In order to achieve desired high level of identification performance, extensive interaction by a trained operator is needed to create the templates, identify potentials about which the program is uncertain, and double-check the program's identifications. The method has been able to reveal some interesting new phenomena related to motor-unit behavior but is far too laborious for routine clinical use, requiring as much as one hour of computation time per second of data.

Moschytz, De Figueiredo, and colleagues [5, 6] have presented an advanced method for decomposing single-channel EMG recorded with standard concentric EMG needle electrodes. This method can extract up to seven sets of simultaneously active MUAP waveforms and firing patterns from partial IPs of moderate complexity. The analysis consist of three steps. The first is the learning phase in which the number of different active MUAPs and their waveforms are determined on the basis of shape-related features, independent of firing times. Next is a decomposition phase which reanalyzes the signal in an attempt to detect all the firings of each identified MUAP. The program attempts to resolve superimpositions using a sophisticated algorithm that is able to optimally scale and align up to three of the MUAP templates to find the best match to each observed superimposition potential.

McGill, Dorfman and Cummins [7, 8, 9] have described a different method of EMG analysis, which they refer to as Automatic Decomposition EMG (ADEMG), which is specifically oriented toward clinical application. ADEMG operates upon single-channel EMG signal of moderate complexity - corresponding to contractile forces of up to 30% MVC - recorded using standard EMG electrodes, and decomposes them into their constituent MUAPs. The analysis is performed in

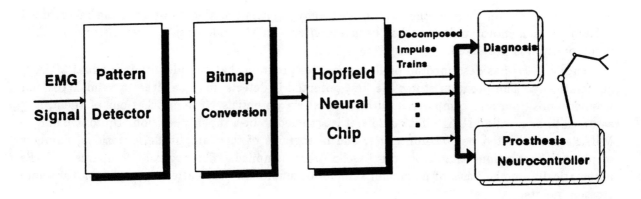

Figure 2: Block Diagram of The Proposed Inverse Neuromuscular System for Diagnosis and Control

nearly real time (less than 1 minute), a speed achieved by not attempting to resolve every occurance of each MUAP and by several computational innovations. Only steady isometric contractions are decomposed, so that MUAP waveshapes and firing rates can be accurately estimated despite incomplete identification. The method is now also available in hardware.

4 Signal Decomposition Using Hopfield Network

A block diagram of the proposed Hopfield network chip-based inverse neuro-muscular decomposition system is shown in Figure 2. A muscle signal is simulated which is composed of five different patterns of action potential trains. The shapes of the simulated action potentials are derived from typical real muscle signals. Signal templates, one from each class of action potentials, are converted into its bipolar bitmap patterns and are used to compute the network weights and biases. This multi-train signal is then corrupted with 20% noise, as compared to the average action potential amplitude, for a normal clinical measurement environment. A moving window-based spike detector is designed for the detection of the presence of action potentials as the window moves along the entire EMG data. The spikes are identified whenever they crossed a predetermined threshold. Once there is a crossing of the threshold value, the detector backs-up of two data points and picks-up a total of 12 consecutive data points to represent the captured action potential. Each detected action potential in the signal is then converted to its equivalent bitmap pattern. This bitmap pattern is then presented to the Hopfield network for iterative stabilization to its closest attractor in the network state space which outputs the recognized signal pattern.

A Hopfield model is used for pattern storage [10]. The captured action potential of 12 data points is converted in to a 2-D bitmap (20X20) using bipolar binary notation. The matrix element is valued a "1" if there is a presence of data value within the space resolution as defined by the bitmap matrix. Otherwise the matrix elements are valued as "-1". The bitmap conversion is the first step before the pattern is to be presented to the Hopfield network. Five different prototype templates are thus converted to their bitmap patterns and are used to compute the weights of a Hopfield auto-associative network.

The noisy EMG signal is then presented to the spike detection system. Once the signal detector detects a signal. the signal is converted to its bitmap pattern and are presented to the Hopfield network for classification. After the network receives the corrupted pattern it goes through iterative

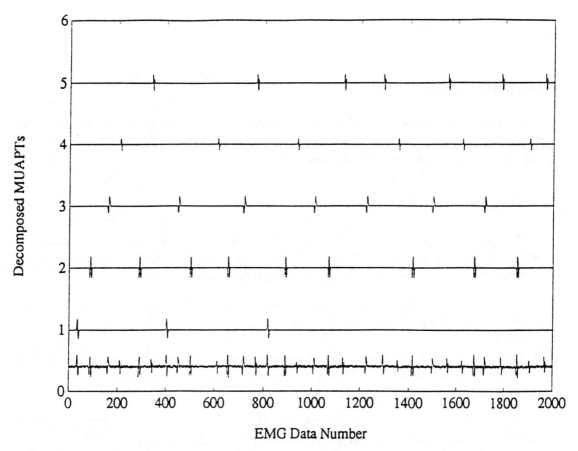

Figure 3: The Corrupted EMG Signal and Its Decomposed MUAPTs

state transition until it stabilizes into a closest attractor. After stabilization, the network stops iteration process and outputs the classification results. The decomposition system graphically plots the corrupted multi-train EMG signal and also plots the classified action potentials into decomposed channels as shown in Figure 3.

5   Results and Conclusions

The EMG signal decomposition is very important for clinical neurophysiologists for diagnosis of various neuro-muscular abnormalities. The firing patterns of individual motor unit can also be used for the study of motor control properties. The decomposition of neuro-muscular signal using a Hopfield network model is a success experiment and can be easily implemented for real-time application using Hopfield neuro-chip. Recognition and decomposition of EMG patterns may also serve an urgent need in deriving biological control algorithms which can be applied to control prosthesis.

From the simulated signal, with 20% added noise, the network has decomposed 30 spikes correctly, into their respective motor channel, out of a total 32 spikes in the corrupted signal. Which gives a success rate of nearly 94%. The success rates with 10% and 40% noise are also found to be 100% and 50% respectively. In this experiment, the prototype templates could also be adaptively updated each time a new action potential is detected. This allows the stored template to adapt the gradual changes during the MUAP recruitment. However, in this experiment the templates, that are stored initially, are not updated. It should also be noted here that the use of bitmap conversion technique eliminates the alignment problem that occurs in time domain template matching technique.

6 Acknowledgements

This work has been conducted in the Center for Neural Engineering (CNE) at Tennessee State University supported by the U.S. Navy Grant No. N00014-92-J-1372. The authors wish to thank them for their support for pursuing this research.

References

[1] J. Bergmans, " Computer-assisted measurement of the parameters of single motor unit potentials in human electromyography", in *New Development in Electromyography and Clinical Neurophysiology*, JE Desmedt (ed), Basel, Karger, 2:482-488,1973.

[2] V. J. Prochazka, B. Conrad and F. Sindermann, " A neuroelectric signal recognition system." *Electroenceph Clin Neurophysiol*, 32:95-97, 1971.

[3] R. LeFever and C. J. De Luca, "A procedure for decomposing the myoelectric signal into its constituent action potentials. Part I. Technique, theory and implementation." *IEEE Trans Biomed Eng*, 29:149-157, 1982.

[4] B. Mambrito and C. J. De Luca, "Acquisition and decomposition of the EMG signal", *Computer-Aided Electromyography*, JE Desmedt (ed), Basel, Karger, 1983.

[5] R. M. Studer, De Figueiredo and G. S. Moschytz, "An algorithm for sequential signal estimation and system identification for EMG signals." *IEEE Trans Biomed Eng*, BME-28:318-324, 1984.

[6] De Figueiredo and A. Gerber, "Separation of superimposed signals by a cross correlation method', *IEEE Trans ASSP*, 31:1084-1089, 1983.

[7] K. C. McGill, K. L. Cummings and L. J. Dorfman, "Automatic decomposition of the clinical electromyogram." *IEEE Trans Biomed Eng*, BME-31:462-468, 1984.

[8] K. C. McGill and L. J. Dorfman, "High resolution alignment of sampled waveforms." *IEEE Trans Biomed Eng.* BME-32:470-477, 1985.

[9] K. C. McGill and L. J. Dorfman, "Automatic decomposition electromyography (ADEMG): validation and normative data in brachial biceps." *Electroencephhalogr Clin Neurophysiol*, 61:453-461, 1985.

[10] J. J. Hopfield, "Neural network and physical systems with emergent collective computational abilities. *Proceedings of the National Academy of Sciences*, 79:2554-2558, 1982.

"Molecular Lesion Spectra as Radiation Signatures"

K. Rupnik and S. P. McGlynn

Department of Chemistry, Louisiana State University, Baton Rouge, LA 70803

Abstract

The Radiation Signature (RS) paradigm takes aim at practical applications of the knowledge provided by molecular studies of radiation-matter interactions in DNA. The central proposition is the idea that the distribution of molecular lesions (i.e., a molecular lesion spectrum, MLS) generated in DNA by exposure to a particular radiation is a characteristic of that causal radiation (i.e., is a RS). We have found that adaptive neural networks provide an efficient way to validate that proposition[1,2]. Feature recognition techniques become necessary when one deals with data bases that are less than optimal, when one quires the minimum number of lesions adequate for signature, or when one wishes to pursue the more tenuous and presumptive connection of a radiation and its clinical outcome. The focus of this work is on the modeling and interpretation of RS's using neural network processing. The specific goals of RS research in the domain of feature extraction and modeling are: 1) to use trained neural networks to extract signatures and markers from molecular lesion sets of various sizes, and to identify these DNA lesions which serve as markers of specific radiation, 2) to investigate which methods, including various neural networks and various architectures, can suggest the molecular lesion sets that are most appropriate for particular purposes, and 3) to use adaptive neural networks for interpretation of results. Although efforts to identify products of radiation that are specific to radiation type and to link these with biological responses are almost a century old, the RS concept has provided the first quantitative confirmation of such causal relations.

1) K. Rupnik, and S. P. McGlynn "Molecular Lesion Spectra as Radiation Signatures" *Spectroscopy Letters,* **26** 5 873 (1993).

2) S. P. McGlynn, K. Rupnik, M. N. Varma and L. Klasinc, "Radiation Signatures and Radiation Markers", Radiation Protection Dosimetry (in press, 1994).

Ability of the 3D Vector Version of the Back-Propagation to Learn 3D Motion

Tohru Nitta

Electrotechnical Laboratory,

1-1-4 Umezono, Tsukuba Science City, Ibaraki, 305 Japan.

Abstract :

The 3D vector version of the back-propagation algorithm (called "3DV-BP") is a natural extension of the complex-valued version of the back-propagation algorithm (called "Complex-BP"). The Complex-BP can be applied to multi-layered neural networks whose weights, threshold values, input and output signals are all complex numbers, and the 3DV-BP can be applied to multi-layered neural networks whose threshold values, input and output signals are all 3D real valued vectors, and whose weights are all 3D orthogonal matrices. It has already been reported that an inherent property of the Complex-BP is its ability to learn "2D motion". This paper shows in computational experiments that the 3DV-BP has the ability to learn "3D motion", which corresponds to the ability of the Complex-BP to learn "2D motion".

1   Introduction

One of the most popular neural network models is the multi-layered network and the related back-propagation training algorithm, called here, "Real-BP" [7]. Back-propagation networks have many successful applications.

The "Complex-BP" is a complex valued version of the back-propagation algorithm, which can be applied to multi-layered neural networks whose weights, threshold values, input and output signals are all complex numbers [1, 3]. This algorithm enables the network to learn complex valued patterns naturally. It has already been reported that an inherent property of the Complex-BP is its ability to learn "2D motion" [1, 3]. And also, the Complex-BP has been applied to the interpretation of optical flow (motion vector field calculated from images) and estimation of motion which are important tasks in computer vision [5, 6].

The "3DV-BP" is a three-dimensional vector version of the back-propagation algorithm which can be applied to multi-layered neural networks whose threshold values, input and output signals are all 3D real valued vectors, and whose weights are all 3D orthogonal matrices [2]. This algorithm is a natural extention of the Complex-BP algorithm. This paper shows in computational experiments that the 3DV-BP has the ability to learn "3D motion", which corresponds to the ability of the Complex-BP to learn "2D motion".

Hereafter, we shall refer to a real valued (usual) neural network used by the Real-BP as a "Real-BP network", a complex valued neural network used by the Complex-BP as a "Complex-BP network", and a three-dimensional vector valued neural network used by the 3DV-BP as a "3DV-BP network".

This paper is organized as follows: Section 2 describes the 3DV-BP algorithm, and Section 3 deals with the empirical analyses of the ability of the 3DV-BP network model to learn 3D motion . The paper will end with our conclusions.

2   The "3DV-BP" Algorithm

This section briefly describes the 3DV-BP algorithm [2]. It can be applied to multi-layered neural networks in which threshold values, input and output signals are all 3D real valued vectors, and whose weights are all 3D orthogonal matrices, and the output function F of a neuron can be defined as

$$F(\boldsymbol{A}) = \begin{bmatrix} f(a_1) \\ f(a_2) \\ f(a_3) \end{bmatrix}, \quad \boldsymbol{A} = \begin{bmatrix} a_1 \\ a_2 \\ a_3 \end{bmatrix}, \tag{1}$$

where $f(u) = 1/(1 + \exp[-u])$, that is, each component of an output $F(\boldsymbol{A})$ of a neuron means the sigmoid function of each component a_m of the net input $\boldsymbol{A}$ to the neuron, respectively ($m = 1, 2, 3$). The learning rule has been obtained by using a steepest descent method.

3 Ability to Learn 3D Motion

We will now present some illustrative examples to show that an adaptive network of 3D valued neurons can be used to learn 3D motion such as rotation, similar transformation, and translation. Due to space limitations, we will restrict the presentation of our results to similar transformations, although similar work has been carried out on rotations, and parallel displacement [4].

We used a 1-6-1 three-layered network, which transformed a point (x_1, x_2, x_3) into another point (x'_1, x'_2, x'_3) in 3-dimensional space. Although the 3DV-BP network generates a value $\boldsymbol{X} = {}^t[x_1\ x_2\ x_3]$ within the range $0 \leq x_1, x_2, x_3 \leq 1$, for the sake of convenience, we present it in the figures given below as having a transformed value within the range $-1 \leq x_1, x_2, x_3 \leq 1$.

We also conducted experiments with a 3-15-3 network with real valued weights and thresholds, to compare the 3DV-BP with the Real-BP. The first component of a 3-vector was input into the first input neuron, the second component was input into the second input neuron, and the third component was input into the third input neuron. The output from the first output neuron was interpreted as the first component of a 3-vector, and the output from the second output neuron was interpreted as the second component, and the output from the third output neuron was interpreted as the third component.

The learning constant ε used in these experiments was 0.5. The initial components of the weights and the thresholds were chosen to be random real numbers between -0.3 and 0.3. We determined that learning finished when

$$\sqrt{\sum_p \sum_{k=1}^N ||\boldsymbol{T}_k^{(p)} - \boldsymbol{O}_k^{(p)}||^2} = 0.05 \tag{2}$$

held, where $||\boldsymbol{x}|| \stackrel{\text{def}}{=} \sqrt{x_1^2 + x_2^2 + x_3^2}$, $\boldsymbol{x} = {}^t[x_1\ x_2\ x_3]$; $\boldsymbol{T}_k^{(p)}$, $\boldsymbol{O}_k^{(p)} \in \boldsymbol{R}^3$ denote the desired output value, the actual output value of the neuron k for the pattern p, i.e. the left side of (2) means the error between the desired and actual output patterns ($\boldsymbol{R}$ denotes the set of real numbers); N denotes the number of neurons in the output layer. We regarded presenting a set of learning patterns to the neural network as one learning cycle. In this connection, time complexity per learning cycle of the 1-6-1 three-layered network for the 3DV-BP was nearly equal to that of the 3-15-3 three-layered network for the standard BP, as seen in Table 1. Furthermore, the space complexity (i.e. the number of parameters) was almost half that of the standard BP.

The experiments described in this section, consisted of two parts - a training step, followed by a test step.

3.1 Learning of a Simple 3D Motion

Figs. 1 and 2 show the result of an experiment on a simple similar transformation.

The training step consisted of learning a set of (3D orthogonal matrix valued) weights and (3D vector valued) thresholds, such that the input set of 11 points (with equal intervals) lying along the straight line

$$
\begin{bmatrix} x \\ y \\ z \end{bmatrix} = t \begin{bmatrix} 1 \\ 1 \\ 1 \end{bmatrix} \qquad (0.0 \leq t \leq 1.0) \tag{3}
$$

gave as output, half-scaled straight line points (Fig. 1). The output training points also lay along the same straight line (equation (3)), but the range was $0.0 \leq t \leq 0.5$. To avoid complexity, we omitted the points and showed only the lines joining them in the figures.

In a second (test) step, the 48 input points (with equal intervals) lying on three squares would hopefully be mapped to an output set of points lying on three half-scaled squares. The actual output test points for the 3DV-BP did, indeed, almost lie on the squares (but, with an error) (Fig. 2).

To compare how a real valued network would perform, the 3-15-3 (real valued) network mentioned above was trained using the same pairs of training points lying along equation (3). The same 48 test points lying on the three squares were then input with this real network. All points were "mapped" onto straight lines, as shown in Fig. 2.

3.2 Learning of a More Complex 3D Motion

This subsection shows that the 3DV-BP can make more complicated transformation.

Fig. 3 shows how the training points mapped onto each other. Those 11 points (with equal intervals) lying along the straight line indicated by "Input Pattern 1", mapped onto points along the same line, but with a scale reduction factor of 2. Those 11 points (with equal intervals) lying along the straight line indicated by "Input Pattern 2" mapped onto points along the same line, but with a scale reduction factor of 10. All the training points lie along the straight line

$$
\begin{bmatrix} x \\ y \\ z \end{bmatrix} = t \begin{bmatrix} 1 \\ 1 \\ 1 \end{bmatrix} \qquad (-1.0 \leq t \leq 1.0), \tag{4}
$$

where "Input Pattern 1" for $0.0 \leq t \leq 1.0$, "Output Pattern 1" for $0.0 \leq t \leq 0.5$, "Input Pattern 2" for $-1.0 \leq t \leq 0.0$, and "Output Pattern 2" for $-0.1 \leq t \leq 0.0$.

In the test step, by presenting the 60 points lying on the three circles $x^2 + z^2 = 1$, $y^2 + z^2 = 1$ and $x^2 + y^2 = 1$, the actual output points took the patterns as shown in Fig. 4.

It appears that this 3DV-BP network has learned to generalize the reduction factor α as a function of the position in three-dimensional space, i.e. a point $^t[x \quad y \quad z]$ is transformed into another point $\alpha^t[x \quad y \quad z]$, where $\alpha(^t[x \quad y \quad z]) \approx 0.5$ for $x, y, z \geq 0$, and $\alpha(^t[x \quad y \quad z]) \approx 0.1$ for $x, y, z \leq 0$.

4 Conclusions

We investigated by computational experiments the characteristics of the 3DV-BP algorithm which is a natural extension of the Complex-BP algorithm. It was learned that the 3DV-BP had the ability to learn "3D motion" such as similar transformation as its inherent property, which corresponded to the ability of the Complex-BP to learn "2D motion". We expect that applications for the 3DV-BP algorithm will be found in such areas as 3D image processing.

Acknowledgements

The author expresses his thanks to Dr.K.Ohta, Director of the Computer Science Division, and Dr.T.Higuchi, Chief of the Computational Models Section, for having an opportunity to do this study and their continual encouragement.

References

[1] Nitta, T. and Furuya, T. (1991). A Complex Back-Propagation Learning. *Transactions of Information Processing Society of Japan*, Vol. 32, No. 10, pp. 1319-1329 (in Japanese).

[2] Nitta, T. (1993). A Three-Dimensional Back-Propagation. *Proc. INNS World Congress on Neural Networks*, Portland, Vol. 3, pp. 572-575.

[3] Nitta, T. (1993). A Complex Numbered Version of the Back-Propagation Algorithm. *Proc. INNS World Congress on Neural Networks*, Portland, Vol. 3, pp. 576-579.

[4] Nitta, T. (1993). Ability of the 3D Vector Version of the Back-Propagation to Learn 3D Motion. *ETL Technical Report*, TR-93-24 (in Japanese).

[5] Miyauchi, M. and Seki, M. (1992). Interpretation of Optical Flow through Neural Network Learning. *Proc. IEEE International Conference on Communication Systems /International Symposium on Information Theory and its Applications*, Singapore, pp. 1247-1251.

[6] Miyauchi, M., Seki, M., Watanabe, A. and Miyauchi, A. (1992). Interpretation of Optical Flow through Neural Network Learning. *Proc. IAPR Workshop on Machine Vision Applications*, Tokyo, pp. 523-528.

[7] Rumelhart, D. E. et al. (1986). *Parallel Distributed Processing*, Vol. 1, p. 547, MIT press.

Network	Time complexity			Space complexity		
	$\times$ and $\div$	+ and $-$	Sum	Weights	Thresholds	Sum
3DV-BP 1-6-1	255	141	396	36	21	57
Standard BP 3-15-3	264	141	405	90	18	108

Table 1 The Computational Complexity of the 3DV-BP and the Standard BP. Time complexity means the sum of the four operations performed per learning cycle. Space complexity means the sum of the parameters (weights and thresholds).

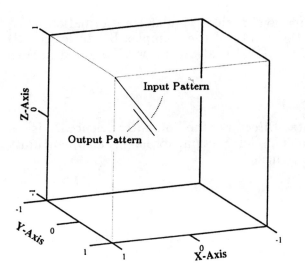

Fig. 1 Learning pattern (Simple transformation).

Fig. 2 (a) Test pattern 1 (Simple transformation).

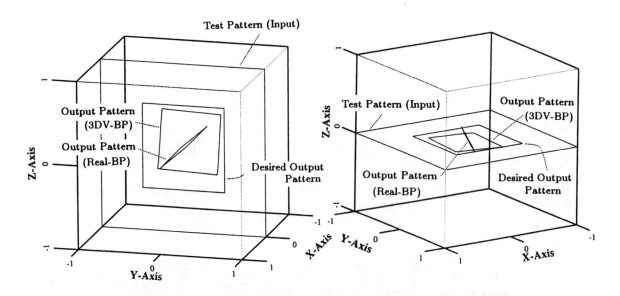

Fig. 2 (b) Test pattern 2 (Simple transformation).

Fig. 2 (c) Test pattern 3 (Simple transformation).

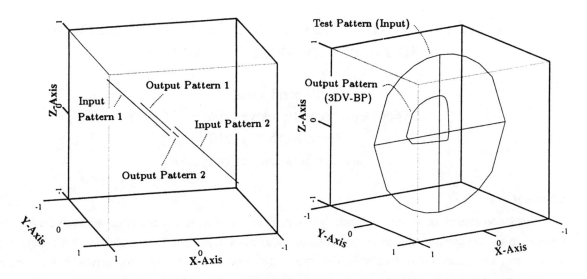

Fig. 3 Learning patterns (Complex transformation).   **Fig. 4 (a)** Test pattern 1 (Complex transformation).

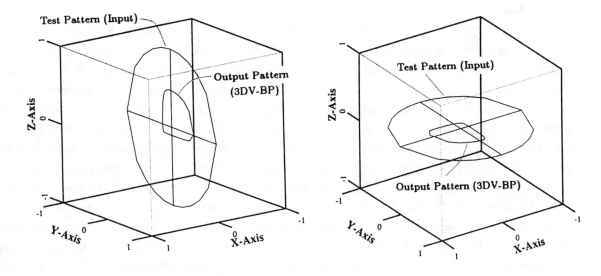

Fig. 4 (b) Test pattern 2 (Complex transformation).   **Fig. 4 (c)** Test pattern 3 (Complex transformation).

Asymptotically stable automaton-like behavior in recurrent neural networks

Robert Fanelli

Physics Department, Brooklyn College of CUNY

Brooklyn, NY 11210

e-mail: rvfbc@cunyvm.cuny.edu

Abstract

Simulation studies confirm the previously observed ability of recurrent neural networks to emulate finite automata in a stable manner while processing arbitrarily long input sequences. First order recurrent networks with two different architectures have been trained to emulate given automata and untrained networks with randomly assigned weights can often spontaneously emulate automata. This behavior is tied to the existence of regions of the network state space which correspond to the states of the automata and are mapped into each other by the inputs to the network. Networks initialized at arbitrary points in the state space and supplied with random input sequences enter these regions in a small number of time steps and then remain in them indefinitely. This automaton structure can be thought of as a generalization of the limit cycle attractor for systems with varying inputs.

Background

Researchers applying recurrent neural networks to the problem of learning regular grammars have consistently found that they accomplish this task by configuring themselves to approximately emulate the finite automata associated with these grammars (Cleeremans, Servan-Schreiber, & McClelland, 1989; Giles, Miller, Chen, Chen, Sun, & Lee, 1992; Omlin, Giles, & Miller, 1992 and others). The points in the network state space visited while processing strings of characters tend to cluster, with the clusters corresponding to the states of the automata. Since there are errors in the output of a recurrent neural network at each time step, it has been generally assumed that these errors should accumulate with time, producing a progressive degradation in performance. Such degradation has been observed when networks have been tested on strings much longer that those on which they were trained. The observed clusters grow, become less well separated and eventually overlap and lose their identity. An exception to this was observed by Manolios & Fanelli (1993). Some recurrent networks trained on relatively short strings maintained their performance and retained well defined clusters that did not grow even when processing strings up to 1,000 characters in length. Zeng, Goodman, & Smyth (1993) seem to have observed similar behavior in one of their networks. Manolios & Fanelli (1993) concluded that the finite automaton like behavior of the network had been somehow encoded in its attractor structure (when considered as a dynamical system) so that it could be retained indefinitely, without degradation. This paper reports on further investigations of this phenomenon and its nature as the generalization of a limit cycle attractor. A simulation study such as this is empirical and thus cannot be definitive or all encompassing. However, it can expose some of the features of the phenomenon and thus provide a basis for theoretical analyses.

Introduction

The study has investigated discrete-time, first order, recurrent neural networks with two architectures, the simple recurrent network of Elman (1990) and an architecture with two recurrent layers, feeding back to each other (Manolios & Fanelli, 1993). The inputs to the networks were restricted to be members of finite sets (*e.g.*

representations of the characters in a character set), but could otherwise vary arbitrarily with time. Systems with no inputs or constant ones normally have well defined equilibrium points, limit cycles or chaotic attractors. Hirsch (1989) has briefly discussed systems with variable inputs, suggesting that in some cases such a system can act like "a rather unreliable finite state automaton." Each different input can be thought of as defining a different mapping of the system state from one time step to the next, thus defining a different dynamics for the system. Repetition of each input thus results in an approach to a distinct set of attractors. Also, any finite sequence of inputs also specifies a dynamics, but with a larger effective time step. Its own attractors will be approached after enough repetitions. There is thus an infinite number of sets of attractors associated with a network and its inputs. In this study, a few of these attractors have been observed and points on them found to be closely associated with stable clusters of network states corresponding to automaton states.

Methods used

Automaton-like behavior can be identified in the following way. As a network processes a sequence of inputs, clusters of network states corresponding to automaton states can remain stable indefinitely, provided that the points in these clusters lie in regions with the following property: In one time step, a point in such a region is mapped by any member of the input set into a point that lies within the same or another such region. A subtractive algorithm for identifying stable regions, based on this property, has been developed. First, the clusters of states observed when a network processes long random strings are used as a guide for choosing initial regions which include them. The remainder of the state space is denoted the excluded region. Then a fixed rectangular grid is imposed on the state space. Each included point on a grid intersection is mapped by each member of the input set to a resulting point. If any of the resulting points lie in the excluded region, the grid point is reassigned to the excluded region. This continues until no more grid points can be excluded. The boundaries of the resulting regions are uncertain because of the finite grid size. The algorithm deals conservatively with this uncertainty by excluding a grid point unless all of its mapped points are entirely surrounded by included grid points. Finally, points whose mappings lie in the stable regions but which are not themselves close to any mapped points are considered not to be part of the asymptotic regions and are removed. The remaining points indicate the stable regions. The results of the algorithm may depend on the initial choice of the regions, so the algorithm can be repeated with different choices to check consistency.

In this paper, sample results for three neural networks are shown. In each case, the network has a single input unit, set to zero or one, so that over time the inputs are bit strings. The number of units representing the states of the networks was held to two, so that the state spaces were two dimensional and could be easily displayed. The first network had an Elman architecture, with two hidden units representing the state. The second had the 2-layer architecture with two state units, one designated for output. These networks were trained with versions of the RTRL algorithm (Williams & Zipser, 1989) on simple bit string grammars. The third was another 2-layer network, randomly initialized and untrained. Each network was studied in the same way. All the networks were tested with a randomly selected state at the start of the processing of each string. First the network was tested with 3 random strings of 1000 0's and 1's and the last 100 states in each case were observed. The clustering of these states served as a guide for the algorithm for finding stable regions. Second, this algorithm was applied. Third, the networks were tested with 9 strings of 100 0's then 9 strings of 100 1's and then 9 strings of 50 01 pairs. These tests located the attractors for single characters and two character sequences, which appeared well in advance of 100 time steps. Fourth, convergence of the networks was tested with 100 strings of 10 random characters, which turned out to be long enough to reach the asymptotic automaton region. With random initial states, this test indicated whether the asymptotic automaton was reached globally or from some basin of attraction.

Elman Architecture

The network was trained as in Fanelli (1993) on a simple bit string grammar which was found easy to learn for this architecture. The grammatical strings are just those that end in the sequence "01". The training set consisted of all strings less than or equal to 4 characters in length, including the null string. Forty nets were initialized randomly and trained for 10,000 epochs each with a learning parameter of 0.01 and a momentum term of 0. The initial states for the nets were chosen randomly during the initialization, then held fixed during training. The network with the smallest root-mean-square (rms) error (0.016) was further trained to a total of 350,000 epochs. Its final rms error was 0.0011. This network was then studied as described above.

Figure 1 shows the stable regions found for this network, which correspond to the three states of the minimal automaton for the grammar. The rectangular shape of the regions is purely a consequence of the coarseness of the grid used in this case. The attractors for single characters and 2 character sequences are also shown and lie within the stable regions. The long random string tests described above yielded clusters of states that all lay within the stable regions also. These are not shown. In the convergence test, the network states reached stable regions within 10 time steps from all 100 initial states, indicating global convergence.

Two-Layer Architecture, Tomita 6 grammar

The network was trained on the sixth grammar of Tomita (1982). The training set used initially consisted of all strings less than or equal to 4 characters in length, including the null string. The initial states for the nets were chosen as described above for the Elman nets. To begin, 182 nets were initialized randomly and trained for 1000 epochs each, with a learning parameter of 0.1 and a momentum term of 0.5. Of these nets, 5 had root-mean-square errors less than 0.1. The best, with an rms error of 0.042 was chosen for further training. It was trained for another 1000 epochs on the same training set, reaching an rms error of 0.027. It was then tested on each of 3 single strings consisting of 1000 random 0's and 1's (different than the strings described above). Its largest rms error was 0.031. The network was trained for another 3000 epochs on the string producing this error, reaching a final rms error of 0.010.

Figure 2 shows the stable regions and 1 and 2 character attractors for this network. There are four stable regions corresponding to an automaton that is reducible to the three state minimal automaton for Tomita 6. The attractors are all limit cycles with two 3 state cycles for single characters and three 2 state cycles for two character sequences, all expected from the grammar itself. The stable regions are larger than in the previous case, with the lower two breaking up into sub-regions. As above, the last 100 states of long strings all lay well within the regions shown. Global convergence to the stable regions within 10 time steps was observed for this network also.

Two-Layer Architecture, untrained

Networks were randomly initialized in the same manner as the other nets, but were not trained. The weight values were uniformly distributed between -2.0 and +2.0. The same studies were performed as on the other nets.

Figure 3 shows results for one such network. They are similar to those already presented, even though the networks were not trained. Once again, later states of long random strings clustered within the stable regions and global convergence within 10 time steps was observed.

Discussion

The above results indicate that stable automaton-like behavior is often a feature of recurrent neural networks running for large numbers of time steps. Untrained nets can display it spontaneously and nets can be trained to approximate particular automata with errors remaining within fixed tolerances. It is likely that this behavior is a feature of other systems also, such as second order neural networks and other kinds of discrete-time dynamical systems. It may be considered as a natural generalization of the limit cycle to systems with discrete time-varying inputs.

The automata observed appear to have a finite number of states at the accuracy scale of this study. However, the sub-regions observed for the second network and other observations suggest that as the grid size (or other scale measure) becomes finer, breakup into still smaller regions may be observed. This raises the possibility that in the limit these regions approach a possibly unbounded number of distinct points. Definitive resolution of this question goes beyond simulation studies and requires a theoretical analysis.

Acknowledgement

It is a pleasure to thank Peter Manolios for many stimulating and helpful discussions and suggestions during the course of this work.

References

Cleeremans, A., Servan-Schreiber, D., & McClelland, J. (1989). Finite state automata and simple recurrent networks. Neural Computation, 1(3), 372.

Elman, J. L. (1990). Finding structure in time. Cognitive Science, 14, 179.

Fanelli, R. (1993). Grammatical inference and approximation of finite automata by simple recurrent neural networks trained with full forward error propagation (Technical Report No. NNRG930811A). Brooklyn College.

Giles, C. L., Miller, C. B., Chen, D., Chen, H. H., Sun, G. Z., & Lee, Y. C. (1992). Learning and extracting finite state automata with second-order recurrent neural networks. Neural Computation, 4, 393-405.

Hirsch, M. (1989). Convergent activation dynamics in continuous time networks. Neural Networks, 2(5), 331-349.

Manolios, P., & Fanelli, R. (1993). First order recurrent neural networks and deterministic finite state automata (Technical Report No. NNRG930901A). Brooklyn College.

Omlin, C. W., Giles, C. L., & Miller, C. B. (1992). Heuristics for the extraction of rules from discrete-time recurrent neural networks. In International Joint Conference on Neural Networks, I (pp. 33-38). Baltimore:

Tomita, M. (1982). Construction of finite-state automata from examples using hill-climbing. In Proceedings of the Fourth Annual Cognitive Science Conference, (pp. 105-108).

Williams, R. J., & Zipser, D. (1989). A learning algorithm for continually running fully recurrent neural networks. Neural Computation, 1(2), 270.

Zeng, Z., Goodman, R. M., & Smyth, P. (1993). Self-clustering recurrent networks. In IEEE International Conference on Neural Networks, 1 (pp. 33-38). San Francisco: IEEE Press.

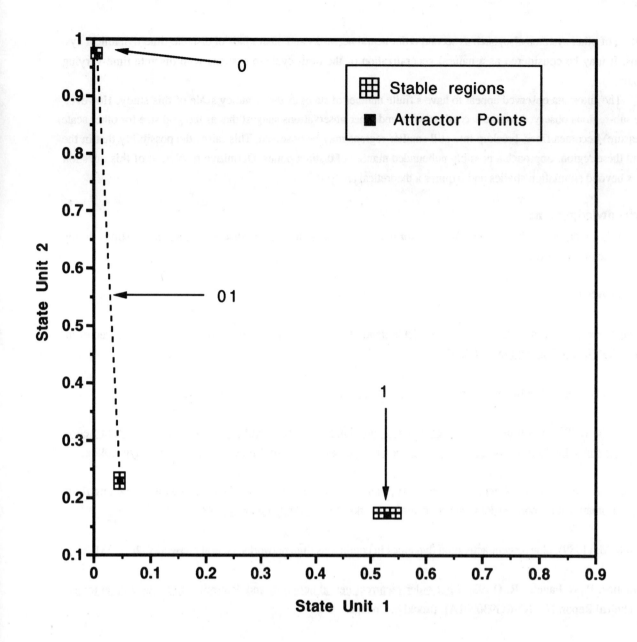

Figure 1. Stable regions and three attractors for an Elman network trained on a simple bit string grammar. Data point symbols are scaled to approximately indicate the grid size used in applying the stable region finding algorithm. The single character attractors are both equilibrium points while the two character attractor is a two state limit cycle. The dotted line traces the cycle and the repeated character sequences associated with the attractors are indicated with arrows. The region at the lower right corresponds to the start state and that at the lower left to the single final state.

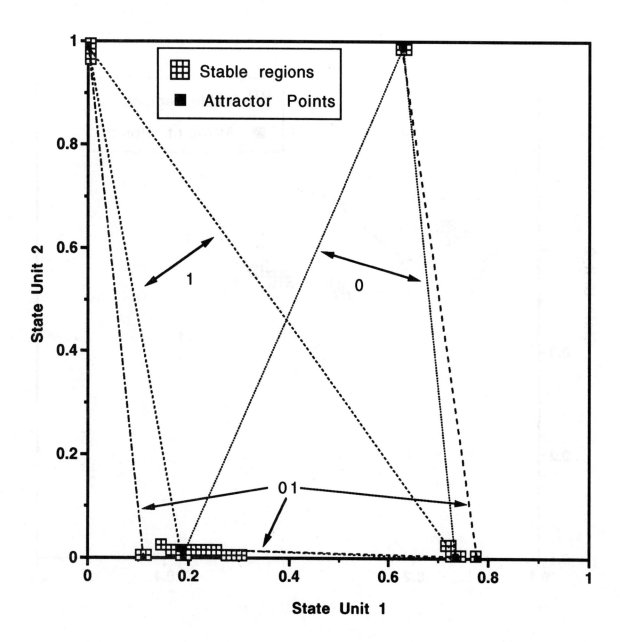

Figure 2. Stable regions and simple attractors for a 2-layer network trained on the Tomita 6 bit string grammar. Data point symbols are scaled to approximately indicate the grid size used in applying the stable region finding algorithm. The two single character attractors are three state limit cycles while the three two character attractors are two state limit cycles. The dotted lines trace the cycles and the repeated character sequences associated with them are indicated with arrows. The "0" cycle is traversed counterclockwise and the "1" cycle clockwise. The automaton is reducible, with the two upper states reducing to the start state which is also the single final state.

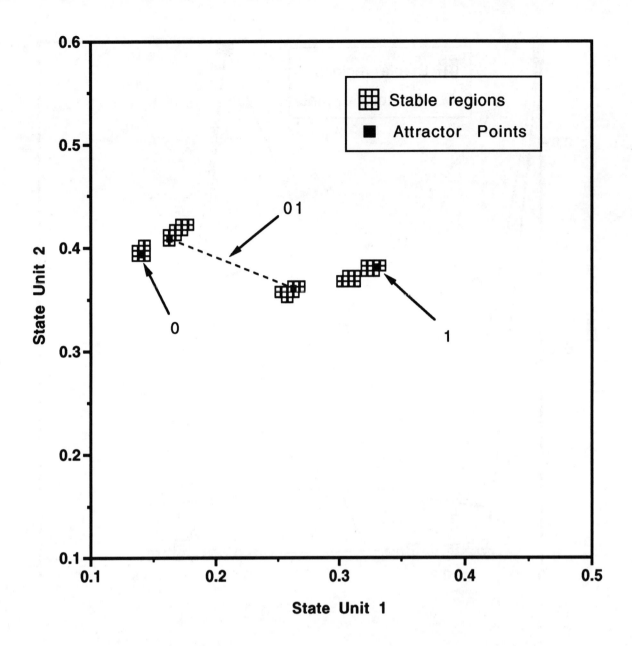

Figure 3. Stable regions and simple attractors for a 2-layer network randomly initialized, but untrained. Data point symbols are scaled to approximately indicate the grid size used in applying the stable region finding algorithm. The two single character attractors are equilibrium points while the two character attractor is a two state limit cycle. The dotted lines trace the cycles and the repeated character sequences associated with them are indicated with arrows.

HAVNET: A NOVEL NEURAL NETWORK ARCHITECTURE FOR TWO-DIMENSIONAL PATTERN RECOGNITION

Ryan G. Rosandich   Cihan H. Dagli

Department of Engineering Management, University of Missouri-Rolla

Rolla, MO 65401

ABSTRACT

A novel artificial neural network architecture is introduced. The network employs the Hausdorff distance as a metric of similarity between two-dimensional patterns. The Hausdorff distance exhibits many properties that are desirable in a pattern recognition context, and the network inherits these advantageous traits. The architecture, learning rule, and recall processing for the network are presented. It is shown that the network internally employs a version of the Voronoi surface to facilitate processing. Preliminary results from applying the network to pattern recognition tasks are encouraging.

INTRODUCTION

This paper introduces a new neural network architecture specifically designed for two-dimensional pattern recognition. Because the network utilizes the Hausdorff distance as a metric of similarity between patterns, and because it employs a learned version of the Voronoi surface to perform the comparison, it has been dubbed the HAusdorff-Voronoi NETwork or *HAVNET*. The choice of the Hausdorff distance as the metric of similarity between input patterns and learned patterns is what makes HAVNET different from most other neural network paradigms.

Some current neural networks treat the input as a vector and the trained weights as another vector, and the measure of similarity becomes the difference between these two vectors [e.g. 1]. The node with an internal weight vector that most closely matches the presented vector generates the highest output response. Unfortunately, transforming a two-dimensional input pattern into a multidimensional vector can produce behavior that is counter-intuitive. Input patterns that appear very similar (to the human eye) to learned patterns for a particular node can generate very poor responses from that node.

Other networks treat two-dimensional input patterns as a matrix, and the measure of comparison between the input matrix and the stored (learned) matrix is computed as a correlation between the two patterns [e.g. 2]. These networks essentially perform template matching. Although these networks perform well when input patterns are identical to learned patterns, slight distortions in the input patterns can drastically reduce the output from the trained node, again producing results that do not agree well with human interpretations of pattern similarity.

One measure of similarity between two-dimensional binary patterns that has been shown to agree closely with human performance is the *Hausdorff distance* [3]. The Hausdorff distance measures the extent to which each point of an input set lies near some point of a model set. Given two finite point sets $A=\{a_1,...,a_p\}$ and $B=\{b_1,...,b_q\}$, the Hausdorff distance is defined as:

$$H(A,B) = \max\{h(A,B), h(B,A)\} \tag{1}$$

Where the function $h(A,B)$ computes the *directed* Hausdorff distance from A to B as follows:

$$h(A,B) = \max_{a \in A}\left\{\min_{b \in B}\left\{\|a-b\|\right\}\right\} \tag{2}$$

Where $\|a-b\|$ is typically the Euclidean distance between points a and b. The directed Hausdorff distance identifies that point in A that is furthest from any point in B and measures the distance from that point to its nearest neighbor in B. If $h(A,B)=d$, all points in A are within distance d of some point in B. The (undirected) Hausdorff distance, then, is the maximum of the two directed distances between two point sets *A* and *B* so that if the Hausdorff distance is *d*, then all points of set *A* are within distance *d* of some point in set *B* and vice versa.

The Hausdorff distance exhibits many desirable properties for pattern recognition. First, it is known to be a metric over the set of all closed, bounded sets [4]. Also, it is everywhere non-negative and it obeys the properties of identity, symmetry, and triangle inequality. In the context of pattern recognition this means that a shape is identical only to itself, that the order of comparison of two shapes does not matter, and that if two shapes are highly dissimilar they cannot both be similar to some third shape. This final property (triangle inequality) is particularly important for reliable pattern classification. It was because of these advantageous properties that the Hausdorff distance was chosen as the similarity metric that is the basis of HAVNET. The architecture, learning rule, and recognition process used in HAVNET are described in detail in the following sections.

NEURAL NETWORK ARCHITECTURE

An overview of the architecture of HAVNET is shown in Figure 1. The neural network behaves as a binary pattern classifier. It takes as inputs two-dimensional binary patterns, it employs feed-forward processing, and it produces analog output patterns. One output is generated by each node, with the analog value indicating the level of match

between the input pattern and the class represented by that node. The neural network consists of three layers, the *plastic layer*, the *Voronoi layer*, and the *Hausdorff layer*. The plastic layer contains neurons with the weights that are trained during the learning process, the Voronoi layer serves to measure the distance between individual points in the input and learned patterns, and the Hausdorff layer uses information from the Voronoi layer to compute the overall level of similarity between the input pattern and the learned pattern. A detailed diagram of the architecture for a single node is shown in Figure 2. The node is shown in a configuration for one-dimensional inputs for reasons of clarity. In the actual network, the input pattern, plastic layer, and Voronoi layer are all two-dimensional.

Learning is employed in HAVNET to adapt the individual nodes to recognize certain classes, and it is conducted by presenting examples of each class to the network during a training phase. Learning in the particular implementation of the network described here is done off-line and in a

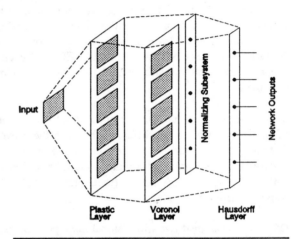

Figure 1. Neural Network Architecture Overview

supervised manner, but it could alternatively employ on-line learning and self-organization. The specific details of how learning and recognition are carried out are presented in the following sections.

NEURAL NETWORK LEARNING

Off-line supervised learning is implemented in the version of HAVNET described here. The network is trained to recognize objects off-line, and the network is informed *a priori* of the class to which each training pattern belongs. Once the network is put into the recognition (on-line) mode, training ceases and recognition response is repeatable and predictable.

The weight matrices that undergo changes during the learning process reside in the plastic layer of the network (the reader may wish to refer to Figures 1 and 2 throughout this discussion). A binary input pattern A^m that is presented to the network during the learning phase is represented as follows:

$$a^m_{x,y} = (1,0) \qquad x=1\ldots X, \; y=1\ldots Y \tag{3}$$

Where: $X,Y =$ *the dimensions of the input pattern*

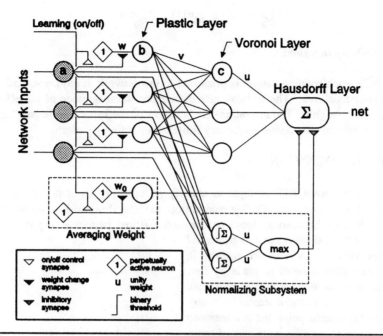

Figure 2. Neural Network Detailed Node Architecture

Prior to learning, each weight matrix W^n of the network is initialized as follows:

$$W^n_{(x+\delta),(y+\delta)} = 0 \qquad n=1\ldots N \tag{4}$$

$$w_0^n = 0 \tag{5}$$

Where: $N =$ *the total number of nodes in the network*

The quantity δ is defined as the *span* of the Voronoi layer, and its meaning will be elaborated upon later. At this point it is necessary only to state that it is a positive integer value that is much less than the dimensions of the input pattern. The weight w_0^n is defined as the *averaging weight* for a node, and it is trained during each training pass regardless of the input pattern. The w_0 weights serve as an indicator of the extent to which each node has received training.

When node n is trained on input pattern m, the change in each of the weights is computed as follows:

$$\Delta w^n_{(x+\delta),(y+\delta)} = a^m_{x,y} \, \alpha \, (1 - w^n_{(x+\delta),(y+\delta)}) \tag{6}$$

$$\Delta w_0^n = \alpha \, (1 - w_0^n) \tag{7}$$

Where: $0 \le \alpha \le 1$ *is the learning rate*

Once the weight change is computed, the weights are updated as follows:

$$W_{(x+\delta),(y+\delta)}^{n(t+1)} = W_{(x+\delta),(y+\delta)}^{n(t)} + \Delta W_{(x+\delta),(y+\delta)}^{n(t)} \qquad (8)$$

$$W_0^{n(t+1)} = W_0^{n(t)} + \Delta W_0^{n(t)} \qquad (9)$$

Where: $t = $ *training iterations*

During the learning phase, each training pattern is presented to the network in sequence, and the appropriate node is trained using the equations above. The learning rate determines the magnitude of the effect that each training exemplar has on the trained weights. The saturation-like behavior of the learning rule (see Equation 4) guarantees that the learning process will reliably converge for any finite set of training patterns.

NEURAL NETWORK RECOGNITION

In the recognition mode, the HAVNET attempts to classify an arbitrary input pattern into one of the classes represented by the trained network nodes. During recognition, the neural network computes a modified version of the directed Hausdorff distance between an input pattern and a stored pattern at a given node. To clarify the explanation of this computation, the concept of a *truncated Voronoi surface* is introduced. A *Voronoi surface* is constructed for a two-dimensional set of points A by first locating the members of A in the x-y plane, and then plotting in the third (z) dimension the distance from any point in the x-y plane to the nearest point that is a member of A [5]. When this distance is not allowed to exceed some value δ, then the surface is defined as a *truncated* Voronoi surface. The plot of the truncated Voronoi surface is sometimes referred to as an egg-carton plot because, if the members of A form a rectangular grid, the resulting plot resembles an egg carton [3]. Figure 3 shows a set of 10 randomly located points, and Figure 4 shows the truncated Voronoi surface for that set, with the maximum distance at $\delta=3$. Note that cone shaped depressions are formed in the surface at the locations of the original points.

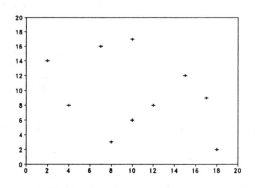

Figure 3. Random Point Set

The Voronoi surface can be used to conveniently compute the directed Hausdorff distance between two point sets. In order to perform the computation between a point set B and the previously defined point set A, the members of B are simply located in the x-y plane, and the z-value above each point represents the distance from that point in B to its nearest neighbor in A. The maximum of these values is the directed Hausdorff distance $h(B,A)$. For neural network purposes it is desirable to compute the inverse of this distance, so that shorter distances result in higher outputs. It is also desirable to threshold this distance at some maximum, so that any distance above that maximum will generate the minimum network output (zero in this case). For these reasons it is desirable for the neural network to model the *inverse* of the truncated Voronoi surface. The truncation distance δ is the *span* of the Voronoi layer of the neural network that was previously referred to.

An example will serve to demonstrate the neural network

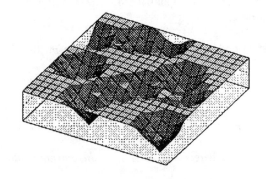

Figure 4. Truncated Voronoi Surface

processing before it is specified in detail. Assume a network with a single node that is designed for 20 x 20 input patterns. Assume further that this node is trained in the manner explained earlier, with a learning rate of $\alpha = 1.0$, to recognize the pattern of points previously presented in Figure 3. After training, the response of the node is measured to input patterns that consist of a single point in one position in the input matrix. That response is then plotted as a function of the position of that point in the input field. Such a plot is shown in Figure 5. This plot demonstrates that, in a single training pass, the network has learned to reproduce the exact inverse of the original truncated Voronoi surface of Figure 4. The network, then, is prepared to compute the *inverse directed Hausdorff distance* between any input pattern and the learned pattern,

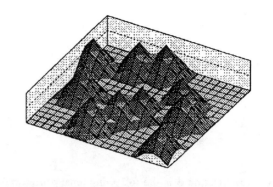

Figure 5. Network Node Response

simply by projecting the points of the input pattern onto this learned surface. Although there are additional complications in practice, this is the essence of how HAVNET conducts pattern recognition. The exact details of the recognition process are given below.

The response of a node n to an input pattern A^m is determined by first computing the output of the plastic layer:

$$b^n_{(x+i),(y+j)} = w^n_{(x+i),(y+j)} \, a^m_{x,y} \tag{10}$$

Where: $x = 1...X$ *input x dimension* $y = 1...Y$ *input y dimension*
$i,j = -\delta...\delta$ *Voronoi layer span* $n = 1...N$ *node number*
w^n = *plastic layer weight for node n* b^n = *plastic layer outputs for node n*

Given the outputs from the plastic layer, the outputs for the Voronoi layer c^n are computed as follows:

$$c^n_{x,y} = \max_j \left\{ \max_i \left\{ v_{i,j} \, b^n_{(x+i),(y+j)} \right\} \right\} \tag{11}$$

The *Voronoi weights* $v_{i,j}$ are the same for all nodes and are computed as follows:

$$v_{i,j} = 1 - \frac{\sqrt{i^2 + j^2}}{\delta + 1} \qquad -\delta \le i,j \le \delta \tag{12}$$

Once the outputs from the Voronoi layer are determined, the responses of the Hausdorff (or output) layer neurons are computed:

$$net^n = \frac{1}{w_0^n \eta^n} \sum_{y=1}^{Y} \sum_{x=1}^{X} c^n_{x,y} \tag{13}$$

Where: w_0^n = *averaging weight for node n* net^n = *output for node n*

The normalizing quantity η^n is determined as follows:

$$\eta^n = \max \left\{ p_a^m, p_w^n \right\} \tag{14}$$

Where:

$$p_a^m = \sum_{y=1}^{Y} \sum_{x=1}^{X} \phi(a_{x,y}) \tag{15}$$

$$p_w^n = \sum_{y=1}^{Y} \sum_{x=1}^{X} \phi(w_{(x+\delta),(y+\delta)}^n) \tag{16}$$

And the function ϕ is the following binary threshold function:

$$\phi(x) = \begin{cases} 1 & if \quad x > 0 \\ 0 & otherwise \end{cases} \tag{17}$$

The final outputs net^n indicate, for each node, the similarity of the input pattern to the patterns that have been learned by that node.

CONCLUSIONS

HAVNET represents a novel neural network that is specifically designed for pattern recognition. The network is well developed and well behaved mathematically, and it is the first known neural network paradigm to take advantage of the Hausdorff distance as a metric of similarity between two-dimensional patterns. In doing so, the network inherits the desirable properties of the Hausdorff distance, and therefore duplicates human performance more accurately than many previous neural network architectures. Furthermore, the network architecture is flexible enough to incorporate self-organization, unsupervised learning, and nearest neighbor competitive or cooperative learning in the plastic layer as required by specific applications. The evaluation of HAVNET on several pattern recognition tasks is presently in progress. Initial results on character recognition, and the learning and recognition of objects from edge images, are encouraging.

REFERENCES

[1]   G.A. Carpenter and S. Grossberg, "A Massively Parallel Architecture for a Self-Organizing Neural Pattern Recognition Machine," *Computer Vision, Graphics, and Image Processing*, Vol. 37 (1987): 54-115.

[2]   K. Fukushima, "Neocognitron: A Neural Network Model for a Mechanism of Visual Pattern Recognition," *IEEE Transactions on Systems, Man, and Cybernetics*, Vol. SMC-13, No. 5 (1983): 826-834.

[3]   D.P. Huttenlocher, G.A. Klanderman, and W.J. Rucklidge, "Comparing Images Using the Hausdorff Distance," *IEEE Trans. on Pattern Analysis and Machine Intelligence*, Vol. 15, No. 9 (1993): 850-863.

[4]   A. Csaszar, *General Topology*. Adam Hilger Publ., 1978.

[5]   D.P. Huttenlocher, K. Keden, and M. Sharir, "The Upper Envelope of Voronoi Surfaces and their Applications," in *Proceedings of the 7th ACM Symposium on Computational Geometry* (1991): 194-293.

THE CORTECONS: A NEW CLASS OF NEURAL NETWORKS FOR TEMPORAL PATTERN ASSOCIATION

Alianna J. Maren
Accurate Automation Corporation
7001 Shallowford Rd., Chattanooga, TN 37421-1716

Eyal Schwartz
Computer Science Department
Radford University, Radford, VA 24142

ABSTRACT

CORTECONS (COntent-Retentive, TEmporally-CONnected neural networks) are a new class of neural network. CORTECONS use a novel energy function, a "free energy" taken from statistical mechanics models of Ising spin glasses, to facilitate a richer range of temporal behaviors than currently are available. This "free energy" includes a *spatial configuration entropy* term in addition to the basic interaction energy that is commonly used. By making the interaction energy dependent on nearest-neighbor interactions only, and by using the spatial configuration entropy, minimizing the network's "free energy" drives the network towards certain *types* of patterns rather than to *specific, stored patterns*. The specific patterns to which the network moves can thus be influenced by a number of factors that allow the influence of previous system states. These include current input, regular and temporally-gated lateral interconnections, unit activation from previous inputs, and other factors. With different implementation strategies, CORTECONS form a class of neural networks that provide a basis for a rich range of temporal pattern association capabilities.

1. DECOUPLING THE DRIVING FORCES: A NEW APPROACH IN NEURAL SYSTEMS DESIGN

One of the greatest challenges in neural network design is to create a class of neural networks with richer *temporal processing and association properties* than are currently existent. The temporal properties of a network are related to two major factors. One is the extent to which either the individual neurons and/or the interconnections can maintain some temporal continuity, or have memory of previous states. The other is the nature of the dynamics which govern network processes. When a network's dynamics are associated with the minimization of an energy function, as in the case of the Hopfield neural network, we can think of the energy minimization as a "driving force" governing the network processes. We can expand our concept of a "driving force" to include the structurally-dependent process of transferring weighted signals between neurons. Such a structurally-embedded "driving force" is the rule in feedforward networks. Current driving forces are *state specific*. That is, they drive the network towards one of a set of known, encoded states.

This paper introduces the novel approach of decoupling the driving forces in a neural network into two forces; one which is state-specific, and another which is non-state-specific. The state-specific driving force is encoded, as usual, within the connection weights of the network. The *non-state-specific driving force is a free energy minimization process* which drives the network towards states with certain *configuration characteristics*, rather than to specific instantiations of such states. The interaction between the two forces produces a class of network which not only has good pattern response capabilities, but which can also exhibit a wide range of *temporal properties* which have not hitherto been found in any neural network. Most significantly, this architecture promises a route to more cortical-like behavior of the artificial neuron assemblage. This leads to the name for the prototype of this new class of neural network, the CORTECON: A COntent-Retentive, TEmporally-CONnected network.

The use of a *free energy function* as a driving force instead of the usual energy function is novel in neural network design. The free energy function contains an entropy term, which combines additively with the energy term to create the free energy. The "free energy" concept has been well established in thermodynamics and statistical thermodynamics. Within the thermodynamics framework, a system approaches equilibrium by minimizing its free energy, rather than just minimizing the simple energy function. The key to minimizing the free energy of the system is to treat the system as an ensemble of bistate units, to which the principles of statistical thermodynamics can be applied. The next section describes the structure and dynamics of a basic CORTECON. The following section gives some particulars of the special type of free energy which is used by the CORTECON. A final section presents some results to date.

2. CORTECONS: NEURAL NETWORKS DRIVEN BY FREE ENERGY MINIMIZATION

CORTECONs are a class of novel neural networks that have as a common element two features: processing units or "neurons" whose activations are dependent on previous states, and the use of "free energy" as a driving function. The basic CORTECON structure is a two-layer neural network consisting of an *input layer* and a *computational layer*, as illustrated in Figure 1. The input layer functions in the usual manner of accepting inputs and propagating them via weighted sums to the computational layer. The computational layer is composed of processing units which receive inputs and Gaussian noise and which also experience activation decay. The *state* of each processing unit is governed by a function of both its activation (due to the previously mentioned factors) and the overall drive to minimize the free energy. The process of minimizing the free energy can alter a unit"s state. To do this, the absolute value of the unit's activation must be less than a predetermined threshold. Units above threshold value are "fixed" on or off, and stay that way until changes in input or activation decay cause the activation to become smaller than the (positive or negative) threshold value. Once a unit's activation is smaller than threshold, it becomes labile, and the free energy minimization process can change that unit's state.

The free energy minimization process is conducted in a manner similar to training a Boltzmann machine. Units in the computational layer are selected at random. If a unit has activation smaller than threshold, it's state is changed, and the free energy for the computational (output) layer is redetermined. If the change results in a lower total free energy, the change is kept. Otherwise, the unit is returned to its previous state. This means that even if a unit is receiving positive activation, and would typically be in an "on" state, the free energy minimization process can turn it off, and vice versa.

Use of free energy minimization for this network is analogous to using a Lyapunov function. The free energy is not a time-dependent function, nor is it a potential energy function in the sense used for most neural network Lyapunov functions. However, it is used in analogy to the free energy minimization process observed in many natural systems. Use of a free energy function of the type described here implies that the network exists at or near an equilibrium state, and that inputs to individual processing units in the network are treated as perturbations on the overall network state. When a perturbing input is received by the network, the network adapts its overall spatial configuration so that it accomodates both to the inputs to each processing unit and to the overall free energy minimization.

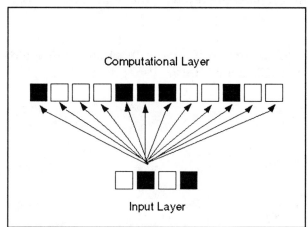

Figure 1: System Architecture for the CORTECON Engine.

3. HELMHOLTZ FREE ENERGY WITH SPATIAL CONFIGURATION ENTROPY

The "computational layer" of this new class of neural network can be modeled as large 1-D or 2-D "grids" of bistate processing units. (A 1-D grid has been used for prototyping the CORTECON.) This grid can be treated as an ensemble of bistate units, and Ising statistical mechanics model can be applied. The basic formalism for the Helmholtz Free Energy (named after H. von Helmholtz, who did much of the pioneering work in this area) is

$$A = E - TS, \qquad (1)$$

where A is the Helmholtz Free Energy, E is the energy, T is the temperature, and S is the entropy. We can express (1) in reduced form, by dividing through by temperature, Boltzmann's constant (k), and the total number of units in the system (N). (Both the latter terms are involved in the expression for entropy.) This yields

$$\underline{A} = \underline{E} - S/(Nk), \qquad (2)$$

where $\underline{A}$ and $\underline{E}$ are the reduced Helmholtz free energy and the reduced energy, respectively.

The equilibrium state of a system (pressure and volume fixed) is defined as the minimum in the Helmholtz free energy. Two processes contribute to this free energy minimization; minimizing the total energy of the system (defined in terms of the energies of individual units and their interactions), and maximizing the entropy of the system. The entropy of a system describes the distribution of its components into the different possible states. Usually the states which are considered for entropy are the energy states of individual units.. An alternative is to consider as different "states" the variety of local spatial configurations of processing units in different states. This can be used to construct an entropy function which drives the system towards an spatial configuration characterized by a distribution of certain types of local patterns. These *micropatterns* are composed of nearest-neighbors and next-nearest-neighbors, which provide respectively three and six distinct types of configurations, as is shown in Figure 2, for configurations composed of units in one of two states, A or B. A "configuration" in terms of the cluster variation theory, on which this work is based, can be either a "pairwise" configuration, e.g. the pair A-B or the pair B-A (both would be counted as the same type of configuration), or as a "triple," e.g., A-B-A. The configurations which appear differently when viewed right-to-left vs. left-to-right are treated as different instantiations of the same configuration, but are weighted doubly with the redundancy parameters β_i and γ_i, as is shown in Figure 2.

The specific Helmholtz free energy equation which is used as a driving function for this class of neural network is given as [Maren et al., 1992: Kikuchi & Brush, 1967]

$$\underline{A} = A/\ NkT = 2\beta\epsilon(-z_1 + z_3 + z_4 - z_6)$$

$$- 2\sum_{i=1}^{3}\beta_i Lf(y_i) + 2\sum_{i=1}^{6}\gamma_i Lf(z_i) \tag{3}$$

$$+ \mu\beta(1 - \sum_{i=1}^{6}y_i z_i) + 4\lambda(z_3 + z_5 - z_2 - z_4)$$

where
  ϵ is the interaction energy between processing units,
  β is the Boltzmann's constant,
  y_i and z_i are the cluster variables, as illustrated in Figure 2,
  β_i and γ_i are cluster variable coefficients that account for redundancy in the way a
  given cluster variable can be measured, and
  μ and λ are Lagrange coefficients.

The term Lf(x) is given as

$$Lf(x) = x ln(x) - x. \tag{4}$$

The first term on the RHS of Eq. (3) is the interaction energy, which is negative when neighboring units are in the same state. The next two terms are the entropy, and express the distribution of the ensemble into different types of local spatial configurations. The variables used to describe these relationships are the nearest-neighbor configurations variables, y_i, and the "triples," z_i, both shown in Fig. 2. The remaining two terms are Lagrangian multiplier terms.

Configuration	Fraction	α_i
A	x_1	1
B	x_2	1

Configuration	Fraction	β_i
A - A	y_1	1
A - B	y_2	2
B - B	y_3	1

Configuration	Fraction	γ_i
A A \/ A	z_1	1
A B \/ A	z_2	2
A A \/ B	z_3	1
B B \/ A	z_4	1
B A \/ B	z_5	2
B B \/ B	z_6	1

Figure 2: The Fraction Variables from Cluster Variation Theory.

4. RESULTS OF NETWORK OPERATIONS

Early studies with the CORTECON (Maren et al., 1992; Maren, 1993) confirmed that the free energy minimization process, as carried out via the stepwise process of "flipping" unit states and testing the new free energy, produced results which met theoretical predictions for the free energy of the computational layer. Recent work has focused on identifying the pattern association abilities of the network, and on introducing design features which give the network unique and interesting temporal capabilities. These design features include additive noise in the computational layer units, exponential activation decay of patterns once input stimulus is removed, and use of *interneurons* to strengthen the activation of units in response to a present pattern, or to enhance temporal association with a succeeding pattern.

Our pattern association studies have confirmed that once the input-to-computational layer connection weights have been briefly trained using a variation of Hebbian learning, it is possible to gain recognizable recall of "prototype" output patterns associated with a given input pattern. Prototype output patterns were identified for each of the randomly established, stored input patterns used in training and testing the network. They were obtained by randomly presenting the different input patterns at least 50 times after network training. The resultant output patterns for each distinct input were stored and averaged. For testing, the inputs were again presented a similar number of times, and the normalized Hamming distance between the resultant output pattern and the corresponding prototype was found. Hamming distances between each of the prototypes (in pairwise manner) was also found. We found that the Hamming distance between the prototypes was typically 3-4 times as large as the Hamming distance between a resultant pattern and its associated prototype. This gives confidence that the unit clustering caused by action of the free energy driving force does not too greatly distort the heteroassociative capabilities of this network.

The combination of free energy (which causes clustering of like units) with learned and sparse lateral connections or *interneurons*, becomes valuable in maintaining output pattern stability during the activation decay which follows when the input pattern is removed. When an input pattern is presented, clusters of like units will develop in the output layer as a result of the free energy minimization. The "core" units of such clusters typically have high activation values, and so are impervious to the random "flipping" of units with less activation. When the input pattern is removed and activation decay begins, the interactions between like nearest neighbors in the clusters help to "persist" the cluster for a longer time than would be so if the free energy minimization process were not present. Further, the interneurons established between the strongest units (whether "on" or "off") are designed to persist the state of the receiving units. This helps them maintain their original state. Interneurons have also been designed to facilitate association and stabilization of temporally-paired patterns.

ACKNOWLEDGEMENTS
This work was supported by a grant from the Thomas F. Jeffress and Kate Miller Jeffress Memorial Trust and by Accurate Automation Corporation IR&D.

REFERENCES

Kikuchi, R., & Brush, S.G. (1967). "Improvement of the cluster-variation method," *J. Chem. Phys.*, **47**, 195-203.

Maren, A.J. (1993). "Free energy as a driving function in neural networks," *Proc. 1993 Symposium on Nonlinear Theory and It's Applications* (Hawaii, December 6-10, 1993).

Maren, A.J., E. Schwartz, & J. Seyfried (1992). "Configurational entropy stabilizes pattern formation in a hetero-associative neural network," *Proc. 1992 IEEE Int'l. Conf. on Systems, Man, & Cybernetics* (Chicago, IL; Oct. 18-21, 1992), 89-93.

Deformed lattice analysing using neural networks

Jürgen Leopold, Holger Günther
Gesellschaft für Fertigungstechnik und Entwicklung e.V. (GFE)
Technische Universität Chemnitz/Zwickau
Lassallestraße 14, D-09117 CHEMNITZ, Germany

Optical methods of measuring in-plane deformations and displacements on the surface of specimen and workpieces are used in many branches of metalworking industry, development, investigation, and science. They are, for example, the method of visioplasticity, interferometric and moire techniques etc. All this methods are based on the optical analysis of resulted grid structures and measure of their interested points or lines. Especially, the method of visioplasticity is often applied in the analysis of large plastic deformations in metal cutting and forming processes and for quality control. An typical example for a visioplastic application (metal cutting analysis) is proposed in Fig.1 below.

The image analysis of deformed grids may help for development and investigation of pairs of workpiece and cutting material, optimized technological conditions and new tool material which may allow cutting without coolants and lubricants or with less use of coolants and lubricants. However, for a comprehensive and economical industrial inset of this methods it's necessary to automatize the recognization of grid points and the analysis of deformations. For the processing of given points exists some programs and software systems like the system VISIO, developed by the Society for Production Engineering and Development (GFE) Chemnitz, but the analysis of large or extrem deformed grid structures continues to be only practicable manually (using microcsopes,digitizers etc.). The described paper will propose a solution for recognize points in large deformed and injured lattices using digital image processing in combination with neural networks.

For the recognition of small or medium deformed lattice structures exists a collection of useful and exactly algorithms. These are, for example, binary image processing, different filters, splines and Fourier Transform. However, if the deformation of the surface is large or extrem, the results of this "classical" algorithms are unexactly or false, because most methods requires a similar form of grid crosses. In addition to this, in consequence of then large deformation the grids are often injured. During the last three years, we have investigated the demeanour of traditional, usual algorithms for lattice analysis like skeletonization of binary images and Fourier Transform in visioplastic experiments (Fig. 1) with a deformation of some hundred percent. Usually the results of this methods are false, and not one of this algorithms has produced evaluable results.

Fig.1: Typical example for a large deformed lattice in visioplastic investigations
      (metal cutting analysis).

In this cause, it's necessary to find a way to search and range the objects automatically, including the learning of new search patterns (auto-adaption). A hopeful way is the usage of procedures of biocomputing, like fuzzy logic and neuronal networks. Particularly some models of neuronal networks appears qualified for problems of pattern recognition, and tentatively experiences confirm the eligibility of this models for the cross analysis in deformed lattices.

In first investigations was choosed the backpropagation model with a sigmoid activation function. This model is applied often in the optical recognition of patterns and characters (OCR). A backpropagation network usually contains three or more neuron layers. The output of each neuron of one layer is connected to an input of each neuron of the next layer; all of this connections are weighted. A source pattern is entering to the inputs of the neurons of the first layer. The network propagates the input pattern layer by layer. Finally, on the outputs of the neurons of the output layer appears the target pattern. A backpropagation network needs an "supervisor" during the learning phase, i.e. the target pattern must be known. Thereupon, for each pair of patterns the network adjust the weights, until the difference between the target pattern and the output pattern is minimal.

manually. It was performed learning cycles, until the average error per pair of pattern was less than 0.1. Usually a backpropagation network needs no more than some hundred cycles.

During the "recall" phase, the part of the image evaluable by the network is moving pixel by pixel, until the complete image is scanned. For each of this sub-images the backpropagation network gives an output value in range between 0 and 1. This value kan be interpret as a "level of comparability" between the learned patterns and the real part of the lattice. All output values will be stored into a file on a harddisk and form a matrix.

This matrix is equal to the filtered image and contains the probabilities of the existence of an object for each picture element. Like an image, thereupon the matrix can be processed using traditional image processing methods. For example, if the location of the crosses is wanted, then the local maxima greater than a threshold (ca. 0,5..0,7) are interpretable as probably crosses. For this problem also exists some algorithms in the classical image analysis.

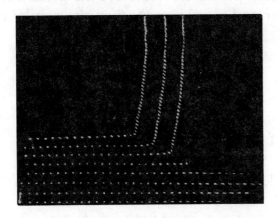

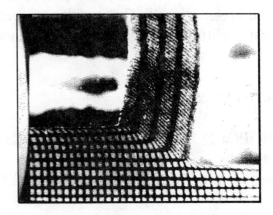

Fig.2: The matrix of output values, shown as image.

Fig.3: Local maxima of the output values in the original image.

An effective simulation of neuronal networks needs a very powerful hardware and a large memory. Usually, for networks in the describted size (some 1000 up to 10.000 connections) are using special hardware features (emulators). However, in this investigations special hardware was not in use. In this cause, some essential restrictions was requisitely. It's desirable to connect each picture element (pixel) in the sub-image evaluable per step to an input neuron. The largest networks creatable into the main memory of an MS-DOS PC contents ca. 13x13 input neurons. However, the recgnition of a complete cross in the applied lattices needs a size of the sub-image by ca. 25x25 pixels. Therefore, ever 2x2 adjacent pixels must be summarize, and the network receives only the average value of this four pixels. In this cause, particulary the quality of small lines in the image is debased.

Nevertheless, the most results of the investigated networks are remarkable. In the parts of small lattice deformations the backpropagation network has all cross points recognized unmistaken and unambiguous, with a deviation of the cross localisation of one pixel maximum. In the large deformed parts (Fig. 3/4) was detected 90% minimum of all the cross points, nevertheless the grids have wide areas injured. This results are better and more exactly than the results of most traditional image analysing methods.

References

LEOPOLD,J; GÜNTHER,H.: Analysis of deformed grids using neural networks;
Symposium "Neuroinformatik 93", 13./14. Mai 1993, Ehrenfriedersdorf

LEOPOLD,J.;LANGER,U.: Experimental and numerical Methods for Micro-Mechanics/Microdynamics - Nanotechnology Hybrid Method; 7th International PRECISION ENGINEERING Seminar Kobe/Japan, 17-23 May 1993

LEOPOLD,J.: Experimental and numerical methods to investigate the cutting process, 19th Leeds - Lyons Symposium on Tribology 1992

LEOPOLD,J.:Hybrid-Method: Visioplasticity and Finite Element Method in Production Engeneering;LUSAS-AMT 1991, Stratford-upon-Avon/UK

LEOPOLD,J.;GÜNTHER,H.: Anwendung der digitalen Bildverarbeitung in Rastertechniken, Wissenschaftliche Schriftenreihe der TU Chemnitz Heft 3/1992

AUTOMATIC TARGET RECOGNITION FROM RADAR RANGE PROFILES USING FUZZY ARTMAP

Mark A. Rubin[1]

Physics Division, Naval Air Warfare Center[2]

China Lake, California 93555

Abstract

We investigate the use of the Fuzzy ARTMAP neural network for automatic classification of targets based on their radar range profiles. Tests on synthetic data indicate that arbitrarily high accuracy may be achieved by increasing sufficiently the number of aspects used during training. Creation of "artificial training sets" by interpolation of input data is examined as a potential means of decreasing the number of training aspects required to achieve a given level of accuracy, and is shown to be of limited effectiveness. The problem of rejecting patterns not present in the training set is also examined.

1 Radar range profiles

A "range profile" of an object is a sort of "one-dimensional picture" of the object, generated from its radar reflection[1, 2, 3]. Imagine, for example, a sharp pulse of electromagnetic energy being directed at an aircraft which is flying directly towards the place where the transmitter of the pulse is located. A receiver, located at approximately the same spot as the transmitter, will not pick up the same sharp pulse which was originally sent out. Radiation reflected from the nose of the aircraft, having less far to travel, will arrive back at the receiver first, followed by reflections off of parts of the interior of the aircraft and the wings, followed finally by reflections from the tail. If the strength of the reflections is recorded in "bins" corresponding to time of arrival—i.e., the initial reflection from the nose, and anything following within a time Δt, is summed and recorded in bin 1, everything arriving between Δt and $2\Delta t$ goes in bin 2, etc.—the resulting histogram of reflected energy forms a pattern which is termed a "radar range profile" or "downrange profile." The bins are referred to as "range bins," since reflections which arrive at the receiver within a time Δt must have come from parts of the target whose respective distances from the receiver differ by no more than $c\Delta t/2$.

Clearly, different aircraft (or other targets) will yield different profiles; so it is natural to consider using these profiles to identify the target. Just as clearly, the profile of a *given* target will change as a function of the relative orientation of the target with respect to the line from the transmitter/receiver to the target. (The overall amplitude of the profile will also change as the distance to the target changes, but this can always be compensated for by applying a normalization procedure to all profiles.) In this regard, range profiles are no different from the usual two-dimensional images of objects formed by optical lenses; e.g., the appearance of the computer monitor before which I am sitting changes somewhat if move my head to the left or right a couple of inches, and changes drastically if I view it from above or the side.

The distinguishing feature of range profiles is that even *small* changes in viewing angle tend to result in large changes in "appearance." Since the object being "viewed" is extended in the directions transverse to the direction of the radar beam, and since the radar is coherent, reflections which fall into the same bin will exhibit interference. This coherent interference is analogous to the speckle observed when viewing an object under laser light, but is of much greater magnitude, due to the differences in the wavelengths of the radiation and the apertures involved. As a result, small changes in viewing direction can produce large changes in the constructive or destructive nature of the interference in the bins, and hence in the shape of the profile. Simulated range profiles of the same target viewed from directions only one degree apart are shown in Fig. 1.

---

[1] email: mark@peewee.chinalake.navy.mil

[2] mailing address

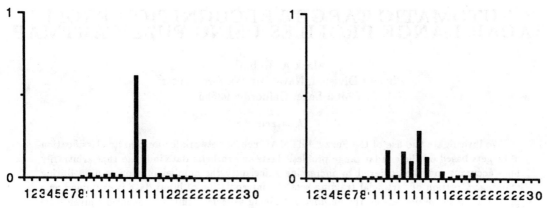

Figure 1: Synthetic range profiles of the first target in Fig. 2, at aspects of 0 (left) and 1 (right) degrees, after normalization.

2 Fuzzy ARTMAP

Since a given target will generally yield very different profiles when viewed from directions differing even slightly, a range-profile classifier must be able to group together input patterns with widely varying characteristics and assign them to a common classification category. At the same time, the large number of different patterns per category requires that the information needed to accomplish the task of classification be recorded in as efficient as a manner as possible. These requirements suggest the application of the Fuzzy ARTMAP neural network[4] to this problem.

The core of Fuzzy ARTMAP is a Fuzzy ART network[5] which performs unsupervised classification of analog vectors with components between 0 and 1. Similar input vectors are associated with the same recognition node, "similarity" being determined by an L_1-like norm. During training, these recognition nodes[3] become associated with nodes representing the categories into which the vectors are to be classified (e.g., type of aircraft). If a vector is presented which matches a recognition node which has, through previous training, become associated with a particular category, the vector is considered to have been classified in that category. During the training phase an *incorrect* category choice by the network causes the network to repeatedly reassign the input vector to different recognition nodes or, if necessary, create an entirely new recognition node. In this way the network learns to make correct predictions for the vectors on which it is trained, while creating only the minimum number of recognition nodes necessary for the task. Storage requirements are thus minimized, and generalization ability is maximized.

3 Data simulation and classification

We consider only two-dimensional targets, so the relation between the direction of the radar beam and the orientation of the target is given by a single aspect angle, which will be taken to be zero when the aircraft is heading directly towards the source of the beam. To generate simulated range profiles, the return signal will be calculated as being produced by 100 point scatterers located randomly within the target, and the far-field approximation will be used. Where not otherwise specified, simulations will be done using the nine "aircraft" shown in Fig. 2. The length of each target is about 10 meters, and the wavelength of the radar is two centimeters. Thirty range bins are used, each covering 2/3 of a meter, so the entire range profile covers 20 meters with returns

---

[3]Layer F_2^a in [4].

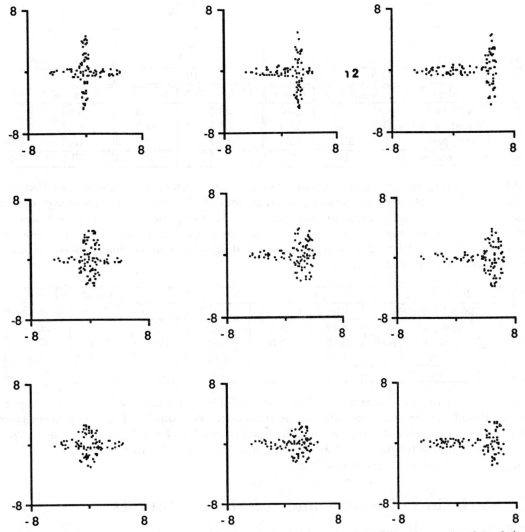

Figure 2: Scattering centers for set of nine targets (three wing positions, three wing lengths).

from the targets filling 15 to 20 of the bins. The profiles are normalized by dividing the value of each bin of the "raw" profile by the sum of all the bins.

The baseline vigilance parameter, which governs the fineness with which the initial unsupervised classification (association with recognition nodes) is made, is kept at its minimum value of zero,[4] as this seems to give the lowest error rate when the network is asked to classify targets of a type which it has been trained to recognize. (See, however, Sec. 7 below.) The voting procedure is also used, in which a set of Fuzzy ARTMAP networks, each of which has been trained with a different random permutation of the training data, vote on the classification of a test input. Unanimity is required for the "voters" to be considered to have made a choice. Comparatively little improvement was found in having an "electorate" of more than two members (again, however, see Sec. 7), and this is the number used unless otherwise stated .

---

[4] As for the few other adjustable parameters of Fuzzy ARTMAP, the choice parameter is set at .0001, and fast learning is used. Complement coding in employed in the Fuzzy ART$_a$ module.

aspect (degrees)	-5 to 5	40 to 50	85 to 95
1a. % abst./all	4.66	28.1	43.5
2a. %(abst. + err.)/all	7.74	35.3	54.7
3a. % err./pred.	3.23	10.1	19.8
4a. av. # nodes	39	106	163.5

aspect (degrees)	-.5 to .5	4 to 5	44.5 to 45.5	49 to 50	89.5 to 90.5	94 to 95
1b. % abst./all	10.1	8.63	22.5	24.6	35.6	21.8
2b. %(abst. + err.)/all	15.7	11.4	28.8	32.5	45.7	42.6
3b. % err./pred.	6.18	3.04	8.07	10.5	15.7	26.5
4b. av. # nodes	16	20	26.5	27	33.5	37.5

Table 1: Training and testing at various aspects. 1a,b: Percentage of abstentions (out of all tests). 2a,b: percentage of abstentions-plus-errors (out of all tests). 3a,b: percentage of errors (out of predictions made). 4a,b: average number of F_2^a recognition nodes (averaged over both voters). Training and testing was on views of the nine targets shown in Fig. 2. Training views were uniformly spaced a tenth of a degree apart. Testing views were randomly chosen within the specified ranges of aspects.

# of targets	3=1 wp × 3 wl			6=2 wp × 3 wl		
aspect (degrees)	-5 to 5	40 to 50	85 to 95	-5 to 5	40 to 50	85 to 95
1. % abst./all	3.79	25.0	6.39	8.68	29.7	26.6
2. %(abst. + err.)/all	5.28	35.6	9.58	12.0	41.2	37.2
3. % err./pred.	1.56	14.2	3.41	3.61	16.3	14.4
4. av. # nodes	8	13.5	10	21	64	66.5

Table 2: Fewer targets. Same as first four rows of Table 1, but using subsets of the targets in Fig. 2. Results in the first three columns are from networks trained and tested on three targets with one wing position and three wing lengths (the first column of Fig. 2); results in the last three columns are from networks trained and tested on six targets with two wing positions and three wing lengths (the first two columns of Fig 2).

4 Variation of aspect and number of targets

Results for the targets of Fig. 2 are given in Table 1. Only the polled results of the two voting networks are given; disagreement was counted as an abstention. The networks were trained on views of each target evenly spaced a tenth of a degree apart. The views with which the networks were tested were randomly chosen. The first four rows of Table 1 show results from networks trained and tested on aspects differing by up to ten degrees. The spread of ten degrees was chosen because this is more or less the accuracy with which the aspect of an aircraft can be estimated at a distance. The last four rows of Table 1 show results for one-degree regions, and illustrate that increasing the angle over which the networks are trained does not in general degrade performance (provided, of course, that number of training views per degree is maintained.) Note also that the number of recognition nodes goes up more slowly than the number of training views, indicating that Fuzzy ARTMAP is economically "reusing" them.

An important question is the scaling of the error rates and network size with the number targets on which the networks are trained. Comparing the first four lines of Table 1, for networks trained on all of the targets of Fig. 2, with the results presented in Table 2 for networks trained on subsets of those targets, we see that the error rates may be either larger of smaller as the number of targets increases; the most important factor in determining the error rate seems to be the particular viewing aspect. The number of recognition nodes increases with increasing number of targets, and apparently at a greater-than-proportional rate.

Tests were also done on different sets of targets, groups of sixteen (four wing positions, four

# of targets	16	25	16	25
aspect (degrees)	-.5 to .5		-5 to 5	
1. % abst./all	21.1	26.1	16.4	20.2
2. %(abst. + err.)/all	27.1	35.9	21.6	25.5
3. % err./pred.	7.56	13.3	6.29	6.64
4. av. # nodes	41.5	88.5	147	322.5

Table 3: More targets. Same as first four rows of Table 1, but trained and tested on larger sets of more-similar targets.

wing lengths) and twenty-five (five wing positions, five wing lengths). The maximum and minimum values of the wing lengths and wing positions were the same as for the nine targets in Fig. 2, so the targets in these larger sets were not only more numerous but geometrically more similar to one another. Results using these target sets, with training views spaced a tenth of a degree apart, are given in Table 3.

5   Separability and variation of training view spacing

Not surprisingly, increasing the number of training views per degree decreases the error rates for a given set of targets. One would like to know: how *fast* does it decrease? And does it go to zero, or approach some greater-than-zero limit? For example, the latter would be the case if, in the space of posssible range profiles (in this case, a 30-dimensional space), the patterns corresponding to different targets formed partly-overlapping clusters. In the regions of overlap it would be impossible to distinguish targets by their range profiles. In principle, this problem *should* occur; there is no a priori reason why two distinct targets, at certain respective viewing angles and for certain bin sizes and wavelengths of illumination, could not have arbitrarily similar range profiles. In practice, for the set of 9 targets in Fig. 2, increasing the number of training-views-per-degree rapidly decreases the error rate (out of predictions made) to zero, and the abstention rate to less than half a percent. (See Fig. 3). Such a "brute force" approach to higher accuracy is not a practical one. (Approaches for increasing accuracy with a fixed number of training views are briefly mentioned in Sec. 8). However, it does suggest that at least there may be no obstacle in principle to reaching high accuracies.

6   Interpolation of input data

One approach to keeping down the number of training views is to create "extra" training data by interpolation. That is, we take two profiles of the same target at nearby aspects, and, assume that profiles taken from in-between aspects will vary smoothly from one of the measured[5] profiles to the other as the aspect is changed, calculate profiles for the in-between aspects. The measured profiles and the interpolates are then used together as the training set, as if a larger set of measurements with more closely-spaced views had been taken.

This procedure is probably better suited to tasks *other* the one at hand, given that the essential characteristic of the problem is the non-smooth variation of the profiles as the aspect is changed. Upon investigation, the approach is found to have some utility when the measured profiles are spaced relatively coarsely (and no more than four or five interpolates are used between pairs of adjacent measured profiles), but to be less effective as the separation of the measured profiles is decreased. (See Fig. 4.) In particular, it does not seem to be a promising avenue for achieving high accuracy.

---

[5] Of course, *all* of the "data" in the present paper is synthetic; we have in mind here a practical implementation where the range profiles are obtained by actual measurement.

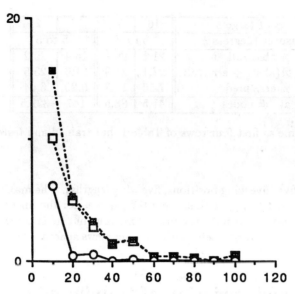

Figure 3: Closer training views. Percentages of abstentions (empty boxes) and abstentions-plus-errors (filled boxes) out of all tests, and percentage of errors out of predictions made (circles), for the nine targets of Fig. 2, as a funtion of numbers of uniformly-spaced training views per degree (abscissa). Testing and training views were at aspects between -.5 and .5 degrees.

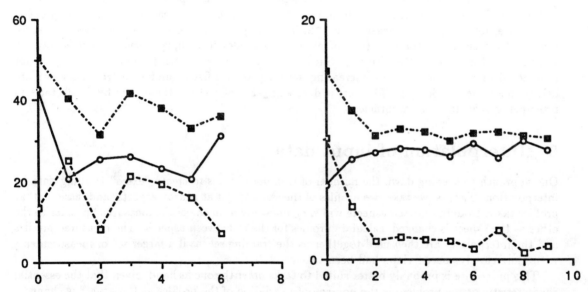

Figure 4: Interpolation. Same as Fig. 3, but using extra interpolated training profiles. Abscissas are numbers of interpolates between each pair of adjacent measured profiles. Left: two measured profiles at -.5 and .5 degrees, resp. Right: eleven measured profiles evenly spaced from -.5 to .5 degrees.

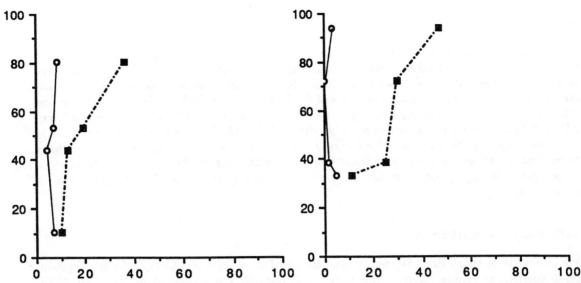

Figure 5: Unknown-target rejection versus known-target error. From bottom to top along each curve, the data points correspond respectively to baseline vigilance values of 0, .925, .95, and .975. All ordinates are percentages of unknown targets which are rejected. Abscissas are percentages of abstentions-plus-errors out of all tests (filled boxes), and percentage of errors out of predictions made (circles), for the nine targets of Fig. 2. Training and testing views are at aspects between -.5 and .5 degrees; training views uniformly spaced a tenth of a degree apart; two voters on the left, four voters on the right "Known" targets are the six targets in the top two rows of Fig. 2, "unknown" targets are the three in the last row. Vigilance was the same during training and testing. (The number of test patterns for unknown target rejection was 500 for each value of baseline vigilance, half the number used or testing in all other runs in this paper.)

7   Rejection of unknown targets

In all of the tests presented so far, the set of training targets has been identical to the set of test targets. So, the task facing the neural network has been to assign a test profile to a target category, *given* that the profile is definitely known to correspond to one of a fixed set of categories. An equally important task is *rejection* of profiles corresponding to *unknown* targets, i.e., targets for which the network has not been trained. In the basic form in which we have been operating it up to this point, Fuzzy ARTMAP has had only one mechanism with which to reject unknown categories: it can abstain because, although each voter has made a choice of classification, their choices have not been unanimous. A simple way of providing another mechanism for rejection is to raise the baseline vigilance.[6] As mentioned above, nonzero baseline vigilance seems to somewhat worsen performance on the known-target recognition task; however, it improves performance on the unknown-target rejection task, a not-unexpected tradeoff. In Fig. 5 the rate of abstentions on unknown targets (ideally 100%) is plotted against both the error rates (out of predictions made) and the combined error-plus-abstention rate on known targets (both ideally 0%).

(Interestingly, the rate of abstention by individual voters is less than 1% for all but the highest level of baseline vigilance (.975) in Fig. 5, and the increase in the ability to reject unknown targets seems due to the increased number of F_2^a nodes which nonzero baseline vigilance causes to be created. At baseline vigilance=.975, abstention by single voters has become significant, accounting for about three-fourths of the total abstentions on unknown targets.)

---

[6]During the testing phase the learning rate is set to zero and no new F_2^a nodes are added, so the network will abstain on test inputs which do not satisfy the vigilance criterion for any of the allocated F_2^a nodes.

8 Outlook

The initial investigations which have been reported above show the promise of Fuzzy ARTMAP for the range profile recognition task. Several modifications of the basic setup employed here suggest themselves as ways of achieving the higher levels of performance required for a production system. Greater accuracy in the recognition of familiar targets could be accomplished by basing classification on a *succession* of profiles[2], rather than a single "snapshot." (An extension of Fuzzy ARTMAP suited to such an approach already exists, ART-EMAP[6]). As for increasing the rate of unknown-target rejection, greater effectiveness might be achieved by utilizing the outputs of many "specialist" networks, all of which are trained on the same training set, but each of which is trained to give only a binary "present" or "absent" response to one specific target. These approaches are under study.

Acknowledgments

We would like to thank Brett Borden, Harold Brooks, Duane Roth and Carey Schwartz for helpful discussions at various stages of this work. This research was supported by the ONR/ASEE postdoctoral fellowship program.

References

[1] B. Borden, Problems in airborne radar target recognition, NAWC preprint (1993), to appear in *Inverse Problems.*

[2] S. Hudson and D. Psaltis, Correlation filters for aircraft identification from radar range profiles, *IEEE Transactions on Aerospace and Electronic Systems,* 29 (1993) 741-748.

[3] C.R. Smith and P.M. Goggans, Radar target identification, *IEEE Antennas and Propagation Magazine,* 35 (1993) 27-38.

[4] G.A. Carpenter, S. Grossberg, N. Markuzon, J.H. Reynolds, and D.B. Rosen, Fuzzy ARTMAP: a neural network architecture for incremental supervised learning of analog multidimensional maps, *IEEE Transactions on Neural Networks,* 3 (5) 698-713.

[5] G.A. Carpenter, S. Grossberg, and D.B. Rosen, Fuzzy ART: fast stable learning and categorization of analog patterns by an adaptive resonance system, *Neural Networks* 4 (1991) 759-771.

[6] G.A. Carpenter and W.D. Ross, ART-EMAP: a neural network architecture for learning and prediction by evidence accumulation, in: *World Congress on Neural Networks,* Portland, Oregon (Lawrence Erlbaum, Hillsdale, NJ, 1993) Vol. III, 649-656.

RECOGNIZING AND DIAGNOSING PSYCHIATRIC DISORDERS USING THE CLINICAL MATRIX

BY

MICHAEL E. SMOLINSKI & FRANK C. LIN
Department of Mathematics and Computer Science
University of Maryland, Princess Anne, MD. 21853, U.S.A.

ABSTRACT

The Clinical Matrix [1] can be used to diagnose many psychiatric disorders. Data collected by clinical physicians can be summarized in such a way that neural networks can be implemented to produce an educated summary as to the proper Clinical Psychiatric Disorder (CPD's). By using neural networks to help make diagnoses based on the numerous symptoms that are inherent to CPD's, there is the possibility for quicker and conceivably more accurate identification of the psychiatric disorder. To consider Neural Networks based on the use of the Clinical Matrix as a tool for the medical community could only enhance the clinical diagnostic procedure.

KEY WORDS

Clinical Matrix, Neural Networks, diagnosis, learning, recalling, robustness, back-propagation, hidden layers, transfer function.

I.   INTRODUCTION

By using the Clinical Matrix to help correlate the large amount of collected data, it is feasible to use much more data within a short period to analyze a given problem. The Clinical Matrix can be applied to neural networks in order to combine the experience of several physicians. This report introduces the use of the Clinical Matrix as it applies to the diagnosis of symptoms relating to various psychiatric disorders. Back-Propagation was chosen for the Clinical Matrix due to its adaptability, learning, and recall characteristics. Learning is the ability of the network to modify the connecting weights in response to stimulus presented at the input. This could also be considered to be the teaching or training of the network. Recalling the network will process the stimulus presented to the network's input and calculate a response at the output.

II. DESCRIPTION OF BACKPROPAGATION NETWORK

Neural networks are well suited for the Clinical Matrix application. Neural networks have the ability to learn, and they can be used to interpret data and calculate a proper response to give a desired output. Also, the Clinical Matrix allows the network to provide the desired output even when the input is imprecise (ie. different physicians place different weights on various symptoms). Since neural networks work better with greater amounts of data, the Clinical Matrix lends itself to using large amounts of clinical data gathered from many physicians. Networks rely on hidden layers and output layers with a specified learning rule and a transfer function that adjusts the output data to what is required (Figure 1) The way in which a network is trained depends upon the type of transfer function and learning rule used with the network. The transfer function is used in conjunction with the PE's (processing elements) and determines the way in which data is propagated from input to output. The various learning rules determine the way in which data is summed and how error is handled to adjust the

connection weights. The weights are recalculated to bring the
actual output to within an acceptable accuracy of the desired
output. Processing elements are used to connect the input and
output functions. A processing element can be considered as a
form of data input and data output. Each PE has associated with
it a path connecting itself to a previous layer and to the next
layer in the network   (Figure 1) The transfer function we used
in the Clinical Matrix is the Sigmoidal function. The Sigmoidal
transfer function is a continuous mapping of input data into a
value between zero and one: i.e.

$$T=(1+e^{-\sigma})^{-1}$$ [1]   where

T is the result of transfer function. The function σ
is given by

$$\sigma = \sum_{j=1}^{d} W_{ij} * X_j$$ [2]

where d is the total number of diseases under consideration

W_{ij} denotes the elements of the clinical matrix in Table
1;

i is the row index label of symptoms (1 to 33);

j is the column index label of psychotic disorders (1
to 7);

and X_j is initially a set of random numbers between 0
and 1.

Figure 1 is a graphical presentation showing the input PE's
(signs and symptoms), the hidden layer PE's, and the output PE's
(psychiatric disorders) along with the associated path which

connects the three layer's. The figure demonstrates a 33xMx7 matrix, where M can equal 6 thru 15. For the purpose of this study, 6 to 15 processing elements in the hidden layer produced equivalent results within the same amount of time.

III. PSYCHIATRIC DISORDERS USED FOR STUDY

The symptoms for several psychiatric disorders concerning schizophrenia can be included in a clinical matrix. These symptoms are shown in Table 1. This table was derived from *Noyes' Modern Clinical Psychiatry.* [6] The 33 psychiatric symptoms were given according to the severity of the symptom for each psychotic disorder. The input data presented to the network is shown in Table 2. In formulating his concept of Psychotic Disorders, Kraepelin classified his cases into different varieties, depending on the predominant symptomatology. Although classification according to reaction type continues to be made, it must be recognized that numerous patients show at one time or another psychopathology characteristic of the individual groups. From the Clinical Matrix, it is obvious that while some psychological disorders exhibit the same symptoms, they vary in the degrees of severity. What makes the use of neural networks so beneficial in this study is that the data can vary slightly between physicians, for instance, and due to the attributes of the Neural Network the same diagnosis will be obtained. Shown in Table 3 is the test data that was input into the network for training and the response that was diagnosed. Although the data included some variation of symptoms that are common to other disorders, and differing weights the network was able to determine the proper response for all pyschotic disorders. This test data demonstrates the robustness of the networks capability to produce a reliable output within an allowable tolerance, in this case 10 percent.

IV. CONCLUSION

Applying the Clinical Matrix to interpret the data obtained during normal clinical interviews could enhance the diagnosis of the subjective interpretation of data. The knowledge of a larger number of physicians should be included in any diagnosis. Various psychiatric disorder interview techniques, such as the *Psychiatric Epidemiology Research Instrument (PERI)* and the *Structured Clinical Interview for DSM-III-R: Psychotic Disorders (SCID-PD)* [5], would likely benefit from using the Clinical Matrix technique. The PERI and the SCID-PD included a survey of homeless men which were screened and diagnosed for psychotic disorders. The interviewer who screened the homeless were mainly graduate students in psychology and social work. The large amounts of data produced in this study is best handled by the clinical matrix. The advantages of this methodology include the speed of interpreted data, the low cost of Personal Computers and also the user friendliness of a properly designed computer program.

PSYCHIATRIC SYMPTOMS CONCERNING PSYCHOTIC DISORDERS

	CATATONIC STUPOR SCHIZO- PHRENIA	CATATONIC EXCITEMENT SCHIZO- PHRENIA	SIMPLE SCHIZO- PHRENIA	HEBEPHRENIC SCHIZO- PHRENIA	PARANOID SCHIZO- PHRENIA	INVOLUTIONAL MELANCHOLIA	MANIC DEPRESSIVE
GRIEF						0.3	
SADNESS						0.1	0.2
ANXIETY						0.5	0.3
SHAME						0.4	0.3
GUILT						0.6	0.2
HELPLESSNESS			0.3		0.2	0.8	0.4
SELF-ESTEEM		0.3		0.8	0.3	0.3	0.2
INHIBITION OF PERSONALITY		0.4	0.7	0.6	0.5	0.7	0.4
INSOMNIA						0.3	
SUSPICIOUS					0.7	0.4	
DOUBT	0.4				0.6	0.2	
INTEREST	0.2		0.3		0.3	0.4	
EATING HABITS	0.6	0.1		0.9		0.4	
LOOSES WEIGHT		0.6				0.4	
RAGE				0.7			0.7
AFFECTIVE REGRESSION				0.7		0.4	0.7
HEALTH SWINGS						0.4	0.7
SLEEPS POORLY		0.7				0.5	0.6
FATIGUE							0.2
ATTENTION	0.1				0.3	0.1	0.1
HALLUCINATIONS		0.2					
EMOTION			0.2		0.6		
DISORDER			0.2				
MOODY			0.5				
INDIFFERENCE	0.3		0.2		0.4		0.4
EMOTION SWINGS	0.2	0.2		0.3			
RESPONSIBILITY		0.2					
SILLINESS		0.5		0.5			
SPEECH		0.4		0.4			
INCOHERENT STUPOR	0.6			0.6			
AUTISTIC LIFE	0.4	0.4		0.7			
PERSONNEL HYGIENE SWINGS	0.1	0.1					0.7
REACTION TO PAINFUL STIMULI	0.2						

TABLE 1

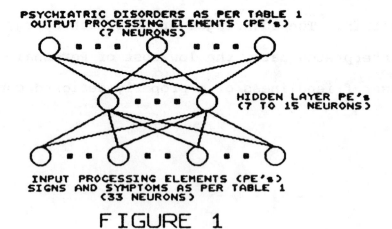

PSYCHIATRIC DISORDERS AS PER TABLE 1
OUTPUT PROCESSING ELEMENTS (PE's)
(7 NEURONS)

HIDDEN LAYER PE's
(7 TO 15 NEURONS)

INPUT PROCESSING ELEMENTS (PE's)
SIGNS AND SYMPTOMS AS PER TABLE 1
(33 NEURONS)

FIGURE 1

TRAINING DATA

TRAINING SET INPUT FILE	DESIRED OUTPUT FILE	PSYCHOTIC DISORDER
0.0 0.0 0.0 0.0 0.0 0.0 0.0 0.0 0.0 0.0 0.0 0.4 0.2 0.6 0.0 0.0 0.0 0.0 0.0 0.0 0.0 0.1 0.0 0.0 0.0 0.0 0.0 0.3 0.2 0.0 0.0 0.0 0.6 0.4 0.1 0.2	1.0 0.0 0.0 0.0 0.0 0.0 0.0 0.0	Catatonic Stupor Schizophrenia
0.0 0.0 0.0 0.0 0.0 0.0 0.0 0.3 0.4 0.0 0.0 0.0 0.0 0.1 0.6 0.0 0.0 0.0 0.0 0.7 0.0 0.0 0.2 0.0 0.0 0.0 0.0 0.2 0.2 0.5 0.4 0.0 0.4 0.1 0.0	0.0 1.0 0.0 0.0 0.0 0.0 0.0 0.0	Catatonic Stupor Schizophrenia
0.0 0.0 0.0 0.0 0.0 0.0 0.3 0.0 0.7 0.0 0.0 0.0 0.3 0.0 0.0 0.0 0.0 0.0 0.0 0.0 0.0 0.0 0.0 0.2 0.2 0.5 0.2 0.0 0.0 0.0 0.0 0.0 0.0 0.0 0.0 0.0	0.0 0.0 1.0 0.0 0.0 0.0 0.0 0.0	Simple Schizophrenia
0.0 0.0 0.0 0.0 0.0 0.0 0.0 0.0 0.8 0.6 0.0 0.0 0.0 0.0 0.9 0.0 0.0 0.7 0.7 0.0 0.0 0.0 0.0 0.0 0.0 0.0 0.0 0.0 0.3 0.0 0.5 0.4 0.6 0.7 0.0 0.0	0.0 0.0 0.0 1.0 0.0 0.0 0.0 0.0	Hebephrenic Schizophrenia
0.0 0.0 0.0 0.0 0.0 0.0 0.0 0.2 0.3 0.5 0.0 0.7 0.6 0.3 0.0 0.0 0.0 0.0 0.0 0.0 0.0 0.0 0.3 0.0 0.6 0.0 0.0 0.4 0.0 0.0 0.0 0.0 0.0 0.0 0.0 0.0 0.0	0.0 0.0 0.0 0.0 1.0 0.0 0.0 0.0	Paranoid Schizophrenia
0.3 0.1 0.5 0.4 0.6 0.8 0.3 0.7 0.3 0.4 0.2 0.4 0.4 0.4 0.0 0.4 0.4 0.5 0.0 0.1 0.0 0.0 0.0 0.0 0.0 0.0 0.0 0.0 0.0 0.0 0.0 0.0 0.0 0.0 0.0	0.0 0.0 0.0 0.0 0.0 1.0 0.0 0.0	Involutional Melancholia
0.0 0.0 0.2 0.3 0.3 0.2 0.4 0.2 0.4 0.0 0.0 0.0 0.0 0.0 0.0 0.0 0.7 0.7 0.7 0.6 0.2 0.1 0.0 0.0 0.0 0.0 0.4 0.0 0.0 0.0 0.0 0.0 0.0 0.7 0.0	0.0 0.0 0.0 0.0 0.0 0.0 1.0	Manic Depressive

TABLE 2

TEST VERIFICATION DATA

TEST INPUT DATA	ACTUAL OUTPUT FILE	PSYCHOTIC DISORDER
0.1 0.0 0.0 0.0 0.0 0.0 0.0 0.0 0.0 0.0 0.0 0.3 0.1 0.4 0.2 0.0 0.0 0.0 0.0 0.0 0.0 0.3 0.0 0.0 0.0 0.0 0.3 0.2 0.0 0.0 0.0 0.2 0.6 0.4 0.2 0.2	.93 .04 .02 .02 .03 .00 .01	Catatonic Stupor Schizophrenia
0.0 0.0 0.0 0.2 0.0 0.0 0.0 0.0 0.2 0.5 0.0 0.0 0.0 0.3 0.3 0.6 0.0 0.0 0.0 0.0 0.6 0.0 0.0 0.2 0.0 0.0 0.0 0.0 0.2 0.2 0.5 0.4 0.0 0.4 0.1 0.0	.01 .94 .02 .02 .01 .03 .00	Catatonic Stupor Schizophrenia
0.0 0.0 0.0 0.0 0.0 0.0 0.3 0.0 0.5 0.0 0.0 0.0 0.3 0.0 0.0 0.0 0.0 0.0 0.7 0.0 0.0 0.0 0.0 0.2 0.2 0.5 0.2 0.0 0.1 0.0 0.0 0.0 0.0 0.0 0.0	.02 .01 .92 .00 .02 .02 .08	Simple Schizophrenia
0.0 0.0 0.0 0.0 0.0 0.0 0.0 0.0 0.7 0.6 0.0 0.0 0.0 0.0 0.9 0.0 0.0 0.6 0.8 0.0 0.0 0.0 0.0 0.0 0.0 0.2 0.0 0.0 0.0 0.3 0.0 0.5 0.5 0.6 0.7 0.0 0.0	.02 .02 .00 .97 .00 .01 .02	Hebephrenic Schizophrenia
0.0 0.0 0.0 0.0 0.0 0.0 0.3 0.3 0.6 0.0 0.4 0.6 0.3 0.0 0.0 0.0 0.4 0.0 0.0 0.0 0.0 0.3 0.0 0.6 0.0 0.0 0.4 0.0 0.0 0.0 0.0 0.0 0.0 0.0 0.0	.02 .01 .03 .00 .90 .02 .03	Paranoid Schizophrenia
0.3 0.1 0.5 0.4 0.6 0.8 0.3 0.7 0.3 0.4 0.2 0.4 0.4 0.4 0.0 0.4 0.4 0.5 0.0 0.1 0.0 0.0 0.0 0.0 0.0 0.0 0.0 0.0 0.0 0.0 0.0 0.0 0.0 0.0	.00 .01 .04 .01 .02 .93 .02	Involutional Melancholia
0.0 0.0 0.0 0.5 0.3 0.2 0.4 0.2 0.4 0.0 0.0 0.0 0.0 0.0 0.0 0.4 0.4 0.7 0.6 0.2 0.1 0.0 0.0 0.0 0.0 0.4 0.0 0.0 0.3 0.0 0.0 0.0 0.6 0.0	.00 .02 .01 .01 .01 .03 .91	Manic Depressive

TABLE 3

REFERENCES:

1. Frank C. Lin.: "The CLINICAL MATRIX as a Diagnostic Tool" Part 1, <u>Computational Medicine TC Newsletter, IEEE Computer Society</u>, Spring (1991).

2. H. M. Baldado M.D., & Frank C. Lin, PhD.; "A Neural Network for Medical Diagnosis", <u>Computational Medicine TC Newsletter, IEEE Computer Society</u>, Fall (1989).

3. Philip D. Wasserman: <u>Neural Computing Theory and Practice</u>, Van Nostrand Reinhold, 1989.

4. Maury Wright: "Design Neural Networks Commands Skill and Savvy", <u>Engineering Design News</u>, December 5, 1991.

5. Susser, Ezra L: "Diagnosis and Screening for Psychotic Disorders in a Study of the Homeless", <u>Schizophrenia Bulletin</u>, Vol. 16, No. 1, 1990 pp 133-137.

6. Lawrence C. Kolb, M.D.: <u>Noyes' Modern Clinical Psychiatry</u>, W.B. Saunders Company, 1968.

Principal Components and Neural Nets

Cris Koutsougeras

Center for Automation, Autonomous and Complex Systems (CA^2CS)
Computer Science Department
Tulane University
New Orleans, LA 70118

Abstract

Principal components analysis has been a valuable tool for statistics, signal processing, and AI applications. The process involves the finding of the eigenvectors of the lumped covariance matrix of a statistical sample. We discuss here the undertaking of computing the principal components with an iterative method based on neural nets. The method consists of training a feed forward neural net structure. The goal which the training attempts to attain relates to Fisher's measure for linear discriminants and so the principal components are attractors for the convergence of the training method.

1.   Introduction

In pattern recognition methods, objects are usually represented as vectors of attribute values. Each attribute is usually a feature which is deemed pertinent to the recognition task. The set of such features which is to be considered is determined a priori and with trial and error methods since it is not always known which features exactly are necessary or sufficient. Thus the vector representations of objects may be long and the corresponding vector space (in terms of which the object space is expressed) may be of high dimensionality. Thus it is necessary to determine alternative representations for the object space, that is, in terms of a different vector space or a different coordinate system of as low dimensionality as possible. The idea is roughly to find a subspace of the original vector space of the least dimensionality in which the various projected vectors are still distinguishable in the proper object classes. This is the idea behind the Karhunen-Loeve transformation, or the principal components analysis. It has been useful in projecting vector spaces of high dimensionality into other spaces of lower dimensionality while at the same time retaining as much of the discriminant information content of the original space.

The process to compute the principal components involves costly matrix operations and a number of efforts have been undertaken to compute them by alternative methods. Such an alternative method based on a rather simple neural network structure is discussed here. It is instructive to provide an outline of the approach here before getting into details.

Fisher's method [2,3,5] is based on the optimization of a certain measure which reflects certain restrictions on the overall statistics of the samples in the projection space (the new vector space which is sought).

The solution to the optimization problem is exactly the eigenvectors of the lumped covariance matrix of the samples. The idea pursued here is to train a feed-forward neural net with a training objective that is similar to Fisher's measure. If this objective is attained then the solution eigenvectors should be reflected in the trained net structure after the training process has converged.

2.   The network based method

Let's assume that we have a feed-forward net in which we feed input vectors X_i and receive corresponding output vectors Y_i. The Y_i's are functions of the X_i's and of the weights associated with the net. The weights in particular are parameters which determine the net's transfer function. As these weights change the Y_i's move around, that is, they represent points which move within the output space. Suppose now that the X_i's are partitioned in object classes and suppose that we would like to identify the network weights which will attain the following goal. In a topological sense, we would like outputs which correspond to inputs of same class to be close to each other (in terms of Eucledian distance), while outputs of different class to be as far apart as possible. Thus, we do not require that outputs approximate any specific target values nor any specific distribution. Outputs are free and can attain any values as long as they attain this aggregate clustering constraint. A similar criterion has been used before for various purposes, like in the Coulomb energy net and in hybrid nets [1,7,9] It turns out that this criterion is significant in many ways. Now, let's assume that we can device a measure $G(W)$, with the net's weights W as parameters, and which reflects the above described goal. That is, we assume that $G(W)$ is a measure of the "goodness" of the topological distribution of the Y_i's (with respect to the above goal). Then we can come up with a training algorithm for identifying the weights W using $G(W)$ as the energy function.

There are a few options regarding an appropriate measure $G(W)$. We can device a distance measure $D(Y_i, Y_j)$ (positive of course!) on pairs of output vectors and then use:

$$G = \sum_{i,j} \alpha_{ij} D(Y_i, Y_j), \qquad where \quad \alpha_{ij} = \begin{cases} 1 & if \quad class(X_i) = class(X_j) \\ -1 & if \quad class(X_i) \neq class(X_j) \end{cases} \tag{1}$$

If α_{ij} is positive then the corresponding term $D(Y_i, Y_j)$ contributes positively to G otherwise it contributes negatively. So G is minimized if the positive terms become very small (output Y_i vectors of same class moving close together), while at the same time negative terms become large (output Y_i vectors of different class moving apart). The obvious way to the optimization of G would be a gradient descent thus the weight parameters should change according to the delta rule: $\Delta W = -\lambda \dfrac{\partial G}{\partial W}$

Let's now turn to a short review of Fisher's linear discriminant method. A statistical sample of classified vectors of some vector space is given. The method seeks to identify a direction (or a line) within the vector space. The goal is that the projections of the given sample set on this direction cluster in as best discriminated class sets as possible. Depending on the choice of this direction the projections of the various class subsets of the sample may overlap or may fall in well separated regions. Often, there may not exist a direction such that the projections of the various classes are well separated and more or less partial overlaps are inevitable. The goal of Fisher's method is to find the best discriminant direction. The problem is formulated as an optimization problem where the measure to be optimized is:

$$\frac{\textit{Sum of squared distances of the mean projections of}}{\textit{Variance of all sample projections}} \quad \textit{all classes from the projection of the overall mean} \tag{2}$$

The directions which optimize this measure in a certain order are the eigenvectors which correspond to the eigenvalues of the lumped covariance matrix of the sample. What is interesting is that this measure is compatible with the one described in the transforming neural net above. If in that net we set the neuron activation functions to be linear, then the output of each neuron is the projection of the neuron's input vector in the direction of the neuron's weight vector. If we apply the training method described above on a single linear neuron, then Fisher's solution should be an attractor of the convergence of the (iterative) training process.

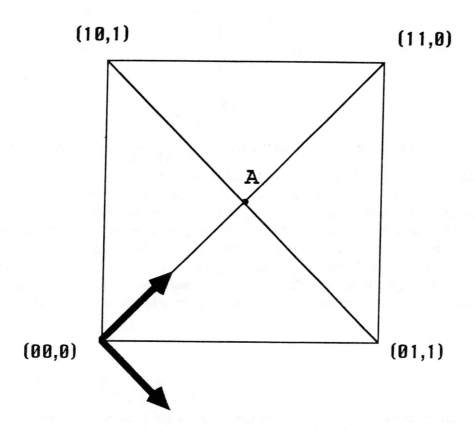

Figure 1. Experimentation on a simple X-OR set.

We used the X-OR problem as one of the standard benchmarks. Inputs 00 and 11 are supposed to produce a target of 0 and inputs 01 and 10 are supposed to produce a target of 1. The activation function of the neuron was set to $f = W'X$. The process was converging to one of the vectors oriented at (1,1) and (1,–1) as shown in figure 1. Both of them are equally good. The reason is simple: the best the net could do was to map the input vectors of a single class to a single output vector and keep the outputs for the vectors of the other class apart from that one. The end result depended on the initial setting of the neuron's weight vector. Then we used 2 linear neurons in a single layer. Since the two neurons operate in parallel without exchanging any information, each one recreates the earlier behavior of a single neuron independently from each other. The resulting weight vectors would end up in the directions (1,1) and (1,–1) independently of each other and often both weight vectors ended up in the same direction (depending on initial values). So we introduced a lateral virtual interaction from one neuron to the second. The interaction was one way from the first to the second. Thus, the first neuron operated freely in trying to optimize $G(W)$ whereas the second under a restriction. The second neuron had to optimize the $G(W)$ function augmented with the correlation of the two weight vectors; so we used $G + W_1' W_2$, thus attempting to reduce also the correlation between the weight vectors. As a result we consistently got the above principal components independently of initial weight values.

To conclude, we should provide some remarks regarding the choice of the distance measure $D(Y_i, Y_j)$. There are a few possibilities for its choice such as:

$$D(Y_i, Y_j) = |Y_i - Y_j|^2 \tag{3}$$

$$D(Y_i, Y_j) = -\frac{1}{|Y_i - Y_j|^2} \tag{4}$$

$$G = \frac{\sum_{ij}^{+} |Y_i - Y_j|^2}{\sum_{ij}^{-} |Y_i - Y_j|^2} \tag{5}$$

$$G = \sum_{ij}^{+} |Y_i - Y_j|^2 + \sum_{ij}^{-} \frac{1}{|Y_i - Y_j|^2} \tag{6}$$

However, the best choice of all of the above was to use $D(Y_i, Y_j) = -\frac{1}{|Y_i - Y_j|^2}$. We found most of the rest to present some technical difficulties, and it turned out that they were not actually capturing or representing the goal which the output distribution is supposed to attain. For example, the choice of $|Y_i - Y_j|^2$ will work well until same class output vectors come sufficiently close. Then their contribution becomes very small relatively to the contribution of the rest terms of dissimilar pairs. So the process tends to sacrifice the "shrinking" of each class in favor of bringing classes apart from each other. So if the change in weights could bring classes further apart at the cost of somewhat spreading a certain class then it would. The choice of (4) was best since it seems to balance these tradeoffs better. We also used the later form with a limiter function (sigmoid) applied on the pairwise distance and obtained faster convergence rates but the ultimate results appeared rather insensitive.

3. Conclusion

We intented here to point out the apparent relation between the principal components analysis and a neural network training method. The significance of this relation lies in the potential to compute the principal components by means of a connectionist method. There are various alternatives associated with this approach and we provided our insight with respect to certain choices as this insight emerges from our preliminary experimentation.

References

[1] Bachmann, C.M., L.N. Cooper, A. Dembo, O. Zeitouni, "A Relaxation Model for Memory with High Density Storage", Proc. Natl. Acad. Sci.USA 21, 7529-7531 Nov. 87

[2] Duda, R., and P. Hart "Pattern Recognition and Scene Analysis", John Wiley & Sons 1973

[3] Fisher, R. A., "The use of multiple measurements in taxonomic problems", Ann. Eugenics, 7, Part II, 179-188 (1936); also in Contributions to Mathematical Statistics (John Wiley, New York, 1950)

[4] Hect-Nielsen, R., "Neurocomputing", Addison-Wesley Publishing Company, 1990.

[5] Johnson, R.A., and D.W. Wichern, "Applied Multivariate Statistical Analysis" 2nd ed. Englewood Cliffs, N.J. : Prentice Hall, 1988.

[6]   Kirkpatrick, S., C.D. Gellat Jr. and M.P. Vecchi, "Optimization by Simulated Annealing," Science, Vol. 220, No. 4598, May 13, 1983.

[7]   Koutsougeras C., and R. Srikanth, "Data transformation for learning in feed-forward neural nets", Proc. Internat. conf. on Tools for AI, Boston, MA. November 1993.

[8]   Koutsougeras, C., and G. Papadourakis, "Coupling Supervised and Unsupervised Techniques in Training Feed-Forward Nets", International Journal of Artificial Intelligence Tools, Vol. 1, pp.37-55, March 1992.

[9]   Scofield, C.L., "Learning Internal Representations in the Coulomb Energy Network", in Proc. IEEE Internat. Conf. on Neural Networks (ICNN '88),New York: IEEE, July 1988.

[10]   Szu, H. and R. Hartley, "Fast Simulated Annealing," Physics Letters A, Vol. 122, No. 3, 4, June 8, 1987.

[11]   Werbos, P.J. "Beyond Regression: New Tools for Prediction and Analysis in the Behavioral Sciences", PhD thesis, Harvard University, 1974.

Pattern Identification by Trajectory Analysis in Autocorrelation Hyperspace

Christopher W. Tyler and Richard Miller
Smith-Kettlewell Eye Research Institute, San Francisco

Introduction

The human pattern recognition system has the property that it is able to identify salient features of arbitrary patterns in a parallel manner and to do so in the presence of masking noise. The question of which features are regarded as salient may depend on the definition of salience; e.g., features having greater contrast, greater overall area or a greater frequency of similar examples than the less salient features. To match such properties of human pattern recognition, we developed an algorithm based on the pattern's autocorrelation function (ACF).

The second order ACF is represented by a 2D array defining the self-similarity of the pattern at all (x,y) displacements; each entry in the array reflects the similarity between the pattern and a translation of it. The third order ACF is represented by a 4D array, each of whose entries reflects the similarity among the pattern and two translations of it. Thus, successive orders of the ACF form a hyperspace of contingent self-similarities.

By seeking high valued entries of the Nth order ACF, one can uncover N-point features that are strongly represented in the overall pattern. However, because of the size of the array involved, (viz., $(m.n)^{N-1}$ entries for an m x n pattern array), direct extraction of high valued entries is intractable for all but the lowest orders for patterns of useful size.

Our solution to the Nth order problem was to develop a procedure for tracking the trajectory through the Nth order ACF by means of a sequence of N-1 constrained maximizations for each intermediate ACF. In this way, each order was reduced to a single point in the projection to the pattern array. This solution has the advantage that computation grows linearly with N as opposed growing with the array size to the power of N. It has the disadvantage that it may well not find globally maximal subpatterns. However, this disadvantage is more than offset by the algorithm's ability to find subpatterns corresponding to perceptually interesting features.

Methods.

To obtain the most salient feature in the image, the algorithm constructs a 2D projection of the of the higher order ACF at non-zero shifts by tracking the trajectory of a maximal non-zero ACF value through the orders. Of course, this procedure is not unique. The particular constraints applied to the definition of the maximum found at each order determine the properties of the algorithm. The shift at each order defines the position of its representation in the 2D trajectory projected onto the pattern array, as depicted for a

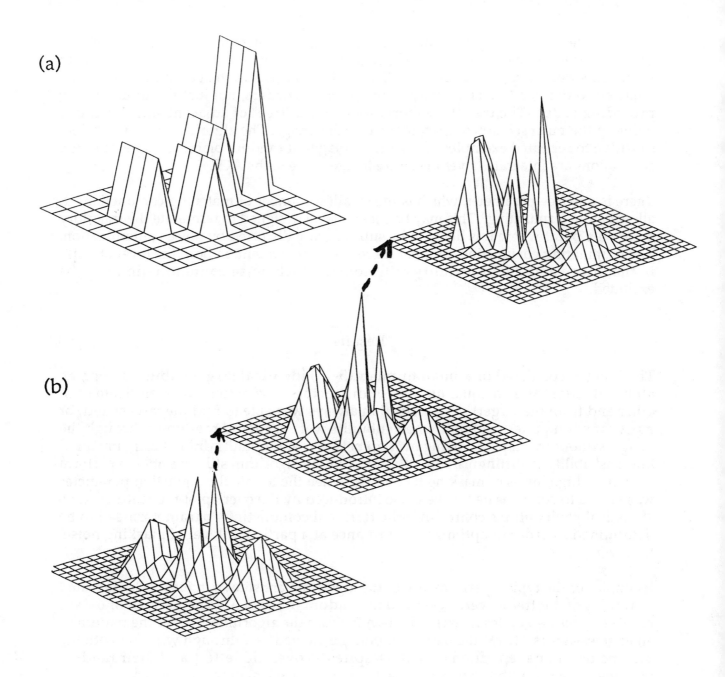

Fig. 1. Depiction of autocorrelation trajectory analysis:
(a). Meshplot of luminance profile of a test image consisting of 4 bars of the same orientation;
(b). Meshplots of the 2nd, 3rd and 4th order ACF surfaces. The central point for zero shift in the 2nd order ACF has been set to zero, so the highest point is one pixel away. The 3rd order ACF at this point is then computed, setting the highest point from the 2nd order (and its reflection) to zero. The trajectory then progresses to the next highest point, which forms the basis for the 4th order ACF at the fixed shifts for 2nd and 3rd order.

specific base image in Fig. 1. To limit the solutions to localized images, only correlated points adjacent to the solution at the previous order were included (as contrasted with the unconstrained trajectory of Fig. 1). The optimum correlation at each order could be adjacent to the positions from any of the previous orders, not just the immediately preceding order. The trajectory therefore forms a "tree" of adjacent shift positions defining the most salient compact feature in the image. The algorithm is nevertheless sensitive to repeated examples of the same images at random placements because the correlations are integrated over the entire image space in the ACF.

There is one free parameter, which is the smallest number of matching conjunctions to allow before terminating. This may be set at a level designed to terminate the trajectory before the point where it is likely to be substantially distorted by noise contamination. The terminating conjunction number therefore is dependent on both the level of noise in the image and the probability criterion at which noise contamination is to be excluded.

Results.

The images consisted of a small number (5-10) identical target subunits (e.g., an alphabet letter) and an equal number of distractors (e.g., letters different from each other and from the target). The algorithm always was able to find the largest and/or most common pattern subunit when subunits were scattered randomly through the image without overlap. Allowing overlap between the subunits dramatically impaired humans' ability to distinguish the subunits, but the algorithm still was able to perform well up to high levels of masking by overlap when the terminal conjunction parameter was varied to compensate for the noise introduced by the overlap of the features. The statistical probabilities controlling the terminal conjunctions parameter need to be determined in order to optimize performance at a particular level of masking noise, however.

Examples of the typical performance of the algorithm are shown in Figs. 1-3. Repeated examples of a letter R were scattered at random in Fig. 1A. (The pattern of 6 Rs is repeated over two cycles in each direction because the algorithm treated the pattern as an edgeless torus. Thus, the pattern should be viewed as a through window with the dimension of one repetition cycle.) Despite the overlaid letters and their random placement, the algorithm can extract the target pattern element without error.

In Fig. 2, a random target pattern of 4 Ss is overlaid by a mask of 6 other letters (B,C,D,E,G & H) placed at random. Human observers can identify the S as the most dominant pattern element with little trouble. The algorithm extracts the features of the S but also detects a tail introduced by the configuration of the masking letters. Such defects differ with each random placement of the targets and masks.

Fig. 3 shows a similar example with 4 Ls in the same set of maskers, but one in which the masker configuration makes it harder for human observers to extract the dominant pattern element without prior knowledge. The algorithm extracts the whole letter but picks up additional elements from the masking.

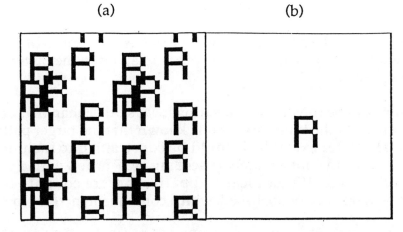

(a)　　　　　　(b)

Fig. 2. ACF trajectory analysis without maskers: (a). Six examples of the letter R were scattered at random. The pattern is repeated over two cycles in each direction and should be viewed as a through window with the dimension of one repetition cycle; (b). The ACF trajectory for (a).

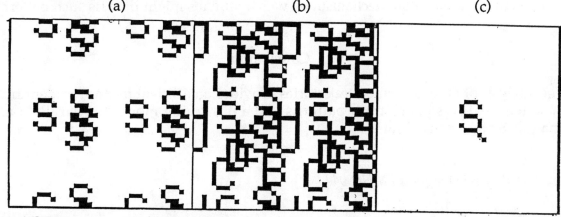

(a)　　　　　　(b)　　　　　　(c)

Fig. 3. ACF trajectory analysis with masking patterns: (a). A random target pattern of 4 Ss in the two-cycle repeat format of Fig. 2; (b). The pattern in (a) is overlaid by a mask of 6 other letters (B,C,D,E,G & H) placed at random. (c). The ACF trajectory for (b).

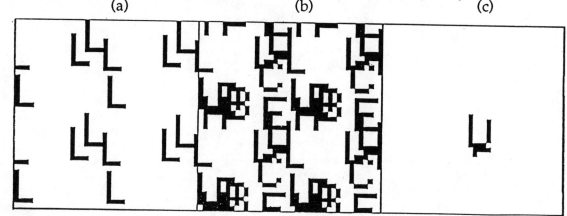

(a)　　　　　　(b)　　　　　　(c)

Fig. 4. ACF trajectory analysis with a strong masking configuration (a). A random target pattern of 4 Ls in the two-cycle repeat format of Fig. 2; (b). The pattern in (a) is overlaid by a mask of 6 other letters (B,C,D,E,G & H) placed at random; (c). The ACF trajectory for (b).

Discussion.

The results illustrate that the ACF trajectory approach is superior to the 2nd order ACF itself because the trajectory is sensitive to the phase relations in the pattern, whereas the ACF is phase insensitive.

The ACF trajectory can be constrained in various ways other than that of adjacency to any previous position in the trajectory. If it is known that the target patterns are one-dimensional "snakes", for example, it could be constrained to include only points adjacent to solution for the immediately preceding ACF order, with a corresponding increase in search speed. If non-localized patterns were sought, the adjacency constraint could be weakened or abolished, with a consequent increase in search time.

The approach to pattern analysis through ACF trajectories is a viable model for human pattern recognition because it could be implemented with local parallel processes in a neuronal network. Because it has global cooperative properties in the way common elements reinforce each other at a distance, the ACF trajectory provides interesting insights into the potential mechanism by which humans might process such patterns.

Conclusion.

The analysis of autocorrelation trajectories provides an efficient means for identification of salient features in arbitrary patterns and a intriguing model for parallel pattern analysis by the human brain.

Supported by NIMH grant #MH49044.

Supervised Learning

Session Chairs: George Lendaris
Soo-Young Lee

ORAL PRESENTATIONS

On Prestructuring ANNs Using *A Priori* Knowledge

George G. Lendaris* and Karl Mathia**
*Professor of Systems Science & Electrical Engineering
**Ph.D. Candidate in Electrical Engineering
Portland State University, P.O. Box 751, Portland, OR 97207
email: [lendaris, mathiak]@sysc.pdx.edu
and
*Visiting Senior Research Engineer (during Sabbatical Leave, 1993-94)
**Staff Research Engineer
Accurate Automation Corp., Chattanooga, TN

Abstract

*This is the next step of work reported in [Lendaris, Zwick & Mathia, 1993]. The objective has been to develop a constructive method that uses certain a priori information about a problem domain to design the starting structure of an artificial neural network (ANN). The method explored is based on a general systems theory methodology (here called GSM) that calculates a kind of structural information of the problem domain via analyzing I/O pairs from that domain. A modularized ANN structure is developed based on the GSM information provided. The notion of performance subset (PS) of an ANN structure is described, and extensive experiments on 3-input, 1-output Boolean mappings indicate that the resulting **modularized-ANN design is 'conservative'** in the sense that the PS of the modularized ANN contains at least all the mappings included in the GSM category used to design the ANN. Partial experiments on 5-input, 1-output Boolean functions indicate further success. The extended experimental results also suggest the possibility of using a measure of the learning curve of specified ANNs on a series of (in this case Boolean) functions to serve as a proxy measure for the complexity of those functions. This proxy measure seems to correlate well with a measure known as Boolean Length. Determining a function's Boolean Length is a non-trivial undertaking; perhaps it will turn out that training an ANN on the function and measuring its learning experience will be a useful measure of function complexity, and easier to determine than the function's Boolean Length.*

1 Background

In the General Systems Theory literature, there is a method we refer to as the general system method (GSM) [Lendaris, Zwick & Mathia, 1993] which provides 'structural knowledge' about a problem via a particular kind of (information-theoretic) analysis of data from that problem domain. A question arises as to whether that GSM structural knowledge can be used as *a priori* information about the problem to assist in designing an artificial neural network (ANN) to be applied to that problem. In the above reference, we presented the idea of using the GSM structural knowledge to design modularized ANNs to learn the mappings implicit in such data (in our case, I/O pairs of a Boolean mapping), and the results of some preliminary experiments. Certain predictions were made, and verified, about the potential benefits of designing an ANN in this way.

The results reported here are based on an extensive set of experiments based on a four-variable (nominal-data) structure. In GSM notation, this is designated an ABCD structure. In our case, due to the input/output nature of our problem context, we impose the notion of causality, and consider this a 3-input, 1-output system, as shown schematically in Figure 1a. The data are all binary, thus this system is mathematically expressed as a Boolean function. The set of $2^{2^3} = 256$ possible Boolean functions (mappings) for such a system has been widely studied, and much is known about them. In the context of elementary cellular automata (ECA) for example, the 256 mappings are grouped into 88 equivalence classes [15]. This latter knowledge was used to select functions with known structural properties for the present ANN exploration.

The focus here is on relations of two different *structural types*: 1) non-decomposable, and 2) decomposable into two relations with one shared variable. In GSM notation, type 1) is expressed as an ABCD structure, and type 2) as an ABD:ACD structure. We define D to represent the output variable of our causal system, and the ABD:ACD notation represents the case of A being the shared variable. Permutations of the input variables A,B,C generate a number of different but topologically equivalent mappings. In GSM, the ABCD structure corresponds to a relation of maximum complexity -- there is no reduction available (within this framework). The ABD:ACD structure, on the other hand, represents the case where there is a (partial) decoupling of variables possible: that is, ABCD may be decomposed into two sub-structures ABD and ACD which are not further decomposable. These two sub-structures are said to *share* variable A.

Consider now the task of designing an ANN to perform a 3-input, 1-output binary mapping. If nothing were known a priori about the specific mapping to be learned, then a typical candidate ANN structure to put into the box of Figure 1a would be a feed-forward type, with perhaps a single hidden layer, and **fully interconnected** [for present purposes, we call this a 'non-decomposed structure']. On the other hand, if *a priori* knowledge were available that the mapping to be learned was of the ABD:ACD type, then an ANN structure that would take into account such *a priori* information is shown in Figure 1b. In this case, we decompose the hidden layer into two sub-structures (the shaded boxes) which are not further decomposable. The number of inputs to each sub-structure is smaller than for the ANN of Figure 1a. [We call this a decomposed structure, or alternatively, a modularized structure.] For a 3-input system, with only 256 total possible mappings, this may seem trivial, but even moving up to just a 5-input system, the ANN related implications start becoming significant. For the 5-input case, the total number of possible maps is Order(billion)! Even for seemingly small numbers of inputs, it is physically not tractable to build ANNs whose performance subspace **PS** (defined below) covers the entire set of possible mappings, so, any constraints discovered in the data that can be translated into correlated constraints on the ANN structure would be most welcome.

2 Notation

We start with a characterization of the ANN as a "black box" that performs a mapping of its inputs to its outputs. Once the inputs and outputs are defined, *conceptually*, there exists a **set of all possible mappings (SAPM)** from the input domain to the output range [e.g., for an n-binary-input, 1-binary-output context, there are 2^{2^n} possible mappings]. For each ANN structure (inside the box) with a given setting of its weight values, the ANN will perform exactly one of these possible mappings. Doing the mental experiment of scanning all possible weight-value combinations in the given ANN, and collecting all the individual mappings performed by the ANN, we call the resulting collection of mappings the ANN's **performance subset (PS)** [8][6]. (For the binary case, if the number of inputs to the ANN exceeds approximately 30, it would be physically impossible to build an ANN whose **PS** contains all $2^{2^{30}}$ mappings, hence the name **sub**set.)

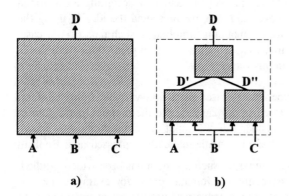

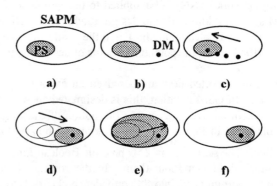

Figure 1. a) Non-decomposed and b) decomposed 3-input, 1-output system. The shaded boxes are implemented as separate ANNs.

Figure 2. Set of all possible mappings (SAPM) and Performance Subset (PS) [shaded areas]. The dot represents the desired mapping (DM).

In Figure 2a, we symbolize the set of all possible maps (**SAPM**) as the region defined by the outermost boundary, and symbolize the **PS** of some given ANN structure as the region defined by the inner boundary (shaded area). In Figure 2b, we add a point DM to represent the mapping corresponding to a problem we wish solved (Desired Mapping) . By our definition of **PS** as the collection of all those mappings it is possible for the given ANN structure to perform (over the set of all its weight values), **it is not possible** for the given ANN structure to perform the mapping DM shown in Figure 2b. Thus, no matter what weight-adjusting algorithm one attempts to use, it would be impossible for that ANN structure to ever learn the mapping at DM. So what is the ANN designer to do? Several strategies suggest themselves for what might be done either before training and/or during training: 1) "move" the point DM until it is inside the given region **PS** (Figure 2c) , 2) "move" the region marked **PS** until it contains the desired mapping DM (Figure 2d), and/or 3) increase the size of **PS** until it contains the point DM (Figure 2e). Strategy 1 may be accomplished by the designer selecting a different representation schema for the inputs and/or outputs, and *de facto*, is accomplished any time a designer selects a representation of the problem such that the ANN structure the designer is working with successfully learns the desired mapping. Strategy 2 is accomplished by selecting a different ANN structure. The authors are aware of two references describing approaches (that appear to) use this strategy on line [5][11] (while this possible strategy was discussed even in the 1960's, a theoretical basis for such an approach is still in its infancy). Strategy 3 is exemplified by the variety of methods that "grow" the starting ANN structure during training. To date, most training strategies assume that DM is already contained within the **PS** of the starting ANN structure (Figure 2f), and the job of the training algorithm is to converge upon DM -- indeed, typical convergence theorems state that a solution will be found *provided it exists*, and using the present vocabulary, this says *provided DM is contained in* ***PS***.

The present paper is concerned with the possibility of using *a priori* information about the problem domain to constructively **prestructure** an ANN with assurance that its **PS** contains the desired mapping (Figure 2f), and in addition, with assurance that the size of its **PS** is relatively small. The reason for the latter desire is that if a given ANN structure learns the training data, then the smaller its **PS**, the better its chance for good generalization performance [8][1]. This latter property is the objective pursued by those methods that do weight 'pruning' [14][12]: they start with an ANN structure whose **PS** is large enough to assure inclusion of their DM, and then shrink the size of the **PS** in a principled way, making it smaller and smaller just to the stage before it no longer contains their DM.

3 Experiments

A set of experiments was performed on the 256 possible 3-input, 1-output Boolean functions, using the partitioning into 88 equivalence classes mentioned in Section 1. A consistent exemplar of each of the classes was selected, yielding a set of 88 functions, and then 1760 experiments were run on these 88 functions [10]. Feedforward ANNs with back-propagation-of-error training were used. All experiments with each structure type used the same starting state, and the same training parameters. The key variable in the experiments were the different mappings to be learned. The training process was stopped at specified increments of training iterations, and the performance of the ANN was evaluated, via counting the number of bits of the output mapping that were correctly learned. The initial experiments reported in [9] focused on just those functions of the ABD:ACD decomposable type, all of which are of GSM structural type 4, and an equivalent number of *non*-decomposable functions (type ABCD), which are of GSM structural type 6. The examples from structural type 6 were selected intuitively to correspond in some plausible way to each of the ABD:ACD functions of type 4. Those preliminary results paved the way to the more extensive experiments described in this paper. These experiments included examples from all six structural types.

First, experiments were run to determine the size hidden layer needed in the non-decomposed ANN structure to learn the examples taken from the ABCD class. We settled on a fully-connected, feed-forward structure with one hidden layer of 4 elements, and this led to a decomposed ANN structure (via removing selected connections) with each sub-structure in the hidden layer comprising 2 elements. The conjecture was that while the non-decomposed (more general) ANN would be able to learn all the mappings (i.e., both the ABCD types and the ABD:ACD types), the modularized ANN would not be able to learn the ABCD mappings. Further, it was conjectured that since the structure of the modularized ANN in some sense mirrored the known structure of the ABD:ACD mappings, the modularized ANN would be able to learn the ABD:ACD mappings 'more easily' than the more general ANN structure would, and (more importantly) it was conjectured that if the two structures were each trained on partial data from an ABD:ACD mapping, then the decomposed ANN would have better generalization performance than the more general ANN structure would (since its performance subset (**PS**) would be smaller).

Let us use the vocabulary introduced in Section 2 to discuss the 6 groupings of functions used in this study. As noted earlier, GSM structural type 6 refers to the most complex case, and thus these functions are expected to require the most general ANN structure, i.e., a fully connected one. The ABD:ACD functions used above are from type 4, and we have noted that the modularized ANN structure of Figure 1b works for these functions. The fully connected ANN structure selected has a performance subset (**PS**) that covers the entire set of 256 possible 3-input, 1-output Boolean mappings (as noted earlier, had the number of inputs been larger than approximately 30, this would not be physically possible). The modularized ANN structure used, however, has a smaller **PS**. The way the modularization was done in this case was to divide up the elements in the hidden layer equally to the two partitions. This can be considered in the same way as we discussed weight pruning earlier to infer that the **PS** of the modularized ANN is a reduced version of the more general ANN's **PS** (in this case, trivially so, since the larger **PS** includes the entire set of possible maps). A question of basic interest in the present research is how does the **PS** of the modularized ANN relate to the set of mappings associated with the various GSM structural types? We know that the **PS** of the modularized structure does not contain some of the mappings of type 6 (when we trained on those mappings that intuitively were among the "hardest" of these, the modularized ANN did not learn them). We also know that the **PS** of the modularized structure contains all of the mappings of type 4 (the ABD:ACD type), as it learned all of these. Since each structural type subsumes the lower types, we expect the **PS** of the modularized ANN structure designed according to structure type 4 requirements to include the mappings corresponding to the lower types. The experiments bore this out.

In addition, however, the full set of experiments show that the **PS** of the modularized ANN structure is in fact larger than just the mappings of GSM structural type 4 (and the subsumed structure types 3, 2 & 1). The modularized ANN was able to learn all the mappings of type 5, and further, some of the mappings of type 6. These results indicate that if we select a modularized ANN structure based on the GSM structural type inferred via GSM analysis of I/O pairs of data from the problem domain, then **the design is "conservative"** in the sense that its **PS** is at least big enough to contain the mappings of the inferred GSM structural type. The fact that the **PS** is larger than just the mappings contained in the inferred GSM set can be explained as follows: the mappings being explored are Boolean, i.e., all variables are binary. While the inputs to the ANN are binary, and the output neurode learns to give binary outputs, the hidden neurode values are not constrained (in our experiments) to binary values. Accordingly, it is clear that the **PS** of the ANN prestructing selected will be larger than the set of mappings of the inferred GSM set. For the 3-input case the size of the ANN's **PS** reached up into structural type 6 (not all of it though). For a number of inputs n, larger than the 3 used here, the number of GSM structural types will be significantly larger than the 6 associated with the n=3 case. Our analysis so far gives us hints suggesting the following speculation: the **PS** of the ANN designed via the GSM structural information (i.e. the selected structure in the GSM lattice) will contain functions within the "neighborhood" of the GSM structure identified. The term neighborhood here is intended to mean within approximately 2 levels further up from the one selected in the GSM lattice of structures. In the 4 variable case (3 inputs, 1 output), since the GSM lattice of structures is so small, the "neighborhood" reached into the top level of the lattice. However, for larger values of n, the GSM lattice will have significantly more levels, so the "neighborhood" could be a rather small fraction of the total range. Accordingly, the relative size of the prestructured ANN's **PS** will be a small fraction of the size of the collection of mappings up to the top of the lattice, and thus the difference between a general ANN's **PS** and that of a prestructured ANN will be greater, and thus the prestructuring will pay even better dividends than those already discussed for the n=3 case. We believe that the principle has been demonstrated, but there remains yet a significant amount of work to analyze even the 5-input case.

We pause here to mention that all the 3-input, 1-output experiments were carried out with a full training set, where the research objective was to observe the learning process. In these cases, the question of generalization was not at issue. But, when we do move on to consider the generalization question, the kind of knowledge available about the functions we are exploring is very useful. Since there is a definite (known) structure for the functions being learned, we are in a position to constructively design a subset of the possible input patterns for training the ANN that theoretically contains enough information to infer the entire mapping. After the ANN trains on this subset, to the extent that its structure really is tailored to the structure of the desired mapping, then we should expect the ANN to generalize well. The better the structural match, the closer to 100% generalization. To carry out a preliminary experiment related to generalization, a set of four 5-input, 1-output functions, decomposable in a way indicated in Figure 3, were crafted. This selection was made because the 3-input case used for the rest of the experiments was judged too limiting for carrying out the desired generalization experiment. By construction of these functions, we were able to select a training set comprising only 50% of the possible input patterns (i.e., just half the mapping) which we knew theoretically contained sufficient information from which to infer the total mapping. This set was used to train both a general (fully connected) 5-input ANN and a modularized 5-input ANN (cf. Figure 3). For the decomposed functions, both structures learned the training set perfectly. However, there was a big difference in the generalization tests: 1) the modularized ANN gave **perfect** responses for the I/O pairs not seen during training, and 2) the general ANN averaged only 55% correct responses (nearly random) on these test inputs. Also, four non-decomposable functions were selected, and both ANN structures trained on them, again using 50% of the possible input patterns. The general ANN learned the training set, while the modularized ANN did poorly. The modularized ANN did poorly at generalizing, and *so did the general* ANN. While these experiments used but a small fraction of the possible mappings in the 5-input, 1-output context, the experimental procedure of constructing a focused experiment and having this give results which support the hypothesis carries reasonable convincing power -- especially since it was constructed such that if the experiment gave negative results (counter-example), it would have significantly undermined the basic premise of the approach.

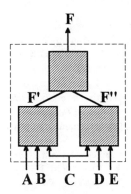

Figure 3. Modularized ANN, implementing a 5-input, 1-output ABCF:CDEF system. Used for generalization test.

4 Proxy Measures for Complexity?

To recapitulate, the assumption is that we start with a set of I/O data for the problem domain, specifically here, binary I/O data. Next, we submit this data to what we are calling GSM structural analysis, and this analysis assigns a structural type to the data (ranging from type 6 to type 1 for the 4-variable case). This structure number is a kind of complexity measure (6 being the most complex), relating to the decomposability of the Boolean function inferred to underlie the given data. This yields a rather coarse coding of the possible 256 functions being considered, and as might be expected, within each category, there will be a gradation of the degree of complexity, if we had a finer way to measure it. Nevertheless, the premise here is that even this rather coarse measure can be put to good use in modularizing ANNs -- where 'good' here relates to improved learning speed, and more importantly, improved generalization performance.

The 88 functions studied in these experiments were sorted according to the 'learning difficulty' experienced by the 1) fully-interconnected ANN and 2) the modularized ANN. In addition, the same functions were sorted according to four different measures in the literature dealing with Boolean functions, namely, the already discussed GSM structural type (range 1-6) [3], and in addition the Lambda-count (range 0-4) [4], Fluency (range 1-9) (theory developed in [15], original idea by Ashby [13]), and Boolean Length (range 1-10) -- this is the minimum number of Boolean operations necessary to represent the binary string (related to Kolmogorov complexity) [15]. Values of these four complexity measures for the 88 Boolean functions selected for our experiments appear in [25]. In comparing these sorted lists, except at the two ends (where all but Lambda basically concurred), it turned out that there was little, if any, correlation between the orderings given by the 4 published measures of complexity. However, there was a good correlation in the orderings provided by the Boolean Length measure and the 'learning difficulty' assigned to each of the ANN structures investigated. The suggestion based on these observations is that certain measures of the learning curve of specified ANN structures might be used as a proxy measure for the complexity of certain classes of functions [10]. The learning curve may be characterized by (at least) two of its attributes: the transient portion and the steady state level. Here the steady state level can be characterized by the number of bits learned (max. of 8 for the 3-input, 1-output case), the transient by the number of training cycles required by the ANN structure to accomplish the learning. Other qualities of the transient suggest themselves via visual analysis, but have not yet been reduced to quantitative expressions.

While the investigation here was based upon Boolean functions that have well documented properties in the literature, there might be a basis for developing this approach to other classes of functions. Thus we have a turn of events. Instead of lamenting the difficulty an ANN has in learning a given task, we might be able to use the learning experience of specified ANN structures as proxy measures for the complexity of certain classes of functions

5 References

[1.] Hertz, J., Krogh, A. & R.G. Palmer, *Introduction to the Theory of Neural Computation*, Addison-Wesley, 1991.

[2.] Kalman, B.L., Kwasny, S.C. & A. Abella, "Decomposing Input Patterns to Facilitate Training," *Proceedings of World Congress on Neural Networks Portland* (WCNN-93), pp. III.503-III.506 Earlbaum, July, 1993.

[3.] Krippendorff, K., *Information Theory: Structural Models for Qualitative Data*, Sage University Paper No. 62, SAGE, 1984.

[4.] Langton C.G., Taylor C. , Farmer J.D. & S. Rasmussen (eds.), *Artificial Life II*, Addison-Wesley, 1992.

[5.] Lee, T-C, *Structure Level Adaptation for Artificial Neural Networks*, Bluer Academic, 1991.

[6.] Lendaris, G.G., "A Proposal for Indicating Quality of Generalization when Evaluating ANNs," *Proc. of IJCNN 1990*, San Diego, IEEE, 1990.

[7.] Lendaris, G.G. & D. Todd, "Use of Structured Problem Domain to Explore Development of Modularized Neural Networks," *Proc. of the IJCNN-92, Baltimore*, pp. III-869-874, IEEE, June 1992.

[8.] Lendaris, G.G. & G.L. Stanley, "Structure and Constraint in Discrete Adaptive Networks," *Proc. of the Nat Electronics Conf*, vol. XXI, pp. 500-505, 1965.

[9.] Lendaris, G.G., M. Zwick & K. Mathia, "On Matching ANN Structure to Problem Domain Structure," *Proc. of the World Congress on Neural Networks - WCNN-93 Portland*, Earlbaum/INNS, July 1993.

[10.] Mathia, K., "Under What Conditions Do Modularized Neural Networks Learn Boolean Functions?", Project Report SySc 651, Portland State University, Portland, Oregon, March 1994.

[11.] Odri, S.V., Petrovacki, D.P. & G.A. Krstonosic, "Evolutional Development of a Multilevel Neural Network," *Neural Networks*, vol. 6, pp. 583-595, Pergamon, 1993.

[12.] Reed, R., "Pruning Algorithms--A Survey," *IEEE Trans. on Neural Networks*, vol. 4, no 5, Sept 1993, pp. 740-747.

[13.] Walker, C.C. & W.R. Ashby, "On Temporal Characteristics of Behavior in Certain Complex Systems," *Kybernetik*, vol. 3, no. 2, pp. 100-108, 1966. [Reprinted in *Mechanisms of Intelligence: Ross Ashby's Writings on Cybernetics*, R. Conant (Ed), Intersystems Publications, pp.93 -110, 1981.

[14.] Weigend, A.S., Rumelhart, D.E. & B.A. Huberman, "Back Propagation, weight-elimination and time series prediction," in *Proc. 1990 Connectionist Models Summer School*, D.Touretzky, J. Elman, T Sejnowski & G. Hinton, Eds., pp. 105-116, 1990, .

[15.] Zwick, M., Shu, H. & B. Gifford, "Complexity and Dynamics of Elementary Cellular Automata", in preparation.

Error Minimization, Generalization, and Hardware Implementability of Supervised Learning

Soo-Young Lee and Dong-Gyu Jeong
Computation and Neural Systems Laboratory
Department of Electrical Engineering
Korea Advanced Institute of Science and Technology
373-1 Kusong-dong, Yusong-gu, Taejon 305-701, Korea
Tel: +82-52-869-3431 / Fax: +82-42-869-3410 / E-mail: sylee@eekaist.kaist.ac.kr

Abstract

The tradeoff between output error minimization and generalization is discussed, and a new learning algorithm is developed to improve generalization and robust classification capability for multi-layer Perceptron. Unlike other methods which reduce network complexity by putting restrictions on synaptic weights, this algorithm increases complexity of the underlying problem by imposing appropriate additional requirements on the hidden-layer neurons, i.e. low output sensitivity to the input values or equivalently saturation of hidden-layer activations. The additional gradient-descent term turns out to be Hebbian, and this new algorithm incorporates both the error back-propagation and Hebbian learning rules. The algorithhm also utilizes full power of existing hardwares to find solution with maximum generalization capability. Computer simulation demonstrates much faster learning convergence as well as improved robustness for classification and hetero-association problems.

1. Introduction

Although multi-layer Perceptron is capable of solving complicated pattern classification and functional approximation problems, good generalization is achievable only with proper combination of the training data size, the underlying problem complexity, and the network complexity. (Hush and Horne 1993) For given number of training data and problem complexity smaller networks are not capable of representing the problem accurately. On the other hand larger networks with too many synaptic weights suffer from poor generalization. To improve the generalization capability in this case, one may put restrictions on the synaptic weights and reduce the network complexity. Synaptic weight pruning (LeCun *et al* 1990), local connections and weight sharing (Fukushima 1988, 1993; Waibel *et al.* 1989; LeCun *et al.* 1990), weight decay (Hanson and Pratt 1989), weight elimination (Weigend *et al* 1990), and soft weight sharing (Nowlan and Hinton 1992) all belong to this approach. However, for many practical hardware implementations the network complexity is already determined by the hardware itself and one would like to fully utilize existing hardware capability. Also it is not easy to modify the network architecture in hardware implementations.

In this paper we propose the other approach, i.e. to increase the underlying problem complexity. By properly imposing additional requirements for low sensitivity on the hidden-layer neurons, the problem complexity is increased to result in better generalization. The neural network architecture and major parameters, e.x. numbers of synapses and hidden-layer neurons, are unchanged during learning. The learning algorithm just utilizes maximum power of the hardware available. Also, the gradient-descent learning algorithm happends to incorporate both the error back-propagation and Hebbian learning rules.

2. Saturation Requirements on Hidden-layer Neurons

One of the most frequent symptom of the poor generalization with overfitting is erroneous high sensitivity of output values on input values. For good generalization and robust classification we would like to reduce the unreasonably-high sensitivity. By applying chain rule one obtains the sensitivity as

$$\frac{\partial y_i}{\partial x_k} = \sum_j W_{ij}^{(2)} f'(h_j) W_{jk}^{(1)}, \tag{1}$$

where $\mathbf{x}$ and $\mathbf{y}$ are input and output vector, respectively, and $W_{jk}^{(1)}$ and $W_{ij}^{(2)}$ are synaptic interconnections. Although our approach can be extended to general multi-layer architecture, only 2-layer Perceptron with linear output neurons is considered here for simplicity. The $f'(.)$ is derivative of Sigmoid nonlinear function at hidden-layer neurons, and $h_j = \sum_k W_{jk}^{(1)} x_k$ is post-synaptic neural activations. From Eq.(1) the sensitivity can be made smaller by forcing the hidden-layer activations to be saturated, i.e. $f'(h_j) \approx 0$, and this additional requirement increases the problem complexity for better generalization. Instead of standard output error we define a new error as

$$E = E_o + \gamma E_h = \frac{1}{M} \sum_s E_o^s + \frac{\gamma}{M} \sum_s E_h^s, \tag{2}$$

where the $E_o^s = \frac{1}{2N_o} \sum_i (t_i^s - y_i^s)^2$ is output error and the $E_h^s = \frac{2}{N_h} \sum_j f'(\hat{h}_j^s)$ is the additional error defined from the hidden-layer neural activations. The t_i^s and y_i^s are target and output values of the ith output neuron for the sth stored pattern, and $\hat{h}_j^s$ is the corresponding post-synaptic value for the jth hidden-layer neuron. Here M, N_o, and N_h are number of stored patterns, number of output neurons, and number of hidden-layer neurons, respectively, and the errors are normalized with these numbers. If the neural activation of the hidden-layer stays at linear region of the Sigmoid function, it becomes sensitive to the input noise and high hidden-layer error E_h^s is assigned. (The above definition of E_h^s results in $\frac{1}{2N_h} \sum_j [1 - f(\hat{h}_j^s)^2]$ for bipolar hyperbolic tangent Sigmoid function and $\frac{2}{N_h} \sum_j f(\hat{h}_j^s)[1 - f(\hat{h}_j^s)]$ for unipolar Sigmoid function.) It is worth noting that both the output error E_o and hidden-layer error E_h are normalized to take similar values, i.e. around 0.5 for bipolar Sigmoid and 0.25 for unipolar Sigmoid, for very small initial synapses and converge to 0 by training. By minimizing the E_h one may push the network into nonlinear region for improved robustness. The γ represents relative significance of the hidden-layer error E_h over output error E_o.

The network is trained by steepest-descent error minimization algorithm as usual. Although the last layer is not affected by this additional error term, the partial derivative of total error E with respect to each weight in the first layer now contains additional term and the weight update becomes

$$\Delta\omega^{(1)}_{jk} = \frac{\eta}{MN_o} x^s_k \, \delta^s_j \, f'\left(\hat{h}^s_j\right) + \frac{2\eta\gamma}{MN_h} x^s_k \, f''\left(\hat{h}^s_j\right) = \frac{\eta}{M}\left(\frac{\delta^s_j x^s_k}{N_o} + \frac{\gamma \hat{h}^s_j x^s_k}{N_h}\right) f'\left(\hat{h}^s_j\right),\qquad (3)$$

where the δ^s_j is back-propagated error on the jth hidden-layer neuron for the sth training pattern as usual. The η is a learning coefficient, and $f''(.)$ is second derivative of the hyperbolic tangent Sigmoid function $f(.)$. The additional term in Eq.(3) happends to follow Hebbian learning rule, and this new learning algorithm incorporates two popular learning algorithms, i.e. the error back-propagation and Hebbian learning rules. It is worth noting that the Hebbian term is also multiplied by $f'\left(\hat{h}^s_j\right)$, which prevents the synaptic weights from indefinite increase or decrease.

With very small initial synaptic values the $\hat{h}^s_j \approx 0$ and the Hebbian term does not contribute much. As learning process goes on by the first error back-propagation term only, the hidden-layer activation values become non-trivial and the Hebbian term starts contributing to push hidden-layer activations to the saturation regions.

Although the author's previous work to merge Hebbian learning and error back-propagation (Koh *et al.* 1990) was based on correlation matrix synapses, this new algorithm represents more general adaptive Hebbian learning. Actually it shares more with Radial Basis Function networks. (Hartman *et al.* 1990; Lee and Kil 1991) Both networks incorporate competetive Hebbian learning for the first layer and error minimization for the second layer. However, instead of localized Gaussian nonlinearity used for the Radial Basis Function network, our network utilizes monotonically increasing global Sigmoid nonlinearity on the hidden-layer neurons, which allows gradient-descent algorithm throughout the whole network with less problems. Also. synaptic weights for both the first layer and second layer are adapted simultaneously here.

3. Simulation Results

The proposed learning algorithm is applied to classification and hetero-association problems. Results for classification of 10 binary patterns are shown in Figures 1 and 2. The numbers of input, hidden, and output layers are set to 35, 30, and 10, respectively. In Fig.1 learning convergences are shown in log-log scale. Fig.1(a) shows the total errors as functions of learning epoch for different γ, i.e. relative significance of the hidden-layer error E_h over output error E_o. The new algorithm converges much faster than standard error back-propagation ($\gamma = 0$), and the trained results are not sensitive on γ. As shown in Figs.1(b) and (c), the output error E_o drops very rapidly after initial learning stage (around 10 epoches in this case), and becomes much smaller than γE_h thereafter. This is the point when the Hebbian learning term in Eq.(3) starts contributing. The dominance of the hidden-layer error at the later stage explains the insensitivity of this algorithm to the γ.

Error correction probabilities after learning are plotted as functions of Hamming distances in Figs. 2 and 3. In Fig.2 results of the same classification problem is plotted, while hetero-association problems is shown in Fig.3. Both input and output layers have 35 binary neurons, and 30 hidden-layer neurons are used in the hetero-association problem. At each Hamming distance, i.e. number of different bits with a stored pattern, 100 test patterns are randomly generated to satisfy the Hamming distance with each of the 10 stored patterns, and their overall performances are collected for the 1000 test patterns. In Figs.2(a) and 3(a) the adaptive training was stopped at $E = 0.03$, while the E was further reduced to 0.001 in Figs.2(b) and 3(b). When the learning was not complete, the correct classification probability is greatly affected by the γ as shown in Figs.2(a) and 3(a). However, when enough learning was performed in Figs. 2(b) and 3(b), the correct classification or association probability becomes much higher and also insensitive to the γ. These figures clearly demonstrate much robust classification and hetero-association capability of the proposed algorithm compared to the standard error back-propagation algorithm ($\gamma = 0$).

The proposed hybrid learning algorithm is being implemented by modular neuro-chip set. The chip-set consists of one synapse chip and one soma chip. Each synapse cell is composed of one capacitor for weight storage, and 3 analog multipliers, one for feed-forward signal flow, another for error back-propagation, and the other for weight update outer-products. In the soma chip the Sigmoid and its derivatives are calculated with current sum. Also, the back-propagated error can be added up with neural activations for the hybrid learning. These chip sets are designed to support modular concepts for generic neuro-computers with on-chip learning capability.

4. Conclusion

In this paper we have presented a new supervised learning algorithm for 2-layer feed-forward neural networks for robust classification and hetero-association problems. By forcing the hidden-

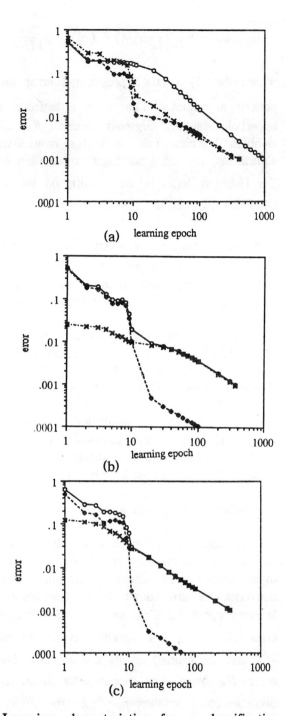

Fig.1 Learning characteristics for a classification problem. (a) Total error vs. learning epoch for classification of 10 random patterns. Here, "o", "●", and "x" denote cases for $\gamma=0$, 0.1, and 0.5, respectively. (b) Error vs. learning epoch for $\gamma=0.1$. (c) Error vs. learning epoch for $\gamma=0.5$. Here, "o", "●", and "x" denote the total error E, output error E_o, and hidden-layer error γE_h, respectively.

III-328

layer neurons saturated, we are able to increase problem complexity and improve generalization capability. Also the gradient-descent algorithm turns out to incorporate Hebbian learning rule, and converges much faster than standard back-propagation algorithm. Extention to general multi-layer architecture seems straightforward. Modular neuro-chip to incorporate this learning algorithm is 9being developed. Also, adaptive modification of the γ, relative significance of the hidden-layer error E_h over output error E_o, is currently being investigated. Starting with arbitrary γ one goes on the learning process. After reaching the steady and slow error reduction stage, the output error may start increasing again due to the relatively high γ value.

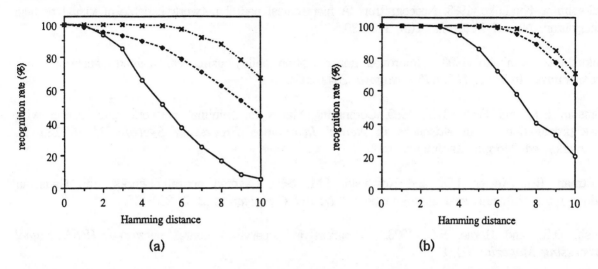

(a)   (b)

Fig.2 Correct classification probabilities as functions of Hamming distance for a classifier problem. (a) at total error E = 0.03 and (b) at E = 0.0001. Here, "o", "●", and "x" denote cases with γ = 0, 0.1, and 0.5, respectively. The γ= 0 case corresponds to standard error back-propagation learning rule.

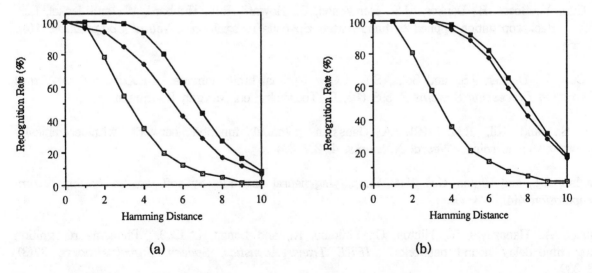

(a)   (b)

Fig.3 Correct association probabilities as functions of Hamming distance for a hetero-association problem. (a) at total error E = 0.03 and (b) at E = 0.0001. Here, "o", "●", and "x" denote cases with γ = 0, 0.1, and 0.5, respectively. The γ= 0 case corresponds to standard error back-propagation learning rule.

This means the network complexity is not large enough both to minimize the output error and to saturate the hidden-layer activations. In this case the γ can be made smaller to keep the output error going down.

Acknowledgement: This research was supported by Korean Ministry of Science and Technology through KAIST as an Advanced Essential Technology Project.

References

Fukushima, Kunihiko. 1988. Neocognitron: A hierarchical neural network capable of visual pattern recognition. *Neural Networks*, 1(2), 119-130.

Fukushima, Kunihiko. 1993. Improved generalization ability using constrained neural network architecture. In *Proc. IJCNN'93-Nagoya*. 2049-2054.

Hanson, S.J., and Pratt., L.Y. 1989. Comparing biases for minimal network construction with back-propagation. In *Advances in Neural Information Processing Systems 1*, 177-185, D. Touretzky, ed. Morgan Kaufmann.

Hartman, E.J., Keeler, J.D., and Kowalski, J.M. 1990. Layered neuralnetworks with Gaussian hidden units with universal approximations. *Neural Computation*, 2(2), 210-215.

Hush, D.R., and Horne, B.G. 1993. Progress in supervised neural networks. *IEEE Signal Processing Magazine* (1), 8-39.

Koh, S.H., Lee, S.Y., Jang, J.S., and Shin, S.Y. 1990. Merging Hebbian learning rule and least-mean-square error algorithm for two layer neural networks. In *Proc. IJCNN'90-WASH* I, 647-650.

Le Cun, Y., Boser, B., Denker, J.S., Henderson, D., Howard, R.E., Hubbard, W., and Jackel, L.D. 1989. Backpropagation applied to handwritten zip code recognition. *Neural Computation*, 1(4), 541-551.

Le Cun, Y., Denker, J.S., and Solla, S.A. 1990. Optimal brain damage. In *Advances in Neural Information Processing Systems 2*, 598-605, D. Touretzky, ed. Morgan Kaufmann.

Lee, S., and Kil, R.M. 1991. A Gaussian potential function network withhierarchically self-organizing learning. *Neural Networks*, 4, 207-224.

Nowlan, S.J., and Hinton, G.E. 1992. Simplifying neural networks by soft weight sharing. *Neural Computation* 4(4), 473-493.

Waibel, A., Hanazawa, T., Hinton, G., Shikano, K., and Lang, K. 1989. Phoneme recognition using time-delay neural networks. *IEEE Trans. Acoustics, Speech, Signal Process.* 37(3), 328-339.

Weigend, A.S., Rumelhart, D.E., and Huberman, B.A. 1990. Back-propagation, weight elimination and time-series prediction. In *Proceedings of the 1990 Connectionist Models Summer School*, 65-80, Morgan Kaufmann.

A Simulated Annealing Based Backpropagation Model Improves the Convergence Rate of the Network

Adel M. Abunawass
Western Illinois University
Macomb, Illinois 61455
E-mail: mfama@uxa.ecn.bgu.edu

Charles B. Owen
Dartmouth College
Hanover, New Hampshire 03755-3551
E-mail: cowen@cs.dartmouth.edu

Original Paper Citation:
Application of Simulated Annealing to the Backpropagation Model Improves Convergence. *Proceedings of the Conference on the Science of Artificial Neural Networks II* (1993), Vol. 1966, pp. 269-276.

Abstract

The Backpropagation technique for learning internal representations in multi-layer neural networks is an effective approach for solution of the gradient descent problem. However, being a deterministic solution, it will attempt to take the best path to the nearest error minima, whether global or local. If a local minima is reached, the network fails to converge and either will not learn or will learn a poor approximation of the solution.

This paper introduces a novel stochastic approach to the Backpropagation model based on Simulated Annealing. The model is designed to provide an effective means of escape from local minima. This technique augments the traditional gradient descent learning scheme with a Metropolis loop. This extension of the algorithm is shown to be modeled as a Markov chain consisting of a Markov neighborhood, a selection function, an acceptance function, and a cooling schedule. The Markov neighborhood is defined as the possible next states of the network and is a combination of the gradient descent weight deltas and a noise injection method. The selection function provides for the probabilistic selection of the proposed next state of the network. Several alternative noise injection methods and selection functions are presented complete with experimental data. The acceptance function determines the probability of acceptance of a new network state. The acceptance function for this model is based on the total network error. Simulated Annealing is highly dependent upon cooling schedules and several alternative cooling schedules are presented. Both static and dynamic approaches to cooling are examined. The prevention of premature quenching is addressed and the selection of desirable quenching conditions are defined.

In experimental results the system is shown to converge with a much higher degree of reliability. It is also shown to converge more reliably and much faster than traditional noise insertion techniques. Due to the characteristics of the cooling schedule, the system also demonstrates a more consistent training profile.

Backpropagation Learning for Systems with Discrete-Valued Functions

Edward Wilson*
Stanford University
Aerospace Robotics Laboratory
Stanford, California 94305
ed@sun-valley.stanford.edu

Abstract

Backpropagation is a powerful learning algorithm, but its restriction to continuously differentiable functions limits its use in many applications. One important example is training a multi-layered neural network of hard-limiting units (signums instead of sigmoids). Another example is a control system that uses discrete-level actuators, such as our free-flying space robot model equipped with on-off gas thrusters.

A new technique is presented that extends backpropagation to allow for discrete-valued functions. Each signum that exists at run-time is temporarily replaced with a sigmoid during training, and noise is injected at the input to the sigmoid. The noise prevents the use of the smooth transition region of the sigmoid as the primary means of solution. The effect is that the sigmoid outputs are close to hard-limited during training so there is not a significant performance reduction when the signums are re-introduced at run-time. The use of differentiable approximating functions allows fast learning due to gradient-based optimization. The noise does not corrupt the gradient estimation algorithm, so no modifications are needed on the backward error propagation.

The viability of this method is verified by applying it to the training of networks with hard-limiting units as well as a complex on-off thruster control problem associated with our free-flying space robot.

1 Introduction

1.1 Optimization with discrete-valued functions

Optimization methods that use gradient information often converge much faster than those that do not. Use of the backpropagation algorithm (BP) [1][2] to get this gradient information for training neural networks (NNs) has made them useful in many applications; however, BP's requirement of continuous differentiability, not only for the network itself, but for anything that the error is backpropagated through (e.g. the plant model in a control problem), limits its applicability.

This is a significant limitation since there are many applications where discrete-valued states arise. For example: on-off thrusters commonly used in spacecraft; other systems with discrete-valued inputs and outputs; and neural networks built with signums (aka hard-limiters or Heaviside step functions) rather than sigmoids. Signum networks may be preferred to sigmoidal ones due to hardware considerations.

In cases like these, one choice is to use an alternative method not restricted to continuously differentiable functions, such as unsupervised learning, simulated annealing, or a genetic algorithm, but these are usually significantly slower to train, because they do not use gradient information.

1.2 Related research

Learning algorithms for single-layer networks date back to 1960, with Widrow's ADALINE [3] and Rosenblatt's Perceptron [4]. Unfortunately, neither of these methods extend directly to multiple layers.

MADALINE Rule I was a two-layer network (one hidden layer) that had a trainable first layer, but the second layer was a fixed logic operation, such as OR, AND, or MAJ (majority) [5]. In MADALINE Rule II, Winter [6] used a heuristic approach which had limited success at training a two-layer network of hard-limiters (ADALINEs). These methods may be classified as "error-correction rules" rather than "steepest-descent rules" (gradient-based) [3].

In recent research aimed at using gradient-based learning for multi-layer signum networks, Bartlett and Downs [7] use weights that are random variables, and develop a training algorithm based on the fact that

---

*Ph.D. Candidate, Department of Mechanical Engineering. Research partially supported by NASA and AFOSR.

the resulting probability distribution is continuously differentiable. The algorithm is limited to one hidden layer, requires all inputs to be 1 or -1, and needs extra computation to estimate the gradient.

Another method is to approximate the discrete-valued functions with linear functions or smooth sigmoids during the learning phase, and switch to the true discontinuous functions at run-time. This is similar to the original ADALINE, where the neuron was trained on its linear output, but in operation, this output passed through a signum function [3]. This method may work in cases where the behavior of the system with sigmoids is close enough to that of the real system; however, this assumption is very often unreliable.

1.3 Outline of paper

There are three major sections in this paper. In Section 2, the technique of learning with noisy sigmoids is explained and the training algorithm is derived. In Section 3, to demonstrate the usefulness of the method for training multi-layered networks of hard-limiters, it is applied to two different problems. In Section 4, to demonstrate application to a complex control problem, it is applied to a thruster-mapping problem involving eight on-off thrusters controlling a 3-dof free-flying space robot.

2 Backpropagation Learning with Noisy Sigmoids

2.1 Training algorithm

We introduce the method of noise injection by applying it to the training of a single hard-limiting neuron, as shown in Figure 1. This neuron could be trained with the ADALINE or perceptron learning rules, but those methods do not extend to multiple layers, while this one does.

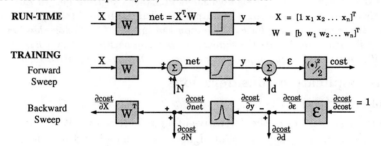

Figure 1: **Training Algorithm**

During training, replace discontinuous signums with sigmoids, and inject noise before the sigmoid on the forward sweep. The backward sweep calculation is the same as standard backpropagation.

The first block diagram in Figure 1 shows the neuron as it appears at run-time, a dot-product and hard-limiter. For simplicity in bookkeeping, the input, X, and weight, W, vectors are augmented to include the threshold bias for the output function. The next two diagrams show the neuron during training, where the signum has been replaced by a smooth sigmoid function. The input, X, is propagated through the forward sweep, finally resulting in an error, ϵ, and a cost. The derivative of this cost is calculated and propagated though the backward sweep, resulting in a $\partial \text{cost}/\partial X$ to be propagated to more units upstream, and a $\partial \text{cost}/\partial \text{net}$ to be used in calculating $\partial \text{cost}/\partial W$, which is used in the weight-update algorithm.

This is almost the same as training a standard neuron with backpropagation – the only difference involves the injection of zero-mean noise, N, immediately before the sigmoid. While the mechanics of the backward sweep are identical, different weight updates result because the forward sweep resulted in a different error.

Note that the noise injection does not corrupt the calculation of $\partial \text{cost}/\partial W$ (just as the desired signal does not). Using an unmodified backward sweep is not only the simplest thing to do, it does precisely the right calculations for estimating the weight gradient.

What makes this method useful is that as the noise level increases to cover the sigmoid's transition region, adaptation with the resulting $\partial \text{cost}/\partial W$ leads to a set of weights that work well for the signum network. To summarize, the training algorithm is:

- Replace the hard-limiters with sigmoids during training
- Inject noise immediately before the sigmoids on the forward sweep
- Use the exact same backward sweep as with standard backpropagation

2.2 Why it works

Without addition of noise, the network may train using values in the sigmoid transition region (roughly -0.8 to 0.8) that will be unavailable at run-time. Simply rounding off at run-time may introduce significant errors. The goal of noise injection is to move neuron activations away from the transition region during training, so round-off error will be small when the discontinuous functions are replaced.

An intuitive reason for adding the noise is to throw the neuron off its transition region, and effectively force it to hard-limit at the high or low value. Figure 2 shows how the neuron output distribution changes as the noise level increases. With no noise, only a single output can result, but as noise increases to cover most of the transition region, the output distribution approaches that of a hard-limiting function. Differentiability is maintained, however, so gradient information will be available to speed up learning. Since the noise has pushed the distribution to approximate a hard-limiting non-linearity, when the hard-limiter is re-introduced at run-time the performance degradation will be small.

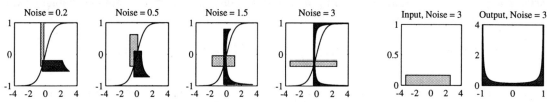

Figure 2: **Effect of Input Noise Level on Sigmoid Output Distribution**
Lightly-shaded region represents the sigmoid input probability distribution (in this case, $-0.3 +$ noise). Darkly-shaded region is the sigmoid output distribution (from -1 to 1), plotted horizontally to correspond to the sigmoid plot. Each distribution has an area of 1. As noise level increases, and the input distribution spreads out, the sigmoid output approaches that of a hard-limiter, while remaining differentiable. At right, input and output distributions are plotted separately.

2.3 Extensions, application considerations

2.3.1 Selection of noise level

One concern is the attenuating effect of the derivative-of-sigmoid function. When back-propagated through many layers of near-saturated sigmoids, the error signal is attenuated and may lead to slow learning. To handle this problem, it may be necessary to be gradual in increasing the noise level - slowly push the outputs from the linear region to the hard-limits, rather than all at once. However, since all the experiments presented here had a single layer of discontinuity, no such gradual increase was required.

For training networks with simple bi-level sigmoids, once the noise reached a sufficient level (roughly 0.5 and 3 in two different applications), there was no degradation if it were increased beyond that level. The only possible drawback is the attenuation effect mentioned above. The required noise level varies in different applications depending upon how sharp the decision boundaries would be with no noise (i.e. if it's a sharp sigmoid to begin with, not much noise is needed to force it off the transition region).

When multi-level sigmoids are used, as seen in Figure 9, there *is* an upper limit to noise level. Too much noise may cause the individual sigmoids to overlap, which in this example would blur out the middle level.

2.3.2 Discrete-valued functions other than bi-level signums

If adapting a system that contains discrete-valued functions that are not simple Heaviside step functions, the method may work if a continuously differentiable approximating function is used. For example, a function whose output can take on multiple discrete values may be approximated by combining multiple sigmoid functions. For the thruster mapping problem described in Section 4, the thruster can take on three states: forward, off, or backward. Two bi-level (-1,1) sigmoids were summed to produce a tri-level (-1,0,1) sigmoid.

2.3.3 Batch-learning

The randomness introduced with the addition of noise could make learning slow because of the reduction in signal-to-noise ratio in the weight gradient estimation. Batch-learning, using the exact same training set from one epoch to the next worked well (considering the "training set" to include the "input set" and "noise set"). Freezing the training set and noise set defines a fixed deterministic cost hyper-surface. With a fixed cost function, on-line tuning of momentum and learning rate can be applied to dramatically improve convergence rate.

2.3.4 Optimization of discrete-valued parameters

Another area where this method has potential is for optimization problems that have discrete valued parameters. For example, a design optimization problem where the task is to select the right DC motor, pipe diameter, or gear ratio from a finite set of discrete-valued options. It is expected that this method will extend well to this family of problems [8].

3 Application to Training Multi-Layer Signum Networks

In this section, this method is shown to extend to multiple layers of hard-limiting units with no modification. Figure 3 summarizes the method; during training, replace each hard-limiter with a sigmoid and zero-mean independent noise source. Note that the sharpness of the sigmoids does not matter *at all* here, since the sharpness factor simply multiplies the weights, and the weights are adapted.

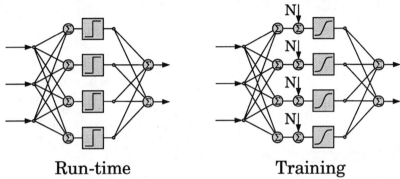

Run-time   Training

Figure 3: **A multi-layer signum network, seen at run-time and during training**

In the first test, an adaptive $3 - 5 - 4$ signum network is trained to emulate the input-output mapping defined by an independent, fixed, $3 - 10 - 4$ sigmoidal network. Fewer hidden neurons are used in the adaptive network to ensure that overfitting will not introduce unnecessary complications. The $3 - 10 - 4$ network's fixed weights were randomly chosen between -2 and 2.

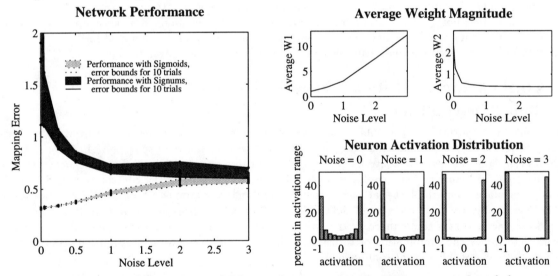

Figure 4: **Direct training of a multi-layer signum network, NN-generated training set**
Left: with higher noise levels, performance on the noisy sigmoidal network approaches that of the signum network, indicating that the noisy sigmoid is a valid (and differentiable!) approximation for the signum. Right: As noise increases, the network adapts to sharpen its sigmoids, causing the first layer weights to increase, and the sigmoid output distributions to approach hard-limiters. Activation distributions were collected over the whole training set, with no noise added.

Performance is shown in Figure 4. Each dot on the graph represents the final performance after a full training run (10,000 epochs or until a local minimum was reached). Seven values for noise level were chosen, and ten different network initial conditions were used at each noise value. With no noise, performance is good for the sigmoidal network, but when the signums are reintroduced at run-time, the error increases dramatically. One point is off the graph at an error of over 6 units. As noise increases, performance on the sigmoid network decreases, as expected, but the signum-network-performance improves, and approaches the sigmoid-network-performance. The weight magnitude and neuron activation distribution plots confirm that as noise increases, the noisy sigmoids behave like hard-limiters. Note that these activation distributions could not have been achieved by manually increasing the sharpness of the sigmoids - this would have had *zero* net effect since the network would adapt the first layer weights to *exactly* counteract the sharpness increase.

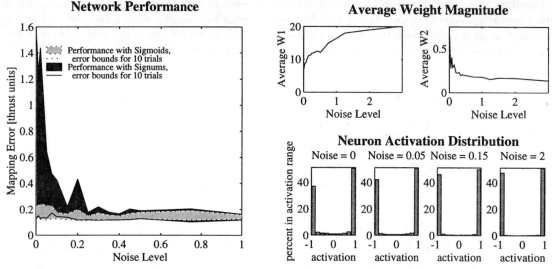

Figure 5: **Direct training of a network of hard-limiters to emulate optimal thruster mapping**

In the second application, the hard-limiting network is trained to emulate the optimal thruster mapping, which will be described in detail in the next section. For now, this mapping is used as an independent second test of the method. A similar dramatic improvement in hard-limiting performance occurs as noise increases past about 0.5. It is not shown on the plot, but good performance is obtained at least up to a noise level of three. The training set for this mapping represents continuous values being mapped to discrete values, so the first-layer weights are high (indicating sharp decision hyper-surfaces), even for *noise = 0*.

4 Application to Robot Thruster Control

4.1 Robot Description

Experiments are performed using a mobile robot, shown in Figure 6, that operates in a horizontal plane, using air-cushion technology to simulate the drag-free and zero-g characteristics of space[9]. The three degrees of freedom (x, y, θ) of the base are controlled using eight thrusters positioned around its perimeter, shown in the upper right of Figure 6. The on-off thrusters substantially complicate the control design, due to their discontinuous nature and the fact that each thruster simultaneously produces both a net force and torque.

The overall objective is to use a set of eight full-on, full-off air jet thrusters to approximate a continuous-valued force vector that is commanded by the position/attitude control law of the mobile robot. The neural network determines the combination of thrusters to fire that will generate a (normalized) resultant force vector as close as possible to that commanded.

4.2 Indirect training, Application of noisy sigmoids

Three different techniques used to solve this thruster mapping problem are summarized in the lower right of Figure 6. The first implementation used an exhaustive search at each sample period to find the thruster pattern minimizing the force error vector [9]. Symmetries are used to reduce the search space, but this method relies on testing every possible thruster pattern to find the one with minimum error. The second method used a neural network that had been trained directly to emulate the optimal mapping produced by the exhaustive search, described in Section 3 and in [10] [11].

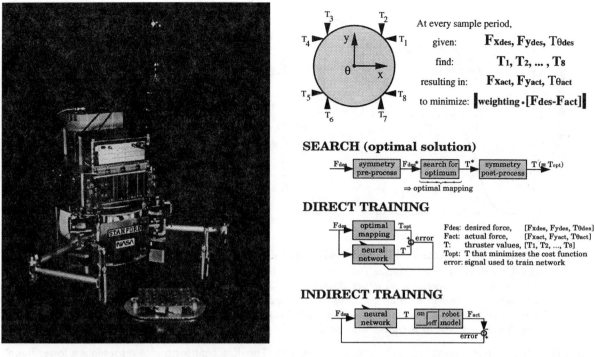

At every sample period,

given: $\mathbf{F_{xdes}, F_{ydes}, T_{\theta des}}$

find: $\mathbf{T_1, T_2, ... , T_8}$

resulting in: $\mathbf{F_{xact}, F_{yact}, T_{\theta act}}$

to minimize: $|\text{weighting} \cdot [\mathbf{F_{des} - F_{act}}]|$

SEARCH (optimal solution)

$\Rightarrow$ optimal mapping

DIRECT TRAINING

Fdes: desired force,   [Fxdes, Fydes, Tθdes]
Fact: actual force,   [Fxact, Fyact, Tθact]
T: thruster values, [T1, T2, ..., T8]
Topt: T that minimizes the cost function
error: signal used to train network

INDIRECT TRAINING

Figure 6: Free-flying robot, Thruster mapping problem definition, Solution methods

Left: The robot is a fully self-contained planar laboratory-prototype of a free-flying space robot complete with on-board gas, thrusters, electrical power, multi-processor computer system, camera, wireless Ethernet data/communications link, and two cooperating manipulators. It exhibits nearly frictionless motion as it floats above a granite surface plate on a 50 micron thick cushion of air. Right: [Desired forces ⇒ Thruster values] mapping: problem definition, solution methods. The on-off thrusters and coupling between forces and torque make this problem difficult.

The third method, indirect training, is presented here and shown in Figure 7. In this case, the optimal mapping is not used, and the NN must learn the mapping through experimentation with the plant model. This requires back-propagation of error through the discontinuous thrusters, which motivated development of the noise injection method presented in this paper.

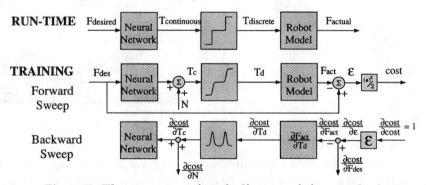

Figure 7: Thruster mapping, indirect training method

Figure 8 shows the result of training with two differentiable thruster models. During training with the continuous thruster models, the NN produces a mapping with a very low error, but when the signums are replaced at run-time, the error is large. This is because the network learned to optimize the solution using outputs that would be unavailable at run-time. The resulting roundoff error is unknown to the NN during training.

Figure 9 shows the results when the thrusters are modelled by *noisy* tri-level sigmoids. With *noise* = 0, error is high, corresponding to the data in Figure 8, but as noise increases, performance approaches that of the

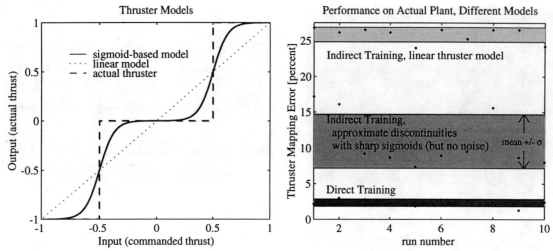

Figure 8: **Results of indirect training, two differentiable thruster models**

The sigmoid-based approximation (without noise) is better than the linear model, but has limited performance. The results from direct training represent a lower limit for comparison. Mapping error is average percent error above the optimal mapping (which results from an exhaustive search of all possible thruster combinations). The shaded areas represent the mean ± σ for ten different runs. 3 − 10 − 4 layered networks were used.

network trained directly (emulating the optimal mapping). The direct-performance represents a lower bound set by the functional complexity of the $3 - 10 - 4$ layered network. The best noise value in this application seems to be around 0.15, and the resulting noisy sigmoid is shown in the left side of Figure 9. Examining this figure, the sigmoid sharpness and noise levels seem to be set correctly according to intuition. As noise increases beyond 0.2, error increases (as the "off" region of the sigmoid becomes blurred) as expected, but the method is fairly robust to the noise value selected.

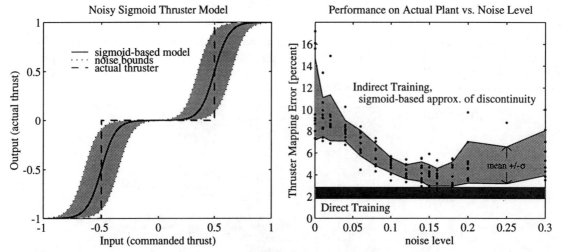

Figure 9: **Results of indirect training, noisy tri-level sigmoid thruster model**

Left: the sharpness (4) and noise level (0.15) for the noisy tri-level sigmoid appear to be intuitively correct. Right: as noise increases, performance approaches that of the network trained directly (emulating the optimal mapping). 3 − 10 − 4 layered networks were used.

A good solution results when noise is added because it prevents the network from using a solution that uses non-saturated portions of the tri-level sigmoid. Such a solution would give a nearly random output and high error during training. The training algorithm must find a solution that works well *despite* the noise addition. This means the expected value of the output must be well into the saturated region to consistently work well. The results approximate the optimal solution very well, and work when the tri-level sigmoids are replaced with tri-level signums.

5 Conclusions

This paper has described a new technique that allows backpropagation learning to work with systems containing discrete-valued functions, despite the discontinuity that exists between discrete values. The modification to backpropagation is very small, simply requiring sigmoidal approximation of the discrete-valued functions, and careful injection of noise into the smooth approximating function on the forward sweep. The noise injection is critical to ensuring that the noisy sigmoid behaves like a signum during training.

Multi-layered networks of hard-limiters require simpler processing hardware than do multi-layered sigmoid networks. Sigmoid networks are commonly used due to their increased functionality as well as the lack of a reliable training algorithm for signum networks. Multi-layered signum networks have now been successfully trained using this noise injection method in two different applications, clearly demonstrating its usefulness in this area.

Application to a complex thruster control problem, with implementation on a laboratory model of a free-flying space robot, has demonstrated the method's realizability and usefulness for on-off control problems.

In each application, the training behavior in the presence of noise has been well-understood, and the algorithm appears to be relatively robust to the amplitude of the injected noise.

Acknowledgements

The author wishes to thank AFOSR and NASA for their support of this research, and Tim McLain, Dr. Larry Pfeffer, Glen Sapilewski, and Prof. Bernard Widrow for their help reviewing the paper.

References

[1] Paul J. Werbos. *Beyond Regression: New Tools for Prediction and Analysis in the Behavioral Sciences.* PhD thesis, Harvard University, Cambridge, MA 02142, August 1974.

[2] David E. Rumelhart, Geoffrey E. Hinton, and Ronald J. Williams. Learning internal representations by error propagation. In David E. Rumelhart, James L. McClelland, and the PDP Research Group, editors, *Parallel Distributed Processing*, page 318. The MIT Press, Cambridge, MA 02142, 1986.

[3] B. Widrow and M.A. Lehr. 30 years of adaptive neural networks: perceptron, madaline, and backpropagation. *Proceedings of the IEEE*, 78(9):1415–42, September 1990.

[4] Frank Rosenblatt. *Principles of Neurodynamics: Perceptrons and the Theory of Brain Mechanisms.* Spartan Books, Washington, D.C., 1962.

[5] M.E. Hoff, Jr. *Learning Phenomena in Networks of Adaptive Switching Circuits.* PhD thesis, Stanford University, Stanford, CA 94305, July 1962. Tech. Rep. 1556-1, Stanford Electron. Labs.

[6] R. Winter and B. Widrow. Madaline rule II: a training algorithm for neural networks. In *IEEE International Conference on Neural Networks*, volume 1, pages 401–408, San Diego CA, July 1988.

[7] P.L. Bartlett and T. Downs. Using random weights to train multilayer networks of hard-limiting units. *IEEE Transactions on Neural Networks*, 3(2):202–210, March 1992.

[8] Timothy W. McLain. Personal communication, 1993.

[9] Marc A. Ullman. *Experiments in Autonomous Navigation and Control of Multi-Manipulator, Free-Flying Space Robots.* PhD thesis, Stanford University, Stanford, CA 94305, March 1993.

[10] Edward Wilson and Stephen M. Rock. Experiments in control of a free-flying space robot using fully-connected neural networks. In *Proceedings of the World Congress on Neural Networks*, volume 3, pages 157–162, Portland OR, July 1993.

[11] Edward Wilson. Experiments in neural network control of a free-flying space robot. In *Proceedings of the Fifth Workshop on Neural Networks: Academic/Industrial/NASA/Defense*, pages 204–209, San Francisco CA, November 1993.

Fuzzy-controlled, Parallel Coordinate Descent in a Backpropagation Net

W.-M. Lippe, Th. Feuring, A. Tenhagen *

– Institut fuer Informatik – WWU Muenster –

Einsteinstr. 62

48149 Muenster, Germany

November 1993

Abstract

In classic backpropagation nets, as introduced by Rumelhart et al.[1], the weights are modified according to the method of steepest descent. The goal of this weight modification is to minimise the error in net-outputs for a given training set.

Basing upon Jacobs' work [2], we point out drawbacks of steepest descent and suggest improvements on it. These yield a backpropagation net, which adjusts its weights according to a parallel coordinate descent method, whose parameters are being fuzzy-controlled.

1 Introduction

The backpropagation net is a multilayer neural net consisting of one input-layer, one output-layer and at least one hidden-layer. The weights $\vec{w} = (w_1, \ldots, w_n)$ of this net are modified by means of the *backpropagation learning rule*, which is supposed to perform steepest descent with the *mean-squared-error*-function $F(\vec{w})$.

To accomplish this, Rumelhart et al. introduced the *generalised delta rule*:

$$\vec{w}^{\text{new}} = \vec{w}^{\text{old}} - \eta \nabla_{\vec{w}} F(\vec{w}) \tag{1}$$

$\nabla_{\vec{w}} F(\vec{w})$ is the gradient of F with respect to $\vec{w}$ and gives the direction of maximum increase relative to $\vec{w}$. $\eta > 0$ is a constant, which is referred to as the *learnrate*. The portion of $-\nabla_{\vec{w}} F(\vec{w})$ by which the weight vector $\vec{w}$ is moved, is determined by the value of this learnrate.

Image(F) can be interpreted as a surface over the space of weight vectors. $F(\vec{w})$ gives the 'height' of this *error surface* at $\vec{w}$. The goal of all weight adjustments is to find a $\vec{w}^*$ for which F takes on a global minimum $F(\vec{w}^*) = F_{\min}$ (typically, $F_{\min} > 0$).

An advantageous property of the method of steepest descent is its global convergence, which may only lead to a local minimum though. Many modifications of the backpropagation algorithm that find a minimum of the error surface more quickly, can only guarantee local convergence. The *Quickprop* algorithm is an example for this; it implements an approximation of Newton's method and its order of convergence is two.

The parallel coordinate descent we propose, which provides each weight with its own learnrate, comes without this disadvantage and it seems to find its way along the error surfaces faster than the original backpropagation algorithm. By introducing a fuzzy control of some descent parameters we are able to further improve the performance of the algorithm.

We will now point out the drawbacks of steepest descent and consider the improvements suggested by Jacobs [2], thereby putting forward coordinate descent and the *delta-bar-delta rule*. Subsequently a hybrid from delta-bar-delta and *momentum version* is introduced and a fuzzy control of this hybrid is explained. In the end we test our new algorithm and compare its performance with that of the generalised delta rule and delta-bar-delta rule.

---

*e-mail: lippe@math.uni-muenster.de, feuring@math.uni-muenster.de, tenhaga@math.uni-muenster.de

2   Problems with the Method of Steepest Descent

The method of steepest descent, which is implemented by the classic backpropagation learning law has some weak points, that take effect on typically shaped error surfaces.

Hecht-Nielsen [3] makes the following statements about the shape of backpropagation error surfaces:

- Many error surfaces have extensive flat areas and troughs with little slope.
- The symmetry of the net weights (each weight vector behaves equivalent to certain permutations of itself) causes many global minima to exist. As a result, most error surfaces appear rough in many dimensions.
- Error surfaces with real local (not global) minima at a 'high' errorlevel do exist. Little is known about the position and number of these minima.

Jacobs [2] closely examined the behaviour of steepest descent on backpropagation error surfaces and reached these conclusions:

- If the error surface is flat in the dimension of one of the weights, the corresponding derivative is (absolutely speaking) small. Because of the gradient-component being that small, changing the corresponding weight by a portion of it (determined by the learnrate η) yields only a slight adjustment of the weight. If the error surface is flat in all dimensions, application of the learning law takes almost no effect. Consequently the progress of the method is very slow in situations like these; it may even stop because of computing-inaccuracies.
- If — on the other hand — the curvature of the error surface is high for some weight-dimensions, a related problem with (absolutely speaking) large gradient-components arises. The weight vector may be moved too far – thus overshooting the minimum.
- The gradient gives the direction of the steepest ascent. But the negative gradient does not necessarily show the shortest way to a minimum. So steepest descent may make a detour on its way to a minimum and thus may encounter more difficulties.

3   Improving the Backpropagation Learning Algorithm

Jacobs [2] discusses some improvements to the generalised delta rule, upon which we enlarge:

3.1   Parallel Coordinate Descent

The learnrate η determines decisively by what amount each weight is adjusted. Because one learnrate for all weights cannot allow for the different curvature of the error surface in each dimension, each weight should be equipped with an individual learnrate.

By using individual learnrates, the learning law no longer moves a point on the error surface in the direction of the negative gradient and therefore no longer performs steepest descent.

Actually, a kind of coordinate descent is now executed. This does not minimise $F(\vec{w})$ directly, but searches for $\min_{w_i}(F(\vec{w}))$ for each component w_i of $\vec{w}$. Unlike 'normal' coordinate descent methods, which change the weights one at a time (for instance the Gauss-Southwell method [4]), this method adjusts all components of $\vec{w}$ in parallel.

The learning law implementing this parallel coordinate descent looks like this (it is derived by slightly changing (1) (to allow for individual learnrates)):

$$\vec{w}^{\text{new}} \quad = \quad \vec{w}^{\text{old}} - \sum_{i=1}^{n} \eta_i E_{i,i} \nabla_{\vec{w}} F(\vec{w}), \tag{2}$$

where n is the dimension of $\vec{w}$; $\eta_i > 0$ is the learnrate corresponding to w_i; $E_{i,i}$ is a $n \times n$ Matrix, with every component $= 0$, except one component with row $=$ column $= i$, which is $= 1$, $(1 \leq i \leq n)$. Now holds:

Theorem 3.1 *If the preliminaries for the convergence of the classic backpropagation algorithm are given, the parallel coordinate descent method will also converge to a minimum of the error surface.*

This can be prooved analogously to the corresponding proof for the backpropagation algorithm (if all η_i are equal the method behaves like steepest descent).

3.2 The Delta-Bar-Delta Rule

Because the error surface curvature (in each dimension) is not the same everywhere, every learnrate η_i should be allowed to vary. This variation can be controlled by the following heuristics:

When the sign of the derivative of a weight is the same on several consecutive steps, the corresponding learnrate should be increased (we suppose the error surface to be flat in this situation). When the sign alternates on consecutive steps, the learnrate should be decreased.

The delta-bar-delta rule was developed by Jacobs [2]. It is a variation of the generalised delta rule and implements the heuristics mentioned above. In fact it consists of two rules: one for weight adjustment and the other for control of the learnrates.

The weights are modified analogous to (2):

$$\vec{w}(t+1) = \vec{w}(t) - \sum_{i=1}^{n} \eta_i(t) E_{i,i} \nabla_{\vec{w}} F(\vec{w}), \tag{3}$$

where $\vec{w}(t)$ is the weight vector's value at time step t and $\eta_i(t)$ is the value of η_i at time step t.

Every learnrate is adjusted according to $\eta(t+1) = \eta(t) + \Delta\eta(t)$, (for convenience we write η instead of η_i) with:

$$\Delta\eta(t) = \begin{cases} \kappa & \text{, if } \bar{\delta}(t-1)\delta(t) > 0 \\ -\phi\,\eta(t) & \text{, if } \bar{\delta}(t-1)\delta(t) < 0 \\ 0 & \text{else} \end{cases} \tag{4}$$

where $\qquad \delta(t) = \dfrac{\partial F(t)}{\partial w(t)} \qquad$ and $\qquad \begin{aligned} \bar{\delta}(t) &= (1-\theta)\delta(t) + \theta\bar{\delta}(t-1) \\ &= (1-\theta)\sum_{i=0}^{t} \theta^i\,\delta(t-i) \end{aligned}$

$\kappa > 0$ and $\phi \in [0,1]$ are constants, θ is $\in [0,1]$, κ, ϕ, θ are the same for every learnrate.

When the sign of the current (step t) derivative and that of the exponential average at step $(t-1)$ are the same ($\approx$ the error surface is flat), the learnrate is increased by κ. When the signs are different ($\approx$ the curvature of the error surface is high) the learnrate is decreased by a portion (determined by ϕ) of itself.

The η_i are decreased exponentially by the $\bar{\delta}$-δ rule, thereby guaranteeing fast decrease and $\eta_i > 0$.

The increase of the learnrates is done linearly to prevent them from increasing too quickly.

The effectiveness of the net depends decisively on κ: Set to an inadequately small value, the increase of the learnrates will take place too slow. If κ is set too large, the algorithm will become very inaccurate. Taking into consideration the existence of extensive flat areas on error surfaces (see (2)), we see the importance of a good choice for κ (in flat areas the first case of (4) takes effect). A 'good choice' for κ can only be made after a couple of experiments.

Ideally, κ should be set to a different (appropriate) value for each weight and each step. Therefore we introduce a fuzzy control of κ in (4).

3.3 The Momentum Version

This modification of the generalised delta rule leaves the (single) learnrate unchanged.

At step t each weight $w(t)$ (no indices for convenience) is adjusted according to:

$$\begin{aligned} w(t+1) &= w(t) + \Delta w(t) \tag{5} \\ \Delta w(t) &= -(1-\alpha)\,\eta\,\frac{\partial F(t)}{\partial w(t)} + \alpha\,\Delta w(t-1) = -(1-\alpha)\,\eta\sum_{i=0}^{t}\alpha^i\,\frac{\partial F(t-i)}{\partial w(t-i)} \tag{6} \end{aligned}$$

where $\alpha \in [0,1]$ (referred to as the *momentum term*) and η is the learnrate. $\Delta w(t-1)$ gives the amount by which the weight w was changed during the previous step. Typically, α is set ≈ 0.9. This is an arbitrary choice and may have to be revised after a couple of experiments.

When the derivatives have the same sign on consecutive steps, the sum in (6) grows larger (causing the change in w to be greater), otherwise it stays small (causing smaller change in w).

The momentum version has chiefly two weak points:

There may exist an upper bound on the sum in (6)(if all derivatives are $= 0$, for instance); thereby the greatest amount by which a weight can be changed is limited, which is not desirable in certain flat areas of the error surface. In addition, the sign of the sum starting at $i = 1$ may differ from the sign of the current derivative; thus — in an extreme situation — w may be moved in the wrong direction.

3.4 The Hybrid Rule

The hybrid rule uses individual, variable learnrates and a momentum term. The learnrates are adjusted according to the learnrate updating rule (4) of the $\bar{\delta}$-δ rule. The momentum version (5) (with individual learnrates) is used as weight modification rule.

Without further changes both methods do not cooperate ideally (which is what Jacobs observed in his comparison of pure $\bar{\delta}$-δ rule with the hybrid rule).

On the one hand the *momentum-term* being large (i.e. $(1 - \alpha)$ is small), causes the learnrate to be less important in determining the weight change – the benefits of the complicated $\bar{\delta}$-δ rule take only little effect. On the other hand the effectiveness of the momentum version on flat areas of the error surface is greater, if α is large, whereas α should be small on areas with high curvature.

4 The Fuzzy Controller

From our observations in **(3.2)**, **(3.3)** and **(3.4)** we draw the following conclusion: The hybrid rule (from **(3.4)**) can be improved strongly by allowing the parameters κ (of the $\bar{\delta}$-δ rule) and α (of the momentum version) to vary. To control these parameters we use a fuzzy controller. The heuristics for adjusting κ and α are easy to implement this way. Also, fuzzy control yields flexible outputs and we do not have to think about exponential and/or linear de- or increases. The heuristics we used in the construction of the controller (see **(App. B)**) are:

The longer the weight vector is in a flat area of the error surface the larger κ and α may be set. κ should be allowed to become large enough, so it can take effect despite of a large α. In areas of high curvature κ and α should be small. We employ a Sugeno-type fuzzy controller [5], which is based upon the 'familiar' IF...THEN rules. In contrast to these 'familiar' constructs the Sugeno-type THEN instructions do not contain any fuzzy sets but *crisp* functions. The output of the controller is the average of these functions' values. As a result of that, no defuzzification has to be performed and the fuzzy controller works faster than the 'familiar' one.

For use in the IF clauses, a couple of fuzzy sets is defined. These describe the current curvature of the error surface (for instance VERYLOW, NOTSURE, HIGH). In a new variable we record how often each case in (4) is selected. This new variable is then used to represent the curvature of the error surface.

4.1 Computational Expense

The new learning law is more complicated to compute than the generalised delta rule. A couple of extra additions, multiplications and comparisons have to be executed. These additional computations take less time than performing one complete training step. The additional expense is justifiable since the faster convergence of our new method decreases the number of training steps which have to be computed.

5 Conclusions

We modified the classic backpropagation algorithm to perform a parallel coordinate descent, based upon Jacobs' ideas. Heuristics about the properties of the error surface further have been implemented in a fuzzy control of the parameters κ and α. The modified net needs far less training steps to 'learn' a training set, without too much extra computations. In addition we still have a method with global convergence.

Appendix A: Two Tests

Our new learning law (referred to as *fuzzy hybrid*) is tested with two different problems. We compare the results of fuzzy hybrid, with the performance of the generalised delta rule and the $\bar{\delta}$-δ rule. The parameters of each rule were set to values that lead to fastest convergence.

1. The net is trained to learn the XOR function. The training was repeated 40 times, starting with a different weight vector each time. The diagram shows the average of the results.

2. The training set consisted of 28 examples of $f(x) = x^2$, where $x \in [1, 10]$. The diagram shows the (typical) results of training the net once.

Note: η_0 and κ_0 are starting values that have to be set by the user.

The y-axis of each diagram is scaled logarithmically.

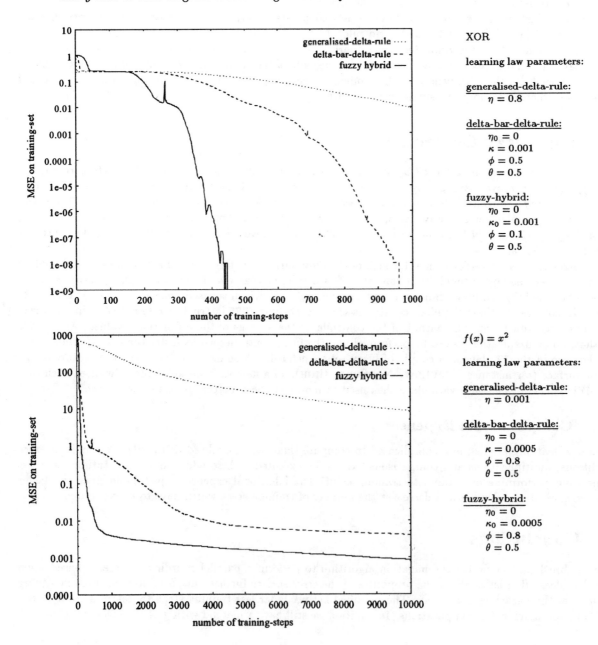

Appendix B: Details of the Fuzzy Controller

The value of the variable c_i describes the curvature of the error surface in the i-th dimension (the corresponding weight is w_i):

$$c_i := \begin{cases} c_i + 1 & \text{, if } \eta_i \text{ was increased by } \kappa, \\ c_i - 5 & \text{, if } \eta_i \text{ was decreased by } -\phi\,\eta_i(t). \end{cases}$$

κ and ϕ are parameters of the $\bar{\delta}$-δ rule and η_i is the learnrate corresponding to w_i.
Additionally, we make certain, that $c_i \in [-1, 100]$.

κ and α are controlled by the following rules:

$$\text{IF } (c_i \text{ is} \left\{ \begin{array}{l} \text{(V)ERYLOW} \\ \text{(L)OW} \\ \text{(N)OTSURE} \\ \text{(H)IGH} \end{array} \right\}) \text{ THEN } \kappa := \left\{ \begin{array}{l} V(c_i) * 100\kappa_0 \\ L(c_i) * 10\kappa_0 \\ N(c_i) * \kappa_0 \\ H(c_i) * \kappa_0/10 \end{array} \right\} ; \ \alpha := \left\{ \begin{array}{l} V(c_i) * 0.9 \\ L(c_i) * 0.7 \\ N(c_i) * 0.3 \\ H(c_i) * 0.01 \end{array} \right\}$$

κ_0 is a starting value that has to be set by the user.
(κ and α are computed newly for each weight at each step, so their values do not have to be stored.)

The four fuzzy sets are defined by:

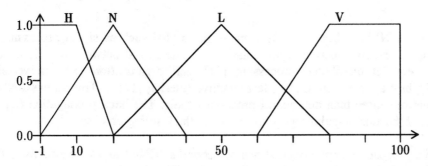

References

[1] Rumelhart, D.E., Hinton, G.E., Williams, R.J.,
"Learning Internal Representations by Error Propagation", in
Rumelhart, D.E., McCleland, J.L. [Eds.], *Parallel Distributed Processing: Explorations in the Microstructure of Cognition*, 1, pp.318-362, MIT Press, Cambridge MA, 1986.

[2] Jacobs, Robert A.,
"Increased Rates of Convergence Through Learning Rate Adaption", in *Neural Networks*, Vol.1, pp.295-307, 1988.

[3] Hecht-Nielsen, Robert,
"The Backpropagation Neural Network", in *Neurocomputing*, pp. 124-137, Addison-Wesley, 1991.

[4] Luenberger, D.G.,
"Coordinate Descent Methods", in *Linear and Nonlinear Programming*, pp. 227-230, Addison-Wesley, 1989.

[5] Sugeno, M., Takagi, T.,
"Fuzzy identification of systems and its applications to modeling and control", in *IEEE Trans. Systems Man Cybernetics*, Vol.15, pp.116–132, 1985.

THE VECTOR BACK PROPAGATION ALGORITHM

M. IBN KAHLA, S. PUECHMOREL, and F. CASTANIE

ENSEEIHT-GAPSE, 2 rue Camichel
31071 TOULOUSE Cedex, FRANCE
Phone : (33)61588350, Fax : (33)61588237
email : IBNKAHLA@LEN7.ENSEEIHT.FR

ABSTRACT

In many domains where the data belongs to a multidimensional vector space, there is a need to have vector representation and vector processing of signals. This paper gives a new tool to do this: The multi-layer vector neural network. In this architecture, the neuron inputs and outputs are vectors, the weights are matrices, and the activation functions are vector functions. The training technique presented in this paper is the vector back propagation algorithm which is a generalization of the scalar back propagation algorithm.

1. INTRODUCTION

Real-valued neural networks (RNN) have been applied to many fields [14] such as signal processing, pattern recognition, vector quantization, function approximation... These neural network models have very interesting properties: Parallel distributed processing [21], self organization [13], universal approximation [4, 9, 11, 17], best approximation [10], fast adaptive filtering [12] ... This allows RNN to have, in general, better performances than non neural processing tools. The back propagation (BP) algorithm [16, 21, 22] is one of the most popular algorithms used for the learning process.

Recently, some authors have proposed complex-valued neural networks (CNN) and extended the BP algorithm to the complex plane [5, 8, 15]. These architectures can be applied to domains where signals have complex representation (e.g. signal processing and digital communications) [5, 6, 7].

In many domains, like array signal processing, the data belongs to a vector space and its treatment needs vector mappings. It is of a great importance, therefore, to have neural networks that allow not only a vector representation of signals, but also a vector processing of them. Scalar-Valued Neural Networks (i.e. RNN and CNN) can not allow both vector representation and vector processing because the activation functions are scalar functions.

In this paper we present the multi-layer vector neural network (MVNN). In this architecture, the neuron inputs and outputs are vectors, the weights are represented by matrices, and the activation functions are vector functions. The training algorithm is called the Vector Back Propagation (VBP) algorithm because it propagates error vector terms in a backwards fashion. The classic BP algorithm [16, 21, 22] corresponds to the VBP when all variables are scalars and the activation functions are defined in the real or the complex domain.

The VBP algorithm can be useful in many applications dealing with vector data like vector quantization, array signal processing, principal component analysis, digital communications over non linear channels (with complex valued signals), speech coding, classification and pattern recognition, vector function approximation, learning under constraints, robotics, parallel distributed processing ...

This paper is restricted to MVNNs, an analogous analysis concerning vector self organisation and associative maps (VSAMs) is discussed in [18]. VSAMs generalise Kohonen feature maps (KFM) and the adaptive resonance theory (ART) to multidimensional vector spaces.

Since vector spaces are linear manifolds, both MVNNs and VSAMs are special cases of the manifold neural network (MNN) presented in [18, 19].

The paper is organized as follows: In part 2 we describe the MVNN architecture. Part 3 gives the VBP learning rule. Finally, some concluding remarks are given in part 4.

2. THE MULTI-LAYER VECTOR NEURAL NETWORK

The letters R and C will denote the set of real and complex numbers, respectively. Let Φ be either R or C. E_K denotes a K dimensional vector space over Φ. $B_K = (e_1, .., e_K)$ denotes the canonic basis of E_K which is supposed to be normed by means of the usual Euclidean metric. $L(E_{K_1}, E_{K_2})$ denotes the field of linear mappings defined from E_{K_1} to E_{K_2}. $F(E_{K_1}, E_{K_2})$ denotes the field of vector functions defined from E_{K_1} to E_{K_2}.

The multi-layer vector neural network consists of many vector units, or vector neurons. A vector neuron is composed of a vector linear combiner Σ and a vector activation function f_{ik} :

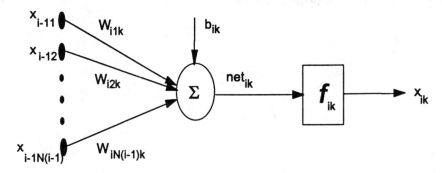

Figure 1 : The vector neuron

Note that the indices i and k are not important here. They refer to the layer index and the neuron index, respectively, see figure 2.

The input $\{x_{i-1j}\}, 1 \le j \le N(i-1)$ is composed of $N(i-1)$ vectors of a vector space $E_{K(i-1)}$. The weights $\{W_{ijk}\}, 1 \le j \le N(i-1)$ are $K(i) \times K(i-1)$ matrices (they correspond to matrix representations of N linear mappings of $L(E_{K(i-1)}, E_{K(i)})$). The bias b_{ik} belongs to $E_{K(i)}$. The linear combiner sums the bias and the input vectors $\{x_{i-1j}\}$ multiplied by the corresponding matrix weights:

$$net_{ik}((x_{i-11}, .., x_{i-1N(i-1)})) = \sum_{j=1}^{N(i-1)} W_{ijk} x_{i-1j} + b_{ik}$$

The activation function f_{ik} maps the vector net_{ik} into a vector x_{ik} :

$$
\begin{aligned}
f_{ik} &: E_{K(i)} \to E_{K(i)} \\
net_{ik} &\to x_{ik} = f_{ik}(net_{ik}) = f_{ik}(\sum_{j=1}^{N(i-1)} W_{ijk} x_{i-1j} + b_{ik}) \quad (1)
\end{aligned}
$$

In the canonic basis $B_{K(i)}$, vector x_{ik} can be written

$$x_{ik} = \begin{bmatrix} f_{ik}^1(net_{ik}) \\ \cdot \\ \cdot \\ f_{ik}^{K(i)}(net_{ik}) \end{bmatrix}.$$

Note that the function f_{ik}^p (corresponding to the direction e_p), is function of the vector net_{ik} (and not of the scalar f_{ik}^p). This is the main difference with SNNs.

f_{ik} can be any vector function (differentiable or not). For example, it can be the generalized characteristic function (in the case of vector spaces defined over R) :

$$x_{ik} = f_{ik}(net_{ik}) = [1...1]^t \quad \text{if } net_{ik}^l > 0 \quad \text{for all } 1 \le l \le K(i)$$
$$= [0..0]^t \quad \text{if } net_{ik}^l \le 0 \quad \text{for all } 1 \le l \le K(i)$$

An other example of f_{ik}, is the multidimensional quadratic sigmoidal function:

$$f_{ik}(net_{ik}) = \begin{bmatrix} th(net_{ik}^t A_1 \, net_{ik}) \\ \vdots \\ th(net_{ik}^t A_{K(i)} \, net_{ik}) \end{bmatrix}.$$

where $\{A_p\}, 1 \le p \le K(i)$ are $K(i) \times K(i)$ matrices and th is the hyperbolic tangent function.

The multi-layer vector neural network is shown in figure 2.

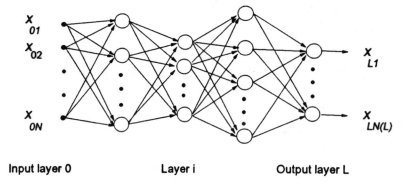

Input layer 0   Layer i   Output layer L

Figure 2 : Multi-layer Vector Neural Network.

In figures 1 and 2, i denotes the layer index, x_{ik} the output of neuron k of layer i, W_{ijk} the matrix weight that links vector x_{i-1j} to neuron k of layer i, $N(i)$ the number of neurons in layer i, and $E_{K(i)}$ the vector space to which belong layer i outputs.

The network works as follows: $N(0)$ vectors (of a vector space $E_{K(0)}$) are fed to the network input and are processed in a feed forward fashion through intermediate vector spaces: Each layer i has in its inputs $N(i-1)$ vectors (of the vector space $E_{K(i-1)}$) and maps them into $N(i)$ vectors (of the vector space $E_{K(i)}$). If we denote by Ψ_i this mapping, then we have

$$\Psi_i : \quad \left(E_{K(i-1)}\right)^{N(i-1)} \rightarrow \left(E_{K(i)}\right)^{N(i)}$$
$$(x_{i-11},...,x_{i-1N(i-1)}) \rightarrow (x_{i1},...,x_{iN(i)})$$

The global network input-output mapping represents a function Ψ which belongs to the set of vector functions $F(E_{K(0)})^{N(0)},(E_{K(L)})^{N(L)})$:

$$\Psi : \quad \left(E_{K(0)}\right)^{N(0)} \rightarrow \left(E_{K(L)}\right)^{N(L)}$$
$$(x_{01},...,x_{0N(0)}) \rightarrow (x_{L1},...,x_{LN(L)})$$

If all variables are scalars ($E_{K(i)} = \Phi$), then the VNN is reduced to an SNN. Therefore, the mapping Ψ_{SNN} belongs to $F(\Phi^{N(0)},\Phi^{N(L)})$.

Many algorithms can be used to train the VNN (in supervised or unsupervised learning procedures), in this paper we describe only the vector back propagation algorithm which is a generalization of the scalar back propagation algorithm. Other algorithms used for SNN (see for instance [14, 16]) can also be generalized to VNN.

3. THE VECTOR BACK PROPAGATION ALGORITHM (VBP)

In supervised learning, $N(0)$ input vectors $\{x_{01},...,x_{0N(0)}\}$ (of a vector space $E_{K(0)}$), and $N(L)$ desired output vectors $\{d_1,...,d_{N(L)}\}$ (of a vector space $E_{K(L)}$), are presented to the neural network at time t. The goal is to adjust the network weights in order to minimize a cost function ξ.

We define the error vectors $\varepsilon_j(t)$ at time t as the difference between the desired output vectors $d_j(t)$ and the output vectors $x_{Lj}(t)$:

$$\varepsilon_j(t) = d_j(t) - x_{Lj}(t) , \quad 1 \le j \le N(L)$$

The cost function is defined as the sum of the norm of these error vectors:

$$\xi = \sum_{j=1}^{N(L)} \left\| \varepsilon_j \right\|^2 = \sum_{j=1}^{N(L)} \bar{\varepsilon}_j{}^t \varepsilon_j = \sum_{j=1}^{N(L)} \sum_{l=1}^{K(L)} \bar{\varepsilon}_j{}^l \varepsilon_j{}^l$$

where $\bar{\varepsilon}_j$ denotes the conjugate of vector ε_j, and ε_j^t denotes the transpose.

Without loss of generality, we suppose that $\Phi = R$. A similar study can be done for the case $\Phi = C$ (one should calculate the derivatives according to the conjugate variables).

We suppose that the vector activation functions are all differentiable.

3.1 Notation

We denote by $J(f_{ik})$ the differential matrix of f_{ik} with respect to vector net_{ik}:

$$J(f_{ik}) = \left[\frac{\partial f_{ik}^p}{\partial net_{ik}^l} \right] , \quad 1 \le p \le K(i) \text{ (line index)} , \quad 1 \le l \le K(i) \text{ (column index)}$$

We denote by $J_{W_{ijk}}(\xi)$ the differential matrix of ξ with respect to the matrix W_{ijk}:

$$J_{W_{ijk}}(\xi) = \left[\frac{\partial \xi}{\partial W_{ijk}^{mn}} \right] , \quad 1 \le m \le K(i) \text{ (line index)} , \quad 1 \le n \le K(i-1) \text{ (column index)}$$

We denote by $J_{b_{ik}}(\xi)$ the gradient of ξ with respect to vector b_{ik}:

$$J_{b_{ik}}(\xi) = \left[\frac{\partial \xi}{\partial b_{ik}^l} \right] , \quad 1 \le l \le K(i) \text{ (line index)}$$

We denote by δ_{ik} the gradient of ξ with respect to vector x_{ik}:

$$\delta_{ik}(\xi) = \left[\frac{\partial \xi}{\partial x_{ik}^l} \right] , \quad 1 \le l \le K(i) \text{ (line index)}$$

3.2 The VBP Algorithm

The VBP algorithm minimizes the cost function ξ by updating weights and biases according to the gradient search technique:

$$W_{ijk}(t+1) = W_{ijk}(t) - \mu J_{W_{ijk}}(\xi) \qquad (2)$$

$$b_{ik}(t+1) = b_{ik}(t) - \mu J_{b_{ik}}(\xi) \qquad (3)$$

μ is a small positive constant.

The term $J_{W_{ijk}}(\xi)$ can be expressed as a function of 3 terms:

$$J_{W_{ijk}}(\xi) = \left(J(f_{ik})\right)^t \delta_{ik} x_{i-1j}^t \qquad (4)$$

The second term of the right hand side (RHS) of (4) δ_{ik}, called error term, depends on the cost function ξ, the other two depend only on layer i parameters (i.e. the activation function and the input vectors).

The term $J_{b_{ijk}}(\xi)$ can be expressed as a function of two terms (5). The first depends only on layer i, the second is the error term δ_{ik}:

$$J_{b_{ik}}(\xi) = \left(J(f_{ik})\right)^t \delta_{ik} \qquad (5)$$

The error terms δ_{ik} are computed efficiently by starting with the output layer:

$$\delta_{Lk} = \begin{bmatrix} \dfrac{\partial \xi}{\partial x_{Lk}^1} \\ \cdot \\ \cdot \\ \dfrac{\partial \xi}{\partial x_{Lk}^{N(L)}} \end{bmatrix} = \sum_{j=1}^{N(L)} \sum_{p=1}^{K(L)} \begin{bmatrix} \dfrac{\partial (\varepsilon_j^p)^2}{\partial x_{Lk}^1} \\ \cdot \\ \cdot \\ \dfrac{\partial (\varepsilon_j^p)^2}{\partial x_{Lk}^{N(L)}} \end{bmatrix} = -2\varepsilon_k \qquad (6)$$

and working backwards through the other layers:

$$\delta_{ik} = \sum_{k'=1}^{N(i+1)} \left(J(f_{i+1k'})W_{i+1kk'}\right)^t \delta_{i+1k'} \qquad (7)$$

The Vector Back Propagation Algorithm:

Step 1. Initialize matrix weights and vector offsets:
   Set all matrix weights to small values (according to a matrix norm), and all vector biases to small values (according to the Euclidean norm).

Step 2. Present inputs and desired outputs:
   Present $N(0)$ input vectors $\left\{ x_{01}, ..., x_{0N(0)} \right\}$ (of a vector space $E_{K(0)}$), and desired output vectors $\left\{ d_1, ..., d_{N(L)} \right\}$ (of a vector space $E_{K(L)}$)

Step 3. Calculate actual outputs:
   Use the formula (1) to calculate the outputs $\left\{ x_{L1}, ..., x_{LN(L)} \right\}$

Step 4. Adapt weights:
   $$w_{ijk}(t+1) = w_{ijk}(t) - \mu \left(J(f_{ik})\right)^t \delta_{ik} x_{i-1j}^t$$
   $$b_{ik}(t+1) = b_{ik}(t) - \mu \left(J(f_{ik})\right)^t \delta_{ik}$$
   δ_{ik} is calculated as follows:
   For the output layer: $\delta_{Lk} = -2(d_k - x_{Lk})$ (a $K(L)$-dim. vector)
   For layer i: $\delta_{ik} = \sum\limits_{k'=1}^{N(i+1)} \left(J(f_{i+1k'})W_{i+1kk'}\right)^t \delta_{i+1k'}$ (a $K(i)$-dim. vector)

Step 5. Repeat by going to step 2.

---

4. CONCLUSION AND FUTURE WORK:

In this paper we have presented the Multi-layer Vector Neural Network (MVNN) whose neuron inputs and outputs are vectors, weights are matrices, and activation functions are vector functions. The Vector Back Propagation (VBP) algorithm, which is a generalization to the scalar one, was also presented. Other algorithms and models used in Scalar-valued Neural Networks (SNN) (see for instance [3, 5, 16, 21]) can also be extended to MVNN. In further communications we try explore the mathematical properties of VNN, like those obtained for SNN (see for instance [1, 10, 20]). Many questions have to be answered: Can the universal approximation [11] be generalized to MVNN, and which activation functions are able to do this? How to extend the learning curve models, studied for SNN (e.g. [2, 12, 13, 20]), to the multidimensional case? Note that the universal approximation of SNN was demonstrated after 1988!

The answers to these questions are not yet known. We think, however, that VNN can be an important tool to treat multidimensional problems (see the computational examples given in [18]).

References :
[1] S. I. AMARI, "Mathematical foundations of neurocomputing", Proc. IEEE, Vol. 78, No. 9, pp. 1443-1463", September 1990.
[2] S. I. AMARI, "A universal theorem for learning curves", Neural Networks, Vol. 6, pp. 161-166, 1993.
[3] J. C. BEZDEK, "A review of probabilistic, fuzzy, and neural models for pattern recognition", Journal of intelligent and fuzzy systems, Vol. 1 (1), pp. 1-25, 1993.
[4] D. S. BROOMHEAD and D. LOWE, "Multivariable functional interpolation and adaptive networks", Complex Systems, 2, 321-355, 1988.
[5] F. CASTANIE, M. IBN KAHLA, and S. PUECHMOREL, "A constrained neural network with complex activation function : application to time-frequency analysis", IEEE int. Conf. on Acoustics Speech and Signal Processing : ICASSP'94, Adelaide, Australia, 1994.
[6] S. CHEN, S. McLAUGHLIN, and B. MULGREW, "Complex-valued radial basis function network Part 1: Network architecture and learning algorithm", Submitted to Signal Processing.
[7] S. CHEN, S. McLAUGHLIN, and B. MULGREW, "Complex-valued radial basis function network Part 2 : Application to digital communication channel equalization", Submitted to Signal Processing.
[8] T. CLARKE, "Generalization of neural networks to the complex plane", Int. Joint Conf. on Neural Networks, IJCNN'90, Vol. 2, pp. 435-440, 1990.
[9] G. CYBENKO, "Approximation by superpositions of a sigmoidal function", Mathematics of control, signals and systems, 2, 303-314, 1989.
[10] F. GIROSI and T. POGGIO, "Networks and the best approximation property", Biological Cybernetics, Springer-Verlag, 63, 169-176, 1990.
[11] K. HORNIK et al., "Multilayer feedforward networks are universal approximators", Neural Networks, Vol. 2, pp. 359-366, 1989.
[12] M..IBN KAHLA, Z. FARAJ, F. CASTANIE, and J. C. HOFFMANN, "Multi-layer adaptive filters trained with back propagation : a statistical approach", Submitted to Signal Processing.
[13] T. KOHONEN, "Self-organization and associative memory", 3rd ed., Springer-Verlag, Berlin, Heidelberg, New York, 1989.
[14] S. Y. KUNG, "Digital neural networks", PTR Prentice Hall, Englewood Cliffs, New Jersy, 1993.
[15] H. LEUNG and S. HAYKIN, "The complex back propagation algorithm", IEEE Trans. Signal Processing, Vol. 39, No. 9, pp. 2101-2104, September 1991.
[16] R. P. LIPPMANN, "An introduction to computing with neural nets", IEEE ASSP magazine, pp. 4-22, April 1987.
[17] T. POGGIO and F. GIROSI, "Networks for approximation and learning", Pro. IEEE, Vol. 78, No. 9, pp. 1481-1497, September 1990.
[18] S. PUECHMOREL, M. IBN KAHLA, and F. CASTANIE, "Manifold neural networks", Submitted to IEEE trans. on Neural Networks, 1993.
[19] S. PUECHMOREL, M. IBN KAHLA, and F. CASTANIE, "The manifold back propagation algorithm", Submitted to IEEE Inter. Conf. on Neural Networks, ICNN'94, Orlando, Florida, June 1994.
[20] H. RITTER, T. MARTINETZ, and K. SCHULTEN, "Neural computation and self organizing maps", Eddition-Wesley Publishing Company, 1992.
[21] D. E. RUMELHART, G. E. HINTON, and R. J. WILLIAMS, "Learning internal representations by error propagation", in D. E. RUMELHART and J. L. McCLELLAND eds., "Parallel distributed processing", Vol. 1, pp. 318-362, MIT Press, Cambridge, MA, 1986.
[22] B. WIDROW and M. LEHR, "30 years of adaptive neural networks : perceptron, madaline, and back propagation", Proc. IEEE, Vol. 78, No. 9, pp. 1415-1442, September 1990

Improving Generalization Performance by Entropy Maximization

Ryotaro Kamimura
Information Science Laboratory
Shohachiro Nakanishi
Department of Electrical Engineering
Tokai University
1117 Kitakaname Hiratsuka Kanagawa 259-12, Japan

Abstract

In the present paper, we propose a method of entropy maximization to improve generalization. For good generalization, the strength or the number of weights must significantly be reduced and the input patterns must be represented over many hidden units. In other words, the cost (represented in the number or the strength of weights) must be as small as possible, while the diversity of hidden unit activity is as large as possible. The diversity can be represented by an entropy (H) with respect to hidden unit activity. The cost (C) can be the average of the squared weights. Then, to obtain the better generalization, the ratio (H/C) must be as large as possible. We formulated a learning rule to maximize this ratio and applied it to the identification of frequencies. The results confirmed that the ratio of entropy to the cost was increased and the generalization performance was greatly improved. In addition, the learning time was significantly improved by using the entropy method.

1 Introduction

Neural networks can create the internal representation or hidden unit activity patterns in the course of the learning. The information, contained in input patterns is recoded in distributed ways or represented over many hidden units. Because of the distributed representation, the networks can appropriately generalize to novel situations [4]. Thus, the improvement of generalization performance depends upon the recoding of input patterns at hidden layer. In addition, it has been well known that a weight decay method and weight pruning contribute significantly to the improvement of the generalization [5],[6], [7], [8]. To achieve good generalization, the number of weights or the strength of weights in networks must be small.

To represent concretely this condition, let us define an entropy function (H) with respect to hidden unit activities,

$$H = -\sum_i p_i \log p_i,$$

where p_i is a normalized hidden unit activity and the summation is over all the hidden units. If this entropy is maximized, all the hidden units are equally or uniformly activated. On the other hand, if this entropy is minimized, only one hidden unit is activated and all the other units are off. To achieve better generalization, entropy must appropriately be increased, that is, hidden units are activated over many input patterns. Now, let us formulate the average cost for each hidden unit or weight strength (C) as

$$C = \frac{1}{M} \sum_i C_i$$

where C_i is the sum of the squared weights into ith hidden unit, M is the number of hidden units. This average cost must be as small as possible and entropy for hidden units must be as large as possible. Thus, if the ratio (G)

$$G = \frac{H}{C}$$

is maximized, the generalization will be improved.

In the following sections, we formulate the maximization method of the ratio of entropy to the cost. Then, we apply the method to the identification of frequencies. We show that the ratio of entropy to the cost is significantly increased and the generalization is greatly improved in all cases. Finally, the comparison with the simple weight decay method is presented.

2   Theory and Computational Methods

2.1   Entropy Function

Let us formulate the entropy maximization for the improvement of generalization performance. Suppose that a network is composed of three layers: input, hidden and output layers. Hidden unit activities are denoted by v_i and input terminals by ξ_j. Then, connections from inputs to hidden units are denoted by w_{ij} and connections from hidden units to output units are denoted by W_{ij}.

A hidden unit produces an output

$$v_i = f(u_i),$$

where u_i is a net input to ith hidden unit and defined by

$$u_i = \sum_{j=1}^{L} w_{ij}\xi_j.$$

where ξ_i is ith element of an input pattern and L is the number of elements in the pattern. An entropy function at hidden layer is defined by

$$H = -\sum_{i=1}^{M} p_i \log p_i, \tag{1}$$

where

$$p_i = \frac{v_i}{\sum_m v_m},$$

where the summation is over all the hidden units.

2.2   Input-hidden Connections

The cost can be measured by the total sum of the squared weights. Thus, the cost for ith hidden unit is defined by

$$C_i = \sum_{j=1}^{L} w_{ij}^2,$$

where the summation is over all the input units (L input units). Thus, the average cost per unit is computed by

$$C = \frac{1}{M}\sum_{i=1}^{M} C_i.$$

A function to be maximized is the ratio of the information entropy to the average cost:

$$\begin{aligned} G &= \frac{H}{C} \\ &= \frac{-M\sum_i p_i \log p_i}{\sum_i \sum_j w_{ij}^2} \end{aligned} \tag{2}$$

By differentiating both sides of this equation, we have

$$\frac{\partial G}{\partial w_{ij}} = \frac{-M(\log p_i + 1)\frac{\sum_m v_m - v_i}{\sum_m v_m}f'(u_i)\xi_j}{\sum_i \sum_j w_{ij}^2}$$
$$-\frac{-2M\sum_i p_i \log p_i}{(\sum_i \sum_j w_{ij}^2)^2}w_{ij}$$
$$= -\frac{M}{C}\phi_i \xi_j - 2M\frac{H}{C^2}w_{ij}. \tag{3}$$

where ϕ_i is defined by

$$\phi_i = (\log p_i + 1)\frac{\sum_m v_m - v_i}{\sum_m v_m}f'(u_i).$$

Update rule is formulated as follows:

$$\Delta w_{ij} = \epsilon\frac{\partial G}{\partial w_{ij}} - \beta\frac{\partial E}{\partial w_{ij}}$$
$$= -\alpha\frac{1}{C}\phi_i \xi_j - 2\alpha\frac{H}{C^2}w_{ij} + \beta\delta_i\xi_j, \tag{4}$$

where $\alpha = \epsilon M$ and δ_i is the ordinary delta for the back-propagation.

2.3 Hidden-Output Connections

Let us formulate a cost for the hidden-output connections. A cost for ith hidden unit is formulated by

$$D_j = \sum_{i=1}^{N} W_{ij}^2,$$

where W_{ij} is a hidden-output connection and the summation is over all the output units (N output units). Thus, an average cost is

$$D = \frac{1}{M}\sum_{j=1}^{M}D_j$$
$$= \frac{1}{M}\sum_{j=1}^{M}\sum_{i=1}^{N}W_{ij}^2 \tag{5}$$

A function to be maximized is defined by

$$F = \frac{H}{D}$$

Differentiating both sides of this equation with respect to W_{ij}, we have

$$\epsilon\frac{\partial F}{\partial W_{ij}} = -2\alpha\frac{H}{D^2}W_{ij}$$

3 Results and Discussion

3.1 Identification of Frequencies

We applied our method to the identification of frequencies[8]. Networks must identify three frequencies of sine waves with phases shifts, different from those of training data sets. First, training data were divided

Table 1: Summary of experiments for network with nine hidden units.

$\alpha(/\log M)$	$G(H/C)$	$F(H/D)$	HD(%)	SSE	Epoch ($\times30$)
0	3.16	6.56	4.44	4.48	192
0.01	3.31	6.35	5.93	4.05	189
0.02	3.66	6.65	0.74	2.24	175
0.03	3.79	6.64	0	2.06	177

into three classess with three different frequencies (2, 4, 6). Each class has ten examplars with sixty-four smaples from sine waves. Thus, the number of input units was sixty-four. The number of output units was three and specific target values were assigned to each output unit, according to the frequency of a class. Let us take an exmaple of frequency 2. The class of frequency 2 have a target output $(0,0,1)$ and input(ξ_i) are given by

$$\xi_i = A\sin(2i\frac{2\pi}{64} + p),$$

where i=1,2,...,64, A=0.8 or 1.0, and p= 2jπ/5, j=1,2,3,4. Total number of training data was thrity exmaplars. Following the specfication of Siestma et al. [8], test data was made with phase shift p= (2j−1)π/5, i=1,2,3,4. However, the amplitudes were set to 0.7, 0.9 and 1.1. Thus, total number of training sets was forty-five, compared with fifteen of Siestma's original data. In addition, input sine waves were modified by using the sigmoid function. Experiments were performed as follows. First, only input-hidden connections were updated so as to increase entropy. Only when the generalization performance was not significantly improved, in addition to the update of input-hidden connections, hidden-output connections were used to increase entropy. Because the update by input-hidden connections were very stable, while the update of all the connections tended to be unstable. Several times, same experiments were perfomed with different intial values for weights, ranging between -0.5 and 0.5. The learning was considered to be finished when the absolute differences between targets and ouputs were all below 0.2. Though the final Hamming distance and the sum of squared errors were dependent upon chosen initial values, approximately the same improvement (relative improvement) in the generalization performance was obtained. Thus, in the following sections, only one typical result was given for each experiment.

3.2 Generalization Performance

Table 1 shows the summary of experimental results, when the number of hidden units was nine. Only input-hidden connections were used to increase entropy. To facilitate the adjustment of the parameter α, values for the parameter α was divided by the maximum entropy: $\log M$. HD means the Hamming distance between targets and outputs, averaged over all the input patterns and all the elements in the patterns and ranged between zero and one. Outputs greater than 0.5 were set to one, while outputs less than or equal to 0.5 were set to zero. One epoch means thirty presentations of input patterns. As can be seen in the table, the ratio of entropy to the average cost (G) increases significantly from 3.16 to 3.79. Average hamming distance between targets and outputs decreases from 4.44 to zero, meaning that the network can produce perfectly targets. In addition, the number of epochs needed to finish the learning decreases as the parameter α decreases.

Then, we increased the number of hidden units from nine to fifteen. Table 2 shows experimental results, when the number of hidden units was fifteen and only input-hidden connections were used to maximize entropy. As the parameter α increases, the ratio of entropy to the cost increases significantly from 5.74 to 8.66 for input-hidden connections and from 11.03 to 18.01 for hidden-output connections. Average Hamming distance decreases from 4.44 to 2.22. Then, we used all the connections to increase the entropy. Table 3 shows experimental results when all the connections were used to increase the entropy. As can be seen in the table, the Hamming distance decreases greatly from 4.44 to zero, meaning that networks can produce targets perfectly. In addition, we can see that the number of epochs for finishing the learning is significantly decreased from 237 epochs (by standard back-propagation) to 119 epochs at the end.

The number of hidden units was increased from fifteen to twenty-one hidden units. In this case, we can also see a significant increase in the generalization performance by entropy maximization. Table 4 shows results when the number of hidden units was twenty-one with updates of input-hidden connections to increase

Table 2: Summary of experiments for networks with fifteen hidden units only with updates of input-hidden connections.

α	G	F	HD	SSE	Epoch
0	5.74	11.03	4.44	3.27	237
0.06	7.72	16.12	2.96	2.26	169
0.12	8.66	18.01	2.22	2.45	154

Table 3: Summary of experiments for networks with fifteen hidden units with updates of all the connections to increase entropy.

α	G	F	HD	SSE	Epoch
0.04	7.22	10.99	4.44	2.65	129
0.08	8.02	13.13	0	2.35	119

the entropy. As the parameter α increases, the ratios of entropy to the average cost significantly increase. The Hamming distance decreases from 10.37 to 3.70. The number of training epochs decreases from 157 to 135 epochs. Then, we used all the connections to decrease the Hamming distance. As can be seen in Table 5, computed with all the connections, the ratio (G) increases, while the ratio(F) does no increase. However, finally Hamming distance decreases and reaches the level of 2.22. The number of epochs also decreases significantly from 157 (by standard back-propagation) to 104 epochs.

3.3 Simple Weight Decay

It has been well known that adding a simple weight decay term increases the generalization performance [6]. Let us compare the performance by entropy method with that by the simple weight decay method. The weight decay method can be formulated as

$$\Delta w_{ij} = -\beta \frac{\partial E}{\partial w_{ij}} - \lambda w_{ij},$$

where w_{ij} means all the connections, including hidden-output connections. Table 6 shows experimental results by using the weight decay method. As can be seen in the table, the minimum Hamming distance(1.48) is larger than the minimum(0) obtained by entropy method. See Table 1. In addition, the number of epochs to be needed for the learning increases significantly, as the parameter λ increases. Even if the sum squared error (SSE) decreases below the minimum level (2.06), obtained by the entropy method, the Hamming distance can not decrease to the minimum level (zero) by the entropy method. As shown in the table, the ratio (G) and (F) increase greatly as the parameter increases. Thus, the weight decay method is only a method to increase the ratio with fixed entropy values.

Table 4: Summary of experiments for networks with twenty-one hidden units only with updates of input-hidden connections to increase entropy.

α	G	F	HD	SSE	Epoch
0	9.51	24.60	10.37	6.36	157
0.2	11.93	29.74	5.93	4.63	137
0.4	14.14	32.15	3.70	3.99	135

Table 5: Summary of experiments for network with twenty-one hidden units with updates of all the connections.

α	G	F	HD	SSE	Epoch
0.10	11.17	17.56	4.44	2.36	164
0.17	12.24	18.04	2.22	2.73	104

Table 6: Summary of experiments for networks with nine hidden units with a simple weight decay method was used.

$\lambda(\times 10^{-5})$	G	F	HD	SSE	Epoch
0.5	3.60	6.11	4.44	3.34	219
1.0	4.62	6.27	1.48	1.78	263
1.5	5.53	6.96	1.48	1.84	304
2.0	6.50	6.96	7.41	3.51	439

4   Conclusion

In this paper, we have proposed an entropy maximization method to improve the generalization performance. To achieve the better generalization, the information, contained in input patterns must be represented over many hidden units. The number and the strength of weights must significantly be small. We have formulated a method to increase the ratio of entropy to the cost (total sum of squared weights). We have shown that the ratios are significantly increased and the generalization performance is greatly improved. In addition, the learning time is significantly improved, compared with the weight decay method. By maximizing entropy, networks try to use as many hidden units as possible to finish the learning.

References

[1] Y. Chauvin, "A backpropagation algorithm with optimal use of hidden units," in *Advances in Neural Information Processing Systems*, D. S. Touretzky, Eds, San Mateo: CA, pp.519-526, 1989.

[2] F. L. Chung and T. Lee, "A node pruning algorithm for back-propagation networks," *International Journal of Neural Systems*, Vol.3, No.3, pp.301-314, 1992.

[3] T. Grossman, "The CHIR algorithm for feed forward networks with binary weights," in *Advances in Neural Information Processing Systems*, D. S. Touretzky, Eds, San Mateo: CA, pp.516-523, 1990.

[4] G. E. Hinton, J. L. MacClelland and D. E. Rumelhart, "Distributed Representations," in *Parallel Distributed Processing*, D. E. Rumelhart, J. L. McClelland, and the PDP Research Group, Cambridge, Massachusetts: the MIT Press, Vol.1, pp.77-109, 1986.

[5] H. H Thodberg, "Improving generalization of nerual networks through pruning," *International Journal of Neural Systems*, Vol.1, No.4, pp.317-326, 1991.

[6] A. Krogh and J. A. Hertz, "A simple weight decay can improve generalization," in *Neural Information Processing Systems*, Vol.4, pp.950-957, Morgan Kaufmann Publishers, 1992.

[7] C. W. Omlin and C. L. Giles, "Pruning recurrent neural networks for improved generalization performance," Revised Technical Report No. 93-6, April 1993, Computer Science Department, Rosselaer Polytechnic Institute, Troy, N. Y.

[8] J. Sietsma and R. J. F. Dow, "Creating artificial neural networks that generalize," *Neural Networks*, Vol.4, pp.67-79, 1991.

The boolean sphere: a geometrical approach to perceptron learning

Raúl Rojas

Freie Universität Berlin
Fachbereich Mathematik und Informatik
Takustr. 9, Berlin 14195

Abstract

We introduce in this paper the *boolean sphere*, a visualization of the solution regions for perceptron learning. Linear threshold elements with n boolean inputs can be used to compute a subset of the 2^{2^n} boolean functions definable on n inputs. Each one of these *linearly separable boolean functions* corresponds to a region on the surface of a sphere defined in weight space. Perceptron learning can be thought of as the process of examining the solution regions on the boolean sphere. The case of two boolean inputs provides a nice graphical illustration of perceptron learning and its convergence. Moreover, symmetry considerations show why perceptrons are more easily trained using bipolar than binary vectors. The boolean sphere allows us to give some estimates of the complexity of learning problems.

1 Perceptrons and linear separability

Linear threshold elements have attracted attention in the last years as building blocks for artificial neural networks and it is in this context that they are called *perceptrons*. Their properties have been extensively studied and there exist learning algorithms to train them efficiently. A perceptron with n inputs $x_1, x_2, \ldots, x_n$ and $n+1$ associated weights $w_1, w_2, \ldots, w_{n+1}$ outputs a one if $x_1 w_1 + \cdots + x_n w_n + w_{n+1} \leq 0$ and a zero otherwise. In our notation $-w_{n+1}$ is what is normally called the threshold of the perceptron. Boolean functions of n arguments computable by a perceptron with $n+1$ parameters are called linearly separable. It is well known that of the 2^{2^n} possible boolean functions of n variables only a vanishing percentage of them is computable by a perceptron when n goes to infinity [1]. This fact can be related to the number of regions delimited in weight-space by the hyperplanes defined by the input vectors in the training set. By defining the *boolean sphere* we can attempt to actually measure the relative sizes of each region. This allows us to make certain predictions regarding the learning difficulties of perceptrons and perceptron networks. Before doing this we have to take a closer look at the solution regions for perceptron learning.

Let us suppose that we want to find the perceptron's parameters for the computation of a given boolean function f of n arguments. There are 2^n different possible inputs which can be enumerated. Let us call f_i the value of f for the i-th input vector. The $n + 1$ parameters for each of 2^n possible inputs must satisfy the inequality

$$x_1^i w_1 + x_2^i w_2 + \cdots + x_n^i w_n \geq 0$$

if $f_i = 1$, or the inequality

$$x_1^i w_1 + x_2^i w_2 + \cdots + x_n^i w_n < 0$$

if $f_i = 0$. Here x_j^i stands for the j-th bit of the i-th input vector. A learning algorithm should be able to find the $n + 1$ necessary weights if they exist.

We can visualize this problem either in the n-dimensional input space as the question of separating the positive from the negative examples with a hyperplane, or we can visualize it in weight space as the problem of finding a point $(w_1, w_2, \ldots, w_{n+1})$ which fulfills the above 2^n inequalities. The first alternative is the traditional approach used in most textbooks. The second alternative is more interesting because it allows us to look at the inner working of training algorithms.

Each one of the inequalities referred above represents a cut through the origin with a hyperplane of dimension n of the $n + 1$ dimensional weight space corresponding to the i-input $x_1^i, \ldots, x_n^i$. Weight space is thus divided into a *positive* and a *negative* halfspace. Weight combinations $(w_1, w_2, \ldots, w_{n+1})$ in the positive halfspace produce the perceptron output $f_i = 1$ for the i-th input. Weight combinations in the negative halfspace produce the perceptron output $f_i = 0$ for the same input.

Perceptron learning amounts to finding a point $(w_1, w_2, \ldots, w_{n+1})$ in weight space which lies in the positive halfspace of the i-th cut whenever $f_i = 1$ and in the negative halfspace whenever $f_i = 0$. This is the *dual view* of perceptron learning, in which learning amounts to finding an interior point in an intersection of halfspaces defined by all possible inputs to the perceptron. Since the boundaries of the solution regions are hyperplanes, the learning problem amounts to finding an interior point of a poltype defined by linear constraints.

Each one of the regions defined by the intersection of halfspaces is a *solution region* for a linearly separable boolean function. Not all solution regions have the same shape and an interesting problem is the relative volume of each one. Since perceptron learning normally starts at a point chosen at random and proceeds looking for the interior of a specific solution region, it is intuitively clear that the smaller this region, the harder learning should be. We discuss this problem in the next section.

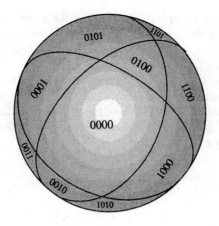

Figure 1: The boolean sphere in three dimensions

2   The boolean sphere

One way of looking at the regions defined by m hyperplane cuts going through the origin in an n-dimensional space, is by requiring that the weight vectors for our perceptron be normalized. This does not affect the perceptron computation and is equivalent to the condition that the tip of all weight vectors should end at the unit hypersphere of dimension n. In this way all the convex regions produced by the m hyperplane cuts define solution regions on the 'surface' of the hypersphere. Figure 1 shows an example for the case of the perceptron with two binary inputs. Since the perceptron uses three parameters, weight space also has this dimension. Note that four possible binary inputs define four cuts, but four cuts in the three dimensional space define only 14 different regions. This means that only 14 of the 16 possible boolean functions of two arguments can be computed by this perceptron.

Figure 1 immediately leads to a conjecture. Since the relative sizes of the solution regions on the boolean sphere represent how difficult it is to learn them, and since our learning algorithm will be asked to learn one of these functions randomly, the best strategy is to try to get regions of about the same relative size. Binary input vectors however lead to unsymmetrical cuts in weight space and the solution regions are of very different size. Symmetrical cuts can be achieved by substituting the binary input vectors by bipolar ones and training the perceptron under this coding. Table 3 was calculated using a Monte Carlo method. A normed weight vector was generated randomly and its associated boolean function was computed. By repeating the experiment many times it was possible to calculate the relative volumes of the solution regions. The table shows that the maximum variation in the relative sizes of the 14 possible regions is given by a factor of 1.33 when bipolar coding is used, whereas in the binary case it is about 12.5. This means that with binary coding some regions are almost an order of magnitude smaller than others. And indeed it has been empirically observed that multilayer neural networks are easier to train using a

Table 1: Relative sizes of the regions on the boolean sphere

Coding	Boolean function number							
	0	1	2	3	4	5	6	7
binary	26.83	2.13	4.18	4.13	4.17	4.22	0.00	4.13
bipolar	8.33	6.29	6.26	8.32	6.24	8.36	0.00	6.22

Coding	Boolean function number							
	8	9	10	11	12	13	14	15
binary	4.28	0.00	4.26	4.17	4.17	4.14	2.07	27.12
bipolar	6.16	0.00	8.42	6.33	8.27	6.31	6.25	8.23

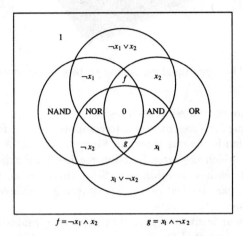

Figure 2: Solution regions on the surface of the boolean sphere

bipolar representation than a binary one. The rationale for this fact is given by the size of the regions in the boolean sphere. It is also possible to show that bipolar coding is optimal under this criterion.

We can go one step further and ask what is the shape of the error function for perceptrons in weight space. Given a boolean function f and a weight vector $w_1, w_2, \ldots, w_{n+1}$ the error function is the number of misclassified input vectors. We can visualize this function for the case of a perceptron with two inputs by projecting the solution regions on the three dimensional boolean sphere in weight space on a plane using an adequate transformation. Figure 2 shows a stylized representation of the result of using a stereographic projection. The great circles on the boolean sphere are projected to ellipses. Since we are only interested in the number of regions and the topological relation between them, we can think of the projection of the great circles of the boolean sphere as circles in the plane. The result is Figure 2, which also shows which boolean functions

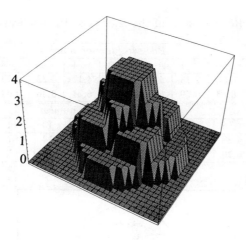

Figure 3: The error function on the surface of the boolean sphere

of two variables are computed in each region.

If we are looking for a weight vector to compute the zero function, the shape of the error function is the one shown in Figure 3. It can be seen that there is a single region in which the error function reaches its maximum, and a single region in which it reaches its minimum. Since there are no local minima, any greedy procedure, like classical perceptron learning, converges to a solution in weight space whenever this exists.

It should be clear from the figure that these conclusions do not depend on the specific function selected for the training process. This visualization of the error function is superior to the one used in [3].

In the case of multilayer networks we can also visualize the form of the error function, like it is shown in Figure 4. In this case a network of two hidden units has been used. The boolean functions of two arguments have been numerated from f_0 to f_{15}. The table shows which function is computed by the first hidden unit (rows) and by the second (columns). It is shown at each place in the table thus defined which function is computed by the output unit. One can think of this diagram as of the surface of the boolean sphere associated with the nine-dimensional weight space of the three unit network used to compute XOR. All solutions for the XOR task are shown in the diagram, and one can see the high symmetry of the solution regions. They are uniformly distributed in weight space, although the volume of each region differs.

3   Conclusions

The relevance of the boolean sphere relies not on its practical application to perceptron or neural networks learning, but in its visualization power to understand how learning algorithms work and why they sometimes fail. The boolean sphere allows us to measure the difficulty of a learning task by relating it to the

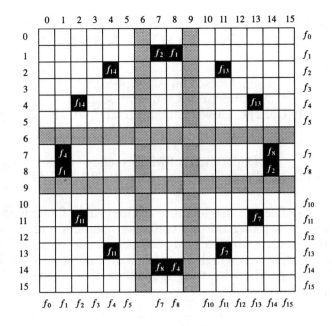

Figure 4: Regions in the boolean sphere for the XOR problem

volume of its solution region in the boolean sphere. With an estimate for this volume it is possible to give an upper bound for stochastic learning of boolean functions. It is easy to compute, for example, that a solution for the XOR problem can be found with probability 0.001 using a network with two hidden neurons and trying around 1800 different weight combinations. This would be uninteresting, were it not for the fact that some authors normally report still larger iterative cycles using fancy algorithms. The boolean sphere is thus a conceptual instrument which allows us to understand neural networks better. As a matter of fact, it has been used implicitly in the Karnaugh maps of logical functions. Simplification of logic expressions amounts in this formalism to the elimination of superfluous hyperplane cuts.

References

[1] Abu-Mostafa, Y., and St. Jacques, J., "Information Capacity of the Hopfield Model", *IEEE Transactions on Information Theory*, Vol. 31, n. 4.

[2] Rojas, R., *Theorie der neuronalen Netze*, Springer-Verlag, Berlin, 1993.

[3] Hush, D.R.,Salas, H.M. and Horne, B., "Error surfaces for multilayer perceptrons", *IEEE IJCNN*, Seattle, 1991, pp. I–759–761.

A CLASSICAL ALGORITHM FOR
AVOIDING LOCAL MINIMA

D Gorse and A Shepherd
Department of Computer Science
University College, Gower Street, London WC1E 6BT, UK

J G Taylor
Department of Mathematics
King's College, Strand, London WC2R 2LS, UK

Conventional methods of supervised learning are inevitably faced with the problem of local minima; evidence is presented that conjugate gradient and quasi-Newton techniques are particularly susceptible to being trapped in sub-optimal solutions. A new classical technique is presented which by the use of a homotopy on the range of the target outputs allows supervised learning methods to find a global minimum of the error function in almost every case.

Introduction

The problems to which neural computing techniques are most frequently applied involve the supervised learning of an input-output mapping, defined implicitly by a set of P input patterns together with their desired outputs. Such tasks can be formulated as error-minimisation problems, where the error function is usually given by

$$E = \frac{1}{P} \sum_{p=1}^{P} E_p = \frac{1}{PN} \sum_{p=1}^{P} \sum_{i=1}^{N} (d_{i,p} - z_{i,p})^2 \qquad (1)$$

where $d_{i,p}$ and $z_{i,p}$ are the desired and actual values of the ith output unit for pattern p, for a network with N output units. E is a function of all the parameters (weights and thresholds) of the network; this parameter list can be written as a multidimensional vector $\overline{w}$. The problem is to change $\overline{w}$ so as to avoid those solutions of the minimisation condition $\partial E / \partial \overline{w} = 0$ which do not correspond to the lowest value of E, the local minima of the error-weight surface. The most commonly used supervised training technique, error backpropagation (BP) (equivalent to gradient descent with a fixed step length) is well known to have difficulties with local minima, especially for non linearly separable problems [1]. What is less well known is that the neural implementations of more efficient classical minimisation algorithms, such as conjugate gradients (CG) or the quasi-Newton method (QN), are even more likely to be trapped in sub-optimal solutions. Table 1 shows the percentage success in reaching a global minimum for 100 (2-2-1) networks learning to solve the XOR problem.

XOR	% reaching global minimum	
method	sigmoid in final layer	linear in final layer
on-line BP	85	95
batched BP	75	96
CG	51	80
QN	34	66

Table 1

XOR is a useful benchmark because it is a non linearly separable problem with known local minima [2], but one which can be solved by a small network with only 9 adaptive weights. Linear outputs in the second layer (as opposed to sigmoidal squashing for both computational layers) improve the percentage success, but there is a clear trend toward worsened performance for the more sophisticated algorithms. Simple on-line BP (without momentum) performs best; this may be due to the method's stochastic features, as discussed in [3].

Trapping in local minima can also be observed for continuous function learning problems. McInerney et al [4] have discovered (by exhaustive search of the error-weight surface) local minima in a (1-2-1) network (with a linear output node) learning the sine function. This problem was also investigated, using the same training set as in [4], and the results are summarised in Table 2.

sine	% reaching global minimum
batched BP	100
CG	96
QN	87

Table 2

These results do not show as high a probability of trapping in local minima as in the XOR example, but there is still a significant correlation between the probability of failure and the convergence speed of the method; the quasi-Newton method, with a 13% failure rate, would probably not be a good choice unless multiple restarts were acceptable.

It is commonly believed - though we do not know of any 'no-go theorem' to this effect - that the only techniques guaranteed to converge to a global minimum with a probability approaching 1 are stochastic in character, with methods based on simulated annealing [5] and, currently, genetic algorithms [6] being among the most popular. However these techniques can be very slow and must be applied carefully in order to ensure a good solution. Is there a way to retain the fast convergence of techniques like conjugate gradients and the quasi-Newton method whilst improving the robustness of these algorithms in the face of local minima? We will present here a new and purely classical method which is guaranteed to succeed in avoiding local minima in almost all cases.

Expanded range approximation (ERA)

The basic idea underpinning this new algorithm is that of a homotopy on the range of the target values d_p (for simplicity we consider just one output node). This range is modified by compressing these values down to their mean value $<d> = \frac{1}{P} \sum_{p=1}^{P} d_p$ and then progressively expanding these compressed targets back toward their original values (hence the epithet 'expanded range approximation', or ERA, we have coined for this approach). We define a modified training set
$$S(\lambda) = \{x_p, d_p(\lambda)\} = \{x_p, <d> + \lambda(d_p - <d>)\}$$
where the $d_p(\lambda)$ are the new, compressed, targets. The problem defined by S(0) is easy for the network to solve (the corresponding error-weight surface can be shown to have only a global minimum); S(1) is the original problem with training set $\{x_p, d_p\}$. The homotopy parameter λ interpolates between these extremes. A λ-parametrised error function can be defined during training on each of the sets $S(\lambda)$ by
$$E(\lambda) = \frac{1}{P} \sum_{p=1}^{P} [<d> + \lambda(d_p - <d>) - z_p(\lambda)]^2 \tag{2}$$
where the $z_p(\lambda)$ are the actual network outputs during this procedure. Setting $\lambda = 1$ gives $E(1) \equiv E$, the error function (1) in the case of a single output node. The ERA method involves first solving the problem $S(\lambda_1)$ for small λ_1, then the problem $S(\lambda_2)$ with $\lambda_2 > \lambda_1$, and so on up to the original problem S(1). We have usually chosen to increase λ by uniform steps of η; an 'N-step ERA' method refers to the progressive solution of the N problems $S(\lambda_n = n\eta)$ for $n = 1..N=1/\eta$ ('1-step ERA' ($\eta=1$) is the conventional single step training technique).

As a first example, the ERA method was applied to the same 100 XOR networks (with sigmoidal output in the final layer) as in Table 1, using the CG algorithm. With 10-step ERA (η=0.1), the success rate improves dramatically from 51% when η=1 to 94%. Figure 1 shows a training curve for a particular set of XOR weights which led to a failure when η=1 (curve (a)), but succeeded with 10-step ERA (curve (b)). The error function plotted for the 10-step ERA case is the square root of $E(1)$, the error with respect to the original, uncompressed targets. The errors $E(\lambda)$ always decrease during ERA steps, but the overall E can show local increases, as is evident from Figure 1.

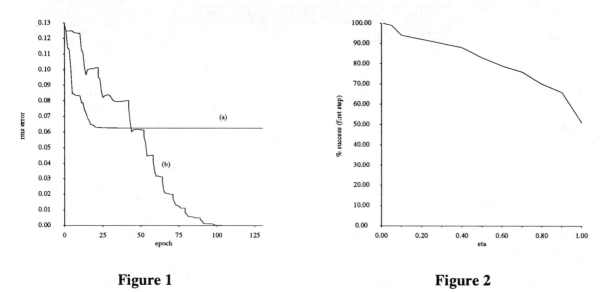

| Figure 1 | Figure 2 |

If the step size η is decreased, the percentage success improves still further: 100-step ERA (η=0.01) is 100% successful in solving the XOR problem. As a second example, 2-step ERA (η=0.5) was applied to the sine problem of Table 2, using the QN method. In this case - a continuous as opposed to binary problem, a linear as opposed to sigmoidal output in the final layer, a different training method - there was also a very significant improvement, from 87% success when η=1 to 100% for 2-step ERA.

It might seem that the ERA technique could become computationally expensive if very many small steps were required. In fact we suspect that it will be possible to make a short cut in many cases. We have so far observed that an ERA simulation which fails to find a global minimum of $E(\lambda_1)$ will not subsequently succeed as the homotopy parameter $\lambda \to 1$. Conversely, however, in our experience a simulation which succeeds at the first step never subsequently fails. This suggests that it is most important to get the first step right, and that subsequent range expansion does not need to be done so carefully. Figure 2 shows the percentage of successes at the first step (successful minimisations of $E(\lambda_1 = \eta)$) as a function of the size of η for the same 100 XOR networks used in the single step (conventional) and 10-step tests. The dependence appears to be roughly linear, with, in this case, 100% success at η=0.01.

All the initial simulations suggested a special role for η, the size of the first step. In order to try to get some further insight into the process, we looked at the trajectories in output space followed for the XOR problem by the $z_p(\lambda_1 = \eta)$, the first-step responses to the four patterns p = 00, 01, 10, 11. Since the initial weights are randomly chosen (from the interval [-1,1]) the trajectories in these experiments begin at some arbitrary point inside the hypercube $[0,1]^4$. The target for η=1 is the point (0,1,1,0); the targets for $\eta < 1$ lie on a line joining this point to (½,½,½,½). By taking pairs of these responses we were able to plot trajectories in the six 2-

dimensional $(z_{p_1}(\eta), z_{p_2}(\eta))$ subspaces during CG training. Figures 3a-d illustrate trajectories in $(z_{00}(\eta), z_{10}(\eta))$ space for $\eta=1.0$ (Figure 3a), $\eta=0.3$ (3b), $\eta=0.2$ (3c), $\eta=0.1$ (3d). A coordinate transformation

$$(x, y) = \frac{1}{\eta}(z_{00} - \tfrac{1}{2}(1-\eta), z_{10} - \tfrac{1}{2}(1-\eta))$$

is used in plotting the diagrams so that the scales are identical, and in each case the target is the top left hand corner. The midpoint on the y-axis represents a local minimum.

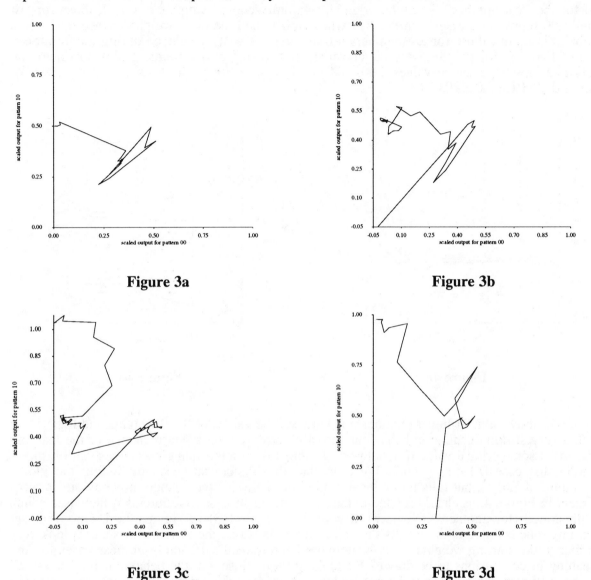

Figure 3a   **Figure 3b**

Figure 3c   **Figure 3d**

Figure 3a shows a conventionally trained ($\eta=1$) network which fails to solve the XOR problem, becoming trapped in the local minimum corresponding to a final response to the four patterns of $z = (0, \tfrac{1}{2}, \tfrac{1}{2}, 0)$. Figure 3b also shows a failure, for $\eta=0.3$, but notice that the trajectory appears to almost escape from the local minimum. Figure 3c shows a success at $\eta=0.2$, but the trajectory still spends a lot of time in the vicinity of the local minimum before escaping. Finally, Figure 3d, with $\eta=0.1$, shows a trajectory which entirely avoids the vicinity of the local minimum, heading more or less directly for the global minimum of $E(\lambda_1 = \eta)$. There appears to be a progressive change of behaviour as η is decreased; this progression is most marked for small values of η.

In order to further investigate this progressive change in the first-step behaviour we looked at the values of the 9 weights which were developed by typical examples of the (2-2-1) XOR networks after minimisation of the first-step error function $E(\eta)$. In Figures 4a,b the weights plotted for the 'test number' -1 are the original, randomly chosen weights $\in [-1,1]$, those for test number 0 represent the solution reached when $\eta=0$ (when the error-weight surface has only a global minimum), those for test numbers > 0 the weights $w(\eta)$ developed during the minimisation of $E(\eta > 0)$ for progressively larger values of η (using a logarithmic scale). In Figure 4a, tests 1, 2, 3, 4 represent η-values 0.001, 0.01, 0.1, 1.0; in Figure 4b, tests 1, 2, 3 represent η-values 0.00001, 0.0001, 0.001.

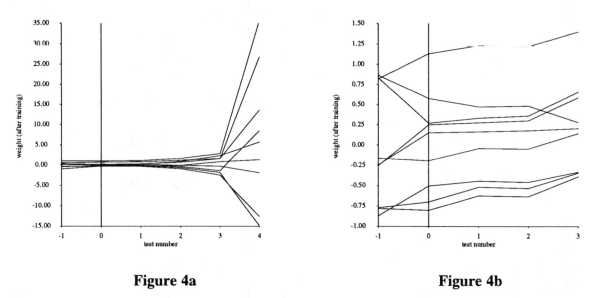

Figure 4a   **Figure 4b**

Figure 4a shows almost linear relationships between the values of the 9 weights and $\log(\eta)$, but with a very striking change in behaviour (possibly representing a phase change of the learning system) at some critical value η_{crit} between 0.1 and 1.0. A somewhat closer investigation shows that in this case $0.1 < \eta_{crit} < 0.2$. We note that this system succeeds in finding the global minimum of $E(0.1)$, but falls into a local minimum of $E(0.2)$; the change in behaviour in $w(\eta)$ evident in Figure 4a is clearly related to the switch from success to failure as η increases which is illustrated (for another XOR network with $0.2 < \eta_{crit} < 0.3$) in Figures 3a-d. One criticism that might be levelled at the results shown in Figure 4a is that the weights for small η look very similar to the starting weights - has the network been trained sufficiently in these cases for any meaningful conclusions to be drawn? By looking more closely at the behaviour for very small η, this criticism can be seen to be unfounded. Figure 4b, which uses a different set of starting weights, shows that in general there is a large difference between the starting weights and the $\eta=0$ solution, but thereafter a much smoother progression with increasing η.

Discussion

This paper has presented results which violate the widespread belief that the only way to avoid local minima in supervised learning problems with complex error-weight surfaces is to use computationally expensive stochastic procedures like simulated annealing or genetic algorithms. If the results presented here can be shown to be securely founded, and the ERA method shown to have wide applicability, there could be a significant changes in the way that supervised learning tasks are approached. We believe that it is possible to construct a rigorous mathematical proof that the ERA method will work in all but pathological (and rare) cases. The details of this proof are too lengthy to be presented here, but the general principles can be outlined. Initially we look at the first ERA step, for which the homotopy parameter $0 < \lambda \ll 1$. For such small λ, the error $E(\lambda)$ of (2) can be expanded as

$$E(\lambda) = E(0) + \lambda E_1 + O(\lambda^2)$$

where

$$E(0) = \frac{1}{P} \sum_{p=1}^{P} [<d> - z_p(0)]^2, \quad E_1 = \frac{1}{P} \sum_{p=1}^{P} (d_p - <d> - z'_p(0)) z_p(0)$$

where the derivative $z'_p(0)$ depends on the particular learning law, but is assumed bounded. It is possible to show that $E(0)$ has only a global minimum. Then we can investigate the shape of the surface $E(\lambda)$ by looking at the effect of the additional term λE_1 for small λ. Outside some small neighbourhood N_0 of the global minimum P_0 of $E(0)$ the effect of this additional term can be made arbitrarily small by choosing λ small enough. In particular it can be shown that no local minima can exist outside N_0, as

$$\lambda \left| \frac{\partial E_1}{\partial \underline{w}} \right| < \left| \frac{\partial E(0)}{\partial \underline{w}} \right| \quad \rightarrow \quad \frac{\partial}{\partial \underline{w}} (E(0) + \lambda E_1) \neq 0$$

Within N_0 the global minimum of $E(0)$ will in general be shifted; there can be degenerate cases where a number of global minima could arise, but this set would be expected to be of measure zero. Continued expansion of the homotopy parameter $\lambda \rightarrow 1$ is handled in a similar way to the first step above. There may be obstructions to performing the homotopy up to $\lambda=1$, but we expect that such cases will be rare. Further investigations are in progress, and will be reported in the literature.

References

[1]   M Gori and A Tesi, "On the problem of local minima in backpropagation", *IEEE Trans. on Pattern Analysis and Machine Intelligence*, 14, 76-86 (1992).

[2]   E K Blum, "Approximation of Boolean functions by sigmoidal networks: Part I: XOR and other two-variable functions", *Neural Computation*, 1, 532-540 (1989).

[3]   C Darken and J M Moody, "Towards faster stochastic gradient search", in: *Advances in Neural Information Systems 4*, Morgan Kaufmann, San Mateo, CA, 1009-1016 (1991).

[4]   J M McInerney, K G Haines, S Biafore and R Hecht-Nielsen, "Error surfaces of multi-layer networks can have local minima", UCSD Tech. Rep. CS89-157, October 1989.

[5]   L Ingber, "Very fast simulated re-annealing", *Mathl. Comput. Modelling*, 12, 967-973 (1989).

[6]   J Holland, *Adaptation in Natural and Artificial Systems*, University of Michigan Press, Ann Arbor, MI (1975).

GLOBALLY OPTIMAL NEURAL LEARNING

J. Barhen[1,2], A. Fijany[1], and N. Toomarian[1]

California Institute of Technology
Pasadena, CA 91109

Abstract: One of the fundamental limitations of current artificial neural network learning paradigms is the susceptibility to local minima during training. Building upon the recently discovered TRUST global optimization methodology, computationally efficient algorithms are presented, that enable overcoming local minima, both for backpropagation schema in feed forward multilayer architectures, and for adjoint-operator learning in recurrent networks. Extensions to TRUST are introduced, that now formally guarantee convergence to a global minimum in the multidimensional case. Results for a standard benchmark are included, to illustrate the theoretical developments.

Introduction

Considerable efforts have recently been devoted to the development of efficient computational methodologies for learning. Even though the primary emphasis has largely been on error-backpropagation algorithms for "feedforward" [1] architectures, the more complex "recurrent" networks [2-5] are currently receiving renewed attention. In particular, the introduction of adjoint-operator formalisms for very fast procesing of static [6] and time-dependent [7] phenomena has opened new avenues in terms of computational efficiency and relevance to real-time applications. The development of such learning algorithms is generally based upon the minimization of an energy-like "neuromorphic" function or functional. The main emphasis of most research to date has been on how to best obtain the gradients [8] of this function or functional with respect to the various parameters of the neural architecture.

The susceptibility to local minima during training remains, however, one of the fundamental limitations of current artificial neural network learning paradigms. Heretofore, local minimization techniques have provided the main operational tools for implementing the corresponding algorithms, with the notable exception of stochastic paradigms such as the "Boltzmann Machine" [9] or "diffusion" processes [10]. This paper presents a new approach to learning, in which the gradient descent mechanism is replaced by a methodology based upon a recently developed global optimization scheme, acronymed TRUST [11]. The deterministic TRUST algorithm formulates global optimization in terms of the flow of a special nonlinear dynamical system. TRUST can be applied both to backpropagation learning and to recurrent networks. Originally [11], we could only guarantee convergence to a global minimum for 1-dimensional problems, eventhough in practice, for all n-dimensional applications, a global minimum was always reached. Here, we introduce a simple extension to TRUST, which now formally guarantees convergence to global minima in the multidimensional case. We demonstrate, on a couple of standard benchmarks, that our approach indeed overcomes encountered local minima, and thereby provides a globally optimal solution to the learning problems under consideration.

([1]) Jet Propulsion Laboratory, 4800 Oak Grove Dr., Tel. (818)354-9218, Fax (818)393-5013, ([2]) Applied Physics Department

Global Optimization

Let $f(x)$ be a twice continuously differentiable scalar function of the variable x defined over an interval of interest. Consider the nonlinear transformation

$$E(x, x^*) = \ln \frac{1}{1 + e^{-[\hat{f}(x) + \varepsilon]}} - \frac{3}{4} \rho (x - x^*)^{4/3} \; H[\hat{f}(x)] \tag{1}$$

where H denotes the Heaviside function, x^* is a fixed value of x, the selection of which will be discussed below, and $\hat{f}(x)$ represents an offset of $f(x)$ by the amount $f(x^*)$. The positive parameters ε and ρ will be specified in the sequel. To highlight the two basic concepts which underlie the TRUST formalism, we rewrite Eq. (1) as

$$E(x, x^*) = E_{sub}(x, x^*) + E_\rho(x, x^*) \tag{2}$$

The sub-energy tunneling function, E_{sub}, is defined as the first term in the right-hand-side of Eq. (1). It has the same relative ordering of local and global minima as $\hat{f}(x)$ since

$$\frac{\partial E_{sub}}{\partial x} = 0 \iff \frac{df}{dx} = 0$$

Furthermore, E_{sub} is monotonically increasing in terms of both $f(x)$ and $\hat{f}(x)$. We want E_{sub} to have the following effects: first, it should suppress $\hat{f}(x)$ to zero for $f(x) > f(x^*)$; second, it should leave $\hat{f}(x)$ nearly unmodified for $f(x) < f(x^*)$. These requirements determine possible values for the parameter ε. Figure 1 illustrates the action of E_{sub} on the function $f(x) = [\sin 2x - x - 1]^2$ with $x^* \simeq -6.80678$ and $\varepsilon = 2$. We see that E_{sub} preserves all properties relevant for optimization. The term E_ρ induces a terminal repeller [12] effect.

The basic idea driving our approach to globally optimal learning is to construct a dynamical system which switches autonomously between two phases: (1) a tunneling phase, where the system flows under the action of a terminal repeller over a sub-energy surface flattened to near zero level for all values of $f(x)$ above a threshold $f(x^*)$; (2) a gradient descent phase, during which the repeller effect is switched off, and which starts whenever a lower energy valley has been reached, to obtain a new threshold $f(x^*)$.

For actual neural learning, f is an error function or functional of a parameter vector $\mathbf{x}$ (including, e.g., the synaptic weights, the potential decay constants and the sigmoidal gains). For the sake of simplicity, the following discussion is limited to one dimension. In this vein, upon application of gradient descent to the E functional, we obtain

$$\dot{x} = -\frac{df(x)}{dx} \frac{1}{1 + e^{\hat{f}(x) + \varepsilon}} + \rho (x - x^*)^{1/3} H[\hat{f}(x)] \tag{3}$$

We assume that the optimization is to take place in a specified domain, D, which, in the multidimensional case, will be taken as a hyperparallelepiped. In the one-dimensional case, D is simply the interval $[x_L, x_U]$. To initiate the optimization process, x^* is chosen to be the lower limit of D, i.e., $x^* = x_L$. This point need not be a local minimum. A repeller is placed at x^*, and the dynamical system (3) is given the initial condition $x^* + \xi$, where ξ is a very small positive perturbation, so that the system flows in the positive direction, i.e., toward the upper limit of D.

The selection of x^* defines a threshold called the zero sub-energy limit, $f(x^*)$, above which $E_{sub}(x, x^*)$ is nearly zero in value and approximately flat. If $\hat{f}(x^* + \xi) < f(x^*)$, the algorithm immediately enters a gradient descent phase, in which the state of the dynamical system flows down the gradient and reaches its first local minimum at $x = x^{1(*)}$. At this point, we set $x^* = x^{1(*)}$ in (3), and perturb x to $x^* + \xi$. Since $x^{1(*)}$ is a local minimum, $f(x) \geq f(x^*)$ in a neighborhood of x^*. Consequently, the repelling term is active. The repeller located at x^* drives the solution across the flattened sub-energy surface, which in effect pushes the system uphill on the surface of the associated objective function. The dynamical system remains in the repelling phase until it reaches a lower valley, where $\hat{f}(x) < 0$. This phase tunnels through all of the state space region with functional values that lie above the last found local minimum, $f(x^{1(*)})$. A lower valley of $E_{sub}(x, x^*)$ is a lower value of $f(x)$ as well. As the dynamical system enters the next valley, the algorithm automatically switches to the second phase, where the terminal repeller term is zero and gradient descent takes over, leading to further minimization of $\hat{f}(x)$. The system will equilibrate at the next lower local minimum, $x^{2(*)}$. We set $x^* = x^{2(*)}$ and repeat the process. If $f(x^* + \xi) \geq f(x^*)$ when the optimization procedure is initiated, the dynamical system will initially enter the tunneling phase. The tunneling will proceed to a lower valley, at which point the algorithm enters a gradient descent phase and follows the behavior discussed above.

The two-phase descent-and-tunneling process continues until a suitable stopping criterion is satisfied. Here, as soon as the lowest local minimum, x_G^*, in D has been reached, the optimization cycle is repeated by placing a repeller at x_G^* and perturbing the system to initiate the next tunneling phase. In this case, the sub-energy transformation flattens $f(x)$ in the entire domain of interest, since $f(x_G^*)$ is the lowest objective function value in D. The perturbed dynamical system, which is now in the repeller tunneling phase, will eventually flow beyond the upper boundary of D. Thus, when the state flows out of the domain boundary, i.e., when $x > x_U$, the last local minimum found is the global minimum of the function in D.

Multidimensional Global Optimization

The one-dimensional algorithm can easily be extended to handle multidimensional problems. Let $f(\mathbf{x})$ be a function of the $M-$ parameter vector $\mathbf{x}$, and define the nonlinear transformation

$$E(\mathbf{x}, \mathbf{x}^*) = \ln \frac{1}{1 + e^{-[\hat{f}(\mathbf{x}) + \varepsilon]}} - \frac{3}{4} \rho \sum_{\mu=1}^{M} (x_\mu - x_\mu^*)^{4/3} \, H[\hat{f}(\mathbf{x})] \qquad (4)$$

The multidimensional sub-energy term is analogous to the one-dimensional sub-energy functional E_{sub}. The portions of the objective function surface which lie above the zero sub-energy limit, $f(\mathbf{x}^*)$, are flattened by the use of the $E_{sub}(\mathbf{x}, \mathbf{x}^*)$ transformation.

Upon application of gradient descent to $E(\mathbf{x}, \mathbf{x}^*)$ in Eq. (4), we obtain the vector differential equation

$$\dot{x}_\mu = -\frac{df(\mathbf{x})}{dx_\mu} \frac{1}{1 + e^{\hat{f}(\mathbf{x}) + \varepsilon}} + \rho (x_\mu - x_\mu^*)^{1/3} \, H[\hat{f}(\mathbf{x})] \qquad (5)$$

The dynamical system (5) has a highly parallel structure and its initial conditions, operation, and stopping criterion are highly analogous to the one dimensional case.

In the multidimensional case, $\mathbf{x}^*$ is initially chosen to be one corner of the hyperparallelpiped D, usually $x_i^* = x_{iL} \; \forall i$. A repeller is placed at $\mathbf{x}^*$. It should be noted that the repelling terms in the multidimensional case can be interpreted as "line" or "hyperplane" repellers, and are active whenever $\hat{f}(\mathbf{x}) \geq 0$. It should also be noted that in the multidimensional tunneling phase the sub-energy gradient is not identically zero. While the repeller terms dominate, the amount of information in the sub-energy gradient helps the state to flow in a direction that ultimately leads to the next lower valley.

In a departure from this paradigm, described in detail in [11], and in order to formally guarantee the convergence to a global minimum in the multidimensional case, we consider here an approach whereby the M-dimensional learning error function (typically $M \geq N^2$, N being the number of neurons in the network) is represented in terms of a single variable. To achieve such a representation, Kolmogorov embeddings [13] could be envisioned, but they result in a computationally complex nonsmooth transform. On the other hand, multidimensional embeddings based on the dense covering of the real plane by an Archimedes' spiral are well known [14]. Using the latter transformation, we can write:

$$f[\; \mathbf{w}_1, \cdots \mathbf{w}_\mu, \cdots \mathbf{w}_M] = f[\alpha_1(\omega), \cdots \alpha_\mu(\omega), \cdots \alpha_M(\omega)] \tag{6}$$

Each synaptic weight $\mathbf{w}_\mu$ has been expressed in terms of a single parameter w, using the Archimedes spiral representation. Specifically, for a 2-dimensional case, we can write

$$\mathbf{w}_1 = \alpha\omega\cos\omega \qquad\qquad \mathbf{w}_2 = \alpha\omega\sin\omega \tag{7}$$

where α is a constant controlling the precision of the computation. TRUST, the fastest known [11] 1-D global optimization algorithm can now readily be applied to the function $f(w)$.

Learning Examples

To illustrate the power of this novel approach, we sek the global minima of the following two functions:

$$f(\; \mathbf{w}_1, \; \mathbf{w}_2) = \left\{ \sum_{i=1}^{5} i\cos[(i+1)\,\mathbf{w}_1 + i] \right\} \cdot \left\{ \sum_{j=1}^{5} j\cos[(j+1)\,\mathbf{w}_2 + j] \right\} \tag{8}$$

and

$$f(\; \mathbf{w}_1, \; \mathbf{w}_2) = [4 - 2.1\mathbf{w}_1^2 + (\mathbf{w}_1^4/3)]\mathbf{w}_1^2 + \mathbf{w}_1\mathbf{w}_2 + 4(\mathbf{w}_2^2 - 1)\mathbf{w}_2^2 \tag{9}$$

The first function is displayed in Fig. 2, and is shown to exhibit a very complex structure. For weights in the domain [-10, +10] x [-10, +10], it possesses 760 local minima. We measure the cost of the global minimzation in terms of the number of function evaluations. Then, under identical operating conditions, we find that the respective costs of the best stochastic method (Aluffi-Pentini [15]), Newton-tunneling (Levy-Montalvo [16]), and interval algorithm (Walster [17]) were 241215, 12160 and 7424, respectively. TRUST, on the other hand reached the global minimum after only 269 function evaluations. The second benchmark, the well known two-dimensional six-hump camelback function, possesses six local minima and two global minima in the domain [-3, +3] x [-2, +2]. Starting at point (-3, -2) it required 10,822 evaluations using the fastest stochastic methods, 1496 evaluations using Newton-tunneling and 168 evaluations via TRUST.

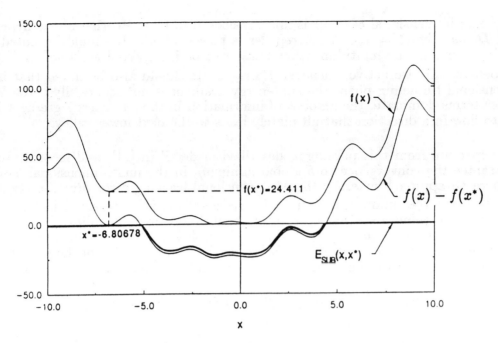

Figure 1: Example of subenergy tunneling transformation

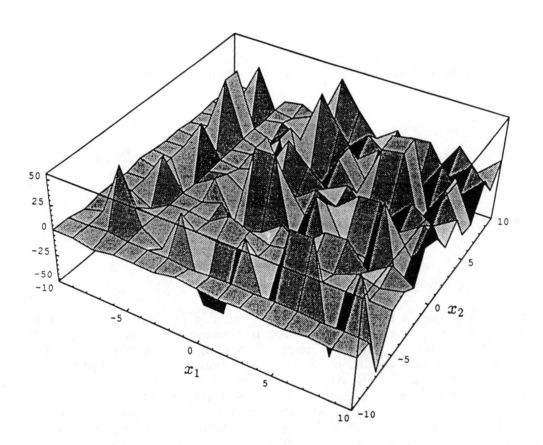

Figure 2: Function defined in Eq. (8) exhibits complex structure with many local minima

REFERENCES

1. Rumelhart, D. E., et al., 1986, *Parallel and Distributed Processing*, MIT Press.

2. Pearlmutter, B. A., 1989, "Learning State Space Trajectories in Recurrent Neural Networks", *Neural Computation, 1* (2), 263-269.

3. Williams, R. J., and Zipser, D., 1989, "A Learning Algorithm for Continually Running Fully Recurrent Neural Networks", *Neural Computation, 1*, (2), 270-280.

4. Barhen, J., Gulati, S., and Zak, M., 1989, "Neural Learning of Constrained Nonlinear Transformations", *IEEE Computer*, 22(6), 67-76.

5. Pineda, F., 1990, "Time Dependent Adaptive Neural Networks", *Adv. Neur. Inf. Proc. Sys.*, 2, 710-718.

6. Barhen, J., Toomarian, N., and Gulati, S., 1990b, "Application of Adjoint Operators to Neural Learning", *Appl. Math. Lett.*, 3 (3), 13-18.

7. Toomarian, N. and Barhen, J., 1992, "Learning a Trajectory Using Adjoint Functions and Teacher Forcing", *Neural Networks, 5*, 473-484.

8. Rohwer, R., 1991, "Time Trials on Second Order and Variable-Learning Rate Algorithms", *Adv. Neur. Inf. Proc Syst., 3*, 977-983.

9. Hinton, G., 1989, "Deterministic Boltzmann Learning Performs Steepest Descent in Weight Space", *Neural Computation, (1)*, 143-150.

10. Guillerm, T.J., Cotter, N.E., 1991, "A Diffusion Processfor Global Optimization in Neural Networks," *IEEE INNS, 1*, 335-340.

11. Cetin, B., Barhen, J., and Burdick, J., 1993, "Terminal Repeller Unconstrained Subenergy Tunneling for Fast Global Optimization", *Journal of Optimization Theory and Applications, 77* (1), 97-126.

12. Zak, M., 1989, "Terminal Attractors in Neural Networks", *Neural Networks, 2*, (4), 259-274.

13. Fisher, A.J., 1986, "A New Algorithm for Generating Hilbert Curves", *Software-Practice and Experience, 16*(1), 5-12 (1986).

14. Cherrualt, Y. and A. Guillez, 1983, *Comptes Rendus de l'Academie des sciences, Paris, 296*(I), 175-178.

15 Alfuffi-Pentini, F., Parisi, V., and Zirilli, F., 1985, *Global Optimization and Stochastic Differential Equations*, Journal of Optimization Theory and Applications, Vol. 47, pp. 1-15.

16 Levy, A.V., and Montalvo, A., 1985, *The Tunneling Algorithm for the Global Minimization of Functions*, SIAM Journal on Scientific and Statistical Computing, Vol. 6, pp. 15-29

17 Walster, G.W., Hansen, E. R., and Sengupta, S. 1985, *Test Results for a Global Optimization Problem, Numerical Optimization, Edited by P.T. Boggs, R. H. Byrd, and R.B. Schnabel, SIAM, Philadelphia, Pennsylvania,.pp. 272-287.*

Covariance Learning Rules for
Stochastic Neural Networks

Javier R. Movellan
University of California San Diego
James L. McClelland
Carnegie Mellon University

In the present article we present two learning rules for symmetric diffusion networks (SDN), a family of networks related to the Boltzmann machines but that work in continuous time with continuous activations. We focus our analysis primarily on a property of SDN's and Boltzmann machines that arises jointly from their stochastic character and the pressence of symmetric connections. This is the fact that they are capable of using covariance information, rather than explicit error information, to drive learning. In essence, symmetric connectivity allows covariances between quantities computed deep inside a network and quantities computed at the output to provide information on how to improve performance. In the following sections we briefly describe SDN's followed by the derivation of the learning rules and simulation experiments.

1   THE DIFFUSION EQUATION

SDN's can be seen as a variant of the continuous Hopfield model (1984) but with hidden units and a stochastic component. Let $\mathbf{a} = [a_1, ...a_n]$ be a real valued activation row vector. Let $\mathbf{W} = [\mathbf{w}_1^T, ..., \mathbf{w}_n^T]$ be a real valued symmetric matrix of connections, where each $\mathbf{w}_i^T$ is the column vector of connections to the ith unit. The evolution of the activations is governed by the following system of stochastic differential equations:

$$da_i(t) = \lambda_i \, drift_i(t) \, dt + \sigma dB_i(t) \; ; \;\; i \in \{1, ..., n\} \tag{1}$$

where λ_i is the processing rate of the ith unit, σ is the diffusion constant, which controls the flow of entropy throughout the network, and $dB_i(t)$ is a Brownian motion differential (Soon, 1973).

Equation 1 is known as a Langevin description of a Markovian diffusion process with a *diffusion matrix* $\sigma \mathbf{I}$ and a *drift vector* $\mathbf{drift}(\mathbf{a}) = [drift_1(\mathbf{a}), ..., drift_n(\mathbf{a})]$. The drift vector is the exact gradient, times a negative sign, of a Hopfield style *Goodness function*

$$G(\mathbf{a}) = \frac{1}{2} \mathbf{a} \mathbf{W} \, \mathbf{a}^T - \sum_{i=1}^{n} \frac{1}{g_i} \int_{rest}^{a_i} f(x)dx \tag{2}$$

where $rest = f(0)$. We call the integral $\int_{rest}^{a_i} f(x)dx$ the *stress* (s_i) of the ith unit. If we use a logit function scaled in the min-max interval, the stress has the following form:

$$s_i = (a_i - min)log(a_i - min) + (max - a_i)log(max - a_i) \tag{3}$$

A known result in Markovian diffusion theory is that processes defined by a Langevin equation satisfy the *forward Fokker-Planck diffusion equation*. In the SDN case, the diffusion equation assumes the following form:

$$\frac{\partial P(\mathbf{a};t|\mathbf{a}_0;t_0)}{\partial t} = -\nabla.(\mathbf{drift(a)}\ P(\mathbf{a};t|\mathbf{a}_0;t_0)\ ) + \frac{\sigma^2}{2}\nabla^2 P(\mathbf{a};t|\mathbf{a}_0;t_0) \quad (4)$$

where $P(\mathbf{a};t|\mathbf{a}_0;t_0)$ represents the probability density of the network being in state $\mathbf{a}$, at time t, given that it was in state $\mathbf{a}_0$ at time $t_0 \leq t$. The symbol $\nabla.$ is the *divergence operator*

$$\nabla.(\mathbf{drift(a)}P(\mathbf{a};t|\mathbf{a}_0;t_0)\ ) = \sum_{i=1}^{n}\frac{\partial}{\partial a_i}(drift_i(\mathbf{a})\ P(\mathbf{a};t|\mathbf{a}_0;t_0)\ ) \quad (5)$$

and ∇^2 is the divergence of the gradient, also known as the *Laplace operator*,

$$\nabla^2 P(\mathbf{a};t|\mathbf{a}_0;t_0) = \nabla.\nabla P(\mathbf{a};t|\mathbf{a}_0;t_0) = \sum_{i=1}^{n}\frac{\partial^2 P(\mathbf{a};t|\mathbf{a}_0;t_0)}{\partial a_i^2} \quad (6)$$

It is easy to show that the Boltzmann probability density function

$$P(\mathbf{a}) = \frac{1}{Z}e^{2G(\mathbf{a})/\sigma^2} \quad (7)$$

makes the left side of equation 4 vanish and is the unique limiting distribution in these networks.

2 COVARIANCE LEARNING RULES

To begin, we partition the activation vector, $\mathbf{a} \in \{A\}$, into an input vector, $\mathbf{x} \in \{X\}$, a vector of hidden unit activations, $\mathbf{h} \in \{H\}$, and an output vector, $\mathbf{y} \in \{Y\}$. So that $\mathbf{a} = [\mathbf{x}, \mathbf{h}, \mathbf{y}]$. The input, hidden, and output sets may be different for different patterns. The central problem is to find the gradient with respect to the weight and gain parameters of an error function in the set of output units when the set of input units is fixed to a particular vector $\mathbf{x}$. Since most of the results are common to both gains and weights, we proceed with our derivations in terms of a generic parameter θ, which can be a weight parameter w_{ij}, or a gain parameter g_k. Let us define a random variable, τ, which we will name the *goodness signal*

$$\tau_{\mathbf{xhy}} = \frac{\partial G_{\mathbf{xhy}}(\theta)}{\partial \theta} \quad (8)$$

From the definition of goodness in equation 2 it is easy to show that for $\theta = w_{ij}$

$$\tau_{\mathbf{xhy}} = (a_i \, a_j)_{\mathbf{xhy}} \tag{9}$$

where $(a_i \, a_j)_{\mathbf{xhy}}$ is the coproduct of the ith and j^{th} elements in the **xhy** vector. For $\theta = g_k^{-1}$

$$\tau_{\mathbf{xhy}} = -\int_{rest}^{(a_k)_{\mathbf{xhy}}} f(x)dx = -s_i$$

We now proceed to derive the learning rules.

2.1 Minimizing Information Gain

In this case the derivations are similar to the Boltzmann machine learning derivations (Ackley *et al.*, 1985) but replacing sums with integrals. However, since SDNs are defined in continuous activation space, we can also derive rules for the gain parameters.

We use as error function a continuous version of the *total information gain* function (Ackley *et al.*, 1985)

$$TIG_{\mathbf{x}}(\theta) = \int_Y P_{\mathbf{x}d}(\mathbf{y}) \, ln(\frac{P_{\mathbf{x}d}(\mathbf{y})}{P_{\mathbf{x}}(\mathbf{y})}) \, d\mathbf{y} \tag{10}$$

where $P_{\mathbf{x}}(\mathbf{y})$ represents the obtained equilibrium probability of output vector **y**, when the input activations are fixed to the vector **x** and $P_{\mathbf{x}d}(\mathbf{y})$ represents the desired probability density of the output vector **y** when the environment is in input state **x**.

Following steps similar to those used in the Boltzmann machine derivations but replacing sums with integrals it can be shown that

$$\frac{\partial TIG_{\mathbf{x}}(\theta)}{\partial \theta} = -\frac{2}{\sigma^2}(E_d(E_{\mathbf{xy}}(\tau)) - E_{\mathbf{x}}(\tau)) \tag{11}$$

where $E_d()$ is the expected value using the desired probability distribution of output vectors; $E_{\mathbf{xy}}(a_i a_j)$ is the expected value of the product of the activations of the ith and j^{th} units when the input units are fixed to pattern **x**, the output units are fixed to pattern **y** and the *hidden units* are free to evolve according to equation 4; $E_{\mathbf{x}}(a_i a_j)$ represents the expected value of this product when the input units are fixed to pattern **x** but the output and hidden units are free, and ϵ is the *step-size* for weight changes. As in the Boltzmann machine, when the network runs with inputs fixed to **x** and outputs fixed to **y**, it is said to be in a fixed (plus) phase. When the inputs are fixed to **x** but the outputs units are not fixed, the network is said to be in a free (minus) phase.

The learning rule for weights is often called contrastive Hebbian Learning (Galland and Hinton, 1989; Movellan, 1990)

$$\Delta w_{ij} = \epsilon \frac{2}{\sigma^2} \left(E_d(E_{\mathbf{xy}}(a_i a_j)) - E_{\mathbf{x}}(a_i a_j) \right) \tag{12}$$

2.2 Minimizing the Error of Average Activations

This rule is the SDN equivalent of the generalized delta rule (Werbos, 1974; LeCun, 1985;Rumelhart *et al.*, 1986) in back propagation networks, based on minimization of the total sum of squares (TSS). This is an appropriate error function for deterministic problems or for deterministic problems with independent noise contamination, where we just need to learn average values of the output units. Since the error of each output unit is combined in an additive manner, we do not lose generality by focusing on the case where there is a unique output unit

$$TSS(\theta) = (E_{\mathbf{x}}(y) - d)^2 \tag{13}$$

where d is a desired real value and $E_{\mathbf{x}}(y)$ the expected value of the output unit when the input units are fixed to $\mathbf{x}$. Using the chain rule

$$\frac{\partial}{\partial \theta} TSS(\theta) = (E_{\mathbf{x}}(y) - d) \frac{\partial}{\partial \theta} E_{\mathbf{x}}(y) \tag{14}$$

Itcan be seen that

$$\frac{\partial}{\partial \theta} TSS(\theta) = Cov_{\mathbf{x}}(\tau; y \delta_y) \tag{15}$$

where $\delta_y = (E_{\mathbf{x}}(y) - d)$; $Cov_{\mathbf{x}}(\tau; y)$ is the covariance between the goodness signal, $\tau_{\mathbf{xhy}}$, and the activation of the output unit y when the inputs are fixed to $\mathbf{x}$. For more than one output unit, the desired gradients can be computed very efficiently using the following relationship

$$\frac{\partial}{\partial \theta} TSS(\theta) = \sum_Y Cov_{\mathbf{x}}(\tau; y \delta_y) = Cov_{\mathbf{x}}(\tau; \sum_Y y \delta_y) \tag{16}$$

The learning rules for gains and weights easily follow

$$\Delta w_{ij} = -\epsilon \frac{2}{\sigma^2} Cov_{\mathbf{x}}(a_i a_j; \sum_Y y \delta_y) \tag{17}$$

$$\Delta g_k^{-1} = \epsilon \frac{2}{\sigma^2} Cov_{\mathbf{x}}(s_k; \sum_Y y \delta_y) \tag{18}$$

2.3 Simulations

We tested the learning rules on a simple exclusive-or problem. Table 1 shows the median number of epochs to criterion and, in parenthesis, the percentage of simulations where criterion was achieved in less than 4000 epochs. These statistics where obtained with 20 runs per cell with random starting weights chosen from a uniform (-1, 1) distribution.

Table 1 shows that CHL was the fastest algorithm in terms of number of epochs, followed by the MEA rule. However, since the CHL rule requires two learning phases, the MEA algorithm had comparable speed in terms of learning phases. There was not a statistically significant difference between the average number of phases, using optimal stepsizes, for the CHL and for the MEA rule ($t(38)=$ 0.19 ; $p \geq 0.05$).

Learning rule	stepsize					
	0.1		0.01		0.001	
CHL	81	(90%)	72	(100%)	308.5	(100%)
MEA	98.5	(100%)	94	(100%)	785.5	(100%)

3 CONCLUSIONS

The work presented here builds on previous work on stochastic networks (Ackley, Hinton and Sejnowski 1985; Geman and Geman, 1984; Smolensky, 1986) and extends it to the continuous case. In particular we have explored the problem of learning in a stochastic network that works in continuous time with continuous activation states. We have presented learning algorithms based on computations of simple covariances that are capable of learning problems that require hidden units. One of the advantages of noise in these networks is that it provides enough information to calculate gradients with respect to weights without explicit back-propagation of error through a network of inverted weights and activation function derivatives. This aspect makes the learning rules attractive for biologically oriented simulations and for hardware implementations.

References

[1] Ackley D, Hinton G and Sejnowski T (1985) A learning algorithm for Boltzmann machines. *Cognitive Science*, 9, 147-169.

[2] Alspector J, Jayakumar A, Luna S (1992) Experimental evaluation of learning in a neural mycrosystem, in Moody, J, Hanson, S, Lippmann R. *Advances in Neural Information Processing Systems*, Vol 4., 871-878.

[3] Geman S, Geman D (1984) Stochastic relaxation, Gibbs distributions and the Bayesian restoration of images. *IEEE Transactions on Patterns Analysis and Machine Intelligence*, 6, 721-741.

[4] Gillespie D (1992) Markov Processes: An introduction for Physical Scientists. San Diego, Academic Press. 1, 143-150.

[5] Hopfield J (1984) Neurons with graded response have collective computational properties like those of two-state neurons. *Proceedings of the National Academy of Sciences U.S.A.*, **81**, 3088-3092.

[6] Y. LeCun (1985) A learning scheme for asymmetric threshold networks. Proc of *Cognitiva*, 323, 533-536.

[7] Smolensky P (1986) Information Processing in Dynamical Systems: Foundations of Harmony Theory. in D. Rumelhart, & J. L. McClelland (1986) *Parallel distributed processing: Explorations in the microstructure of cognition. Volume 1: Foundations.* Camgbridge, Mass: M. I. T. Press.

[8] Werbos P (1974) Beyond Regression: New tools for prediction and analysis in the behavioral sciences. Ph.D. Thesis. Harvard University.

Network Reciprocity: A Simple Approach to Derive Gradient Algorithms for Arbitrary Neural Network Structures.

Eric A. Wan[*] and Françoise Beaufays[†]

Abstract

Deriving backpropagation algorithms for time-dependent neural network structures typically requires numerous chain rule expansions, diligent bookkeeping, and careful manipulation of terms. In this paper, we show how to use the principle of *Network Reciprocity* to derive such algorithms via a set of block diagram manipulation rules. Examples are provided that illustrate the simplicity of the approach. Algorithms are derived for a variety of structures, including feedforward and feedback systems.

Network Adaptation and Error Gradient Propagation

Adapting a feedforward multilayer neural network structure amounts to finding the set of variable weights W that minimizes the cost function:

$$J = \sum_{k=1}^{K} \mathbf{e}(k)^T \mathbf{e}(k), \tag{1}$$

where the sum is taken over K samples in a training sequence, and $\mathbf{e}(k)$ is the error vector.

In certain problems (*e.g.*, time series prediction, system identification), a desired output is specified at each time step; in others (*e.g.*, terminal control), the desired output is defined only at final time $k = K$. Therefore, we define the error vector $\mathbf{e}(k)$ as the difference between the desired and the actual output vectors when a desired output is available, and as zero otherwise.

According to gradient descent, the contribution to the weight update at each time step is

$$\Delta W(k) = -\mu \, \frac{\partial J}{\partial W(k)}, \tag{2}$$

where μ controls the learning rate. Note we evaluate $\partial J / \partial W(k)$ rather than the instantaneous gradient $\partial(\mathbf{e}^T(k)\mathbf{e}(k))/\partial W(k)$. This is essential for the desired Network Reciprocity result.

At the architectural level, a variable weight[‡] w_{ij} may be isolated between two points in a network with corresponding signals $a_i(k)$ and $a_j(k)$ (*i.e.*, $a_j(k) = w_{ij}\, a_i(k)$). Using the chain rule, we get

$$\frac{\partial J}{\partial w_{ij}(k)} = \frac{\partial J}{\partial a_j(k)} \frac{\partial a_j(k)}{\partial w_{ij}(k)} = \frac{\partial J}{\partial a_j(k)}\, a_i(k), \tag{3}$$

and the weight update becomes

$$\Delta w_{ij}(k) = -\mu\, \delta_j(k)\, a_i(k), \tag{4}$$

---

[*]Dept. of Electrical Engineering and Applied Physics, Oregon Graduate Institute of Science and Technology, P.O.box 91000, Portland, OR 97291.

[†]Dept. of Electrical Engineering, Stanford University, Stanford, CA 94305-4055. This work was sponsored by EPRI under contract RP8010-13 and NSF under grant NSF IRI 91-12531.

[‡]The general case of a variable coefficient, $a_j(k) = f(w_{ij}, a_i(k))$, is treated in [5,6].

where we define the error gradient

$$\delta_j(k) \triangleq \frac{\partial J}{\partial a_j(k)}. \tag{5}$$

The error gradient $\delta_j(k)$ depends on the entire topology of the network. Reported methods for deriving the delta terms rest on chain rule expansions, which must be carefully applied for the specific network topology. In the next section, the method of Network Reciprocity is introduced as a means for finding the delta terms without algebraic derivation. A set of simple block diagram rules are used to construct a *reciprocal network*, which then directly specifies the adaptive algorithm.

Construction of a Reciprocal Network

An arbitrary multilayer network can be represented as a block diagram whose building blocks are: summing junctions, branching points, univariate functions, multivariate functions, and delay operators.

The *reciprocal network* is constructed by reversing the flow direction in the original network, labeling all resulting signals $\delta_i(k)$, and performing the following operations.

1. *Summing junctions are replaced with branching points.*

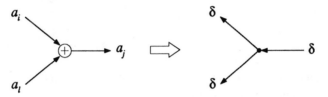

2. *Branching points are replaced with summing junctions.*

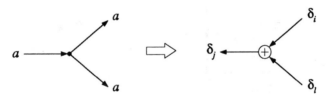

3. *Univariate functions are replaced with their derivatives.*

$$a_i(k) \longrightarrow \boxed{f(\ )} \longrightarrow a_j(k) \qquad \Longrightarrow \qquad \delta_i(k) \longleftarrow \boxed{f'(a_i(k))} \longleftarrow \delta_j(k)$$

Explicitly, $\delta_i(k) = f'(a_i(k))\,\delta_j(k)$, where $f'(a_i(k)) \triangleq \partial a_j(k)/\partial a_i(k)$. We have included the time index k to emphasize the linear *time-dependent* transmittance. Special cases are:

- Weights, $a_j = w_{ij}\,a_i$, in which case $\delta_i = w_{ij}\,\delta_j$.

$$a_i \xrightarrow{\ w_{ij}\ } a_j \qquad \Longrightarrow \qquad \delta_i \xleftarrow{\ w_{ij}\ } \delta_j$$

- Activation function: $a_n(k) = tanh(a_j(k))$. In this case, $f'(a_j(k)) = 1 - a_n^2(k)$.

$$a_j(k) \longrightarrow \boxed{tanh(\ )} \longrightarrow a_n(k) \qquad \Longrightarrow \qquad \delta_j(k) \longleftarrow \boxed{1 - a_n^2(k)} \longleftarrow \delta_n(k)$$

III-383

4. *Multivariate functions are replaced with their Jacobians.*

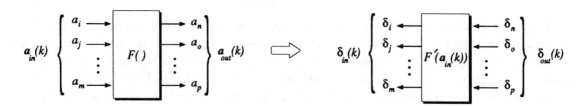

Explicitly, $\delta_{in}(k) = F'(\mathbf{a}_{in}(k))\,\delta_{out}(k)$, where $F'(\mathbf{a}_{in}(k)) \triangleq \partial\mathbf{a}_{out}(k)/\partial\mathbf{a}_{in}(k)$ corresponds to a matrix of partial derivatives. For shorthand, $F'(\mathbf{a}_{in}(k))$ will be written simply as $F'(k)$. Note this rule replaces a nonlinear function by a *linear time-dependent* transmittance. Important cases include:

- Product junctions, $a_j(k) = a_i(k)\,a_l(k)$, in which case $F' = [a_l(k)\ a_i(k)]^T$:

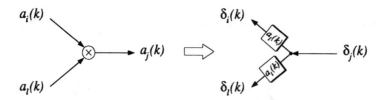

- Layered networks, in which case the product $F'(\mathbf{a}_{in}(k))\,\delta_{out}(k)$ is found directly by backpropagating δ_{out} through the network:

5. *Delay operators are replaced with advance operators.*

$$a_i(k) \longrightarrow \boxed{q^{-1}} \longrightarrow a_j(k) = a_i(k{-}1) \quad \Longrightarrow \quad \delta_i(k) = \delta_j(k{+}1) \longleftarrow \boxed{q^{+1}} \longleftarrow \delta_j(k)$$

Explicitly, $a_j(k) = q^{-1}a_i(k) = a_i(k-1)$ is transformed into $\delta_i(k) = q^{+1}\delta_j(k) = \delta_j(k+1)$. This forces the reciprocal system to be noncausal and is crucial for maintaining the topological equivalence between the original network and its reciprocal. Making the system causal is an implementation issue that must be addressed for each specific examples.

These 5 rules allow direct construction of the reciprocal network from the original network. Note there is a topological equivalence between the two networks. By reversing the signal flow, output nodes in the original network become input nodes in the reciprocal network. These inputs are then set at each time step to $-2e_i(k)$. The signals $\delta_j(k)$ that propagate through the reciprocal network correspond to the terms $\partial J/\partial a_j(k)$ necessary for gradient adaptation. The exact equations are "read-out" directly from the reciprocal network. A formal proof that this *always* provides the correct derivation may be found in [5,6].

Examples

Backpropagation

We start be rederiving standard backpropagation [3] using the principles of Network Reciprocity. Figure 1 shows a hidden neuron feeding other neurons and an output neuron in a multilayer network. For consistency with traditional notation, we have labeled the summing junction signal s_i^l rather than a_i, and added superscripts to denote the layer. In addition, since the multilayer networks are static structures, we omit the time index k.

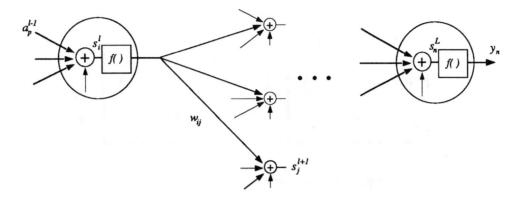

Figure 1: **Block diagram construction of a multilayer network.**

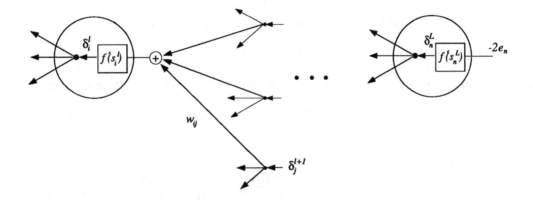

Figure 2: **Reciprocal multilayer network.**

The reciprocal network shown in Figure 2 is found by applying the construction rules of the previous section. From this figure, we may immediately write down the equations for calculating the delta terms:

$$\delta_i^l = \begin{cases} -2e_i \, f'(s_i^L) & l = L \\ f'(s_i^l) \cdot \displaystyle\sum_j \delta_j^{l+1} \cdot w_{ij}^{l+1} & 0 \le l \le L - 1. \end{cases} \tag{6}$$

By Equation 4 the weight update is given by

$$\Delta w_{ij}^l = -\mu \, \delta_j^l \, a_i^{l-1}. \tag{7}$$

III-385

These are precisely the equations describing standard backpropagation. It should be emphasized that this approach provided a *formal* derivation requiring no chain rule expansions.

Cascaded Neural Networks

Let us now turn to the more complicated example of two cascaded neural networks as illustrated in Figure 3. The inputs to the first network are samples from a time sequence $x(k)$. Delayed outputs of the first network are fed to the second network. Typically, the last network represents the model of some physical system, and the first network is used to prewarp or equalize the driving signal.

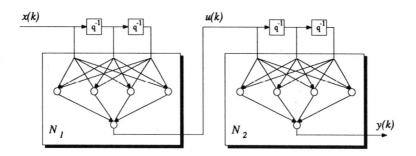

Figure 3: Cascaded neural network filters.

The cascaded networks are defined as

$$u(k) = \mathcal{N}_1(W_1, x(k), x(k-1), x(k-2)), \tag{8}$$

$$y(k) = \mathcal{N}_2(W_2, u(k), u(k-1), u(k-2)), \tag{9}$$

where W_1 and W_2 represent the weights parameterizing the networks, $x(k)$ is the input, $y(k)$ the output, and $u(k)$ the intermediate signal. Given a desired response for the output y of the second network, it is a straightforward procedure to use backpropagation for adapting the second network. It is not obvious, however, what the effective error should be for the first network. In this case, the chain rule is simple enough to apply directly to find the instantaneous error gradient:

$$\frac{\partial e^2(k)}{\partial W_1} = -2e(k)\frac{\partial y(k)}{\partial W_1} \tag{10}$$

$$= -2e(k)\left[\frac{\partial y(k)}{\partial u(k)}\frac{\partial u(k)}{\partial W_1} + \frac{\partial y(k)}{\partial u(k-1)}\frac{\partial u(k-1)}{\partial W_1} + \frac{\partial y(k)}{\partial u(k-2)}\frac{\partial u(k-2)}{\partial W_1}\right]$$

$$= \delta_1(k)\frac{\partial u(k)}{\partial W_1} + \delta_2(k)\frac{\partial u(k-1)}{\partial W_1} + \delta_3(k)\frac{\partial u(k-2)}{\partial W_1}, \tag{11}$$

where we define

$$\delta_i(k) \stackrel{\triangle}{=} -2e(k)\frac{\partial y(k)}{\partial u(k-i)} \qquad i = 1, 2, 3.$$

The δ_i terms are found simultaneously by a single backpropagation of the error through the second network. Each product $\delta_{i+1}(k)\partial u(k-i)/\partial W_1$ is then found by backpropagation applied to the first network with $\delta_{i+1}(k)$ acting as an error. However, since the derivatives used in backpropagation are time-dependent, *separate* backpropagations are necessary for each $\delta_{i+1}(k)$. These equations, in fact, imply backpropagation through an *unfolded* structure as illustrated in Figure 4. In situations where there may be hundreds of taps in the second network, this approach leads to a very inefficient adaptation algorithm.

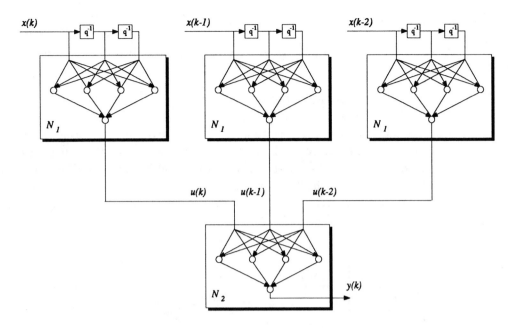

Figure 4: Cascaded neural network filters unfolded-in-time.

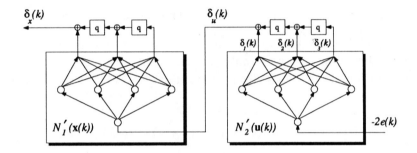

Figure 5: Reciprocal network for cascaded neural filters.

A more efficient algorithm for finding the delta terms may be arrived at by returning to the method of Network Reciprocity. The original cascaded networks are transformed into the reciprocal structure shown in Figure 5. Simply by labeling the desired signals, gradient relations may be written down directly:

$$\delta_u(k) = \delta_1(k) + \delta_2(k+1) + \delta_3(k+2), \tag{12}$$

with

$$[\delta_1(k)\ \delta_2(k)\ \delta_3(k)] = -2e(k)\,\mathcal{N}_2'(\mathbf{u}(k)), \tag{13}$$

i.e., each $\delta_i(k)$ is found by backpropagation through the output network, and the δ_i's (after appropriate advance operations) are summed together. The weight update is given by

$$\Delta W_1(k) = -\mu\,\delta_u(k)\,\frac{\partial u(k)}{\partial W_1(k)}, \tag{14}$$

in which the product term is found by a *single* backpropagation with $\delta_u(k)$ acting as the error to first network. Equations can be made causal by simply delaying the weight update for a few time steps. Clearly generalization to an arbitrary number of taps is also straightforward. This new algorithm is far more efficient than the earlier direct gradient calculation method: we completely avoided backpropagation through a redundant unfolded network.

Backpropagation-Through-Time

So far, we have examined only feedforward structures. Figure 6 illustrates a recurrent network described by

$$\mathbf{y}(k) = \mathcal{N}(\mathbf{x}(k), \mathbf{y}(k-1)), \tag{15}$$

where $\mathbf{x}(k)$ are external inputs, and $\mathbf{y}(k)$ represents the *vector* of outputs that form feedback connections. $\mathcal{N}$ is a multilayer neural network. If $\mathcal{N}$ has only one layer of neurons, every neuron output has a feedback connection to the input of every other neuron and the structure is referred to as a *fully recurrent network* [9]. Typically, only a select set of the outputs have an actual desired response. The remaining outputs have no desired response (error equals zero) and are used for internal computation.

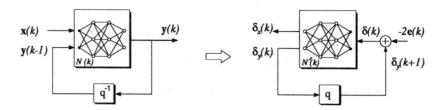

Figure 6: **Recurrent network and backpropagation-through-time.**

Calculating the gradients for such a structure can be extremely complicated. A weight perturbation at a specified time step affects not only the output at future time steps, but future inputs as well. However, applying the Network Reciprocity rules (see Figure 6) we find immediately:

$$\begin{aligned}
\boldsymbol{\delta}(k) &= \boldsymbol{\delta}_y(k) - 2\mathbf{e}(k) \\
&= \mathcal{N}'(k+1)\boldsymbol{\delta}(k+1) - 2\mathbf{e}(k).
\end{aligned} \tag{16}$$

Note the causality constraints require these equations to be run backward in time. These are precisely the equations describing *backpropagation-through-time*, which have been derived in the past using either ordered derivatives [8] or Euler-Lagrange techniques [2]. Network Reciprocity is by far the simplest and most direct approach.

Other examples

Backpropagation-through-time has been modified for a variety of neural control problems [1]. Suppose the state-space model of a dynamic system is given and a neural controller is to be built to drive the plant. The overall structure is related to the recurrent network seen in the previous section, in which $\mathbf{y}(k)$ is the plant state vector, and $\mathbf{x}(k)$ is the output of an additional neural controller taking as inputs past states $\mathbf{y}(k-1)$. Again, Network Reciprocity provides a direct derivation of the adaptation algorithm.

A more general case is obtained by passing the state vector and the driving signal through tapped-delay lines before entering the controller and/or plant model. Deriving the adaptation algorithms for the resulting ARMA (AutoRegressive Moving Average) networks would be extremely difficult without using Network Reciprocity.

Related to cascaded networks are structures that distribute time delays through the entire network. Such architectures include *FIR neural networks* [6,7] (where the synaptic connections of the traditional multilayer neural network are replaced by FIR (Finite Impulse Response) filters), *time-delay neural networks* [4] (where time-delays are introduced between the hidden layers of a feedforward neural network), IIR (Infinite Impulse Response) structures, and lattice filters. For such networks, direct chain rule expansions or equivalent unfolded structures are extremely complicated. In all cases, Network Reciprocity provides a quick and easy way to derive the desired adaptation algorithm.

Bibliography

1. W.T. Miller III, R.S. Sutton, P.J. Werbos, editors. *Neural Networks for Control.* MIT Press, Cambridge, MA, 1990.

2. E. Plumer. *Optimal Terminal Control Using Feedforward Neural Networks.* Ph.D. dissertation. Stanford University, Aug. 1993.

3. D.E. Rumelhart, J.L. McClelland, and the PDP Research Group. *Parallel Distributed Processing: Explorations in the Microstructure of Cognition.* Vol. 1. MIT Press, Cambridge, MA, 1986.

4. A. Waibel, T. Hanazawa, G. Hinton, K. Shikano, and K. Lang. Phoneme recognition using time-delay neural networks. *IEEE Transactions on Acoustics, Speech, and Signal Processing.* Vol. 37(3), March 1989, pp. 328-339.

5. E. Wan and F. Beaufays. Network Reciprocity: A Unified Approach to Derive Gradient Algorithms for Arbitrary Neural Network Structures. Submitted to *Neural Computation.*

6. E. Wan. *Finite Impulse Response Neural Networks with Applications in Time Series Prediction.* Ph.D. dissertation. Stanford University, Nov. 1993.

7. E. Wan. Time series prediction using a connectionist network with internal delay lines. In A. Weigend and N. Gershenfeld, editors, *Time Series Prediction: Forecasting the Future and Understanding the Past,* Addison-Wesley, 1993.

8. P. Werbos. Generalization of backpropagation with application to a recurrent gas market model. *Neural Networks.* Vol. 1, 1988, pp. 339-356.

9. R.J. Williams and D. Zipser. A learning algorithm for continually running fully recurrent neural networks. *Neural Computation.* Vol. 1(2), 1989, pp. 270-280.

Efficient Learning through Cooperation*

R. Venkateswaran
rvenkate@eecs.wsu.edu

Zoran Obradović
zoran@eecs.wsu.edu

School of Electrical Engineering and Computer Science
Washington State University, Pullman WA 99164-2752

Abstract

A new algorithm has been proposed which uses cooperative efforts of several identical neural networks for efficient gradient descent learning. In contrast to the sequential gradient descent, in this algorithm it is easy to select learning rates such that the number of epochs for convergence is minimized. This algorithm is suitable for implementation on a parallel or distributed environment. It has been implemented on a network of heterogeneous workstations using p4. Results are presented where few learners cooperate and learn much faster than if they learn individually.

1 Introduction

The goal of supervised learning from examples is generalization using some preclassified inputs (training set). Learning in neural networks is achieved by adjusting the connection strengths (*weights*) among processors, so that the outputs reflect the class of the input patterns. One popular method of adjusting the weights is gradient descent learning through back-propagation [8]. Unfortunately, in the back-propagation algorithm, a number of parameters have to be appropriately specified. If parameters are not appropriate, the algorithm can take a long time to converge or may not converge at all [7]. Due to local minimum problem, an appropriate learning rate significantly affects the quality of the generalization and the number of epochs for convergence [2]. Selection of an appropriate learning rate is a computationally expensive experimental problem that can be solved satisfactorily for small networks only [5].

The goal of this paper is to speed-up learning with improved accuracy using systems composed of several neural networks of the same topology that concurrently run the standard back-propagation algorithm. Our approach is different from the approach in [6] where each network learns a subset of training examples. In our system, the various networks periodically communicate with each other and cooperate in learning the entire training set. If any of the processes gets stuck in a local minimum site, the rest of the processes help in moving it out of this predicament. The algorithm also works well if any process gets stuck in a plateau or a ridge.

In Section 2, we propose this new cooperative learning algorithm, followed by experimental results in Section 3 and analysis in Section 4.

2 Cooperative Learning Algorithm

In our algorithm, several processes run the standard back-propagation algorithm concurrently. All processes work on neural networks of identical topology, each using a local copy of the training set. These processes are called the *slave* processes. A *master* process initiates these slaves and controls them. The slaves communicate only with the master. The master initializes its *hypothesis* (the weights and the bias values of the neurons) and broadcasts it to the slaves. The slaves adjust this hypothesis using back-propagation. Each slave uses its own learning rate that is different from the learning rates of other slaves and hence, the adjusted hypothesis in each of the slaves is different.

---

*Research sponsored in part by the NSF research grant NSF-IRI-9308523.

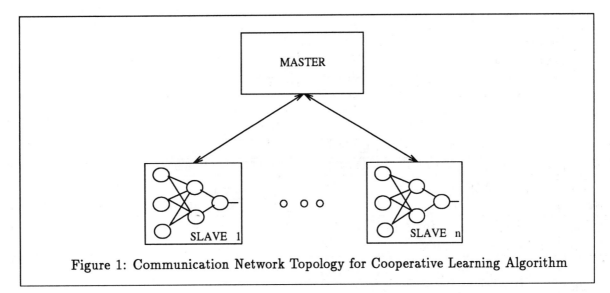

Figure 1: Communication Network Topology for Cooperative Learning Algorithm

Periodically, the slaves cooperate by exchanging information. The period between two cooperations is called an *era*.

The algorithm is suitable for implementation on a distributed platform since the communication graph is simple and the total number of communications is small (Figure 1). Our implementation uses *p*4 which supports parallel programming for both distributed environments and highly parallel computers [1]. It helps to create the master and the slave processes and provides easy means of communication between them. Another advantage of using *p*4 for neural networks implementation is its ability to port directly from a distributed to a highly parallel platform [4].

2.1 Epoch-based Cooperation

In *epoch-based cooperation*, the slaves communicate their learned weights back to the master after a specified number of epochs (one *era*). Since all slaves use the identical topology, the master forms a new hypothesis after each era by averaging these weights. For each link between neurons, the new weight is the average of the weights of that link as computed by the slaves. This hypothesis is broadcast to the slaves and they proceed with back-propagation for the next era starting from this new hypothesis. When any of the slaves has learned the training set to satisfaction, the hypothesis learned by this slave is output and learning is completed.

2.2 Time-based Cooperation

One disadvantage of the epoch-based cooperation is that the slaves on faster machines finish their era earlier but they have to wait for the slowest slave to finish its era. So, in a heterogeneous environment, the slowest machine is a bottle-neck and one cannot take advantage of faster machines. For such heterogeneous environments, we propose another approach called the *time-based cooperation*. Here, the era is specified as a duration of time rather than number of epochs. Since all slaves run for the same duration, no machine will be idle.

2.3 Cooperation with Dynamic Learning Rates

In this approach, we start with the cooperative algorithm (epoch or time based) using initial learning rates spread uniformly in (0,1) range. After few eras, the range of the learning rates is reduced. New values for the learning rates are chosen uniformly around the value of the learning

	Problem :	To classify 'A', 'I' and 'O'.	
	Dimensionality :	2	Number of Classes : 3
	Architecture :	2-9-3	Size of Training Set : 16
	Percentage Learned :	100%	Era : 50 epochs

One Node	η	0.01	0.05	0.1	0.125	0.15	0.175	0.2
	Epochs	8708	1819	1295	1179	1419	>10000	>10000

Two Nodes	$\eta1$, $\eta2$	0.05 , 0.15	0.1 , 0.15	0.01 , 0.15	0.05 , 0.175
	Epochs	1099	1040	1374	985

Three Nodes	$\eta1,\eta2,\eta3$	0.05 , 0.10 , 0.15	0.01 , 0.1 , 0.2
	Epochs	1149	1148

Four Nodes	$\eta1$, $\eta2$, $\eta3$, $\eta4$	0.05 , 0.1 , 0.15 , 0.2
	Epochs	946

Figure 2: Epoch-based Cooperation for Pattern Classification Problem

rate of the slave which currently generalizes the best. The advantage of this approach is that the selection of an optimal learning rate becomes completely automatic.

3 Results

Two benchmark problems are used for experimentation. The experiments are performed by varying the number of slaves from one to four. Both the epoch-based and the time-based cooperation are tested.

3.1 Pattern Classification Problem

The problem is to classify three patterns, 'A', 'I' and 'O', formed in a 4-by-4 grid, using a feedforward network. Figure 2 gives the results of the epoch-based cooperation for this problem. In this figure, One Node table gives the number of epochs required to learn the training set using sequential back-propagation algorithm with various learning rates. The number of epochs to learn the training set using the cooperative system of two slaves with various pairs of learning rates is given in Two Nodes table. Here, one slave uses the learning rate $\eta1$ and the other uses $\eta2$. Similarly, other tables show results for cooperative systems of three and four slaves respectively.

3.2 Two-Spirals Problem

This hard benchmark problem consists of two classes of points arranged in two interlocking spirals that go around the origin [3]. The goal is to develop a feed forward network that classifies all the training points correctly. The results of the epoch-based cooperative learning algorithm on a training set of 40 points are given in Figure 3.

Figure 4 gives results of the time-based cooperative algorithm. In one experiment, the cooperative algorithm using two slaves is run on a homogeneous system consisting of two DEC3100

Problem : Two-Spirals Problem.
Dimensionality : 2 Number of Classes : 2
Architecture : 2-5-1 Size of Training Set : 40
Percentage Learned : 100% Era : 100 epochs

One Node	η	0.05	0.1	0.15	0.2	0.25	0.3	0.35	0.4	0.5
	Epochs	>30000	8799	3683	2593	2238	1727	>30000	>30000	>30000

Two Nodes	$\eta1 , \eta2$	0.05 , 0.35	0.15 , 0.35	0.25 , 0.35	0.05 , 0.5
	Epochs	2691	2122	1777	1920

Three Nodes	$\eta1,\eta2,\eta3$	0.1 , 0.3 , 0.5	0.15 , 0.25 , 0.35
	Epochs	1775	2103

Four Nodes	$\eta1 , \eta2 , \eta3 , \eta4$	0.1 , 0.2 , 0.3 , 0.4
	Epochs	2498

Figure 3: Epoch-based Cooperation for Two-Spirals Problem

Problem : Two-Spirals Problem.
Dimensionality : 2 Number of Classes : 2
Architecture : 2-5-1 Size of Training Set : 40
Percentage Learned : 100% Era : 400 msec

Two Nodes	$\eta_{DEC1} , \eta_{DEC2}$	0.05 , 0.35	0.15 , 0.35	0.25 , 0.35	0.05 , 0.5
	Cooperations	40	34	28	27

(a)

Two Nodes	η_{DEC} , η_{HP}	0.05 , 0.35	0.15 , 0.35	0.25 , 0.35	0.05 , 0.5
	Cooperations	6	6	6	5

(b)

Two Nodes	η_{HP} , η_{DEC}	0.05 , 0.35	0.15 , 0.35	0.25 , 0.35	0.05 , 0.5
	Cooperations	22	6	7	21

(c)

Figure 4: (a) Homogeneous and (b,c) Heterogeneous System for Cooperative Learning

workstations. The slave on one of the workstations uses learning rate η_{DEC1} while the other slave on the other workstation uses η_{DEC2}. The number of cooperations required for convergence using various pairs of learning rates are given in Figure 4 (a). In the other experiment two slaves are run on a heterogeneous system consisting of the faster HP9000/735 and the slower DEC3100 workstation. In the pair of learning rates given in Figure 4 (b) the left value is used by the slave on the DEC3100 and the right value by the slave on the HP9000/735.

Similar results are obtained for training set of 80 points. Here, the range of good learning rates for the sequential algorithm is smaller than for 40 points.

4 Analysis of Experimental Results

4.1 Epoch-based experiments

Let η_{min} be the learning rate that minimizes the number of epochs for convergence in standard back-propagation. From the experiments it can be observed that if the learning rates for the slaves in the cooperative algorithm are chosen such that $\eta < \eta_{min}$ for some slaves, and $\eta > \eta_{min}$ for the remaining slaves, then, in general, the cooperative algorithm needs significantly smaller number of epochs to converge. For instance, suppose that there are two slaves using learning rates η_1 and η_2. In order to get a performance better than the sequential algorithm, we choose the learning rates η_1 and η_2 so that $\eta_1 < \eta_{min} < \eta_2$. For the pattern classification problem, it is easy to see from One Node table in Figure 2 that the fastest convergence for the sequential algorithm takes 1179 epochs with $\eta = 0.125$. By setting $\eta_1 = 0.05$ and $\eta_2 = 0.175$, the cooperative learning algorithm takes only 985 epochs for convergence. Without any cooperation, the algorithm takes 1819 and 10000 epochs for convergence for $\eta = 0.05$ and $\eta = 0.175$ respectively. Similarly, in Figure 3, the fastest convergence for the sequential algorithm takes 1727 epochs for $\eta = 0.3$. With the learning rate set to 0.25 and 0.35 the non-cooperative algorithm takes 2238 and 30000 epochs respectively. But, with cooperation, the convergence takes 1777 epochs, which is very close to the fastest sequential convergence.

In sequential back-propagation, learning rates less than and greater than η_{min} exist if the number of epochs for convergence is a non-monotonic function of the learning rate, which is true for many real-life problems. For these problems, cooperative algorithm will work better, provided appropriate learning rates are selected. The XOR problem is an example where the number of epochs is a monotone decreasing function of the learning rate. So, for this problem, cooperative learning does not give a better performance.

4.2 Time-based experiments

Here, the time between two cooperations (one era is 400ms in our experiments) is fixed. So, the total time for convergence of the time-based cooperation is proportional to the product of the number of cooperations and the execution time of one era. From the Figure 4, it can be observed that the time-based cooperation executed on a heterogeneous system with one fast and one slower machine converges much faster than on a homogeneous system with two slower machines. Also, the algorithm is more efficient if the slave with the higher learning rate is assigned to the faster machine (see Figure 4 b,c). It is clear that the slave on the faster machine executes more epochs per era than the slave on the slower machine. So, if the slave with the smaller learning rate is assigned to the faster machine, the weights computed by the two slaves are not very far apart. Consequently, averaging is not so beneficial in this case.

5 Conclusion

The cooperative learning algorithm proposed here has given promising results. In general, for the back-propagation algorithm, it is very hard to find learning rates for which the algorithm converges in minimum number of epochs. In our algorithm, we can easily select the learning rates such that the number of epochs for convergence is close to this minimum or even better. This approach can be used to improve any gradient descent algorithm. It can be easily implemented on a parallel machine or a network of heterogeneous workstations using $p4$.

The experimentation using cooperation with dynamic learning rates is still under investigation with promising preliminary results. We are also experimenting with a more sophisticated way of combining slave hypotheses (instead of averaging), which might further improve the performance.

References

[1] R.Butler and E.Lusk, "*User's Guide to the p4 Parallel Programming System*," Argonne National Lab., November, 1992.

[2] J.P.Cater, "Successfully Using Peak Learning Rates of 10 (and greater) in Back-Propagation Networks with the Heuristic Learning Algorithm," *IEEE First Int. Conference on Neural Networks*, vol. 2, pp. 645-651, 1987.

[3] S.Fahlman and C. Labiere, "The Cascade Correlation Learning Architecture," *Advances in Neural Information Processing Systems*, vol. 2, Morgan Kaufmann, pp. 524-532, 1990.

[4] J. Fletcher and Z. Obradovic, "Parallel and Distributed Systems for Constructive Neural Network Learning," *IEEE Second Intl. Sym. on High Performance Distributed Computing*, pp. 174-178, 1993.

[5] J.Hertz et al, "*Introduction to the Theory of Neural Computation,*" Addison Wesley, 1991.

[6] R.Jacobs et al, "Adaptive Mixture of Local Experts," *Neural Computation*, vol. 3, no. 1, pp. 79-87, 1991.

[7] S.J.Orfanidis, "Gram-Schmidt Neural Nets," *Neural Computation*, vol.2, pp. 116-126, 1990.

[8] D.E.Rumelhart, G.E.Hilton and R.J.Williams, "Learning Internal Representations by Error Propagation," *Parallel and Distributed Processing*, Eds. D.E.Rumelhart and J.L.McClelland, Cambridge, MA, MIT Press, 1986.

Growing Neural Tree Networks Using AMIG Learning[*]

Jae H. Yoo and Ishwar K. Sethi
Vision and Neural Networks Laboratory
Department of Computer Science
Wayne State University
Detroit, MI 48202

Abstract

This paper presents a new top-down method for growing neural tree networks using a gradient search for the best hyperplane that maximizes the information measure called AMIG (average mutual information gain). Previous information based learning methods are limited to binary classification problems and requires square computation time for calculating the probabilities by using activation values of all training data for each learning epoch. Our method removes these restrictions to allow learning in multicategory problems and has linear computation time for calculating the probabilities by using the incremental estimation for each learning epoch. We give the interpretation to the new learning method as compared to the delta rule or LMS rule. A set of experimental results is presented to demonstrate the performance of the proposed neural tree network.

1. Introduction

Neural tree networks are feedforward networks that perform classification in a manner similar to the traditional decision tree classifiers. There are several methods for the design of neural tree networks/decision tree classifiers using concepts of information theory ([SeS82], [Qui86], [BiS89], [CiL92], [Set91], [SeY93a, b]).

Information gain has been used as the object function of optimization to generate neural networks sequentially ([BiS89], [CiL92]) and to prune neural networks [FaE92]. Bichsel and Seitz [BiS89] propose a method to generate neural networks of hard nonlinearity neuron. They provide a learning algorithm which combines a structured pattern search and a simulated annealing for the modified object function of information gain. They also suggest that the gradient method using soft nonlinearity neurons is preferable when all local minimums are close in value to the global minimum. This suggestion has been adopted by Cios and Liu [CiL92] to generate feedforward neural networks similar to the cascade correlation net of Fahlman and Lebiere [FaL90]. However, these methods ([BiS89], [CiL92]) are limited to binary classification problems and required to have square computation time for calculating the probabilities by using activation values of all training data for each learning epoch. In contrast, the delta rule that minimizes the LMS (least mean square) error has linear computation time for calculating activation values for each learning epoch. Our method removes these restrictions to allow learning in multicategory problem with linear computation time for calculating the probabilities for each learning epoch of training data presentation.

Our usage of the mutual information gain of a partition is based on the framework of the AMIG tree induction algorithm of Sethi and Sarvarayudu [SeS82]. The AMIG learning algorithm based tree induction method is capable of generating good multicategory, multifeature split neural trees irrespective of class population unbalance in the training data.

2. Learning rule using the information gain as the object function

Our weight adaptation rule is based on the gradient search of the best hyperplane which will maximize the AMIG information measure of partitioning. The derivation of the weight adaptation rule is fully discussed in [Yoo93]. Given patterns from C classes and a partitioning P that divides the pattern space into R mutually exclusive partitions, the AMIG information measure of partitioning, $I(P)$, is written as:

$$I(P) = \sum_{i=1}^{R} \sum_{j=1}^{C} p(r_i, c_j) \log_2 \frac{p(c_j | r_i)}{p(c_j)}. \tag{1}$$

We use the sigmoid function to the gradient search in the weight adaptation rule as

$$g(x) = 1 / (1 + \exp(-2w^t x)), \tag{2}$$

where the feature vector and the weight vector are augmented.

We treat the sigmoid function as a continuous or *fuzzy* count of a frequency for the estimation of the probability that the given input belongs to the positive region of the hyperplane. In contrast, the sign function is a

[*] The material presented here is based upon the work supported by the National Science Foundation under the grant IRI-9002087.

binary or crisp count of a frequency for the estimation of the same probability as suggested in [BiS89]. There is a similar fuzzy count of a frequency in the so-called "fuzzy k-nearest neighbor classifiers" ([Joz83],[KiH92]). Using this sigmoid function, we can estimate the appropriate probabilities as

$$p(c_j) = \sum_{x \in C_j} 1 / N_{total}, \qquad (3)$$

$$p(r_2, c_j) = \sum_{x \in C_j} g(x) / N_{total}, \qquad (4)$$

$$p(r_2) = \sum_{all\ x} g(x) / N_{total}, \qquad (5)$$

$$p(r_1, c_j) = p(c_j) - p(r_2, c_j), \qquad (6)$$

$$p(r_1) = 1 - p(r_2). \qquad (7)$$

We can maximize the information measure of hyperplane partitioning ($R = 2$) or equivalently minimize the conditional class entropy by using the gradient search on the continuous probability defined by the sigmoid function. The gradient contains the following four components for each weight variable w_k:

$$\frac{\partial I(P)}{\partial w_k} = \sum_{i=1}^{2} \sum_{j=1}^{C} \frac{\partial p(r_i, c_j)}{\partial w_k} \log_2 p(c_j|r_i)$$

$$- \sum_{i=1}^{2} \sum_{j=1}^{C} \frac{\partial p(r_i, c_j)}{\partial w_k} \log_2 p(c_j) \qquad (8)$$

$$+ \sum_{i=1}^{2} \sum_{j=1}^{C} \frac{p(r_i, c_j)}{\log_e 2} \frac{1}{p(c_j|r_i)} \frac{\partial p(c_j|r_i)}{\partial w_k}$$

$$- \sum_{i=1}^{2} \sum_{j=1}^{C} \frac{p(r_i, c_j)}{\log_e 2} \frac{1}{p(c_j)} \frac{\partial p(c_j)}{\partial w_k}.$$

The second term amounts to zero since $p(r_1, c_j) + p(r_2, c_j) = p(c_j)$ is an invariant of the weight change. The third term amounts to zero since both the summation of the joint probabilities $p(r_i, c_j)$ and the summation of the marginal probabilities $p(r_i)$ equal one. The last term also amounts to zero since $p(c_j)$ is an invariant of the weight change. We write the weight updating rule as:

$$\Delta w_k = \frac{\rho}{N_{total}} 2\ g(x)(1- g(x))\ x_k\ (\log_2 \frac{p(c_j|r_2)}{p(c_j|r_1)}), \qquad (9)$$

where ρ, is the learning coefficient. This weight updating rule gives us the extension of Cios and Liu's formulation [CiL92] with regard to the multicategory problem. Moreover, we can give the interpretation of the weight change rule when compared to the nonlinear delta rule by using sigmoid function:

$$\Delta w_k = \rho\ 2\ g(x)(1- g(x))\ x_k\ (T - g(x)). \qquad (10)$$

The desired output, T, is fixed in the delta rule for each class. However, there is no explicit desired output in the new learning rule. Instead, the ratio of conditional probabilities, $p(r_2 \mid c_j) / p(r_1 \mid c_j)$ decides the majority region for each class. That is, if the ratio is greater than one, region r_2 will be the majority region for the class. Otherwise if the ratio is less than one, region r_1 will be the majority region for the class. This ratio gives us a modification to the usual decision of finding a majority region which is based on the ratio of joint probabilities, $p(r_2, c_j) / p(r_1, c_j)$ ([SeY93a], [SeY93b]).

When the ratio of conditional probabilities equals one, it is necessary to break the symmetry by using the probability estimation of the law of succession [BuB74],. If the ratio of conditional probabilities still equals one and the information measure nearly equals zero, we will replace the log ratio factor by a random number in (-1, 1). If the activation function $g(x)$ is saturated to either 0 or 1 and the information measure nearly equals zero, then the gradient will equal zero. This state corresponds to the flat region of the energy surface discovered by Bichsel and Seitz [BiS89]. The object function can be modified to remove the flat region such that:

$$J = I(P) - \frac{\varepsilon}{I(P) + \varepsilon}, \qquad (11)$$

where ε has a small positive value. If the activation function $g(x)$ is saturated to either 0 or 1 and the information measure nearly equals zero, then the weight updating rule becomes:

$$\Delta w_k = 2\rho\ (0.5 - g(x))\ x_k\ \frac{\varepsilon}{(I(p) + \varepsilon)}. \qquad (12)$$

After taking limit $\varepsilon \to 0$ with $I(p) \ll \varepsilon$, we have

$$\Delta w_k = 2\rho\ (0.5 - g(x))\ x_k. \qquad (13)$$

We give the interpretation on this weight updating rule as compared to the delta rule. It is difficult for the delta rule to escape the flat region of an energy surface since the activation function $g(x)$ is saturated to either 0 or 1 and the amount of weight change is close to zero; whereas it is not difficult for the AMIG delta rule since the saturated activation function gives the maximum momentum for escaping the flat region. The sign of the factor $(0.5 - g(x))$ of equation (13) points the direction toward the center of the data cluster of class c_j in the projection of x_k feature.

After adjusting the scaling factor of equation (9) to be comparable with that of the LMS rule of equation (10), we have:

$$\Delta w_k = \frac{\rho}{\log_2 \frac{N(c_j) + 1}{N(c_j) + C} (N_{total} - N(c_j) + C)} \, 2 \, g(x)(1 - g(x)) \, x_k \, \log_2 \frac{p(c_j|r_2)}{p(c_j|r_1)} \tag{14}$$

Here, we use the probability estimation of the law of succession to arrive at the maximum ratio $(N_{total} - N(c_j) + c)$ $(N(c_j) + 1) / (N(c_j) + C)$ in order to scale the LRCP factor within the interval $(-1.0, 1.0)$. With these two weight updating rules (equations (13) and (14)), we are able to complete the learning method by using the gradient search of maximum information measure or minimum conditional class entropy.

The calculation of the probabilities takes $O(m^2)$ times (m is the number of the training examples) for each iteration. This is because of batch estimation of the probabilities using all training examples. We see that it is more desirable to have the linear time to compute the probabilities by using the previous estimation. Applying the recurrence relation of the estimation of a sample mean m after introducing $n+1$ th sample x_{n+1} [DuH73] to the class mean of sigmoid function

$$\langle g(x) \rangle = \frac{\sum\limits_{x \in c_j} g(x)}{\sum\limits_{x \in c_j} 1} = \frac{p(r_2, c_j)N_{total}}{p(c_j)N_{total}} \tag{15}$$

we have

$$p(r_2, c_j)_{new} = \frac{p(c_j)N_{total}}{p(c_j)N_{total} + 1} p(r_2, c_j)_{old} + \frac{1}{p(c_j)N_{total} + 1} p(c_j)g(x) . \tag{16}$$

Based on the above discussion, our new learning algorithm is as follows:

Algorithm 1 The gradient search of the maximum information measure using the incremental estimation of probabilities.

Input : Training examples $\{x_k, l_k\}$ where x_k is an augmented vector and l_k is its class label being $l_k \in \{1, 2, ..., c_k\}$.

Output : A weight vector **w** that best divides all training examples into two groups.
1. For each class, calculate $p(c_j)$ and the max log ratio of conditional probabilities, $LRCP_{max}(c_j) = log_2$ $((N_{total} - N(c_j) + c) (N(c_j) + 1) / (N(c_j) + C))$.
2. Initialization: Randomly initialize the current weight vector, **w**. Initialize the iteration counter to zero. Calculate $I(P)$, the information measure for the initial weight vector.
3. Do the following until the weight change (WC) is less than the tolerance or the iteration counter is over the limit.
    3.1. Set $iteration\_count = iteration\_count + 1$. Set WC to zero.
    3.2. Shuffle the training data.
    3.3. For all training examples, do the following.
        3.3.1. Calculate $p(r_2, c_j)$ by using previous estimation and sigmoid function.
        3.3.2. Calculate $p(r_1, c_j)$, $p(r_2)$ and $p(r_1)$.
        3.3.3. Calculate $I(P)$, the information measure.
        3.3.4. Calculate LRCP (the log ratio of conditional probabilities), $log_2(p(c_j | r_2) / p(c_j | r_1))$ by the law of succession.
        3.3.5. If $I(P) = 0.0$ and $g(x_k) (1 - g(x_k)) = 0.0$ then
            3.3.5.1. Set $dw := 2\rho (0.5 - g(x_k)) x_k$.
        3.3.6. Else if $I(P) = 0.0$ and LRCP $= 0.0$ then
            3.3.6.1. Set $LRCP := random(-1.0, 1.0)$.
            3.3.6.2. Set $dw := 2\rho g(x_k) (1 - g(x_k)) x_k LRCP$.
        3.3.7. Else
            3.3.7.1. Set $dw := 2\rho g(x_k) (1 - g(x_k)) x_k LRCP / LRCP_{max}(c_j)$.
        3.3.8. Set $w := w + dw$.
        3.3.9. Set $WC = WC + norm(dw)$.
End of Algorithm 1.

3. Using AMIG learning rule for neural tree networks

In this section, we describe a top-down design method for generating multifeature-split decision trees or neural tree networks for problems having data from multiple classes. The suggested method can be considered as an extension of the AMIG decision tree algorithm. To specify a top-down decision tree induction method, three aspects need to be considered: (1) a method for generating and evaluating possible multifeature splits, (2) a criterion for determining when to stop the tree from growing, and (3) a way for assigning a class label to each terminal partition or node of the decision tree. The last aspect of a top-down decision tree design method is the simplest to deal with. Invariably, the majority rule (i.e., the class most heavily represented in a terminal partition) is used to label the terminal nodes. Our method also follows the same majority rule. We discuss the remaining two aspects below.

Beginning with the root node, the AMIG delta learning algorithm of the previous section is used in our tree induction method to generate the best multifeature splits successively. Each selected split gives rise to two data subsets each of which is again handled in a similar fashion. As tree induction proceeds, the number of applicable training vectors for the partitioning algorithm starts decreasing. With decreasing sample size, the issue of properly estimating the information measure becomes important [BuB74]. In our method, we, therefore, use the following expression for estimating the information measure of a partition

$$I(P) = \sum_{i=1}^{2} \sum_{j=1}^{C} \frac{n_{i,j}}{N} log_2 \frac{(n_{i,j} + 1) N}{(row(x_i) + c) col(c_j)} \tag{17}$$

where $n_{i,j}$ is number of examples in the partition x_i with class c_j, $row(x_i)$ is number of examples in the partition x_i, $col(c_j)$ is number of examples in the class c_j, and N is total number of training examples.

To determine when to stop tree growing, we follow a two step approach that combines controlled tree growth with pruning. This approach involves dividing the available training patterns into two subsets. One subset of training patterns is used to develop the tree to the desired extent. The other subset is used to prune the grown tree. To control the growth of the tree, we follow the procedure used in the AMIG algorithm. According to this procedure, the minimum amount of information that must be provided by the tree is given as

$$I_{min} = - \sum_{j=1}^{c} p(c_j) log_2 p(c_j) + p_e log_2 p_e + (1 - p_e) log_2 (1 - p_e) - p_e log_2 (c - 1) \tag{18}$$

where p_e is the acceptable error rate. Letting I_k as the amount of information associated with the weight vector of the k-th internal node, the cumulative information given by a tree having L terminal nodes is given as

$$I(T) = \sum_{k=1}^{L-1} s_k I_k \tag{19}$$

where s_k is the fraction of training examples that pass through the k-th internal node. Thus by keeping a check on the cumulative information measure of the tree, we determine when to stop tree growing. Once the tree is grown to the extent that it provides information exceeding I_{min}, we prune it using the pruning subset of the training patterns to size T, $T \geq c$ with c being the number of classes, with the pruning criterion being that the pruned tree should have least possible performance difference on tree growing and pruning subsets of the training data. We first search the pruning point that is the first minimum after the number of categories - two way minimum - in the total tree performance graph. If there is no such pruning point, we find the maximum jump after the number of categories - one way minimum - of performance difference on tree growing and pruning subsets of the training data. We have found this simple pruning to provide trees of good classification accuracy compared to more expensive pruning methods([BFO84], [GRD91]).

Although the AMIG delta learning based algorithm has a smoother energy surface than the LMS rule as shown in [Yoo93], it is not guaranteed to find a tree having performance equal to or better than that of the single feature split decision trees. This is due to the fact that the AMIG delta rule can be stuck to a local optimal solution.

4. Performance Evaluation

In this section, we report on two experiments that were conducted to evaluate the performance of the suggested multiclass multifeature split neural tree procedure using the AMIG delta learning algorithm. In each experiment, the acceptable error rate was set to zero to control tree growth. Unless stated otherwise, all the available training vectors were used for tree growing and all available test vectors were used for tree pruning. In all experiments, the classification performance was measured as

$$P_{cc} \cong \frac{1}{C} \sum_{j=1}^{C} \frac{1}{T_j} \sum_{i=1}^{T_j} b_{j,i} \tag{20}$$

where b_{jk} is the Boolean-valued classification score of the k-th sample of the j-th class. This equally weighted class average of correct classification yields a more meaningful performance measure compared to the simple correct classification count measure because the performance of size one tree is always *1/C* where *C* is the number of pattern classes. At each stage of tree building, the iteration count limit for AMIG delta learning was set to *10 * max {n, d}* where *n* is the number of available training examples at a given tree stage and d is the dimension of training vectors. To compare different trees on the basis of their size and linearity of the structure, average tree size was calculated for each case using the following relationship

$$T_{avg} = \frac{1}{L} \sum_{j=1}^{L} d_j \qquad (21)$$

where *L* is the number of terminal nodes in a tree and d_j is the depth of the *j-th* terminal node.

To carry out the assessment of the proposed method, three methods were used for each data set. These are: (1) The single feature split AMIG procedure, (2) The multifeature split decision tree using AMIG delta learning rule, and (3) backpropagation network with one hidden layer.

The first experiment was designed to evaluate the performance of the proposed method in a problem with highly uneven class populations. This experiment was performed using THINNING data set which was generated by the application of step one of the thinning algorithm due to Zhang and Suen [ZhS84]. The THINNING data set consists of 256 8-bit feature vectors that represent various possibilities of an 8-neighborhood in a binary image with the central pixel of the neighborhood being one. The class label for each combination represents the thinning decision whether the central point of the neighborhood should be marked for deletion or not. Of the 256 combinations, there are 222 combinations for which the central point is marked for deletion; the remaining 34 combinations correspond to maintaining the central point. The entire data set was used as the training data in this experiment. Table 1 shows the performance of the four tree methods. The average size column in Tables 1-2 contains two entries. The first entry denotes the number of terminal nodes and the second entry denotes the value of T_{avg} as defined in equation (21). The backpropagation network, BP has only one entry denoting the number of nodes in the hidden layer. It is seen from the Table 1 that the proposed procedure, ADR has a comparable performance to backpropagation network, BP. While the single feature decision tree, AMIG, provides slightly lower performance compared to ADR, the suggested procedure, it has much higher number of terminal nodes and larger average tree size.

The second experiment was designed to evaluate the performance of the proposed method in multicategory problems using VOWEL data. The VOWEL data set represents a difficult classification task of speaker independent recognition of the 11 steady state vowels [Rob89]. It consists of utterances from 15 speakers, eight males and seven females, each repeating six times each vowel. Each utterance constitutes a pattern in the form of a 10-dimensional vector whose components are based on log area ratios derived from linear predictive analysis. The entire set is divided into two subsets of 528 training vectors, corresponding to four male and four female speakers, and 462 test vectors, corresponding to remaining speakers. The nearest neighbor recognition rate for this data is 56.28% in the original data and 49.13% in the normalized data. The results of the second experiment are summarized in Table 2 for the VOWEL data. It is observed that the AMIG delta learning rule, ADR has better performance than that of the single feature decision tree, AMIG. The BP net results are similar to those of Robinson's Ph.D. dissertation [Ron89].

Summarizing the results, it can be seen that the proposed AMIG delta rule based multiclass, multifeature decision tree induction method (ADR) gives another comparable way of neural tree network construction.

5. Conclusion

A method for growing neural trees has been described in this paper. This method is based on a modified delta rule called the AMIG delta rule that performs the gradient ascent search on the AMIG object function in a multiclass environment. The best two-way grouping is automatically decided by the ratio of conditional class probabilities due to a partitioning hyperplane and updated by the incremental estimation of probabilities. It is contrast to the conventional majority region criterion by the ratio of joint class probabilities due to a partitioning hyperplane. The log ratio of conditional class probabilities due to a partitioning hyperplane (LRCP) replaces the factor of (Target - Output) in the usual delta rule. The incremental estimation of probabilities make the AMIG delta rule comparable to the delta rule in terms of the time complexity. The performance of the proposed method has been reported using two data sets. In each case, it has been shown that the suggested method has better performance than that of comparable methods.

References

[BFO84] L. Breiman, J. Friedman, R. Olshen, and C. J. Stone, *Classification and Regression Tree*. Belmont, CA: Wadsworth Int. Group, 1984.

[BiS89] M. Bichsel and P. Seitz, "Minimum class entropy: a maximum information approach to layered networks," *Neural Networks*, vol. 2, pp. 133-144, 1989.

[BuB74] G. A. Butler and H. Barry Ritea, "Estimation of mutual information in two-class pattern recognition," *IEEE trans. Comput.*, vol. C-23, pp. 410-420, Apr. 1974.

[CiL92] K. J. Cios and N. Liu, "A machine learning method for generation of a neural network architecture: a continuous ID3 algorithm," *IEEE Trans. on Neural Networks*, vol. 3, no. 2, pp. 280-291, Mar., 1992.

[DuH73] R. O. Duda and P. E. Hart, *Pattern Classification and Scene Analysis*, John Wiley & sons, Inc., New York, 1973.

[FaE92] W. Fakhr and M. I. Elmasry, "Mutual information training and size minimization of adaptive probabilistic neural networks," *IEEE Int. Symp. on Circuits and Systems*, pp. 61-64., 1992.

[FaL90] S. E. Fahlman and C. Lebiere, "The cascade-correlation learning architecture," In *Advance in Neural Information Processing System II*, ed. D. S. Touretzky, pp. 524-532, San Mateo: Morgan Kaufmann, 1990.

[GRD91] S. B. Gelfand, C. S. Ravishankar, and E. J. Delp, "An iterative growing and pruning algorithm for classification tree design," *IEEE Trans. Pattern Anal. Mach. Intell.*, vol. 13, pp. 163-174, 1991.

[Joz83] A. Jozwik, "A learning scheme for a fuzzy k-NN rule," in *Pattern Recognition Letter*, vol. 1, pp. 287-289, July, 1983.

[KiH92] V. T. Kissiov and S. T. Hadjitodorov, "A fuzzy version of the k-NN method," in *Fuzzy Sets and System*, vol. 49, pp. 323-329, 1992.

[Qui86] J. R. Quinlan, "Induction of decision trees," *Machine Learning*, vol. 1, pp. 81-106, 1986.

[Rob89] A. J. Robinson, *Dynamic Error Propagation Network*, Ph.D. Thesis, Cambridge University Engineering Department, 1989.

[SeS82] I. K. Sethi and G. P. R. Sarvarayudu, "Hierarchical classifier design using mutual information," *IEEE Trans. Patt. Anal. Machine Intell.*, vol. PAMI-4, pp. 441-445, 1982.

[Set91] I. K. Sethi, "Decision tree performance enhancement using an artificial neural network implementation," in *Artificial Neural Networks and statistical Pattern Recognition Old and New Connections*, I. K. Sethi and A. K. Jain (Eds.), pp. 71-88, Elsevier Science Publishers B. V., 1991.

[SeY93a] I. K. Sethi and J. H. Yoo, "Design of multicategory multifeature split decision tree using perceptron learning," accepted for publication in *Pattern Recognition*, 1993.

[SeY93b] I. K. Sethi and J. H. Yoo, "Modified pocket algorithm for single perceptron training in a multicategory environment," *World Congress on Neural Networks (WCNN '93 Portland)*, vol. 4, pp. 33-38, 1993.

[Yoo93] J. H. Yoo, *Symbolic Rule Extraction from Artificial Neural Networks*, Ph.D. dissertation in Computer Science, Wayne State University, Detroit, MI, 1993.

[ZhS84] T. Y. Zhang and C. Y. Suen, "A fast parallel algorithm for thinning digital patterns," Comm. ACM, vol. 27, pp. 236-239, 1984.

Table 1. Performance results for THINNING data.

	Avg Size	Accuracy
AMIG	45, 6.0	95.58
ADR	17, 3.85	97.17
BP	12	100.00

Table 2. Performance results for VOWEL data.

	Before pruning			After pruning		
	Avg Size	Training	Testing	Avg Size	Training	Testing
AMIG	25, 4.96	74.81	37.88	23, 4.87	73.29	38.09
ADR	13, 3.85	84.28	50.65	12, 3.67	83.52	50.65
BP				22	82.95	48.26

An Adaptive Structure Neural Network Using an Improved Back-Propagation Learning Algorithm

K. Khorasani and H.F. Yin
Department of Electrical and Computer Engineering
Concordia University
1455 De Maisonneuve Blvd. W., Montreal, Quebec, H3G 1M8, Canada

[**Abstract**] An improved back-propagation algorithm is proposed in this paper. The initial weights and learning rates are set differently for individual hidden layer units. In this algorithm the variance of the hidden layer units are set to be different. An error analysis is given for removing the unnecessary hidden units from the network. A procedure for dynamically adjusting the structure of the network is proposed. Numerical examples are given to illustrate the utility of the proposed methods.

1   Introduction

Back-propagation (B-P) algorithm is the most commonly used neural network model [1,2]. Back-propagation allows us to train the weights in a feedforward network of arbitrary structure by following a gradient steepest decent path in weight space, where the energy surface is usually defined by the mean squared error between desired and actual outputs of the network. There have been many examples of successful use of back-propagation for performing different tasks [3,4,5].

Unfortunately, back-propagation has some problems. Firstly, the energy surface may have many local minima, so the algorithm can not always be guaranteed to converge to the optimal solution. The second problem is that it is difficult to analyze the behavior of hidden units in a multilayered network. Consequently it is not easy to estimate the exact number of the hidden units required for a given problem before the network is trained. The third problem is that back-propagation algorithm is often slow.

The weights of the network after training depend on several factors. Among them one may mention the randomly chosen initial weights and the sequence of training examples. The hidden units have approximately equal variance [6,7]. For some problems, such as image coding and compression, these factors may reduce the usefulness of the B-P. This is due to the fact that the bits must be allocated evenly among the weights of the network and noise cannot be eliminated by removing the units with lowest variance. If the network is designed with too many hidden units then the additional error introduced is spread evenly throughout the units and cannot be easily detected or removed by looking at the signal to noise ratio of the individual units. If the network does not have enough hidden units, then the learning procedure may never converge. There are algorithms in the literature [8,9] that can add or delete hidden units from the network. However, it is not easy to decide when and where the structure of the network should be changed. Since the variance of the hidden units is at the same level, a large error could be introduced by removing any hidden unit from the network.

In this paper, we give an improvement to the back-propagation algorithm(IB-P). For a three layer network with one hidden layer, the initial variance of the weights and the learning rates are set differently for different hidden layer units. The algorithm results in the hidden units having different variances, therefore, the hidden layer units have different degrees of importance. A procedure for dynamically adjusting the network architecture is also proposed. Application of the proposed methods to solve pattern recognition and function approximation problems are demonstrated.

2 The B-P Algorithm and its Improvements

The back-propagation learning algorithm is summarized by the following equations. The forward propagation algorithm is defined as $net_{pj} = \sum_i w_{ji}o_{pi}$, $o_{pj} = f_j(net_{pj})$. The back-propagation algorithm is $\Delta_p w_{ji} = \eta \delta_{pj} o_{pi}$. The error signal is given by

$$\delta_{pj} = \begin{cases} (t_{pj} - o_{pj})f_j'(net_{pj}) & \text{If the neuron is an output unit} \\ f_j'(net_{pj})\sum_k \delta_{pk}w_{kj} & \text{If the neuron is not an output unit.} \end{cases}$$

The B-P algorithm is improved as follows: First, we set the initial weights randomly with different variances. For the weights that connect to the hidden layer unit k, the variance is set to $V_k = V_0/\alpha^k$ where $0 < \alpha \le 1$. The weights can be produced by any random distribution. In above equations, the learning rate η is constant. We also choose the learning rate to be different for different hidden layer units. For a three layer network with one hidden layer, the weight adjustment for hidden neuron k is changed into $\Delta_p w_{ji} = \eta_k \delta_{pj} o_{pi}$. The learning rate η_k is now given by $\eta_k = \eta_0/\alpha^k$, where η_0 is a positive constant and $0 < \alpha \le 1$.

In this algorithm, the weights that connect to the first hidden units are adjusted most, i.e. the first hidden neuron is the most important one. After the utility of the first hidden neuron is exhausted, the second neuron becomes more significant, etc. If for instance the network needs m hidden units for training, the hidden neurons after the mth one are adjusted with a very small variance. Therefore, these hidden neurons can be removed from the network without affecting the performance significantly. The last hidden neuron is the least important one.

The activation function for all the neurons is selected as $f(x) = \frac{2}{1+e^x} - 1$. Since $f'(x) = (1 + f(x))(1 - f(x))/2 \le 1/2$, it is easy to prove that $|f(x)| \le |x/2|$ and $|f(x + \Delta x) - f(x)| \le |\Delta x/2|$. For the ith hidden neuron, we have $|o_{pi}| = |f(net_{pi})| \le |net_{pi}|/2 = |\sum_j w_{ji}o_{pj}|/2 \le W_o I/2$, where $W_o = \sum_j |w_{ji}|$, $I = max_j o_{pj}$. The input from neuron i to output neuron k is $w_{ik}o_{pi}$. If the hidden neuron i is removed, the change of the output in neuron k is $|\Delta o_{ik}| = |f(net_{pk}) - f(net_{pk} - w_{ik}o_{pi})| \le |w_{ik}o_{pi}|/2$, and $|\Delta o_{ik}| \le |w_{ik}|W_o I/4 \le (|w_{ik}| + W_o)^2 I/16 = S_{ik}^2 I/16$, where $S_{ik} = (W_o + |w_{ik}|)$ is the sum of the absolute value of the weights from the input neurons to the hidden neuron and from hidden neuron to the output neuron. If $I = 1$, $|\Delta o_{ik}| \le S_{ik}^2/16$. Therefore, if a hidden neuron is deleted from a trained network, the change of the output in neuron k depends on S_{ik}. If the network has only one output neuron, S_{ik} is written as S_i.

For pattern classification a training set is correctly classified if the largest output error over the entire set is less than one. Let β designate the maximum error between the output and target output for the trained network over the entire sample space. The hidden neuron i is deleted from the network if $S_i < 4\sqrt{1 - \beta}$. If the hidden neuron i is one of the neurons that can not be removed from the network, regardless of the learning rate and the initial weights, then we have $S_i \ge 4\sqrt{1 - \beta}$.

3 An Adaptive Structure Neural Network

An adaptive structure neural network is achieved through adjusting the number of neurons in the hidden layers dynamically. By using the IB-P learning algorithm, the hidden neurons have different variances. If a hidden neuron has small S_{ik} relative to the other neurons, it can be removed from the network dynamically. For pattern classification problems, if e_m defined as the maximum error between the desired output and the output of the network over the entire training set is less than 1, then the result is considered as correct classification. The maximum error introduced by removing neuron i from the network is $e_{ri} \le S_i^2/16$. After node i is removed, e_{Ti} the maximum difference between the desired output and network output, becomes $e_{Ti} \le e_m + e_{ri} \le e_m + S_i^2/16$. If $S_i < 4\sqrt{1 - e_m}$, then $e_{ri} < e_m + (1 - e_m) = 1$. Therefore, if $S_i < 4\sqrt{1 - e_m}$, node i can be removed and the network can still provide a correct classification.

For a function approximation problem, a positive number ν which is larger than the expected error is selected. If the actual error e_m of the network is less than ν and $S_i < 4\sqrt{\nu - e_m}/\sqrt{I}$, we can remove the hidden neuron i from the network. The maximum error introduced by removing the hidden neuron i from the network is $e_{ri} \leq S_i^2 I/16 = \nu - e_m$. After neuron i is removed, the maximum output error is $e_{Ti} \leq e_m + e_{ri} \leq e_m + \nu - e_m = \nu$. So even if the hidden neuron i is removed the actual output error remains less than ν.

4   Experimental Results

4.1   XOR and Parity Problem

As a benchmark example we solve XOR problem to test our algorithm. It is well known that a network with two hidden nodes can correctly solve the problem. To train our network we start with 4 hidden units using the improved B-P algorithm with $\eta = 0.5$ and $\alpha = 5.0$. The following results are obtained. Figure 1 shows the change of S_i. After the network is trained 5200 steps, we have $S_0 = 14.1, S_1 = 13.1, S_2 = 1.47$, and $S_3 = 0.038$. According to (7), if we remove hidden unit 2 we get $|\Delta o_2| < 1.47^2/16 = 0.14$. Similarly if we remove hidden unit 3 we get $|\Delta o_3| < 0.00006$. Therefore, hidden unit 3 contributes very little to the outputs of the network. Consequently the network gives a correct classification with hidden neuron 2 deleted.

For parity problem with 3 inputs, if the network has 3 hidden neurons we found 4 cases out of 300 cases of getting trapped in local minima by using the original B-P algorithm with random initial weights. All 300 learning cases are convergent using improved learning algorithm with $\alpha = 5$. For parity problem with 4 inputs and with 5 hidden units after the network has been trained with $\alpha = 5.0$ and $\eta = 0.5$, the sum of the absolute values of the weights is given in the following table for 8 learning procedures with random initial weights. We can see that there is large difference between the variance of the necessary hidden units and the variance of the unnecessary hidden units, while there is no big difference among the variance of necessary hidden units.

case number	S_0	S_1	S_2	S_3	S_4
1	10.220725	7.223655	5.098019	0.294625	0.054301
2	9.609260	8.124382	5.240492	0.044274	0.041409
3	9.338788	7.360354	4.720688	0.092741	0.032782
4	9.338788	7.360354	4.720688	0.092741	0.032782
5	9.819942	8.174868	5.250357	0.132380	0.025526
6	12.271564	11.087083	7.780679	6.153959	0.140350
7	8.238710	7.184856	5.073183	0.089974	0.025867
8	10.716545	8.312218	5.125797	0.478817	0.046587

Figure 2 shows the change of the weights if we train a network with four hidden neurons and $\alpha = 5$ for a four input parity problem using dynamic structure method. We can see that hidden neurons 3 and 4 are removed within 100 steps.

4.2   Function Approximation

A neural network can also be used to approximate a function. As an example consider the function $f(x) = sin(2\pi x)cos(6\pi x)/3 + 2\pi x/9$. When we use a network with 9 hidden neurons to approximate this function after 45000 training steps with B-P algorithm the output function of the network is shown in Figure 3(a). The sum of the absolute value of weights S_i after the network is trained is given by $S_0 = 31.47, S_1 = 3.56, S_2 = 5.15, S_3 = 18.11, S_4 = 4.98, S_5 = 5.84, S_6 = 6.00, S_7 = 5.30, S_8 = 5.21$. Figures 3 (b), (c) and (d) show the outputs of network with node (1), (3) and (5) removed, respectively. When IB-P method is used to train the network with 9 hidden neurons, with $\eta = 0.5$ and $\alpha = 2.0$, the results are shown in Figure 4. The sum of the absolute value of the weights S_i after the network is trained is given by $S_0 = 8.11, S_1 = 18.79, S_2 = 27.54, S_3 = 5.79, S_4 = 4.07, S_5 = 0.083, , S_6 = 0.093, S_7 = 0.0092, S_8 = 0.0035$. We can see that the last 4 hidden units have a very little contribution to the output and therefore can be deleted from the network. Figure 4 (a) shows the response of the trained network and the desired output. Figure 4(b) shows the output of the network with the last four hidden units removed. If we use the adaptive structure algorithm that removes the hidden units dynamically we get the following results. The network selected has 8 hidden units at the beginning of training with ν set to 0.1. Figure 5(a) shows the change of the sum of absolute value of weights. Figure 5(b) shows the network output before the structure is changed at about 44000 steps. Figure 5(c) shows the network output immediately after the last 3 neurons are removed. Figure 5(d) is the result of the final network with 5 hidden neurons at the end of training cycle.

5   Conclusion

The algorithm proposed in this paper improves some problems of the back-propagation algorithm. After a network is trained, we clearly see which and how many hidden units are needed to solve the given problem. According to the analysis given in this paper , we can remove the hidden neurons from the network both staticly and dynamically. The algorithms proposed in the paper are applicable for solving problems such as pattern recognition, function approximation, image compression, etc.

References

[1] Rumelhart, D. E., McClelland, J. L., Parallel Distributed Processing: Exploration in the Microstructure of Cognition MIT Press(1986).

[2] Rumelhart, D. E., Hinton, G. E., Williams, R. J., "Learning Representations by Back-propagating errors. Nature, 323, 1986."

[3] Touretzky, D.S., Hinton D.E." A Distributed Connectionist Production System", Cognitive Science, Vol.12, pp.423-466, 1988.

[4] D.G. Bounds, P.J.Lioyd, B.Mathew, and G. Waddell," A Multilayer Perceptron Network for the Diagnosis of Low Back Pain,", Proc. 2nd IEEE Intl. Conf. on Neural Networks, vol.2, PP.481-489, San Diego, CA, July 1988.

[5] Gallant, S.I. "Connectionist Expert System", Commun. Acm, Vol.31, No.2, pp152-169, Feb. 1988.

[6] Baldi,. P., Hornik, K., "Neural networks and principal component analysis: Learning from example without local minima", Neural Network, 2,53-58. 1987.

[7] Cottrell, G. A., Munro, P., Ziper,D. " Learning internal representation from gray-scale images: An example of extensional programming", In proceeding of the 9th Annual Conference of the Cognitive Science Society (pp.461-473). 1987.

[8] Lee, T. C., Perterson, A. M., " SPAN: A Neural Network That Grows," Proceedings of IJCNN'89: International Joint Conference on Neural Networks, June 1989.

[9] Lee, T. C., Structure Level Adaptation for Artificial Neural Networks, Kluwer Academic Publishers,1991.

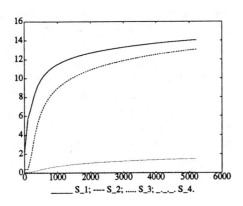

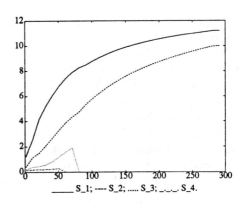

Figure 1: The sum of the absolute values of weights

Figure 2: The sum of the absolute values of weights using adaptive structure scheme

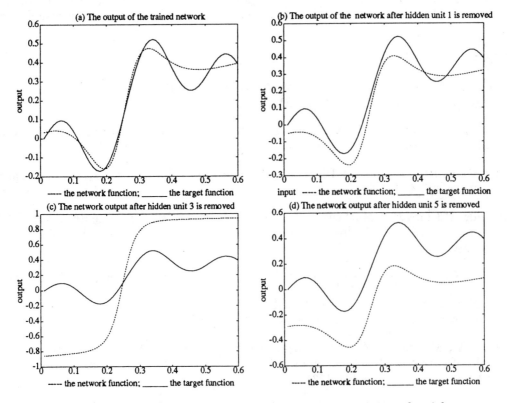

Figure 3: The output of the network using B-P training algorithm

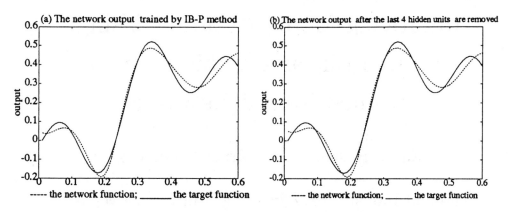

Figure 4: The output of the network using IB-P training algorithm

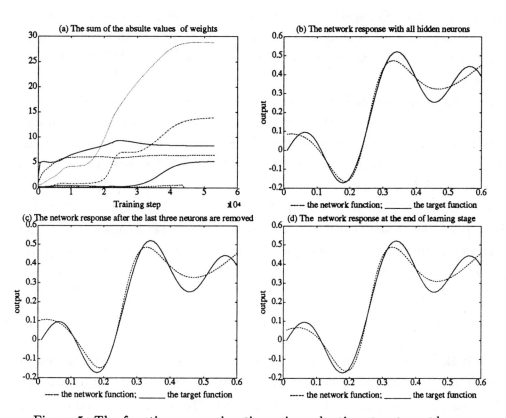

Figure 5: The function approximation using adaptive structure scheme

Improving Model Accuracy Using Optimal Linear Combinations of Trained Neural Networks

Sherif Hashem*   Bruce Schmeiser

School of Industrial Engineering, Purdue University,
1287 Grissom Hall, W. Lafayette, IN 47907–1287

Abstract

Neural network (NN) based modeling often requires trying multiple networks with different architectures and training parameters in order to achieve an acceptable model accuracy. Typically, only one of the trained networks is selected as "best" and the rest are discarded.

We propose using optimal linear combinations (OLCs) of the corresponding outputs of a set of NNs as an alternative to using a single network. Modeling accuracy is measured by mean squared error (MSE) with respect to the distribution of random inputs. Optimality is defined by minimizing the MSE, with the resultant combination referred to as MSE-OLC.

We formulate the MSE-OLC problem for trained NNs and derive two closed-form expressions for the optimal combination-weights. An example that illustrates significant improvement in model accuracy as a result of using MSE-OLCs of the trained networks is included.

Reference

S. Hashem and B. Schmeiser. Improving model accuracy using optimal linear combinations of trained neural networks. Technical Report SMS92–16, School of Industrial Engineering, Purdue University, 1992. Accepted by *IEEE Transactions on Neural Networks*.

*Currently at Pacific Northwest Laboratory, Battelle Boulevard, P.O. Box 999, MS K1–87, Richland, WA 99352, USA. E-mail: s_hashem@pnl.gov

This work was supported by PRF Research Grant 6901627 from Purdue University and by NSF Grant DMS–8717799.

Projection Learning for Multilayer Neural Networks

John Alberg

Department of Mathematics
Williams College
Williamstown, Mass. 01267

Abstract

We derive a simple constructive algorithm for determining hidden layer weights in a single hidden layer neural network based on an algebraic condition necessary for the existence of the output layer weights. The algorithm adds nodes iteratively—performing a simple optimization with the addition of each node—until the algebraic condition is met. Consequently, the difficult problem of specifying the number of hidden units *a priori* is eliminated. The optimization of each node is only as computationally taxing as the simplest forms of the Hebb rule and hence should enable fast training of networks with this architecture.

The Problem

Let the class of single hidden layer feedforward networks mapping all $\mathbf{x}$ in $\Re^m$ into $\Re$ be defined by

$$\psi_n(\mathbf{x}; \boldsymbol{\theta}) = \sum_{j=1}^{n} v_j \sigma(\tilde{\mathbf{x}}^T \mathbf{w}_j), \tag{1}$$

where n is the integer number of hidden units, $\mathbf{w}_j$ in $\Re^{m+1}$ is the weight vector from the input units to the jth hidden unit, v_j in $\Re$ is the weight from the jth hidden unit to the output node, $\boldsymbol{\theta} = (v_1, \ldots, v_n, \mathbf{w}_1, \ldots, \mathbf{w}_n)$, $\tilde{\mathbf{x}} = (1, \mathbf{x})^T$ is the augmented input vector, and $\sigma: \Re \to \Re$ is the hidden unit transfer function which is continuous and always increasing(i.e., $\sigma'(\cdot) \geq 0$). In particular, we are concerned with finding the network parameters $\boldsymbol{\theta}$ and n, such that this network realizes a given input-output map. Which is to say, assume we are given a set of input-output pairs $\mathcal{T} = \{(\mathbf{x}_1, z_1), (\mathbf{x}_2, z_2), \ldots, (\mathbf{x}_N, z_N)\}$, typically called the *training set*, then we want to find a $\hat{\boldsymbol{\theta}}$ and an $\hat{n}$ such that $\psi_{\hat{n}}(\mathbf{x}_k; \hat{\boldsymbol{\theta}}) = z_k$ for all $k = 1, \ldots, N$.

To do this, one typically constructs a cost function of the form $E(\boldsymbol{\theta}) = \frac{1}{2} \sum_{k=1}^{N} (z_k - \psi_{\hat{n}}(\mathbf{x}_k; \boldsymbol{\theta}))^2$, where $\hat{n}$ is determined *a priori*, and attempts to minimize it with respect to $\boldsymbol{\theta}$ using a gradient descent. This type of optimization has been made popular by the back–propagation algorithm(see Rumelhart *et al.* (1986)). Unfortunately, there are many problems associated with this technique, a few of which are: local minima on the surface of $E(\boldsymbol{\theta})$ can cause the gradient search can get "stuck"; updating the hidden layer weights necessitates summations over the all the output units weights and is thus computationally taxing; and determining $\hat{n}$ *a priori* is a difficult problem. Hence we present an alternative approach.

To begin, consider the $N \times m$ matrix X, whose row vectors are given by the N augmented input training patterns $\tilde{\mathbf{x}}_1, \tilde{\mathbf{x}}_2, \ldots, \tilde{\mathbf{x}}_N$, and the $N \times n$ matrix Y with column vectors

$$\mathbf{y}_j = \boldsymbol{\sigma}(X\mathbf{w}_j), \tag{2}$$

where $j = 1, \ldots, n$ and $\boldsymbol{\sigma}: \Re^N \to \Re^N$ is given by $\boldsymbol{\sigma}(\mathbf{a}) = (\sigma(a_1), \sigma(a_2), \ldots, \sigma(a_N))^T$. Notice that the kth row vector of Y represents the states of the hidden units on the kth training pattern. Furthermore, note that each column vector $\mathbf{y}_j$ is in the image of $L[X]$ under $\boldsymbol{\sigma}$, where $L[A]$ is the linear subspace spanned by the column vectors of A. For sake of brevity, we will thus think of each $\mathbf{y}_j$ as an element drawn from the set $\Sigma[X] = \boldsymbol{\sigma}(L[X])/\{\mathbf{0}\}$ rather than specifying it by a particular $\mathbf{w}_j$. We have removed the zero vector from $\Sigma[X]$ because, as we will see latter, we want to exclude the trivial solution.

From equation 1, the output of the network $\psi(\mathbf{x}_k)$ is a linear sum of the states of the hidden units on the kth training pattern weighted with the parameters $v_1, v_2, \ldots, v_n$—which is to say, the N dimensional vector of outputs over the training set is given by $(\psi(\mathbf{x}_1), \psi(\mathbf{x}_2), \ldots, \psi(\mathbf{x}_N))^T = Y\mathbf{v}$, where $\mathbf{v}$ is in $\Re^n$. Hence a network can realize the training set when there exists a solution $\hat{\mathbf{v}}$ such that

$$Y\hat{\mathbf{v}} = \mathbf{z}, \tag{3}$$

where $\mathbf{z} = (z_1, z_2, \ldots, z_N)^T$. From linear algebra, $\hat{\mathbf{v}}$ exists if and only if $\mathbf{z}$ is in the subspace spanned by the column vectors of Y. Therefore we wish to choose a solution set $\hat{\mathbf{y}}_1, \hat{\mathbf{y}}_2, \ldots, \hat{\mathbf{y}}_n$ from $\Sigma[X]$ which spans a linear subspace containing $\mathbf{z}$. An efficient method of choosing such a solution is given herein. Similar methods are given in Bärmann and Biegler-König(1992) and Fujita(1992).

Projection Operators

We will begin by introducing some of the tools necessary for our construction and analysis. In particular, we are interested in the projection operator[1].

Definition 1 *An $n \times n$ real matrix P is a projection operator if and only if P is symmetric, $(P^T = P)$, and P is idempotent, $(P^2 = P)$.*

Furthermore, the $n \times n$ projection matrix[2] P projects onto a subspace S of $\Re^n$. Hence for $\mathbf{a}$ in $\Re^n$, $P\mathbf{a} = \mathbf{a}$ if and only if $\mathbf{a}$ is in S.

Definition 2 *If the $n \times n$ projection matrix P projects onto the subspace S in $\Re^n$, then the $n \times n$ matrix $P_c = I_n - P$, where I_n is the $n \times n$ identity matrix, projects onto the orthogonal complement $S^\perp$ of S.*

Hence for $\mathbf{a}$ in $\Re^n$, $P_c\mathbf{a} = \mathbf{a}$ if and only if $\mathbf{a}$ is in $S^\perp$.

We now define the map $\rho_n: \Re^n \to \Re^n \times \Re^n$ such that $\rho_n(\mathbf{a}) = \mathbf{a}(\mathbf{a}^T\mathbf{a})^{-1}\mathbf{a}^T$, for all $\mathbf{a}$ in $\Re^n$. Since $\rho_n(\mathbf{a})$ is both symmetric and idempotent it is a projection matrix. We also note that if some vector $\mathbf{b}$ in $\Re^n$ is a scalar multiple of $\mathbf{a}$, i.e., $\mathbf{b} = \alpha\mathbf{a}$ for some $\alpha \in \Re$, then $\rho(\mathbf{a})\mathbf{b} = \alpha\rho(\mathbf{a})\mathbf{a} = \alpha\mathbf{a}(\mathbf{a}^T\mathbf{a})^{-1}\mathbf{a}^T\mathbf{a} = \alpha\mathbf{a} = \mathbf{b}$, and hence $\rho_n(\mathbf{a})$ projects onto the one dimensional subspace spanned by the vector $\mathbf{a}$. Now suppose we are given an $n \times n$ matrix P which projects onto the subspace spanned by the vectors $\mathbf{a}_1, \mathbf{a}_2, \ldots, \mathbf{a}_m$ in $\Re^n$. Then,

---

[1] A thorough treatment of projection operators is given in S. Roman 1992.

[2] We will use the terms projection operator and projection matrix interchangeably.

for any vector $\mathbf{b}$ in $\Re^n$, the augmented projection matrix P' which projects onto the space spanned by the vectors $\mathbf{a}_1, \mathbf{a}_2, \ldots, \mathbf{a}_m, \mathbf{b}$ is given by

$$P' = P + \rho_n(P_c \mathbf{b}). \tag{4}$$

This result is proven in the appendix of O. Fujita 1992. We now use this relation to define a projection operator recursively based on some initial "reference vector". Which is to say, given a sequence of vectors $\{\mathbf{a}_1, \mathbf{a}_2, \ldots\}$ in $\Re^n$ and a reference vector $\mathbf{r}$ in $\Re^n$, let the recursive sequence $\{P^1, P^2, \ldots\}$ of $n \times n$ projection matrices be defined by the relation $P^{j+1} = P^j + \rho_n(P_c^j \mathbf{a}_j)$, where $P^1 = \rho_n(\mathbf{r})$. Using equation 4, one can easily verify by induction that P^{j+1} projects onto the subspace spanned by the vector $\mathbf{r}, \mathbf{a}_1, \mathbf{a}_2, \ldots, \mathbf{a}_j$.

A Construction

We now construct the set of linearly independent vectors $\hat{\mathbf{y}}_1, \hat{\mathbf{y}}_2, \ldots, \hat{\mathbf{y}}_n$, where $n \leq N$, which span a subspace that includes $\mathbf{z}$. As above, define the recursive sequence $\{P^1, P^2, \ldots\}$ of $N \times N$ projection matrices by the relation $P^{j+1} = P^j + \rho_N(P_c^j \hat{\mathbf{y}}_j)$, where $\mathbf{z}$ is our reference vector(i.e., $P^1 = \rho_N(\mathbf{z})$), $\hat{\mathbf{y}}_j$ is drawn from the set $\Sigma[X]$ such that it is not in the subspace spanned by the vectors $\hat{\mathbf{y}}_1, \hat{\mathbf{y}}_2, \ldots, \hat{\mathbf{y}}_{j-1}$, and $\mathbf{z}$ is defined as in equation 3. We then have that P^{j+1} projects onto the subspace spanned by the vectors $\mathbf{z}, \hat{\mathbf{y}}_1, \ldots, \hat{\mathbf{y}}_j$ for all $j = 1, 2, \ldots$.

Theorem 1 *There exists a positive integer $n \leq N$ such that $P^n \hat{\mathbf{y}}_n = \hat{\mathbf{y}}_n$, where P^n is given by the recurrence relation above. Furthermore, $\mathbf{z}$ is in the space spanned by the vectors $\hat{\mathbf{y}}_1, \hat{\mathbf{y}}_2, \ldots, \hat{\mathbf{y}}_n$.*

Proof. Since P^j projects onto the space spanned by the vectors $\mathbf{z}, \hat{\mathbf{y}}_1, \ldots, \hat{\mathbf{y}}_{j-1}$, if $P^j \hat{\mathbf{y}}_j \neq \hat{\mathbf{y}}_j$ then, by induction on j, the vectors $\mathbf{z}, \hat{\mathbf{y}}_1, \ldots, \hat{\mathbf{y}}_j$ are linearly independent. Now suppose that for all $j = 1, 2, \ldots, N$, $P^j \hat{\mathbf{y}}_j \neq \hat{\mathbf{y}}_j$. Then the set of $N+1$ vectors $\mathbf{z}, \hat{\mathbf{y}}_1, \ldots, \hat{\mathbf{y}}_N$ in $\Re^N$ are linearly independent. Yet the largest number of linearly independent vectors in $\Re^N$ is N and hence there must be some $n \leq N$ such that $P^n \hat{\mathbf{y}}_n = \hat{\mathbf{y}}_n$. Furthermore, this implies that $\hat{\mathbf{y}}_n$ is in the subspace spanned by the vectors $\mathbf{z}, \hat{\mathbf{y}}_1, \ldots, \hat{\mathbf{y}}_{n-1}$ and thus there must exist scalars α_j, $j = 0, 1, \ldots, n-1$ such that $\hat{\mathbf{y}}_n = \alpha_0 \mathbf{z} + \sum_{j=1}^{n-1} \alpha_j \hat{\mathbf{y}}_j$. If $\alpha_0 = 0$ then obviously $\hat{\mathbf{y}}_n$ is in the subspace spanned by the vectors $\hat{\mathbf{y}}_1, \hat{\mathbf{y}}_2, \ldots, \hat{\mathbf{y}}_{j-1}$ which contradicts our assumption. Hence letting $\alpha_n = -1$, we have

$$\mathbf{z} = \sum_{j=1}^{n} \frac{\alpha_j}{-\alpha_0} \hat{\mathbf{y}}_j,$$

and thus $\mathbf{z}$ is the space spanned by the vectors $\hat{\mathbf{y}}_1, \hat{\mathbf{y}}_2, \ldots, \hat{\mathbf{y}}_n$.

$\square$

We now need a method of choosing each $\hat{\mathbf{y}}_j$ so that the following conditions hold:

1. $\hat{\mathbf{y}}_j$ is not in the subspace spanned by $\hat{\mathbf{y}}_1, \hat{\mathbf{y}}_2, \ldots, \hat{\mathbf{y}}_{j-1}$.

2. $P^j \hat{\mathbf{y}}_j = \hat{\mathbf{y}}_j$ if such a $\hat{\mathbf{y}}_j$ in $\Sigma[X]$ exists.

Condition 1 ensures that theorem 1 holds and condition 2 ensures a minimal n in the sense that if there is a vector in $\Sigma[X]$ which satisfies the theorem then it will be chosen over any other vector. Note that if

> **The Subspace Projection Algorithm.**
>
> Given a set $(\mathbf{x}_1, z_1), (\mathbf{x}_2, z_2), \ldots, (\mathbf{x}_N, z_N)$, of training patterns, let the kth row vector of the $N \times m$ matrix X be $(1, \mathbf{x}_k^T)$, $k = 1, \ldots, N$. Furthermore let $\mathbf{z} = (z_1, z_2, \ldots, z_N)^T$ and $\mathbf{y}_j = \sigma(X\mathbf{w}_j)$ for all $j = 1, 2, \ldots,$ where $\mathbf{w}_j$ is in $\Re^{m+1}$ and σ is defined as in equation 2. Let the $N \times N$ projection matrices P^1 and P_c^1 be defined as $\rho_N(\mathbf{z})$ and $I_N - P^1$ respectively, where $\rho_N(\mathbf{a}) = \mathbf{a}(\mathbf{a}^T\mathbf{a})^{-1}\mathbf{a}^T$ for all $\mathbf{a}$ in $\Re^N$.
>
> For $j = 1, 2, \ldots$:
>   Let $\boldsymbol{\pi}_i = P_c^j \mathbf{x}_i$ for all $i = 1, \ldots, n$.
>   While $\frac{1}{2}\|P_c^j \mathbf{y}_j\|^2$ is not minimum:
>   For $i = 1, \ldots m$:
> $\Delta w_{ij} = -\eta \mathbf{y}_j^T \boldsymbol{\pi}_i$.
> $w_{ij} = w_{ij} + \Delta w_{ij}$.
>   End For.
>   End While.
>   Let $P^{j+1} = P^j + \rho_N(P_c^j \mathbf{y}_j)$.
>   Let $P_c^{j+1} = I_N - P^{j+1}$.
> End For when $P^j \mathbf{y}_j = \mathbf{y}_j$.

Figure 1: An algorithm for finding the hidden layer weights in a single hidden layer neural network.

$P^n \hat{\mathbf{y}}_n = \hat{\mathbf{y}}_n$ for some n then $P_c^n \hat{\mathbf{y}}_n = \mathbf{0}$ and hence condition 2 holds if for each $j = 1, 2, \ldots$, we choose $\hat{\mathbf{y}}_j$ such that

$$\|P_c^j \hat{\mathbf{y}}_j\| = \min_{\mathbf{y} \in \Sigma[X]} \left\{ \|P_c^j \mathbf{y}\| \right\}. \tag{5}$$

This condition can be approximated by a gradient descent algorithm. To this end, consider the cost function

$$E(\mathbf{w}_j) = \frac{1}{2}\|P_c^j \mathbf{y}_j\|^2, \tag{6}$$

where $\mathbf{w}_j$ is the weight vector of the jth hidden unit and $\mathbf{y}_j$ is defined in equation 2. Equation 6 can be optimized by iteratively changing the components of $\mathbf{w}_j$ towards the direction of the negative gradient of $E(\mathbf{w}_j)$. To do this, we change w_{ij} for all $i = 1, \ldots, m$ by Δw_{ij} according to

$$\Delta w_{ij} = -\eta \mathbf{y}_j^T \boldsymbol{\pi}_{ij}, \tag{7}$$

where η in $\Re^+$ is the step size, $\boldsymbol{\pi}_{ij} = P_c^j \mathbf{x}_i$, and $\mathbf{x}_i$ is the ith column vector of X.

It should be noted that equation 7 is, as learning rules go, very simple—i.e., it is no more complicated than the simplest forms of the Hebb rule. To see this, note that $\boldsymbol{\pi}_{ij}$ is constant with respect to $\mathbf{w}_j$ and hence for each w_i the rule involves only a linear sum of the states of the hidden units on each training pattern weighted with the elements of π_{ij}. The only computationally taxing part of the construction are done when a new hidden unit is added. The complete algorithm is given in figure 1. Unfortunately, this optimization does not ensure that condition 1 holds. Yet simulations have shown that if we initialize the weights to large random values and let $\sigma(\cdot) = tanh(\cdot)$, then the gradient descent defined in equation 7 will find a $\hat{\mathbf{y}}_j$ which "fills out" the subspace defined by P^j. Hence $\hat{\mathbf{y}}_j$ should not be completely contained in any subspace of $span\{\mathbf{z}, \hat{\mathbf{y}}_1, \ldots, \hat{\mathbf{y}}_{j-1}\}$—or equivently, not in the subspace spanned by the vectors $\hat{\mathbf{y}}_1, \hat{\mathbf{y}}_2, \ldots, \hat{\mathbf{y}}_{j-1}$.

References

Bärmann, F., & Biegler-König, F.(1992).On a Class of Efficient Learning Algorithms for Neural Networks. *Neural Networks*,**5**, pp. 139–144.

Fujita, O.(1992). Optimization of the Hidden Unit Function in Feedforward Neural Networks. *Neural Networks*, **5**, 755–764.

Roman, S.(1992). *Advanced Linear Algebra* (Chap. 8, pp. 145–154). Springer–Verlag.

Rumelhart, D.E., Hinton, G.E., & Williams, R.J.(1986). Reprinted in *Parallel Distributied Processing: the Microstructure of Cognition*(Chap 8, pp. 319–362). MIT Press, 1988.

Analysis of Input Vector Space for Speeding Up Learning in Feedforward Neural Networks[1]

Chidchanok Lursinsap
Center for Advanced Computer Studies
University of Southwestern Louisiana
Lafayette La 70504 USA

Vasana Coowanitwong
Department of Mathematics
Chulalongkorn University
Bangkok 10330 Thailand

Abstract

Although several new learning rules have been proposed, the space and time complexities of these two bottlenecks remain. The bottlenecks occur because all the existing learning techniques are based on a single large neural structure. In this paper, we approach the solution to this problem by analyzing the input vector space and, then, partition this space into subspaces. Each subspace will be learned by a small neural network with a simple learning rule. We also speed up the learning process by reducing the number of training vectors down to $O(mn)$ instead of 2^n, where m is the number of vectors having output targets equal to ones and n is the number of input bits. The reduction is based on the concept of *guard ring* vectors. The experimental results show that our learning can be speeded up by 2-30 times over the non-partition process. However the number of neurons used in our approach is uncontrollable. In some cases, the number is reduced but in some cases it is increased.

1   Introduction

In any supervised neural network model such as backpropagation [2], there are two major bottleneck problems: perfect recognition and convergence rate. The perfect recognition problem concerns two main factors. One factor is the generalization of the training set. The training set and the actual data set must be very similar within a small variance range. If the variance between these sets is high the chance that an input vector will be misrecognized is also high. Currently, for a binary space, the size of a training is in the order of 2^n where n is the size of each input vector. For a training set, it composes of two subsets. The first subset consists of all vectors whose target outputs are equal to ones while the second subset consists of all vectors whose target outputs are equal to zeros. The training time complexity will possibly be exponential in some cases. In this paper we reduce this time complexity down to polynomial time by using *guard ring concept*. Another factor concerning the perfect recognition is the structure of the network. Generally, a network is composed of layers of neurons. The recognition capability of a network depends upon this structure and the number of neurons in each layer [5]. The convergence rate problem concerns the learning rule of the network. Several learning rules have been proposed. All the classical rules are summarized in [6]. Estimation of the feasible required number of neurons in the hidden layer are in [3,5]. If the number of the hidden neurons is too few the network can partially recognize the input vectors. On the contrary, if the number of the hidden neurons is over the actual requirement, it will create redundancy problem. These redundant neurons when implemented on a chip will consume power. To overcome these bottleneck problems the whole network should be partitioned into subnetworks by analyzing the input vector space. For each subnetworks only a simple learning rule is employed. The contributions of this paper are: 1. concept of 0-1 surface projection, 2. input space slicing algorithm, 3. guard ring pattern concept, and 4. maximum subnetwork sharing concept.

The paper consists of eight sections. Section 2 discusses the analysis concept of parallel training. Section 3 discusses the input vector slicing algorithm. Section 4 discusses and provides the bound on the number of

---

[1] This work is partially supported by Department of Mathematics, Chulalongkorn University, Bangkok, Thailand and by National Science Foundation, USA under grant NSF-ADP-04

guard ring patterns. The technique to combine all the subnetworks is given in Section 5. Section 6 discusses the multiple output case. Section 7 gives the experimental results. Section 8 concludes the paper.

2 Analysis Concept of Parallel Training

One solution to these bottleneck problems previously mentioned is by analyzing the input vector space and, then, slicing this space into many subspaces. Then, each subspace will be learned by each separated subnetwork concurrently. The space that we study in this paper will be a binary space. The definition of these two spaces and the distance metrices are as follows.

Definition 1 *A binary space of dimension m is a space consisting of a set of vectors. Each vector $V = (v_1, v_2, \ldots, v_m)$ and for each bit $v_i \in \{0,1\}$.*

Definition 2 *A bit distance $B(V_i, V_j)$ between binary vectors V_i and V_j is equal to the number of bit pairs such that the ath bit pairs $v_{i,a} \neq v_{j,a}$, for all a's and $v_{i,a} \in V_i$ and $v_{j,a} \in V_j$.*

Definition 3 *Binary vectors V and W are adjacent if $B(V, W) = 1$.*

Definition 4 *A Eucledian distance $D(V_i, V_j)$ between real vectors V_i and V_j is equal to $\| V_i - V_j \|$.*

The size of the binary space is equal to 2^m and all possible vectors in the space form a hyperspace cube. Each V is located at the corner of this cube. The bit distance between any two adjacent vectors is equal to one and it is also equal to the Eucledian distance.

2.1 Separability in Binary Space

We consider this situation. Given a binary space S whose vectors belong to either class A or class B. We want to find the conditions that guarantee the separability of S into two classes A and B in n dimensions by a hyperplane. n can be any value. The problem of separability has been reported in [1,7,8]. The PAC learning model and developed an algorithm to learn n input vectors under given k hidden threshold units is considered in [1]. These n vectors are learned by a single network consisting of k hidden threshold units. The time complexity of this technique is $O(kn^3 + nk^2\epsilon^{-1} + k^2\epsilon^{-3})$. A sufficient condition that a set of regions can be separated by a 2-layer feed forward network using threshold units is shown in [7]. The relation among the number of hidden layer nodes, the complexity of a multiclass discrimination problem, and the number of input vector needed for a good learning are summarized in [8]. They did not consider the location distribution of each vector. Unlike these proposed concepts and algorithms we analyze the grouping characteristics of the input vectors and slice them into *minimum* number of subgroups. Each subgroup must be perfectly separated from the others. To achieve the minimum number of subgroups, some subgroups must be combined into one subgroup to preserve the condition that the new group is separable from the others. Before discussing the technique for slicing a group into subgroups we will consider the conditions when two groups in n dimensional space can be separated. These conditions which are different from those in [9] are summarized as follows.

Lemma 1 *Given a space S consists of two groups, A and B. The members of these two groups are randomly scattered. If there exists a hyperplane, H, passing through S and the projection of the vectors in S onto this hyperplane creates a group vector of either ABA or BAB pattern then A and B cannot be separated by any hyperplane.*

Definition 5 *$P_i^1(V) : B^n \to B^n$ is a surface-1 projection on the ith dimension of a vector $V = (v_1, v_2, \ldots, v_n)$ if $v_i = 1$.*

Definition 6 $P_i^0(V) : B^n \to B^n$ *is a surface-0 projection on the* i^{th} *dimension of a vector* $V = (v_1, v_2, \ldots, v_n)$ *if* $v_i = 0.$

From the definitions of projections above, it is obvious that $P_i^0(V)$ is adjacent to V if the ith bit of V is 1 and $P_i^1(V)$ is adjacent to V if the ith bit of V is 0. Given a binary space S. Let $\{V_i\}$ be a set of vectors in group A and the rest in group $S - A$. Suppose $P_i^1\{V_j\}$ and $P_i^0\{V_j\}$ are applied to every V_j in A. $P_i^1\{V_j\}$ and $P_i^0\{V_j\}$ may produce some new vectors not originally in A which implies that these new vectors must be in $S - A$. We conclude following results.

Theorem 1 *In the* i^{th} *dimension, if both* $P_i^1\{V_j\}$ *and* $P_i^0\{V_j\}$, *where* $V_j \in A$, *produce some new vectors not originally in* A *then* A *is inseparable from* $S - A$ *by a hyperplane in the* i^{th} *dimension.*

Proof Consider $P_i^1\{V_j\}$ first. If it generates some new vectors in $-A$ it means that there must be some vectors in $S - A$ adjacent to those vectors in A whose bits are changed from 0 to 1 by projection. Similarly, $P_i^0\{V_j\}$ implies that there must be some vectors in $S - A$ adjacent to those vectors in A whose bits are changed from 1 to 0 by projection. Therefore A is sandwiched by some vectors in $S - A$. By Lemma 1, A and $S - A$ are inseparable by a hyperplane. $\square$

Theorem 2 *In the* i^{th} *dimension, if only either* $P_i^1\{V_j\}$ *or* $P_i^0\{V_j\}$, *where* $V_j \in A$, *produces some new vectors not originally in* A *then* A *is separable from* $S - A$ *by a hyperplane in the* i^{th} *dimension.*

Proof If either $P_i^1\{V_j\}$ or $P_i^0\{V_j\}$ produces some vectors in A and $S - A$ it implies that A is not sandwiched by any vectors in $S - A$. Thus A and $S - A$ are separable in the ith dimension. $\square$

Theorem 3 A *is separable from* $S - A$ *by a hyperplane if for every* i^{th} *dimension only either* $P_i^1\{V_j\}$ *or* $P_i^0\{V_j\}$, *where* $V_j \in A$, *produces some new vectors not originally in* A.

Proof The result follows directly from Theorems 1 and 2. If in some dimension i some vectors of A are sandwiched by some vectors of $S - A$ then it is obvious that these vectors of A are inseparable from $S - A$ by a hyperplane. $\square$

Theorem 4 *(Generalized exclusive-OR). If every pair* V_i *and* V_j *of class* A *has* $B(V_i, V_j) \geq 2$ *then class* A *is inseparable from class* B.

Proof If every pair V_i and V_j has $B(V_i, V_j) \geq 2$ it means that all paths that connect V_i and V_j of class A must pass some adjacent vectors V_{k1} and V_{k2} in $S - A$ on different paths. When V_i and V_j are projected on both surfaces are executed it will create a sandwich situation. Therefore V_i and V_j cannot be in the same group and cannot be separated from $S - A$ by a hyperplane. $\square$

The following table illustrates how the surface-0 and surface-1 projections are performed. We designate symbols $s - 0$ and $s - 1$ to represent surface-0 and surface-1 projections, respectively. The bold vectors are vectors not in the given set. Let $\{101, 100, 110, 010, 011\}$ be a given vector set. In the first dimension, the projection creates a new vector $\{111\}$ only on surface-1. In the second dimension the projection creates two new vector pairs, namely $\{111,000\}$ and $\{111,001\}$ and in the third dimension the projection creates two new vector pairs, $\{001,111\}$ and $\{111,111\}$. By applying the above Theorems we can conclude that this given vector set cannot be separated from the other vectors $\{111,000,001,001\}$ in this 3-dimensional space by using a hyperplane.

Given	*Dimension 1*		*Dimension 2*		*Dimension 3*	
patterns	*s-0*	*s-1*	*s-0*	*s-1*	*s-0*	*s-1*
101	100	101	101	**111**	000	100
100	100	101	100	110	000	100
110	110	**111**	100	110	010	110
010	010	011	**000**	010	010	110
011	010	011	**001**	011	011	**111**

3 Input Vector Set Slicing Concept

If class A cannot be separated by from class $S - A$ we need to slice class A into subclasses further such that each subclass, A_i, is separable from $S - A_i$ by a hyperplane. The previous Theorems can be applied to test the separability of A_i from $S - Ai$. Class A is sliced into many subclasses by conditionally grouping each vector in A into subclasses. There are two conditions that must be considered during the slicing and grouping process. The first condition occurs after 0/1 surface projection. In class A, two vectors V_i and V_j cannot be grouped in the same subclass if there exists a sandwich condition that is $P_k^0(V_i) \notin A$ and $P_k^1(V_j) \notin A$ or $P_k^1(V_i) \notin A$ and $P_k^0(V_j) \notin A$ exist. The second condition concerns the transformation of the given vector set after the 0/1 surface projection. To group any vectors, V_i and V_j together, V_i must be able to transform to itself of to V_j. To prevent the first condition to occur each vector must be able to transform to the other vectors within the same group. For example, let $A = \{101, 111, 110, 001, 000, 010\}$. We name a=101, b=111, c=110, d=001, e=000, f=010. It can be seen that if vectors b, d, and f are in the same group vector b cannot be transformed to vectors d and f. Similarly, vector d cannot be transformed to vectors b and f and vector f cannot be transformed to vectors b and d. We call the first condition *conflicting* and the second condition *transformable*.

A valid group occurs if there are *transformable* and *non − conflicting* conditions for any pair of vectors in that group. Let $\{v_1, v_2, \ldots, v_m\}$ be a set of given input vectors. The transformability between any two vectors V_i and V_j occurs when $B(V_i, V_j) = 1$.

Slicing Algorithm

1. For all input vectors, perform surface-0 and surface-1 projections in all dimensions.
2. Select v_1. Let g be the group index. Set $g = 1$.
3. Select all v_i's such that $B(v_i, v_1) = 1$ and there is no *conflict* between any v_i and v_1. Assign v_i in the same group as v_1.
4. Set $g = g+1$. Select a new v_i not grouped in any group as the first vector of a new group g.
5. Select all v_k not grouped in any group such that $B(v_k, v_i) = 1$ and there is no *conflict* between any v_k and v_i. Assign v_k in the same group as v_i.
6. Repeat steps 4 and 5 until all vectors are grouped.

From the above example $\{101, 111, 110, 001, 000, 010\}$, after the slicing algorithm the valid groups are $\{101, 111, 110\}$ and $\{001, 000, 010\}$.

Theorem 5 *The time complexity of the slicing algorithm is $O(m^2)$, where m is the number of given input vectors.*

Proof Consider the worst case. For any vector, V_i, being considered, we must compare this vector with the other given vector, V_j, if $B(V_i, V_j)$ do not conflict. The maximum number of V_j's that must be considered is equal to m. Therefore the maximum number of comparison is less than or equal to m^2 which means that the time complexity is $O(m^2)$. $\square$

4 Minimal Number of Guard Ring Vectors

It is necessary to use both vectors in class A and class B to train any subnetwork. If we use both classes the number of training vectors will be equal to 2^n where n is the number of input vector bits. The essential number of additional vectors used to train with the vectors in class A is $O(mn)$ where m is the number of vectors with respect to nucleus p and n is the number of input bits is given in [10]. The additional vectors act as guards protecting all vectors in class A from those in class B. These additional vectors are taken from class B. The concept of guard ring vectors can be applied to our case. The difference between our case and [10] is there is no nucleus vectors for grouping other vectors whose bit distances are equal to one in our case. In our case all vectors are grouped in the same group if they generate only surface-0 projection vectors or surface-1 projection vectors. Our approach is more general than theirs. Let m be the number of vectors in a separable group, n the number of bit in each vector, d the number of vector pairs having bit distance of one, and b the number of vectors having bit distance of two. The number of guard ring vectors is summarized as follows.

Theorem 6 *The number of guard ring vectors is equal to $mn - 2d - b$*

5   Combining Subnetworks

All subnetworks must be combined to form one network. The combining technique is based on the fact that each subnetwork generates a single output one at a time. These outputs from subnetworks must be combined in such a way that when one of the subnetworks generates an output the output will appear at the output layer of the combined subnetworks. Let's consider the case when the combined subnetworks has only one output one output at the output layer. Suppose that there are m subnetworks. At any time only one subnetwork generates an output. Thus the possible output vectors of m bits generated by these subnetworks are $\{100...000, 010...000, \cdots, 000...001\}$. We need one neuron to learn these outputs and generate an 1's when one of them appears. To train the output neuron to recognize these vectors may take many epochs. The easier approach to this training is by considering the complement of this situation. Instead of letting the output neuron generate an 1's when it recognizes these output vectors we let it generate an 0's and let it generate an 1's when it recognizes vectors $\{000...000\}$. The output vectors $\{100...000, 010...000, \cdots, 000...001\}$ will become the guard ring vectors for vector $\{000...000\}$.

6   Multiple Outputs

The slicing technique previously discussed can be extended to multiple output case. The objective of multiple output case is to obtain the minimum number of subnetworks or the maximum sharing of subnetworks for all outputs. For an output, the way to group the input vectors with respect to this output is not unique. This fact can be applied to obtain the maximum sharing of subnetworks. Therefore the solution to achieve the maximum sharing is to generate all possible slicing group and find those common subgroups.

7   Experimental Results

The comparison is performed by using the classical backpropagation learning rule proposed in [2]. The reason that we did not use any recent complex learning techniques such as the one in [4] because we want to emphasize on the slicing algorithm and projection testing technique rather than the learning algorithm itself. We want to signify the point that another approach to speed up the learning time besides improving the learning rule is by slicing the the input vectors and using a simple learning rule to learn these in parallel. We compare two critical factors, the learning speed and the area saved between the unsliced and sliced input vector approaches. The total sum square error lays inbetween 0.001 to 0.007. On the speed comparison between sliced and unsliced network cases, we try to use the minimum number of neurons in both cases. For the sliced network case, by the above Theorems, the minimum number of neurons is always achieved. On the other hand, for the unsliced network case, the fewer the number of neurons are used the longer the training time is achieved. The meaning of each symbol in the comparison table is as follows: Ns symbolizes the total minimum number of neurons; Is symbolizes the size of each input vector; Os symbolizes the size of each output vector; Es symbolizes the number of epochs; SNs symbolizes the number of subnetworks; NsS symbolizes the number of neurons in each subnetworks; $E-range$ symbolizes the range of epochs of all subnetworks; $\%Sp$ symbolizes the speedup ratio which is equal to the number of epochs by unsliced network and the number of epochs of sliced network; $\%N\ change$ symbolizes the percent of number of neurons change between sliced and unsliced approaches. The plus sign means the number of neurons is increased while the minus sign means the number of neurons is decreased.

Ex	Unsliced				Sliced				
	Ns	Is	Os	Es	SNs	NsS	E-range	%Sp	%N change
1	17	5	1	2288	3	12	686-1037	2.21	-29.41
2	9	3	1	988	2	8	628-748	1.32	-11.11
3	9	3	3	25260	5	13	474-772	36.61	+44.44

8   Conclusion

We presented another approach to speed up the learning process. Based on the experiments, the learning process is speeded up by 2-30 times. Although the partitioning algorithm has a polynomial time the area complexity is varied from case to case which is difficult to predict. Generally, it can be deduced from the experiments that the higher the speed the more the neurons are required. The comparison speed in the above table may be varied depending on several parameters such as learning rate, initial weight vectors, and the steepness of the sigmoidal function.

References

[1] E.B. Baum, "Neural Net Algorithms That learn in Polynomial Time From Example and Queries", IEEE Transactions on Neural Networks, Jan 1991.

[2] D.E. Rumelhart, G.E. Hinton, and R.J. William, "Learning Internal Representations by Error Propagation", Parallel Distributed Processing, D.E. Rumelhart and J.L. McClelland, Eds. Cambridge, MA, MIT Press 1986.

[3] Y. Yu and R. Simmon, "Extra Output Biased Learning", Proceedings of the International Joint Conference on Neural Networks, 1990.

[4] M.R. Azimi-Sadjadi, S. Sheedvash, and F.O. Trujillo, "Recursive Dynamic Node Creation in Multi layer Neural Networks", IEEE Transactions on Neural Networks, March 1993.

[5] R. Hecht-Nielson, "Kolmogorov's Mapping Neural Network Existence Theorem", Proceedings of the International Joint Conference on Neural networks, New York 1987.

[6] R.P. Lippman, "An Introduction to Computing With Neural Nets", ASSP Magazine, April 1987.

[7] R. Shonwiler, "Separating the vertices of N-Cube by Hyperplanes and its Applications to Artificial Neural Networks", IEEE Transactions on Neural Networks, March 1993.

[8] K.G. Mehrotra, C.K. Mohan, and S. Sanka, "Bounds on the Number of Samples Needed for Neural Learning", IEEE Transactions on Neural Networks, Nov. 1991.

[9] S.T. Hu, *Threshold Logic*, Univ. of California Press 1965.

[10] C. Lursinsap and J. Kim, "Parallel Learning for Backpropagation Network in Binary Field", International Symposium on Circuits and Systems, 1991.

AN APPROACH FOR COMBINATORIAL OPTIMIZATION PROBLEM BASED ON LEARNING IN THE RECURRENT RANDOM NEURAL NETWORK

Jose AGUILAR

EHEI. UFR de Mathématiques et d'Informatique. Université René Descartes
45, Rue des Saints Pères. Paris. 75006. France
phone: (33.1) 47.03.31.27   fax: (33.1) 42.86.22.31
email: jose@ehei.ehei.fr   and aguilar@ing.ula.ve

ABSTRACT Recently, some fast and flexible neural networks have been proposed to attempt to solve efficiently hard optimization problems. With the intent to represent more closely the major features of biological neural systems and to mimic their behavior, a neural network model, called the Random Neural Network (RNN), has been introduced by Gelenbe and has been used in solution of optimization and recognition problems. Lately, a supervised learning procedure which is mainly based on the minimization of a quadratic error function, is proposed for the recurrent RNN model. In this paper we explore the relationship between the RNN model applied to optimization and the network learning, specifically for acyclic graph partitioning problem. This new approach links these two domains known as learning and optimization.

1. INTRODUCTION

Many optimization problems become intractable when the number of suboptimal solutions grows exponentially with the size of the problem. Such problems belong to the class of NP-complete problems, i.e., no algorithm is know which provides an exact solution to the problem in a computational time which is a polynomial in the size of the problem input. In the past, researchers have developed heuristic methods that provided suboptimal solutions in a time that is proportional to a polynomial in the size of the problem. But the solutions provided by heuristic methods are often unacceptable for problems involving large size graphs which are unfortunately the most frequent in practical applications.

Recently, some fast and flexible neural networks have been proposed to attempt to solve efficiently hard optimization problems. With the intent to represent more closely the major features of biological neural systems and to mimic their behavior, a neural network model, called the Random Neural Network (RNN), has been introduced by Gelenbe [2, 6] and has been used in solution optimization [7] and recognition problems. Lately, a supervised learning procedure which is mainly based on the minimization of a quadratic error function, is proposed for the recurrent RNN model [9]. In this paper we explore the relationship between the RNN model applied to optimization and the network learning, specifically for acyclic graph partitioning problem. This new approach links these two domains known as learning and optimization. The general idea is that the network learns to minimize the cost.

This work is organized as follows. In section 2, we present the partitioning graph problem. Section 3 presents the RNN of Gelenbe, the basic learning algorithm and their application to optimization problem. Section 4 compares the recurrent RNN model with other methods. Remarks concerning the future works and concluding are provided in section 5.

2. DEFINITION OF GRAPH PARTITIONING PROBLEM

The problem consists in dividing a graph in several subgraphs, so as to minimize the costs of connection between them. The idea is to divide the nodes of the graph in several distinct subsets so as to minimize the links between the subsets, that is the sum of the arcs whose joined nodes are in different subset is minimal. The graphs are acyclic and directed. We can complicate the problem with a weight for the arcs. In this case, we must minimize the sum of the weights between the subsets. Also, we can add a weight to the nodes and define again what we want to minimize according to the particular characteristics of problem in study. We have an example of a particular definition of graph in [7], for the problem of parallel program partitioning.

In a very general way, to place the problem on a mathematical formulation, the following definition is necessary: the graphs are sets of nodes joined by arcs. It can be defined as follows:

$\Pi = (N, A)$ where, Π is a directed graph,

> N is a set of n nodes on which we can associate a weight function $Q : N \rightarrow R$. In ours studies $Q(i) = 1$ for $i = 1, ..., n$,
>
> $A = a_{ij}$, are node pairs that define the arcs. It's known as adjacency matrix, and it defines the arc weight of Π.

The problem consists in dividing the graph in K different subgraphs $\Pi = \{\Pi_1, ..., \Pi_K\}$, according to certain constraints. The classic constraints are:

- The subgraphs must have a specify size $N_{\Pi_1}, ..., N_{\Pi_k}$, or must have a weight sum of nodes less than a

given value $\qquad \forall \atop \Pi_k \quad N_{\Pi_k} <$ given value $\qquad$ where, $N_{\Pi_k} = \sum_{i \in \Pi_k} Q(i) \qquad$ for k=1...K

- The arcs with extremities in different subgraphs must be minimal, or the weight sum of arcs which join nodes which are in different subgraphs must be mimimized

$$\sum_{i,j \in D} a_{ij} < \text{must be mimimized} \qquad D=\{i \in \Pi_k \ \& \ j \in \Pi_l \ \& \ l \neq k\}$$

The cost function associates a real value to every subgraph configuration. It permits to calculate the cost of a subgraphs configuration, according to the constraints defined in the cost function. To study this problem as a graph partitioning optimization problem, we use the cost function:

$$F = \sum_{i,j \, \in \, D} a_{ij} + b \left(\sum_{k=1}^{K} (N_{\Pi_k} - n/_K)^2 \right) / K \qquad (1)$$

This cost function was defined in [10] as the minimization of the interconnection and imbalance costs. This later constraint consists on minimizing the node variance between the subgraphs.

The balance factor (b) defines the importance of the interconnection cost with respect to imbalance cost, and N_{Π_k} is the tasks number in $\Pi_k \ \forall \ k=1 .. K$.

The graph partitioning problem is reduced to find a subgraph configuration with minimum value for the cost function: $\qquad \qquad F1 = MIN(F) \qquad\qquad\qquad\qquad\qquad (2)$

3. THE RANDOM NEURAL NETWORK

A. Random Network Model

The Random Network (RNN) model has been introduced by Gelenbe [2, 6] in 1989. Signals in this model take the form of impulses which mimic what is presently known of inter-neural signals in biophysical neural networks.

We shall recall here the principal characteristics of the RNN. The model consists of a network of n neurons in which positive and negative signals circulate. Each neuron accumulates signals as they arrive, and can fire if its total signal count at a given instant of time is positive. Firing then occurs at random according to an exponential distribution of constant rate, and signals are sent out to other neurons or to the outside of the network. Each neuron i of the network is represented at any time t by its input signal potential $k_i(t)$.

Positive and negative signals have different roles in the network. A negative signal reduces by 1 the potential of the neuron to which it arrives (inhibition) or has no effect on the signal potential if it is already zero; while an arriving positive signal adds 1 to the neuron potential. Signals can either arrive to a neuron from the outside of the network or from other neurons. Each time a neuron fires, a signal leaves it depleting the total input potential of the neuron. A signal which leaves neuron i heads for neuron j with probability $p^+(i,j)$ as a positive signal, or as negative signal with probability p-(i,j), or it departs from the network with probability d(i). Clearly we shall have: $\qquad \sum_{j=1}^{n} [p^+(i,j)+p^-(i,j)] + d(i) = 1$ for $1 \leq i \leq n$.

Positive signals arrive to the ith neuron according to a Poisson process of rate $\Lambda(i)$. Negative signals arrive to the ith neuron according to a Poisson process of rate $\lambda(i)$. The rate at which neuron i fires is r(i).

The main property of this model is the excitation probability of a neuron i, q(i). It is defined as:

$$q(i) = \lambda^+(i)/(r(i)+\lambda^-(i)) \qquad\qquad\qquad (3)$$

where, $\quad \lambda^+(i) = \sum_{j=1}^{n} q(j)r(j)p^+(j,i)+\Lambda(i) \qquad \Lambda(i)=$ arrival rate of external positive signals,

$\qquad \lambda^-(i) = \sum_{j=1}^{n} q(j)r(j)p^-(j,i)+\lambda(i) \qquad \lambda(i)=$ arrival rate of external negative signals.

If a unique non-negative solution exists to equation (3) such that each $q(i) \leq 1$, then the stationary probability distribution is $\qquad p(k) = \prod_{i=1}^{n} (1-q(i))q(i)^{k(i)} \qquad\qquad$ k(t) : vector of signal potentials at time t.

To guarantee the stability of the RNN, the following is a sufficient condition for the existence and uniqueness of the solution in the equation (3) $\qquad \Lambda(i) + \sum_{j=1}^{n} r(j)p^+(j,i) < r(i) + \lambda(i)$

B. Relation between the RNN Model and the Network Learning to Optimization Problems

i) Learning in the recurrent RNN model:

In the RNN model, the weight parameter $w^+(i,j)$ and $w^-(i,j)$ are defined as:

$$w^+(i,j) = r(i)p^+(i,j) \qquad\qquad w^-(i,j) = r(i)p^-(i,j)$$

and
$$r(i) = \sum_{j=1}^{n} [w^+(i,j) + w^-(i,j)]$$

They represent rates at which positive and negative signals are sent out from any neuron i to neuron j. Gelenbe has proposed an algorithm in [9] for choosing the set of network parameters W in order to learn a given set of m input-output pairs (Ω, β) where the set of successive inputs is denoted:

$$\Omega = \{\Omega_1, ..., \Omega_m\} \qquad\text{where}\qquad \Omega_m = \{\Lambda_m, \lambda_m\}$$

and
$$\Lambda_m = (\Lambda_m(1), ..., \Lambda_m(n)) \qquad\qquad \lambda_m = (\lambda_m(1), ..., \lambda_m(n))$$

The successive desired outputs are the vector $\beta = \{\beta_1, ..., \beta_m\}$, where $\beta_m = (\beta_m(1), ..., \beta_m(n))$ and $\beta_m(i) \in [0,1]$ correspond to the desired output vectors. The network approximates the set of desired output vectors in a manner which minimizes a cost function E_m:

$$E_m = \frac{1}{2} \sum_{i=1}^{n} a_i \big(q(i) - \beta_m(i)\big)^2 \qquad\qquad a_i \geq 0$$

The algorithm lets the network learn both n by n weights matrices $W_m^+ = \{w_m^+(i,j)\}$ and $W_m^- = \{w_m^-(i,j)\}$ by computing for each input Ω_m, a new value w_m^+ and w_m^-, using gradient descent. The rule to update the weights may be written as:

$$w_m(u, v) = w_{m-1}(u, v) - \mu \sum_{i=1}^{n} a_i \big(q_m(i) - \beta_m(i)\big) \left[\frac{\partial q(i)}{\partial w(u, v)}\right]_m \qquad (4)$$

where, $\mu > 0$ is some constant $\qquad q_m(i)$ is calculated using Ω_m and $w_m(u,v) = w_{m-1}(u,v)$ in (3)

$[\partial q(i) / \partial w(u,v)]_m$ is evaluated of the values $q(i) = q_m(i)$ and $w(u,v) = w_{m-1}(u,v)$ in (4)

The complete learning algorithm for the network is:
- Initiate the matrices W_0^+ and W_0^- in some appropriate manner. Choose a value of μ in (4).
- For each successive value of m:
  - Set the input-output pair (Ω_m, β_m)
  - Repeat
    - Solve the equation (3) with these values
    - Using (4) and the previous results, update the matrices W_m^+ and W_m^-

Until the change in the new values of the weights is smaller than some predetermined valued.

ii) Optimization using RNN model:

In the RNN model, $q(i)$ depends on $\Lambda(i)$, $\lambda(i)$, $p^+(j,i)$, $p^-(j,i)$, $r(i)$ and the other $q(j)$s. The weight between neurons is characterized by $p^+(j,i)$, $p^-(j,i)$ and $r(i)$. The update of these parameters is logical in the learning phase. In the optimization, of every iteration we redefine the network without a change in the weights. By this way, $p^+(j,i)$, $p^-(j,i)$ and $r(i)$ are fixed and depend on the nature of combinatorial problem. Besides, in the optimization problem the relationship between two neurons is competitive or cooperative, that is either $p^+(j,i)$ or $p^-(j,i)$ is null. Of course, if there are not interaction between them, both $p^+(j,i)$ and $p^-(j,i)$ are null. On the other hand, emission of external signals is not interesting to optimization, it is better to employ the signals to inhibit or to excite the neighbor neurons, that is $d(i)$ is null. The fire rate $r(i)$ is obtained by the reciprocity of effect between neurons. When two neurons i and j are excited and i emits signals to j, the excitation or inhibition that i exerts over j must be the same as excitation or inhibition that i receives.

If the weights are fixed, the only way to lead the network from one stationary state to another one is to act over the inputs. This state of the RNN model is defined by $(q(i), ..., q(n))$. The use of two externals flows to every neuron permits a complex scaling of an external positive flow to an external negative flow [8]. In optimization, the use of two flows is not interesting. We consider $\lambda(i)$ as null so that the neurons only receive external positive signals, representing the preference that the neuron belongs to the solution. By this way, $q(i)$ and $\Lambda(i)$ become the variables of the RNN model.

We define a dynamic of external positive signals in RNN model, in order to find the state that gives the minimal energy in the network. Using the technique of gradient descent, the dynamic of external excitation signal is defined as: $\qquad \Lambda(u)^{m+1} = \Lambda(u)^m - \mu\, [\partial E / \partial \Lambda(u)]^m \qquad\qquad$ in the m-th iteration $\qquad (5)$

where E is the energy function of the system state.

This equation describes the control that is necessary to apply to the system to minimize the energy function. The optimization with RNN model is the same as problem of optimal control. This method uses a technique of learning, where the network learns to minimize the energy function.

The general algorithm for the RNN model in optimization problem with learning is:

- Initialize $\Lambda(i)$ in some appropriate manner
- Repeat
  - Solve the equation (3)
  - Using (5) and the previous results, update $\Lambda(i)$.

  If $\Lambda(i)$ is outside of $[0, r(i)]$, replace for the nearest bounds
Until the change in the new value of $q(i)$ is smaller than some predetermined valued.

iii) Application of the RNN model in partitioning problem:

We use the two solutions presented in [7] for this problem. We like study in this work the capability of the RNN model as dynamic method using gradient descent. The two solutions in [7] are defined as following:

In the first solution (RNN1), we study the space of possible solutions. To model this, we use $nK+K$ neurons of two types. There are nK neurons of type $N_1(i,k)$ that represent one element of the solution space, where i is the node T_i and k the partition Π_k; and K neurons of the type $N_2(k)$, which represent the load regulator of partition Π_k.

a) For N_1, if $q_1(i,k) \approx 1$ this solution is admitted. There are negative links between: $N_1(i,k)$ and $N_1(i,z)$ where $k \neq z$ (with incompatibles solutions, with probability $p_1^-((i,k),(i,z)))$, $N_1(i,k)$ and $N_1(i,z)$ where $k \neq z$ and $a_{ij}=1$ (successor nodes which are in different partitions, with $p_1^-((i,k),(j,z))$ probability) and, $N_1(i,k)$ and $N_2(k)$ (the node i belongs to partition k with regulator k, with probability $p_1^-((i,k),k))$. There are excitation links between $N_1(i,k)$ and $N_1(j,k)$ where $a_{ij}=1$ (the successor nodes which are in the same partition, with probability $p_1^+((i,k),(j,k)))$.

b) For $N_2(k)$, if $q_2(k) \approx 0$ the partition has arrived to its maximal capacity. There are only positive links between: $N_2(k)$ and $N_1(i,k)$ for $i= 1 \ldots n$ (the regulator k with the nodes belonging to partition k, with probability $p_2^+(k,(i,k)))$ and, $N_2(k)$ and $N_2(z)$ where $k \neq z$ (the other load regulator, with probability $p_2^+(k,z))$.

The equations of the system are:

$$q_1(i,k)=X1/Y1 \quad \text{and} \quad X1=\sum_{z=k}\sum_{j \neq i \& aji=1} q_1(j,z)r_1(j,z)p_1^+((j,z),(i,k)) + q_2(k)r_2(k)p_2^+(k,(i,k))$$

$$Y1=r_1(i,k) + \sum_{z \neq k}\sum_{j=1 \& (aji= 1 \text{ or } j=i)}^{n} q_1(j,z)r_1(j,z)p_1^-((j,z),(i,k)) \qquad (6)$$

$$q_2(k) = X2/Y2 \quad \text{and} \quad X2 = \Lambda_2(k) + \sum_{z \neq k} q_2(z)r_2(z)p_2^+(z,k)$$

$$Y2 = r_2(k) + \sum_{i=1}^{n} q_1(i,k)r_1(i,k)p_1^-((i,k),k)$$

And, the model parameters:

$$d_1(i,k)=d_2(k)=\lambda_1(i,k)=\lambda_2(k)=\Lambda_1(i,k)=0 \qquad \Lambda_2(k)= n/K$$

$$r_1(j,z) p_1^+((j,z),(i,k)) = r_1(j,z) p_1^-((j,z),(i,k)) = r_1(i,k) p_1^-((i,k),k) =1$$

$$r_2(k) p_2^+(k,(i,k)) = r_2(z) p_2^+(z,k) = 1$$

In the second solution (RNN2), we start with an initial solution that we will try to improve. To model this, we use $n+K$ neurons of two types: n neurons, $N_1(i,k)$, represent the k partition to which the node i belongs; and K neurons, $N_2(k)$, represent the load regulator for every partition.

a) For N_1, if $q_1(i,k) \approx 1$ the task i is accepted in the k partition. There are positive links between $N_1(i,k)$ and $N_1(j,k)$ where $a_{ij}=1$ (the successor nodes if are in the same partition with probability $p_1^+((i,k),(j,k)))$. There are negative links between: $N_1(i,k)$ and $N_1(j,z)$ where $k \neq z$ and $a_{ij}=1$ (the successor nodes if are in different partitions, with probability $p_1^-((i,k),(j,z)))$ and, $N_1(i,k)$ and $N_2(k)$ (the node i belongs to partition k with regulator k, with probability $p_1^-((i,k),k))$.

b) For $N_2(k)$, if $q_2(k) \approx 0$, the partition has arrived to its maximal capacity. There are only positive links between: $N_2(k)$ and $N_1(i,k)$ for $i= 1 \ldots n$ (the regulator k with the nodes belonging to partition k, with probability $p_2^+(k,(i,k)))$ and, $N_2(k)$ and $N_2(z)$ where $k \neq z$ (the other load regulator, with probability $p_2^+(k,z))$.

The equations of the system are:

$$q_1(i,k)=X3/Y3 \quad \text{and} \quad X3=\sum_{z=k}\sum_{j \neq i \& aji=1} q_1(j,z)r_1(j,z)p_1^+((j,z),(i,k))+q_2(k)r_2(k)p_2^+(k,(i,k))$$

$$Y3= r_1(i,k) + \sum_{z \neq k}\sum_{j \neq i \& aji=1} q_1(j,z)r_1(j,z)p_1^-((j,z),(i,k)) \qquad (7)$$

$$q_2(k) = X4/Y4 \quad \text{and} \quad X4 = \Lambda_2(k) + \sum_{z \neq k} q_2(z)r_2(z)p_2^+(z,k)$$

$$Y4 = r_2(k) + \sum_{i \in k} q_1(i,k)r_1(i,k)p_1^-((i,k),k)$$

III-423

And the model parameters:

$d_1(i,k)=d_2(k)=\lambda_1(i,k)=\lambda_2(k)=\Lambda_1(i,k)=0$ $\qquad\qquad$ $\Lambda_2(k)= n/K$

$r_1(j,z)p_1{}^+((j,z),(i,k)) = r_1(j,z)p_1{}^-((j,z),(i,k)) = r_1(i,k)p_1{}^-((i,k),k) = 1$

$r_2(k)p_2{}^+(k,(i,k)) = r_2(z)p_2{}^+(z,k) = 1$

iv) Application of the recurrent RNN model in the partitioning problem:

In this article, we use a method where the neural network learns to optimize based in an improves to RNN model. To define the dynamic of external positive signals in RNN model, in order to find the state that gives the minimal energy in the model, we introduce $\Lambda_1(i,k)$ as control parameter in the system equations (6) and (7), and use the cost function (1) as energy function (E). The new system equations for RNN1 is

$q_1(i,k)=X1/Y1$ $\quad$ and $X1=\Lambda_1(i,k) + \sum_{z=k}\sum_{j\neq i\&aji=1}q_1(j,z)r_1(j,z)p_1{}^+((j,z),(i,k)) + q_2(k)r_2(k)p_2{}^+(k,(i,k))$

$\qquad\qquad$ Y1 is identical to Y1 in the system equation (6) $\qquad\qquad\qquad\qquad$ (8)

$q_2(k)$ is identical to $q_2(k)$ in the system equation (6)

and, for RNN2 is

$q_1(i,k)=X3/Y3$ $\quad$ and $X3=\Lambda_1(i,k) +\sum_{z=k}\sum_{j\neq i\&aji=1} q_1(j,z)r_1(j,z)p_1{}^+((j,z),(i,k))+q_2(k)r_2(k)p_2{}^+(k,(i,k))$

$\qquad\qquad$ Y3 is identical to Y3 in the system equation (7) $\qquad\qquad\qquad\qquad$ (9)

$q_2(k)$ is identical to $q_2(k)$ in the system equation (7)

To search value optimal to $\Lambda_1(i,k)$ and $\Lambda_2(k)$, starting with an initial value $\Lambda_1{}^0(i,k)$ and $\Lambda_2{}^0(k)$, we use the gradient decent: $\qquad\qquad$ $\Lambda_1{}^m(u,v) = \Lambda_1{}^{m-1}(u,v)- \mu\,[\partial E/\partial\Lambda_1(u,v)]^m$ $\qquad\qquad\qquad$ (10)

and $\qquad\qquad\qquad\qquad$ $\Lambda_2{}^m(v) = \Lambda_2{}^{m-1}(v)- \mu\,[\partial E/\partial\Lambda_2(v)]^m$ $\qquad\qquad\qquad\qquad$ (11)

which guarantee that $E^m \leq E^{m-1}$

The energy function (E) for the graph partitioning problem, according to the equation (1) is

$$E = \sum_{i,j\,\in\,D} a_{ij}\, q_1(i,k)\, q_1(j,l) + b\,(\sum_{k=1}^{K}(N_{\Pi_k}q_2(k) - n/K)^2)\,/\,K \qquad\qquad (12)$$

where $D=\{i\in\Pi_k\ \&\ j\in\Pi_l\ \&\ l\neq k\}$

To determine $\partial E/\partial\Lambda_1(u,v)$ and $\partial E/\partial\Lambda_2(v)$ we use the equations (8), (9), (10), (11) and (12)

$\partial E/\partial\Lambda_1(u,v) = [\sum_{i\neq j}(a_{ij}\mathbf{1}[i>j] + a_{ji}\mathbf{1}[i<j]\,)\,q_1(i,k)]\,\partial q_1(i,k)/\partial\Lambda_1(u,v)$

$\partial E/\partial\Lambda_2(v) = (b/K)\,[\,2\sum_{k=1}^{K}(N_{\Pi_k}{}^2 q_2(k) - N_{\Pi_k}(n/K))\,]\,\partial q_2(k)/\partial\Lambda_2(v)$

where $\quad \partial q_1(i,k)/\partial\Lambda_1(u,v) = 1/Y_{k1}\,[1-C_1]^{-1}$

$\qquad\qquad \partial q_2(k)/\partial\Lambda_2(v) = 1/Y_{k2}\,[1-C_2]^{-1}$

and $\ C_1=[\sum_{z=k}\sum_{j\neq i\&aji=1}r_1(j,z)p_1{}^+((j,z),(i,k))]/Y_{k1}-[X_{k1}\sum_{z\neq k}\sum_{j=1\&(aji=1\ or\ j=i)}^{n}r_1(j,z)p_1{}^-((j,z),(i,k))]/Y_{k1}{}^2$

$\quad C_2 = \sum_{z\neq k}q_2(z)r_2(z)\,/\,Y_{k2}$ $\qquad\qquad$ for RNN1 k1 = 1 and k2 = 2 or, K1 = 3 and K2 = 4 for RNN2.

4. PERFORMANCE EVALUATION

We compare the random neural model with the approximate methods studied in [10]: genetic algorithm (GA), simulated annealing (SA) and kernighan's heuristic (H). We have used the parameters that give the better performance in every method, according to the results of the work [10]. We have used a SUN SPARCstation IPC with 16M of memory and a matrix as data structure. The graphs used are defined for the number of nodes (N) and the average degrees of the nodes (D). The execution time is in seconds.

For graph of little size ($\leq$ 15 nodes) simulated annealing and recurrent RNN model gives the optimal solution (table 1). In general, the result quality and the execution time are approximately the same. The difference between the exact solution and the results of the approximate methods is little and the execution time similar. For graph of 50 or more nodes the approximate methods are more interesting, because they have a reasonable execution time to find a suboptimal solution. Recurrent RNN model that starts with an initial solution gives the best results. In general, the qualities of the results of recurrent RNN model and simulated annealing method are similar, but recurrent RNN models execution times are a lot less.

Recurrent RNN model gives better results than RNN model that not uses gradient descent, because in the first model the network learns to optimize. The improve of the results is very important. The RNN model that starts with an initial solution gives better results than the RNN model that uses all solution space.

b	N	K	D	EXAC		H		SA		GA		RNN1		RNN2		RNN1-rec		RNN2-rec	
				Tim	Cos	Tim	Cos	Time	Cost	Time	Cost	Time	Cost	Time	Cos	Time	Cos	Time	Cos
0	10	2	2	7	0	6	2	13	0	6	2	11	0	7	0	6	0	4	0
1	10	2	2	3	2.5	4	2.5	8	3.5	3	2.5	6	2.5	6	4	5	2.5	4	2.5
1	15	2	2	85	2.5	5	5.5	7	3.5	4	4.5	11	5.5	6	6.5	5	5	5	4
1	50	5	5			10	15	148	9.5	48	15	10	11	8	18	7	10.5	7	7.5
0	100	5	5		0	22	66	6983	17	399	0	37	0	43	0	63	0	52	0
1	100	5	5			15	66.8	6610	35.8	356	58.8	33	63.5	47	65	65	52.8	54	32.5

TABLE 1. Results of the simulations

5. CONCLUSIONS

The experiments we have run show that the results obtained by each approximate method vary widely depending on the type and size of the graphs considered. In our study all the methods give good results, but recurrent RNN model gives the best results for large graph with short execution time. In RNN model, the approaches that start with an initial solution give the better results.

The use of learning algorithm for optimization problem in RNN networks, improves the previous results obtained with this model. The news results are better or same as the results of simulated annealing (this method gave the best results in [10]), and the execution time is similar to RNN network without feedback control. The problem in recurrent RNN networks, is the number of variables (μ, threshold) that are necessary to control.

The execution time for the Genetic Algorithm and Simulated Annealing are very large. For Genetic Algorithm, the reason is that generation calculations take relatively much more time. It is necessary to determine the better combination of genetics operators, to decrease the number of necessary generations to reach the suboptimal solution. For Simulated Annealing, since it is not possible determine coherent movements of nodes in every temperature level that decrease the energy, the solution is evaluated in a relatively longer time. The Genetic Algorithm and the Random Neural Model are easy to implement on a parallel machine, and this can considerably improve the speed obtained with these methods.

Future research will apply these algorithms in the optimization of the parallel program speedup; will examine other combinatorial optimization methods for the solution of design problems in distributed systems (tasks assignment, files allocation, ...); will consider a combination of the Random Neural Model and Genetic Algorithms; and will implement these algorithms on parallel machines.

REFERENCES

1. HOPFIELD, J. and TANK, D. "Neural computation of decisions in optimization problem", Biolog. Cybern., N° 52, 1985.
2. GELENBE, E. "Random neural networks with positive and negative signals and product form solution", Neural Computation Vol. 1, No. 4, 1989.
3. GELENBE, E. "Stable random neural networks", Neural Computation, Vol. 2, No. 2, 1990.
4. Fang, L. and Li, T. "Design of Competition-Based Neural Networks for Combinatorial Optimization", International Journal of Neural Systems, Vol. 1, No 3, 1990.
5. HERAULT, C. and NIEZ, J. "Neural networks and combinatorial optimization: a study of NP-complete graph problems", Neural networks: Advances and Applications (E. Gelenbe editor), North Holland, 1991.
6. GELENBE, E. "Theory of the random neural network model", Neural networks: Advances and Applications (E. Gelenbe editor). North-Holland, 1991.
7. AGUILAR, J. "Comparison between the random neural network model and other optimization combinatorial methods for large acyclic graph partitioning problem" Proceedings of the 7th International Symposium on Computer & Information Sciences, ISCIS VII, Antalya, Turkey, 1992.
8. PEKERGIN, F. "Optimisation Combinatoire par le calcul neuronal et parallelisme optimal". PHD thesis. Rene Descartes University, Paris, France, 1992.
9. GELENBE, E. "Learning in the recurrent Random Neural Network", Neural Computation, Vol. 5, No. 5, 1993.
10. AGUILAR, J. "Combinatorial Optimization Methods. A study of graph partitioning problem", Proceedings of the Panamerican Workshop on Applied and Computational Mathematics, PWACM, Caracas, Venezuela, 1993.

A Double-Well Potential Energy Function
Resolving Bistable Ambiguity Figures by Neural Networks

Harold H. Szu
Naval Surface Warfare Center
Dahlgren Division, Code B44
Silver Spring, Maryland 20903

Feng Lu
The American University, Department of Physics
4400 Massachusetts Avenue, Washington, D.C. 20016

ABSTRACT

The LMS energy function becomes less useful for the class of bistable ambiguity figures, because the desired output is ambiguous. A revised back error propagation network based on Haken Synergetic Computer's polynomial energy function, e.g., ξ^4 field, is proposed for the recognition of bistable reversible figures. The training of the network follows a modified supervised delta learning rule of interconnected weights. The test of "reversible figures" is subsequently controlled by the double well potential phase transition tuning parameter given test image data. The effects of the tuning parameter changing potential from a sing well into a double well are illustrated. We demonstrate that the networks trained with the new energy function generally have better performance in training speed and classification of patterns than the standard back error propagation networks trained by the least mean square energy.

Keywords: Reversible figures, bistable, neural networks, phase transition.

1. INTRODUCTION

Recent advances in top down design of artificial neural networks have yielded improvement in recognition of objects belonging to identifiable and therefore labelled classes. The reversible figure, vase/face (Figure 1. pattern 1), problem represents a different challenge, where the date can not be *a prior* defined. One picture can belong equally to two different classes depending on the perception environmental conditions. We could classify it as either a vase or two old men facing each other. Since both interpretations are correct, a network is forced to either converge on a single pattern or separate the pattern into two unrelated classes. A single minimum energy function such as LMS, must merge these two interpretations into one class or several classes. We adapt the single order parameter double well potential function of Haken's Synergetic Computer[1][4] as the Artificial Neural Network energy function, with Haken's attention parameter as the phase tuning parameter to resolve reversible figures. The energy function could evolve into a double potential well with appropriate attention parameters. The separate minimums could be used to represent the two feature patterns of the bistable figures. We assume a standard back error propagation network using three layers of sigmoidal nodes. Connections are made from the bottom layer to the hidden layer and then from the hidden layer to the output layer with no local recurrent or intralayer connections. We test our network using reversible figure input patterns and patterns with small symmetry-breaking perturbations and noises.

2. GENERIC BPN TRAINING RULE

We begin with a standard feed-forward back error propagation network architecture with the uplink W_{ij} between the output layer neurons (in,out) = (u,v) and the hidden layer neurons (in,out) = (u',v') and lower link W_{ij}' between the hidden layer neurons and the input layer neurons (in,out) = (u",v"). From the gradient descending learning rule, we could derive the following BPN weights update rule by keeping the energy function E until the last step of its substitution.

For general E, the weights between output layer and hidden layer are given as:

$$W_{ij}(t+1) = W_{ij}(t) + \Delta W_{ij} \tag{1}$$

$$\Delta W_{ij} \equiv \delta_i v_j' \Delta t \tag{2}$$

where
$$\delta_i \equiv -\frac{\partial E}{\partial u_i} = -\frac{\partial E}{\partial v_i} v_i(1 - v_i) \tag{3}$$

For the weights between hidden layer and input layer:

$$W_{ij}'(t+1) = W_{ij}'(t) + \Delta W_{ij}' \tag{4}$$

$$\Delta W_{ij}' = (\delta_i')(v_j'')(\Delta t) \tag{5}$$

where
$$\delta_i' \equiv -\frac{\partial E}{\partial u_i'} = \frac{dv_i'}{du_i'}\Sigma_j \delta_j W_{ij} \tag{6}$$

These are the generic delta training rule based on an unspecified energy function. It could be seen that the δ_i is the key element of the six equations. It has been shown that the least mean square energy function, minimum misclassification error functions, and minimax energy functions are all valid for backpropagation type networks. All these different functions have limitations. The least mean square technique is most common and deeply rooted in our thinking because it is most general. This technique has earned its place in history for its ability to find best fit for a wide variety of data sets. The MME technique helps to separate overlapping features that cause confusion between two distinct classes of objects and are generally more appropriate for automatic target recognition problems [8]. The development of minimax gives us another tool for determination of unknown feature vectors necessary for class separation.

3.   QUARTIC POTENTIAL ENERGY FUNCTION TRAINING RULE

The general quartic energy function in terms of Haken's order parameters ξ has the following forms,

$$V = A\xi^4 + B\xi^3 + C\xi^2 + D\xi + E \tag{7}$$

Using the case of Hopf bifurcation (A=1/4, B=0, C=-λ/2, D=0, E=0) when $\lambda < 0$ the potential energy V has a single minimum at the origin $\xi = 0$. When $\lambda > 0$ a double well exists with the minimum located at $\xi = \pm\sqrt{\lambda}$ and a minimum value of -λ^2/4. We are now left with

$$V = -\frac{\lambda}{2}\xi^2 + \frac{1}{4}\xi^4 \tag{8}$$

This energy function is of the same form as the single *order parameter* potential function of Haken's Synergetic computers. By adapting Haken's potential function as our networks training energy function, we can derive our specific weights update rules. We will use the attention parameter λ as the phase tuning parameter to see its effects on the network performance.

For $\lambda > 0$, we set
$$\xi_\pm = \sqrt{\Sigma(T_i - v_i)^2} \pm \sqrt{\lambda} \tag{9}$$

Where T_i is the target output value of output neuron i, V_i is the actual output value of the output neuron. When $T_i = V_i$, $\xi = \pm\sqrt{\lambda}$ are the two attractor positions representing face and vase respectively. Substituting both definition (9) and the new energy function (8) into the arbitrary energy function delta training rule formula (3), we have

$$\delta_i^\pm = \xi(\xi \pm \sqrt{\lambda})(T_i - v_i)v_i(1 - v_i) \tag{10}$$
where $\xi = \xi_\pm$

For $\lambda < 0$, we set $\xi = \sqrt{\Sigma(T_i - v_i)^2}$ so

$$\delta_i=(\xi^2-\lambda)(T_i-v_i)v_i(1-v_i) \qquad (11)$$

The substitution of these specific δ_i into the general weights update rule Eqs.(3,6) yields the corresponding training rule.

4. SIMULATIONS

To test our energy function we break down the reversible figure of face/vase into a two-dimensional binary array. Using a 30 X 30 pixels picture gives us sufficient resolution to identify both figures in the pattern. All the training pattern and testing pattern are listed in Figure 1. We use pattern 1 and pattern 2 as the training patterns for face and vase respectively. Pattern 3 through pattern 8 are the perturbed test pattern, pattern 9 through pattern 14 are used to test the connectivity performance of the trained networks. The face and vase figures each have 450 pixels, while the perturbation figure apple and earrings each have 60 pixels. To train on this pattern, we use 900 input neurons. We vary the number of hidden layer nodes to ensure generality, but limit ourselves to no more than one percent of the input.   Our output layer consists of two nodes, each representing the presence of one attractor. Weights are allowed to train until convergence and test patterns are then identified. The performance are then compared to the non-modified LMS networks. We add momentum term in the training algorithm of both network to accelerate the training speed, with the learning coefficient set to 0.15 and momentum coefficient set to 0.075 the general form of our learning formula is

$$W_{ij}(t+1)=W_{ij}(t)+0.15\delta_i v_j+0.075\Delta W_{ij}(t-1) \qquad (12)$$

Initial weights are random values between ±0.015. The network stopping training condition is $E_r = \Sigma(T_i-v_i)^2 < 0.01$

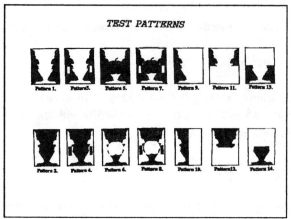

Figure 1. Training and testing patterns. Pattern 1 & 2 are the two training patterns for the memory networks.

We test the typical LMS energy neural network converging speed while varying the number of hidden units, The result is shown in Figure 2. When hidden unit number equals to 1, 2, 3, 5, there is no convergence. When hidden unit number equals to 4, the network converges after 25 iteration, with 6 hidden units, number of iterations drops to 19. But because each iteration takes more time with 6 hidden units than with 4 hidden units, so the actual speed may not improve much. As we will see later that all the network trained poorly when there are 5 hidden units. This suggests that the number of the hidden units should be kept as symmetry with input units number and output units number. Since we have even numbers of input and output units, the hidden units should be even number too.

We then test the training speed of the double well potential energy($\lambda > 0$) neural network(Figure 3). Comparing with Figure 2, now we can have networks convergence with 3, 4, 5 and 6 hidden units by choosing proper λ values. This reveals better converge ability of the double well neural networks. The best overall performance is at 4 hidden units and λ equals to 14 and 16, where the networks converged only after 10 iterations, that is about 150% faster than the LMS network. Generally, by increasing λ value, we could have faster convergence. But there is a limit on the increase. After certain value of λ the network can not converge. We believe this is because of the general gradient descend training method... with bigger λ, we have steeper gradient, bigger correction of weights after each iteration. So the network will be faster to reach the energy landscape minimum. But when the step becomes too big, it leads oscillation within the potential well, the system will be trapped in a middle state and never converge to the minimum. This explanation could be further confirmed by observing the evolution of the E_r value after each iteration during the training. For the normal converged training, we observe that the change of the E_r value ΔE_r is quite big initially. It becomes smaller and smaller after each iteration. We can see a clear trend moving toward zero until that E_r reaches a preset stopping condition. In the case of big λ, we observed a very big E_r value changes initially and then drops abruptly to a very small values. The trend did not converge toward zero but an intermediate value, i.e. the system was trapped in a spurious intermediate state.

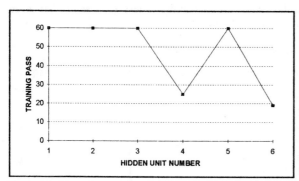

Figure 2. The effect of different hidden layer neuron numbers on the training speed of a typical <u>LMS</u> back error propagation network. Training pass equaling sixty means non-converged training.

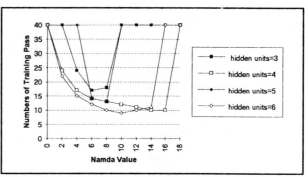

Figure 3. The effect of different phase tuning parameter λ values and hidden layer unit numbers on the converging speed of double potential well energy trained memory networks.

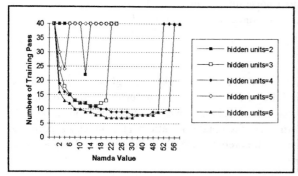

Figure 4. The effect of different phase tuning parameter λ values and hidden layer unit numbers on the converging speed of a <u>single</u> potential well energy.

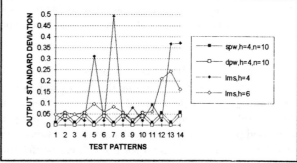

Figure 5. The comparison of the output standard deviation of four different networks: a LMS with four hidden units, a LMS with six hidden units, a single potential well with four hidden units and λ = 10, a double potential well with four hidden units and λ = 10. It shows that these two LMS networks have much bigger standard deviation errors for all test patterns.

Figure 4. shows the training speed of the single well potential neural network ($\lambda < 0$). Compare with the double potential well network, we have pretty much the same date structure, but a bigger range of the converging λ value. This is due to that the double potential well is separated by a middle point at V=0, such that only one side of the double well become rather shallow. With a bigger λ value, the training step could easily jump over the middle point and get stuck in the opposite well. Since the single potential well has no such tendency, it can accept a much bigger λ values. Another interesting aspect of this single well network is that we now can have two hidden unit that still converge.

To test the ability of recognition ability among these three networks, we run all fourteen test patterns through these three networks, the result is showed in Figure 5. It is clear that the network trained by using Haken's ξ^4 potential energy has much better performance in recognizing the symmetry-breaking perturbed patterns. The standard deviation ($\sqrt{(\sum(T_i - v_i)^2)/2}$) of all fourteen test patterns is less than 0.06. This is because the first two patterns are the actual training patterns while the standard deviation value of all the other test pattern should use this value as the reference, keeping this in mind, we can see that all twelve perturbed patterns are perfectly recognized. The recognition ability of the LMS neural networks is quite different. In case of four hidden units, the LMS NN has a very big error in recognizing pattern #5,7,13 and 14. However for six hidden units, it improves a little, but still has a fairly big error in recognizing pattern #12, 13 and 14. Also we notice that the poor performance occurs at different patterns for different cases of 4 hidden units and 6 hidden units. These tests show that large fluctuation occur at the phase transition critical point known as the critical fluctuations.[1]

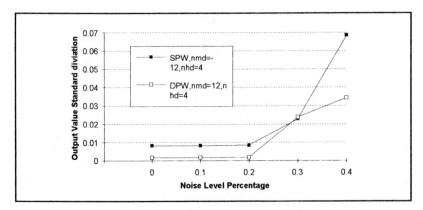

Figure 6. The performance of the networks under noise input conditions. The single potential well and the double potential well trained networks both did well for up to forty percent noise level input.

To test the ability of fault tolerance in this quartic potential energy networks, we add noise to the binary input pattern by randomly reversing the input pixel value and then we look at the output error standard deviation errors. We tested a single potential well with four hidden units and λ=-12. Also, we tested a double potential well with four hidden units and λ=12. In both cases the test pattern is the face pattern (pattern 1). Both cases exhibit a pretty good performance in recognizing noise patterns. For up to 40 percent noise, the output standard deviation is under 0.07, which is very good for Haken's energy function.

6.   CONCLUSION

Adapting Haken's single order parameter potential function as the training energy on the back error propagation neural network, we get much improved performance both in the training speed and recognition of symmetry-breaking and noisy patterns. We can manipulate tuning parameters to move double well attractors further apart or closer together depending on our model of the environment. Moving the tuning parameter toward zero, we will see an increased fluctuation, this is believed to be due to the phase transition phenomena. Since the LMS energy function is very close to the phase transition point, we observe an increased fluctuation as expected. This leads us to believe that although the LMS energy is the most common used training energy function, it is less desirable to be used to recognize perturbed and noisy patterns. Also by using the LMS training energy, the network becomes slow and difficult to converge. When $\lambda > 0$, we succeed in training the network to converge to both attractors with each representing a pattern, the double well model shows a slightly better accuracy in recognizing perturbed patterns than single well ξ^4 energy model, though have much better performance than LMS energy model. When $\lambda < 0$, we get a single potential well that is much steeper than the LMS single well. To train a network toward its minimum energy point, it is desirable to have big jumps initially, but while the system moves close to the minimum point, the jump steps become smaller and smaller until it converges. This cannot be done by adjusting learning rates, because it is fixed along the training. But by using this ξ^4 single potential well, the step size becomes proportional to the slope naturally, through the δ_i Eqs(3,6) where the energy slope varies more than those of LMS. Therefore, the gradient descent is very big initially, and then becomes smaller and smaller when it closes to the minimum. The LMS potential well has a much flatter basin than the ξ^4 single well, so its average gradient descent is much smaller than $\xi4$ single well. Therefore we observe much improved performance in the training speed and the pattern recognitions. Current interests[11-14] in vision ambiguity figures have been led to the present investigation using the standard neural network approach to test the ability to resolve the ambiguity under symmetry-breaking perturbation as well as partial & noisy imagery input. We believe that the double well potential energy by Haken's synergetic computing is a performer when coupled with neural networks.

REFERENCES

[1] Ditzinger, A. Fuchs, T., and Haken, H. (1992): Synergetic Approach to Phenomena of Perception in Neural and Artificial Systems, Springer Proceedings in Physics, Vol.69.

[2] Freeman, J.A., Skapura, D.M. (1991): Neural Networks: Algorithms, Applications, and Programming Techniques, Addison-Wesley Publishing Company, Massachusetts.

[3] Grossberg, S., Wyse, L. (1991): "A Neural Network Architecture for Figure-Ground Separation of Connected Scenic Figures", Neural Networks, Vol. 4, pp. 723-742.

[4] Haken, H. (1991): Synergetic Computers and Cognition: a Top-Down Approach to Neural Networks, Springer-Verlag (1991)

[5] Intrator, N., Cooper, L. N. (1992): "Objective function formulation of the BCM theory of visual cortical plasticity: Statistical connection, stability conditions," Neural Networks Vol. 5 pp. 3-17 .

[6] Rumelhart, D. R., McCelland, J. L., (1986): Parallel distributed Processing: Exploration in the Microstructure of Cognition, MIT Press.

[7] Sheng, Y., Roberg, D., Szu, H., Lu, T. (1993): "Optical Wavelet Matched Filters for Shift-invariant Pattern Recognition", Optics Letters, Vol. 18, No. 4.

[8] Szu, H. H., Telfer, B. (1991): "Minimum Misclassification Error Performance Measure for Layered Networks of Artificial Fuzzy Neurons," IJCNN-91 Seattle.

[9] Szu, H. H., Lu, F., Landa, J. S.,<1993>:" Artificial Neural Networks and Haken Synergetic Computer Hybrid Approach for Solving Bistable Reversible Figures" Springer-Verlag proceedings.

[10] Werbos, P. (1974): "Beyond regression: New tools for prediction and analysis in the behavioral science," Ph.D thesis Harvard University.

[11] Kawamoto, A. H., Anderson, J. A. (1985)" A Neural Network Model of Multistable Perception" Acta Psychoolgic, North-Holland.

[12] Grossberg, S.(1993) " 3-D Vision and Figure-Ground Separation by Visual Cortex", Perception and Psychophysics.

[13] Teranishi, M., Ohnishi, N., Sugie, N.(1993) "Subjective Contours are Useful for Extracting Contours with Very Weak Contrasts", IJCNN-93, Nagoya.

[14] Giuseppe Caglioti (1992): The Dynamics of Ambiguity. Springer-Verlag.

PERFORMANCES OF A PERCEPTRON WITH SLOPE LEARNING BACKPROPAGATION ALGORITHM

Didier GUERIOT
IRP, TROP Laboratory
68000 MULHOUSE, FRANCE
Tel : + 33 89 59 82 00
Fax : +33 89 32 76 01

Eric MAILLARD
GESMA
29240 BREST-NAVAL, FRANCE
Tel : + 33 98 22 71 62
Fax : +33 98 22 72 13

ABSTRACT : In this paper, we present an optimized backpropagation algorithm for multilayer perceptrons in order to increase speed learning by improving the adaptability to different problems. Thus, we introduced a new parameter allowing us to tune the slope of neuron sigmoid function. Two algorithms result: the first one has a common slope, set before the network begins to learn, the other one considers all the slopes as variables of the system and learns them like weights. Comparisons between these algorithms and Fahlman quickprop are performed on an encoder/decoder benchmark and then, on a base provided by a texture analysis on sonar images in order to recognize sea-bed nature. Slope learning algorithm seems to be more efficient in application where there is a sensible evolution of the slope value during the training phase.

I. INTRODUCTION

Multilayer perceptrons (MLP) associated with backpropagation algorithms are used in many applications such as classification or data compression because of their ability in matching to the problems by a supervised training, and their adaptability to generalize from partial information. Although this model is efficient in a running phase, the time consumed by such a learning algorithm often grows with the complexity of the problem. Thus, our approach has two goals in optimizing backpropagation algorithm: increasing learning speed while using an adaptive method, whose settings do not depend on the learning data. We obtain good results by a slope learning of the last layer neuron sigmoid function.

In order to validate our algorithm whose theory and development are given in [1], we compare its performances with two other backpropagation algorithms (Rumelhart's basic one [2] with optimum parameters and optimized one called "quickprop" from Fahlman [3]) when running on two kinds of problem. The first one, benchmark proposed by Fahlman, belongs to the encoder/decoder family problem with a man-made database, while the second one uses a learning base resulting from texture analysis computations on sea-bed sonar images.

II. SYNTHETIC VISION OF THE ALGORITHMS

Updates occurred on a variable x during the training phase may be summarized with the next general formula

$$\Delta x(t) = -\eta . \frac{\partial E}{\partial x(t)} + \alpha . \Delta x(t-1)$$ (1)

where

$$\bullet E = \frac{1}{2} \sum_{p=1}^{nb\_pattern} \sum_{i=0}^{N_{K+1}-1} \left(s_i - x_i^{(K+1)}\right)^2,$$

- $\dfrac{\partial E}{\partial x(t)}$ is the error derivative for x(t),

- and η, α, the learning rate and momentum.

We also use an extended definition of the neuron sigmoid function f by adding a parameter λ that tunes the slope of f at the origin (for standard neuron, $\lambda = 1$).

$$f(t) = \frac{1.0}{1.0 + e^{-\lambda t}} \tag{2}$$

II.1. Rumelhart algorithm [2] :

Only the weights between neurons are considered as variables of the system, and modified according to equation (1) with η as learning rate and α as momentum. Each neuron uses the same slope λ. With notations of figure 1, we obtain:

$$\Delta w_{ij}^{(k-1,k)}(t) = -\eta . \frac{\partial E}{\partial w_{ij}^{(k-1,k)}(t)} + \alpha . \Delta w_{ij}^{(k-1,k)}(t-1) \tag{3}$$

where $\dfrac{\partial E}{\partial w_{ij}^{(k-1,k)}(t)} = \lambda . \delta_j^{(k)} . x_i^{(k-1)}$

- $\delta_j^{(k)} = x_j^{(k)}.(1-x_j^{(k)}).(s_j - x_j^{(k)})$ if layer k is the output layer

- $\delta_j^{(k)} = x_j^{(k)}.(1-x_j^{(k)}). \displaystyle\sum_{p=1}^{N_{k+1}} \lambda . \delta_p^{(k+1)} . w_{jp}^{(k,k+1)}$ otherwise

II.2. Fahlman quickprop algorithm [3] :

Various optimizations are introduced in order to prevent some neurons from getting stuck in the zero state (for instance, when $x_j^{(k)}$ is close to 0.0 or 1.0 so is $\delta_j^{(k)}$: "flat spot") but the major one consists in reducing the cost of $\Delta w(t)$ computation by using only the local second order information.

$$\Delta w(t) = \frac{S(t)}{S(t-1)-S(t)} . \Delta w(t-1) \tag{4}$$

where S(t) and S(t-1) are the current and previous values of $\dfrac{\partial E}{\partial w}$.

As Fahlman says, the new value of Δw is only a crude approximation to the optimum value for the weight, but when applied iteratively, this method is surprisingly effective.

II.3. Learning slope algorithm [1] :

In addition to the weights, our algorithm introduces the slope of each neuron sigmoid function as a variable of the network, allowing the slope to be updated in relation to the network evolution, and preventing the user from setting the slopes manually. Thus, we obtain for the slopes updates:

$$\Delta \lambda_i^{(k)}(t) = -\nu . \frac{\partial E}{\partial \lambda_i^{(k)}(t)} + \kappa . \Delta \lambda_i^{(k)}(t-1) \tag{5}$$

where $\dfrac{\partial E}{\partial \lambda_i^{(k)}(t)} = \delta_i^{(k)} . net_i^{(k)}$

- $\delta_i^{(k)} = x_i^{(k)} . (1 - x_i^{(k)}) . (s_i - x_i^{(k)})$ if layer k is the output layer

- $\delta_i^{(k)} = x_i^{(k)} . (1 - x_i^{(k)}) . \displaystyle\sum_{p=1}^{N_{k+1}} \lambda_p . \delta_p^{(k+1)} . w_{ip}^{(k,k+1)}$ otherwise

III . EXPERIMENTS AND RESULTS

Stochastic gradient is effectively employed in basic and learning slope algorithms (i.e. network variables are updated after each pattern presentation, using an approximation E_p of the global energy E, to calculate the errors).

$$E_p = \frac{1}{2} \sum_{i=0}^{N_{K+1}-1} \left(s_i - x_i^{(K+1)} \right)^2$$

Two experiments are achieved to compare the results brought by our algorithm, with basic and quickprop algorithm. The first one based on an encoder/decoder problem completely defined, is used by Fahlman in his paper [3] by way of benchmark. The second one resulting of a less artificial approach, applies all these algorithms on patterns provided by a texture analysis on sonar images.

Many computations are needed to compare the performances of these algorithms for a given problem. First, we prepared 10 different weight initializations in order to make a series of learning with the same initial states. Then for each algorithm, we go over all its coarsely discretized parameter space in order to find the optimum combination that provides the fastest series of learning.

III.1. Fahlman benchmark : M-N-M encoder (10-5-10 encoder)

A neural network encoder consists in a 3-layer network for which output results are the same as input patterns. Then the encoded information is recovered by looking at the values of the hidden layer (bottleneck of the network). The artificial training base is realized by a set of M patterns 'u':

$\{ i \in [0, M-1]$ $, u_i \in R^M / u_i = (x_0, ..., x_{M-1}), x_0 = ... = x_{i-1} = x_{i+1} = ... = x_{M-1} = 0.0, x_i = 1.0 \}$

We implemented quickprop algorithm and what we obtained corroborate Fahlman results. The hyperbolic arctangent error function was not used in this algorithm but the standard sum-of-squares one. End criterion based on a minimal distance (here 0.3) between network outputs and wished results is preserved and applied to the other algorithms.

Basic Rumelhart Algorithm						
η	α	Initial λ	Max	Min	Ave	S.D.
0.6	0.75	2.0	36	17	24.3	7.27

Quickprop Algorithm						
η	α	Range	Max	Min	Ave	S.D.
1.5	1.75	2.0	72	13	22.1	8.9

Slope Learning Algorithm								
η	α	ν	κ	Initial λ	Max	Min	Ave	S.D.
1.0	0.75	0.4	0.75	0.75	50	27	37.6	7.29

We observe that a classical MLP with optimum parameters including a fixed slope obtains quite the same results as the quickprop algorithm. The impact of setting the slope is obvious since its optimum value is 2.0.

In this case, our algorithm is slower than the other ones because it has not enough time to learn the slope. This phenomenon is due to the weak slope variation during the learning phase as it is shown in figure 2.a (slope range in [2.4,3.0]). Therefore for this specific problem, the initial slope setting correspond to the problem constant optimum slope so much so that learning slope do not really improve the speed training phase. Even if crude performances are not so high as other ones, we observe a quite good homogeneity of the training speeds that may highlight a better endurance stability. All that remarks must be confirmed by an application on more complex and realistic problems.

III.2. Learning sea-bed natures according to texture analysis parameters

In order to validate more efficiently our algorithm, we used a database constituted by patterns stemmed from parameters that characterize the sea-bed natures by a texture analysis applied to sonar images. Practically, we extract 290 sub-images from data collected by sonar [4], each image representing only one kind of bottom among four classes: dunes, ripples, sand and stones (figure 3). Many methods allow us to discover structural information on the texture of these images [5]. Cooccurrence matrices are well known concentrating spatial organization of pairs of pixels in a texture, according to a polar shifting vector (distance, angle). Thus, we calculate 9 matrices on each sub-image, each matrix corresponding with a value for the distance of the shifting vector (from 1 to 9) in four privileged directions [6]. To characterize the properties of a matrix, we compute 6 parameters such as homogeneity, entropy, correlation, ... which allow quite good discrimination between textures.

Finally, the 3-layer network used for this application, has 54 neurons for the input layer (a learning pattern is a 54-dimensional vector), 25 neurons for the hidden layer and 4 for the output layer (4 classes must be learned). The training is realized with 10 patterns of each class (on the whole 40 patterns), randomly chosen among the base.

Basic Rumelhart Algorithm						
η	α	λ	Max	Min	Ave	S.D.
0.4	0.75	1.25	99	72	85.4	8.38

Slope Learning Algorithm								
η	α	ν	κ	λ	Max	Min	Ave	S.D.
1.0	0.75	0.6	0.0	1.0	88	77	82.0	4.05

Unfortunately, we were not able to obtain any results for the quickprop algorithm because its state did not satisfy the end criterion after 200 epochs, despite several runs for each parameter combination. Optimum slope for Basic Rumelhart Algorithm is still different from 1.0; it emphasizes the usefulness of such a parameter. The major interest of this application comes from the wide evolution of the slope values during training phase (between 0.35 and 1.5). The figure 2.b shows a training phase where slopes were initialized to 1.8 in order to present the impact of such a learning (see the fall of the global error when slopes begin to be learnt).

IV . CONCLUSION

The stability of this algorithm for a series of training (weak standard deviation value), constitutes an interesting characteristic provided by the slope learning, and proves its better adaptability to different pattern distributions.

Figure 2.b obviously shows that each neuron requires a different slope variable. Learning these slope variables allows us to set only two parameters (learning rate & momentum) instead of one initial slope value per last layer neuron. The profit is peculiarly appreciable when the number of output classes increases. We also observe that learning slope do not need a very fine tuning of its two parameters.

Resulting in training speed optimization, this algorithm offers an other approach to a more adaptive learning strategy.

V . REFERENCES

[1] E. Maillard, D. Gueriot "Learning the sigmoid slope to increase the convergence speed of the perceptron", submitted to WCNN'94, San Diego

[2] D. Rumelhart, J. Mc Clelland (eds.) : Parallel Distributed Processing, vol. 1&2, D. Rumelhart, J. Mc Clelland eds, MIT Press, 1986

[3] S.E. Fahlman, "Faster-Learning Variations on Backpropagation : an empirical study", in *Proc. 1988 Connectionists models summer school*, 1989, pp.38-51

[4] P. Cervenka, C. de Moustier, "Sidescan Sonar Image Processing Techniques" , IEEE Journal of Oceanic Engineering, Vol. 18, No. 2, April 1993

[5] R.M. Haralick , "Statistical and structural approaches to texture", Proceedings of the IEEE, Vol. 67, No. 5, May 1979

[6] R.M. Haralick, K. Shanmugam, Its'hak Dinstein, "Textural features for Image Classification", IEEE Transactions on Systems, Man and Cybernetics, Vol. SMC-3, No. 6, November 1973.

VI . FIGURES

Couche   Couche   Couche
(k-1)   k   (k+1)

K hidden layers (0, 1, ..., K, K+1).
N_k : Number of neurons in layer k
$n_{k,i}$: Neuron i of the layer k
s_i : Wished output for $n_{i,K+1}$
$w_{ij}^{(k,k+1)}$: Weight of neuron between $n_{i,k}$ and $n_{j,k+1}$

Figure 1 : Notations for algorithms

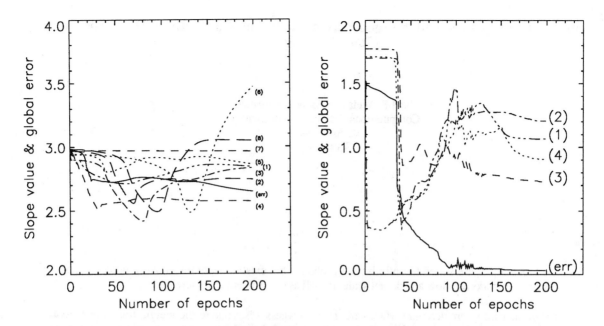

Figure 2 : Last layer neuron slopes & global error evolution during training phase
a. : Encoder/decoder problem
b. : Sea-bed texture parameters

Figure 3 : Sea-bed sonar sub-images (dunes, stones, sand, ripples)

Tangent Hyperplanes and Subgoals as a Means of Controlling Direction in Goal Finding

Michael K. Weir and António Fernandes
Computational Science Department
St. Andrews
Scotland

Abstract

Gradient based techniques are suited to optimisation problems but existing techniques using gradient descent surfaces for neural networks are slow and do not scale up well as the problem size increases.

We argue that in the case where descent surfaces are used, slowness arises due to the weight transitions having weakly controlled directional properties. We present here an approach for feedforward networks which does not use descent surfaces. Instead, tangent hyperplanes are used with subgoals to provide strongly controlled directions for weight transitions. The extra control comes from best-fit approximations to a set of local solution manifolds which are computed directly using a linear solution system. The technique is fully automated with no critical problem dependent parameters.

Results on the benchmarks of XOR and the 2-spirals problem show substantial improvements in feasibility, robustness, and training speed when compared to descent techniques such as back-propagation and conjugate gradient descent.

1. Introduction

Gradient descent techniques are commonly used to train feedforward networks. However, these techniques have been found to be slow and sometimes unreliable especially for larger problems [1].

With these techniques, a goal weight state is typically viewed as a minimum of an error-weight surface. In order to be effective, gradient descent methods require their travel surfaces to be regular to various degrees in directions towards such states. For a steepest descent method such as standard back-propagation [2], the regularity takes the form of circular bowls or linear troughs. More sophisicated descent methods can rely on less regularity to make for a benign surface. When momentum is used with back-propagation for example, oscillatory directions may be suppressed [2], though only to a limited extent. Another technique, Conjugate Gradient Descent, assumes the travel surface is an approximation to a quadratic surface. While there are clear improvements in training speed for this technique [3], the improvements in general have not been substantial enough for the method to be seen as overcoming the problem of slow or infeasible training for large training sets.

We would argue that the reason for hostile surfaces occurring lies in the way the surfaces are generated for feedforward nets. For each I-O pattern there is a gradient vector pointing in the direction of steepest descent for the respective error-weight surface. These vectors are summed to produce an overall vector for an overall error-weight surface. Although we have found empirically that each component vector provides an accurate direction to a surface minimum, the vector sum is not nearly as precise.

In fact, there is no theoretical geometric basis for a vector sum to point at the goal. That is, the number and direction of the component vectors are arbitrary as a set in relation to what is required for their sum to point correctly. Consequently, we suppose that a weak point in gradient descent methods is the way the individual vectors are combined. We provide instead a method of combining individual gradient information that is not based on the vector sum and has a geometrically grounded ability to point towards desired goals.

2.   Tangential Solution

In the introduction, a goal weight state was viewed as a minimum of an overall error-weight surface. Figure 1(a) provides an example of this view for a linear net with a single minimum. A different perspective will be taken here. For each individual I-O pattern there is a set of weight states that will have zero error. We will call such a set a *solution manifold*. This suggests another view of a goal weight state as a point which has least error in the sense of being closest to all the solution manifolds. If there is a common intersection of all the solution manifolds then the solution will be exact, i.e. the set of I-O patterns will have no error at the intersection. Figure 1(b) illustrates this for a linear net. Otherwise the solution will be inexact. The goal states from the manifold and surface views are the same if the error is measured as the distance away from the solution manifolds.

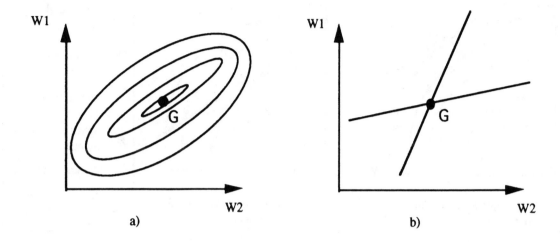

Figure 1.
Two views of a goal weight state for a linear 2-1 net (without bias) that has an exact solution.
a) The contours of an error-weight surface with the goal indicated by G.
b) The individual solution manifolds with the goal at their intersection.

The approach taken here has to deal with a set of non-linear rather than linear solution manifolds for non-linear feedforward networks with hidden units. This will be done by taking a linear approximation to the non-linear manifolds for sufficient iterations. We will restrict ourselves to providing the simplest general method for feedforward networks. A single hidden layer is sufficient for any I-O mapping [4] and we adopt this architecture.

A further restriction will be to confine the methodology to networks with a single output unit initially before considering multiple output units. Each solution manifold for this type of network has dimension (N−1) in an N-D weight space. The linear approximation to the manifold at some point on it is then the tangent hyperplane at that point. The set of such hyperplanes constitutes a linear approximation to the set of solution manifolds. A point which is closest to the set of hyperplanes in terms of the total distance away from the hyperplanes is therefore this set's approximation to a goal weight state. This approximation will be accurate if the initial weight state is close enough to the goal. The degree of closeness required is directly related to the degree of curvature of the solution manifolds. The more non-linear they are, the closer the goal has to be for a good approximation to be expected.

In order to guarantee a good approximation then, a desired state needs to be nearby. Yet the goal which is the solution to the user problem may only have states which are far away. Consequently, a nearby subgoal is attempted with the chain of subgoals used leading to the final goal. In this way, a good initial approximation to the goal weight state is not needed by the method. A subgoal weight state is similar to the final goal weight state in that although it has a known desired output state, its position in weight space is unknown until it is achieved. It differs from the final goal in that it may be set to be closer to the current state than any goal weight state. The requirements for a subgoal are that it must be close enough to the present weight state in order to generate a good linear approximation to the subgoal and yet also far enough away to allow significant progress to be achieved towards the goal.

2.1 Subgoal aiming

As mentioned in the introduction, the gradient vector for an individual I-O pattern provides an accurate direction to a minimum in the pattern's surface. A point W_{SGP} on the solution manifold for a subgoal I-O pattern P is therefore found using line search in the direction of the individual I-O pattern's gradient vector from the current weight state W_C (Figure 2(a)). The aim is to use such points to approximate W_{SG} (Figure 3).

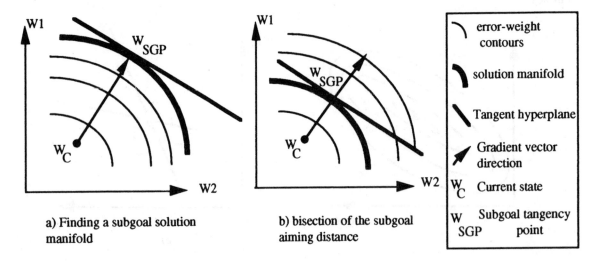

a) Finding a subgoal solution manifold

b) bisection of the subgoal aiming distance

Figure 2.
In a) the subgoal contour or solution manifold found is thickened.
In b) a contour at half the distance relative to the existing subgoal contour is selected as being the next subgoal solution manifold.

The tangent hyperplane approximating the solution manifold at W_{SGP} is then determined. The set of such hyperplanes for all the patterns' solution manifolds constitutes a linear approximation to the latter. The linear equations corresponding to the set of hyperplanes may be solved using Singular Value Decomposition [5]. SVD provides a candidate solution weight state W_{SVD} in both the exact and the inexact cases (Figure 3). In the inexact case, SVD yields an optimal solution in Least Mean Square terms. That is, the solution has the Least Mean Square error where error is measured as the total distance away from the tangent hyperplanes.

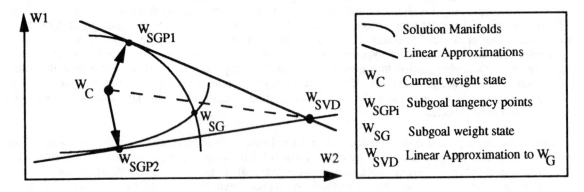

Figure 3.
Subgoal aiming.

2.2 Subgoal testing, setting, and chaining

The weight state W_{SVD} has data associated with it that is used in testing whether the subgoal it is aimed at is close enough to W_C. Besides the weight state itself, there is the actual output produced by W_{SVD} in response to the training inputs. There is also the subgoal output being targeted. This subgoal output is the output produced by each W_{SGP} in response to the training inputs for each pattern P. The aim is to see if such output can be found in a single weight state nearby with W_{SVD} being the candidate. The data is tested using three heuristic criteria. The first two criteria need to be satisfied for W_{SG} to deemed to be close enough. We have:

$$\forall i: \left| w_{Ci} - w_{SVDi} \right| < L_w \tag{1}$$

where w_i is the ith component of a weight state, and L_W is a constant real value, and also

$$\forall P: \left| o_{CP} - o_{SGP} \right| < L_o \tag{2}$$

where O_{CP} and O_{SGP} are the current and subgoal output values respectively for a pattern P, and L_O is a constant real value.

If the first two criteria are satisfied, the third criterion tests the closeness achieved by a candidate weight transition for progress. There are two alternatives for satisfaction.

$$\sum_P \left(o_{CP}(t) - o_{SGP}(t) \right)^2 > \sum_P \left(o_{CP}(t+1) - o_{SGP}(t) \right)^2 \tag{3}$$

$$\sum_P \left(o_{CP}(t+1) - o_{SGP}(t+1) \right)^2 < M \tag{4}$$

where the times t and $t+1$ refer to the beginning and end of the weight transition respectively, and M is a small constant set a priori by the user.

The first alternative, (3), is a test for progress achieved towards the goal. If this alternative is satisfied, the candidate subgoal is acceptable and is set as the subgoal. When progress has not been achieved, the candidate subgoal is failed. There then remains the decision as to whether to seek a new candidate for the existing subgoal. If the second alternative fails, this signals that there is still potential progress to be had and so a new candidate is sought. If the alternative is satisfied, the potential progress is too small to be worth pursuing further. The candidate is set as the subgoal, and a weight transition is triggered to move the process on and seek a new subgoal.

The first candidate subgoal for being set is the goal itself in case it is close enough. The subgoal aiming procedure described above is invoked and a candidate solution weight state attempting the candidate subgoal is found. This subgoal is tested using the data from the attempt on it, and the three heuristic criteria, for being close enough.

When the subgoal is not close enough and is failed, we halve the distances involved in the subgoal aiming. In the first instance, the distances between W_C and the solution manifolds are halved and the target output reset according to the outputs found at this distance (Figure 2(b)). This resetting provides a new candidate subgoal in output terms.

The distance bisection process is repeated until a candidate subgoal and solution weight state are found that satisfy the heuristic criteria. A subgoal is then deemed to have been set. Also, the solution state is taken to be the single attempt made on this subgoal. One iteration in our method has then been completed. A new subgoal is now set using the goal as a starting candidate again and the process repeated until the resultant subgoal chain converges the weight state to be sufficiently close to the goal in output terms.

In the description of the method above, each time a new candidate subgoal is aimed at during the setting of the next subgoal, we theoretically have to compute a completely new set of tangent hyperplanes to determine a new W_{SVD}. In practice though, we compute only one set of hyperplanes from scratch for this stage.

When the subgoal is close enough, there is not only a good match between the linear and non-linear solution but also a good degree of parallelism in the contours. Consequently, we may suppose the tangent hyperplanes at the candidate subgoal solution manifolds to be parallel in the direction of the gradient vector for an I-O pattern without loss. The hyperplane which is orthogonal to the gradient direction at W_C is computed once and then translated to each candidate subgoal solution manifold as required.

This simplification also gives us another major benefit. Since we set the subgoals for each pattern at the same fractional distance from their solution manifolds, all candidate subgoal attempts lie on the line connecting W_C and W_{SVD} (see Figure 3) where W_{SVD} is the state found by taking the goal as the candidate subgoal. Therefore we only need to use SVD once per iteration to compute the direction in which the subgoal attempts lie. The fractional distance being used then completes the determination of the position of each attempt.

3. Experiments

We present results comparing our technique with standard back-propagation (using momentum) for the common benchmarks of the XOR problem and the 2 spirals problem [1],[6]. We suggest that the results reflect an ability to find a good goal direction not present in gradient descent methods. The low number of iterations needed for each problem together with an insignificant failure rate indicate the robustness of the technique.

The 2 spirals problem represents a bridge between our version of the minimal problem of XOR and real world problems. In particular, it can be used to give an indication of how the method will scale up. We successfully attempted this problem with a fixed 2-50-1 architecture. This architecture is unsuited to deal with such a non-linear problem, at least as far as gradient descent is concerned. We could not find a solution weight state for this single layer architecture using standard back-propagation.

The same failure to train is reported by Baum & Lang. They were in fact unable to find a solution using either standard back-propagation or conjugate gradient methods even when they used a larger 2-60-1 architecture. Lang & Witbrock managed to solve the problem using a jumped 2-5-5-5-1 architecture, but also reported failure when training with architectures with fewer hidden layers.

These failures for the 2-spirals problem with conventional gradient descent methods and our zero failure rate lead us to the conclusion that our method scales up relatively better. We see the significance of our results in showing the method to be powerful in finding directions in networks not especially suited to deal with a problem.

The tolerance mentioned in the parameters for standard back-propagation represents the maximum acceptable difference between output and target for terminating training. The parameter settings for heuristics are shown to not be critically problem dependent here by choosing a common setting for both the XOR and the 2-spirals problems. We set L_W to 1.0, L_O to 0.1, and M to 0.001. The iterations indicate the number of direction changes made and are not otherwise comparable to those of standard back-propagation as computations.

Table 1. XOR Problem

Method	Learning rate	training average	iterations std. deviation	failure rate
SBP	1.00	188	102	131
TP	-	10	3	2

Parameters
Trials: 1000; Output tolerance: 0.01; Targets: 0.8, 0.2; Initial weight range: [-1, +1]; momentum (for SBP): 0.9

Table 2. 2-Spirals Problem

Method	Learning rate	training average	iterations std. deviation	Failure rate	Av. Real Time
TP	-	445	209	0	253.69

Parameters
Trials: 10; Output tolerance: 0.35; Targets: 0.95, 0.05; Initial weight range: [-1, +1].

4. Multiple Output Units

The method described as the basis for the demonstrator experiments is suited to networks with single output units. In particular, it is based on the solution manifolds having a dimensionality $(N-1)$ in an N-D weight space. The solution manifold for networks with multiple output units is $(N-r)$-D though, with r being the number of output units. The method may be extended to cope with this difficulty relatively straightforwardly, since such a solution manifold may be seen as the intersection of r $(N-1)$-D solution manifolds derived from the r combinations of an I/O pair and each output unit. Consequently, a tangent hyperplane may be computed for each of the r output units. These sets of hyperplanes constitute the linear approximation to the non-linear system of equations required by the approach.

5. Conclusion

A geometrical basis for finding an optimum combination of gradient vectors has been given using tangent hyperplanes and subgoals. The method is seen to provide strongly controlled directioning resulting in a lower number of direction changes during training and lower failure rates. The method has also indicated a good scaling up through its solutions to the 2-spirals problem.

The approach provides a training algorithm for feedforward networks with single hidden layers and hence is capable of providing any I-O mapping. Nevertheless, some problems may be better solved using networks having more than one hidden layer and this extension is currently under further investigation.

6. References

[1] - Baum, E.B., Lang, K.J. *Constructing Hidden Units using Examples and Queries.*, In "Neural Information Processing Systems 3 1990", pp 904-910, 1991.

[2] - Rumelhart, D.E., McClelland J.L. and the PDP Research Group. *Parallel Distributed Processing.* Vol. I. The MIT Press, Cambridge, 1986.

[3] - Johanson, E.M., Dowla, F.U., Goodman, D.M. *Back-propagation Learning for Multilayer Feed-Forward Neural Networks using the Conjugate Gradient Method.* International Journal of Neural Systems, Vol. 2, No. 4 pp 291-301, 1992.

[4] - Hornik, K., Stinchcombe,M. and White,H., *Multilayer Networks are Universal Approximators*, Neural Networks, 2 pp 359-366, 1989.

[5] - Press, W.H., Teukolsky, S.A., Vetterling, W.T., Flannery, B.P. *Numerical Recipes - The Art of Scientific Computing*, 2nd ed. Cambridge University Press, 1992.

[6] - Lang, K. J. and Witbrock, M. J. *Learning to Tell Two Spirals Apart*, Proceedings of the 1988 Connectionist Models Summer School, Morgan Kaufmann, pp 52-59, 1988.

Soft-Monotonic Error Functions

Martin Møller and Jan Depenau
Terma Elektronik A/S, Hovmarken 4, DK-8520 Lystrup, Denmark
and
Computer Science Department, Århus University,
Ny Munkegade, Build. 540, DK-8000 Århus C, Denmark

Abstract

It is well known that the least mean square error function and the entropy error function are Bayes optimal. Satisfying Bayes optimality criteria does not give any information about convergence properties, trajectories in weight space (e.g., if training often leads to local minima or flat regions in weight space), or generalization ability when trained on smaller sets of data. The problem with these error functions is that they are not monotonic with respect to classification, i.e., minimization of the error functions does not imply minimization of misclassifications.

This paper proposes two new error functions, that exhibits a form of soft-monotonicity, where the monotonic behavior is dependent on the values of certain parameters associated with the functions. Through several experiments, it is shown that these functions can improve convergence and generalization.

1 Introduction

Error functions like least mean square and cross-entropy, are known to be Bayes optimal in the sense that minimization with these functions produce solutions that approach the greatest lower bound on generalization error as the training set approaches infinity. But when the training set is small this approximation can be poor [Buntine 91], and it is sparse it is necessary to impose constraints on the network solutions. This is in a Bayesian perspective the same as choosing appropriate priors which is strongly related to penalty terms or regularizers in statistical literature.

The problem with the least mean square error function can be illustrated by the following simple figure [Hampshire 92]. Consider a network with two output units having output between 0 and 1. The outputs are mapped onto the x- and y-axis respectively. If the desired target pattern is (1 0) then all outputs to the right of the line $y = x$ can be considered correct. If and only if the contours of equal error are straight lines parallel to $y = x$, then there exist no regions with misclassification and lower error than other regions with correct classification. Hampshire defines error functions that satisfy such a condition to be *monotonic*. Hampshire strongly suggests that non-monotonic behavior in training can be the cause for the often seen "overlearning", i.e., where the recognition performance on a disjoint test set peaks and then degrades, while training set performance continues to improve.

The problem with suboptimal solutions exists in the form of local minima, which in practice often are very flat regions in error space. Suboptimal solutions in flat regions are often characterized by having a few patterns classified very wrong and many correct. The regions are flat because the network gradients are small for extreme wrong outputs. Minimization of the least mean square error function might very well converge to such regions because the training algorithms are *greedy*

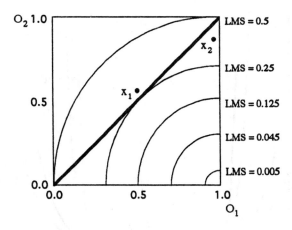

Figure 1: Illustration of *non-monotonicity*. The x-axis is the output from the first unit and the y-axis is the output from the second. The curves corresponds to regions with equal least mean square error on target pattern (1 0). Clearly, there are regions where the network misclassifies, but where the error is lower than in other regions where the network classifies correctly. For example, the error in the point x_1 is lower than the error in x_2. For a monotonic error function, the contours would have to be straight lines.

algorithms, updating weights in the direction of fastest error decrease, and no mechanism in the error function prevents the update of weights into these regions.

This paper defines two new error functions that satisfies a *soft-monotonic* condition in the sense that the functions are asymptotically monotonic in the limit for certain parameters associated with the functions.

2 Imposing constraints on network solutions

Instead of insisting on strict monotonicity, we can define error functions that satisfy a *soft-monotonic* condition, where a certain parameter controls the *degree* of monotonicity. The main idea is to incorporate appropriate constraints into the error function, so that the weights are constrained away from bad regions in weight space.

A way to avoid suboptimal solutions is to strictly minimize the number of misclassifications. Hampshire defines such an approach that works for binary classification problems [Hampshire 92]. We present a more general approach that involves a soft minimization of misclassifications.

Since good solutions are characterized not only by low average error but also by having as many patterns with low error as possible, a good idea would be to include both terms in the error function. One possible approach is to define an error function that penalizes errors of large magnitude.

$$E(\bar{w}) = \frac{1}{2} \sum_{p,j} e^{-\alpha(o_{pj} - t_{pj} + \beta)(t_{pj} + \beta - o_{pj})} \tag{1}$$

where α and β are positive parameters. The derivative to (1) with respect to a given o_{pj} is

$$\frac{dE(\bar{w})}{do_{pj}} = -\alpha(t_{pj} - o_{pj})e^{-\alpha(o_{pj} - t_{pj} + \beta)(t_{pj} + \beta - o_{pj})} \tag{2}$$

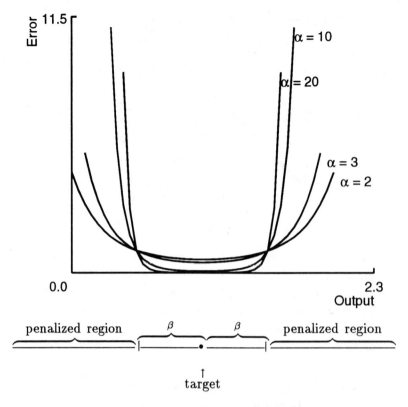

Figure 2: The function of the α and β parameter.

It is easy to see that the global minimum for (1) is when $t_{pj} = o_{pj}$, $\forall p, j$. The function of α and β is illustrated through figure 2. β defines the width of the acceptable error around the desired target and α controls the steepness of the exponentially growing error in the penalized regions outside the interval. If α is small equation (2) resembles the derivative of the least square function. But the higher α gets the more active is the constraint imposed on the penalized regions. When no errors are in the penalized regions β is decreased, so that the outputs are pulled towards the targets. A high α value gives large partial error derivatives inside the penalized regions and small partial error derivatives when outside the regions. So the higher the α value the more the errors will tend to arrange themselves inside the region around the target. This gives a sort of balanced distribution of the errors. For regression problems it is well known in statistics that a balanced set of errors can yield better generalization, this is often referred to as *variance heterogeneity* [Seber and Wild 89]. It is an open question whether this is true also for classification problems.

In the limit when α increases to infinity, the exponential error function is monotonic. Surely, for a fixed number of patterns in the training set, we can select a large enough α so that the error function is monotonic. The problem is how large α should be to ensure monotonicity in a given problem. Selecting too high a α slows down the convergence, because of too hard constraints imposed on the acceptable paths down to the minimum. On the other hand, too small a α results in non-monotonic behavior of the error function. One promising approach would be to adapt α similarly to the penalty parameters in constrained optimization, starting with a small α and then successively increasing α during training. This approach has not been tried yet. It seems that just setting α to a "reasonable" size yields good results.

Notice that the exponential error function also works for non-classification problems and that the soft-monotonicity condition can be obtained for any accuracy required by adjustment of the β parameter.

A more direct way of balancing errors is to minimize the variance of the magnitude of the errors. This can be done by adding the variance as a penalty term to an existing error function like least square.

$$E(\bar{w}) = \frac{1}{NP} \sum_j^N \sum_p^P (t_{pj} - o_{pj})^2 + \eta \frac{1}{NP} \sum_j^N \sum_p^P \left((t_{pj} - o_{pj})^2 - \frac{1}{PN} \sum_i^N \sum_q^P (t_{qi} - o_{qi})^2 \right)^2 \quad (3)$$

where η is a positive penalty parameter, N the number of output units and P the number of patterns. The derivative to (3) is

$$\frac{dE(\bar{w})}{do_{pj}} = -\frac{1}{NP} (t_{pj} - o_{pj}) \left(2 + 4\eta \frac{PN-1}{PN} \left((t_{pj} - o_{pj})^2 - \frac{1}{PN} \sum_i^N \sum_q^P (t_{qi} - o_{qi})^2 \right) \right) \quad (4)$$

From (4) we observe, that while the exponential error function can be used in both online and offline training mode, the minimum variance error function can only be applied in offline mode.

3 Experiments

In this section, we compare the least mean square error function, the exponential error function and the minimum variance error function.

To be able to see how the different error functions compare on problems with varying input dimensions some artificial data were generated. For dimension N a set of 4N *centerpoints*, each a N-bit string, was randomly chosen. Around each centerpoint a set of 9 *distortions* was generated using a Gaussian distribution to determine whether to flip a bit or not. This gives a total of 40N patterns. Each centerpoint and its distortions were then randomly assigned to one out of two possible classes.

It is widely recognized that the class of conjugate gradient algorithms are well suited for learning algorithms because of their ability to gain second order information without too much calculation work [Battiti 92]. One, the Scaled Conjugate Gradient algorithm [Møller 92a], has especially low calculation costs, and has for that reason been used in the experiments to follow.

3.1 Training

The three error functions were tested on dimension 8,10,12,14,16 and 18 running 5 different runs on each dimension using a 3 layer network with N hidden units. The training was first terminated when all patterns were classified correctly or until a resonable limit was reached. Table 1 summarizes the average results obtained. α was set to 1. The initial β was set to 0.9 and then halfed every time no errors were inside the penalized regions. The penalty parameter η was set to 1-2.

In the runs with the least mean square error function only a few global solutions was found with a 100% correct classification. Training on the other two error functions, however, yielded optimal solutions in all runs. The exponential error function seems to give the fastest convergence, but this might be because of the actual values of α, β and η.

Dim	Least Mean Square				Exponential Error				Variance Error			
	Epoch		Correct		Epoch		Correct		Epoch		Correct	
	μ	σ	μ	σ	μ	σ	μ	σ	μ	σ	μ	σ
8	487	73	.984	.004	76	3	1	0	82	13	1	0
10	493	15	.983	.008	112	19	1	0	147	23	1	0
12	413	54	.988	.000	109	10	1	0	111	10	1	0
14	478	37	.993	.002	77	12	1	0	81	5	1	0
16	490	24	.994	.001	75	1	1	0	94	13	1	0
18	447	46	.996	.004	78	7	1	0	89	4	1	0

Table 1: Average results on artificial data. μ = mean and σ = standard deviation.

3.2 Generalization

In this section we investigate the generalization ability of network solutions found by minimization of the different error functions. Again some artificial data were generated, this time with continuous input constrained between 0 and 1. We chose dimension 10 with 20 centerpoints, 50 distortions per centerpoint and 4 possible output classes. The average overlap between the centerpoints was 4%, meaning that 4% of the distortions were nearer other centerpoints than the one they were generated from. The set of patterns was then split in to a training set, validation set and a test set of equal size. When applying the k-nearest neighbor technique on the data we got a max performance of 94.26% on the validation set giving 93.69% on the test set (k=5). Because of the way the data is generated we would not expect the neural network solution to do much better than that. We ran the following experiments. SCG was tested on the least square error function, the exponential error function and the minimimum variance error function. 5 different runs were made for each test. When the classification rate of the validation set was at it highest the number of iterations run and the classification rate of the test set were recorded.

The results are illustrated in figure 4. We observe the same trend for both the exponential error function and the minimum variance error function. The higher the α and η values the better the generalization. For η equal to 30 there is a decrease in generalization. At this point the constraint towards low variance was too strong. Unfortunatly, this gain in generalization is done at the expense of the convergence rate as the figure also show. This is, however, not surprising since high α and η values impose a tougher constraint on the acceptable path down to the minimum. The minimum variance- and the exponential error function gives approximately the same maximum generalization performance as the k-nearest neighbor. At this maximum generalization point the convergence rate of the minimum variance error funtion is slightly higher than the convergence rate of the exponential error function.

4 Conclusion

This paper has shown that imposing appropriate constraints on network solutions can improve convergence and generalization. We have proposed two new error functions that impose such constraints. We do not claim that these functions are in any way optimal, but we do believe that our results illustrates the neccesity of adding such constraints. Minimization with the new error functions produce in average better solutions with respect to generalization than the least mean square error function.

The quality of the solutions found with the new error functions depends heavily on the values of the constraint parameters α and η. We have not addressed the problem of choosing optimal

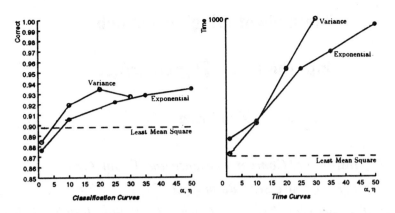

Figure 3: Results on the test set using the exponential error function and the minimum variance error function with different α and η values.

values of α and η. Several heuristic methods could be applied, like starting with a small value and then slowly increase. More sophisticated techniques, like the ones used to estimate appropriate regularization parameters, might also be usable in this context.

It would be interesting to know how the distribution of the errors on the training set influence the generalization ability. Our results indicate that the more balanced the distribution is, i.e, the more equal the errors are in magnitude, the better generalization one can expect. It remains to future work to actually prove the relationship between expected generalization and error distribution.

Acknowledgements

Many thanks to Wray Buntine, Scott Fahlman and Brian Mayoh for their helpful comments. Thanks also to John Hampshire for sharing some of his thesis results with us before publishing. The second author is supported by Terma Elektronik A/S and the Danish Academy of Technical Sciences (ATV).

References

[Battiti 92]   R. Battiti (1992), *First and Second-Order Methods for Learning: between Steepest descent and Newton's Method*, Neural Computation, Vol. 4 (2), pp. 141-167.

[Buntine 91]   W. Buntine and A.S. Weigend (1991), *Bayesian Back-Propagation*, Complex Systems, Vol. 5, pp. 603-643.

[Hampshire 92]   J.B. Hampshire (1992), *A Differential Theory of Learning for Statistical Pattern Recognition with Connectionist Models*, Ph.D. Thesis, School of Computer Science, Carnegie Mellon University.

[Møller 93]   M. Møller (1993), *A Scaled Conjugate Gradient Algorithm for Fast Supervised Learning*, Neural Networks, June, Vol. 6, No. 4, pp. 525-533.

[Seber and Wild 89] G.A.F. Seber and C.J. Wild (1989), *Non-linear Regression*, John Wiley and Sons, New York.

Methods of Digging Tunnels

into the Error Hypersurface

Xun Liang

Institute of Computer Science and Technology
Peking University, Beijing 100871, P.R.China
Department of Automation, Tsinghua University, Beijing 100084, P.R.China

In the past several years, feedforward neural networks were developed rapidly, especially a number of papers improved the Back Propagation algorithms. However, generally speaking, they used gradient descent techniques on the error hypersurface. In this talk, we mainly discuss the methods of digging tunnels into the error hypersurface. Two digging methods are presented: one is digging horizontally, another is digging down into the error hypersurface. Both methods use structure variation idea. Since multilayer perceptron (MLP) training intrinsically solves a nonlinear problem, and MLPs are white boxes in which the weights and thresholds can be added, deleted and renewed purposely, it is unnecessary to always use the traditional gradient descent techniques.

Our idea is as follows: (1) An MLP is trained with a relatively small number of hidden neurons using traditional gradient descent techniques until the algorithm is trapped in local minima. (2) A tunnel is digged horizontally to move the MLP to another isohypse position on the error hypersurface and use gradient descent techniques again. This digging method can be called rotation transformation, in which a hidden neuron is added by certain rules and the Perceptron Convergence Theorem is used, then an original hidden neuron is removed according to the correlation of the outputs in the hidden layer. Hence the number of hidden neurons will not increase. (3) Or a tunnel is digged down into the error hypersurface. This digging method is also called the compensation method, in which hidden neurons are also added. But whenever a hidden neuron is added, its input and output weights and threshold are calculated definitely rather than iterated. Thus, it ensures the global convergence.

Hardware Supervised Learning for Cellular and Hopfield Neural Networks

M. Balsi

No.E.L. - Nonlinear Electronics Laboratory
University of California at Berkeley, CA 94720 USA[1]

Abstract - Hardware *implementation of learning algorithms for recurrent neural networks is considered. Recurrent back-propagation and diffusion optimization are modified so as to work on-line, and circuit realization scheme is proposed. A new error function is defined, specifically suitable for continuous input - discrete output mapping tasks. Simulation results are presented for a simple cellular neural network problem.*

1. Introduction

Supervised learning for Neural Networks (NNs) is a very complex optimization problem, that is generally solved by lengthy computations on digital (conventional or parallel) computers. For this reason, large computing resources (time and/or power) are required, so that in many cases real-time problems are hardly accessible.

Therefore, it is desirable to realize fully parallel hardware implementation of NNs that include learning in the same system, which would also allow for real-time on-line adaptability of the net.

Several authors have studied implementation of learning algorithms; however, only few results have been published concerning supervised learning for feedforward networks. Back-Propagation (BP) was implemented by H. Eguchi *et al.* (1991) by using pulse frequency encoding for signals. In this technique, multiplication and addition/nonlinear squashing are performed by very simple circuitry (AND and OR gates, respectively). Concerning fully analog implementations, M. Hasler (1993) proposed a continuous-time realization of BP by use of a resistive circuit (the adjoint of the NN).

In this paper, the problem of hardware learning for recurrent NNs is addressed. The author in aware of no feasible solution proposed to date. Application of Recurrent Back-Propagation (RBP), and of Diffusion Optimization is considered. The main advantages of these algorithms, in view of hardware realization, are: continuous time operation; calculation of weight corrections performed locally; no memory required (no batch operation). Possible circuit implementations are proposed, and results of simulations performed on Cellular Neural Networks reported.

2. Definitions and Notations

2.1 Hopfield and Cellular Neural Networks

In order to fix notations, define a Hopfield Neural Network (HNN - Hopfield, 1984) as follows:

$$\tau_X \frac{dx_i}{dt} = -x_i + \sum_j W_{ij} y_j + u_i$$

$$y_i = f(x_i); \quad f(-x) = -f(x); \quad f'(x) \geq 0; \quad \lim_{x \to \pm\infty} f(x) = \pm 1$$

Vector x will be called state of the network, y is output, u is input, or threshold, and matrix W is the weight matrix. Function f is a sigmoidal, or squashing function.

Define Cellular Neural Network (CNN - Chua and Yang, 1988) as a HNN in which neurons are only connected to neighbors, and weights are defined in a uniform way over the network. Without loss of generality, we consider a CNN in which neurons are arranged on a planar square grid, and indexed by double indices. Neurons are connected, whose indices do not differ more than r. Relevant equations are written as follows:

---

[1] On leave from: Dipartimento di Ingegneria Elettronica, Università "La Sapienza" di Roma, via Eudossiana, 18 - 00184 Roma Italy. E-mail: mb@tce.ing.uniroma1.it

$$\tau_X \frac{dx_{ij}}{dt} = -x_{ij} + \sum_{kl \in N_r(ij)} W_{k-i;l-j} y_{kl} + \sum_{kl \in N_r(ij)} B_{k-i;l-j} u_{kl} + I$$

$$y_{ij} = f(x_{ij}); \quad f(x) = \frac{1}{2}(|x+1| - |x-1|)$$

In this case, input vector u, weighted by control matrix B, is considered distinct from bias I. $N_r(ij)$ is a function yielding the set of indices of neighbors of neuron ij, which is a square of side $(2r+1)$ centred on ij.

It is apparent that in this case there are only a small number of independent weights, which can be arranged into $(2r+1) \times (2r+1)$ matrices W and B, plus a scalar bias I. If, on the contrary, weights are allowed to vary independently over the network, the corresponding network will be called a General CNN (GCNN).

2.2 <u>Learning problem</u>

We shall consider use of HNNs and CNNs as mappers from the continuous space $X^0 \times U$ of initial states and inputs into the space $Y^\infty = ([-1, -1+\epsilon] \cup [1-\epsilon, 1])^N$ (where N is the number of neurons) of saturated outputs; ϵ is a small positive number, and when f is piece-wise linear, $Y^\infty = \{-1, 1\}^N$. Define $X^\infty = [(-\infty, -x_{sat}] \cup [x_{sat}, +\infty)]^N$, where x_{sat} is a positive number, so that $y \in Y^\infty$ when $x \in X^\infty$ (for CNNs, $x_{sat}=1$).

Under suitable conditions on weights and derivative of f (Hopfield, 1984; Chua and Yang, 1988), the network is asymptotically stable, and equilibria belong to Y^∞. We shall assume that such conditions are enforced.

The learning task considered consists of realizing a given mapping $\mathfrak{m}: X^0 \times U \to Y^\infty$, given a set of learning examples (training set) $\mathfrak{B} = \{x_0^\mu, u^\mu, \zeta^\mu; \mu = 1, 2, \ldots, M\} \subset X^0 \times U \times \{-1, 1\}^N$ (i.e. a set of triplets formed by initial state, input, and desired output). We are not addressing here the problem of generalization, however we note that in the case of CNNs a single learning example ($M=1$) may be enough to define a task, because, due to the space-invariant property of the cloning template, it is in some sense equivalent to as many independent examples as there are neighborhood-sized subsets contained in it.

The training set is the only information given to the algorithm, besides network topology. In fact, external control and data communication should be minimized, in order to exploit the full speed of parallel analog computation. For the same reason, emphasis is put on simplicity of realization, rather than on computing time; all calculations are to be done locally, and if memory is required, it should also be local, and preferably analog.

2.3 <u>Recurrent Back-Propagation and Diffusion Learning</u>

RBP, defined by F. Pineda (1987), is analogous to BP for recurrent networks. Unlike BP, it is defined in continuous time, and does not need separate forward- and back-propagation phases, which simplifies circuit timing issues. It can be realized by adding to the network an adjoint net that has the same topological properties. RBP changes weights dynamically by making their time derivatives proportional to the opposite of the derivative of error function with respect to the weight considered:

$$\tau_W \frac{dW_{ij}}{dt} = -\frac{\partial E}{\partial W_{ij}}$$

Relevant equations for RBP for HNNs are as follows (Pineda, 1987; Balsi, 1993):

$$\tau_W \frac{dW_{ij}}{dt} = \sum_{\mu \in \mathfrak{B}} z_i^\mu \bar{y}_j^\mu$$

$$z_i^\mu - \sum_j W_{ji} f'(\bar{x}_i^\mu) z_j^\mu = -\frac{\partial E}{\partial \bar{x}_i^\mu}$$

The first equation describes weight dynamics, while the second represents the adjoint BP network, which appears to be a resistive net, with the same connection topology as the forward net, except for direction reversal of connections, as seen from weight matrix transposition. Symbol $\bar{x}^\mu$ denotes equilibrium state reached by applying initial state and input of example μ. E is error function, to be defined below.

Diffusion optimization (Geman and Hwang, 1986) can be seen as a gradient descent method with added noise, which decreases slowly, so that parameters converge in probability to global minimizers of the error function. Continuous annealing (a discrete-time version of diffusion, or, from another point of view, a continuous-space version of simulated annealing) has been used by a few authors (Hoptroff and Hall, 1989) for NN learning; Wong (1991) used diffusion learning for stochastic HNNs both as a means of obtaining global convergence during operation and for learning, also hinting at hardware realization. His method, however, is not immediately translated to deterministic networks, as those considered here.

Diffusion learning can be defined for the HNN as follows:

$$\tau_W \frac{dW_{ij}}{dt} = -\frac{\partial E}{\partial W_{ij}} + Tw$$

where $w(t)$ is a white noise, which is (in a weak sense) the time derivative of a Wiener process (Pugachev and Sinitsyn, 1987). It is apparent, that the diffusion algorithm may be obtained by adding a noise term to RBP learning equations.

3. Error Function - Realization Issues - Modified Equations

For the learning problem stated in section 2.2, we chose to use a new "tailor-cut" error function. In fact, when a traditional output-based function is used, shallow error surfaces arise, especially when output function is piece-wise linear, as is the case with CNNs. However, using a state-based function, while effectively improving from this point of view (Schuler, 1993), adds unwanted additional constraints to the output, which may even prevent a working solution from being reached.

In order to have the advantages of both approaches, without their disadvantages, the new error function is defined as follows:

$$E = \sum_{\mu} \sum_{i} E_i^{\mu} = \sum_{\mu} \sum_{i} \left[\delta^{(-3)}\left(1 + \rho_{min} - \zeta_i^{\mu} \bar{x}_i^{\mu}\right) + \delta^{(-3)}\left(-1 - \rho_{max} + \zeta_i^{\mu} \bar{x}_i^{\mu}\right) \right]$$

Error is written as a sum of errors over individual neurons (indexed by i) and examples (indexed by μ).

$\delta^{(-i)}$ is the third integral of the Dirac pulse, e.g.:

$$\delta^{(-3)}(x) = \begin{cases} 0 & \text{if } x < 0 \\ \frac{1}{2}x^2 & \text{else} \end{cases}$$

$1 + \rho_{min} \geq x_{sat}$ is minimum acceptable magnitude of equilibrium state value, while $1 + \rho_{max}$ is its maximum. The second term, involving maximum state, may be omitted, but it has the advantage of preventing weights from drifting towards bigger and bigger values, especially when the algorithm is implemented in such a way as to be sensible to the time integral of error, which is reduced when outputs are saturated earlier.

The quadratic form has the advantage of causing error derivatives to be piece-wise linear, simplifying implementation. In fact, relevant function to be implemented is the following:

$$f_E\left(\zeta_i^{\mu}, \bar{x}_i^{\mu}\right) = -\frac{\partial E_i^{\mu}}{\partial \bar{x}_i^{\mu}} =$$

$$= \zeta_i^{\mu}\left[-\delta^{(-2)}\left(1 + \rho_{min} - \zeta_i^{\mu} \bar{x}_i^{\mu}\right) + \delta^{(-2)}\left(-1 - \rho_{max} + \zeta_i^{\mu} \bar{x}_i^{\mu}\right)\right]$$

A generic error component E_i^{μ} (solid line), and function f_E, are plotted in figure 1 for $\zeta=1$.

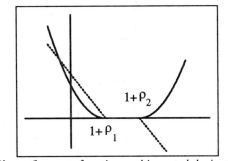

Figure 1 - *error function and inverted derivative*

Learning equations, as written in section 2.3, imply batch processing of examples, which would mean memorizing corrections and separating forward and backward propagation phases. Simplified operation is obtained by exploiting integration over time, while presenting examples in a (deterministic or stochastic) succession, keeping each example steady for a prescribed period.

At the same time, instead of using equilibrium states, transient states are used. Period of example presentation should be long enough for the network to relax, and to stay steady at equilibrium for a time long enough to make negligible wrong contribution to weight correction due to transient. In this functioning mode, the algorithm is actually sensible to the integral of error over time, so that faster solutions are preferred. With a little addition to the system, effect of transient may be masked by interrupting learning for a suitable time after a new example is presented. This may be obtained by fixing error signals at zero.

With these considerations in mind, learning equations will be written as follows for diffusion (RBP is obtained in the same form for $T=0$):

$$\tau_W \frac{dW_{ij}}{dt} = z_i y_j + Tw$$

$$z_i - \sum_j W_{ji} f'(x_i) z_j = f_E(\zeta_i, x_i)$$

The following equations define diffusion learning (and, for $T=0$, RBP) for CNNs. In this case, parameters to be learned are not only state weights, but also input (control) weights and bias.

$$\tau_W \frac{dW_{ij}}{dt} = \sum_{kl} z_{kl} y_{k+i;l+j} + Tw$$

$$z_{ij} - \sum_{kl \in N_r(ij)} W_{i-k;j-l} f'(x_{ij}) z_{kl} = f_E(\zeta_{ij}, x_{ij})$$

$$\tau_B \frac{dB_{ij}}{dt} = \sum_{kl} f_E(\zeta_{ij}, x_{ij}) u_{k+i;l+j} + Tw$$

$$\tau_I \frac{dI}{dt} = \sum_{ij} f_E(\zeta_{ij}, x_{ij}) + Tw$$

4. Proposed Hardware Realization

In figure 2, realization of a HNN with hardware learning is presented schematically, by making use of transconductance amplifiers. One neuron is considered, with only one connection represented. Output function is here supposed to be piece-wise linear, so that a controlled switch is sufficient to realize multiplication by its derivative, whose only possible values are 0 and 1 (figure 3(b)). In weight adaptation section, a controlled source is driven by resistor noise, to produce the stochastic term for the diffusion algorithm. This is obviously just a way of representing the necessary operation, while its actual realization should be considered at a stage where technology is chosen.

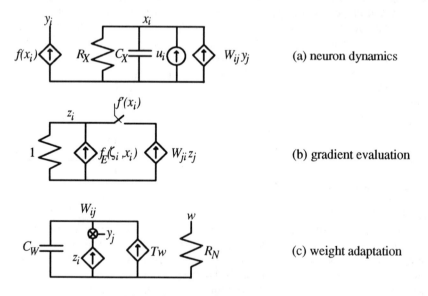

(a) neuron dynamics

(b) gradient evaluation

(c) weight adaptation

Figure 2 - hardware implementation

5. Simulation Results

Simulations were performed on CNNs. In a previous paper (Balsi, 1993), I reported results concerning application of RBP to GCNNs. In that case, individual weights are not subject to as many constraints as for CNNs. For the latter, in fact, global functioning is only governed by a few parameters, forming the cloning template. This is reflected in learning equations, where a global connection pattern arises (summations over all neurons are present), that is not present in the case of GCNNs or HNNs, where learning equations are local.

When applied to CNN learning, RBP proved very prone to get stuck into local minima, so that learning was successful only when starting weights were very close to a valid solution. In fact, correct functioning was obtained only when starting weights guaranteed correct sign of equilibrium points.

For this reason, I tried using random presentation of examples as a way of climbing out of the said local minima, as proposed by many authors for BP (Heskes *et al.*, 1992). In this way, the CNN can correctly learn what is generally called "noise filtering" cloning template. This functionality consists of bringing to negative final output all those neurons that have positive initial state, but are surrounded by negative output neurons, while leaving everything else as it is. The name is due to the fact, that by associating light intensity of pixels of an image with the outputs of neurons of a planar CNN, isolated lighted pixels are removed, and the image smoothed.

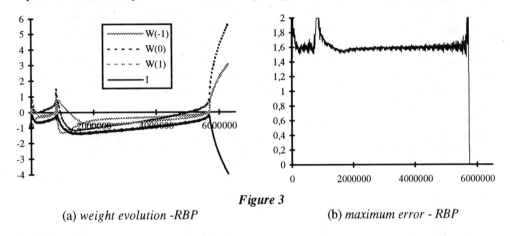

Figure 3

(a) *weight evolution -RBP* (b) *maximum error - RBP*

Figure 3 shows evolution of weight values (a) and maximum error as a function of time, measured in neuron time constants τ_X, obtained in a simulation of a one-dimensional 5-neuron CNN, performed by integrating equations with a modified Runge-Kutta-Merson algorithm, with 32 examples. Simulation was interrupted after error had stayed at zero for a while; weights would have actually settled at larger values because of parameters chosen (large ρ_{max}), but representing them would make the figure less readable.

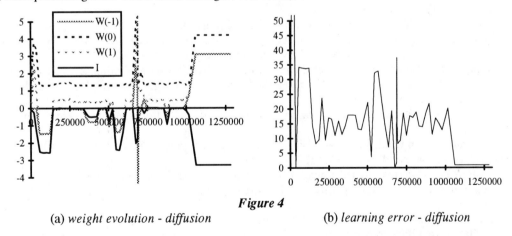

Figure 4

(a) *weight evolution - diffusion* (b) *learning error - diffusion*

As it is said above, a CNN task may also be specified by a single example, which simplifies control and communication very much. As in this case random motion cannot be obtained from the data, it is necessary to use

III-455

diffusion learning, which provides built-in, controlled stochasticity. In fact, by using the diffusion algorithm, an 11-neuron CNN was taught the same noise filtering task with a single example. Figure 4(a) shows weight evolution during learning, while figure 4(b) shows learning error E. Computed cloniong templete works correctly in all cases.

In both cases, it is apparent that the role of gradient force is keeping steady those correct weight patterns that are actually found by random motion.

6. Conclusions, Open Problems, Perspectives.

Supervised learning algorithms for recurrent networks were adapted for hardware realizability, and tested by simulation. The case presented is very simple, because of complexity of simulation; however, it proves feasibility of the methods presented. In fact, results were obtained under realistic constraints: in particular, limited range and bandwidth of electronic circuits. These preliminary results, therefore, encourage further research towards realization of a completely analog network, capable of real-time on-line learning.

One of the main open problems is caused by limitation of weight and state values, due to supply voltage constraints, that, in some cases, causes the algorithm to get stuck, for a possibly long time, on wrong solutions. Methods to avoid such failures should still be investigated. Further investigation should also explore practical circuit implementation. In relation to this issue, some aspects of the algorithms (e.g. pattern presentation schemes, noise exploitation) might be adapted to physical constraints.

A particular issue concerns CNNs. In fact, as noted above, cloning template learning involves global evaluation of the problem being solved, while the network only has local information flowing. This issue poses serious difficulties to learning in cases characterized by diffusion of information over the whole network. Solution to such problems goes beyond the scope of this paper.

Continuation of the work will aim at designing a practical system. The purpose is twofold: making a complete adaptive neural machine, to be applied to real-time problems, and realizing a learning system to be used in development of special-purpose networks. This last case might be of interest in particular in the case of CNNs, where uniformity of the system makes solutions found on small nets immediately scalable to large problems.

7. Acknowledgement

Assistance and support of Prof. L.O. Chua during my stay at the University of California at Berkeley, where this research was performed, is gratefully acknowledged.

8. References

Balsi M., "Recurrent Back-Propagation for Cellular Neural Networks", in: H. Dedieu (ed.), "ECCTD'93 - Circuit Theory and Design", Elsevier, Amsterdam, 1993, 677.

Chua L.O., Yang L., "Cellular Neural Networks: Theory", IEEE Trans. Circ. Syst., CAS-35(10), 1257 (1988).

Eguchi H., Furuta T., Horiguchi H., Oteki S., Kitaguchi T., "Neural Network LSI Chip with On-Chip Learning", Proc. of Int. Joint Conf. on Neural Networks, Seattle, WA, July 8-12, 1991, vol. I, 453.

Geman S, Hwang C.-R., "Diffusions from Global Optimization", SIAM J. Control Optim., 24(5), 1031 (1986).

Hasler M., "The Backpropagation Learning Algorithm Realized by an Analogue Circuit", Int. j. circ. th. appl., 21, 177 (1993).

Heskes T.M., Slijpen T.P., Kappen B., "Learning in Neural Networks with Local Minima", Phys. Rev. A, 46(8), 5221 (1992)

Hopfield J.J., "Neurons with Graded Response Have Collective Computational Properties like those of Two-State Neurons", Proc. Nat. Acad. Sci. USA, 81, 3088 (1984).

Hoptroff R.G., Hall T.J., "Learning by Diffusion for Multilayer Perceptron", Electronics Lett. 25(8), 531 (1989).

Pineda F., "Generalization of Back-Propagation to Recurrent Neural Networks", Phys. Rev. Lett. 59(19), 2229 (1987).

Pugachev V.S., Sinitsyn I.N., "Stochastic Differential Systems", J. Wiley & sons, Chichester, 1987.

Schuler A.J., "State-Based Backpropagation-Through-Time for CNNs", in: H. Dedieu (ed.), "ECCTD'93 - Circuit Theory and Design", Elsevier, Amsterdam, 1993, 33.

Wong E., "Stochastic Neural Networks", Algorithmica, 6, 466 (1991).

Speed and Area Improvement by Reduced Operation Backpropagation

Kan Boonyanit
LSI Logic Corporation
1525 McCarthy Blvd., MS G-813
Milpitas, CA 95035

Allen M. Peterson
STAR Lab, Department of Electrical Engineering
Stanford University
Stanford, CA 94305

Abstract

There have been numerous proposed algorithms to speed up the learning time of backpropagation. However, most of them do not take into consideration the amount of hardware required to implement the algorithm. Without suitable hardware implementation, the real promise of neural network applications will be difficult to achieve. There is a need for special purpose hardware, particularly in specialized integrated circuits to serve in high performance real-time applications. This paper proposes an adapted backpropagation algorithm to be judged by the measure of speed and area if it is implemented with digital VLSI. Since multiply dominates computation and is expensive in hardware, the approach is to reduce the number of multiplies in the backward path of backpropagation algorithm by setting some neuron errors to zero. This paper proves the convergence theorem by the general Robbins-Monro process, a stochastic approximation process. It is valid if neuron errors are set to zero randomly and the learning rate decreases with time. However, setting the neuron errors to zero randomly is slow compared to the standard algorithm. So, this paper proposes why neuron errors should be set to zero according to their magnitudes. The theory is confirmed with simulation results of a character recognition problem by minimizing errors only and a function approximation problem with testing patterns to monitor generalization performance. Finally, hardware implementation is discussed and the area comparison is shown. The conclusion is that the reduced operation algorithm performance in terms of speed and area is superior to a standard backpropagation algorithm.

Introduction

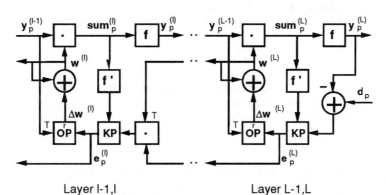

Figure 1: Data flow diagram of backpropagation

A data flow diagram of backpropagation [1] algorithm is shown in figure 1. It was first shown in [2]. In the diagram, data are expressed as vectors and matrices so that all operations can be written as vector-vector and matrix-vector products. $\mathbf{sum}_p^{(l)}$ and $\mathbf{y}_p^{(l)}$ is a vector where each component $sum_{pj}^{(l)}$ and $y_{pj}^{(l)}$ is an input and an output of neuron j in layer l with pattern p, respectively. $\mathbf{d}_p$ is a desired output vector with similar definition. $\mathbf{w}^{(l)}$ and $\Delta\mathbf{w}^{(l)}$ is a weight and a change of weight matrix where each component $w_{ji}^{(l)}$ and $\Delta w_{ji}^{(l)}$ is a weight and a change of weight connection between neuron i in layer l-1 to neuron j in layer l, respectively. $\mathbf{e}_p^{(l)}$ is a neuron error vector where each component $e_{pj}^{(l)}$ is an error term associated with neuron j in layer l with pattern p. The matrix-vector multiplication is represented by •. **KP** is a Kronecker product or a term by term multiplication of two equal length vectors. **OP** is an outer product of a column and a row vector to expand a matrix. **f** is a sigmoid function and **f** ' is its derivative. T represents a transpose and r is the learning rate.

The data flow diagram can be used to estimate the number of multiplications required which is a good indication of the complexity of the hardware needed to implement the algorithm because multiplication is expensive and dominates the whole computation. For simplicity, assume that all layers have the same number of neurons, N. In the forward path, between each layer, there are N^2 multiplies represented by •. In the backward path, • takes N^2 multiplies, the same as the forward path. **KP** needs N multiplies and **OP** needs $2N^2$ multiplies (including the multiplies of the learning rate, r, and assuming the weights are updated after each pattern). Except for the last layer which has $2N^2 + N$ multiplies, there are $3N^2 + N$ multiplies for the backward computation between layer l-1 and l. Consequently, the number of multiplications in the backward path is about three times that in the forward path.

Since the backward path requires considerably more multiplications, we propose an approach to reduce them. In figure 1, if we set some elements of $e_p^{(l)}$ in each layer to zero, the number of multiplies is reduced. Since $e_p^{(l)}$ is computed recursively for each layer, the number of multiplications is reduced for all layers. Again, assume that all layers have N neurons and that K of them are kept. N-K out of N components of $e_p^{(l)}$ are set to zero. In the backward path, • now requires KN multiplies. **KP** still needs N multiplies and **OP** needs 2KN multiplies. The total number is reduced from $3N^2 + N$ to $3KN + N$, about a factor of N/k. Undoubtedly, this reduction changes the normal backpropagation algorithm. The proof is presented next.

General Robbins-Monro Process

The general Robbins-Monro process with exogenous noise [3] will be used to prove the reduced operation backpropagation. For the proof, the process is given by

$$\mathbf{w}_{n+1} = \mathbf{w}_n + a_n h(\mathbf{w}_n, z_n) \tag{1}$$

where $\mathbf{w}_n$ is the state of the process at the nth estimate of the optimal value of $\mathbf{w}$. The sequence $\{\mathbf{w}_n\}$ is assumed to be bounded w.p.1. z_n is a random variable which is independent of the state $\mathbf{w}_n$ and its past values. The sequence $\{z_n\}$ is called exogenous noise.

There are three conditions (C1.1, C1.2, and C1.3) to be satisfied for a convergence w.p.1 of the sequence $\{\mathbf{w}_n\}$. They are

C1.1   h is a bounded measurable R^r-valued function. It is continuous in $\mathbf{w}$, uniformly in z on bounded $\mathbf{w}$ sets.

C1.2   For each $\varepsilon > 0$ and each $\mathbf{w}$

$$\lim_{n \to \infty} P\{\sup_{m \ge n} | \sum_{i=n}^{m} a_i(h(\mathbf{w}, z_i) - \bar{h}(\mathbf{w})) | \ge \varepsilon\} = 0$$

C1.3 $\{a_n\}$ is a sequence of positive real numbers such that $a_n \to 0$ and $\sum_{i=0}^{n} a_i = \infty$ as $n \to \infty$.

With the three required conditions satisfied, the sequence $\{\mathbf{w}_n\}$ (if bounded w.p. 1) will be interpolated into a continuous parameter process and have the same asymptotic properties as those of the solution to an ordinary differential equation

$$\frac{d\mathbf{w}_t}{dt} = \bar{h}(\mathbf{w}_t) \tag{2}$$

Application To Reduced Operation Algorithm

The general Robbins-Monro process can now be applied to prove the convergence of the reduced operation proposal. Equation (1) is the equation to update all the weights in the weight space. That is if we define $\mathbf{w}_n$ to be a state of the neural network at the nth update. The formula used to update weights per state $\mathbf{w}_n$ is

$$h(\mathbf{w}, z_i) = (h(w_{11}^{(1)}, z_i), \dots, h(w_{jk}^{(l)}, z_i) \dots, h(w_{N_L N_{L-1}}^{(L)}, z_i))^T \tag{3}$$

where each component is used to update each weight. We define the random variable z_i as

$$z_i = (s_{i,1}^{(1)}, s_{i,2}^{(1)}, \dots, s_{i,j}^{(1)}, \dots, s_{i,1}^{(L)}, s_{i,2}^{(L)}, \dots, s_{i,N_L}^{(L)}, p_i) \tag{4}$$

where $s_{i,j}^{(l)}$ is a selection variable. For the ith update, $s_{i,j}^{(l)}$ is 1 if the corresponding error $e_{pj}^{(l)}$ is selected. It is 0, otherwise. The selection is random and pattern independent. Each error in the same layer has an equal chance of being selected. Another random variable is p_i which is the index for pattern p in the ith update. We choose at random (uniformly) an integer $p_i \in \{1, 2, \dots, P\}$ where P is the total number of patterns in the training set. From now on, we will use p_i in place of p to emphasize randomness of pattern selections.

Now, we can write the formula to update a weight in term of a modified error term. That is

$$h(w_{jk}^{(l)}, z_i) = v_{pij}^{(l)} y_{pik}^{(l-1)} \tag{5}$$

where the modified error term $v_{pij}^{(l)}$ is derived in the same recursive manner as $e_{pij}^{(l)}$ of normal backpropagation algorithm. It is always multiplied by $s_{i,j}^{(l)}$. For the output layer L

$$v_{pij}^{(L)} = e_{pij}^{(L)} s_{i,j}^{(L)} = (d_{pij} - y_{pij}^{(L)}) f'(sum_{pij}^{(L)}) s_{i,j}^{(L)} \tag{6}$$

and for a hidden layer l

$$v_{pij}^{(l)} = \sum_{h=1}^{N_{l+1}} v_{pih}^{(l+1)} w_{hj}^{(l+1)} f'(sum_{pij}^{(l)}) s_{i,j}^{(l)} \tag{7}$$

We will write $h(w_{jk}^{(l)}, z_i)$ for a few layers explicitly in terms of all $s_{i,j}^{(l)}$ it depends on so that later proofs will be easier to understand. For the output layer L

$$h(w_{jk}^{(L)}, z_i) = (d_{pij} - y_{pij}^{(L)}) f'(sum_{pij}^{(L)}) s_{i,j}^{(L)} y_{pik}^{(L-1)} \tag{8}$$

for layer L-1

$$h(w_{jk}^{(L-1)}, z_i) = \sum_{h=1}^{NL} e_{p;h}^{(L)} s_{i,h}^{(L)} w_{hj}^{(L)} f'(sum_{p;ij}^{(L-1)}) s_{i,j}^{(L-1)} y_{p;k}^{(L-2)}$$ (9)

and for layer L-2

$$h(w_{jk}^{(L-2)}, z_i) = \sum_{h=1}^{NL-1} \sum_{g=1}^{NL} e_{p;g}^{(L)} s_{i,g}^{(L)} w_{gh}^{(L)} f'(sum_{p;ih}^{(L-1)}) s_{i,h}^{(L-1)} w_{hj}^{(L-1)} f'(sum_{p;ij}^{(L-2)}) s_{i,j}^{(L-2)} y_{p;k}^{(L-3)}$$ (10)

The next step is to show that C1.1, C1.2, and C1.3 are satisfied. C1.1 is satisfied if we we assume that each weight is bounded. C1.3 can be satisfied by choosing the learning rate appropriately such as $a_n = c/n$ where c is a positive real number. The most difficult one is C1.2. First, we define

$$\overline{h}(w) = E[h(w, z_i)]$$ (11)

where E is expectation. We also define

$$Y_i = h(w, z_i) - \overline{h}(w)$$ (12)

So we have to show that

$$\lim_{n \to \infty} P\{\sup_{m \geq n} |\sum_{i=n}^{m} a_i Y_i| \geq \varepsilon\} = 0$$ (13)

[3] shows, by using the martingale inequality of Doob, that (13) holds if $E |\sum_{i=0}^{n} a_i Y_i|^2 < \infty$ as $n \to \infty$, and if $\sum_{i=0}^{n} a_i Y_i$ is a martingale sequence. Also, assume that $\sum_{i=0}^{n} a_i^2 < \infty$ as $n \to \infty$.

$E |\sum_{i=0}^{n} a_i Y_i|^2 < \infty$ as $n \to \infty$ since $h(w, z_i)$ is bounded as in C1.1. We need to prove that $\sum_{i=0}^{n} a_i Y_i$ is a martingale sequence which is to show that

$$E[\sum_{i=0}^{n} a_i Y_i | \sum_{i=0}^{n-1} a_i Y_i] = \sum_{i=0}^{n-1} a_i Y_i$$ (14)

From (11) and (12), we have

$$E[Y_i] = E[h(w, z_i) - \overline{h}(w)] = E[h(w, z_i)] - \overline{h}(w) = 0$$ (15)

We use (14), (15), and the fact that Y_i are i.i.d. random variables w.r.t. i from the definition of z_i to write

$$E[\sum_{i=0}^{n} a_i Y_i | \sum_{i=0}^{n-1} a_i Y_i] = E[\sum_{i=0}^{n-1} a_i Y_i | \sum_{i=0}^{n-1} a_i Y_i] + E[a_n Y_n | \sum_{i=0}^{n-1} a_i Y_i]$$

$$= \sum_{i=0}^{n-1} a_i Y_i + a_n E[Y_n] = \sum_{i=0}^{n-1} a_i Y_i$$

This shows that (14) holds and completes the proof that $\sum_{i=0}^{n} a_i Y_i$ is a martingale sequence. If we choose a_n such that $\sum_{i=0}^{n} a_i^2 < \infty$ as $n \to \infty$, C1.2 is satisfied. Note that $a_n = c/n$ as in C1.3 works here.

The last step is to solve the ODE (2), but first we have to derive $\overline{h}(w)$ or $E[h(w, z_i)]$ where each component $E[h(w_{jk}^{(l)}, z_i)]$ can be derived as follows. For the output layer L from (8)

$$E[h(w_{jk}^{(L)}, z_i)] = E[(d_{p;ij} - y_{p;ij}^{(L)}) f'(sum_{p;ij}^{(L)}) y_{p;k}^{(L-1)}] E[s_{i,j}^{(L)}]$$ (16)

The term inside the first expectation on the right hand side of (16) is the negative error gradient of the weight in the last layer with pattern p. Since we select a pattern randomly with a uniform distribution the expectation becomes $-1/P \partial E_T / \partial w_{jk}^{(l)}$ where E_T is the total error. The expectation on $s_{i,j}^{(l)}$ is by its definition the probability that the error $e_{pj}^{(l)}$ is selected. The probability must be the same for all neurons within the same layer. We define the probability as $q^{(l)}$. Consequently, (16) becomes

$$E[h(w_{jk}^{(L)}, z_i)] = -\frac{1}{P} \frac{\partial E_T}{\partial w_{jk}^{(L)}} q^{(L)}$$ (17)

Applying the same procedure for the output layer L to the hidden layer L-1 of (9) yields

$$E[h(w_{jk}^{(L-1)}, z_i)] = E[\sum_{h=1}^{NL} e_{p;h}^{(L)} w_{hj}^{(L)} f'(sum_{p;ij}^{(L-1)}) y_{p;k}^{(L-2)}] E[s_{i,h}^{(L)} s_{i,j}^{(L-1)}]$$

$$= E[e_{p;ij}^{(L-1)} y_{p;k}^{(L-2)}] E[s_{i,h}^{(L)}] E[s_{i,j}^{(L-1)}]$$ (18)

In deriving (18), for simplicity, we assume, w.l.o.g., that $s_{i,j}^{(l)}$ is layer independent, i.e. errors are set to zero independently from each layer. Again the term inside the expectation on the right hand side of (18) is the negative error gradient of the weight in the hidden layer L-1 with pattern p. Hence,

$$E[h(w_{jk}^{(L-1)}, z_i)] = -\frac{1}{P} \frac{\partial E_T}{\partial w_{jk}^{(L-1)}} q^{(L)} q^{(L-1)}$$ (19)

$E[h(w_{jk}^{(L-2)}, z_i)]$ can be derived in the same way. Once we take the expectation of all $s_{i,j}^{(l)}$, the rest of the expectation is just the negative error gradient of the weight in the hidden layer L-2 with pattern p. From (10), the result is

$$E[h(w_{jk}^{(L-2)}, z_i)] = -\frac{1}{P}\frac{\partial E_T}{\partial w_{jk}^{(L-2)}} q^{(L)} q^{(L-1)} q^{(L-2)} \tag{20}$$

In fact, from the recursive nature of (7), for any layer l, we can conclude that

$$E[h(w_{jk}^{(l)}, z_i)] = -\frac{1}{P}\frac{\partial E_T}{\partial w_{jk}^{(l)}} q^{(L)} q^{(L-1)}...q^{(l)} \tag{21}$$

Notice that output layer L has the highest expected value (in absolute value) with a factor of only $q^{(L)}$ whereas the lower the hidden layer (less l), the lower the expected value because of more factors of $q^{(l)}$. It should be as expected since some neuron errors are set to 0 in each layer. They are propagated back and become less accurate.

Now we can solve (2). w_t is a column vector with each component a weight. Let's index it from 1 to D where D is the total number of weights in the network, i.e. $w_t = (w_1, ... , w_k, ... , w_D)^T$. We have

$$\frac{dw_t}{dt} = (\frac{dw_1}{dt}, ... , \frac{dw_k}{dt}, ... , \frac{dw_D}{dt})^T \tag{22}$$

From (21), define $c^{(l)}$ as $(1/P) q^{(L)} q^{(L-1)}...q^{(l)}$. Furthermore, define $c_k = c^{(l)}$ for all corresponding weights w_k of layer l. For example, $c_1 = c_2 = c^{(l)}$ if w_1 and w_2 are both in layer 1. From (11) and (21), we can now write

$$\bar{h}(w_t) = (-c_1\frac{\partial E_T}{\partial w_1}, -c_2\frac{\partial E_T}{\partial w_2}, ... , -c_k\frac{\partial E_T}{\partial w_k}, ... , -c_D\frac{\partial E_T}{\partial w_D})^T \tag{23}$$

From (2), (22) equals (23), we have

$$\frac{dw_k}{dt} = -c_k\frac{\partial E_T}{\partial w_k} \tag{24}$$

Let's examine dE_T/dt, the change of total error with time. Using the chain rule, we write

$$\frac{dE_T}{dt} = \sum_{k=1}^{D} \frac{\partial E_T}{\partial w_k}\frac{dw_k}{dt} \tag{25}$$

Substitute (24) into (25) yields

$$\frac{dE_T}{dt} = \sum_{k=1}^{D} -c_k\left[\frac{\partial E_T}{\partial w_k}\right]^2 \tag{26}$$

The differential equation (2) has the name of autonomous functional-differential equation. [4] covers it in great detail. For our case, a simplified explanation is as follows.

Since c_k is greater than zero by its definition, dE_T/dt in (26) is negative. Hence, E_T decreases in t and because E_T is always greater than or equal to zero, it has a limit. Moreover, E_T is differentiable, so we can conclude that $dE_T/dt \rightarrow 0$. From (23) and (26), $dE_T/dt = 0$ if and only if $h(w_t) = 0$. That means $dw_t/dt = 0$ or w_t is at a fixed point. Consequently, we can conclude that w_t reaches a local minimum w^* if there exists one, the same condition for a normal backpropagation algorithm. This completes the convergence proof of the reduced operation backpropagation algorithm.

Largest K Algorithm

In the last section, setting some of the errors to zero randomly has been shown to converge, but the rate of convergence is not known. In this section, we propose that the largest K errors in absolute value in each layer are kept and the rest are set to zero. K can vary from layer to layer. This is intended to reduce the number of iterations. The reasons can be briefly explained as follows.

The vector used in a stochastic update of the backpropagation algorithm is the instantaneous negative gradient of a particular pattern. Let's call it g_p. The sum over all the patterns is g which points in the direction of a negative gradient of the total error in the weight space. For a batch update, g is used as the vector. In the reduced operation method, the vector in the update is $h(w,z_i)$. Let's call it h_p. If we use a batch update, it is h instead and the convergence proof is still valid, but there will be no 1/P factor in (21) since pattern p is not random. We update the weights after all patterns have been presented. Batch update will be discussed first since it is easier to understand. At a particular point on the error surface, g and h can be calculated. If we want a descent direction to guarantee that E_T can be reduced after the update from that point, the directional derivative of E_T must be negative, i.e. the dot product of the gradient, which is $-g$, and h is negative or equivalently, the inner product $g^T h > 0$. This has a maximum when $h = g$. That is what happens in normal backpropagation even though it does not guarantee to reach the local minimum faster since normally g does not point to the local minimum. Nevertheless, we want the angle between g and h to be less than $90°$ so that, at least, we will be able to reduce E_T with appropriate learning rate.

In the reduced operation method by selecting the errors randomly, $\mathbf{g}^T\mathbf{h}$ is sometimes less than zero, but on the average over a long period of time, descent directions are achieved. The same is true for a stochastic update of normal backpropagation where we use $\mathbf{g}_p$ in stead of $\mathbf{h}$. To understand why the errors should be chosen according to their magnitudes instead of chosen randomly, consider a case for a batch update with only one pattern (P=1) and one layer (output layer). $\mathbf{g}^T\mathbf{h}$ is bounded to be non-negative since $\mathbf{h}$ is just $\mathbf{g}$ with some components set to zero. If we select K errors, $\mathbf{g}^T\mathbf{h}$ is maximized when the largest K errors in magnitude are chosen. With L>1 and P>1, it is less obvious to see, but choosing the errors according to their magnitudes will maximize the chance of moving in the descent directions. For a stochastic update, the idea is similar. We try to make $\mathbf{h}_p$ as close to $\mathbf{g}_p$ as possible, i.e. to maximize $\mathbf{g}_p{}^T\mathbf{h}_p$. so that E_T is reduced faster. This can be achieved by selecting the largest K errors.

Simulation Results Discussion

Due to limited space, two simulation results will be summarized. In both problems, a small constant learning rate is used in place of a decreasing learning rate as the theory suggests because the latter is very slow to converge in practice. The network has two hidden layers (L=3) and is fully connected. The first simulation is a classification problem where we train the network to recognize English characters. The objective is to minimize total error E_T only, i.e. we look at the problem as a non-linear optimization problem. In most runs (different initial weights), selecting the largest K errors reduces E_T faster than selecting the errors randomly. The smaller K becomes (selecting fewer errors), the bigger the convergent speed difference between the two selection methods is. For selecting K errors randomly, the larger K is, the faster the network converges in most cases. Normal backpropagation is the fastest (requires minimum number of iterations). However, for selecting the largest K errors, normal backpropagation is not necessarily the fastest. In may runs, K=N/2 is sometimes the fastest. For stochastic update, with 50 different initial weights and the stopping criteria that E_T reaches the point when the average error for each output is 10%, we have that, on the average, selecting the largest K=N/2 indeed requires 75% of the total number of iterations compared to that of normal backpropagation. Obviously, K=N/2 requires less number of · and **OP** operations in the backward path for each iteration. So, it actually takes less than 75% of the time in real chip (for this particular problem). This is possible since in normal backpropagation moving in the negative gradient direction with a finite step length is not guaranteed to reduce total error the most.

The second simulation is a continuous function approximation problem. Testing patterns are used to monitor the network generalization performance instead of training patterns only as in the first one. Noise is also injected to increase the network ability to generalize. The performance is measured by the number of iterations it takes to have overtraining, i.e. when testing errors go up, and by the total error at the time. Selecting the largest K errors (K=N/2) performs very well against the normal algorithm in term of generalization with and without noise injection. On the average, the plots are very similar. Again, selecting the largest K errors requires less number of · and **OP** operations for each iteration.

Hardware Implementation and Comparison

We proposed a detailed efficient hardware implementation [5]. The proposed architecture resembles the data flow diagram in figure 1. Basically, each operation becomes a unit, all working simultaneously. The pipelined chip has parallel MACs (Multiply-Accumulators) in the MAC unit to handle matrix-vector multiplications (· operations). The Manchester carry chain based largest K unit was also proposed. It comprises of many cells. Each cell executes two phases of operations during each cycle: compare and shift. The number stored in each cell is compared to the input which enters the unit serially each cycle. Shifting and storing will occur according to the comparison result. The largest K unit with N cells, in Y cycles, can output the largest X out of Y numbers as long as Y-X <= N. By adding the largest K unit to the chip, the number of · operations can be reduced. Each cell takes about one-tenth of an area of a multiply-accumulator since we only need a carry out to compare two numbers. We performed SPICE simulations to show its feasibility for use in a high speed neural network processor chip such as the Stanford Boltzmann machine [6], a 125 MHz deeply pipelined digital CMOS processor.

The actual number of cycles to train a network depends on the architecture of the hardware, i.e. how we allocate resources for the chip. For comparison purpose, the assumption is that the chip is very large, to handle a real world problem, so that memory and processor area dominate the total area. If the number of parallel MACs (M) in the MAC unit is large, the assumption is valid since many operations in figure 1 do not scale up with M. Only memory unit (to store weights and their changes) and the following units, which are counted as processor, scale up with M: multipliers for the **OP** operations in the **OP** unit, multipliers and adders for the weight update unit, and the largest K unit. The actual area ratio of memory to processor depends on many factors such as the number of patterns/second that we want the chip to process. The Stanford Boltzmann machine has about equal area for memory and processor. Higher ratio means that the chip can handle bigger problem, but it takes longer time to finish.

For normal backpropagation algorithm, there are M MACs in the MAC unit. We choose to have M multipliers for the **OP** unit, M multipliers and M adders for the weight update unit to multiply each weight by the learning rate and update it. The number is reasonable since the **OP** unit and the weight update unit must keep up with the MAC unit particularly the weight update unit. It must be fast to update all the weights in a stochastic update. Otherwise, the MAC unit can stall. Assume that each pattern presentation takes 1 unit of time for the forward path to complete all the • operations and produce outputs. The backward path will also require about 1 unit of time to complete all the • operations. Assume that weight update takes an additional 1 unit of time after the backward path finishes to access the weight memory and update all the weights before new pattern can be presented. The total time for normal backpropagation is 3 units of time for each pattern presentation in the learning mode. The X1 architecture by Adaptive Solutions [7], one of the most powerful neural network processors, requires 6 units of time for learning relative to feedforward computations. Since our proposed hardware is for the backpropagation algorithm only, 3 units of time should be reasonable to assume.

For the reduced operation algorithm in the case of selecting half the errors, we can trade off between speed and area. Let's consider the case where there are M MACS. In this case, the **OP** unit has M/2 multipliers, and the weight update unit has M/2 multipliers and M/2 adders. The largest K unit needs M/2 cells to select the largest M/2 out of M errors. In terms of the unit of time, it is clear that this scheme takes 1 unit of time for the forward path, but only takes 0.5 units of time for the backward path. With M/2 multipliers for the **OP** unit, it requires the same amount of time as the normal case with M multipliers since only half the weight matrix is expanded in the **OP** operations. The same reason applies for calculating new weight values, i.e. M/2 multipliers and M/2 adders in the weight update unit are sufficient. However, it will take an additional 0.5 instead of 1 unit of time to update the weights since only half the weight memory is accessed. Consequently, the total time to learn one pattern is 2 units of time. That means it takes 2/3 of the time of normal algorithm for each iteration. The total number of iterations is shown to be less than or about the same as that of a normal algorithm. The speed up could be done in many ways without increasing the hardware complexity and area such as varying the learning rate dynamically.

We can now compare the area of both methods. The area is estimated by the number of transistors since all, counted as processor, can be considered logic and have the same area density per transistor. The weight, activation, and learning rate values are assumed to be 8 bits. Also, assume that the accumulator can accumulate additional 8 bits beyond the MSB of a 17-bit product between a weight and an activation value with no overflow. The number of transistors for each resource is estimated in detail in [5]. An 8x8-bit multiply-accumulator has 2240 transistors. An 8x8-bit multiplier has 1910 transistors. An 8-bit adder has 290 transistors. One cell of an 8-bit largest K unit has 200 transistors (including the control.) For normal algorithm, the total number of transistors is thus $(2240 + 1910 + 1910 + 210)M = 6350M$. For the reduced operation algorithm, the total number of transistors is $2240M + (1910 + 1910 + 210 + 200)M/2 = 4395M$.

Now, the area saving can be computed. Since the memory area assumption is the same for both methods, the area saving comes from the processor part only. The saving ranges from 6% to 20% when the memory to processor area decreases from 4 to 0.5. In fact, we can also trade off the speed and area by varying M. In conclusion, the reduced operation algorithm is indeed better than the normal backpropagation by speed and area comparison. The saving in the area can be allocated for the weight memory or other resources. Or it can be used to reduce the size of the chip to increase yield and reduce power consumption.

Acknowledgement

This research was supported, in part, by the NASA CASIS project under NASA grant NAGW-419. The research was conducted while Kan Boonyanit was a doctoral candidate in the EE Department at Stanford University.

References

[1] Rumelhart, D. E., and McClelland J. L. (Eds.), "Parallel Distributed Processing: Explorations in the Microstructure of Cognition," Vol.1, MIT Press, Cambridge, MA, pp.318-362, 1986.

[2] Groot, A. J. De, and Parker, S. R., "Systolic Implementation of Neural Networks," Proc. SPIE, High Speed Computing II, Vol.1058, 1989.

[3] Kushner, Harold J., and Clark, Dean S., "Stochastic Approximation Methods for Constrained and Unconstrained Systems," Springer-Verlag, NY, 1978.

[4] Hale, Jack K., "Sufficient Conditions For Stability and Instability of Autonomous Functional Differential Equations," Journal of Differential Equations 1, pp.452-482, 1965.

[5] Boonyanit, Kan, "Reduced Operation Backpropagation Neural Network: Algorithms and Implementation," Ph.D. Thesis, Stanford University, 1993.

[6] Murray, M., Burr, J. B., Stork, D. G., Leung, M., Boonyanit, K., Wolff G. J., and Peterson, A. M., "Deterministic Boltzmann Machine VLSI Can be Scaled Using Multi-Chip Modules," Proceedings of the International Conference on Application Specific Array Processors, Berkeley, CA, 1992.

[7] Hammerstrom, Dan, "A VLSI Architecture for High-Performance, Low-Cost, On-Chip Learning," Proceedings of International Joint Conference on Neural Networks, Vol.2, pp.537-544, 1990.

Fault Tolerant Radial Basis Function Networks

P. Bapat, M.V. Hegde and M. Naraghi-Pour

Department of Electrical and Computer Engineering

Louisiana State University, Baton Rouge, LA 70803

email: bandit@bandit.ee.lsu.edu

Abstract

This paper investigates the incorporation of fault tolerance at the learning stage into Radial Basis Function (RBF) networks. The approach is particularly attractive since the cost of fault detection and correction in a practical VLSI implementation of such networks could be prohibitive due to the large number of neurons and connections. The RBF networks considered are applied to the task of analog function approximation. A fairly general fault model is considered wherein faulty neurons are assumed to be stuck at a random value. Two new learning methods based on regression are proposed to learn the weights and one new regression based learning method is proposed to learn the centers. The methods explicitly take into account the mean squared error in the objective function in the presence of faults and use stepwise selection methods to choose the regressors. Simulation results are presented which show that a considerable improvement in fault tolerance can be achieved over the non-fault-tolerant learning algorithm.

1 Introduction

We consider the fault-tolerance behavior of the class of feed-forward networks known as Radial Basis Function (RBF) networks. The RBF networks studied are utilized for the purpose of analog function approximation. Let $S = \{(\mathbf{x}(j), y(j)) \in R^n \times R \mid j = 1, 2, 3, \ldots, N\}$ be a set of data points which is a subset of the graph of a function, $f(\mathbf{x})$. By using the set S to learn, it is desired to find an RBF network such that when given input $\mathbf{x}(j)$, it produces an output which is, in some sense, close to $y(j)$.

The use of RBF networks for solving analog function approximation problems was analyzed by [9] and also by [5]. RBF networks have been applied to this task in [1], [4], [7], [6] and [8]. In [8] it is shown that RBF networks are a special case of *regularization* networks. Fault tolerant training of feedforward networks with backpropagation training algorithm is considered in [10], [11] and [12].

We study the fault tolerance of an RBF network with respect to the failures of the hidden units. The output of a faulty unit i is assumed to be stuck at a random value Z_i which is uniformly distributed over an interval defined by the minimum and maximum values the unit can assume, (in our case, 0 and 1, respectively). The measure of fault tolerance used is the mean squared error of the calculated outputs of the RBF. We assume that the hidden units fail independently with some probability p. Let W_i be a random variable indicating whether unit i has failed or not. W_i takes the value 1 if the unit has failed and 0 otherwise. Thus, W_i is 1 with probability p and 0 with probability $1 - p$. Furthermore, the Z_i's and W_i's are assumed to be independent of each other.

2 Fault Tolerance Learning: (FTL1)

In the following we define our notation. Let
$\{\mathbf{x}(j) \in R^n, \, j = 1, 2, 3, \ldots, N\}$ be the set of input points,

$\{y(j) \in R, \ j = 1, 2, 3, ..., N\}$ be the corresponding set of output points,

$c_i \in R^n, \ i = 1, 2, 3, ..., M$ be the centers for the radial basis functions,

$\sigma^2(i), \ i = 1, 2, 3, ..., M$, be the variance corresponding to the ith radial basis function,

r_{ij} be the output of the ith hidden unit for the jth data point, i.e., $r_{ij} = exp\left(-\frac{\|x(j) - c_i\|^2}{\sigma_i^2}\right)$. We define $r_{0j} = 1, \ j = 1, 2, 3, ..., N$.

Let $\theta_i, \ i = 0, 1, 2, ..., M$, be the connection weight from the ith hidden unit to the output unit.

$\epsilon(j), \ j = 1, 2, 3, ..., N$, dnotes the error between $y(j)$ and the actual output produced by the network. Thus,

$$y(j) = \sum_{i=0}^{M} \theta_i \ r_{ij} + \epsilon(j), \quad \text{for} \quad j = 1, 2, 3, ..., N.$$

To put the above equation into matrix form, we define,

$\mathbf{Y} = [y(1), y(2), ..., y(N)]^T$, as the desired output vector,

$\mathbf{R} = [R_0, R_1, ..., R_M]$, the regression matrix, where $R_i = [r_{i1}, r_{i2}, ..., r_{iN}]^T$ represents a column vector of the outputs of the hidden unit i for the data points $y(1), y(2), ..., y(N)$,

$\Theta = [\theta_0, \theta_1, ..., \theta_M]^T$, the weight vector,

$\mathbf{E} = [\epsilon(1), \epsilon(2), ..., \epsilon(N)]^T$, the error vector. Then

$$\mathbf{Y} = \mathbf{R}\Theta + \mathbf{E}. \tag{1}$$

The error signals $\epsilon(j)$'s are treated as random variables which are assumed to be uncorrelated with the regressors and independent of each other. The least squares method minimizes the expectation of the squared error $\mathbf{E}^T \mathbf{E}$ with respect to Θ.

In the first fault tolerant algorithm called FTL1, the elements of the regressor matrix $\mathbf{R}$ are modified to take into account the possibility of failures of the hidden units. We denote this modified regressor matrix by $\mathbf{R}_f$. The $(i, j)^{th}$ element of $\mathbf{R}_f$ is given by

$$r_{f_{ij}} = r_{ij}(1 - W_i) + W_i \ Z_i.$$

Note that if the ith unit is not faulty ($W_i = 0$), then $r_{f_{ij}} = r_{ij}$. On the other hand if the ith unit is faulty ($W_i = 1$), then $r_{f_{ij}} = Z_i$. The regression equation $\mathbf{Y} = \mathbf{R}_f \ \Theta_f + \mathbf{E}_f$ is then used to estimate Θ_f which minimizes the expected mean squared error, $\mathbf{E}_f^T \ \mathbf{E}_f$. We get an estimate of Θ_f as

$$\hat{\Theta}_f = [\mathbf{R}_f^T \ \mathbf{R}_f - \mathbf{S} + (1 - p)\mathbf{Q} + \mathbf{P}]^{-1} \ \mathbf{R}_f^T \ \mathbf{Y}.$$

where

$$\mathbf{S} = \begin{bmatrix} R_{f_0}^T R_{f_0} & 0 & 0 & \cdots & 0 \\ 0 & R_{f_1}^T R_{f_1} & 0 & \cdots & 0 \\ \vdots & & \ddots & & \vdots \\ 0 & 0 & 0 & \cdots & R_{f_M}^T R_{f_M} \end{bmatrix}$$

$$\mathbf{Q} = \begin{bmatrix} R_0^T R_0 & 0 & 0 & \cdots & 0 \\ 0 & R_1^T R_1 & 0 & \cdots & 0 \\ \vdots & & \ddots & & \vdots \\ 0 & 0 & 0 & \cdots & R_M^T R_M \end{bmatrix}$$

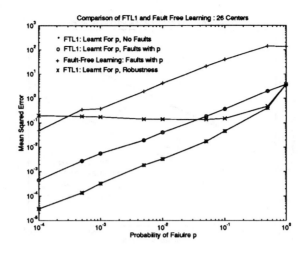

Figure 1: Comparison of FTL1 and Fault Free Learning : 26 Centers.

$$\mathbf{P} \;=\; \frac{Np}{12} \begin{bmatrix} 1 & 0 & 0 & \cdots & 0 \\ 0 & 1 & 0 & \cdots & 0 \\ \vdots & & \ddots & & \vdots \\ 0 & 0 & 0 & \cdots & 1 \end{bmatrix}.$$

We use the following simulations framework for performance evaluation. Simulations for all the methods are carried out for the task of approximating a sinc function, namely $y = \operatorname{sinc}(x) = \sin(2\pi x)/2\pi x$, where the range of x is $[-1, +1]$. The set of data points is formed by choosing 41 equally spaced points over the range of x.

We run two types of simulations for measuring the immunity of the network to faults. With the independent probability of failure, p, for each hidden unit, the network is run over all the data points and the mean squared error is measured. This step is repeated 10,000 times and the average mean squared error (which is a measure of fault tolerance) is evaluated. To measure robustness, instead of assigning a probability of failure to the hidden units, the units are made to fail one at a time. Thus one of the hidden units is made faulty (stuck at a random value Z), and the network is run for all the data points. The mean squared error is measured. This step is repeated till each of the hidden units is made faulty once. The average mean squared error is then calculated which is a measure of robustness of the system to a failure of one unit. In addition, since the probability of failure is very low in practice, we consider only one failure.

The performance of the network is plotted in Figures 1 and 2. In Figure 1 we compare the performance of fault free learning with that of FTL1 algorithm. In FTL1 learning the network was trained for the value of p given on the horizontal axis. The performance of the network is then evaluated for three cases: 1) when no faults occur (fault-free), 2) faults occur with probability p (faults with p), 3) One hidden unit has failed (robustness). For fault-free training the performance is evaluated assuming faults occur with probability p. In Figure 2, the FTL1 algorithm is used for training assuming a fixed value of p (given in the figure). The performance is then evaluated for the value of p given on the axis.

From these figures we can observe the following.

- As expected, the network trained with FTL1 results in a lower mean squared error than the one trained with fault free learning for the probability of failure under consideration.

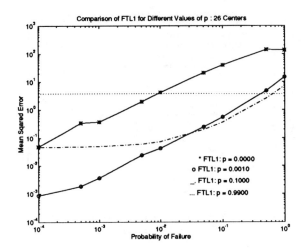

Figure 2: Comparison of FTL1 for Different Values of p : 26 Centers.

- The response to different values of probability of failure becomes more and more flat as the value of p for FTL1 is increased. Thus, over a range of probability of failures less than p, the network exhibits very small deviation in the mean squared error from that in the fault free case.

- In all the simulations we have run, FTL1 always outperforms fault-free learning and the improvement increases as the number of centers increase. This can be attributed to the following. We have observed that as the number of centers increases, the values of the weights become very large in the case of fault free learning. Consequently, failure of one hidden unit causes a large error in the computed output. On the other hand, with FTL1 the values of the weights remain small even as the number of centers increases. This phenomenon is similar to the weight control scheme of [12].

3 Fault Tolerance Learning: (FTL2)

In practice, we often do not have apriori knowledge of the probability of failure p. Also we are more interested in studying performance of the network in presence of failures. Further, assuming that failure is a very low probability event, we would be interested in failure of at most one hidden unit.

FTL2 is a learning algorithm which concentrates on one hidden unit failure. It does not depend on the probability of failure p of the hidden units. In FTL2, we consider all the possible cases in which one hidden unit is faulty and the case in which none of the units is faulty. The expectation of the sum of the mean squared errors over all these cases is minimized. The estimate Θ_f minimizes the expectation of the total mean squared error.

Denote $\mathbf{R}_{fl}$ as the regressor matrix representing the case in which the lth hidden unit is faulty. This matrix is obtained by replacing the lth column of regressor matrix $\mathbf{R}$ by Z_l. Since the columns of $\mathbf{R}_f$ are indexed from 0 through M, denote $\mathbf{R}_{f(M+1)}$ as the regressor matrix for the case of no failures. Thus we have,

$$\mathbf{Y} = \mathbf{R}_{fl}\,\Theta_f + \mathbf{E}_l \quad \text{for } l = 0, 1, 2, ..., M, M+1$$

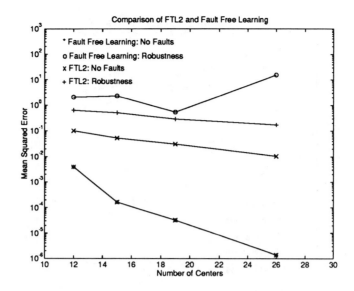

Figure 3: Comparison of FTL2 and Fault Free Learning.

The estimate of Θ_f is found from minimizing the following expression.

$$\sum_{l=0}^{M+1} \mathbf{E}_l^T \, \mathbf{E}_l = \sum_{l=0}^{M+1} \left(\mathbf{Y} - \mathbf{R}_{fl} \, \Theta \right)^T \left(\mathbf{Y} - \mathbf{R}_{fl} \, \Theta_f \right).$$

We get

$$\hat{\Theta}_f \;=\; \left[\sum_{l=0}^{M+1} \mathbf{R}_{fl}^T \, \mathbf{R}_{fl} + \mathbf{P}' \right]^{-1} \sum_{l=0}^{M+1} \mathbf{R}_{fl}^T$$

where $\mathbf{P}' = \mathbf{P}/p$. The networks were trained using fault free learning as well as FTL2. The fault tolerance and robustness simulations were run on each of the networks and the results are shown in Figure 3. From this figure we can observe that

- In the presence of one unit failure, FTL2 shows a considerable improvement in performance over fault free learning.

- As the number of centers increases, the robustness of fault free case can actually worsen as there is no control over it as opposed to FTL2 which guarantees an improvement in robustness. This is similar to the case of FTL1.

4   Choice of Centers for Improving Robustness : LSR Method

In this section, we suggest a stepwise method to choose the centers based on robustness considerations. The method is called LSR since it uses an algorithm similar to Least Squares and is designed for improving Robustness. We assume that the network is to be trained with FTL2 to achieve an improvement in robustness.

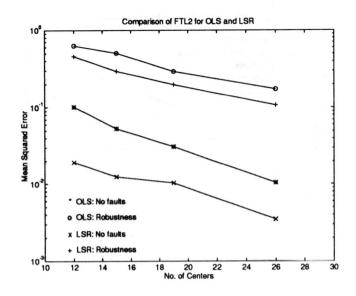

Figure 4: Comparison of LSR and OLS with FTL2 as Learning Algorithm.

All the data points are possible candidates for the centers to be chosen. Let C denote the set of data points chosen to be the centers. Initially, the set C is empty. In each step of the algorithm one data point is added to the set C. At the kth step we calculate the value of the objective function for FTL2 using each of the data points not in the set C as a center along with the $(k-1)$ data points which are in the set C. The data point which results in the minimum value of the objective function is added to the set C. The algorithm is terminated when the value of the objective function is within the given acceptable limit.

The choice of the centers using the method described was compared with the OLS method [3] for different numbers of centers. In Figure 4 we plot the mean squared error as a function of the number of centers. It should be noted that here we are using the FTL2 algorithm for both LSR and OLS. Therefore, the difference in performance is only due to the choice of the centers.

From this figure, it can be see that

- The network whose centers are chosen using LSR and trained with FTL2 results in a better performance than the one using OLS for selecting the centers both when there are no faults as well as when one fault occurs.

5 Conclusions

From the discussions and the results presented in the previous sections we can note the following.

If the probability of failure p for hidden units is specified apriori, then the network learnt with FTL1 performs better than the network learnt with fault-free learning in terms of fault tolerance. This means that in the presence of failures the network trained with FTL1 will result in a lower mean squared error than the network trained with OLS.

FTL2 which does not need the value of p can be used for achieving an improvement in robustness. Also FTL2 is more practical than FTL1 since it does not consider the probabilistic nature of faults but rather considers the performance of the network given that a fault has occurred.

We can achieve better robustness for a given number of centers, when the centers are selected from a set of data points by the LSR method instead of the OLS method and FTL2 is used for learning the weights. The reason being that LSR is based upon FTL2 itself, which is a learning method for improving robustness as opposed to OLS which is not based on fault tolerance learning.

If it is required that the mean squared error be within specified limits under fault free and one fault cases, then using FTL2 and appropriate number of centers, this criterion can always be met.

References

[1] D. S. Broomhead and D. Lowe, "Multivariable Functional Interpolation and Adaptive Networks",*Complex Syst.*, vol. 2, pp. 321-355, 1988.

[2] A. E. Bryson and Y. C. Ho, *Applied Optimal Control*, Blaisdell, New York, 1969.

[3] S. Chen, C. F. N. Cowan and P. M. Grant, "Orthogonal Least Squares Learning Algorithm for Radial Basis Function Networks", *IEEE Transactions on Neural Networks*, vol. 2, no. 2, pp. 302-309, 1991.

[4] A. Lepedes and R. Farber,"How Neural Nets work", *Neural Information Processing Systems*, D. Z. Anderson,(Ed.), A. P., New York, 1988.

[5] C. A. Micchelli,"Interpolation of Scattered Data: Distance Matrices and Conditionally Positive Definite Functions", *Construct. Approx.*, vol. 2, pp. 11-22, 1986.

[6] J. Moody and C. Darken,"Fast Learning in Networks of Locally Tuned Processing Units", *Neural Computation*,vol. 1, no. 2, pp. 281-294, 1989.

[7] Niranjian and F. Fallside,"Neural Networks and Radial Basis Functions in Classifying Static Speech Patterns", *Cambridge University Engineering Dept. Technical Report*, CUED/F-IFENG/TR22, 1988.

[8] T. Poggio and F. Girosi,"Networks for Approximation and Learning", *Proceedings of the IEEE*, vol. 78, no. 9, 1990.

[9] M. J. D. Powell,"Radial Basis Functions for Multivariable Interpolation: A Review", *Algorithms for Approximation*, J. C. Mason and M. G. Cox, (Ed.), Clarendon Press, Oxford, 1987.

[10] C. H. Sequin and R. Clay,"Fault Tolerance in Feed-forward Artificial Neural Networks", *TR-90-031*, July 1990.

[11] C. Neti, M.H. Schneider and D.E. Young, "Maximally Fault Tolerant Neural Networks and Nonlinear Programming," *Proceedings of IJCNN*, vol. II, pp. 483-496, June 1990.

[12] M. Naraghi-Pour, M. Hegde and P. Bapat, "Fault Tolerance Design of Feedforward Networks," *Proceedings of WCNN*, vol. III, pp. 568-571, July 1993.

A Neural Network Learning Theory and Modified RBF Net Generation

Asim Roy and Raymond Miranda, Dept. of Decision and Information Systems
Arizona State University, Tempe, AZ 85287

Abstract

This paper presents a new neural network learning theory that is much more brain-like than classical connectionist learning. Unlike connectionist learning, the algorithms here both design and train networks and do so in polynomial time. They are also immune to other learning problems (local minima, oscillation, catastrophic forgetting). This paper shows how a RBF-like net can be generated under this theory for classification problems.

1. Introduction - A Robust and Efficient Learning Theory

The science of artificial neural networks (ANN) needs a robust theory for generating neural networks. Lack of a robust learning theory has been a significant impediment to the field. A rigorous theory for ANN should include learning methods that adhere to the following stringent performance criteria and tasks: 1. <u>Perform Network Design Task</u>: A neural network learning method must be able to design an appropriate network for a given problem, since it is a task performed by the brain. A pre-designed net should not be provided to it as part of its external input, since it never is an external input to the brain. 2. <u>Robustness in Learning</u>: The method must be robust so as not to have the problems of local minima, oscillation and catastrophic interference and/or similar learning difficulties. The brain does not exhibit such problems. 3. <u>Quickness in Learning</u>: The method must be quick in its learning and learn rapidly from only a few examples, much as humans do. For example, an on-line method that learns from only 10 examples is quicker than one that needs a 1,000 examples. 4. <u>Efficiency in Learning</u>: The method must be computationally efficient in its learning when provided with a finite number of training examples. It must be able to both design and train an appropriate net in polynomial time. That is, given n examples, the learning time must be a polynomial function of n. 5. <u>Generalization in Learning</u>: The method must be able to generalize reasonably well so that only a small amount of network resources is used. That is, it must try to design the smallest possible net. This characteristic must be an explicit part of the algorithm.

This theory defines learning principles that are obviously much more brain-like than those of classical connectionist theory. Judging by these algorithmic characteristics, connectionist learning is not very powerful or robust. First of all, it does not even address the issue of network design, a task that should be central to any learning theory. It is also plagued by efficiency (lack of polynomial time complexity, need for excessive number of teaching examples) and robustness problems (local minima, oscillation, and catastrophic interference), problems that are partly acquired from its attempt to learn without using memory. Classical connectionist learning, therefore, is not very brain-like at all. Several algorithms have been previously developed for perceptrons that satisfy these learning principles (Roy et al. [1991, 1993], Mukhopadhyay et al. [1993]). The algorithm presented here shows RBF-type nets can also be constructed using these same learning principles.

2. Radial Basis Function (RBF) Nets - Background

RBF nets belong to the group of kernel function nets that utilize simple kernel functions whose responses are essentially local in nature. The net has one hidden and one output layer. Each hidden node is a kernel function. An output node computes the weighted sum of the hidden node outputs. The gaussian function is a popular kernel function. The design and training of a RBF net consists of 1) determining how many kernal functions to use, 2) finding their centers and widths, and 3) finding the weights that connect them to an output node.

The following notation is used. An input pattern is given by the N-dimensional vector $x, x = (X_1, X_2, \ldots, X_N)$. K denotes the total number of classes. The method is for supervised learning where the training set $x_1, x_2, \ldots, x_n$ is a set of sample patterns with known classification. The input $F_j(x)$ to the jth output node is given by $F_j(x) = \sum_{q=1}^{Q} h_{jq} G_q(x)$, $G_q(x) = R(\| x - C_q \|, w_q)$. Here, Q is the number of hidden nodes, $G_q(x)$ is the response function of the qth hidden node, R is a radially asymmetric kernel function, $C_q = (C_{q1} \ldots C_{qN})$ and $w_q = (w_{q1} \ldots w_{qN})$ are the center and widths of the qth kernel function, and h_{jq} is the weight connecting the qth hidden node to the jth output node. There is one output node for each class. Here, an asymmetric gaussian is chosen as the kernel function: $G_q(x) = exp(-\sum_{j=1}^{N}(C_{qj} - X_j)^2 / w_{qj}^2)$. Several RBF algorithms have been proposed recently. Significant contributions include those by Powell [1987],

Moody and Darken [1989], Broomhead and Lowe [1988], Musavi et al. [1992], Platt [1991] and others.

3. Basic Ideas and the Algorithm

The basic idea is to cover a class region with a set of gaussians. A function $F(x)$ is said to cover a certain class region if it is slightly positive ($F(x) \geq \epsilon$) for patterns in that class and zero or negative for patterns outside that class. Let p_k gaussians be required to cover a certain class k. The covering function $F_k(x)$, being a linear combination of p_k gaussians, will be $F_k(x) = \sum_{q=1}^{p_k} h_q G_q(x)$, where $G_q(x), q = 1, \ldots, p_k$, is the qth gaussian used to cover class k and h_q the corresponding connection weight. A pattern x, therefore, will be in class k if $F_k(x) \geq \epsilon_k$ and not in class k if $F_k(x) \leq 0$. Hence, the RBF net is modified to add thresholding at the output node. Furthermore, when the effect of a gaussian unit is small, it is ignored. This requires truncated gaussian units as follows: $G'_q(x) = G_q(x)$ if $G_q(x) \geq \phi, = 0$ otherwise, where $G'_q(x)$ is a truncated gaussian function and ϕ a small constant. In experiments, ϕ was set to 10^{-4}. Thus, the function $F_k(x)$ is redefined as $F_k(x) = \sum_{q=1}^{p_k} h_q G'_q(x)$. Thus the modified RBF net has truncation at the hidden nodes and thresholding at the output nodes.

In general, let p_k be the number of gaussians required to cover class $k, k = 1, \ldots, K$, $F_k(x)$ be the covering function (mask) and $G_1^k(x), \ldots, G_{p_k}^k(x)$ be the corresponding set of gaussians. Then a pattern x' will belong to class j if and only if its mask $F_j(x)$ is at least slightly positive, and the masks for all other classes are zero or negative. Here, each mask $F_j(x)$ will have its own threshold value ϵ_j as determined during its construction. In mathematical notation, a pattern x' is in class j, if and only if $F_j(x') \geq \epsilon_j$ and $F_k(x') \leq 0$ for all $k \neq j, k = 1, \ldots, K$. If all masks have values equal to or below zero, the input cannot be classified. If masks from two or more classes have values above their ϵ-thresholds, then also the input cannot be classified, unless the maximum of the mask values is used to determine class.

Let TR_C be the set of pattern vectors of any class k whose masking is desired and TR_{NC} be the corresponding set of non-class k vectors, where $TR = TR_C \cup TR_{NC}$ is the total training set. Suppose $m(= p_k)$ gaussians are available to cover the class. The following linear program is solved to determine the m weights $h = (h_1, \ldots, h_m)$ for the m gaussians that minimize the classification error:

$$\text{Minimize } \alpha \sum_{i \epsilon TR_C} d_i + \beta \sum_{i \epsilon TR_{NC}} d_i \tag{1}$$

subject to

$$F_k(x_i) + d_i \geq \epsilon_k, \; i \epsilon TR_C, \tag{2}$$

$$F_k(x_i) - d_i \leq 0, \; i \epsilon TR_{NC} \tag{3}$$

$$d_i \geq 0, \; i \epsilon TR, \tag{4}$$

$$\epsilon_k \geq \text{a small positive constant, } h \text{ in } F_k(x) \text{ unrestricted in sign,} \tag{5}$$

where d_i's are external deviation variables and α and β are the weights for the in-class and out-of-class deviations, respectively.

3.1 Generation of Gaussian Units

Here, gaussians are not purely local units. A variety of overlapping gaussians are created for masking. Though both "fat" and "narrow" gaussians can be created, the "fat" ones are created first in an attempt to generalize better using broad territorial features. Thus, the gaussians are generated incrementally and as new gaussians are generated, the LP model (1)-(5) is solved for each class using all of the gaussians for that class and the resulting network evaluated. Whenever incremental change in the error rate (training and testing) becomes small or overfitting occurs on the training set, masking of a class is complete.

The gaussians for a given class k at any stage h are randomly selected in the following way. First, a majority criteria is specified for that stage. Denote this majority criteria by M_h^k for the kth class at stage h. A M_h^k of 60% means that at least 60% of the patterns covered by a gaussian's core (within one standard deviation) should belong to class k. M_h^k starts at 50% and can go up to 100%. To generate a gaussian, randomly select a pattern x_g of class k from the training set and search for all other patterns in some δ-neighborhood of x_g. This δ-neighborhood is actually an ellipsoid defined by different widths in different directions. Let V_i be the set of patterns within the δ-neighborhood of ith such initial vector x_g^i. If the set V_i satisfies the majority criteria, it can be used to create a gaussian. If a gaussian is created from V_i, the centroid of its pattern vectors become the center C_i and the standard deviation of their distances from C_i in direction j becomes w_{ij}, the width in direction j. Whether a gaussian is defined or not, the patterns in V_i are removed from the training set. This process of randomly picking a pattern x_g of class k from the remaining training set and searching for patterns in its δ-neighborhood is then repeated. A set of gaussians $(j = 1, \ldots, Q_h)$ can be found at the hth stage by repeating this process until the remaining training set is empty of class k vectors.

The procedure described above is embellished slightly whereby the δ-neighborhood is allowed to grow until it reaches a certain maximum size of δ_{max} or until it no longer satisfies the majority criteria. Let δ_r be the width of the elliptical δ-neighborhood at growth stage r, $\delta_r = (\delta_{r1}, \ldots, \delta_{rN})$. So the process of generating a gaussian starts with an initial δ, δ_0, and then increases δ by a fixed increment $(\delta_r = \delta_{r-1} + \Delta\delta)$ where $\Delta\delta = (\Delta\delta_1, \ldots, \Delta\delta_N)$. So, in this embellished method, the gaussians at any stage h are randomly selected as follows. Randomly select a pattern x_g of class k from the remaining training set and search for all other patterns in the δ_0-neighborhood of x_g. Let V_i^r be the set of patterns within the δ_r-neighborhood of ith such initial vector x_g^i. A neighborhood can be grown only if the current pattern set V_i^r from the δ_r-neighborhood satisfies the majority criteria and if $\delta_r \neq \delta_{max}$. If the current set V_i^r fails on the majority criteria, the previous set V_i^{r-1} is used to create a gaussian. The center and widths of a gaussian are determined in the same manner as before. Once a gaussian is defined from a pattern set (V_i^r or V_i^{r-1}), that set is removed from the remaining training set. This process of randomly picking a pattern vector x_g of class k from the remaining training set and growing the largest possible gaussian around it is then repeated. A set of gaussians $(j = 1, \ldots, Q_h)$ for class k is found at the hth stage by repeating this process until the remaining training set is empty of class k patterns.

3.2 The Algorithm

The algorithm is summarized below. The following notation is used. I and R denote the initial and remaining training sets, respectively. δ_{max} is the maximum neighborhood radius and δ_r is the neighborhood width at the rth step of neighborhood growth. $\Delta\delta$ is the δ_r increment at each step. V_i^r is the set of patterns within the δ_r-neighborhood of ith initial vector x_g^i. $P_i(k)$ denotes the percentage of class k members in V_i^r. N_i^r denotes the number of vectors in V_i^r. h is the stage counter, θ_h is the minimum percentage of class k members in V_i^r in stage h and $\Delta\theta$ is the increment for θ_h at each stage. Q_j corresponds to the number of gaussians created in stage j and $p_h = \sum_{j=1}^h Q_j$ is the total number of gaussians till stage h. C_{kl} and w_{kl} are the center and widths respective of the lth gaussian unit of class k. TRE_h and TSE_h are the training and testing set errors, respectively, at the hth stage for class k. β is the minimum number of points required to form a gaussian and $\sigma = (\sigma_1, \ldots, \sigma_N)$ the standard deviations of the distances from the centroid in various directions for class k. δ_{max} is set to some multiple of σ. The fixed growth step in each direction $i, \Delta\delta_i$, is set to σ_i/L, where L is the desired number of growth steps. L was set to 25 for computational experiments.

The Gaussian Masking (GM) Algorithm
(1) Initialize class counter: $k = 0$.
(2) Increment class counter: $k = k + 1$. If $k > K$, stop. Else, initialize gaussian counter: $j = 0$.
(3) Initialize stage counter and constants: $h = 0, \delta_{max} = \alpha\sigma, \Delta\delta_i = \sigma_i/L, \Delta\theta =$ some constant (e.g. 10%).
(4) Increment stage counter: $h = h + 1$. Increase majority criteria: if $h > 1, \theta_h = \theta_{h-1} + \Delta\theta$; otherwise $\theta_h = 50\%$. If $\theta_h > 100\%$, go to (2).
(5) Select gaussian units for the hth stage: $i = 0, R = I, Q_h = 0$.
    (a) Set $i = i + 1, r = 1, \delta_r = \Delta\delta$.
    (b) Select an input pattern vector x_g^i of class k at random from R, the remaining training set.
    (c) Search for all pattern vectors in R within a δ_r-neighborhood of x_g^i. Let this set of vectors be V_i^r.
        (i) If $P_i(k) < \theta_h$ and $r > 1$, set $r = r - 1$, go to (e); (ii) if $P_i(k) > \theta_h$ and $r > 1$, go to (d) to expand neighborhood; (iii) if $P_i(k) < \theta_h$ and $r = 1$, go to (h); (iv) if $P_i(k) > \theta_h$ and $r = 1$, go to (d).
    (d) Set $r = r + 1, \delta_r = \delta_{r-1} + \Delta\delta$. If $\delta_r > \delta_{max}$, set $r = r - 1$, go to (e). Else, go to (c).
    (e) Remove the set V_i^r from $R : R = R - V_i^r$. If $N_i^r < \beta$, go to (g).
    (f) Set $j = j + 1$. Compute the center C_{kj} and widths w_{kj} of the jth gaussian for class k. $Q_h = Q_h + 1$. C_{kj}=centroid of the set V_i^r, and

w_{kj}=standard deviations of the distances from their centroid of the patterns in V_i^r

(g) If R is not empty, go to (a), else go to (6).

(h) Remove the set V_i^r from $R : R = R - V_i^r$. If R is not empty, go to (a), else go to (6).

(6) From the set p_h, eliminate similar gaussians (i.e. those with very close centers and widths). Let p_h' be the new set of gaussians after this elimination.

(7) Solve LP (1)-(5) for class k mask using p_h' number of gaussians.

(8) Compute TSE_h and TRE_h for class k. (a) If $TSE_h < TSE_{h-1}$, go to (4); (b) If $TSE_h > TSE_{h-1}$ and $TRE_h > TRE_{h-1}$, go to (4); (c) Otherwise, overfitting has occurred. Use the mask generated in the previous stage as class k mask. Go to (2) to mask next class.

Other stopping criteria, like maximum number of gaussians used or incremental change in TSE, can also be used. Polynomial time convergence of the GM algorithm can be proven in a manner similar to Roy et al. [1993].

4. Computational Results

All problems were solved on a SUN Sparc2 workstation. Linear programs were solved using Roy Marsten's OB1 interior point code from Georgia Institute of Technology. The dual log barrier penalty method of OB1 was used. The weights in LP (1)-(5), α and β, were set to 1 in all cases.

Several well-known problems were solved using this method. Only a few results are reported here. A 2-class, 2-dimensional problem, described in Musavi et al. [1992], was solved where the first class has a zero mean vector with identity covariance matrix and the second class has a mean [1,2] and a diagonal covariance matrix with values 0.01 and 4. The estimated optimal error rate is 6%. The GM algorithm obtained an error rate of 8.75% using only 11 gaussians (up to 80% majority gaussians). Musavi et al. [1992] achieved an error rate of 9.26% with 86 gaussians. The GM algorithm used 200 points for training. Mangasarian et al. [1990] describes a breast cancer diagnosis problem. The data, from University of Wisconsin Hospitals, contains 608 cases, each case having 9 measurements with values between 1 and 10. Of the 608 cases, 379 were benign and the rest malignant. Of the 608, 405 were used for training and rest used for testing. An error rate of 4.43% was obtained by the GM algorithm using 7 gaussians. Mangasarian et al. [1990] report average error rates of 2.56% and 6.10% with their MSM1 and MSM methods respectively.

Acknowledgement

This research was supported, in part, by the National Science Foundation grant IRI- 9113370.

References

1. Broomhead, D., & Lowe, D. (1988). Multivariable function interpolation and adaptive networks, *Complex Systems*, 2, 321-355.

2. Mangasarian, O.L., Setiono, R. and Wolberg, W.H. (1990). Pattern Recognition Via Linear Programming: Theory and Application to Medical Diagnosis. In T.F. Coleman and Y. Li, editors, Proceedings of the Workshop on Large-Scale Numerical Optimization, Cornell University, Ithaca, New York, Oct. 19-20, 1989, pp. 22-31, Philadelphia, PA, 1990, SIAM.

3. Moody, J. & Darken, C. (1989). Fast Learning in Networks of Locally-Tuned Processing Units, *Neural Computation*, 1(2), 281-294.

4. Mukhopadhyay, S., Roy, A., Kim, L.S. & Govil, S. (1993). A Polynomial Time Algorithm for Generating Neural Networks for Pattern Classification - its Stability Properties and Some Test Results. *Neural Computation*, Vol. 5, No. 2, pp. 225-238.

5. Musavi, M.T., Ahmed, W., Chan, K.H., Faris, K.B. and Hummels, D.M. (1992). On the Training of Radial Basis Function Classifiers. *Neural Networks*, 5, 4, 595-603.

6. Platt, J. (1991). A Resource-Allocating Network for Function Interpolation. *Neural Computation*, Vol. 3, No. 2, pp. 213-225.

7. Powell, M.J.D. (1987). Radial Basis Functions for Multivariable Interpolation: A Review. In: *Algorithms for Approximation*, J.C. Mason, M.G. Cox, eds. Clarendon Press, Oxford.

8. Roy, A. & Mukhopadhyay, S. (1991). Pattern Classification Using Linear Programming. *ORSA Journal on Computing*, Winter, 3, 1, 66-80.

9. Roy, A., Kim, L.S. & Mukhopadhyay, S. (1993). A Polynomial Time Algorithm for the Construction and Training of a Class of Multilayer Perceptrons. *Neural Networks*, Vol. 6, No. 4, pp. 535-545.

Some Further Results on L_2 Convergence Rate of RBF Networks and Kernel Regression Estimators

Adam Krzyzak[1] and Lei Xu[2]
1. Dept. of Computer Science, Concordia Univ. Canada
2. Dept. of Computer Sciences, The Chinese Univ. of Hong Kong, HK

Abstract   *Some further results are proposed for the L_2 convergence rates of Kernel Regression Estimators (KRE) and Radial Basis Function (RBF) nets given in Xu, Krzyzak & Yuille (1992&93). Instead of studying the convergence properties of the L2 error, here we study the convergence properties of the MISE (Mean Integrated Square Error). It will be shown that the upper bounds for the convergence rate of MISE are tighter than those for convergence rate of L_2 error given in Xu, Krzyzak & Yuille (1992&93), under milder conditions.*

1. Introduction

A number of theoretical results on Radial Basis Function (RBF) networks have been obtained, see Xu, Krzyzak & Yuille (1993) for a long list of references. It has been shown that the RBF net can be naturally derived from the *regularization theory* (Poggio & Girosi, 1989; Yuille & Grzywacz, 1989), and that RBF nets have the universal approximation ability (Hartman, Keeler & Kowalski, 1989; Park & Sandberg, 1991&1993) as well as the so-called best approximation ability (Girosi & Poggio, 1989). In addition, RBF nets can also be related to *Parzen Window* estimators of probability density (it can be considered a special example of an RBF net) and *probabilistic neural networks* (Specht, 1990) which are based on Parzen window estimator.

Recent theoretical studies on RBF nets gave convergence rates of approximation and generalization error in terms of the size of RBF nets (i.e., the number of basis functions) (Xu, Krzyzak, Yuille, 1992 &93; Girosi & Anzellotti, 1992; and Corradit & White, 1992). In Xu, Krzyzak, Yuille (1992&93), the connection between RBF nets and the *Kernel Regression Estimator (KRE)* has been established. It has been shown that KRE can be regarded as a particular kind of an RBF net. Using theoretical results about KRE, a number of interesting theoretical results for RBF nets have been obtained. First, upper bounds have been given for the pointwise and L_2 convergence rates of the approximation error with respect to the number n of basis functions; An example of such bound is $O(n^{-2\alpha/(2\alpha+d)})$ for the L_2 convergence rate on approximating function $R(x)$ in the Lipschitz function class. , or $O(n^{-2q/(2q+d)})$ for L_2 convergence rate on approximating function $R(x)$ in the class of functions which have order-q ($q \geq 1$) square integrable derivatives t , where d is the dimension of x. Second, the learnability of RBF nets has been proved by showing the existence of a consistent estimator for RBF nets constructively. Third, upper bounds have also been provided for the pointwise and L_2 convergence rates of the best consistent estimator for RBF nets as n and N (the number of the learning samples, $N \geq n$) tend to ∞. Examples of such bounds are $O(n^{-2\alpha/(2\alpha+d)})$, $N \geq n$ or $O(n^{-2q/(2q+d)})$, $N \geq n$ for L_2 convergence rates for the two function classes described above. Fourth, some theoretical results on selecting the appropriate size of the receptive field of the radial basis function have been provided too. Nearly in the same period, Girosi & Anzellotti (1992) and Corradit & White(1992) also proposed some results on RBF net convergence rates of the approximation error. However, their studies differ from Xu, Krzyzak & Yuille (1992&93) in several aspects: (1) the unnormalized RBF net has been considered instead of the normalized RBF nets considered by Xu, Krzyzak & Yuille (1992&93); (2) the tools used were totally different; (2) the results of Girosi & Anzellotti (1992) and Corradit & White(1992) concern only convergence rate of the approximation error; while Xu, Krzyzak & Yuille (1992&93) study much more than just approximation error; (4) the conditions assumed and the detailed results are also different, though the rates obtained in Xu, Krzyzak & Yuille (1992&93), Girosi & Anzellotti (1992), and Corradit & White(1992) are consistent.

This paper propose some further complementary results for those obtained in Xu, Krzyzak & Yuille (1992&93) on the L_2 convergence rates of KRE and RBF nets. Given a vector-valued regression function $R(x) = [r^{(1)}(x), \cdots, r^{(m)}(x)]^T$, let network with output estimate $f_{n,N}(x)$ be trained by a training set $D_N = \{X_i, Y_i\}_1^N$, where N is the number of training samples and n is the size of the network, e.g., the number of hidden neurons in the network. In Xu, Krzyzak & Yuille (1992&93), we have studied the convergence properties of the L_2 error $\varepsilon^2 = \int_U |R(x) - f_{n,D_N}(x)|^2 d\mu(x)$, where $|z(x)| = \sum_{i=1}^m |z^{(i)}(x)|$ for $z(x) = [z^{(1)}(x), \cdots, z^{(m)}(x)]^T$, and U is the domain of x, and μ denotes the measure on x. This error is a random variable because the training samples are random varaibles. Thus, the convergence properties given in Xu, Krzyzak & Yuille (1992&93) are described in terms of 'almost surely', ' in probability'. In this paper, we study the convergence properties of the MISE error:

$$e_2 = E_{D_N}[(R(X_1) - f_{n,N}(X))^2 \,[], \qquad (1)$$

where $X_1 \in D_N$. This error is not a random variable. We will show that the upper bounds for the convergence rate of e_2 are tighter than those for the L_2 convergence rate of ε^2 given in Xu, Krzyzak & Yuille (1992&93), under milder conditions.

2. RBF Net, KRE and Convergence Properties

As in Xu, Krzyzak & Yuille (1992&93), we consider the RBF nets of the following normalized version (Moody

& Darken, 1989; Nowlan, 1990; Jones et al, 1991):

$$f_n(x) = \frac{\sum_{i=1}^n w_i \phi([x - c_i]^t \Sigma^{-1} [x - c_i])}{\sum_{i=1}^n \phi([x - c_i]^t \Sigma^{-1} [x - c_i])} \tag{2}$$

where $\phi(r^2)$ is a prespecified basis function satisfying certain weak conditions. The most common choice is the Gaussian function, $\phi(r^2) = e^{-r^2}$ with $\Sigma = \sigma(n)^2 I$, but a number of alternatives can also be used, (e.g., several choices are listed in Poggio & Girosi, 1989). c_i is called the center vector and $w_i \in R^m$ is a weight vector. Σ is a $d \times d$ positive matrix which controls the receptive field of the basis functions $\phi([x - c_i]^t \Sigma^{-1} [x - c_i])$.

Xu, Krzyzak & Yuille (1992&93) has shown that this type of RBF nets has close connections to the *Kernel Regression Estimator (KRE)* studied in the statistical literature.

Let (X, Y) be a pair of random vectors in $R^d \times R^m$ and $R(x) = E\{Y|X = x\}$ be the corresponding regression function. Let μ denote the probability measure of X. Moreover, let $\mathcal{D}_n^g = \{X_i, Y_i\}_1^n$ be a set of independent identically distributed samples drawn from (X, Y). The kernel regression estimate of $R(x)$ is defined as follows:

$$g_n(x) = g_n(x, \mathcal{D}_n^g) = \frac{\sum_{i=1}^n Y_i K(\frac{x - X_i}{h_n})}{\sum_{i=1}^n K(\frac{x - X_i}{h_n})} \tag{3}$$

which is the weighted average of Y_i for approximating the conditional mean of Y under a given $X = x$ with weights depending nonlinearly on X_i. Here, h_n is usually called a *smoothness parameter* and is a positive number that depends on the number of samples n. $K \geq 0$ is a μ integrable kernel on R^d. When the kernel $K(x)$ is spherical symmetry, we can rewrite eq.(3) as:

$$g_n(x) = \frac{\sum_{i=1}^n K(\frac{\|x - X_i\|}{h_n}) Y_i}{\sum_{i=1}^n K(\frac{\|x - X_i\|}{h_n})} \tag{4}$$

It is not difficult to see that by letting

$$K(r) = \phi(r^2), \ \Sigma = h_n^2 I, \ \sigma(n)^2 = h_n^2, \ and \ w_i = Y_i, \ c_i = X_i, \ i = 1, \cdots, n \tag{5}$$

eq.(4) is identical to eq.(2). That is, a spherically symmetrical kernel $K(r^2)$ is just a special instance of radial basis function model eq.(2) with a hyper-spherically shaped receptive field specified by the matrix $\Sigma = h_n^2 I$, and with the weight vectors $w_i, i = 1, \cdots, n$ being simply assigned to the specified values $Y_i, i = 1, \cdots, n$. It is interesting to notice that the assumption of hyper-spherically shaped receptive fields is commonly used in the existing studies of RBF nets (Broomhead & Lowe, 1988; Chen, Cowan & Grant, 1991; Moody & Darken, 1989; Poggio & Girosi, 1989; Xu, Klasa & Yuille, 1992).

With this connection, we can obtain upper bounds for the convergence rates of RBF nets via the convergence rates of KRE.

To make our statements more precise, we first review some mathematical terms.

Given a vector-valued function $f(x) = [f^{(1)}(x), \cdots, f^{(m)}(x)]^T$, and a sequence $\{f_n(x)\}_1^\infty$, let

$$e_x(f, f_n) = |f(x) - f_n(x)|, \quad \rho_U^2(f, f_n) = \int_U |e_x(f, f_n)|^2 d\mu(x), \tag{6}$$

where $|z(x)| = \sum_{i=1}^m |z^{(i)}(x)|$ for $z(x) = [z^{(1)}(x), \cdots, z^{(m)}(x)]^T$, U is the domain of x, and μ denotes the measure on x. For any $\epsilon > 0$, if there exists a specific n_0 such that $\rho_U^2(f, f_n) < \epsilon$ for any $n > n_0$, then f_n is said to converge in L_2 to f. Given a positive sequence ξ_n which tends to zero as $n \to \infty$, the convergence rate of ξ_n is said to be of $O(r(n))$, if there is an explicit positive function $r(n)$ of n with $r(n) \to 0$ as $n \to \infty$ (e.g., $r(n) = n^{-q}, q > 0$) such that $a_n \xi_n / r(n) \to 0$ as $n \to \infty$ for any sequence of positive numbers $\{a_n\}$ which satisfies $a_n \to 0$ as $n \to \infty$. Using $\rho_U^2(f, f_n)$ to replace ξ_n, we get the definition for L_2 convergence rate.

A *function approximation scheme* is a device of a set $\mathcal{F}$ of functions supported on R^d. Usually, this device consists of a number of components so that the set $\mathcal{F}$ can be characterized by this number (say n), that is, we can denote it by $\mathcal{F}_n$. Examples of such devices are multilayer networks with n hidden sigmoid units and RBF nets with n radial basis functions. Let $\mathcal{F}_U = \bigcup_{n=1}^\infty \mathcal{F}_n$, then the function approximation scheme is said to have the property of *universal approximation* (Hornik, Stinchocombe & White, 1989) if $\mathcal{F}_U$ is *dense* in the space of the continuous functions $C[U]$ defined on some domain U of R^d; or in other words, if for any continuous function $f(x)$ supported on U, there exists a specific $\hat{f}_n \in \mathcal{F}_n$ such that $\hat{f}_n(x)$ converges to $f(x)$ *uniformly*. Similarly, for any function $f(x)$ of a given a function class $\mathcal{F}_c(U)$ supported on U, if there exist a specific $\hat{f}_n \in \mathcal{F}_n$ such that $\hat{f}_n(x)$ converges to $f(x)$ in the L_2 sense, we say that the function approximation scheme has the property of L_2 approximation for the function class $\mathcal{F}_c(U)$.

These properties describe the *approximation ability* of one set of functions to another set of functions. For a given function $f(x)$, the properties *only* say that there exists, in the set $\mathcal{F}_n$ defined by the function approximation scheme, a function that can approximate $f(x)$ well as $n \to \infty$. They say nothing about how to find such a function. Usually, $\mathcal{F}_n$ is characterized by a set Θ of unspecified parameters. Each specified value $\hat{\Theta}$ of Θ determines a $\hat{f}_n(x)$ in $\mathcal{F}_n$. The value $\hat{\Theta}$ (thus $\hat{f}_n(x)$) is obtained based on a set of observed samples $\mathcal{D}_N = \{X_i, Y_i\}_1^N$ of a given function $f(x)$. Usually these observed samples $X_1, Y_1, \cdots, X_N, Y_N$ are identical and independent random variables with $f(x)$ being their regression function, i.e., $f(X_i) = R(X_i) = E(Y_i|X_i)$. Such a $\hat{f}_n(x)$ is called an estimator of $R(x)$. To explicitly indicate its dependence on $\mathcal{D}_N$, we denote it by $\hat{f}_{n,N}(x)$. An examples of such estimators is KRE, a specific RBF net obtained via eq.(5). Since $\mathcal{D}_N$ are random samples, $\hat{f}_{n,N}(x)$ is also random variable. In this case, the convergence behavior is described by a property called *statistical consistency* which describes how the estimator approaches the regression function $R(x) = E(Y|X = x)$ as the number of samples tends to infinity. An estimator $\hat{f}_{n,N}(x)$ is said to be L_2 consistent in probability if it converges in L_2 sense to $R(x)$ in probability.

Although useful, the convergence properties of *universal approximation*, L_2 approximation and *statistical consistency* give no descriptions on the rates of $f_n(x)$, $f_{n,N}(x)$ converge to $f(x)$ with respect to the number n, N, i.e., the size of the hidden layer and the size of training sequence. Since KRE is a particular specified RBF net and its $g_n(x)$ belongs to the set $\mathcal{F}_n$ that is defined by the RBF net eq.(2), we can explore the convergence rates of RBF nets through investigating the convergence rates of KRE. It was through this thought line, Xu, Krzyzak & Yuille (1992&93) obtained a number of results on the convergence rates of RBF nets.

This paper will provide some complementary results. We further study the convergence properties of the following MISE error

$$e_2^g = E_{D_N}[(R(X_1) - g_n(X_1))^2], \quad for\ KRE$$
$$e_2^f = E_{D_N}[(R(X_1) - f_{n,N}(X_1))^2], \quad for\ RBF.$$

where D_N is the training set. By taking expectation on $\frac{1}{N}\sum_{i=1}^N (R(X_1) - f_{n,N}(X_1))^2$, we see that it becomes $E_{D_N}(R(X_1) - f_{n,N}(X_1))^2$ when $X_1, \cdots, X_N$ are i.i.d random variables. In other words, This error can also be regarded as the estimation error of the networks on the traning set D_N.

3. Main results
Theorem 1 (KRE's convergence)

Let $EY^2 < \infty$, and

$$c_1 I_{S_{0,r}} \le K(x) \le c_2 I_{S_{0,R}}, \quad 0 < r < R < \infty, c_1, c_2 > 0$$

$$h \to 0, \quad nh^d \to \infty$$

where I_A denote indicator of set A and $S_{x,r} = \{y : \|y - x\| \le r\}$. For $g_n(x)$ given by eq.(4), we have

$$E(R(X_1) - g_n(X_1))^2 \to 0 \ \ as \ \ n \to \infty.$$

The above Theorem shows that KRE estimator $g_n(x)$ given by eq.(4) converges in the MISE sense. In comparison with Theorem 2 of Xu, Krzyzak, Yuille (1992 & 93), we can observe that the condition $E|Y|^{2+s} < \infty \ \ s > 0$ has been relaxed into $EY^2 < \infty$. The following theorem gives the MISE convergence rate of KRE estimator $g_n(x)$ given by eq.(4).

Theorem 3 (KRE's convergence rate)

Let μ denote the probability measure of X with a compact support, and

$$c_1 I_{S_{0,r}} \le K(x) \le c_2 I_{S_{0,R}}, \quad 0 < r < R < \infty, c_1, c_2 > 0$$

$$h \to 0, \quad n^{s/(s+2)} h^d \to \infty \quad as \quad n \to \infty$$

$$E|Y|^{2+s} < \infty \quad s > 0$$
$$|R(x) - R(y)| \le \beta \|x - y\|^\alpha, \quad 0 < \alpha \le 1, \quad \beta > 0$$

For $g_n(x)$ given by eq.(4), we have

$$E(R(X_1) - g_n(X_1))^2 = O\left(n^{-\frac{2\alpha s}{(2+s)(2\alpha+d)}}\right).$$

Let $t = 2 + s$ and put it into Theorem 4, then the condition $E|Y|^{2+s} < \infty \ \ s > 0$ becomes $E|Y|^t < \infty \ \ t > 2$. Correspondingly, the rate becomes $O\left(n^{-\frac{2\alpha(t-2)}{t(2\alpha+d)}}\right)$. Now we are ready to compare with the rate $O\left(n^{-\frac{2}{s} - \frac{2\alpha}{(2\alpha+d)}}\right)$—the one given in Theorem 6(B) of Xu, Krzyzak, Yuille (1992 & 93). Let $t = s$ and noticing that $\frac{2\alpha}{2\alpha+d}\frac{2}{s} < \frac{2}{s}$, we have $\frac{2\alpha(s-2)}{s(2\alpha+d)} > \frac{2\alpha}{(2\alpha+d)} - \frac{2}{s}$. That is, the rate given in Theorem 2 is is tighter than the one given in Theorem 6(B) of Xu,

Krzyzak, Yuille (1992 & 93). In addition, comparing the requirements $E|Y|^s < \infty$ $s > 2$ with $E|Y|^s < \infty$ $s > 2 + \frac{d}{\alpha}$, we see that the condition has also been relaxed.

From the above theorems about the KRE estimator $g_n(x)$ given by eq.(4), we can observe that that for a given function $f(x) = R(x)$ we can construct a specific RBF net $f_n \in \mathcal{F}_n$ by simply letting the parameters Θ to assume the values provided by the samples $D_n = \{X_i, Y_i\}_1^n$ with D_n being a randomly selected subset of D_N, in the same way as it was done for the KRE eq.(4). As a result, this $f_{n,n}$ will converge in MISE to $f(x)$ with the same convergence properties as described by Theorems 1–2. Recalling that such a specific $f_{n,n}$ may not be the best $f_{n,N}^*, N \geq n$, so the convergence rate of the best $f_{n,N}^*, N \geq n$ given by RBF net will be not worse than the rate provided by Theorem 2. That is, we can get upper bounds for the convergence rates of $f_{n,N}^*, N \geq n$. These bounds are described more precisely in the following theorems.

Theorem 3 (RBF's convergence)

Let $EY^2 < \infty$, and

$$c_1 I_{S_{0,r}} \leq \phi(x) \leq c_2 I_{S_{0,R}}, \quad 0 < r < R < \infty, c_1, c_2 > 0$$

$$h \to 0, \quad nh^d \to \infty.$$

Let $f_{n,N}^*(x)$ denote the one in $\mathcal{F}_{n,N}$ that approximates $R(x)$ best. We have

$$E(R(X_1) - f_{n,N}^*(X_1))^2 \to 0 \qquad \text{as } n \to \infty$$

where $\mathcal{F}_{n,N}$ denotes the set of functions defined by the RBF nets eq.(2) and trained by the training set of N samples.

Theorem 4 (RBF's convergence rate)

Let μ denote the probability measure of X with a compact support, and

$$c_1 I_{S_{0,r}} \leq \phi(x) \leq c_2 I_{S_{0,R}}, \quad 0 < r < R < \infty, c_1, c_2 > 0$$

$$h \to 0, \qquad n^{s/(s+2)}h^d \to \infty \quad as \quad n \to \infty$$

$$E|Y|^{2+s} < \infty \quad s > 0$$
$$|R(x) - R(y)| \leq \beta \|x - y\|^\alpha, \quad 0 < \alpha \leq 1, \quad \beta > 0.$$

Let $f_{n,N}^*(x)$ denote the one in $\mathcal{F}_{n,N}$ that approximates $R(x)$ best. We have

$$E(R(X_1) - f_{n,N}^*(X_1))^2 = O(n^{-\frac{2\alpha s}{(2+s)(2\alpha+d)}}).$$

References [1] Broomhead, D.S., and Lowe, D., (1988), Multivariable functional interpolation and adaptive networks, *Complex Systems 2*, 321-323. [2] Chen, S., Cowan, C.F.N., and Grant, P.M., (1991), Orthogonal least squares learning algorithm for Radial basis function networks, *IEEE Trans. on Neural Networks 2*, 302-309. [3] Corradit, V. and White, H., (1992), Regularized neural networks: some convergence rate results, Manuscript, Dept. of Economics, UCSD, San Diego, Sept., 1992. [4] Devroye, L., and Krzyzak, A. (1989), An equivalence theorem for L_1 convergence of the kernel regression estimate, *J. of Statistical Planning and Inference 23*, 71-82. [5] Girosi, F., and Poggio, T., (1989), Networks and the best approximation property, *M.I.T. AI Memo. No.1164*, MIT, 1989. [6] Girosi, F., and Anzellotti, (1992), Convergence rates of approximation by translates, *M.I.T. AI Memo. No.1288*, MIT, Cambridge, March, 1992. [7] Hartman, E.J., Keeler, J.D, and Kowalski, J.M. (1990), Layered neural networks with Gaussian hidden units s universal approximations, *Neural Computation 2*, 210-215. [8] Hornik, K., Stinchocombe, S., and White, H.,(1989), Multilayer feed-forward networks are universal approximators, *Neural Networks 2*, 359-366. [9] Moody, J., and Darken, J., (1989), Fast learning in networks of locally-tuned processing units, *Neural Computation 1*, 281-294. [10] Nowlan, S.J., (1990), Max likelihood competition in RBF networks, *Tech. Rep. CRG-Tr-90-2, Dept. of Computer Sci., U. of Toronto.* [11] Park, J., and Sandberg, I., W. (1991), Universal approximation using radial-basis-function networks, *Neural Computation 3*, 246-257. [12] Park, J., and Sandberg, I., W. (1993), Universal approximation using radial-basis-function networks, *Neural Computation 5*, [13] Specht, D.F., (1990), Probabilistic neural networks, *Neural Networks 3*, 109-118. [14] Xu, L., Klasa, S., and Yuille, A.L., (1992), Recent Advances on Techniques Static Feedforward Networks with Supervised Learning, *International Journal of Neural Systems*, Vol.3, No.3, pp.253-290, 1992. [15] Xu, L., Krzyzak, A. and Oja, E., (1993), Rival Penalized Competitive Learning for Clustering Analysis, RBF net and Curve Detection, *IEEE Trans. on Neural Networks*, Vol.4, No.4, pp636-649. [16] Xu, L., Krzyzak, A., and Yuille, A.L., (1992), On Radial Basis Function Nets and Kernel Regression: Approximation Ability, Convergence Rate and Receptive Field Size, Technical report No. 92-4, Harvard Robotics Laboratory, Harvard University, Feb., 1992. [17] Xu, L., Krzyzak, A., and Yuille, A.L., (1993), On Radial Basis Function Nets and Kernel Regression: Statistical Consisteney, Convergence Rates and Receptive Field Size, *Neural Networks*, in press. [18] Yuille, A.L., and Grzywacz, N.M., (1989), A mathematical analysis of the motion coherence theory, *Int. J. of Computer Vision 3*, 155-175.

Weighted Neural Network Models for Nonlinear Regression with Fixed and Random Effects

Momiao Xiong[1] and Ping Wang[2]

December 5, 1993

Department of Mathematics and Molecular Biology[1], University of Southern California, LA. CA 90089
Department of Information and Decision Sciences[2], James Madison University, Harrisonburg, VA 22807.

Abstract General nonlinear mixed effects models for repeated measurement data have a wide range of applications in medicine, pharmecokinetics, business and economics, but may have a complicated covariance structure. Traditional neural network models for nonlinear regression can not be directly applied to the nonlinear regression with fixed and random effects. In this paper, we propose a novel neural network model with weighted sum of square error. Iterative algorithm between estimation of fixed effects parameter and variance components is presented. A modified backpropagation scheme is investigated with encouraging simulation results.

1 Introduction

There has been a great deal of increasing interests in general nonlinear mixed effects models for repeated measures data in which data are generated on individuals over time or under fixed conditions. Regression with fixed and random effects plays an important role in biomedical research including pharmacokinetics, bioassay, and clinical trials, business and economics (Vonesh and Carter, 1992). Since individuals are assumed to constitute a random sample from a population of interests, the observed data have nonconstant correlation among them. Traditional neural network models for nonlinear regression can not be directly applied to the nonlinear regression with mixed effects(Blum, 1992; Freeman, 1994).

In this paper, we propose a novel neural network model for nonlinear regression with mixed effects. The model allows for incomplete or unbalanced data and a variance-covariance structure. The response is expressed as a Sum of nonlinear functions of fixed effects and linear functions of random effects. The objective function is a weighted sum of square errors. The estimates of unknown population parameters are obtained by an iterative algorithm. A modified backpropagation scheme involving weight matrix imposed on sum of square errors is presented. Finally, the model is applied to the growth of orange trees over time.

2 The Model

It is assumed that there are P distinct individuals ($p = 1, ..., P$) and whose responses can be expressed as the following general nonlinear mixed effects model:

$$Y_p = f(X_p, W) + Z_p \beta_p + \epsilon_p, p = 1, \ldots, P \tag{1}$$

where $Y_p = [Y_{p1}, \ldots, Y_{pr_p}]^T$ is an $r_p \times 1$ vector of repeated measurements from the pth individual; $X_p = [X_{p1}, \ldots, X_{pr_p}]^T$ is an $r_p \times k$ matrix of known explanatory variables; W is a vector of unknown parameters; $f(X_p, W)$ is a nonlinear response function; Z_p is an $r_p \times m$ full-rank matrix of known constants. β_p is a

m-vector of unobserved random regression coefficients with mean zero and covariance matrix Ψ ; and ϵ_p the r_p random error vector with mean zero and variance matrix $\sigma^2 I_{rp}$.

The nonlinear function $f(X_p, W)$ can be approximated by a neural network. The bias units always have an output of one and they are connected to all units on their respective layer. Units on all layers calculate their net-input values. For the hidden-layer units:

$$net_{pj}^h = \sum_{i=1}^{k} W_{ji}^h X_{pi}^{(l)} + \theta_j^h \tag{2}$$

and for the output-layer units

$$net_p^o = \sum_{j=1}^{L} W_j^o O_j \tag{3}$$

We assume that output function in each units takes a sigmoid function. Then the output of the j-th unit in the hidden layer is

$$O_j = f_j^h(net_{pj}^h) = \frac{1}{1 + e^{-net_{pj}^h}} \tag{4}$$

3 Estimation Procedure

Let

$$e_p = Z_p \beta_p + \epsilon_p \tag{5}$$

Then, equation (1) can rewritten as

$$Y_p = f(X_p, W) + e_p, p = 1, \ldots, P \tag{6}$$

It is easy to see that the variance matrix of random vector e_p is given by

$$V_p = Var(e_p) = Z_p \Psi Z_p^T + \sigma^2 I_p \tag{7}$$

Let

$$V_p^{-1} = A_p = \begin{pmatrix} A_{11}^p \ldots A_{1r_p}^p \\ \ldots\ldots\ldots \\ A_{r_p 1}^p \ldots A_{r_p r_p}^p \end{pmatrix} \tag{8}$$

Because of heteroscedasticity of random vector e_p we use the weighted least square method to estimate the weights of neural networks.

The weighted objective function is

$$E = \frac{1}{2} \sum_{p=1}^{P} (Y_p - f(X_p, W))^T A_p (Y_p - f(X_p, W)), \tag{9}$$

or

$$E = \frac{1}{2} \sum_{p=1}^{P} \sum_{l=1}^{r_p} (y_{pl} - f(X_{pl}, W)) \sum_{k=1}^{r_p} A_k^{(p)} (y_{pk} - f(X_{pk}, W)). \tag{10}$$

The estimation procedure is as follows.

Step 1:

The first stage of the procedure is to obtain the nonlinear ordinary least square estimator(OLS), $W^{(o)}$, by minimizing the residual sum of squares

$$E(W, I_{r_p}) = \frac{1}{2} \sum_{p=1}^{P} (Y_p - f(X_p, W))^T I_{r_p} (Y_p - f(X_p, W)). \tag{11}$$

This stage provides an initial estimator $W^{(o)}$ and may be implemented by ordinary Backpropagation algorithm.

Step 2:

After substituting the estimated residuals

$$\hat{e}_p^{(k)} = y_p - f(x_p, \hat{W}^{(k)}), p = 1, ..., P. \tag{12}$$

into equation (5), we obtain the following random coefficient linear equation:

$$\hat{e}_p^{(k)} = Z_p \beta_p + \epsilon_p, p = 1, ..., P. \tag{13}$$

Thus, the least square estimation $\hat{\beta}_p^{(k)}$ and $\hat{\sigma}_p^{(k)}$ are given by

$$\hat{\beta}_p^{(k)} = (Z_p^T Z_p)^{-1} Z_p^T \hat{e}_p^{(k)} \tag{14}$$

and

$$\hat{\sigma}_p^{(k)} = \frac{1}{r_p - m} \hat{e}_p^{(k)} (I_{rp} - Z_p (Z_p^T Z_p)^{-1} Z_p^T) \hat{e}_p^{(k)} \tag{15}$$

respectively.

Step 3:

It follows from equation (13) and equation (14) that

$$\hat{\beta}_p^{(k)} = \beta_p + (Z_p^T Z_p)^{-1} Z_p^T \epsilon_p. \tag{16}$$

Since $\beta_p \sim N(0, \Psi)$, the least square estimator $\hat{\Psi}^{(k)}$ is given by

$$\hat{\Psi}^{(k)} = S - \frac{1}{P} \sum_{p=1}^{P} \hat{\sigma}_p^{(k)} (Z_p^T Z_p)^{-1}, \tag{17}$$

where

$$S = \frac{1}{P-1} \sum_{p=1}^{P} (\hat{\beta}_p^{(k)} - \bar{\beta}_p^{(k)})(\hat{\beta}_p^{(k)} - \bar{\beta}_p^{(k)})^T, \tag{18}$$

and

$$\bar{\beta}_p^{(k)} = \frac{1}{P} \sum_{p=1}^{P} \hat{\beta}_p^{(k)}. \tag{19}$$

Step 4.

Define

$$A_p^{(k)} = [Z_p \hat{\Psi}^{(k)} Z_p^T + (\hat{\sigma}^{(k)})^2 I_{rp}]^{-1}. \tag{20}$$

The weighted least square estimation $\hat{W}^{(k+1)}$ of weights W of neural networks are obtained by minimizing

$$E(W, A_p^{(k)}) = \frac{1}{2} \sum_{p=1}^{P} (Y_p - f(X_p, W^{(k)}))^T A_p^{(k)} (Y_p - f(X_p, W^{(k)})). \tag{21}$$

The minimization of $E(W, A_p^{(k)})$ is implemented by modified Backpropagation, for detail, see Appendix. If $||W^{(k+1)} - W^{(k)}|| \leq e$, a prespecified error, then stop, otherwise go to step 1.

4 An Example

The proposed neural network model is applied to fitting the data on the growth of orange trees over time given in Draper and Smith(1981). The data are presented in Fig.1 and consist of seven measurements of the trunk circumference on end of five orange trees. It turns out that the neural network model fits the data very well. The marginal correlation between observations on the same individual is quite high and is greater at the larger time points. This reflects the large variability between trees are compared to within trees.

Appendix

Suppose that the global error surface is given by

$$E(W, A) = \frac{1}{2} \sum_{p=1}^{P} \sum_{l=1}^{r_p} \sum_{k=1}^{r_p} A_{lk}(y_{pl} - f(X_p^{(l)}, W))(y_{pk} - f(X_p^{(k)}, W)). \tag{22}$$

Let

$$E_{plk} = \frac{1}{2} A_{lk}(y_{pl} - f(X_p^{(l)}, W))(y_{pk} - f(X_p^{(k)}, W)), \tag{23}$$

and

$$e_{ij} = y_{ij} - f(X_i^{(j)}, W). \tag{24}$$

Then

$$\frac{\partial E_{plk}}{\partial W_j^o} = -\frac{1}{2} A_{lk}(O_j(X_p^{(l)})e_{pk} + O_j(X_p^{(k)})e_{pl}, \tag{25}$$

where $O_j(X_p^{(l)})$ and $O_j(X_p^{(k)})$ are the output for unit j in the hidden layer when $X_p^{(l)}$ and $X_p^{(k)}$ are input to the neural network respectively.

Similarly, we can find the gradient of the error surface with respect to the hidden-layer weights:

$$\frac{\partial E_{plk}}{\partial W_{ji}^h} = -\frac{1}{2} A_{lk}(O_j'(X_p^{(l)})X_{pi}^{(l)}e_{pk} + O_j'(X_p^{(k)})X_{pi}^{(k)})e_{pl}, \tag{26}$$

where

$$O_j'(X_p^{(l)}) = O_j(X_p^{(l)}(1 - O_j(X_p^{(l)}), \tag{27}$$

$$O_j'(X_p^{(k)}) = O_j(X_p^{(k)}(1 - O_j(X_p^{(k)}), \tag{28}$$

and

$$\frac{\partial E_{plk}}{\partial \theta_j^h} = -\frac{1}{2} A_{lk}[O_j(X_p^{(l)}(1 - O_j(X_p^{(l)})e_{pk} + [O_j(X_p^{(k)}(1 - O_j(X_p^{(k)})e_{pl}. \tag{29}$$

Hence

$$W_j^o(t + 1) = W_j^o(t) + \eta \frac{1}{2} A_{lk}(O_j(X_p^{(l)})e_{pk} + O_j(X_p^{(k)})e_{pl}, \tag{30}$$

$$W_{ji}^h(t+1) = W_{ji}^h(t) + \eta\frac{1}{2}A_{lk}[(O_j(X_p^{(l)})(1 - O_j(X_p^{(l)}X_{pi}^{(l)}e_{pk} + O_j(X_p^{(k)})(1 - O_j(X_p^{(k)}))X_{pi}^{(k)}e_{pl}], \quad (31)$$

$$\theta_j^h(t+1) = \theta_j^h(t) + \eta\frac{1}{2}A_{lk}[O_j(X_p^{(l)}(1 - O_j(X_p^{(l)})e_{pk} + [O_j(X_p^{(k)})(1 - O_j(X_p^{(k)})e_{pl}. \quad (32)$$

References

Blum, A. (1992), Neural networks in C++, An object-oriented framework for building connectionist systems, John Wiley and Sons, Inc. New York.

drapper, N.R. and Smith, H. (1981), Applied regression analysis, wiley, New York.

Freeman, J.A. (1994), Simulating neural networks with Mathematica, Addison-Wesley Publishing Company, New York.

Vonesh, E.F. and Carter, R.L. (1992), Mixed-effects Nonlinear regression for unbalanced repeated measures, Biometrics, 48, 1-17.

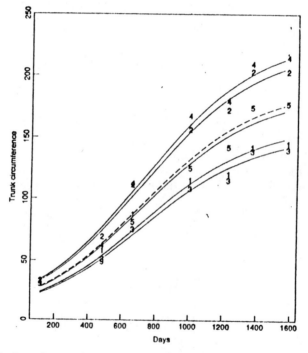

Figure 1. Trunk circumference (in millimeters) of five orange trees: Data and individual fitted curves from RML estimation. Dashed line represents the mean curve.

Supervised Learning

**Session Chairs: George Lendaris
Soo-Young Lee**

POSTER PRESENTATIONS

Weight Decay
as a Process of Redundancy Reduction

Ryotaro Kamimura
Information Science Laboratory
Shohachiro Nakanishi
Department of Electrical Engineering
Tokai University
1117 Kitakaname Hiratsuka Kanagawa 259-12, Japan

Abstract

In the present paper, we attempt to show that the weight decay method, used frequently to improve the generalization performance, is a method to decrease the redundancy in networks. To confirm our hypothesis of the weight decay as a process of the redundancy reduction, we performed two experiments: the inference of regular English verbs and the inference of regular and irregular verbs with the grammatical determination. In both cases, we could explicitly see that the redundancy was decreased, proportional to the generalization errors, when the weight decay term was added. Thus, we think that the weight decay is only a special case of more general redundancy reduction methods for the improvement of the generalization performance.

1 Introduction

Many techniques have been proposed to improve the generalization performance of neural networks [1], [2], [5], [9]. The weight decay method has been well known in the circle of neural networks and widely used to improve the generalization performance. However, we have little knowledge on the reason why the decay term can improve the generalization performance. One possible answer was proposed by Krogh and Hertz [3]. They argued that the decay term suppressed irrelevant parts of the weight vectors and the effects of static noises.

We think that the weight decay can decrease the redundancy in networks and thus tries to maximize the possible information for new patterns. In other words, networks try to minimize the information content, specific to training input patterns. Redundancy is usually defined by the difference between maximum entropy and observed entropy:

$$R = \frac{H^{max} - H}{H_{max}} \qquad (1)$$

where H^{max} is a maximum entropy and H is an observed entropy. Thus, using this redundancy, our objective is to show that networks try to minimize this redundancy R by using the weight decay term for the improvement of the generalization performance. Finally, one of the difficult problems is to define an information or redundancy for networks. We have defined an entropy for the internal representation. Thus, to reduce the redundancy corresponds to the reduction of the redundancy, defined for the internal representation.

2 Theory and Computational Methods

Let us formulate an entropy function for the internal representation. Suppose that a network is composed of three layers: input, hidden and output layers. Hidden unit activities are denoted by v_i and input terminals by ξ_j. Then, input-hidden connections are denoted by w_{ij} and hidden-output connections are denoted by W_{ij}.

A hidden unit produces an output

$$v_i^k = f(u_i^k),$$

where f is a logistic function define by

$$f(u_i^k) = \frac{1}{1 + e^{-u_i^k}}$$

and where u_i^k is a net input to ith hidden unit and defined by

$$u_i^k = \sum_{j=1}^{L} w_{ij} \xi_j^k.$$

where ξ_i^k is ith element of an input pattern and L is the number of elements in the pattern. An entropy for kth input pattern is defined by

$$H_k = -\sum_i p_i^k \log p_i^k, \tag{2}$$

where

$$p_i^k = \frac{v_i^k}{\sum_m v_m^k},$$

where the summation is over all the hidden units. Averaging over all the input patterns, we have

$$H = -\frac{1}{N} \sum_k^N \sum_i^M p_i^k \log p_i^k, \tag{3}$$

where M is the number of hidden units and N is the number of input patterns. The redundancy is defined by the difference between the maximum entropy and the observed entropy. That is,

$$\begin{aligned}
R &= \frac{H_{max} - H}{H_{max}} \\
&= \frac{N \log M + \sum_k^N \sum_i^M p_i \log p_i}{N \log M}.
\end{aligned} \tag{4}$$

2.1 Weight Decay as a Process of Information Minimization

Weight decay method is a very popular method, used to improve the generalization performance. For the weight decay, the sum of the squared weights:

$$C = \frac{\lambda}{2} \sum_{ij} w_{ij}^2$$

must be minimized. Differentiating both sides of this equation, we have,

$$-\frac{\partial C}{\partial w_{ij}} = -\lambda w_{ij}.$$

Now, let us see how the information is changed as the weight is close to zero. It is easily verified that

$$\lim_{w_{ij}\to 0} \left[\frac{N\log M + \sum_k^N \sum_i^M p_i^k \log p_i^k}{N\log M}\right] = 0 \quad for \ \forall i, j.$$

Thus, as the weights approaches zero, the redundancy also approaches zero. In other words, the weight decay method is considered to be one of methods to minimize the redundancy.

3 Results

3.1 Data and Network Architectures

In experiments, we trained networks to produce correct past tense forms, given various verb stems of artificial languages, close to English. All the artificial languages were composed of strings: CVC, CCV, and VCC, where V is a vowel, and C is a consonant. Each string was represented in a phonological representation with eight bits, used by Plunkett et al. [6]. The number of training patterns was 100 for the regular verbs and 200 for the irregular verbs. The number of validation patterns was 500 and testing patterns was also 500 patterns for all the experiments. The number of input, hidden, and output units was 18, 30, 20 respectively for the inference of regular verbs and 18, 30, 21 respectively for the inference of regular and irregular verbs with grammatical determination. Networks started to learn with initial random values (-0.25, 0.25). The parameter for the momentum term was fixed to 0.9 for all the experiments. The learning was performed by using the so-called *Batch* learning, meaning that weights were updated after processing all the input patterns. The learning was considered to be finished, only when the epoch was 200. If the over-training was observed, the learning was stopped immediately before the over-training (BP-stop-learning).

3.2 Redundancy and Generalization Errors

Figure 1 shows the generalization errors (an upper figure) and the redundancy (a lower figure), computed with standard BP and weight decay for the inference of regular verbs. In this case, only if the Hamming distance between outputs and targets was zero, the trial of networks was considered to be a success. Generalization errors were normalized, ranging [0,1]. As you can see from the figure, the generalization errors by standard BP remain constant, meaning that the standard BP could not generalize at all, though the errors for the training patterns were completely zero. On the other hand, the generalization errors by the weight decay is decreased gradually. Let us see a lower figure. It is easy to see that in direct proportion to the generalization errors, the redundancy is decreased, when the weight decay is used. Except the first stages of the training epochs, the redundancy is decreased, in direct proportion to the generalization errors.

Then, we used irregular verbs in addition to regular verbs and attempted to determine the well-formedness of obtained strings. Figure 2 shows generalization errors (an upper figure) and the redundancy (a lower figure), computed with standard BP and with weight decay. As you can see from the figure, by using standard BP, generalization errors remain constant. On the other hand, by using the weight decay method, the generalization errors are decreased significantly. A lower figure shows the redundancy, computed with standard BP and the weight decay. The redundancy, computed with standard BP is decreased very slowly. On the other hand, the redundancy, computed with the weight decay, is quickly decreased. Thus, these results show that the generalization errors are in direct proportion to the redundancy and the weight decay is a method to decrease the redundancy.

4   Conclusion

In the present paper, we have attempted to show that the redundancy is decreased by using the weight decay method and the weight decay method is only a method to minimize the redundancy in neural networks. The weight decay is a popular method to improve the generalization. However, we have observed that there are some cases in which the decay method is not so effective. In these cases, we think that the direct redundancy reduction with the weight decay method is effective in improving the generalization performance.

References

[1] R. A. Jacobs and M. I. Jordan, "Computational consequences of a bias toward short connections," *Journal of cognitive neuroscience*, Vol.4, No.4, pp323-336, 1992.

[2] H. H Thodberg, "Improving generalization of neural networks through pruning," *International Journal of Neural Systems*, Vol.1, No.4, pp.317-326, 1991.

[3] A. Krogh and J. A. Hertz, "A simple weight decay can improve generalization," in *Neural Information Processing Systems*, Morgan Kaufmann Publishers, San Mateo: CA, Vol.4, pp.950-957, 1992.

[4] V. A. Marchman, "Constraints on Plasticity in a Connectionist Model of the English Past Tense," *Journal of Cognitive Neuroscience*, Vol.5, No.2, pp.215-234, 1993.

[5] C. W. Omlin and C. L. Giles, "Pruning recurrent neural networks for improved generalization performance," Revised Technical Report No. 93-6, April 1993, Computer Science Department, Rensselaer Polytechnic Institute, Troy, N. Y.

[6] K. Plunkett, V. Marchman, and S. L. Knudsen, "From Rote Learning to System Building: Acquiring Verb Morphology in Children and Connectionist Nets," in *Connectionist Models: Proceedings of the 1990 Summer School*, D. S. Touretzky, J. L. Elman and G. E. Hinton, (Eds), Morgan Kaufmann Publishers, Inc, San Mateo: California, pp.201-219, 1990.

[7] D. E. Rumelhart and J. L. MacClelland, "On Learning the Past Tense of English Verbs," in *Parallel Distributed Processing*, J. L. MacClelland, D. E. Rumelhart and the PDP Research Group, The MIT Press, Cambridge: Massachusetts, pp.216-271, 1986.

[8] J. Sietsma and R. J. F. Dow, "Creating artificial neural networks that generalize," *Neural Networks*, Vol.4, pp.67-79, 1991.

[9] A. S. Weigend, D. E. Rumelhart, and B. A. Huberman, "Generalization by weight-elimination with application to forecasting," in *Neural Information Processing Systems*, Morgan Kaufmann Publishers, San Mateo: CA, Vol.4, pp.950-957, 1992.

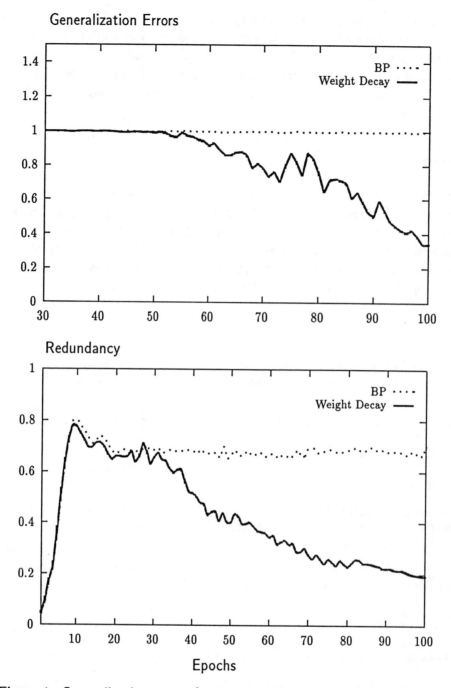

Figure 1: Generalization errors (upper figure) and Redundancy (lower figure), computed for the inference of regular verbs. The learning rate and the parameter λ for the weight decay were set to 0.1 and 0.005 respectively.

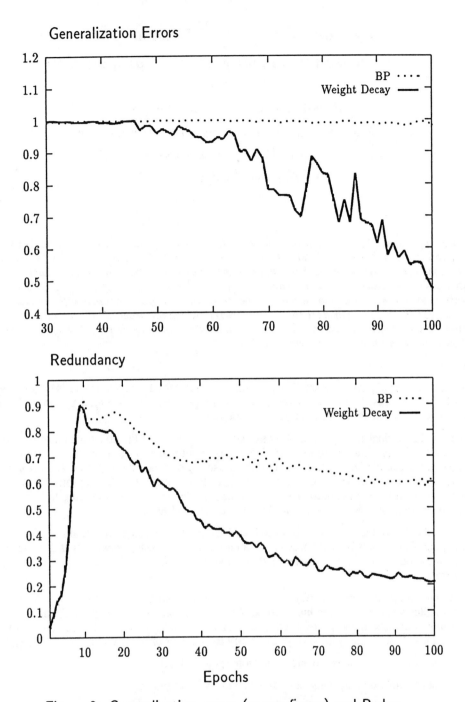

Figure 2: Generalization errors (upper figure) and Redundancy (lower figure), computed for the inference of regular and irregular verbs with grammatical determination. The learning rate and the parameter λ for the weight decay were set to 0.05 and 0.005 respectively.

Dynamic Creation of Hidden Units with Selective Pruning in Backpropagation

Siew-Foong Lim and Seng-Beng Ho

Department of Information Systems and Computer Science

National University of Singapore

Lower Kent Ridge Road, Singapore 0511

Republic of Singapore

Abstract: *Many approaches have been devised to vary the number of hidden units in a backpropagation-based neural network in a systematic way to obtain a more efficient network. This paper presents an approach that adds hidden units and then selectively removes them to determine a more efficient network for a particular problem. The addition phase adds hidden units one at a time until a convergence criterion is satisfied. The selective pruning process selects the least important hidden unit to be removed based on the weights associated with the hidden units. This is an improvement over a previous method (Hirose et. al. 1990) in which the order of hidden unit chosen for removal is fixed. Simulations using Boolean test cases were carried out on a backpropagation network with one hidden layer and the results show improvements over the previous method.*

1. Introduction

The backpropagation (BP) algorithm (Rumelhart, Hinton and Williams 1986; Webos 1974) opened a new way for training multi-layer networks. It provides a solution to some problems encountered by single layer perceptrons (Minsky and Papert 1988) and works well in many applications.

However, the original BP algorithm does not address the issue of the construction of the optimal network architecture necessary for the learning of the intended input-output mapping for a particular problem. In particular, the near-optimal number of hidden units in the network is usually obtained through trial-and-error experimentation which is ad hoc and often time-consuming. Some solutions to this problem have been proposed that involve the use of mechanisms that permit the network to grow and shrink, i.e., by creating or removing hidden unit(s) or hidden layer(s) during the process of training (e.g., Ash 1989; Hirose et. al. 1991).

An optimal network facilitates the construction of an internal representation that is appropriate for learning the desired mapping. This avoids both the problem of a larger than necessary network that does not generalize well (Denker et. al. 1987) and the problem of a network that is too small and that does not possess enough power to learn the mapping correctly.

Very often, an optimal network may be difficult to obtain, but a near-optimal network or a more efficient network with a smaller number of hidden units can be obtained through one of the methods that modify the number of hidden units in a systematic manner until such a network is found. These methods (e.g., Ash 1989; Hirose et. al. 1991; Sietma and Dow 1988) employ three ways to modify the number of hidden units:

    i)   start with fewer units and add some more (pure adding),

    ii)   start with too many units and take some away (pure pruning), or

    iii)   start with fewer units and after adding, take the redundant units away.

A pure adding approach, such as the Dynamic Node Creation method (Ash 1989), adds hidden units one at a time to the network. A certain desired accuracy of the network is specified and addition of a node is carried out when the accuracy is not reached and further training does not bring about any further improvement of the accuracy. This is repeated until the desired accuracy is achieved. Conversely, a pure pruning technique starts with a network that is larger than appropriate and removes redundant nodes (e.g., Sietma and Dow 1988).

Methods such as that of Hirose, Yamashita and Hijiya (Hirose et. al. 1991, henceforth referred to as the Hirose algorithm) combine addition and removal of hidden units. First, addition is carried out until the network has learnt a set of weights for the correct mapping. Any redundant units can then be pruned off to achieve a more efficient size. The most recently added hidden unit is chosen for removal first.

In a method that uses addition of hidden nodes followed by pruning of the network, an effective pruning technique is essential to ensure that no added hidden units are removed wrongly. This prevents extra effort that would be needed to retrain the network if important hidden units were wrongly pruned.This paper describes such an effective pruning approach in the context of an addition cum removal method that represents an improvement over the pruning method used in the Hirose algorithm.

We use the same method as that of the Hirose algorithm (described in Section 2) for the addition of hidden units. However, in the pruning phase, instead of using a fixed removal order for the hidden units (i.e., removing the most recently added hidden unit first) like in the Hirose algorithm, which could result in some problems as described in Section 3, our method selectively removes the hidden units based on their importance. This method is described in Section 4. Simulations with Boolean test cases were carried out in a network with one hidden layer and the results are presented in Sections 5 and 6.

2. The Hirose Algorithm

In the addition phase, the algorithm starts with one hidden unit. Weight corrections are the same as those in the BP algorithm. E, the total error between the target and the actual output is expressed as

$$E \ = \ \frac{1}{2} \sum_{p} \sum_{j} (t_{pj} - o_{pj})^2$$

where t_{pj} is the desired output of an output unit j for pattern p, o_{pj} is the actual output of output unit j for pattern p, and the sum is taken over the set of output units for the set of training patterns.

E is checked after every 100 weight corrections. If it decreases by less than 1% of its previous value (i.e., the error 100 weight corrections ago), a new hidden unit is added. However, if E decreases by more than 1%, no hidden unit is added and the weights are corrected another 100 times. The criterion for convergence is when E is less than 0.01.

When a new hidden unit is added, the initial weights between the added hidden unit and the other units in the input and output layers are assigned random values.

The algorithm enters the reduction phase as soon as the network converges. The most recently added hidden unit is removed. Training continues with the pruned network. If the hidden network converges again, another hidden unit is removed. This procedure is repeated until the network no longer converges, whereby the algorithm judges the present network to be incapable of learning the mapping. Hence the required number of hidden units is one plus the present number of hidden units.

3. Effects of Order of Removal in Hirose Algorithm

In the Hirose algorithm, the most recently added hidden unit is removed first. A question arises as to how the network's performance will be affected if another hidden unit is removed first instead.To answer that, we investigated the effect of changing the order of removal of hidden units using the PAR2 problem (parity problem with an input pattern of size 2, or XOR). The simulation resulted in 4 hidden units at the end of the addition phase. The weights of the network before the reduction phase are shown in Figure 1.

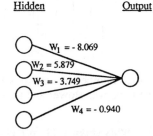

Hidden   Output

Figure 1. Weights between the hidden and output layer of a PAR2 simulation before reduction phase.

In one trial, the most recently added hidden unit was removed first and in another, the initial hidden unit that the network started with was removed first. The behaviors of the network are graphed in Figure 2 and Figure 3 respectively.

Both removals resulted in 2 hidden units. However, when the initial hidden unit was removed first (Figure 3), the network took more than twice as long a time than in the case of the other to converge before the next hidden unit could be removed. Also, the error after the removal of the first hidden unit rises to a much higher level compared to that in the case where the most recently added hidden unit was the first to be removed.

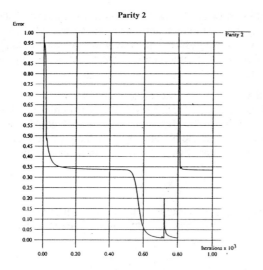

Figure 2. Graph of total error E versus the number of iterations for PAR2 when the 4th (most recently added) hidden unit was removed first. Hidden units were added at iterations 300, 400, and 500. Pruning took place at iterations 711, 723, and 800. The final architecture thus required 2 hidden units.

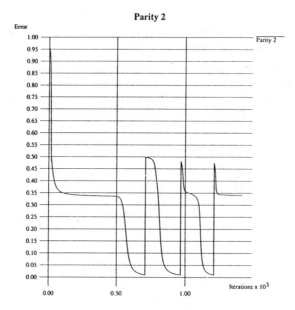

Figure 3. Graph of total error E versus the total number of iterations for PAR2 when the initial hidden unit was removed first. Removal of subsequent hidden units was slower and the errors immediately after the removal of the hidden units were higher.

Comparing the absolute values of weights (Figure 1), W1 is the largest weight and W4 is the smallest compared to the rest of the weights. Thus, the first hidden unit is likely to be the most important hidden unit. In this example, the most recently added unit happened to be the least important unit. In general, this may not be the case. Hence, using a fixed removal order gives rise to the possibility of removing an important unit which contributes significantly to the input/output mapping. This results in the longer time needed for convergence. There is also the possibility that the removal of the wrong node would result in a less optimal network - i.e., one with more nodes than necessary.

4. Selective Pruning

We introduce a modified method called *selective pruning* that improves on the fixed removal order method by taking into consideration the magnitudes of the weights between the hidden and output layer before pruning.

The idea of selective pruning is to remove the hidden unit that contributes the smallest total weight to the output units. That is, the hidden unit corresponding to

$$\min_{i} \left(\sum_{j}^{H} | w_{ji} | \right)$$

is pruned, where wji is the weight associated with the connection between a hidden unit i and the output unit j, and H is the total number of hidden units.

The absolute value of each weight is considered since it is undesirable to remove a hidden unit with a large negative weight (as well as one with a large positive weight) since this weight contributes significantly to the inhibitory signal sent to the output node.

The selective pruning technique involves three steps:

1) Remove the hidden unit with the smallest sum of absolute weights associated with the connections to the output units. This sum is computed according to Eq 1.

2) Train the network with the remaining hidden units.

3) Repeat 1) and 2) until the network can no longer converge.

5. Simulations Results Obtained for PAR4

Figures 4 and 5 illustrate the results obtained with PAR4 (parity problem with input pattern size 4) using the Hirose fixed pruning method and the selective pruning method respectively. Both simulations were based on the same set of initial weights.

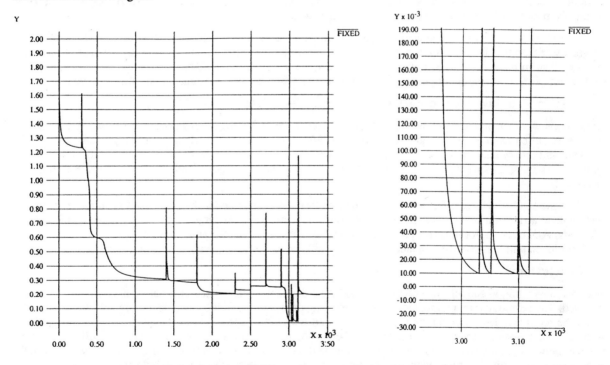

Figure 4. Fixed Pruning applied to PAR4. 8 hidden units were added and 3 hidden units were removed. The graph on the right shows an enlarged portion of the pruning process.

III-495

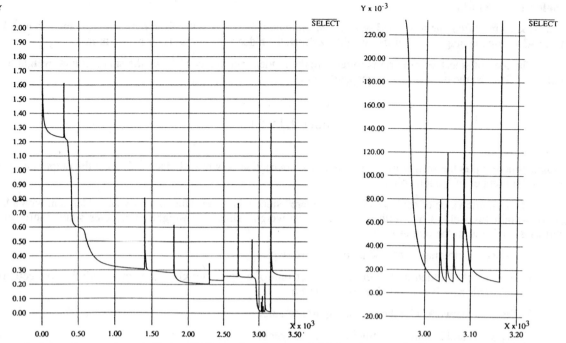

Figure 5. Selective pruning applied to PAR4, using the same initial weights as in Figure 4. 4 units were pruned. The graph on the right shows an enlarged portion of the pruning process.

In both simulations, 8 hidden units were added. Selective pruning removed 4 hidden units, in contrast to Hirose fixed pruning which removed 3 hidden units. The enlarged portions of both pruning processes show that within the same 100 iterations, selective pruning removed more hidden units, compared to Hirose fixed pruning. Hence, the removal of subsequent hidden units is faster in selective pruning.

Also, the figures show that with selective pruning, the error immediately after pruning a hidden unit rose to a level lower than that in fixed pruning. This is because the unit removed in selective pruning contributed less to the mapping than in the case of fixed pruning. Thus these two illustrations show that selective pruning removes *more* hidden units *faster* without driving the error up, due to the fact that the correct redundant unit was removed.

6. Selective Pruning Applied to Other Boolean Test Cases

Simulations were carried to test how well selective pruning works for the other Boolean test cases. Boolean tests cases were culled from Rumelhart and McClelland (1986, chapter 8). These include the parity, symmetry, encoder problem, and binary addtion with carry. A total of 50 trials were carried out for the same set of initial weights in the range (-1, 1) using learning rate 0.7 and momentum 0.7. The average number of hidden units arrived at is tabulated in Table 1.

The table shows that the selective pruning method performed better than the fixed pruning procedure in being able to arrive at a smaller number of hidden units on the average. The largest improvements are in the cases of PAR6 and ADD3. Also, for selective pruning, removing of subsequent hidden units took place very much faster after the first hidden unit was removed. In many cases. this could be as fast as requiring only 1 or 2 iterations.

7. Conclusions

In a combined addition and selective pruning method the redundant hidden units added during the training process are removed. The selective pruning method considers the magnitudes of the trained weights before selecting the hidden unit to be removed. The method removes the hidden unit with the smallest total of the absolute weights associated with the connections to the output units. This has been shown to 1) remove more hidden units, resulting in a more efficient network; 2) increase the likelihood that redundant hidden units are removed, and consequently 3) reduce the effort needed to retrain the pruned network which results in faster removal of subsequent hidden units.

The above method overcomes the problems faced by a method that uses a fixed removal order of hidden units. For more complex architectures consisting of more hidden units and more weight corrections, removing the "right" hidden units is especially important. Rather than removing the hidden units in a fixed manner, it would be more efficient if the algorithm is capable of removing redundant hidden units in a non-arbitrary and effective manner.

	Fixed Pruning	Selective Pruning
PAR2	2.08	2.02
PAR4	4.94	4.34
PAR5	6.46	5.31
PAR6	12.60	8.20
SYM4	3.04	2.94
SYM6	2.33	2.02
ADD2	4.03	4.00
ADD3	9.15	8.77
ENC16	4.00	4.00

Table 1. Average number of hidden units for Hirose fixed pruning method (in which the most recently added hidden unit is removed) and selective pruning method (in which the hidden unit with the smallest total of the absolute weights associated with all its connections to the output units is removed). Both simulations were based on the *same* set of initial weights in the range (-1, 1).

References

Ash, T. (1989) Dynamic node creation. *Connection Science,* 1(4), 365-375.

Denker, J., Schwartz. D., Wittner, B., Solla, S., Howard, R., Jackel, R. and Hopfield, J. (1987) Large Automatic learning, rule extraction and generalization. *Complex Systems I,* 877-922.

Hirose, Y., Yamashita, K. and Hijiya S. (1991) Backpropagation algorithm which varies the number of hidden units. *Neural Networks,* **4,** 61-66.

Minsky, M. and Papert, S. (1988) *Perceptrons.* Cambridge, MA: MIT Press.

Rumelhart, D.E., Hinton, G.E. and Williams, R.J. (1986) Learning internal representations by error propagation. In J.L. McClelland, R.E. Rumelhart and the PDP Research Group (eds.), *Parallel Distributed Processing, Vol 1.* Cambridge, MA: MIT Press.

Sietma, J. and Dow, R. (1988) Neural net pruning - why and how. *Proceedings of IEEE International Conference on Neural Networks,* **I,** 325-333.

Webos, P.J. (1974) *Beyond Regression: New Tools for Prediction and Analysis in the Behavioral Sciences.* Ph.D. Thesis, Harvard University.

A Self-Pruning Constructive Algorithm Based on Linear-Programming

F. M. Frattale Mascioli & G. Martinelli
INFO-COM Dept. - University of Rome
Mail Address: INFO-COM Dept.; via Eudossiana, 18; 00184 Roma - ITALY
Telephone: + 39-6-44585488/9; Fax: + 39-6-4873300
e-mail: mascioli@infocom.ing.uniroma1.it

Abstract— A constructive training algorithm for supervised neural network, based on a linear-programming procedure, is presented. It builds two-layer single-output networks that implement any consistent training set of binary or real-valued examples. The algorithm can incorporate a self-pruning technique; in fact it can determine the percentage variation of the examples which are satisfied by the construction of any further hidden neuron. Simulations show satisfactory results.

1   Introduction

In the present paper we propose a constructive training algorithm for supervised single hidden layer neural networks. The algorithm is guaranteed to implement any consistent training set of binary or real-valued examples classified into two classes. It extends the constructive algorithm based on a linear-programming approach presented in ref. [1] and results similar to the 'sequential' training algorithm of Marchand *et al.* [2], without the restriction of binary input only. Our approach is based on the following remarks:

1) For classification problems on a point set, it is known that a single hidden layer is sufficient to implement any task [3]. In fact, the hidden neurons define the hyperplanes which separate the decision region that is an approximate version of the true decision region for the problem;

2) Hyperplanes coincident or very close to the previous ones are determined step-by-step by means of a procedure inspired by the 'simplex method';

3) Our constructive algorithm is inherently self-pruning, since it is able to measure the importance of each hyperplane to the total solution of the given problem. Therefore, we have all the information necessary for applying a simple and effective pruning of the neurons and for obtaining a simultaneous control of the resulting generalization capability of the net.

2   The Proposed Algorithm

The proposed algorithm is based on the constructive procedure described in ref. [1]. That procedure builds a cascade scheme which satisfies all the examples of a training set by a suitable number of neurons. In order to understand the method, it is necessary to summarize the procedure followed in determining the cascade. Let us denote by type 1 and 0 respectively the examples of the training set belonging to the two possible classes. In correspondence to step k, the k-th neuron of the cascade is determined by carrying out the three following substeps:

i) determination of the residual training set. The number of examples decreases at each step (i.e., we have a convergence to zero-errors);

ii) determination of the hyperplane in the input space, which allows to correctly classify all the examples of one type and the maximum number of the other type. This substep is carried out by a linear programming procedure based on the simplex method. Namely, at each application of the procedure a 'feasible set' of the linear inequalities, that correspond to the training examples suitably modified, is found;

iii) determination of the connection weights and the threshold of the k-th neuron from the previous hyperplane.

The cascade obtained at the end of the k-th step satisfies a certain percentage of examples of the original training set, say P_k. It is important to note that $P_k \geq P_{k-1}$.

The proposed method builds a single hidden layer network by means of two applications of the previously described procedure. It starts by applying this procedure to the given training set. The neurons of the resulting cascade, with the same connection weights and thresholds, constitute the first layer of the neural network we are constructing. Some of these neurons can be eliminated by the pruning technique discussed in sect. 3. Then, we determine the outputs of the neurons of the first layer corresponding to all the inputs of the original training set. These outputs take on the values {1,0} since the activation function of the neurons of the cascade is hard. The set of input-output pairs identified by the calculated outputs of the first layer neurons (as inputs for the second layer) and by the original desired outputs constitutes a new binary training set. Since it is always possible to solve a classification problem on a point set by only one hidden layer, the new training set is characterized by linearly separable binary examples. Hence, a second application of the linear-programming procedure on this linearly separable training set constructs a single neuron that constitutes the second layer of the network.

3   Pruning and Generalization Capability

The generalization capability of the two-layer network regards its operation with respect to examples outside the training set. It can be strongly hampered by wrong examples present in the training set, since the training algorithm will try to accommodate them in contrast with the remaining ones. Consequently, a robust training algorithm should be able to detect wrong examples and to neglet them.

The algorithm proposed in the present paper can be easily tailored to incorporate this performance, since it is possible to measure the importance of each neuron to the formation of the decision region. In fact, when we apply the cascade procedure for determining the hidden layer, we can simultaneously determine the percentage variation of the training examples which are satisfied by the addition of any further neuron. It is evident that, when the percentage is very close to 100%, the remaining examples to be satisfied are very different from the previous already satisfied. This difference is usually due just to the presence of wrong examples. A reasonable strategy in this case is consequently to prune away the final neurons of the cascade by retaining only those which guarantee a desired threshold on the percentage of satisfied examples.

As an illustration of this point, we consider the simple case of classifying two regions in a plane separated by a straight line. The training set is constituted by examples concerning with 18 points uniformly located in the first region and other 18 similarly located in the other region. One of those examples is then set to the wrong label. In Fig. 1 these points are represented by black or white dots together with the lines corresponding to the neurons which the cascade procedure successively determines. The lines are labelled 'a', 'b', and 'c' in order of succession. We see from the figure that line 'a' is such that the points are correctly classified independently from the error. The first neuron of the cascade attains a percentage of correct classification equal to 97,2% (35 over 36 examples of the training set). This percentage does not vary when a further neuron is added. In fact, the line corresponding to this neuron, i.e. 'b', is not sufficient to separate the wrong point. Only where we add the last neuron, which introduces line 'c', the percentage rises to 100%. However, it is evident the overfitting operated by the cascade algorithm, when we try to arrive to a zero-error solution. It is also clear the simple and effective pruning technique which we can implement by controlling the percentage of training examples satisfied by the cascade scheme during its construction. It is sufficient to stop the construction by pruning away the successive neurons, when the percentage of satisfied examples attains a suitable threshold.

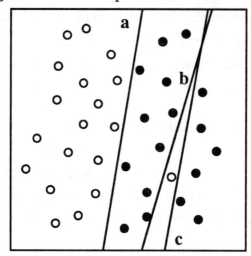

Fig. 1: Example related to the adopted pruning technique (classification on a set of 36 points).

4   Simulations

In order to illustrate the proposed algorithm, we will describe in the following simulations both with binary examples and with real-valued ones.

Random Boolean functions: To test the robustness of the algorithm, we have generated at random 100 Boolean functions on 6 input bits. As expected, a single hidden layer network was always found. The average number of hidden neurons found was 7.37±1.06, which is very close to the one obtained by Marchand *et al*. [2] (7.28±0.82) and significantly better than the results reported in ref. [4] (20.5±3.9) and [5] (about 18 units in 4 layers).

Parity functions: We remark that, in the case of Parity functions (tested from N=2 to N=8), the algorithm constructed networks with a number of hidden neurons equal to $\lceil N/2+1 \rceil$. The only algorithm with a similar performance, that we aware of, is Cascade-Correlation [6].

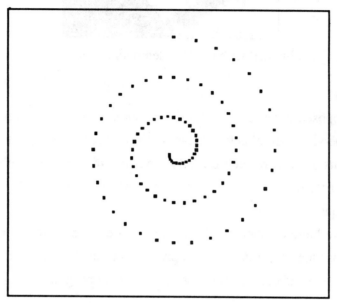

Fig. 2: The twin spirals problem training set (194 pixels distributed in two interlocking spirals).

Twin spirals: The twin spirals problem (separating 194 points from two interlocking spirals, see Fig. 2) requires a highly nonlinear classification of real-valued patterns; therefore is an extremely hard problem for algorithms of the Back-Propagation family to solve [7]. The proposed algorithm found a solution with 20 hidden neurons. We consider to be satisfactory the resulting decision region (see Fig. 3) The time required for building the network (with a 486-based computer) was less than five minutes. We note that a solution of the same problem with Cascade-Correlation [6] and Upstart [8] required about one hour of elaboration time in the same conditions. Finally, we remark that the only other solution to twin spirals in a single hidden layer architecture, that we are aware of, has 50 hidden units [9].

Fig. 3: The decision region obtained with a 20 hidden neurons network.

5   Conclusions

By relying on the proposed constructive algorithm, some of the inconveniences impairing the determination of a supervised neural network can be circumvent. In particular, the architecture and the connection weights are determined directly from the training set without trials and time-consuming iterative procedures. Also the generalization capability can be controlled by a very simple pruning technique.

In the present case we have considered the cascade procedure which is based on a modified simplex method. Consequently, a possible improvement can be obtained by using the neural networks proposed in the technical literature for solving linear programming [10—12].

Acknowledgements— This work was supported by MURST and CNR. The authors thank G. Demurtas for experimental co-operation.

References

[1] G. Martinelli, F.M. Mascioli: *"Cascade perceptron"*, IEE Electronics Letters, Vol. 28, pp. 947-949, 1992.

[2] M. Marchand, M. Golea, and P. Rujàn: *"A convergence theorem for sequential training in two-layer perceptrons"*, Europhysics Letters, Vol. 11, 1990, pp. 487-492.

[3] S.C. Huang, Y.F. Huang: *"Bound on the number of hidden neurons in multilayer perceptrons"*, IEEE Trans. on NN, Vol. 2, 1991, pp. 47-55.

[4] M. Golea and M. Marchand: *"A growth algorithm for neural network decision trees"*, Europhys Lett., 12, 1990, pp. 205-210.

[5] M. Mezard and J.P. Nadal: *"Training in feedforward layered networks: the tiling algorithm"*, J. Phys. A, 22, 1989, pp. 2191-2203.

[6] S.E. Fahlman, C. Lebiere: *"The cascade-correlation training architecture"*, Adv. in Neur. Inf. Proc. Sys. 2, D.S. Touretzky, Los Altos, Morgan-Kaufman, 1990, pp. 524-532.

[7] K.J. Lang and M.J. Witbrock: *"Training to tell two spirals apart"*, Proc. of the 1988 Connectionist Models Summer School, Morgan Kaufmann, 1988.

[8] M. Frean: *"The upstart algorithm: a method for constructing and training feedforward neural networks"*, Neural Computation, Vol. 2, 1990, pp. 198-209.

[9] E.B. Baum and K.J. Lang: *"Constructing hidden units using examples and queries"*, NIPS3, 1990, pp. 904-910.

[10] D.W. Tank, J.J. Hopfield: *"Simple neural optimization networks: an A/D converter, signal decision circuits and a linear programming circuit"*, IEEE Trans. on CAS, Vol. 22, 1986, pp. 533-541.

[11] A. Rodrigues-Vasquez, et alii: *"Switched-capacitor neural networks for linear programming"*, Electronics Letters, Vol. 24, 1988, pp. 496-498.

[12] A. Cichocki, R. Umbehanen: *"Neural networks for solving systems of linear equations and related problems"*, IEEE Trans. on CAS - I:FTA, Vol. 39, 1992, pp. 124-138.

Aspects of Generalization and Pruning

Jan Depenau and Martin Møller

TERMA Electronik AS, Hovmarken 4 , DK-8520 Lystrup, Denmark

and

DAIMI, Computer Science Department, Aarhus University,

Ny Munkegade, Bldg. 540, DK-8000 Aarhus C, Denmark

Abstract

It is well known that the generalization ability of a neural network can be improved by reducing the network's complexity. Pruning methods based on the idea of eliminating weights of a well working feed-forward network have proved to be successful. The theoretical background of pruning is established through a mathematical model of generalization. A short description of three of the most popular pruning methods, Optimal Brain Surgeon (OBS) [Hassibi et al. 93], Optimal Brain Damage (OBS) [LeCun et al. 90] and Magnitude Based Pruning (MAG) is given. These three methods have experimentally been tested on standard benchmark problems known as the MONK's problems [Thrun et al. 91]. It is shown that there is no theoretical evidence for choosing one of the methods compared to the other. This was confirmed by the experiments showing that all methods were capable of reducing the number of weights of a well working network, but none of the methods was the best every time. However, OBS was the most robust, stable and fastest method although it could be caught in a local minimum. Both MAG and OBD showed a fluctuating performance according to number of weights they could remove when the initialized conditions or learning parameters were changed.

1 Introduction

The main goal with a neural network classifier is to get a system that is able to classify unknown data correctly, i.e. a system with a good generalization ability. Vapnik (1992) and many others have shown the relation between the capacity of a network and its generalization ability. Further it is also known that the capacity of a feed-forward network somehow is related to the number of units and weights in a network. But it is often impossible to determine the exact capacity of a neural network. In order to overcome this problem various, more or less mathematically based, methods have been proposed. A group of methods focus on successively building a network while others try to reduce the number of units or weights in a well working network. This paper focuses on the latter group of methods known as prunings. Through a description of generalization the foundation of pruning is established. Three of the most popular methods are described and tested on a benchmark problem.

2 Learning and Generalization

This section describes generalization and how it is related to a feed-forward network. The learning paradigm considered here is supervised learning. The error between the output $\mathbf{y} = f_w(\mathbf{x})$ and the desired output $\mathbf{t} = f^d(\mathbf{x})$ is normally calculated by an error function $E(\mathbf{y}, \mathbf{t})$ often, but not necessarily, the Least Mean Square error between $\mathbf{y}$ and $\mathbf{t}$. Hence **bold** script will denote a vector or a matrix. The learning error on a set of known data, the training set $\{\mathbf{x}_i, \mathbf{t}_i\}, 1 \le i \le m$, is defined as

$$E_L(\mathbf{W}) = \frac{1}{m} \sum_{i=1}^{m} E(\mathbf{y}_i, \mathbf{t}_i) \tag{1}$$

and measures the dissimilarity between f_w and f^d, within the restricted domain of input patterns in the training set. Note that it is a function of weights in the weight space $\mathbf{W}$.

However, the error of interest is the expected error on unknown data, the test set. This error is called the generalization error and is defined as an average over the full distribution of input-output pairs, and can be expressed as:

$$E_G(\mathbf{W}) = \int E(\mathbf{y}_i, \mathbf{t}_i) P(\mathbf{x}, \mathbf{t}) d\mathbf{x} d\mathbf{t}. \tag{2}$$

where $P(\mathbf{x}, \mathbf{t})$ is the joint probability distribution formed by $P(\mathbf{x})$ describing the distribution of data in the input space and $P(\mathbf{t}|\mathbf{x})$ describing the functional dependence, so $P(\mathbf{x}, \mathbf{t}) = P(\mathbf{t}|\mathbf{x}) P(\mathbf{x})$. The generalization error is the expectation value of error for an arbitrary $(\mathbf{x}, \mathbf{t})$ point drawn from the $P(\mathbf{x}, \mathbf{t})$ distribution.

The real goal of learning is to minimize the generalization error. But the joint probability distribution $P(\mathbf{x}, \mathbf{t})$ is unknown and the only available information is contained in the training set. In order to solve this problem the generalization error is replaced by the learning error, computed empirically on the basis of data available in the form of a training set.

For simplicity the following description is restricted to the binary case, where data from an N-dimensional space are to be classified as belonging to one out of two possible classes. This means that $\mathbf{y} \in \{0, 1\}$ and that the mapping function f_w is an indicator function. The error function $E(\mathbf{t}, \mathbf{y})$ is also assumed to be an indicator function. This means that $E(\mathbf{t}, \mathbf{y}) = 0$ if $f_w(\mathbf{x}) = \mathbf{t}$, and $E(\mathbf{t}, \mathbf{y}) = 1$ otherwise, so $E_G(\mathbf{W})$ is the probability of error, and $E_L(\mathbf{W})$ is the frequency of error on the training set.

Inspired by the Bernoulli theorem Vapnik (1982;1992) found that with a probability larger than $(1 - \eta)$, simultaneously for all possible configurations $\{\mathbf{W}\}$ the following relation between $E_G(\mathbf{W})$ and $E_L(\mathbf{W})$ independent of $P(\mathbf{x}, \mathbf{t})$ would be valid:

$$E_G(\mathbf{W}) \le E_L(\mathbf{W}) + C(\frac{m}{h}, E_L, \eta) \tag{3}$$

where $C(\frac{m}{h}, E_L, \eta)$ is a confidence interval, a function which depends on m, the number of training patterns, h the capacity of the network, E_L the learning error and η the accuracy parameter corresponding to the probability. The confidence interval is defined as:

$$C(\frac{m}{h}, E_L, \eta) = 2\Psi(\frac{m}{h}, \eta) \left(1 + \sqrt{\frac{E_L}{1 + \Psi(\frac{m}{h}, \eta)}}\right), \tag{4}$$

where

$$\Psi(\frac{m}{h}, \eta) = \frac{1}{m} \left((\ln 2\frac{m}{h} + 1)h - \ln \eta\right)$$

is essentially a function of the ratio $\frac{m}{h}$.

The only unknown parameter at this point is the capacity h, known as the VC-dimension. This parameter is very important because it is related to the architecture of the network. The capacity for a feed-forward network will correspond to the number of units and number of weights and thresholds (Baum et al. 89).

The size of m, the data in the training set will normally be limited by the problem domain or by the supervisor in order to learn something in a reasonable time. For a fixed number m, the learning error will decrease monotonically as the capacity h increases. Unfortunately the confidence interval of equation (4) is a monotonically increasing function of h at a fixed m. This indicates that there will be an optimal h_{opt} where the generalization error will have a minimum. If an optimal capacity h_{opt} of the network could be found, the number of units and the number of weights and thresholds would be known. So far nothing is said about the values of these parameters. It seems likely that there will be several weight constellations W_i from W that could implement the desired function. This corresponds to the curve-fitting situations where it is known that an n- polynomial to some extent would fit points from a N-polynomial where $N \gg n$. It would be possible to find several coefficient constellations that would be equally valid. This was confirmed by Denker et al.(1988) in what they call a perturbation analysis. They took a well working network ($E_L = 0$), and perturbed the network, moving the weights to a new point in the weight space, and re-trained it. They found that the network was quite able to re-solve the task, returning to $E_L = 0$, but did not do so by undoing the perturbation. In fact, it moved in some other direction and settled on a new point W_i in the weight space.

A class of experimental methods used to find a h close to the optimal h_{opt} is known as pruning and will be described in the next section.

3   The theory and ideas behind pruning

The main idea behind all pruning methods is to keep the learning error $E_L(W)$ for a well working feed-forward network as low as possible and at the same time to reduce the complexity i.e. number of weights.

One of the simplest methods for reducing the complexity in a neural network is called Magnitude Based pruning (MAG). The method is based on the idea of eliminating the weakest connection, i.e. the weight with the smallest magnitude. For the simplest MAG version the algorithm is: *delete the weight with smallest magnitude and retrain the network, repeat until a certain stop criterion is fulfilled.* There are several more or less sophisticated versions of this method. A widely used form is the weight decay (Herzt et al.) gradually decreasing the magnitude of the weights doing training (not necessarily eliminating any weights).

The next two methods called Optimal Brain Damage (OBD) and Optimal Brain Surgeon (OBS) have a more mathematical approach using information from the second order derivatives of the error function to perform pruning. They both use the Taylor expansion to express an estimate of how the training error will change as the weights are perturbed.

$$\delta E_T \approx \sum_i \mathbf{G}_i \delta \mathbf{w}_i + \sum_i \frac{1}{2} \delta \mathbf{H}_{ii} \delta \mathbf{w}_i^2 + \sum_{i \neq j} \frac{1}{2} \mathbf{H}_{ij} \delta \mathbf{w}_i \delta \mathbf{w}_j + (\|\mathbf{W}\|^3)$$

where $\mathbf{G}$ is the gradient $\frac{\partial E_T}{\partial w_i}$ and $\mathbf{H}$ is the hessian $\frac{\partial^2 E_T}{\partial w_i \partial w_j}$.

Both methods make the assumptions that the network is trained to a point where the gradient is zero so the first term in the equation can be neglected and that the "quadratic" approximation assumed that the cost function is nearly quadratic also holds so that the last term in the equation can be neglected.

The OBD method additionally assumes that δE caused by deleting several parameters is the sum of the δE's caused by deleting each parameter individually so the off-diagonal part of the second order term is zero. The equation is then reduced to

$$\delta E_L = \frac{1}{2}\delta \mathbf{H}_{ii}\delta \mathbf{w}_i^2$$

The δE_L term is called saliency and expresses the change in the cost function due to the eliminations of weights. The algorithm is: *delete the weight with smallest saliency and retrain the network, repeat until a certain stop criterion is fulfilled.*

The OBS does not assume that the off-diagonal of the Hessian is zero. Instead it reformulates the goal. The elimination of $\mathbf{w}_j$ can be expressed as: $\delta \mathbf{w}_j + \mathbf{w}_j = 0$ or $\mathbf{e}_j^T \delta \mathbf{w} + \mathbf{w}_j = 0$ where e_j is the unit vector in the weight space corresponding to (scala) weight $\mathbf{w}_j$. The goal is then to solve:

$$\min_j \left(\min_{\delta \mathbf{w}}(\frac{1}{2}\delta \mathbf{w}_j^T \mathbf{H} \delta \mathbf{w}_j) \right) \quad ; \text{ such that } \quad \mathbf{e}_j^T \delta \mathbf{w} + \mathbf{w}_j = 0$$

or expressed in terms of Lagrange Multiplier

$$\delta E_L = \frac{1}{2}\delta \mathbf{w}_j^T \mathbf{H} \delta \mathbf{w}_j + \lambda(\mathbf{e}_j^T \delta \mathbf{w} + \mathbf{w}_j)$$

By taking functional derivatives the foll owing equations appear:

$$\delta \mathbf{w} = (\frac{\mathbf{w}_j}{\mathbf{H}_{jj}^{-1}})\mathbf{H}^{-1}\delta \mathbf{e}_j^T \quad \text{and} \quad \delta E_L = \frac{1}{2}(\frac{\mathbf{w}_j^2}{\mathbf{H}_{jj}^{-1}})$$

The δE_L term is again called saliency and expresses the change in the cost function due to the eliminations of weights. The $\delta \mathbf{w}$ indicates how all weights should be adjusted, according to the elimination of a weight. This means that the network does not demand retraining. The only "learning" parameter involved is an α which comes from using a particular data vector and the Sherman-Morrison formular in calculations of the Invers Hessian. The algorithm is: *delete the weight with smallest saliency and adjust the other weights according to $\delta \mathbf{w}$, repeat until a certain stop criterion is satisfied.*

4 Test and experiments

The three methods were tested on the MONK's problems (Thrun et al. 1991). They designed 3 fully connected networks trained by a backpropagation with weight decay (BPWD) that outperformed all other approaches (network and rule-based) on these problems in an extensive machine learning competition. The goal here was to find how many weights could be eliminated by the different methods and still perform as well as Thrun et al. did. The result from these experiments is shown in table 1.

Comment to MONK 1: The MAG used a standard backpropagation with weight decay with learning rate $\eta = 0.1$ and decay rate $\gamma = 0.00001$. It needed only 3 epochs to perform as well as the OBS and was better with 22 epochs. The OBD used the same learning procedure as MAG with learning rate $\eta = 0.1$ and decay rate $\gamma = 0.0001$, but needed 300 epochs to perform as well as the MAG. Both methods were, however, highly sensitive to changes in the learning parameters (Epochs, η, γ). This is contrary to OBS, which shows the same performance as long as α was kept between 10^{-3} and 10^{-7}.

Comment to MONK 2 and MONK 3: The learning parameters for MAG and OBD were respectively: epochs = 10, $\eta = 0.1$ and $\gamma = 10^{-6}$ and epochs = 100, $\eta = 0.1$ and $\gamma = 10^{-4}$. Other

	BPWD	MAG	OBD	OBS
MONK 1	58	13	13	14
MONK 2	39	15	26	15
MONK 3	39	6	9	4

Table 1: Number of weights needed for MAG, OBD and OBS to make the same performance as the Backpropagation with weight decay (BPWD) found by Thrun et al.(1991), on the MONK's problems.

combinations of learning parameters were tried but the best performance was obtained with the above-mentioned parameters. The result with these parameters is shown in table 1. It will be possible to optimize their performance, by training other parameter combinations.

Many similar tests were made on these MONK's problem given new start conditions. The new start conditions were created by training the original network from random weights so the weight-start-position of the test network would differ from test to test.

The result was the same, all methods were capable of reducing the number of weights, and none of the methods was the best every time. Adjusting the parameters in the learning algorithm, MAG and OBD performed as well as the OBS and sometimes better. However, OBS was by far the most robust, stable and fastest method.

5 Discussion and Conclusion

In section 2 it was shown that there could be many possible weight constellations (points in the weight space) that would yield equally valid generalizations for an optimal or nearly optimal capacity.

Although OBD and OBS have established a mathematical foundation to get a good estimate of the saliency, they still do not make a quantitative statement of how well they improve the generalization. From equation (3) it can be justified that they will improve the generalization. The same is also true for the magnitude based method. So it seems there is no theoretical evidence that one method will improve the generalization more than the other. Experimentally this was confirmed by showing that there were several optimal solutions to the same problem.

But the experiments also showed that OBS was by far the most stable and robust. If it was not the best it was always close to the best. The way OBS works is that it will stay close to the local minimum from where it begins the pruning, try to remove one weight and then project the error surface to a space one dimension smaller that the previous. This means that it will stay at the same local minimum error in the surface. This will work very well as long as the local minimum from where OBS starts is close to the global minimum. But if the original (start) minimum error is not the smallest local error OBS will never find this point because it does not retrain. Both OBD and MAG will be able to find such new local minimum all depending of their learning algorithm. Hassibi et al. (1992) has shown through an example of a 5 node solution to the XOR problem that only the OBS will always be able to remove the right weight while both OBD and especially MAG often fails to do so. The reason OBS works perfectly here is that the minimum error at the start is equal to the global minimum. This is often the case for smaller networks and OBS will probably be the best in these cases.

The general problem with the strategies used by MAG and OBD is that they are one step predictors, which means that they take one "optimal" step, recalculate the conditions and take another "optimal" step. There are no guaranties that these two steps together are optimal. How optimal the steps are all together will depend on the recalculations of the conditions which are directly dependent on the learning algorithm and its parameters. These methods are therefore unstable. This explains how both MAG and OBD were able to perform better than OBS on the Monk 1 problem while OBS in general is more stable that the others.

To choose among these different methods, considerations of the memory requirement, computing time, etc. should be made. For real life application, where the complexity might be very large the following pruning scheme seems reasonable. Starting with MAG until the network has a size that will allow the use of OBS, and use some effort in order to find "good" local minimum. When such a minimum is found OBS should be used to do the rest of the pruning. When OBS stops the network should be retrained in order to get $\delta E = 0$ and OBS should be started again.

Acknowledgements

We thank Brian Mayoh for valuable comment to the draft version and Barka Hassibi for kindly providing us with his original OBS code. The first author is supported by TERMA Electronic AS and the Danish Academy of Technical Sciences (ATV).

References

[Baum et al. 89]   Baum, E.B. and D. Haussler (1989). What Size Net Gives Valid Generalization? Neural Computation 1 151-160.

[Denker et al. 87]   Denker, J., D. Schwartz, B. Wittner, S. Solla, R. Howard, L. Jackel, and J. Hopfield (1987). Large Automatic Learning, Rule Extraction, and Generalization Complex Systems 1 877-922.

[Hassibi et al. 93]   Hassibi, B, Stork, D. (1993). Second order derivatives for network pruning: Optimal Brain Surgeone. Advances in Neural Information Processing Systems V (Denver 1993). ed. S.J. Hanson et al., 164-171. San Mateo: Morgan Kaufmann.

[Hertz et al. 91]   Hertz, J. Krogh, A. and Palmer, R. (1991), Introduction to the Theory of Neural Computation. Addison Wesley: 115 - 162.

[Le Cun et al. 90]   Le Cun., J.S. Denker, and S.A. Sollar (1990). Optimal Brain Damage. Advances in Neural Information Pr ocessing Systems II (Denver 1989). ed. D.S. Touretzky, 598-605. San Mateo: Morgan Kaufmann.

[Thrun et al. 91]   Thrun, S.B. and 23 co-authors (1991). The MONK's Problems - A performance comparison of different learning algorithms, CMU-CS-91-197 Carnegie-Mellon U. Department of Computer Science Tech Report

[Vapnik 82]   Vapnik, V.N. (1982). Estimation of Dependences Based on Empirical Data. Berlin: Springer-Verlag.

[Vapnik 92]   Vapnik, V.N. (1992). Principles of Risk Minimization for Learning Theory Advances in Neural Information Processing Systems IV (Denver 1992). ed. J.E.Moddy et al., 831-838. San Mateo: Morgan Kaufmann.

Sequential Classification By Perceptrons and Application to Net Pruning of Multilayer Perceptron

Kou-Yuan Huang

Institute of Computer and Information Science
National Chiao Tung University, Hsinchu,
Taiwan, 30050, R.O.C.

Abstract

Using the important property of the approximating a posteriori probability functions of the classes in the outputs of the trained multilayer perceptrons, we propose the technique for the implementation of sequential classification by perceptron and multilayer perceptron, and application to the node growing in the number of input nodes of percetron and the number of hidden nodes of the multilayer perceptron. A measurement for the ordering of hidden nodes of the trained multilayer perceptron is also proposed. The ordering of the hidden nodes comes from the contribution of each hidden node. Using the node growing technique, the minimum number of hidden nodes can be obtained in the training and used in the classification. The technique can also apply to the single layer perceptron. In the experiment, the typical "XOR" problem is applied. The balance between the reduction of hidden nodes and classification results is quite good.

Introduction

When performing the back-propagation algorithm on multi-layer perception, the number of layers and the number of the hidden nodes in layers have to be determined. Related papers [1] have shown that the feed-forward networks with one hidden layer are capable of accurate approximation to an arbitrary mapping provided that sufficient hidden nodes are available. So two-layer perceptron is used in this study. Too many hidden nodes in the two-layer perceptron may take longer computation time. Too small hidden nodes may not slove the problem. As for how many nodes should be used in the hidden layer, no absolute criteria can be followed. It seems to depend on the problems to be confronted with.

One feasible method of obtaining a neural networks with an appropriate number of hidden nodes for a particular problem is to start with a larger net, then prune it to the desired size. Many previous issues of research has mentioned it [2]. Such a smaller net, owing to the reduction of synaptic connections, is more efficient in both forward computations and learning.

Sequential classification (SC) is quite important in statistical pattern recognition. Its application to pattern classification was mentioned by Fu [3], and could be employed widely to a number of fields such as industrial process and biomedical diagnosis. The property of keeping the balance between the misclassified error and the cost of feature measurements makes SC a feasible method with practical importance and theoretical interest. By taking feature measurements sequentially and terminating the sequential process (making a decision) when the proper stopping criterion is achieved, a desirable accuracy of classification can be obtained and the cost of taking feature measurements is also acceptable. In this study, SC schemes applied to back-propagation trained single-layer and two-layer perceptrons are proposed for dynamically pruning the network. The number of hidden nodes can be reduced. The minimum number of hidden nodes can also be determined.

Sequential Classification by Two-layer Perceptron

In this study, we adopt an important key property. The outputs of the output nodes of the multilayer perceptron are approximating the posteriori probability functions of the classes being trained [4], it can be seen that

$$O_i \approx P(\omega_i|X) \tag{1}$$

Here, O_1 and O_2 are the outputs of the first and second output nodes. ω_1 and ω_2 are the class 1 and 2. X is the input vector.

There are m output nodes in the output layer to denote the classes. At the n-th stage of the process, the vector H of the hidden nodes is $< h_1, h_2, \ldots, h_n >$. The graph representation of the n-th step in this sequential classification process is presented in Figure 1.

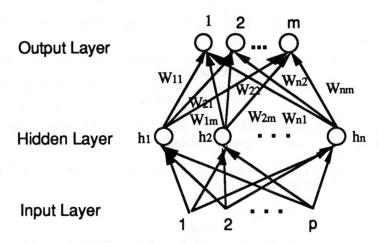

Figure 1 The n-th step in this sequential classification process.

The generalized sequential probability ratio $U_n(\omega_s|X)$ of taking n hidden nodes is computed as follows [3]:

$$U_n(\omega_s|X) = \frac{p_n(X|\omega_s)}{\left[\prod_{k=1}^{m} p_n(X|\omega_k)\right]^{\frac{1}{m}}} = \frac{p_n(\omega_s|X)p(X)/p(\omega_s)}{\left[\prod_{k=1}^{m} p_n(\omega_k|X)p(X)/p(\omega_k)\right]^{\frac{1}{m}}}$$

$$= \frac{\left[\prod_{k=1}^{m} p(\omega_k)\right]^{\frac{1}{m}}}{p(\omega_s)} \frac{p_n(\omega_s|X)}{\left[\prod_{k=1}^{m} p_n(\omega_k|X)\right]^{\frac{1}{m}}} \approx \frac{\left[\prod_{k=1}^{m} p(\omega_k)\right]^{\frac{1}{m}}}{p(\omega_s)} \frac{O_s}{\left[\prod_{k=1}^{m} O_k\right]^{\frac{1}{m}}} \tag{2}$$

Consider that the sigmoidal function is the activation function, then

$$U_n(\omega_s|X) \approx \frac{\left[\prod_{k=1}^{m} p(\omega_k)\right]^{\frac{1}{m}}}{p(\omega_s)} \frac{\left[\prod_{k=1}^{m} \left(1 + \exp\left(-\sum_{j=1}^{n} W_{jk}h_j - \theta_k\right)\right)\right]^{\frac{1}{m}}}{1 + \exp\left(-\sum_{j=1}^{n} W_{js}h_j - \theta_s\right)} \tag{3}$$

Where W_{jk} is the weight from the j-th hidden node to the k-th output node. h_j is the output of the j-th hidden node. θ_k is the bias of the k-th output node. And the modified stopping boundary is taken as

$$g_s(n) = \log \left(\frac{1 - e_{ss}}{\left[\prod_{k=1}^{m} (1 - e_{sk}) \right]^{\frac{1}{m}}} \right) \left(1 - \frac{n}{N} \right)^{r_s} \qquad (4)$$

Then, $\log U_n(\omega_s | X)$ is compared with the stopping boundary of the s-th pattern class, $g_s(n)$, if

$$\log U_n(\omega_s | X) < g_s(n), \quad s = 1, 2, ..., m \qquad (5)$$

X is not considered in the class ω_s. Repeat the rejection condition until one class is left. Then the pattern X is assigned to the class.

Algorithm 1
Sequential classification with growing of hidden nodes for m-class problem on two-layer network

Input : A back-propagation "trained" two-layer network with ordered hidden nodes and a set of "testing" patterns.

Output : The classification result of every testing pattern by sequential classification of MLP.

Step 1. Present an input pattern.
Present an input vector X in the input layer.

Step 2. Set the selected number of hidden nodes starting from one.
n=1, where n is the number of the seleted hidden nodes.

Step 3. Calculate the computed outputs through the selected hidden nodes.

Calculate the computed output of k-th output node from the n selected hidden nodes.

$$O_k = \frac{1}{1 + \exp(-\sum_{j}^{n} W_{jk} h_j - \theta_k)}$$

where W_{jk} is the weight between the j-th hidden node to the k-th output node. θ_k is the bias of the k-th output node.

Step 4. If a sufficient or desirable accuracy of classification is not achieved, add one hidden node and go to step 3.
Set class s = 1
repeat {
  Calculate the sequential probability ratio

$$U_n(\omega_s | X) \approx \frac{\left[\prod_{k=1}^{m} p(\omega_k) \right]^{\frac{1}{m}}}{p(\omega_s)} \frac{O_s}{\left[\prod_{k=1}^{m} O_k \right]^{\frac{1}{m}}}$$

  If $U_n(\omega_s | X) > g_s(n)$, go to step 5.
  else s=s+1
} until s > m

Add one hidden node, $n = n+1$ and go to step 3.
Step 5. Repeat by Going to Step 1. Go to step 1 until all the testing patterns are classified.

Ordering of Hidden Nodes on Neural Networks

In this study, differing from the K-L expansion method in feature ordering, a technique based on the property of neural networks is used. The hidden nodes of the two-layer perceptron, essentially, behave as the general feature extractors except for their non-linearities. A concept can be realized that a feature measurement is more important if it can separate more training samples. Hence the classification ability of a node can be measured depending on the separability of the training samples between their desired class and the others by just consider it in the layer.

For a two-layer perceptron in m-class case, consider that the activation function is a sigmoidal function, and the j-th hidden node has the classification error φ_{sjk} of the k-th output node for the s-th learning sample.

$$\varphi_{sjk} = D_k - \frac{1}{1 + \exp(-W_{jk}O_j + \theta_k)} \qquad (6)$$

Where D_k is the desired output of the training samples for the k-th output node. O_j is the output of the j-th hidden node. W_{jk} is the weight from the j-th hidden node to the k-th output node. θ_k is the bias (threshold) of the k-th output node. From (6), the j-th hidden node contributes the total mean square error ψ_j for all m output nodes. And from all n training sample, ψ_j is

$$\psi_j = \frac{1}{m \times n} \sum_{s=1}^{n} \sum_{k=1}^{m} \varphi_{sjk}^2 \qquad (7)$$

Sort the nodes and let $\psi_1 > \psi_2 > \cdots > \psi_h$, where h is the number of hidden nodes.

A node with small mean square error indicates that it is helpful to correct classification, while one with large mean square error shows the contrary. In the sequential classification process, the nodes should be taken according to the ascending order of their mean square error for the purpose of terminating the process earlier.

Experiments

The experiment is the classification of "XOR" problem. We use four training patterns to train this two-layer network. After back-propagation training, we take $100*100 = 10,000$ testing patterns for classification. They form a square in a two-dimensional space with their X and Y coordinates which are from (- 0.5, - 0.5) to (1.5, 1.5) and increase by 0.02. Through the SPRT procedure of the sequential classification, the used hidden nodes of 2-3-2 two-layer perceptron are shown in Table 1. The classification results for the 2-3-2, 2-4-2, 2-5-2, 2-6-2, 2-7-2, 2-8-2 and 2-9-2 two-layer perceptrons are shown in Figure 2. The overall reduction of the net size can be seen in Table 2.

Total No. of testing samples.	10000		
No. of hidden nodes used in the SPRT procedure.	1	2	3
No. of classified samples with used hidden nodes	4802	3685	1513
Average number of taken hidden nodes on the SPRT procedure.	1.6711		

Table 1 Used hidden nodes for 2-3-2 two-layer perceptron with sorted hidden nodes.

**2-3-2
(network)**

2-4-2

2-5-2

2-6-2

2-7-2

2-8-2

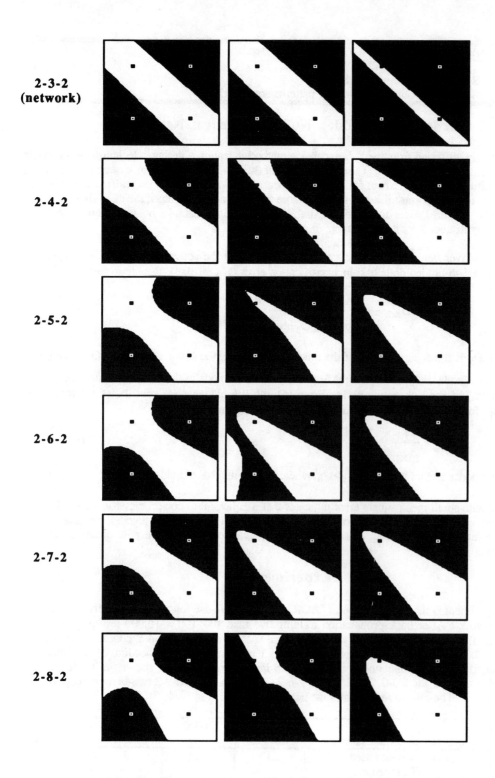

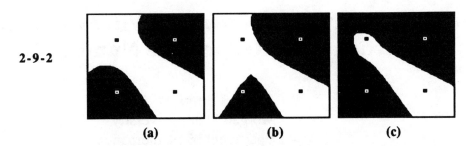

(a) **(b)** **(c)**

Figure 2. The classification results of the "XOR" problem. (a) shows the classification result by using all the hidden nodes for each network. (b) is the classification result of taking unsorted hidden nodes by SC. (c) is the classification result of taking sorted hidden nodes by SC.

No. of hidden nodes used in the SPRT process.	3	4	5	6	7	8	9
Average No. of used hidden nodes in the SPRT process.	1.67	1.70	1.67	1.67	1.68	1.98	1.81
Reduced rate of network	44.3%	57.5%	66.6%	72.2%	76%	75.3%	79.9%

Table 4. Net pruning results for the two-layer perceptron with sorted hidden nodes.

Conclusions and Discussion

In this paper, the implementation of sequential classification by percetron and multilayer percetron is proposed and an efficient net pruning effect is achieved. An important key property is adopted in the derivation of sequential classification. This property is that the outputs of the multilayer perceptron are approximating the posteriori probability functions of the classes being trained. The formular for the ordering of hidden nodes of multilayer perceptron or input nodes of perceptron is proposed.

In the experiments, our method gets a good result to prune multi-layer network. The results of pruning the 2-4-2, 2-5-2, 2-6-2, 2-7-2 two-layer networks to 2-2-2 two-layer networks are the minimum number of hidden nodes used in the classification of the "XOR" probelm which is the same as the derivation of Mirchandani and Cao [5].

The proposed algorithm can be applied in the single layer perceptron with 2-class and multi-class problems. If the number of hidden layers is more than 1, then our proposed technique may also be applied. The pruning procedures start from the hidden layer close to the output and sequentially prune the hidden layer backward to the input.

References

[1]   R. P. Lippmann, " An introduction to computing with neural nets," IEEE ASSP Magazine, vol. 4, April 1987, pp.4-22.

[2]   E. D. Karnin, "A simple procedure for pruning back-propagation trained neural networks," IEEE Transactions on Neural Networks, vol. 1, no. 2, 1990, pp.239-242.

[3]   K. S. Fu, Sequential Methods in Pattern Recognition and Machine Learning, Academic Press, New York, 1968.

[4]   D. W. Ruck et al., "The multilayer perceptron as an approximation to a Bayes optimal discriminant function," IEEE Transactions on Neural Networks, vol. 1, no. 4, 1990, pp. 296-298.

[5]   Gagan Mirchandani and Wei Cao, "On hidden nodes for neural nets," IEEE Transactions on Circuits and Systems, Vol. 36, No.5, May 1989, pp.661-664.

Layered Neural Networks With Horizontal Connections Can Reduce The Number of Units

J.Smid
Morgan State University
Department of Mathematics
Baltimore, MD 21239
and
Research and Data Systems Corporation
Greenbelt, MD 20770

Abstract

We define *layered networks with horizontal connections* as networks having units that receive inputs from the lower layer and also from the previous units of the same layer. We show that architecture with horizontal connections does not require as many units in the hidden layers as the plain layered architecture in order to approximate a function.

1. Introduction

Performance of a learning network depends both on the architecture and the algorithm of the network. For example, the Cascade Correlation (Cascor) algorithm performs better for both the two spiral problem [Fahlman 1991] and simple applications [Blonda 1993] than does the Backpropagation algorithm. Cascor is an example of the multilayer architecture with horizontal connections and an incremental algorithm. One reason for the superior performance of this architecture is the ability to capture regions where the function being modeled is constant with a fewer units. In this paper we demonstrate that architectures with horizontal connnections require fewer units compared with the plain multilayer architecture.

The multilayer perceptron network with k units in a single hidden layer computes functions

$$\bar{f}(x) = \sum_{j=1}^{k} w_j H(a_j x - c_j) \qquad (1)$$

This network was proved [Leshno et al.1993] to be a universal approximator. The function (1) can approximate any continuous function $f(x) = [0,1]^n \to R$ provided that H is a non-polynomial activation function satisfying mild conditions. Another architecture [Blum1991], a constructive one, requires a three-layer network. We use Blum's technique to demonstrate that nets with two hidden layers and with horizontal connections require fewer units.

2. Approximation by a network with two hidden layers

Approximation capabilities of two hidden layer networks were studied and estimates of rates of approximation were derived [Blum1991]. For simplicity, let us assume that $f \in L_2([0,1]^2)$. Piecewise constant functions on rectangular partitions of $[0,1]^2$ are dense in $L_2([0,1]^2)$. A function $f \in L_2([0,1]^2)$ can be approximated by a piecewise constant function $\overline{f}$. This function can be modeled by a two-hidden-layers network

$$\overline{f} = \sum wI \qquad (2)$$

where the summation is over all rectangular boxes and

$$I = H\left[\sum_{i=1}^{n=4} [H(x_i - b_{left\ i}) + H(b_{right\ i} - x_i)] - 2n + 0.5 \right] \qquad (3)$$

is the indicator function (one hidden-layer network) for an n-dimensional rectangular box ($a_i < b_{left\ i} < x_i < b_{right\ i}, 1 \le i \le n = 4$) of a rectangular partition of $[0,1]^2$. The H is the left-hand continuous Heaviside function, $H(z) = 1, for\ z > 0, \quad H(z) = 0, \quad z \le 0$.

Note that the activation function H can be a general sigmoid σ. The Blum's approximation results and the results that follow for Heaviside functions hold for

general sigmoids, $\sigma(z) \to 1\ as\ z \to \infty, \sigma(z) \to 0\ as\ z \to -\infty$.
This stems from the fact that a general rescaled sigmoid converges to a Heaviside function,

$\sigma(nz) = 1\ for\ z > 0, 0\ for\ z < 0, \quad \sigma(0)\ for\ z = 0\ as\ n \to \infty$

and consequently $\|\sigma(nz) - H(z)\|_{L^2} \to 0$.

3. Layered networks with horizontal connections

Definition. Networks with horizontal connections have units that receive inputs from the lower (input) layer and also from the previous units of the same layer

$$\sigma_k = \sigma_k (a_k x - b_k + \sum_{l<k} b_{lk} \sigma_l) \quad (4)$$

Note that a network with horizontal connections suggests an incremental algorithm. In the n+1st iteration a new unit is added and all $w, b_{jn+1}, a_{n+1}, b_{n+1}$ coefficients are calculated and the other coefficients associated with the first n units are kept unchanged. Examples of incremental algorithms are the Cascade Correlation [Falman 1990] and the projection pursuit algorithm [Jones 1992].

In two dimensional case, n=2, the function

$$I = H(b_2 - a_2 x_2 + \sum_{k=1}^{m} b_{12k} H(x_1 - b_{1k})) \quad (6)$$

is the indicator function of a set which is a union of vertical rectangular strips, fig.1. Similarly, the function

$$I = H(b_1 - a_1 x_1 + \sum_{k=1}^{m} b_{21k} H(x_2 - b_{2k})) \quad (7)$$

is the indicator function of a set which is a union of horizontal rectangular strips. By replacing units

$$H(x_i - b_{left\ i}) + H(b_{right\ i} - x_i) \quad (8)$$

with (6),(7), the indicator functions of a piecewise rectangular region, we obtain a two layer network. This network can model non-convex figures, e.g. a semicircle fig.1b.

4. Estimate for the upper bound of units needed in three-layer networks with horizontal connections

Following Blum (1991) let us assume that we have a square mesh of size $1/m$ for dimension n=2. Then we need m^2 units (3) in the second hidden layer and $4(m+1)$ units (8) in the first hidden layer of the plain multilayer net. The total number units for a two-hidden-layer network is $m^2 + 4(m+1)$.

Some piecewise constant functions can be conveniently implemented by units with horizontal connections. To illustrate that a net with horizontal connections can reduce the requirement on the number of units in the second hidden layer, let us consider the indicator function of a 2-dimensional chessboard pattern (black=1, white=0, with an even number of rows), fig.2. Two successive lines of squares can be implemented by two units (each with one hidden layer), e.g. the indicator function of the first two lines of the chessboard (a 'zigzag' function) can be defined as follows

$$I_1 = H_1(1/m - x_2 + (1/m)\sum_{k=1}^{m} b_k H(x_1 - k/m))$$

$$I_0 = H_1(x_2 - (1/m)\sum_{k=1}^{m} b_k H(x_1 - k/m))$$

$$b_1 = 0, \quad b_k = 1, for \quad k \quad even, \quad b_k = -1, for \quad k \quad odd$$

$$I_{zigzag\_01} = H[I_0 + I_1 - 2 + 0.5]$$

Similarly we can construct an indicator function for other zigzag indicator functions. This process requires two units per zigzag, or m units for the second layer, rather than m^2 units when we model (using plain units of type (3)) one square at a time. The two-hidden layer network for the chessboard requires only $m + 4(m+1)$ units. Similarly we can construct two-hidden-layer networks, with fewer units, computing indicator functions for other geometric figures, e.g. semi circles, spirals.

We can reduce the number of required units for any nonconvex indicator function:

Theorem. A function $f \in L^2([0,1]^n$ which is a constant on a nonconvex measurable subset S can be represented by a two-hidden-layer network with horizontal connections. This network has fewer units in the second hidden layer than the plain network (2).

Proof: The function f can be approximated with arbitrary precision by a piecewise constant function $\bar{f}$, where the nonconvex set S is approximated by a piecewise rectangular region, $\bar{S}$. The boundary of $\bar{S}$ consists of at least one L-shaped set of 3 rectangles (fig. 6) or of the saddle type pairs of rectangles (fig. 3) where the function.is constant across the L-shaped set. A one-hidden-layer unit with horizontal connections can represent the indicator function of an entire set of four rectangles (either fig. 3 or fig. 6) whereas with a plain architecture, 4 units (one for each rectangle) are required. The indicator function of an L-shaped set of 3 rectangles is represented by $I_{Lshape} = H[x_1 - b_1 + b_1 H(b_2 - x_2)]$.

The saddle-type representation is shown below.

5. Examples of two-layer networks
Blum (1991) showed that a saddle type function cannot be implemented by a two layer net with a linear output unit. However, if we admit horizontal connections we can construct a one-hidden-layer solution.

5.1 XOR example
An indicator function of a strip
$$f(x) = \begin{cases} 0 & for \quad x_2 \le 0.25 \\ 0 & for \quad x_2 > 0.5 \\ 1 & for \quad 0.25 < x_2 \le 0.5 \end{cases}$$
is implemented by a two layer net,
$$f_{strip} = H(x_2 - b_1 - (1 - b_1)H(x_2 - b_2)), b_1 = 0.25, b_2 = 0.5$$
Rotation and slight rescaling of this strip results in a two layer net, fig.4,
$$f_{xor} = H(b_1 - x_2 - x_1 + (2.5 - b_1)H(x_2 - b_2)), b_1 = 0.25, b_2 = 0.5$$
that separates points (0,0), (1,1), of the unit square, from points (0,1), (1,0).

5.2 Saddle type function implementation
Besides an XOR function, the two layer network with horizontal connections can implement a saddle type function, fig.3,
$$f(x) = \begin{cases} 1 & for \quad x_1 < 0.5, x_2 < 0.5 \\ 1 & for \quad x_1 \ge 0.5, x_2 \ge 0.5 \\ 0 & otherwise \end{cases}$$

The net implementing this function has 4 units and a linear output unit

$$f_{saddle} = H(b - x_2 - bH(x_1 - a)) + H(x_2 - b - (1 - b)H(a - x_1))$$

III-519

References

Blum,E.,K., Li,L.,K. (1991). Approximation Theory and Feedforward Networks, *Neural Networks*, **4**, 511-515.

Fahlman,S.E., Lebier,C. (1991). The Cascade-Correlation Learning Architecture. In D.Touretzky, editor, *Advances in Neural Information Processing Systems 2*, pp.524-532, Morgan Kaufmann.

Jones,L.,K. (1992) A Simple Lemma on Greedy Approximation in Hilbert Space and Convergence Rates for Projection Pursuit Regression and Neural Network Training. *The Annals of Statistics*, Vol. 20, No.1,pp. 608-613.

Leshno,M.(1993), Multilayer Feedforward networks With a Nonpolynomial Activation Function Can Approximate Any Function. *Neural Networks*, Vol.6,pp.861-867

Blonda,P., Pasquariello,Q., Smid,J. (1993) Comparison of Backpropagation, Cascade-Correlation and Kohonen Algorithms for Cloud Retrieval, *Proceedings of Int.Joint Conference on Neural Networks*, Nagoya, Japan.

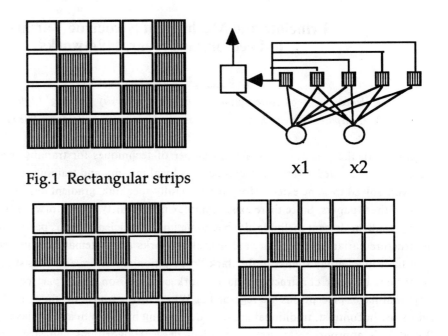

Fig.1 Rectangular strips

Fig.2 A chessboard function   Fig.2b A semi circle

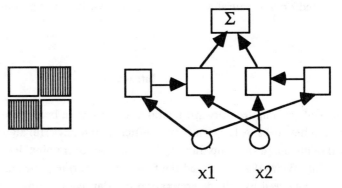

x1   x2

Fig.3 The saddle type function net

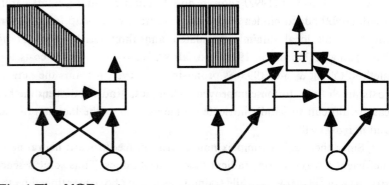

Fig.4 The XOR net   Fig.4b The L-shape net

Principle and Methods of Structrue Variation
in Feedforward Neural Networks

Xun Liang[2,1]   and Shaowei Xia[1]

1. Department of Automation, Tsinghua University, Beijing 100084, P.R.China
2. Computer Research Center, Peking University, Beijing 100871, P.R.China

Abstract: In the past several years, a number of techniques for training feedforward neural networks were presented. Many problems such as local minima and training speed have been discussed and were solved to some extent. However, generally speaking, gradient descent methods were used in most of these papers. Since there exists complex nonlinearity in feedforward neural networks, training by gradient descent methods alone is sometimes inefficient. In this paper, principle and methods of structure variation in feedforward neural networks are systematically presented. They also have their basis in anatomy similar to the Back Propagation algorithm and consist of three parts: network expansion, network construction and network compression. Each part contains several methods. Here multilayer preceptrons are regarded as White Boxes whose weights and thresholds are controlled by us. In contrast, traditional gradient descending methods treat multilayer perceptrons as Black Boxes. It is appropriate to use the gradient descent algorithms and structure variation methods alternately. This combined method has been discussed by several papers. In this paper it will be studied comprehensively and systematically.

Key Words: Feedforward neural networks, structure variation, dig tunnels, global minima, hidden neurons

1. Introduction

The techniques of training feedforward neural networks have been studied and improved since the resurge of neural networks. A large amount of efficient and powerful algorithms have been presented to avoid local minima and speed up training in most cases of training. For example, for algorithms to speed up learning, Weir (1991) analyzed the function of learning rates in Back Propogation and improved the training speed by self-determination of adaptive learning rates. Shoemaker *et al* (1991) discussed trinary quantization of weight updating. For the techniques of avoiding local minima, Wessels & Barnard (1992) showed how to choose initial weights carefully, Hirose *et al* (1991) and Tsaih (1992) added hidden neurons during training to skip from local minima. Among the methods for avoiding local minima, simulated annealing (Kirkpatrick *et al*, 1983; Atkin *et al*, 1989; Nakayama & Normura, 1992) is a fairly effective one, but it costs too much time. The homotopy method (Yang & Yu, 1993) is promising, however, it trains the network many times and therefore costs much time. In these improved techniques, gradient descent methods are mainly used so that it can be difficult to handle intricate problems such as the location of the global minimum at a "deep and narrow well".

Since there exists complex nonlinearity in feedforward neural networks, it seems that it will be inefficient always to use gradient descent techniques. Thus some researchers turned to changing the structrue of the network while training, as in the above mentioned method of adding hidden neurons given by Hirose *et al* (1991) and Tsaih (1992). Nadel (1989), Hoehfeld & Fahlman (1992) added hidden neurons which are connected to the preceding hidden neurons and to the input layer, during training or construction.

In this paper, we will summarize and develop the structrue variation methods by dividing them into three parts: network expansion, network construction and network compression. Due to space limits, only our results about structure variation are briefly outlined in this paper (for details see Liang (1993)).

The idea of structure variation has its anatomical basis. According to anatomy, the learning process is not finished only by the variation of the intensity and polarity of connections among the neurons. When learning becomes difficult, new neurons come into the biological network to aid learning, i.e., the network expands. In fact, One neuron memorizing one pattern is a special case of one neuron memorizing several patterns or several neurons memorizing several patterns, which is similar to some construction processes. On the other hand, in the process of thinking, not only the intensity and polarity of connections but also the structure of the biological network is always changing in order to comprehend and master the knowledge, which leads to a compression of the network. Network expansion means learning while network compression means digesting. These processes are also similar to the learning process of human beings. For example, when we first learn a subject, we feel that there is so much for us to learn, but several years later, we will feel that the subject has narrowed down into a few key points. In summary, when we learn knowledge, not only the intensity and polarity of connections among the neurons change, but also the structure of the network varies. Therefore, the idea of structure variation is based on anatomy.

This paper is organized as follows: Since the method of network compression will be used repeatedly in the later sections, it will be introduced in section 2, as well as the relevant proofs of its generalization. Based on these results, the idea and technique of second learning and rotation transformation are developed, the latter showing ways to skip out of local minima by digging tunnels horizontally into the error hypersurface. In section 3, some construction methods for both binary and real training patterns, particularly for the parity problem and the encoder problem, are given. In the method of construction for the encoder problem, only one hidden neuron is used and the values of connection weights and thresholds are polynomially increasing so that it is convenient to realize both in programs and circuits. A statistical technique for fabricating multilayer perceptrons is also discussed. In section 4, the principle and method for network expansion are presented, in which we intrinsically dig tunnels down with an inclination into the error hypersurface, and by which one can dig tunnels down into the error hypersurface from local minima to the global one. Section 5 concludes the paper.

In practice, the methods of network expansion, network construction and network compression ought to be used alternately, e.g., in the process of second learning and rotation transformation, both expansion and compression are involved. After construction, in general, network compression should be considered. That is to say, the methods of structure variation ought to be taken as a whole rather than in separate parts, and it will be powerful and efficient if we combine these methods, or even with gradient descent algorithms in training.

2. Method of Network Compression

In this section, firstly a method of pruning away the redundant hidden neurons is reviewed systematically and mathematically. Secondly the necessary and sufficient condition of the generalized value of change during the pruning process is given, as well as some relevent theorems. Thirdly, the steps of learning the patterns in the testing set which is called the second learning is addressed, and the change of generalization ability during second learning is proved. Finally, the method of rotation transformation is discussed.

2.1. Pruning away redendunt hidden neurons

In recent years, some methods of pruning away the redundant connections were published. Some papers used connection constraints during training and removed the small value connections after training, e.g., Yasui (1992), Qin & He (1992). Using the linear dependency, some researchers presented the method of general compression (Arai, 1989; Sperduti & Starita, 1992; Liang & Xia, 1993). Although this method seems trival and obivous, it is the starting point of some useful methods.

2.2. Generalization analysis during compressing

While pruning away the redundant neurons, generalization ability may vary. In this subsection, we discuss in which case it varies and in which case it does not. Two lemmas and six theorems are proved. See Liang & Xia (1993) and Liang (1993) for details.

2.3. Second learning

See Liang & Xia (1993) for details.

2.4. Rotation transformation

Provided that the network is not at the global minimum, then adding a hidden neuron and pruning away an old neuron in the same layer is the process of rotation transformation. In this process, the outputs errors are not changed, so we dig tunnels horizontally into the error hypersurface. Since a hidden neuron is added and then another is deleted, rotation transformation will not change the scale of the network. See Liang (1993) for details.

3. Methods of Network Construction

We think that construction is one part of the structure variation methods because the memory of training patterns is finished mainly by structure variation rather than by weights and thresholds adjustment. Construction procedures can also be found in the human's brain.

Although using Kolmogorov Theorem (1957), Hecht−Nielson (1987) gave the existence proofs, he (1990) admitted that since it is no constructive proof, it is not useful in practice. It followed that many papers dicussed the construction methods (Arai, 1989 & 1993; Huang & Huang, 1990; Kruglyak,1990; Stork, 1992; Stork & Allen, 1992 & 1993; Brown, 1993; Korn, 1993; Liang *et al*, 1993; Liang & Xia, 1993a & 1993b; etc). For the binary training patterns, Arai (1989 & 1993), Liang *et al* (1993) constructed their three−layer perceptrons. For the real training patterns, Huang & Huang (1990), Liang & Xia (1993a) gave some different construction methods. Besides, some researchers studied the construction for two special training sets: parity problem and encoder problem. For the parity problem, Stork & Allen (1992) constructed a multilayer perceptron with minimal numbers of free parameters, and replied to Brown (1993) and Korn (1993) respectively in his letter to the editor (1993). We shall present a new construction with fewer connections than before for the parity problem. For the encoder problem, Kruglyak (1990) constructed a feedforward neural network solving the N−bit encoder problem with just two hidden units. In a recent letter Stork & Allen (1993) presented a constructive method to the N−bit encoder problem with just one hidden unit, which gives the minimal network architecture to this problem. However, in their method, the input weights and output thresholds are exponentially increasing as N increases, which leads to inpracticality in designing learning algorithms. In our improved method (Liang & Xia, 1993b), the weights and thresholds are polynomially increasing as N increases, thus it may be more useful to learning algorithm designers.

In this section, only our methods are introduced. We will first breifly introduce the general analytic express for the binary training patterns, which is convenient to be extended to solve some problems, such as parity problem. In subsection 3.2, constructions for real training patterns are discussed. Parity problem and encoder problem are constructed respectively in subsection 3.3 and 3.4.

subsection 3.5 gives a statistical fabricating technique.

3.1. Construction for binary training patterns

See Liang *et al* (1993).

3.2. Construction for real training patterns

See Liang & Xia (1993a).

3.3. Construction for the parity problem

Minsky & Papert (1969) gave a construction for the parity problem. Liang (1993) gave his construction for the parity problem whose construction process is just like cutting the N-cube hierarchically from a vertex. Recently, Setiono & Hui (1993) announced that some N-bit parity problem can be realized by less than N hidden neurons. We have tested and confirmed their result.

Besides, interestingly, using the wave-like monotone increasing activation function, Stork & Allen (1992) gave the minimal architecture with 2 hidden units for stardard three-layer perceptrons (referring to the later four conditions Stork & Allen stated (1992), although strictly speaking, the network given by Stork & Allen (1992) also violates their third condition: the unit step function of the output unit is not a *strictly* mononically increasing function).

Inspired by Stork & Allen (1992) and Minor (1993), Fig.1 depicts a four-layer network with an equal number of free parameters and with similar generalization as the network of Stork & Allen (1992), but with fewer connections than those of Stork & Allen (1992) and Minor (1993). This network also satisfies the three conditions that Stork (1993) repeated later and gives fewer connections than before for standard multilayer perceptrons.

3.4. Construction for the encoder problem

See Liang & Xia (1993b).

3.5. Statistical fabricating method

See Liang & Xia (1993c).

4. Methods of Network Expansion

In this section, compensating methods for multilayer perceptrons, which are very difficult to train by traditional

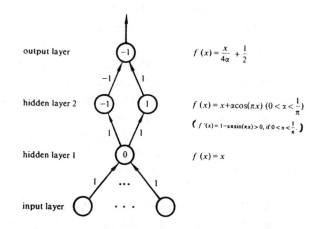

Fig.1. An N-1-2-1 feedforward network that solves the N-parity problem. The values in the units are the thresholds.

Back Propagation methods, are presented. For a three-layer perceptron trapped in local minima the compensating methods can correct the wrong outputs one by one until all outputs are right, so that the three-layer perceptron can skip from local minima to a global minimum. The compensation methods use principle of network expansion. A hidden neuron is added as compensation for a binary input three-layer perceptron trapped in a local minimum; and one or two hidden neurons are added as compensation for a real input three-layer perceptron. For a more than three-layer perceptron, the second hidden layer from behind will be temporarily treated as the input layer during compensation, hence the above methods can also be used. In compensating, whenever a hidden neuron is added its input and output weights and threshold are calculated definitely rather than iterated, so the global convergence is guaranteed and a lot of time is saved. If the global minimum on the error hypersurface is in the "narrow and deep well", the multilayer perceptron can be moved there by compensating. See Liang & Xia (1993d & 1993e) for details.

5. Conclusions and Further Work

In this paper, the principle and methods of structure variation are presented and developed, which consist of three parts: network expansion, network construction and network compression. Each part comprises several methods and its applications such as second learning and rotation transformation. This idea also has an anatomical basis like the Back Propagation method. In practice, it is appropriate to combine several structure variation methods and even combine them with conversional gradient descent techniques.

Obviously there is still a lot of work to do in the field of structure variation methods. Consequently, further work includes developing and completing the methods of structure variation, laying a more solid foundation for this idea, and testing these combined techniques in applications.

References

Arai, M. (1989). Mapping ability of three-layer neural networks. *Proc. of IEEE Int. Conf. on Neural Networks*. Washington D.C. vol. I, pp.419-423.

Arai, M. (1993). Bounds on the number of hidden units in binary-valued three-layer neural networks. *Neural Networks*. vol.6, pp.855-860.

Atkin, G. K., Bowcock, J. E. & Queen, N. M. (1989). Solution of a distributed deterministic parallel networks. *Pattern Recognition*. vol.22, pp.461-466.

Brown, D. A. (1993). Solving the N-bit parity problem with only one hidden unit. *Neural Networks*, vol.6, pp.607-608.

Hecht-Nielson, R. (1987). Kolmogorov's mapping neural network existence theorem. *Proc. of Int. Conf. on Neural Networks*. New York: IEEE Press. vol.III, pp.11-14.

Hecht-Nielson, R. (1990). *Neurocomputing*. California: Addition-Wesley Publishing Company. pp.122-124.

Hirose, Y., Yamashita, K. & Hijiya, S. (1991). Back-propagation algorithm which varies the number of hidden units. *Neural Networks*. vol.4, pp.61-66.

Hoehfeld, M & Fahlman, S. E. (1992). Learning with limited numerical precision using the cascade-correlation algorithm. *IEEE trans. on Neural Networks*. vol.3, pp.602-611.

Huang, S. & Huang, Y. (1991). Bounds on the number of hidden neurons in multilayer perceptrons. *IEEE trans. on Neural Networks*. vol.2, pp.47-55.

Kirkpatrick, S., Gellatt, C. D. & Vecchi, P. (1983). Optimization by simulated annealing. *Science*. vol.220, pp.671-680.

Kolmogorov, A. N. (1957). On the representation of continuous functions of many variables by superposition of continuous functions of one variable and addition. *Dokl. Akad. Nauk USSR*. vol.114, pp.953-956.

Korn, A. (1993). Letter to the editor. *Neural Networks*, vol.6, pp.608.

Kruglyak, L. (1990). How to solve the N bit encoder problem with just two hidden unit, *Neural computation* vol.2, pp.399-401.

Liang, X. (1993). *Structure Variation in Feedforward Neural Networks: Theory and Practice (Ph.D. Thesis)*. Tsinghua University.

Liang, X., Ni, E. & Xia, S. (1993). Knowledge Base based on neural networks. *Int. Conf. on Systems Science & Systems Engineering*. Beijing. pp.830-832.

Liang, X. & Xia, S. (1993). Second learning of generalized multilayer perceptrons. *IEEE Region* 10

Conf. on Computer, Communication, Control & Power Eng. Beijing. pp.763–766.

Liang, X. & Xia, S. (1993a). Construction of multilayer perceptrons with real training patterns. *Chinese Neural Networks Congress.* Xian. pp.334–338.

Liang, X. & Xia, S. (1993b). How to solve N-bit encoder problem practically with just one hidden unit. Submitted to *Neurocomputing.*

Liang, X. & Xia, S. (1993c). Analysis of ststistical training method. *Int. Joint Conf. on Neural Networks.* Nagoya. pp.1657–1660.

Liang, X. & Xia, S. (1993d). A method of getting global minima necessarily in binary input multilayer perceptrons. *Proc. of World Congress on Neural Networks.* Portland. vol.III, pp.606–609.

Liang, X. & Xia, S. (1993e). A method of getting global minima necessarily in multilayer perceptrons. *Proc. of World Congress on Neural Networks.* Portland. vol.III, pp.609–613.

Nadel, J.-P. (1989). Study of a growth algorithm for a feedforward network *Int. J. of Neural Systems.* vol.1, pp.55–59.

Minor, J. M. (1993). Parity with two layer feedforward nets. *Neural Networks,* vol.6, pp.705–707.

Minsky, M. L. & Papert, S. (1969). *Perceptrons: An Introduction to Computation Geometry.* Cambridge: MIT Press.

Nakayama H. & Nomura M. (1992). Methods for getting global minima in back-propagation. *Proc. of Int. Joint Conf. on Neural Networks.* Beijing. vol.Ⅱ, pp.434–440.

Qin, H. & He, Z. (1992). Variable step BP algorithm which prunes away redundant connections dynamically. *Proc. of Int. Joint Conf. on Neural Networks.* Beijing. vol.Ⅱ, pp.441–445.

Setiono, R. & Hui, L. C. K. (1993). Some n-bit parity problems are solvable by feed-forward networks with less than n hidden units. *Proc. of Int. Joint Conf. on Neural Networks.* vol.1, pp.305–308.

Shoemaker, P. A., Carlin, M. J. & Shimabukuro, R. (1991). Back propagation learning with trinary quantization of weight updates. *Neural Networks.* vol.4, pp.231–241.

Sperduti, A. & Starita, A. (1992). Using linear dependency in the weight space to reduce the size of a feed-forward network. *Proc. of Int. Joint Conf. on Neural Networks.* Beijing. vol.Ⅱ, pp.460–461.

Stork, D. G. & Allen, J. D. (1992). How to solve the N-bit parity problem with two hidden units. *Neural Networks,* vol.5, pp.923–926.

Stork, D. G. (1993). N-bit parity networks: a reply to Brown and Korn. *Neural Networks,* vol.5, pp.609.

Stork, D. G. & Allen, J. D. (1993). How to solve the N-bit encoder problem with just one hidden unit, *Neurocomputing* vol.5, pp.141–143.

Tsaih R. R. (1992). A learning procedure for the back propagation networks that guarantees obtaining the desired solution. *Proc. of Int. Joint Conf. on Neural Networks.* Beijing. vol.Ⅱ, pp.771–780.

Weir, M. K. (1991). A method for self-determination of adaptive learning rates in back propagation. *Neural Networks.* vol.4, pp.371–379.

Wessels, L. F. A. & Barnard, E. (1992). Avoiding false local minima by proper initialization of connections. *IEEE trans. on Neural Networks.* vol.3, pp.899–905.

Yang L. & Yu W. (1993). Backpropagation with homotopy. *Neural Computation.* vol.5, pp.363–366.

Yasui, S. (1992). A new method to remove redundant connections in Backpropagation neural networks: introduction of parametric lateral inhibition fields. *Proc. of Int. Joint Conf. on Neural Networks.* Beijing. vol.Ⅱ, pp.360–367.

Block-Recursive Least Squares Technique for Training Multilayer Perceptrons

E.D. Di Claudio R. Parisi G. Orlandi
INFOCOM Dept. - University of Rome "La Sapienza"
Via Eudossiana 18, 00184 Roma - Italy
Phone: +39-6-44585837, Fax: + 39-6-4873300
email orl@infocom.ing.uniroma1.it

Abstract

A novel learning technique is described as a faster and more reliable alternative to the classical backpropagation method. The approach is based on the application of Least Squares criterion to a linearized system at each step of the learning procedure. The squared error at the output of each layer immediately before the non linearity is minimized over the entire training set by a Block Recursive Least Squares algorithm. The optimal weights (in the sense of minimal 2-norm of the error) are computed for each layer by using the QR decomposition.

The high performance of the new algorithm has been verified in several experimental trials, yielding considerable improvements from the point of view of both the accuracy and the speed of convergence.

1-Introduction

The multilayer perceptron is one of the most commonly used types of feed-forward neural networks and it is used in a large number of applications. Its strength resides in its capacity of mapping arbitrarily complex non-linear functions by a convenient number of layers of sigmoidal non-linearities. The backpropagation algorithm (BP) is still the most used learning algorithm; it consists in the minimization of the Mean-Squared Error (MSE) at the network output performed by means of a gradient descent on the error surface in the space of weights.

The backpropagation algorithm suffers from a number of shortcomings; above all the relatively slow rate of convergence and the final misadjustment that can not guarantee the success of the training procedure in real applications. Great efforts have been made to overcome these limitations by introducing some heuristic modifications to the basic BP algorithm [1][2]. Anyway these methods require an accurate tuning of learning parameters in order to obtain satisfactory performance.

Recently a new class of algorithms has been developed, based on Least Squares concepts [3] applied to the solution of a linearized system for each layer of the network. These techniques generally offer more reliable training procedures and much higher convergence rates[4][5][6]. The Block Recursive Least Squares (BRLS) training algorithm allows to obtain considerable improvements from the point of view of both the numerical accuracy and the speed of convergence. Its numerical stability is enhanced by the use of QR decomposition [3] and by the fact that the algorithm works directly on data, without forming any correlation matrix.

2-Description of the algorithm

The presence of the non-linearity makes it difficult to apply to multilayer perceptrons a number of techniques so popular in the field of adaptive filtering [7]. A kind of linearization is needed in order to make available to the problem of learning a large number of experimented and efficient algorithms.

The algorithm herein presented is based on the idea of separating each layer of the network in a linear part (the multiplication by the weights) and a non-linear one (the activation functions). Defining the error immediately before the non-linearity allows to use the method of QR Recursive Least Squares ([3] [7]) to update the weights of each layer.

In the backpropagation algorithm the output error at step n is defined as:

$$E(n) = \sum_p E_p(n) \tag{1}$$

where Ep is the output squared error for the p-th pattern.

The weights are updated by computing the derivatives of E according to the formula:

$$\Delta w_{ij}^{(k)}(n) = -\eta \frac{\partial E(n)}{\partial w_{ij}^{(k)}(n)} \tag{2}$$

where wij(k) is the weight from the i-th neuron in layer (k-1) to the j-th neuron in layer (k) and η is the learning rate.

The learning rule thus derived is :

$$w_{ij}^{(k)}(t+1) = w_{ij}^{(k)}(t) + \eta e_{pj}^{(k)} x_{pi}^{(k-1)} \tag{3}$$

where epj(k) is the error signal for the j-th unit in layer (k) and xpi(k-1) is the output of the i-th unit in layer (k-1), relatively to the p-th input pattern. The error signal is computed as:

$$e_{pj}^{(L)} = f'(y_{pj}^{(L)})(d_{pj} - x_{pj}^{(L+1)}) \tag{4}$$

for the output layer, and as:

$$e_{pi}^{(k)} = f'(y_{pi}^{(k)}) \sum_j e_{pj}^{(k+1)} w_{ij}^{(k+1)} \tag{5}$$

for all the other layers. In these formulas dpj is the j-th desired target output for the p-th pattern, ypi(k) is the input to the generic non linearity, being f'() the derivative of the non-linear activation function, typically the sigmoidal one. L is the number of layers.

The error signals above defined can be used to form a linear system for each layer of the network; after each presentation of a learning epoch, this system can be solved in the LS sense yielding the optimal weights.

The new algorithm can be formulated in matrix notation in the following way. Let P be the length of a generic epoch. For each layer the following matrices are defined:

$$
\mathbf{X}(n) = \begin{pmatrix} \mathbf{x}_1^T(n) \\ ... \\ \mathbf{x}_P^T(n) \end{pmatrix}; \quad \mathbf{Y}(n) = \begin{pmatrix} \mathbf{y}_1^T(n) \\ ... \\ \mathbf{y}_P^T(n) \end{pmatrix}; \quad \mathbf{E}(n) = \begin{pmatrix} \mathbf{e}_1^T(n) \\ ... \\ \mathbf{e}_P^T(n) \end{pmatrix}
\tag{6}
$$

where the layer index has been omitted and n indicates the generic iteration. In these expressions x_i^T, y_i^T and e_i^T are the input, output and error row vectors relative to the linear part of the generic layer, for the i-th learning pattern (T indicates the matrix transposition operation). Moreover we indicate with $\mathbf{Q}(n)$ and $\mathbf{R}(n)$ the matrices deriving from the QR decomposition of the system coefficient matrix [3].

The BRLS algorithm consists of the following steps:

1- the weights are randomly initialized;

2- the triangular matrix $\mathbf{R}$ is initialized to $\mathbf{R}(0)=diag(\varepsilon)$, where ε is a properly chosen small value;

3- each pattern of the current epoch is presented to the network and forward propagated through it; during this phase the matrices $\mathbf{X}(n)$ and $\mathbf{Y}(n)$ for each layer are formed;

4- for each pattern, the output of the network is compared to the desired output; the error signals (4) and (5) at the output of the linear part of each layer are computed. For each layer the perturbation matrix $\mathbf{E}(n)$ is formed ;

5- after the presentation of an entire training epoch, for each layer the following linear system is formed:

$$
\begin{pmatrix} \lambda^{1/2}\mathbf{R}(n-1) \\ (1-\lambda)^{1/2}\mathbf{X}(n) \end{pmatrix} \mathbf{W}(n) = \begin{pmatrix} \lambda^{1/2}\mathbf{C}(n) \\ (1-\lambda)^{1/2}(\mathbf{Y}(n)+\eta\mathbf{E}(n)) \end{pmatrix}
\tag{7}
$$

where η is the learning rate (measuring the entity of the perturbation on matrix $\mathbf{Y}$) and λ is the forgetting factor. This system is solved for $n>0$ by performing first a QR decomposition of the coefficient matrix, yielding the matrices $\mathbf{Q}(n)$ and $\mathbf{R}(n)$. In (7) $\mathbf{C}(1)=0$ while for $n>1$ $\mathbf{C}(n)$ is computed from the formula:

$$
\mathbf{Q}^T(n-1)\begin{pmatrix} \lambda^{1/2}\mathbf{C}(n-1) \\ (1-\lambda)^{1/2}(\mathbf{Y}(n-1)+\eta\mathbf{E}(n-1)) \end{pmatrix} = \begin{pmatrix} \mathbf{C}(n) \\ \mathbf{D}(n) \end{pmatrix}
\tag{8}
$$

Then a procedure of backsubstitution on matrix $\mathbf{R}(n)$ yields the optimal set of weights, in the sense of the minimal 2-norm of the weight solution matrix $\mathbf{W}(n)$;

6- if the global output error with the new weights is still higher than a specified threshold the procedure is repeated from point 3 by appending a new epoch (e.g. the QR decomposition is recursively performed as new data come); otherwise the training has terminated successfully.

The QR decomposition (performed with either the Householder transformation or the Givens rotations) gives to the algorithm stability and robustness from a numerical point of view. In some cases it can be replaced by a Singular Value Decomposition (SVD), yielding a complete control over the internal structure of matrix X and the regularity of the weight matrix W, at the expenses of a higher computational cost.

3-Experimental results

The performance of the BRLS algorithm have been evaluated in several problems: parity (2,3 and 4 bits), generalized XOR, pattern recognition (circle in a square and character recognition). In all cases comparison with backpropagation has been made on the basis of a proper number of trials with different configurations of initial weights and different values of learning parameters. Main results of this analysis are much faster rates of convergence and higher accuracy of the new algorithm in approximating the desired outputs.

Fig. 1 reports the MSE as a function of the number of iterations in a typical case for the XOR problem; both the rapidity of convergence (about 30 iterations to get MSE<0.01) and its depth (MSE~10-4 after 100 iterations) can be verified.

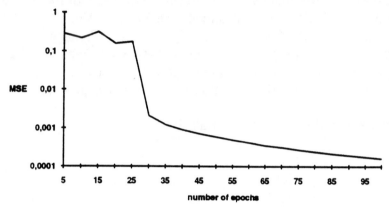

Fig. 1 : MSE versus number of epochs for XOR problem

The algorithm has shown also the ability of forming sharper transition regions. This property is shown in fig. 2 referring to the circle in a square problem.

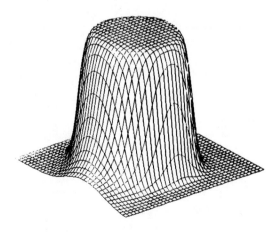

Fig. 2 : 3D output for circle in a square problem

III-531

The possibility of varying the length P of the training epoch (differently from other LS-based algorithms) is a peculiar feature of BRLS algorithm. Its efficacy is proved by the good performance of the algorithm in problems where the training patterns are totally randomly selected during the learning phase. Moreover, with respect to previous approaches ([4] [5] [6]) the numerical stability is enhanced by the fact that the proposed procedure works only on raw data matrices, without forming any correlation matrix.

References

[1]T.P.Vogl, J.K.Mangis, A.K.Rigler, W.T.Zink, D.L.Alkon, "Accelerating the Convergence of the Back-Propagation Method", Biological Cybernetics 59,257-263, 1988.

[2]R.A.Jacobs, "Increased Rates of Convergence Through Learning Rate Adaptation, Neural Networks", Vol. 1, pp. 295-307, 1988.

[3]G.H.Golub, C.F.van Loan, "Matrix computations", John Hopkins Universiy Press, Second edition, 1989.

[4]S.Kollias, D.Anastassiou, "An Adaptive Least Squares Algorithm for the Efficient Training of Artificial Neural Networks", IEEE Trans. on Circuits and Systems, Vol. 36, no. 8, August 1989.

[5]R.S.Scalero, N.Tepedelenlioglu, "A Fast New Algorithm for Training Feedforward Neural Networks", IEEE Transactions on signal processing, Vol.40, No. 1, January 1992.

[6]M.R.Azimi-Sadjadi, R.-J.Liou, "Fast Learning Process of Multilayer Neural Networks Using Recursive Least Squares Method", IEEE Transactions on signal processing, Vol.40, No. 2, February 1992.

[7]S.Haykin, "Adaptive filter theory", Prentice Hall, 1991.

Batch Parallel Training of Simple Recurrent Neural Networks *

Peter J. McCann and Barry L. Kalman

Department of Computer Science, Washington University, Campus Box 1045, St. Louis, Missouri 63130-4899

pjm3@cs.wustl.edu

barry@cs.wustl.edu

Abstract

A concurrent implementation of the method of conjugate gradients for training Elman networks is discussed. The parallelism is obtained in the computation of the error gradient and the method is therefore applicable to any gradient descent training technique for this form of network. The experimental results were obtained on a Sun Sparc Center 2000 multiprocessor. The Sparc 2000 is a shared memory machine well suited to coarse-grained distributed computations, but the concurrency could be extended to other architectures as well.

1 Introduction

It takes an exceptionally large amount of computer time to train recurrent networks because of the added complexity of the derivative calculations. In this work, we focus on one type of recurrent network, Elman's Simple Recurrent Network [1], and we present a way to distribute the gradient computation.

Figure 1 shows a variant of an Elman SRN. This is a partially recurrent neural network capable of learning sequence information. The context units hold copies of the hidden unit activations from the previous pattern presentation, and therefore the output of the network can depend not only on the current input but also on the entire input history.

Our network architecture includes "skip connections" that bypass the hidden layer. It has been determined experimentally that these connections allow for faster network training. They provide an alternate set of parameters for the linearly separable, or perceptron, portion of the problem. See [2] for a more complete discussion of the rationale for these connections.

Each input sequence is an ordered set of patterns because of the recurrent connections in the network. These allow the network to learn sequence information and base its output on the history of the inputs presented to it. At the beginning of a sequence, we can set the feedback activations to zero, so that they have no impact on the output during the first pattern presentation. We have found empirically that this is the best choice for the initial conditions. See [2] for a more detailed discussion. During subsequent presentations, the feedback units are copied back from the hidden layer and provide the context needed

---

*This material is based upon work supported by the National Science Foundation under Grant No. IRI-9201987. Thanks to Dr. Mark Franklin and the Washington University Computer and Communications Research Center for the use of their Sparc Center 2000 multiprocessor. The Sparc Center 2000 was purchased in part with funds from NSF CISE Instrumentation Grant 9022560.

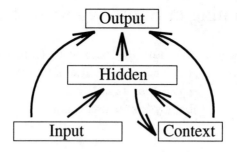

Figure 1: An Elman Simple Recurrent Network.

to make decisions about later input patterns. Typically, we will present the network with many of these sequences during training, in hopes that its performance will generalize across the set of all possible sequences in some reasonable way.

Some notational conventions:

t_{po}	The target of output unit o when the network is presented with pattern p.
a_{po}	The activation of unit o when the network is presented with pattern p.
b_i	The bias value of unit i.
w_{ij}	The weight from unit i to unit j.
$\mathcal{F}$	The set of all feedback (context) units.
$\mathcal{O}$	The set of all output units.
$\mathcal{P}$	The set of input sequences.

We are using an epoch based training method, so the error function is a sum over all patterns of some function of the targets and the actual activations, defined as:

$$\Phi = \sum_{p \in \mathcal{P}} \sum_{o \in \mathcal{O}} e(t_{po}, a_{po}).$$

Any gradient-descent based method of minimizing the error function will need to calculate the gradient. That is, we need to take a derivative of our error function with respect to each of the parameters of the network. Taking Y to be some weight or bias in the network, we have

$$\frac{\partial \Phi}{\partial Y} = \sum_{p \in \mathcal{P}} \sum_{o \in \mathcal{O}} \frac{\partial e(t_{po}, a_{po})}{\partial Y}. \tag{1}$$

For efficiency, we should obviously propagate each pattern through to the outputs and then calculate the $\frac{\partial \Phi}{\partial Y}$ contribution from this pattern for every parameter in the network, summing each term into a global sum for that parameter. The propagation steps also must be performed in a certain order due to the sequence information inherent in the patterns. However, we can break up the patterns along sequence boundaries, and present the sequences themselves in an arbitrary order. This is where opportunities for concurrency arise.

2   Concurrency

We can partition the set of patterns into subsets where each subset is itself ordered, but requires no context from any other subset. That is,

$$\mathcal{P} = \{s_1, s_2, \ldots s_N\},$$

where we can define $\text{len}(s_i)$ to be the number of patterns in sequence i. The input sequences might be of different lengths, and so we need a strategy for assigning sequences to processors so that the computation is as load-balanced as possible. To accomplish this, we first sort the sequences in nonincreasing order by $\text{len}(s_i)$, and then assign each sequence in turn to the least loaded processor. We assume that the load is proportional to the number of pattern presentations required and therefore to the total length of all sequences assigned to a processor so far.

After sequences have been assigned to processors, we need to make some additional modifications to the sequential code. Since each processor will be doing independent forward propagation, we will need a separate copy of the network activations for each job. Since each processor will be computing a local sum of the gradient components, we will need a separate copy of all the $\frac{\partial \Phi}{\partial Y}$ variables for each job. However, the results are to be computed using only one set of weights, and so all of the w_{ij} and b_i values can be shared.

The derivative calculation for recurrent networks is quite computationally intense. It scales as $O(\|\mathcal{F}\|^4)$ for calculating the derivatives with respect to weights that connect input units to hidden units. See [2] for the details of these calculations.

Note that certain implementations of second order methods may require a line search along the descent direction indicated by the gradient in order to find a minimum in that direction. Our conjugate gradient trainer uses such a search, and we have found that a derivative-free line search involving only evaluations of Φ is the most efficient. The above partitioning of input patterns can be used equally well to speed up this forward propagation.

3   Results

Our conjugate-gradient trainer is implemented using the available C libraries for multi-threaded execution on the Sun Sparc Center 2000 multiprocessor system. There are currently eight processors available on the system, but with a coming operating system upgrade, this number should increase to twenty. The Sparc 2000 has a shared memory architecture with two high bandwidth packet buses. A message-passing implementation would require duplication and update of the w_{ij} and b_i values in the local memory of each node.

Our test problem was a (192+9)-13-2 network, meaning 192 inputs, 9 feedback units, 13 hidden units, and 2 outputs. The goal was to identify the language spoken in a ten-second sample of audio. The network was presented with successive 400 millisecond overlapping frames of bandpass filtered sound and trained to differentiate between English and French speakers. The training patterns consisted of 41 sequences which were divided over processors as evenly as possible. Table 1 shows the division of labor. There was a total of 15,457 patterns in all 41 sequences.

Processor	Number of Sequences Assigned							
8								6
7							6	5
6						7	6	5
5					9	7	6	5
4				11	8	7	6	5
3			14	10	8	7	6	5
2		21	14	10	8	7	6	5
1	41	20	13	10	8	6	5	5
	1	2	3	4	5	6	7	8
	Number of Processors Used							

Table 1: Division of Labor

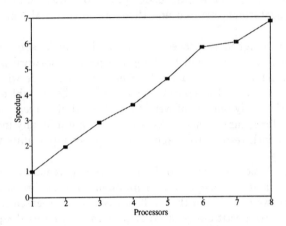

Figure 2: Speedup of a derivative, or backpropagation, epoch as function of processors used.

Figure 2 shows the speedups obtained for a derivative epoch. Speedup was experimentally measured and is the ratio between the execution time of the sequential version and the execution times of each multiprocessor version. It includes all overhead for adding each portion of the derivatives into a grand sum for each network parameter. A derivative evaluation, in the sequential version, takes approximately 24 minutes for this problem.

Figure 3 shows the speedups obtained for the derivative free forward evaluation of the error. A forward evaluation, in the sequential version, takes approximately 13 seconds for this problem. Typically, about ten forward evaluations are required per conjugate gradient epoch to perform the line search. The speedups obtained here are smaller because the computation is smaller, and the overhead of concurrent memory access tends to drown out the advantages gained. The data point for 6 processors represents an unusually efficient use of time. This is probably because the assignment of sequences, as shown in Table 1, is unusually smooth, and the smaller computation is more sensitive to this than the derivative calculation.

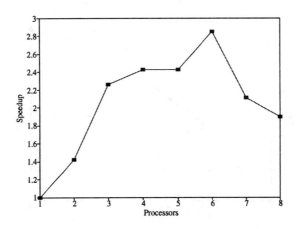

Figure 3: Speedup of a linesearch epoch as function of processors used.

Figure 4 shows the overall speedups obtained for a conjugate gradient epoch. The speedups take into account time from the sequential portion of the code that computes the conjugate gradient directions. A training epoch, in the sequential version, takes approximately 27 minutes for this problem. This time is dominated by the derivative calculation, and so good overall speedup can be obtained by making that portion of the code concurrent. Note, however, that forward evaluation is also important, as indicated by the data point for 6 processors.

Typically, a single training run will require hundreds of epochs. The overall speedup presented here therefore represents significant savings in time over the sequential version. By reducing the turnaround time, a greater number of network architectures can be investigated, and connectionist research can be more effective.

4   Conclusion

Our previous work focused on the possibilities for concurrency in one portion of the derivative calculation. This allowed us to achieve some speedup, but it was limited by the size of the network architecture used, and did not allow concurrent computation of the forward propagation step. Our current trainer, although it was more difficult to implement, allows us to partition the set of inputs, which is typically large. This lets us use the available hardware more efficiently.

While the training of recurrent networks, even of simple ones, introduces myriad new complexities over feedforward network training, our algorithm contains opportunities for concurrency. These opportunities can be taken advantage of after a careful and thorough study of the data dependencies involved. Reducing the real time elapsed during a training run is of great benefit to those undertaking connectionist research projects. It means that more experiments can be conducted in less time than with sequential methods.

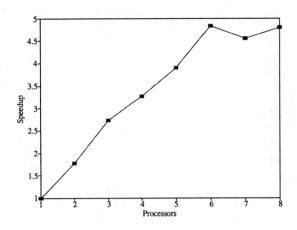

Figure 4: Overall speedup as function of processors used.

References

[1] Elman, J.L. (1990). Finding Structure in Time. *Cognitive Science* **14**, 179-211.

[2] Kalman, B.L., and Kwasny, Stan C. (1993). TRAINREC: A System for Training Feedforward and Simple Recurrent Networks Efficiently and Correctly. Technical Report WUCS-93-26, St. Louis: Department of Computer Science, Washington University.

[3] Kalman, B.L., and Kwasny, Stan C. (1992). Why Tanh: Choosing a Sigmoidal Function. *Proceedings of the International Joint Conference on Neural Networks* (Baltimore 1992), vol. IV, 578-581. New York: IEEE.

[4] Kalman, B.L., and Kwasny, Stan C. (1991). A Superior Error Function for Training Neural Nets. *Proceedings of the International Joint Conference on Neural Networks* (Seattle 1991), vol. II, 49-52. New York: IEEE.

[5] Kramer, A., and Sangiovanni-Vincentelli, A. (1989). Efficient Parallel Learning Algorithms for Neural Networks. *Advances in Neural Information Processing Systems 1*, ed. D.S. Touretzky, 40-48. San Mateo: Morgan Kaufman.

LEARNING THE SIGMOID SLOPES TO INCREASE THE CONVERGENCE SPEED OF THE MULTILAYER PERCEPTRON

Eric MAILLARD
GESMA
29240 BREST-NAVAL, FRANCE
Tel : +33 98 22 71 62
Fax : +33 98 22 72 13

Didier GUERIOT
IRP, TROP laboratory
68000 MULHOUSE, FRANCE
Tel : +33 89 59 82 00
Fax: +33 89 32 76 01

ABSTRACT : A time constant is introduced as a variable in the decision function of the perceptron neuron. It is shown that a time constant carefully chosen dramatically improves the performance of the backpropagation algorithm on a benchmark. A new learning algorithm including the time constant as a variable is developed in this study. Two versions of the algorithm are detailed. The difference between them lies in the set of neurons to which the new algorithm is applied. Both versions exhibit improved convergence rate when compared to a backpropagation algorithm using optimum fixed time constant.

I INTRODUCTION

One of the most popular decision function for the neurons of a multilayer perceptron (MLP) is the so-called sigmoid function defined by:

$$y_j = \frac{1.0}{1.0 + e^{-net_j}} \quad \text{with} \quad net_j = \sum_{i=0}^{n} w_{ji} x_i + \theta_j$$

where:
- w_{ji} is the synaptic weight from neuron i of layer l to neuron j of layer l+1,
- θ_j is a bias term
- y_i is the output of neuron i.
- n is the number of neurons of layer l.

Using this decision function, the poor performances of the MLP on the XOR problem have been a strong motivation of research for improved versions [1][2] of the classical backpropagation (BP) [3]. A simple variation of the decision function allows the MLP to achieve convergence in an average of 42 epochs over 100 runs of the XOR problem. A time constant λ scales the network input to the neuron (i.e. net_j) before passing through the non-linear decision function:

$$y_j = \frac{1.0}{1.0 + e^{-\lambda \, net_j}}$$

"Trial and error" method was used to choose a proper time constant. This approach is time consuming and would be even more consuming should each neuron have its own time constant. In section II, the time constant is introduced and its effects on the discrimination capabilities of a neuron analyzed. In section III, a new algorithm based on BP is derived in full length. Each neuron uses an individual time constant learned during training. In section IV, the dynamic of the time constants is studied and we draw the conclusion that the output layer neurons alone should make use of an individual time constant thus reducing the computational burden induced by the introduction of this variable in BP. Finally a comparison of the new learning algorithms with a standard version of the MLP is carried out on a 2-D artificial data in section V. Section VI concludes this paper by discussing the robustness of the algorithms.

II TIME CONSTANT AND DISCRIMINATION

While used on classification applications, the sigmoid function exhibits the advantage over the symmetric $\tanh(net_j / 2)$ function that it can be interpreted as a loose membership function varying from 0 to 1. The critic of slower convergence of the sigmoid function emphasizes the need for fast learning algorithms. Consider a single perceptron neuron trained on a two-class discrimination problem according to an algorithm aimed at minimizing an error function defined by :

$$E(t) = \frac{1}{2}(d(t) - y(t))^2$$

where d(t) is the desired output at time t and y(t) is the actual output of the neuron at time t.

While learning unfolds, this neuron must deal with two opposite goals : on one side, the update of its weights is maximum when the output of the neuron is near 0.5 and on the other side, its objective value for each pattern is either 0 or 1, those values prevent any update of the weights. Adding a time constant to the decision function of the neuron helps acting on its sensibility to input patterns. The variation of the output value according to different values of the time constant is illustrated in Fig. 1. A decision function with a large constant tends to approximate a Boolean decision function while the same function with a small constant looks like a quite linear function. Clearly the time constant must be carefully chosen in order to achieve fast and efficient training. One may also wonder whether a fixed time constant is well suited for learning since during the process of training the behavior of the network is bounded to change.

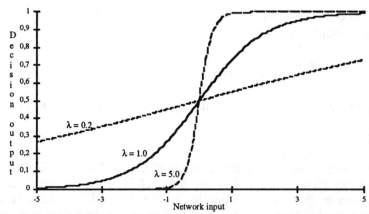

Fig. 1 : Influence of the time constant on the shape of the decision function.

The XOR problem was referred to as a toy problem, the decision of introducing a time constant must not be taken on the sole basis of the performance of a neural network with two hidden neurons and one output neuron. When dealing with a real problem, such as texture classification, the size of the network is an order of magnitude larger than that of the previous one. No a priori knowledge ensures the existence of a single optimum time constant shared by all the neurons, it may turn out that each neuron needs a specific time constant. Empirical search for these optimum values may soon become intractable. This emphasizes the need for learned time constants.

III FORMAL DERIVATION OF THE NEW ALGORITHM

Since the time constants will be learned, and according to their effects on the decision function curve, they will be referred to as slopes from here on. The notations are defined in Fig. 2. The output of any neuron is defined by :

$$y_i = \frac{1}{1 + e^{(-\lambda_i \, net_i)}}$$

The error function for pattern p is defined by :

$$E_p = \frac{1}{2} \sum_k \left(d_k^p - y_k^p\right)^2$$

where d_k^p is the desired output for neuron k and y_k^p is the actual one when presented the pattern p.

Weight updating rule is computed according to:

$$\Delta w_{jk} = -\eta \, \frac{\partial E_p}{\partial w_{jk}}$$

In order to preserve the consistency of the BP learning algorithm, slope learning is achieved according to :

$$\Delta \lambda_k = -v \, \frac{\partial E_p}{\partial \lambda_k}$$

For the neurons of the output layer it comes :

$$\frac{\partial E_p}{\partial w_{kj}} = -(d_k - y_k) \, \lambda_k \, y_k \, (1 - y_k) \, y_j \tag{1}$$

$$\frac{\partial E_p}{\partial \lambda_k} = -(d_k - y_k) \, net_k \, y_k \, (1 - y_k) \tag{2}$$

For the neurons of any hidden layer it comes :

$$\frac{\partial E_p}{\partial w_{kj}} = -\sum_k (d_k - y_k) \, y_k \, (1 - y_k) \, w_{kj} \, \lambda_k \, y_j \, (1 - y_j) \, \lambda_j \, y_i$$

$$\frac{\partial E_p}{\partial \lambda_k} = -\sum_k (d_k - y_k) \, y_k \, (1 - y_k) \, w_{kj} \, \lambda_k \, y_j \, (1 - y_j) \, net_j$$

Detailed formal derivation of the learning algorithm is given in appendix (for sake of simplicity the momemtun term is not introduced here).

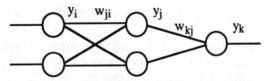

Fig. 2 : Notations used in the derivation of the new algorithm.

Some learning algorithms need to evaluate the exact energy function before any weight update : the entire training set must be propagated forward, and the error for each pattern estimated, between each backward propagation . Since the introduction of a time constant do not alter the core of BP, the new algorithm takes advantage of the so-called stochastic gradient algorithm. After forward propagation of a pattern, the weights and slopes are updated.

IV ANALYSIS OF THE SLOPE DYNAMIC

A test on artificial data is used to analyze the dynamic of the slopes. Several runs were performed on two-dimensional difficult data. One representative run is depicted in Fig. 3. Although the neural network used on this test is a two-layer one, preliminary results on networks with many hidden layers confirm the analysis drawn below. Furthermore, some additional runs with random initial values of the time constants show that these values do not have much effect on the following evolution.

An empirical study shows that the slopes of the hidden-layer neurons do not vary much during learning. The only variation is a slow increase of these slopes. This can be explained by considering the presumed goal of the neurons of any hidden layer. These neurons try to separate patterns according to their class : a stiffer slope gives a finer separation.

The slopes of the last-layer neurons decrease at the beginning of learning then increase until convergence is achieved. The initial decrease of these slopes can be analyzed as a search for information in order to ignite the process of decision-surface positioning. Once those decision surfaces are coarsely positioned, stabilization becomes the goal of the output neurons. The increasing slopes prevent broad variation of the weights by saturating the output of the neurons. Due to the backward process of updating, small variations of the weights of the last layer neurons prevent large variations of the weights of the hidden layers neurons.

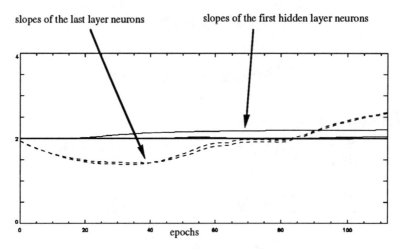

Fig. 3 : Dynamic of the slopes

V OPTIMUM VERSION OF THE NEW ALGORITHM

The new algorithm as defined in section II, adds a computational burden to the already slow and heavy BP algorithm. Although the updating laws of the weights and of the slopes share a common part, it would be useful to keep the additional computation to a minimum. The analysis of the dynamic of the slopes suggests a way to achieve this goal. Since the slopes of the hidden-layer neurons do not vary much, those neurons may not need an individual variable slope. A minimum algorithm including slope learning for the neurons of the last layer is derived. The updating laws for those neurons are identical to the previous ones : (1) and (2) . In order to preserve adaptation ability, a common slope γ that can be set to any arbitrary value is kept in the decision function of the hidden-layer neurons. The updating law for their weights is :

$$\frac{\partial E_p}{\partial w_{ji}} = - \sum_k (d_k - y_k) y_k (1 - y_k) w_{kj} \lambda_k y_j (1 - y_j) \gamma \, y_i$$

The performance of the minimum algorithm is analyzed on the problem used previously in order to appreciate the loss induced by the simplification. A general robustness test was performed. A standard MLP with a common slope for every neuron trained consecutively with classical BP (CBP) , BP with individual slopes for every neuron (EBP) and BP with individual slopes for the output layer neurons (OBP) , was trained 10 times for 2300 combinations of the learning parameters chosen to span the whole parameter space. Results are described in the next section.

VI CONCLUSION AND DISCUSSION

A new algorithm for the MLP has been presented. The introduction of a variable slope in the decision function of the neurons increases the convergence speed. The additional computation burden induced by the new algorithm, lead us to an empirical study of the slope dynamic that points out the uselessness of the variable slope for the neurons of hidden layers. A minimum algorithm was then derived. It exhibits good performance results on both artificial and real data classification problems. A detailed performances analysis can be found in [4]. Preliminary studies of the robustness of the algorithms show that while the maximum number of achieved convergence is obtained by EBP : 42.1% (pointing out its robustness to parameters variation), the performance of OBP : 39.6% is quite equivalent and anyway much better than those of the CBP : 26.5%.

VII APPENDIX

Notations are defined by Fig. 2. Derivation deals with a two layers network for the sake of simplicity (extension to higher dimension network is immediate). The output of the last layer neurons is :

$$y_k = \frac{1.0}{1.0 + \exp\left(\lambda_k \, net_k\right)} \quad \text{with} \quad net_k = \sum_{j=1}^{m} y_j \, w_{kj} + \theta_k$$

The output of the neuron of a hidden layer is given by :

$$y_j = \frac{1.0}{1.0 + \exp\left(\lambda_j \, net_j\right)} \quad \text{with} \quad net_j = \sum_{i=1}^{n} y_i \, w_{ji} + \theta_j$$

Updating of the variables (weights and slope) of a last layer neuron follows :

$$\Delta w_{kj} (t+1) = - \eta \, \frac{\partial E_p}{\partial w_{kj}} + \alpha \, \Delta w_{kj} (t)$$

$$\Delta \lambda_k (t+1) = - \nu \, \frac{\partial E_p}{\partial \lambda_k} + \kappa \, \Delta \lambda_k (t)$$

where :

$$\frac{\partial E_p}{\partial w_{kj}} = \frac{\partial E_p}{\partial net_k} \cdot \frac{\partial net_k}{\partial w_{kj}}$$

$$= \frac{\partial E_p}{\partial net_k} \cdot y_j$$

III-543

$$\frac{\partial E_p}{\partial \, net_k} = \frac{\partial E_p}{\partial \, o_k} \cdot \frac{\partial \, y_k}{\partial \, net_k}$$

$$= - (d_k - y_k) \cdot y_k \, (1 - y_k) \, \lambda_k$$

and :

$$\frac{\partial E_p}{\partial \lambda_k} = \frac{\partial E_p}{\partial \, y_k} \cdot \frac{\partial \, y_k}{\partial \lambda_k}$$

$$= - (d_k - y_k) \cdot (y_k \, (1 - y_k) \, net_k)$$

Updating of a hidden layer neuron variable follows :

$$\Delta w_{ji} \, (t+1) = - \eta \, \frac{\partial E_p}{\partial \, w_{ji}} + \alpha \, \Delta w_{ji} \, (t)$$

$$\Delta \lambda_j \, (t+1) = - \nu \, \frac{\partial E_p}{\partial \lambda_j} + \kappa \, \Delta \lambda_j \, (t)$$

with :

$$\frac{\partial E_p}{\partial \, w_{ji}} = \frac{\partial E_p}{\partial \, net_j} \cdot \frac{\partial \, net_j}{\partial \, w_{ji}}$$

$$= \frac{\partial E_p}{\partial \, net_j} \cdot y_i$$

$$\frac{\partial E_p}{\partial \, net_j} = \frac{\partial E_p}{\partial \, o_j} \cdot \frac{\partial \, y_j}{\partial \, net_j}$$

$$= - \sum_k \delta_k \, w_{kj} \cdot y_j \, (1 - y_j) \, \lambda_j$$

and

$$\frac{\partial E_p}{\partial \lambda_j} = \frac{\partial E_p}{\partial \, y_j} \cdot \frac{\partial \, y_j}{\partial \lambda_j}$$

$$= - \sum_k \delta_k \, w_{kj} \cdot (y_j \, (1 - y_j) \, net_j)$$

REFERENCES

[1] Jacobs R. : "Increased rates of convergence through learning rate adaptation", Neural Networks, 1, pp 295-307, 1988

[2] S.E. Fahlman, "Faster-Learning Variations on Back-propagation : an empirical study", in *Proc. 1988 Connectionists models summer school*, 1989, pp.38-51.

[3] Rumelhart D., Mc Clelland J. (eds.): Parallel Distributed Processing, vol. 1&2, D. Rumelhart , J. Mc Clelland eds, MIT Press, 1986.

[4] Didier Gueriot, Eric Maillard, "Performances of a perceptron with slope learning backpropagation", submitted to WCNN'94 San Diego.

The Constraint Based Decomposition Training Architecture

Sorin Draghici, Department of Computational Science,
University of St Andrews, North Haugh, St Andrews, KY16 9SS, UK

Abstract. Constraint based decomposition (CBD) is a variation of the "divide and conquer" method. The CBD algorithm is composed by a weight updating rule (any algorithm able to train a single layer net), a pattern presentation algorithm and a method for constructing the network. CBD finds an architecture able to solve the problem and trains it at the same time. The search for the solution is performed by reducing the dimensionality of the weight space and that of the training set. The training is performed on subnets with subgoals and the weights found in one subgoal training will be conserved and form a part of the final solution. The training is performed exclusively on the simplest possible type of net: one layer, one neuron and though the resulting net is as powerful as a multilayer perceptron. The pattern subsets contain always n-1 correctly classified and one misclassified pattern. The computation involved is very simple. No derivatives are calculated and no preprocessing is needed.

1. Introduction

Many training algorithm for feedforward multilayer networks, have important drawbacks. Some of them are inherently slow and can be trapped in local minima. For most of them, it is necessary to start the training with the correct architecture. In the following, some factors influencing the training process are reviewed and a new algorithm is proposed that addresses these factors. This algorithm is based on constraint satisfaction and constructs the network during training.

Architectural issues. It is well known that the training difficulty increases with the complexity of the architecture, in particular with the number of layers.

A certain architectural complexity is required because one layer networks cannot solve problems that are not linearly separable. At the same time, multilayer networks, are hard to train and their training may fail. If the network has more than one hidden layer, other problems such as the attenuation of the error signal appear [Lang, 1988].

Deciding the architecture of a multilayer perceptron for a given I/O training set is a problem in itself. Many algorithms work with a fixed architecture. Therefore, the correct architecture has to be chosen before training starts. If training fails it is not clear if this is because of an insufficient architecture or another cause. If the architecture is too rich, the solution weight state will have neurons which provide unnecessary information and/or neurons which do not contribute to the solution [Sietsma, 1991].

Dimensionality of the weight space. The training problem can be posed as that of finding the minimum of an error surface over a weight space. Independently of the algorithm used, this problem becomes more difficult as the number of dimensions of the weight space increases. Wilensky and Neuhaus (Wilensky, 1990) report that even for a simple, linearly separable problem like discrimination between two N dimensional gaussians, the training time increases both with the number N of dimensions for the same architecture and with the number of hidden units for the same dimensionality of the input space.

The pattern set. Falhman and Lebiere in [Falhman, 1990] identified the moving target problem as one of the causes of the training problems for a multi-layer architecture. This effect is determined by the presence in the training set of many different tasks to be accomplished. In this situation, more than one hidden unit will try to tackle the same task. Only after one of the tasks is accomplished by one or more hidden neurons, will other neurons be redirected to other sources of error. This is one of the reasons for which the standard training is slow. This effect can be eliminated if there is only one source of error in the training set and only one hidden unit to be trained. The training problem is even simpler if the net does not have hidden units.

There are perhaps counter-examples for one or more of the statements above. These should be taken more like assumptions justified by some experiments rather than irrefutable truth. However they are useful in understanding the technique which is being proposed. As far as these factors are concerned, the ideal training problem is to train an architecture with only one layer, only one neuron and to have a unique source of error in the training set. This is what the CBD techniques addresses.

2. Time based decomposition (TBD) vs. constraint based decomposition (CBD).

A possible approach to solving a problem is "divide and conquer". Split the task into many simpler tasks and solve each of them. There are two fundamentally different methods for splitting a complex goal into sub-goals: history based decomposition and constraint based decomposition.

Let us consider for instance a robot (with a humanoid anatomy) situated in the middle of a room with the task to open the door. The task is complex. The robot has to move towards the door. Perhaps at the same time, it will move its arm, raising it from its normal position along the body towards the level of the door knob. Concurrently, it will move its fingers preparing them to grasp the door knob. During this complex movement, the head and the eyes must move in such a way that the door knob is kept in the centre of the visual field independently of the position of the body.

Let us suppose we ask a human to perform the task. We are going to record this solution which is one of the many possible solutions and use it to teach our robot. The solution will be a sequence of intermediate positions, a path P in the space S of all the possible positions. We call this path a solution path. Now, we could sample this path by choosing a number of intermediate positions: $(p_1, p_2,...,p_n)$. This is a discrete solution path. The first subgoal of the system is to reach the first point on the path, the second is to reach the next point and so on. Any complex task for which we know (or could design) a path can now be learned. This type of decomposition will be called time based decomposition.

There exists, however, another possibility to split the task into sub-tasks. For the robot to accomplish the task, a set of constraints must be satisfied e.g. the robot must be near the door (i.e. the distance between the robot's mass centre and the door knob must be less than the arm's length), the hand must be at the height of the door knob, the fingers must be open so that grasping the knob is possible, etc. The task is characterised by a set of constraints $(r_1, r_2,...,r_p)$. This set of constraints does not depend on the path in the position space the subject used to reach the final state.

One could consider a constraint space with one dimension for each constraint in the constraint set. Fig. 1 shows a possible training path for a time based decomposition. The variables characterising the constraints vary all at the same time. In each step, each of them will come closer to the value which characterises the solution.

Fig. 2 shows a training path for a constraint based decomposition. The subgoals are defined such that the first one includes the first constraint, the second one the first two constraints and so on. The first step of the training takes the net into the subspace corresponding to the first constraint. The search for the solution of the second subgoal will be performed in the subspace ss1 which is a subspace with n-1 dimensions of the n dimensional constraint space. The search for the solution of the next subgoal will be performed in a subspace with n-2 dimensions and so on.

3. Theoretical framework

Definition. A **constraint** is a condition necessary but not sufficient for the solution. There must be possible for the solution to be expressed as a set of non-contradictory constraints.

Definition. A **task** is defined by a set of constraints $(r_1, r_2,...,r_j)$. This set of constraints defines a point p in the constraint space. The solution of a task is a point W in the weight space which satisfies the given set of constraints.

Observation: In a constraint based decomposition the number of constraint variables varies but if a variable appears in a subgoal it will contains the final value of that variable (the value characterising the solution). In a time based decomposition, the number of constraint variables remains constant and equal to the number of constraints of the problem but their values vary at each stage.

Definition. Given a task defined by the set of constraints $(r_1, r_2,...,r_n)$, a **time based decomposition (TBD)** is a discrete solution path $P=(p_1, p_2,...,p_n)$ with the property that p_1 is the initial point, p_n is the solution and each state p_i satisfies a set of constraints $(r^i_1, r^i_2,...,r^i_n)$.

Definition. Given a task defined by the set of constraints $(r_1, r_2,...,r_n)$, a **constraint based decomposition (CBD)** is a discrete solution path $P=(p_1, p_2,...,p_p)$ with the property that p_1 is the initial point, p_n is the solution and each state p_i satisfies the constraints $(r_1, r_2,...,r_i)$.

4. Constraint definition. CBD as a method to perform a dimensionality reduction in the weight space.

For present implementation purposes, a constraint is defined as obtaining the correct output for patterns situated in a limited region of the input space or equivalently the construction of the desired I/O surface above a limited region of the input space. When the output is the correct one, the constraint is satisfied.

This definition satisfies the conditions for a constraints because:

a) The whole I/O surface can be cut into pieces corresponding to disjoint regions of input space $\{a_1, a_2, ...a_3\}$. In order for the I/O surface S to be the goal I/O surface Sg, S must be equal to Sg in all of the regions $a_1, a_2, ...a_3$. Therefore, $S = Sg|a_i$ (the condition that S be equal to Sg in the limited area a_i) is a necessary but not sufficient condition.

b) The solution i.e. the goal I/O surface can be expressed as a set of non-contradictory constraints: S is a solution if and only if $S = Sg|a_i$ for any i from 1 to n, where n is the number of areas the input space has been cut into. Due to the fact that a_i are disjoint by definition, the constraints cannot be contradictory.

The CBD training starts by training the first subgoal which requires the satisfaction of the first constraint. The second subgoal will ask the satisfaction of the first two constraints. Therefore, the search for the solution of the second subgoal is performed in a subspace with n-1 dimensions of the n dimensional constraint space.

The interesting case is when the reduction of dimensionality in the constraint space can be put into correspondence to a reduction of dimensionality in the weight space. In this case, the weights found in one subgoal training will be preserved unchanged and will be a part of the final solution. Having as few dimensions in the weight space as possible was one of the characteristics of the ideal training situation.

The shape and the size of the regions of input space used in defining the constraints is very important. The shape and the size chosen should depend on the problem. Ideally this should be done automatically, by the training algorithm.

Search directed by subgoals

The search directed by subgoals characterises a situation in which there is only a weak coupling between the constraint space and the weight space. A reduction of dimensions in the constraint space could but does not necessarily correspond to a reduction of dimensions in the weight space.

The simplest form in which the CBD idea can be implemented is to define the subgoals by splitting the training set into subsets. This is roughly equivalent to splitting the input space into disjoint regions and taking as a training set of a subgoal, the patterns in this region. A constraint is getting the correct output for a subset of the training set. A subgoal is the training of a increasing number of constraints.

In order to check the effects of this CBD, one could simply train (with a standard weight change algorithm) the subgoals corresponding to the chosen constraints. In constraint space, the net is asked to reach the first subgoal. From this point, the net is trained with the second subgoal. No measures to ensure that the net will remain in the subspace corresponding to the first subgoal are taken. The question is whether the net will be able to preserve the information obtained by the training of the first subgoal in the training of the second one.

This will be shown by the evolution of the error for the patterns in the first subset during the training of the second subgoal and so on. If this error remains small, it will mean that the search for the solution to the second subgoal is directed by the subspace corresponding to the first one. If the error goes up, it will mean that the first few weight changes in the second training session have thrown the net far from the subspace corresponding to the first subgoal and the first training was useless.

This experiment could show the importance of the pattern presentation algorithm. If the result of the training can be substantially changed by changing the pattern presentation algorithm, a training algorithm must be seen as the combination of a weight changing algorithm and a pattern presentation algorithm rather than a weight changing algorithm alone. A substantial change would be for instance the success of the CBD pattern presentation algorithm in some problem where the batch pattern presentation algorithm fails. Both should use the same weight updating rule.

The CBD pattern presentation algorithm tries to ensure that, for each training, the position of the initial weight state in relation to the position of the goal is good. This is achieved by training exclusively on pattern sets containing mostly patterns that the net is already able to respond to correctly.

Search restricted by subgoals. The CBD net.

In the case of a search restricted by subgoals, there is a strong connection between the constraint space and the weight space. A reduction of dimensions in the constraint space is put into a direct correspondence with a reduction of dimensions in the weight space. The weights found by training a subgoal will become a part of the final solution.

Since the purpose is to train only few weights at a time and to keep those weights unchanged afterwards, the idea of constructing the net during the training comes naturally in one's mind. The CBD algorithm is formed by a CBD pattern presentation algorithm, a construction mechanism for building the net and a weight change algorithm for a single layer perceptron (delta rule for instance).

To illustrate the CBD algorithm, let us consider the example of a classification problem. Without loss of generality, we shall consider only two classes C1 and C2 in an n dimensional input space. The problem is defined by a set of patterns for each class. There are two output units O1 and O2, one for each class.

The CBD algorithm starts with the input units, one hidden unit and the bias unit (permanently set to 1). For the classification problem one can use threshold units with (-1,+1) output range and 0 threshold. For problems in which a precise analogue output is desired, one can use a different type of activation function with the same algorithm.

Let $C_1 = \left\{ x_1^{C1}, x_2^{C1}, ..., x_m^{C1} \right\}$ be the set of patterns in the class C1 and $C_2 = \left\{ x_1^{C2}, x_2^{C2}, ..., x_n^{C2} \right\}$ be the set of patterns in class C2.

The first stage is to construct a hidden layer (the hyperplane layer) which has a hidden unit for each hyperplane necessary for the separation of the regions belonging to different classes. The result of this stage is a set of hyperplanes h_1, h_2, ..., h_k and a set of terms T_i of the form T_i=sign(h_1)h_1...sign(h_k)h_k, Cj) where sign(h_i) can be 1,-1 or nil and j can be 1 or 2. This is equivalent to building a piecewise linear boundary between classes.

Each hyperplane divides the space into two regions one positive and one negative. A hyperplane and its sign form a factor. A factor is used to represent the corresponding half-space determined by the hyperplane. A term is obtained by performing a logical and between factors. Not all the hyperplanes must contribute with a factor to all the terms. Finally, a logical or is performed between terms in order to obtain the expression of the solution for each class.

The algorithm for the first stage (building and training the hyperplane layer) is presented in fig. 7.

The algorithm is presented as a recursive procedure. Its parameters are: a region of the space (initial value = whole space), the training set divided into two sets, one for each class (initial value = the whole training set) and a factor (initial value = nil). The factor describes the region and nil corresponds to the whole space.

The CBD algorithm starts by building a subgoal with only two patterns, one from each class. A unit (which will become a hidden unit in the final net) will be added and trained such as it separates the two patterns. This training problem is the simplest problem one can have: only one layer and only one unit. It is assumed that this training will succeed. Let h be the hyperplane obtained by this training. This hyperplane will be saved. A new pattern (from any class) will now be added to the current subgoal. The same unit will be trained again. The training problem is again the simplest possible: one layer, one unit and the pattern set contains only one misclassified example. If the training succeeds, the pattern will remain in the current subgoal and the new hyperplane will be used subsequently. If the training fails, the old hyperplane will be restored and the pattern will be deleted from the current subgoal. The process continues until all the patterns in the training set have been considered. In the simplest case, the failure of a training is detected by imposing a timeout condition in number of epochs or monitoring the weight changes and stopping the training when the error evolution becomes asymptotic.

The hyperplane resulted at the end of this process will divide the space into two half-spaces h+ and h-. If h+ contains only patterns in the same class Cj, h+ will be added to the current factor and the result classified as class Cj. The region resulted will be the intersection between the initial region and h+. Therefore, the factor characterising the new region will be (factor and h+). If h+ is not homogeneous (it contains patterns in both classes) the algorithm will be applied again to h+ region. The same is done for h-.

The next stage is very simple and does not need training at all. CBD builds another layer with a unit for each term T_i=sign(h_1)h_1...sign(h_k)h_k. Let us consider the unit associated with T_i. The bias weight w_bias, will be set at an arbitrary negative value (e.g. -0.5). The unit will be connected only with the units corresponding to those hyperplanes in T_i. The values of the weights will be all equal to x where x is the solution of the following inequality:

$$\begin{cases} x > \dfrac{threshold + bias\_weight}{fan\_in} \\ x < \dfrac{threshold + bias\_weight}{fan\_in - 2} \end{cases}$$

where fan_in is the number of hyperplanes present in T_i. The first inequality ensures that the unit will be turned on if all of the units are in the state required by the sign of their corresponding factors. The second inequality ensures that the unit will remain off if even a single unit has the wrong activation. For the chosen type of neurons, the threshold is 0. In this formula, the bias_weight represents the absolute value of the bias weight. The sign of each weight will be the sign of the corresponding hyperplane in T_i. This unit implements a logical and and will be turned on if and only if the input pattern is in the region characterised by T_i.

There will be a unit for each term in the solution given by the algorithm. Finally, another layer of weights will implement a logical or. This layer will contain a unit for each class (2 units in this case) and each unit will be connected with the terms corresponding to its class on the previous layer. The weight can have any value greater than the threshold (any positive value for 0 threshold).

In conclusion, the CBD algorithm builds a net with 3 layers of active weights. The first layer implements hyperplanes which separates the patterns into regions containing only patterns in the same class. The second layer implements a logical **and** between different hyperplanes. In the set theory language this layer implements an **intersection** between half-spaces given by different hyperplanes. Each unit on this layer will be activated only by input patterns situated in a homogeneous regions of the input space and can be associated with their output class. The third layer implements a logical **or** between units on the second layer. In other words it performs the **reunion** of different regions corresponding to the same class. The typical final architecture of the net is presented in fig. 3.

Another option is to use only two layers. The first one is built in the same way and the second one is trained with the "delta" rule or any other well-known learning algorithms for single layer networks. Because the hyperplanes are in the correct position, the problem is now separable in the hidden layer activation space and the training can succeed.

The CBD algorithm can be easily extended to cope with more than two classes. The training speed can be further reduced by performing an simple on-line analysis of the current subgoal and the current solution but these enhancements are beyond the scope of the present paper.

Experiments.

1. Search directed by subgoals. Pattern presentation algorithm.

The experiments were done with a classification network with a 128-20-36 architecture. The net is used to classify characters of the English alphabet (10 digits and 26 letters).

The training patterns were obtained from images of car number plates. The image is segmented into number plate and background and the number plate is segmented into characters. Each character area is binarised and divided into 8 by 16=128 rectangles and a mean luminance value is calculated for each rectangle. These 128 luminance values are normalised and the result of this normalisation constitutes the input to the net. The output is a vector of 36 elements with all elements zero but the one corresponding to the character presented.

Due to various character sets used in the number plates, different illumination conditions and different positions of the camera with respect to the car, the differences between various instances of the same character are rather large in spite of various normalisations performed. As a consequence, various instances of the same character will be spread over a large volume in the input space. The training set contains 180 patterns.

Two types of experiments were performed. The first type compares the training of a constraint based decomposition approach with respect to the standard training approach. The second type of experiments investigates in more detail the behaviour of the constraint based decomposition and shows that the search is indeed directed by the subgoals.

A. Constraint based decomposition versus standard training.

The standard approach of training the whole training set is compared with a constraint based decomposition approach. The weight changing mechanisms is the generalised delta rule [McClelland,1986].

In each trial, two networks were initialised with the same initial weight state and used the same values of the above parameters during the whole training process. One network used the classical technique of training with the whole set of patterns and the other was trained with a constraint based decomposition of the training set. Subsequently, the standard training was tried with different parameters (especially learning rate) but it was never successful.

The standard approach training fails to converge in 15000 epochs whereas the CBD training converges to an error limit of 0.3 in approx. 13200 epochs and to an error limit of 0.2 in approx. 13600.

As the final performances of the net depend ultimately on the error limit for the last sub-goal only, the speed of the training can be dramatically increased if a higher error limit is used to detect the end of a sub-goal training. An error limit of approx. 0.75 for the subgoals reduces the total training time (in epochs) by approximately a half. This intermediate error limit depends very much on the problem.

Note that an epoch for the whole training set necessitates the calculation of the weight changes determined by the entire number of training patterns whereas a epoch for a sub-goal training set necessitates only the calculation for the number of the patterns in the sub-goal training set. Therefore, the CPU time needed for an epoch in the standard technique will be much longer than the time needed for an epoch for any sub-goal but the last one which is the whole training set.

As discussed in the introduction, the results of the generalised delta rule as a weight updating algorithm can be improved using various techniques. Their combination can also be used with a constraint based decomposition pattern presentation algorithm. It is believed that the use of most of the techniques would not affect essentially the overall result of the comparison.

A strict constraint based decomposition would ask sub-goals formed by adding the characters one by one i.e. the first sub-goal is implemented by a training set formed with instances of the first character, the second with instances of the first two characters, etc. This is this is inefficient because all the units in the output layer whose class is not present in the current subgoal will tend to have 0 weights. In this conditions the distance in weight space between the initial position and the solution would be very large for each subgoal. Without any other precautions, the CBD pattern presentation algorithm would not be able to help the training. For this reason, the first subgoal was built with a pattern from each class ensuring that the first subgoal offers a fair start.

B. Investigating the search directed by subgoals

Fig. 4 shows the evolution of the error during an CBD training session. Note that the error goes up at the beginning of the training of each subgoal but the error does not accumulate from a subgoal to another.

In fig. 5 the evolution of the error during a subgoal training is plotted against the number of epochs. Both the error over the current subgoal and the error over the previous subgoal are plotted. This graphs shows that even when the error over the current subgoal training set is large due to the presence of the newly added patterns, the error over the previous sub-goal training set remains small which shows that the search takes places in the sub-space of the target space determined by the previous subgoal. Therefore, in this case, the subgoal manages to direct the search for the solution.

These experiments show the role of the pattern presentation algorithm. Both the standard training and the CBD training used the same weight change algorithm. However, the standard training fails systematically on this problem whereas the CBD can be successful. However, the success of the pattern presentation algorithm itself depends too much on the subgoal definition which must be done manually. Although in this case there was an improvement, the CBD pattern presentation algorithm by itself does not guarantees the success.

2. Search restricted by subgoals. CBD training algorithm (architecture and pattern presentation)

The full CBD algorithm has been tested with linearly inseparable problems containing the XOR training set. An example is presented in fig. 6. The figure contains both the training set and the hyperplanes the algorithm found in solving the problem.

The architecture resulted at the end of the training used 5 hyperplanes of the form $w_1x+w_2y+w_{bias}=0$. The solution is:

$$C1 = h_o + \bar{h}_0 h_1 h_2 + \bar{h}_0 h_1 \bar{h}_2 h_3 h_4$$

$$C2 = \bar{h}_0 h_1 \bar{h}_2 h_3 \bar{h}_4 + \bar{h}_0 h_1 \bar{h}_2 h_3 + \bar{h}_0 h_1$$

The horizontal bar means the sign of the correspondent hyperplane is minus and the hyperplanes with sign = nil are missing from the expression of the solution.

The solution is interpreted in the following way: a pattern will be classified as C1 if it determines (a positive activation of the neuron associated with h_0) or (a negative activation of the neuron associated with h_0) and (a positive activation of the neuron associated with h_1) and (a positive activation of the neuron associated with h_2) or...etc. Logical and has a higher priority than logical or. As previously described, the expressions for C1 and C2 can be seen as a reunion of regions obtained by intersecting half-spaces determined by different hyperplanes.

Discussion

The characteristics of the CBD architecture and training algorithm are:

1. The CBD training algorithm is composed by a weight updating algorithm for a single layer (delta rule, for instance), the CBD pattern presentation algorithm and the CBD construction method.

2. CBD has the abilities of a multilayer perceptron but the training is performed exclusively in subnets with a minimal architecture containing only one layer and one neuron. This is the simplest possible training problem from the point of view of the architecture (the best possible situation for the first two factors in section 1: only one layer so one can use a simple weight update rule and only one neuron so that number of dimension of the weight space is minimum).

3. CBD trains exclusively training sets with n examples of which n-1 are already correctly classified. This is the simplest possible training problem from the point of view of the training set and this eliminates the herd effect. Furthermore, all the training sets have less patterns than the original set and most of them have only very few patterns. This is a reduction of the training set's dimensionality.

4. CBD finds automatically an architecture able to solve the problem. The algorithm guarantees the absence of useless units (whose outputs are not actually used in performing the classification). Although the architecture found by the net is often the minimal one, the algorithm does not offer guarantees in this sense. However, the convergence is guaranteed.

5. The computation involved in training is very simple. No first or second order derivatives are used. No preprocessing is needed. The training is very fast and the resulting network is able to solve linearly inseparable tasks.

6. The fact that the first hidden layer is not fully connected to the **and** layer avoids the interference between hyperplanes which is one of the difficulty faced by a fully connected net.

7. CBD can be used for incremental learning, in which a trained network is asked to adapt itself at new patterns. The CBD net will train only the smallest possible region(s) of the input space which contain the new pattern(s). The hyperplanes introduced to satisfy the new patterns will not affect the classification of other regions.

8. The CBD pattern presentation algorithm can be used with any training algorithm. Combined with the standard backpropagation weight updating algorithm it gives an improvement over the standard training but the results are not always guaranteed.

Relation to other work.

The main differences between CBD and older training algorithms are the solutions to the training problems brought by performing the training only in the simplest architecture and the simplest training set.

Training only one neuron at a time and gradually building the net are present in the Cascade Correlation (CC) net proposed by Falhman and Lebiere in [Falhman, 1990]. However, CC algorithm uses the whole pattern set and the resulting architecture is different. CC builds feature detectors which could be useful in some problems. However, further research must be done in order to compare the performances of CBD and CC.

The idea of positioning the hyperplanes in the right places is present in several other techniques such as entropy nets and query learning. The entropy nets use a decision tree to classify the regions and two layers one for logical **and** and one for logical **or**. These layers are similar to those use by CBD. However, the building of the decision tree can be a very lengthy process because it involves testing very many candidate questions for each node in the tree. For instance, the CART (Classification and Regression Trees) uses a standard set of candidate questions with one candidate test value between each pair of data points. At each node, CART searches through all the variables, finding the best split for each. Then the best of the best is found (see [Breiman, 1984]). This can be a very time consuming process.

Query learning is more efficient but it requires the existence of an oracle able to give the correct classification for any point in the input space. In the usual case of learning from examples, where only a limited number of data points is available, this is not possible. The query learning algorithm is presented in [Baum, 1990] and [Baum, 1991].

CBD builds up the I/O surface gradually, one region after another. The idea of locally constructing the I/O shape is present in all RBF algorithms (see [Moody, 1989], [Musavi, 1992], [Poggio, 1990]). In RBF's case, one unit with a localised activation function will ensure the desired response for a small region of the I/O space. However, there are situations in which a hyperplane net is better than an RBF net. Furthermore, for an RBF net to be efficient, a preprocessing stage must be performed and parameters like radii of the activation functions, their shape and orientation, the clustering, etc. must be calculated. For some problems the simplicity of CBD could be preferred.

The idea of building the solution by combining partial solutions was proposed by Hinton and Anderson in [Hinton, 1981]. However, the combining method proposed there is a simple sum of the weight matrices and it works only for orthogonal patterns. This can be seen as a particular case of CBD in which a constraint is one pattern. In this special case, each subspace of the constraint space is characterised by a unique weight state (a partial solution). The set of partial solutions can be combined to give a unique weight state which satisfies all the constraints and therefore is the solution. In constraint space, the above technique is equivalent to finding the subspaces corresponding to each pattern and directly calculating their intersection which is the solution.

There are few algorithms which ensure the convergence of the training process. The upstart algorithm [Frean, 1990] builds a hierarchical structure (which can be eventually reduced to a 2 layer net) by starting with a unit and adding daughter units which cater for the misclassifications of the parents. Sirat and Nadal proposed a similar algorithm in [Sirat, 1990] However, both of them work for on/off units only. Mezard and Nadal proposed a tiling algorithm which starts by training a unit on the whole training set. The training is stopped when the units produces the correct target on as many units as possible. This pseudo-solution weight state is given by the pocket algorithm which assumes that if the problem is not linearly separable the algorithm will spend most of its time in a region giving the fewest errors. The pocket algorithm simply monitors the weight change and stops the training after some chosen time t. It is very inefficient to start with the whole training set because most of the time the training will fail and the pocket algorithm does not offer any guarantees regarding the optimality of the weight state obtained. A short description of these techniques can be found in [Hertz, 1991].

Romaniuk and Hall [Romaniuk, 1993] proposed a divide and conquer net which builds up the network. Their divide and conquer strategy starts with one neuron and the entire training set. If the problem is linearly inseparable (usually), the first training is bound to fail and this is detected by a time-out condition. In comparison, CBD starts with the minimum problem which is guaranteed to have a solution. The divide and conquer technique also requires a pre-processing stage in which the nearest neighbour is found for each pattern in the training set. The architecture given by the divide and conquer algorithm is similar to that of a Cascade Correlation network, with each unit connected to all the input units. However, the architecture of the DCN network depends on the initial weight state which can be inconvenient in some cases.

The extentron, proposed by Baffes and Zelle in [Baffes, 1992] builds up a network using the idea that a problem which is not linearly separable in the original input space becomes so in a space with more dimensions. A unit is used to separate at least one pattern and any other subsequent units will be connected to it as well as to all input patterns. This cascade connection means that for highly non-linear problem such as 2-spirals, the last few hidden units, will have to solve a problem in a higly dimensional space (2 dimensions of the input space plus n dimensions of the first n hidden units). Although a perceptron training, the training can be more difficult because of the possible large number of dimensions.

Acknowledgements

I would like to thank Dr. Mike Weir for help in putting the results of this work in the form of a paper. I also thank Gary Polhill, Dr. Mike Livesey and especially Martin Balchin and Mark Child for their invaluable comments on early versions of this paper.

Bibliography

[Baffes, 1992] - Baffes, P.T., J.M. Zelle - Growing layers of perceptrons: introducing the extentron algorithm

[Baum,1991] - Baum, E. B. - Neural net algorithms that learn in polynomial time from examples and queries, IEEE Transactions of Neural Networks 2(1), January, 1991.

[Baum,1990] - Baum, E. B., K.J. Lang - Constructing hidden units using examples and queries, NIPS 1990, pp. 904-910.

[Breiman, 1984] - Breiman L., J.H. Friedman, R.A. Olsen, C.J. Stone - Classification and regression trees, Wadsworth &Brooks, (1984).

[Denoeux, 1993] - Denoeux T., R. Lengelle - Initialising backpropagation networks with prototypes, Neural Networks, vol. 6, 351-363, (1993).

[Fahlman, 1990] - Fahlman, S.E. and C. Lebiere - The cascade correlation architecture, Technical report, Carnegie Mellon University, CMU-CS-90-100, (1990).

[Frean, 1990] - The Upstart algorithm: A Method for Constructing and Training Feedforward Neural Networks, Marcus Frean, Neural Computation 2, 198-209, 1990

[Hertz, 1991] - Hertz, J., A. Krogh, R.G. Palmer - Introduction to the theory of neural computation, Addison Wesley, 1991

[Hinton,1981] - Hinton, G., J. Anderson - Parallel models of Associative Memory, Hillsdale, NJ: Lawrence Erlbaum Associates, (1981).

[Lang ,1988] - Lang K.J, M.J. Witbrock - Learning to tell two spirals apart, Proceedings of the 1988 Connectionist Models Summer School, Morgan Kaufmann.

[McClelland, 1986] - McClelland, J.J., D. Rumelhart et. al. - Parallel Distributed processing, MIT Press, 1986

[Moody, 1989] - Moody, J., C.J. Darken - Fast learning in networks of locally-tuned processing units. Neural Computation 1, 281-294, (1989).

[Musavi, 1992] - Musavi, M.T., W. Ahmed, K.H.Chan, K.B. Faris and D.M. Hummels - On the training of radial basis function classifiers, Neural Networks, vol. 5, 595-603, (1992).

[Poggio, 1990] - Poggio, T., F. Girosi - Networks for approximation and learning. Proceedings of the IEEE, vol. 78, no. 9, 1481-1497, September 1990.

[Romaniuk, 1993] - Romaniuk, S.T., L.O. Hall - Divide and Conquer Neural Networks, Neural Networks, Vol. 6, pp. 1105-1116, 1993

[Sietsma, 1991] - Sietsma, J.S., R.J.F. Dow - Creating artificial neural networks that generalise, Neural Networks, Vol.4, pp. 67-79, 1991

[Sirat, 1990] - Sirat, J.-A., J.-P. Nadal, Neural Trees: A new tool for classification. Preprint, Laboratoires d'Electronique Philips, Limeil-Brevannes, France

[Wilensky,1990] - Wilensky, G.D., J.A. Neuhaus - Scaling of back-propagation training time to large dimensions.

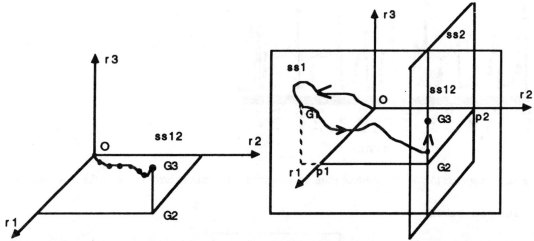

Fig. 1. A history based training (in restriction space). The network is trained with intermediate targets. Each intermediate target (sub-goal) is characterised by the same number of restrictions as the original training set.

Fig. 2. A restriction based decomposition (in target space). Each subgoal asks the satisfaction of one restriction more than the previous sub-goal. The search for a solution of a sub-goal is performed in a sub-space of the restriction space.

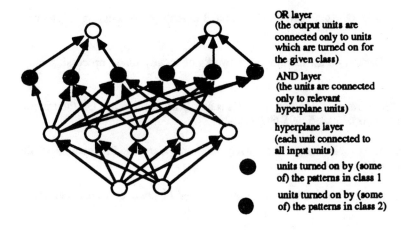

OR layer
(the output units are
connected only to units
which are turned on for
the given class)

AND layer
(the units are connected
only to relevant
hyperplane units)

hyperplane layer
(each unit connected to
all input units)

⬤ units turned on by (some
of) the patterns in class 1

⬤ units turned on by (some
of) the patterns in class 2

Fig. 3. The complete architecture of a CBD network. The picture shows the solution of the problem presented in fig. 6.

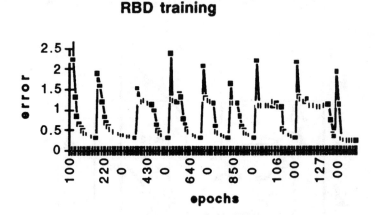

RBD training

Fig. 4. Each peak corresponds to start of a subgoal training. The sudden increase in error is due to the new patterns.

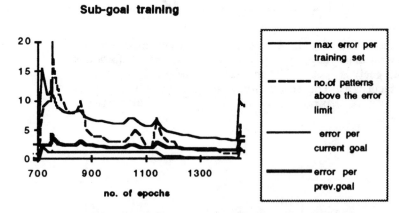

Sub-goal training

max error per training set

no.of patterns above the error limit

error per current goal

error per prev.goal

Fig. 5 The evolution of the error during a subgoal training. The total error increases as the new patterns are added. However, the error for the patterns in the previous subgoal remains fairly small even if it becomes greater than the error limit which is 3. This shows that the training path remains in the vicinity of the subspace of the restriction space determined by the previous subgoal i.e. the training is directed by the previous subgoal.

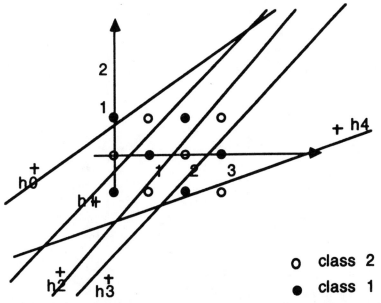

o class 2

● class 1

Fig. 6. An example of a I/O set. The architecture obtained at the end of the training uses 5 hyperplanes.

separate (region, C1=set of patterns in C1, C2=set of patterns in C2, factor) **is**
    • Build a subgoal S with patterns x_1^{C1} and x_1^{C2} taken at random from C1 and C2. Delete x_1^{C1} and x_1^{C2} from C1 and C2.
    • Add a hidden unit and train it to separate x_1^{C1} and x_1^{C2}. Let h be the hyperplane which separates them.
    • **For each** pattern p in C1 U C2.
        • Add p to the current subgoal S
        • Save h in h_copy
        • Train with the current subgoal S
        if not success then
            • Restore h from h_copy
            • Remove p from S
    • Let new_factor = factor **and** (h,'+')
    • **If** the positive half-space determined by new_factor contains only patterns in the same class Cj
        then
            • Classify new_factor as Cj
        else
            • Delete from C1 and C2 all the patterns which are not in h+. Store the result in new_C1 and new_C2.
            • Separate(h+, new_factor, new_C1, new_C2, new_factor)
    • Let new_factor = factor **and** (h,'-')
    • **If** the negative half-space determined by new_factor contains only patterns in the same class Cj
        then
            • Classify new_factor as Cj
        else
            • Delete from C1 and C2 all the patterns which are not in h-. Store the result in new_C1 and new_C2.
            • Separate(h-, new_factor, new_C1, new_C2, new_factor)

Fig. 7 The CBD algorithm for building and training the hyperplane layer.

Integration of On-Line and Batch Versions of the EBP Algorithm and Its Three Cost-Effective Approximate Implementations

Yao-Ching Liu
Electrical and Computer Engineering
University of Miami
Coral Gables, FL 33124
e-mail: ycliu@impala.ir.miami.edu

Dilip Sarkar
Mathematics and Computer Science
University of Miami
Coral Gables, FL 33124
e-mail: sarkar@cal.cs.miami.edu

Abstract

The EBP (error back-propagation) is now the most used learning algorithm for FFANNs (feedforward artificial neural networks). There are two versions of the EBP algorithm — *on-line* and *batch*. The on-line version updates weights after presentation of every training pattern. On the other hand, the batch version of the EBP algorithm accumulates weight-corrections for all the training patterns, and then updates all weights. Each version has its advantages and disadvantages when compared on the basis of learning time and convergence rate. In this paper, we propose a method for integrating on-line and batch versions of the EBP algorithm into one algorithm. We also propose and study three approximate implementations of the integrated EBP algorithm. Our simulation study of the integrated EBP algorithm for the XOR problem has shown smaller learning time and better convergence rate than those of the Quickprop algorithm proposed by Fahlman. All three approximate implementations of the integrated EBP algorithm for the binary version of the Majority-XOR problem have shown very favorable performances in comparison with extensive study data available in the literature.

1 Introduction

Artificial Neural Networks (ANNs) are mathematical models developed to mimic certain information storing and processing capabilities of the brain of higher animals. Although the interest of the research community in ANNs as a means for intelligent computing had existed for over 30 years (see [WL90]), there is little doubt that Rumelhart, McClelland, and the PDP research group are credited with revitalizing of wide interest in it [RM+86]. The different models and their applications can be found in many books and in such surveys as [Hin89, Lip87, WL90]. This paper concentrates only on Feedforward ANNs (FFANNs) and Error Back Propagation (EBP) learning algorithms for them. Basic elements of the theory, as pointed out by le Cun [lC88], can be traced back to the book of Bryson and Ho [BH69]. It was more explicitly stated by Werbos [Wer74], Parker [Par85], le Cun [lC86], and Rumelhart-Hinton-Williams [RHW86]. The EBP is now the most popular learning algorithm for multilayer FFANNs, because of its simplicity, because of its power to extract useful information from examples, and because of its capability of storing information implicitly in the connecting links in the form of weights.

Despite its power, the original version of the EBP learning algorithm has been of great concern to practical users for many reasons: *i*) it is extremely slow if does converge, *ii*) it may get stuck in local minima before learning all the examples, *iii*) it is sensitive to initial conditions, and *iv*) it may start oscillating etc. Several methods have been proposed to improve the performance of EBP algorithm. Important methods to speedup the EBP algorithm have been surveyed in [Sar92], and are very briefly discussed next.

Efforts to Speedup the EBP Algorithm Rumelhart, Hinton, and Williams [RHW86] have insightfully argued that a relatively smaller learning rate coefficient makes learning slow, but too large a value causes oscillation preventing the network from learning the task, and have suggested adding a momentum term in the weight updating rule which dynamically increases or decreases the *effective value* of the learning rate coefficients depending on the nature of the energy surface. Further analysis and experimental study on the effect of momentum coefficient on improvement of learning can be found in [Bat92, EO92, Jac88, Tol90, Wat88]. Although a limited *effective* dynamic range of learning rate coefficient is obtained by adding a momentum term, in most practical cases it is not good enough to cover requirements of all types of energy surfaces that may have a wide range of gradient values, and hence various methods have been reported to directly adapt learning rate coefficient [Bat89, DO88, Jac88, PS91, Tol90, Wei91]. Some of these methods keep one learning coefficient for each weight [DO88, Jac88, Tol90], and others keep only one learning rate coefficient for all weights [Bat89, PS91, Wei91]. Conjugate gradient method or some approximations to it, when used with the EBP algorithm, have shown considerable improvement in learning speed [Bat89, Bat92, Kin92]. Yet another method for fast learning with the EBP algorithm is to use new (other than standard sum-of-the-squared error) energy functions [EO92, AS92]. The size of the learning set affects the learning rate and could be considered in selecting learning rate coefficient [vON92]. Other suggested methods for improving learning rate include rescaling of error at every layer [RIV91], and using expected outputs instead of actual outputs to compute weight correction [Sam91]. In the next section, following [RHW86] the original version of EBP algorithm is presented.

2 Original EBP Algorithm

Error back-propagation (EBP) learning rule (popularly known as back-propagation algorithm) which is also known as the Generalized Delta Rule (GDR) was proposed by Rummelhart, Hinton, and Williams in their seminal work [RHW86]. In the EBP learning algorithm, following the presentation of an input vector X_m and a target vector T_m (for $m = 1...P$), the rule for updating weight w_{jk}^l of the link connecting kth node in a layer l to the jth node in the subsequent layer $l+1$ is given by:

$$\Delta w_{jk}^l = -\eta \times \Delta_{w_{jk}^l} E_i, \tag{1}$$

where η is a constant known as the learning rate coefficient and $\Delta_{w_{jk}^l}$ is the partial derivative with respect to w_{jk}^l and E_i is the energy function. Rumelhart, Hinton, and Williams [RHW86] in their original EBP algorithm used the sum-of-the-squared error as the energy function.

$$E_{ba} = \frac{1}{2} \sum_{m=1}^{P} \sum_{n=1}^{n_o} (t_{mn} - y_{mn})^2 \tag{2}$$

where n_o is the number of units in the output layer, t_{mn} and y_{mn} are target output and actual output, respectively. The energy function, E_p can be defined for only one training pattern pair (x_p, d_p) as follows.

$$E_p = \frac{1}{2} \sum_{n=1}^{n_o} (t_{pn} - y_{pn})^2 \tag{3}$$

There are two versions of the EBP algorithm, *on-line* and *batch*. In the on-line EBP algorithm, the weights are updated using the error corresponding to every training pattern. This method uses energy function defined by equation 3. However, in the batch EBP algorithm, the weights are updated after accumulating errors corresponding to all input patterns, and thus makes use of the energy function defined by equation 2.

Values of several parameters are of importance for implementation. The initial value of weights should be small and randomly chosen [RHW86] to avoid the symmetry problem. The η value plays a very important role. A smaller value of η makes learning slow, but too large a value will cause oscillation preventing the network from learning the task [RHW86]. In practice, most effective value of η depends on the problem. For example, Fahlman [Fah88] has reported 0.9 as value of learning rate coefficient for one problem, while Hinton [Hin87] has reported 0.002 as the value of learning rate coefficient for another problem. This variation in the value of learning rate coefficient for faster training of FFANNs has drawn the attention of many researchers.

3 Integration of On-Line and Batch EBP Algorithms

In this section, we propose a method for integrating on-line and batch versions of the EBP algorithm. The integrated algorithm attempts to take best features of both on-line and batch EBP algorithms. We believe, it would increase convergence rate and reduce learning time. Since, an exact implementation of this novel version of the EBP algorithm requires considerably higher computation time, several methods for its approximate implementation are also proposed. Before proceeding further some notations are introduced to make the presentation concise and precise. Since the same method will apply to all the weights, without causing any confusion we drop the subscripts and superscripts from Δw_{jk}^l.

The on-line version of the EBP algorithm updates weights after presentation of each pattern, and hence if two patterns have weight corrections opposite in sign, they tend to cancel each other's effort. The batch version of the EBP algorithm avoids this problem by accumulating weight-corrections for all patterns and then making only one update at the end. This, however, may risk the possibility where the sum of all weight corrections is zero but the network has not learnt many examples. Under this situation the on-line algorithm may be of use since weight correction for one pattern at a time reduce error for that pattern.

The proposed algorithm defines energy function by combining energy functions of on-line and batch EBP algorithms. A new energy function E_{I_p} for the novel EBP is as follows:

$$E_{I_p} = \beta \times E_p + \frac{1}{P} E_{ba} \tag{4}$$

where β is a positive constant. For a given pattern p, the weight updating rule is given by:

$$\Delta w = -\eta \times (\beta \times \Delta_w E_p + \frac{1}{P} \Delta_w E_{ba}) \tag{5}$$

Thus, for updating weights for a input pattern, it is necessary to compute weight correction for all the patterns. This integrated energy function in computing weight corrections considers the effect of all the patterns. Thus, for example, if overall weight correction for a weight w due to all the patterns is negative, but weight correction due to a pattern p is positive, then the net weight correction will be lower, and vice versa. This gives the algorithm some sense of fairness. The amount of learning for a pattern is reduced if it has adverse effect on the whole set of patterns. On the other hand, the amount of weight correction for a given pattern is increased if it has a favorable advantage on the whole set of patterns. Yet another way to see the effect of the new learning algorithm is that it increases the dynamic range of learning-rate coefficient. When the value of $\Delta_w E_p$ and ΔE_{ba} are opposite in sign, the effective learning rate is lower; but when $\Delta_w E_p$ and ΔE_{ba} are same in sign, the effective learning rate is higher. Next, three methods for approximate implementation of the proposed algorithm is presented.

4 Three Cost-Effective Approximate Implementations

Average of the Last Cycle (ALC) In this method weight corrections for each weight is accumulated for all the patterns to be taught during the last cycle. The average of this accumulated correction is divided by the number of patterns to obtain approximate value of $\frac{1}{P} \Delta_w E_{ba}$. A Pascal-like description of this is given next.

average-del-weight {approximation of $\frac{1}{P} \Delta_w E_{ba}$ for the next cycle } := 0;
while not trained **do**
begin
        cum-del-weight {for a weight w} := 0;
        for $i := 1$ **to** P { number of patterns } **do**
                begin cum-del-weight := cum-del-weight $+ \Delta w$; **end**
        average-del-weight {approximation of $\frac{1}{P} \Delta_w E_{ba}$ for the next cycle } := cum-del-weight$/P$;
end

Our experience is that this very simple to implement method works well when the number of patterns to be taught is not 'too large'.

Modified Average of the Last Cycle (MALC) In this method, at the beginning of each cycle $\frac{1}{P} \Delta_w E_{ba}$ is the average value of weight corrections for all the patterns during the last cycle. For subsequent patterns $\frac{1}{P} \Delta_w E_{ba}$ is approximated by subtracting $\frac{1}{P}$th of the current value and then adding $\frac{1}{P}$th of the Δw for the last pattern. A Pascal-like description of this procedure is as follows:

approx-average-del-weight {approximation of $\frac{1}{P} \Delta_w E_{ba}$ at the beginning of the next cycle } := 0;
while not trained **do**

begin

    cum-del-weight {for a weight w} := 0;

    for i := 1 **to** P { number of patterns } **do**

    begin

        cum-del-weight := cum-del-weight + Δw;

        approx-average-del-weight {approximation of $\frac{1}{P}\Delta_w E_{ba}$ for the next pattern}

                := $(1 - 1/P)$ * approx-average-del-weight + $(\Delta w)/P$;

    end

    approx-average-del-weight {approximation of $\frac{1}{P}\Delta_w E_{ba}$ at the beginning of the next cycle }

        := cum-del-weight/P;

end

This method requires additional computation for updating the approximated value of $\frac{1}{P}\Delta_w E_{ba}$ after presentation of each pattern. However, when the number of patterns to be taught is large, this approximation method might reduce learning time to a great extent. Thus, the additional computation is justified for teaching a large number of patterns to a network.

Weighted Average of Last and Current Cycle (WALCC) In this method the approximation of $\frac{1}{P}\Delta_w E_{ba}$ after presentation of i patterns is given by $(P - i)/P$ times the average weight correction for the last cycle plus i/P times the average weight correction for the i patterns in the current cycle. A Pascal-like description of this method is shown next.

approx-average-del-weight {approximation of $\frac{1}{P}\Delta_w E_{ba}$ for the next pattern } := 0;

while not trained **do**

begin

    cum-del-weight {for a weight w} := 0;

    for i := 1 **to** P { number of patterns } **do**

    begin

        cum-del-weight := cum-del-weight + Δw;

        approx-average-del-weight {approximation of $\frac{1}{P}\Delta_w E_{ba}$ for the next pattern}

                := $(1 - i/P)$ * average-cum-del-weight + (cum-del-weight/i) $*$ (i/P);

    end

    average-del-weight {approximation of $\frac{1}{P}\Delta_w E_{ba}$ at the beginning of the next cycle }

        := cum-del-weight/P;

end

In the next section simulation results for approximate implementations of the integrated EBP algorithm is reported.

5 Simulation Results and Discussion

The performance of the algorithms presented in the earlier section was studied through simulation. We compare the performance of our algorithms with the data in [Fah88, CT91]. Since the Quickprop algorithm in [Fah88] has shown dramatic improvements and benchmark data are also available, we first compared our results with it.

The data in Table 1 for Standard EBP and ALC implementation of Integrated EBP algorithms are for 10 different initialization of the network. In three instances the Standard EBP learning algorithm failed to stop. We excluded them in our average computation. The data for the Quickprop algorithm is for 100 trials [Fah88]. As can be seen from Table 1, Integrated algorithm outperformed both the standard EBP with momentum and the Quickprop algorithms in learning speed and convergence rate.

algorithm	learning rate	momentum or β	restart	maximum epochs	minimum epochs	average epochs
Standard EBP	5.5	1.2	3	214	82	140.9
Quickprop [Fah88]	4.0	1.0	14	66	10	24.22
Integrated EBP	1.2	$\beta = 0.83$	0	34	12	19.4

Table 1   Comparison of Performance of Integrated EBP Algorithm with
That of Quickprop and Standard EBP Algorithms

In [CT91] it was reported that for Majority-XOR problem (see description next) the standard EBP algorithm with momentum converged only 86.84% of the times with a cutoff of 50,000 epochs. Thus, we believe that it would be a good problem to compare our algorithms' convergence with their results. Next we briefly describe the Majority-XOR and then the simulation results.

Majority-XOR (M-XOR)   This is one of the problems Cohn and Tesauro used to see 'can neural networks do better than Vapnik-Chervonenkis bounds?' [CT91]. It is an extension of the linearly separable majority function. Majority is a Boolean predicate in which the output is '1' if and only if more than half of the bits are '1'. Majority-XOR is a Boolean function of N bits where output of the function is '1' if and only if Nth bit disagrees with the majority of the first $N-1$ bits. Following [CT91], in our study the input was 26-bit binary patterns and output was one-bit binary value. The network had three hidden units and presented 600 patterns until it learnt all or 400 epochs expired. Table 2 summarizes empirical observations from simulations.

implementation	learning rate	β	restart	maximum epochs	minimum epochs	average epochs
ALC	0.125	2.4	0	393	145	207.45
MALC	0.125	2.4	1	259	134	201.11
WALCC	0.125	2.4	1	324	136	206.58

Table 2   Comparison of Performance of Three Approximate
Implementations of the Integrated EBP Algorithm

With 20 different initializations each of the three implementations was tested. As can be seen from Table 2, both MALC and WALCC implementations failed to stop only one in 400 epochs out of 20 trials. If we consider all 60 trials of the three implementation, it turns out that 96.7% of the times the integrated EBP algorithm converged even with a cutoff of 400 epochs. This is a significant improvement over the study reported in [CT91], where it was reported that only 86.84% of the times Standard EBP algorithm with momentum terms converged with a cutoff of 50,000 epochs.

References

[AS92]   M. Ahmad and F. M. A. Salam. Dynamic learning using Exponential energy function. In *Proceedings of the International Joint Conference on Neural Networks*, 1992.

[Bat89]   R. Battiti. Accelerated backpropagation learning: Two optimization methods. *Complex Systems*, 3, 1989.

[Bat92]   R. Battiti. First- and second-order methods for learning: Between steepest descent and newton's method. *Neural Computation*, 4, 1992.

[BH69]   A. E. Bryson and Y. C. Ho. *Applied Optimal Control*. Waltham Mass, 1969.

[CT91]   D. Cohn and G. Tesauro. Can neural networks do better than the Vapnik-Chervonenkis bounds? In *Advances in Neural Information Processing Systems 3*. Morgan Kaufmann, 1991.

[DO88]   M. R. Devos and G. A. Orban. Self learning backpropagation. In *Proceedings of the NeuroNimes*, 1988.

[EO92]   H. A. C. Eaton and T. L. Olivier. Learning coefficient dependence on training set size. *Neural Networks*, 5, 1992.

[Fah88]   S. E. Fahlman. An empirical study of learning speed in back-propagation networks. Technical Report CMU-CS-88-162, Carnegie Mellon University, 1988.

[Hin87]   G. E. Hinton. Learning translation invariant recognition in massively parallel networks. In *Lecture Notes in Computer Science*. Springer-Verlag, 1987.

[Hin89]   G. E. Hinton. Connectionist learning procedures. *Artificial Intelligence*, 40, 1989.

[Jac88]   R. A. Jacobs. Increased rate of convergence throught learning rate adaptation. *Neural Networks*, 1988.

[Kin92]   J. A. Kinsella. Comparison and evaluation of variants of the conjugate gradient method for learning in feed-forward neural networks with backward error propagation. *Network*, 3, 1992.

[lC86]   Y. le Cun. Learning process in an asymmetric threshold network. In *Disordered Systems and Biological Organization*. Springer-Verlag, 1986.

[lC88]   Y. le Cun. A theoretical framework for backpropagation. In *Proceedings of the 1988 Connectionist Models Summer School*, 1988.

[Lip87]   R. P. Lippmann. An introduction to computing with neural network. *IEEE ASSP Magazine*, 1987.

[Par85]   D. B. Parker. Learning logic. Technical report, MIT, 1885.

[PS91]   Y. M. Pirez and D. Sarkar. Back-propagation with controlled oscillation of weights. Technical Report TR-CS-01-91, University of Miami, 1991.

[RHW86]   D. H. Rumelhart, G. E. Hinton, and R. J. Williams. Learning internal representation by error propagation. In *Parallel Distributed Processing: Explorations in the microstructures of cognition*, volume 1. MIT Press, 1986.

[RIV91]   A. K. Rigler, J. M. Irvine, and T. P. Vogl. Rescaling of variables in back propagation learning. *Neural Networks*, 4, 1991.

[RM+86]   D. E. Rumelhart, J. L. McClelland, et al. *Parallel Distributed Processing: Explorations in the microstructures of cognition*, volume 1. MIT Press, 1986.

[Sam91]   T. Samad. Back propagation with expected source values. *Neural Networks*, 4, 1991.

[Sar92]   D. Sarkar. Methods to speedup error back propagation learning. Technical Report TR-CS-01-92, University of Miami, 1992.

[Tol90]   T. Tollenaere. SuperSAB: Fast adaptive back propagation with good scaling properties. *Neural Networks*, 3, 1990.

[vON92]   A. van Ooyen and B. Nienhuis. Improving the convergence of the back-propagation algorithm. *Neural Networks*, 1992.

[Wat88]   R. Watrous. Learning algorithms for connectionist networks: Applied gradient methods for non-linear optimisation. Technical Report MS-SIS-88-62, University of Pennysylvania, 1988.

[Wei91]   M. K. Weir. A method for self-determination of adaptive learning rates in back propagation. *Neural Networks*, 4, 1991.

[Wer74]   P. J. Werbos. *Beyond regression: New tool for prediction and analysis in the behavioral sciences.* PhD thesis, Harvard University, 1974.

[WL90]   B. Widrow and M. A. Lehr. 30 years of adaptive neuarl networks: Perceptron, madline, and backpropagation. *Proceedings of the IEEE*, 78, 1990.

Backpropagation Algorithm Modification Reducing Number of Local Minima and Convergence Time

Charles T. Kendrick, Ph. D.
University of Alaska, Fairbanks
Fairbanks, Ak, 99775–1110
Kendrick@acad5.alaska.edu

Abstract

This paper presents a modification to the backpropagation algorithm which improves network development time in two areas. The modification reduces the number of times the network convergence settles into a local minima during training. It simultaneously speeds convergence. Experimental results are given which demonstrate the improvement gained in both of these areas: speed of convergence is 3 to 5 times faster than with the standard BPN algorithm and for many of the experimental cases, local minima are almost totally eliminated.

1. Introduction

The backpropagation neural network has been used for both classification problems and for generalization problems. This paper investigates the problem of local minima in the context of generalization problems, although the results obtained should be equally applicable to classification problems. (For a background on the use of Neural Networks in generalization problems, see [Shekhar].)

A neural network "learns" a function from a set of input/output pairs representing the function. As the learning algorithm progresses, it is possible that the network learns a less than optimal function as its best approximation to the function over the full domain for which the network is developed. At a local minimum, the algorithm makes no further progress on approximating the function since any small change to the weights of the network will increase the error found by applying the training patterns to the network. There has been considerable discussion on the problem of local minima and methods to remove them, e.g. Paul Werbos's presentation at WCNN, '93 [Werbos.] Some methods have proved to be quite effective in removing local minima but are too costly in terms of convergence speed. The Boltzman machine is one such attempt to avoid local minima but often has unacceptably long convergence time. For a discussion of Boltzman machines, see [Ackley].

Others have examined how the number of training patterns or the number of hidden layers in a network effect local minima. In some cases dealing with function classification networks, increasing the number of hidden layers increases the number of local minima [Perugini]. In the generalization networks examined in this paper, this does not seem to be the case. However, the complexity of the function to be generalized is a factor.

The convergence time which I investigate is simply a count of the number of training cycles needed before the network's error on the training set is at some minimally acceptable level. Each cycle consists of the application of all the input patterns and of the weight adjustments after each pattern.

2. Algorithm Modification

The backpropagation algorithm is undoubtedly the most commonly used neural network implementation today. The description of the algorithm can be found in many books and articles [Rumelhart, or in Hecht-Nielsen].

The architecture for this paper consisted of a three-layer network. The transfer function for the nodes of the hidden layer was the sigmoid transfer function, $1/(1 + e^{-x})$, where x is the weighted sum of the inputs to the nodes plus the bias term. Then output nodes simply yielded an affine combination of the hidden nodes including the output node's bias.

The usual BPN algorithm is a gradient descent on the error surface, which is a manifold over the "weight space" of the network. Any given weight configuration fixes the average error of the network over all testing or training patterns. The backpropagation algorithm describes a method to determine at each node the partial derivative of the error value with respect to each weight at that node. A small modification of the weight is then made in the direction that will minimize the error. Local minima on this weight surface are one of the banes of the technique.

The algorithm described in this paper avoids local minima by changing the weight surface itself. First, define the transfer function for a hidden node to be:

$$s(\,I, node\_max, node\_min\,) = \frac{(node\_max - node\_min)}{(1 + e^{-I})} + node\_min$$

Note that a change in node_max or node_min does not simply change the position on the error surface for a given input or set of inputs — it changes the shape of the error surface. Changes in these parameters have a markedly different type of effect on the output of a node for a given input vector than those changes which occur when either an input weight is changed or the bias value is changed.

The actual change to the backpropagation algorithm is given as follows:

- Define the transfer function for each sigmoid as in the equation above where each node keeps node_max and node_min in its local memory. At initialization, these are set to 1 and 0 respectively.
- On learning, if sum is the accumulated, weighted, backpropagated errors to a node, then the node_max is updated by the formula:

  node_max += node_max_delta = η * sum * logistic + α * node_max_delta

  where η is the learning rate, α is the momentum rate and

  logistic = $1/(1 + e^{-I})$ with I being the usual weighted input to the node.
- Node_min is similarly updated by the formula:

  node_min += node_min_delta = η * sum * (1 – logistic) + α * node_min_delta.

3. Test Cases

Currently, the efficacy of the algorithm has been verified on a number of generalization problems for mappings from $\mathbf{R}^1 \to \mathbf{R}^1$. Runs were made on linear, quadratic and cubic polynomial equations and also on a Bessel function. The Mathematica plots at the top of the next page show the functions that were used for training the networks for this paper.

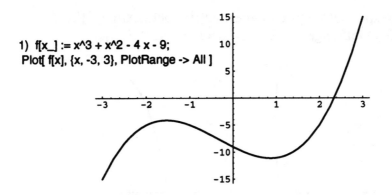

1) f[x_] := x^3 + x^2 - 4 x - 9;
   Plot[f[x], {x, -3, 3}, PlotRange -> All]

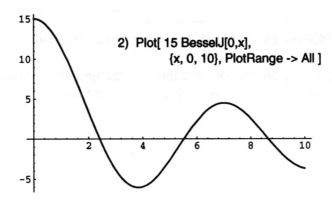

2) Plot[15 BesselJ[0,x],
   {x, 0, 10}, PlotRange -> All]

I used 15 * BesselJ[0,x] so the range of the two functions is similar thus facilitating comparison of results.

For each function, the training set consists of the functional values for the integers in the domain of the functions. Thus there were 7 training points for the cubic function and 11 training points for the Bessel function.

4. Result: Effect on Local Minima

Look at the cubic function first. The following table summarizes the number of local minima for various architectures with the two contrasting algorithms:

Number of Local Minima: Cubic Function

Hidden Nodes	# tests	"Standard" BPN	"Modified" BPN
3	200	200	9
5	200	113	1
7	200	7	0
9	200	1	0
11	200	0	0

Although there are several local minima configurations for the network, the following graph shows a typical output from a network that is in a local minima. (In this case the max and min on all nodes was set to 1 and 0, respectively.)

Plot[netoutput[netweights, hidmaxmin[[i]], outmaxmin[[i]],{x}],
{x, -3, 3}, PlotRange -> All, PlotLabel -> "Plot" (i/2)]

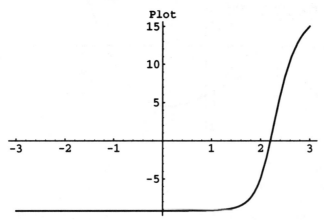

Local Minima for Network Learning Cubic Function

Similarly, there are a number of local minima configurations when the network is trying to approximate the Bessel function. One of these configurations is:

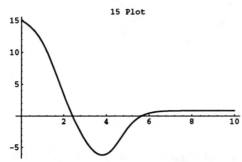

Local Minima for Network Learning Bessel Function

The following table shows the improvement made in the number of local minima in convergence to the Bessel function in various network architectures. The modified BPN algorithm shows markedly better convergence.

Number of Local Minima: Bessel Function

Hidden Nodes	# tests	"Standard" BPN	"Modified" BPN
3	100	100	27
5	100	100	8
7	100	93	7
9	100	63	7
11	100	42	1

Not only does the modified BPN algorithm decrease the number of local minima, it simultaneously reduces the number of cycles necessary for convergence. This is described in the next section.

5. Result: Effect on Speed of Convergence

I checked the speed of convergence by running the network up to 10,000 cycles, where one cycle was a presentation of all the training patterns. The network was said to converge when, for a cycle, the maximum absolute error over all training patterns was less than 0.5. The plots below for 100 runs show the number of cycles it took for the network to converge by this criterion. Note that the network was in a local minimum for most (but not all) of the cases where it had not converged in 10,000 cycles.

Test runs with 5 hidden nodes; Cubic Function; Modified BPN

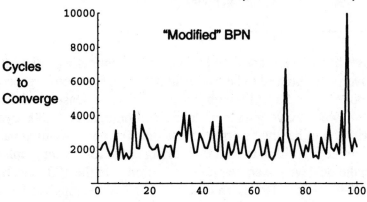

Test runs with 5 hidden nodes; Cubic Function; Standard BPN

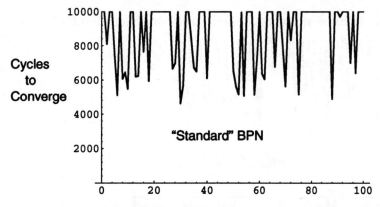

As the nodes in the hidden layer increased, the modified BPN algorithm more consistently gave convergence times in the 1900 to 2000 cycles range. With 11 hidden nodes, the convergence statistics on the number of cycles it took to converge were:

Mean = 2034, Median = 1954, Standard deviation = 338.5

The standard BPN algorithm continued to improve with more hidden nodes, but even for 11 hidden nodes, the results were not that good. The statistics in this case are:

Mean = 6533, Median = 6546, Standard deviation = 970.5

The chart on the next page shows graphically the poor convergence results even in this case.

Test runs with 11 hidden nodes; Cubic Function; Standard BPN

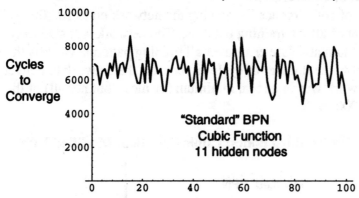

The results on the Bessel function are not final but are very encouraging. The limit of 10,000 cycles allowed for convergence proved to be too stringent. The best convergence was achieved with the 11–hidden node networks. Although it was clear that at least 58 of the runs with the standard BPN algorithm were converging to a global minimum, after 10,000 cycles not one of the 100 runs met the criterion of having an error of less than 0.5 on all training patterns. The increased speed of the modified algorithm is seen by looking at the following graph showing cycles at which that algorithm did achieve the convergence criterion. On the 100 runs, the median time to converge was 9036 cycles. The mean time of 8580.7 is meaningless because of the number of trials cut off after 10,000 cycles. Likewise, the standard deviation of 1646.2 does not tell much; it would be somewhat larger if we upped the cutoff limit.

Test runs with 11 hidden nodes; Bessel Function; Modified BPN

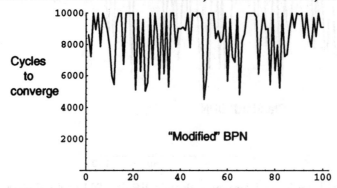

6. Conclusions and Discussion

This easily implemented modification to the backpropagation algorithm shows much promise in avoiding local minima and simultaneously speeding the rate of convergence during neural network training. It is recognized that the $R^1 \to R^1$ mappings that were tested here are relatively simple. Work is now in progress to verify these results with actual problem data. At UAF we have implemented a neural network to aid lightening forecasting in Alaska and had problems getting convergence and avoiding local minima. We are starting to test this algorithm on a more extensive system which has 16 inputs, 30 to 60 hidden nodes and one output and is to be trained on lightening data. Because the algorithm is based on the fundamental idea of avoiding local minima by modifying the error surface instead of simply finding a path on the error surface to a global minima, we believe that these results are extensible to much larger systems.

References

Robert Hecht-Nielsen, *Neurocomputing*, Addison–Wesley, 1990.

N.K. Perugini, W.E. Engler, "Neural Network Learning Time: Effects of Network and Training Set Size," *ICJNN International Joint Conference on Neural Networks"*, **2**, 395–401, 1989.

D. E. Rumelhart, G.E. Hinton and R.J. Williams, "Learning Internal Representations by Error Propagation," *Neurocomputing, Foundations of Research, (James A. Anderson and Edward Rosenfeld, Eds)*, The MIT Press, 1988.

Shashi Shekhar and Minesh B. Amin, "Generalization by Neural Networks," *IEEE Trans. on Knowledge and Data Engineering*, **4** (2), 177–185, 1992.

Paul J. Werbos, "Supervised Learning: Can it Escape Its Local Minimum?, " *Proceedings of World Congress On Neural Networks*, **3**, 358–363, 1993.

D.H. Wolpert, "A Benchmark for How Well Neural Nets Generalize," *Biological Cybernetics*, **61**, 303–313, 1989.

Condition Number as a Convergence Indicator in Backpropagation

Jagesh V. Shah and Chi-Sang Poon

Harvard-MIT Division of Health Sciences and Technology
Massachusetts Institute of Technology
Cambridge, Massachusetts, 02139.

Abstract

A system matrix is introduced through a reformulation of the backpropagation training algorithm. The condition number of this matrix is a good indicator of training convergence. The structure of the system matrix can also be exploited to accelerate convergence. This is illustrated via the addition of derivative noise, the use of a cross entropy cost function and the addition of hidden units.

1 Introduction

Backpropagation of errors [12, 8] is the most popular training algorithm for feedforward artificial neural networks [3]. Its popularity is a result of its simplicity and easy implementation on digital computers. A major disadvantage of backpropagation is its slow convergence [7]. Presently, there exists a myriad of algorithms which increase the convergence rate of backpropagation [10, 1, 9, 11, 2]. However, many are based on ad hoc modifications which perform well under simulation of specific examples, but offer little in the way of analysis. To design algorithms which have better convergence rates it is important to understand the factors underlying training dynamics.

This paper reformulates the backpropagation training algorithm into a linear algebraic framework. As a result, analysis of training dynamics is simpler and linear techniques can be used to predict algorithm performance.

In section 2 the *system matrix*, $\mathbf{A}(\mathbf{w})$, is defined. It represents the core of this analysis. In section 3 the use of the condition number of a matrix as a related notion of linear independence is discussed. The condition number of the system matrix is used to quantify the training process. Simulation results in section 4 illustrate the use of condition number as a convergence indicator.

In section 5, the matrix formulation is used to predict the performance of various algorithms. These include the use of derivative noise [2] and the use of the cross entropy cost function [10, 11]. The addition of hidden units is also analyzed for convergence performance.

2 Construction of the System Matrix, $\mathbf{A}(\mathbf{w})$

This section outlines the construction of the system matrix from the basic backpropagation of errors [8] weight update formulae.

Consider a multilayer perceptron with I inputs, H hidden units and one output unit. The training set consists of P patterns and the training cost function is chosen to be the sum of squared error, i.e. $E(\mathbf{w}) = \frac{1}{2}\sum_{l=1}^{P}\left(t^l - o^l\right)^2$. t^l is the target output for the input pattern $\mathbf{x}^l$, and o^l the corresponding network output. The superscripts denote the pattern number. The vector $\mathbf{w}$ represents the weight vector of the network. It is comprised of Ω, the weights from the hidden units to the output unit and Λ, the weights from input to hidden nodes. Individual weights in Ω are denoted $\Omega_i, i = 1, \ldots, H + 1$. Weights in Λ are further divided into $\Lambda_i, i = 1, \ldots, H$, the weight vectors from the input nodes to the ith hidden unit. A particular weight that connects hidden node i and input j is denoted $\lambda_{i,j}$. The Ω_{H+1} and $\lambda_{i,I+1}$ weights in $\mathbf{w}$ represent the bias weights which have an activation of unity.

As prescribed by the backpropagation algorithm the weight vector $\mathbf{w}$ is updated according to the gradient descent rule i.e. $\Delta\mathbf{w} = -\eta\nabla_{\mathbf{w}}E(\mathbf{w})$. where η represents the step size or learning rate.

The weight update rules can be written explicitly as

$$\Delta\Omega_i = \eta\sum_{l=1}^{P} f'(\overline{h_o^l})h_i^l(t^l - o^l) \tag{1}$$

$$\Delta\lambda_{i,j} = \eta\sum_{l=1}^{P} f'(\overline{x_i^l})x_j^l \cdot f'(\overline{h_o^l})\Omega_i(t^l - o^l) \tag{2}$$

$\overline{x_i^l}$ is the activation for hidden node i and $\overline{h_o^l}$ is the activation for the output node. h_i^l is the output of hidden node i and x_j^l is the jth component of the input pattern. The terms h_{H+1}^l and x_{I+1}^l are unity, for the update of the bias weights. In addition, $f(\cdot)$ is the nodal activation function and $f'(\cdot)$ its first derivative. Throughout this discussion it is assumed that $f(\cdot)$ is at least once continuously differentiable, bounded and monotonically increasing. The sigmoid function $f(x) = 1/(1 + e^{-x})$ is an example of such a function. This function is used in all simulations presented.

The update equations can be interpreted as a set of linear equations in the term $(t^l - o^l)$. Let $e^l(\mathbf{w}) = t^l - o^l$ and $\mathbf{e}(\mathbf{w}) = [e^1(\mathbf{w}) \ldots e^P(\mathbf{w})]^T$. $\mathbf{e}(\mathbf{w})$ is the error vector. The weight update equations can now be rewritten as

$$\Delta\mathbf{\Omega} = \eta\mathbf{A}_{\mathbf{\Omega}}(\mathbf{w})\mathbf{e}(\mathbf{w}) \tag{3}$$

$$\text{where } [\mathbf{A}_{\mathbf{\Omega}}(\mathbf{w})]_{qr} = [f'(h_o^r)h_q^r]_{qr} \tag{4}$$

$$\Delta\mathbf{\Lambda}_i = \eta\mathbf{A}_{\mathbf{\Lambda}_i}(\mathbf{w})\mathbf{e}(\mathbf{w}) \tag{5}$$

$$\text{where } [\mathbf{A}_{\mathbf{\Lambda}_i}(\mathbf{w})]_{qr} = [f'(x_i^r)x_q^r f'(h_o^r)\Omega_i]_{qr} \tag{6}$$

$[\mathbf{A}]_{qr} = [a_{qr}]_{qr}$ is used to denote a matrix $\mathbf{A}$, with element a_{qr} at row q and column r. These equations can be further accumulated into one matrix equation for the simultaneous update of all the weights in $\mathbf{w}$. When equations 4 and 6 are combined, the result is

$$\Delta\mathbf{w} = \eta\mathbf{A}(\mathbf{w})\mathbf{e}(\mathbf{w}), \text{ where } \mathbf{A}(\mathbf{w}) = \begin{bmatrix} \mathbf{A}_{\mathbf{\Omega}}(\mathbf{w}) \\ \mathbf{A}_{\mathbf{\Lambda}_1}(\mathbf{w}) \\ \vdots \\ \mathbf{A}_{\mathbf{\Lambda}_H}(\mathbf{w}) \end{bmatrix} = \begin{bmatrix} \mathbf{A}_{\mathbf{\Omega}}(\mathbf{w}) \\ \mathbf{A}_{\mathbf{\Lambda}}(\mathbf{w}) \end{bmatrix} \tag{7}$$

$\mathbf{A}(\mathbf{w})$ is the system matrix.

We assume that $P \leq (H+1) + H(I+1)$, that is, the number of training patterns is less than the number of weights and biases in the network. This assumption holds for many applications in which artificial neural networks have been used.

3 Condition Number of $\mathbf{A}(\mathbf{w})$ and Network Convergence

This section discusses the use of the condition number as a relative measure of rank in a matrix. The result is an interpretation of the system matrix which is illustrated through simulation.

The condition number of a matrix is the ratio of the largest and smallest singular values of a matrix [6]. A large condition number corresponds to a matrix which has columns which are *nearly* linearly dependent. This implies that rank of the matrix is *nearly* deficient. The condition number provides *relative* information about the linear dependence of the columns of a matrix rather than the *absolute* information given by the rank (i.e. either dependent or independent).

Using this linear dependence approach equation 7 can be rewritten as

$$\Delta\mathbf{w} = \sum_{l=1}^{P} \mathbf{a}^l(\mathbf{w})e^l(\mathbf{w}) \tag{8}$$

where $\mathbf{a}^l(\mathbf{w})$ is the lth column of $\mathbf{A}(\mathbf{w})$ and $e^l(\mathbf{w})$ is the scalar error for the lth pattern. The term $\mathbf{a}^l(\mathbf{w})e^l(\mathbf{w})$

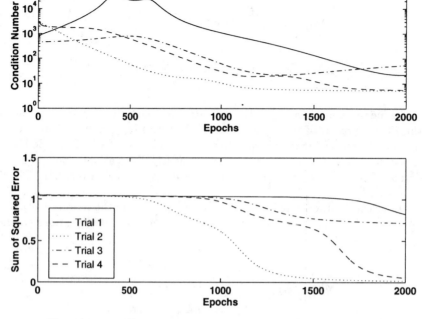

Figure 1: Condition Number and Network Error Trajectories

represents the gradient of the cost function for the lth pattern. Thus equation 8 is the vector sum of P gradient vectors.

The linear dependence of the columns of $\mathbf{A(w)}$ (i.e. the rank) determines the number of directions that $\Delta\mathbf{w}$ can take. If the rank of $\mathbf{A(w)}$ is deficient, then the directions of $\Delta\mathbf{w}$ are restricted, in fact there exists a subspace of error vectors, $\mathbf{e(w)} \neq \mathbf{0}$, which will result in $\Delta\mathbf{w} = \mathbf{0}$. The algorithm has become stuck in a local minimum. If, however, the rank of $\mathbf{A(w)}$ is full, then $\Delta\mathbf{w} \neq \mathbf{0}$ for $\mathbf{e(w)} \neq \mathbf{0}$ and the training error continues to decrease. Note that if $\mathbf{e(w)} = \mathbf{0}$ the global solution has been reached. For this analysis strict gradient descent is always guaranteed, thus there is no possibility of limit cycle behaviour.

Because of the continuous nature of the activation functions, it is unlikely that the system matrix will lose rank. However in the neighbourhood of a local minima, the columns of $\mathbf{A(w)}$ will become *nearly* linearly dependent. Thus it is appropriate to use the condition number as a measure of the linear dependence of the columns of $\mathbf{A(w)}$.

4   Simulation Examples

To study the linear dependence of the columns of $\mathbf{A(w)}$, the condition number of the system matrix and the training error of an Exclusive-Or (one layer of two hidden units) network were tracked (see figure 1). The graphs show that the condition number and error fall together. This is a result of the columns of $\mathbf{A(w)}$ becoming *more* linearly independent. In trials where convergence was not attained the condition numbers remained higher than those of the converged trials. Extended simulation runs revealed that high condition numbers may be associated with local minima. Note that one of the trials showed an increase in condition number with continued training and thus may be stuck in a local minimum.

Final solution optimality was also characterized using the condition number. A set of trials were run for a fixed duration. The condition number of the system matrix was then calculated for each trial. The convergence criteria was a sum of squared error less than 0.05. Five hundred Exclusive-Or networks (as above) were simulated. Figure 2 shows the results of the simulation. Of the 500 trials, 299 converged and 201 did not. The bars represent the mean condition number of the final system matrix. Note that for the converged trials the final condition number of the system matrix is much smaller. This indicates a strong correlation between network convergence to a globally optimal solution and a low system matrix condition number.

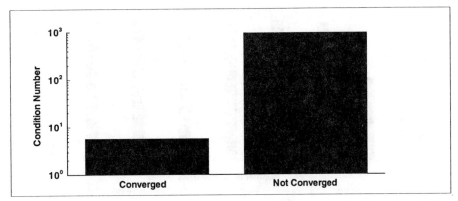

Figure 2: Mean condition numbers of converged and unconverged trials after 10000 epochs

5   Enhancing convergence by conditioning A(w)

Simulation results have indicated that there is a strong correlation between a low condition number and final solution optimality. In this section algorithms that use this relationship are discussed.

5.1   Increasing the condition number of A(w)

Before examining the algorithms, it is useful to outline some of the properties of the system matrix that they exploit.

In examining the rank of the system matrix only the columns were considered for linear independence. The rank calculation can also be viewed as an examination of linearly independent rows of the system matrix. In particular, many of the rows of the submatrix $A_\Lambda(w)$ are linearly dependent. To see this note equation 6. The lth column of $A_{\Lambda_i}(w)$ shares the term $f'(\overline{x_i^l})f'(\overline{h_o^l})\Omega_i$. Since $f'(\cdot) > 0$ for any finite argument, $f'(\overline{x_i^l})f'(\overline{h_o^l})\Omega_i$ can be eliminated from each column without changing the rank of $A_{\Lambda_i}(w)$. Thus $\mathcal{R}(A_{\Lambda_i}(w)) = \mathcal{R}([x_q^r]_{qr})$ where $\mathcal{R}(\cdot)$ is the rank operator. Note that the simplified matrix is independent of i, implying $\mathcal{R}(A_\Lambda(w)) = \mathcal{R}(A_{\Lambda_i}(w))$. Thus, many of the rows of $\mathcal{R}(A_\Lambda(w))$ do not contribute to increasing the condition number of $A(w)$. This is an inherent redundancy in backpropagation that can be exploited to increase convergence performance.

This simplification can also be performed for $A_\Omega(w)$. However, the resulting rank is the same as that of $A_\Omega(w)$. This is because the terms of the simplified matrix are functions of the network weights which change over the training period. Thus no rows can be eliminated due to linearly dependency.

5.2   Derivative Noise

One ad hoc method of achieving the modulation of the elements of $A_\Lambda(w)$ is to randomize them by adding noise. If the terms in the matrix are disturbed using noise more rows can potentially contribute to the condition number. At the same time, however, the guarantee of strict gradient descent is lost. As a result this method can be very sensitive to the magnitude of noise used. In spite of this, the noise method has been shown to prove effective by Falhman [2] who used the noise to prevent saturation of the derivative of the activation function. When a small amount of noise was added to the derivatives, the networks converged faster and were less likely to get stuck in local minima. In other words, by keeping more rows linearly independent, the algorithm could proceed without being impeded by local minima.

5.3   Cross Entropy versus Sum of Squared Error

Another method of increasing convergence performance is to increase the magnitude of the weight update vector. Thus a larger step is taken down the error surface during each weight update, resulting in faster convergence.

The system matrix, $A(w)$, can be simplified by eliminating the term $f'(\overline{h_o^l})$ from each column. This is in direct analogy with the simplification of $\mathcal{R}(A_{\Lambda_i}(w))$. The sigmoidal activation function, $f(x) = 1/(1+e^{-x})$,

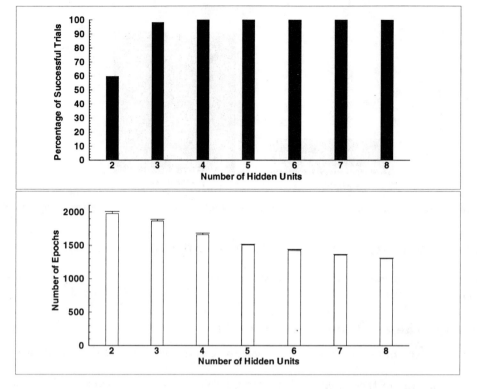

Figure 3: Effect of number of hidden units on network convergence

has the property that $0 < f'(x) < 1$. That is $f'(\overline{h_o^l})$ has the effect of attenuating the matrix elements and thus the magnitude of the weight update vector. The removal of this term should accelerate convergence.

This approach has been used in training algorithms that have a cross entropy [10] type cost function. The cross entropy cost function has the form

$$E(\mathbf{w}) = \sum_{l=1}^{P} \left\{ t^l \ln \frac{t^l}{o^l} + (1 - t^l) \ln \frac{(1 - t^l)}{(1 - o^l)} \right\} \tag{9}$$

for a single output network.

When weight update equations are calculated for this cost function, the result is a system matrix without the $f'(\overline{h_o^l})$ term. These algorithms yield faster convergence when compared with the sum of squared error cost function as shown in [10] and [11].

5.4 Increasing number of hidden units

The condition number of $\mathbf{A}(\mathbf{w})$ can also be increased by increasing the number of rows. In particular, adding rows to $\mathbf{A}_\Omega(\mathbf{w})$ is equivalent to adding more hidden units to the network. It follows that more hidden nodes should increase the possibility of obtaining a better conditioned system matrix. A similar redundancy approach is taken by Izui and Pentland [5]. They show that when redundant nodes (input and hidden) are added to the network they speed up convergence. In figure 3 the number of converged networks is plotted for the Exclusive-Or example with varying hidden layer sizes. Note the increase in the percentage of converged networks as the number of hidden units is increased. In fact, with four or more hidden units all the trials converged. Figure 3 also shows the number of epochs required to achieve the convergence criterion. As the number of hidden units increases the number of epochs needed to achieve convergence decreases.

6 Conclusions

In this paper, a linear algebraic formulation has been described that is useful in predicting the convergence performance of algorithms that are based on backpropagation of errors.

Simulations showed the correlation between the training error and system matrix condition number trajectories.

The enhanced performance of algorithms with derivative noise [2] a nd cross entropy cost functions [10, 11] were predicted using the matrix formulation. In addition, improved performance due to additional hidden units was predicted by the formulation and illustrated through simulation. The approach is similar to that found in [5].

7 Acknowledgements

We thank the SCOUT consortium at MIT for use of the Connection Machine CM-5 in the many numerically intensive simulations. This work was supported in part by the National Science Foundation under Grant BCS-9216419. J. V. Shah was partially funded by a fellowship from the Canadian Natural Sciences and Engineering Research Council.

References

[1] E. Barnard. Optimization for training neural nets. *IEEE Transactions on Neural Networks*, 3(2), 1992.

[2] S. E. Fahlman. Faster-learning variations of back-propagation: an empirical study. In D. Touretzky, G. Hinton, and T. Sejnowski, editors, *Proceedings of the 1988 Connectionist Models Summer School at Carnegie Mellon University*, pages 38–51, San Mateo, California, June 1988. Morgan Kaufmann.

[3] D. Hammerstrom. Working with neural networks. *IEEE Spectrum*, pages 46–53, July 1993.

[4] J. Hertz, A. Krogh, and R. G. Palmer. *Introduction to the Theory of Neural Computation*, volume 1 of *Santa Fe Institute Studies in the Sciences of Complexity*. Addison-Wesley, Reading, Massachusetts, 1991.

[5] Y. Izui and A. Pentland. Analysis of neural networks with redundancy. *Neural Computation*, 2:226–238, 1990.

[6] T. Kailath. *Linear Systems*. Prentice Hall, Englewood Cliffs, New Jersey, 1980.

[7] J. F. Kolen and A. K. Goel. Learning in parallel distributed processing networks : computational complexity and information content. *IEEE Transactions on Systems, Man and Cybernetics*, 21(2), 1991.

[8] D. E. Rumelhart, G. E. Hinton, and R. J. William. Learning internal representations by error propagation. In D. E. Rumelhart, J. L. McClelland, and the PDP Research Group, editors, *Parallel Distributed Processing : Explorations in the Microstructure of Cognition. Volume 1 : Foundations*, volume 1, chapter 8. The MIT Press, Cambridge, Massachusetts, 1986.

[9] R. Scalero and N. Tepedelenlioglu. A fast new algorithm for training feedforward neural networks. *IEEE Transactions on Signal Processing*, 40(1), 1992.

[10] S. A. Solla, E. Levin, and M. Fleisher. Accelerated learning in layered neural networks. *Complex Systems*, 2:625–640, 1988.

[11] A. van Ooyen and B. Nienhuis. Improving the convergence of the backpropagation algorithm. *Neural Networks*, 5:465–471, 1992.

[12] P. Werbos. *Beyond regression: New tools for prediction and analysis in the Behavioural Sciences*. PhD thesis, Division of Applied Sciences, Harvard University, Cambridge, Massachusetts, 1974.

Speeding Up the Training Process of the MLNN by Optimizing the Hidden Layers' Outputs

Mingsheng Zhao, Youshou Wu, and Xiaqin Ding

Department of Electronic Engineering
Tsinghua University, Beijing 100084, China

Abstract—A new rapid and efficient learning algorithm (OHLO Algorithm) is proposed in this paper. In the process of learning, the hidden layers' outputs are optimized. Experiments on XOR problem, 3 bit parity problem and circle decision area forming problem show that the convergence stability and the training speed of the method proposed are better than that of standard BP.

I. INTRODUCTION

In recent years, MLNN with the standard BP algorithm has been applied to many scientific fields successfully. However, applications are limited because of the slowness of learning process. Research for method of speeding up supervised learning for MLNN is very important in both practice and theory. Many techniques have been studied to speed up back propagation, such as dynamic adaptation of learning parameters [2,5], optimizing weights based on Kalman Filter principle [4] and conjugate gradient algorithm [1,3]. The convergence speed of all the methods presented which based on the back propagation principles reported to achieve several to ten times faster than the standard BP.

Here we address a new learning algorithm in which learning for MLNN can also be regarded as parameters estimation for a multi–inputs and multi–outputs nonlinear system. But the new method use different principles for learning compared to that of the standard BP. Layer by layer optimization which optimizing both weights and inputs of a certain layer is adopted, in which the optimized inputs are taken as the desired outputs of previous layer. We name it the OHLO (Optimizing Hidden Layers' Outputs) algorithm. This algorithm can perform simple computations and accelerate the learning speed of MLNN considerably.

The new algorithm is introduced in detail in Section II; the simulation results tested on XOR problem, 3 bit parity problem and circle decision area forming problem are shown in Section III; In Section IV, some important conclusions are given.

II. LAYER BY LAYER OPTIMIZING HIDDEN LAYERS' OUTPUTS LEARNING ALGORITHM

Let us assume any layer of MLNN, such as the mth layer, consisting of L inputs, which are $y_{p1}, y_{p2}, \dots, y_{pL}$, respectively. Denoted as:

$$Y_p = (y_{p1}, y_{p2}, \cdots y_{pL}) \tag{1}$$

where p is referred to the pth pattern of training set. p = 1,2,3...P. Usually, $y_{pL} = -1$.

Outputs of the mth layer which are $O_{p1}, O_{p2},...,O_{pN}$, is denoted as:

$$O_p = (O_{p1}, O_{p2},...,O_{pN}) \tag{2}$$

The mapping of input vector Yp to output vector Op implemented by the mth layer can be expressed as:

$$O_p = f(W Y_p) \tag{3}$$

where W is the weights matrix of the mth layer neurons, it is a $N \times L$ matrix.

f(•) is a nonlinear activation function of neuron, typically, it is sigmoid function, as:

$$f(x) = \frac{1}{1 + e^{-x}} \tag{4}$$

Assume the desired responses of the mth layer for pth training pattern to be $d_{p1}, d_{p2},...,d_{pN}$, which is denoted as:

$$d_p = (d_{p1}, d_{p2},...,d_{pN}) \tag{5}$$

The squared errors of the mth layer outputs for the pth training pattern is defined as:

$$E_p = \frac{1}{2} \| d_p - O_p \|^2 = \frac{1}{2} \sum_{n=1}^{N} (d_{pn} - O_{pn})^2 \tag{6}$$

The global error function E for all training patterns is:

$$E = \sum_{p=1}^{P} E_p = \frac{1}{2} \sum_{p=1}^{P} \| d_p - O_p \|^2 = \frac{1}{2} \sum_{p=1}^{P} \sum_{n=1}^{N} (d_{pn} - O_{pn})^2 \tag{7}$$

Sub−algorithms and formulae used in this method are introduced as following:

A.   Weights Optimizing

The function of this sub−algorithm is to minimize the output squared errors of a certain layer, such as the mth layer, by optimizing this layer's weights when the inputs are fixed. The steepest descent combined with line−searching technique is adopted here.

The weights adjustment formula is

$$\triangle W = - \mu \nabla E_w \tag{8}$$

Where $\mu > 0$, $\mu \in R$.

$$\frac{\partial E}{\partial W_{ij}} = -\sum_{p=1}^{P} (d_{pi} - O_{pi}) O_{pi} (1 - O_{pi}) y_{pj} \tag{9}$$
$$i = 1,2,\ldots,N; j = 1,2,\ldots,L.$$

μ in (8) is known as learning rate. It is a tuned parameter. Selecting proper μ, we can get local minimum of the error function along the gradient direction. Line—searching technique is used for solving this problem

B.   Inputs Optimizing

The function of this sub—algorithm is to minimize the output squared errors of a certain layer by optimizing this layer's inputs when the weights are fixed. Then we take the optimized inputs of the mth layer as the desired outputs of the (m−1)th layer.

Because the outputs of neurons take value in the range of (0,1), steepest descent and constrained line—searching techniques are adopted here.

By the definition of gradient, we get

$$\nabla E_Y = \left(\frac{\partial E}{\partial y_{p1}}, \frac{\partial E}{\partial y_{p2}}, \cdots, \frac{\partial E}{\partial y_{p,L-1}}, 0 \right)^T \tag{10}$$

Where

$$\frac{\partial E}{\partial y_{p1}} = \frac{\partial \left[\frac{1}{2} \sum_{p=1}^{P} \sum_{n=1}^{N} (d_{pn} - O_{pn})^2 \right]}{\partial y_{p1}} = -\sum_{n=1}^{N} (d_{pn} - O_{pn}) O_{pn} (1 - O_{pn}) W_{nl} \tag{11}$$
$$p = 1,2,\ldots,P; l = 1,2,\ldots,L - 1.$$

According to the steepest descent principle, the inputs adjustment formula is

$$\triangle Y = -\eta \nabla E_Y \tag{12}$$

Where $\eta > 0$, $\eta \in R$.

η in (12) is named as inputs optimizing rate.

Use the line—searching technique to seek the optimal η. Notice that the object function in line—searching procedure is different from that in weights optimizing procedure. Constrained object function with a constrained term add to Equ. (7) should be used here. We select the added constrained term Ec as

$$E_C = \sum_{p=1}^{P} \sum_{l=1}^{L-1} (|y_{pi} - 0.5|)^2 \tag{13}$$

C.   Layer By Layer Optimizing For MLNN

The first step of the training process of this algorithm is to optimize the weights $(W^{(M)})$ of the Mth layer (output layer). After this step, optimize the inputs $(Y^{(M)})$ of this layer using the sub−algorithm discussed in section B with the newly weights, then take the input vectors of the Mth layer $(Y^{(M)})$ as the desired output vectors $(d^{(M-1)})$ of the (M−1)th layer. Do the same optimizations for the (M−1)th layer, the (M−2)th layer, ... , until reach the first layer. Because the inputs of first layer are the inputs of training pattern vectors, only weights optimizing is needed to take into account. After one training cycle is finished, if the output error of the networks is not satisfied with the requirement, start a new training cycle from the Mth layer, iterate repeatedly layer by layer, stop learning when networks is converged.

Learning algorithm can be summarized as following:

step 1: $\eta > 0$, $\eta > 0$, Emax chosen;

Weights are initialized at random value;

m = M; Set initial iterate number q = 0;

step 2: Training step starts here

The training pattern is presented and the layers' outputs computed.

step 3: Optimize weights of layer m. Take optimized weights using the method discussed in section A as the new weights of layer m.

step 4: If m = 1, then go to step 6; Otherwise, optimize inputs of layer m using the method introduced in section B as the desired responses of layer m−1.

step 5: Set m = m−1, go to step 3;

step 6: Total error is computed, $E = \sum_{p=1}^{p} E_p$;

step 7: The training cycle is completed, set q = q+1; If E > Emax, then set m = M, and initiate the new training cycle by going to step 2; If E < Emax, stop training. Output weights $W^{(m)}$, (m = 1,2,...,M), iteration number q and total error E.

It is very interesting to point out, owing to the independence of weights and inputs optimization in every layer, all the iteration processes can be proceeded from the input layer to the output layer, or vice versa, except for the first iteration.

III. EXPERIMENT RESULTS

The XOR problem, the 3 bit parity problem and circle decision area forming problem are used in our experiment for the comparision of the performances of the proposed algorithm with that of the traditional BP algorithm. Table I∼ III are the results of our test.

Circle Decision Area Forming (CDAF) Problem

The CDAF problem used in our tests may be defined as follows: if the input pattern X fallen inside a certain circleof radius r = 1, the desired output is 1; Otherwise, when the input is outside the concentric circle with a little bit too large radius, say r = 1.1, the desired output is 0. Let the training patterns be the points on the two circles of every 45 degree. 16 sampled training patterns and their desired responses can be expressed as following:

$$(x1,x2,d) = \{ (1 * \cos(3.14 / 4 * i), 1 * \sin(3.14 / 4 * i), 1);$$
$$(1.1 * \cos(3.14 / 4 * i), 1.1 * \sin(3.14 / 4 * i), 0);$$
$$i = 0,1,2,...7\}$$

Three kinds of MLNN architecture have also been used in this experiment. Simulation results are listed in table III.

Table I   Comparing experiments results from the XOR problem

Networks	Two layers				Three Layers		Four Layers	
Structure	2->2->1		2->5->1		2->5->3->1		2->5->4->3->1	
Algorithm	OHLO	BP	OHLO	BP	OHLO	BP	OHLO	BP
Iterations	60	16140	46	12120	65	12399	44	15422
MSE Error	0	10^{-5}	0	10^{-5}	0	10^{-5}	0	10^{-5}

Table II.   Comparing experiments results from the 3 bit parity problem

Networks	Two layers				Three Layers1		Four Layers	
Structure	3->3->1		3->8->1		3->5->3->1		3->5->4->3->1	
Algorithm	OHLO	BP	OHLO	BP	OHLO	BP	OHLO	BP
Iterations	78	12566	71	6921	104	4910	66	53000
MSE Error	0	10^{-5}	0	10^{-5}	0	10^{-5}	0	10^{-5}

Table III   Comparing experiments results from the CDAF problem

Networks	Two layers				Three Layers		Four Layers	
Structure	2->3->1		2->10->1		2->5->3->1		2->5->4->3->1	
Algorithm	OHLO	BP	OHLO	BP	OHLO	BP	OHLO	BP
Iterations	2022	145300	1402	30156	1598	124520	541	67000
MSE Error	0	10^{-5}	0	10^{-5}	10^{-5}	10^{-5}	10^{-4}	10^{-4}

The results show that the convergence property is more sensitive to the initial weights in BP algorithm, than that of OHLO algorithm. Furthermore, in the OHLO, learning process converges with higher speed and stability. Especially, when the squared errors is less than 10^{-1} in OHLO, learning begins to converge very quickly, As in the learning process of BP algorithm, when the squared errors decrease to a certain degree, the convergence speed is getting slower and slower, and the error is hardly to become zero.

Although the time required for one iteration by OHLO is about 6 times of that required by BP, The total number of iterations for convergence of OHLO is 2–3 order of magnitude less than that of BP with the same MLNN architecture and initial weights. So OHLO can yield an acceleration of about 1–2 order of magnitude compared to BP tested on above three problems.

We can also conclude from the experiments that local minimum problem exists too in OHLO as it does in BP. But the probability of meeting local minimum resolution is less.

IV. CONCLUSIONS

In this paper, we proposed a learning algorithm for training MLNN by Optimizing the Hidden Layers' Outputs (OHLO), which is different from Back Propagation Principle and get more effective than the standard BP algorithm. Simulation results show that OHLO is an order of magnitude or more faster than standard BP and converge more stably when tested on the XOR problem, 3 bit parity problem and circle decision area forming problem.

OHLO is suitable for MLNN with any layers proved by our experiments. Optimizing layer by layer independently make the new method more simple to realize with parallel processing.

Another advantage of OHLO is full–automated, includes no critical user–dependent parameters with respect to BP in which the values of these parameters are often crucial for the success of the algorithm. So the new method is more easy for practical applications.

Of course, local minimum problem can not be eliminated completely in OHLO, It is a problem remained to be solved.

REFERENCES

1. Battiti, R & Masulli, F.(1990)."BFGS optimization for fast and automated supervised learning", INCC 90 Paris, Intl. NN Conf., 2, 757–760.
2. Jacobs, R.A.(1988)."Increased rated of convergence through learning rate adaption", Neural Networks,1(4),295–307.
3. Moller, M.F. (1993), "A scales conjugate gradient algorithm for fast supervised learning", Neural Networks, Vol.6, pp.525–533.
4. R.S. Scalero and N.Tepedelenlioglu,"A fast new algorithm for training feed forward neural networks"IEEE Trans. on SP Vol.40,No. 1, 1992, pp.202–210.
5. Vogl,T.P. et al.(1988)."Accelerating the convergence of the back–propagation method",Biological Cybernetics, 59, 257–263.

Investigating the GA/Back Propagation Trade-Off

in the GANNet Algorithm

David W. White
MRJ, Inc.
10455 White Granite Drive
Oakton, Virginia 22124
dwhite@mrj.com

Abstract: Designing and training neural networks are very difficult tasks, requiring much trial and error, and the standard layered network architectures do not map naturally into hardware. This paper investigates a novel genetic algorithm which is used to design the topology and find the link weights for a layered, feedforward neural network. The topologies are not limited either in the number of layers or in the number of nodes per layer. A robust, global search is conducted by the genetic algorithm over both the link weight and topology spaces, after which back propagation can be used to quickly find the desired link weights. Thus, both the GA and back propagation can be used to their greatest advantage: the global search of the GA can find the approximate area of a solution, and back propagation can then quickly find the local optimum. The point at which the GA should be terminated and back propagation should be employed is illustrated for two example problems.

Keywords: neural network, genetic algorithm, multilayer perceptron

Introduction

Creating an appropriate neural network for a given application is a multivariate optimization problem with few (if any) reliable guidelines. Typically, a guess is made of the required topology, often using some rule of thumb, and training is attempted. If training fails, it may be that the network is too large, too small, or the initial point in the weight space was too poor to allow the network to learn the task. Therefore, the designer has gained little knowledge to guide the next attempt, which can result in a large amount of trial and error before success is obtained.

One multivariate optimization technique which has recently gained a great deal of attention is the genetic algorithm (GA). The virtue of the GA is that the relationship between the parameters to be optimized and the evaluation function need not be known for the GA to be successful. This is very fortunate, since the relationship of neural network parameters and the network's success in learning the task at hand is definitely unknown. Another virtue of the GA is that the evaluation function can be crafted to optimize those features of the solution which are most important. For more information on GAs, see [Gol89].

In the GANNet algorithm, the "parameter string" is a neural network. Each allele is a node of the neural network with its input links. This includes the transfer function type (which is either sigmoid or Gaussian), transfer function slope, scale, and offset, the input link weights, and the index of the node of origin on the previous layer for each link. Thus, each allele is a feature detector (since that node will respond to some set of features in the input vectors) and therefore the search is conducted in "feature detector space", rather than link weight space or topology space. In short, the algorithm searches for the proper set of feature detectors to solve the problem at hand.

Although the algorithm finds solution networks a large percentage of the time, the time required to reach a solution is not bounded, and as with all GAs, no convergence theorem exists. Therefore, it may be advantageous to terminate the GA before a satisfactory solution network has been found, and use back propagation (or whatever local algorithm is preferred) on the best network to find the solution more quickly. For this purpose, two example problems were chosen: the well-known exclusive-or problem, and a synthetic binary problem. A synthetic problem was devised which would be simple enough to allow the results to be easily understood, yet pose enough challenge to rise above the trivial. For this purpose, a binary problem with eight inputs and one output was chosen, with the output being the following binary function of the inputs:

$$O = I7 \ \& \ ((I3 \ \& \ I5) \ | \ (I4 \ \& \ I6))$$

I0, ..., I7 are the individual inputs, "&" is the logical AND function, and "|" is the logical (inclusive) OR function. Inputs I1, I2, and I8 are not used to compute the output. All trials used whole population replacement, two point crossover, the "mutate nodes" mutation operator [Whit93], and a distributed GA (as in [WS90]) with 20 subpopulations of ten individuals each.

Results

First, the difference between the desired error (2%) and the best initial error was calculated. The difference is divided by 10 to produce "checkpoints" at every 10% of error reduction, from merely using the best initial network (0%) to allowing the GA to reduce the error to the desired 2% threshold (which is 100% of the error to be eliminated). At each checkpoint, the best performing network is trained using back propagation. If the genetic operators are performing as desired, the number of hidden nodes should show a decrease with the amount of the original error the GA is allowed to eliminate, since the topology search of the GA will have had more time to find better topologies. Table 1 presents the averages recorded over ten trials, and Figure 1 shows a graphical representation (which is a bit easier to grasp).

Error	Success Rate (%)	Number of Generations	Number of Epochs	Number of Layers	Number of Hidden Nodes	
0	90	0	257	2.4	4.6	
10	80	1.6	233	2.3	2.8	
20	-	-	-	-	-	*
30	50	4	519	2	1.5	*
40	100	4.5	4.5	1.5	0.5	*
50	100	15	11	1.8	1	*
60	100	17.3	4.7	1.7	1	*
70	100	5	4.6	1.8	1	
80	100	13	3.7	1.5	0.8	
90	100	21.6	2.1	1.7	0.9	
100	100	39.5	0.3	1.7	0.9	

Table 1

GA/Back Propagation Trade-Off for the Exclusive-Or Problem
An asterisk (*) indicates that there are fewer than five data points.

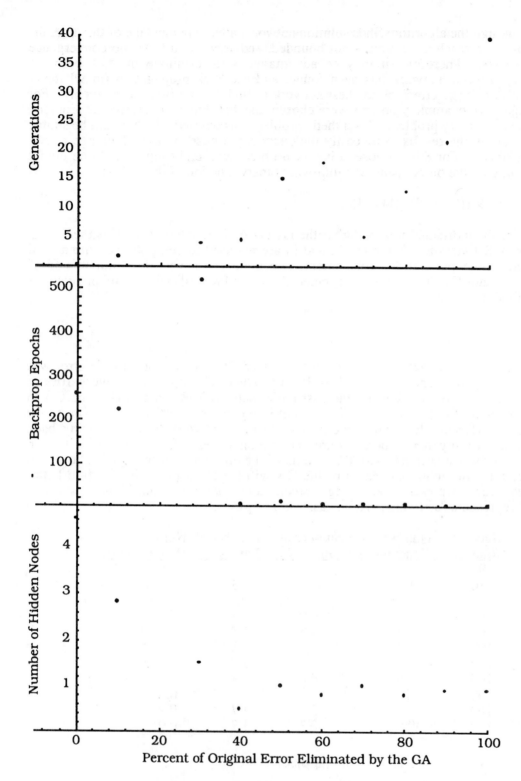

Figure 1.

Exclusive-Or GA/Backprop Trade-Off

These results indicate that the genetic topology search is performing as desired. The graph shows a clear trade-off between the number of GA generations and the number of back propagation epochs and network size. An optimal trade-off point seems to be around the point at which the GA has eliminated 80% of the original error. After this point, the GA spends a lot of time settling in on the final solution. There also seems to be an optimum at the 40% mark, but too few data points exist in this region to reach any conclusion. The major network size reduction seems to be in reducing the first 40% of the error, which makes some sense, since a "cheap" way to increase fitness is to decrease network size (thereby decreasing the node penalty used in the evaluation (or fitness) function). It so happens that this problem is simple enough to be solved by the smaller networks.

The virtue of allowing Gaussian nodes in the networks is also demonstrated by these results, since 3 of the ten trials resulted in networks with no hidden layers at all (using a single Gaussian node as the output), and five of the other trials had hidden layers consisting of a single Gaussian node. Thus, in cases where a subfunction of the output is of a Gaussian form naturally (as in this case), the ability to include Gaussian nodes in the networks allows far more compact topologies than networks with only sigmoid nodes.

Next, the synthetic problem was used, with the same procedure as before. Table 2 presents the test data, with Figure 2 showing the graphical representation. The initial networks tended to be small, because all of the networks performed rather poorly, so the discriminating feature was the size of the network (via the node cost in the fitness function). Unfortunately, these networks also tended to perform poorly, as evidenced by the low convergence rates. Once the network performance became the discriminating feature, the network size began to grow, and the convergence rate increased as well. There seems to be a definite optimal crossover point at around 80% error reduction, where the network size is still relatively small and the performance is good, as well. After that, the GA is straining to find an optimum performing network, and increases the size of the network to achieve it. This shows the tendency of the GA to find a neighborhood of the solution relatively quickly, but to have great trouble in finding the actual solution, as can be seen from the fact that the number of generations rapidly increases as the GA converges on a solution. In Figures 1 and 2, the independent variable is the percent of the original error the GA is allowed to eliminate before the switch to back propagation is made.

Error	Success Rate (%)	Number of Generations	Number of Epochs	Number of Layers	Number of Hidden Nodes
0	50	0	504	2	3
10	-	-	-	-	-
20	-	-	-	-	-
30	38	1	633	2	3
40	0	1.6	1000	2	2.6
50	60	2.3	456	2	3
60	50	4.5	561	2	3.2
70	70	7.6	353	2.3	6.7
80	100	12.9	51	2.3	6.4
90	90	17.9	172	2.4	7.2
100	100	40.9	5.5	2.7	8.0

Table 2

GA/Back Propagation Trade-Off for the Synthetic Problem

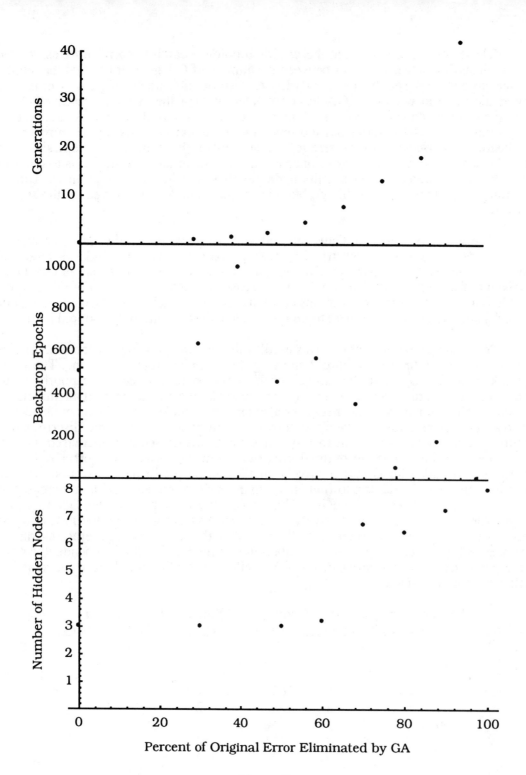

Figure 2

Synthetic Problem GA/Backprop Trade-Off

Conclusion

This paper has investigated a new genetic algorithm which develops neural networks. The trade-off between the global genetic search and a local search algorithm (in this case back propagation) was investigated, with the result that after 80% of the original error has been eliminated, the rate of progress of the genetic algorithm decreases rapidly, and a switch to the local algorithm yields faster solutions. In fact, on harder problems, the GA will actually increase the size of the networks to reduce the last bit of error, which is hardly a desirable effect.

Acknowledgement

The author acknowledges Professor Panos Ligomenides for his guidance and encouragement, and MRJ, Inc., for their support.

References

[Gol89]   D.Goldberg, *Genetic Algorithms in Search, Optimization & Machine Learning,* Addison-Wesley, 1989.

[Whit93]   D.White, "GANNet: A Genetic Algorithm for Searching Topology and Weight Spaces in Neural Network Design", Ph.D. Dissertation, University of Maryland at College Park, 1993.

[WS90]   D.Whitley and T.Starkweather, "Optimizing Small Neural Networks Using a Distributed Genetic Algorithm", *Proceedings of the International Joint Conference on Neural Networks*, Jan. 1990, Vol. I, pp. 206 - 209. Washington, D.C., IEEE, January 1990.

Restart Concept for
Error Backpropagation with Gains Algorithm

Kang S. BYUN and Sung Y. BANG
Computer Science and Engineering Department
Pohang Institute of Science and Technology
San 31, Hyoja-dong, Pohang
790-784, South Korea

Abstract

Restart concept is found in Conjugate Gradient method to find the best error decreasing vectors when it fails to reach a minimum. We applied this restart concept to the error backpropagation with gains algorithm and obtained a good result. This paper reports the idea and the experimental results. We apply the restart procedure to the error backpropagation with gains learning not only periodically but also when the error did not decrease during the previous learning epoch. The restart procedure resets the gains and the bias and the learning is continued. The experiments using parity and encoder problems showed that the proposed approach is about 10 times faster in learning time than the conventional error backpropagation with momentum algorithm.

1. Background

1. 1. Summary of BPG

There have recently been growing interests in the extension of the conventional error backpropagation with momentum(BP) algorithm[1]. Our interest here is mainly in error backpropagation with gains(BPG)[2] algorithm and the neural implementation of the conjugate gradient(CG) algorithms[3,4]. Conjugate gradient algorithms are generally much faster and can result in an impressively low error level. But these algorithms also are particularly vulnerable to being trapped in local minima. Especially, line search efficiency and initial weights set are critical to the success of conjugate gradient algorithms[4,5].

BPG algorithm has several advantages over BP algorithm; it is faster in lowering standard deviation of error over the entire training pattern set than BP during the learning phase[6]. For some problems BPG is much less likely to become trapped in local minima[7,6]. And it was shown that BPG is 2.2 times on the average faster in some parity and encoder problems[2].

However BPG has a shortcoming too: its error-decreasing rate becomes slow in the later learning phase which is the fact common to all gradient descent learning algorithms. The focus of our effort was directed to overcoming the learning slow-down phenomena generally observed in the gradient descent learning algorithms including BP and BPG.

1. 2. Restart procedure of CG method

The learning problem of neural networks can be formulated as an optimization problem in numerical analysis. Among the techniques of numerical analysis which can be used to train the neural networks, conjugate gradient method is relatively easy to implement and inexpensive in computational cost.

CG tries to directly reach a minimum on the error surface by using quadratic approximation, saving search effort otherwise required by gradient descent calculations. But due to the gap between the real shape of the error surface and the approximation of the weights of the minimum, this method usually fails to directly reach a minimum and hence need more trials of approximation.

When it fails, this method uses restart procedure to again guess the best error-decreasing direction vectors from the last gradient descent direction. Then the regular learning operation is continued. We apply this restart concept of CG method to BPG by developing a restart procedure that is suitable to BPG.

2. Restart Procedure

2.1. When to restart and when to stop restarting

Restart concept in BPG algorithm[2] is based on the idea from the restart in CG method; the improvement on the navigating directions of error surface in weights space.

We use the BPG algorithm without momentum. A restart process is taken periodically for every 2N epochs of learning where N is the number of the weights in the network. In addition, when the error did not decrease during the last learning epoch, a restart process is also taken even during the period mentioned above. The choice of a length of the period is heuristic, at this moment. We found after many experiments that 2N is about the optimal at least for those problems mentioned later.

Although restart process is taken periodically from the beginning of the learning as described above, it is not always necessary to continue the process forever. More specifically, we can stop restarting as soon as the learning reaches a classifiable state. **A classifiable state is a learning stage of the network where every node** of the output layer can classify all input patterns into the correct pattern classes according to the signs of their net inputs. For example, suppose that a node of the output layer is to classify the inputs to the class A and the non-class A patterns, and that now the net inputs of the input patterns are grouped to the two separate sets as shown in Fig. 1(a), then we say that the node is in a classifiable state. And further the network is in a classifiable state of learning if all nodes of the output layer are in classifiable state. **As soon as we reach a classifiable state of learning, a certain large (fixed) momentum rate(e.g. 0.9) is given to the gain of each node and each weight so that the learning can be finished more quickly[11.12] to the desired error level. At the same time we multiply a certain constant(e.g. 1.4) to every weight so that we would not lose the route to a minimum just found[9].** The value 1.4 above is justified as follows. If you take 0.9 for a momentum rate, then the largest overshoot possible from the current position is $0.9 * 0.25 = 0.225$ where 0.25 is the largest derivative value of the activation function $f(x)= 1 / (1+\exp(-x))$. Therefore any small value close to but greater than 1.225 can be used as the multiplier for weights. Here we picked up 1.4.

Here we assume that the initial weights are randomly generated from the real range [-0.5, +0.5]. And each weight vector is normalized in length. Also we assume that the network architecture is always 2-layer feed-forward. Let a_i^S be the activation of the i-th node of the layer S, and let $a^S = \begin{bmatrix} a_1^S \cdots a_n^S \end{bmatrix}^T$ be the column vector of activation values in layer S. The input layer is the layer 0. Let w_{ij}^S be the weight on the connection from the j-th node in layer S-1 to the i-th node in layer S, and let $w_i^S = \begin{bmatrix} w_{i1}^S \cdots w_{im}^S \end{bmatrix}^T$ be the column vector of weights from layer S-1 to the i-th node in layer S. The given weights set is partitioned into K vectors if there are K processing nodes in the network. The net input to the i-th node of layer S is defined as $net_i^S = \langle w_i^S, a^{S-1} \rangle = \sum_k w_{ik}^S a_k^{S-1}$, and let $net^S = \begin{bmatrix} net_1^S \cdots net_n^S \end{bmatrix}^T$ be the column vector of net input values in layer S. Then the activation of a node is given by the function of its net input, $a_i^S = f\left(g_i^S net_i^S \right)$, where f is conventional sigmoid function[1], and g_i^S is a real number called the gain of the node.

If the initial weight vectors are sufficiently small, then the distribution of the net inputs to an output node shall be in the unsaturated region[10]. An unsaturated region is an area where the derivative of the sigmoid activation function $f(x)= 1 / (1+\exp(-x))$ is not very small(e.g. not less than a tenth of the maximum value of the derivative function) so that the error-correcting signal propagated back is significant and hence the learning proceeds relatively fast.

Therefore we want to keep all net inputs to the output node in the unsaturated region until the network comes to a classifiable state.

By varying the bias of a output node according to the range of its activation, the corresponding net input distribution is stabilized and the center of corresponding net input distribution comes near the origin of the net input axis of the activation function so that we can prevent a premature saturation in the early learning phase. And at the same time we can also diminish the sensitivity of the initial weights.

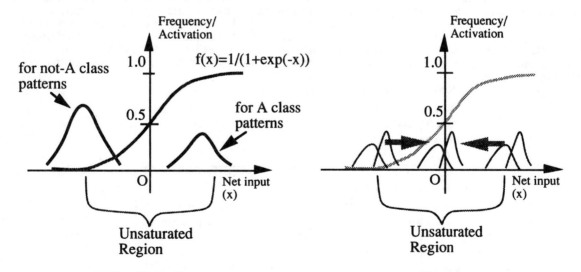

(a) Classifiable State　　　　　　　　　　　　　(b) Bias Adjustment

Fig. 1. The net input distribution, unsaturated region, and the re-configuring the bias in a output node

2.2 How to restart

We set the bias of each output node to the value 0.5 at the initial point of learning and, during each following restart process, the bias is set to the median value of the activation distribution of the output node.

We set the gain of each processing node to 1.0 at the restart process as well as at the initial setting of the learning. Now we describe specifically what to do for each restart. Let pat_{qi} be the i-th component of the q-th input pattern pat_q, m be the number of components in an input patterns, and p be the number of input patterns to be used for learning. Systematically,

$$pat_q = \left[pat_{q1} \cdots pat_{qm}\right]^T, pat_{qi} \ni \{0,1\}, \forall i \ni \{1,2,3,\cdots,m\} \wedge \forall q \ni \{1,2,3,\cdots,p\}.$$

Let the output of k-th processing node of the output layer according to the q-th input pattern be O_{qk}, and the set of the outputs for all input patterns be $\{O_k\}$. A restart process consists of 2 steps: bias adjustment and gain reset.

Step 1: Set the bias of k-th output node $bias_k = \left(\min\{O_k\} + \max\{O_k\}\right)/2$.

Step 2: Reset the gain of each processing node.

$$g_i^S = 1.0, \forall i \ni \{1,2,\cdots,l\} \text{ (cf. l is the number of nodes in S-th layer.)}$$

3. Experiments

We are interested in the comparison of the learning time between the conventional BP[1] and the BPG with restart process proposed in this paper. For this purpose we used XOR, 5-bit parity, and 4-bit encoder-decoder problems. We tried each problem 15 times with initial weights randomly generated within the real range of [-0.5, +0.5] each time. The basic network architecture used is feed-forward fully connected 2-layer (hidden layer and output layer for both cases). The notation of network structure x-y-z is used here to tell that the network has x nodes in the input layer, y nodes in the hidden layer, and z nodes in the output layer.

For XOR and 5-bit parity problems, we used 2-2-1 and 5-5-1 network structures respectively. For 4-bit encoder problem, we used 4-4-1 network structure. For the learning by conventional BP algorithm, we set the learning rate to 0.7 and the momentum rate to 0.9. For the learning by the BPG with restart, we set the learning rate for weight change to 1.0 and the learning rate for gain change to 1.0. And the momentum rates for both weight and gain were set to 0's.

In case of the BPG with restart, we multiplied each connection weight by 1.4 and set the momentum rates for both weight and gain change to 0.9 in order to accelerate the further learning, as described above, as soon as we reached a classifiable state. We witnessed through three experiments that the learning always converged to a lower error level without deviating from the point where a classifiable state was reached. The experimental results are summarized in 3 graphs and 3 tables. A failure means that the error level could not be reached within 3000 learning epochs starting with the given initial weights. From the results it is evident that the consistency in good performance with the BPG with restart and that the learning speed with BPG with restart is about 10 times faster than that of BP.

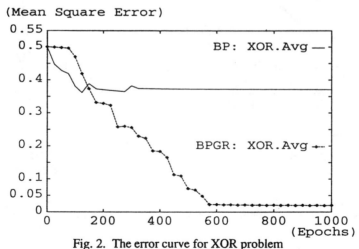

Fig. 2. The error curve for XOR problem

Table. 1. XOR Problem, Avg. Epochs (No. of Failures) / Std. Dev.

Mean Squared Error	Conventional BP	BPGR
0.50	19.23(2)/ 27.26	26.67(0)/ 29.53
0.10	175.00 (14)/ 0.0	319.64(1)/156.75
0.05	375.00 (14)/ 0.0	319.64(1)/156.75

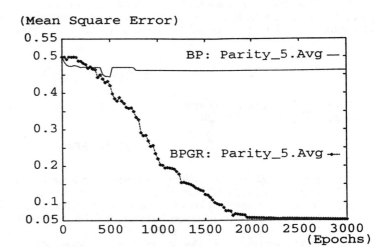

Fig. 3. The error curve for 5-bit Parity problem

Table. 2. 5-bit Parity Problem, Avg. Epochs (No. of Failures) / Std. Dev.

Mean Squared Error	Conventional BP	BPGR
0.50	6.82 (4)/ 11.23	41.67 (0)/ 96.90
0.10	N.A.* (15)/ N.A.	1048.21 (1)/486.02
0.05	N.A. (15)/ N.A.	1078.13 (7)/485.80

(* N.A. means 'Not Applicable'.)

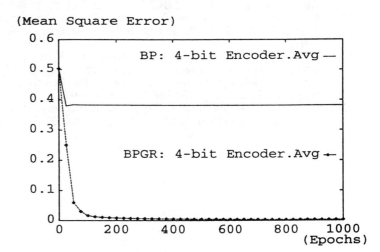

Fig. 4. The error curve for 4-bit Encoder problem

Table. 3. 4-bit Encoder Problem, Avg. Epochs (No. of Failures) / Std. Dev.

Mean Squared Error	Conventional BP	BPGR
0.50	13.33 (0) / 12.47	13.33 (0) / 12.47
0.10	N.A.* (15)/ N.A.	63.33 (0) / 22.11
0.05	N.A. (15)/ N.A.	105.00 (0) / 64.03

(* N.A. means 'Not Applicable'.)

4. Conclusion

We introduced a restart concept for BPG learning algorithm. We described when to restart the learning as well as when to stop the restart operations.

We provided some of the reasons why such restart operations help speed up the learning. We introduced the concept of a classifiable state in order to identify the learning stage where no more restart operations are necessary. We showed that a further speedup can be attained by applying a different strategy from the point of the classifiable state. Computer simulations indicated a significant improvement in the learning time with our proposed method for XOR, 5-bit parity and 4-bit encoder problems. This preliminary results showed that the new algorithm is about 10 times faster than the conventional BP algorithm.

Acknowledgment

This work was supported by grants KT 93-45 from Korea Telecom and KOSEF 92-21-00-05 from Korea Science and Engineering Foundation.

References

[1]   D.E. Rumelhart, J.L. McClelland, and PDP Research Group, "Parallel Distributed Processing: Explorations in the Microstructure of Cognition," vol. 1, MIT Press, pp. 322-330, 1986.

[2]   John K. Kruschke and Javier R. Movellan, "Benefits of Gain: Speeded Learning and Minimal Hidden Layers in Back-Propagation Networks," IEEE Transactions on Systems, Man, and Cybernetics, Vol.21,No.1, pp.273-280, Jan./Feb. 1991

[3]   E. M. Johansson, F. U. Dowla and D. M. Goodman, "Backpropagation Learning for Multilayer Feed-Forward Neural Networks using the Conjugate Gradient Method," International Journal of Neural Systems, vol.2, no.4, pp. 291-301, 1992.

[4]   Martin Fodslette Moeller, "A Scaled Conjugate Gradient Algorithm for Fast Supervised Learning," Neural Networks, vol.6, pp. 525-533, 1993.

[5]   D. Gorse, A. Shepherd, and J. G. Taylor, "Tracking Global Minima by Progressive Range Expansion," Proc. WCNN, INNS, vol.4, pp. 350-353, July, 1993.

[6]   Raoul Tawel, "Does the Neuron "LEARN" like Synapse?," Advances in Neural Information Processing Systems I, Ed. by David S. Touretzky, Morgan Kaufmann, pp. 169-176, 1989.

[7]   Kang S. BYUN and Sung Y. BANG, "Improving Learning Speed using Restart Concept in Error Backpropagation networks with Gains," Proc. of The Third Joint Conference/Exhibition on A.I. and Neural Networks, and Fuzzy Systems, pp. 49-53, Oct., Seoul, Korea, 1993.

[8]   Qi Jia and Shiro Usui, "An Equivalent Relation Concerning the Gain in Back-Propagation Algorithms," Proceedings of IJCNN, P.H.E.I., vol. II, pp.387-392, Beijing, China, Nov.3-6, 1992.

[9]   L. Y. Pratt, J. Mostow, and C. A. Kamm, "Direct Transfer of Learned Information Among Neural Networks," AAAI-91, Proceedings of Ninth National Conference on AI, vol. 2, pp. 584-589, July, 1991.

[10] Youngjik Lee, Sang-Hoon Oh, and Myung Won Kim, "The Effect of Initial Weights on Premature Saturation in Back-Propagation Learning,," Proceedings of IJCNN, IEEE, pp. I-765 -- I-770, 1991.

[11] Marvin L. Minsky, Seymour A. Papert, "The Perceptron Convergence Theorem," Perceptrons (Expanded Edition), pp. 164-168, MIT Press, 1988.

[12] P. Frasconi, M. Gori, and A. Tesi, "Backpropagation for Linearly-Separable Patterns: a Detailed Analysis," Proc. of IEEE ICNN, vol. 3, pp. 1818-1822, San Francisco, California, March 28 - April 1, 1993.

Learning Algorithm for a Piecewise Linear Neural Network

Mark J. Brady

3M Company
Applied Research Group
3M Center 260-6A-08
St. Paul, MN 55144-1000

email: brady@neuro.med.umn.edu

Abstract

A new classifier neural network architecture and corresponding learning algorithm is introduced. The hypothesis space for this algorithm is the set of all piecewise linear separations. Properties that are desirable in neural network architectures in general are discussed and related to the present design. The algorithm is shown to be consistent. A means for reducing the size of the model produced by the learning algorithm, and a rationale for performing such a reduction are given.

1. Introduction

In this paper, a classifying neural network and learning algorithm which generate piecewise linear models is presented. The learning problem to which this algorithm is applied is that of learning concepts, about which no a priori knowledge is available, except perhaps that the concept is representable as a open subset of the input space. As is the case with most learning classifiers, the learning algorithm accepts a set of samples from the input space along with the correct classification of those samples and produces or configures a network which effectively partitions the input space into regions which represent two or more classes. Configuration of the net includes actions such as determining the number of nodes or neurons, determining the connectivity, and determining the synaptic weights.

The introduction of any new learning algorithm or network should be accompanied by a description of its desirable properties. The standard used to evaluate the network introduced in this paper is summarized below. However, in order to describe these properties, some preliminary definitions must be given.

<u>Definition:</u>   *Concept* - A set of points in the network's input space. Given samples and counter-examples of this set, a network's learning algorithm attempts to set parameters or synaptic weights in the network such that novel points, which are also in the concept, are recognized.

<u>Definition:</u>   *Sample* - A point from the input space, paired with information regarding membership in some concept c.

Definition: *Hypothesis* - The set of all points in the input space which are classified as belonging to the concept, after the network has been trained.

Definition: *Hypothesis Space* - The set of all hypotheses which can be generated by a given learning algorithm when presented with concepts from a given concept class.

Definition: *Consistent Learning Algorithm* - A learning algorithm is consistent if the network it configures is guaranteed to correctly classify all members of the example training set.

Desirable properties of classifying neural networks may now be listed as follows:

Property 1)   The hypothesis space of the learning algorithm should be large enough to model a broad range of potential concepts. While the concept space of a given problem domain need not match the hypothesis space generated by the learning algorithm used, a large concept space does require a correspondingly large hypothesis space. An example of a large hypothesis space is the set of all open sets. In fact, it is doubtful that any neural net-like system can produce a useful hypothesis if the concept space is larger than the set of all open sets.

An example of a small hypothesis space is the classic example of linear separations or half spaces. Few problems with interesting applications can be reduced to such simplicity. These limited hypothesis spaces can only be used to construct models for small concept recognition problems. A small concept class is indicative of having some specific knowledge of the nature of the concept to be learned. In these cases, it may be argued that a generally applicable and powerful learning system is not required.

The size of the hypothesis space is determined by the nature of the network architectures produced by the learning algorithm rather than by the specifics of the learning algorithm itself. For example, it is known that multilayer nets with linear units having sigmoidal activation functions have a very large hypothesis space (Funahashi, 1989). However, this does not mean that there exists an algorithm which can configure such a net so that it will reliably learn complex concepts. Therefore at least one additional property is required.

Property 2)   The network, after training should have a high probability of correctly classifying samples from its input space. This requirement is obvious, although formulating it precisely and knowing when the requirement has been met, is far from obvious.

One precise formulation of this property is the notion of polynomial learnability, also known as probably almost correct (PAC) learnability.

Definition: *Polynomially Learnable* - Let s be an upper bound on **size**(c), where **size**() is some concept complexity measure. A concept class **C** is polynomially learnable if there exists a polynomial time algorithm A that accepts samples from $c \in$ **C** according to an arbitrary probability distribution over the sample space, and returns a hypothesis h (i.e. the network is trained), such that for all $0 < \varepsilon, \delta < 1$ and $s \geq 1$, there exists a sample size $m(\varepsilon,\delta,s)$, polynomial in $1/\varepsilon$, $1/\delta$ and s, such that given a random sample set of size $m(\varepsilon,\delta,s)$, A produces, with probability at least $1-\delta$, a hypothesis h that has error at most ε. (Valiant, 1984)

In essence, the polynomial learnability requirement demands that reliable learning can be achieved with a practical number of examples. Furthermore, it sensibly allows the number of examples to grow as the complexity of the concept or the stringency of the reliability is increased.

The definition of polynomially learnable concept classes is, of course, only a definition and therefore it does not provide a means for determining whether a particular algorithm can polynomially learn concepts from a particular concept class. A theorem which may be helpful in this regard is provided by Blumer et al. (1989). Blumer's theorem states, in part, that a concept class **C** is polynomially learnable if there is an Occam algorithm for **C**.

Definition: *Occam Algorithm* - A learning algorithm *A* is Occam if:

i)   *A* runs in polynomial time p(m).

ii)   *A* is consistent.

iii)   Let $C^A_{s,m}$ be the set of all hypotheses produced by *A* when *A* is given m samples with respect to a concept c in C, where **size**(c) < s. The VC dimension (Haussler and Welzl, 1987) of $C^A_{s,m}$ must be less than $p(s)m^\alpha$. p(s) is some polynomial in s and α is a constant in [0,1).

Property 3)   The algorithm should run in an amount of time which makes use of the algorithm practical. Convention from the theory of computing places the boundary between practical and impractical as being between the polynomial time algorithms and the exponential time algorithms. Time functions are measured in the input size, which in our case is the number of samples provided for training. Polynomial time properties are included in the definitions of polynomially learnable and Occam algorithm above.

Combining desirable property (1) with Occam definition items (ii) and (iii), one can see that a learning algorithmist seeks an algorithm with $C^A_{s,m}$ large enough so that consistency with respect to a large concept class is possible, yet $C^A_{s,m}$ is not so large that its VC dimension exceeds $p(s)m^\alpha$. In this paper it will be shown that, no matter how large C is, the algorithm presented can always produce a consistent hypothesis. Furthermore, in the spirit of reducing the VC dimension of $C^A_{s,m}$ the learning algorithm includes a means of reducing the number of linear separations which make up the entire piecewise linear separation. The number of linear separations is related to the VC dimension. It is not difficult to show that the VC dimension of the set of all piecewise separations, having k linear separations, is $\geq$ k(n+1).

2. Piecewise Linear Neural Networks

A piecewise linear separation is a suitable approximator of certain concept classes. If the concept is an open set which is separated from non-concept points by piecewise continuous manifolds, or hypersurfaces, then those manifolds may be approximated by multiple bounded hyperplanes. The resulting set of bounded hyperplanes form a separation which is piecewise linear.

Algorithms exist for determining a single linear separation when the sample points are so separable (Rosenblatt, 1962; Karmarkar, 1984). These algorithms are well known. In the case of Karmarkar, the algorithm is polynomial time. The primary difficulties in extending single linear separations to piecewise linear separations lie in determining which linearly separable subsets of the sample set should be grouped together and in determining which regions of the input space are associated with each linear separation.

The simplest possible case one may consider is that of two samples, $\bar{x}_a$ and $\bar{x}_b$, of opposite class, one belonging to the concept and one not belonging. In order to approximate the surface which bounds the concept and separates the point one may employ the following observation: a line segment connecting any two points of opposite type must include a point which is on the surface. A point on the segment must be selected as well as a surface model type and orientation. Since the simplest sufficient model of any phenomenon tends to be superior, the simplest possible assumptions are made, namely: the model surface type is a hyperplane, the orientation of the plane is given by normal vector $\bar{x}_a - \bar{x}_b$, and the point shared by the hyperplane and the line segment is chosen to be $(\bar{x}_a + \bar{x}_b)/2$. Nilsson (1965) generalized this idea from point pairs to point cluster pairs. The present algorithm generalizes the idea of generating hyperplanes from point pairs to the case of an arbitrary number of sample points which are not necessarily clustered and not necessarily linearly separable.

3. Target Network Architecture

The network architecture which is trained by the learning algorithm is shown in figure 1. The learning algorithm determines the number of nodes as well as the synaptic weights. There are five node types in the net: **m**, **z**, **g**, **n**, and **M**. There is a plurality of (**m**, **z**, **g**, **n**) 4-tuples while **M** is unique. The **m**, **z**, and **n** nodes each store a vector having the same dimension, n, as the input space. Input vector $\bar{I}$ enters the system and is distributed to all **m** and **z** nodes. **z** computes $\bar{\Delta} = \bar{I} - \bar{z}$ while **m** computes the magnitude $|\bar{\Delta}|$. Each m directs its output $|\bar{\Delta}|$ to node M where the minimum of all $|\bar{\Delta}|$s is computed. The minimum is then broadcast back to the **m** nodes which compare the minimum with $|\bar{\Delta}|$. If m's output matches the minimum, **m** outputs an open-gate signal to gate node **g**. Gate node **g** then passes z's output to node **p** which is a perceptron. Only one perceptron receives input in response to net input $\bar{I}$. The perceptron performs the usual dot product between its input and the stored synaptic weight vector. The dot product is compared to a threshold which is always zero and the network outputs zero or one depending on the comparison. The input to the network is thus classified as belonging to a concept or not.

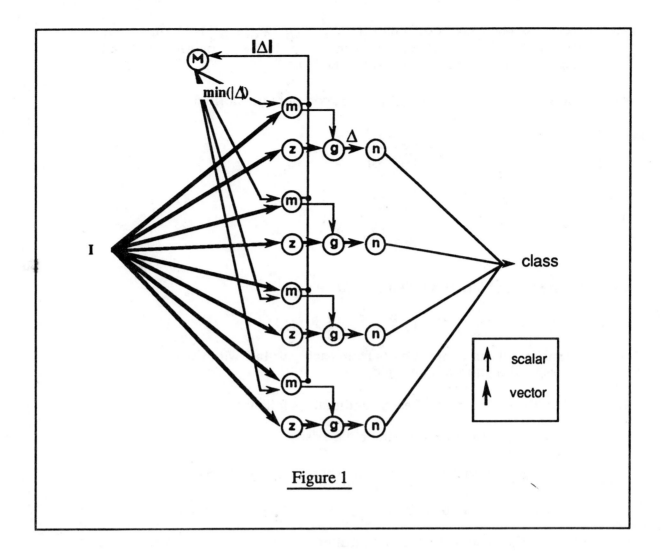

Figure 1

4. Learning Algorithm

The learning algorithm proceeds as follows:

1)   Acquire N sample points and their classifications :

$S \equiv \{ (\vec{X}_i, C_i) \mid i=1...N, C_i = A \text{ or } B\}$, the set of classified samples

$A \equiv \{\vec{X}_i \mid C_i = A \}$, the set of all samples having type A

$B \equiv \{\vec{X}_i \mid C_i = B \}$, the set of all samples having type B

2)   For each $(\vec{X}_a, C_a) \in S$, find $(\vec{X}_b, C_b)$ such that $C_a \neq C_b$ and $|\vec{X}_a - \vec{X}_b| \leq |\vec{X}_a - \vec{X}_k|$ for all k where $C_a \neq C_k$. In other words, find the nearest neighbor of opposite type. Call the resultant set of pairs of classified samples P.

3) Order the elements in each pair $[(\vec{X}_a, C_a), (\vec{X}_b, C_b)]$ such that   the first element is a class A pair and the second is a class B   pair if not already so ordered. Remove redundant elements from P.

4) For each $[(\vec{X}_a, C_a), (\vec{X}_b, C_b)] \in P$, compute the normal

$$\vec{n} \equiv \frac{(\vec{x}_a - \vec{x}_b)}{|\vec{x}_a - \vec{x}_b|}$$

and the midpoints

$$\vec{z} = \vec{m} \equiv \frac{(\vec{x}_a + \vec{x}_b)}{2}$$

Define a set of 5-tuples called *candidate posts*

$$C \equiv \{ (\vec{X}_a, \vec{X}_b, \vec{n}, \vec{z}, \vec{m}) \}$$

comprised of the sample points from each pair in P with their corresponding normals and midpoints.

5) Adjust the midpoint $\vec{z}$ of each candidate as follows:

At least one of the two following balls exists:

G_a= uniform ball about $\vec{X}_a$, where $\vec{X}_a$'s NNOT is $\vec{X}_b$.

G_b= uniform ball about $\vec{X}_b$, where $\vec{X}_b$'s NNOT is $\vec{X}_a$.

a) If they both exist then do nothing.

b) If the uniform ball G_a exists, set

$$s \equiv \min\{(\vec{x} - \vec{x}_b) \bullet \vec{n} | \vec{x} \in G_a\}$$

c) $\vec{z}$ is then changed to $\vec{x}_b + \frac{s}{2}\vec{n}$.

d) If the uniform ball G_b exists, set

$$s \equiv \min\{(\vec{x}_a - \vec{x}) \bullet \vec{n} | \vec{x} \in G_b\}$$

e) $\vec{z}$ is then changed to $\vec{x}_a - \frac{s}{2}\vec{n}$.

6)   The candidate posts compete to be included in the final post set:

Definition- A candidate *classifies* a point $\vec{x}$ as being in **A** or in **B** as follows: if $(\vec{x} - \vec{z}) \bullet \vec{n} > 0$ then $\vec{x}$ is classified as being in **A**. Otherwise $\vec{x}$ is classified as being in **B**. Note that $\vec{x}$ being classified as in **A** (or **B**) does not necessarily imply that $\vec{x}$ must actually be in **A** (or **B**).

Definition- The *popularity* of a candidate is equal to the number of samples in the largest ball centered at $\vec{m}$ such that no sample in the ball is incorrectly classified.

Definition - For a given $\vec{x}$, let **G** be the largest ball, centered at $\vec{x}$, which contains no candidates which misclassify $\vec{x}$. A *proxy* candidate for $\vec{x}$ is the most popular candidate in **G**.

a)   Compute the popularity of each candidate.

b)   For each sample point $\vec{x}$, find a proxy candidate.

c)   Remove any candidate from the candidate list if it is not a proxy for some sample.

d)   If some removals occur, go to (b).

e)   The remaining candidate posts are the *posts* and are used to define the weights of the classification network. The vectors $\vec{m}$ are stored in the network's **m** nodes, the vectors $\vec{z}$ are stored in the **z** nodes and the vectors $\vec{n}$ are stored as the weights of the perceptron nodes **n**.

5. Consistency
Definition: *NNOT* - Nearest neighbor of opposite type.

Definition: *Uniform Ball of a Point*- The open ball centered at a sample and having radius equal to the distance from that sample to the sample's NNOT. Uniform balls contain only samples of the type found at center, if any.

Definition: *Candidate Post of a Sample Point* - In the algorithm, each sample point $\vec{x}$ generates a post P by first defining a NNOT for $\vec{x}$. $\vec{x}$ and the NNOT then define a midpoint and so on. In this manner, each sample has assigned to it a unique candidate post. P is referred to as the candidate post of sample $\vec{x}$. If the candidate survives the competition to become a post, then P is referred to as the *post of a sample point* $\vec{x}$.

Definition: *Uniform Ball of a Post*- Let $\vec{x}_a$ and $\vec{x}_b$ be the samples which generate post P. From the algorithm for the construction of a post, we know that there is a ball of radius $|\vec{x}_a - \vec{x}_b|$ and centered at either $\vec{x}_a$ or $\vec{x}_b$ which uniformly contains points of the center type. This ball, of which there is at least one and possibly two, is the uniform ball of the post.

<u>Theorem:</u>   The learning algorithm is consistent .

Proof:
By lemma 1, the network which may be generated using candidate posts defined after $\vec{z}$ adjustment and before candidate competition is consistent. It remains to show that the process of candidate competition preserves consistency. To see that this is the case, note that in the algorithm, for each sample the corresponding proxy is chosen such that no other candidate which is closer to the sample will misclassify it. Therefore, if some other candidate is chosen as a proxy for some other sample point, and if that proxy is closer to the original sample than its own proxy, the new proxy will also correctly classify the original sample. Hence, the closest post, as determined by $\vec{m}$, correctly classifies each sample. This is all that is required for consistency of the network.
Q.E.D.

<u>Lemma 1:</u>   In the algorithm, following the adjustment of the $\vec{z}$ vectors, a network formed using the candidate posts as weights is consistent.

Proof:
A sample will always be correctly classified by its own post. Therefore, for misclassification to occur, a sample must be closer to the $\vec{m}$ point of another post and that other post must misclassify the sample. Such potential situations may be broken down into two cases.

Case 1) *The uniform balls of P_j and $\vec{x}_{ak}$ are of the same type.* Let P_j be the post which potentially misclassifies sample $\vec{x}_{ak}$. Both P_j and $\vec{x}_{ak}$ have associated with them a uniform ball. If these uniform balls are of the same type, then by lemma 2, $\vec{x}_{ak}$ is in the uniform ball of P_j. Since the $\vec{z}$ vector of P_j has been adjusted to ensure that all points in P_j's uniform ball are properly classified, $\vec{x}_{ak}$ is properly classified.

Case 2) *The uniform balls of P_j and $\vec{x}_{ak}$ are of different types.* By lemma 3, $\vec{x}_{ak}$ cannot be closer to $\vec{m}_j$ than it is to $\vec{m}_k$. Therefore there can be no misclassification.

Since, in both cases there is no misclassification, the network is consistent.
Q.E.D.

Lemma 2: Let $(\vec{x}_{ak}, \vec{x}_{bk}, \vec{m}_k, \vec{n}_k, \vec{z}_k)$ and $(\vec{x}_{aj}, \vec{x}_{bj}, \vec{m}_j, \vec{n}_j, \vec{z}_j)$ be candidate posts produced by the algorithm. If has a uniform ball and if $\vec{x}_{ak}$ is closer to $\vec{m}_j$ than it is to $\vec{m}_k$, and if $\vec{x}_{aj}$ has a uniform ball, then $\vec{x}_{ak}$ is in the uniform ball of $\vec{x}_{aj}$.

Proof by contradiction: Let $\vec{x}_{aj} \equiv (x_{a,j,1}, ..., x_{a,j,n})$. Likewise for $\vec{x}_{ak}$, $\vec{x}_{bk}$, and $\vec{x}_{bj}$. Let $r \equiv |\vec{x}_{ak} - \vec{x}_{bk}|$.

*)   Assume that $\bar{x}_{ak}$ is closer to $\bar{m}_j$ than it is to $\bar{m}_k$ and $\bar{x}_{ak}$ is *not* in the uniform ball of $\bar{x}_{aj}$.

By the definition of a midpoint,
1) $x_{m,j,i} = (x_{a,j,i} + x_{b,j,i})/2$

Without loss of generality one may place $\bar{x}_{ak}$ at the origin. $\bar{x}_{ak}$ is closer to $\bar{m}_j$ than it is to $\bar{m}_k$ may be expressed as:

2) $\sqrt{\sum_i x_{m,j,i}^2} < r/2$ or $\sum_i x_{m,j,i}^2 < r^2/4$

By the definition of "uniform ball":

3) $\sqrt{\sum_i x_{b,j,i}^2} > r$ or $\sum_i x_{b,j,i}^2 > r^2$

$\bar{x}_{ak}$ is *not* in the uniform ball of $\bar{x}_{aj}$ can be written as:

4) $\sqrt{\sum_i x_{a,j,i}^2} > \sqrt{\sum_i (x_{a,j,i} - x_{b,j,i})^2}$ or $\sum_i x_{a,j,i}^2 > \sum_i (x_{a,j,i} - x_{b,j,i})^2$

Combining (1) & (2) gives:

5) $\sum_i \left[(x_{a,j,i} + x_{b,j,i})/2\right]^2 < r^2/4$ or $\sum_i \left[(x_{a,j,i} + x_{b,j,i})\right]^2 < r^2$

Expanding (4) & (5):

6) $\sum_i x_{a,j,i}^2 > \sum_i (x_{a,j,i}^2 - 2x_{a,j,i}x_{b,j,i} + x_{b,j,i}^2)$

7) $\sum_i \left[x_{a,j,i}^2 + 2x_{a,j,i}x_{b,j,i} + x_{b,j,i}^2\right] < r^2$

Add (3) to (6):

8) $\sum_i (x_{a,j,i}^2 + x_{b,j,i}^2) > r^2 + \sum_i (x_{a,j,i}^2 - 2x_{a,j,i}x_{b,j,i} + x_{b,j,i}^2)$

Which implies:

9) $\sum_i 2x_{a,j,i}x_{b,j,i} > r^2$

Using (3), (9), and the fact that $x_{a,j,i}^2$ is positive, one has:

10) $\sum_i \left[x_{a,j,i}^2 + 2x_{a,j,i}x_{b,j,i} + x_{b,j,i}^2\right] > r^2$

which contradicts (7). Therefore, statement (*) must be false.
Q.E.D.

Lemma 3: Let ($\vec{x}_{ak}, \vec{x}_{bk}, \vec{m}_k, \vec{n}_k, \vec{z}_k$) and ($\vec{x}_{aj}, \vec{x}_{bj}, \vec{m}_j, \vec{n}_j, \vec{z}_j$) be candidate posts produced by the algorithm. If $\vec{x}_{ak}$ has a uniform ball and if $\vec{x}_{bj}$ has a uniform ball, then $\vec{x}_{ak}$ cannot be closer to $\vec{m}_j$ than it is to $\vec{m}_k$.

Proof by Contradiction:

The radius of $\vec{x}_{ak}$'s uniform ball must be less than $\left|\vec{x}_{ak} - \vec{x}_{bj}\right|$. Likewise for $\vec{x}_{bj}$'s uniform ball. By the definition of midpoint, $\vec{m}_k$ is on the sphere centered at $\vec{x}_{ak}$ and of radius $\left|\vec{x}_{ak} - \vec{x}_{bj}\right|/2$. Call the interior of this sphere B. If $\vec{x}_{ak}$ is closer to $\vec{m}_k$ than it is to $\vec{m}_k$ then $\vec{m}_j$ must be in the ball B. However, $\vec{m}_j$ in B implies $\left|\vec{x}_{bj} - \vec{x}_{aj}\right| > \left|\vec{x}_{ak} - \vec{x}_{bj}\right|$. This would, in turn, imply that $\vec{x}_{ak}$ is in the uniform ball of $\vec{x}_{bj}$. Since this is impossible, $\vec{x}_{ak}$ must not be closer to $\vec{m}_j$ than it is to $\vec{m}_k$.

Q.E.D.

6. Conclusion

A learning algorithm for a piecewise linear network has been presented. It has been proven that this algorithm can consistently learn an arbitrary training set from a large concept class. While this paper stops short of proving the algorithm is Occam, it does show one means of reducing the model size. In forthcoming work, the algorithm will be shown to be polynomial. Future efforts will also include an attempt to show that this algorithm, or a variant of it, is an Occam algorithm.

References

Blumer, A., Ehrenfeucht, A., Haussler, D., Warmuth, K. 1989. Learnability and the Vapnick-Chervonenkis Dimension. *J. of the ACM* 36(4), 929-965.

Funahashi, K. 1989. On the approximate realization of continuous mappings by neural networks. *Neural Networks* 2, 183-192.

Haussler, D., and Welzl, E. 1987. Epsilon nets and simplex range queries. *Disc. Comput. Geometry* 2, 127-151.

Karmarkar, N. 1984. A polynomial time algorithm for linear programming. *Combinatorica* 4, 373-395.

Nilsson, N. 1965. *Learning machines.* McGraw-Hill, New York.

Rosenblatt, F. 1962. *Principles of neurodynamics.* Spartan Books, New York.

Valiant, L.G. 1984. A theory of the learnable. *Commun. ACM* 27(11), 1124-1142.

PATTERN RECOGNITION USING A FASTER NEW ALGORITHM FOR TRAINING FEED-FORWARD NEURAL NETWORKS

Mario Mastriani, Ph.D.

Secretaría de Investigación y Doctorado (SECID)
Facultad de Ingeniería de la Universidad de Buenos Aires (FIUBA)
C.C. N° 4394, (1000) C.C., Buenos Aires - ARGENTINA
TELEFAX: (54-1) 97-5658
E-Mail: posmaster@ieeear.edu.ar

ABSTRACT - A fast and robust algorithm is presented for training multilayer feedforward neural networks as an alternative to the backpropagation algorithm. The number of iterations required by the new algorithm to converge is less than 10% of what is required by the backpropagation algorithm. Also, it is less affected by the choice of initial weights and setup parameters.

The algorithm uses a modified form of the backpropagation algorithm to minimize the mean-squared error between the desired and actual outputs with respect to the inputs to the nonlinearities. This is in contrast to the standard algorithm which minimizes the mean-squared error with respect to the weights.

The new algorithm will be called *"Predictor of Linear Output"* (PLO), in terms of its function.

Estimated linear signals, generated by the modified backpropagation algorithm, are used to produce an updated set of weights through a system of linear equations (which has an easy resolution) at each node.

I. INTRODUCTION

The feedforward neural networks are used in a number of applications, e.g., control, see [6] and [7]. Because of the hidden layers, they have overcome many limitations of single layer perceptrons. These types of networks are trained ahead of time, using known input/output data. Once trained, the network weights are frozen and unknown data can be run through the network.

The classical method for training a multilayer perceptron is the backpropagation algorithm [1]-[3] which is an iterative gradient algorithm designed to minimize the mean-squared error between the desired output and the actual output for a particular input to the net.

Although it is successfully used in many cases, the backpropagation algorithm suffers from a number of shortcomings. One such shortcomings is the rate at which the algorithm converges. Many iterations are required to train small networks for even the simplest problems. For large network structures and data sets, it may take days or weeks in order to train the network. A training algorithm that reduces this time would be of considerable value.

It is the purpose of this paper to present a new alternative algorithm which is considerably faster than the backpropagation algorithm [1]-[3] and has the added advantage of being less affected by poor initial weights and setup parameters (another shortcoming of the backpropagation algorithm). Besides, the new algorithm is robust and much simpler to build and to understand than another modifications of backpropagation [4] with less computational complexity and more speed of convergence and quality of output.

Estimated linear signals, generated by the modified backpropagation algorithm, are used to produce an updated set of weights through a system of linear equations (which has an easy resolution) at each node.

Training patterns are run through the network until convergence is reached.

II. PREDICTOR OF LINEAR OUTPUT

Before beginning with the functional description of the algorithm, let us state some pertinent definitions on the basis of Fig.1:

SAE = sigmoid[1] adaline element

μ = learning rate. Its selection controls stability and speed of convergence

k = time index or the cycle number

Also $(.)^T$ denotes the transpose of a vector or a matrix.

For a single SAE: (in Fig.1(a))

d_k = desired response at time k

$\mathbf{W}_k = [w_{0,k}, w_{1,k}, \ldots, w_{n,k}]^T$ is the weight vector at time k

$\mathbf{X}_k = [+1, x_{1,k}, \ldots, x_{n,k}]^T$ is the present input pattern vector (IPV) at time k

s_k = linear output at time k, being $s_k = \mathbf{W}_k^T \mathbf{X}_k = \mathbf{X}_k^T \mathbf{W}_k$ (1)

y_k = sigmoid output at time k, being $y_k = sgm(s_k)$ (2)

$\tilde{\epsilon}_k = d_k - y_k$ is the sigmoid error at time k   (3)

For an isolated SAE of a multilayer net: (in Fig.1(b))

$X_k^{(i)} = (+1, x_{1,k}^{(i)}, x_{2,k}^{(i)}, \ldots, x_{n,k}^{(i)})^T$ is the pattern vector of ith layer at time k; e.g., for the output of the jth SAE, will be

$x_{j,k}^{(i)} = sgm(s_{j,k}^{(i)})$ (4)

$W_{j,k}^{(i)} = (w_{j0,k}^{(i)}, w_{j1,k}^{(i)}, w_{j2,k}^{(i)}, \ldots, w_{jn,k}^{(i)})^T$ is the weight vector of ith layer and j^{th} SAE at time k.

$\tilde{\epsilon}_k^{(i)} = (\tilde{\epsilon}_{1,k}^{(i)}, \tilde{\epsilon}_{2,k}^{(i)}, \ldots, \tilde{\epsilon}_{n,k}^{(i)})^T$ is the back-propagated error vector to the ith layer at time k.

$s_k^{(i)} = (s_{1,k}^{(i)}, s_{2,k}^{(i)}, \ldots, s_{n,k}^{(i)})^T$ is the linear output vector of the ith layer at time k; e.g., for the jth SAE, it will be

$s_{j,k}^{(i)} = (W_{j,k}^{(i)})^T X_k^{(i-1)}$ (5)

Note: In both cases, the first premise is to randomize all present weights.

I.- <u>PLO applied to a single SAE</u>: in Fig.1(a), we can see the implementation of the PLO-algorithm for a single neuron in detail. The algorithm is $s_{k+1} \triangleq s_k + \mu \hat{V}_k$ (6)

where $\hat{V}_k \triangleq -\partial E_k / \partial s_k$ (7)

is the instantaneous error gradient for this element with respect to linear output "s_k", and

$$E_k = \tfrac{1}{2} (\tilde{\epsilon}_k)^2 \qquad (8)$$

is the mean square of the sigmoid error. Therefore, replacing Eq.(8) in Eq.(7), we have:

$$\hat{V}_k = -\tfrac{1}{2} \, \partial(\tilde{\epsilon}_k)^2 / \partial s_k =$$
$$= \tilde{\epsilon}_k \; sgm'(s_k) \qquad (9)$$

This particular gradient is coincident with the square error derivative associated to a single SAE (see pp. 1434 in [1]), $\delta_k = -\tfrac{1}{2} \, \partial(\tilde{\epsilon}_k)^2 / \partial s_k =$
$$= \tilde{\epsilon}_k \; sgm'(s_k) \qquad (10)$$

Such as, Eq(9) and Eq(10) are similars, substituting Eq(10) into Eq(6) gives

_____

[1] The term ''sigmoid'' is usually used in reference to monotonically increasing ''S-shaped'' functions, such as the hyperbolic tangent. The sigmoid function, will be represented with the term '' sgm '', while '' sgm' '' will be its derivative wich respect to s_k (linear output).

$$s_{k+1} \stackrel{\Delta}{=} s_k + \mu \, \delta_k =$$

$$= s_k + \mu \, \tilde{\epsilon}_k \, \text{sgm'}(s_k) \tag{11}$$

besides,
$$s_{k+1} = W_{k+1}^T X_{k+1} = X_{k+1}^T W_{k+1} \tag{12}$$

and being $[X_{k+1}(X_{k+1})^T]$ a square and positive semidefinite matrix, then, by equational handling we will have

$$W_{k+1} = s_{k+1} X_{k+1} / |X_{k+1}|^2 \tag{13}$$

II.- <u>PLO applied to an isolated SAE of multilayer net:</u> in Fig.1(b), we can see, in detail, the implementation of the PLO-algorithm for an isolated neuron of multilayer net. This technique is based on the square error derivative associated with the jth neuron in the ith layer (see pp.1433-1434 in [1]),

$$\delta_{j,k}^{(i)} = -\tfrac{1}{2} \, \partial E_k / \partial s_{j,k}^{(i)} =$$

$$= \text{sgm'}(s_{j,k}^{(i)}) \, \tilde{\epsilon}_{j,k}^{(i)} \tag{14}$$

where
$$\tilde{\epsilon}_{j,k}^{(i)} = \sum_{m=1}^{N^{(n)}} W_{mj,k}^{(i+1)} \delta_{m,k}^{(i+1)} \tag{15}$$

is the back-propagated error up to the jth neuron of the ith layer; and

$$E_k = (\epsilon_k)^2 = \sum_{m=1}^{N^{(n)}} (\tilde{\epsilon}_{mk})^2 = \sum_{m=1}^{N^{(n)}} (d_{mk} - x_{mk}^{(n)})^2 \tag{16}$$

The instantaneous sum squared error $(\epsilon_k)^2$ is the sum of the squares of the errors at each of the $N^{(n)}$ outputs of the network ``$x_{mk}^{(n)}$'' and each one the desired responses ``d_{mk}'' for the nth layer, i.e., the last layer. $N^{(i+1)}$ will be the number of neurons of the layer $(i+1)^{th}$. Finally, the estimate linear signal of the neuron j^{th} and of the ith layer will be
$$s_{j,k+1}^{(i)} = s_{j,k}^{(i)} + \mu \, \delta_{j,k}^{(i)} = s_{j,k}^{(i)} + \mu \, \tilde{\epsilon}_{j,k}^{(i)} \text{sgm'}(s_{j,k}^{(i)}) \tag{17}$$

Here too, being $[X_{k+1}^{(i-1)}(X_{k+1}^{(i-1)})^T]$ a square and positive semidefinite matrix, then,

$$W_{j,k+1}^{(i)} = s_{j,k+1}^{(i)} X_{k+1}^{(i-1)} / |X_{k+1}^{(i-1)}|^2 \tag{18}$$

III. PATTERN RECOGNITION

We consider the training of a neural network to recognize patterns presented to its input. Although many different experiments were performed with several data sets and different networks structures, it is presented here only a limited number because of space considerations.

The input pixels are set to a level of -0.5 or +0.5. It is important to note that these levels are considered to be analog values rather than digital binary values. Although it is presented here experiments with patterns of two levels, similar results are obtained with patterns of various gray levels.

The output is likewise treated as analog. Therefore, the network is considered trained not only when the output agrees in sign with the desired output but also in absolute value.

The 7 x 7 pixel patterns in Fig.2 are the inputs to a 2 layer feedforward perceptron with 16 nodes in the hidden layer. The desired output of the network is a 2, 3, or 4 binary word depending upon the number of patterns used to train the network.

Fig.3 shows the mean-squared error versus the iteration number for both algorithms during training for the 7 x 7 example. Table I presents numerically the performance comparison of the two algorithms shown in Fig.3. This comparison takes into account the computational efficiency of each algorithm as well as the number of iterations required for the algorithm to reach a specified mean-squared error. The result is a time ratio of the two algorithms when run on a sequential machine. A mean-squared error convergence of slightly less than 0.25 was chosen since this value is the maximun that can be used and still produce correct results, assuming that the outputs are eventually passed through a hard limiter to produce a binary word.

The algorithm has been implemented in TurboC++ 3.0 (C), Borland (R), on a Pentium™ Processor-66 Mhz PC/AT.

IV. CONCLUSIONS

It has been presented in this paper a new algorithm wich is faster and robuster than the standard backpropagation algorithm in training in training multilayer perceptrons.

The algorithm presented here convergences in less than 10% of the time it takes for the backpropagation algorithm.

Testing performed on 3 layer networks and networks with more neurons per layer, had equally impressive results. In one experiment (not shown) with 39 neurons in first and second layers and 1 neuron in the output layer, the backpropagation algorithm took approximately 20000 iterations to reach the same mean-squared error that the new algorithm achieved in 200.

Also, the new algorithm is more predictable in its training. In Fig.3, it be notice that the backpropagation algorithm tends to reach a certain mean-squared error and remain there for quite a while making little or no progress.

At some point, it either rapidly converges, or jumps to a new level where it would again make little or no progress for quite a while. In contrast, the new algorithm continues to make steady progress toward improving the mean-squared error throughout the training period.

Finally, the convergence of the backpropagation algorithm depends heavily on the magnitude of the initial weights. If chosen incorrectly, the algorithm takes a long time to converge. The new algorithm seems to be less sensitive to the initial weight setting.

V. REFERENCES

[1] B. Widrow and M. A. Lehr, ''30 Years of adaptive neural networks: Perceptron, Madaline and backpropagation,'' Proc. IEEE, vol. 78, pp. 1415- 1442, Sept. 1990.

[2] R. P. Lippman, "An introduction to computing with neural networks," *IEEE ASSP* Mag., vol. 4, no. 2, Apr. 1987.

[3] D. E. Rumelhart and J. L. McClelland, "Parallel Distributed Processing, vol.1, Cambridge, MA: M.I.T. Press, 1986.

[4] R. S. Scalero, "A fast new algorithm for training feedforward neural networks," Ph.D. dissertation, Florida Institute of Technology, 1989.

[5] S. S. Haykin, Adaptive Filter Theory. Englewood Cliffs, NJ: Prentice-Hall, 1986.

[6] M. Mastriani, ''Self-Restorable Stochastic Neuro-Estimation using Forward-Propagation Training Algorithm,'' Proc. of Inter. Neural Network Society, (WCNN '93 Portland) World Congr.on Neural Network, Portland, Oregon, Vol. I, July 11-15, 1993, pp. 404-411.

[7] M. Mastriani, ''Self-Restorable Stochastic Neurocontrol using Back-Propagation and Forward-Propagation Training Algorithms,'' Proc. Inter. Conference on Signal Processing Applications & Technology, (ICSPAT '93), Santa Clara, CA, Vol. II, Sept. 28 - Oct. 1, 1993, pp.1058-1071.

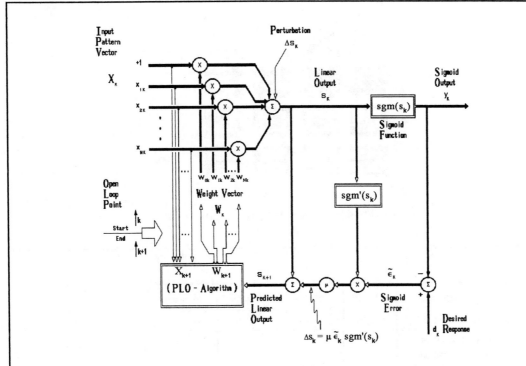

Fig.1(a) - PLO applied to a single SAE.

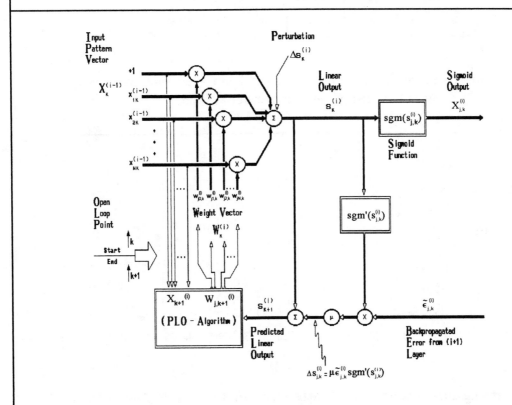

Fig.1(b) - PLO applied to an isolated SAE of a multilayer net.

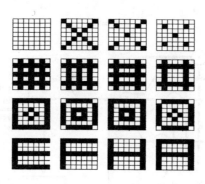

Fig. 2 - Seven-by-seven patterns used for training.

7 x 7 Patterns	4 Patterns	8 Patterns	12 Patterns	16 Patterns
16 Input Nodes	(2 Outputs)	(3 Outputs)	(4 Outputs)	
New algorithm iterations	4	5	12	14
Back-Porpagation iterations	64100	167800	21150	53200
Iteration ratio	16025.00	33560.00	1762.50	3800.00
Comp. ratio	0.9391	0.9459	0.9526	0.9526
Total improve.	15049.07	31744.40	1678.95	3619.88

Table 1 - Improvement Ratio of the New Algorithm over BackPropagation with the MSE Convergence Set at 0.25.

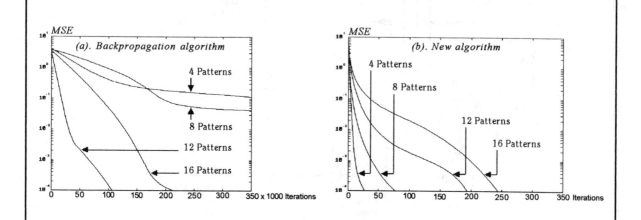

Fig. 3 - Learning curves for a 2 layer pattern recognition network with 16 nodes in the hidden layer. Seven-by-seven patterns were used for training.

COMPUTATIONAL EXPERIENCE WITH A QUASI NEWTON BASED TRAINING OF THE FEEDFORWARD NEURAL NETWORK

L. E. K. Achenie
Department of Chemical Engineering, U-222
University of Connecticut
191 Auditorium Road
Storrs, CT 06269

ABSTRACT:

This paper reports on computational experience with a quasi-Newton based strategy for the supervised training of feed forward neural networks. Coupled with a generalized formulation of the logistic function and explicit box constraints on network variables, it is shown that up to three orders of magnitude fewer function evaluations than the delta rule, and up to an order of magnitude fewer function evaluations than certain conjugate gradient implementations can be obtained.

INTRODUCTION

The ability of neural networks to generalize based only on a set of training data has been extensively documented in the open literature in recent years (see for example Rumelhart 1986 [5]). Supervised training of a feedforward neural network is usually achieved through the solution of an appropriate nonlinear program. Subsequently training times are affected by the nonlinear programming algorithms used. Some of these algorithms are (i) simulated annealing, (ii) the delta rule, (iii) conjugate gradients, (iv) heuristics, (v) Kalman filter techniques and (vi) Newton-based strategies.

The overall goal of this paper is to address the training of the feedforward network using successive quadratic programming. In the suggested framework, one can handle network training while incorporating explicit bound (or box) constraints on key network parameters such as weights. In the oral presentation, I will also report on the implementation of the algorithm on a network of workstations using Scientific Computing's Linda parallel processing software.

THE FEED FORWARD NETWORK

A typical feed forward neural network consists of s layers of neural elements (an input layer, $s - 2$ hidden layers and one output layer) as illustrated in Figure 1 with $s = 3$. In the j-th layer there are M_j processing elements which are interconnected with elements in the $(j - 1)$-th and $(j + 1)$-th layers. Associated with the interconnection between the k_{j-1}-th element of layer $(j - 1)$ and the k_j-th element of layer j is the weighting factor W_{k_{j-1}, k_j}.

A generalized logistic function, σ which maps the cumulative input, X to the output, Y of a processing element is defined as follows:

$$Y = \sigma(X) = (1 + e^{P(X)})^{-1} - C \qquad (1)$$

In this paper, $P(X)$ is restricted to the family of polynomials. Thus $P(X) = \sum_{q=0}^{m} \alpha_q X^q$. The choice of $m = 1$, $\alpha_1 = -1$ and $C = 0.5$ corresponds to the more conventional form of the logistic function. Here α_0 corresponds to the bias term. A subset of the $\alpha's$ together with the network weights, W_{ij}, may be used as training parameters (i.e. design variables).

The choice of $m = $ odd integer results in a monotonic basis function. In contrast, the choice of m, even integer, results in a non monotonic (bell shaped) basis function. The bell shaped function (from preliminary trials) seems to do better on two dimensional pattern recognition problems in which points (members) in a class span non contiguous regions (see for example Example 3). The properties of the new basis are still being investigated and will be reported fully in another paper.

Let us define σ as follows

$$Y = \sigma(X) = (1 + e^{P(X)})^{-1} - C \qquad (2)$$

where $P(X)$ is a function of X.

Network training is achieved by solving the following nonlinear program for the optimal values of Q which is a subset of network parameters, C, W (weights) and parameters associated with $P(X)$. Thus

$$\min_Q J = \sum_{n=1}^N \sum_{k_s=1}^{M_s} \left(Y_{n,k_s} - \hat{Y}_{n,k_s} \right)^2 \tag{3}$$

$$subject \quad to$$

$$Y_{n,k_1} = a_{n,k_1} \tag{4}$$

$$Y_{n,k_j} = \sigma(X_{n,k_j}) \tag{5}$$

$$X_{n,k_j} = \sum_{k_{j-1}=1}^{M_{j-1}} W_{k_{j-1},k_j} Y_{n,k_{j-1}} \tag{6}$$

$$Q_{lower} \leq Q \leq Q_{upper} \tag{7}$$

where $a_{n,k_1} = n$-th training data set (input to k_1-th element) and $[Q_{lower}, Q_{upper}]$ are bounds on Q. In addition, the performance objective, J is the sum of squares of the deviation of the network output, Y_{n,k_s} from the expected or desired output, $\hat{Y}_{n,k_s}$. At the solution of the nonlinear program, the two outputs are close to each other. There are several variations of the form of J. For example, the root mean square deviation and the weighted residual have been used in the open literature.

The inclusion of the simple bounds on the training parameters leads to better conditioning of the training algorithm since the weights, for instance, do not become excessively large.

QUASI-NEWTON BASED TRAINING

Typically a feedforward network is trained using the delta rule (or error backpropagation (Rumelhart, 1986 [5]). A different approach is taken in this paper. Here, the analytic expressions which have been derived for the gradients of the feedforward network (see Appendix) have been used directly to solve the feedforward training problem as posed in Equation 3. Gradient information for the training algorithm was obtained two ways, by adjoints and by perturbation. The adjoint method was at least an order of magnitude faster than perturbation by central differences.

The solution procedure uses a Successive Quadratic Programming algorithm (Han, 1977 [2], Biegler, 1985 [1]) that employs low rank hessian updating schemes like BFGS. For convenience, I will refer to the SQP training of the feedforward network with the new logistic function as SQPN. The training algorithm is illustrated in Figure 2.

TEST PROBLEMS

Unfortunately, due to space limitations, only a selection of example problems are presented and discussed. In the following test problems, a subset of the $\alpha's$ together with the network weights, W_{ij}, have been used as training parameters (i.e. design variables). In particular, I have consistently employed α_0 as a design variable since it plays the role of the bias. Each simulation was performed on a SUN SparcStation, an IBM RS/6000 model 320H or model 530H. Unless otherwise stated, the initial values for the design variables were randomly generated using the time of day as the seed.

Example 1: Parity Problem

In the parity problem (Makram, 1989 [3]), the output is required to respond with a positive sign for an odd number (N) of $+1's$ inputs and with a negative sign otherwise. Thus there are 2^N training sets for the N-parity problem. The problem was solved for $N = 2, 3, 4, and\ 5$ respectively. The network consisted of the input layer (N neurons), one hidden layer ($N + 1$ neurons) and an output layer (1 neuron). For comparison, m was chosen to be 1 and α_1 was set to -1. In addition, the weights and α_0 were used as training parameters.

Table 1 summarizes the results of several training runs using $N + 1$ hidden nodes, the same number used by Makram-Ebeid[1] et al. SQPN yields up to five times fewer function evaluations

---

[1]The values reported for SQPN are averaged over a few runs from random initial points. BCG is Bounded

(network sweeps) than the Bounded Conjugate Gradients approach of Makram-Ebeid et al. In addition SQPN results in up to 2300 times fewer function evaluations than their implementation of the delta rule.

Table 2 compares the use of α_0 to that of α_1 as design variables. α_0 does better than α_1 for the parity examples. This may be due to the greater sensitivity of the logistic function to α_1 (second term in polynomial tends to dominate first term) compared to α_0. Thus the latter may lead to better conditioned training than α_1.

Example 2: Nonlinear Identification

This nonlinear identification example was proposed by Narendra and Parthasarathy [4]. Here the network is trained to identify the following nonlinear model of a plant.

$$y_p(k+1) = f[y_p(k), y_p(k-1)] + u(k) \tag{8}$$

$$f[y_p(k), y_p(k-1)] = \frac{y_p(k)y_p(k-1)[y_p(k) + 2.5]}{1 + y_p^2(k) + y_p^2(k-1)} \tag{9}$$

Training sets were made up by taking one hundred samples of $u(k)$ (assuming that $u(k)$ is i.i.d random signal uniformly distributed in the interval [-2,2]) and evaluating the corresponding y_p. The network was trained to predict $[y_p(k+1)]$ given $[y_p(k-1), y_p(k)]$ using a 2-20-10-1 network (i.e. 2 inputs, 2 hidden layers with 20 and 10 elements respectively, and 1 output). Narendra et al employed the same architecture and used only weights (total of 250 variables) as the decision variables. Thus in order to do a fair comparison I used only weights as the decision variables.

I trained the network by repeatedly using data from the first 100 time steps. Thus the network saw a smaller set of training data than was used by Narendra et al. who trained the network for 100000 time steps in order to obtain good prediction. From Table 3, just over 300 function evaluations, equivalent to 31100 (311 *times* 100) time steps, were needed to make the objective (square error = 0.004) small enough for good prediction. The trained network was validated by letting it predict y_p for the next 100 time steps. From Figure 3, the prediction is very good.

Example 3: 2-D Pattern Recognition

In this two dimensional example (Shah, 1990 [6]) points are classified as belonging to class A or B as illustrated in Figure 4.

Five hundred training points were randomly generated for classes A and B respectively. This pattern recognition problem is a nonlinearly separable problem that requires two hidden layers according to Kolmogorov. The problem was solved using two hidden layers, and ten elements in each hidden layer.

Shah et al. solved this problem[2] using three training methods, namely the error backpropagation (delta rule), the global extended Kalman filter algorithm and the multiple extended Kalman filter algorithm. They used network output of 0.9 (0.1) for points belonging to class A (B).

In addition to using [0.9, 0.1] for [A, B], [0.5, -0.5] were used for another set of runs. Table 4 (also Figures 5 and 6) summarizes results from the literature (Shah et al.) and ours. Values had to be estimated from the plots given in the literature in order to make specific comparisons. The multiple extended Kalman filter algorithm performed about as well as SQPN at the 25-iteration mark. No data beyond the 25-iteration mark was provided in the literature.

The table shows that SQPN reduces the square error twice as much as either error backpropagation, the global extended Kalman filter and the multiple extended Kalman filter. The table and Figures 5 and 6 also show that a polynomial index of 2 (in the logistic function) speeds up convergence compared to an index of 1 for this particular example. Similarly, the use of [0.5, -0.5] ($C = -0.5$ in logistic function) to represent membership in region A or B is worse than the use of [0.9, 0.1] ($C = 0$ in logistic function). Since -0.5 and 0.5 are asymptotic values of the logistic function, their use to represent class membership leads to relatively large values of the weights, thus resulting in numerical problems.

Conjugate Gradients. Makram et al. attained Training Objective values close to 0.01.

[2]Account is taken of the fact that our objective function expression, J is twice that of Shah et al.

DISCUSSION AND FUTURE WORK

The quasi-Newton training strategy have been shown to yield significantly fewer function iterations in the training of the feed forward network than similar strategies described in the open literature. Since CPU times were not reported in the literature, and since invariably different computing platforms were employed by various researchers for the simulations, it is impossible to compare the performance of the algorithms in terms of CPU times. However, the number of function evaluations is an appropriate and acceptable measure of speed and for all practical purposes independent of the computing platform.

The adjoint method of evaluating the gradients lends itself to implementation on a parallel computer. The generalized logistic function introduced in this paper shows considerable promise in this research effort into neural network speed up. The properties of this novel function are still research issues that are being resolved.

Box constraints on the decision variables were included as explicit constraints for the following reasons: (i) numerical difficulties, for example floating underflows due to large network parameters and poorly scaled training sets, are minimized and (ii) since they are linear, once they are satisfied at the first iteration, they will be satisfied for subsequent iterations. The main disadvantage with using explicit constraints is the large set of constraints that may result. To get around the dimensionality problem, logarithmic barrier function and penalty function approaches lump these box constraints with the objective function. However, the log barrier approach will either avoid the bounds on the decisions or get very close to the bounds at the risk of introducing numerical difficulties. With penalty function approaches, often a trade off is made between satisfying the box constraints and minimizing the original objective. If a proper adaptation scheme is not chosen for the penalty parameter, then poor training will result.

One main disadvantage that one can anticipate in SQPN is that, since storage of Hessian information is required in the SQP approach, it is expected that for large networks (on the order of perhaps 1000 weights), the quasi-Newton based approach will not be feasible. Limited memory quasi-Newton methods, as well as conjugate gradients with thrust region approaches are being investigated for such large scale problems. I am also looking into decomposing the hessian into reasonably sized submatrices.

Although not discussed in this paper, analytic expressions have been derived for the hessian of the feedforward network. These are being used directly in SQPN to reduce the need to employ low rank hessian updating schemes like BFGS.

ACKNOWLEDGEMENT

NSF grant # CTS-9211691 and The University of Connecticut Research Foundation's support for this work is gratefully acknowledged.

APPENDIX

Proposition 1 *The gradient of performance objective , J, with respect to the decision variables is given by*

$$\frac{\partial J}{\partial W_{k_{j-1},k_j}} = \sum_{n=1}^{N} \lambda_{n,k_j} \left(\frac{\partial \sigma}{\partial X_{n,k_j}} \right) Y_{n,k_{j-1}} \tag{10}$$

$$\frac{\partial J}{\partial \alpha_{k_j}^q} = \sum_{n=1}^{N} \lambda_{n,k_j} \left(\frac{\partial \sigma}{\partial \alpha^q} \right) \tag{11}$$

$$\frac{\partial J}{\partial C_{k_j}} = -\sum_{n=1}^{N} \lambda_{n,k_j} \tag{12}$$

$$q = 0 \ldots m$$
$$j = 2 \ldots s$$
$$k_p = 1 \ldots M_p$$

with

$$\lambda_{n,k_j} = \sum_{k_{j+1}=1}^{M_{j+1}} \lambda_{n,k_{j+1}} \left(\frac{\partial \sigma}{\partial X_{n,k_{j+1}}} \right) W_{k_j,k_{j+1}} \tag{13}$$

$$\lambda_{n,k_s} = \frac{\partial J}{\partial Y_{n,k_s}} \tag{14}$$

where

$$n = 1 \ldots N : k_s = 1 \ldots M_s,$$
$$j = 1 \ldots (s-1) : k_j = 1 \ldots M_j$$

In the interest of space the proof will appear in another paper, and can be obtained from the author. The gradients obtained above have been compared with calculations via perturbation (finite differences) and the accuracy of the results agree.

References

[1] Biegler, L. T. and Cuthrell, J. E. Improved Infeasible Path Optimization for Sequential Modular Simulators - II: The Optimization Algorithm. *Comp. & ChE.*, 9(3), 1985.

[2] Han, S. P. A Globally Convergent Method for Nonlinear Programming. *J. Opt. Theory Appl.*, 22(3):297–309, 1977.

[3] Makram-Ebeid, S., Sirat, J. A. and Viala, J. R. A Rationalized Error Back-Propagation Learning Algorithm. *International Joint Conference on Neural Networks*, II:373–380, 1989.

[4] Narendra, K. S. and Parthasarathy, K. Identification and Control of Dynamical Systems Using Neural Networks. *IEEE Trans. on Neural Networks*, 1:4–27, 1990.

[5] Rumelhart, D. E., Hinton, G. E. and Williams, R. J. Learning Representations by Back-Propagating Errors. *Nature*, 323:533–536, 1986.

[6] Shah, S. and Palmieri F. MEKA - A Fast, Local Algorithm for Training Feedforward Neural Networks. *International Joint Conference on Neural Networks*, 1990.

Table 1: Example 1: Comparison with Makram-Ebeid et al

N-Parity	Delta Rule Fxn Eval	BCG Fxn Eval	SQPN Fxn Eval	SQPN Objective
2	> 2000	≈ 50	26	0.002
3	> 20000	≈ 60	74	0.0002
4	> 80000	≈ 500	82	0.0010
5	> 1000000	≈ 750	108	0.0030

Table 2: Example 1: # of Iterations: Comparison of α_0 and α_1

N-Parity	α_0 (best) Iterations	α_0 (Average) Iterations	α_1 (best) Iterations	α_1 (Average) Iterations
2	26	26	16	34
3	31	31	21	38
4	31	41	36	50
5	36	43	36	86

Table 3: Example 2: Summary

Objective	Function Evals	Gradient Evals	Iterations
21.6742	1	1	1
12.0330	66	10	12
1.2211	146	40	42
0.9034	221	70	72
0.0040	311	100	102

Table 4: Example 3: Square Error (J) in 25 Iterations

	J (initial)	J (final)	% reduction
Error Backpropagation	≈ 400	≈ 300	25
Global Extended Kalman Filter	≈ 250	≈ 140	56
Multiple Extended Kalman Filter	≈ 216	≈ 48	78
SQPN ([A, B] = [0.5, -0.5])	475	153	68
SQPN ([A, B] = [0.9, 0.1])	410	89	78
SQPN ([A, B] = [0.9, 0.1], m = 2)	410	83	80
SQPN ([A, B] = [0.9, 0.1], 1st param)	345	82	76

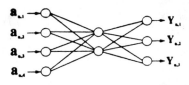

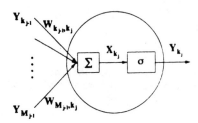

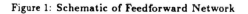

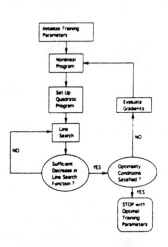

Figure 1: Schematic of Feedforward Network

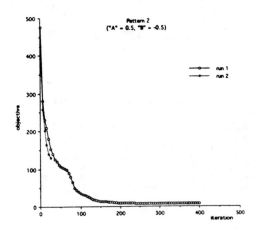

Figure 2: Schematic of Training Algorithm

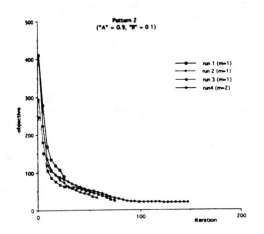

Figure 3: Example 2: Prediction of Data not in Training Set

Figure 4: Example 3

Pattern 2
("A" - 0.5, "B" - -0.5)

run 1
run 2

Figure 6: Example 3: Training - [A, B] = [-0.5, 0.5]

Pattern 2
("A" - 0.9, "B" - 0.1)

run 1 (m=1)
run 2 (m=1)
run 3 (m=1)
run4 (m=2)

Figure 5: Example 3: Training - [A, B] = [0.9, 0.1]

NEURAL NETWORKS SHARING KNOWLEDGE AND EXPERIENCE

S. Zein-Sabatto, W. R. Hwang, and D. R. Marpaka
College of Engineering and Technology
Department of Electrical and Computer Engineering
Tennessee State University, Nashville, TN 37209

Abstract

In this paper a new neural network architecture suitable for building robust neurocontrollers is proposed and tested. The concept of the new architecture is developed around the idea of sharing intelligence of a neural network between knowledge and experience. The architecture consists of two specialized sub-networks; one provides the knowledge and the other provides experience. The two sub-networks are connected in a feedforward configuration to form an intelligent neural network. The advantage of such a neural network architecture is that the experience sub-network constantly updates the knowledge sub-network with experience information creating dynamic intelligence. This makes the overall neural network adaptively changing its knowledge to accommodate changes in the environment.

I. Introduction

Noise and disturbance are the sources of problems in any control system. In the control theory the problem of noise and disturbance have been studied and solution are considered. A way to suppress noise in a control loop is to insert a filter in the path of such noise [1]. Adaptive controllers have been successfully designed and used to compensate for disturbance or minor changes in system dynamics [2,3]. One of the shortcoming of filtering the noise and adapting controller parameters is the limited range of operation over which the scheme is valid. Other shortcoming is the robustness of such a controller. When the level of noise or disturbance becomes high, the performance of an adaptive controller or filter is expected to degrade [4].

In the past decade, use of neural networks has gained interest in the field of control systems [5,6]. Several neurocontrollers have been designed and implemented [7,8]. The pronounce features of a traditional neurocontroller are robustness and computation speed. Neurocontrollers provide fast computation due to the fact that they are parallel processing devices when implemented in hardware. Neurocontrollers are robust in the sense that partial failure in their structure (processing element or connection's weight) does not necessary lead to significant degradation in their performance. However, current neural networks implemented as neurocontroller are sensitive to noise and disturbance. When the level of noise or disturbance increases a neural network is expected to predict the target with some uncertainty. Therefore building an adaptive neurocontroller capable of on-line filtering of high level of noise and disturbance is of interest to control engineers. A purpose for designing adaptive neurocontrollers is to implement an on-line learning procedure. In such a training procedure a neural network learns as it predicts. Reinforcement learning is one way for implementing on-line training of a neural network [9]. In the reinforcement learning a neural network learns from previous experience. However, several training cycles may be needed before the network learns new changes in the environment. This make it difficult to implement for complex control problems in real-time.

Our concept of building an adaptive neurocontroller is based on sharing information between knowledge (constant intelligence) and experience (adaptive intelligence) neural networks. In this architecture, first the knowledge is acquired by training a neural network on the nominal behavior of the system. Then the experience is developed by training anther neural network to learn the amount of adjustment of the knowledge needed when the system is subjected to noise or disturbance. Finally, the experience network is used to supplement the knowledge neural network. Hence, the overall neural network intelligence is always up-to-date and will not render absolute as changes (noise or disturbance) take place in the system.

II. Biological Learning

Intelligent biological systems, e.g., human beings and monkeys, accumulate their intelligence over periods of time. Some times, it is difficult to precisely identify the level of intelligence of a person at a given instance of time. However, the performance of a person can be observed over a range of actions. The measure of intelligence of a person becomes more decisive when the complexity of the task assigned to the person increases. Teaching a person to perform certain task is known as gaining knowledge. If the knowledge of a person is enhanced with time, the person is said to be gaining experience. These biological facts lead to the following conclusions: First, intelligence consists of two components; knowledge and experience. A natural progression of the two components is that knowledge comes first then experience is gained at later stage of time. Second, experience should always supplement and not replace knowledge to maintain intelligence. Certain amount of knowledge should always be kept constant without alteration. Finally, knowledge is normally acquired during learning stage (off-line) and experience is gained through out experimentation (on-line). Figure 1 illustrates our understanding of such biological learning.

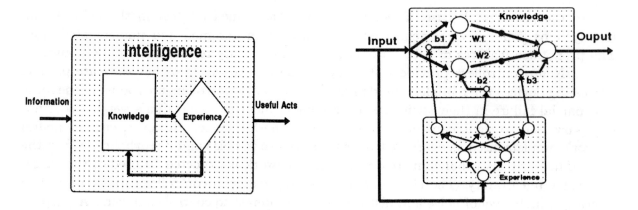

Figure 1. (a) Biological Intelligence, (b) Computational Intelligence

III. Neural Network Architecture

The concept of biological learning is translated into a neural network architecture using reverse engineering techniques. The proposed neural network architecture is developed keeping in mind the basic principles of biological learning. It is known in the sensory motor control system, for example, a motor signal generated by a motor neuron and transmitted through the neuron postsynaptic is influenced by another motor signal derived from the same stimuli of the original neuron and transmitted though out an inhibitory interneuron. The interneuron is connected in a loop with respect to the original neuron. This neuron exhibits time delay, frequency modulation, and/or combination of both. It can influence the original motor neuron in excitatory or inhibitory mode [10]. The loop interaction between the two motor neurons is a form of implementation of knowledge and experience in biological systems. The motor neuron represents knowledge and the interneuron is a representation of experience. Figure 2 shows biological interaction between two motor neuron. This biological interaction between neurons is translated into a computational neuron with constant trained weights and variable biases. The actual value of the biases for a computational neuron is determined by another feedforward neuron similar to that of biological system. The feedforward neuron acts on the same input data of the computational neuron and predicts proper biases in accordance with the current input data.

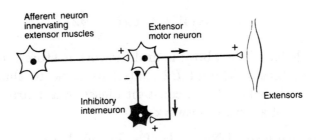

(Courtesy of Kandel, "Principles of Neural Science")
Figure 2. Interaction Between Biological Neuron

IV. Adaptive Neural Network

Generalization of the knowledge-experience computational neuron can be extended to a complete neural network architecture. An intelligent neural network with knowledge and experience components is constructed from two sub-neural networks. A knowledge neural network surrounded by an experience neural network. First the experience neural network reads input data then it predicts the proper biases for the knowledge neural network. The knowledge neural network in turn reads input data and the set of biases form the experience network then it predicts the expected output of the intelligent neural network. The following is a mathematical analysis of the proposed neural network to demonstrate the interaction between knowledge and experience in a sharing intelligence neural network.

Traditional Neural Network: The performance of a multilayers neural network can be described in the testing (non-training) mode by the function

$$Y(t) = \aleph(W \times X(t) + B) \tag{1}$$

where $\aleph$ define a neural network with weight matrices W and bias vectors B. The input and output of the network are $X(t)$ and $Y(t)$ respectively. For a two layer neural network with unipolar sigmoid function in the 1st layer and linear function in the output layer equation 1 can be expressed as a Matlab function

$$Y(t) = pureline(W2, (tansign(W1, X(t), B1), B2) \tag{2}$$

where $B1$ and $B2$ are constant biases found during the training of the neural network. Equation 2 can be simplified as

$$Y(t) = pureline(W2, A1(t), B2) \tag{3}$$

where $A1(t) = 1/(1 + e^{-\alpha(t)})$ with

$$\alpha(t) = W1 \times X(t) + B1 \tag{4}$$

the final output of the neural network is therefore expressed by

$$Y(t) = K(W2 \times A1(t) + B2) \tag{5}$$

It is clear that the knowledge of the above neural network is stored in the weight matrices $W1$ and $W2$. While the biases $B1$ and $B2$ contribute little to that knowledge. In the following section, we will show how these constant biases of a neural network can be used to enhance the knowledge of a neural network.

Knowledge and Experience Neural Network: The knowledge of a neural network can be enhanced by making the biases of the network dependent on the input data. In this case equation 4 can be written in the following form

$$\alpha(t) = W1 \times X(t) + \widetilde{B}1 \tag{6}$$

where the bias vector $\widetilde{B}1$ is a variable vector and can be predicted by the experience neural network as follows

$$\widetilde{B}1 = WE1 \times X(t) + BE1 \tag{7}$$

where $WE1$ and $BE1$ represent the weights and biases of the experience neural network. Substituting equation 7 into equation 6 results

$$\alpha(t) = (W1 + WE1)X(t) + BE1 \tag{8}$$

similar equation can be derived for the final output of the neural network

$$Y(t) = K(W2 \times A1(t) + WE2 \times X(t) + BE2) \tag{9}$$

Equations 8 and 9 reveal the fact that intelligence of the neural network has been distributed between the knowledge of the network ($W1, W2$) and the experience of the network ($WE1, WE2$). Furthermore, equation 9 shows that the experience of the network is made sensitive to the input data ($WE2 \times X(t)$) so that it can accommodate any change such as noise and disturbance in the outside environment of the network. A disadvantage of such neural network is that complete parallelism has been lost by the amount of delay-time required by the experience neural network to reach steady state values of the biases.

VI. Results Presentation

An intelligent neural network with shared knowledge and experience architecture has been designed and trained. The knowledge network consists of one hidden layer with five neurons, two input nodes and 41 output nodes. The experience neural network consists of one hidden layer with 10 neurons, two input nodes and 46 output nodes. The knowledge neural network was trained to predict a two-dimension function of the form $F(x_1, x_2) = e^{-2(x_1^2 + x_2^2)}$. This function represents a hat shape function. The knowledge network was trained on clean set of input data and tested on input data corrupted with up to 15% noise. The first test was done without adding the experience network, keeping the original biases learned by the knowledge neural net constant. The second test was done by supplying different set of biases to the knowledge network at different level of noise. Those biases were predicted by the experience neural network. Results show no significant deference between the two tests for low level of noise. However, the deference is the network performance becomes more significant as the level of noise increases. Figure 3 (a,b, and c) shows the prediction error of the intelligent neural network for the three cases with only 15% noise. Figure 3-d shows the sum of squared errors for all levels of noise. An improvement of 100% is noticed at 15% level of noise.

VII. Conclusion

This study indicates that intelligence of a neural network can be improved by training two specialized sub-neural networks and connecting them in a feedforward form. The proposed neural network architecture is proven to be more robust as the level of noise or disturbance increases. This could be very useful in control applications such as designing of neurocontrollers for systems that exhibit high level of noise or disturbance.

Acknowledgement

This work is supported by NASA Lewis Research Center under NASA grant No. NAG3-1471. This effort is also a part of the research activities conducted in the Center for Neural Engineering (CNE) at Tennessee State University. CNE is supported by the U.S. Navy Grant No. N00014-92-J-1372. The authors wish to thank both NASA and ONR for their support for pursuing this research.

References

[1] Sorenson, H. W., "Kalman Filering: Theory and Application," IEEE Control Systems Society Press, 1985.

[2] Iserman, R., "Parameter Adaptive Control Algorithms-A Tutorial," IEEE Systems, Man, and Cybernetics Society Press, 1986.

[3] Amerongen, J.V., "Adaptive Steering for Ships-A Model Reference Approach," IEEE Systems, Man, and Cybernetics Society Press, 1986.

[4] Kallstrom, C.G., "Adaptive Autopilot for Tankers," IEEE Systems, Man, and Cybernetics Society Press, 1986.

[5] Narendra, K.S., "Intelligent Control," IEEE Computer Society Press, pp. 440-441, 1992.

[6] Werbos, P.J., "An Overview of Neural Networks for Control," IEEE Computer Society Press, pp. 442-443, 1992.

[7] Psaltis, D., Sideris, A., and Yamamura, A. " A Multilayered Neural Network Controller," IEEE Computer Society Press, pp.479-483, 1992.

[8] Saeren, M., and Soquet, A., "Neural Controller Based on Back-Propagation Algorithm," IEEE Computer Society Press, pp.484-496 1992.

[9] Barto, A.G.. "Reinforcement Learing and Adaptive Critic Methods," Handbook of INtelligent Control, Van Norstrand Reinhold, NY. 1992.

[10] Kandel, E.R., Schwarts, J.H., and Jessell, T.M., "Priciples of Neural Science," Elsevier Science Publishing Co., NY., 3rd edition, 1991.

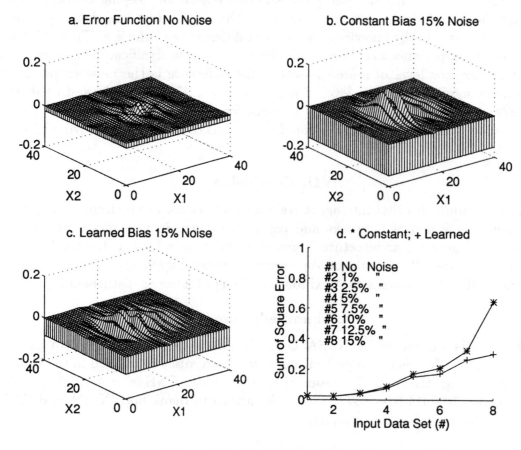

Figure 3. Simulation Results

An ART2-BP Supervised Neural Net

Wu-Yuan Tsai*, Heng-Ming Tai** and Albert C. Reynolds***

*Computer Science Department (tsai@euler.mcs.utulsa.edu)
**Electrical Engineering Department
***Petroleum Engineering Department

The University of Tulsa
600 S. College Ave.
Tulsa, OK 74104-3189

ABSTRACT

Backpropagation feedforward neural networks have been applied to pattern recognition and classification problems. However, under certain conditions the backpropagation net classifier can produce non-intuitive, non-robust and unreliable classification results. The backpropagation net is slower to train and is not easy to accommodate new data.

To solve the difficulties mentioned above, an unsupervised/supervised type neural net, namely, ART2-BP net, is proposed. The idea is to use a low vigilance parameter in ART2 net to categorize input patterns into some classes and then utilize a backpropagation net to recognize patterns in each class. Advantages of the ART2-BP neural net include (1) improvement of recognition capability, (2) training convergence enhancement, and (3) easy to add new data. Theoretical analysis and example are given to illustrate these advantages.

INTRODUCTION

Pattern recognition and classification are potentially useful approaches for interpreting data generated by industrial systems such as chemical, manufacturing, and well testing processes. Possible applications include sensor data interpretation, model identification and validation. Neural networks, especially backpropagation networks[1], have been applied to many pattern recognition problems including the classification of sonar targets[2] and sensor interpretation[3].

Application of back-propagation networks to well test model identification in reservoir engineering has been studied by several researchers[4,5]. These results have shown that the feedforward backpropagation network classifier has the ability to learn a set of pressure derivative curves and can often generalize to new cases of known models. Nevertheless, several difficulties were uncovered when more models are included in the net decision space and when more training curves are added to the training set[4]. For example, in our simulation, 16 models and 30 pressure derivative data curves per model were used for training. It took more than 12 hours on a 486-PC for the backpropagation net to learn[6]. Moreover, it can not correctly recognize models with similar features. Furthermore, the backpropagation net is not robust since it is not easy to add new models.

*This work is partially supported by **TUPREP** at University of Tulsa funded by 12 major oil companies in the world.*

In this paper, we propose a novel neural net to remedy the aforementioned difficulties. This network, called the *ART2-BP net*, uses an ART2 net[7] to sort a large number of input patterns into several classes. Then the three-layer BP net associated with each class node in the output layer of the ART2 net is trained using a 2nd-order backpropagation algorithm[8] for further classification. Advantages of the ART2-BP net include shorter training time, improved training and classification abilities, and capability of easily accommodating new models.

Analysis on the advantages the ART2-BP neural net provide is given in Section II. The learning algorithm using a conjugate gradient method is derived. A nonlinear mapping technique[11] employed for better classification will also be shown. A well testing model recognition problem is used for the performance comparison.

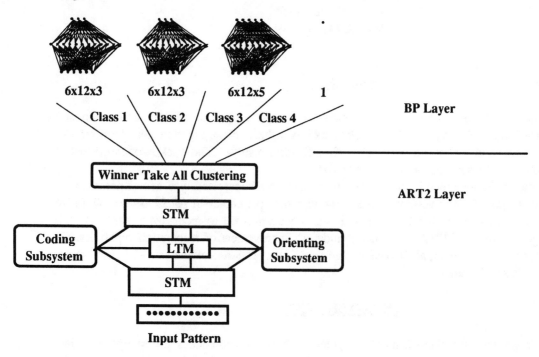

Figure 1. The ART2-BP neural net.

The ART2-BP NEURAL NET

The ART2-BP neural network is shown in Figure 1. In this architecture, backpropagation nets are placed directly on the output layer of an ART2 net. First, top-down weights and bottom-up weights of ART2 are modified by the training examples. Then the three-layer BP net associated with each class node is trained using a 2nd-order backpropagation algorithm[8] for further classification. It offers several advantages over the ART2 net as well as the backpropagation net. Advantages include (1) improvement of recognition capability, (2) training convergence enhancement, and (3) easy to add new data. These will be elucidated later on.

The training-recognition procedure of the ART2-BP net can be described as follows. Input patterns are clustered into classes through the unsupervised learning process provided by ART2 layer. At this stage coarse classification was carried out such that patterns with similar features were clustered together. Patterns in each class are then forwarded to the BP layer for fine classification. In this phase, training is efficient because faster learning algorithm is employed. Furthermore, classification is effective since fewer patterns are used.

ART2 is a category learning system that self-organizes a sequence of input patterns into various recognition categories or classes. For detailed mechanism of ART2, please refer to reference 7. Vigilance parameter used in ART2 plays a pivotal role. High vigilance parameter will enable ART2 to explicitly distinguish patterns with similar features, but the net will not be able to recognize or classify patterns corrupted with noise or distorted features. On the other hand, if the vigilance parameter value is too small, almost all patterns will be categorized as a single class.

The backpropagation algorithm[1], on the other hand, is a supervised learning. Though a great deal of applications using feedforward neural networks with the backpropagation algorithm have been reported, several disadvantages were also mentioned. These include slow training, convergence failure during training, and inability for the trained neural net to accurately distinguish patterns with similar features.

To lesson some of the drawback of using the delta learning rule or even with the momentum term[9], a three-layer feedforward neural network with conjugate gradient learning algorithm is employed. Using this method, efficient learning rate can be selected and global minimum of the error surface can be found. Further, the least squared error can be reduced to less than 10^{-6} in a few iterations. All these will improve the training convergence quality and reduce the training time dramatically. The updated weights under the conjugate gradient method can be expressed as follows.

$$w_{k+1} = w_k + \alpha_k R_k, \qquad R_k = -E'(w_k)$$

$$\alpha_k = \frac{P_k^T R_k}{P_k^T E''(w_k) P_k}, \qquad P_{k+1} = R_{k+1} + \frac{\|R_{k+1}\|^2 - R_{k+1}^T R_k}{P_k^T R_k} P_k$$

where $P_k = [p_{1k}, p_{2k}, ..., p_{nk}]$ is a conjugate basis with respect to the Hessian matrix $E''(w_k)$.

Advantages of this ART2-BP neural net[6] are analyzed in the following.

1. Recognition capability improvement.

It is known[10] that all the input patterns, exemplar patterns and synaptic vectors can be normalized and mapped into a unit R^n sphere. After applying a nonlinear mapping scheme developed by Sammon[11], those normalized vectors are mapped from an R^n space to an R^2 space as shown in Figure 2. This nonlinear mapping the characteristics of preserving the inherent structure of the data. In this figure, D_1, D_2, ..., and D_5 denote classes categorized by ART2 and m_1, m_2, ..., and m_5 are centroids of D_1, D_2, ..., and D_5, respectively. x denotes the test pattern and θ is the angle between the test pattern and the centroid of Class D_3. Note that $D_j \in R^n$ and $R^n = \bigcup_{j=1}^{5} D_j$, $D_i \cap D_j = \emptyset$ if $i \neq j$. By analyzing the competitive learning mechanism in ART2, we find that the winning synaptic vector m_j of ART2 equals the centroid of the Class D_j. This means that m_j defines the deterministic center of mass of the class D_j:

$$m_j = \frac{\int_{D_j} x p(x) dx}{\int_{D_j} p(x) dx}, \qquad \text{where } P(x) \text{ represents a probability distribution of the pattern } x.$$

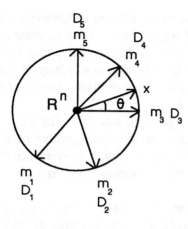

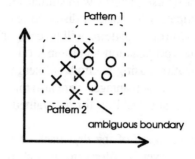

Fig. 2. Centroids of classes in ART2 net.   Fig. 4. Ambiguous windows.

Ranges of this class is bounded by $[x_{max}, x_{min}]$. These bounds depend on the vigilance parameter used in ART2. Small vigilance parameter increases the range of the class. In other words, more patterns will be clustered into the same class if a smaller vigilance parameter value is employed in ART2.

At this stage, we apply a backpropagation net to classify patterns categorized in the same class. Suppose there are six patterns $t_1, t_2, t_3, \ldots, t_6$ in Class D_1 which has centroid m_1 as shown in Fig. 3. Now we assign each pattern a specific vector in the output layer of the BP net. For example, $[0.9, 0.1, 0.1, 0.1, 0.1, 0.1]$ is used to represent t_1 and $[0.1, 0.9, 0.1, 0.1, 0.1, 0.1]$ is for t_2, etc. By using the Sammon's nonlinear mapping algorithm, $t_1, t_2, t_3, \ldots, t_6$ will be located around a circle as depicted in Fig. 3(b). This means that these six patterns can be easily classified by the BP type neural net in that explicit boundary can be formed.

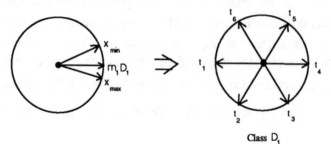

Fig. 3. Six patterns in Class D_1 are mapped into explicitly classified pattern by Sammon's technique.

As elucidated in the above from a theoretic viewpoint, the ART2-BP net would significantly improve the recognition performance. Figure 4 shows the case when two patterns are intertwined. The proposed ART2-BP neural net can be trained to classified these two patterns, but not the ART2 net or the backpropagation net.

2. Training convergence enhancement.

After clustering by ART2, fewer patterns will be located in the same class. Thus, when applying the BP net to each class, training time is dramatically reduced. Since explicit decision surfaces can be found, problems caused by premature convergence and convergence to local minima are diminished. Therefore, in the recalling phase, the BP net being trained can produce satisfactory results.

3. Easy to add new data.

When a new exemplar pattern is added, it will be either categorized into one of the existing classes or a new class by ART2. Then only the class having this new pattern need to be retained. This feature is very important from the extendibility viewpoint. On the contrary, if only the BP net is applied, it has to be retrained using the whole (old and new) patterns. This is very time consuming and may cause some convergence problems. Furthermore, the larger the number of patterns, the worse the performance of the ART2 or the BP net. From this point, we may claim that the ART2-BP net can handle much more data than the ART2 net or the BP net does.

A Well Testing Model Recognition Problem

In a pressure transient test a signal of pressure vs. time is recorded. This signal is plotted as derivative curves which are used in the interpretation process. The signal on these curves is usually deformed and shaped by some underlying mechanisms in the formation and the wellbore. Since more than one interpretation model can produce the same signal, this approach can lead to misleading results. Thus to correctly identify these models from the signatures present on the derivative plot is of great importance.

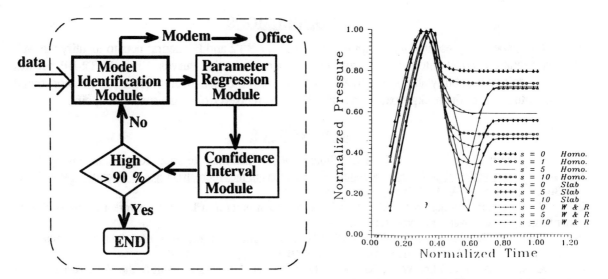

Fig. 5. Software implementation.   Fig. 6. Pressure curves for training.

A software package in C++ has been developed in a PC-486 environment. This program is interactive and user-friendly. Not only can it identify the model reflected by given data, it also provides an initial guess of reservoir properties as the input to an analysis program. A schematic diagram for a complete recognition process is shown in Figure 5. Time-dependent pressure data collected from hardware module are fed into the computer for recognition. The ART2-BP neural net is implemented in the Model Identification Module. After the model is identified, regression techniques are utilized for parameter estimation. In the Confidence Interval Module, statistical characteristics of the identified model are calculated to verify the results.

For the well testing model recognition problem considered here, ten pressure curves shown in Fig. 6 were used. They belong to three different models with various skin factors. The three models are homogeneous reservoir and dual porosity reservoir (slab model and Warren & Root model). Each pressure derivative curve in the training set was normalized and then sampled at 12 points as the input pattern. Note that the same normalization method must be used for all curves including the training curves and the test unknown curves to avoid curves being shifted, enlarged or reduced. A vigilance parameter of value 0.9 was used in ART2.

This ten-pattern data set was used to train the BP net and the ART2-BP net. The $12 \times 24 \times 10$ backpropagation net did not converge after more than ten thousand iterations. This problem is also encountered in the work of Al-Kaabi and Lee[4]. Nevertheless, the ART2-BP net did learn and successfully identify those curves. ART2 categorized the first five curves in Fig. 6 into Class 1 and the other five into Class 2. Then a smaller $12 \times 24 \times 5$ BP net was utilized in each class. Three curves were used for recognition. The test results are shown in Table I. The first row shows that the test curve was recognized as a homogeneous reservoir with skin factor s equal to either 0 or 5.

TABLE I Test Results

Test curve	Output of ART2 (Class)	Output of BP (Activation)
Homogeneous, s=3	1	0.010 0.822 0.944 0.002 0.003
Slab, s=3	1	0.002 0.002 0.317 0.322 0.705
Warren & Root, s=3	2	0.023 0.035 0.345 0.654 0.002

CONCLUSIONS

This paper has presented a new approach based on ART2 and BP neural nets to identify the well test interpretation model automatically from the pressure derivative curves. The ART2-BP net has better recognition capability and is easy to accommodate new models. Moreover we have demonstrated that the limitations of the backpropagation network can be relaxed from a theoretic viewpoint.

REFERENCES

1.   Rumelhart, D.E., Hinton, G.E. and Williams, R.J., "Learning Internal Representations by Error Propagation," In Parallel Distributed Processing : Explorations in the Microstructures of Cognition, Vol. 1, pp. 318-362. Cambridge, MA : MIT Press, 1986.
2.   Gorman, R.P. and Sejnowski, T.J., "Analysis of hidden units in a layered network trained to classify sonar targets," *Neural Networks*, vol. 1, pp. 75-89, 1988.
3.   Naidu, S., Zafiriou, E. and McAvoy, T.J., "Use of neural networks for sensor failure detection in a control system," *IEEE Control Systems Magazine*, vol. 10, No. 3, pp. 49-55, 1990.
4.   Al-Kaabi ,A. U. and Lee W. J., "Using Artificial Neural Networks to Identify the Well Test Interpretation Model," paper SPE 20332, the *5th SPE Petroleum Computer Conference*, Denver, June 25-28, 1990.
5.   Houze, O.P. and Allain, O.F., "A hybrid artificial intelligence approach in well test interpretation," paper SPE 24733, the *67th SPE Annual Technical Conf. and Exhi.*, Washington, D.C., Oct. 4-7, 1992.
6.   Tsai, W.Y., "An Intelligent Well Testing Machine to Automate Pressure Transient Analysis," M.E. Report, Department of Petroleum Engineering, University of Tulsa, 1993.
7.   Carpenter, G.A. and Grossberg, S., "ART2 : Self-organization of Stable Category Recognition Codes for Analog Input Patterns," *Applied Optics*, Vol. 26, pp. 4919-4930, Dec. 1987.
8.   Moller, M.F., "A scaled conjugate gradient algorithm for fast supervised learning," Preprint, Computer Science Department, University of Aarhus, Denmark, 1990.
9.   Pao, Y.H., Adaptive Pattern Recognition and Neural Networks, Addison-Wesley, Reading, MA, 1989.
10.   Hecht-Nielsen, R., "Counterpropagation Networks," *Applied Optics*, vol. 26, pp. 4979-4985, 1987.
11.   Sammon, Jr. J., "A Nonlinear Mapping for Data Structure Analysis," *IEEE Transactions on Computers*, vol. C-18, pp. 401-409, May 1969.

On A Unified Geometrical Interpretation of Multilayer Feedforward Networks
Part I : The Interpretation

Hauhua Lee

GE Corporate Research and Development Center, Schenectady, N.Y. 12301

Prabhat Hajela

Rensselaer Polytechnic Institute, Troy, N.Y. 12180

Abstract:

The present paper consists of two parts. In the first part, a unified geometrical interpretation of the behavior of multilayer feedforward networks (MFN) is presented. The inputs and outputs of training samples can be represented as two separated matrices and an MFN is a mechanism that successively transforms the input matrix into the desired output matrix, via the intermediate matrix (or matrices) associated with hidden layer(s). By thinking of the matrix as a multidimensional pliable object, the successive matrix transformation can then be compared to a sequence of *stretchings* and *squeezings* of the imaginary object. This interpretation holds for both binary and continuous function mappings, as well as for mappings where both input and output space are multidimensional, i.e., not being limited to n–to–1 mappings. More importantly, this interpretation provides a whole new perspective to several important yet still unanswered questions about MFN. In particular, the generalization capability of MFN seems to be the result of certain symmetry within the underlying mapping function. In the second part, implications of the interpretation will be elaborated specifically in regards to quantifying mapping nonlinearity. Novel schemes will be suggested to quantify the mapping nonlinearity based upon the spatial characteristics of training samples, and provide guidelines to avoid hard–learning situations by reducing the mapping nonlinearity of training samples. Illustrative examples and results of numerical experiment are presented in support of the interpretation concepts.

1. Introduction

Multilayer feedforward networks (MFN) have been the most widely explored of all neural network paradigms. In regards to explaining the behavior of MFN, previous publications such as [Nilsson], [Lippmann] and [Pao] have provided primitive interpretations in terms of decision boundaries and decision regions from a mapping perspective. However, these interpretations are only good for classification problems, where the mappings are n–to–1 and with binary or discrete outputs. In this paper, a novel and unified interpretation of MFN is presented to assign a more physical sense to the MFN. This interpretation is valid not only for both binary and continuous function mappings, but also for the mappings where both input and output space are multidimensional (not being limited to n–to–1 mappings).

The inputs and outputs of training samples can be represented as two separated matrices, corresponding to the input and output states of an imaginary multidimensional pliable object. Geometrically, MFN can be thought of as a mechanism that successively *reshapes* such an imaginary *training object* from its input state to its output state, via the intermediate state(s) associated with the hidden layer(s). The weight matrix (including the activation function) between two adjacent layers corresponds to a *reshape* operation, which consists of two basic actions, *stretching* and *squeezing*. Mathematically, *stretching* corresponds to the dot product, and *squeezing* corresponds to the processing through an activation function. Each of the hidden and output node is associated with a weight vector that corresponds to a column vector in the associated weight matrix. The weight vector indicates the direction of *stretching* and *squeezing*, as well as the strength of *stretching*. Subsequently, the training of an MFN can be thought of as the process to find an appropriate way that can successively reshape the training object from its input state to its desired output state. On the other hand, the prediction behavior of MFN can be thought of as the result of a successive reshaping of the continuum training object.

This interpretation may shed light on several important yet unanswered questions in MFN, such as what constitutes a hard learning case, why MFN can generalize, and what is hidden in the hidden layers. This paper does not intend to tackle the problem of deciding the number of hidden nodes/layers; instead, it suggests certain guidelines for the preprocessing of raw training samples. The *distribution angle* and *maximum distribution gradient* are introduced to gauge the mapping nonlinearity. Prior to the training, one may preprocess the raw samples so that the mapping nonlinearity is reduced in order to facilitate the training.

The paper is organized into two parts. Part I focuses on the unified interpretation of MFN, with an illustrative example and discussions about the implications of the interpretation. Novel schemes for quantifying mapping nonlinearity will be presented separately in Part II.

2. MFN : Successive Matrix Transformation

MFN is often explained in biological terms such as neurons, axons, synapse, etc., for its analogy to the neural system of living beings. Mathematical descriptions can be found in standard texts on the subject. [Lippmann, Kosko, Pao]. Here, MFN is first described from the perspective of matrix transformations and then associated with specific interpretations.

MFN is known to be able to approximate any mapping function, represented by a set of mapping samples (also called training patterns), to any degree of accuracy[Honic]. Let the mapping function be denoted as $f : R^m \rightarrow R^n$, and the samples given as $(\mathbf{I}_i, \mathbf{O}_i)$, where $\mathbf{O}_i = f(\mathbf{I}_i)$, $i=1,..,p$, $\mathbf{I}_i \in R^m$, and $\mathbf{O}_i \in R^n$. (In practice, the input and output of samples are usually scaled to either binary hypercubics $[0,1]^m/[0,1]^n$, or bipolar hypercubics $[-1,1]^m/[-1,1]^n$, rather than being used with infinite spaces.) The input and output parts of samples can be represented as two separate matrices, denoted as $[I]_{p \times m}$ and $[O]_{p \times n}$ respectively, where p is the number of samples, m and n are the dimensions of input and output spaces. Suppose a single hidden layer MFN is trained with samples $(\mathbf{I}_i, \mathbf{O}_i)$, $i=1,..,p$. It is clear that when an input vector $\mathbf{I}_i$ is presented to this MFN, $\mathbf{I}_i$ is first transformed into an intermediate vector $\mathbf{H}_i$ at the hidden layer, and then into the output vector $\mathbf{O}_i$. Similarly, when the entire input matrix $[I]_{p \times m}$ is presented to the MFN, $[I]_{p \times m}$ is first transformed into the intermediate matrix, $[H]_{p \times q}$ (where q is the number of hidden nodes), and then into the output matrix $[O]_{p \times n}$. Hence, an MFN is, in fact, a successive matrix transformation mechanism.

The successive matrix transformation in an MFN can be compared to *"playing dough"* in hyperspace. Each layer in an MFN can be associated with a multidimensional space of which the dimension equals the number of nodes in the layer. For a specific layer, a group of vectors (i.e., a matrix) can be thought of as a group of points in the associated multidimensional space. One can imagine the whole group of points as a multidimensional object which is constructed by connecting every point with each other using a rubber stick. The rubber sticks allow the imaginary object to be arbitrarily pliable. In this manner, the successive matrix transformation can be thought of as a successive reshaping process of the imaginary pliable object. Mathematically, a matrix with dimension $p \times q$ represents a specific state of the imaginary pliable object, where p is the total number of vectors and q is the space dimension (i.e., the number of nodes in the layer). In this research, such object is referred to as *training object*, and the matrix is referred to as the *state matrix* of the training object. Hence, in the MFN example above, the three matrices [I], [H] and [O], represent the three states, input, intermediate and output, of the training object. The reshaping operation can be decomposed into two basic actions, *stretching* and *squeezing*, which can be mathematically associated with the dot product and the processing through an activation function, as elaborated next.

3. Stretching and Squeezing

The principle of the matrix transformation (or reshaping) between any two adjacent layers is identical, regardless of any layer being an input, output or hidden one. Therefore, in Figure 1, two adjacent layers are used to explain *stretching* and *squeezing*. The two layers are referred to as the source layer, SL, and the target layer, TL, instead of input/output layer. Suppose there are p samples, and the numbers of nodes in SL and TL are s and t respectively. The matrices $[S]_{p \times s}$ and $[T]_{p \times t}$ then denote the source and target states of the training object. Note that in practice, it is preferable to add a bias node in SL to help the training, as explained later. Hence, $[S]_{p \times s}$ is augmented as $[S]_{p \times (s+1)}$, in which the last column is a unity vector. Accordingly, the weight matrix between SL and TL is denoted as $[W]_{(s+1) \times t}$.

Now one may look into the function of a target node. In Figure 1, the target node N_t is associated with a weight vector $\mathbf{W}_t$, i.e., a column vector of the weight matrix. Two mathematical operations performed inside a target node. First, the dot product between the associated weight vector and an input source vector, $\mathbf{W}_t \bullet \mathbf{S}_p$, and second, the processing through an activation function of $\mathbf{W}_t \bullet \mathbf{S}_p$. When a state matrix of a training object is presented to a target node, the effect

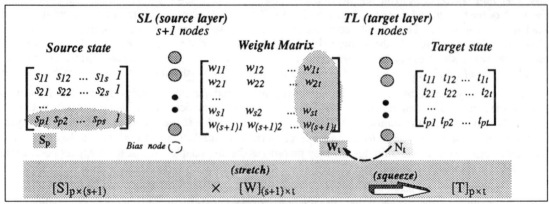

Figure 1. Operations between two adjacent layers.

is equivalent to stretching and then squeezing the object along the direction of the weight vector associated with the target node. The length of weight vector is equivalent to the magnitude of stretching.

Dot Product as Stretching

Conceptually, applying a dot product between a weight vector and each point vector on the pliable object is equivalent to *stretching* the object along the direction of the weight vector. This is explained in Figure 2, where there are a weight vector W_t, a point vector S_p, and an imaginary neutral plane that is perpendicular to W_t and passes through the origin. The dash line marks the location of the neutral plane, d is the distance from S_p to the neutral plane (i.e., the projection of S_p on W_t), and θ is the angle between S_p and W_t. Then

$$d = |S_p| \cos \theta.$$

On the other hand,

$$W_t \bullet S_p = |W_t| \, |S_p| \cos \theta$$
$$= |W_t| \, d.$$

Therefore, after applying a dot product between a weight vector W_t and every point vector on the training object, the distance from every point to the neutral plane is scaled up by $|W_t|$. In other words, all points are stretched away from the neutral plane (in both sides of the plane), except for those points on the neutral plane being unaffected. Note that $|W_t|$ is often greater than 1, thus results in the stretching effect. In case $|W_t|$ equals 1, the projected lengths do not change. If $|W_t|$ is less than 1, the projected length actually shrinks. In practice, if $|W_t|$ is relatively small (e.g., ≤ 1), one may conclude that the associated node is redundant and can be removed. (Trimming redundant hidden nodes is a separate subject and is not pursued in this research.)

To be more precise, the dot product between a weight vector W_t and every point vector on the training object essentially converts every point vector into the value that equals the projected length of the point vector on W_t and enlarged by $|W_t|$. The multiplication between a state matrix, $[S]_{p \times (s+1)}$, and a weight matrix, $[W]_{(s+1) \times t}$, can then be realized as the process that converts each s-dimensional point v_{si} into a t-dimensional point v_{ti} via the dot products between each v_{si} and the t column vectors in $[W]$. Subsequently, the training object can be imagined as being stretched from s-dimensional one to t-dimensional one, by stretching the object along t directions at one time. Such a simultaneous stretch is referred to as *hyperstretch*, which is different from an intuitive stretch because of the change of object dimensionality – one might need some imagination to perceive the hyperstretch. However, intuitively one can perceive that the hyperstretch can result in a nonlinear distortion of the topological appearance of training object, because of the nonlinear change of the relative distances among training points.

The function of the bias node in SL now becomes clearer. Adding a bias node at SL is equivalent to placing the object in an added dimensionality space where the stretch is made. For an s-dimensional object, the stretch can be made in $(s+1)$dimension (e.g., a 2D object is to be stretched in a 3D space). It is intuitively perceivable that given the extra dimension for stretching, it should be easier to achieve desired distortions of training object.

Activation Function as Squeezing

Figure 3 shows a typical sigmoid activation function, $y = 1/(1 + e^{-x/T})$, where T is a constant (referred to as *temperature*). The activation function is also called threshold or squash function. This function converts a 1D infinite space into a unit region [0, 1], and the origin is mapped into the center (i.e., 0.5). In Figure 3, the region marked by $[-x, x]$ can be defined as an *effective region*. The space inside the effective region is nonlinearly normalized to (0,1), while the space outside the region is *squashed* nearly to the boundary of the region. For the activation function with $T = 1$, the effective region is approximately [-4.5, 4.5], which maps to [0.01, 0.99]. Note that the activation function only accepts a scalar input. When it is applied to a state matrix of a training object, it is applied to each element of the matrix. Therefore an n-dimensional space is squeezed into an n-dimensional hypercubic $[0, 1]^n$.

Schematical examples are helpful in visualizing the multidimensional squeezing effect. Figure 4 shows a 2D example, where three arbitrary objects, A, B and C are squeezed to a, b and c respectively. Note the difference in scales as well as

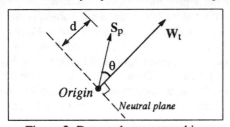

Figure 2. Dot product as stretching

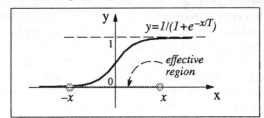

Figure 3. A sigmoid activation function

III-627

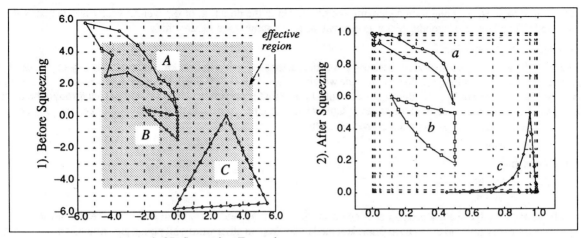

Figure 4. 2D Squeezing Example.
The objects *A, B* and *C* are squeezed to *a, b* and *c* respectively.
Note the difference in scales and the nonlinear change of grids.

the nonlinear change of grids locations. The entire R^2 space (only region $[-6, 6]^2$ is shown) is squeezed into $[0, 1]^2$; the origin $(0,0)$ is mapped into the new center, $(0.5, 0.5)$. The effective region in this case is approximately $[-4.5, 4.5]^2$. One sees that the space distortion increases sharply with respect to the distance from the origin, and gets saturated approximately around the boundary of the effective region. For example, object *B* has the least distortion, and object *A* has less distortion for the portion closer to the origin. For objects *A* and *C*, the portions lying outside the effective region are distorted dramatically, and are squashed to near the boundary of the effective region. Specifically, comparing *A* with *a*, it seems that the portion of *A* lying outside the effective region is chopped off, although none of the points on *A* are actually lost. Such a *pseudo–chopping* may help to perceive the change of topological feature when an *over-stretched* multidimensional object is squeezed (*overstretched* pertains to those portions of an object that are stretched to outside of the effective region).

As a scalar operation, the activation function really needs no direction to apply. In this paper, squeezing is associated with the direction of stretching because conceptually squeezing effect occurs exactly in the same direction of stretching. Similar to the concept of *hyperstretching*, a *hypersqueezing* refers to a set of squeezings associated with the multiple directions in a weight matrix.

4. Illustrative Example

The well–known 2–bit XOR problem is used to illustrate the successive hyperstretchings and hypersqueezings. The problem is to approximate the mapping where the four points, $(0,0)$, $(0,1)$, $(1,0)$ and $(1,1)$ map to 0, 1, 1, and 0 respectively. These four samples, labeled as p1, p2, p3 and p4, are trained by an MFN with two hidden nodes organized in a single hidden layer. Figure 5 shows the various state matrices of the training object, M_a, M_b, M_c, M_d, M_e and M_f, together with the two weight matrices associated with the hidden layer and output layer, $[W]^{(1)}$ and $[W]^{(2)}$. M_a is the input state matrix, where the last column is a unity vector associated with the bias node. M_b results from the hyperstretching of M_a by $[W]^{(1)}$. M_c is obtained by squeezing M_b (i.e., each component in M_b is processed through the activation function), and including a unity column vector for the bias node. Next, the stretching by $[W]^{(2)}$ is applied to M_c and yields M_d. Finally, M_d is squeezed to M_e, which is the predicted output state and is very close to the desired output, M_f.

As a counterpart of Figure 5, Figure 6 shows the successive reshaping process of the training object. The object is marked by p1, p2, p3, p4, and dashed lines. The weight vectors applied to stretch the object are shown in M_a and M_c. (The weight vectors are not shown with exact scale, rather they show the approximate application directions.) Figure 6–M_a is a 3D view of the training object, where one can visualize the effect of the bias node: the 2D object is placed in the space with an extra dimension and shifted to the unity location in that dimension. Figure 6–M_b and 6–M_c show the 2D view of the training object, where p1 and p4 nearly coincides with each other. In 6–M_c, the third dimension is not shown and corresponds to the axis that is perpendicular to the figure plane and passes through the origin. In 6–M_d and 6–M_e, the object is shown on a straight line for the object has been squeezed to a 1D space. One can observe that the topological appearance of the training object is evolved gradually from the input state to the output state. Obviously, visualization of the successive reshaping process would be difficult, if not impractical, when the object dimension is greater than three.

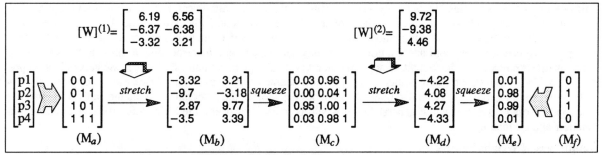

Figure 5. Successive matrix transformation of the 2–bit XOR problem

M_a, input state; M_b, M_c and M_d, intermediate states after a stretching, a squeezing, and another stretching; M_e, predicted output state; M_f, desired output state; $[W]^{(1)}$ and $[W]^{(2)}$, weight matrices for hidden layer and output layer.

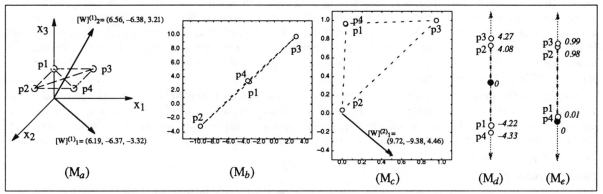

Figure 6. Successive reshaping of the training object of the 2–bit XOR problem

The training object is associated with the state matrices M_a, M_b, M_c, M_d, and M_e in Figure 5.
The weight vectors associated with $[W]^{(1)}$ and $[W]^{(2)}$ are shown in states M_a and M_c.

5. Implications of the Interpretation

Although the illustrated XOR problem is an n–to–1 binary mapping function, the interpretation also holds for mappings that are continuous and multidimensional (i.e., n–to–m). This is obvious since, firstly, the intermediate state matrices actually possess real numbers even for binary mappings, and secondly, the interpretation is independent of the dimension of state matrix. With this interpretation, the training of MFN can be interpreted as the process to find out how to reshape the training object from the input state to the desired output state, i.e., to decide the directions, strengths, and perhaps the repetition times, of hyperstretchings and hypersqueezings. On the other hand, the use of MFN for prediction can be thought of as the result of successive reshaping: a novel input is marked in the continuous input space, when the entire input space is reshaped to the output state, the marked location represents the predicted output.

From Figure 6, one can observe that during the sequence of reshaping, the topological appearance of the training object is evolving toward that of the desired state. The evolving principle is that after each reshaping operation, those points that are close to (or far away from) each other in the desired output state tend to be pulled closer (or pushed further away) to each other. This observation will be elaborated in the next section, where novel schemes for quantifying mapping nonlinearity are presented based on this observation. Discussed below are a few more implications of the interpretation.

Generalization with MFN

The property of *generalization* in MFN has been particularly elusive. Mathematically, generalization is different from *interpolation* in that interpolation always predicts an outcome based upon the neighboring samples, while generalization allows the prediction to be made on the basis beyond the neighboring samples. Take the n–bit XOR problem as an example. The interpolation tends to predict a wrong outcome due to the fact that in the input space, each point always has an output value that is opposite to that of its immediate adjacent points. Hence if the prediction is based on neighboring samples, it tends to yield an outcome that is similar to that of its neighboring points, i.e., a false one. On the other hand, it is well known that the MFN can predict satisfactorily with such problems: it can overpass the neighboring barrier to achieve the generalization.

This property can be explained from the viewpoint of reshaping the training object. For the n–bit XOR problem, if one marks each training point at input state with the corresponding output value (either 0 or 1), the mapping function must exhibit certain symmetry. Due to this symmetry, those regions with insufficient number of training points will also be reshaped in a correct manner and hence a novel input may get mapped into a correct output through the symmetrical relationship with respect to the weight vectors. In other words, it is this symmetry that makes the generalization possible. Should the input state training points be insufficient to characterize the symmetry (if such symmetry exists) of the underlying mapping function, generalization would not be possible. On the other hand, should the underlying mapping function possess no symmetry, the generalization would be meaningless and the MFN would behave like a regular function approximator.

Uniqueness of Weight Vectors

Another frequently asked question is "For a trained MFN, is the set of weight vectors unique? If not, what is the relationship between the feasible solutions?" The first question can be restated as "Is the set of intermediate states of a trained MFN unique?" to exclude the situations where the weight matrices consist of different permutation of weight vectors. From the perspective of successive reshaping, it seems that the answer must be negative, i.e., the set of intermediate states is not necessarily unique. In the sequence of reshaping, one may distort the training object more strongly in certain reshaping directions, while compensate with less distortion in other directions. Consequently, it would result in different sets of intermediate states. From this point of view, redundant hidden nodes in an MFN can be thought of as unnecessary stretchings/squeezings, which would obviously result in different intermediate states in addition to causing undesirable over–fitting effects.

The relationship between all feasible sets of weight vectors can be explained from the perspective of optimization (i.e., the minimization of the error function). Since the feasible intermediate states appear to be *continuously reshapable* to each other, the corresponding weight vectors must exhibit a form of ridges in the weight space. In other words, the global minimum of the error function appears to be hyper–ridges that have infinite number of minimum, rather than a valley with a unique minimum.

Linear Separability

With the presented interpretation, the linear separability[Nilsson, Pao] can be interpreted as the feasibility of reshaping a training object from the source state to the target state with only a fixed number of stretchings and squeezings (i.e., one hyperstretching and one hypersqueezing), where the number equals the number of output nodes (or the target space dimension). Obviously, if the topological appearance of input and output states differ from each other considerably, the fixed number of stretchings/squeezings can not achieve the desired transformation. In such situations, the successive reshaping is required where one has freedom to apply more stretchings/squeezings, and/or repeat hyperstretchings/hypersqueezings (the number of repetitions is corresponding to the number of hidden layers). For a trained MFN, one finds that any two adjacent states automatically satisfy the linear separability.

6. Concluding Remarks

The essence of the geometrical interpretation is that the training samples are regarded as two states, input and output, of an imaginary training object which is multidimensional and pliable. The weight matrix between two adjacent layers, including the activation function, is associated with a reshaping operation: the matrix multiplication is thought of as a hyperstretching and the activation function is thought of as a hypersqueezing. By successive hyperstretchings and hypersqueezings, the training object is transformed from the input state to the desired output state, through the intermediate states associated with hidden layers. This interpretation is valid for multidimensional (n–to–m) mappings including classification problems, as well as for both binary and continuous mappings. A 2–bit XOR problem was illustrated to show the successive reshaping process. The evolving principle in a trained MFN is observed as follows: the points that are close to (far away from) each other in the desired output state tend to get closer to (further away from) each other after each reshaping operation. This interpretation may have solved many mysteries about MFN. In particular, the generalization of MFN seems to be the result of certain symmetry within the underlying mapping function. In the second part of this paper, the interpretation will be extended to introduce novel schemes for quantifying mapping nonlinearity based on the spatial characteristics of mapping samples.

Reference

[Hornik] K. Hornik, M. Stinchcombe and H. White, Multilayer Feedforward Networks are Universal Approximators, Neural Networks, Vol. 2, pp 359–366, 1989.

[Kosko] B. Kosko, Neural Networks and Fuzzy Systems, Prentice–Hall, Inc., N.J., 1992.

[Lippmann] R.P. Lippmann, An Introduction to Computing with Neural Nets, IEEE, ASSP Mag. pp. 4–22, April 1987.

[Nilsson] N.J.Nilsson,The mathematical Foundations of Learning Machines, Morgan Kaufmann Publishers, Inc.1990.

[Pao] Y.–H. Pao, Adaptive Pattern Recognition and Neural Networks, Addison–Wesley Inc. 1989.

On A Unified Geometrical Interpretation of Multilayer Feedforward Networks
Part II: Quantifying Mapping Nonlinearity

Hauhua Lee
GE Corporate Research and Development Center, Schenectady, N.Y. 12301
Prabhat Hajela
Rensselaer Polytechnic Institute, Troy, N.Y. 12180

Abstract:

This is the second of a two–part paper. The geometrical interpretation of MFN presented in Part I allows the mapping nonlinearity to be quantified based on the spatial characteristics of training samples. The normalized *object distribution vector* (ODV) is introduced as a generic representation of a multidimensional object. This representation is independent of the dimension, as well as the size, location and orientation, of the object. Based on ODV, two types of measurement are suggested to gauge the mapping nonlinearity between mapping samples: the *distribution angle* α, and the *maximum distribution gradient* β_{max}. To facilitate the training process (or avoid hard–learning situations), one should try to reduce α and β_{max} during the preparation of training samples. The schemes are supported by results of numerical experiments, including an elaborated one–to–one and continuous mapping example.

1. Introduction

This is the second of a two–part paper. In Part I, a unified geometrical interpretation of the behavior of multilayer feedforward networks (MFN) was presented. There, MFN was shown to be a successive matrix transformation mechanism, where a matrix can be thought of as representing a state of the imaginary training object. The successive matrix transformation was shown to be analogous to a sequence of hyperstretchings and hypersqueezings of the training object. This interpretation holds for both binary and continuous function mappings, and for mappings where both input and output spaces are multidimensional. More importantly, the interpretation has opened up a new perspective to the problem of quantifying mapping nonlinearity, a perspective in view of the spatial characteristics of training samples. Conventionally, efforts on quantifying mapping nonlinearity (also called mapping complexity) have been made from a statistical view point. For example, [Baum] suggested a relationship between the number of training samples and the number of hidden nodes. More recently, [Koiran] derived a stricter relationship between the two numbers by taking into account a specific spatial characteristic of the training samples, the smallest distance between two samples that have different outputs (for classification problems). Unfortunately, these results do not help much in practice as one still must struggle with determining appropriate numbers of hidden nodes/layers and accommodate slow training (or hard–learning) when dealing with complex applications such as [Lee]. In this regard, the second part of this paper concentrates on exploring how one can possibly facilitate a training process, or avoid hard–learning situations.

This paper suggests that the mapping nonlinearity which the training samples exhibit should be an effective indicator for the degree of learnability (or trainability). Moreover, it is the spatial characteristics of the training samples that is essential to the mapping nonlinearity, far more so than merely the number of samples. (In this regard, the work of [Koiran] is more meaningful than [Baum]). In this paper, the mapping nonlinearity is used as an antonym of *mapping similarity*, i.e., the similarity between inputs and outputs of mapping samples. The normalized *object distribution vector* (ODV) is introduced as a generic representation of a multidimensional object. Two types of similarity measurement are suggested based on ODV: the *distribution angle,* α, and the *maximum distribution gradient,* β_{max}. These schemes are supported by results of numerical experiments, including a continuous one–to–one mapping example.

2. Quantifying Mapping Nonlinearity

Part I has shown that during the sequence of reshaping, the training object is so twisted that its topological appearance becomes more and more *similar* to that of the desired output state. If such similarity between any two states can be somehow quantified, the same schemes can be used to gauge the similarity (or nonlinearity) in any mapping set. However, it is not straightforward to quantify the similarity between any two states of a training object, for the dimensionality could be different in the associated states. In addition, the overall size of the object is scaled up and down by *stretchings* and *squeezings*. In this paper, it is assumed that the similarity measure is independent of the size as well as the dimensionality of the training object. Hence, to conduct the similarity measure, one has to first represent the state of the multidimensional training object in a way that is independent of the object size and dimensionality. The normalized *object distribution vector* (ODV) is introduced for this purpose.

Object Distribution Vector (ODV)

The ODV is defined as a vector to characterize the distribution of all point vectors on a training object. The components of an ODV are obtained by sequentially enumerating all distances between every pair of training points. Given a training object V_{obj} that is represented by n point vectors:

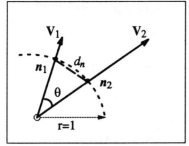 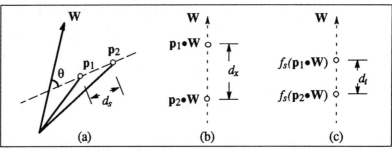

Figure 1. Euclidean distance *vs.* Angle.　　　Figure 2. A hard learning case.

(a)souce state; (b)after stretching; (c) after squeezing.

$$V_{obj} \equiv \{\mathbf{p}_i \mid i=1,...,n, \mathbf{p}_i \in R^m\}$$

then

$$ODV(V_{obj}) \equiv \{d_{ij} \mid d_{ij} = \text{distance between } \mathbf{p}_i \text{ and } \mathbf{p}_j; \mathbf{p}_i, \mathbf{p}_j \in V_{obj}; i > j; i,j=1,...,n\}.$$

The number of components in an ODV equals $n(n-1)/2$, where n is the number of point vectors in the associated object. It is important to note that the ODV representation is independent of the dimensionality of object: an ODV essentially transforms an m-dimensional object that has n point vectors into a point vector in an $n(n-1)/2$ dimensional space, regardless of the dimensionality m. Moreover, ODV is not affected if the entire object V_{obj} is translated or rotated in the associated space. If all components in V_{obj} are scaled linearly, the associated ODV will also be scaled in the same manner. Hence, a normalized ODV is a representation that is invariant to the location, orientation, and size, in addition to the dimensionality, of its associated object. Subsequently, the similarity measure between two states of a training object becomes the similarity measure between two point vectors (the associated ODVs) that have the same dimension.

In the numerical experiments conducted, it was found that the ODV can be modified in a specific way to improve the performance of similarity measure. A simple approach is to subtract the minimum component in an ODV from every component (i.e., all components are down-shifted so that the minimum is 0). Such a modified ODV, denoted as MODV, is more appropriate for the similarity measure with binary mappings.

Distribution Angle: α

The Euclidean distance is a common measure of the similarity between two point vectors.[Kohonen] Suppose V_1 and V_2 are two ODVs; n_1, n_2 represent the normalized vectors of V_1 and V_2 respectively. One can find that the Euclidean distance between n_1 and n_2 (denoted by d_n) is a function of the angle between V_1 and V_2 (denoted by θ). This relationship is explained in Figure 1, where

$$\cos \theta = V_1 \bullet V_2/(|V_1| \, |V_2|)$$
$$n_1 \equiv V_1/|V_1|$$
$$n_2 \equiv V_2/|V_2|$$
$$|n_1 - n_2|^2 = |n_1|^2 + |n_2|^2 - 2n_1 \bullet n_2$$
$$= 1 + 1 - 2 (V_1/|V_1|) \bullet (V_2/|V_2|)$$
$$= 2(1 - \cos \theta).$$

i.e., $d_n^2 = 2(1-\cos \theta)$.

Therefore, the similarity measure between two states of a training object is conceptually equivalent when using either the Euclidean distance between the associated normalized ODVs, or the angle between the associated ODVs. The *angle* measure is more intuitive and is adopted in this research, referred to as the *distribution angle*, α. From the standpoint of reshaping, the smaller the α between two states, the more similar the two, and the more likely that the transformation between the two requires fewer number of stretchings and squeezings. (The distribution angle that is measured based on MODV is referred to as *modified distribution angle*, α_m.)

Distribution Gradient: β

Apart from the distribution angle, the *maximum distribution gradient* is introduced as another type of mapping nonlinearity based on ODV. One can identify a specific hard learning situation as explained in Figure 2. Suppose $\mathbf{p}_1$, $\mathbf{p}_2$ represent two points in the source state, and W is a weight vector. During the reshaping operation by W, the two points are stretched to $\mathbf{p}_1 \bullet W$ and $\mathbf{p}_2 \bullet W$ first, and then squeezed to $f_s(\mathbf{p}_1 \bullet W)$ and $f_s(\mathbf{p}_2 \bullet W)$, where f_s is the activation function:

$$f_s(x) = 1/(1 + e^{-x}). \tag{1}$$

Let d_s, d_x and d_t denote the distance between the two points at the source state, the state after stretching by W, and the state after squeezing, respectively, i.e.,

$$d_s = |\,\mathbf{p}_1 - \mathbf{p}_2\,|, \tag{2a}$$
$$d_x = |\,\mathbf{p}_1 \bullet \mathbf{W} - \mathbf{p}_2 \bullet \mathbf{W}\,|, \tag{2b}$$
and $$d_t = |\,f_s(\mathbf{p}_1 \bullet \mathbf{W}) - f_s(\mathbf{p}_2 \bullet \mathbf{W})\,|. \tag{2c}$$

Equation (2b) can be rewritten as
$$d_x = |\,\mathbf{p}_1 - \mathbf{p}_2\,|\,|\mathbf{W}|\cos\theta, \tag{3}$$

i.e., $$|\mathbf{W}| = \frac{d_x}{|\,\mathbf{p}_1 - \mathbf{p}_2\,|\cos\theta}. \tag{4}$$

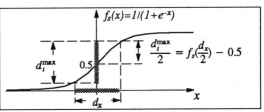

Figure 3. Relationship between d_x and d_t.

The relationship between d_x and d_t is explained in Figure 3. For an object with length d_x, the maximum length after squeezing should be $d_t{}^{max} = 2(f_s(d_x/2) - 0.5)$, which is obtained when the center of the object coincides with the origin. If the center of the object is placed elsewhere other than the origin, the length after squeezing will always be smaller. Therefore,
$$d_t \leq d_t{}^{max} = 2(f_s(d_x/2) - 0.5). \tag{5}$$

The equality holds when the origin coincides with the center point between $\mathbf{p}_1$ and $\mathbf{p}_2$. Substitute (1) into (5) and get
$$d_x \geq 2\,ln\,((1 + d_t)/(1 - d_t)) \tag{6}$$

Substitute (2a) and (6) into (4),
$$|\mathbf{W}| \geq \frac{2\,ln\,((1 + d_t)/(1 - d_t))}{d_s \cos\theta}. \tag{7}$$

Equation (7) shows the required magnitude of the weight vector that can reshape, by stretching and squeezing, two points from source state to target state. This magnitude depends on the angle θ and the distances between two points at source and target states, d_s and d_t. From the perspective of θ, one sees that the most efficient weight vector (i.e., with the smallest magnitude) for reshaping the target points is in the direction parallel to the difference of the two point vectors at the source state (i.e., when $\theta = 0$). In such cases, equation (7) becomes
$$|\mathbf{W}| \geq \frac{2\,ln\,((1 + d_t)/(1 - d_t))}{d_s}. \tag{8}$$

This equation shows that under two situations the magnitude of weight vector, $|\mathbf{W}|$, will increase dramatically: (a) when d_t approaches 1 for a fixed d_s, and (b) when d_s approaches 0 for a fixed d_t (note that d_t is within [0, 1] and $d_s > 0$). Situation (a) is less sensitive to $|\mathbf{W}|$ because the value of the numerator in equation (8) increases slowly with respect to d_t. For example, with tolerance 0.1%, a desired d_t of value 1 can accept a predicted d_t of 0.999. The numerator is then $2ln((1+0.999)/(1-0.999)) = 15.2$, which is not too large. The major concern is with situation (b), which shows that if there is a pair of sample points whose d_s is small while the corresponding d_t is not small enough, it will require a very large weight vector to reshape (i.e., *separate*) the two points. If such a weight vector is not offered by any weight matrix in MFN, either one of the two samples will never be *learned* by the network, i.e., one or the other will be a stubborn sample. On the other hand, if one purposely includes such an outstanding weight vector in a weight matrix in order to learn the stubborn samples, it is likely that the overall performance of the hyperstretching will be deteriorated, as the outstanding vector may tend to dominate the overall direction of the associated hyperstretching. Hence, it is clear that a mapping with this type of stubborn samples is hard to learn. Note that in equation (8) the d_t could equal 1. To avoid the problem of division by 0 and only emphasize situation (b), this research suggests using an alternative, the ratio between d_t and d_s, as a rough and quick estimation of equation (8),
$$|\mathbf{W}| \geq d_t / d_s. \tag{9}$$

Equation (9) expresses the hard learning situation as when *the ratio between d_t and d_s is large*. In other words, it is difficult to reshape two training points whose distance at source state is small while at desired output state is large. This is consistent with one's intuition: if similar inputs yield similar outputs, it is easy to learn; if similar inputs give rise to quite different outputs, the learning would be difficult. Based on equation (9), the *Distribution Gradient Vector*, DGV, is introduced below for the purpose of checking the existence of stubborn samples. The *"gradient"* refers to the ratio of the similarity (in terms of *distance*) between the source state and the target state. Let $\mathbf{V}_s$ and $\mathbf{V}_t$ represent the ODV of a training object at source state and target state, i.e.,
$$\mathbf{V}_s = \{s_i \mid s_i \in R, s_i > 0, i=1,..., n\},$$
$$\mathbf{V}_t = \{t_i \mid t_i \in R, t_i \geq 0, i=1,..., n\}.$$

Then the associated DGV is defined as the vector which consists of the ratio between every pair of source state distance s_i and target state distance t_i:
$$DGV\,(\mathbf{V}_s, \mathbf{V}_t) = \{g_i \mid g_i = t_i/s_i, t_i \in \mathbf{V}_t, s_i \in \mathbf{V}_s, i=1,..., n\}.$$

In this research, the g_i is converted to an angle by the function tan^{-1} (arc–tangent) and is denoted as β. The maximum component of DGV is denoted as β_{max}, and is suggested as the second type of measure for mapping nonlinearity. Empirically, it was found that during the preparation of training samples, one should avoid a large β_{max} (e.g., no more than a threshold, 88 degrees).

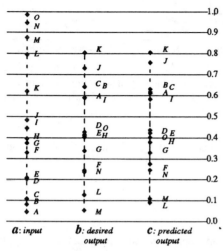

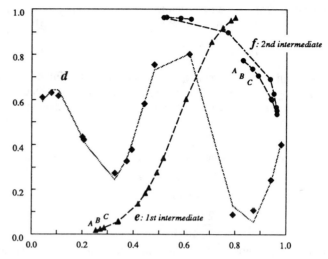

Figure 4. Successive Reshaping Example for a 1x2x2x1 MFN.

a, input state; *b*, desired output state; *c*, predicted output state; *d*, input/output mapping; *e*, the first intermediate state; *f*, the second intermediate state.

label	Input State	Inter. State 1	Inter. State 2	Predicted Output	Desired Output
A	0.0429	(0.2545 0.0162)	(0.8306 0.7719)	0.6078	0.5879
B	0.0793	(0.2729 0.0214)	(0.8677 0.7347)	0.6284	0.6403
C	0.1064	(0.2872 0.0263)	(0.8905 0.7052)	0.6145	0.6414
D	0.2009	(0.3402 0.0537)	(0.9417 0.6027)	0.4325	0.4257
E	0.2062	(0.3433 0.0559)	(0.9435 0.5976)	0.4200	0.4093
F	0.3284	(0.4185 0.1339)	(0.9647 0.5337)	0.2714	0.2412
G	0.3740	(0.4477 0.1811)	(0.9643 0.5496)	0.3255	0.3371
H	0.3939	(0.4606 0.2054)	(0.9626 0.5651)	0.3772	0.4014
I	0.4427	(0.4924 0.2750)	(0.9530 0.6250)	0.5797	0.5871
J	0.4816	(0.5178 0.3398)	(0.9375 0.6901)	0.7534	0.7291
K	0.6181	(0.6054 0.6005)	(0.7708 0.8970)	0.8007	0.8013
L	0.7919	(0.7072 0.8547)	(0.5178 0.9634)	0.0866	0.1253
M	0.8735	(0.7494 0.9178)	(0.5279 0.9649)	0.1058	0.0512
N	0.9429	(0.7819 0.9506)	(0.5834 0.9606)	0.2418	0.2351
O	0.9827	(0.7991 0.9634)	(0.6253 0.9562)	0.3986	0.4141

Table 1. Raw data of 15 training samples

Figure 5. Distance Matrix and ODV for the input state of the 1x2x2x1 example.

	$Inter_1$	$Inter_2$	Out_p	Out_d
Input	8.9	25.8	41.2	41.6
$Inter_1$		20.4	41.0	41.4
$Inter_2$			38.3	38.6
Out_p				6.2

Table 2. Distribution angles for the 1x2x2x1 example. ($Inter_1$ and $Inter_2$ are for the 1st and 2nd intermediate state; Out_p and Out_d are for the predicted and desired output state.)

3. Numerical Experiments and Discussions

Extensive numerical experiments have been conducted to validate the proposed schemes for quantifying mapping nonlinearity. Selected results of the experiments are presented here: an MFN model that approximates a continuous one–to–one mapping is used to illustrate the evolution of training object. In addition, the distribution angle α is verified with several MFN models.

Evolution of Training Object

Figure 4 illustrates the successive reshaping of a one–to–one and continuous mapping. There are 15 training samples, trained by an MFN with a configuration 1x2x2x1.The use of two hidden layers and each with two hidden nodes was intentional – in this manner, the intermediate states of training object are 2D and therefore

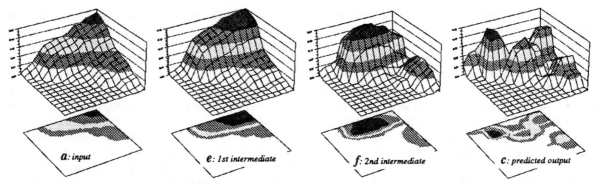

Figure 6. Evolution of ODVs.
a input state; *e* the first intermediate state; *f* the second intermediate state; *c* predicted output state.

can be visualized easily. The 15 samples, labeled from *A* to *O*, are listed in Table 1 with the input state, the desired output state, the predicted output state, as well as the two intermediate states at hidden layers (after stretching and squeezing).

The data in Table 1 is shown schematically in Figure 4, where there are 6 curves (including 3 straight lines) marked as *a*, *b*, *c*, *d*, *e* and *f*. Curves *a*, *b* and *c* represent the input, the desired output and the predicted output states, respectively – they are shown with straight lines since they are associated with 1D space. The minor deviations between *b* and *c* are negligible, i.e., the desired output and predicted output are considered equivalent to each other. Curves *d*, *e* and *f* are drawn inside a unit square. Curve *d* shows the mapping relationship between the inputs and outputs (solid line marks the desired outputs and squares mark the predicted outputs). By taking the horizontal axis as the input state and the vertical axis as the output state, one can visualize the mapping relationship. In this case, it shows a wave–like form. (In fact, the underlying mapping function is in the form of $y=x \cdot \sin x$. The samples are randomly chosen from within $[0, 4\pi]$ and both inputs and outputs are normalized to $[0, 1]$). The mapping relationship is not always visualizable – it is easy to visualize only when the output space is 1D and the input space is below 3D. At this point, one is advised to not be distracted by the mapping curve, since the mapping relation is indeed unrelated to the explanation of successive re-shapings. Instead, curve *e* and *f* are what need to be emphasized: *e* and *f* correspond to the first and second intermediate state of the training object respectively.

In Figure 4, the imaginary training object is shown with a single dash line connecting all training points sequentially, from point *A* to point *O*. Note that on curves *e* and *f* only the first three points, *A*, *B* and *C*, are labelled and one can easily trace the remaining points. Now the successive reshaping of the training object can be represented by four curves sequentially, i.e., $a \rightarrow e \rightarrow f \rightarrow c$. One may observe how the training object is *folded* and *twisted* from the input state to the output state – the points that are close to (or far away from) each other at output state tend to get closer to (or further away from) each other during the reshaping process. This is exactly the evolution principle observed in the previous section.

The reshaping process can be also visualized from the perspective of ODVs. Figure 5 shows how the ODV associated with input state is obtained. By listing all the distances between every pair of points, one can come up with a distance matrix. (Figure 5 only shows a portion of the entire distance matrix for the input state.) Apparently, this matrix is symmetric and its diagonal elements are all 0. Hence, essentially the ODV is defined as the upper (or lower) triangular portion of the distance matrix (no need to include the diagonal). One can display this triangular matrix in a 3D view, e.g., by attaching two axes along the directions of row and column of the matrix, and the third axis to show the magnitude of elements. In this manner, the ODVs associated with curves *a*, *e*, *f*, and *c* in Figure 4 are shown in Figure 6, where each ODV is shown as a 3D view as well as a 2D contour plot. The sample sequences are the same at both column and row directions, i.e., from point *A* to point *O*, as shown in Figure 5. Such sequence resulted in a single smooth hump in the 3D view of the input state ODV. Obviously, the appearance of ODV is directly affected by the sample sequence in both the row and column directions. It is important to note that, in Figure 6, the evolution principle can be recognized more easily in view of the heights of elements. The elements that are *high* (or *low*) in output state tend to become *higher* (or *lower*) during the reshaping process.

α, α_m and β_{max}

The distribution angle α is defined for measuring the similarity between two ODVs. Table 2 lists the α values between each pair of ODVs that are associated with the five states of the 1x2x2x1 MFN. The notations $Inter_1$ and $Inter_2$ refer to the first and second intermediate states; Out_p and Out_d refer to the predicted and desired output states. The α is listed in degree. The smaller the α, the more similar the two ODVs. The data on the first row exhibits a trend of increasing (from left to right), which means that the input state is most similar to its adjacent state, the first intermediate state, and becomes more and more dissimilar to the states after more reshapings. In fact, the data on same rows and columns all follow the same trend (decreasing from top to bottom in a column). Therefore, it appears that α is a rational measure for the similarity between two states of a training object.

In Table 3, the same set of training samples are trained by two different MFNs. With the 1x10x1 MFN, α follows the uniform increasing/decreasing trend well. However, with the 1x8x8x1 MFN, the trend is *disturbed* by data such as 19.6 and 39.7. This disturbance must be due to the fact that the 1x8x8x1 MFN indeed contains too many redundant hidden nodes that lead to the undesired over–reshaping effect (recall that 1x2x2x1 is sufficient with two hidden layers).

Table 4 shows α for a binary mapping example, the 4–bit XOR problem. The training samples used are the full set of mapping points (i.e., $2^4=16$ samples). The net configuration is 4x3x1. Both the regular distribution angle α and the modified distribution angle α_m are tabulated and the convergence trend is better with α_m. In fact, in several other experiments with boolean mappings, α_m always performs better than α. However, for continuous mappings, the difference in performance between α and α_m is not significant.

In another experiment, the 4–bit XOR problem was trained by a 4x2x1 MFN, where an insufficient number of hidden nodes were intentionally used (i.e., 2 hidden nodes) in order to obtain an under–fitting intermediate state. It was found that during the training process, the maximum distribution gradient β_{max} of output state *vs.* intermediate state increased sharply when the training process was reaching a saturation point – in terms of *gradient angle*, β_{max} was approaching 90 degrees.

MFN: 1x10x1		Inter.	Out$_p$	Out$_d$
	Input	10.1	41.5	41.6
	Inter.		38.6	38.7
	Out$_p$			2.6

MFN: 1x8x8x1		Inter$_1$	Inter$_2$	Out$_p$	Out$_d$
	Input	7.0	17.1	41.4	41.6
	Inter$_1$		19.6	39.7	39.8
	Inter$_2$			41.0	41.1
	Out$_p$				2.0

Table 3. Distribution Angle α for MFNs 1x10x1 and 1x8x8x1.

Regular Distribution Angle				Modified Distribution Angle			
	Inter.	Out$_p$	Out$_d$		Inter.	Out$_p$	Out$_d$
Input	38.0	46.85	46.9	Input	46.4	59.5	59.6
Inter.		50.7	50.8	Inter.		50.7	50.8
Out$_p$			0.3	Out$_p$			0.3

Table 4. Distribution Angle α and α_m for 4–bit XOR mapping (MFN: 4x3x1)

4. Conclusion

Based on the geometrical interpretation presented in Part I, this paper introduced the normalized *object distribution vector* (ODV) as a generic representation of the multidimensional training objects. This representation is independent of the dimension, size, location and orientation of the associated object. Based on ODV, two types of measurement are suggested to gauge the mapping nonlinearity between any pair of source/target states. The first type is the *distribution angle* α and the second is the *maximum distribution gradient* β_{max}. With α and β_{max}, one can then try to reduce the mapping nonlinearity within the mapping samples so as to facilitate the training process or avoid hard–learning situations.

Acknowledgement

The authors would like to thank Professor Mark Embrechts at Rensselaer Polytechnic Institute for providing the BP software, *metaneural*, and Dr. W.–J. Hsueh at GE Corporate Research and Development Center for suggestions that helped improve the paper. Partial support received under grant NAG 3–1196 from the NASA Lewis Research Center is gratefully acknowledged.

Reference

[Baum] E. B. Baum, On the capabilities of multilayer perceptrons, Journal of Complexity, 4, pp. 193–215.

[Kohonen] T. Kohonen, Self–Organization and Associative Memory,3rd. ed. Springer–Verlag Berlin Heidelberg,1989.

[Koiran] P. Koiran, On the Complexity of Approximating Mappings Using Feedforward Networks, Neural Networks, Vol. 6. pp. 649–653, 1993.

[Lee] H. Lee and P. Hajela, Vector Clustering for Neural Networks Based Prediction of Geometrical Characteristics, The 3rd International Conference on the Application of Artificial Intelligence of Civil and Structural Engineering, Edinburgh, UK, August 17–19, 1993.

Unbounded Reinforcement for the Associative Reward-Penalty Algorithm

R. Neville & T.J. Stonham

Dept Elec Eng, Brunel University, Uxbridge, Middx

Email Add: Richard.Neville@brunel.ac.uk

Abstract

We describe an extension to the Associative Reward-Penalty, or A_{R-P}, algorithm for solving nonlinear supervised learning tasks utilising multi-layer feed-forward networks. We introduce a variant of the A_{R-P} algorithm, called the 'Unbounded' reinforcement A_{R-P}. The method utilises a quantised real-valued reinforcement, which is a payoff metric optimised by an associated Critic Net.

1 Introduction

The underlying principle of the Associative Reward-Penalty, A_{R-P}, algorithm is that a binary (scalar) reward signal is broadcast globally across a network. The reinforcement signal "r" is then utilised by each unit in the net, to determine their weight updates. The premise is that the stochastic nodes in the net are given credit or reinforcement if the net gives a 'successful' output. The net is given a debit or penalized if its output is wrong [1]. The initial research of Barto [2] defines the reward signal $r \in [0, 1]$ in his P-model as:

$$r = 1 \ \textit{with probability} \ 1 - e_o \ \textbf{or} \ r = 0 \ \textit{with probability} \ e_o \tag{1}$$

where the error e_o is the mean-square output error of the net.

This means the reinforcement is deduced solely as a function of the output error and the present input stimuli, which we term *primary* information. The scalar reward has a very low information content and as such can not give credit to a good action as precisely as Barto's [2] S-model, where the reward signal $0.0 \le r^{\Re} \le 1.0$ is a real-valued variable, defined by:

$$r^{\Re} = 1 - e_o \tag{2}$$

The S-model requires a large bandwidth signal to be broadcast to all the units in a net. This has significant repercussions if one is considering mapping the S-model to hardware, as the reward signal would not be a single binary control line, if one considers a network as being supervised by an external training environment (R) that provides input stimuli to the network and monitors the output action of the net. It is of interest to note that the A_{R-P} algorithms do not utilise *secondary* information, such as past data obtained from the environment R. In this paper, we describe an extension to the A_{R-P} algorithm which uses *secondary* information which is based on tracing the frequency of 'stimuli' occurrence and then using this to derive a prediction of the reinforcement.

2 The Sigma-pi Neuron Model

The neuron model we utilise has previously been termed a Sigma-pi unit [3] , these units are similar to pRAM units [4] and as they are RAM based they may be placed in the same category as PLN units [5] or the more recent GNU units [6]. We use the stochastic model Direct Output Node (DON). The activation of the DON, for the Analogue case, is defined as:

$$a = \frac{1}{2^n} \sum_{\mu} \sigma(S_\mu) \prod_{i=1}^{i=n} (1 + \bar{\mu}_i z_i) \tag{3}$$

where z_i defines a set of probability distributions for an input address formed from a set of Boolean variables $\{X_i\}$, given by

$$P_{\underline{\mu}}(\underline{x}_i) = \frac{1}{2}(1 + \underline{\mu}_i z_i) \tag{4}$$

Given $x \in \{x_1, x_2, ...x_i\}$ is a binary input vector which may be represented as a set of bits in positions x_1 to x_i. The site address $\mu \in \{\mu_1, \mu_2, ...\mu_i\}$ is represented by a set of bits in positions μ_1 to μ_i. The site value S_μ is addressed by the binary string μ. The site value S_μ stores a value $S_\mu \in \{-S_m, S_m\}$. Then for the stochastic model

$$a = \sum_{\mu} \sigma(S_\mu)P(\mu) = < \sigma(S_\mu) > \tag{5}$$

The output y of the DON is defined as equal to the activation a and

$$P(\underline{y} = 1|\eta) = \sigma(S_\mu) = \frac{1}{1 + e^{\frac{-S_\mu}{\rho}}} \tag{6}$$

Then the output $y = < \sigma(S_\mu) >$. The output behaviour of these units is similar to that of Boltzmann units [7].

3 Training Artificial Neural Networks by Error minimisation

The goal of the learning regime is to minimise a mean-square output error term:

$$\forall_{I_v} \quad e_o = \frac{1}{N_V} \sum_{I_V} [y_t^j - \sigma(S_\mu^j)]^2 \tag{7}$$

where $[.]^2$ is the square error per input stimuli, defined on the output. This is summed over all Nv output units or visible units. The sum is over the set I_v of these visible units. The error is the difference between the target response y_t^j of output j for a given input/output pattern pair, and the sigmoidal value of the site $\sigma(S_\mu^j)$, where μ specifies a site address.

3.1 Unbounded Reinforcement A_{R-P} Training

The external reward has been previously defined in (1), where $r_{(t)} \in [0, 1]$ is a binary scalar value. The external reinforcement, in the case of unbounded Reinforcement, is then scaled:

$$r'_{(t)} = (2 * r_{(t)}) - 1 \tag{8}$$

where $r'_{(t)} \in [-1, +1]$ is of the form utilised by Barto, Sutton and Anderson [8]. The scaled reward signal is then used to derive an improved or internal reinforcement signal, given by:

$$\hat{r}_{(t)} = r'_{(t)} + \gamma P_{v(t)} - P_{v(t-1)} \tag{9}$$

where $P_{v(t)}$ is the present prediction and $P_{v(t-1)}$ the past prediction. It should be noted that this is not the same as Barto's [8] original work, where he uses the prediction values $P_{(t)}$ and $P_{(t-1)}$. We use the present and previous prediction values for the given site address v. The coefficient $0.0 < \gamma \leq 1.0$ has previously been termed the "discount factor" by Barto et. al. [8]. The prediction value is updated by:

$$\Delta P_{v(t+1)} = \beta \hat{r}_{(t)} \bar{x}_{v(t)} \tag{10}$$

where $0 < \beta < 1$ is a positive constant determining the rate of change of $P_v(.)$. All the input eligibility traces are updated using:

$$\forall_u \qquad \bar{x}_{u(t+1)} = \lambda \bar{x}_{u(t)} + (1 - \lambda)x_v \tag{11}$$

for all input addresses $0 \leq u \leq \eta$, where η is the maximum input address (i.e. for an 8-tuple $\eta = [(2^8) - 1]$ or 255 decimal or FF hexidecimal), and where lambda $0 < \lambda < 1$ determines the eligibility traces decay rates. The binary value x_v is a trigger for the eligibility trace, and when the site v is addressed $x_v = 1$ and all other non-addressed traces are updated with $x_{\bar{v}} = 0$. The internal reinforcement $\hat{r}_{(t)}$ is then re-scaled

$$r^*_{(t)} = \frac{1}{2}(\hat{r} + 1.0) \tag{12}$$

which denotes a quantised real-valued reinforcement $-1.0 \leq r^*_{(t)} \leq +2.0$, that is defined as the **unbounded** $r^*_{(t)}$ internal reinforcement which permits penalisation even when $\lambda = 0$.

The net is then trained substituting $r_{(t)} = r^*_{(t)}$ which is the **unbounded** internal reinforcement, while the standard A_{R-P} regime utilises r defined in (1). Then each node j, given site address μ, updates its site value according to the following equation:

$$\Delta S^j_\mu = \alpha[y^j - \sigma(S^j_\mu)]r_{(t)} + \alpha\lambda[1 - y^j - \sigma(S^j_\mu)](1 - r_{(t)}) \tag{13}$$

4   Discussion of Theory

In the original work of Barto [2] he utilises a scalar Reinforcement signal. In the above we replace this with a quantised Reinforcement signal based on the present external Reinforcement and past and present prediction values. We utilise the Adaptive Critic Element (ACE) of Barto, Sutton and Anderson [8] to maximise $r_{(t)}$ over time by maximising $r^*_{(t)}$ in the immediate future. Barto's method may be thought of as a 'temporal difference' (T.D.) method [9] as he utilises data that relates to the past and present events to enable a payoff metric to be optimised, where the payoff was used as a "prediction" or "expectation" of a future Reinforcement [10]. The prediction values are calculated with reference to the ACE's input eligibility traces, where the eligibility is a trace of events over time [8].

The eligibility trace may be described as follows; given a pathway between two neurons, the pathway is said to reach maximum eligibility a short time after the occurrence of a nonzero input signal on that pathway. The input eligibility traces are averages ($\bar{x}$), where the bar ($\bar{\cdot}$) denotes an exponential average over time. Each input to the Adaptive Critic Element is given its own trace in Barto's original study.

In our case we store the eligibility values in an n-tuple. The input eligibility $\bar{x}_{v(t)}$ is interpreted as; given an 'i' bit input vector $\{x_1, x_2, ...x_i\}$, which addresses location 'v' in an eligibility n-tuple, giving an eligibility $\bar{x}_{v(t)} \in [0, +\bar{x}_n]$, that is specified as a 'q' bit number, having $D = \bar{x}_n + 1$ discrete levels. Hence if $\bar{x}_n = 8$ then $\bar{x}v_{(.)} = \{0.125n \mid n = 0, 1, ...N\}$ where $N = 1.0/0.125 = \bar{x}_n$. These input eligibility traces increase when the input is active, and decrease to zero with time in the absence of future activity.

The adaptive critic is utilised to predict an internal Reinforcement, the procedure the adaptive critic follows is; given an external reward $r_{(t)}$ signal at time t, the critic then deduces an internal Reinforcement $r^*_{(t)}$ signal based on the external Reinforcement $r_{(t)}$ and the present $P_{v(t)}$ and past $P_{v(t-1)}$ predictions. The future prediction value is then derived as a function of the input eligibility trace. Finally all the input eligibility traces are updated. One should note that the predictions are quantised and stored in an n-tuple in the same manner as the eligibility trace. Where $P_{(.)} \in [0, +P_n]$, giving $D = P_n + 1$ discrete levels, which are stored as a q bit number. Hence if $P_n = 8$ then $P_{(.)} = \{0.125n \mid n = 0, 1, ...N\}$ where $N = 1.0/0.125 = P_n$. The internal reinforcement $r^*_{(t)}$ is calculated using $P_{(t)}$ and $P_{(t-1)}$, hence the unbounded reward signal is defined as $r^*_{(.)} \in [-r_n, +2r_n]$ giving $D = 3r_n + 1$ discrete levels, which is a q bit number. Then the unbounded reward utilised in (13) is defined as $r^*_{(.)} = \{0.125n \mid n = -N, ...0, 1, ...2N\}$, given $N = r_n$ and for all our simulations $P_n = \bar{x}_n = r_n = 8$.

5 Simulation Results

5.1 The 8-3-8 encoder

We utilise the 8-3-8 encoder of Hinton et. al. [11], which they used for their research into the Boltzmann machine, it is a simple abstraction of the recurring task of communicating information among various components of a parallel network. We use this to benchmark the learning algorithms, because it is clear what the optimal solution is and it is non-trivial to discover it.

The encoder is made up of two groups of visible units, designated $v1$ and $v2$, representing the two systems that wish to communicate their states. It should be noted, that the $v1$ units are passive, just used to communicate their inputs to the next layer of the encoder. Each group has V units. In the simple formulation we consider here, $v1$ and $v2$ are not directly connected but both are connected to a group of H hidden units, with $H < V$, so h may act as a limited capacity channel through which information about $v1$ must be transmitted with optimal coding. In all our simulations we begin by setting all the site values at the start of the training to $S_\mu = 0$, then $\sigma(S_\mu) = 0.5$, giving $P(Y = 1 \mid \mu) = 0.5$, i.e. 50% probability of the output Y obtaining a value "1", i.e. no prior information has been bestowed on the network. Hence finding a solution to such a problem requires that the two visible groups come to agree upon the meaning of a set of codes without any prior conventions for communicating through h.

5.2 Experimental Delimitations

The results presented show a graph of the error $\bar{e}_o$ where

$$\bar{e}_o = \frac{1}{N_{th}} \sum_{n=1}^{n=N_{th}} \frac{1}{N_p} \sum_{k=1}^{k=N_p} e_o \tag{14}$$

is the average error over $N_{tn} = 100$ trained networks, after 6000 training cycles have elapsed, over all N_p training patterns, where e_o is the mean-squared output error (7) of each training vector. The training vector set used were hexidecimal numbers $\{F0, 78, 3C, 1E, 0F, 87, C3, E1\}$, hence $N_p = 8$. The training set was randomly ordered for each sample and a different seed was given to the stochastic operator of the net at the start of each training session. The training vectors each have four adjacent set-bits. This means that there are 192 valid codes, which represent 0.0011% of all possible code solutions. For all the experiments $\rho = 0.3$, $\lambda = 0.0$, $S_m \in [-10, +10]$ and $P_n = \bar{x}_n = r_n = 8$.

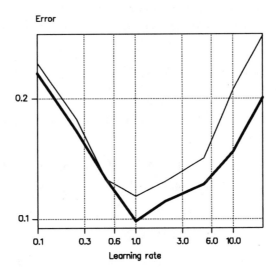

Figure 1   Average log error $\bar{e}_o$ versus log α, for Sigma-pi based 838-encoder with 8 training vectors having four set-bits. (The graph shows the average error $\bar{e}_o$, over 100 nets, after the networks have been trained for 6000 cycles. The lighter solid line shows the error for the standard scalar $r \in [0, 1]$ Reinforcement A_{R-P}. The heavy solid line shows the error for the unbounded internal reinforcement $-1.0 \le r_{(}t)^* \le +2.0$.)

The plot of log error $\bar{e}_o$ against log α is shown in Figure 1. The learning rates used were $\alpha = 0.1, 0.25, 0.5, 1.0, 2.0, 5.0, 10.0$ & 20.0 . The graph shows that unbounded A_{R-P} reduces the average percentage error over all eight learning rates, when compared with standard A_{R-P}, by 10%.

6   Concluding Remarks

The unbounded Reinforcement Associative Reward Penalty A_{R-P} gives increased efficiency of training when compared to the standard A_{R-P}. This we hypothesize is due to the fact that the unbounded reward signal is able to reward/penalise the net to a higher degree. If, for example, the external reward is a penalty signal and the temporal difference between the predictions is a negative quantity (i.e. $P_{v(t)} < P_{v(t-1)}$), then the internal reinforcement is reduced, and the net is then penalised to a greater degree. The converse is also true, as the internal Reinforcement would be increased if the external Reinforcement signal is a reward and the temporal difference between the predictions is positive (i.e. $P_{v(t)} > P_{v(t-1)}$). It is of interest to note that the unbounded A_{R-P} training methodology permits penalisation of the net even when the penalty coefficient is set to zero, as the internal reward signal may be negative, normally the net is only penalised if the penalty coefficient λ is non-zero.

References

[1] M.L. Minskey and S.A. Papert. *Perceptrons: An Introduction to Computational Geometry.* The MIT Press, 1969. ISBN 0-26263111-3.

[2] A.G. Barto and M.I. Jordan. Gradient following without back-propagation in layered networks. In *Proceedings 1st IEEE Conference on Neural Networks*, pages II.629–II.636. IEEE, 1987.

[3] K.N. Gurney. Training nets of hardware realizable sigma-pi units. *Neural Networks*, 5:289–303, 1992.

[4] D. Gorse and J.G. Taylor. A continuous input ram-based stochastic neural model. *Neural Networks*, 4:657–665, 1991.

[5] I. Aleksander. Canonical neural nets based on logic nodes. In *1st IEE International Conference on Artificial Neural Networks*, pages 110–114, 1989.

[6] I. Aleksander. Weightless neural tools: Towards cognitive macrostructures. In *CAIP Neural Network Workshop*, New Jersey, 1990. Rutgers University.

[7] G.E. Hinton D.H. Ackley and T.J. Sejnowski. A learning algorithm for boltzmann machines. *Cognitive Science*, 9:147–169, 1985.

[8] R.S. Sutton A.G. Barto and C.W. Anderson. Neuronlike adaptive elements that can solve difficult learning problems. *IEEE Transactions on systems, man, and cybernetics*, SMC-13(5):834–846, September/October 1983.

[9] P.J. Werbos. *Handbook of Intelligent Control: Neural, Fuzzy and Adaptive Approaches*, chapter Approximate Dynamic Programming for real-time control and neural modelling, pages 493–525. Van Nostrand, USA, 1992. ISBN 0-442-30857-4.

[10] C.E. Myers. *Learning with delayed Reinforcment in an Exploratory Probabilistic Logic Neural Network.* PhD thesis, Imperial College of Science, The University of London, Department of Electrical Engineering, 1990.

[11] T.J. Sejnowski G.E. Hinton and D.H. Ackley. Boltzmann machines: Constraint satisfaction networks that learn. Technical Report CMU-CS-84-119, Carnegie Mellon University, Pittsburgh, PA, 1984.

Fuzzy encoding as a preprocessing method for artificial neural networks

N. Pizzi and R. L. Somorjai
Institute for Biodiagnostics
National Research Council Canada
435 Ellice Avenue, Winnipeg, MB, Canada, R3B 2Y6

ABSTRACT

Fuzzy encoding is the process of determining the respective degrees to which a datum belongs to a collection of fuzzy sets and subsequently using these membership grades in place of the original datum. This procedure is similar to 1-of-n intervalization encoding except that gradual transitions occur at interval boundaries.

This paper examines the efficacy of fuzzy encoding the input data presented to artificial neural networks employing the back-propagation algorithm. A general problem is described and defined in two, three, four, and twenty dimensions. Performance results obtained from two groups of trained artificial neural networks are compared and contrasted: one group used non-encoded data and the other used the corresponding fuzzy encoded data. The networks using the fuzzy encoded data consistently attained superior classification rates compared to their non-encoded counterparts. Moreover, these results were achieved using significantly fewer iterations.

Finally, performance results obtained using this process on a set of "real-world" data, namely, 1-dimensional magnetic resonance spectra of thyroid biopsies, are discussed and compared with results obtained using other techniques. Once again, the fuzzy encoded networks outperformed the corresponding non-encoded networks. However, when some conventional enhancements were made to the networks, the performance of the non-encoded networks improved appreciably while the fuzzy-encoded networks suffered some performance degradations.

1. INTRODUCTION

The artificial neural network (ANN) paradigm has consistently demonstrated its effectiveness as a robust classification technique. The back-propagation network (BPN) [1] has served as a workhorse and a touchstone for many fruitful inquiries. This paper investigates the utility of fuzzy encoding as a preprocessing method for BPNs.

The BPN architecture that is used in this investigation has the following characteristics. The transfer function, tr, is the logistic function,

$$tr(x) = (1 + e^{-x})^{-1} \tag{1}$$

and the global error function, E, is

$$E = 0.5 \sum_k ((d_k - o_k)^2) \tag{2}$$

where the d_k's and o_k's are the respective components of the desired and actual outputs and the weight changes are calculated using the standard gradient descent strategy

$$\Delta w_{ji}^{[l]} = -\alpha (\partial E / \partial w_{ji}^{[l]}) \tag{3}$$

where α, the learning coefficient, is set to 0.9. No momentum term is used.

Fuzzy set theory is an extension of Boolean set theory developed by Zadeh [2]. Fuzzy encoding involves taking a single input value and intervalizing it across a collection of fuzzy sets, thereby producing a list of degrees of membership for each of the fuzzy sets. In other words, if we have n fuzzy sets and f_i is the membership function for the ith fuzzy set then the list of values for an input value x is $\{f_1(x), f_2(x), ..., f_n(x)\}$. Selecting intervals for the fuzzy sets is usually an experimental or heuristic process and is similar to the techniques used in standard 1-of-n intervalization encodings. The purpose of intervalization is to reduce the effects of noise in the data as well as to transform the problem in such a way that a non-linear regression model such as BPN can provide better solutions. The fuzzy membership functions are easily defined once the intervals have been selected because the definition corresponds to 1-of-n intervalization with the addition of gradual transitions at the respective interval boundaries.

2. THE CLASSIFICATION PROBLEM

Data were generated that fell into two classes: those points that were bounded by a set of hyperplanes and those that were outside the region. Figure 1a illustrates the problem in two dimensions. A point, (x_1, x_2), is considered to be class 1 if $-0.75 < x_1 < 0.75$ and $-0.75 < x_2 < 0.75$, otherwise, it belongs to class 0. Four lines, H1 through H4, perfectly separate the two classes. For an n-dimensional problem, a point $(x_1, x_2, ..., x_n)$ is considered to be class 1 if $-0.75 < x_i < 0.75$ for all i=1, 2, ..., n or class 0 otherwise. Further, 2n hyperplanes will perfectly separate the two classes. In the ideal case, a BPN will find the 2n hyperplanes. It should be noted that (at least) 2n processing elements (PEs) in the hidden layer are needed, corresponding to the 2n hyperplanes.

However, in practice a BPN may not find these hyperplanes. Figure 1b illustrates a suboptimal solution for the 2-dimensional problem using three lines. In this case, one of two events will have occurred: one of the hidden PEs will have weights that are similar to one of the other three PEs in the hidden layer (in which case it will duplicate the functionality of the other PE); or, the weights of one of the PEs are near zero in which case it contributes negligibly to the outcome. It should be noted that even when only three hyperplanes are used, a BPN may converge to a point where a majority of the vectors will be correctly classified. However, this benefit may also be considered a disadvantage – when it begins to converge to a solution, a BPN is not able to escape from the associated local minimum to determine if better solutions exist. This is a result of the gradient descent strategy — the error cannot increase, thus when the algorithm begins to converge towards a solution it cannot diverge from it.

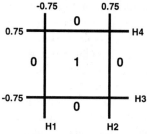
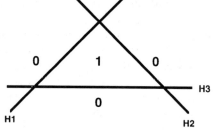

Figure 1: a) The Problem in Two Dimensions   b) A Non-Ideal Solution

3. CONVENTIONAL ENHANCEMENTS TO THE BPN

A number of enhancements may be made to BPNs that: increase the rate of convergence; increase robustness; or improve the accuracy of the final results [3]. Using the hyperbolic tangent function as the transfer function instead of the logistic function typically improves the performance of a BPN. The transfer function's output is a multiplier in the weight update formula. The logistic function's range of [0, 1] may cause a bias towards learning larger values. However, the hyperbolic tangent function is bipolar, hence this will not occur. A gain term, g, may also be introduced into the sigmoid,

$$tr(x) = (1 + e^{-xg})^{-1} \qquad (4)$$

A large gain value may increase the rate of convergence but at the same time makes the BPN more susceptible to pitted error surfaces and may cause wild oscillations during learning.

Different learning and momentum rates may be used for each layer and/or after each of a set of predetermined number of iterations. A typical scenario is to use large learning and momentum values for the initial layers and/or the initial sets of iterations and successively smaller values for subsequent layers and/or sets of iterations. The end effect of this modulated learning strategy is to search for gross data features at the initial layers and/or during the initial sets of iterations and successively refine these detected features by subsequent layers and/or sets of iterations.

A number of preprocessing techniques may also be applied to the data before presentation to a BPN. Data may be scaled and normalized in order to avoid saturation of the sigmoid by large input values (with respect to other input values). Uniform or gaussian noise may also be added to the ANN in order to make the system more robust. Principal component analysis may be performed. Fuzzy encoding falls into the preprocessing category of enhancements and its efficacy will be examined in section 6.

4. IDEAL SOLUTIONS

Figure 1a suggests that the ideal solution for the n-dimensional problem requires exactly 2n hyperplanes. If a step function is used as the transfer function

$$tr(x) = \begin{cases} 1, x > 0 \\ 0, x \le 0 \end{cases} \qquad (5)$$

then the solution is straightforward. For each dimension, i, we have a pair of hidden PEs corresponding to the pair of hyperplanes used for that dimension. The weights for the corresponding coordinate, x_i, are set to 1. The weights are set to 0 for the remaining coordinates. The weight value between the first PE and the output node is 1 and -1 for the second. The bias for the first PE is 0.75 and -0.75 for the second. Finally, the bias for the output PE is -(n-e), where e is a small real. If x_i is bounded by the corresponding hyperplanes then the sum of the pair of PEs is large, otherwise, it tends towards 0. If all coordinates, x_1, x_2, ..., x_n, are bounded by their respective hyperplanes then the sum of the outputs of the 2n hyperplanes is large.

Of course, a BPN cannot use the step function as a transfer function because the gradient descent strategy requires a differentiable transfer function. Moreover, because the logistic function produces continuous values between 0 and 1, it smoothes the output values instead of providing a discrete, non-continuous jump from 0 to 1. The smoothing nature of the sigmoid tends to affect the results such that data points near the boundaries become misclassified. One way to compensate for this is to use a gain term with the logistic function. As the gain term approaches infinity the logistic function tends towards a step function. Unfortunately, large gain terms usually cause the BPNs to wildly oscillate. However, if we use the logistic function without any gain, we can still get an ideal solution if we change the bias values and input weights for the hidden PEs (figure 2). In fact, the larger values (two orders of magnitude) tend to produce the same results as those where a large gain term is used. The advantage, though, is that this approach does not tend to cause wild oscillations.

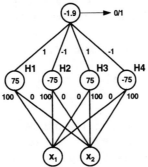

Figure 2: An Ideal 2D Solution Using the Logistic Function

5. FUZZY ENCODED BPNS

In the experiments, four triangular fuzzy sets were selected at intervals of [-1,-0.5], [-0.5,0], [0,0.5], and [0.5, 1], respectively. The fuzzy membership functions are:

$$f_1(x) = 0 \vee (1 - 2|x+.75|), \quad f_2(x) = 0 \vee (1 - 2|x+.25|), \quad f_3(x) = 0 \vee (1 - 2|x-.25|), \quad f_4(x) = 0 \vee (1 - 2|x-.75|) \quad (6)$$

where x is the input, and $\vee$ and $\wedge$ are the *max* and *min* operators, respectively. Figure 3 shows the architecture of a fuzzy encoded BPN comparable to the non-encoded BPN shown in figure 2. Additional runs were made using 8 triangular fuzzy sets for each input value (see section 6). It is fairly straightforward to derive a formula to generate a collection of fuzzy membership functions. First, select the number of fuzzy sets, n, that are to be used. Let l_i be the left boundary and r_i the right boundary of the ith fuzzy set. Let b be the boundary value at the intersection of the fuzzy sets. For simplicity, b is constant for each intersection. Let w be the width of the top of the trapezoid of the fuzzy sets. Finally, let x be the non-encoded input value. Then,

$$f_i(x) = 1 \wedge (0 \vee (1 + w - 2 \frac{1+w-b}{r_i - l_i}|x - 0.5(l_i + r_i)|)) \quad (7)$$

It should be noted that if w=0 then the f_i's correspond to triangular fuzzy sets (see figure 4).

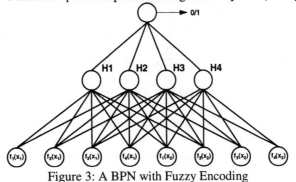

Figure 3: A BPN with Fuzzy Encoding

When b is at least 0.5 then there exists a strict 1–1 correspondence between the fuzzy encoding and the original input value. Since a particular fuzzy encoding can be produced by only one input value, the fuzzy encoding of the data does not change the nature of the problem. If b is less than 0.5 then we have a 1–many correspondence and the information content of the fuzzy encoding is reduced and hence the nature of the problem is changed. Furthermore, because of the relationship across each fuzzy set, the encoding does not introduce any extra degrees of freedom into the problem. As a matter of fact, there are situations when the dimensionality of our specific problem can be reduced. Also, even though more connections are introduced into the BPN than with the associated NE experiments, no additional data are required to train it.

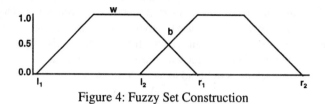

Figure 4: Fuzzy Set Construction

6. EXPERIMENTAL DETAILS

The generated data were neither scaled nor normalized. For each specific n-dimensional problem, one hidden layer was used that contained 2n PEs. After some initial trials, the number of iterations was fixed for each set of experiments in order to more accurately compare the performance of a BPN using non-encoded (NE) data versus the corresponding BPN using fuzzy encoded (FE) data.

The data range for the classification problem is [-1, 1] and is discretized in intervals of 0.1. Apart from ensuring that vectors were randomly selected from the entire pool, the overriding constraint was to ensure that there was an equal number of class 0 and class 1 vectors in the training sets. For each 2-, 3-, 4-, and 20-dimensional case, 100 training and testing sets were generated in order to provide a more statistically accurate set of observations. Each set was then fuzzy-encoded and paired with its corresponding non-encoded set. For each experiment, a fixed number of iteration was used. After the training phase stopped, the test sets were run through the BPNs to determine how well they performed. The weights were also recorded for subsequent analysis. For purposes of this discussion, some representative experiment pairs were selected from the 2--dimensional cases.

In the 2-dimensional case, the NE version of experiment 87 (figure 5a) that yielded perfect classifications, is very similar in structure to the BPN found in figure 3. That is, the relative magnitudes are similar and the signs identical for each respective weight and bias value. This suggests that each hidden PE corresponds to a unique and significant hyperplane. The NE version of experiment 31 (figure 5b) produced an accuracy rate of 86%. Note that the PE, H4 (shaded), contributed little to the final outcome. In this case only three hyperplanes are used thereby degrading overall performance. The NE version of experiment 23 produced poor results. This is to be expected since three of the hidden PEs duplicate the functionality of the remaining hidden PE and this implies that only one hyperplane is used. In the FE versions of all the experiments, perfect results were achieved. The structures of the corresponding BPNs suggest that the information content is more uniformly distributed through each BPN.

Tables 1i–iv list the overall classification rates (averaged over 100 runs) and the iteration count for several different experiments. In all cases the FE BPNs that used four fuzzy sets attained their classification rates with an iteration count of roughly an order of magnitude less than their NE counterparts. Moreover, when eight fuzzy sets were used an additional order of magnitude reduction in the number of iterations was achieved. These significant reductions do not precisely translate to corresponding increases in speed because there are roughly 4 times the number of computations that have to be performed for the FE BPNs using four fuzzy sets (8 times for the FE BPNs using 8 fuzzy sets). Nevertheless, taking this fact into account, the FE BPNs performance were still many times better. It should also be noted that when 8 fuzzy sets were used the FE BPNs were somewhat sensitive to overtraining. That is, as the iteration count increased, their performance with respect to classification success was slightly degraded.

Table 1i clearly indicates that the FE BPNs outperformed their NE BPNs counterparts for the 2-, 3-, 4-, and 20-dimensional cases.

Table 1ii lists performance results when varying amounts of gaussian noise were added to the first coordinate of the 2-dimensional data sets. The FE BPNs produced comparable or more accurate classifications with far fewer iterations. It should also be noted however that NE BPNs tended to produced better results than their noise-free counterparts. This suggests that the introduction of noise is indeed a useful enhancement to BPNs.

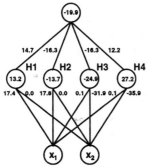
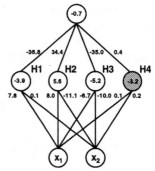

Figure 5: a) NE BPN with Four Hyperplanes   b) NE BPN with Three Hyperplanes

The distribution of the training data in all of the previous experiments was uniform. Additional experiments were run for the 2-dimensional case to determine how well the two types of networks performed if the training data were not uniformly distributed. Training data were carefully reselected to ensure non-uniform distributions: two distinct bimodal distributions and two distinct skewed distributions. Results in table 1iii indicate that FE BPNs again consistently outperformed NE BPNs and with far fewer iterations.

		NE	Iters	FE-4	Iters	FE-8	Iters
i) 2	dimensions	86	300	100	50	100	5
3	dimensions	83	600	100	100	99	10
4	dimensions	90	2000	100	200	99	100
20	dimensions	85	5000	98	500	98	200
ii) 2D	Noise (5%)	100	400	99	90	99	9
	Noise (10%)	99	400	99	90	99	9
	Noise (20%)	81	400	99	90	98	9
	Noise (30%)	92	1500	92	400	97	50
	Noise (40%)	88	1500	90	400	90	50
iii) 2D	Bimodal I	39	2000	97	60	99	5
	Bimodal II	95	2000	92	60	98	5
	Skewed I	80	2000	100	60	97	5
	Skewed II	87	2000	100	60	97	5
iv)	Choline I	64	1400	92	3	84	0.1
	Lipid I	80	4000	88	5	88	0.4
v)	Choline II	96	600	96	10	76	1
	Lipid II	100	2000	92	25	80	3

Table 1: Classification Results (as percentages) averaged over 100 runs
(FE-4=fuzzy-encoded data using 4 fuzzy sets, NE=non-encoded data
FE-8=fuzzy-encoded data using 8 fuzzy sets, Iters=number of iterations (x1,000))

7. A REAL-WORLD PROBLEM

One-dimensional magnetic resonance (MR) spectra were obtained at 360 MHz for 25 thyroid biopsies: 16 papillary carcinomas and 9 normal. Two spectral regions were analyzed: the main lipid CH_2 and CH_3 peaks, 0.64–2.59 ppm; and the choline-like species, 2.59–3.41 ppm. Analysis was based on 170 input points for the choline region and 400 input points for the lipid region. It has been demonstrated in [4] that an ANN can be constructed that produces a robust classification of thyroid biopsies given their MR spectra. The inputs to the ANN were the ten best principal components of the original data that accounted for 97% of the total variance. In this paper, BPNs using the original spectral regions are used without any preprocessing (principal component analysis) and compared with BPNs using the corresponding FE spectral regions. Twenty experiments were run for each case described below. Unlike the results discussed previously that were based solely on the test data, the average performance results listed in tables 2iv–v are based on all of the data (due to the scarcity of the data).

Four fuzzy sets were constructed for each input coordinate and the FE data were generated (680 and 1600 input points for the choline and lipid regions, respectively). In order to effect uniform coverage, quartiles were computed for each coordinate and the fuzzy sets were constructed around them (see figure 6). The intersection, b, was set to 0.5 for all sets. Subsequently, eight fuzzy sets were constructed by dividing each quartile in half. Table 2iv lists the performance results. Once again FE BPNs outperformed their NE counterparts. What is particularly surprising is the rate of convergence for the FE BPNs (for instance, the NE BPNs used to classify the lipid regions are 800 times slower than the corresponding NE BPNs).

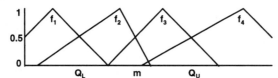

Figure 6: Fuzzy Sets for Magnetic Resonance Data

Finally, comparisons were made using BPNs with some enhancements: momentum term; modulated learning; hyperbolic tangent function instead of the logistic function; and data scaling. In this case, the FE BPNs using four fuzzy sets performed as well as their NE BPN counterparts for the choline region but slightly poorer results were obtained for the lipid region (table 2v). Although convergence still occurred much more quickly with the FE BPNs, the NE BPNs converged approximately twice as quickly with enhancements as without, whereas the FE BPNs converged roughly 3–5 times more slowly. Moreover, when 8 fuzzy sets were used, the overall classification rates were significantly poorer. Since data scaling occurred after the data were fuzzy encoded, the information content of the FE data may have actually changed, thereby affecting the nature of the problem. It was noted that when at least one of the BPN enhancements was deactivated, the FE BPNs performance results approached those found in the FE BPNs without any enhancements. This sensitivity of FE data to conventional BPN enhancements warrants further study.

8. FUTURE ACTIVITIES

A number of research activities need to be pursued to further test the effectiveness of fuzzy encoding, not the least of which is further experimentation employing "real-world" data. Trapezoidal fuzzy sets may be used to determine if they are of any additional benefit. The 1–1 correspondence is lost and this will affect the information content of the input values but the resulting BPN may become more robust. Further analysis is required concerning the sensitivity of FE data to BPN enhancements. Methods, other than uniform coverage per input unit, need to be examined for the selection of the type and number of fuzzy sets. For example, a clustering method such as fuzzy c-means [5] or Kohonen self-organizing maps [6] may be used to intervalize the data.

This paper has demonstrated the efficacy of fuzzy encoding input data for artificial neural networks that employ the back-propagation algorithm. Compared to their NE counterparts, FE BPNs consistently produced superior classification results with dramatically improved rates of convergence. Additional areas of inquiry need to be examined, especially employing "real-world" data, but the initial results are extremely promising. In particular, since the volume of MR spectral data used for clinical diagnosis is growing rapidly, a variety of multivariate techniques such as ANNs need to be used in order to quickly and accurately classify them. Fuzzy encoding should be considered as another tool in this arsenal.

9. REFERENCES

1. Rumelhart, D. E. and McClelland, J. L., Parallel Distributed Processing, vol. 1, MIT Press, Mass., 1986.
2. Zadeh, L. A., "Outline of a new approach to the analysis of complex systems and decision processes", IEEE Transactions on Systems, Man and Cybernetics, SMC-1, 1973, pp. 28–44.
3. Lippmann, R. P., "An introduction to computing with neural networks", IEEE ASSP Mag., April 1987, 4–22.
4. Somorjai, R. L. Pizzi, N., Nikulin, A., Jackson, R., Mountford, C. E., Russell, P, Lean, C. L., Debridge, L., Smith, I. C. P., "Thryoid Neoplasms: Classification by Means of Consensus Multivariate Analysis of ^{1}H MR Spectra", 12th Annual Scientific Meeting of the Society of Magnetic Resonance in Medicine, New York, 1993.
5. J. C. Bezdek, R. Ehrlich, and W. Full, "FCM: the fuzzy c-means clustering algorithm", *Computers and Geosciences*, vol. 10, 1984, 191–203.
6. Kohonen, T., Self-Organization and Associative Memory, Springer-Verlag, New York, 1989.

Improving Generalization with Symmetry Constraints

by

N. Scott Cardell, Wayne H. Joerding, and Ying Li
Washington State University, Pullman, WA 99164

Abstract[1]

This paper presents research on the benefits of using *a priori* information about the symmetry of cross-partial derivatives to improve generalization. We show how to impose the symmetry constraint on a global training algorithm and demonstrate its efficacious use with a problem in economics.

1. Introduction

This paper presents preliminary results from our research into imposing *a priori* information on feedforward neural networks. We take as an example the imposition of symmetry constraints suitable when using a feedforward network to approximate a system of nonlinear equations derived as the gradient of some known or unknown function. This problem can arise in many fields. For example, in geology detection of magnetic anomalies depends on the gradient of a gravitational potential function. In economics, the condition for profit maximization sets the gradient of the production function equal to the real input prices. In electrical engineering, the non-linear behavior of a MOSFET device depends on the gradient of the device response function with respect to drain and gate source voltages. In each of these cases observations on the gradient of a non-linear response function can represent important, or even the only, information about the phenomena of interest, such as in the magnetic anomaly example.

The universal approximation capabilities of feedforward networks make them good candidates for a semi-nonparametric approach to modeling non-linear functions, but traditional implementations ignore *a priori* information about the problem implied by the symmetry of cross-partial derivatives. In this paper, we show how to impose symmetry constraints and demonstrate their usefulness in an example taken from economics.

2. Symmetry in gradient vector equations

Let $\psi^* : \mathbb{R}^{k_0} \to \mathbb{R}$ represent a twice differentiable function of k_0 inputs, and $\Psi^*(\mathbf{x}) \equiv \nabla \psi^*(\mathbf{x})$ its k_0 dimensional gradient vector. If we were to observe a sample $(o_n, \mathbf{x}_n)$, where $o_n = \psi^*(\mathbf{x}_n) + e_n$, $n = 1, \ldots, N$, e_n a mean zero noise term, then we could use the data to train a network to approximate the unknown function *and* its derivatives on a compact set (see, for example, Hornik, Stinchcombe, and White (1989, 1990)). Sometimes, however, we do not observe a number o_n, but instead observe a vector $\mathbf{y}_n = \Psi^*(\mathbf{x}_n) + \mathbf{e}_n$ where $\mathbf{e}_n$ represents a vector of mean zero noise terms. In other cases we observe both o_n and $\mathbf{y}_n$.

---

[1]This research was partially funded by National Science Foundation Grant No. SES-9022773.

In either of these cases, approximating the unknown response functions ψ and/or Ψ can benefit from using the *a priori* information that the Hessian matrix for $\psi^*(\mathbf{x})$, defined by the $k_0 \times k_0$ Jacobian $\nabla \Psi^*(\mathbf{x})$, must be a $k_0 \times k_0$ *symmetric* matrix. In other words, the symmetry of cross-partial derivatives defines a property that a network approximation of $\Psi^*(\mathbf{x})$ should also satisfy.

In this paper we consider using a single hidden layer feedforward network to approximate Ψ when one only observes $\mathbf{y}_n$.[2] Let $\Psi(\mathbf{x})$ represent a feedforward network with k_0 inputs, $k_2 = k_0$ outputs, and connection weights W. We seek to approximate $\Psi^* : \mathbb{X} \to \mathbb{R}^{k_0}$ for some set $\mathbb{X} \subset \mathbb{R}^{k_0}$ using the network Ψ. The above reasoning demonstrates that we should require $\Psi(\mathbf{x})$ to satisfy symmetry for all $\mathbf{x} \in \mathbb{X}$. We define $\Psi(\mathbf{x}) \equiv W_1 F(W_0 \mathbf{x})$ as a single hidden layer network with k_1 hidden units and connection weights $W = (W_0, W_1)$, where the W_i's represent $k_{i+1} \times k_i$ weight matrices, $\mathbf{F}(W_0 \mathbf{x}) \equiv (f(\mathbf{w}_{0,1} \mathbf{x}), \ldots, f(\mathbf{w}_{0,k_1} \mathbf{x}))^\top$, a vector of activation functions, and $\mathbf{w}_{0,h}$ represents the hth row of W_0. Let $w_{k,\ell,i}$ represent the (ℓ, i) element of W_k, $f' \equiv \frac{\partial f(z)}{\partial z}$ and $f_i' \equiv f'(\mathbf{w}_{0,i} \mathbf{x})$ for some $\mathbf{x} \in \mathbb{X}$. Then

$$
\begin{aligned}
\nabla \Psi(\mathbf{x}) &= \mathbf{F}'(W_0 \mathbf{x}) W_1^\top, \quad \text{where} \quad \mathbf{F}' \equiv \frac{\partial \mathbf{F}}{\partial \mathbf{x}} \\
&= \begin{pmatrix} f_1' \mathbf{w}_{0,1}^\top & f_2' \mathbf{w}_{0,2}^\top & \cdots & f_{k_1}' \mathbf{w}_{0,k_1}^\top \end{pmatrix} W_1^\top \\
&= W_0^\top \begin{pmatrix} f_1' & 0 & \cdots & 0 \\ 0 & f_2' & \cdots & 0 \\ \vdots & \vdots & \ddots & \vdots \\ 0 & 0 & \cdots & f_{k_1}' \end{pmatrix} W_1^\top.
\end{aligned} \tag{1}
$$

Let $\psi_{ij}(\mathbf{x})$ define the (i, j) term of $\nabla \Psi(\mathbf{x})$. Then

$$
\psi_{ij}(\mathbf{x}) = \sum_{\ell=1}^{k_1} w_{0,\ell,i} f'(\mathbf{w}_{0,\ell} \mathbf{x}) w_{1,j,\ell}. \tag{2}
$$

Therefore symmetry requires that

$$
\psi_{ji}(\mathbf{x}) - \psi_{ij}(\mathbf{x}) = \sum_{\ell=1}^{k_1} f'(\mathbf{w}_{0,\ell} \mathbf{x})[w_{0,\ell,j} w_{1,i,\ell} - w_{0,\ell,i} w_{1,j,\ell}] = 0 \tag{3}
$$

for $i = 1, \ldots, k_0 - 1$ and $j = i + 1, \ldots, k_0$. We can express the $\frac{k_0(k_0-1)}{2}$ constraints defined by (3) more compactly by

$$
\omega_{i,j}^\top \mathbf{F}'(W_0 \mathbf{x}) \equiv 0 \text{ for all } \mathbf{x} \in \mathbb{X} \begin{cases} i = 1, \ldots, k_0 - 1 \\ j = i + 1, \ldots, k_0 \end{cases} \tag{4}
$$

where $\mathbf{F}'(\mathbf{x}) \equiv (f'(\mathbf{w}_{0,1} \mathbf{x}), \ldots, f'(\mathbf{w}_{0,k_1} \mathbf{x}))^\top$ and $\omega_{i,j}$ represents a $k_1 \times 1$ vector of the $[w_{0,\ell,j} w_{1,i,\ell} - w_{0,\ell,i} w_{1,j,\ell}]$ terms from (3).

---

[2] We defer the more general problem in which one observes both o_n and $\mathbf{y}_n$ to future work.

Cardell, Joerding, and Li (1993) show that under fairly general conditions (4) can be satisfied if and only if $\omega_{i,j} \equiv 0$. From the definition of $\omega_{i,j}$ we see that this requires

$$w_{0,\ell,j} w_{1,i,\ell} = w_{0,\ell,i} w_{1,j,\ell} \qquad \text{for} \qquad \begin{cases} \ell &= 1, \ldots, k_1, \\ i &= 1, \ldots, k_0 - 1, \\ j &= i+1, \ldots, k_0. \end{cases} \tag{5}$$

Or, alternatively,

$$w_{1i\ell} = \beta_\ell w_{0\ell i} \qquad \text{for} \qquad \begin{cases} \ell &= 1, \ldots, k_1, \\ i &= 1, \ldots, k_0 \end{cases} \tag{6}$$

for some $k_1 \times 1$ vector of constants $\beta = (\beta_1, \ldots, \beta_{k_1})^\top$.

The universal approximation capabilities of feedforward networks, as described in Carroll and Dickinson (1989), Cybenko (1989), Hornik et al. (1989, 1990), and Ito (1991, 1992), explain much of their usefulness. Thus, we do not want to lose these capabilities when imposing the symmetry constraints described in (6). The Symmetry constraints require satisfying equality conditions, and so pose somewhat more danger of reducing the universal approximation capability than do inequality constraints. (See Gallant Gallant (1982), p307, for an example using inequality constraints.) This derives from the reduced dimension of the function space that satisfies the symmetry constraint. That is, because functions satisfying equality constraints occupy a lower dimension subspace of the unconstrained function space, there may not exist a network that satisfies the symmetry constraint and comes arbitrarily close to any function with a symmetric Hessian matrix. Fortunately, it turns out that networks satisfying the kind of constraints defined in (6) possess the same type of approximation capability described in Hornik et al. (1989, 1990), see Cardell et al. (1993).

Finally, we note that one can use results in Cardell et al. (1993) with the results in White (1990) to show that a constrained network that minimizes the sum of squared errors converges consistently to the gradient system $\nabla \Psi^*(\mathbf{x})$. Thus, there exist appropriate growth rates for the number of hidden units to insure that trained networks converge almost surely to the true gradient system.

3. Training

Training seeks values for the weights that minimize the sum-of-squared errors $SS = \sum_{n=1}^N (\mathbf{y}_n - \Psi(\mathbf{x}_n))^\top (\mathbf{y}_n - \Psi(\mathbf{x}_n))$ subject to the constraints (6). The constraints in (6) provide a straightforward extension for many training methods but especially so for hybrid methods such as described in Li, Joerding, and Genz (1993) or Webb and Lowe (1988). At each iteration these hybrid methods update the W_0 matrix and then solve k_2 systems of overidentified linear equations, $\{y_{i,n} = \mathbf{w}_{1,i}\mathbf{F}(W_0\mathbf{x}_n), n = 1, \ldots, N\}$, $i = 1, \ldots, k_2$ to compute the W_1 weights given W_0.

We can take the same approach to the constrained problem by altering the nature of the linear least squares sub-problem. Specifically, we solve a system of linear equations with the typical equation

$$y_{i,n} = (\beta^\top, \theta^\top)[w_{0,1,i}f(\mathbf{w}_{0,1}\mathbf{x}_n + \mu_1), \ldots, w_{0,k_1,i}f(\mathbf{w}_{0,k_1}\mathbf{x}_n + \mu_{k_1}), I_1(i), \ldots, I_{k_1}(i)]^\top, \tag{7}$$

where $n = 1, \ldots, N$, $i = 1, \ldots, k_2$ and μ_i represents a bias parameter for the ith hidden unit and $\theta = (\theta_1, \ldots, \theta_{k_2})^\top$ represents bias parameters for each of the output units, and $I_1(i), \ldots, I_{k_1}(i)$ form a vector of indicator variables such that $I_h(i) = 1$ if $i = h$, 0 otherwise. Thus, instead of having k_2 systems of equations with N equations each and a total of $k_1(k_0 + 1) + k_2(k_1 + 1)$ parameters, the constrained sub-problem has a single system of $k_2 \times N$ equations and $k_1(k_0 + 1) + k_1 + k_2$ parameters. Since computation time in the sub-problem increases as the square of the number of parameters, each iteration of the constrained algorithm takes more time than the unconstrained algorithm.

4. Example

Presumably, the use of *a priori* information can improve the ability of a network to generalize out of sample. (See Joerding and Meador (1991) for more discussion.) To demonstrate this effect we take an example from our own field of economics. A well-known result in economic theory concludes that a profit-maximizing firm sets the gradient of the production function with respect to factor inputs (such as capital and labor) equal to the real input prices. Sometimes economists do not observe output levels of a firm but do observe input levels and real factor prices. From these data economists can recover some characteristics of the unobserved production process by relating input prices to factor input levels, in other words, by approximating a relationship of the form $\mathbf{y}_n = \Psi^*(\mathbf{x}_n) + \mathbf{e}_n$. To make the best use of expensive data and to improve generalization the network approximator to Ψ^* should satisfy the symmetry constraints described above.

Of course, the *a priori* information must be correct for it to benefit generalization. We also expect *a priori* information to have the most value for small sample sizes. Thus, for our demonstration we generate a modest amount of data from a known data-generating process (DGP) and then seek to approximate that process with various single hidden layer feedforward networks. Specifically we generate 10 different samples of 50 observations each from the gradient of $\psi(\mathbf{x}) \equiv x_1^2 x_2^8$ where x_1 represents capital and x_2 represents labor inputs. The input data come from random selection of points in the square $[1, 20] \times [1, 20]$. We then use these data to train networks with 2,4,6,...,28 hidden units, measuring the approximation error (AE) of the resulting networks by summing the absolute deviation of the network from the true value at each point on a mesh covering the domain of the input data. Lines on the mesh have a .5 spacing.

As noted above, the number of free weights grows more quickly in the unconstrained networks than in the constrained. Thus, we limit training of unconstrained networks to 26 hidden units. This results in the number of free weights varying from 12 to 132 for the unconstrained networks and from 10 to 88 for the constrained. We train the network using a hybrid algorithm based on simulated annealing to find a global minimum to the sum-of-squares function, see Li et al. (1993). Taken together we have 130 observations on the approximation error for unconstrained networks and 140 observations on constrained networks. We then fit these AE values to quadratic and cubic equations in the number of hidden units, H, and the number of free parameters, K. Plots of these fitted polynomials are displayed in Figures 1 and 2. Note, although this is not clear in the picture, the N line lies everywhere above the N_c line in the right side panel of Figure 2. Also, the N cubic lines decline for very low numbers of hidden units and free parameters, an anomaly that does not appear in a quartic polynomial.

The plots show that the symmetry constraint lowers the approximation error almost uniformly and postpones the onset of degraded approximation as the number of hidden units increases. The postponement effect shows up most strongly when plotted against the number of hidden units (left side of figures). Because the number of hidden units is the only complexity control parameter in a feedforward network, this represents an important advantage for constrained networks.

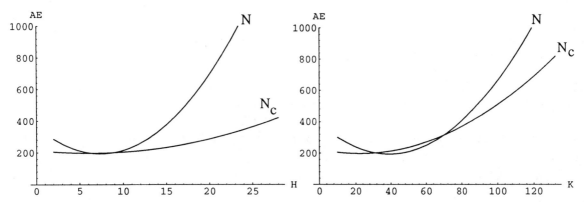

Figure 1: Quadratic approximation of approximation error, AE, for unconstrained N, and constrained, N_c, networks as a function of the number of hidden units, H, and the number of free parameters K.

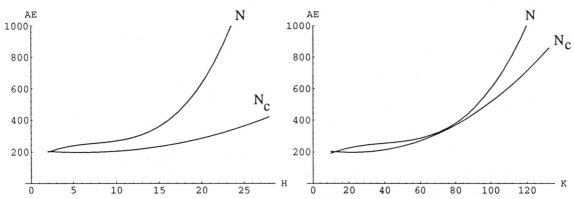

Figure 2: Cubic approximation of approximation error, AE, for unconstrained N, and constrained, N_c, networks as a function of the number of hidden units, H, and the number of free parameters K.

References

Cardell, N. S., Joerding, W. H., & Li, Y. (1993). Symmetry constraints for feedforward network models of gradient systems. Tech. rep., Washington State University, Department of Economics, Pullman, WA 99164.

Carroll, B. W., & Dickinson, B. D. (1989). Construction of neural net using the radon transform. In *Proceedings of the International Joint Conference on Neural Networks*, Vol. I, pp. 607–611.

Cybenko, G. (1989). Approximation by superpositions of a sigmoidal function. *Mathematical Control Signal Systems, 2*.

Gallant, A. (1982). Unbiased determination of production technologies. *Journal of Econometrics, 20*, 285–323.

Hornik, K., Stinchcombe, M., & White, H. (1989). Multilayer feedforward networks are universal approximators. *Neural Networks, 2*, 359–366.

Hornik, K., Stinchcombe, M., & White, H. (1990). Universal approximation of an unknown mapping and its derivatives using multilayer feedforward networks. *Neural Networks, 3*(5), 551–560.

Ito, Y. (1991). Approximation of functions on a compact set by finite sums of a sigmoid function without scaling. *Neural Networks, 4*(6), 817–826.

Ito, Y. (1992). Approximation of continuous functions on $\mathbf{r}^d$ by linear combinations of shifted rotations of a sigmoid function with and without scaling. *Neural Networks, 5*(1), 105–116.

Joerding, W. H., & Meador, J. L. (1991). Encoding a priori information in feedforward networks. *Neural Networks, 4*(6), 847–856.

Li, Y., Joerding, W. H., & Genz, A. (1993). Global estimation of feedforward neural networks with hybrid lls/simulated annealing. In *Proceedings of the World Congress on Neural Networks*, pp. 443–447 New York. IEEE Press.

Webb, A., & Lowe, D. (1988). A hybrid optimization strategy for adaptive feed-forward layered networks. Tech. rep. 4193, Royal Signals and Radar Establishment Memorandum, Ministry of Defence, Malvern, UK.

White, H. (1990). Connectionist nonparametric regression: Multilayer feedforward networks can learn arbitrary mappings. *Neural Networks, 3*(5), 535–549.

The Error Absorption for Fitting an Under-fitting (Skeleton) Net

Zhengrong Yang

Shanghai Institute of Metallurgy, Academia Sinica, 865 ChangNing Rd., Shanghai, 200050, P. R. CHINA

Abstract

The macro and micro mechanism of error absorption have been developed for fitting an under-fitting (skeleton) net in this paper. The theoretic analysis and experimental results are also given in this paper.

1. Introduction

In past few years, a lot of researchers have paid attention to the improvement of the generalisation performance of neural networks. For example, Mozer [1] proposed a skeletonization method at the Colorado University in 1989. He determined the functionality or relevance of individual hidden and input units using the knowledge in the net. His basic idea was training the net to a certain criterion, computing the measurement of relevance, and trimming the least relevant units. Yann [2] developed a method called the "Optimal Brain Damage" at the AT&T Bell Laboratory in 1990. He derived a nearly optimal schemes for adapting the size of a neural network using the information-theoretic ideas. Weigend [3] introduced the information theoretic idea of minimum description length into the weight elimination of the neural network at the Stafford University in 1991. Ramachandran [5] removed the superfluous hidden units based on their information measures, which borrowed from decision tree induction techniques at the Texas University in 1992. Zimmermann [6] designed the active and deactivate test variables for elimination process at the Siemans Coperation in 1992.

All methods mentioned above skeletonized an over-fitting neural network with different measurements. There are two problems associated with them. The first is how to choose an initial (over-fitting) net, which will affect the process of skeletonization. For example, if 100 hidden units is an optimal solution, the initial net with 300 hidden units will have longer process of skeletonization than the initial net with 200 hidden units. In general, it is difficult to choose the suitable initial net, although there were some papers describing how to choose the optimised structure. The second is that there are some abysses and many local minimum's in the training process [7]. If one chooses a larger initial net, there will be larger possibilities that the training sinks into an abyss or sticks at a local minimum such that the final net still has lower generalisation performance.

Sethi [8] has developed a new type of skeleton neural network. This net has no redundant weights for error absorption. If one trains this skeleton net, the generalisation performance will not be higher because of the absence of redundant weights for error absorption. Our experiments have shown that if we train this skeleton net with some added redundant weights, the generalisation performance will be improved to some degree. A skeleton net is called the under-fitting net and the process of adding some redundant weights on the skeleton net is called the fitting process. In this paper, a detail analysis of the error absorption mechanism and the experimental results are presented.

2. The Macro Mechanism of Error Absorption

The mechanism of error absorption is composed by two parts: macro mechanism and micro mechanism. Most back-propagation neural networks use the algorithm proposed by Rumelhart [9] for their weights updating:

$$\Delta \vec{w} \propto \frac{\partial E}{\partial \vec{w}}.$$

The structure information of a net is described as:

$$a_j = f_j(x_j) \qquad x_j = \sum_h w_{hj} a_h$$

$$a_h = f_h(x_h) \qquad x_h = \sum_i w_{ih} a_i \,,$$

where, $A = \{\{a_i\},\{a_h\},\{a_j\}\}$ is the activate-space of the input units, hidden units, and output units, $W = \{\{w_{ih}\},\{w_{hj}\}\}$ is the weight-space of the weights between the input layer and hidden layer and the weights between the hidden layer and output layer, and $F = \{\{f_h\},\{f_j\}\}$ is the function-space of the hidden units and output units. The uniform activate function is the sigmoid function:

$$f_h = f_j = \frac{1}{1 + e^{-\Sigma}}.$$

The deduced weight-updating formulas are:

$$\Delta w_{hj} = \eta \frac{\partial E}{\partial w_{hj}} = \eta \frac{\partial E}{\partial x_j} a_h = \eta \frac{\partial E}{\partial a_j} f_j' a_h$$

$$\Delta w_{ih} = \eta \frac{\partial E}{\partial w_{ih}} = \eta (\sum_j \frac{\partial E}{\partial a_j} f_j' w_{hj}) f_h' a_i \,.$$

From these weight-updating formulas, one can find out that the error occurring at an output unit will be absorbed through the weight-space by the units at the lower layers. In fact, the error occurring at any output unit is synthesised from the units at the lower layers through the weight-space during the forward-propagation. The weight-updating is a back-error propagation process, which propagates the errors occurring at the output units back to the units at the lower layers and modifies the weight-space by the gradient descent method.

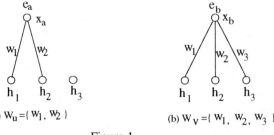

(a) $W_u = \{ w_1, w_2 \}$ (b) $W_v = \{ w_1, w_2, w_3 \}$

Figure 1

Consider a net, which just has one output and two layers as shown in figure 1. In figure 1 (a) the output error e_a is absorbed by the hidden units h_1 and h_2 through the weight-space W_u. While in figure 1 (b), the output error e_b is absorbed by the hidden units h_1, h_2 and h_3 through the weight-space W_v. The activate values of x_a and x_b at the next time step can be obtained as follows:

$$a_{x_a}^{t+1} = f[(w_1 + \Delta w_1)a_{h1} + (w_2 + \Delta w_2)a_{h2}] = \frac{1}{1 + e^{-[\eta \frac{\partial E}{\partial x_a'}(a_{h1}^2 + a_{h2}^2)]} * e^{-\Sigma}} = \frac{1}{1 + k_a * e^{-\Sigma}}$$

$$a^{t+1}_{x_b} = f[(w_1 + \Delta w_1)a_{h1} + (w_2 + \Delta w_2)a_{h2} + (w_3 + \Delta w_3)a_{h3}] = \cfrac{1}{1+e^{-[\eta\frac{\partial E}{\partial x^t_b}(a^2_{h1}+a^2_{h2}+a^2_{h3})]}*e^{-\Sigma}} = \cfrac{1}{1+k_b*e^{-\Sigma}}$$

here, k_a and k_b are weight-independent coefficients. Because of

$$k_b > k_a > 1 \qquad if(\frac{\partial E}{\partial x} < 0)$$

$$k_b < k_a < 1 \qquad if(\frac{\partial E}{\partial x} > 0),$$

then

$$e^{t+1}_b < e^{t+1}_a.$$

That is, the error at x_a will decay faster than at x_a. It can be concluded that larger weight-space can improve the error absorption more than smaller weight-space. This was supported by experimental results shown in figure 2. It is clear from figure 2 that the redundant net (the net with some redundant weights) converges faster than the one without redundant weights. This is called the macro mechanism of error absorption.

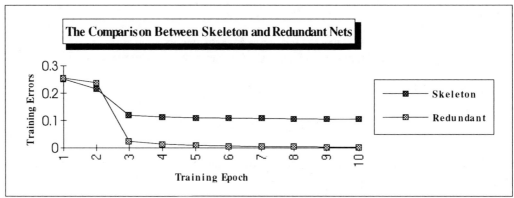

Figure 2

3. The Micro Mechanism of Error Absorption

If there are more than one output units in a net, the output unit with the largest error will have the largest contribution to the net error and, this kind of output unit should be selected for adding redundant weight at first. This is because through the redundant weight, the error at this output unit can be absorbed partially by a unit at the lower layer. After the output unit is chosen, which unit at the lower layer has to be selected to connect to this output unit should be considered. Consider the situation shown in figure 3:

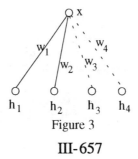

Figure 3

III-657

Given the wanted activate values of h_3 and h_4 are $\hat{a}_{h_3}$ and $\hat{a}_{h_4}$ respectively. If $da_{h_4} > da_{h_3}$, a_{h_4} will have larger deviation from $\hat{a}_{h_4}$, and a_{h_3} will have smaller deviation from $\hat{a}_{h_3}$ (The derivatives on the units at the lower layer can be obtained by BP method). In qualitative view, h_4 has less ability to let the error on x parasite in it or has less ability to absorb the error on x because its error is already larger. In quantitative view, we can deduce a derivation on x:

$$da_x^{t+1}(h_i) = \frac{k_{h_i} * e^{-\Sigma}}{(1 + k_{h_i} * e^{-\Sigma})^2} * (w_i - 2a_{h_i}) * da_{h_i}.$$

Given the approximate condition that there is no big difference among w_i s and among a_{h_i} s. Because of $da_{h_4} > da_{h_3}$, then,

$$da_x^{t+1}(h_3) < da_x^{t+1}(h_4).$$

That is, connecting to the unit with the smallest derivation at the lower layer will result in better error absorption.

4. The Performance Measurements

In this paper, two important measurements used to measure the performance were:

(a) Training Error:

$$TRE = \Sigma (\hat{x} - x)^2,$$

where, $\hat{x}$ is the target output vectors of the training patterns and x is the actual output vectors responding to the input vectors of the training patterns;

(b) Generalisation Performance:

$$GP = (1 - \frac{failures}{total\ tests}) * 100\%,$$

where, the "failures" is the number of the decision failures when a trained net is used for diagnosis or reasoning.

5. Algorithm

The algorithm is shown as follows:

Step 1. Constructing a skeleton net with expert knowledge;
Step 2. Preparing training data and test data;
Step 3. Determining the optimised training parameters;
Step 4. Training;
Step 5. If the generalisation performance is satisfied, goto step 7, else go on;
Step 6. Applying the error absorption into the net, goto step 4;
Step 7. Stop.

6. The Experimental Results

Below, we present three experiments and their simulation results. The first and the last ones are classification problems. The second one is an optimisation problem. All of them have the same characteristic in that the initial skeleton net can be obtained by some expert knowledge.

Figure 4 gives the experimental results of partitioning the plane points into two fields and the problem itself is a XOR problem [8]. Figure 4 (a) presents the simulation result with the error absorption mechanism. Figure 4 (b) gives the simulation result without this mechanism. The fitting epochs are five for both them. Clearly, with the error absorption mechanism, the generalisation performance has increased up to 90%, as shown in figure 4 (a). But without the error absorption mechanism, the generalisation has decreased down to 76%. Meanwhile, the training error decays with the error absorption mechanism more than without the error absorption mechanism. For example, the training error reaches 0.008 in figure 4 (a), while one just reaches 0.017 in figure 4 (b). Figure 5 shows the results of finding a minimum value among some values. Figure 5 (a) and (b) illustrate the simulation results with and without the error absorption mechanism respectively. The fitting epochs are six both for them. In figure 5 (a), the total tendency of generalisation performance has increased up to 98.5%, while in figure 5 (b), the generalisation performance oscillations greatly. Figure 6 presents the same experiment as figure 4, but with the momentum factor in the net. Figure 6 (a) and (b) present the simulation results with and without the error absorption mechanism respectively. Because of the function of momentum, the difference is smaller between the methods with and without the error absorption mechanism. However, adding momentum factor means increasing the computational cost and space cost.

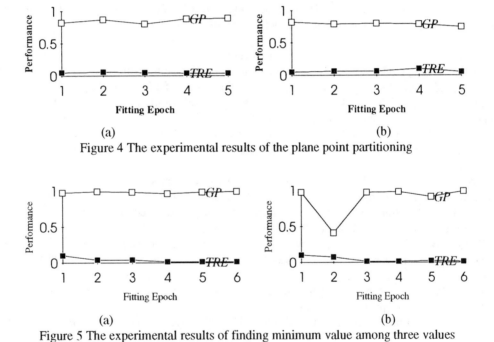

(a)   (b)

Figure 4 The experimental results of the plane point partitioning

(a)   (b)

Figure 5 The experimental results of finding minimum value among three values

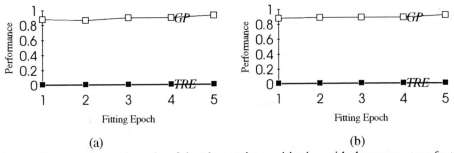

(a)   (b)

Figure 6 The experimental results of the plane point partitioning with the momentum factor

7. Conclusion

This paper has presented a new method for improving the generalisation performance of neural networks. The mechanism of error absorption was developed for fitting an under-fitting (skeleton) net. The experimental results have shown that it is very useful for one type of problems. where the initial skeleton net can be constructed by the expert knowledge, and the training technique is used to overcome the drawback of incomplete knowledge of expert. With this new method, sinking into the abyss can be avoided and the generalisation performance improvement time is obviously reduced.

Acknowledgement

*The author would like to thank **Professor G. Musgrave** (head of dept. of EE & E, brunel university) for his guidance and thank **Dr. Richard Neville and Mr Thomas A. Tawiah** (dept. of EE & E, brunel university) for their kindly discussion and support about this research.*

Reference

1. Michael C. Mozer, Paul Smolensky, "Skeletonization: a technique for trimming the fat from a network via relevance assessment", Advances in Neural Information Processing Systems, Vol. 1, 1989, pp107-115

2. Yann Le Cun, John S. Denker, Sara A. Solla, "Optimal Brain Damage", Advances in Neural Information Processing Systems, Vol. 2, 1990, pp598-605

3. Andreas S. Weigend, David E. Rumelhart, Bernardo A. Huberman, "Generalisation by weight-elimination with application to forecasting", Advances in Neural Information Processing Systems, Vol. 3, 1991, pp875-882

4. Anders Krogh, John A. Hertz, "A simple weight decay can improve generalisation", Advances in Neural Information Processing Systems, Vol. 4, 1992, pp950-957

5. Sowmya Ramachandran, Lorien Y. Pratt, "Information measure based skeletonization", Advances in Neural Information Processing Systems, Vol. 4, 1992, pp1080-1087

6. F. Hergert, W. Finnoff, H. G. Zimmermann, "A comparison of weight elimination methods for reducing complexity in neural networks", 1992 International Joint Conference on Neural Networks, ppIII-980-987

7. Sankar K. Pal, et al, "Multilayer perceptron, fuzzy sets, and classification",, IEEE trans. on neural networks, vol. 3, no. 5, September 1992, pp683-697

8. Ishwar K. Sethi, "Entroy Nets: From Decision Trees to Neural Networks", Proc. IEEE 1990, pp1605-1613

9. D. E. Rumelhart, "Parallel distributed processing, vol. 1, foundations", Cambridge, MA:MIT press, 1986

Active Data Selection and Subsequent Revision
for Sequential Learning with Neural Networks

Hiroshi YAMAKAWA, Daiki MASUMOTO, Takashi KIMOTO, and Shigemi NAGATA

FUJITSU LABORATORIES LTD.
1015 Kamikodanaka, Nakahara-ku, Kawasaki 211, Japan

yamakawa@flab.fujitsu.co.jp daiki@flab.fujitsu.co.jp kimoto@flab.fujitsu.co.jp nagata@flab.fujitsu.co.jp

Abstract

We propose a neural network system that sequentially obtains I/O sample data. The system selects useful sample data as training data, in what we call active data selection (ADS), and interpolates errors between training data and the network output, called subsequent revision (SR). ADS removes sample data if doing so only causes small errors. To speed up ADS, we ignore errors generated by the network and consider only those from SR.

We found that ADS steadily decreases errors and that SR gives suitable output, even if the neural network's learning is still not adequate. Simulation demonstrated the ability of the network to learn a sine function from sample data distributed unevenly in the input space.

1. Introduction

Adaptive I/O systems that interpolate sample data are classified to two typical techniques -- storage or learning. Storage techniques, e.g., the k nearest neighbors method, simply store sample data without learning until the data is interpolated and output. Although techniques of this type dispense with learning, memory and processing requirements and the response time tend to increase with the amount of sample data. Although learning techniques, e.g., the gradient descent method for a layered neural network, express I/O relationships compactly and shorten the response times, more time is needed for adaptation due to the increased learning workload.

Combined techniques with sample data selection have also been proposed. In some studies [1, 2, 3], the output is superimposed Gaussian functions associated with the sample data and constants or linear functions. If the system performs well with new sample data, the parameters are updated using the gradient descent method. If the system performs poorly, the data is used to add new Gaussian functions. The criteria for selecting useful data is studied in other situations [4, 5]. Oka proposed the system which chooses the appropriate output of back-propagation or memory-based learning sub systems [6].

We combine a layered neural network, which learns by back-propagation, with storage techniques. Active data selection (ADS) selects useful training data from sequentially given sample data. The training data is used for neural network learning and subsequent revisions (SR), which adjust the network output by interpolating errors between the training data and network output. ADS selects training data based on the principle that more errors occur when useful data is removed. ADS limits the amount of training data stored, which prevents memory and processing requirements from increasing. The training data chosen by ADS steadily decreases errors. SR adjusts the network output, to compensate for insufficient network learning and enable the system to adapt quickly. The single-layered superposition of Gaussian functions [1, 2, 3] is sufficiently easy to enable sample data to be evaluated for selection. The complex output of a layered neural network, however, makes it difficult to evaluate sample data. To speed up selection, ADS considered only SR errors and ignored those of the neural network to reduce the network learning workload.

2. System
2.1 SR

The proposed system generates an input-related output while adapting itself to sequentially given sample data (Figure 1). When input vector x is given, adjustment $e(x)$ is added to the neural network output $f_N(x)$ in the adder to give an adjusted output $f(x)$.

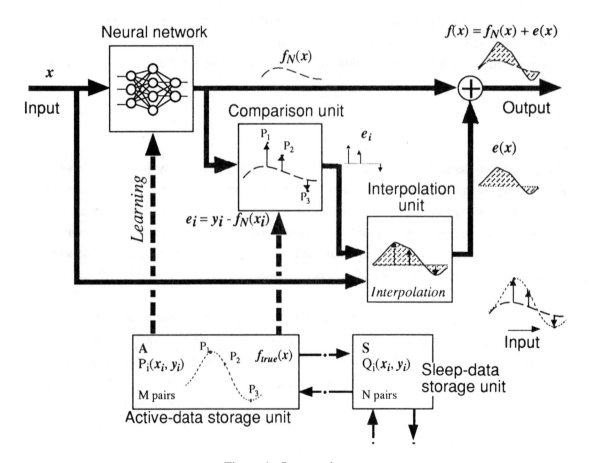

Figure 1. Proposed system

$$f(x) = f_N(x) + e(x) \tag{1}$$

The three-layered network learns by back-propagation [7] using dataset **A** which is stored in the active-data storage unit. Dataset $\mathbf{A} = (P_1, P_2, ..., P_M)$ is the set of sample data $P_i = (x_i, y_i)$ that represents up to M I/O pairs.

The comparison unit generates a set of errors e_i (i = 1 to M),

$$e_i = y_i - f_N(x_i) \tag{2}$$

$$e(x) = e(x: P_1, P_1, ..., P_M) = \frac{\sum_{i=1}^{M} e_i \, W_i(x) \exp\left(-\frac{|x - x_i|^2}{\sigma^2}\right)}{\sum_{i=1}^{n} W_i(x)} \tag{3}$$

$$\begin{array}{ll} & (x \neq x_i) \\ e(x) = e_i & (x = x_i) \end{array}$$

$W_i(x)$: Weight of error e_i at x

x_i, x_j: Input of sample data

σ: Exponential damping coefficient of output

which are the differences between the neural network output $f_N(x_i)$ and the output y_i of data P_i.

To make the output $f(x)$ equal the sample data y_i, the interpolation unit derives the adjustment $e(x)$ for any input x from the set of output errors e_i. The adjustment $e(x)$ is the weighted average of e_i.

The weight $W_i(x)$ is proportional to inverse distance from sample data's input x_i to x ($|x-x_i|$) with exponential damping (Figure 2).

$$W_i(x) = \frac{\exp\left(-\frac{|x - x_i|}{D_r}\right)}{|x - x_i|} \prod_{j=1}^{M} \left(\frac{|x - x_j|^2 + |x_i - x_j|^2 - |x - x_i|^2}{2|x - x_j||x_i - x_j|}\right) \tag{4}$$

D_r: Exponential damping coefficient of weight

The subjoined multiplication modulates the weight $W_i(x)$ to make the adjustment $e(x)$ smooth in the neighborhood of the sample data's input. The weight $W_i(x)$, corresponding sample data P_i, is seriously affected by the other sample data P_j, when x_j exist between x_i and x. The exponential damping in Eq.(3) suppresses the adjustment $e(x)$ in the distance from any sample data.

This interpolation method is suitable for multidimensional inputs, and follows the sample

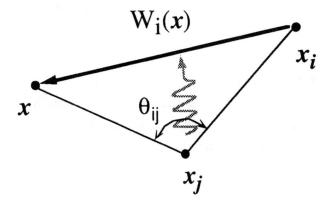

Figure 2. Interpolation method

data smoothly. Because of the storage technique, the response process and time of the interpolation unit increase with the size of dataset **A**, but adapts rapidly.

2.2 ADS

The active-data storage unit holds dataset $A = (P_1, P_2,..., P_M)$, which contains up to M pairs of sample data $P_i = (x_i, y_i)$ (i=1 to M), for use in the neural network learning and SR. As the network fetches new data, it removes no longer needed data to maintain the size of the dataset. This is supported by the sleep-data storage unit and dataset S stored in it.

If the sample data does not include noise, we must consider the difference between the output and sample data output, selection criterion 1, and the ease with which the output is estimated from adjacent sample data, selection criterion 2. Squared error Δe_i^2,

$$\Delta e_i^2 = |e_i - e(x_i: P_1, P_2, ..., P_{i-1}, P_{i+1}, ..., P_M)|^2 \qquad (5)$$

which is the squared difference between the errors e_i of the data P_i and the adjustment $e(x_i)$ without data P_i, was used as the evaluation criteria (Figure 3). This includes the two selection criteria above. The larger the value, the more useful the data is. ADS is fast, because this does not involve the workload associated with network learning.

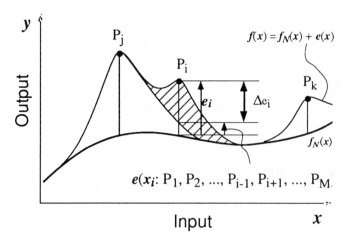

Figure 3. Evaluation criteria

3. Experiment

Simulation demonstrates that ADS enables the neural network to retain data with a suitable distribution, even when sample data is unevenly distributed. Our simulation involved learning a single-input, single-output sine function:

$$y = (1 + \sin(2\pi x))/2 \qquad (6)$$

where input x and output y are in the range [0.0, 1.0].

The simulation used 500 sample data (x_i, y_i) satisfying Eq. (6); 90% of the sample data appeared in input area A [0.0, 0.5] and the remaining 10% in input area B [0.5, 1.0]. The data distribution in each area was uniform. As the control a network system without ADS was tested. The control discarded data on a FIFO basis.

The neural network consists of three layers with a 1-6-1 structure. The active-data storage unit holds up to ten sample data and the sleep-data storage unit up to five. Each time the neural network fetches new data, 30 network learning iterations follow.

4. Results

Squared error E, relative to output $f(x)$, is represented by:

$$E = \frac{1}{V} \int [f(x) - f_{true}(x)]^2 \, dV \qquad (7)$$

where $f(x)$:   Output

$f_{true}(x)$: True function output

Squared errors of the system with ADS decrease steadily. Without ADS, the errors do not decrease as much (Figure 4). SR also decreases the errors and so compensates for slow learning in the neural network. The system outputs were measured based on 500 sample data (Figure 5). Without ADS, large differences from $f_{true}(x)$ occur in input area B [0.5, 1.0], where the probability of data appearing is low. ADS, however, decreases errors in both areas.

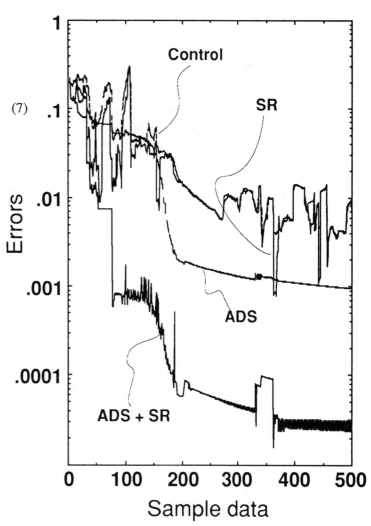

Figure 4. Squared errors
$D_r^2 = 0.10, \sigma = 0.10$

5. Conclusion

We proposed a neural network system which is combined with storage technique. Active data selection (ADS) selects useful training data from sequentially given sample data. The training data is used for neural network learning and subsequent revisions (SR), which adjust the network output by interpolating errors between the training data and network output.

Simulation demonstrates abilities of the system. The training data chosen by ADS steadily decreases the errors. SR adjusts the output to compensate for insufficient network learning and gives an adequate result. The proposed neural network system responds and adapts rapidly to sequential learning.

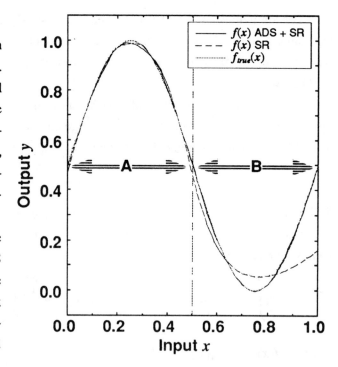

Figure 5. Outputs after obtaining
500 sample data
$D_r^2 = 0.10$, $\sigma = 0.10$

REFERENCES

[1] J. C. Platt (1991). "A resource allocating network for function interpolation," *Neural Computation*, **3**(2), 213-225

[2] J. C. Platt (1991). "Learning by combining memorization and gradient descent," In R. P. Lippmann, J. E. Moody and D. S. Touretzky, eds., *Neural Information Processing Systems* 3. Morgan Kaufmann

[3] V. Kadirkamanathan and M. Niranjan (1992). "A function estimation approach to sequential learning with neural networks," CUED/F-UNIFYING/TR.111.

[4] M. Plutowski and H. White (1991). "Active selection of training examples for network learning in noiseless environments," *Dept. Computer Science, UCSD TR 90-011.*

[5] D. J. C. MacKay (1992). "Information-based objective functions for active data selection," *Neural Computation*, 4(4), 590-604

[6] N. Oka, and K. Yoshida (1992). "Combining back-propagation and memory-based learning,"*6th conference of Japanese Society for Artificial Intellligence*, **8-5**, 377-380, (in Japanese).

[7] D. E. Rumelhart, G. E. Hinton, and R. J. Williams (1986). "Learning internal representations by error propagation," *in Parallel Distributed Processing: Explorations in the Microstructure of Cognition*, Vol 1, D. E. Rummelhart and J.L.McClelland (eds), MIT Press, Cambridge MA

INPUT DATA TRANSFORMATION FOR BETTER PATTERN CLASSIFICATIONS WITH FEWER NEURONS

Yasuhiro Ota
Bogdan Wilamowski
Electrical Engineering Department
University of Wyoming
Laramie, WY 82071, USA

Abstract:

Ordinary discriminant functions for pattern separations are normally linear. Neural networks with one-layer architecture can classify only linearly separable patterns, and thus multilayer neural networks are required for separation of nonlinearly separable patterns. In this paper, an improved formulation of discriminant functions with fewer neurons is proposed. This is accomplished by introducing an additional dimension to a set of input patterns.

I. Introduction:

A pattern is the quantitative description of an object, phenomenon, or event. A classification of patterns can be spatial or temporal. Examples of the former case are pictures, video images, and characters. Examples of the latter case include speech signals, seismograms, and electrocardiograms, which normally involve ordered sequences of data appearing in time. The goal of pattern classification is to assign a physical object, phenomenon, or event to one of the prespecified classes. The mechanism of pattern recognition (classification) in the human brain seems to be almost impossible to reveal it. However, an artificial intelligence classifying system consists of an input transducer which provides the input pattern data to the feature extractor [1]. Typically, inputs to the feature extractor are sets of data vectors that belong to a certain category.

Several designs have been presented in the past for classifying patterns using n-dimensional discriminant functions. The efficient classifiers, in general, are described by discriminant functions that are nonlinear functions of input patterns [2][3]. As was described by Marvin Minsky and Seymour Papert one-layer neural networks have very limited ability for pattern classifications [4]. They can classify only linearly separable patterns; therefore, multilayer neural networks are required for separation of nonlinearly separable patterns. This paper discusses how to reduce the number of neurons with an effective nonlinear pattern classification. The formulation of the input data transformation method is described in Section II, and the simulation of a proposed network design is shown in Section III. Section IV concludes the design and gives suggestions of possible future studies applicable to this design.

II. Structure of Pattern Classifications

First, the assumption is made that both a set of n-dimensional input patterns $\{x_1, x_2, \cdots, x_P\}$ and the desired classification for each input pattern $\{d_1, d_2, \cdots, d_P\}$ are known. The size P of the pattern set is finite and usually much larger than the dimensionality n of the pattern space. In many practical cases, it is assumed that P is much larger than the number of categories (classes) R. The goal is to classify input patterns into R categories. For given input patterns $\{x_1, x_2, \cdots, x_P\}$ with R categories, each category of input patterns normally has a center of gravity, and it can be found by

$$x_{CG_R} = \frac{x_{R_1} + x_{R_2} + \cdots + x_{R_k}}{k} \tag{1}$$

where the subscript CG_R stands for the center of gravity for the R-th category with k input data in that category. Once the centers of gravity for each category are defined, the radii r_R of circles (or spheres) that enclose all the input data that belong to a certain category can be found from the following equation:

$$r_R = \left| x_{R_k} - x_{CG_R} \right|_{\max} \tag{2}$$

One more parameter, D_{MAX}, must be defined in order to transform n-dimensional input data into $(n+1)$-dimensions. The maximum distance of an input point from the origin, D_{MAX}, is used to scale all the input data in transforming them into new $(n+1)$-dimensional input arrays. Finally, the series of the following equations is utilized for the transformation of input patterns.

$$
\begin{aligned}
z_1 &= \cos\alpha_1 \\
z_2 &= \sin\alpha_1 \cos\alpha_2 \\
z_3 &= \sin\alpha_1 \sin\alpha_2 \cos\alpha_3 \\
&\vdots \qquad\qquad \vdots \\
z_n &= \sin\alpha_1 \sin\alpha_2 \cdots \sin\alpha_{n-1} \cos\alpha_n \\
z_{n+1} &= \sin\alpha_1 \sin\alpha_2 \cdots \sin\alpha_{n-1} \sin\alpha_n
\end{aligned} \tag{3}
$$

where z_i ($i = 1, 2, \cdots, n+1$) are the new $(n+1)$-dimensional transformed input data space and the arguments α_j ($j = 1, 2, \cdots, n$) are defined by

$$\alpha_j = \left(\frac{x_j}{D_{MAX}} \right) \pi \tag{4}$$

Notice that $(n+1)$-dimensional input data are mapped such that

$$\sum_{i=1}^{n+1} z_i^2 = 1 \tag{5}$$

By employing relations (3) and (4) all the n-dimensional input data including the centers of gravity of all the R categories can be transformed. In order to find discriminant functions for the separation of patterns, equations of decision surfaces (separation planes) are required. Notice that the $(n+1)$-dimensional data at the center of gravity represent the normal vector of a separation plane; i.e.,

$$\hat{\mathbf{n}}_R = \begin{bmatrix} z_{CG_{R_1}} & z_{CG_{R_2}} & \cdots & z_{CG_{R_{n+1}}} \end{bmatrix} \tag{6}$$

Once some point which lies on this separation plane is known, the equation of the plane can be established. The point which lies on the boundary, r_R, of the original n-dimensional pattern should be mapped onto the edge of the boundary in the $(n+1)$-dimensional pattern, and hence this point, z_{EDGE_R}, shoucld be used in formulating the equations of the discriminant functions. Thus, the discriminant functions can be given by

$$\hat{\mathbf{n}}_R^T \left(\mathbf{z} - \mathbf{z}_{EDGE_R} \right) = 0 \tag{7}$$

The above transformation can be used, not only for the condition with linear separability of patterns, but also for the case of linearly nonseparable patterns. The analytical weights for the neuron being activated for the R-th category can then be given as

$$\mathbf{W}_R = \begin{bmatrix} z_{CG_{R_1}} & z_{CG_{R_2}} & \cdots & z_{CG_{R_{n+1}}} & -\sum_{i=1}^{n+1} z_{CG_{R_i}} z_{EDGE_{R_i}} \end{bmatrix} \tag{8}$$

III. Simulation Results

The following simple example will allow the reader to gain better insight into the discussion of the pattern classification issue. Now consider looking at two-dimensional patterns ($n=1$) with two categories ($R=2$). Initially, seventeen patterns were assigned in two-dimensional pattern space according to their membership in sets as follows:

Class 1 ($\mathbf{d}_1 = +1$): $\left\{ \begin{bmatrix} 5 \\ 5 \end{bmatrix}, \begin{bmatrix} 3 \\ 4 \end{bmatrix}, \begin{bmatrix} 5 \\ 4 \end{bmatrix}, \begin{bmatrix} 6 \\ 5 \end{bmatrix}, \begin{bmatrix} 4 \\ 3 \end{bmatrix}, \begin{bmatrix} 4 \\ 4 \end{bmatrix}, \begin{bmatrix} 7 \\ 5 \end{bmatrix} \right\}$

Class 2 ($\mathbf{d}_2 = -1$): $\left\{ \begin{bmatrix} 0 \\ 0 \end{bmatrix}, \begin{bmatrix} 2 \\ 1 \end{bmatrix}, \begin{bmatrix} 9 \\ 3 \end{bmatrix}, \begin{bmatrix} 1 \\ 10 \end{bmatrix}, \begin{bmatrix} 5 \\ 0 \end{bmatrix}, \begin{bmatrix} 8 \\ 8 \end{bmatrix}, \begin{bmatrix} 2 \\ 8 \end{bmatrix}, \begin{bmatrix} 5 \\ 10 \end{bmatrix}, \begin{bmatrix} 10 \\ 4 \end{bmatrix}, \begin{bmatrix} 12 \\ 9 \end{bmatrix} \right\}$

In order to classify the given patterns into two categories with the ordinary decision lines, discriminant functions, at least four decision lines and a two-layer neural network are necessary as shown in Figure 1. On the other hand, only one neuron is necessary to perform the same function if the proposed design is employed since it is possible to separate the two categories with one circle as shown in Figure 2. Figure 3 illustrates the given input data after they have been transformed into three-dimensional patterns.

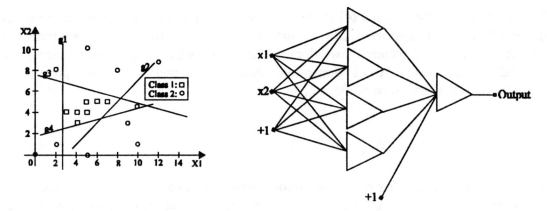

Figure 1. Two-Dimensional Input Patterns with Ordinary Discriminant Functions and the Two-Layer Neural Network.

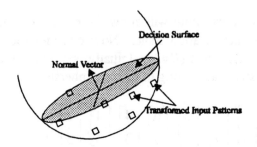

Figure 2. Two-Dimensional Input Patterns with the Improved Model and the Single-Neuron Network.

Figure 3. Input Patterns After the Transformation.

For the given single-neuron network, the analytical weight vector can be found by utilizing relation (8). This vector is given as

$$W_{1_{analytical}} = [\ 0.5305\ \ 0.5180\ \ 0.6710\ \ -0.8008\ ]$$

The popular error back-propagation training algorithm [5][6] (delta training for a single-layer network) can also be utilized to compute the optimal weight vector. The performance of the neural network will then be compared with both the analytical and the delta training weights. Initial weights for training are randomly chosen as in the normal procedure, and the total output error does converge towards zero as shown in Figure 4. After the training of the network with 500 iterations, the delta-trained weight vector is found to be

$$W_{1_{delta}} = [\ 0.4448\ \ 0.5034\ \ 0.7408\ \ -0.7890\ ]$$

Testing of pattern classifications is achieved with the two weight vectors listed above, and the results are tabulated in Figure 5. Figure 6 illustrates the mesh plots of the actual input-output nonlinear mappings in the original pattern space.

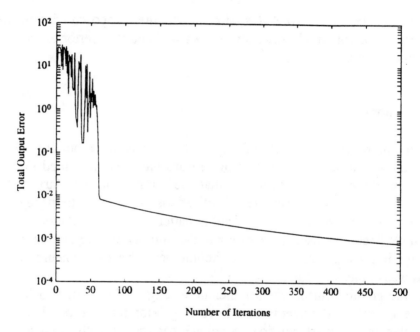

Figure 4. Total Output Error of the Neural Network with the Delta Training.

Test Input Pattern	Desired Output	Analytical Method		Delta Training	
		Output	% Error	Output	% Error
[4 5]	1	0.9226	7.74	0.9141	8.59
[12 11]	-1	-1.0000	0.00	-1.0000	0.00
[0 10]	-1	-0.9847	1.53	-0.9959	0.04
[9 1]	-1	-0.9963	0.37	-0.9927	0.73
[5 6]	1	0.8857	11.43	0.9923	7.78

Figure 5. Test Results of the Neural Network.

III-671

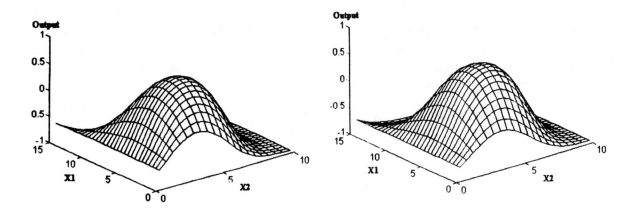

Figure 6. Actual Output Transfer Characteristics: (a) Using the Analytical Weight Vector and (b) Using the Weight Vector with the Delta Training.

As can be seen from this simulation, the proposed design of input data transformation for pattern classifications works well and is superior to the ordinary pattern classification designs.

IV. Conclusions

An improved technique of input data transformation for effective pattern classification with a minimum number of neurons has been presented in this paper. The simulation results clearly demonstrated that the number of necessary neurons could be effectively minimized with accurate classifications of input patterns by introducing an additional dimension (freedom) for the input patterns. The simulation revealed that even with a simple linearly nonseparable example the number of neurons required was reduced by using the improved method. In fact, the number of necessary neurons for the example case used was reduced by four.

Some possible further studies include testing of this design to higher dimensions with more complicated patterns that have a greater number of classifying categories although this input transformation technique can be virtually applied to any pattern classification problems of any dimensions..

References

[1]   J. M. Zurada, <u>Introduction to Artificial Neural Systems</u>., West Publishing Company, St. Paul, MN., 1992

[2]   H. C. Andrews, <u>Introduction to Mathematical Techniques in Pattern Recognition</u>., Wiley Interscience, New York, NY., 1972.

[3]   B. Widrow and M. A. Lehr, "30 Years of Adaptive Neural Networks: Perceptron, Medaline, and Backpropagation," *IEEE Proceedings*, vol. 78, no. 9, pp. 1415-1442, Sept. 1990.

[4]   M. Minsky and S. Papert, <u>Perceptrons</u>., MIT Press., Cambridge, MA., 1969.

[5]   K. Hornik, M. Stinchcombe, and H. White, "Multilayer Feedforward Networks Are Universal Approximations," *Neural Networks*, vol. 2, pp. 359-366, 1989.

[6]   E. D. Karin, "A Simple Procedure for Pruning Back-Propagation Trained Neural Networks," *IEEE Trans. on Neural Networks*, vol. 1, no. 2, pp. 239-242, 1990.

Fundamentals of the Bootstrap Based Analysis of Neural Network's Accuracy.

Alex S. Katz [1]
Simon Katz [2]
Norma Lowe [1]

[1] Baxter Healthcare Corporation, Edwards CVS Division,
17221 Red Hill Ave. MS-33, Irvine, CA 92714
(714) 250-2546
(714) 250-3579 FAX
[2] University of Southern California, Geology Dept., Los Angeles, CA 90033

Abstract.

Neural networks and bootstrap methodologies were combined into a single system (NNB), creating a powerful predictive neural engine together with the means of statistical estimation of the accuracy of the prediction errors. The NNB system was tested on clinical data obtained from a clinical trial of implanted artificial heart valves. The system correctly predicted 78% of the valve related deaths in the time period of 1981-1991, for a patient sample of 789, based solely on the information available preoperatively. Distribution of the prediction error and its variation in relation to selection of the training set was observed and analyzed, based on 1300 bootstrap replications of the neural net's cycle of training and testing. Expectation of the prediction error along with the confidence intervals and prediction intervals for the error were computed.

Introduction.

Artificial adaptive neural networks provide a powerful tool that has been used successfully in image processing, pattern recognition, natural phenomena prediction and signal processing [1,3,5,6]. The encouraging results of application of the neural techniques to a number of problems poses a question of estimation of reliability of the neural networks' performance. Because of the neural systems' nonlinearity and structural complexity, the classical statistical theory provides little help in analyzing the performance and accuracy of predictions of neural nets. This gap may be successfully filled using such methods of computational statistics as bootstrap.

The bootstrap is a computer-based method of statistical inference for assigning measures of accuracy to statistical estimates[8,9]. Bootstrap methods can assess accuracy measures such as biases, prediction errors and confidence intervals[7,8]. The bootstrap algorithm generates a large number of bootstrap samples, obtained by resampling with replacement of the original data. For each bootstrap sample a corresponding bootstrap replication of the statistic of interest is calculated[7-10]. The accuracy measures of interest are then estimated from these bootstrap replications. For instance, if $s(\bar{x})$ is the statistic of interest, and its standard error is to be estimated, then the bootstrap estimate SE_{boot} can be computed according to the following formula:

$$SE_{boot} = \left\{ \sum_{b=1}^{B} [s(\mathbf{x}^{*b}) - s(\cdot)]^2 / (B-1) \right\}^{1/2} \tag{1}$$

Where $s(\cdot) = \sum_{b=1}^{B} s(\mathbf{x}^{*b}) / B$ (2)

B is the number of bootstrap replications, and x^{*b} is a bootstrap resampling of the original data $\mathbf{X} = (x_1, x_2, ..., x_n)$

Application of the bootstrap methodology provides the means of estimating the standard error and computing prediction intervals, as well as confidence intervals for the estimated mean of the error of neural network's prediction [2]. This approach combines powerful prediction capabilities, provided by the neural networks, with the ability of estimating the results of prediction and prediction errors, which in its turn enables us to optimize the predictive mechanism, minimizing the error and maximizing its predictive power. Additionally, this approach allows for further optimization of the neural network and increasing its predictive capability and accuracy of prediction.

Bootstrap estimation of prediction errors.

Available data Ω consists of pairs (input, expected output) $(\overline{\mathbf{x}}_i, \overline{\mathbf{z}}_i)$. Ω is randomly divided into two non empty subsets Ω_{tr} and Ω_{ts}, such that

$$\Omega_{tr} \bigcup \Omega_{ts} = \Omega$$
$$\Omega_{tr} \mid \Omega_{ts} = \varnothing \tag{3}$$

Bootstrap training and testing samples $\omega_{tr}(j)$ and $\omega_{ts}(j)$ are generated from Ω_{tr} and Ω_{ts}, where j is the index of the bootstrap replication.

A neural network is defined by the vector of its parameters $\mathbf{u}$, and the output F of the neural net is a function of the net's input and parameters: $F = F(\mathbf{u}, \mathbf{x})$.

For each bootstrap sample of the training set $\omega_{tr}(j)$ the neural net is initialized and trained to minimize the approximation error

$$\varepsilon(\mathbf{u}, j) = \sum_{\mathbf{x}_i \in \omega_{tr}(j)} \| F(\mathbf{u}, \mathbf{x}_i) - \mathbf{z}_i \|^2 \tag{4}$$

The parameter vector $\mathbf{u}_j$ of this neural network is defined by the following characteristic equation

$$\varepsilon(\mathbf{u}_j, j) = \underset{\mathbf{u}}{Min}\ \varepsilon(\mathbf{u}, j) \tag{5}$$

The corresponding bootstrap estimate of the neural net's prediction error computed over $\omega_{ts}(j)$ is

$$\xi(\mathbf{u}_j) = \sum_{\mathbf{x}_i \in \omega_{ts}(j)} \| F(\mathbf{u}_j, \mathbf{x}_i) - \mathbf{z}_i \|^2 \tag{6}$$

After generating bootstrap samples $\omega_{tr}(j)$ and $\omega_{ts}(j)$ of the training and testing sets for $j \in [1, J]$, and estimating the network's prediction errors $\xi(\mathbf{u}_j)$, random variable statistics may be computed per (1) and (2) and distribution parameters for $\xi(\mathbf{u}_j)$ may be estimated and analyzed.

The expectation of the prediction error may be estimated as the average of bootstrap estimates for $\xi(\mathbf{u}_j)$.

$$\bar{\xi} = \frac{1}{J}\sum_{j=1}^{J}\xi\,(\mathbf{u}_j) \qquad (7)$$

Standard error of the prediction error may be estimated as

$$se_{\xi\,boot} = \{\sum_{j=1}^{J}[\xi(u_j)-\bar{\xi}]^2/(J-1)\}^{1/2} \qquad (8)$$

Depending on the size of the training set and the empirical distribution of the estimate of the measure of interest (prediction error $\xi\,(\mathbf{u}_j)$ in our case), confidence intervals for the actual value of the estimated parameter may be estimated by different methods. In this study the bootstrap percentile method was used. If $\xi^{*(\alpha)}$ is the $100\cdot\alpha$ percentile of J bootstrap replications $\xi^*\,(j)$, $j=1,...,J$, then the interval of intended coverage $1-2\alpha$ is obtained by

$$(\xi_{lo},\,\xi_{up}) = (\xi^{*(\alpha)},\,\xi^{*(1-\alpha)}) \qquad (9)$$

Neural network architecture.

A fully connected feed-forward backpropagation neural network was integrated into the NNB system for this study in the manner described in the Experiment Design section. Eight variables, available preoperatively on both the patients and the implanted devices, were used as the network's inputs. Since the neural net had to be able to train on small samples, the cost function $C(\mathbf{A})$, characterizing the efficiency of the net, had to be modified into $C'(\mathbf{A})$, where

$$C(\mathbf{A}) = \sum\{N(\mathbf{X}_k)-D(k)\}^2 \qquad (10)$$

$$C'(\mathbf{A}) = C(\mathbf{A}) + \delta^2\|\mathbf{A}\|^2, \qquad (11)$$

$\mathbf{A}$ is the vector of the neural net's parameters, $\mathbf{X}_k$ is the k-th vector of input parameters, $N(\mathbf{X}_k)$ is the output of the neural net, and $D(k)$ is the expected output of the net.

Experiment Design.

The neural net -- bootstrap methodology was tested on clinical data obtained from a clinical trial of patients implanted with artificial heart valves. Seven hundred eighty-nine (789) patients implanted with Carpentier-Edwards ® Pericardial bioprosthesis have been followed from 1981. The aim of this study was to predict which patients would develop device-related complications, serious enough to cause death, in the time interval from 1981 to 1991, based only on preoperative patients' information and the implanted devices' characteristics.

Patient records were divided into two groups -- Ω_1 containing patients' records indicating a "positive" response, i.e., death from a valve related complication between 1981 and 1991; and Ω_2 containing records with "negative" responses, i.e., no valve-related death. A predetermined number (30) of "positive" responses were randomly selected with replacement from Ω_1 and assigned to the training set. An equal number of "negative" responses were randomly selected from Ω_2 and added to the training set. From the remaining records, both "positive" and "negative", random sampling with replacement was used again for selecting testing records. Sampling of "negative" and "positive" responses for the training set was performed independently, in order to compensate for the relatively small proportion of the "positive" responses (60 out of 776). The neural net was synthesized using data from the training set. The data from the testing data-set was then used for estimation of the neural net efficacy, errors of prediction and optimization of the neural net. Then training and testing sets were reselected, the network retrained, and the prediction error estimated. A single NNB cycle included a bootstrap

network retrained, and the prediction error estimated. A single NNB cycle included a bootstrap generation of the training and testing sets, synthesis of the NN, testing NN and estimation of the prediction accuracy. After repeating the process for 1300 cycles, the calculated errors were accumulated and analyzed. Since the NNB system included the neural network, which had to be synthesized, trained and tested hundreds of times, the process, being very computationally intensive, called for a very efficient adaptive neural network. The neural net for the NNB system was designed and developed by MultiSpectrum Technologies, Inc. of Santa Monica, California.

Classification methodology.

When the trained network predicted a valve related death, where no such event was indicated by the clinical records, we called it "false alarm". On the other hand, if a patient died from a valve related complication and the event was not predicted by the network, we called it "missed event". Two separate errors of prediction were computed for each cycle of NNB. The errors were calculated as ratios of incorrectly predicted events (either "false alarms" or "missed events") to the expected number of events of the same type, as indicated by the clinical records. These two errors were then averaged to obtain a single score representing the prediction accuracy for a given NNB cycle.

A step-function $S(h, z)$, taking values 0 and 1, was used for evaluating the networks' output. It transformed the networks' continuous output into a dichotomous variable -- predicted event or predicted no-event.

$$S(h,z) = 1, \quad z \geq h \tag{12}$$
$$S(h,z) = 0, \quad z < h \tag{13}$$

Then correct predictions are defined as

$$S(h,z) = 1 \text{ for } \mathbf{x} \in \Omega_1 \text{ or } S(h,z) = 0 \text{ for } \mathbf{x} \in \Omega_2 \tag{14}$$

False alarms, according to our definition are then described as

$$S(h,z) = 1 \text{ for } \mathbf{x} \in \Omega_2 \tag{15}$$

and missed events

$$S(h,z) = 0 \text{ for } \mathbf{x} \in \Omega_1 \tag{16}$$

The threshold of the step-function -- h -- is one of the networks' parameters, and modifying its value, the error rates may be adjusted.

Results.

In Figure 1 the rates of "false alarms" and "missed events" are plotted against the step-function's threshold h. As the value of the threshold increases, the number of "missed events" increases as well, while the number of false alarms goes down. In Figure 3 the relationship between the averaged error of prediction and the step-function's threshold is investigated. In this case the averaged error of prediction attained its minimum when $h = 0.44$, and the value of the error is below 0.23, which gives us approximately 78% accuracy in prediction. Figure 2 presents a histogram of the averaged errors, obtained from 1300 NNB cycles for a fixed value of the step-functions' threshold $h = 0.44$. Based on the values of the bootstrap replications of the NNB-generated averaged error, parameters of the error distribution were estimated and both the prediction interval for the NN error and confidence interval around its mean were constructed [2,7,8,10]. The mean of the averaged error was estimated at 0.22 (SE mean = 0.0015) and the

Conclusion.

Neural networks and bootstrap were combined into one algorithm to bring the best of the two worlds together: a powerful predictive engine of the neural nets' paradigm and the proven ways of statistical methods for assessing prediction accuracy. This combination of the two methods also proved to be effective for further optimization of the neural network and increasing its predictive power. Based on the preoperative information only, 78% of patients were correctly classified by the neural network into two groups: those that would die from an implanted device related cause and those that would not. The averaged error of prediction was 22% (+/-5%) and the prediction interval for the prediction error was estimated to be (14%, 32%) at the 95% confidence level.

References.

1. Katz AS, Katz S, Wickham E, Quijano RC. Prediction of valve related complications for artificial heart valves using adaptive neural networks. J. Heart Valve Dis. 1993, Vol.2, No.5: 504-508

2. Katz AS, Katz S, Lowe N, Quijano RC. Neural network -- bootstrap hybrid methodology for prediction of complications for patients implanted with artificial heart valves. J. Heart Valve Dis. Jan.1994, (in print)

3. Katz S, Aki K. Experiments with a neural net based earthquake prediction. Proceedings of Int'l AGU Meeting 1992 Vol.73, No.43:366

4. Katz S, Katz AS. Adaptive multichannel filters. Proceedings of Int'l SEG conference 1990:541-543

5. Domay E, van Hemman JL, Shulten KS. Models of neural networks. Springer-Verlag, 1991

6. Kosko B. Neural networks for signal processing. Prentice Hall, 1992

7. Efron B. Nonparametric standard error and confidence intervals, 1981 Can J. Statist, 139-172

8. Tibshirani R. Bootstrap confidence intervals. Computer Sci. and Statist., 1986, Amer Statist Assoc, Washington DC, 267-276

9. Stine RA. Bootstrap prediction intervals for regression. J Amer Statist Assoc, 1985, 80:1026-1031

10. Hall P. Performance of bootstrap balanced resampling in distribution function and quantile problems. 1990, Prob Th Rel Fields, 85:239-267

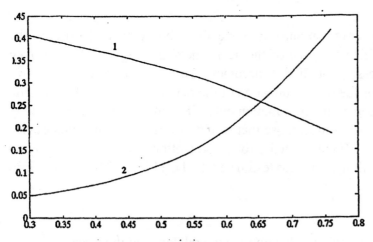

Figure 1: False alarms and missed events vs. threshold.
curve 1 - false alarms
curve 2 - missed events

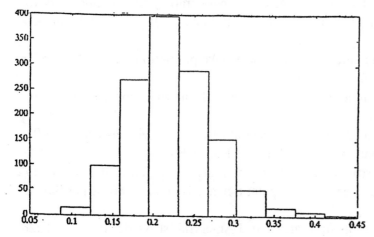

Figure 2: Histogram of 1300 bootstrap replications of the averaged error of ANN prediction.

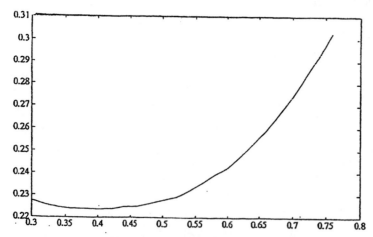

Figure 3: Averaged error of the ANN prediction vs. threshold.

III-678

A Study of the Effect and Effectiveness of Noise Injection during Neural Network Training

Adel M. Abunawass
Western Illinois University
Macomb, Illinois 61455
E-mail: mfama@uxa.ecn.bgu.edu

Charles B. Owen
Dartmouth College
Hanover, New Hampshire 03755-3551
E-mail: cowen@cs.dartmouth.edu

Original Paper Citation:
A Statistical Analysis of the Effect of Noise Injection during Neural Network Training. *Proceedings of the Conference on the Science of Artificial Neural Networks II* (1993), Vol. 1966, pp. 362-371.

Abstract:

It is commonly accepted that the modification of the weights during training of an Artificial Neural Network can be augmented by addition of a random element chosen from various distributions. This technique, commonly referred to as Noise Injection, allows the training process to stochastically traverse a larger area of the sample space, as well as escape from local minima. Numerous noise distributions and intensities are used and training can be shown, experimentally, to be more reliable.

The original paper examined the effect of noise injection on the training cycle of feed-forward neural networks. Emphasis was placed on the gradient descent weight modification technique of the Backpropagation model. Statistical examination was made of the distribution of the effect within the topology of the weight space, upon the outputs of individual units, and on the total error of the network. Since the weights of the network can be considered together as an n-tuple, injection of noise can be statistically examined within that n-dimensional space. It was shown that, for stochastically independent random distributions, the effect on this weight space is dependent upon the number of weights in the network. The multivariate distribution of the vector modification during training becomes increasingly distorted as the network size increases, such that noise injection has a more significant, and less stable effect, as network size increases. For each individual nodal output it can be shown that the random distribution of change in the output of the node is a function of the multivariate distribution of all weights preceding the neuron, the applied pattern, and the neuron activation function. This distribution was also shown to be dependent upon network size.

The effect on error output of the network is a composite function of the effect on each output unit. This distribution was examined in detail. The paper looked at the common independent uniform and normal noise distribution injection in detail. Problems with these traditional approaches were examined and an alternative noise injection method based on an n-tuple vector modification was proposed that was less dependent on network size. The study found that uniformly distributed noise led to faster convergence but less reliable than that of normally distributed noise. Additionally, generalization of the sine wave provided (overall) better approximation when the noise was normally distributed than when the noise was uniformly distributed.

Minimum Information Principle: Improving Generalization Performance by Information Minimization

Ryotaro Kamimura

Information Science Laboratory

Toshiyuki Takagi

Department of Electrical Engineering

Shohachiro Nakanishi

Department of Electrical Engineering

Tokai University

1117 Kitakaname Hiratsuka Kanagawa 259-12, Japan

Abstract

In the present paper, we propose a minimum information principle for the improvement of the generalization performance. This principle states that the information about input patterns must be as small as possible for improving the generalization performance under the condition that the network can produce targets with appropriate accuracy. The information is defined by the difference between maximum entropy or uncertainty and observed entropy. Borrowing a definition of fuzzy entropy, the uncertainty function is defined for the internal representation and represented by the equation: $-v_i \log v_i - (1 - v_i) \log(1 - v_i)$, where v_i is a hidden unit activity. After having formulated an update rule for the minimization of the information, we applied the method to a problem of language acquisition: the inference of the past tense forms of regular verbs. Experimental results confirmed that by our method, the information was significantly decreased and the generalization performance was greatly improved.

1 Introduction

Many techniques have been developed for the improvement of the generalization performance. One of the most popular methods consists in the reduction of complexity in network architectures, for example, addition of weight decay or weight pruning, [4], [6], [7]. If network architectures are too complex, they can store everything including noises in addition to the necessary part of input patterns. If the complexity is too small, it is impossible to learn input patterns. Thus, it is necessary to adjust the complexity of network architectures to given problems.

Let us see the complexity problem from an informational theoretical point of view. Suppose that the complexity represents a kind of information capacity of networks. If the information regarding training input patterns is excessively stored, meaning that networks store every details of training patterns, the generalization performance is not improved. Thus, the reduction of complexity shows that the information about training patterns is appropriately stored in network architectures so as to improve the generalization performance.

In the present paper, we would like to show that for the improvement of the generalization performance, the information to be stored in network architectures should be as small as possible, under the condition that networks can learn the training input patterns with appropriate accuracy. This statement is referred to as *Minimum Information Principle* for the improvement of the generalization performance.

For demonstrating this hypothesis of the minimum information principle, let us define the information, stored in network architecture. Information can be defined by the difference between maximum entropy and observed entropy:

$$I \;\; = \;\; H^{max} - H \tag{1}$$

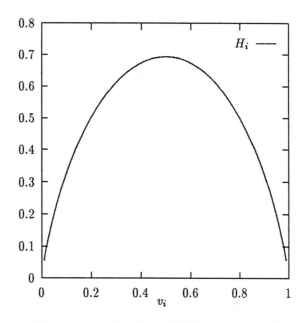

Figure 1: Entropy as a function of hidden unit activity v_i.

where H^{max} is a maximum entropy and H is an observed entropy. The information means how much uncertainty is decreased by training networks with training patterns. Using this information, our objective is to show that the information must be as small as possible for the improvement of the generalization performance, under the condition that networks can produce targets with appropriate accuracy.

2   Theory and Computational Methods

We have defined an entropy for the internal representation. Following Bridal and Deco [1], [2], we suppose that an activity of a hidden unit represents a probability that a given input pattern belongs to a certain class. If v_i represents an activity of ith hidden unit, this activity means the probability that a given input patterns belongs to the class i. Suppose that the ordinary sigmoid activation function (0,1) is used to produce outputs. The most uncertain state is a state in which the hidden unit produces an activity close to 0.5. In this case, it is impossible to tell whether the input pattern belongs to class i or not. On the other hand, the most certain state is a state in which the hidden unit produces an activity close to 1 (the input pattern certainly belongs to the class) or 0 (the input pattern does not belong to the class). If H_i represents this uncertainty, one of the possible candidates is formulated as follows:

$$H_i = -v_i \log v_i - (1 - v_i) \log(1 - v_i).$$

This equation is equivalent to the well-known *fuzzy entropy* [3]. As you can see from Figure 1, the function H_i reaches the maximum, when the activity v_i is 0.5, the most uncertain state.

With this entropy function, the information is defined by

$$I_i = H_i^{max} - H_i.$$

This information means the information content, stored in a hidden unit for an input pattern. Using this definition of information, our objective is to minimize this information as much as possible, under the condition that networks can produce targets with appropriate accuracy.

Our entropy function is defined with respect to a hidden unit activity and shows uncertainty or ambiguity of the function of the hidden unit. Our learning rule is to maximize this uncertainty or ambiguity as much as possible.

Let us formulate an entropy function for the internal representation. Suppose that a network is composed of three layers: input, hidden and output layers. Hidden unit activities are denoted by v_i and input terminals by ξ_j. Then, input-hidden connections are denoted by w_{ij}.

A hidden unit for kth input pattern produces an output

$$v_i^k = f(u_i^k),$$

where f is a sigmoid activation function, defined by

$$f(u_i^k) = \frac{1}{1 + e^{-u_i^k}}$$

and where u_i is a net input to ith hidden unit and defined by

$$u_i^k = \sum_j w_{ij} \xi_j^k.$$

where ξ_i is ith element of an input pattern. An entropy is defined by

$$H = -\sum_k^K \sum_i^M [v_i^k \log v_i^k + (1 - v_i^k) \log(1 - v_i^k)], \tag{2}$$

where K is the number of input patterns and M is the number of hidden units. Using this entropy, the information content is defined by

$$
\begin{aligned}
I &= H^{max} - H \\
&= KM \log 2 + \sum_k \sum_i [v_i^k \log v_i^k + (1 - v_i^k) \log(1 - v_i^k)],
\end{aligned}
\tag{3}
$$

where M is the number of hidden units. Now, suppose that the squared error function can be defined by

$$E = \frac{1}{2} \sum_k \sum_i (\zeta_i^k - o_i^k)^2,$$

where ζ_i^k is a target for an output o_i^k. Using this error function, total function to be minimized is formulated as follows:

$$F = \alpha I + \beta E,$$

where E is the squared error function. Differentiating both sides of this equation, we have the following update rule:

$$
\begin{aligned}
\Delta w_{ij} &= -\frac{\partial F}{\partial w_{ij}} \\
&= \sum_k (\alpha \phi_i^k + \beta \delta_i^k) \xi_j^k
\end{aligned}
\tag{4}
$$

where

$$\phi_i^k = v_i^k(1 - v_i^k) \log\left(\frac{1 - v_i^k}{v_i^k}\right)$$

and δ is an ordinary delta for the back-propagation.

3 Results and Discussion

3.1 Data and Network Architectures

We applied our information minimization method to the well-known problem of language acquisition [5]. This problem is quite significant from a linguistic point of view and it is easy to compare our results with the

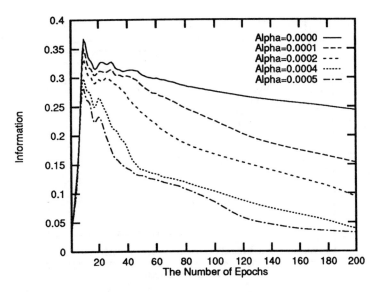

Figure 2: Information as a function of the number of epochs for five different values of the parameter α.

previous results on the past tense acquisition. Details on the training and testing patterns are omitted for the simplicity of the explanation. We attempt only to show how networks were trained to produce targets.

In this problem, networks are trained to produce correct past tense forms. For example, a string /pat/ is given to the networks. From the grammar of our artificial language, the correct past tense form is /patid/. Thus, networks must produce this correct past tense form after finishing the learning.

In actual problems, input strings were represented in the phonological representation [5] and the number of input units was 18 units. The number of hidden units was 20. The number of output units was 20 for the inference of regular verbs. The number of training patterns was 100 and the number of testing patterns was 500. Networks started to learn with initial random values (-0.25, 0.25). The parameter for the momentum term was fixed to 0.9 for all the experiments. The learning was performed by using the so-called *Batch* learning, meaning that weights were updated after processing all the input patterns. The learning was considered to be finished, only when the epochs were 200.

3.2 Inference of Regular Verbs

In this section, we attempt to show that by increasing the value of the parameter α, the information, stored in the internal representation is decreased and the generalization performance is significantly improved.

Figure 2 shows the information as a function of the number of epochs, when the number of hidden units was 20. The information was normalized by the following equation:

$$
\begin{aligned}
I^{nrm} &= \frac{I}{H_{max}} \\
&= 1 + \frac{1}{KM \log 2} \sum_{k}^{K} \sum_{i}^{M} [v_i^k \log v_i^k + (1 - v_i^k) \log(1 - v_i^k)].
\end{aligned} \tag{5}
$$

Thus, the range of this normalized information is [0,1]. If the information is 1, the information is maximized. On the other hand, if the information is zero, the information is minimized. As you can see from the figure, the information is increased quickly at the first part of the learning, and then decreased gradually. As the parameter α is increased, the information is more significantly decreased and close to zero, minimum information state. This shows that the information minimization method is quite effective to decrease the information content in the internal representation.

Now, let us see how the generalization errors can be improved by using the method of information minimization. Figure 3 and Figure 4 show training and generalization errors as a function of the number

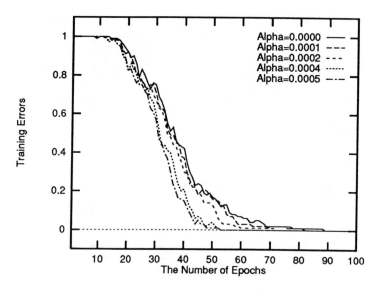

Figure 3: Training errors as a function of the number of epochs
for five different values of the parameter α.

of epochs respectively. Training errors (T^{nrm}) and generalization errors(G^{nrm}) were computed by using Hamming distance between targets and outputs at output units. For example, the generalization errors (G^{nrm}) are normalized as follows:

$$G^{nrm} = \frac{1}{SN} \sum_{k}^{S} \sum_{i}^{N} [A(o_i^k)(1 - \zeta_i^k) + (1 - A(o_i^k))\zeta_i^k],$$

where o_i^k is an output at ith output unit for kth input pattern for the testing patterns, ζ_i^k is its target, N is the number of output units, S is the number of testing patterns, and $A(x)$ is 1 for $x \geq 0.5$ and 0 for $x < 0.5$. Let us see Figure 3 for the training errors. As you can see from the figure, training errors are decreased gradually and finally zero both for the standard back-propagation (α=0) and information minimization method. Little difference can be seen in the training errors. However, for the testing data, a big difference can be seen. Figure 4 shows generalization errors for the testing data. As the parameter α is increased, the information is decreased significantly. We can clearly see that the generalization is much improved by using the information minimization.

4   Conclusion

In the present paper, we have proposed the minimum information principle. This principle states that for the good generalization performance, the information stored in network architecture must be as small as possible, under the condition that networks have the sufficient capacity to learn the input patterns with appropriate accuracy. We have formulated the entropy function for the internal representation and the update rule to minimize the information content. By applying the method to the problem of language acquisition, we have demonstrated that the generalization is really improved by minimizing the information content, stored in the internal representation. We think that many techniques concerning the improvement of the generalization performance can be incorporated into the framework of the minimum information principle.

References

[1] J. Bridle, D. MacKay and A. Heading, "Unsupervised classifier, mutual information and phantom targets," in *Neural Information Processing Systems*, Morgan Kaufmann Publishers, San Mateo: CA, Vol.4, pp.1096-1101, 1992.

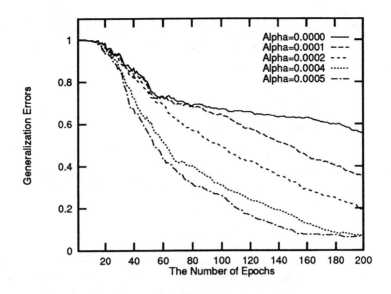

Figure 4: Generalization errors as a function of the number of epochs for five different values of the parameter α.

[2] G. Deco, W. Finnof and H. G. Zimmermann, "Elimination of overtraining by a mutual information network," in *Proceeding of the International Conference on Artificial Neural Networks*, Springer-Verlag, pp.744-749.

[3] M. Mizumoto, *Fuzzy Theory and its Application*, (in Japanese), Science Publishers, Tokyo.

[4] C. W. Omlin and C. L. Giles, "Pruning recurrent neural networks for improved generalization performance," Revised Technical Report No. 93-6, April 1993, Computer Science Department, Rensselaer Polytechnic Institute, Troy, N. Y.

[5] K. Plunkett, V. Marchman, and S. L. Knudsen, "From Rote Learning to System Building: Acquiring Verb Morphology in Children and Connectionist Nets," in *Connectionist Models: Proceedings of the 1990 Summer School*, D. S. Touretzky, J. L. Elman and G. E. Hinton, (Eds), Morgan Kaufmann Publishers, Inc, San Mateo: California, pp.201-219, 1990.

[6] H. H Thodberg, "Improving generalization of neural networks through pruning," *International Journal of Neural Systems*, Vol.1, No.4, pp.317-326, 1991.

[7] A. S. Weigend, D. E. Rumelhart, and B. A. Huberman, "Generalization by weight-elimination with application to forecasting," in *Neural Information Processing Systems*, Morgan Kaufmann Publishers, San Mateo: CA, Vol.4, pp.950-957, 1992.

Improved learning of backpropagation neural networks using an alternative data clustering algorithm

Igor Dvorchik and Howard R. Doyle

From the Section of Computational Medicine, Pittsburgh Transplant Institute, University of Pittsburgh School of Medicine, Pittsburgh PA, 15213

ABSTRACT

We propose a method that scales data to a range that is appropriate for presentation to a neural network, and takes into consideration its actual probability distribution. This method can be applied to any data set, even when there is no prior knowledge of its underlying distribution. We have found that such data transformation greatly improves learning in a standard backpropagation network, and allows the network to learn difficult, linearly non-separable problems that resist more traditional methods.

INTRODUCTION

When training a feed-forward, multilayer neural network there are several issues that arise, with data representation being one of major importance. To represent real numbers we must consider how to scale and, if necessary, transform the data. Scaling is certainly called for in networks whose outputs are other than binary, and, in general, learning is probably improved by limiting the range the learning algorithm must traverse. Transformations, on the other hand, should be considered whenever the variables have a highly asymmetrical distribution, or greatly uneven variances. Linear scaling under these circumstances could lead to loss of information, as the data are unevenly compressed or expanded. A common approach consists of performing a preliminary exploratory analysis of the data, and then applying a suitable transformation.

We propose a method that scales the data to any range appropriate for presentation to a neural network, while at the same time letting us cluster it in a way that can make it more meaningful. We have found that such data transformation improves learning in a standard backpropagation network, allowing the network to learn difficult, non-linearly separable problems that resist more traditional methods.

TRANSFORMATION ALGORITHM

The purpose of the transformation is to create a one-to-one correspondence between the actual data and its transformed (scaled and clustered) values, based upon the data's probability distribution. The proposed algorithm can be used on any bounded, real valued input vectors with a finite number of elements.

Let $X = (x_{min}, \ldots x_{max})$ be a vector of the actual data, distributed in ascending order, with x_{min} and x_{max}, minimum and maximum values, respectively. We now divide this range on N equal segments, of lengths λ_k, where

$$\lambda_k = (x_{max} - x_{min}) / N, k = 1,2,\ldots N \qquad \text{(Eq. 1)}$$

The normalization function ϕ transforms all segments of the actual data, λ_k to the corresponding clustered segments of normalized data, $\tilde{\lambda}_k$, according to the expression:

$$\phi(\lambda_k) = \widetilde{\lambda}_k + D_k \qquad \text{(Eq. 2)}$$

where:

$$\widetilde{\lambda}_k = C * L * P_k \qquad \text{(Eq. 3)}$$

$$D_k = (1 - C) / (N - 1), k = 1, 2, \dots N - 1, \quad D_N = 0 \qquad \text{(Eq. 4)}$$

Where P_k is the probability that an actual data value, which belongs to the input vector X, is located in a segment λ_k, L is the length of the normalized input vector, and C is a compression factor. Although the data can be normalized between any real numbers, for the purposes of this work the members of the input vector will be normalized between 0 and 1 and, therefore, $L = $. The number of clusters is defined by N; and the value of the compression factor, C, defines the lengths of the normalized segments $\widetilde{\lambda}_k$ and spaces D_k between them [eq. (3) and (4)], with $0 < C \leq 1$

Since $\sum\limits_{k=1}^{N} P_k = 1$, the sum of all transformed segments $\widetilde{\lambda}_k$ equals $\sum\limits_{k=1}^{N} C * L * P_k = C * L$

$$\text{(eq.5)}$$

All members $(x_1^k, \dots x_n^k)$ inside the segment λ_k of the input vector X are homotheticaly transformed to the members $(\widetilde{x}_1^k, \dots \widetilde{x}_n^k)$ of the normalized segment $\widetilde{\lambda}_k$, correspondingly to the distance between them and the origins of the segments λ_k and $\widetilde{\lambda}_k$ respectively, with a coefficient of similitude equal $\lambda_k / \widetilde{\lambda}_k$. Hence, if $x_o \in \lambda_k$ then its transformed value $\widetilde{x}_o \in \widetilde{\lambda}_k$ and:

$$\frac{(\widetilde{x}_o - \widetilde{x}_{k-1})}{(x_o - x_{k-1})} = \frac{\widetilde{\lambda}_k}{\lambda_k} \qquad \text{(Eq. 6)}$$

where:

$\widetilde{x}_{k-1}$ and x_{k-1} are the values of the origins of the normalized segment $\widetilde{\lambda}_k$ and actual data segment λ_k, respectively.

From equation (6), and using equations (1-5), we derive a one-to-one correspondence between any actual value x_o belonging to the segment λ_k, and its transformed value $\widetilde{x}_o$ belonging to the segment $\widetilde{\lambda}_k$:

$$\widetilde{x}_o = \widetilde{x}_{k-1} + \frac{P_k * C * L * (x_o - x_{k-1})}{(x_{max} - x_{min}) / N} \qquad \text{(Eq. 7)}$$

Where:

$$\widetilde{x}_{k-1} = x_{k-1} + L * C * \sum_{j=1}^{k-1} P_j + \frac{L * (1 - C) * (k - 1)}{N - 1} \qquad \text{(Eq. 8)}$$

and:

$$x_{k-1} = x_{min} + \frac{(x_{max} - x_{min}) * (k - 1)}{N} \qquad \text{(Eq. 9)}$$

$\widetilde{x}$ — the transformed value, corresponding to the real value x, which belongs to the $k - th$ segment.

P_j, P_k — the probabilities of distribution of the variable x on the j and k segments, respectively.

N — the number of segments that the variable has been divided into.

x_{min}, x_{max} - minimum and maximum values of the variable, respectively.

x_{k-1} — the coordinate of the origin of the $k - th$ segment.

L — the length of the normalized input vector.

C — a compression factor.

As shown by equation (3), the length of the normalized data segments depends linearly on the probability that data are observed at the corresponding actual data segments; therefore, the normalization is carried out without loss of "non-significant" data values, which could prove important in real-life problems. Moreover, this is accomplished without the need for prior knowledge regarding the underlying distribution.

The number of segments is determined by N, which can take any integer value ≥ 1, and it is arrived at either empirically or through the use of more formal methods, such as cluster analysis. The compression factor, C, adds flexibility to the representation because it determines the lengths of the normalized segments and of the spaces, free of data, between them. Hence, it allows presentation of data to the neural network as either distinctly quantized data sets, $C \approx 0$, or as individual data members, $C \approx 1$. By tailoring the values of N and C to the individual variables, one can arrive at the best possible representation for any given data set.

Another point that bears emphasis is that this transformation is independent from the internal network structure, making it possible to present data so transformed to any neural network, regardless of the architecture.

EXPERIMENTAL METHODS.

To test the effect on network performance of the transformation algorithm we trained a series of multilayer, backpropagation networks to predict outcome following liver transplantation. The data set used was gathered from 155 liver transplantations, and has been described in detail [Doyle, et al., 1994]. Initially, ten different training/testing data sets were prepared by random subsampling of the original data. The training sets consisted of 138 examples, while the testing sets had 17 examples, with the proportions of both outcomes (i.e., success and failure) being the same in both. By applying the preceding algorithm to these data, three separate transformed data groups were generated (using 2, 4, and 10 intervals, respectively, and a compression factor of 0.9). A fourth group consisted of data that were linearly scaled.

The networks used in these experiments had the same architecture, namely 19 input neurons, a single hidden layer with two neurons, and one output neuron. There were a total of 40 networks (one for each training/testing set), and each network was trained 10 times, using different initial random weights. The following parameters were compared:

- The number of networks which were able to completely learn their training sets in the course of 70,000 epochs

- Minimal training RMS errors

- Mean RMS error, for all networks and those which learned their training sets completely

Results were compared using one-way analysis of variance (Scheffe test), with the level of significance set at 0.05.

RESULTS

Table 1 shows the summary results:

TABLE 1

Transformation	Complete	Min-RMS	Mean-RMS	Complete-RMS
Linear	39	0.031	0.079	0.045
2-intervals	26	0.024	0.097	0.042
4-intervals	54	0.020	0.074	0.032
10-intervals	75	0.020	0.052	0.028

Where:

- Complete - Number of networks that learned their training set completely in the course of 70,000 epochs (n=100).

- Min-RMS - The minimal training RMS error

- Mean-RMS - The mean of training RMS errors

- Complete-RMS - Mean of training RMS errors among the networks that learned their training set completely in the course of 70,000 epochs

The performance of those networks working with data transformed using 10 intervals was superior to that of those using linearly transformed data, in all the categories examined (one-way analysis of variance).

CONCLUSION

Our results suggest that employment of the proposed transformation improves learning in backpropagation neural networks. This introduces another degree of freedom when developing a neural network model, which is independent of network architecture, and offers the possibility of representing data in a manner that more closely reflects its underlying distribution.

Since the number of possible proposed transformations is theoretically infinite, the obvious question arises: how to chose the best one for a particular input variable? Although we are not able to answer this question at present, we see our future work in this exploring the following issues:

- Using well-established clustering algorithms (K-means, Melting, etc.) to choose the most appropriate number of intervals

- Study the effects of different compression factors as we vary the number of intervals

- Develop "toy" networks to determine, for different variables belonging to a given domain, what is the best combination of compression factor and number of intervals.

REFERENCES

Doyle HR, Dvorchik I, Mitchell S, et al. Predicting outcomes after liver transplantation. A connectionist approach. Ann Surg (in press).

Analysis of Unscaled Contributions in Cross Connected Networks

Thomas R. Shultz
shultz@psych.mcgill.ca

and

Yuriko Oshima-Takane
yuriko@hebb.psych.mcgill.ca

Department of Psychology
McGill University
Montréal, Québec, Canada H3A 1B1

ABSTRACT

Contribution analysis is a useful tool for the analysis of cross-connected networks such as those generated by the cascade-correlation learning algorithm. Networks with cross connections that supersede hidden layers pose particular difficulties for standard analyses of hidden unit activation patterns. A contribution is defined as the product of an output weight and the associated activation on the sending unit. Previously such contributions have been multiplied by the sign of the output target for a particular input pattern. The present work shows that a principal components analysis (PCA) of unscaled contributions yields more interesting insights than comparable analyses of contributions scaled by the sign of output targets.

1 INTRODUCTION

Solutions learned by neural networks are often quite difficult to understand because of the complex non-linear properties of neural nets and the common use of distributed representations. Standard techniques of network analysis, based either on a network's weights or its hidden unit activations have been somewhat limited. The most notable features of weight diagrams are often the complexity of the pattern of weights and its variability across multiple networks learning the same problem. Statistical analysis of activation patterns on hidden units is limited to nets with a single hidden layer without cross-connections.

Cross connections are direct connections that bypass intervening hidden layers. They are known to increase learning speed in back-propagation networks (Lang & Witbrock, 1988) and are a standard feature of some generative learning algorithms, such as cascade-correlation (Fahlman & Lebiere, 1990). Because such cross connections carry so much of the work load, any analysis restricted to hidden unit activations provides at best a partial picture of the network solution.

Contribution analysis appears to be a useful technique for multi-layer, cross connected nets. Sanger (1989) defined a contribution as the triple product of an output weight, the activation of a sending unit, and the sign of the output target for that input. Contributions are potentially more informative than either weights alone or hidden unit activations alone since they take account of both weight and sending activation. Shultz and Elman (1994) used principal components analysis to reduce the dimensionality of such contributions in several different types of cascade-correlation nets.

The present work explores whether it is preferable to employ contributions that are scaled by the sign of their output targets or to use unscaled contributions in network analysis. Sanger (1989) recommended scaling contributions by the signs of output targets in order to determine whether the contributions helped or hindered the network's solution. However, since target signs are not available to networks except as error correction signals, it could be argued that it is more natural to use unscaled contributions in analyzing knowledge representations.

Understanding the knowledge representations in network solutions may be useful in a variety of contexts. It is surely useful in the area of cognitive modeling, where the mere ability of nets to simulate psychological phenomena does not suffice. It is also critically important to determine whether the representations developed by networks bear any systematic relation to the representations employed by human subjects (McCloskey, 1991).

2 PRINCIPAL COMPONENTS ANALYSIS OF CONTRIBUTIONS

In contrast to Sanger's (1989) three-dimensional array of contributions (output unit x hidden unit x input pattern), we begin with a two-dimensional output weight x input pattern array of contributions. This is more efficient than the slicing technique used by Sanger to focus on particular output or hidden units and yet allows identification of the roles of specific contributions (Shultz & Elman, 1994).

We subject the correlations among contributions across input patterns to PCA, a statistical technique that identifies dimensions of variation (Flury, 1988). A component is a line of closest fit to a set of points in multi-dimensional space. PCA summarizes a multivariate data set in a few components by capitalizing on correlations among the variables.

Here we apply PCA to contributions taken from networks learning either continuous XOR or arithmetic comparisons. The contribution matrix for each net is subjected to PCA with 1.0 as the minimum eigenvalue for retention. Varimax rotation is applied to improve the interpretability of the solution. Component scores are plotted to indicate the function of the components and component loadings are examined to determine the roles of particular contributions.

3 APPLICATION TO THE CONTINUOUS XOR PROBLEM

The classical binary XOR problem has too few training patterns (four) to require contribution analysis. We construct a continuous version of the XOR problem by dividing the input space into four quadrants. Input values are incremented in steps of 0.1 starting from 0.1, yielding 100 x, y input pairs. Quadrant a has values of x less than 0.55 combined with values of y above 0.55. Quadrant b has values of x and y greater than 0.55. Quadrant c has values of x and y less than 0.55. Quadrant d has values of x greater than 0.55 combined with values of y below 0.55. Problems from quadrants a and d produce a positive output target, whereas problems from quadrants b and c yield a negative output target.

Three cascade-correlation nets are trained on continuous XOR. Each net generates a unique solution, recruiting either five or six hidden units and taking from 541 to 765 epochs. PCA of unscaled contributions yields three components rather than the two yielded by PCA of scaled contributions (Shultz & Elman, 1994). Plots of rotated component scores for the 100 training patterns are less dense but more interesting for unscaled than for scaled contributions.

Two-dimensional plots of component scores for net 1 are shown in Figure 1 and labeled according to their respective quadrant. Figure 1a, plotting scores on components 1 and 3, shows that component 1 reflects the second input dimension (quadrants a and b vs. quadrants c and d). Figure 1b, plotting scores on components 2 and 3, shows that component 2 reflects the first input dimension (quadrants b and d vs. quadrants a and c). Both Figures 1a and 1b reveal that component 3 separates the quadrants with a positive output target (a and d) from those with a negative output target (b and c). Similar results were obtained for the two other nets. In contrast, plots of component scores for scaled contributions indicated interactive separation of the four quadrants, but with no clear individual roles for the two components (Shultz & Elman, 1994).

Figure 2 plots the rotated component scores for this net. Such plots can be examined to determine the role of each contribution in the network. For example, input 2 and hidden units 1, 5, and 6 all participate in the job done by component 1, namely the representation of the second input dimension.

4 APPLICATION TO COMPARATIVE ARITHMETIC

Arithmetic comparison tasks require nets to compare sums or products to some value and then output whether the sum or product is greater than, less than, or equal to that comparative value. The fact that several psychological simulations using neural nets involve problems of linear and non-linear arithmetic operations enhances interest in this sort of problem (McClelland, 1989; Shultz, Schmidt, Buckingham, & Mareschal, in press).

Addition and multiplication tasks each involve three linear input units. The first two input units each code a randomly selected integer in the range from 0 to 9, inclusive, and the third input unit codes a randomly selected comparison integer. For addition problems, comparison values range from 0 to 19, inclusive; for multiplication, comparison values range from 0 to 82, inclusive. Two output units code the results of the comparison. Target outputs of +- represent that the results of the arithmetic operation are *greater than* the comparison value, targets of -+ represent *less than*, and targets of ++ represent *equal to*. For problems involving both addition and multiplication, a fourth input unit codes the type of arithmetic operation to be performed: 0 for addition, 1 for multiplication.

Nets trained on either addition or multiplication have 100 randomly selected training patterns, with the restriction that 45 of them have correct answers of *greater than*, 45 have correct answers of *less than*, and 10 have correct answers of *equal to*. These constraints reduce the skew of comparative values in the high direction on multiplication problems. Nets trained on both addition and multiplication receive 100 randomly selected addition problems and 100 randomly selected multiplication problems. There are three addition nets, three multiplication nets, and three nets trained on both addition and multiplication.

4.1 ADDITION RESULTS

Each of the three nets learning addition problems recruited a single hidden unit. They took between 155 and 169 epochs to learn. PCA of unscaled contributions in each net yields three significant components, unlike the two components obtained with scaled contributions.

Component score plots, such as that for net 1 in Figure 3, indicate that component 1 distinguishes *less than* from *greater than* answers. Problems with *equal to* answers were not isolated by the three components. Components 2 and 3 are particularly sensitive to variation in the size of the first and second integers to be added, respectively. This was revealed by examining extreme component scores on these components, either greater than 1.0 or less than -1.0. Problems with extremely negative component 2 scores had a mean of 8.41 for the first integer and 5.36 for the second integer. Problems with extremely positive component 2 scores had a mean of 1.00 for the first integer and 5.52 for the second integer. This indicates that component 2 is primarily sensitive to the size of the first integer input. In contrast, component 3 was sensitive to the size of the second integer input with means of 1.48 for extremely negative component scores and 8.36 for extremely positive component scores. The means on the first integer input did not vary much with extremity of component 3 score: 4.70 vs. 4.05. Similar results obtained for the other two nets.

PCA of scaled contributions had produced two components that were sensitive only to answer type and not to variation in integer input. As with the continuous XOR problem, the plots of component scores were denser for scaled contributions, but not as revealing (Shultz & Elman, 1994).

4.2 MULTIPLICATION RESULTS

Multiplication is a much more difficult problem for nets with additive activation functions, as revealed by the fact that the nets learning multiplication comparisons required from 832 to over 1000 epochs and recruited between six and eight hidden units. Runs were terminated when they reached 1000 epochs. PCA applied to the contributions in these nets yields from 4 to 6 significant components. Plots of rotated component scores for two of the four components from net 3 are presented in Figure 4. This plot shows that most of the separation of *greater than* from *less than* outputs was accomplished by component 2. Component 1 served to make this distinction for the remaining problems. Problems with *equal to* answers were not isolated by any of the four components.

Component 1 also served to represent variation in the second input. Problems with extremely high scores on component 1 have a mean second input of 8.57; those with extremely low scores on component 1 have a mean second input of 0.56. Component 3 serves a similar role for the first input. Problems with extremely high scores on component 3 have a mean first input of 8.11; those with extremely low scores on component 3 have a mean first input of 1.10. The role of component 4 is opaque. Basically similar results were obtained for the other two multiplication nets. In contrast, PCA of scaled components were less revealing, except for offering a clear separation of answer types (Shultz & Elman, 1994).

4.3 RESULTS FOR NETS DOING BOTH ADDITION AND MULTIPLICATION

Learning to do both addition and multiplication is even more difficult than multiplication alone. None of the three nets quite reached victory by 1000 epochs, but each did come close. Either seven or eight hiddens units were recruited. PCA of contributions yields five components in each of the three nets. Besides the familiar distinctions between problem types and variation in integer inputs found in nets doing either addition or multiplication, it is of interest to determine whether nets doing both operations distinguish between adding and multiplying.

Figure 5 shows rotated component scores for three components from net 3. Component 1 separates *greater than* from *less than* answers. Component 5 and, to a lesser extent, component 4 separate adding from multiplying. The role of component 4 is not very clear from Figure 5, but various two-dimensional plots of component 4 reveal that it separates adding vs. multiplying for problems with *less than* answers.

Components 2 and 3 handle variation in the first and second input integers, respectively. Problems with extremely positive component 2 scores have a mean first input integer of 8.53; problems with extremely negative component 2 scores have a mean first input integer of 0.84. Problems with extremely positive component 3 scores have a mean second input integer of 8.55; problems with extremely negative component 3 scores have a mean second input integer of 1.05. Problems with *equal to* answers are not isolated by any of the components. Results for the other two nets learning both multiplication and addition comparisons are essentially similar to these. In contrast, PCA of scaled contributions had produced three components that interactively separated the three answer types and operations, but did not represent variation in input integers (Shultz & Elman, 1994).

5 DISCUSSION

As with continuous XOR, there is considerable variation among networks learning comparative arithmetic problems. Yet with all of this variation, it is apparent that the nets learn to separate arithmetic problems according to features afforded by the training set. Nets learning either addition or multiplication differentiate the problems according to answer types and nets learning both arithmetic operations supplement these answer distinctions with the operational distinction between adding and multiplying. Variation along the integer input dimensions is also well represented.

This research confirms earlier conclusions that PCA of network contributions is a useful technique for understanding the performance of networks constructed by the cascade-correlation learning algorithm (Shultz & Elman, 1994). Because cascade-correlation nets typically possess multiple hidden layers and are fully cross connected, they are difficult to analyze with more standard methods emphasizing activation patterns on the hidden units alone. Examination of their weight patterns is also problematic, particularly in larger networks, because of the highly distributed nature of the net's representations.

Analyzing contributions, in contrast to either hidden unit activations or weights, is a naturally appealing solution. Contributions capture the influence coming into output units both from adjacent hidden units and from distant, cross connected hidden and input units.

The present work also suggests that analyzing unscaled contributions yields more useful results than does the analysis of contributions that are scaled by the output targets. This is particularly true in terms of sensitivity to various input dimensions and to operational distinctions between adding and multiplying. Plots of component scores based on unscaled contributions are typically not as dense as those based on scaled contributions but seem to be more revealing of what information the network is representing. Including target outputs in these analyses is not only unrealistic, but also obscures at least part of what networks represent, such as variation along important input dimensions. A drawback of using unscaled contributions is that contributions from the bias unit are ignored for lack of variation. This may explain why the present analyses fail to isolate arithmetic problems with *equal to* outcomes.

Because PCA of contributions can identify the role of contributions from particular hidden units, it should be useful in predicting the results of lesioning experiments with neural nets. Once the role of a hidden unit has been identified by its association with a particular principal component, then it could be predicted that lesioning this unit would impair whatever function is served by the component. PCA of network contributions obtained from cognitive modeling could also be a useful source of psychological hypotheses.

Acknowledgments

This research was supported by the Natural Sciences and Engineering Research Council of Canada.

References

Fahlman, S. E., & Lebiere, C. (1990.) The Cascade-Correlation learning architecture. In D. Touretzky (Ed.), *Advances in neural information processing systems 2*, (pp. 524-532). Mountain View, CA: Morgan Kaufmann.

Flury, B. (1988). *Common principal components and related multivariate models.* New York: Wesley.

Lang, K. J., & Witbrock, M. J. (1988). Learning to tell two spirals apart. In D. Touretzky, G. Hinton, & T. Sejnowski (Eds)., *Proceedings of the Connectionist Models Summer School*, (pp. 52-59). Mountain View, CA: Morgan Kaufmann.

McClelland, J. L. (1989). Parallel distributed processing: Implications for cognition and development. In Morris, R. G. M. (Ed.), *Parallel distributed processing: Implications for psychology and neurobiology*, pp. 8-45. Oxford University Press.

McCloskey, M. (1991). Networks and theories: The place of connectionism in cognitive science. *Psychological Science*, 2, 387-395.

Sanger, D. (1989). Contribution analysis: A technique for assigning responsibilities to hidden units in connectionist networks. *Connection Science*, 1, 115-138.

Shultz, T. R., & Elman, J. L. (1994). Analyzing cross connected networks. In J. D. Cowan, G. Tesauro, & J. Alspector (Eds.), *Advances in Neural Information Processing Systems 6*. San Francisco, CA: Morgan Kaufmann.

Shultz, T. R., Schmidt, W. C., Buckingham, D., & Mareschal, D. (In press). Modeling cognitive development with a generative connectionist algorithm. In G. Halford & T. Simon (Eds.), *Developing cognitive competence: New approaches to process modeling*. Hillsdale, NJ: Erlbaum.

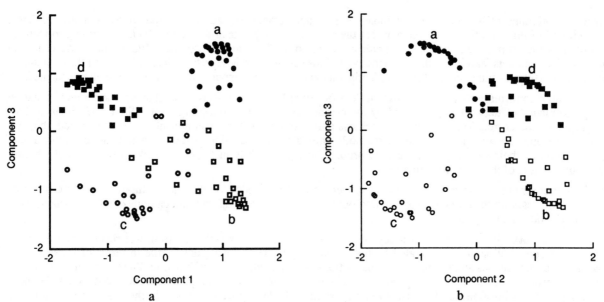

Figure1. Rotated component scores for a continuous XOR net. 1a. Components 1 and 3. 1b. Components 2 and 3.

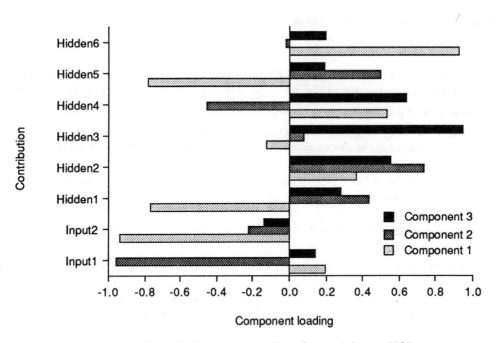

Figure 2. Component loadings for a continuous XOR net.

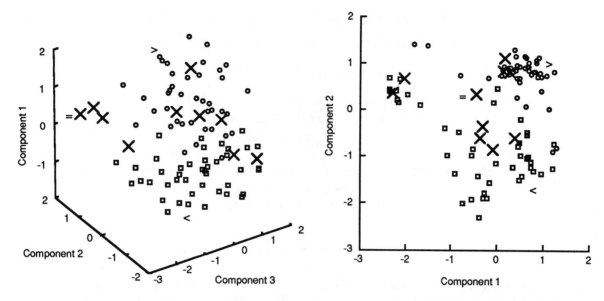

Figure 3. Rotated component scores for an addition net.

Figure 4. Rotated component scores for a multiplication net.

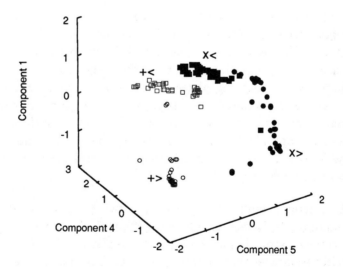

Figure 5. Rotated component scores for a net doing both addition and multiplication.

Genetic Algorithm Approach to Fault-Tolerant Neural Networks Design

C. R. Chow,[1] C. H. Chu,[1] M. Naraghi-Pour,[2] and M. Hegde[2]

[1]CENTER FOR ADVANCED COMPUTER STUDIES
THE UNIVERSITY OF SOUTHWESTERN LOUISIANA
LAFAYETTE, LA 70504
and
[2]DEPARTMENT OF ELECTRICAL AND COMPUTER ENGINEERING
LOUISIANA STATE UNIVERSITY
BATON ROUGE, LA 70803

Abstract

A learning algorithm, referred to as concurrent training, based on genetic algorithms for a neural network with connected modules is described. The algorithm does not require the knowledge of training sets for each module so that all modules can be trained concurrently. For an N-module system, N separate pools of chromosomes are maintained and updated. The concurrent training algorithm is applied to train multilayered feedforward networks by considering each layer of connections to be a 1-layer network module. The algorithm is tested using the 4-bit parity problem and a linearly nonseparable classification problem. Experiment results are presented and the learning behavior and performance is analyzed.

1   Introduction

Supervised learning of feedforward networks is typically in the form of a search in the weight space for a set of weights which minimizes the difference between the computed and the target outputs for a given input. The optimization method used most often in this role is the gradient descent search, such as in the variations of the backpropagation learning algorithm. After the network has completed the learning phase, faults in the components of the network may lead to incorrect output being computed. In this paper, the design of fault-tolerant feedforward networks is considered by incorporating a measure of fault-tolerance in the optimization criterion during learning. Since the optimization function will not be convex, the use of an alternative optimization method known as genetic algorithms to train multilayered feedforward networks in the supervised learning mode is described.

Previous work in designing fault-tolerant neural networks have included: including faults during training [1], min-max fault-tolerance learning [2], fault-tolerance through weight control, and fault-tolerance through strict learning and strict operation [3]. The method used in the present paper explicitly separates the classification error from the errors due to faults in the optimization function. Let $\{(\xi^\mu, \tau^\mu) : \mu = 0, 1, \cdots, N - 1\}$ be the training set, where ξ^μ and τ^μ denote the μth input and target output, respectively. Let ζ^μ denote the output of a network in response to the input pattern ξ^μ. The mean-squared classification error

$$E_n = \sum_\mu (\zeta^\mu - \tau^\mu)^2$$

is typically the measure to be minimized in a training algorithm. Suppose the network has M hidden units; let ζ_m^μ, $m = 0, \cdots, M-1$, be the network output in response to ξ^μ when the mth hidden unit is faulty. The error due to faults is defined to be:

$$E_f = \sum_\mu \max_m (\zeta_m^\mu - \tau^\mu)^2.$$

The overall optimization criterion in our training algorithm is then:

$$E = E_n + \lambda E_f,$$

where λ is a scalar constant and is set at 0.4 in our experiments. It is noted that in this paper the attention is restricted to faults occurring in the hidden units; nevertheless, the concepts can be generalized to failures in the links or units in other layers by extending E_f to cover all faults.

Genetic algorithms (GAs) are stochastic optimization algorithms [4] in which a solution to the combinatorial problem of interest is represented by a binary string, referred to as a chromosome. A fitness value is defined for each chromosome based on the cost associated with the corresponding solution. A population of chromosomes is maintained, and a new generation is formed by selecting mating pairs with superior fitness values. Genetic operators, such as crossover or mutation, are applied to the mating pairs to form offsprings, which would be improved, or better fit, solutions. This process is repeated until an acceptable solution appears in one of the generations.

Genetic algorithms have been used to train multilayered neural networks. In some approaches (e.g., [5]), the network architecture is fixed and the network weights are encoded as a chromosome with which a GA is used to search for the optimal weights. In others (e.g., [6]), a GA is used to assist some other training techniques such as back-propagation by defining the network architecture, by finding the initial weights for back-propagation, or parameters used in other training methods. In this approach, GA is used to augment the main training method by finding a set of favorable constraint domains. In [7], a GA is used to train a neural network and to construct the network architecture simultaneously. In [8], a GA is used to train a large scale neural network system by training each component subnetwork or module separately provided that the training sets are available for all modules.

The concurrent training algorithm used in this project sets the synaptic weights using a genetic algorithm search, in which multiple strands of chromosomes are used to encode a phenotype [9]. A neural network that consists of N layers could be encoded as N chromosomes.

2 Experiments and Results

The concurrent training of fault-tolerant neural networks is validated by using the 4-bit parity problem, so that there are a total of 16 input-target pattern pairs. While all inputs are encoded using binary digits 1 and -1, the weights, and hence the chromosomes, are encoded with binary digits 0 and 1.

The experiments for training fault-tolerant neural networks were conducted by setting $\lambda = 0.4$ in the optimization function. As a control, the experiments were repeated with the same GA parameters while setting $\lambda = 0.0$ in the optimization function, thus removing the fault-tolerance inclusion property of the training algorithm. The network to be trained in each experiment set are 2-layer fully connected networks, each with four input units and one output unit. Different numbers of hidden units are considered (viz. 4, 6, 8, and 10), to observe the effect of increasing hidden units on fault-tolerance. Because the training algorithm is stochastic in nature, seven runs were made for each parameter setting, with the number of iterations set at a constant 200 generations for each run.

The results of the experiments are summarized in Tables 1 and 2. in which the number of generations it took for the best network to evolve, the number of classification error and the number of errors due to faults of the best network, are tabulated against the number of hidden units in the network. In Tables 1 and 2, the minimum and the average of the number of errors in the seven runs, respectively, are shown. In both tables, part (a) refers to the case where fault-tolerance is included ($\lambda = 0.4$) while part (b) refers to the case when $\lambda = 0$, so that the number of errors due to faults of the network is not used in the training.

Two factors are of interest here: the learning behavior and the effectiveness of training with fault-tolerance inclusion. The learning behavior is first considered. When fault-tolerance is not used in the training, the number of generations required to obtain an optimal network decreased rather rapidly from about 60 to 32 as the number of hidden units was increased from 4 to 10, as can be expected. When fault-tolerance is included in training, however, the number of generations required to obtain an optimal network increased gradually from about 90 to 110 as the number of hidden units was increased. More time is needed because more training constraints were imposed, although it was observed that some runs converged early and some very late.

Next, the effectiveness of fault-tolerance inclusion training is studied. Consider a network with 4 hidden units, without including fault-tolerance in the training, it makes on average 5.43 (out of 16) output errors with a single fault in the network. Increasing the number of hidden units did not produce more fault-tolerant networks, as shown in Tables 1(b) and 2(b). With fault-tolerance included in the training, a network with 4 hidden units makes on average 2.86 output errors. The number of errors due to fault decreases to an average of 0.14 when 10 hidden units are used.

The capacity of the neural networks trained with single fault-tolerance inclusion to handle multiple faults is further tested. Networks with 10 hidden units are trained, again with $\lambda = 0.4$ for testing and with $\lambda = 0.0$ for control. One to five hidden units were set to fail in these experiments. There are C_n^{10} combinations of having n faults, $n = 1, \cdots, 5$, out of 10 hidden units; all combinations were tested and the maximum, average, and minimum errors of all combinations were recorded. The experiments were repeated for seven times, and the corresponding maximum, average, and minimum errors were averaged over these runs.

The results are shown in Table 3, where each row contains averaged results from seven runs. It can be seen that networks trained with fault tolerance inclusion have less maximum errors than networks trained without fault tolerance inclusion; i.e., such fault tolerance networks perform better in the worst case scenario in which serveral "important" hidden unit fail. Their overall average performances are also better than their counterparts. As can be expected, networks trained with fault tolerance inclusion do not handle multiple faults as effective as single fault. Multiple faults are handled in both cases by sheer redundancy. This could be attributed to the nature of the error functions defined for the training.

3   Concluding Remarks

A training algorithm is presented which includes a fault-tolerance component as part of the optimization criterion. Since the combined error function is not convex, a genetic algorithm is used to search for the optimal weights. The representation of the network in a genetic algorithm is considered, and a scheme where different layers of the networks are distributed on different chromosome strands is proposed and analyzed. Experiment results are used to show the learning behavior as well as the effectiveness of the new training algorithm to produce networks that can handle single as well as multiple faults.

Acknowledgments

This work is supported in part by the National Science Foundation and the Louisiana Board of Regents under grants no. NSF/LEQSF(1992-96)-ADP-04 and no. LEQSF(1992-94)-RD-A-28.

References

[1] C. H. Séquin and R. D. Clay, "Fault tolerance in artificial neural networks," in *Proceedings of the International Joint Conference on Neural Networks*, vol. I, pp. 703–708, June 1990.

[2] C. Neti, M. H. Schneider and E. D. Young, "Maximally fault tolerant neural networks and nonlinear programming," in *Proceedings of the International Joint Conference on Neural Networks*, vol. II, pp. 483–496, June 1990.

[3] M. Naraghi-Pour, M. Hegde, and P. Bapat, "Fault tolerance design of feedforward networks," in *Proc. World Congress in Neural Networks*, vol. III, pp. 568–571, July 1993.

[4] D. E. Goldberg, *Genetic Algorithms in Search, Optimization, and Machine Learning*. Reading, Mass.: Addison Wesley, 1989.

[5] D. J. Montana and L. Davis, "Training feedforward neural networks using genetic algorithms," in *Proceedings of the International Joint Conference on Artificial Intelligence*, vol. 1, pp. 762–767, 1989.

[6] R. K. Belew, J. McInerney, and N. Schraudolph, "Evolving networks: Using the genetic algorithm with connectionist learning," Tech. Rep. CS90-174, University of California at San Diego, Computer Science and Engineering Department, June 1990.

[7] J. R. Koza, "Genetic generation of both the weights and architecture for a neural network," in *Proceedings of the International Joint Conference on Neural Networks*, pp. 397–403, 1991.

[8] H. de Garis, "Genetic programming: Building artificial nervous systems with genetically programmed neural network modules," in *Neural and Intelligent Systems Integration* (B. Soucek, ed.), New York: Wiley, 1991, pp. 207–234.

[9] C. H. Chu and C. R. Chow, "A genetic algorithm approach to supervised learning in multilayered feedforward network," in *1993 Proc. World Congress on Neural Networks*, Portland, Ore., July 1993, vol. IV, pp. 744–747.

Table 1. Best performance of concurrent training attained in seven runs.

Number of hidden units	Number of generations	Number of classification errors	Number of fault errors
4	135.00	0.00	3.00
6	188.00	0.00	1.00
8	106.00	0.00	0.00
10	68.00	0.00	0.00

(a) With fault-tolerance inclusion in learning ($\lambda = 0.4$).

Number of hidden units	Number of generations	Number of classification errors	Number of fault errors
4	98.00	0.00	5.00
6	92.00	0.00	3.00
8	22.00	0.00	3.00
10	24.00	0.00	3.00

(b) Without fault-tolerance inclusion in learning ($\lambda = 0.0$).

Table 2. Average performance of concurrent training attained in seven runs.

Number of hidden units	Number of generations	Number of class-fication errors	Number of fault errors
4	92.29	1.71	2.86
6	102.14	0.14	1.71
8	103.43	0.00	0.57
10	107.29	0.00	0.14

(a) With fault-tolerance inclusion in learning ($\lambda = 0.4$).

Number of hidden units	Number of generations	Number of class-fication errors	Number of fault errors
4	61.43	1.14	5.43
6	44.71	0.00	4.43
8	45.14	0.00	4.57
10	32.86	0.00	4.43

(b) Without fault-tolerance inclusion in learning ($\lambda = 0.0$).

Table 3. Average of the performance of concurrent training in seven runs with multiple faults.

Number of Faulty Units	Number of Combinations	Average of Maximum Errors	Average of Minimum Errors	Average of Average Errors
1	10	0.14	0.00	0.11
2	45	4.71	0.00	1.38
3	120	5.57	0.14	2.09
4	210	6.43	0.14	2.82
5	252	7.14	0.14	2.99

(a) With fault-tolerance inclusion in learning ($\lambda = 0.4$).

Number of Faulty Units	Number of Combinations	Average of Maximum Errors	Average of Minimum Errors	Average of Average Errors
1	10	4.43	0.00	1.79
2	45	5.57	0.00	2.64
3	120	7.00	0.00	3.33
4	210	7.57	0.43	3.89
5	252	8.14	0.71	4.45

(b) Without fault-tolerance inclusion in learning ($\lambda = 0.0$).

An Analysis on the Learning Rule in the Complex Back-Propagation Algorithm

Tohru Nitta

Electrotechnical Laboratory,

1-1-4 Umezono, Tsukuba Science City, Ibaraki, 305 Japan.

Abstract:

In this paper, the characteristics of the learning rule in the "Complex-BP", a complex numbered version of the back-propagation algorithm, are investigated. The results of this study may be summarized as follows: (a) the error back propagation has a structure which is concerned with two-dimensional motion, (b) the unit of learning is complex-valued signals flowing in neural networks, (c) the learning rule is structured to avoid a "standstill in learning". Ultimately, learning speed is improved. In addition, the number of parameters needed is only about half that of the standard BP.

1 Introduction

The purpose of this paper is to investigate the characteristics of the learning rule in the complex-valued version of the back-propagation algorithm "Complex-BP" [2, 3]. We have obtained the following results on the inherent properties of the Complex-BP algorithm. (a) The error back propagation has a structure which is concerned with two-dimensional motion. (b) The unit of learning is complex-valued signals flowing in neural networks. (c) The learning rule is structured to avoid a "standstill in learning". Ultimately, the average convergence speed is improved. In addition, the required number of weights and thresholds (called "learning parameters" here) is only about half that of the standard back-propagation algorithm or "Real-BP" [5]. Thus it seems that the Complex-BP algorithm is well suited for learning complex-valued patterns.

2 The "Complex-BP" Algorithm

This section will briefly describe the Complex-BP algorithm [2, 3]. It can be applied to multi-layered neural networks in which weights, threshold values, input and output signals are all complex numbers, and the output function f_C of a neuron is defined as

$$f_C(z) = f_R(x) + i f_R(y), \tag{1}$$

where $z = x + iy$, i denotes $\sqrt{-1}$ and $f_R(u) = 1/(1 + \exp(-u))$, that is, the real and imaginary parts of the output of a neuron refer to the sigmoid functions of the real part x and the imaginary part y of the net input z to a neuron, respectively. The learning rule was obtained using a steepest descent method.

Note that there is another formulation of a complex-valued version [1] in which the output function is a complex-valued function $f_C(z) = 1/(1 + \exp(-z))$, where $z = x + iy$.

3 Characteristics of Learning

In this section, the characteristics of learning in the Complex-BP algorithm are discussed.

3.1 Structure of Learning Rule

First of all, we investigated the structure of the learning rule in the Complex-BP algorithm, using the three-layered (complex-valued) neural network described below as an example. We used w_{ml} for the weight between the input neuron l and the hidden neuron m, v_{nm} for the weight between the hidden neuron m and the output neuron n, θ_m for the threshold of the hidden neuron m, and γ_n for the threshold of the output neuron n. We let I_l, H_m, O_n denote the output values of the input neuron l, the hidden neuron m, and the output neuron n. We also let $\delta^n = T_n - O_n$ be the error between the output value O_n of the output neuron n and the desired output value T_n for the output neuron n.

Let Δx^R, Δx^I be the real and imaginary parts of the magnitude of change of a learning parameter x, respectively; i.e., $\Delta x^R = Re[\Delta x]$, $\Delta x^I = Im[\Delta x]$, where $Re[z]$, $Im[z]$ denote the real and imaginary parts of a complex number z, respectively. Then, the learning rule can be expressed as:

$$\begin{bmatrix} \Delta v_{nm}^R \\ \Delta v_{nm}^I \end{bmatrix} = \begin{bmatrix} Re[H_m] & Im[H_m] \\ -Im[H_m] & Re[H_m] \end{bmatrix} \begin{bmatrix} \Delta \gamma_n^R \\ \Delta \gamma_n^I \end{bmatrix} = |H_m| \begin{bmatrix} \cos \beta_m & \sin \beta_m \\ -\sin \beta_m & \cos \beta_m \end{bmatrix} \begin{bmatrix} \Delta \gamma_n^R \\ \Delta \gamma_n^I \end{bmatrix}, \quad (2)$$

$$\begin{bmatrix} \Delta \gamma_n^R \\ \Delta \gamma_n^I \end{bmatrix} = \varepsilon \begin{bmatrix} A_n & 0 \\ 0 & B_n \end{bmatrix} \begin{bmatrix} Re[\delta^n] \\ Im[\delta^n] \end{bmatrix}, \quad (3)$$

$$\begin{bmatrix} \Delta w_{ml}^R \\ \Delta w_{ml}^I \end{bmatrix} = \begin{bmatrix} Re[I_l] & Im[I_l] \\ -Im[I_l] & Re[I_l] \end{bmatrix} \begin{bmatrix} \Delta \theta_m^R \\ \Delta \theta_m^I \end{bmatrix} = |I_l| \begin{bmatrix} \cos \phi_l & \sin \phi_l \\ -\sin \phi_l & \cos \phi_l \end{bmatrix} \begin{bmatrix} \Delta \theta_m^R \\ \Delta \theta_m^I \end{bmatrix}, \quad (4)$$

$$\begin{bmatrix} \Delta \theta_m^R \\ \Delta \theta_m^I \end{bmatrix} = \begin{bmatrix} C_m & 0 \\ 0 & D_m \end{bmatrix} \sum_n \begin{bmatrix} Re[v_{nm}] & Im[v_{nm}] \\ -Im[v_{nm}] & Re[v_{nm}] \end{bmatrix} \begin{bmatrix} \Delta \gamma_n^R \\ \Delta \gamma_n^I \end{bmatrix}$$

$$= \begin{bmatrix} C_m & 0 \\ 0 & D_m \end{bmatrix} \sum_n |v_{nm}| \begin{bmatrix} \cos \varphi_{nm} & \sin \varphi_{nm} \\ -\sin \varphi_{nm} & \cos \varphi_{nm} \end{bmatrix} \begin{bmatrix} \Delta \gamma_n^R \\ \Delta \gamma_n^I \end{bmatrix}, \quad (5)$$

where $A_n = (1 - Re[O_n])Re[O_n]$, $B_n = (1 - Im[O_n])Im[O_n]$, $C_m = (1 - Re[H_m])Re[H_m]$, $D_m = (1 - Im[H_m])Im[H_m]$, $\beta_m = \arctan(Im[H_m]/Re[H_m])$, $\phi_l = \arctan(Im[I_l]/Re[I_l])$, and $\varphi_{nm} = \arctan(Im[v_{nm}]/Re[v_{nm}])$.

In expression (2), $|H_m|$ refers to a similar transformation (reduction, magnification) of the distance between a point and the origin in the Euclidean plane, and $\begin{bmatrix} \cos \beta_m & \sin \beta_m \\ -\sin \beta_m & \cos \beta_m \end{bmatrix}$ a clockwise rotation of a point by β_m degrees about the origin. Thus, the linear transformation called two-dimensional motion is performed in equation (2). Hence, we find that the magnitude of change in the weight between the hidden and output neurons $(\Delta v_{nm}^R, \Delta v_{nm}^I)$ can be obtained via the above linear transformation (two-dimensional motion) of $(\Delta \gamma_n^R, \Delta \gamma_n^I)$ which is the magnitude of change in the threshold of the output neuron. Similarly, the magnitude of change in the threshold of the hidden neuron $(\Delta \theta_m^R, \Delta \theta_m^I)$ can be obtained by applying the two-dimensional motion concerning v_{nm} (the weight between the hidden and output neurons) to $(\Delta \gamma_n^R, \Delta \gamma_n^I)$ which is the magnitude of change in the threshold of the output neuron (equation (5)). Finally, $(\Delta w_{ml}^R, \Delta w_{ml}^I)$ can be obtained by applying the two-dimensional motion concerning I_l to $(\Delta \theta_m^R, \Delta \theta_m^I)$ (equation (4)). Thus, it seems to be quite reasonable to assume that the error propagation in the Complex-BP has a structure based on two-dimensional motion.

The two-dimensional structure of the error propagation described above makes its appearance as the following mechanism: the unit of learning in the Complex-BP algorithm is complex-valued signals flowing in neural networks. For example, Δv_{nm}^R and Δv_{nm}^I comprise both the real part ($Re[H_m]$, $Re[O_n]$) and the imaginary part ($Im[H_m]$, $Im[O_n]$)

of complex-valued signals (H_m, O_n) flowing in neural networks, respectively (equation (2)). That is, there is a relation through ($Re[H_m]$, $Re[O_n]$) and ($Im[H_m]$, $Im[O_n]$) between Δv_{nm}^R and Δv_{nm}^I. Similarly, there are relations between Δw_{ml}^R and Δw_{ml}^I (equation (4)), and between $\Delta \theta_m^R$ and $\Delta \theta_m^I$ (equation (5)). Therefore, in the Complex-BP algorithm, the real and imaginary parts of learning parameters are modified, based on both the real and imaginary parts of complex-valued signals flowing in neural networks, respectively. From these facts, we may conclude that "complex-valued signals" flowing in neural networks are a unit of learning in the Complex-BP algorithm.

3.2 Improving Learning Speed

As we have seen in the previous subsection, the error propagation of the Complex-BP algorithm has a structure based on two-dimensional motion, which also means that the unit of learning is complex-valued signals flowing in neural networks. Furthermore, we will find in this subsection that this structure improves learning speed.

The derivative $(1 - f_R(u)) f_R(u)$ of the sigmoid function $f_R(u)$, which is the output function of each neuron, appears in the learning rule of the Real-BP. The value of the derivative asymptotically approaches 0 as the absolute value of the net input u to a neuron increases. Hence, as $|u|$ increases to make the output value of a neuron exactly approach 0.0 or 1.0, the derivative $(1 - f_R(u)) f_R(u)$ shows a small value, which causes what is called a *standstill in learning*. This phenomenon is called "getting stuck in a local minimum" if it continuously takes place for a considerable length of time, and the error between the actual and desired output values remains large. As is generally known, this is the mechanism of *standstill in learning* in the standard back-propagation algorithm.

On the other hand, two kinds of derivatives of the sigmoid function appear in the learning rule of the Complex-BP algorithm (equations (2)-(5)): one is the derivative of the real part of an output function ($(1 - Re[O_n])Re[O_n]$, $(1 - Re[H_m])Re[H_m]$), the other is that of the imaginary part ($(1 - Im[O_n])Im[O_n]$, $(1 - Im[H_m])Im[H_m]$). The learning rule of the Complex-BP algorithm basically consists of two linear combinations of them:

$$\alpha_1(1 - Re[O_n])Re[O_n] + \beta_1(1 - Im[O_n])Im[O_n], \tag{6}$$
$$\alpha_2(1 - Re[H_m])Re[H_m] + \beta_2(1 - Im[H_m])Im[H_m], \tag{7}$$

where $\alpha_k, \beta_k \in \mathbf{R}$ ($k=1,2$), $\mathbf{R}$ denotes the set of real numbers. Note that expression (6) shows a very small value when both $(1 - Re[O_n])Re[O_n]$ and $(1 - Im[O_n])Im[O_n]$ are very small values. Hence, there is a possibility that expression (6) does not show an extremely small value even if $(1 - Re[O_n])Re[O_n]$ is very small, because $(1 - Im[O_n])Im[O_n]$ is not always small in the Complex-BP algorithm (whereas the magnitude of learning parameter updates inevitably becomes quite small, if $(1 - f_R(u)) f_R(u)$ is quite small in the Real-BP algorithm). In this sense, the real factor ($(1 - Re[O_n])Re[O_n]$, $(1 - Re[H_m])Re[H_m]$) makes up for the imaginary factor ($(1 - Im[O_n])Im[O_n]$, $(1 - Im[H_m])Im[H_m]$) showing an abnormally small value, and vice versa. Thus, compared with the updating rule of the Real-BP, that of the Complex-BP has a structure that reduces the probability for *standstill in learning* to occur. This indicates that the learning speed of the Complex-BP is faster than that of the Real-BP. This will be confirmed by computational experiments on complex-valued patterns in the following subsection.

3.3 Learning Speed

In this subsection, the learning speed of the Complex-BP algorithm is studied for some simulated examples on complex-valued patterns.

In general, learning speed should be examined from the perspective of computational complexity (time and space complexities). We assume here that "time complexity" means the sum of four operations for real numbers, and "space complexity" the sum of learning parameters (weights and thresholds).

The average of learning cycles needed for convergence by the Complex-BP was compared with that of the conventional back-propagation technique, using the neural networks in which the time complexities per learning cycle of two techniques were almost equal. In addition, the space complexity was also examined.

In the experiments, the initial real and imaginary components of the weights and the thresholds were chosen to be random real numbers between -0.3 and $+0.3$. We determined that learning finished when

$$\sqrt{\sum_{p} \sum_{k=1}^{N} |T_k^{(p)} - O_k^{(p)}|^2} = 0.10 \tag{8}$$

held, where $T_k^{(p)}$, $O_k^{(p)} \in C$ denote the desired output value, the actual output value of the neuron k for the pattern p, i.e. the left side of equation (8) denotes the error between the desired and actual output patterns, C denotes the set of complex numbers; N denotes the number of neurons in the output layer. We regarded the presentation of one set of learning patterns to the neural network as one learning cycle.

Experiment 1
First, a set of simple (complex-valued) learning patterns shown in Table 1 was used to compare the performance of the Complex-BP algorithm with that of the standard back-propagation algorithm. We used a 1-3-1 three-layered network for the Complex-BP, and a 2-7-2 three-layered network for the standard BP. Table 2 shows that their time complexities per learning cycle were almost equal.

In the experiment for the Real-BP, the real component of a complex number was input into the first input neuron, and the imaginary component was input into the second input neuron. The output from the first output neuron was interpreted to be the real component of a complex number; the output from the second output neuron was interpreted to be the imaginary component.

The average number of iterations required for convergence of 50 trials for each of 6 learning rates (0.1, 0.2, $\cdots$, 0.6) was adopted as a criterion of the evaluation. Although we stopped learning at the 50,000th iteration, all trials succeeded in converging. The result of the experiments is shown in Fig. 1.

Experiment 2
Next, we carried out an experiment using the set of (complex-valued) learning patterns shown in Table 3. The learning patterns were defined according to the following two rules:- (a) the real part of "Complex number 3" (output) is 1 if "Complex number 1" (input) is equal to "Complex number 2" (input), otherwise it is 0; (b) the imaginary part of "Complex number 3" is 1 if "Complex number 2" is equal to either 1 or i, otherwise it is 0.

The experimental task was the same as in Experiment 1 except for the layered network structure: a 2-4-1 three-layered network was used for the Complex-BP method while a 4-9-2 three-layered network was used for the standard method. Table 4 shows that their time complexities per learning cycle were equal.

In the experiment for the Real-BP, the real and imaginary components of "Complex number 1" and the real and imaginary components of "Complex number 2" were input into the first, second, third and fourth input neurons, respectively. The output from the first output neuron was interpreted to be the real component of a complex number; the output from the second output neuron was interpreted to be the imaginary component.

We stopped learning at the 100,000th iteration. The results of the experiments are shown in Fig. 2. For reference, we show the rate of convergence in Table 5.

We can conclude from these experiments that the Complex-BP exhibits the following characteristics in learning complex-valued patterns :- the learning speed is several times faster than that of the conventional technique (Figs. 1 and 2), while the space complexity (i.e. the number of learning parameters) is only about half that of the standard BP (Tables 2 and 4).

We can assume that the structure of reducing "standstill in learning" by the linear combinations (equations (6) and (7)) of the real and imaginary components of the derivative of an output function, described in the previous subsection, causes the characteristics described above.

4   Conclusions

We investigated the fundamental characteristics of the Complex-BP algorithm and found that the Complex-BP had some inherent properties. In particular, the average convergence speed was superior to that of the Real-BP. In addition, the number of learning parameters needed was only about half that of the standard BP. It is interesting that such characteristics appeared only by extending neural networks to complex numbers.

Acknowledgements

The author wishes to thank Drs. T.Yuba, K.Ohta, T.Furuya and T.Higuchi for providing the opportunity for this study.

References

[1] Kim, M. S. et al. (1990). Modification of Backpropagation Networks for Complex-Valued Signal Processing in Frequency Domain. *Proc. IJCNN*, Vol.3, June, pp.27-31.

[2] Nitta, T and Furuya, T. (1991). A Complex Back-Propagation Learning. *Transactions of Information Processing Society of Japan*, Vol.32, No.10, pp.1319-1329 (in Japanese).

[3] Nitta, T. (1993). A Complex Numbered Version of the Back-Propagation Algorithm. *Proc. INNS World Congress on Neural Networks*, Portland, Vol. 3, pp.576-579.

[4] Nitta, T. and Furuya, T. (1993). Characteristics of Learning in the Complex Back-Propagation Learning Algorithm. *Transactions of Information Processing Society of Japan*, Vol.34, No.1, pp.29-38 (in Japanese).

[5] Rumelhart, D. E. et al. (1986). *Parallel Distributed Processing*, Vol.1, MIT Press.

Input pattern	Output pattern
0	0
i	1
1	$1 + i$
$1 + i$	i

Table 1   Learning patterns [Experiment 1].

Network	Time complexity			Space complexity		
	$\times$ and $\div$	$+$ and $-$	Sum	Weights	Thresholds	Sum
Complex-BP 1-3-1	78	52	130	12	8	20
Real-BP 2-7-2	90	46	136	28	9	37

Table 2   Computational complexity of the Complex-BP and the Real-BP [Experiment 1].

Input pattern		Output pattern
Complex number 1	Complex number 2	Complex number 3
0	0	1
0	i	i
i	i	$1+i$
i	1	i
1	1	$1+i$
i	0	0
$1+i$	$1+i$	1
$1+i$	i	i

Table 3 Learning patterns [Experiment 2].

Network	Time complexity			Space complexity		
	$\times$ and $\div$	+ and $-$	Sum	Weights	Thresholds	Sum
Complex-BP 2-4-1	134	92	226	24	10	34
Real-BP 4-9-2	150	76	226	54	11	65

Table 4 Computational complexity of the Complex-BP and the Real-BP [Experiment 2].

Network	Learning rate					
	0.1	0.2	0.3	0.4	0.5	0.6
Complex-BP 2-4-1	100	96	88	92	90	98
Real-BP 4-9-2	0	22	64	78	90	100

Table 5 Rate of convergence [Experiment 2].

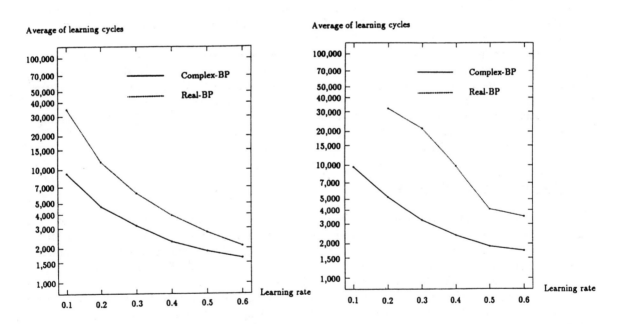

Fig. 1 Average of learning speed [Experiment 1]. Fig. 2 Average of learning speed [Experiment 2].

Identification of Finite State Automata in Simple Recurrent Networks

J. Ludik   E. van der Poel   I. Cloete

jludik@cs.sun.ac.za   evp@cs.sun.ac.za   ian@cs.sun.ac.za

Computer Science Dept., University of Stellenbosch, Stellenbosch 7600, South Africa

Abstract

In this paper we explore the Elman recurrent network by constructing and identifying finite state automata (FSA) for the addition task. By constructing a Mealy machine for addition, non-deterministic elements in the training data were identified. The training performance of different training strategies were investigated with non-deterministic data versus deterministic data. To identify a FSA for addition, we analyze the internal representations of the network by using Hierarchical Cluster Analysis as well as suggesting Sammon Transformation Analysis as a superior clustering technique as opposed to the more familiar Principal Component Analysis. These techniques together with the Mealy machine clearly identify the states of the finite state machine for addition.

1 Introduction

Elman [Elman, 1990] introduced a simple recurrent architecture that has the potential to master an infinite set of sequences by copying the pattern of activation of the hidden units onto a set of context units which feed into the hidden layer along with the inputs. In this paper we show that the Elman simple recurrent network (SRN) can learn to mimic closely a finite state machine (FSM), both in its behaviour and in its state representation. We start by constructing a Mealy machine for the addition task to aid in identifying the finite state machine of the network dynamics. The Mealy machine also enabled us to identify non-deterministic elements in the training data. As a spin-off experiment we investigated the training performance of different training strategies for training with non-deterministic data versus training with deterministic data.

To analyze the internal representations of the Elman network, we have used not only familiar techniques such as Hierarchical Cluster Analysis, which describes the static representation of the network dynamics, and Principal Component Analysis, which gives a more dynamic representation of network, but also introduce a fairly unfamiliar technique called Sammon Transformation Analysis, which depicts network dynamics also in a more dynamical fashion. We show further how the results of these techniques coincide and are congruent with the Mealy Machine drafted in section 3, and also clearly identify the states of a Moore machine for addition.

2 Addition Experiment

The aim of the *addition* experiment [Cottrell & Tsung, 1991] is to learn to sequentially add two base four numbers. Each base four number is given a two-digit binary representation. The Elman SRN is confined to one column of digits at a time. It has five inputs, one indicating the end of the input and four representing the one column of digits, 16 hidden and 16 context units, and six output units representing the sum (two units) of the one column of digits and the four possible actions (four units). Actions are to write the sum, to remember or output the carry, shift to the next column of digits, and indicate if done. The network is trained to produce a sequence of outputs, having an action and result field, according to the following program:

```
while not done do begin
  output(WRITE, low_order_result);
  if sum>radix then output(CARRY,'00');
  output(NEXT,'00');
end
if carry_on_previous_input then output(WRITE,'01');
output(DONE,'00');
```

Since the Elman SRN is required to learn a sequence of inputs and for each input a different sequence of outputs as well as looping, the addition task is quite complex.

3 Mealy Machine for Addition

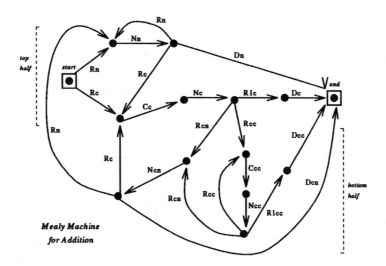

Figure 1: Mealy Machine for Addition

A Mealy machine was constructed to characterize the addition task more precisely and to help identify the finite state machine of the network dynamics. A *Mealy machine* is a 5-tuple (S, A, T, O, f), where S is a finite set of states, A is a finite set called an input alphabet, $T : S \times A \to S$ is the transition function, O is the output alphabet, and $f : S \times A \to O$ is the output function. For the simple recurrent network of the addition problem the input patterns are the input alphabet of the Mealy machine, whilst the target output patterns are the output alphabet.

The Mealy machine in Figure 1 describes all the input-output combinations in the addition problem. Each transition represents a specific group of input-output transitions, which is specified in Tables 1 and 2. The top half of the Mealy machine describes the input-output combinations involved in zero or one carry, whereas the bottom half depicts those input-output transitions involved in more than one carry (top and bottom halves indicated in the figure).

The *result* input-output combinations are denoted by Rx, where x is the type of result action indicated by N, C, D, CN, CC, and CD. R_N is the result actions that lead to *next* actions, whereas R_C actions lead to *carry* actions. R_{CN} and R_{CC} are result actions, which incorporate the changes in the result field due to carry actions earlier in the current temporal pattern. They represent result actions that respectively lead to next and carry actions. R_D and R_{CD} are the final result actions that lead to *done* actions, where the former is part of a temporal pattern that only includes one carry, while the latter's temporal pattern includes more than one carry.

The *carry* input-output combinations are denoted by Cx, where x is the type of carry action indicated by C and CC. C_C is the first carry actions in a temporal pattern, while C_{CC} indicates the successive carry actions.

The *next* input-output combinations are denoted by Nx, where x is the type of next action indicated by N, C, CN, and CC. N_N is next actions contained in a temporal pattern with no carry actions earlier in the temporal pattern, whereas N_C actions indicate one carry action earlier in the temporal pattern. N_{CN} and N_{CC} are next actions which indicate more than one carry action earlier in the temporal pattern. They differ in that the latter's preceding action is a carry (C_{CC}), whilst in the former's case it is a result action (R_{CN}).

The *done* input-output combinations are denoted by Dx, where x is the type of done action indicated by N, C, CN, and CC. D_N is done actions that are preceded by a next action (N_N), whereas D_C actions are preceded by a result action (R_D) which is due to a carry action. D_{CC} is done actions which are performed after more than one carry and preceded by a result action (R_{CD}). D_{CN} is done actions which are performed after at least one carry and preceded by a next action (N_{CN}).

Table 1 specifies the Mealy machine transitions for temporal patterns that include zero or one carry action, whereas the temporal patterns of Table 2 include more than one carry. In both tables only the

Input	Output							
	R_N	R_C	N_N	C_C	N_C	D_N	R_D	D_C
0000	100000		001000			000100		
0001	100010		001000			000100		
0010	100010		001000			000100		
0011		100000		010000	001000		100001	000100
0100	100001		001000			000100		
0101	100011		001000			000100		
0110	100011		001000			000100		
0111		100001*		010000	001000		100001*	000100
1000	100001		001000			000100		
1001	100011		001000			000100		
1010	100011		001000			000100		
1011		100001*		010000	001000		100001*	000100
1100	100010		001000			000100		
1101		100000		010000	001000		100001	000100
1110		100000		010000	001000		100001	000100
1111		100010		010000	001000		100001	000100

Table 1: Mealy machine transitions for zero or one carry. The * indicates a non-deterministic transition.

Input	Output							
	R_{CN}	R_{CC}	N_{CN}	C_{CC}	N_{CC}	D_{CN}	R_{CD}	D_{CC}
0000	100001		001000			000100		
0001	100011		001000			000100		
0010	100011		001000			000100		
0011		100001*		010000	001000		100001*	000100
0100	100010		001000			000100		
0101		100000		010000	001000		100001	000100
0110		100000		010000	001000		100001	000100
0111		100010		010000	001000		100001	000100
1000	100010		001000			000100		
1001		100000		010000	001000		100001	000100
1010		100000		010000	001000		100001	000100
1011		100010		010000	001000		100001	000100
1100	100011		001000			000100		
1101		100001*		010000	001000		100001*	000100
1110		100001*		010000	001000		100001*	000100
1111		100011		010000	001000		100001	000100

Table 2: Mealy machine transitions for more than one carry. The * indicates a non-deterministic transition.

one column of digits (the top and bottom digits) are shown as input. The *end-of-input* bit of the input is not shown, because it is zero for all actions except for the done actions (D_N, D_C, D_{CN} and D_{CC}) when its value is one.

4 Training: Non-determinism versus Determinism

All the Mealy machine transitions in Tables 1 and 2 are deterministic, except those marked with a star. In Table 1 there is a non-deterministic choice between the result actions R_C and R_D when the input is 0111 and 1011, i.e. similar output patterns corresponding to different result actions exist for a specific input. In Table 2 the non-deterministic choice is between the result actions R_{CC} and R_{CD} when the input is 0011, 1101, and 1110. One way to make these choices deterministic is to change the *end-of-input* bit into a one for R_D and R_{CD} in order to distinguish them uniquely from respectively R_C and R_{CC}. Thus every output pattern corresponding to an action is uniquely mapped onto a specific input pattern. This is also logically plausible, since R_D and R_{CD} are the only result actions leading to done actions. The next interesting step was to determine the difference in training performance when training with non-deterministic data (not an unique input-output mapping) versus deterministic data (an unique input-output mapping). The training performance of different training strategies were investigated for these two cases.

The first training strategy, *Combined Subset Training* (CST) [Cottrell & Tsung, 1991], consists of dividing the training set into random subsets, where training occurs on combined larger subsets. The next training strategy, *Increased Complexity Training* (ICT) [Ludik & Cloete, 1993], differs from the first by dividing the training set not into random subsets, but into subsets of increasing complexity, each one having a termination criterion. We have also proposed two *incremental* training strategies called *Incremental Subset Training* (IST) and *Incremental Increased Complexity Training* (IICT) [Cloete & Ludik, 1994]. These strategies incrementally increase subset size and consist of two nested loops: *(a)* an inner loop which decrements the RMS termination values in a linear fashion for the incremental subsets until the desired RMS criterion is reached; *(b)* an outer loop which repeats until successful generalization on an independent test set. For IST training occurs on incremental subsets of random complexity, whereas IICT's incremental subsets increase in complexity. These four training strategies were compared to

| Training | Non-deterministic | | Deterministic | | Improvement of |
Strategies	Updates	Improvement compared to FST	Updates	Improvement compared to FST	Determinism vs Non-determinism
IST	22582	53.3%	10995	47%	51.3%
IICT	23340	51.6%	17841	14%	23.6%
ICT	26180	46%	18450	11.1%	29.5%
CST	28495	41%	18760	9.6 %	34.2%
FST	48405	-	20745	-	57.1%

Table 3: A comparison of *addition* simulation results for the non-deterministic and deterministic cases

Fixed Set Training (FST), where a network is trained with a fixed set of training patterns. The *addition* simulation results for the non-deterministic and deterministic cases are summarized in Table 3.

In the non-deterministic case, all four training strategies improved the number of updates by more than 40% compared to FST, IST being the pick of the strategies by achieving 53.3%. In the deterministic case, IST again performed very well by improving performance by 47% compared to FST. There is a substantial difference in training performance when training with non-deterministic data versus training with deterministic data. This is confirmed by the results in the last column of Table 3, where all the training strategies performed much better with the deterministic data. Noteworthy results are those of IST and FST, which obtained improvements of respectively 51.3% and 57.1%. We suspected that training would be easier with the deterministic data, but were quite surprised at the vast improvements. Especially, when one considers that only one bit in 149 input patterns was changed out of a possible 2305 input patterns with a length of 11 bits (that is only about 0.6% change in the total fixed training set). These results emphasize the importance of identifying the finite state machine of the training data in order to eliminate the non-deterministic elements, if possible.

5 Analysis of Internal Representations

In this section we analyze the hidden unit activations by using Sammon Transformation Analysis, Principal Component Analysis, and Hierarchical Cluster Analysis. We show further how the results of these techniques identify the states of a Moore machine for addition.

For analyzing purposes we have used the weight matrices of the best training strategy, IST, in the classification process of 8-10 column addition. We have extracted the 16 hidden unit activations over time, as the Elman network processed the classification data, which consisted of ten temporal patterns constituting 233 single input patterns.

5.1 Sammon Transformation Analysis

Sammon Transformation Analysis (STA) [Sammon, 1969] is a data transformation technique that maps multidimensional vectors onto two or three dimensional vectors, whose intervector distances tend to approximate those of the multidimensional vectors.

In Figure 2(a) we show the projection of the hidden units vectors onto two dimensions as the network is doing the 233-step addition. The clusters formed by the projected hidden unit activations correspond vividly to the different types of actions that the network are required to learn. Six clusters can be identified that correspond to the main transitions of the four different actions, namely *Next-Result(NR)*, *Result-Next (RN)*, *Carry-Next (CN)*, *Result-Carry (RC)*, *Result-Done (RD)*, and *Next-Done (ND)*. Along the x-axis the network is distinguishing between a *Next* that follows a *Carry (CN)* versus one that follows a *Result* action *(RN)*. Along the y-axis the network is distinguishing between a *Done* that follows a *Result (RD)* versus one that follows a *Next* action *(ND)*.

Figure 2(b) illustrates the correspondence between the STA data and the Mealy Machine transitions in the previous section. The following mapping exists between the transition clusters in Figure 2(a) and the Mealy Machine transitions: $NR = \{R_N, R_C, R_D, R_{CN}, R_{CC}, R_{CD}\}$; $RN = \{N_N, N_{CN}\}$; $CN = \{N_C, N_{CC}\}$; $RC = \{C_C, C_{CC}\}$; $RD = \{D_C, D_{CC}\}$; and $ND = \{D_N, D_{CN}\}$. Another interesting result is the clear-cut separation between clusters that represent actions involved in a carry and clusters representing actions not involved. Figure 2(b) also shows the existence of two groups of actions in the NR cluster, namely a no-carry group $\{R_N, R_{CN}\}$ and a carry-group $\{R_C, R_D, R_{CC}, R_{CD}\}$. The fact

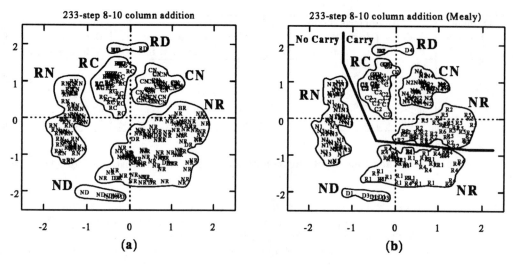

Figure 2: Sammon Transformation Analysis of 233-step 8-10 column addition – (a) transition graph (b) Mealy machine correspondence

that this was not evident in Figure 2(a) shows the importance of using finite state automata, such as a Mealy machine, in the analysis process.

5.2 Principal Component Analysis

Principal Component Analysis (PCA) is a technique whereby multidimensional vectors are mapped onto a new set of orthogonal linear vectors, where the first principal component is such that the projections of the given points onto it have maximum variance among all possible linear coordinates; the second principal component has maximum variance subject to being orthogonal to the first; and so on. In Figure 3(a) we show the projection of the hidden units vectors onto the plane of the first two principal components as the network is doing the 233-step addition. The figure illustrates the correspondence between the PCA data and the Mealy Machine transitions, which is similar to the STA correspondence. The *Result* actions are generally in the left half of the space, wheras the *Next*s and *Carry*s are in the right half. Along the second principal component the network is distinguihing between a *Next* that follows a *Carry (CN)* versus one that follows a *Result* action. Clusters that represent actions involved in a *Carry* can be *linearly* separated from clusters representing actions not involved.

Graphs similar to Figure 2(a) were also generated; again six clusters were identified that correspond to the main transitions of the four actions. We have also obtained similar results by plotting the first principal component at time t versus $t+1$, which basically gives a mapping from the context vector to the next hidden vector.

By comparing Figures 2(a) and 3(a), it is quite evident that STA produces superior clustering results as opposed to PCA for this experiment. We conjecture that this will be the case for other experiments as well, since STA preserves in a certain sense the intervector distances, whereas PCA discards them.

5.3 Hierarchical Cluster Analysis

Hierarchical Cluster Analysis (HCA) is a method of finding the optimal partition of training vectors according to some similarity measure, such as Euclidian distance. The matrix of Euclidean distances between each pair of hidden activation vectors of the 233-step addition served as input to a cluster analysis program. In the graphical results of this analysis, each leaf in the tree corresponds to a particular transition from one action to another. From this graphs, the activation patterns are grouped according to the six main transitions between the different actions, as was the case with STA and PCA. We have also plotted graphs illustrating the correspondence between the HCA data and the Mealy machine transitions, which is similar to the STA and PCA correspondences.

5.4 Identification of Moore Machine

The STA, PCA, and HCA clustering analysis techniques show clearly how the hidden activations classify the main transitions of the four different actions. The clusters obtained with these techniques correspond

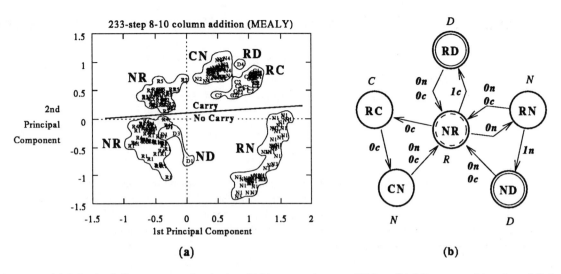

Figure 3: (a)Principal Component Analysis of 233-step column addition (b) Moore machine for addition

to the states of a Moore machine, which is an appropriate FSM, since it is easier to construct the complete machine from these clusters. The remaining task was to determine the Moore machine's input and output alphabet, as well as its transition and output functions. Figure 3(b) presents the graphical representation of the Moore machine, which describes the hidden layer dynamics for addition. The six transitions between actions are the states $S = \{NR, RC, CN, RN, ND, RD\}$, where NR is the start state and RD and ND the final states. The input symbols of the input alphabet $A = \{0c, 0n, 1c, 1n\}$ are represented in such a manner that 0 or 1 indicates respectively *not-end-of-input* and *end-of-input*, and c and n respectively *carry* and *no-carry*. The output alphabet is defined by $O = \{R, C, N, D\}$, where the output symbols respectively are *Result, Carry, Next,* and *Done*. Each state of the Moore machine correspond to Mealy machine transitions, as described in section 5.1.

6   Conclusions

We have investigated the Elman recurrent network by constructing a Mealy machine for addition and identifying a Moore machine that corresponds with the internal representations of the network. The construction of the Mealy machine also enabled us to identify non-deterministic elements in the training data. We have demonstrated with five training strategies that training is much easier (in two cases more than 50%) with deterministic data as opposed to non-deterministic data, even though the difference in the two training sets was only 0.6%. IST, the best training strategy, improved performance in the non-deterministic case by 53% compared to fixed set training and in the deterministic case by 47%.

We have analyzed the internal representations of the network by using Hierarchical Cluster Analysis and suggesting Sammon Transformation Analysis as a superior clustering technique when compared with Principal Component Analysis. We have also showed how the clusters formed by these techniques clearly identify the states of a Moore machine for addition.

References

[Cloete & Ludik, 1994]   Cloete, I., Ludik, J., "Incremental Training Strategies", submitted for publication, 1994.

[Cottrell & Tsung, 1991]   Cottrell, G.W., Tsung, F.S., "Learning Simple Arithmetic Procedures", *High-Level Connectionist Models*, eds. J.A. Barnden, J.B. Pollack, in the series Advances in Connectionist and Neural Computation Theory, Vol. 1, pp.305-321, 1991.

[Elman, 1990]   Elman, J.L., "Finding Structure in Time", *Cognitive Science*, Vol. 14, pp. 179-211, 1990.

[Ludik & Cloete, 1993]   Ludik, J., Cloete, I., "Training Schedules for improved convergence", *IJCNN'93*, Nagoya, Japan, pp. 561-564, October 1993.

[Sammon, 1969]   Sammon, J.W. Jr., "A Nonlinear mapping for Data Structure Analsysis", *IEEE Transactions on Computers*, C-18(5):401–409, May 1969.

Estimating Lipschitz Constants of Feedforward Neural Networks

Zaiyong Tang and Gary J. Koehler †
Division of Bus & Eco, Concord College, Athens, WV 24712
†Dept. of Decision & Info Sci, Univ of Florida, Gainesville, FL. 32611

Abstract

We show that the standard criterion function of a feedforward neural network is Lipschitzian. Procedures are developed to compute efficiently local Lipschitz constants over subsets of the weight space. Local Lipschitz constants can be used to compute lower bounds on the optimal solution. They can also be used to identify weight subregions that do not contain promising solutions, hence reduce the search space.

1   Introduction

The backpropagation (BP) algorithm and its many variations are the most popular training algorithms for feedforward neural networks (FNNs). However, those gradient based training algorithms have some limitations. One of them is obtaining only local minimum solutions. A local minimum may or may not represent an acceptable solution.

Empirical results have shown that with ample hidden units embedded in the network, BP can usually escape a local minimum (Rumelhart et al., 1986) probably due to large degrees of freedom. However, increasing hidden units in the network may not be an appealing idea, since an unnecessarily large number of hidden units is likely to decrease the generalization capability of the network (Kruschke and Movellan, 1991; Baum and Haussler, 1989) and may cause overfitting problems (Weigend et al., 1990). In this paper, we show that an FNN is Lipschitzian. Thus various Lipschitz optimization methods (e.g., Piyavskii, 1972; Horst and Tuy, 1990) can be applied to neural network training. This approach would overcome the problem of converging to a local minimum and yield a globally optimal solution (Tang and koehler, 1993a).

2   An FNN is Lipschitzian

Lipschitz optimization deals with the global optimization of a wide class of functions—the Lipschitz functions. In the following, we first give the definition of Lipschitz functions. Then we show that the standard sum-of-square error (SSE) of an FNN is Lipschitzian.

Definition 2.1 (Lipschitz function) *A continuous function $F : M \to R, M \subseteq R^S$ is a Lipschitz function if there exists a constant $L = L(F, M) > 0$ such that*

$$|F(x) - F(y)| \leq L\|x - y\|, \quad \forall\, x, y \in M$$

where S is a positive integer and L is called a Lipschitz constant.

Knowing the Lipschitz constant of a function F provides a way of computing lower bounds on the global minimum of F. Suppose we want to minimize F over M, let $\delta(M) \equiv max \{\|x-y\| \,|\, x, y \in M\}$ be the diameter of M. From the definition of Lipschitz function, we have

$$F(y) \geq F(x) - L\|x - y\| \geq F(x) - L\delta(M), \quad \forall x, y \in M.$$

If $F(x)$ is known for some $x \in M$, then $F(x) - L\delta(M)$ gives a lower bound to the global minimum of F over M. The following lemmas are needed before we develop the procedures that give easily computable lower bounds on the Lipschitz constant for an FNN.

Lemma 2.1 Let $f_i : R^n \to R$, $i = 1, 2, ..., k$, be Lipschitzian with Lipschitz constants L_i, respectively. Then $F : R^n \to R$, given by $F = \sum_i f_i$ is also Lipschitzian, and a Lipschitz constant of F is given by $L_F = \sum_i L_i$.

Lemma 2.2 Let $x \in R^n$, and $F(x) = f(g(x))$, where $f : R \to R$, $g : R^n \to R$ are Lipschitzian with Lipschitz constant L_f and L_g, respectively. Then $F(x)$ has a Lipschitz constant L_F given by $L_F = L_f L_g$.

Lemma 2.3 Let $x \in R^n$, the l_p norm on R^n, for $1 \le p < \infty$, satisfies

$$\|x\|_p \le \|x\|_1 = \sum_{i=1}^{n} |x_i|$$

Lemma 2.4 Let $x \in R^n$, and $F(x) = f(g(x))$, where $f : R^m \to R$ is Lipschitzian with Lipschitz constant L_f, $g : R^n \to R^m$ with components $g_i, i = 1, 2, ..., m$ being Lipschitzian with Lipschitz constant L_{g_i}. Then $F(x)$ has a Lipschitz constant L_F given by $L_F = L_f \sum_{i=1}^{m} L_{g_i}$.

In the following discussion, we assume the standard sigmoid activation function f (with range $(0, 1.0)$) is used. The transfer function is a linear function of the inputs from the previous layer with a constant term (the bias). L is used to denote a Lipschitz constant with subscripts identifying the corresponding functions.

For a single-output FNN with one hidden layer, the output of the network is

$$o = f(w, x) = f\left(\sum_{j=1}^{h} w_j f_j \left(\sum_{i=1}^{n} w_{ij} x_{ij} + w_{0j}\right) + w_0\right)$$

where h is the number of hidden units, and f_js are activation functions in the hidden layer. Note that the output o can be written as a composite function $o = f(g(w, x))$, where

$$g = \sum_{j=1}^{h} w_j f_j \left(\sum_{i=1}^{n} w_{ij} x_{ij} + w_{0j}\right) + w_0$$

Applying Lemma 2.2, we have

$$L_o = L_f L_g.$$

L_f is given by

$$
\begin{aligned}
L_f &= max\ \|\nabla_g f(w, x)\| \\
&= max\ \gamma f(1 - f), \quad \forall w \in W.
\end{aligned}
\tag{1}
$$

The function g can be rewritten as $g_o(f^H)$, where $g_o : R^h \to R$ transfers the hidden layer output to the output layer input. g_o can be written as

$$g_o = W_H f^H + w_0$$

where W_H is the set of weights between the hidden layer and the output layer, and w_0 is the output unit bias. $f^H : R^n \to R^h$ maps the output from the input layer to the input of the hidden layer. The components of f^H are given by

$$f_j^H = f_j(\sum_{i=1}^{n} w_{ij}x_{ij} + w_{0j}), \quad j = 1, 2, ..., h.$$

Applying Lemma 2.4, we have

$$L_g = L_{g_o} \sum_{j=1}^{h} L_{f_j^H}$$

where L_{g_o} is given by

$$\begin{aligned} L_{g_o} &= max \; \|\nabla_f g_o\| \\ &= max \; (1 + \sum_{j=1}^{h} f_j^2)^{\frac{1}{2}}. \end{aligned} \tag{2}$$

Note that f_j^H in the hidden layer is equivalent to the output function of an FNN without a hidden layer. We have

$$L_{f_j^H} = max \; \gamma f_j(1 - f_j)(1 + \sum_{i=1}^{n} x_i^2)^{\frac{1}{2}}.$$

Putting the above together, we have, for a single hidden layer FNN,

$$L_o = max \; \gamma f(1-f) \; max \; (1 + \sum_{j=1}^{h} f_j^2)^{\frac{1}{2}} \sum_{j=1}^{h} max \; \gamma f_j(1-f_j)(1 + \sum_{i=1}^{n} x_i^2)^{\frac{1}{2}} \tag{3}$$

and, with $F = \sum_p F_p = \frac{1}{2}\sum_p (t_p - o_p)^2$,

$$L_{F_p} = max \; |t_p - o_p|L_{o_p}, \quad \forall w \in W, \tag{4}$$

where L_{o_p} is given by Equation 3 with the input X_p. We observe that f and f_js are functions of the weights and the maximization is taken over the whole weight space, although, with the layered structure, f_js depend only on hidden layer weights. Recall that $L_F = \sum_p L_{F_p}$, thus

$$\begin{aligned} L_F &= \sum_{p=1}^{P} L_{F_p} \\ &= \sum_{p=1}^{P} |t_p - o_p| \; max \; (1 + \sum_{j=1}^{h} f_j^2)^{\frac{1}{2}} \sum_{j=1}^{h} max \; \gamma f_j(1-f_j)(1 + \sum_{i=1}^{n} x_i^2)^{\frac{1}{2}}. \end{aligned} \tag{5}$$

Hence, we have developed a procedure for estimating the Lipschitz constant for FNNs with a single output unit and a single hidden layer.

Equation 3 can be used in estimating the Lipschitz constant for a general three layer FNN (Which is the most widely used NN structure). Let k be the index for the output processing units, then for each output unit o_k, we have

$$L_{o_k} = max \; \gamma f_k(1 - f_k) \; max \; (1 + \sum_{j=1}^{h} f_j^2)^{\frac{1}{2}} \sum_{j=1}^{h} max \; \gamma f_j(1-f_j)(1 + \sum_{i=1}^{n} x_i^2)^{\frac{1}{2}}. \tag{6}$$

Consider the criterion function

$$F = \sum_{p=1}^{P} F_p = \frac{1}{2} \sum_{p=1}^{P} \sum_{k=1}^{K} (t_{pk} - o_{pk})^2,$$

for each training pattern p, $F_p = f_s(f_o)$, where $f_s : R^K \to R$ maps the network output to a performance measure, and $f_o : R^h \to R^K$ maps the hidden layer output to the input to the output layer. Observe that each component of f_o is equivalent to the output function of a three layer FNN with a single output, the case discussed in the above subsection. Let $o_k, k = 1, 2, ..., K$ denote the component function of f_o, o_k is Lipschitzian with Lipschitz constant L_{o_k} given by 6. By Lemma 2.4, the Lipschitz constant for F_p is

$$L_{F_p} = L_{f_s} \sum_{k=1}^{K} L_{o_k}$$

where L_{f_s} is given by

$$
\begin{aligned}
L_{f_s} &= max \ \|\nabla_o F_p\| \\
&= max \ (\sum_{k=1}^{K} (t_{pk} - p_{pk})^2)^{\frac{1}{2}}.
\end{aligned}
\tag{7}
$$

Thus for the criterion function F, we have a Lipschitz constant (using Lemma 2.1 again)

$$L_F = \sum_{p=1}^{P} max \ (\sum_{k=1}^{K} (t_{pk} - p_{pk})^2)^{\frac{1}{2}} \sum_{k=1}^{K} L_{o_k} \tag{8}$$

This leads to the following proposition.

Proposition 2.1 *The criterion function representing a three layered feedforward neural network is Lipschitzian with a Lipschitz constant given by Equation 8.*

Extension of the procedure to estimating Lipschitz constant for an FNN with more than one hidden layers can be carried out by applying the basic lemmas recursively, as illustrated above.

3 Compute Local Lipschitz Constants

The procedures outlined above allows us to compute Lipschitz constant over subsets of the weight space. Furthermore, the estimation of Lipschitz constant is computationally efficient. For clarity of exposition, we will consider computing the Lipschitz constant of a three layer FNN with a single output unit. Using Equation 3, we can compute the Lipschitz constant of the criterion function with a given training pattern p by

$$
\begin{aligned}
L_o &= max \ \gamma f(1-f) \ max \ (1 + \sum_{j=1}^{h} f_j^2)^{\frac{1}{2}} \sum_{j=1}^{h} max \ \gamma f_j (1 - f_j)(1 + \sum_{i=1}^{n} x_i^2)^{\frac{1}{2}} \\
L_{F_p} &= max \ |t_p - o_p| L_o, \quad \forall w \in W.
\end{aligned}
$$

Four maximization problems need to be solved over a given weight subset. Solving those problems may seem to be difficult as the functions are nonlinear and nonconvex. However, by exploiting the properties of the sigmoid activation function and the special structure of the FNN, we can effectively solve those problems over a weight subset, when the weight subset is a hyper-rectangle in

Table 1: Lipschitz Constant over Weight Subsets

Weight Subset	Hyper-rectangle vertices	Lipschitz Constant
W_0	LV=(-10 -10 -10 -10 -10 -10 -10 -10 -10) UV=(10 10 10 10 10 10 10 10 10)	1.20388
W_1	LV=(0 0 0 0 0 0 -10 -10 -10) UV=(10 10 10 10 10 10 10 10 10)	0.89769
W_2	LV=(5 0 0 0 0 0 0 0 0) UV=(10 10 10 10 10 10 10 10 10)	0.01584
W_3	LV=(5 0 0 5 0 0 0 0 0) UV=(10 5 5 10 10 10 10 10 10)	0.00793
W_4	LV=(0 5 5 5 5 0 5 5 0) UV=(5 10 10 10 10 5 10 10 5)	0.00792
W_5	LV=(0 5 0 0 0 0 0 0 0) UV=(5 10 5 10 10 10 10 10 10)	0.17889
W_6	LV=(0 5 0 5 0 0 0 0 0) UV=(5 10 5 10 5 10 10 10 10)	0.01167
W_7	LV=(0 0 0 0 0 0 -5 -5 -5) UV=(5 5 5 5 5 5 5 5 5)	0.89769
W_8	LV=(2.5 2.5 0 0 0 0 0 0 0) UV=(5 5 5 5 5 5 5 5 5)	0.05438
W_9	LV=(2.5 2.5 2.5 2.5 0 0 0 0 0) UV=(5 5 5 5 5 5 5 5 5)	0.00880
W_{10}	LV=(-5 -5 -5 -5 -5 -5 -5 -5 -5) UV=(0 0 0 0 0 0 0 0 0)	0.74146

the weight space. Details of solving those maximization problems are given in (Tang and Koehler 1993b).

Let us apply the above procedure to estimating the Lipschitz constant of the $2 \times 2 \times 1$ XOR network. Assuming $\gamma = 1$, applying Equation 5, a theoretic global Lipschitz constant can be computed by

$$
\begin{aligned}
L_F &= \sum_{p=1}^{4} |t_p - o_p| \ max \ (1 + \sum_{j=1}^{h} f_j^2)^{\frac{1}{2}} \sum_{j=1}^{h} max \ \gamma f_j (1 - f_j)(1 + \sum_{i=1}^{n} x_i^2)^{\frac{1}{2}} \\
&= \frac{h}{16}\sqrt{1+h}(1 + \sqrt{2} + \sqrt{2} + \sqrt{3}) \\
&= \frac{\sqrt{3}}{8}(1 + 2\sqrt{2} + \sqrt{3}) \\
&= 1.20388.
\end{aligned}
\tag{9}
$$

This is obtained by overestimating—assuming the weight set is essentially unbounded, we take $|t_p - o_p| = 1$, $f(1 - f) = 1/4$, and $\sqrt{1 + \sum_{j=1}^{h} f_j^2} = \sqrt{1 + h}$. By actually maximizing those terms over a given weight subset, we get much smaller local Lipschitz constants than the global one for each partition element.

Table 1 shows that the local Lipschitz constants vary significantly over different weight subregions. These subregions are hyper-rectangles identified by the lower vertex (LV) and upper vertex (UV). With $W_0 \equiv \{w \in R^9 \mid -10 \le w_i \le 10, i = 1, 2, ..., 9\}$, the local Lipschitz constant is approximately equal to the global Lipschitz constant. However, for some still relatively large weight subsets (e.g., W_3 and W_4) the Lipschitz constants are quite small. Those local Lipschitz constants may be used to estimate lower bounds on the global criterion function. They may also be used in identifying subregions in the weight space that do not contain promising global optimal solutions. Hence search space can be reduced

4   Conclusions

We studied the Lipschitz properties of the feedforward neural networks. We have shown that the sum-of-squared error criterion function of a feedforward neural network is Lipschitzian. The special structure of feedforward neural networks makes it possible to estimate the Lipschitz constant in a recursive procedure. Furthermore, by exploiting the structure of the network and the property of the sigmoid activation function the computation of local Lipschitz constant can be efficiently carried out.

Local Lipschitz constant can be used either to compute lower bounds on the optimal solution, or to describe approximately the topology of weight subsets. It is well known that the error surface of a feedforward neural network is composed mainly by flat plateaus and some deep valleys that contain local or global minimum solutions. Our procedure provides a way to identify those flat areas and may be used to reduce the search space in neural network training.

References

Baum, E. and Haussler, D. 1989. What size net gives valid generalization? *Neural Computation*, 1:151–160.

Horst, R. and Tuy, H. 1990. *Global Optimization: Deterministic Approaches*. Springer-Verlag, Berlin.

Kruschke, J. K. and Movellan, J. R. 1991. Benefits of Gain: Speeded Learning and Minimal Hidden Layers in Back-Propagation Networks. *IEEE Transactions on Systems, Man, and Cybernetics*, 21(1):273–280.

Piyavskii, S. 1972. An algorithm for finding the absolute extremum of a function. *USSR Comput. Math. and Math. Phys.*, pages 57–67.

Rumelhart, D., Hinton, G., and Williams, R. 1986. Learning internal representations by error propagation. In Rumelhart, D. and McClelland, J., editors, *Parallel Distributed Processing*, volume 1, chapter 8, pages 318–362. MIT Press, Cambridge.

Tang, Z. and Koehler, G. J. 1993a. Deterministic global optimal fnn training algorithms. *Neural Networks*, to appear.

Tang, Z. and Koehler, G. J. 1993b. Lipschitz property of feedforward neural networks. Technical report, Division of Business and Economics, Concord College, Athens, WV. submitted to *Operations Research*.

Weigend, A., Huberman, B., and Rumelhart, D. 1990. Predicting the future: A connectionist approach. Technical Report Stanford-PDP-90-01, Stanfor University, Stanford, CA.

Some Remarks about Boundary Creation by Multi-Layer Perceptrons

Konrad Weigl and Marc Berthod*

INRIA - B.P. 93 - 06902 Sophia Antipolis Cedex France

Abstract. In the present pater, we challenge the classical concept that hidden-layer neurons form necessarily individual segments of boundaries between classes when used for classification: in order to fulfull such a purpose, the majority of the output values of the neurons must be close to 0 or 1 for the input samples given. We introduced in [7] [8] [9] a new learning algorithm, *Projection Learning*: Given enough neurons, the weights from input to hidden layer computed by that algorithm are so small that nowhere does any output from the hidden layer get into the proximity of the upper or lower bound. The function approximation and classification is thus not formed by individual neurons forming boundary segments, but by the linear or non-linear superposition of the outputs of the neurons of the hidden layer. We introduce briefly the new algorithm, compare it to classical algorithms such as backpropagation, show the relevant statistics of the output values of the hidden-layer neurons in a real-world example, and conclude upon the relevancy of the findings.
Keywords: Tensor Theory, Projection Operators, Metric Tensors, Radial Basis Functions, Multi-layer perceptrons

1 The general approach

In the present paper we shall concentrate on the mathematical aspects. Refer to the papers above and [10] for the paradigm. The aim of approximation is modelized by the aim to minimize a function $E = \sum_{k=1}^{M}(F(x_k) - A(x_k))^2$, $F(x_k)$ being the function to be approximated, $A(x_k)$ the approximating function, x_k the set of input values, $k \in \{1,..,n\}$, $g_i, i \in \{1,..,N\}$ the set of arbitrary differentiable functions computed by the N hidden-layer neurons, and $g_i(x_k), k \in \{1,..,M\}, i \in \{1,..,N\}$ the output values computed by the hidden-layer neurons for given inputs x_k. We shall assume a linear output neuron[2]. The problem belongs to the class of separable non-linear least squares [3] [4] [5]. The difference to backpropagation is that we are computing the weights from hidden-layer to output layer *directly* at each step for given input- to hidden-layer weights, have proven that this approach is exact (cf. [10] for details), and shown that it is fast, see below.

---

* email: weigl@sophia.inria.fr berthod@sophia.inria.fr
  Correspondence to: Konrad Weigl
[2] We have shown in [10] the extension to a non-linear output neuron with invertible activation function; extension to multiple output neurons is trivial

2 The algorithm step by step

After initialization, the steps in the learning loop, thus per iteration, are then the following:

1) Compute the output values $g_i(x_k)$ of all the filters/nodes/hidden-layer-neurons i for all the input samples $x_k, k \in 1, .., M$;

2) Multiply pairwise $g_i(x_k)$ with $g_j(x_k)$, and sum over all these products $g_i(x_k)g_j(x_k)$, $k \in 1, .., M$; this gives us the scalar g_{ij}. Do this for all filters i, j; These scalars g_{ij} are the components of the covariant metric tensor, which is a symmetric and real matrix. Invert the matrix by any method, e.g. neural, of your choice [10]. This gives us the contravariant metric tensor.

3) Multiply all the output samples given $F(x_k), k \in 1, .., M$ with the corresponding filter outputs $g_i(x_k), k \in 1, .., M$ computed above. Sum over all these products $F(x_k)g_i(x_k)$, $k \in 1, .., M$; this gives us the covariant component A_i. Repeat for all the filters.

4) Multiply the contravariant metric tensor obtained above, which is a matrix, with the vector formed by all the covariant components A_i; this gives us the vector of contravariant components A^i [3]. Multiplying now all the filters $g_i(x_k)$ with the corresponding A^i, and summing up over all the indices i, gives us the function approximation for the network and input sample x_k, called $A(x_k)$:

$$A(x_k) = \sum_i A^i g_i(x_k) \tag{1}$$

Thus we can now compute the distance E:

$$E = \sum_{k=1}^{M} (F(x_k) - A(x_k))^2 \tag{2}$$

5) We have to differentiate E with regards to the parameters/weights of the nodes/basisfunctions; thus we need, by the chain rule, for example, to differentiate w.r.t. the parameters of the filter j, called $params_j$:

$$\frac{dE}{dparams_j} = \sum_x (F(x_k) - A(x_k))^2 \frac{d(F(x_k) - A(x_k))^2}{dparams_j} \tag{3}$$

implies [4]:

$$\frac{dE}{dparams_j} = \sum_x 2(F(x_k) - \sum_i A^i g_i(x_k))(A^j \frac{dg_j(x_k)}{dparams_j}) \tag{4}$$

$\frac{dg_j}{dparams_j}$ depends on the type of basis function used, obviously; for a sigmoid, it is for example: [6] $\frac{dg_j(x_k)}{dparams_j} = g_j(x_k)(1 - g_j(x_k))x_k$ for the computation of a

---

[3] The superscripts are not power exponents!

[4] We have shown in [10] that the terms depending upon $\frac{dA^j}{dparams_j}$ cancel out

non-bias input, and $\frac{dg_j(x_k)}{dparams_j} = g_j(x_k)(1 - g_j)$ to cmpute the bias weight.
6)Once we have computed $\frac{dE}{dparams_j}$ for all parameters, we can compute:

$$\frac{dparams_j}{dt} = -\frac{dE}{dparams_j} \tag{5}$$

and compute one step via gradient descent or other; then we reiterate the loop with steps 1) - 6), until the minimal distance has been found. Figure 1 shows the evolution of the training of the network on the XOR-function, while figure 2 shows comparisons of computation time of our algorithm with standard gradient descent compared to backpropagation with standard gradient descent.

3   Measurements on taught network

For an individual neuron with sigmoidal activation function to operate as a segment of a boundary between classes, its output must be close to 0 or one for a major part of the input samples.

We have applied thus the algorithm described to a real-world classification task with two classes, namely the detection of inhabited areas on satellite images [12], using from three to thirty hidden-layer neurons and a linear output neuron. Computation time to convergence was between 46 and 149 seconds on a Sparc 10.

The networks were then tasked to classify the testset, which consisted of an 384x384-pixels image, i.e. roughly 147,000 samples. We made then individual histograms of the outputs of all the individual hidden-layer neurons for the 147,000 samples given, one histogram per network with a given number of neurons. Figure 3 shows the results: From top left to bottom right, the number of neurons, and the number of learning iterations is increasing. In hindsight, this is obvious: The more neurons, the more chance that the manifold which they span in function space is close to the function to be approximated, and the greater thus the chance that the error/distance is small. We can see that therefore, with a small number of neurons, the neurons have to adapt, and effectively form boundaries, as we can see from the distribution peak at zero for small number of neurons; when the number of neurons increases, however, their output values tend to gather around the original random initialization value: Thus in no way do individual neurons form boundaries, and only the linear superposition of the outputs allows for the approximation of the function. This means that the neurons with randomly chosen parameters are able to span such a manifold, and thus represent such a function, if there are enough of them. This is a result akin to the *coarse-coding* paradigm of Rumelhart [6], the *population coding* concept of Gaal [2], or the *frame* concept of Daubechies [1] etc., though we are in no way projecting here to a higher dimensional space, as these authors are doing.

4 Conclusion

The present study would have been impossible with backpropagation, which would have modified the parameters of the hidden-layer neurons before any sensible statistical analysis could have taken place; only by using an approach akin to ours, which computes the optimal hidden- to output-layer weights for given input- to hidden layer weights, are we able to determine how many neurons are indeed necessary to form a boundary:

If the output values tend to stay close to the initial values, the number of hidden-layer neurons is higher than necessary; only if the distribution of output values converges towards the upper and/or lower limit do these neurons function as class limiters. In all other cases, a presumably highly redundant superposition of the outputs of still randomly-distributed hidden-layer neurons fullfills the approximation task.

References

1. Daubechies, I., Ten Lectures on Wavelets, SIAM, Philadelphia, Pennsylvania, 1992
2. Gaál, G., Population Coding by Simultaneous Activities of Neurons in Intrinsic Coordinate Systems Defined by their Receptive Field Weighting Functions, in: Neural Networks, Vol. 6, pp. 499-515, 1993
3. Golub, G.H., and Pereyra, V., The Differentiation of Pseudo-inverses and Nonlinear Least-Squares Problems Whose Variables Separate, SIAM, J. Numer. Analysis, Vol. 10, No. 2, April 1973, pg. 413-431
4. Kaufman, L., A Variable Projection Method for Solving Separable Nonlinear Least Squares Problems, BIT 15 (1975), pg. 49-57
5. Krogh, F.T., Efficient Implementation of a Variable Projection Algorithm for Nonlinear Least-Squares Problems, Numerical Mathematics, Communications of the ACM, March 1974, Vol. 17, Number 3.
6. Rumelhart, D.E., McClelland, J.L., et al., Parallel Distributed Processing, Vol. 1, MIT-press, 1986
7. Weigl, K., and Berthod, M., Metric Tensors and Dynamical Non-Orthogonal Bases: An Application to Function Approximation, invited talk, in Proc. WOPPLOT 1992, Workshop on Parallel Processing: Logic, Organization and Technology, Springer Lecture Notes in Computer Sciences, to be published.
8. Weigl, K., and Berthod, M., Non-orthogonal Bases and Metric Tensors: An Application to Artificial Neural Networks, in New Trends in Neural Computation, Proc. IWANN'93, International Workshop on Artificial Neural Networks, Springer Lecture Notes in Computer Sciences, vol. 686.
9. Weigl, K., and Berthod, M., Non-orthogonal Bases and Metric Tensors, invited talk, in: Workshop on Neural Networks, Huening H. et al. eds, Aachen 1993, Verlag der Augustinus Buchhandlung, ISBN 3-86073-140-8
10. Weigl, K., and Berthod, M., Neural Networks as Dynamical Bases in Function Space, research report INRIA no. 2124.
11. Weigl, K., and Berthod, M., Projection Learning: Alternative Approaches to the Computation of the Projection, submitted to ESANN'94, Brussels, Belgium

12. Weigl, K., Giraudon, G., and Berthod, M., A Fast New Neural Network Learning Algorithm and an Application to the Detection of Inhabited Areas on Satellite Images, submitted to the conference on Computer Vision and Pattern Recognition, Seattle, Washington, 1994

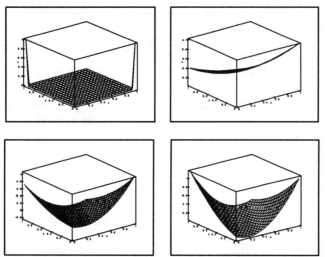

Fig. 1: Evolution of the system; two sigmoidal filters, four samples; top left image shows the original XOR-function; the remaining images, top left linewise to bottom right, show the evolution of the system. Data: 188 iterations, 760 msecs on Sparc 10

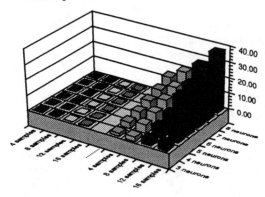

Fig. 2: Time to convergence, averaged over 20 runs each: Projection learning on left, backpropagation on right: Both same initial random weights, convergence time in secs

III-724

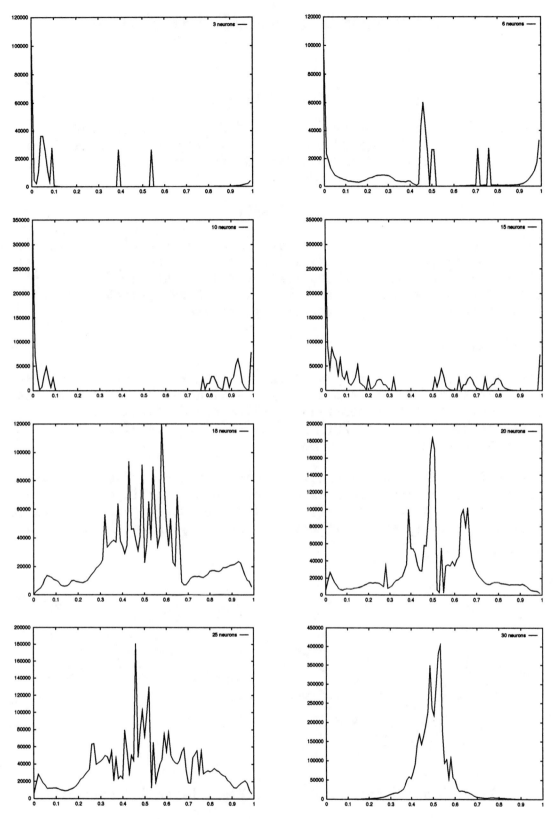

Fig. 3. From top left to bottom right, increasing number of neurons of the hidden layer; computation time varies between 46 and 149 seconds for a final convergence to between 1% and 3% max. error

PERFORMANCE OF NEURAL NETWORK LOOP

Zhang, Yongjun

Institute of Command and Technology, COSTIND
P. O. Box 3380 Ext. 72, Beijing, P. R. China
Tel: +86-1-6755329/5610, Fax: +86-1-2567363

ABSTRACT

This paper analyzes the performance of the neural network loop and gives relationship between stored patterns M and probability of input element p. The analysis shows that If neural nodes N is sufficiently large than the stored pattern M, with high probability the neural network loop converges to stored pattern vectors.

1. Introduction

The classification of stationary random signals and associated signatures may be performed using neural network techniques. The bidirectional associative memory (BAM) [k87], and Hopfield network [L87] can do these works. The papers [Z91] give an architecture of neural network loop which perform associative memory.

The basic system that we shall discuss is shown in Fig. 1. we assume one layer of simple model neurons projects to another layer. Suppose we have three sets of N neurons, called X, Y and Z, where every neuron in set X projects to every neuron in set Y. A neuron j in set X is connected to

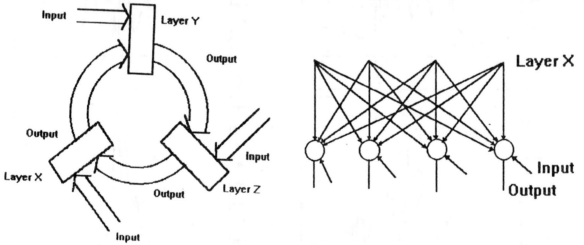

Fig. 1 Three Layer Network   Fig. 2 Layer X Architecture

every neuron i in set Y by way of a modifiable synapses with strength $w_{xy}(i, j)$, forming an $N \times N$ connectivity matrix W_{xy}. Similarly, we can obtain the connectivity matrices W_{yz}, and W_{zx}. Fig. 2 shows the architecture of layer X. It receives the input signals from layer Z or external input and projects the outputs to layer Y. The nodes sum the weighted iuputs from layer X or external input, and then passes the result through a hard limiting function. Using follow learning rule, we can obtain the weight matrices W_{xy}, W_{ys} and W_{zx}.

$$W_{xy} = \sum_{m=1}^{M} Y(m) X(m)^T \tag{1}$$
$$W_{ys} = \sum_{m=1}^{M} Z(m) Y(m)^T \tag{2}$$
$$W_{zx} = \sum_{m=1}^{M} X(m) Z(m)^T \tag{3}$$

where $X(m) = \{x_1(m), \ x_2(m), \ldots x_N(m)\}^T$
$Y(m) = \{y_1(m), \ y_2(m), \ldots y_N(m)\}^T$
$Z(m) = \{z_1(m), \ z_2(m), \ldots z_N(m)\}^T$

2. Performance

From a input vector, such as $X(m)$, we can associate other two corresponding samples[Z91] $Y(m)$ and $Z(m)$ stored patterns in NNL. It is especially useful when input a partial vector. We can recall other two vector samples correctly. This proved that NNL has the ability of fault tolerance and ability against noise.

It can be proved easily that NNL performs task finished by Hopfield and BAM neural networks[Z91]. So NNL has the similar properties which Hopfield and BAM have[Z91]. The paper[Z91] has proved that when $q_0 = p_0 = 1/2$, NNL can converge with high probability, where

$$q_0 = P\{x_i^{(m)} = 1\} = P\{y_i^{(m)} = 1\} = P\{z_i^{(m)} = 1\} \tag{4}$$
$$p_0 = P\{x_i^{(m)} = -1\} = P\{y_i^{(m)} = -1\} = P\{z_i^{(m)} = -1\} \tag{5}$$

are the probability distribution of $x_1(m)$、 $y_1(m)$ and $z_1(m)$.

Now we analyzes convergence of NNL when $q_0 \neq p_0 \neq 1/2$. If NNL is addressed by multiplying the matrix W_{xy} (or W_{yz}, W_{zx}) with one of state vectors, say $X(m_0)$ (or $Y(m_0), Z(m_0)$), it yields the estimate

$$
\begin{aligned}
u_i &= \sum_{j=1}^{N} W_{xy}(i,j) x_j^{(mo)} \\
&= \sum_{j=1}^{N} \sum_{m=1}^{M} y_i^{(m)} x_j^{(m)} x_j^{(mo)} \\
&= N y_i^{(mo)} + \sum_{m \neq mo} \sum_{j=1}^{N} x_j^{(mo)} x_j^{(m)} y_i^{(m)} \\
&= N y_i^{(mo)} + s
\end{aligned}
\tag{6}
$$

Where $s = \sum_{m \neq mo} \sum_{j=1}^{N} x_j^{(m)} x_j^{(mo)} y_i^{(m)}$.

u_1 consists of the sum of two terms, the first is corresponding output vector amplified by N, the second is a linear combination of the remaining stored vectors and it represents an unwanted cross-talk term. The value of s is the sum that M-1 term add randomly, In order to recall corresponding stored vectors correctly, We hope the absolute of the first term is larger than that of the second one. First, let's discuss every term of the second term in Eq. (6). Let

$$s_j^{(m)} = x_j^{(mo)} x_j^{(m)} y_i^{(m)} \tag{7}$$

Suppose probability distribution of $s_j^{(m)}$ are

$$P\{s_j^{(m)} = 1\} = p$$
$$P\{s_j^{(m)} = -1\} = q$$

Where p+q=1. For all $s_j^{(m)}$ i=1, 2, ...,N, m=1, 2, . . . , M m $\neq$ m_0 the probability that there are n $s_j^{(m)}$ are equal to 1 is

$$P\{s=2n-N(M-1)\}=C_{N(M-1)}^n p^n q^{N(m-1)-n}$$
$$=p^n q^{N(M-1)-n} [N(M-1)]! / (n! [N(M-1)-n]!)$$

Suppose s is random variable with mean value m_s and variance σ_s. We can obtain

$$m_s=N(M-1)(p-q) \tag{8a}$$
$$\sigma_s^2=4N(M-1)pq \tag{8b}$$

The magnitude of s can be represented as

$$\sqrt{E\{s^2\}}=\sqrt{4N(M-1)pq+[N(M-1)]^2(p-q)^2}$$

Now we shall discuss $E\{s^2\}$ versus p and rewrite $E\{s^2\}$ as

$$G(p)=E\{s^2\}=4N(M-1)p(1-p)+N(M-1)^2(2p-1)^2 \tag{9}$$

Use the following derivative.

$$G'(p)=4N(M-1)(1-2p)+4N(M-1)^2(2p-1)=0$$

We can obtain p=1/2. Substituting p=1/2 into Eq. (9). We have G(1/2) = N(M-1).So when p=q=1/2, G(p) reaches its minimum value N(M-1) and in this condition the network has the highest capacity.

Now discuss $E\{s^2\}$ versus p_0 and from Eq. (5-7) we have

$$p=2p_0q_0^2+p_0(q_0^2+p_0^2) \tag{10}$$
$$q=q_0(q_0^2+p_0^2)+2p_0^2q_0 \tag{11}$$

$E\{s^2\}$ versus p_0 determined by Eqs. (9-11).

Figs. 3-4 give curves $\sqrt{G(p)}$ versus p and p_0 respectively. From the figures we can know that although in a small domain of p $\sqrt{G(p)}$ is larger than N/2, in a broad domain $\sqrt{G(p)}$ of p_0 is larger than N/2. It is

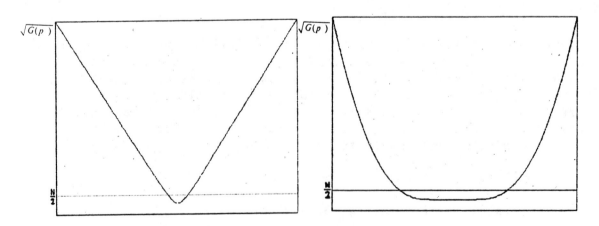

Fig. 3 $\sqrt{G(p)}$ versus p   Fig. 4 $\sqrt{G(p)}$ versus p_0

that we expect. In this domain the network can converge to correct pattern vectors. Because equations (10-11) convert the narrow domain of p into the broad domain of p_O. We can see this point from figure 5. equation 9 determine relationship between stored pattern number M and p. When $\sqrt{G(p)}$ becomes large with p, the second term of equation (9) is much larger than the first one. Equation becomes

$$G(p) \approx N(M-1)^2(2p-1)^2$$

The condition that $\sqrt{G(p)}$ is larger than N/2 becomes

$$|p-q| \leqslant 1/[2(M-1)] \tag{12}$$

Figure 3 has also given this relationship.

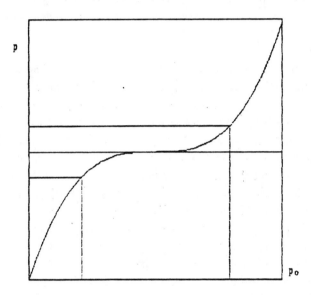

Fig. 5 p versus p_O

3. Conclusion

This paper analyzes the performance of neural network loop and obtain the conclusion that although in a narrow domain of p the network can converges to correct patterns, in a broad doamin of p_O the network can converges to correct one. This result quarantees the convergence of the network.

References

[k87] Bart Kosko. Adaptive bidirectional associative memories, Applied Optics, Vol. 26, No. 23, December 1987.
[L87] Richard P. Lippmann, An Introduction to Computing with Neural Nets, IEEE ASSP Magazine, April 1987.
[Z91] Zhang, Yongjun and Chen, Zongzhi, "A New architecture of Neural Network, IJCNN, Vol. 1, 1991.

A Binary-input Supervised Neural Unit that Forms Input Dependent Higher-order Synaptic Correlations

Marifi Güler and Erol Şahin
Department of Computer Engineering
Middle East Technical University
06531 Ankara, Turkey
E-mails: mguler@trmetu.bitnet, erol@ceng.metu.edu.tr

Abstract: *This paper introduces a neural unit, similar to a sigma-pi unit, that can learn and generalize linearly inseparable binary input vectors. Learning effectively decides a higher-order polynomial suitable to the problem being trained. The unit generalizes in accordance with the relation specified by that polynomial, and hard problems like the parity problem are generalized easily. In training the neural unit, a gradient-descent based supervised learning algorithm is adopted.*

1. INTRODUCTION

The threshold mechanism in a McCulloch and Pitts neuron is not the only nonlinearity that plays an important role in information processing in the brain. Over the years, a substantial body of evidence has grown to support the presence of nonlinear synaptic connections and multiplicative-like operations. We refer the reader to the review article by Koch and Poggio [1]. The introduction of polynomial or sigma-pi units [2][3] have motivated the research to investigate the computational abilities of neural units with nonlinear synaptic connections. The output of a polynomial unit is a function of the linear sum of some monomials, where each monomial is the product of some number of inputs x_i and a weight parameter e.g. $wx_1^2x_3x_4^3$. It has been argued that networks based on sigma-pi units may be more powerful and have other advantages with respect to the more traditional threshold-based networks [4][5]. The backpropagation algorithm is commonly adopted to train the polynomial networks [2][6] and usually the terms upto second-order are used and higher-order terms are ignored. However, for many problems like the parity problem, higher-order terms play the most decisive role and cannot be ignored. Even though invariance properties may be used for certain problems, in general, learning algorithms do not specify which of the higher-order monomials are the most relevant ones and, therefore, to be taken into consideration for the problem in hand.

In attempt to obtain a neural unit that can do nonlinear separation, another approach known as the Gaussian potential function network (GPFN) has been proposed [7]. GPFN is capable of performing forward mappings as a pattern classifier and approximates an arbitrary many-to-one continuous function by a potential field synthesized over the domain of the input space by a number of Gaussian computational units called Gaussian Potential Function Units (GPFU's). The synthesis of a potential field is accomplished by learning the location and shape of individual GPFU's, as well as determining the minimum necessary number of GPFU's via a gradient-descent based supervised learning algorithm.

The reason for much of the excitement about neural networks is their ability to generalize to new situations, and a neural network that is efficient in learning is not necessarily good at generalizing. After being trained on a number of examples of a relationship that interpolates and extrapolates from the examples in a sensible way. But what is meant by *sensible* generalization is often not clear. How does a neural network -or a human for that matter- choose the 'right' one among almost infinitely many possible generalizations? As an example, one could train a neural network with six or seven of the eight parity relations in three dimensions, and it would be very unlikely that any of the known type of networks would actually generalize to full parity. A child with a reasonable IQ will, however, discover the relation as multiplication, or as evenness or oddness, and generalize correctly. Perhaps, discovering a relation through learning, and generalizing accordingly is the *sensible* generalization, and that is what the neural unit we introduce does for binary inputs.

2. THE MODEL NEURAL UNIT

The infinite polynomial sum representing the postsynaptic polarization potential of a sigma-pi unit [2] can be written as a finite sum in case of the binary inputs as follows:

$$\phi(\vec{X}) = \omega_0 + \sum_{k=1}^{N} \sum_{j_1=1}^{N-k+1} \sum_{j_2=j_1+1}^{N-k+2} \cdots \sum_{j_k=j_{k-1}+1}^{N} \omega_{j_1 j_2 \ldots j_k} x_{j_1} x_{j_2} \ldots x_{j_k} \tag{1}$$

Here, N is the dimension of the input vectors $\vec{X} = (x_1, x_2, \ldots, x_N)$, and ω's are the weight parameters. The value of x_i $(i = 1, 2, \ldots, N)$ is either $+1$ or -1. A term like $x_2^3 x_4^2 x_7$ in the infinite polynomial has been absorbed into the term $x_2 x_7$ since each x_i is binary and that is what made it possible to obtain a finite polynomial. For example, for $N = 2$, Eq. (1) yields $\phi(\vec{X}) = \omega_0 + \omega_1 x_1 + \omega_2 x_2 + \omega_{12} x_1 x_2$.

The output of the neural unit, $S(\vec{X})$, is binary $(+1$ or $-1)$ and given as:

$$S(\vec{X}) = sgn(\phi(\vec{X})) \tag{2}$$

$S(\vec{X})$ will not be affected if we ignore some of the weights, and the corresponding terms, with relatively smaller absolute values in $\phi(\vec{X})$, which is important since $\phi(\vec{X})$ contains 2^N weight parameters and naturally, we do not want to compute all. But how do we detect the most relevant terms, that is the terms with relatively larger absolute values?

$\phi(\vec{X})$ can be written as a linear sum of some *"product terms"* as follows:

$$\phi(\vec{X}) = \sum_{j=1}^{L} (H_1^j + M_1^j x_1)(H_2^j + M_2^j x_2) \ldots (H_N^j + M_N^j x_N) \tag{3}$$

Here, H_k^j and M_k^j are some coefficients to be determined and L is some finite integer. Note that a product term contains all the terms in Eq. (1) when it is expanded, but some of the weights in that expansion are dependent on the others. However, the sign of $\phi(\vec{X})$ is important, not its exact value, and this provides some degrees of freedom. If more degrees of freedom is required, then we add new product terms, that is we increase L, which releases some of the dependent weights.

In order to compute the coefficients H_k^j and M_k^j we define a cost function as:

$$E = \sum_{p} (d_p - \phi(\vec{X}_p))^2 \tag{4}$$

where the sum is over the training patterns. $\vec{X}_p$ and d_p denote the training pattern p and its desired output respectively. The cost function is minimized using the gradient-descent method which, for pattern p implies:

$$\Delta H_k^j = \eta\gamma(d_p - \phi(\vec{X}_p)) \prod_{i=1, i \neq k}^{N} (H_i^j + M_i^j x_i^p)$$

$$\Delta M_k^j = \eta\gamma(d_p - \phi(\vec{X}_p)) x_k^p \prod_{i=1, i \neq k}^{N} (H_i^j + M_i^j x_i^p) \tag{5}$$

where $k = 1, 2, \ldots, N$. Initially, random values are assigned to H_k^j and M_k^j. γ is a parameter set in the simulations as $\gamma = 0.1$ if $sgn(\phi(\vec{X}_p)) = d_p$, $\gamma = 1$ otherwise. It has the effect of focusing on getting the sign of $\phi(\vec{X})$ right before paying attention to the magnitude. The learning rate η is not taken as a constant but, instead, is adjusted automatically during the learning process as:

$$\Delta\eta = \begin{cases} +a & \text{if } \Delta E < 0 \text{ consistently} \\ -b\eta & \text{if } \Delta E > 0 \\ 0 & \text{otherwise} \end{cases} \tag{6}$$

where a and b are appropriate constants. The meaning of consistently is based on last K steps. In the simulations, a, b and K are set as $a = 0.05$, $b = 0.3$ and $K = 10$. Such an automatic adjustment of η has been proposed by various authors, e.g. [8][9], for the backpropagation algorithm, which we have adopted here.

The value of $\phi(\vec{X})$ is unbounded which may lead "blow-ups" during the learning process. We have, however, avoided this, imposing a constraint as $|H_k^j| < 1$ and $|M_k^j| < 1$, during the simulations.

It is important that we add new product terms gradually. That is, we start with one product term and if after certain number of cycles the error E does not fall below a required limit then add few more (one or two not twenty) product terms and apply the algorithm again. As far as the learning is concerned, there is no need to the gradual addition of the product terms; in any case the neural unit will learn. However, if new terms are not added gradually we may get a different generalization. A trivial example is the XOR problem. If we train three of the four patterns using two product terms, then, depending on the random initial values of the coefficients in the algorithm, it may generalize the fourth pattern to $+1$ or -1. But if one product term is used then the fourth pattern will be generalized to the full XOR. This is because, with two product terms, even if $E = 0$, the degree of freedom is sufficient that there exists two different set of coefficients (one corresponding to the full XOR and the other corresponding to the linearly separable solution) which can accomodate the three patterns that are trained. Hence, gradual addition of the product terms effectively detects the most relevant terms mentioned earlier, and forces the neural unit to find a relation as simple as possible.

3. SIMULATIONS

In the simulations, after the addition of a new product term, all the coefficients are set to random values and 1000 cycles of training is applied. If after 1000 cycles the error does not fall below the required limit another product term is added and the same steps are repeated. Therefore, a pattern set that employed L product terms is trained for $1000L$ cycles maximum. There is a trade-off between the number of product terms and the error limit. We have taken the error limit as $0.05N_p$, where N_p is the number of training patterns, good enough for *sensible* generalization.

Learning

2^N distinct vectors in N dimensions with various random desired outputs are taken and the neural unit is tested upto $N = 7$. It has learned all of the 2^N input vectors completely. The number of the product terms it has employed varied a lot, as expected, depending on the desired outputs. The maximum number of product terms employed in $2, 3, 4, 5, 6$ and 7 dimensions are $4, 4, 5, 6, 9$ and 17 respectively. These numbers are, in fact, higher than they should be. For example, for $N = 2$ the maximum number should be 2. We interpret this as an artifact of the gradient-descent method's local minima problem. However, note that the storage requirement can be eased up ignoring some coefficients, without affecting $S(\vec{X})$, that are close to 0.

Generalization

Example 1: Parity problem deserves a special attention as it is usually considered as the most

x_1	x_2	x_3		d_p
1	-1	1	→	-1
-1	1	-1	→	1
-1	-1	1	→	1
-1	1	1	→	-1
1	1	-1	→	-1
1	-1	-1	→	1

Table 1: Training pattern set used for the parity generalization in $3D$

x_1	x_2	x_3	x_4		d_p
-1	-1	-1	1	→	-1
-1	1	-1	1	→	1
-1	-1	1	1	→	1
1	-1	1	-1	→	1

Table 2: Training pattern set for the parity generalization in $4D$

difficult problem for most of the existing models and usually cannot be generalized. The neural unit is trained with the $3D$ pattern set shown in Table 1.

The neural unit discovered the parity relation with one product term as

$$\phi(\vec{X}) = (-0.01 + 0.99x_1)(0.03 - 0.97x_2)(0.06 - 0.99x_3)$$
$$\cong 0.95x_1x_2x_3$$

hence generalized all the untrained input vectors accordingly. Note that, although the problem is a linearly separable one, the parity relation is discovered by the neural unit because it requires just one monomial whereas the linearly separable solution requires three monomials. Similarly, the neural unit learned to generalize to the $4D$ parity relation after training it with the $4D$ pattern set shown in Table 2.

Example 2: The problem considered here is the discovery of the Boolean function $f(\vec{X}) = (x_1 \vee x_2) \wedge (x_3 \vee x_5)$ where $\vee$ and $\wedge$ represent conjunction (binary or) and disjunction (binary and) respectively, x_4 being redundant input. The neural unit is trained with 25 of the 32 patterns and formed the polynomial

$$\begin{aligned}
\phi(\vec{X}) = & (0.79 - 0.01x_1)(-0.90 - 0.33x_2)(-0.89 - 0.31x_3)(0.92 + 0.01x_4)(0.83 + 0.28x_5) + \\
& (0.32 - 0.49x_1)(0.35 - 0.48x_2)(-0.51 - 0.84x_3)(-0.63 + 0.18x_4)(-0.31 + 1.00x_5) + \\
& (-0.78 - 0.10x_1)(0.95 + 0.14x_2)(0.49 - 0.84x_3)(0.88 - 0.04x_4)(0.49 - 0.86x_5) + \\
& (-0.51 + 0.94x_1)(-0.58 + 0.57x_2)(-1.00 - 0.23x_3)(-0.86 - 0.09x_4)(-0.89 - 0.43x_5) \\
\cong & \ 0.08 + 0.41x_1 + 0.39x_2 + 0.37x_3 + 0.36x_5 \\
& -0.44x_1x_2 + 0.16x_1x_3 + 0.18x_2x_3 + 0.18x_1x_5 + 0.16x_2x_5 - 0.38x_3x_5 \\
& -0.13x_1x_2x_3 - 0.12x_1x_2x_5 - 0.10x_1x_3x_5 - 0.11x_2x_3x_5 + 0.07x_1x_2x_3x_5
\end{aligned}$$

x_1	x_2	x_3	x_4		d_p
-1	-1	1	1	$\rightarrow$	-1
1	-1	1	-1	$\rightarrow$	1
1	-1	1	1	$\rightarrow$	-1
-1	-1	-1	-1	$\rightarrow$	-1
1	1	1	1	$\rightarrow$	-1
-1	1	1	-1	$\rightarrow$	1
1	1	-1	-1	$\rightarrow$	-1
1	1	1	-1	$\rightarrow$	-1
1	1	-1	1	$\rightarrow$	-1
-1	1	-1	1	$\rightarrow$	1

Table 3: Training pattern set in $4D$

where in the approximation monomials with weights less than 0.05 in absolute value are omitted, which does not affect $S(\vec{X})$. Hence, $S(\vec{X})$ is independent of x_4, as it should be. The neural unit generalized the remaining 7 patterns in consistency with the Boolean function $f(\vec{X})$.

Example 3: The neural unit is trained with the 10 patterns, shown in Table 3, that are generated using the Boolean function $f(\vec{X}) = (x_1 \oplus x_2) \wedge (x_3 \oplus x_4)$ where $\oplus$ represents the XOR operation.

The neural unit comes up with the relation

$$
\begin{aligned}
\phi(\vec{X}) &= (-0.95 + 0.06x_1)(-0.94 + 0.82x_2)(0.07 + 0.75x_3)(0.04 - 0.77x_4) + \\
&\quad (-0.05 - 0.93x_1)(-0.64 - 0.62x_2)(-0.93 + 0.00x_3)(0.89 - 0.01x_4) \\
&\cong -0.49x_1 - 0.48x_1x_2 - 0.52x_3x_4 + 0.45x_2x_3x_4 \\
&\cong 0.5(-x_1 - x_1x_2 - x_3x_4 + x_2x_3x_4) \\
&= -0.5x_1(1 + x_2) - 0.5x_3x_4(1 - x_2)
\end{aligned}
$$

which can be interpreted as:

$$
\phi(\vec{X}) = \begin{cases} -x_3x_4 & \text{if } x_2 = -1 \\ -x_1 & \text{if } x_2 = +1 \end{cases}
$$

and is represented by the Boolean function:

$$
\phi(\vec{X}) = (\bar{x_1} \wedge x_2) \vee ((x_3 \oplus \bar{x_4}) \wedge \bar{x_2})
$$

which is a simpler relation than the one used in generating the pattern set.

4. CONCLUSION

In this paper we have introduced a binary-input supervised neural unit that, through learning, forms higher-order synaptic correlations expressed by a polynomial. Consequently, it can learn and generalize linearly inseparable input vectors. The gradient-descent based learning algorithm is such that the terms in the polynomial that reflect an existing relation in the input vectors are highlighted (i.e. assigned higher absolute weight values), and then generalization is done in accordance with that existing relation discovered. We do not, however, think that the learning algorithm used is the most efficient algorithm one can find, and we are currently working on this point.

References

[1] Koch,C. and Poggio, T., Multiplying with synapses and neurons, *In: "Single Neuron Computation" McKenna T., Davis J. and Zornetzers (eds.) 1992, Chap 12, pp 315-345*

[2] Rumelhart, D.E. and McClelland, J., *Parallel Distributed Processing: Explorations in the Microstructure of Cognition. Vol. 1., 1986, MIT Press, Cambridge, Massachussets*

[3] Volper, D.J. and Hampson, S.E., Learning using specific instances, *Biological Cybernetics, 57, 1987, pp 57-71*

[4] Durbin, R. and Rumelhart, D.E., Product Units: A Computationally Powerful and Biologically Plausible Extension to Backpropagation Networks, *Neural Computation, 1, 1989, pp 133-142*

[5] Mel, B.W., The Sigma-Pi Model Neuron: Roles of the Dendritic Tree in Associative Learning, *Soc. NeuroScience Abstr., 16, 1990, pp 205.4*

[6] Shin, Y.C. and Sridnar, R., Network Configurations and Training Speeds of Second-Order Neural Networks, *Proc. WCNN'93, Vol. I, 1993, pp 585-588*

[7] Lee, S., Supervised Learning with Gaussian Potentials, *In: "Neural Networks for Signal Processing", Kosko, B. (ed), 1992, Chap. 7, pp 189-227*

[8] Jacobs, R.A., Increased Rates of Convergence Through Learning Rate Adaptation, *Neural Networks, 1, 1988, pp 295-307*

[9] Vogl, T.P., Mangis, J.K., Rigler, A.K., Zink, W.T. and Alkon, D.L., Convergence of the Backpropagation Method, *Biological Cybernetics, 59, 1988, pp 257-263*

Adaptive Tessellation CMAC

Jonathan Chey[†], Department of Cognitive and Neural Systems
Boston University, 111 Cummington St, Boston, MA 02215

Abstract

An adaptive tessellation variant of the CMAC architecture is introduced. Adaptive tessellation is an error-based scheme for distributing input representations. Simulations show that the new network outperforms the original CMAC at a variety of learning tasks, including learning the inverse kinematics of a two-link arm.

1 Introduction

The cerebellar model articulation controller (CMAC) is a supervised learning algorithm inspired by the architecture of the cerebellum [1, 2]. It has been successfully applied to a number of tasks which require a quick, computationally efficient algorithm. For example, Miller and others have used CMAC for various robotic control tasks [9, 10, 11].

CMAC is essentially a continuous valued *perceptron*: a general model of neural learning and performance [12]. A perceptron consists of three layers of neurons: *sensory* (S), *association* (A) and *response* (R). Nodes in each layer compute a weighted sum of their inputs. Sensory nodes (S-nodes) transduce input signals, which activate Association nodes (A-nodes) through a fixed mapping. A-nodes activate response nodes through modifiable weights to generate output. Error signals drive weight modification between the A and E layers using the least-mean squares law or delta rule [16].

Since the perceptron calculates a linear transform of input to output, there are many mappings that cannot be represented by a given perceptron, in particular, those that are not linearly separable. However, it is possible to increase the utility of a perceptron by using specific S-A mappings given *a-priori* knowledge of the mapping.

CMAC is an instance of a perceptron that implements a specific S-A mapping called *expansion-recoding*. In expansion-recoding each input, represented as a pattern of activity over the S-nodes, activates a fixed subset of the A-nodes. These subsets are chosen so that an equal number of A-nodes are activated for every input (expansion) and so that nearby inputs activate overlapping subsets (generalisation). The number of A-nodes activated by any particular input determines the granularity, or resolution of the mapping and the overlap between adjacent inputs determines how smoothly this mapping changes and, therefore, the amount of generalisation. The choice of the S-A mapping instantiates a hypothesis: that the complexity or non-linearity of the target mapping is such that it can be adequately represented by the chosen expansion-recoding.

This paper will refer to the choice of particular S-A mapping as the choice of a *tessellation* scheme for the input space. Figure 1 shows schematically possible tessellation schemes for a two-dimensional input space.

2 Adaptive Tessellation

The choice of an S-A mapping is critical for the performance of a perceptron. One might therefore ask whether such a mapping must be fixed or whether it can be altered during the course of learning. If the mapping can be selected automatically during training, the designer need not choose the input quantisation and generalisation.

[†]Supported in part by ARPA ONR N00014-92-J-4015, NSF IRI-90-00530, ONR N00014-91-J-4100, & Boston University Presidential Graduate Fellowship.

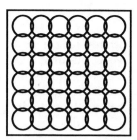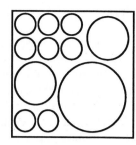

Figure 1: Possible input space tessellations. Each circle represents a portion of the input space which activates an association node. The scheme on the left is appropriate for a mapping which changes rapidly and in which generalisation is not required, the middle scheme is appropriate for a more uniform mapping in which outputs can be generalised between adjacent areas of the input space and the adaptive scheme on the right demonstrates a non-uniform distribution appropriate for a non-uniform mapping.

To approximate such a function to a required level of accuracy, CMAC must allocate enough nodes to quantise the entire input space at the degree of granularity required by the most complex region. An *adaptive tessellation* algorithm is one in which the number of nodes and their position in input space varies during training. Such an algorithm can approximate a function more accurately with less nodes by allocating those nodes in accordance with the structure of the function.

There are many ways to perform an adaptive tessellation and the scheme described here was chosen not for optimality but to show that a simple heuristic can be of use. In this scheme A-nodes are allocated during training to regions in which the error is high. The network is initialised with a single node which represents the entire input space. After some period of training this node is *split* into a number of sub-nodes. The sub-nodes are further broken down at regular intervals during the training. Thus, the network operates on two time scales: a short time scale corresponding to the regular CMAC training schedule and delta rule, and a long time scale corresponding to the allocation of new input representations.

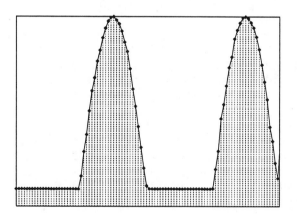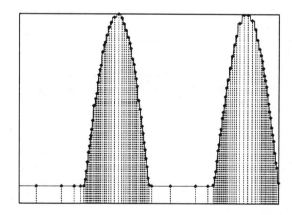

Figure 2: Functional approximations produced by two networks, CMAC (left) and and adaptive tessellation variant (right). The function to be approximated is a sinusoid in part of its domain and constant in other parts. Both networks utilise same number of A-nodes (100). The location of the A-nodes (in the input space or functional domain) are marked; note that in the adaptive network they are sparse in the uniform regions and more concentrated in the sinusoidal regions. Also, within each sinusoidal region, the distribution is biased by the gradient of the curve.

The node to be split is chosen by considering the accumulated error statistics over all nodes and locating the source of the highest error. The result of this process is a node distribution that is concentrated in regions where the error was highest during training. Figure 2 shows an example of such a distribution for a function which is uniform over part, but not all, of its domain.

3 Simulation: Inverse Kinematics

Learning the inverse kinematics of a two-link arm is a simple problem that illustrates some of the advantages and disadvantages of the new architecture in comparison to the original CMAC. Assume that an arm is moved randomly by assigning its two joint angles; the resultant position of its end-effector is used as input and the joint angles as target values for learning. Such a scheme has been postulated to form a part of motor learning [5, 8]. The problem itself is simple; of interest is the accuracy that can be achieved with a limited representation and without extensive domain knowledge.

In order to compare performance parameters were selected that produced reasonable performance from both networks, although these parameters were not optimal for either. All parameters were kept constant and the same learning rates, number of nodes, number of trials and data were used for both networks. Three levels of generalisation were used for CMAC; no generalisation was performed in the adaptive tessellation network. Figure 3 shows the time course of network errors during training of both networks. It can be seen that the adaptive network reaches a lower average error than the conventional CMAC network at any level of generalisation.

The learning task in this simulation was kept as simple as possible by restricting the movement of the arm in such a way that only a portion of the input space was spanned. This subspace was chosen so as to avoid singularities associated with a complete revolution of the arm and within it only a single arm configuration was associated with each end-effector position.

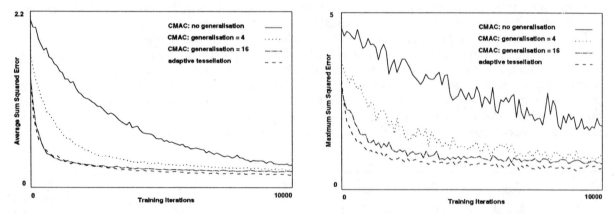

Figure 3: Average (left) and maximum (right) mean squared error from networks trained on the two-link arm inverse kinematics problem. Each graph compares performance of the adaptive tessellation network with CMAC networks utilising three different levels of generalisation. Each generalisation level specifies how many A-nodes are activated by each input.

However, the mapping to be learned still involves some complexities. One is a singularity at the origin of the arm, where multiple positions of the first joint correspond to a single location. Another is the increase in the effect of a joint angle change at extreme distances from the origin. Both of these factors influence the distribution of input representations in the adaptive network, as can be seen in Figure 4. Note that this distribution does not simply reflect the input distribution — it also takes into account the distribution of errors.

4 Discussion

Adaptive tessellation has been identified as an error based mechanism for varying the mapping between sensory and association units in a perceptron. Other models also perform such variations, for example, back-propagation [13]. If adaptive tessellation lies on a spectrum of flexibility in input mappings, at one end of which are simple perceptrons using fixed linear mappings and at the other end of which are models such as back-propagation, which allow continuous modification of all hidden unit (A-node) weights, then it should be located somewhere in the middle of this range.

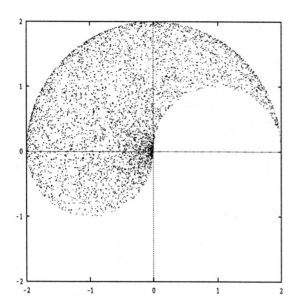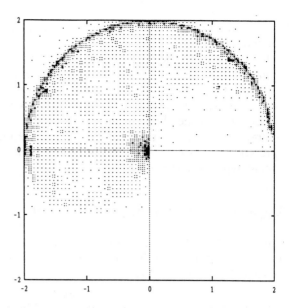

Figure 4: Distribution of input vectors (left) and A-nodes (right) from the adaptive tessellation network trained on the inverse kinematics problem. Each input vector represents a point in the two dimensional space around the arm centre, assumed to be located at the origin. Since the arm links are each one unit long, the arm can reach any point lying within a two unit radius circle of the origin, but its motion is restricted by generating joint angles in the range zero to π. The input distribution shows the result of a uniform random selection of joint angles from this range. The distribution of A-nodes is influenced by the input distribution but is more heavily concentrated around the origin and the edges of the workspace, as these are the regions that generate high errors. The same number of points are shown in each plot.

Like back-propagation, adaptive tessellation CMAC distributes its A-nodes (hidden layer units) in accordance with the error statistics. However, in order to do so, it utilises a heuristic rather than the generalised delta rule. Similar heuristics have been found useful in conjunction with back-propagation, for example, the cascade correlation algorithm [4] is a back-propagation variant which allocates new (hidden) units while the error remains above a given threshold.

The use of a heuristic implies applicability to particular classes of problems. Adaptive tessellation is particularly suited to the learning and representation of functions which contain regions of uniformity and regions of high variation. It is less well suited to functions which vary continuously.

Self-organising feature maps (SOFM) [6,7,15] employ a heuristic which performs an adaptive tessellation using cooperative interactions between nodes. However, this tessellation is based on the relative densities of inputs, rather than an error measure, resulting in greater concentration of nodes solely around areas in which inputs are frequently sampled. A variant of the SOFM algorithm uses error-based distribution of nodes and, like adaptive-tessellation CMAC, breaks down existing nodes when errors are high within the regions represented by those nodes [14]. This model uses a mixture of techniques: it follows the conventional SOFM algorithm to distribute nodes according to the input space densities, then replaces each node which performs at level worse than a fixed threshold by a new set of nodes. The system is used for classification and performance is measured by analysing the number of incorrect classifications made by a given node.

Another system which utilises a heuristic similar to that employed by adaptive tessellation is ARTMAP [3]. ARTMAP allocates new categories specifically when no satisfactory category exists, *i.e.*, when the existing classification scheme would incorrectly classify an input. The new category is placed at the location of the input vector which caused the error.

So adaptive tessellation can be viewed as a particular heuristic technique for choosing an input representation. It is more powerful and more complex than the fixed representation used in conventional CMAC but simpler and faster than techniques such as back-propagation. Although it sacrifices the easy array implementation that CMAC employs, it can be implemented in a computationally efficient manner (see Appendix).

Performance of the adaptive tessellation network could be improved by implementing some form of generalisation. Linear generalisation, implemented by averaging in CMAC, would allow the network the approximate functions with linear regions. More complex curve fitting could be performed by using the nodes to represent points on a spline or other curve types. As always, the optimal generalisation strategy will depend on the shape of the function; the best performance will always be achieved by selecting a generalisation strategy that is based on *a priori* knowledge of the function. The variation in size of regions represented by A-nodes in the adaptive tessellation architecture would automatically restrict generalisation to small regions where errors are high and widen it where errors are low.

Appendix: The Adaptive Tessellation Algorithm

Input and Output: Input is a series of M-dimensional real valued vectors, $\bar{i}$. Output is an N-dimensional vector, $\bar{o}$. Input and output vectors used for training are assumed to be drawn from a function to be approximated, $f : M \rightarrow N$.

Data Structure: Although the network architecture could be implemented in many different ways, all simulations described in this paper were implemented using a tree data structure. The tree is composed of two types of nodes: *output nodes* and *split nodes*. Each output node stores an output vector $\bar{x}$ and an accumulated error measure e. Each split node stores an input space weight vector $\bar{w}$.

Every split node has 2^M branches. Each branch represents a rectangular region of the input space one side of which is defined by the weight vector of the parent and the other sides of which are implicitly defined by neighbouring regions. Thus, a split node divides the input space into 2^M hypercubes around the point represented by its weight vector. The split nodes define the distribution of input representations.

Output nodes are always found at the leaves of the tree, *i.e.*, have no children. They correspond to the A-nodes of the network; their output vectors are the weight vectors connecting the A layer to the R layer.

Initialisation: The tree is initialised by constructing a single output node at the root which is initially responsible for the entire input space. Its output vector is initialised randomly.

Output: Each input is classified by traversing the tree, comparing the input vector to the weight vectors of the split nodes. The appropriate branch of the tree is followed and further comparisons made if another split node is encountered. This process is continued until an output node (leaf) is reached, whereupon the associated output vector $\bar{x}$ becomes the network output.

Training: The network is trained by presenting it with a series of input/output pairs, $\bar{i}$ and $\bar{o}$. Each of these pairs is assumed to represent an instance of the mapping, *i.e.*, $f(\bar{i}) = \bar{o}$. The network output in response to $\bar{i}$ is calculated as described above, call this $\bar{x}$. The error measure, $\bar{o} - \bar{x}$, is used to update the output vector of the unit which responded to the input using the delta rule:

$$\bar{x}' = \bar{x} + \eta \left(\bar{o} - \bar{x} \right)$$

where η is a learning rate. The summed square error, $\sum_{i=1}^{N}(\bar{o}_i - \bar{x}_i)^2$, is added to the accumulated error associated with the output node, e.

After a certain time period, the tree is reorganised and new split and output nodes added. Each such reorganisation allocates one new split node and 2^M new output nodes at the place in the input space where error was maximal, *i.e.*, the output node with the greatest e. The new split node replaces this output node and has 2^M new output node children, each one of which inherits the output vector of the replaced output node. All error statistics are zeroed after this splitting process.

References

[1] J.S. Albus. Data storage in the cerebellar model articulation controller (CMAC). *Transactions of the ASME, Journal of Dynamic Systems, Measurement and Control*, 97:228–233, September 1975.

[2] J.S. Albus. A new approach to manipulator control: the cerebellar model articulation controller (CMAC). *Transactions of the ASME, Journal of Dynamic Systems, Measurement and Control*, 97:220–227, September 1975.

[3] G. A. Carpenter, S. Grossberg, and J. H. Reynolds. ARTMAP: Supervised real-time learning and classification of nonstationary data by a self-organising neural network. In G. A. Carpenter and S. Grossberg, editors, *Pattern Recognition by Self-Organising Neural Networks*, chapter 15, pages 504–544. MIT Press, Cambridge, MA, 1991.

[4] S. E. Fahlman and C. Lebiere. The cascade-correlation learning architecture. In D. S. Touretzky, editor, *Advances in Neural Information Processing Systems 2*, pages 524–532, San Mateo, CA, 1990. Morgan Kaufamnn Publishers.

[5] P. Gaudiano and S. Grossberg. Vector associative maps: Unsupervised real-time error based learning and control of movement trajectories. *Neural Networks*, 4:147–183, 1991.

[6] S. Grossberg. Adaptive pattern classification and universal recoding I: Parallel development and coding of neural features. *Biological Cybernetics*, 23:121–134, 1976.

[7] T. Kohonen. *Self-Organisation and Associative Memory*. Springer-Verlag, Berlin, third edition, 1989.

[8] M. Kuperstein. INFANT neural controller for adaptive sensory-motor coordination. *Neural Networks*, 4:131–145, 1991.

[9] W.T. Miller. Real-time application of neural networks for sensor-based control of robots with vision. *IEEE Transactions on Systems, Man and Cybernetics*, 19(4):825–831, July/August 1989.

[10] W.T. Miller, F.H. Glanz, and L.G. Kraft. Application of a general learning algorithm to the control of robotic manipulators. *The International Journal of Robotics Research*, 6(2):84–95, 1987.

[11] W.T. Miller, R.P. Hewes, F.H. Glanz, and L.G. Kraft. Real-time dynamic control of an industrial manipulator using a neural-network-based learning controller. *IEEE Transactions on Robotics and Automation*, 6(1):1–9, February 1990.

[12] F. Rosenblatt. *Principles of Neurodynamics*. Spartan, New York, 1962.

[13] D. E. Rumelhart, G. E. Hinton, and R. J. Williams. Learning internal representations by error propagation. In D. E. Rumelhart and J. L. McLelland, editors, *Parallel Distributed Processing*, volume I, chapter 8, pages 318–362. MIT Press, Cambridge, MA, 1986.

[14] M. Sabourin and A. Mitiche. Modeling and classification of shape using a Kohonen associative memory with selective multiresolution. *Neural Networks*, 6:275–283, 1993.

[15] C. von der Malsburg. Self-organisation of orientation selective fields in the striate cortex. *Kybernetik*, 14:85–100, 1973.

[16] B. Widrow and M. E. Hoff. Adaptive switching circuits. In *IRE WESCON Convention Record*, pages 96–104, New York, 1960. IRE.

A Bias Architecture With Rank-Expanding Algorithm For Neural Networks Supervised Learning Problem

JiYang Luo

Department of Computer Science and Engineering

Wright State University, Dayton, OH 45435

Abstract:

A fast learning algorithm which can adaptively decide the architecture and synaptic weights of a neural network for any training set is presented here. It aims to use least hidden nodes in only one hidden layer and map the input-output patterns within any required precision. For any N-pattern training set, a maximum of N-r bias nodes are enough to learn all the patterns within required precision (r is the rank, usually the number of dimensions, of the input patterns). In this algorithm, the inverse of activation function is applied to the output data, thus the nonlinear part of the output layer is traversed and can be ignored in the succeeding learning process. Then we try to map the input data linearly to the traversed output data. If the mapping has greater error than required, then we add a hidden bias node, append each input pattern with the corresponding output of the added node, thus to increase the rank of the updated input. PseudoInverse is applied to achieve least square error linear mapping. The process of adding a hidden bias node is repeated until required mapping precision is achieved.

1. Introduction:

Supervised Learning Neural Network is a feed forward network. It picks up an input pattern, feeding forward (usually via some hidden layers), and achieves corresponding output pattern on the output layer.

We call it *supervisedlearning* because we desire to get specific output patterns from it for some input patterns. These input-ouput patterns constitute the training set.

We can see there are only two types of operators in a neural network: matrix operators W's and a nonlinear activation operator. In this paper, we use the following nonlinear activation operator:

$$\sigma : x \rightarrow \frac{e^x - e^{-x}}{e^x + e^{-x}}.$$

We expect the architecture and learning algorithm of this type of networks to :

1. Learn all the patterns in the training set quickly with small error;

2. Adaptively decide the architecure and do not use many hidden layers and nodes;

3. Predict the outputs of other patterns;

4. Can be easily implemented into electronic circuits, etc.

This neural networks model has great potential for applications in various areas. But up to now, we still don't have an architecture or learning algorithm that can satisfy these expectations. Especially, slowness of learning and difficulty to decide a proper architecure are major drawbacks to those who wish to apply Neural Networks.

In the method presented here, at least we can satisfy expectations 1 and 2 very well. We can decide a Neural Network with small quantity of hidden nodes, get their weights quickly, and with the network, each input pattern in the training set can be mapped to the desired output almost exactly, the error within any required precision. The architecture is also good for implementation, because only one type of neuron is used in the architecture.

2. Algorithms Description:

With this learning algorithm, the desired outputs are traced back through the nonlinear part with the inverse of the activation function,

$$\sigma^{-1} : x \rightarrow \frac{1}{2} ln \frac{1+x}{1-x}$$

and then we try to solve the problem linearly.

Denote the input patterns to be $A_{N,n}$, N is the number of patterns, n is the number of input dimensions. And denote the output patterns to be $T_{N,m}$, m is the number of output dimensions. We apply σ^{-1} to each element of T and get $B_{N,m}$. The range of $\sigma(x)$ is (-1,1), to apply σ^{-1}, we should chop those output values of $1, -1$ a little (within error tolerance).

We hope to map A to B with a weight matrix W, i.e. find W such that $A \cdot W = B$. To have exact solution of the linear equations, we require that each column of $B : \beta^j, j = 1..m$ should be linear combination of columns of $A : \alpha^i, i = 1..n$ with scalers $w_{i,j}$. That is, we require A should have the same rank with $[A|B]$.

For any A, B with N patterns, we have $rank(A) <= rank([A|B]) <= N$. When $rank(A) = rank([A|B])$, we can find exact solution W for $A \cdot W = B$. If $rank(A) < rank([A|B])$, we would first add a constant bias node "1", append it to each input pattern. This would most probably increase the rank of updated input patterns by one. If still $rank(A) < rank([A|B])$, then we can expand $rank(A)$ by appending Linear-Independent columns to A. These columns must be derived from input patterns in A. We would add hidden nodes and obtain these columns as their output vectors. To achieve least nodes, we add them one by one, each one choosing its weights such that its output vector would be linear independent to the columns of A, and the space spanned by this column and columns of A will cover the space spanned by columns of B most. To get weights for such a hidden neuron, an approach is to apply the method used by Fahlman and Lebiere [3], attempting to maximize the the covariance between the new unit's output and the residual error we are trying to eliminate.

In this first algorithm, gradient descent method is applied to approach maximum covariance, it still consumes some time. For those applications where learning speed is more emphasized, a simplified method can be applied. Instead of training the hidden neuron's weights, just have the weights randomly. When $rank(A) < rank([A|B]) <= N$, the space spanned by columns of A is only a very small part of the $N - dimension$ space. The weights are random, and the nonlinear activation function *distorts* the sum of the weighted inputs , so we're almost certain to have each new column of the hidden neuron's outputs to be Linear-Independent with the columns of A.

From the constraint of $rank(A) <= rank([A|B]) <= N$, we can see at most $N - r$ linear-independent vectors are needed for exact learning of the training set. It is the upper bound of the number of hidden nodes needed.

In either way above, the bias nodes are hidden nodes with fixed weights, and they are arranged in the same hidden layer. The output vector of each hidden node is attached to the corresponding input patterns, thus to increase the rank of updated inputs. PseudoInverse is then applied to train the weights for the output layer. PseudoInverse is a direct method that achieves least square error solution in a few matrix operations, it is much faster than gradient descent method which tries step by step to optimize the weights for least suqare error solution. This is the major reason that we speed up training rapidly.

3. Algorithms:

Algorithm 1: *(Bias Nodes with Maximum Covariance)*

1. Arrange data of the input patterns in matrix form: A. Arrange data of the output patterns in matix form: T. Each pattern in a row.

2. Add a constant bias node "1". Update A by appending a column of all "1" as its last column.

3. Decide precision of learning:e. Chop those elements of T to be within $[-1+e, 1-e]$: if any element is larger than $1-e$, let it be $1-e$; if any element less than $e-1$, let it be $e-1$.

4. Set W_bias to be empty.

5. $B = \sigma^{-1}(T)$;

6. $A^+ = (A^T \cdot A)^{-1}$;

7. $W = A^+ \cdot B$;

8. $E = |B - A \cdot W|_2 / (N * m)$;

9. If $(E_i = e)$ stop. Else go to step 10.

10. Add a hidden node with random weights connecting every input dimension and the constant bias node.

11. Update the weights of the hidden node with gradient descent method to approach maximum covariance(Refer to [3]).

12. Append the weights of this hidden node to W_bias as its last column.

13. Form a vector of outputs of the hidden node corresponding to each input pattern. Update A by appending this vector as its last column.

14. Goto step 6.

Algorithm 2: *(Bias Nodes with Random Weights)*

Void step 11 in algorithm 1.

4. Related works:

The idea of this Bias Architecture and Rank-Expanding Algorithm was inspired after studying the work of Friedrich Biegler-König and Frank Bärmann [2], and the work of Scott E. Fahlman and Christian Lebiere [3].

A Bias Architecture is a Cascade-Architecture in the sense that the weights for the bias nodes are fixed and then we combine the input patterns with bias outputs to train the ouput layer.

But the Cascade-Correlation Algorithm adds hidden nodes one by one, each in a different layer,*i.e.* each new node is a deeper layer, while we put bias nodes in the same hidden layer, thus to reduce the responding time. And we apply PseudoInverse to train the output layer directly, instead of applying gradient descent as carried out in [3], therefore the training can be much more rapidly.

In the second method of adding bias nodes with random weights, another difference is that the Cascade-Correlation Algorithm adds hidden nodes by maximizing the covariance, here we don't train the weights for the hidden nodes, just have the weights randomly, only to expand the rank of the input and to have more weights involved for output, so as to achieve an exact solution in the linear part. This helps to reduce training time while still mapping the input-output exactly, but it might require some more bias nodes.

The method of separating linear and nonlinear parts on each layer of nodes in the network was presented in [2]. But they didn't discuss the network architecture, they adopted conventional multi-layer network. When the nonlinear part on one layer is separated, there are still nonlinear parts on the other layers involved. In their Least Squares Backpropagation Algorithm, linear least squares computation (PseudoInverse) is applied back and forth through the multilayers repeatedly, trying to diminish the error. But usually, after one or two iterations the error will remain and not go on decreasing, and they suggested to use Backprop or other learning algorithm to further reduce the error, which again would be time consuming.

The authors claimed a special case under which they could achieve exact solution using LSB: *Especially if the network includes a hidden layer with more nodes than the number of exmples to be learned and if the number of nodes in succeeding layers decreases monotonically, the presented algorithm in general finds an exact solution.* But they didn't explain the reason. In fact, when adopting conventional multilayered neural network, if the *last* hidden layer has no less hidden nodes than N, the number of examples to be learned, then we can achieve exact solution in general. Similarly, the weights for the hidden layers were randomly given, so the output columns of the nodes (more than N) in the last hidden layer are evenly distributed in the N dimension space, and the rank of these columns together would most probably be N, thus we can achieve exact solution in the output layer.

5. Conclusions:

With this Bias-Architecture, we separate the hidden layer and the output layer in training. so we can traverse the nonlinear part of the output layer with the inverse of activation function, then no other nonlinear problem remains, and we transfer the problem of neural networks that combines both linear and nonlinear parts to the problem of solving linear equations, which is a more familiar topic to us, and has a good method of PseudoInverse for us to apply.

The first algorithm of training the hidden neurons to have maximum covariance is an approach to obtain an architecture with minimum hidden nodes. The second algorithm aims to further speed up training by adopting hidden nodes with random weights, which can also serve to expand the rank of combined inputs. But it might require some more nodes than the first algorithm do.

We still expect more numerical analysis. There may be some faster, better ways to find the best weights for the bias nodes to achieve least number of nodes, each time appending vectors that helps best to expand the space to include the output vectors.

References:

[1] Jacek M. Zurada,"Introduction to Artificial Neural Systems" West Publishing Company, 1992

[2] Friedrich Biegler-König and Frank Bärmann "A Learning Algorithm for Multilayered Neural Networks Based On Linear Least Squares Problems" Neural Networks, Volume 6, Number 1, 1993

[3] Scott E. Fahlman and Christian Lebiere, "The Cascade-Correlation Learning Achitecture" Neural Information Processing Systems, 2,1990

[4] Kevin G. Kirby, "Connections and Transformations:Seven Lectures on Neural Computation" Unpublished lecture notes, Computer Science and Engineering, Wright State University,1992

[5] R. W. Farebrother, "Linear Least Squares Computations" Marcel Dekker, Inc. New York

[6] William W. Hager ,"Applied Numerical Linear Algebra" Prentice Hall, Eaglewood Cliffs, New Jersey

Eigenvalue Acceleration Technique for
Back Propagation Artificial Neural Networks

B. Nassersharif and Sadhu Prasad
National Supercomputing Center for Energy and Environment
University of Nevada, Las Vegas
Las Vegas, Nevada 89154-2048
e-mail: bn@nye. nscee. edu, sadhu@nye. nscee. edu.

ABSTRACT

One of the widely used neural network models is the back propagation (BP) artificial neural system (ANS). It is a multilayer, heterogenous, supervised, feed-forward ANS paradigm. Slow convergence of the BP learning algorithm hampers its use for problems with a complex and/or large feature space. We have developed a simple and scalable acceleration technique which preserves the convergence characteristics of the BP ANS paradigm. The convergence or divergence of the system is detected by the dominant eigenvalue for each layer. We have discovered a relationship between the speed of convergence and the dominant eigenvalues. As the eigenvalue deviates from 1, the temperature of the network is adjusted to over come the local minima. Numerical experiments indicate a reduction in the learning time for large complex problems.

Introduction

The back propagation (BP) artificial neural network (ANN) algorithm is widely used because of its simplicity and applicability to various problems. Pattern Recognition, combinatorics and controls are some of the major areas of its application. However, slow off-line learning hinders its application to many problems with a large and complex feature space. The training of the BP paradigm involves a fixed learning schedule. During training the system searches for a minimum error surface in the weight space. The error surface is usually degenerate with numerous flat spots, valley and other unevenness. To aid the convergence of the system various parameters of the learning schedule should be varied in a controlled fashion for the faster convergence. The purpose of this research is to develop an acceleration technique for the BP paradigm. One of our main goals was to achieve acceleration without altering the BP algorithm.

Theory of Back Propagation Paradigm

The BP ANN algorithm traces back to 1956, when Rosenblatt(1962) introduced the first connection model called the perceptron, which uses the delta learning rule. The delta learning rule calculates error at the output processing units using simple Euclidean distance in 1-dimensional space. The actual output is calculated using the forward propagation rule given by:

$$O_{pj} = f\left[\sum_i \left(W_{ij}\left(I_i - \theta\right)\right)\right]$$

where,

$$f(x) = \begin{cases} 1 & \text{if } x \geq 0 \\ -1 & \text{othewise} \end{cases}$$

The delta rule is not restricted to binary values. The BP paradigm can also be extended for continuous signals in discrete time.

Generalized Delta Rule

The generalized delta rule was proposed to solve the problems of learning in a feed-forward network with a nonlinear activation function. It is a powerful learning algorithm. It carries out an approximation of a bounded mapping $f: \left(A \subset R^n \rightarrow R^m \right)$ using the training pairs (x_1, y_1), (x_2, y_2), ..., (x_n, y_n) with the mapping of $y_k = f(x_k)$, where, f is an unknown implicit function which the system evolves through the adaptation of its internal representation. The error is iteratively propagated back through the hidden network layers towards the input layer. The weights are adjusted using

$$\Delta_p w_{ji} = \eta \delta_{pj} O_{pi},$$

where,

$$\delta_{pj} = \begin{cases} f'_j(net_{pj}) \sum_k \delta_{pk} w_{kj} & \text{for hidden layer node,} \\ (t_{pj} - O_{pj}) f'_j(net_{pj}) & \text{for output units.} \end{cases}$$

The delta rule is applied iteratively until the network converges.

Minsky and Papert (1969) have pointed out that, for any recurrent architecture, an equivalent feed-forward ANS exists. The generalized delta rule is therefore, applicable to feed-forward as well as equivalent recurrent network systems.

Acceleration technique using the Dominant Eigenvalue of the Iteration Matrix

Back Propagation [Rumelhart(1986)] is a powerful supervised learning algorithm for multilayer feed-forward ANNs. It is an estimating system that stores generalized solution of arbitrary pattern pairs, using the gradient descent error correction procedure. It is extremely popular and has been used for a variety of input/output mapping tasks in the pattern recognition and classification problems. The BP learning procedure is off-line. It has a very slow convergence characteristic. The expanding problem complexity have forced researchers to discover new algorithms to accelerate convergence.

The theory of linear iterative methods provide a treasure of acceleration algorithms. However, the artificial neural systems are inherently nonlinear in operation. Therefore, any direct use of linear system acceleration techniques, to accelerate the ANS, is neither feasible nor practical. Here, we have developed a new technique to monitor and predict the evolution of the connection strength. We adjust the temperature of the activation function of the processing elements for faster convergence.

Consider a feed-forward multilayer ANS architecture. The mapping, done by the network, up to the first hidden layer is linear. For a piecewise linear model, the mapping from the input layer to the output layer, can be assumed linear. Therefore the set of weights, in the first hidden layer, evolves linearly. Any non-linearity or abrupt change in the error surface is detected by rapid variation of the dominant eigenvalue calculated for the iteration matrix of the first hidden layer. The iteration matrix is calculated as follows:

The weight update is given by;

$$W_j^{(p+1)} = W_j^{(p)} + \eta \delta_j I_p.$$

Without loss of generality, we can assume $\eta = 1$. The iterative learning rule can be written as

$$W_j = \left(T_T^p - W_j I_p \right)^T I_p.$$

For the first hidden layer, the iteration matrix G is I_p times an identity matrix for the first hidden layer. The iteration matrix G is a square and a symmetric and positive definite matrix. For the network to converge, all eigenvalues (λ) of the iteration matrix must be less then 1.

We may use the residuals (change in weights) to estimate the dominant eigenvalue of the iteration matrix, obtained by successive approximations, is given by the following equation

$$\lambda_1 = \frac{\sum_i \left[r_i^{(n+1)} \right]^2}{\sum_i \left[r_i^{(n)} \right]^2}.$$

The above Equation is similar to Rayleigh's quotient formula.

Consider the feed-forward ANN architecture, the weights between the first hidden layer units and the input buffer do not contain any nonlinearity. Therefore, they map the input patterns presented at the input buffer linearly to the first hidden layer during the forward pass. Hence we may apply the theory, discussed earlier to accelerate the convergence of the BP algorithm. The piece-wise linear assumption rules out the use of any linear system for acceleration of the linear systems. However, the dominant eigenvalue of the iteration matrix can be used as a parameter to monitor the evolution of the network. The contention is also supported by the fact that, any generate mapping is fairly continues and therefore linear within small intervals.

We have also observed that the dominant eigenvalue of the other layers follow the dominant eigenvalue of the first hidden layer. Thus, the selected eigenvalue reflects the convergence state of the overall network.

The dominant eigenvalue of the first hidden layer may be used to monitor the evolution of the network. The cooling of the system is proportional to the dominant eigenvalue of the iteration matrix. Whenever the system eigenvalues move away from the desired value, the deviation is used to raise the energy of the system. The dominant eigenvalue greater than one indicates that the system is ascending in the weight space.

At this juncture, the energy of the system is raised, in a step, to some higher level. The system starts descending in the weight space again using the gradient descent algorithm.

The acceleration Algorithm

The specific steps of the new algorithm are as follows

1. The back propagation network topology and the learning parameter values are selected.
2. Random values in the range of [-0. 5, 0. 5] are assigned to the connected weights.
3. For each input pattern new activation value for the each processing unit in the forward pass is calculated.
4. The output error, using the least mean squared error criterion for the output buffer processing units, is calculated and the error is propagated backwards.
5. The connection strength is adjusted using the correlation technique.
6. After one complete presentation of the input set (an epoch), the eigenvalue of the first hidden layer matrix is calculated.
7. The temperature of the network is adjusted as follows:
   a. If the eigenvalue of iteration matrix is greater than one then the temperature of the network is increased inversely proportional to the eigenvalue.
   b. If the eigenvalue continues to remain below one then the temperature is reduced gradually.
9. Steps 3 through 7 are iterated until convergence criterion is satisfied.

Results and Discussion

The eigenvalue technique is evaluated for the problems widely used for benchmarking. Currently there are no accepted standards for benchmarking neural networks. However, the XOR problem is mostly used because of its historical importance. Parity 3 through parity 5 are good cases for checking scalability and response of any acceleration technique to increasingly complex problems. The results obtained during the test runs and the analysis of the results with the description of the problem is presented below. For all the tests we took the average of the eigenvalues for different intervals in order to reduce the effect of noise.

XOR Problem

The Exclusive problem is a linearly inseparable problem. The two input, one output training pairs are shown in Table 1.

Table 1: XOR problem input/output groups

Input 1	Input 2	Output
0	0	0
0	1	1
1	0	1
1	1	0

Parity n problems are the extension of the parity 2 problem with increasing number of the input attributes. The feature space grows complex with the number of inputs. The number of patterns grows exponentially with the number of input attributes. Table 2 shows the input/output patterns pairs for the parity 3 problem.

Table 2:

Problem	BP	EVAT
XOR	459	159
Parity 3	2048	269
Parity 4	4056	1565

From the table we see that there is a significant reduction in the convergence rate by the new technique that we have developed

Conclusions

A new technique for the acceleration of the back propagation paradigm was developed and evaluated. The motivation of the work was to develop an acceleration technique without altering the convergence properties of the standard BP paradigm. Another goal was to simplify the training procedure by reducing the degrees of freedom. Generally, the choice of learning parameters is critical to convergence time. The complex interactions of the parameters necessitates thorough knowledge of the problem features. Thus eigenvalue acceleration technique reduces the complexity of training the BP paradigm. The goal was to devise a general technique to monitor the energy state of the neural system. It can help in deciding the optimal energy state for the system. We have successfully shown that using the dominant eigenvalue of the iteration matrix of the first hidden layer, optimal energy of the system can be decided. This information is used to accelerate the convergence of the system towards lower energy level.

The technique developed here for acceleration of the BP paradigm does not alter the algorithm. Also, it does not use any special feature of the algorithm. Thus, the method may be applicable to any feed-forward ANS architecture. Further research is being done in this area for increasing the acceleration of the BP paradigm. Also we have observed a relation between the speed of convergence of the network and eigenvalues. This relation has shown that there is a reduction in the time of convergence rate of the network. Based on numerical experiments our future work will focus on a more rigorous derivation of the mathematical relationships and numerical experimentation with more complex problems.

References

Rumelhart, D. E. & McClelland D. (1986). Learning internal representation by error propagation, Parallel Distributed Processing: Exploration in the Microstructure of Cognition. MIT press, 1986, I, 318-362.

Minai, A. A. (1990). Acceleration of backpropagation through learning rate and momentum rate adaptation. IJCNN, I, 676-679.

Minsky, M. and Papert, s. (1969). Preceptrons. MIT Press, Cambridge MA.

Lipmann, R. P. (1987). An introduction to computing with neural networks. IEEE ASSP magazine, 4, 4-21.

Forward Propagation ($FP-1$) Algorithm in Multilayer Feedforward Network

Jian Zhan and Fu Li
Department of Electrical Engineering
Portland State University
Portland, OR 97207-0751

Abstract

This paper proposes a new forward propagation algorithm ($FP-1$) in multilayer feedforward network. The new approach is a constructive algorithm transferring errors forward while not changing the established structure, neurons, and the trained weights in the network. The concept of $FP-1$ mapping space is defined in which the program of approximation is just to get inversion of vectors and determine the $FP-1$ areas. Several new definitions are introduced, such as $FP-1$ areas, nonlinear distribution chart, global and local approximation, etc. Using $FP-1$ algorithm, for the arbitrary mapping $R_i^n \to R_i^m$, we can know accuracy of every neuron in network is able to arrive, and understand every step of approximation. $FP-1$ algorithm includes an important principle how to decompose the given mapping into global and local components and then to solve the problem by using global and local approximation. The purpose of this paper is to provide basic idea of *Forward Propagation*, specifically $FP-1$ mapping space is emphasized.

1 Introduction

Although BP algorithm is used broadly in many applications, intrinsic mechanism of neurons in the network, training methods and convergence behavior are imperfectly understood, and huge amount of computer time are consumed, especially during training. With impressive successes across a wide variety of applications, this approach prompts many questions that have to be answered.

1. How many hidden units should be used for the given mapping. In this sense, is that possible for us to define or classify the given mappings to different mapping spaces which can be established in neural network with different complexity or difficulty?

2. Why can the nonlinear neurons used in network approximate the given mapping with arbitrary precision? What is real behavior or important but still unknown principles in the network?

3. What concrete types of nonlinear neurons are best to be used in the network according actual applications or data set, and how to choose them?

4. Can we know the errors of every step of approximation or construct the hidden layer neurons definitely to eliminate the errors to arbitrary desired accuracy?

5. Is the BP algorithm the only approach to implement feedforward multilayer network? whether or not there are other algorithms to implement the mapping more efficiently and easily?

This paper will address these issues, and more importantly, it will explore and present a new ideas of *Forward Propagation* (FP) approach, in which the errors are propagated forward and then we can know where the "bottleneck" of approximation happens. The algorithm proposed in this paper is the first algorithm in series of FP approach. For this reason, it is denoted as $FP-1$ algorithm. In fact, the FP approach provides detail information at every step of forward approximation and unveils many interesting features in mapping f: $R_i^n \to R_i^m$. Another important theory proposed in this paper is to decompose global problems into local ones, and then to fit together local components solved to satisfy the global properties needed.

2 Algorithm of Feedforward Propagation

The idea of $FP-1$ algorithm is based on:

1. First to construct two layer neural net. The linear and nonlinear optimal algorithms are used to approximate the given mapping input and target data set.

2. If two layer neural net can not reach the given precision, the third layer is established and the remained errors are erased in neurons in third layer.

3. If the desired accuracy is not satisfied in third layer, the hidden neurons are needed to continue to reduce the errors until the given precision arrives.

An important feature in FP is that the previously trained weights and nonlinear function g_j are not changed while the third or hidden neurons are added, just the coefficients of the new neurons are implemented.

2.1 First two layer linear approximation

As mentioned above, for a given mapping $R_i^n \to R_i^m$ $i = 1, ..., r$, $n < r$, the task is decomposed as $R_i^n \to R_i$ problem at first. The two layer network is constructed shown in Fig.1.

In order to induce the idea of $FP-1$, the linear optimal approximation will be used, and the algorithm of least mean square (LMS) developed by Widrow and Hoff is briefly described here.

Assuming there are r input vectors X_i with n dimensions corresponding to r output Y_i $i = 1, ..., r$, $n < r$ with m dimensions, there is linear estimation,

$$y_{ji}^{sl} = \sum_{k=1}^{n} x_{ik} w_{jk} \qquad i = 1, ..., r \qquad j = 1, ..., m \tag{1}$$

and desired output is y_{ji}, linear output in second layer is y_{ji}^{sl}, the mean squared error function is

$$E(W_j) = (1/2) \sum_{i=1}^{r} (y_{ji} - y_{ji}^{sl})^2 = (1/2) \sum_{i=1}^{r} (y_{ji} - \sum_{k=1}^{n} x_{ik} w_{jk})^2 \qquad j = 1, ..., m \tag{2}$$

The gradient at any point on the surface is obtained by differentiating $\partial E(W_j)/\partial w_{jk}$ with respect to the parameter vector W_j, where W_j is the weight vector from input to jth neuron in second layer:

$$\frac{\partial E(W_j)}{\partial w_{jk}} = - \sum_{i=1}^{r} (y_{ji} - y_{ji}^{sl}) x_{ik} \qquad j = 1, ..., m \quad k = 1, ..., n \tag{3}$$

The LMS can, therefore, be written as

$$w_{jk}(t) = w_{jk}(t-1) + \mu(-\frac{\partial E(W_j)}{\partial w_{jk}}) = w_{jk}(t-1) + \mu \sum_{i=1}^{r} (y_{ji} - y_{ji}^{sl}) x_{ik} \qquad j = 1, ..., m \quad k = 1, ..., n \tag{4}$$

Eq.(4) determines w_{jk} under criterion of LMS. From this point of view, the weights of two layers are decided in linear optimal approximation. Let us take mapping 1 shown below as an example.

$$Mapping 1$$

$$
\begin{bmatrix}
-.55 & -.7 & -.95 & -.78 & -.65 \\
-.4 & -.44 & -.38 & -.2 & -.51 \\
-.32 & -.4 & -.38 & -.43 & -.19 \\
-.21 & -.03 & .05 & -.18 & .03 \\
.38 & .18 & .21 & -.12 & -.13 \\
.31 & .19 & .21 & -.07 & .15 \\
.39 & .23 & .31 & .41 & .25 \\
.5 & .68 & .13 & .5 & .41 \\
.71 & .44 & .68 & .6 & .78 \\
.48 & .5 & .82 & .73 & .19
\end{bmatrix}
\Longrightarrow
\begin{bmatrix}
-.15 \\
-.38 \\
-.75 \\
-.21 \\
.09 \\
.18 \\
.45 \\
.53 \\
.8 \\
-.52
\end{bmatrix}
\tag{5}
$$

After iterative calculation, the mean square error is 0.6645. The target, actual output and error values are shown in Tab.1

target	-.15	-.38	-.75	-.21	.09	.18	.45	.53	.8	-.52
app. result	-.238	-.419	-.095	-.18	.286	.087	.28	.674	.708	-.173
error	.088	.039	-.655	-.029	-.196	.094	.17	-.144	.091	-.347

Tab.1

2.2 Nonlinear distributive chart and nonlinear function g_j

After the linear approximation in first step, we come to the important issue, how to choose nonlinear function g_j.

Definition 2.1 Let $M \to N(X_i \in M, y_i \in N)$ be arbitrary given mapping $\varphi : R_i^n \to R_i$ $i = 1,...,r$, $n < r$, after linear optimal estimation (LMS), there are actual linear output y_i^{sl} and set $V, y_i^{sl} \in V$. there still exists mapping $g_j : V \to N$, then g_j is called nonlinear function for the given mapping φ, and the curve of relationship between y_i^{sl} and y_i is denoted nonlinear distributive chart (NDC).

This definition describes that an arbitrary mapping, $\varphi : R_i^n \to R_i$, in jth neuron of second layer, which can be decomposed into two steps: linear mapping and nonlinear mapping. The relationship between y_i^{sl} and y_i unveils information of what kind nonlinear function should be used as shown in Fig.2. Although NDC varies in different domains, we can concentrate on a class of sigmoid functions in $FP - 1$ by choosing coefficients a_j, b_j, c_j, d_j in formula (6) in jth neuron. Since the domain discussed in $FP-1$ is x_i and $y_i \in [-1, 1]$, we define sigmoid function in

$$g_j = y_{ji}^{snl} = \frac{c_j}{1 + exp(-(y_{ji}^{sl} + a_j)/b_j)} - d_j \qquad i = 1,...,r \qquad j = 1,...,m. \tag{6}$$

Where the y_{ji}^{sl} is jth neuron output of linear approximation in second layer, and y_{ji}^{snl} is jth output of nonlinear function g_j in second layer, the sum of squared errors are

$$E = (1/2)\sum_{i=1}^{r}(y_{ji} - y_{ji}^{snl})^2 \qquad j = 1,...,m \tag{7}$$

The partial derivatives of E with respect to variables a_j, b_j, c_j, d_j are

$$\frac{\partial E}{\partial a_j} = \sum_{i=1}^{r} e_{ji} \frac{c_j\ exp(-(y_{ji}^{sl} + a_j)/b_j)}{b_j(1 + exp(-(y_{ji}^{sl} + a_j)/b_j))^2} \qquad j = 1,...,m. \tag{8}$$

$$\frac{\partial E}{\partial b_j} = \sum_{i=1}^{r} e_{ji} \frac{c_j exp(-(y_{ji}^{sl} + a_j)/b_j)}{b_j^2(1 + exp(-(y_{ji}^{sl} + a_j)/b_j))^2} \qquad j = 1,...,m. \tag{9}$$

$$\frac{\partial E}{\partial c_j} = -\sum_{i=1}^{r} e_{ji} \frac{1}{1 + exp(-(y_{ji}^{sl} + a_j)/b_j)} \qquad j = 1,...,m. \tag{10}$$

$$\frac{\partial E}{\partial d_j} = -\sum_{i=1}^{r} e_{ji} \qquad j = 1,...,m. \tag{11}$$

where $e_{ji} = y_{ji} - y_{ji}^{snl}$, y_{ji} is desired output in jth node, then the algorithm of adapting $a_j(t), b_j(t), c_j(t), d_j(t)$ is given by

$$a_j(t) = a_j(t-1) + \mu(-\frac{\partial E}{\partial a_j(t-1)}) \tag{12}$$

$$b_j(t) = b_j(t-1) + \mu(-\frac{\partial E}{\partial b_j(t-1)}) \tag{13}$$

$$c_j(t) = c_j(t-1) + \mu(-\frac{\partial E}{\partial c_j(t-1)}) \tag{14}$$

$$d_j(t) = d_j(t-1) + \mu(-\frac{\partial E}{\partial d_j(t-1)}) \tag{15}$$

Fig.3 shows nonlinear distributive chart(NDC) and Tab.2 illustrates the values after nonlinear approximation in mapping 1. The squared error is reduced from 0.6645 of linear mapping to 0.5505 of nonlinear mapping, with $a_1 = -0.11, b_1 = 0.42, c_1 = 2.1, d_1 = 1.02$.

target	-.15	-.38	-.75	-.21	.09	.18	.45	.53	.8	-.52	Tab.2
app. result	-.383	-.557	-.223	-.321	.244	-.001	.237	.642	.669	-.313	
error	.233	.177	-.527	.111	-.154	.181	.213	-.112	.131	-.207	

2.3 Construction of the third layer and determination threshold nonlinear function

If two layer net can not reach the given precision, the third layer should be established.

Definition 2.2: Let w_{ji}^{s-t} be the weights between second and third layer, $w_{ji}^{s-t} = 1$ if $i = j$, the connections with $w_{ji}^{s-t} = 1$ from second to third layer are denoted main information channels.

One of important features in FP is the concept of the main information channels which is much different from general network. The main information channels keep the previous achievements transferred. The remained errors are considered as the target set approximated in the third layer. Since the error set should be divided several subsets which are easily eliminated, based on the idea of FP, the subthird layer notion is introduced here,

Definition 2.3: Assuming there are m output nodes in third layer for the given mapping $R_i^n \to R_i^m$. If there are neurons between second and third layer, each of them has $m-1$ weights w_{ji}^{s-t} $(j = 1, ..., m\ i = 1, ..., m-1)$ and nonlinear threshold function g_j, these neurons are denoted subthird neurons.

The purpose of subthird layer is to focus and erase the specified error subset, which is local area processing. The subthird layer is constructed in Fig.4, the dark circles represent subthird neuron. The approximated results of subthird and hidden neurons are summarized in third layer to reach global approximation, each of them focuses on specified error subset. The basic idea of FP is to separate error set into several subsets, and according to the given accuracy of approximation, the error subsets will be erased one by one, by the subthird and the hidden neurons until the desired precision is gotten. Assuming there are m output neurons and r mapping pairs,

Definition 2.4: Let $\sigma_j = [e_{j1}, e_{j2}, ..., e_{jr}]$ be error set in jth neuron of second layer and σ_j is transferred to third layer through main information channel, if there exists relationship $|e_{j1}| \geq |e_{j2}| \geq ... \geq |e_{jr}|$, the set σ_j is called absolute partial order error set.

After the approximation of second layer, the error set is transferred to third neurons totally and rearranged to absolute partial order error set. Since there is one connection being main information channel, in which weight equals to one, there are $m-1$ weights needed to be determined in every neuron of subthird layer. The error subset $\sigma_j^{sub} = [e_{j1}, ..., e_{j(m-1)}]^T$ is selected to be reduced first in jth node of third layer, which are maximum absolute values in error set σ_j. Meanwhile there must be a subset $Y_j^{sub} = [Y_{j1}^{snl}, ..., Y_{j(m-1)}^{snl}]^T$ and $Y_{ji}^{snl} = [y_{i1}^{snl}, ..., y_{i(m-1)}^{snl}]$ $(j = 1, ..., m\ i = 1, ..., m-1)$ in second layer corresponding to $\sigma_j^{sub} = [e_{j1}, ..., e_{j(m-1)}]^T$ in subthird layer, and then we can get $W_j^{s-t} = [Y_j^{sub}]^{-1}\sigma_j^{sub}$, where W_j^{s-t} is the weight vector from second layer to jth neuron of subthird layer, so that there are only $m-1$ variables. On the other hand, the threshold function should be decided by subset σ_j^{sub} There are three kinds of possible distributions in subset σ_j^{sub}. Let a_1 be negative minimum, b_1 be negative maximum, a_2 be positive minimum, b_2 be positive maximum in subset σ_j^{sub}. Fig.5-7 demonstrate the three kinds of distributions.

Definition 2.5: Let error set be $\sigma_j = [e_{j1}, ..., e_{jr}]$ in jth neuron of third layer, which is absolute partial order set. Choosing the first $m-1$ elements to form subset $\sigma_j^{sub} = [e_{j1}, ..., e_{j(m-1)}]$, there must exist one of distributions shown in Figs.5-7, the dark areas in these figures are called $FP-1$ areas, and is denoted Λ_j in jth neuron.

The $FP-1$ areas Λ_j, in fact, define the active intervals for the nonlinear threshold function. This definition actually gives the way of how to decide the threshold function.

For example, the mapping 1 absolute partial order error set is shown in Tab.3.

e_{11}	e_{12}	e_{13}	e_{14}	e_{15}	e_{16}	e_{17}	e_{18}	e_{19}	$e_{1(10)}$
-.5274	.2328	.213	-.2074	.1813	.1767	-.1542	.1311	-.1115	.1108

Tab.3

The subset σ_1^{sub} is $[-.5274, .2328, .213, -.2074]$, which is case 1 shown in Fig.5. Now there exist $FP-1$ areas $a_1 = -.5274 - \varepsilon$, $b_1 = -.2074 + \varepsilon$, $a_2 = .213 - \varepsilon$, $b_2 = .2328 + \varepsilon$, $(0 < \varepsilon << 1)$. The threshold function of jth neuron in subthird layer is,

$$y_{ji}^{s-t} = \sum_{k=1}^{m-1} y_{ik}^{snl} w_{jk}^{s-t} \qquad i = 1, ..., r, \qquad \begin{cases} a_1 \leq y_{ji}^{s-t} \leq b_1 \\ a_2 \leq y_{ji}^{s-t} \leq b_2 \end{cases} \tag{16}$$

$$y_{ji}^{s-t} = 0 \qquad\qquad\qquad\qquad\qquad \text{otherwise}$$

where y_{ji}^{s-t} is the jth neuron output in subthird layer $(j = 1, ..., m\ i = 1, ..., r)$, which is sifted by threshold function g_j. It is obvious that this nonlinear threshold function is defined by $FP-1$ areas, which are decided by σ_j^{sub}. For the convenience of discussion we use Λ_j to represent the threshold function in jth neuron of subthird layer. This threshold function is able to erase error subset σ_j^{sub} under condition of the mapping of other elements $e_{ji} \notin \Lambda_j$ not falling into the $FP-1$ areas, because W_j^{s-t} is derived by Y_j^{sub} and σ_j^{sub}, in output set $Y_j^{s-t} = [y_{j1}^{s-t}, ..., y_{jr}^{s-t}]$ there must be $m-1$ elements y_{il}^{s-t} $(l = 1, ..., m-1) \in \sigma_j^{sub}$. If the other elements y_{ik}^{s-t} $(k = 1, ..., r-m+1) \notin \sigma_j^{sub}$ do not get into Λ_j decided by σ_j^{sub}, this threshold function can erase subset σ_j^{sub}, otherwise, is appears more complicated mapping space, which will be discussed in $FP-2$.

Definition 2.6: Let mapping $R_i^{m-1} \to R_i$ $(i = 1, ..., r, \ m-1 < r)$ be $\Phi : Y_j = [Y_{j1}^{snl}, ..., Y_{jr}^{snl}]^T \to \sigma_j^{s-t} = [e_{j1}, ..., e_{j(m-1)}, \hat{e}_{jm}, ..., \hat{e}_{jr}]^T$ from second to subthird layer, and there is absolute partial order error set $\sigma_j = [e_{j1}, ..., e_{jr}]$ in neuron of the third layer. If there exist subset $\sigma_j^{sub} = [e_{j1}, ..., e_{j(m-1)}]^T$ $(m-1 < r, \ e_{ji} \in \sigma_j)$, which is the first $m-1$ elements of σ_j, and corresponding subset is $Y_j^{sub} = [Y_{j1}^{snl}, ..., Y_{j(m-1)}^{snl}]^T$ $(Y_{ji}^{snl} \in Y_j)$, then there must exist $FP - 1$ areas Λ_j and $W_j^{s-t} = [Y_j^{sub}]^{-1}\sigma_j^{sub}$ $(|Y_j^{sub}| \neq 0)$. The linear mapping $\sigma_j^{s-t} = Y_j W_j^{s-t}$ is gotten, there is relationship $\sigma_j^{sub} \in \sigma_j^{s-t}$, also there is a subset $\hat{\sigma}_j = \sigma_j^{s-t} - \sigma_j^{sub} = [\hat{e}_{jm}, ..., \hat{e}_{jr}]$. If the subset $\hat{\sigma}_j$ settles outside $FP - 1$ areas Λ_j, the linear mapping $(\Phi, Y_j, W_j^{s-t}, \Lambda_j)$ is called $FP - 1$ local mapping space, and is denoted Ψ, σ_j^{s-t} is called the checking set, $\hat{\sigma}_j$ is called the generated subset.

An important type of mapping space is described in Definition 2.6, in which the error subset σ_j^{sub} can be totally eliminated by (16), while other elements $e_{ji} \notin \sigma_j^{sub}$ are not influenced, checking set σ_j^{s-t} is used to find out whether the given mapping is $FP - 1$ local mapping space. More important are, for local $FP - 1$ mapping space Ψ, the complexity of algorithm relates only to the inversion of $m - 1$ vectors and decision of Λ_j instead of searching in state space, this is a non-recursive and analytic approach.

Let us look at example of mapping 1 again. Assuming $m = 5, m - 1 = 4, j = 1, [Y_1^{sub}]^{-1}$ corresponding to σ_1^{sub} in the first neuron of subthird layer is given in (17). and $n = 5, r = 10$. From absolute partial order error set in Tab.3, the error subset $\sigma_1^{sub} = [-.5274, .2328, .213, -.2074]^T$.

$$[Y_1^{sub}]^{-1} = \begin{bmatrix} -.4 & -.25 & .19 & .58 \\ .14 & -.25 & .28 & .18 \\ .49 & .81 & .22 & -.01 \\ .54 & .82 & .23 & -.02 \end{bmatrix}^{-1} = \begin{bmatrix} 1.2856 & -1.8366 & -42.8905 & 42.1995 \\ .0538 & -.6255 & 10.488 & -9.3149 \\ -2.8985 & 6.231 & 59.1355 & -57.6946 \\ 3.5834 & -3.5774 & -44.5292 & 43.988 \end{bmatrix} \tag{17}$$

$W_1^{s-t} = [Y_1^{sub}]^{-1}\sigma_1^{sub} = [-18.9949, 3.9922, 27.6068, -21.332]$. If $\varepsilon = .001$, the $FP - 1$ areas Λ_1 are $a_1 = -.5284, \ b_1 = -.2064, \ a_2 = .212, \ b_2 = .2338$.

By calculating the checking set $\sigma_1^{s-t} = Y_1 W_1^{s-t} = [-.5274, .2328, .213, -.2074, 1.2024, .4832, -18.0361, 6.4508, -.6905]$, where the generated subset $\hat{\sigma}_1 = [1.2024, .4832, -18.0361, 6.4508, -.6905]$ and no generated elements $\hat{e}_{1i} \in \hat{\sigma}_1$ fall into $FP - 1$ areas. The result of adding threshold function into global entity in the third layer is in Tab.4.

target	-.75	-.15	.45	-.52	.18	-.38	.09	.8	.53	-.21	
app.result	-.75	-.15	.45	-.52	-.0013	-.5567	.2442	.6689	.6415	-.3208	Tab.4
error	.0	.0	.0	.0	.1813	.1767	-.1542	.1311	-.1115	.1108	

The total squared error is .1298. The NDC is shown in Fig.8. From this figure the degree of nonlinearity has been changed and become closer to the straight line and more smooth. Hence, the nonlinear threshold function of subthird neuron contributes much to reduce nonlinearity and errors of global approximation. In the instance of mapping 1, the W_1^{s-t} with respect to Y_1^{sub} and σ_1^{sub} results in no generated elements $\hat{e}_{1k} \in \hat{\sigma}_1$ getting into $FP - 1$ areas, which is $FP - 1$ local mapping space. If the primary local mapping is not $FP - 1$ local mapping space, some generated elements $\hat{e}_{1k} \in \hat{\sigma}_1$ getting into $FP - 1$ areas are able to effect the previously established approximation. In the other words, the unexpected $\hat{e}_{1k} \in \hat{\sigma}_1$ settled into $FP - 1$ areas make the corresponding error e_{1k} in the third layer increase. The strategy used in $FP - 1$ algorithm is to compare the deleted absolute values of errors with the increased errors. If $(1/2)\sum_l |e_{jl}^{del}| \geq \sum_k |\hat{e}_{jk}^{inc}|$, the algorithm of $FP - 1$ local mapping space is available continuously. The notion of half $FP - 1$ local mapping space, therefore, is introduced.

Definition 2.7: Let mapping $R_i^{m-1} \to R_i$ $(i = 1, ..., r, m-1 < r)$ be non $FP - 1$ local mapping space. After implementing linear mapping $(\Phi, Y_j, W_j^{s-t}, \Lambda_j)$ in definition 2.6, there must exist subset $\sigma_j^{sub} = [e_{j1}, ..., e_{j(m-1)}]$ $(m-1 < r, \ e_{ji} \in \sigma_j)$, and generated subset $\hat{\sigma}_j^{sub} = [\hat{e}_{j1}, ..., \hat{e}_{jk}]$ $(\hat{e}_{jk} \in \hat{\sigma}_j)$, and $\hat{e}_{jk}$ gets into $FP - 1$ areas Λ_j. If $(1/2)\sum_l |e_{jl}^{del}| \geq \sum_k |\hat{e}_{jk}^{inc}|$, this given mapping $R_i^{m-1} \to R_i$ is called half $FP - 1$ local mapping space, and is denoted $\hat{\Psi}$.

The concept of the half $FP - 1$ local mapping space, in fact, provides the looser condition in implementing $FP - 1$ algorithm. The only difference between Ψ and $\hat{\Psi}$ is that $\hat{\Psi}$ reduces the errors less than Ψ does. From mathematics point of view, $\hat{\Psi}$ reveals more intricate topological mapping relationship. Up to now the two types of primary local mapping spaces Ψ and $\hat{\Psi}$ are defined and the corresponding algorithms are also provided. The $FP - 1$ is based on these two primary local mapping space. Other more sophisticated local mapping space will be introduced in the future discussion of $FP - 2$.

2.4 Determination of hidden neurons

If the process above can not reach the desired accuracy, the hidden neurons should be added.

Definition 2.8: If a hidden neuron is only connected to one output neuron and the corresponding weight equals to 1, this hidden neuron is denoted the direct hidden neuron (DHN).

From $FP-1$ basic idea, the hidden neuron, in fact, only contributes to the local area for the specified output node in the process of approximation. The direct hidden neuron actually transfers information to the connected output node. Let us use mapping 1 to demonstrate the algorithm in hidden layer.

1. The remained errors in Tab.4 should be rebuilt in the absolute partial order error subset σ_j^h, then the first n maximum absolute values in σ_j^h are selected as error subset σ_j^{subh1} to be reduced through hidden neuron, here, σ_j^{subh1} means this error subset eliminated by the first hidden neuron linked to jth output node. W_j^{h1} vector with n variables needs to be decided. Tab.5 shows the rebuilt absolute partial order error set σ_1^h and $n = 5$ in mapping 1.

target	.18	-.38	.09	.8	.53	-.21	-.75	-.15	.45	-.52
app. result	-.0013	-.5567	.2442	.6689	.6415	-.3208	-.75	-.15	.45	-.52
error	.1813	.1767	-.1542	.1311	-.1115	.0	.0	.0	.0

Tab.5

In Tab.5, error subset $\sigma_1^{subh1} = [.1813, .1767, -.1542, .1311, -.1115]^T$. The $FP-1$ areas Λ_1^{h1} are $a_1 = -.1543$, $b_1 = -.1114$, $a_2 = .131$, $b_2 = .1814$.

2. Using $W_1^{h1} = X_{h1}^{-1}\sigma_1^{subh1}$ to set W_1^{h1}, which is weight vector between input and first hidden neuron, X_{h1} is input subset $X_{h1} \in X$, which corresponds to σ_1^{subh1}. With same algorithm in subthird layer, the inversion X_{h1}^{-1} and W_1^{h1} can be gotten. $W_1^{h1} = [.5788, .1725, 1.9783, .6433, -2.6756]$.

3. Using $\sigma_1^{(h-t)1} = XW_1^{h1}$ to check out whether or not other vectors are able to get into the $FP-1$ areas Λ_1^{h1}. If not, it is local $FP-1$ mapping space, here, the $\sigma_1^{(h-t)1}$ is the checking set of first hidden neuron in first output node.

$\sigma_1^{(h-t)1} = [.1813, .1767, -.1542, .1311, -.1115, -.2239. -.7742, -1.0811, .4735, 1.9475]^T$. No generated elements $\hat{e}_{1k}^{h1} \in \sigma_1^{(h-t)1} - \sigma_1^{subh1} = \hat{\sigma}_1^{(h-t)1}$ get into Λ_1^{h1}. Therefore, this is local $FP-1$ mapping space and the nonlinear threshold function is established from the hidden neuron to jth output node,

$$y_{ji}^{h-t} = \sum_{k=1}^{n} x_{ik}w_{jk}^{h1} \qquad i = 1, ..., r, \qquad \left\{ \begin{array}{l} a_1 \le y_{ji}^{h-t} \le b_1 \\ a_2 \le y_{ji}^{h-t} \le b_2 \end{array} \right. \tag{18}$$

$$y_{ji}^{h-t} = 0 \qquad\qquad\qquad otherwise$$

Because it is $FP-1$ mapping space, this nonlinear threshold function only allows subset $\sigma_1^{(h-t)1}$ passing through the hidden neuron to eliminate error subset in the third layer, then in the jth output node the result of final approximation is in Tab.6.

target	.18	-.38	.09	.8	.53	-.21	-.75	-.15	.45	-.52
app. result	.18	-.38	.09	.8	.53	-.3208	-.75	-.15	.45	-.52
error	.0	.0	.0	.0	.0	.1108	.0	.0	.0	.0

Tab.6

The total squared error is .0123. The NDC is shown in Fig.9. In general, this method of adding hidden neuron can be repeated again and again, until the given precision arrives. Fig.10 shows the architecture of mapping 1 neural network, the grey circle is the threshold function.

Definition 2.9: With the given approximation precision, if all of the local mappings from second to third layer and all of direct hidden neurons are $FP-1$ local mapping space, or half $FP-1$ local mapping space, the given mapping $R_i^n \rightarrow R_i^m$ $i = 1, ..., r$, $n < r$ is called global $FP-1$ mapping space, and is denoted Π.

If the given mapping $R_i^n \rightarrow R_i^m$ is global $FP-1$ mapping space Π, we can know and even control the accuracy of approximation in every step, and therefore we are able to control the entire program of approximation.

3 Remarks and Conclusion

Due to the page limit, we can not provide more simulations, the *mapping* 1 is only a simple example. What is the meaning of $FP-1$ algorithm in mathematics? Although BP is used broadly, one important problem is not given much attention by researchers, that is if the configuration of general multilayer perceptron is reasonable. In the other words, connecting every neuron with every neuron in next layer is unreasonable. This is a key problem. In fact, an arbitrary nonlinear mapping can be viewed as a global mapping and its local constituents, that means some neurons play the roles in global region, while others focus on some special local areas, depending on the given mapping data set or applications. The main idea of FP serial algorithm is how to decompose the given mapping into global and local mappings and to decide which neurons focus on which areas. It is undoubtable that many questions will arise with the emergence of $FP-1$. Some of them need to be proved in mathematics. The FP serial algorithms put emphasis on the way of how to realize them.

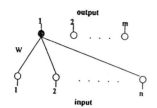

Fig.1 The mapping of $R_i^n \to R$ in two layer network

Fig.2 Linear and approximation result of two layer nets of mapping 1

Fig.3 Linear and nonlinear approximation of two layer nets of mapping 1

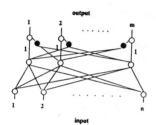

Fig.4 The architecture of three layer nets

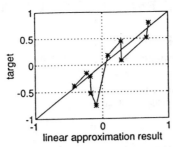

Fig.5 The distribution of threshold function in case 1

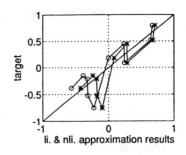

Fig.6 The distribution of threshold function in case 2

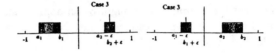

Fig.7 The distribution of threshold function in case 3

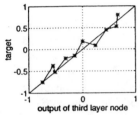

Fig.8 Nonlinear distribution chart in third layer of mapping 1

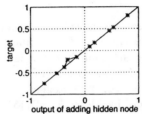

Fig.9 The nonlinear distribution chart after adding a hidden neuron

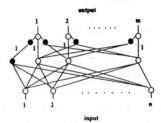

Fig.10 The architecture of adding a hidden neuron in three layer nets

III-759

SPECULATIONS ON THE EVOLUTION OF LEARNING

Dr. John R. Alexander, Jr.
Computer and Information Sciences Department
Towson State University
Towson, MD, 21204
E7C1ALE@TOE.TOWSON.EDU

ABSTRACT

All artificial neural nets (ANN) learning schemes assume the existence of an untrained pool of neurons whose weights are modified, so that after training, the net of which they are a part may solve some problem - pattern recognition for example. But biologically, this untrained pool of neurons seems a contradiction. In a living organism, these untrained neurons serve no survival purpose prior to their training. It is difficult therefore to explain their presence. It seems highly unlikely that a single mutation simultaneously produced this untrained pool and their training rule. How did both untrained pool and the training rule evolve? I discuss the applicability of a two-layered net which employs probability data about the environment as weights. This net (or a similar one) might be an appropriate tool to help answer the question posed above. I have seen no publications in the ANN literature that address the problem of how learning could have evolved.

I. Introduction

A.   History. Reggia [14] explored connectionist models which employed "virtual" lateral inhibition, and included the activation of the receiving node in the equations for the flow of activation. Ahuja [2] extended these concepts to include summing the total excitatory and inhibitory flow into a node. He thus introduced the concept that the change of activation of a node depended on the integral of the flow into that node and not just the present activation levels of the nodes to which it is connected. Both Reggia's and Ahuja's models used probability data for the weights. Ahuja's model was further extended by Alexander [4], [5] in the RX model to allow both the weights and the activations of Ahuja's model to be negative, and further, Alexander's model included the prior probabilities of all nodes. Although these equations have been discussed elsewhere, [4] [5] [6] they are discussed here in light of the new use for which they are proposed in this article.

B.   Overview. Section II of this paper contains a complete listing of the RX equations and describes their development. The convergence of the system is discussed in Section III. Section IV briefly describes the experiments testing the RX system. Section V offers a conjecture on a biologically plausible answer to the question raised above by employing the RX equations, and summarizes and concludes this article.

II. The RX Equations

A.   Details of the net and its usage The net is two-layered, with the J lower level being the input nodes to the N upper level nodes. The processing units depict a "local" or one-unit-one-concept representation. Thus far, the net has been used in pattern recognition applications, lower level nodes serving as features and the upper level nodes representing the possible pattern classes. The values of the upper level nodes are on [0,1] and called $a_i(t)$. The prior probability of the ith node's existence is called $\overline{a}_i$. Values of $a_i(t)$ greater than $\overline{a}_i$ indicate a higher than average chance of occurrence of the concept presented by node i, and those lower, indicate a less than average chance. The lower level nodes (called m_j) are on [-1,1]. Let the range of possible input values to a node be between some Min_j and Max_j. Call the average Ave_j. Let $Observ_j$ be the observed value. Then define:

$$m_j = \frac{[Observ_j - Ave_j]}{[Max_j - Ave_j]} \qquad If\ Observ_j > Ave_j \qquad (1)$$

$$m_j = \frac{[Observ_j - Ave_j]}{[Ave_j - Min_j]} \qquad \text{Otherwise} \qquad (2)$$

When m_j assumes the value 1, then the feature represented by m_j is present, with probability one. When m_j is -1 the feature is absent with probability one. A value of zero indicates that no information exists concerning the absence or presence of the feature (m_j.)

Two sets of weights exist. The first is called w_{ij}, and in absolute value indicates the probability of occurrence, if positive, and non-occurrence, if negative, of the upper level node (the ith node), given the existence of the lower level node (the jth node). The second weight is called v_{ij}, and in absolute value indicates the probability of occurrence, if positive, and non-occurrence, if negative, of the lower level node (the jth node), given the existence of the upper level node (the ith node).

Two auxiliary functions are to be associated with each $a_i(t)$. The function which conveys the excitatory activation is called $Exc_i(t)$, and the one which conveys the inhibitory activation is called $Inh_i(t)$. They are the sums of all the excitatory and inhibitory flow of activation into node $a_i(t)$. The strategy used in defining these functions is to build them as bounded monotone-increasing functions, defined by their derivatives. The monotone-increasing characteristic of the $Exc_i(t)$ term will be achieved by defining it as a product of strictly positive terms in the equation for its derivative. One of these terms is a function of all the $a_i(t)$ and is the variable forcing term. It will for the present be called ForcingFunction and the equations presented shortly. There will be one such function for each lower level (j) node, hence a sum need be taken over all the j nodes connected to any given i node. The bounded characteristic is achieved by including in the equation a factor of the form $[N - Exc_i(t)]$. The choice of N as the bound to which $Exc_i(t)$ approaches is somewhat arbitrary. The differential equation defining $Exc_i(t)$ is then:

$$\dot{Exc}_i(t) = K_1 * \bar{a}_i * [N - Exc_i(t)] * \sum_j ForcingFunction_{ij} \qquad (3)$$

Where K_1 is a constant of proportionality. ForcingFunction is a function of all the $a_i(t)$. The $\bar{a}_i$ term as a factor reflects the prior probability of the concept represented by $a_i(t)$ in a meaningful way. $Inh_i(t)$ is defined in a similar fashion.

Since m_j may be above or below average (positive or negative) and the weights w_{ij} may each be either positive or negative, four separate cases may occur. Only four cases can occur, since the signs of the v_{ij} are the same as the w_{ij}. These cases are: (1) weight positive with activation positive; (2) weight negative with activation positive; (3) weight positive with activation negative; and (4) both weight and activation negative. As will be shown, all activation transfers (both excitatory and inhibitory) will be calculated as positive, with the inhibitory being subtracted from the excitatory to calculate the total for each case used by the equations in calculating the $a_i(t)$. Each of the four cases will have a term calculated using the w_{ij} weights (called OUT_{ij}), and each of these will have a term of opposite sign (offsetting) calculated with the v_{ij} weights (called out_{ij}).

We require two equations per upper level node to describe the change of activation, one when $a_i(t)$ is greater than $\bar{a}_i$, and one when less. Thus for $a_i(t) > \bar{a}_i$:

$$\dot{a}_i(t) = K_3 * c_u * [1 - a_i(t)] * [Exc_i(t) - Inh_i(t)] \qquad (4)$$

When $a_i(t) <= \bar{a}_i$

$$\dot{a}_i(t) = K_3 * c_l * [\quad a_i(t)] * [Exc_i(t) - Inh_i(t)] \qquad (5)$$

Above K_3 is a constant of proportionality, and the c_u and c_l are needed to keep the derivative continuous at $\bar{a}_i$. The values of c_l and c_u are:

$$c_u = 1 / (1 - \bar{a}_i),$$
$$c_l = 1 / \bar{a}_i.$$

The complete list of equations to be used with the above is now given.

$$\dot{Exc}_i(t) = K_1 * \bar{a}_i * [N - Exc_i(t)] * \sum_j [k_{11} * OUTPP_{ij}(t) + k_{12} * outpm_{ij}(t) + k_{13} * outmp_{ij}(t) + k_{14} * OUTMM_{ij}(t)] \tag{6}$$

$$\dot{Inh}_i(t) = K_2 * \bar{a}_i * [N - Inh_i(t)] * \sum_j [k_{21} * outpp_{ij}(t) + k_{22} * OUTPM_{ij}(t) + k_{23} * OUTMP_{ij}(t) + k_{24} * outmm_{ij}(t)] \tag{7}$$

Here $k_{11}, \ldots k_{24}$ are included for generality.

$$OUTPP_{ij}(t) = \frac{W_{ij} * |a_i(t) - \bar{a}_i|}{\sum_l W_{lj} * |a_i(t) - \bar{a}_i|} * m_j \tag{8}$$
$$When\, W_{ij} > 0; m_j > 0$$

$$OUTPM_{ij}(t) = \frac{W_{ij} * |a_i(t) - \bar{a}_i|}{\sum_l W_{lj} * |a_i(t) - \bar{a}_i|} * |m_j| \tag{9}$$
$$When\, W_{ij} > 0; m_j < 0$$

$$OUTMP_{ij}(t) = \frac{W_{ij} * |a_i(t) - \bar{a}_i|}{\sum_l W_{lj} * |a_i(t) - \bar{a}_i|} * m_j \tag{10}$$
$$When\, W_{ij} < 0; m_j > 0$$

$$OUTMM_{ij}(t) = \frac{W_{ij} * |a_i(t) - \bar{a}_i|}{\sum_l W_{lj} * |a_i(t) - \bar{a}_i|} * |m_j| \tag{11}$$
$$When\, W_{ij} < 0; m_j < 0$$

$$outpp_{ij}(t) = \frac{\sum_{k \neq i} V_{kj} * |a_k(t) - \bar{a}_k|}{\sum V_{ij} * |a_1(t) - \bar{a}_1|} * m_j * |a_i(t) - \bar{a}_i| \tag{12}$$
$$When\, V_{ij} > 0, M_j > 0$$

$$outpm_{ij}(t) = \frac{\sum_{k \neq i} V_{kj} * |a_k(t) - \bar{a}_k|}{\sum V_{ij} * |a_1(t) - \bar{a}_1|} * |m_j| * |a_i(t) - \bar{a}_i| \tag{13}$$
$$When\, V_{ij} > 0, m_j < 0$$

$$outmp_{ij}(t) = \frac{\sum_{k \neq i} V_{kj} * |a_k(t) - \bar{a}_k|}{\sum V_{ij} * |a_1(t) - \bar{a}_1|} * m_j * |a_i(t) - \bar{a}_i| \qquad (14)$$
$$When V_{ij} < 0, m_j > 0$$

$$outmm_{ij}(t) = \frac{\sum_{k \neq i} V_{kj} * |a_k(t) - \bar{a}_k|}{\sum V_{ij} * |a_1(t) - \bar{a}_1|} * |m_j| * |a_i(t) - \bar{a}_i| \qquad (15)$$
$$When V_{ij} < 0, m_j < 0$$

As written, with absolute value signs included, only positive addends appear in the summation term, which is itself a multiplicand in the equations for $Exc_i(t)$ and $Inh_i(t)$, hence they are both monotone non-decreasing functions as required.

We first offer some comments on the RX system of equations described in Section II. above. The RX net is more biologically plausible than a perceptron. Consider the following:

a - Unexcited cortical neurons spontaneously fire at some resting average rate [1] [10]. Information is only transmitted when these neurons vary from their average values. This attribute is simulated in the RX equations by having each node possess an average value, at which it assumed to be operating. Activation will flow only when the activation of the lower level nodes is above or below their averages.

b - A highly excited cortical neuron is more likely to fire upon the arrival of an excitatory action pulse than is one at its resting activation level [1]. This property is simulated in the RX equations by making the new activation level of the receiving node functionally depend on the product of the activations of the sending (m_j) and the receiving nodes ($a_i(t)$).

c - The RX system calculates the activation of a receiving node by using the integral of excitatory and inhibitory inputs rather than by the instantaneous values of the nodes from which it receives input. It is for this reason, of course, that the system consists of 3*N rather than N equations.

The RX equations handle the lateral inhibitory effects (on-center, off-surround) of neurons in the same layer by "virtual" lateral inhibition [14] in the RX system: that is, intra-layer inhibitory effects are implemented without actual connections between these nodes. This has overcomes two problems - (1) the number of connections grows rapidly with N (the number of nodes on the upper level) and (2) it is difficult to measure (or estimate) these weights.

III.   Convergence of the RX Equations. The demonstration of the convergence of the RX equations is given in [4]. While it is shown that these equations are convergent almost everywhere, it could not be shown that they converge in an ϵ volume around the critical points. To complicate matters even more, the critical points form a continuous set. As is to be expected in such cases, the demonstration of convergence is long and somewhat difficult. Note that the RX set contains 3*N equations, i.e. N terms in $a_i(t)$, N terms in $Exc_i(t)$ and, N terms in $Inh_i(t)$. The root of the difficulty is that the first N terms of the diagonal of the Jacobian matrix for the RX system are zero, (i.e. N, or one third of the eigenvalues are zero). As yet, the RX equations do not include decay terms. But their inclusion would greatly simplify the proof of convergence since, were they included, all terms of the diagonal of the Jacobian matrix would be negative.

IV.   Testing of the RX Equations. Also in [4] the RX equations were coded and this system extensively tested. Testing included (1) general behavior testing in which their predictions were compared with expected behavior, (2) accuracy by comparisons to special cases that allowed the equations to be integrated in closed form, (3) comparison with similar runs of the IA (Interactive Activation) system of Rumelhart and McClelland [11], and (4) comparison of the results of a radar identification problem with the backpropagation net [16]. They have continued to undergo other tests of their utility [7]. In all cases the RX equations showed themselves on a par with the nets to which they were being compared.

V.   On the evolution of intelligence. Consider again the question raised in the Abstract. - How is the existence of a pool of untrained neurons to be explained in a biologically plausible way? The pool of neurons serves no survival purpose, prior to its training.

Kuffler, Nichols and Martin [10] imply that the brain is primarily a controller. In the <u>Outline of a Theory of Intelligence</u>, Albus [3] states that "...first and foremost, the brain is a controller." But consider the history of the study of artificial neural networks. From Rosenblatt [15] in <u>Neurodynamics</u> "At the time the first perceptron was proposed, the writer was primarily concerned with the problem of memory storage in biological systems..." Clearly Minsky and Papert [13] were concerned with memory, since their surface concern was Rosenblatt's book. The recent revival of the connectionist or artificial neural network field started afresh in 1982 with Hopfield's [9] paper "Neural Networks and Physical Systems with Emergent Collective Computational Abilities." This paper discussed how information could be stored in a certain type of net - again a concern about memory. Although the trend is shifting to the study of control mechanisms [17], the initial studies were mainly on memories.

Fossil records suggest that the use of neurons to transmit control signals existed before their use in memories. It could be argued that the use of memories differentiates lower life forms from higher ones. In the lower forms, the input or signals sensed by the receptor neurons are sent directly to the motor neurons. Little or no computation is performed on the incoming signal prior to its transmittal to the motor neuron which causes some action to be performed. On the other hand, in higher forms of life, from sensors, incoming signals are sent through sequences of cell assemblies where specific processing is performed before the response is sent to the motor neurons to control actions. Albus [3] has suggested that it is in the specific processing that memories might be needed. Stated alternately, lower forms of life respond to given input signals in a predetermined way - the response is hardwired. In higher forms, the possible effects of various behaviors are examined in view of the existent environment, and the most appropriate behavior selected and executed.

In [5] the author suggested that the RX system of equations might be used in a control scenario as follows. Consider the net displayed in Fig 1.   The lower level nodes are labeled m_j and represent presence (or absence) of an external event or stimulus to an organism. The upper level nodes represent possible responses by that organism. Note that m_1 is excitatory to a_1 and inhibitory to a_2, while m_2 is excitatory to a_2 and inhibitory to a_1. Let the responses be mutually exclusive - for example, the decision to run to escape from a predator or freeze and hope not to be observed. The weights w_{11}, w_{12}, w_{21}, and w_{22}, and the activations of m_1 and m_2 will determine what action the organism will take. We may ignore the v_{ij} weights for the present, since they will not change in what follows. As an alternative to the exercise of a rule to modify the weights (learning), the weights may be determined as follows. We assume the existence of some statistical distribution of these weights for all new offspring. Assuming that the organism's biological neural net processes in a similar fashion to the RX net, then an organism possessing the weights that match most closely the actual survival probabilities will have a higher chance of survival (and hence chance to reproduce) than will all others. Further, assuming the weight's values passed on in the genes will be distributed with a mean near the value of the parents, as generations go by the mean of the population weights will tend to approach that which leads to the highest survival probability. Clearly, the above is highly speculative; however, if such phenomena actually exists, perhaps it should be called "Darwinian learning."

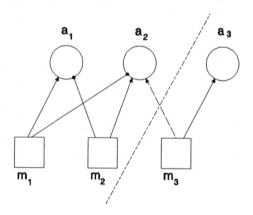

Now assume that a mutation affords the connection from sensor m_3 to one of the action nodes, say a_2. Further, assume that m_3 indicates the presence of an event that, in combination with the presence of the event signified by m_2, makes a_2 a better choice than a_1, i.e. continuing the above example, the ability of the prey to smell the predator might indicate than the wind is from predator to prey. Hence the predator probably can't smell the prey. Then, as long as w_{32} is positive, this mutant connection will tend to make the organism behave in a way that enhances its chance of survival.

In [7] the author studied a fuzzy logic controller designed to determine the appropriate control valve setting required to maintain water at a constant height in a tank with variable inflow and outflow. In this study, the defuzzified centroid, which gave the value for the appropriate control valve setting, was subjected to increasing random noise. The ultimate test in this series was to replace the calculated setting with a positive random number on the range of control valve settings if the defuzzified setting was positive, otherwise a negative random number on this range. Even under these extreme conditions the controller still worked.

Summary. From the above, we can build a plausible explanation of how neurons are added to elementary organisms with small populations of neurons. Although I started with a pool of two in the example above, there is no reason why the I could not have begun with just one neuron. If mutations randomly add connections, some of these connections will be those which could aid in survival. Assuming that the genes will pass these added connections down to the next generation with random variations in the weights, and that the RX net is a close model of actual biological processing, then those organisms lucky enough to inherit weights which contribute to their fitness to survive will have a better chance of passing, through their genes, these weights on to their offspring. From the example of control of the height of water in the tank, we see that just a little guidance can help a great deal in control problems. I suspect that this is true in case of evolution. I offer the following answer to the question posed in the abstract. Organisms possessing neurons serving control functions might, by mutation, beneficially combine the afferent signals of sensory neurons or interneurons in the control paths and thereby improve the survival probability of the organism. The effect of this mutation is to produce a more highly coupled or connected set of neurons. This increased connectivity might allow the emergence of memory in addition to the enhanced control function.

Discussion. The above is highly speculative. "Much of what has been presented is hypothesis and argument by analogy" [3]. No biological evidence exists for any of the hypotheses presented in Section V. The reason for examples being demonstrated with the virtually unknown RX net of the author's familiarity with this net (his dissertation work). Certainly, more biologically plausible models are readily available [12]. Perhaps further review will reveal that major biological implausibilities exist in the above.

Yet, the author feels there is merit in work such as the above. Daniel Gardner [8], and the editors of the series of which this book is a member, posit the theme that "Third Generation Neural Networks Should be Neuromorphic". A step towards biological plausibility seems a step in the right direction.

References

[1]   Abeles M. (1982) **Local Cortical Circuits An Electrophysiological Study.** Springer-Verlag. New York.

[2]   Ahuja S., Soh W., Schwartz A. (1988) **A Connectionist Processing Metaphor for Diagnostic Reasoning.** International Journal of Intelligent Systems.

[3]   Albus,J.S. **Outline for a Theory of Intelligence,**IEEE Transactions on Systems, Man and Cybernetics, vol.21, no.3, May-June 1991.

[4]   Alexander, J.R. (1991) **An Analysis of the General Properties and Convergence of a Connectionist Model Employing Probability Data as Weights and Parameters.** PhD Dissertation. University of Maryland Baltimore County, Baltimore MD.

[5]   Alexander, J.R. (1992) **An Artificial Neural Net Employing Probability Data as Weights and Parameters** 1992 IEEE Systems, Man and Cybernetics Proceedings.

[6]   Alexander, J.R. (1992) **A Connectionist Model Employing Probability Data as Weights and Parameters.** Intelligent Engineering Systems Through Artificial Neural Networks, Vol 2. ASME Press, New York NY.

[7]   Alexander, J.R. (1993) **Calculating the Centroid of a Fuzzy Logic Controller Using an Artificial Neural Net** Intelligent Engineering Systems Through Artificial Neural Networks, Vol 3. ASME Press, New York NY.

[8] Gardner, D. Editor (1993) **The NEUROBIOLOGY of NEURAL NETWORKS** The MIT Press. Cambridge Massachusetts.

[9] Hopfield J. (1982) **Neural Networks & Physical Systems with Emergent Collective Computational Abilities.** Proc.Natl.Acad. Sci.USA.

[10] Kuffler,S.W.,Nichols, J.G., & Martin, R.H., (1984). **From Neuron to Brain.** (2nd Ed.) Sunderland, MA: Sinauer Associates.

[11] McCelland J. & Rumelhart D. (1988) **Explorations in Parallel Distributed Processing. A Handbook of Models, Programs, and Exercises.** MIT Press. Cambridge, Mass.

[12] McGergor R.J. (1987). **Neural and Brain Modeling.** Academic Press. San Diego. Cal.

[13] Minskey, M.L., Papert, S.A. (1988) **Perceptrons.** The MIT Press. Cambridge. Mass.

[14] Reggia J. (1985). **Virtual Lateral Inhibition in Parallel Activation Models of Associative Memory.** Proceedings Ninth International Conference on Artificial Intelligence pp 244-248.

[15] Rosenblatt F. (1962) **Principles of Neurodynamics.** Spartan. New York.

[16] Sigillito, V. G., Wing, S.P., Hutton, L.V., and Baker, K.V. (1989). **Analysis of Radar Returns from the Inosphere Using Neural Networks.** Johns Hopkins APL Technical Digest, Vol 10, Num 3.

[17] Werbos, P.J. April 1993, **Neurocontrol and Elastic Fuzzy Logic: Capabilities, Concepts, and Applications,** IEEE Transactions on Industrial Electronics, Vol 40, No 2.

EFFECTS OF ACTIVATION FUNCTIONS IN MULTILAYER NEURAL NETWORK FOR NOISY PATTERN CLASSIFICATION

Kazuyuki HARA†   Kenji NAKAYAMA† ‡

†Graduate School of Nat. Sci. & Tech., Kanazawa Univ.
‡Faculty of Tech., Kanazawa Univ.

2–40–20 , Kodatsuno , Kanazawa , 920 JAPAN
E–mail : nakayama@haspnn1.ec.t.kanazawa-u.ac.jp

ABSTRUCT This paper discusses properties of activation functions in multilayer neural network applied to multi-frequency classification. A rule of thumb for selecting activation functions or their combination is proposed. The sigmoid, Gaussian and sinusoidal functions are employed due to their unique space division properties. Properties of each function and their combinations are discussed based on the internal representation, that is the distributions of the hidden unit inputs and outputs and classification rates with and without noise. The sigmoid function is not effective for a single hidden unit. On the contrary, the other functions can provide good performance. When several hidden units are employed, the sigmoid function becomes useful. However, the convergence speed is still slower than the others. The Gaussian function is sensitive to the additive noise, while the others are rather insensitive. When noise is not included, the Gaussian function is most useful for the convergence rate and the classification accuracy. On the other hand, the additive noise is included, the sigmoid and sinusoidal functions become more effective. These properties are not straight in the combinations. However, their property still remain, and it is possible to select the optimum activation function. This selection also depends on the patterns to be classified.

I INTRODUCTION

Advantage of multilayer neural networks (NNs) trained by the back-propagation (BP) algorithm is to extract common properties, features or rules, which can be used to classify data included in several groups [1]. Especially, when it is difficult to analyze the common features using conventional methods, the supervised learning, using combinations of the known input and output data, becomes very useful.

We studied the multi-frequency signal classification using multilayer neural network[5]-[7]. Since the frequencies are assigned alternately to several groups, it is very difficult to distinguish the waveforms within a short period, and the limited number of samples by conventional methods. The following advantages of the NN over conventional methods were confirmed. The neural network can classify the signals using a small number of samples and a short observation period with which Fourier transform can not classify. The number of calculation is sufficiently smaller than the convolution calculation, required in digital filters.

In the previous work, a sigmoid function was used. However, it is not always optimum. Therefore, properties of activation functions are investigated in this paper. For this purpose, some typical functions are taken into account. They include a sigmoid

function, a radial basis function[2] and a periodic function. They will be compared with each other in classifying multi–frequency signals. Effects of noisy signals will be also discussed in the training and classification processes.

As a result, a rule of thumb for selecting the suitable functions and the combination of several kinds of functions will be provided.

II MULTI-FREQUENCY SIGNALS

Multi–frequency signals are defined by

$$x_{pm}(n) = \sum_{r=1}^{R} A_{mr} \sin(\omega_{pr} nT + \phi_{mr}) \quad (1)$$

$$n = 1 \sim N , \ \omega_{pr} = 2\pi f_{pr}$$

T is a sampling period. M samples of $x_{pm}(n), m = 1 \sim M$, are included in the group X_p as follows.

$$X_p = \{x_{pm}(n), m = 1 \sim M\}, p = 1 \sim P \quad (2)$$

In one group, the same frequencies are used.

$$F_p = [f_{p1}, f_{p2}, \ldots, f_{pR}] Hz, p = 1 \sim P \quad (3)$$

Amplitude A_{mr} and phase ϕ_{mr} are generated as random numbers, uniformly distributed in following ranges.

$$0 < A_{mr} \leq 1, \quad 0 \leq \phi_{mr} < 2\pi \quad (4)$$

III MULTILAYER NEURAL NETWORK

3.1 Network Structure and Equations

A single-layer neural network is taken into account. N samples of the signal $x_{pm}(n)$ are applied to the input layer in parallel. The nth input unit receives $x_{pm}(n)$. Connection weight from the nth input to the jth hidden unit is denoted w_{nj}. The input and output of the jth hidden unit are given by

$$net_j = \sum_{n=0}^{N-1} w_{nj} x_{pm}(n) + \theta_j \qquad (5)$$

$$y_j = f_H(net_j) \qquad (6)$$

Letting the connection weight from the jth hidden unit to the kth output unit be w_{jk}, the input and output of the kth output unit are given by

$$net_k = \sum_{j=0}^{J-1} w_{jk} y_j + \theta_k \qquad (7)$$

$$y_k = f_O(net_k) \qquad (8)$$

The activation function of the output layer is the sigmoid function.

The number of output units is equal to that of the signal groups P. The neural network is trained so that a single output unit responds to one of the signal groups.

3.2 Training and Classification

Signals are categorized into training and untraining sets, denoted X_{Tp} and X_{Up}, respectively. Their elements are expressed by $x_{Tpm}(n)$ and $x_{Upm}(n)$, respectively.

The neural network is trained by using $x_{Tpm}(n)$, m = $1 \sim M_T$, for the pth group. Here, M_T is the number of the training data. After the training is completed, the untrained signals $x_{Upm}(n)$ are applied to the NN, and the output is calculated. For the input signal $x_{Upm}(n)$, if the pth output y_p has the maximum value, then the signal is exactly classified. Otherwise, the network fails in classification.

IV SELECTION OF ACTIVATION FUNCTIONS

What kinds of activation functions should be selected is very important. At the same time, it is a very difficult problem. In this paper, the following typical functions are selected for the hidden layer.

When binary target can be considered, then the sigmoid function can be used in the output layer.

Sigmoid function:

$$y_j = f_{sig}(net_j) = \frac{1}{1 + e^{-(net_j)}} \qquad (9)$$

Sinusoidal function:

$$y_j = f_{sin}(net_j) = \sin(\pi net_j) \qquad (10)$$

Gaussian function:

$$y_j = f_{gau}(net_j) = e^{-net_j^2} \qquad (11)$$

The input vectors are distributed in a N-dimensional space. Three functions divide the space as follows:

$$f_{sig}(net_j) \begin{cases} > \alpha_+, & net_j > T_{sig} \\ < \alpha_-, & net_j < T_{sig} \end{cases} \qquad (12)$$

$$f_{sin}(net_j) \begin{cases} > \alpha_+, & |net_j - (2n\pi + \frac{\pi}{2})| < T_{sin} \\ < \alpha_-, & |net_j - (2n\pi + \frac{3}{2}\pi)| < T_{sin} \end{cases} \qquad (13)$$

$$f_{gau}(net_j) \begin{cases} > \alpha_+, & |net_j| < T_{gau} \\ < \alpha_-, & |net_j| > T_{gau} \end{cases} \qquad (14)$$

Here, n is integer.

These space division fundamental, and independent to each other. This is an idea behind selecting the above three functions.

Next step of selecting activation functions is how to combine them. It is also highly dependent on the distribution of the input signals, and is very hard to determine before hand. For this reason, both the homogeneous function and the composite functions are investigated.

V SIMULATION OF TRAINING AND CLASSIFICATION WITHOUT NOISE

5.1 Multi-frequency Signals

The number of frequency components is R = 3, and the signal groups is P = 2, respectively. The frequency components are located alternately between the groups as follows: $F_1 = [1, 2, 3]$ Hz for Group 1 (#1) and $F_2 = [1.5, 2.5, 3.5]$ Hz for Group 2 (#2). The sampling frequency is 10 Hz, that is T = 0.1 sec. The number of samples N is 10. Therefore, the observation interval is 1 sec.

5.2 Training and Classification

$x_{Tpm}(n)$, m = $1 \sim 200$ and $x_{Upm}(n)$, m = $1 \sim 1800$ are used. Simulation results are shown in Table 1. The training converged using three hidden units for all activation functions. In the case of the Gaussian and the sinusoidal function, the training almost converged with one hidden unit. Detailed discussion will be provided in Sec. 7.

Table 1:Classification rates by three functions[%]

Activation Function	Hidden Unit	Training		Untraining	
		#1	#2	#1	#2
Sigmoid	1	44.5	100	47.9	100
	3	100	100	97.4	100
Sinusoidal	1	86.0	99.0	79.8	99.0
	3	100	100	92.6	100
Gaussian	1	99.5	100	98.1	100
	3	100	100	99.1	99.9

VI SIMULATION USING THREE ACTIVATION FUNCTIONS

6.1 Additive Noise

White noise, denoted $noise(n)$, is generated as random number, and is added to the signal $x_{pm}(n)$. Noisy signal $x'_{pm}(n)$ is given by

$$x'_{pm}(n) = x_{pm}(n) + noise(n) \tag{15}$$

6.2 Training and Classification

The noisy multi-frequency signals are used for training. N is 10 and M is 200 for each group. After training, untraining signals with white noise are applied, and classification rates are evaluated. White noise is uniformly distributed in the range ±0.5. The results are shown in Table 2. Columns with (A) and (B) list the recognition rates using the training signals without and with white noise, respectively. The NN trained without noise is also used for comparison. From these results, it can be confirmed that training using noisy signals is useful to achieve robustness.

Table 2: Classification rates using training signals
(A) without and (B) with white noise [%]

Activation Function	Hidden Unit	(A)		(B)	
		#1	#2	#1	#2
Sigmoid	1	47.0	52.9	92.8	28.5
	3	97.3	8.4	82.6	78.0
Sinusoidal	1	80.2	20.9	61.7	87.7
	3	65.9	36.2	79.9	82.7
Gaussian	1	98.2	4.8	71.7	65.9
	3	85.3	46.3	79.8	70.2

6.3 Convergence Rates

Figure 1 shows learning curves obtained using the three hidden units. The NN with the Gaussian function can converge faster than the other. However, the error does not well decreased. The NN with the sinusoidal function can also converge faster. At the same time, the error can be well decreased. A convergence rate using the sigmoid function is slow. However, the error can reach to the same level as in using the sinusoidal function.

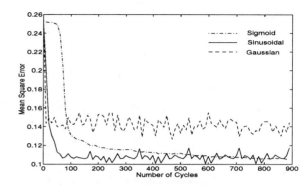

Figure 1: Learning curves

VII Convergence Property Using Single Hidden Unit

7.1 Pure Multi-frequency Signals

The NNs trained without noise are further investigated by hidden unit input and output distribution. Figure 2 illustrates this distribution, using the sigmoid (a1), the sinusoidal (b1) and the Gaussian functions (c1).

In the case of the sigmoid function, the data #1 and the data #2 have to be located the right or left side. This is a fundamental space division property of the sigmoid function. Thus, the network have to adjust the weights, with which the hidden unit input data are completely separated into the right or the left side. The data #2 is concentrated at the edge of the α_+ as shown in Eq.(12), but the data #1 is distributed widely. From this result, the distribution of the hidden unit inputs generated by the multi-frequency signals cannot satisfy the requirements given by Eq.(12).

In the case of the sinusoidal function, the hidden unit inputs of the data #2 locate near one of the peaks and the data #1 distributed widely. The sinusoidal function have large differential coefficient except for the peak. Then the data #2 can be shifted around one of the peaks fast. On the other hand, the data #1 can locate in the region of $f_{sin}(net_j) < \alpha_-$. Therefore, the requirement of the fundamental division property given by Eq.(13) is satisfied by the multi-frequency signals.

In the case of the Gaussian function, the data #2 locate around the peak. Differential coefficients around the peak are large, then, the data #2 can be shifted toward this area very fast. Most of the data #1 are distributed both sides.

From these results, the hidden unit inputs of the multi-frequency signals can be concentrated on a narrow range for one group, and the other is distributed widely for the other group.

Thus, the space division property of the Gaussian

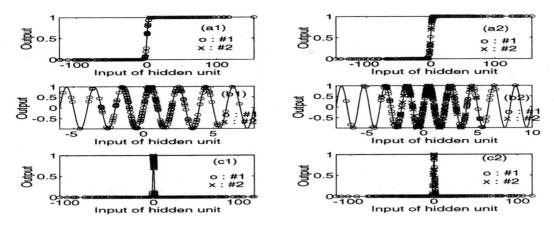

Figure 2: Hidden unit input and output distributions

function is best match with the distribution of the multi-frequency signals. This function can provide the best accuracy as shown in Table 1.

7.2 Noisy Multi-frequency Signals

In Figure 2, (a2), (b2) and (c2) correspond to the hidden unit inputs and output distributions, in which random noise is added. The network is trained by using the pure multi-frequency signals. After the training, the untrained noisy signals are applied to the NN. The distribution of the hidden unit inputs are easily spread by adding the noise.

In the case of the sigmoid, the data #2 distributed widely. However, the most of the data #2 still remain in its own region. Because it has wide stable regions. This is a reason why it can provide better accuracy than the others.

In the case of the Gaussian, the data #2 distributed over the other region. Because a single peak is very narrow. Then these data easily move over the other group's region. Thus, the accuracy is decreased by adding the noise.

The sinusoidal case, the data #2 also widely distributed. However, the sinusoidal function is a periodic function, having several narrow stable regions. Thus, it can provide higher accuracy than that of the Gaussian function.

VIII Convergence Property Using Several Hidden Units

8.1 Homogeneous Activation Funtions

Figures 3, 5 and 7 show distributions of the hidden unit inputs and outputs. The NNs are trained by using the signals without noise. The sigmoid, the sinusoidal and the Gaussian functions are separately used. For each figure, (a), (b) and (c) correspond to one of the hidden unit. (a1), (b1) and (c1) are the response for the data #1, and (a2), (b2) and (c2) are for the data #2.

From these figures, there are two type of distributions, that is concentrated and dispersed distributions. One of two groups locates at near the peak of the functions and the other is widely spread. The overlap of the distributions between the two groups cause miss classification.

In Fig.3, it is very interesting that the data #2 locate at the middle of the slope. Since this region is not a stable region, it can be expected that accuracy is easily degraded by adding the noise. As shown in Table 2, it is true. The classification rates are 97.3% for the data #1 and 8.4% for the data #2. Accuracy for the data #2 is greatly reduced.

Figures 4, 6 and 8 show distribution of the inputs of the two output units. In these figures, (a) and (b) correspond to the data #1 and the data #2, respectively. The region of overlap of the solid and the doted lines will cause miss classification. We can investigate from these figures, how the hidden units separate the signals into two groups. In the case of the data #2 is applied, there are no overlap. So, the hidden unit input space is well separated. In the case of the data #1 is applied, there are some overlap. These overlaps cause miss classification. These results are consistent with the accuracies shown in Table 1.

From the figures, the input space of the output units are well separated by the sigmoid and sinusoidal function. So, it can be concluded that three hidden units cooperate to make the distribution of the inputs to the output unit to be linearly separable.

8.2 Composite Activation Functions

Three functions can be combined in the same hidden layer. This combination is called 'Composite Activation Function' in this paper.

Table 3 shows classification rates using the multifrequency signals without noise. In this table, the symbols D through J correspond to the combination of the functions.

The combination C, having three Gaussian functions, achieves the best accuracy. The convergence rate is also the fastest among three functions. The combination D, having all activation functions, achieves better accuracy than the others except for C. However, I and J, which include two Gaussian functions, are worse than D.

K through M are compared with E through J. E and F are better than K. Then adding both the sinusoidal and the Gaussian to the sigmoid can improve the performance. H is better than L, but G is worse than L. Then adding the Gaussian to the sinusoidal can improve, while the sigmoid can not do.

In the most of the combinations, the Gaussian achieves better accuracy. Then, property of each function does not appear straightly in the combinations.

Table 4 shows classification rates of the network trained using the noisy signals. Training itself did not converge in all cases. This means that the accuracy is not 100% for all combinations of the functions. The network using the homogeneous activation function A and B has higher accuracy than the others. However, C does not achieve better accuracy than the others. Then the homogeneous activation function can not always achieve better accuracy than the composite activation functions.

Table 3: Classification rates using signals without noise

	Combination			Training		Untraining		
	Sig	Sin	Gauss	#1	#2	#1	#2	Ave.
A	3	0	0	100	100	97.4	100	98.7
B	0	3	0	100	100	92.6	100	96.3
C	0	0	3	100	100	99.1	99.9	99.5
D	1	1	1	100	100	100	98.3	99.1
E	2	1	0	99.5	100	96.6	98.4	97.5
F	2	0	1	100	100	97.4	100	98.7
G	1	2	0	93.5	98.5	83.8	97.3	90.6
H	0	2	1	100	100	99.9	97.8	98.9
I	1	0	2	100	100	96.2	99.6	97.9
J	0	1	2	100	100	97.3	98.9	98.1
K	2	0	0	99.0	100	94.0	100	97.2
L	0	2	0	86.0	95.5	86.8	97.3	92.1
M	0	0	2	99.5	98.5	99.4	98.8	99.1

The network using the composite activation function J has higher accuracy, while C and I have worse accuracy than the others. G and H also provide good accuracy. E and F achieve worse accuracy while A provides good one.

K through M are compared with E through J. G and H are better than L. Then adding the sigmoid or the Gaussian to the sinusoidal works well. K is better

than E and F. Then adding both the sinusoidal and the Gaussian to the sigmoid does not work well.

The sinusoidal and sigmoid functions achieve good accuracy in the most of the combinations. However, the sinusoidal combination does not always achieve better accuracy. Thus, property of each function is not straight in the combination, as previously discussed in the no additive noise case.

Table 4: Classification rates using signals with noise

	Combination			Training		Untraining		
	Sig	Sin	Gauss	#1	#2	#1	#2	Ave.
A	3	0	0	83.5	86.0	82.6	78.9	80.8
B	0	3	0	84.5	89.0	79.9	82.7	81.3
C	0	0	3	87.0	81.5	79.8	70.2	75.0
D	1	1	1	77.0	92.5	69.1	84.3	77.6
E	2	1	0	88.5	77.0	80.9	67.8	74.4
F	2	0	1	78.5	98.5	63.8	85.9	74.9
G	1	2	0	74.0	92.5	69.4	87.0	78.2
H	0	2	1	79.0	92.5	72.3	84.3	78.3
I	1	0	2	84.0	87.5	73.5	75.9	74.7
J	0	1	2	84.5	82.0	81.0	78.5	79.8
K	2	0	0	91.5	70.5	81.3	69.3	75.3
L	0	2	0	80.3	83.0	79.1	73.6	76.4
M	0	0	2	75.5	85.0	74.6	76.1	75.4

IX CONCLUSIONS

Properties of the activation functions for multifrequency signal classification has been discussed using multilayer neural network supervised by BP algorithm. The Gaussian function can provide the highest performance for the signals without noise. However, it is sensitive to the additive noise. The sigmoid function is not useful for a single hidden unit. If several hidden units are used, then the sigmoid function becomes useful, and is insensitive to the additive noise. The sinusoidal function is useful for noisy signal.

References

[1] D.E.Rumelhart and J.L.McCelland et al, "Parallel Distributed Processing", MIT Press, 1986.

[2] Philip D. Wasserman,"Advanced Methods in Neural Computing", Van Nostrand Reinhold, pp.147–155, 1993.

[3] G.Veciana and A.Zakhor, "Neural Net-Based Continuous Phase Modulation Receivers", IEEE Transaction on communications, vol.40, No.8, 1992.

[4] J.Karhunen, J.Joutsensalo, "Tracking of sinusoidal frequencies by neural network learning algorithms", IEEE, CH2977-7/91/0000-3177, 1991.

[5] K.Hara and K.Nakayama, "Multi–frequency signal classification using multilayer neural network trained by backpropagation algorithm (in Japanese)", Tech., Rep. IEICE, NC92–75, pp.47–54, 1992.

[6] K.Hara and K.Nakayama, "High resolution of multi- frequencies using multilayer networks trained by back-propagation algorithm", Proc. WCNN'93, Portland Oregon, vol.IV, pp.675–678, 1993.

[7] K.Hara and K.Nakayama, "Classification of multi–frequency signals with random noise using multilayer neural networks", Proc. IJCNN'93, Nagoya Japan, vol.I, pp.601–604, 1993.

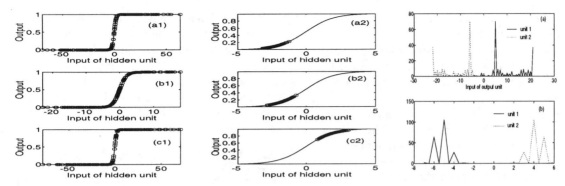

Figure 3: Distribution of sigmoid hidden unit outputs

Figure 4: Distribution of output unit inputs

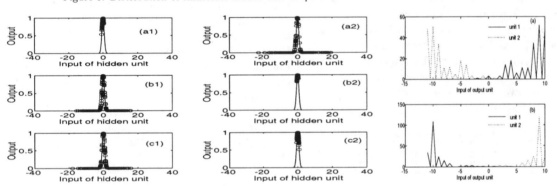

Figure 5: Distribution of sinusoidal hidden unit outputs

Figure 6: Distribution of output unit inputs

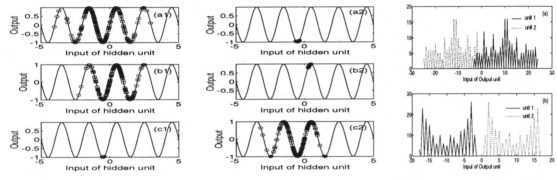

Figure 7: Distribution of Gaussian hidden unit outputs

Figure 8: Distribution of output unit inputs